Bowman, 1953BC, 2½" x 3¾"

Bowman, 1954, 2½" x 3¾"

Bowman, 1955, 2½" x 3¾"

**Bowman, 1989,
2½" x 3¾"**

LARRY MILBOURNE I-F/SHORT

Donruss, 1981, 2½" x 3½"

CLINT HURDLE of

Donruss, 1982, 2½" x 3½"

RYNE SANDBERG

Donruss, 1983, 2½" x 3½"

Donruss, 1984, 2½" x 3½"

DARRYL STRAWBERRY OF

MARK LANGSTON P

Donruss, 1985, 2½" x 3½"

Gene Florence's
Standard
BASEBALL CARD
Price Guide
Revised 3rd Edition

Collector Books
A Division of Schroeder Publishing Co., Inc.

The current values in this book should be used only as a guide. They are not intended to set prices, which vary from one section of the country to another. Auction prices as well as dealer prices vary greatly and are affected by condition as well as demand. Neither the Author nor the Publisher assumes responsibility for any losses that might be incurred as a result of consulting this guide. Baseball cards illustrated are for identification purposes and have been photographed from the author's collection.

FOREWORD

For me baseball card collecting has graduated from a hobby to a major portion of my antique business. When I opened my Grannie Bear Antiques shop in July, 1976, one of the first things I stocked along with Depression era glassware and comic books was baseball cards. I knew if I could get the kids to come into my shop the parents would have to bring them and spend some time with the antiques while the kids were shopping. I started several new glass collectors as well as baseball card collectors.

From that beginning I started to attend baseball card shows and later to sell at these shows including the first and second National shows in California and Michigan. Unfortunately, my books on glassware and other collectibles began to take more of my time and conflict with some of the larger baseball card shows. I have only been able to attend a few shows each year as a dealer, but the card business in my shop is rivaling my glassware business in volume.

This book explores the world of baseball cards from the beginning of the modern era of bubble gum cards (1948) to the present day cards containing holograms to foil reproductions. I will pass along my thoughts on collecting and grading from the standpoint of dealer and collector since I wear both hats. I hope you enjoy the book which is my thirty-fifth book on collectibles since 1972.

ACKNOWLEDGMENTS

Many people have been instrumental in getting this book in print! My publisher, Bill Schroeder (not the ball player), has encouraged me for years to write a book on baseball cards. I'm sure Steve Quertermous, my editor, got more indoctrination into the world of computers and baseball cards than he ever wanted. He went "above and beyond". I thank him for his time and work! I know his wife "enjoyed" all those phone calls at home which could not wait. The staff at Collector Books always play a major role in my work; but a special thanks to Sherry Kraus for making all these listings into workable pages. Without these dedicated folks this book might still be an idea rather than a reality.

My wife and family have endured stacks of cards, boxes and printouts literally taking over the house. Every time I thought I could put the cards back in storage, a new question (or a dozen) would arise and back to the sets I would go. I have used over 50,000 listings in this book. Just finding each card to insert in the copy from all those sets was days of work.

Cathy, my wife, typed new sets into the computer listings to help out. Marc, my younger son, kept me going by continually asking, "Aren't you through, yet?" You'd be surprised at how motivating a question like that can be!

My Mom, Grannie Bear, and my Dad spent days opening cards and putting sets together, so I could list the new cards. She also proofed new card listings and caught many of our computer errors before they got completely out of hand.

A special thanks to Oscar Combs of Cats' Pause and Paul Holloran of Baseball Cards and Comics in Lexington for helping me obtain some sets for use in this book.

Few people ever realize the magnitude of work that goes into writing a book. In my case, it's always been a cooperative effort. I could never have written the books without wonderful support systems. Thank you everyone!

Identification Section

Bowman, 1948, 2¹⁄₁₆" x 2½"

Bowman, 1949, 2¹⁄₁₆"x 2½"

Bowman, 1950, 2¹⁄₁₆" x 2½"

Bowman, 1951, 2¹⁄₁₆" x 3⅛"

Bowman, 1952, 2¹⁄₁₆" x 3⅛"

Bowman, 1953BW, 2½" x 3¾"

4

Donruss, 1986, 2½" x 3½"

Donruss, 1986, Rookies, 2½" x 3½"

Donruss, 1987, 2½" x 3½"

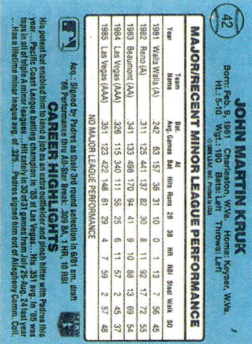

Donruss, Rookies, 1987, 2½" x 3½"

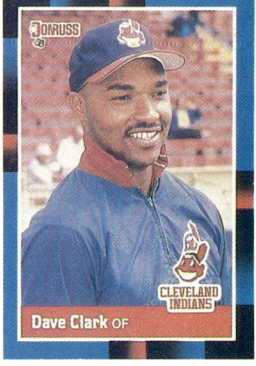

Donruss, 1988, 2½" x 3½"

Donruss, 1988, Rookies, 2½" x 3½"

Donruss, 1988, Baseball's Best 2½" x 3½"

Donruss, 1989, 2½" x 3½"

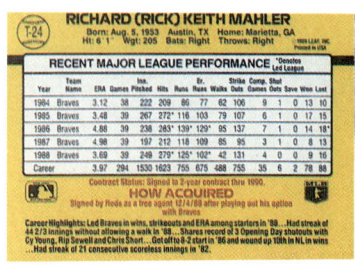

Donruss, 1989, Traded, 2½" x 3½"

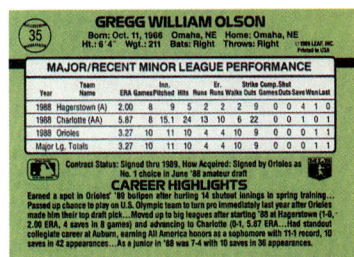

Donruss, 1989, Rookies
2½" x 3½"

Donruss, 1990, 2½"x 3½"

Donruss, 1989, Baseball's Best
2½" x 3½"

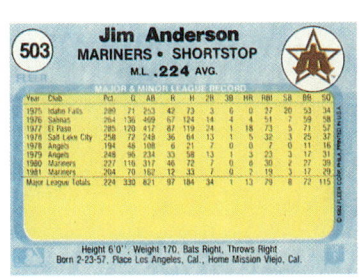

Fleer, 1981, 2½" x 3½"

Fleer, 1982, 2½" x 3½"

Fleer, 1983, 2½" x 3½"   Fleer, 1984, 2½" x 3½"   Fleer, 1984 Update, 2½" x 3½"

Fleer, 1985, 2½" x 3½"

Fleer, 1985, Update, 2½" x 3½"   Fleer, 1986, 2½" x 3½"   Fleer, 1987, 2½" x 3½"

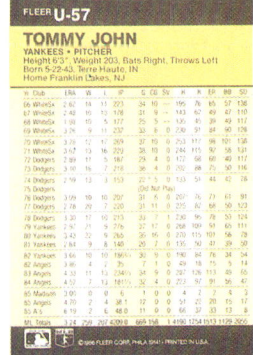

Fleer, 1986 Update, 2½" x 3½"

Fleer, 1987 Update, 2½" x 3½"   **Fleer, 1988, 2½" x 3½"**   **Fleer, 1988 Update, 2½" x 3½"**

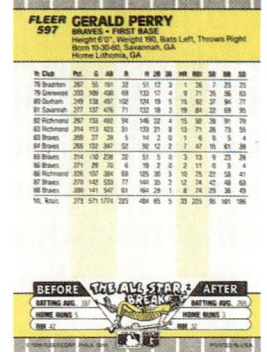

Fleer, 1989, 2½" x 3½"

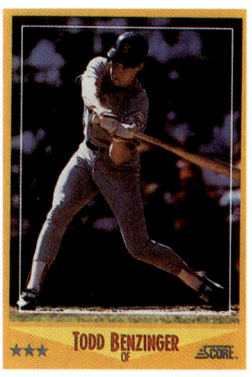

Fleer, 1989 Update, 2½" x 3½"   **Fleer, 1990, 2½" x 3½"**   **Score, 1988, 2½" x 3½"**

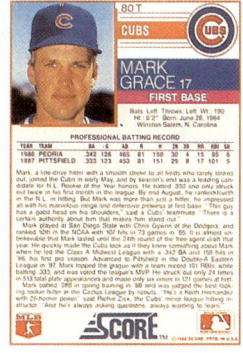

Score, 1988, Traded, 2½" x 3½"

Score, 1989, 2½" x 3½"   Score, 1989, Traded, 2½" x 3½"   Score, 1990 2½" x 3½"

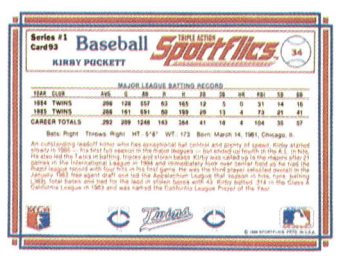

Sportflics, 1986, 2½" x 3½"

Sportflics, 1986 Rookies,
2½" x 3½"

Sportflics, 1987, 2½" x 3½"

Sportflics, 1987 Rookies,
2½" x3½"

Sportflics, 1988, 2½" x 3½"

Topps, 1951 Red
Back, 2" x 2⅝"

Sportflics, 1989, 2½" x 3½"   Sportflics, 1990, 2½" x 3½"

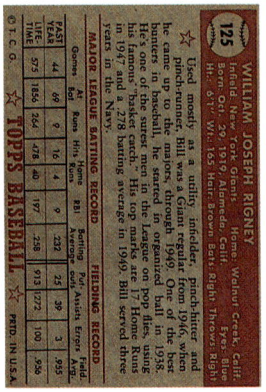

Topps, 1951 Blue
Back, 2" x 2⅝"

Topps, 1952, 2⅝" x 3¾"

Topps, 1953,
2⅝" x 3¾"

Topps, 1954,
2⅝" x 3¾"

Topps, 1955, 2⅝" x 3¾"

Topps, 1956, 2⅝" x 3¾"

Topps, 1957, 2½" x 3½"   Topps, 1958, 2½" x 3½"   Topps, 1959, 2½" x 3½"

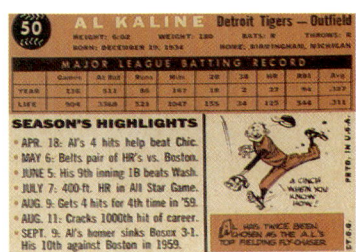

Topps, 1960, 2½" x 3½"

Topps, 1961, 2½" x 3½"   Topps, 1962, 2½" x 3½"   Topps, 1963, 2½" x 3½"

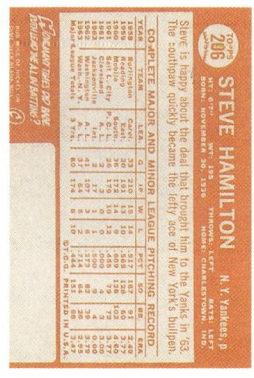

Topps, 1964, 2½" x 3½"

Topps, 1965, 2½" x 3½"   Topps, 1966, 2½" x 3½"   Topps, 1967, 2½" x 3½"

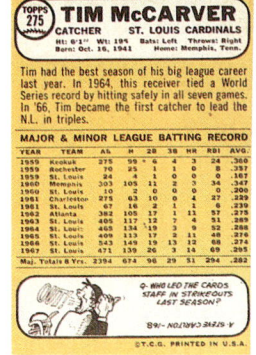

Topps, 1968, 2½" x 3½"

Topps, 1969, 2½" x 3½"   Topps, 1970, 2½" x 3½"   Topps, 1972, 2½" x 3½"

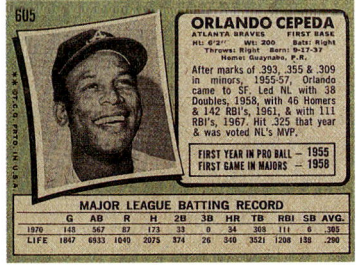

Topps, 1971, 2½" x 3½"

Topps, 1973, 2½" x 3½"   Topps, 1974, 2½" x 3½"   Topps, 1975, 2½" x 3½"

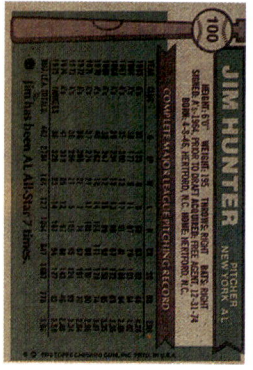

Topps, 1976, 2½" x 3½"

Topps, 1977, 2½" x 3½"   Topps, 1978, 2½" x 3½"   Topps, 1979, 2½" x 3½"

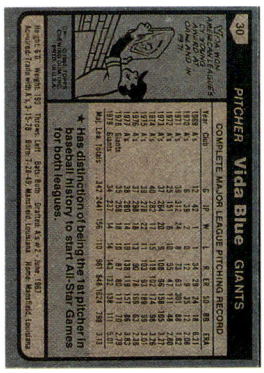

Topps, 1980, 2½" x 3½"

23

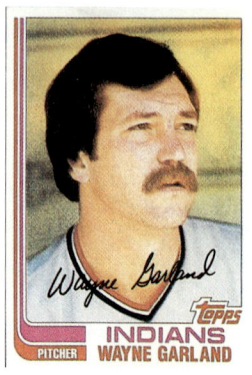

| Topps, 1981, 2½" x 3½" | Topps, 1981 Traded, 2½" x 3½" | Topps, 1982, 2½" x 3½" |

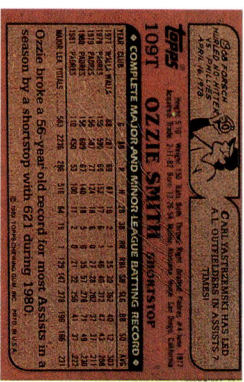

Topps, 1982 Traded, 2½" x 3½"

Topps, 1983, 2½" x 3½"   Topps, 1983 Traded, 2½" x 3½"   Topps, 1984, 2½" x 3½"

Topps, 1984 Traded, 2½" x 3½"

Topps, 1985, 2½" x 3½"   Topps, 1985 Traded, 2½" x 3½"   Topps, 1986, 2½" x 3½"

Topps, 1986 Traded, 2½" x 3½"

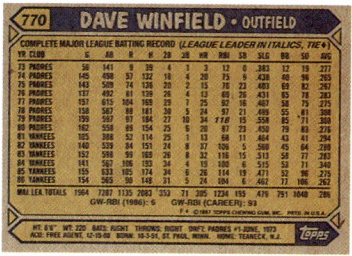

Topps, 1987, 2½" x 3½"

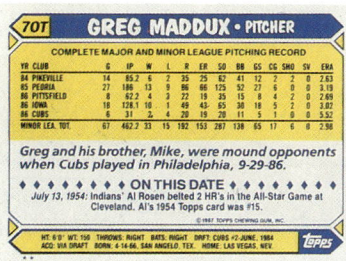

Topps, 1987 Traded, 2½" x 3½"

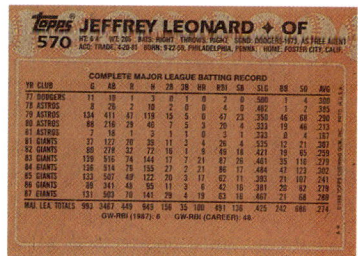

Topps, 1988, 2½" x 3½"

Topps, 1988 Big Baseball, 2½" x 3½"

Topps, 1988 Traded, 2½" x 3½"

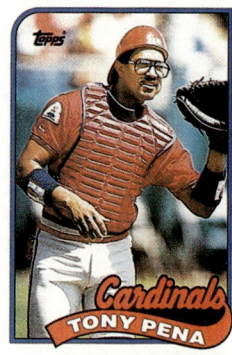

Topps, 1989, 2½" x 3½"

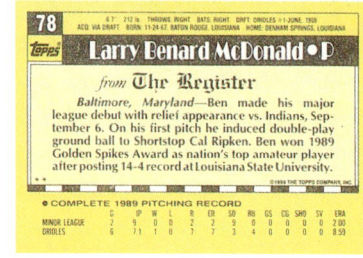

Topps, 1989, Major League Debut, 2½" x 3½"

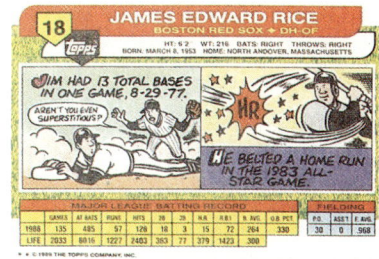

Topps, 1989 Big Baseball, 2½" x 3½"

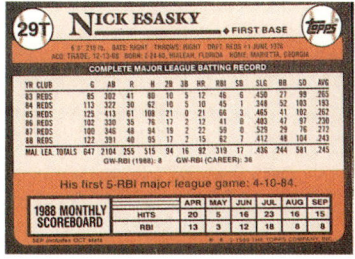

Topps, 1989 Traded, 2½" x 3½"

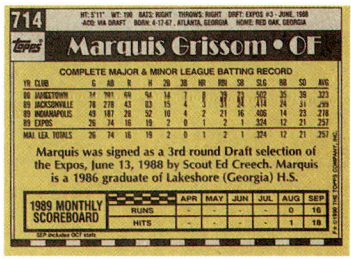

Topps, 1990, 2½" x 3½"

Upper Deck, 1989, 2½" x 3½"

Upper Deck, 1990, 2½" x 3½"

INTRODUCTION

The third book in any series of books is supposed to be easier than the first ones. That has never been true in writing glass books; and I wondered about baseball card books. Although things went smoother than I had imagined, the magnitude of the listings of cards is getting out of hand. There are almost 5,000 new listings this year from the five major companies without going into the small sets issued for individual stores.

The additional listings only became a problem when the new lists were merged with the old and all the alphabetical listings went back to "pure" form again. That means that different first names used over the years became a major nightmare. I hope to have these all corralled soon. Spaces and punctuation have a tendency to be read by the computer in ways that you really did not mean for it to do. If you move names to the correct place in your list, they go right back the next time you turn on the computer.

There are six columns for each entry and each of these can lead to a problem if entered incorrectly. Errors on cards of players who only have one card in the listing are the most difficult to find. I will not even mention the typing mistakes which were missed until the third or later proofing! If you find errors of omission or of any other kind, please let me know. The 50,000 listings with six columns each make over 300,000 entries to be written and proofed.

I first seriously thought about writing a baseball guide in the late 1970's. However it soon became apparent to me that I didn't have the necessary equipment to handle all the sorting of data, and there weren't enough hours in my life to do it manually! So, I put the ideas on hold.

In 1980 my publisher approached me about doing a baseball card book; but again, the idea was dropped due to the lack of a computer that could handle the alphabetical listings I felt were needed. The following year my first computer came and I wrote my next ten books on it; but sorting on it was almost slower than by hand. It took five minutes to sort through two hundred listings and then it would throw out several at the end of the paper - unsorted. Needless to say, that computer would not do what I needed for a card book of this magnitude.

"Macintosh II" arrived in April 1988 and with It the reality that thousands of Topps listings could be sorted! Of course, it has taken several years to gain the user knowledge that takes the computer only minutes to sort. Increased memory has helped, but as the card lists continue to grow at 5,000 entries a year, I am going to have to re-evaluate the way I am now doing the book - else we'll have an expensive and unwieldy tome on our hands.

HOW TO USE THIS BOOK

Traditionally, the trouble I found with other baseball card guides was that it took too long to find a card of a specific player in them - and you had to have quite a bit of prior knowledge about the card itself before you could hope to find it. Also, you had to flip through pages searching from year to year for all the cards of a specific player. I have had numerous dealers in collectibles tell me that they have avoided buying baseball cards because the guides were impossible to use for someone with little or no knowledge of cards. Therefore, I tried to make a book that's "user friendly" as they say in computer circles.

The format of this book is designed to be easily used by baseball card dealers and collectors as well as those who are just beginning to learn about the magic of card collecting. All listings are alphabetical by player as well as divided alphabetically by company of issue. It is not necessary to know the year of manufacture in order to find the value of a card listed in this book! The name of the player is all you have to find!

FINDING A CARD'S VALUE
This section is for someone who knows a little about cards.

Pick a card. Look at the name of the manufacturer (Bowman, Donruss, Fleer, Score, Sportflics, Topps or Upper Deck) on the card to determine in which section to look up the name. Turn to that company's section of the book-also listed alphabetically. Find the name of the player on the card. Under each player's name will be a listing of one or more cards. Find the number on the card and match it with a number listed in the book under the No. column. (On vary rare occasions will a player have the same number for more than one year. In that case look at the statistical data listed. If 1961 is the last date listed in the record of the player, then, it is likely the card is 1962).

If you are confused about the year a card was made, turn to the color section which will help identify any cards you can not figure out by year. This section will familiarize you with the different colored backs and fronts of each year shown in this book (1948-90). Every card of each player is listed in one place so that you can get a checklist of any player by card company manufacturer. This is especially handy for dealers who are constantly asked for a "Don Gullett" or a "Joe Nuxhall" card. Finding a "rookie" card is simple. It will be the first listing for that player under each company. Since true "rookie" card status is debated among dealers and collectors alike, most people consider the first regular issued card (available to the public in retail outlets) as the true "rookie" card which eliminates "Traded" and "Update" cards as "rookie" cards.

All players cards are listed even if the player is only one of several players shown on the card. For example, Don Mattingly is on eight cards in the 1986 Sportflics set and each is listed and priced.

There are two prices listed for every one of the 50,000 plus listings. The first price column is **VG** which is a very good condition card and the next column is **EX/MT** which is excellent to mint. **ALL PRICES IN THIS BOOK ARE RETAIL.** (There will be an explanation of grading following this section).

A STEP BY STEP GUIDE TO FINDING A CARD'S VALUE
This is for someone who knows absolutely nothing about cards.

1. Pick a card.

2. Determine manufacturer of card. There are several different manufacturers of baseball cards and here is the best way to determine each:

BOWMAN - All cards copyrighted Bowman or B.G.H.L.I. on back except some 1950 cards which say "No. 181-252 in the series of Baseball Picture Cards". 1989 cards say "Bowman" on front with a red "B" over a green baseball diamond. (see page 35)

DONRUSS - All Donruss cards have a Donruss logo on front. (see page 54)

FLEER - 1981-1984 Fleer name found on back of card and from 1985 Fleer name on the front also. (see page 112)

SCORE & SPORTFLICS - Score written on front and Sportflics written on back of each year. (see page 170)

TOPPS - 1951 cards are baseball game pieces with red or blue backs and no other identification. Topps is written somewhere on back of all cards from 1952 to1970 except 1958,1959, 1960 which along with 1971 to 1975 have only copyright **T.G.C.** on the back. 1976 to 1978 all have Topps copyright on back and 1979 to date all have a Topps logo on the front. (see page 199-201)

UPPER DECK- 1989 cards have Upper Deck logo on front and Upper Deck hologram on back. (see page 417)

3. Turn to the alphabetical listing of the company determined in No. 2 above and find the player's name. Now look at the number of the card (found on the back of the card, usually in upper left.) Find the card's number in the No. column in the book. Follow this line to give you the year and price in VG (very good) and EX/MT (excellent/mint) condition of the card. (An explanation of grading follows this section.)

4. In case of a number being the same in two years (which rarely happened) there are three choices. You can turn to the color section (pp 4-30) to locate the card year. You can look for a copyright; or you can look at statistical information of the previous year on the card . The latter does not always work as oft times the card will only say last year or lifetime stats. After a while the knowledge of which year a card was issued will become the easiest part of learning about the cards!

GRADING

Everyone thinks he has excellent or better cards, but usually those you put in the cigar or shoe box as a youngster fit the VG category **if you took some care with them.** The latest cards in an accumulation of several years are generally the ones in the best condition. It seems the older you got the better you treated your "treasures".

There are more arguments between buyer and seller over grading than any other concept in collecting. **The grade of a card does not change whether the buyer or the seller owns the card.**

This book only prices cards in two grades because most of the cards collected over the years fit the the grades VG or EX/MT.

VG - very good means a card that has been handled but not torn, cut or flawed. There may be some slight rounding of the corners and there may be gum or wax stains on the card. There may even be a hairline crease caused during manufacture. The original luster is usually gone, but there should be no tack holes, ink stains, rubber band marks or tape. The card may be slightly off center, but not cut badly by the factory.

EX/MT - excellent/mint means a card that is **almost perfect**. The card may have a slight wear overall and may have an ever so slightly rounded corner or yellowing of the border. There should be no gum or wax stains visible. The card should be nicely centered. Early cards have to pass the same criteria as newer cards. Many forty-year-old people are in better shape than others. The same can be said for cards! Age of the card is no excuse for lowering grading standards.

There are other grades. **MINT** grading is a field unto itself. There are special boxes to measure centering. It reminds me of the old days of coin grading; so I can only say that a mint card has to be perfect in every way by today's grading standards. Most of the sets I put away as "mint" in the late 1970's would have a difficult time being graded mint today!

Cards that are less than very good are not sought by collectors or dealers unless they are harder to find cards or cards of well known players. They have little value.

COLLECTING, SELLING and PRICING

I am often asked what to collect. Today, I suggest buying the factory sets that each of the companies issue. First, buy the Topps, Fleer and Donruss since those sets are now all factory sealed. **Leave them sealed! Do not open them!** If you want to look at your collection and play with it, then buy the regular sets. The factory sets that are sealed will be like the sealed proof coins of yesteryear. If sealed, they sold over and over again. Everyone assumed that they were perfect. If opened, there was a possibility of tarnished coins which lowered the value. The same holds true with factory sealed baseball sets. If unopened, all cards are assumed to be there in mint condition. If someone opens the set, and disproves that all the cards are there or that some are badly off-center, then the set value is greatly reduced.

Selling your cards is another story. Find a reliable dealer who will even show you what your cards are worth. Remember, a dealer has to make a profit in order to stay in business. Most dealers will pay from fifty to sixty per cent of the retail price for star cards and cards they need. They will pay very little for cards not needed for stock or common cards. Condition of the cards is a main concern! Personally, I do not buy later cards in less than EX/MT condition and few cards in less than VG no matter what the age. It is easier to sell mint sets of the later years, but it usually takes about five years to make a handsome profit.

There are only so many of the older cards available. If you have some baseball cards packed away in a shoe box in the attic, basement or your closet, better remove all those rubber bands and look up the values of the treasures you stored. Wall Street and big business are still TALKING COLLECTIBLES. It's time to start taking better care of them!

BOWMAN GUM, INC. 1948-1955; 1989

The Bowman Company produced a black and white set of forty-eight cards in 1948. These cards were packed with Blony bubble gum. For a penny you got a piece of bubble gum and one card. As a child, I hated these older cards when I started collecting because they were black and white. I refused to add any of these to my collection by trading because they were not in color like those I was then buying. In fact, I was highly insulted in 1953 when Bowman again put out black and white cards after issuing cards in color.

The 1954 set is the easiest to complete for a new collector if card #66 is collected as Jimmy Piersall and not Ted Williams. There are two #66 cards with the Ted Williams card considered scarce. In my travels, I have come to believe it is only scarce in Mint condition.

The 1955 Bowman set is probably the most popular and the next easiest to assemble. If you collect either the 1954 or 1955 sets in less than excellent condition, you should be able to complete these sets without a lot of difficulty.

Bowman cards are easily identified by beginning collectors. Their smaller size makes these earlier cards stand out in a collection of cards.

Topps shocked the baseball card collecting world in 1989 when they announced that they were bringing back the Bowman name on a set of 484 cards measuring the 2½" x 3¾" of many of the early Bowman sets. Topps bought out the Bowman company in 1955 and had never used the name until then. The listing for these cards is separate from the original Bowman cards of 1948-1955. In 1990 Topps announced that there would be a Bowman set, but that the cards would be of the standard 2½" x 3½" size.The 1990 cards were unavailable as we went to press.

1948 - 48 black & white cards measuring 2¹⁄₁₆" x 2½" (Bowman copyright 1948 on back)

1949 - 240 cards with black and white photo on pastel background measuring 2¹⁄₁₆" x 2½" (Bowman copyright 1949 on back)

1950 - 252 color cards measuring 2¹⁄₁₆" x 2½" (Bowman copyright 1950 on back of most cards; some cards only say "No. 181-252 in the series of Baseball Picture Cards")

1951 - 324 color cards measuring 2¹⁄₁₆" x 3⅛" (copyright Bowman 1951 back of card)

1952 - 252 color cards measuring 2¹⁄₁₆" x 3⅛" (copyright 1952 Bowman Gum Division, Haelan Laboratories, Inc. back of card)

1953BC - 160 color cards measuring 2½" x 3¾" (copyright B.G.H.L.I. on back lower left cornor)

1953BW - 64 black and white cards measuring 2½" x 3¾" (copyright B.G.H.L.I. on back lower left corner)

1954 - 224 color cards measuring 2½" x 3¾" (copyright B.G.H.L.I. on back top left corner)

1955 - 320 color (TV screen) cards measuring 2½" x 3¾" (copyright B.G.H.L.I. on back lower left corner)

1989 - 484 color cards measuring 2½" x 3¾" (Bowman on front with a large red B over a baseball diamond; copyright 1989 Bowman Gum, Inc. on back right corner)

The only abbreviation used in the Bowman section of card listings is in the 1953 cards. As shown above I have used **BC** and **BW** to distinguish between the color and black and white cards of that year.

Although Bowman only survived until 1955 with eight sets issued, these baseball cards with a piece of bubble gum enclosed marked the beginning of many kids' fantasies of being in the Major Leagues and one day having their own picture on a card.

The listing for each card shown appears immediately following the photograph.

Player	Year	No.	VG	EX/MT
Aaron, Hank	55B	179	$40.00	$160.00
Aber, Al	55B	24	$ 1.50	$ 4.50
Abrams, Cal	51B	152	$ 4.00	$14.00
Abrams, Cal	52B	86	$ 3.00	$10.50

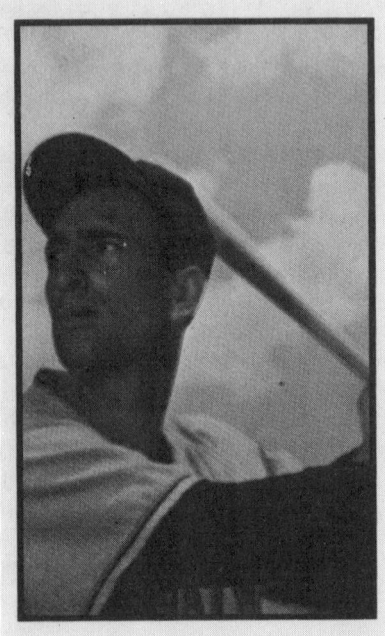

Player	Year	No.	VG	EX/MT
Abrams, Cal	53BC	160	$18.00	$125.00
Abrams, Cal	54B	91	$ 1.50	$ 4.50
Abrams, Cal	55B	55	$ 1.50	$ 4.50
Adams, Bobby	51B	288	$12.00	$37.50
Adams, Bobby	52B	166	$ 3.00	$10.50
Adams, Bobby	53BC	108	$ 6.00	$21.50
Adams, Bobby	54B	108	$ 1.50	$ 4.50
Adams, Bobby	55B	118	$ 1.50	$ 4.50
Adcock, Joe	51B	323	$13.00	$42.00
Adcock, Joe	52B	69	$ 3.25	$12.50
Adcock, Joe	53BC	151	$ 8.75	$28.00
Adcock, Joe	54B	96	$ 1.75	$ 6.50
Adcock, Joe	55B	218	$ 1.75	$ 6.25
Addis, Bob	53BC	94	$ 6.00	$21.50
Aloma, Luis	51B	231	$ 4.00	$14.00
Aloma, Luis	54B	134	$ 1.50	$ 4.50
Alston, Tom	55B	257	$ 3.50	$12.00
Amalfitano, Joe	55B	269	$ 3.50	$12.00
Antonelli, Johnny	50B	74	$ 2.25	$ 9.00
Antone!li, Johnny	51B	243	$ 3.50	$12.00
Antonelli, Johnny	54B	208	$ 1.75	$ 6.50
Antonelli, Johnny	55B	124	$ 1.75	$ 6.50
Appling, Luke	49B	175	$20.00	$80.00
Appling, Luke	50B	37	$12.50	$45.00
Arft, Hank	49B	139	$ 3.00	$10.50
Arft, Hank	51B	173	$ 4.00	$14.00
Arft, Hank	52B	229	$ 3.75	$14.50
Ashburn, Richie	49B	214	$125.00	$400.00
Ashburn, Richie	50B	84	$18.00	$55.00
Ashburn, Richie	51B	186	$15.00	$40.00
Ashburn, Richie	52B	53	$ 6.00	$22.50
Ashburn, Richie	53BC	10	$ 7.75	$30.00

Player	Year	No.	VG	EX/MT
Ashburn, Richie	54B	15	$ 3.00	$10.00
Ashburn, Richie	55B	130	$ 3.25	$12.50
Astroth, Joe	51B	298	$12.00	$37.50
Astroth, Joe	52B	170	$ 3.00	$10.50
Astroth, Joe	53BC	82	$ 6.00	$21.50
Astroth, Joe	54B	131	$ 1.50	$ 4.50
Astroth, Joe	55B	119	$ 1.50	$ 4.50
Atwell, Toby	53BC	112	$ 6.00	$21.50
Atwell, Toby	54B	123	$ 1.50	$ 4.50
Atwell, Toby	55B	164	$ 1.50	$ 4.50
Avila, Bobby	51B	188	$ 3.50	$12.00
Avila, Bobby	52B	167	$ 3.00	$10.50
Avila, Bobby	53BC	29	$ 6.00	$21.50
Avila, Bobby	54B	68	$ 1.50	$ 4.50
Avila, Bobby "Roberto"	55B	19	$ 1.50	$ 4.50
Baczewski, Fred	54B	60	$ 1.50	$ 4.50
Baczewski, Fred	55B	190	$ 1.50	$ 4.50
Baker, Floyd	49B	119	$ 3.00	$10.50
Baker, Floyd	50B	146	$ 2.25	$ 9.00
Baker, Floyd	51B	87	$ 4.00	$14.00
Baker, Floyd	53BW	49	$ 6.50	$21.50
Baker, Gene	55B	7	$ 1.50	$ 4.50
Ballanfant, E. Lee	55B	295	$ 3.00	$12.00
Bankhead, Dan	51B	225	$ 4.00	$14.00
Banks, Ernie	55B	242	$75.00	$300.00
Banta, Jack	50B	224	$ 2.25	$ 9.00
Barlick, Albert J.	55B	265	$12.50	$40.00
Barney, Rex	48B	41	$ 6.00	$17.50
Barney, Rex	49B	61	$ 2.25	$ 9.00
Barney, Rex	50B	76	$ 2.25	$ 9.00
Barney, Rex	51B	153	$ 4.00	$14.00
Barrett, Red	49B	213	$16.00	$65.00
Bartell, Dick	55B	234	$ 3.50	$12.00
Batts, Matt	51B	129	$ 4.00	$14.00
Batts, Matt	52B	216	$ 3.00	$10.50
Batts, Matt	53BW	23	$ 6.50	$21.50
Batts, Matt	54B	183	$ 1.50	$ 4.50
Batts, Matt	55B	161	$ 1.50	$ 4.50
Bauer, Hank	50B	219	$ 9.00	$37.50
Bauer, Hank	51B	183	$ 4.00	$16.00
Bauer, Hank	52B	65	$ 4.50	$17.50
Bauer, Hank	53BC	44	$95.00	$285.00
Bauer, Hank	53BC	84	$ 6.00	$24.50
Bauer, Hank	54B	129	$ 3.50	$12.00
Bauer, Hank	55B	246	$ 3.75	$14.50
Baumholtz, Frank	49B	21	$ 3.50	$12.00
Baumholtz, Frank	52B	195	$ 3.00	$10.50
Baumholtz, Frank	54B	221	$ 1.50	$ 4.50
Baumholtz, Frank	55B	227	$ 3.50	$12.00
Beard, Ralph	55B	206	$ 1.50	$ 4.50
Beard, Ted	51B	308	$12.00	$37.50
Bearden, Gene	49B	57	$ 2.25	$ 9.00
Bearden, Gene	50B	93	$ 2.25	$ 9.00
Bearden, Gene	51B	284	$12.00	$37.50
Bearden, Gene	52B	173	$ 3.00	$10.50
Belardi, Wayne	55B	36	$ 1.50	$ 4.50
Bell, Dave "Gus"	51B	40	$ 4.25	$14.00
Bell, Gus	53BW	1	$18.00	$100.00
Bell, Gus	54B	124	$ 1.50	$ 4.50
Bell, Gus	55B	243	$ 2.25	$ 9.00
Berardino, John	51B	245	$ 4.00	$14.00
Bernier, Carlos	54B	171	$ 1.50	$ 4.50
Berra, Larry 'Yogi'	48B	6	$90.00	$350.00
Berra, Yogi	49B	60	$70.00	$260.00
Berra, Yogi	50B	46	$75.00	$295.00
Berra, Yogi	51B	2	$72.50	$290.00
Berra, Yogi	52B	1	$50.00	$550.00
Berra, Yogi	53BC	121	$150.00	$480.00
Berra, Yogi	53BC	44	$95.00	$285.00
Berra, Yogi	54B	161	$30.00	$110.00
Berra, Yogi	55B	168	$25.00	$100.00
Berry, Charles	55B	281	$ 3.00	$12.00
Berry, Connie "Neil"	49B	180	$16.00	$65.00
Berry, Neil	50B	241	$ 2.25	$ 9.00
Berry, Neil	51B	213	$ 4.00	$14.00

Player	Year	No.	VG	EX/MT	Player	Year	No.	VG	EX/MT
Berry, Neil	52B	219	$ 3.75	$14.50	Brown, Tom	49B	178	$16.00	$65.00
Bevan, Hal	53BW	43	$ 6.50	$21.50	Brown, Tommy	52B	236	$ 3.75	$14.50
Bevins, Floyd	48B	22	$12.00	$37.50	Brown, Tommy	53BC	42	$ 6.00	$21.50
Bickford, Vern	49B	1	$ 7.00	$60.00	Bruton, Bill	54B	224	$ 6.50	$21.50
Bickford, Vern	50B	57	$ 6.50	$22.00	Bruton, Bill	55B	11	$ 1.50	$ 4.50
Bickford, Vern	51B	42	$ 4.00	$14.00	Bucha, Johnny	54B	215	$ 1.50	$ 4.50
Bickford, Vern	52B	48	$ 3.00	$10.50	Buhl, Bob	55B	43	$ 1.50	$ 4.50
Bickford, Vern	54B	176	$ 1.50	$ 4.50	Burdette, Lou	52B	244	$11.00	$42.50
Bilko, Steve	51B	265	$12.00	$37.50	Burdette, Lou	53BW	51	$10.50	$42.00
Bilko, Steve	54B	206	$ 1.50	$ 4.50	Burdette, Lou	54B	192	$ 1.75	$ 6.50
Bilko, Steve	55B	88	$ 1.50	$ 4.50	Burdette, Lou	55B	70	$ 1.75	$ 6.50
Blackburn, Jim	49B	160	$16.00	$65.00	Burgess, Forrest	51B	317	$12.00	$40.00
Blackburn, Jim	51B	287	$12.00	$37.50	Burgess, Forrest 'Smokey'	52B	112	$ 3.25	$12.50
Blackwell, Ewell	48B	2	$ 6.00	$17.50	Burgess, Forrest "Smoky"	53BC	28	$ 6.00	$21.50
Blackwell, Ewell	50B	63	$ 9.00	$36.00	Burgess, Forest "Smokey"	54B	31	$ 1.75	$ 6.50
Blackwell, Ewell	51B	24	$ 3.75	$15.00	Burgess, Forrest "Smoky"	55B	209	$ 1.75	$ 6.25
Blatnick, Johnny	49B	123	$ 3.00	$10.50	Burtschy, Ed	55B	120	$ 1.50	$ 4.50
Blaylock, Marv	55B	292	$ 3.50	$12.00	Busby, Jim	51B	302	$12.00	$37.50
Bloodworth, Jimmy	51B	185	$ 4.00	$14.00	Busby, Jim	52B	68	$ 3.00	$10.50
Bockman, Eddie	49B	195	$16.00	$65.00	Busby, Jim	53BC	15	$ 6.00	$21.50
Boggess, L. R. "Dusty"	55B	297	$ 6.50	$18.00	Busby, Jim	54B	8	$ 1.50	$ 4.50
Bolling, Frank	55B	204	$ 1.75	$ 6.50	Busby, Jim	55B	166	$ 1.50	$ 4.50
Bolling, Milt	54B	130	$ 1.50	$ 4.50	Byrd, Harry	53BC	38	$ 6.00	$21.50
Bolling, Milt	55B	48	$ 1.00	$ 6.00	Byrd, Harry	54B	49	$ 1.50	$ 4.50
Bollweg, Don	54B	115	$ 1.50	$ 4.50	Byrd, Harry	55B	159	$ 1.50	$ 4.50
Bollweg, Don	55B	54	$ 1.50	$ 4.50	Byrne, Tommy	51B	73	$ 3.50	$12.00
Bonham, Ernie	49B	77	$ 3.50	$12.00	Byrne, Tommy	52B	61	$ 3.00	$10.50
Boone, Ray	51B	54	$ 4.00	$14.00	Byrne, Tommy	55B	300	$ 3.50	$12.00
Boone, Ray	52B	214	$ 3.00	$10.50	Cain, Bob	50B	236	$ 2.25	$ 9.00
Boone, Ray	53BC	79	$ 6.00	$21.50	Cain, Bob	51B	197	$ 4.00	$14.00
Borowy, Hank	49B	134	$ 3.00	$10.50	Cain, Bob	52B	19	$ 3.25	$12.50
Borowy, Hank	50B	177	$ 2.25	$ 9.00	Cain, Bob	53BC	56	$ 6.00	$21.50
Borowy, Hank	51B	250	$ 4.00	$14.00	Cain, Bob	54B	195	$ 1.50	$ 4.50
Boudreau, Lou	49B	11	$11.50	$40.00	Campanella, Roy	49B	84	$100.00	$450.00
Boudreau, Lou	50B	94	$ 7.50	$31.50	Campanella, Roy	50B	75	$20.00	$210.00
Boudreau, Lou	51B	62	$ 7.50	$31.50	Campanella, Roy	51B	31	$60.00	$195.00
Boudreau, Lou	53BC	57	$10.50	$28.00	Campanella, Roy	52B	44	$45.00	$150.00
Boudreau, Lou	55B	89	$ 5.00	$12.50	Campanella, Roy	53BC	46	$80.00	$240.00
Bowman, Roger	55B	115	$ 1.50	$ 4.50	Campanella, Roy	54B	90	$35.00	$100.00
Boyd, Bob	54B	118	$ 1.50	$ 4.50	Campanella, Roy	55B	22	$25.00	$100.00
Boyer, Cloyd	51B	228	$ 4.00	$14.00	Candini, Milo	51B	255	$12.00	$37.50
Boyer, Cloyd	53BC	115	$ 8.50	$30.00	Carrasquel, Alfonso Chico	51B	60	$ 4.00	$14.00
Boyer, Cloyd	55B	149	$ 1.50	$ 4.50	Carrasquel, Chico	52B	41	$ 3.00	$10.50
Branca, Ralph	49B	194	$22.50	$85.00	Carrasquel, Chico	53BC	54	$ 6.00	$21.50
Branca, Ralph	50B	59	$ 9.00	$37.50	Carrasquel, Chico	54B	54	$ 1.50	$ 4.50
Branca, Ralph	51B	56	$ 3.50	$12.00	Carrasquel, Al "Chico"	55B	173	$ 1.50	$ 4.50
Branca, Ralph	52B	96	$ 4.25	$14.00	Casey, Hugh	49B	179	$16.00	$65.00
Branca, Ralph	53BW	52	$ 7.00	$32.00	Castiglione, Pete	50B	201	$ 2.25	$ 9.00
Brazle, Al	49B	126	$ 3.00	$10.50	Castiglione, Pete	51B	17	$ 4.00	$14.00
Brazle, Al	50B	126	$ 2.25	$ 9.00	Castiglione, Pete	52B	47	$ 3.00	$10.50
Brazle, Al	51B	157	$ 4.00	$14.00	Castiglione, Pete	54B	174	$ 1.50	$ 4.50
Brazle, Al	52B	134	$ 3.00	$10.50	Cavarretta, Phil	49B	6	$ 2.25	$ 9.00
Brazle, Alpha	53BC	140	$ 8.50	$30.00	Cavarretta(Cavaretta), Phil	50B	195	$ 3.00	$12.00
Brazle, Al	54B	142	$ 1.50	$ 4.50	Cavarretta, Phil	51B	138	$ 4.00	$14.00
Brazle, Al	55B	230	$ 3.50	$12.00	Cavarretta, Phil	52B	126	$ 3.25	$12.50
Brecheen, Harry	49B	158	$16.00	$65.00	Cavarretta, Phil	53BC	30	$ 6.00	$21.50
Brecheen, Harry	50B	90	$ 2.25	$ 9.00	Cavarretta, Phil	55B	282	$ 3.50	$12.00
Brecheen, Harry	51B	86	$ 3.50	$12.00	Cerv, Bob	55B	306	$ 2.25	$ 9.00
Brecheen, Harry	52B	176	$ 3.00	$10.50	Chakales, Bob	55B	148	$ 1.50	$ 4.50
Brewer, Tom	55B	178	$ 1.50	$ 4.50	Chambers, Cliff	50B	202	$ 2.25	$ 9.00
Brideweser, Jim	53BC	136	$ 8.50	$30.00	Chambers, Cliff	51B	131	$ 4.00	$14.00
Brideweser, Jim	55B	151	$ 1.50	$ 4.50	Chambers, Cliff	52B	14	$ 3.25	$12.50
Bridges, Rocky	53BW	32	$ 6.50	$21.50	Chambers, Cliff	54B	126	$ 1.50	$ 4.50
Bridges, Rocky	54B	156	$ 1.75	$ 6.50	Chapman, Sam	49B	112	$ 3.00	$10.50
Bridges, Rocky	55B	136	$ 1.50	$ 4.50	Chapman, Sam	50B	104	$ 2.25	$ 9.00
Brissie, Leland "Lou"	49B	41	$ 2.25	$ 9.00	Chapman, Sam	51B	9	$ 4.00	$14.00
Brissie, Lou	50B	48	$ 6.50	$22.00	Chesnes, Bob	49B	13	$ 3.50	$12.00
Brissie, Lou	51B	155	$ 4.00	$14.00	Chesnes, Bob	50B	70	$ 6.50	$22.00
Brissie, Lou	52B	79	$ 3.00	$10.50	Chipman, Bob	49B	184	$16.00	$65.00
Brosnan, Jim	55B	229	$ 2.25	$ 9.00	Chipman, Bob	50B	192	$ 2.25	$ 9.00
Brown, Bobby	49B	19	$ 5.00	$22.00	Chipman, Bob	52B	228	$ 3.75	$14.50
Brown, Bobby	50B	101	$ 6.50	$21.50	Chiti, Harry	53BC	7	$ 6.00	$21.50
Brown, Bobby	51B	110	$ 3.50	$13.00	Chiti, Harry	55B	304	$ 3.50	$12.00
Brown, Bobby	52B	105	$ 3.25	$12.50	Christman, Mark	49B	121	$ 3.00	$10.50
Brown, Hector "Skinny"	55B	221	$ 1.50	$ 4.50	Church, Emory "Bubba"	51B	149	$ 4.00	$14.00

Player	Year	No.	VG	EX/MT	Player	Year	No.	VG	EX/MT
Church, Bubba	52B	40	$ 3.00	$10.50	Dark, Al	50B	64	$ 9.00	$36.00
Church, Bubba	53BC	138	$ 8.50	$30.00	Dark, Al	51B	14	$ 3.50	$12.00
Church, Bubba	55B	273	$ 3.50	$12.00	Dark, Al	52B	34	$ 4.25	$14.00
Chylak, Nestor	55B	283	$ 3.00	$12.00	Dark, Al	53BC	19	$ 4.25	$16.00
Clark, Allie	49B	150	$16.00	$65.00	Dark, Al	54B	41	$ 3.00	$10.50
Clark, Allie	50B	233	$ 2.25	$ 9.00	Dark, Al "Alwin"	55B	2	$ 1.75	$ 6.50
Clark, Allie	51B	29	$ 4.00	$14.00	Darnell, Bob	55B	39	$ 1.50	$ 4.50
Clark, Allie	52B	130	$ 3.00	$10.50	Dascoli, Frank	55B	291	$ 3.00	$12.00
Clark, Allie	53BC	155	$ 8.50	$30.00	De Maestri, Joe	54B	147	$ 1.50	$ 4.50
Clark, Mel	53BC	67	$ 6.00	$21.50	De Maestri, Joe	55B	176	$ 1.50	$ 4.50
Clark, Mel	54B	175	$ 1.50	$ 4.50	Delock, Ivan	52B	250	$ 3.75	$14.50
Clark, Mel	55B	41	$ 1.50	$ 4.50	Delock, Ivan	55B	276	$ 3.50	$12.00
Coan, Gil	49B	90	$ 3.50	$12.00	Delsing, Jim	51B	279	$12.00	$37.50
Coan, Gil	50B	54	$ 6.50	$22.00	Delsing, Jim	52B	157	$ 3.00	$10.50
Coan, Gil	51B	18	$ 4.00	$14.00	Delsing, Jim	53BW	44	$ 6.50	$21.50
Coan, Gil	52B	51	$ 3.00	$10.50	Delsing, Jim	54B	55	$ 1.50	$ 4.50
Coan, Gil	53BC	34	$ 6.00	$21.50	Delsing, Jim	55B	274	$ 3.50	$12.00
Coan, Gil	54B	40	$ 1.50	$ 4.50	DeMars, Billy	50B	252	$ 5.00	$60.00
Coan, Gil	55B	78	$ 1.50	$ 4.50	DeMars, Billy	51B	43	$ 4.00	$14.00
Cole, Dave	52B	132	$ 3.00	$10.50	Dente, Sam	50B	107	$ 2.25	$ 9.00
Cole, Dave	53BW	38	$ 6.50	$21.50	Dente, Sam	51B	133	$ 4.00	$14.00
Cole, Dick	54B	27	$ 1.50	$ 4.50	Dente, Sam	53BC	137	$ 8.50	$30.00
Cole, Dick	55B	28	$ 1.50	$ 4.50	Dickey, Bill	51B	290	$40.00	$160.00
Coleman, Gerry (Jerry)	49B	225	$19.00	$85.00	Dickson, Murry	49B	8	$ 3.50	$12.00
Coleman, Jerry	50B	47	$ 9.00	$36.00	Dickson, Murry	50B	34	$ 6.50	$22.00
Coleman, Jerry	51B	49	$ 4.00	$14.00	Dickson, Murry	51B	167	$ 4.00	$14.00
Coleman, Jerry	52B	73	$ 3.50	$12.00	Dickson, Murry	52B	59	$ 3.00	$10.50
Coleman, Jerry	54B	81	$ 1.75	$ 6.50	Dickson, Murry	54B	111	$ 1.50	$ 4.50
Coleman, Jerry	55B	99	$ 1.75	$ 6.50	Dickson, Murry	55B	236	$ 3.50	$12.00
Coleman, Joe	50B	141	$ 2.25	$ 9.00	Diering, Charles "Chuck"	50B	179	$ 2.25	$ 9.00
Coleman, Joe	51B	120	$ 4.00	$14.00	Diering, Chuck	51B	158	$ 4.00	$14.00
Coleman, Joe	55B	3	$ 1.50	$ 4.50	Diering, Chuck	52B	198	$ 3.00	$10.50
Coleman, Ray	50B	250	$ 2.25	$ 9.00	Dillinger, Bob	49B	143	$ 3.00	$10.50
Coleman, Ray	51B	136	$ 4.00	$14.00	Dillinger, Bob	50B	105	$ 2.25	$ 9.00
Coleman, Ray	52B	201	$ 3.00	$10.50	Dillinger, Bob	51B	63	$ 4.00	$14.00
Collins, Joe	52B	181	$ 3.25	$12.50	DiMaggio, Dom	49B	64	$ 6.25	$21.50
Collum, Jack	54B	204	$ 1.50	$ 4.50	DiMaggio, Dom	50B	3	$ 9.00	$35.00
Collum, Jack	55B	189	$ 1.50	$ 4.50	Ditmar, Art	55B	90	$ 1.50	$ 4.50
Conlan, J. B. "Jocko"	55B	303	$18.00	$55.00	Dittmer, Jack	54B	48	$ 1.50	$ 4.50
Consuegra, Sandalio	51B	96	$ 4.00	$14.00	Dittmer, Jack	55B	212	$ 1.50	$ 4.50
Consuegra, Sandalio	52B	143	$ 3.00	$10.50	Dixon, Hal H.	55B	309	$ 3.00	$12.00
Consuegra, "Sandy"	53BC	89	$ 6.00	$21.50	Dixon, John "Sonny"	55B	211	$ 1.50	$ 4.50
Consuegra, Sandy	54B	166	$ 1.50	$ 4.50	Dobernic, Jess	49B	200	$16.00	$65.00
Consuegra, Sandy	55B	116	$ 1.50	$ 4.50	Dobson, Joe	49B	7	$ 3.50	$12.00
Coogan, Dale	50B	244	$ 2.25	$ 9.00	Dobson, Joe	50B	44	$ 6.50	$22.00
Cooper, Walker	48B	9	$ 4.00	$14.00	Dobson, Joe	51B	36	$ 4.00	$14.00
Cooper, Walker	49B	117	$ 3.00	$10.50	Dobson, Joe	53BC	88	$ 6.00	$21.50
Cooper, Walker	50B	111	$ 2.25	$ 9.00	Doby, Larry	49B	233	$25.00	$100.00
Cooper, Walker	51B	135	$ 4.00	$14.00	Doby, Larry	50B	39	$13.00	$39.00
Cooper, Walker	52B	208	$ 3.00	$10.50	Doby, Larry	51B	151	$ 5.50	$18.00
Cooper, Walker	53BW	30	$ 6.50	$21.50	Doby, Larry	52B	115	$ 3.00	$10.50
Corwin, Al	52B	121	$ 3.00	$10.50	Doby, Larry	53BC	40	$ 4.50	$17.25
Corwin, Al	53BC	126	$ 8.50	$30.00	Doby, Lary	54B	84	$ 1.75	$ 6.50
Corwin, Al	53BC	149	$ 8.50	$30.00	Doerr, Bobby	49B	23	$ 8.00	$35.00
Corwin, Al	54B	137	$ 1.50	$ 4.50	Doerr, Bobby	50B	43	$10.00	$40.00
Corwin, Al	55B	122	$ 1.50	$ 4.50	Donatelli, A. J.	55B	313	$ 3.00	$12.00
Courtney, Clint	53BC	70	$ 6.00	$21.50	Donnelly, Sylvester	49B	145	$16.00	$65.00
Courtney, Clint	54B	69	$ 1.50	$ 4.50	Donnelly, Sylvester	50B	176	$ 2.25	$ 9.00
Courtney, Clint	55B	34	$ 1.50	$ 4.50	Donnelly, Sylvester "Blix"	51B	208	$ 4.00	$14.00
Cox, Billy	49B	73	$ 6.50	$21.50	Dorish, Harry	51B	266	$12.00	$37.50
Cox, Billy	50B	194	$ 4.25	$14.00	Dorish, Harry	54B	86	$ 1.50	$ 4.50
Cox, Billy	51B	224	$ 4.00	$14.00	Dorish, Harry	55B	248	$ 3.50	$12.00
Cox, Billy	52B	152	$ 3.25	$12.50	Dressen, Charlie	51B	259	$11.00	$35.00
Cox, Billy	53BW	60	$ 6.50	$27.50	Dressen, Charlie	52B	188	$ 3.00	$10.50
Cox, Billy	54B	26	$ 1.75	$ 6.50	Dressen, Charlie	53BC	212	$12.00	$42.50
Cox, Billy	55B	56	$ 1.50	$ 4.50	Drews, Karl	49B	188	$16.00	$65.00
Crandall, Del	50B	56	$ 9.00	$36.00	Drews, Karl	53BC	113	$ 8.50	$30.00
Crandall, Del	51B	20	$ 3.50	$12.00	Drews, Karl	54B	191	$ 1.50	$ 4.50
Crandall, Del	54B	32	$ 1.75	$ 6.50	Dropo, Walt	50B	246	$ 3.00	$12.00
Crandall, Del	55B	217	$ 1.75	$ 6.25	Dropo, Walt	52B	169	$ 3.50	$12.00
Crawford, Rufus	55B	121	$ 1.50	$ 4.50	Dropo, Walt	53BC	45	$ 6.00	$21.50
Crosetti, Frank	52B	252	$15.00	$145.00	Dropo, Walt	54B	7	$ 1.50	$ 4.50
Cusick, John	52B	192	$ 3.00	$10.50	Dropo, Walt	55B	285	$ 3.00	$12.00
Daniels, Jack	53BC	83	$ 6.00	$21.50	Dubiel, Walt	51B	283	$12.00	$37.50
Dark, Al	49B	67	$ 4.75	$18.50	Durocher, Leo	50B	220	$ 9.00	$35.00

Player	Year	No.	VG	EX/MT	Player	Year	No.	VG	EX/MT
Durocher, Leo	51B	233	$ 9.00	$35.00	Evans, Al	51B	38	$ 4.00	$14.00
					Evers, Hoot	49B	42	$ 2.25	$ 9.00
					Evers, Walter	50B	41	$ 6.50	$22.00
					Evers, Walter	51B	23	$ 4.00	$14.00
					Evers, Walter	52B	111	$ 3.00	$10.50
					Evers, Walter	53BC	25	$ 4.50	$17.25
					Evers, Walter "Hoot"	54B	18	$ 1.50	$ 4.50
					Fain, Ferris	48B	21	$ 4.00	$11.50
					Fain, Ferris	49B	9	$ 2.25	$ 9.00
					Fain, Ferris	50B	13	$ 6.50	$22.00
					Fain, Ferris	52B	154	$ 3.25	$12.50
					Fain, Ferris	54B	214	$ 1.75	$ 6.50
					Fannin, Cliff	49B	120	$ 3.00	$10.50
					Fannin, Cliff	50B	106	$ 2.25	$ 9.00
					Fannin, Cliff	51B	244	$ 4.00	$14.00
					Feller, Bob	48B	5	$32.00	$120.00
					Feller, Bob	49B	27	$24.00	$90.00
					Feller, Bob	50B	6	$35.00	$120.00
					Feller, Bob	51B	30	$20.00	$85.00
					Feller, Bob	52B	43	$19.00	$65.00
					Feller, Bob	53BC	114	$70.00	$195.00
					Feller, Bob	54B	132	$17.00	$55.00
					Feller, Bob	55B	134	$16.00	$52.50
					Fernandez, Chico	55B	270	$ 3.50	$12.00
					Ferrick, Tom	51B	182	$ 4.00	$14.00
					Ferriss, Boo	49B	211	$16.00	$65.00
					Fitzgerald, Ed	49B	109	$ 3.00	$10.50
					Fitzgerald, Ed	50B	178	$ 2.25	$ 9.00
					Fitzgerald, Ed	52B	180	$ 3.00	$10.50
					Fitzgerald, Ed	54B	168	$ 1.50	$ 4.50
					Fitzgerald, Eddy	55B	208	$ 1.50	$ 4.50
					Fitzsimmons, Fred	52B	234	$ 3.75	$14.50
					Flaherty, John	55B	272	$ 3.00	$12.00
					Flowers, Bennett	55B	254	$ 3.50	$12.00
					Fondy, Dee	52B	231	$ 3.75	$14.50
					Fondy, Dee	53BW	5	$ 6.50	$21.50
Durocher, Leo	52B	146	$ 8.50	$30.00	Fondy, Dee	54B	173	$ 1.75	$ 6.50
Durocher, Leo	53BC	55	$ 7.50	$29.00	Fondy, Dee	55B	224	$ 1.50	$ 4.50
Dusak, Erv	51B	310	$12.00	$37.50	Ford, Ed "Whitey"	51B	1	$95.00	$850.00
Dyck, Jim	53BC	111	$ 6.00	$21.50	Ford, Ed "Whitey"	53BC	153	$95.00	$355.00
Dyck, Jim	54B	85	$ 1.50	$ 4.50	Ford, Ed "Whitey"	54B	177	$19.00	$85.00
Dykes, Jimmy	51B	226	$ 3.50	$13.00	Ford, Ed "Whitey"	55B	59	$17.00	$70.00
Dykes, Jimmy	52B	98	$ 3.00	$10.50	Fornieles, Mike	55B	266	$ 3.50	$12.00
Dykes, Jimmy	53BC	31	$ 6.00	$21.50	Fowler, Dick	49B	171	$16.00	$65.00
Early, Jake	49B	106	$ 3.50	$12.00	Fowler, Dick	50B	214	$ 2.25	$ 9.00
Easter, Luke	51B	258	$10.00	$30.00	Fowler, Dick	52B	190	$ 3.00	$10.50
Easter, Luke	52B	95	$ 3.25	$12.50	Fox, Howard "Howie"	50B	80	$ 2.25	$ 9.00
Easter, Luke	53BC	104	$ 6.00	$21.50	Fox, Howie	51B	180	$ 4.00	$14.00
Easter, Luke	54B	116	$ 1.50	$ 4.50	Fox, Howie	52B	125	$ 3.00	$10.50
Edwards, Bruce	48B	43	$ 6.00	$17.50	Fox, Howie	53BC	158	$ 8.50	$30.00
Edwards, Bruce	49D	206	$16.00	$65.00	Fox, Nelson "Nellie"	51B	232	$16.25	$55.00
Edwards, Bruce	50B	165	$ 2.25	$ 9.00	Fox, Nellie	52B	21	$ 5.50	$20.00
Edwards, Bruce	51B	116	$ 4.00	$14.00	Fox, Nellie	53BC	18	$ 9.75	$35.00
Edwards, Bruce	52B	88	$ 3.00	$10.50	Fox, Nellie	54B	6	$ 2.75	$11.50
Edwards, Hank	49B	136	$ 3.00	$10.50	Fox, Nellie	55B	33	$ 2.75	$11.50
Edwards, Hank	50B	169	$ 2.25	$ 9.00	Freeman, Hershell	55B	290	$ 3.50	$12.00
Edwards, Hank	52B	141	$ 3.00	$10.50	Freese, George	55B	84	$ 1.50	$ 4.50
Elliott, Bob	48B	1	$ 5.50	$65.00	Fricano, Marion	54B	3	$ 1.50	$ 4.50
Elliott, Bob	49B	58	$ 2.25	$ 9.00	Fricano, Marion	55B	316	$ 3.50	$12.00
Elliott, Bob	50B	20	$ 6.50	$22.00	Friend, Bob	52B	191	$ 3.00	$10.50
Elliott, Bob	51B	66	$ 4.00	$14.00	Friend, Bob	53BC	16	$ 6.00	$21.50
Engeln, William R.	55B	301	$ 3.00	$12.00	Friend, Bob	54B	43	$ 3.00	$10.50
Ennis, Del	50B	31	$ 6.50	$22.00	Friend, Bob	55B	57	$ 1.75	$ 6.50
Ennis, Del	51B	4	$ 3.50	$12.00	Friend, Owen	50B	189	$ 2.25	$ 9.00
Ennis, Del	52B	76	$ 3.50	$12.00	Friend, Owen	51B	101	$ 4.00	$14.00
Ennis, Del	53BC	103	$ 6.00	$21.50	Friend, Owen	54B	212	$ 1.50	$ 4.50
Ennis, Del	54B	127	$ 1.75	$ 6.50	Friend, Owen	55B	256	$ 3.50	$12.00
Ennis, Del	55B	17	$ 1.75	$ 6.50	Frisch, Frank	50B	229	$10.00	$42.50
Erskine, Carl	51B	260	$25.00	$100.00	Frisch, Frank	51B	282	$19.00	$60.00
Erskine, Carl	52B	70	$ 5.50	$20.00	Furillo, Carl	49B	70	$12.00	$42.50
Erskine, Carl	53BC	12	$ 9.25	$35.00	Furillo, Carl	50B	58	$11.50	$42.00
Erskine, Carl	54B	10	$ 3.25	$12.50	Furillo, Carl	51B	81	$ 8.00	$26.00
Erskine, Carl	55B	170	$ 3.25	$12.50	Furillo, Carl	52B	24	$ 6.00	$19.50
Evans, Al	49B	132	$ 3.00	$10.50	Furillo, Carl	53BC	78	$12.00	$42.50
Evans, Al	50B	144	$ 2.25	$ 9.00	Furillo, Carl	54B	122	$ 3.25	$12.00

Player	Year	No.	VG	EX/MT	Player	Year	No.	VG	EX/MT
Furillo, Carl	55B	169	$ 3.75	$13.00	Goodman, Billy	53BC	148	$ 8.50	$30.00
Galan, Augie	48B	39	$ 6.00	$17.50	Goodman, Billy	54B	82	$ 1.00	$ 5.00
Galan, Augie	49B	230	$16.00	$65.00	Goodman, Billy	55B	126	$ 1.50	$ 4.50
Garagiola, Joe	51B	122	$17.00	$55.00	Gordon, Joe	49B	210	$16.00	$65.00
Garagiola, Joe	52B	27	$14.00	$40.00	Gordon, Joe	50B	129	$ 2.25	$ 9.00
Garagiola, Joe	53BC	21	$15.00	$42.50	Gordon, Sid	48B	27	$ 4.00	$14.00
Garagiola, Joe	54B	141	$ 9.50	$25.00	Gordon, Sid	49B	101	$ 3.50	$12.00
Garcia, Mike	50B	147	$ 4.25	$14.00	Gordon, Sid	50B	109	$ 2.25	$ 9.00
Garcia, Mike	51B	150	$ 3.50	$12.00	Gordon, Sid	51B	19	$ 4.00	$14.00
Garcia, Mike	52B	7	$ 4.25	$14.00	Gordon, Sid	52B	60	$ 3.00	$10.50
Garcia, Mike	53BC	43	$ 4.50	$17.25	Gordon, Sid	53BC	5	$ 6.00	$21.50
Garcia, Mike	54B	100	$ 1.75	$ 6.50	Gordon, Sid	54B	11	$ 1.50	$ 4.50
Garcia, Mike	55B	128	$ 1.75	$ 6.50	Gordon, Sid	55B	163	$ 1.50	$ 4.50
Gardner, Billy	55B	249	$ 3.50	$12.00	Gore, Arthur J.	55B	289	$ 3.00	$12.00
Garver, Ned	49B	15	$ 3.50	$12.00	Gorman, Tom	53BW	61	$ 6.50	$21.50
Garver, Ned	50B	51	$ 6.50	$22.00	Gorman, Tom	54B	17	$ 1.50	$ 4.50
Garver, Ned	51B	172	$ 4.00	$14.00	Gorman, Thomas D.	55B	293	$ 3.00	$12.00
					Graham, Jack	50B	145	$ 2.25	$ 9.00
					Grammas, Alex	55B	186	$ 1.50	$ 4.50
					Grasso, Mickey	51B	205	$ 4.00	$14.00
					Grasso, Mickey	52B	174	$ 3.00	$10.50
					Grasso, Mickey	53BC	77	$ 6.00	$21.50
					Grasso, Mickey	54B	184	$ 1.50	$ 4.50
					Gray, Ted	49B	10	$ 3.50	$12.00
					Gray, Ted	50B	210	$ 2.25	$ 9.00
					Gray, Ted	51B	178	$ 4.00	$14.00
					Gray, Ted	52B	199	$ 3.00	$10.50
					Gray, Ted	53BC	72	$ 6.00	$21.50
					Gray, Ted	54B	71	$ 1.50	$ 4.50
					Gray, Ted	55B	86	$ 1.50	$ 4.50
					Greengrass, Jim	54B	28	$ 1.50	$ 4.50
					Greengrass, Jim	55B	49	$ 1.50	$ 4.50
					Greenwood, Bob	55B	42	$ 1.50	$ 4.50
					Grieve, William T.	55B	275	$ 3.00	$12.00
					Grim, Bob	55B	167	$ 1.50	$ 4.50
					Grimm, Charlie	53BC	69	$ 6.00	$21.50
					Grimm, Charlie	55B	298	$ 3.50	$12.00
					Grissom, Marv	55B	123	$ 1.50	$ 4.50
					Gromek, Steve	49B	198	$16.00	$65.00
					Gromek, Steve	50B	131	$ 2.25	$ 9.00
					Gromek, Steve	51B	115	$ 4.00	$14.00
					Gromek, Steve	52B	203	$ 3.00	$10.50
					Gromek, Steve	53BW	63	$ 6.50	$22.00
					Gromek, Steve	54B	199	$ 1.50	$ 4.50
					Gromek, Steve	55B	203	$ 1.50	$ 4.50
					Groth, Johnny	50B	243	$ 2.25	$ 9.00
					Groth, Johnny	51B	249	$ 4.00	$14.00
					Groth, Johnny	52B	67	$ 3.00	$10.50
					Groth, Johnny	54B	165	$ 1.50	$ 4.50
					Groth, Johnny	55B	117	$ 1.50	$ 4.50
					Guerra, Mickey "Mike"	49B	155	$16.00	$65.00
					Guerra, Mike	50B	157	$ 2.25	$ 9.00
					Guerra, Mike	51B	202	$ 4.00	$14.00
					Gumbert, Harry	49B	192	$16.00	$65.00
Garver, Ned	52B	29	$ 3.25	$12.50	Gumbert, Harry	50B	171	$ 2.25	$ 9.00
Garver, Ned	53BC	47	$ 6.00	$21.50	Gumpert, Randy	49B	87	$ 3.50	$12.00
Garver, Ned	54B	39	$ 3.00	$10.50	Gumpert, Randy	50B	184	$ 2.25	$ 9.00
Garver, Ned	55B	188	$ 1.50	$ 4.50	Gumpert, Randy	51B	59	$ 4.00	$14.00
Gernert, Dick	53BW	11	$ 6.50	$21.50	Gumpert, Randy	52B	106	$ 3.00	$10.50
Gernert, Dick	54B	146	$ 1.50	$ 4.50	Gustine, Frank	49B	99	$ 3.50	$12.00
Gettel, Allen	51B	304	$12.00	$37.50	Hacker, Warren	51B	318	$12.00	$37.50
Giel, Paul	55B	125	$ 1.50	$ 4.50	Hacker, Warren	53BC	144	$ 8.50	$30.00
Gilbert, Harold	50B	235	$ 2.25	$ 9.00	Hacker, Warren	54B	125	$ 1.50	$ 4.50
Gilliam, James "Junior"	54B	74	$ 1.75	$ 6.50	Hacker, Warren	55B	8	$ 1.50	$ 4.50
Gilliam, Junior	55B	98	$ 1.75	$ 6.50	Haefner, Mickey	49B	144	$ 3.00	$10.50
Ginsberg, Joe	53BC	6	$ 6.00	$21.50	Haefner, Mickey	50B	183	$ 2.25	$ 9.00
Ginsberg, Joe	54B	52	$ 1.50	$ 4.50	Hall, Bob	55B	113	$ 1.50	$ 4.50
Glaviano, Tommy	51B	301	$12.00	$37.50	Hamner, Granny	50B	204	$ 2.25	$ 9.00
Goetz, Lawrence J.	55B	311	$ 3.00	$12.00	Hamner, Granny	51B	148	$ 4.00	$14.00
Goliat, Mike	50B	205	$ 2.25	$ 9.00	Hamner, Granny	52B	35	$ 3.25	$12.50
Goliat, Mike	51B	77	$ 4.00	$14.00	Hamner, Granny	53BC	60	$ 6.00	$21.50
Goodman, Billy	49B	39	$ 3.00	$12.00	Hamner, Granny	54B	47	$ 1.50	$ 4.50
Goodman, Billy	50B	99	$ 2.25	$ 9.00	Hamner, "Granville" Granny	55B	112	$ 1.50	$ 4.50
Goodman, Billy	51B	237	$ 4.00	$14.00	Hamner, Ralph	49B	212	$16.00	$65.00
Goodman, Billy	52B	81	$ 3.00	$10.50	Hansen, Andy	53BW	64	$10.00	$40.00

Player	Year	No.	VG	EX/MT
Harris, Bucky	51B	275	$11.00	$35.00
Harris, Bucky	52B	158	$ 3.75	$12.50
Harris, Bucky	53BW	46	$10.00	$27.50
Harris, Mickey	49B	151	$16.00	$65.00
Harris, Mickey	50B	160	$ 2.25	$ 9.00
Harris, Mickey	51B	311	$12.00	$37.50
Harris, Mickey	52B	135	$ 3.00	$10.50
Hartsfield, Roy	51B	277	$12.00	$37.50
Hartsfield, Roy	52B	28	$ 3.25	$12.50
Hartung, Clint	48B	37	$ 6.00	$17.50
Hartung, Clint	49B	154	$16.00	$65.00
Hartung, Clint	50B	118	$ 2.25	$ 9.00
Hartung, Clint	51B	234	$ 4.00	$14.00
Hatfield, Fred	52B	153	$ 3.00	$10.50
Hatfield, Fred	53BC	125	$ 8.50	$30.00
Hatfield, Fred	54B	119	$ 1.50	$ 4.50
Hatfield, Fred	55B	187	$ 1.50	$ 4.50
Hatten, Joe	49B	116	$ 1.60	$ 6.00
Hatten, Joe	50B	166	$ 2.25	$ 9.00
Hatten, Joe	51B	190	$ 4.00	$14.00
Hatten, Joe	52B	144	$ 3.00	$10.50
Hatton, Grady	49B	62	$ 2.25	$ 9.00
Hatton, Grady	50B	26	$ 6.50	$22.00
Hatton, Grady	51B	47	$ 4.00	$14.00
Hawes, Roy Lee	55B	268	$ 3.50	$12.00
Haynes, Joe	49B	191	$16.00	$65.00
Haynes, Joe	51B	240	$ 4.00	$14.00
Haynes, Joe	52B	103	$ 3.00	$10.50
Hearn, Jim	49B	190	$16.00	$65.00
Hearn, Jim	50B	208	$ 2.25	$ 9.00
Hearn, Jim	51B	61	$ 4.00	$14.00
Hearn, Jim	52B	49	$ 3.00	$10.50
Hearn, Jim	53BC	76	$ 6.00	$21.50
Hearn, Jim	55B	220	$ 1.50	$ 4.50
Heath, Jeff	49B	169	$16.00	$65.00
Hegan, Jim	50B	7	$ 6.50	$22.00
Hegan, Jim	51B	79	$ 4.00	$14.00
Hegan, Jim	52B	187	$ 3.00	$10.50
Hegan, Jim	53BC	102	$ 6.00	$21.50
Heintzelman, Ken	49B	108	$ 3.50	$12.00
Heintzelman, Ken	50B	85	$ 2.25	$ 9.00
Heintzelman, Ken	51B	147	$ 4.00	$14.00
Heintzleman, Ken	52B	148	$ 3.00	$10.50
Hemus, Solly	52B	212	$ 3.00	$10.50
Hemus, Solly	53BC	85	$ 6.00	$21.50
Hemus, Solly	54B	94	$ 1.50	$ 4.50
Hemus, Solly	55B	107	$ 1.50	$ 4.50
Henrich, Tommy	48B	19	$ 4.50	$11.00
Henrich, Tommy	49B	69	$ 6.50	$21.50
Henrich, Tommy	50B	10	$12.00	$40.00
Henrich, Tommy	51B	291	$16.00	$50.00
Henry, Bill	55B	264	$ 3.50	$12.00
Hermanski, Gene	49B	20	$ 3.50	$12.00
Hermanski, Gene	50B	113	$ 2.25	$ 9.00
Hermanski, Gene	51B	55	$ 4.00	$14.00
Hermanski, Gene	52B	136	$ 3.00	$10.50
Higbe, Kirby	49B	215	$16.00	$65.00
Higbe, Kirby	50B	200	$ 2.25	$ 9.00
Hiller, Frank	52B	114	$ 3.00	$10.50
Hitchcock, Billy	51B	191	$ 4.00	$14.00
Hitchcock, Billy	52B	89	$ 3.00	$10.50
Hoak, Don	55B	21	$ 1.75	$ 6.50
Hoderlein, Mel	54B	120	$ 1.50	$ 4.50
Hodges, Gil	49B	100	$30.00	$130.00
Hodges, Gil	50B	112	$19.00	$75.00
Hodges, Gil	51B	7	$19.00	$72.50
Hodges, Gil	52B	80	$14.00	$45.00
Hodges, Gil	53BC	92	$27.50	$105.00
Hodges, Gil	54B	138	$12.50	$50.00
Hodges, Gil	55B	158	$11.50	$40.00
Hoeft, Billy	53BW	18	$ 6.50	$21.50
Hoeft, Billy	54B	167	$ 1.50	$ 4.50
Hoffman, Bobby	49B	223	$16.00	$65.00
Holcombe, Ken	51B	267	$12.00	$37.50
Holmes, Tommy	49B	72	$ 4.25	$14.00
Holmes, Tommy	50B	110	$ 3.00	$12.00
Honochick, George "Jim"	55B	267	$ 8.00	$34.50
Hooper, Bob	51B	33	$ 4.00	$14.00
Hooper, Bob	52B	10	$ 3.25	$12.50
Hooper, Bob	54B	4	$ 1.50	$ 4.50
Hooper, Bob	55B	271	$ 3.50	$12.00
Hopp, Johnny	49B	207	$16.00	$65.00
Hopp, Johnny	50B	122	$ 2.25	$ 9.00
Hopp, Johnny	51B	146	$ 3.50	$12.00
Houtteman, Art	50B	42	$ 6.50	$22.00
Houtteman, Art	51B	45	$ 4.00	$14.00
Houtteman, Art	53BC	4	$ 6.00	$21.50
Houtteman, Art	54B	20	$ 1.50	$ 4.50
Houtteman, Art	55B	144	$ 1.50	$ 4.50
Howard, Elston	55B	68	$ 4.25	$14.00
Howell, Homer "Dixie"	51B	252	$ 4.00	$14.00
Howell, Homer 'Dixie'	52B	222	$ 3.75	$14.50
Howerton, Bill	50B	239	$ 2.25	$ 9.00
Howerton, Bill	51B	229	$ 4.00	$14.00
Howerton, Bill	52B	119	$ 3.00	$10.50
Hubbard, Cal	55B	315	$12.50	$40.00
Hudson, Sid	50B	17	$ 6.50	$22.00
Hudson, Sid	51B	169	$ 4.00	$14.00
Hudson, Sid	52B	123	$ 3.00	$10.50
Hudson, Sid	53BW	29	$ 6.50	$21.50
Hudson, Sid	54B	194	$ 1.50	$ 4.50
Hudson, Sid	55B	318	$ 3.50	$12.00
Hughes, Jim	55B	156	$ 1.50	$ 4.50
Hughson, Tex	49B	199	$16.00	$65.00
Hunter, Bill	54B	5	$ 1.50	$ 4.50
Hunter, Bill	55B	69	$ 1.50	$ 4.50
Hurley, Edwin H.	55B	260	$ 3.00	$12.00
Hutchinson, Fred	49B	196	$19.00	$85.00
Hutchinson, Fred	50B	151	$ 3.00	$12.00
Hutchinson, Fred	51B	141	$ 3.50	$12.00
Hutchinson, Fred	52B	3	$ 3.00	$10.50
Hutchinson, Fred	53BC	132	$ 7.50	$25.00
Irvin, Monte	51B	198	$12.50	$50.00
Irvin, Monte	52B	162	$ 9.00	$29.50
Irvin, Monte	53BC	51	$10.00	$35.00
Jackowski, William A.	55B	284	$ 3.00	$12.00
Jackson, Ransom "Randy"	52B	175	$ 3.00	$10.50
Jackson, Randy	53BW	12	$ 6.50	$21.50
Jackson, Randy	54B	189	$ 1.50	$ 4.50
Jackson, Randy	55B	87	$ 1.50	$ 4.50
Janowicz, Vic	54B	203	$ 1.50	$ 4.50
Janowicz, Vic	55B	114	$ 1.50	$ 4.50
Jansen, Larry	48B	23	$ 4.00	$14.00
Jansen, Larry	49B	202	$16.00	$65.00
Jansen, Larry	50B	66	$ 6.50	$22.00
Jansen, Larry	51B	162	$ 4.00	$14.00
Jansen, Larry	52B	90	$ 3.00	$10.50
Jansen, Larry	53BW	40	$ 6.50	$21.50
Jansen, Larry	54B	169	$ 1.75	$ 6.50
Jeffcoat, Hal	51B	211	$ 4.00	$14.00
Jeffcoat, Hal	52B	104	$ 3.00	$10.50
Jeffcoat, Hal	53BW	37	$ 6.50	$21.50
Jeffcoat, Hal	54B	205	$ 1.50	$ 4.50
Jeffcoat, Hal	55B	223	$ 1.50	$ 4.50
Jensen, Jackie	51B	254	$22.50	$95.00
Jensen, Jackie	52B	161	$ 5.25	$19.75
Jensen, Jackie	53BC	24	$ 6.00	$22.00
Jensen, Jackie	54B	2	$ 2.00	$ 7.00
Jethroe, Sam	50B	248	$ 3.00	$12.00
Jethroe, Sam	51B	242	$ 4.00	$14.00
Jethroe, Sam	52B	84	$ 3.00	$10.50
Jethroe, Sam	53BC	3	$ 6.00	$21.50
Johnson, Billy	48B	33	$ 4.00	$14.00
Johnson, Billy	49B	129	$ 3.00	$10.50
Johnson, Billy	50B	102	$ 2.25	$ 9.00
Johnson, Billy	51B	74	$ 3.50	$12.00
Johnson, Billy	52B	122	$ 3.00	$10.50
Johnson, Don	53BW	55	$ 6.50	$21.50
Johnson, Don	55B	101	$ 1.75	$ 6.50
Johnson, Earl	49B	231	$16.00	$65.00

BOWMAN

Player	Year	No.	VG	EX/MT	Player	Year	No.	VG	EX/MT
Johnson, Earl	50B	188	$ 2.25	$ 9.00	Kell, George	51B	46	$ 6.25	$25.00
Johnson, Earl	51B	321	$12.00	$37.50	Kell, George	52B	75	$ 9.50	$30.00
Johnson, Ernie	54B	144	$ 1.50	$ 4.50	Kell, George	53BC	61	$11.50	$35.00
Johnson, Ernie	55B	157	$ 1.00	$ 5.00	Kell, George	54B	50	$ 3.75	$14.50
Johnson, Ken	51B	293	$12.00	$37.50	Kell, George	55B	213	$ 3.75	$14.50
Jok, Stan	55B	251	$ 3.50	$12.00	Keller, Charlie	49B	209	$19.00	$85.00
Jolly, Dave	55B	71	$ 1.50	$ 4.50	Keller, Charlie	50B	211	$ 2.25	$ 9.00
Jones, Ray	52B	215	$ 3.00	$10.50	Keller, Charlie	51B	177	$ 3.50	$12.00
Jones, Sheldon	48B	34	$ 7.50	$28.00	Kellner, Alex	49B	222	$16.00	$65.00
Jones, Sheldon	49B	68	$ 2.25	$ 9.00	Kellner, Alex	50B	14	$ 6.50	$22.00
Jones, Sheldon	50B	83	$ 2.25	$ 9.00	Kellner, Alex	51B	57	$ 4.00	$14.00
Jones, Sheldon	51B	199	$ 4.00	$14.00	Kellner, Alex	52B	226	$ 3.75	$14.50
Jones, Vernal	50B	238	$ 2.25	$ 9.00	Kellner, Alex	53BC	107	$ 6.00	$21.50
Jones, Willie	49B	92	$ 3.50	$12.00	Kellner, Alex	54B	51	$ 1.50	$ 4.50
Jones, Willie	50B	67	$ 6.50	$22.00	Kellner, Alex	55B	53	$ 1.50	$ 4.50
Jones, Willie	51B	112	$ 4.00	$14.00	Keltner, Ken	49B	125	$ 3.00	$10.50
Jones, Willie	52B	20	$ 4.50	$17.50	Keltner, Ken	50B	186	$ 2.25	$ 9.00
Jones, Willie	53BC	133	$ 8.50	$30.00	Kemmerer, Russ	55B	222	$ 1.50	$ 4.50
Jones, Willie	54B	143	$ 1.50	$ 4.50	Kennedy, Bill	49B	105	$ 3.50	$12.00
Jones, Willie	55B	172	$ 1.50	$ 4.50	Kennedy, Bob	51B	296	$12.00	$37.50
Joost, Eddie	48B	15	$ 4.00	$14.00	Kennedy, Monte	49B	237	$16.00	$65.00
Joost, Eddie	49B	55	$ 2.25	$ 9.00	Kennedy, Monte	50B	175	$ 2.25	$ 9.00
Joost, Eddie	50B	103	$ 2.25	$ 9.00	Kennedy, Monte	51B	163	$ 4.00	$14.00
Joost, Eddie	51B	119	$ 4.00	$14.00	Kennedy, Monte	52B	213	$ 3.00	$10.50
Joost, Eddie	52B	26	$ 3.25	$12.50	Keriazakos, Gus	55B	14	$ 1.50	$ 4.50
Joost, Eddie	53BC	105	$ 6.00	$21.50	Kerr, Buddy	48B	20	$ 7.50	$28.00
Joost, Eddie	54B	35	$ 1.50	$ 4.50	Kerr, Buddy	49B	186	$16.00	$65.00
Joost, Eddie	55B	263	$ 3.50	$12.00	Kerr, Buddy	50B	55	$ 6.50	$22.00
Judson, Howie	50B	185	$ 2.25	$ 9.00	Kerr, John "Buddy"	51B	171	$ 4.00	$14.00
Judson, Howie	51B	123	$ 4.00	$14.00	Kinder, Ellis	50B	152	$ 2.25	$ 9.00
Judson, Howie	52B	149	$ 3.00	$10.50	Kinder, Ellis	51B	128	$ 4.00	$14.00
Judson, Howie	53BW	42	$ 6.50	$21.50	Kinder, Ellis	54B	98	$ 1.50	$ 4.50
Judson, Howie	55B	193	$ 1.50	$ 4.50	Kiner, Ralph	48B	3	$25.00	$95.00
Kaline, Al	55B	23	$19.00	$60.00	Kiner, Ralph	49B	29	$18.00	$55.00
Katt, Ray	54B	121	$ 1.50	$ 4.50	Kiner, Ralph	50B	33	$17.50	$55.00
Katt, Ray	55B	183	$ 1.50	$ 4.50	Kiner, Ralph	52B	11	$11.50	$45.00
Kazak, Eddie	50B	36	$ 6.50	$22.00	Kiner, Ralph	53BC	80	$21.00	$60.00
					Kiner, Ralph	54B	45	$ 8.75	$30.00
					Kiner, Ralph	55B	197	$ 7.50	$24.00
					King, Charles	55B	133	$ 1.50	$ 4.50
					King, Clyde	51B	299	$12.00	$37.50
					King, Clyde	52B	56	$ 3.00	$10.50
					Klaus, Bill	55B	150	$ 1.50	$ 4.50
					Klippstein, Johnny	51B	248	$ 4.00	$14.00
					Klippstein, Johnny	54B	29	$ 1.50	$ 4.50
					Klippstein, Johnny	55B	152	$ 1.50	$ 4.50
					Kluszewski, Ted	50B	62	$12.00	$45.00
					Kluszewski, Ted	51B	143	$ 5.75	$18.00
					Kluszewski, Ted	53BC	62	$10.00	$35.00
					Kokos, Dick	49B	31	$ 3.50	$12.00
					Kokos, Dick	50B	50	$ 6.50	$22.00
					Kokos, Dick	51B	68	$ 4.00	$14.00
					Kokos, Dick	54B	37	$ 1.50	$ 4.50
					Kolloway, Don	49B	28	$ 3.50	$12.00
					Kolloway, Don	50B	133	$ 2.25	$ 9.00
					Kolloway, Don	51B	105	$ 4.00	$14.00
					Kolloway, Don	52B	91	$ 3.00	$10.50
					Konstanty, Jim	50B	226	$ 4.25	$14.00
					Konstanty, Jim	51B	27	$ 3.50	$12.00
					Konstanty, Jim	53BW	58	$ 6.50	$22.00
					Konstanty, Jim	55B	231	$ 3.00	$12.00
					Koshorek, Clem	53BC	147	$ 8.50	$30.00
					Koslo, Dave "George"	48B	48	$10.00	$50.00
					Koslo, Dave	49B	34	$ 3.50	$12.00
					Koslo, Dave	50B	65	$ 6.50	$22.00
					Koslo, Dave	51B	90	$ 4.00	$14.00
					Koslo, Dave	52B	182	$ 3.00	$10.50
					Kozar, Al	49B	16	$ 3.50	$12.00
					Kozar, Al	50B	15	$ 6.50	$22.00
					Kramer, Jack	49B	53	$ 2.25	$ 9.00
					Kramer, Jack	50B	199	$ 2.25	$ 9.00
					Kramer, Jack	51B	200	$ 4.00	$14.00
					Kretlow, Lou	52B	221	$ 3.75	$14.50
					Kretlow, Lou	53BC	50	$ 6.00	$21.50
					Kretlow, Lou	54B	197	$ 1.50	$ 4.50

Player	Year	No.	VG	EX/MT
Kazak, Eddie	51B	85	$ 4.00	$14.00
Kell, Everett	52B	242	$ 3.75	$14.50
Kell, George	49B	26	$12.00	$42.50
Kell, George	50B	8	$13.00	$42.00

Player	Year	No.	VG	EX/MT	Player	Year	No.	VG	EX/MT
Kretlow, Lou	55B	108	$ 1.50	$ 4.50	Lockman, Carroll "Whitey"	48B	30	$ 9.00	$28.00
Kryhoski, Dick	49B	218	$16.00	$65.00	Lockman, Whitey	49B	2	$ 3.50	$12.00
Kryhoski, Dick	50B	242	$ 2.25	$ 9.00	Lockman, Whitey	50B	82	$ 2.25	$ 9.00
Kryhoski, Dick	52B	133	$ 3.00	$10.50	Lockman, Whitey	51B	37	$ 3.50	$12.00
Kryhoski, Dick	53BC	127	$ 8.50	$30.00	Lockman, Whitey	52B	38	$ 3.00	$10.50
Kryhoski, Dick	54B	117	$ 1.50	$ 4.50	Lockman, Whitey	53BC	128	$ 8.50	$30.00
Kuenn, Harvey	54B	23	$ 5.50	$20.00	Lockman, Whitey	54B	153	$ 1.75	$ 6.50
Kuenn (Kueen), Harvey	55B	132	$ 1.75	$ 7.00	Lockman, Whitey	55B	219	$ 1.50	$ 4.50
Kuzava, Bob	50B	5	$ 5.50	$20.00	Loes, Billy	52B	240	$ 6.50	$32.00
Kuzava, Bob	51B	97	$ 4.00	$14.00	Loes, Billy	53BC	14	$ 6.00	$21.50
Kuzava, Bob	52B	233	$ 3.75	$14.50	Loes, Billy	54B	42	$ 1.50	$ 4.50
Kuzava, Bob	53BW	33	$ 6.50	$21.50	Loes, Billy	55B	240	$ 2.25	$ 9.00
Kuzava, Bob	55B	215	$ 1.50	$ 4.50	Logan, Johnny	54B	80	$ 1.75	$ 6.50
La Palme, Paul	53BW	19	$ 6.50	$21.50	Logan, Johnny	55B	180	$ 1.50	$ 4.50
La Palme, Paul	54B	107	$ 1.50	$ 4.50	Lohrke, Jack	48B	16	$ 7.00	$27.00
La Palme, Paul	55B	61	$ 1.50	$ 4.50	Lohrke, Jack	49B	59	$ 2.25	$ 9.00
Labine, Clem	54B	106	$ 1.75	$ 6.50	Lohrke, Jack	51B	235	$ 4.00	$14.00
Lade, Doyle	49B	168	$16.00	$65.00	Lohrke, Jack	52B	251	$ 4.00	$16.50
Lade, Doyle	50B	196	$ 2.25	$ 9.00	Lohrke, Jack	53BW	47	$ 6.50	$21.50
Lade, Doyle	51B	139	$ 4.00	$14.00	Lollar, Sherman	50B	142	$ 4.25	$14.00
Lake, Eddie	49B	107	$ 3.50	$12.00	Lollar, Sherman	51B	100	$ 4.00	$14.00
Lake, Eddie	50B	240	$ 2.25	$ 9.00	Lollar, Sherman	52B	237	$ 4.00	$16.50
Lake, Eddie	51B	140	$ 4.00	$14.00	Lollar, Sherman	53BC	157	$ 8.50	$30.00
LaManno, Ray	49B	113	$ 3.00	$10.50	Lollar, Sherman	54B	182	$ 1.75	$ 6.50
Landrith, Hobie	54B	220	$ 1.50	$ 4.50	Lollar, Sherman	55B	174	$ 1.50	$ 4.50
Landrith, Hobie	55B	50	$ 1.50	$ 4.50	Lombardi, Vic	51B	204	$ 4.00	$14.00
Lanier, Max	50B	207	$ 2.25	$ 9.00	Lopat, Ed	49B	229	$32.00	$110.00
Lanier, Max	51B	230	$ 4.00	$14.00	Lopat, Ed	50B	215	$ 6.75	$18.00
Lanier, Max	52B	110	$ 3.00	$10.50	Lopat, Ed	51B	218	$ 5.50	$20.00
Larsen, Don	54B	101	$ 1.75	$ 7.50	Lopat, Ed	52B	17	$ 5.50	$19.50
Larsen, Don	55B	67	$ 3.50	$12.00	Lopata, Stan	49B	177	$16.00	$65.00
Lary, Frank	55B	154	$ 1.50	$ 4.50	Lopata, Stan	50B	206	$ 2.25	$ 9.00
Law, Vernon	51B	203	$ 3.50	$12.00	Lopata, Stan	51B	76	$ 4.00	$14.00
Law, Vernon	52B	71	$ 3.25	$12.50	Lopata, Stan	54B	207	$ 1.50	$ 4.50
Law, Vernon	54B	187	$ 1.75	$ 6.50	Lopata, Stan	55B	18	$ 1.50	$ 4.50
Law, Vernon	55B	199	$ 1.50	$ 4.50	Lopez, Al	51B	295	$14.00	$45.00
Lawrence, Brooks	55B	75	$ 1.50	$ 4.50	Lopez, Al	53BC	143	$14.00	$45.00
Lehman, Ken	55B	310	$ 3.50	$12.00	Lopez, Al	55B	308	$ 8.50	$30.00
Lehner, Paul	49B	131	$ 3.00	$10.50	Lown, Omar	52B	16	$ 3.25	$12.50
Lehner, Paul	50B	158	$ 2.25	$ 9.00	Lown, Omar "Turk"	53BC	154	$ 8.50	$30.00
Lehner, Paul	51B	8	$ 4.00	$14.00	Lown, Turk	54B	157	$ 1.50	$ 4.50
Lemon, Bob	49B	238	$55.00	$200.00	Lowrey, Harry	49B	22	$ 3.50	$12.00
Lemon, Bob	50B	40	$15.00	$48.00	Lowrey, Harry	50B	172	$ 2.25	$ 9.00
Lemon, Bob	51B	53	$11.00	$39.50	Lowrey, Harry "Peanuts"	51B	194	$ 4.00	$14.00
Lemon, Bob	52B	23	$11.00	$39.50	Lowrey, Peanuts	52B	102	$ 3.00	$10.50
Lemon, Bob	53BW	27	$25.00	$77.50	Luna, Memo	54B	222	$ 1.50	$ 4.50
Lemon, Bob	54B	196	$ 5.50	$17.75	Lund, Don	54B	87	$ 1.50	$ 4.50
Lemon, Bob	55B	191	$ 4.50	$14.00	Lupien, Ulysses	49B	141	$ 3.00	$10.50
Lemon, Jim	55B	262	$ 2.25	$ 9.00	MacDonald, Bill	51B	239	$ 4.00	$14.00
Lenhardt, Don	53BC	20	$ 6.00	$21.50	Maddern, Clarence	49B	152	$16.00	$65.00
Lenhardt, Don	54B	53	$ 1.75	$ 6.50	Maglie, Sal	51B	127	$ 4.25	$14.00
Leonard, Dutch	48B	24	$ 9.00	$30.00	Maglie, Sal	52B	66	$ 4.25	$14.00
Leonard, Dutch	49B	115	$ 3.00	$10.50	Maglie, Sal	53BC	96	$ 5.50	$20.00
Leonard, Dutch	50B	170	$ 2.25	$ 9.00	Maglie, Sal	54B	105	$ 1.75	$ 6.50
Leonard, Dutch	51B	102	$ 4.00	$14.00	Maglie, Sal	55B	95	$ 1.75	$ 6.50
Leonard, Dutch	52B	159	$ 3.00	$10.50	Majeski, Hank	49B	127	$ 3.00	$12.00
Leonard, Dutch	53BW	50	$ 6.50	$21.50	Majeski, Hank	50B	92	$ 2.25	$ 9.00
Leonard, Emil "Dutch"	55B	247	$ 3.50	$12.00	Majeski, Hank	51B	12	$ 4.00	$14.00
Lepcio, Ted	54B	162	$ 1.50	$ 4.50	Majeski, Hank	52B	58	$ 3.00	$10.50
Liddle, Don	55B	146	$ 1.50	$ 4.50	Majeski, Hank	55B	127	$ 1.50	$ 4.50
Limmer, Lou	55B	80	$ 1.50	$ 4.50	Malzone, Frank	55B	302	$ 2.25	$ 9.00
Lindell, Johnny	48B	11	$ 4.00	$14.00	Mantle, Mickey	51B	253	$950.00	$3750.00
Lindell, Johnny	49B	197	$16.00	$65.00	Mantle, Mickey	52B	101	$365.00	$1200.00
Lindell, Johnny	50B	209	$ 2.25	$ 9.00	Mantle, Mickey	53BC	44	$95.00	$285.00
Lindell, Johnny	54B	159	$ 1.50	$ 4.50	Mantle, Mickey	53BC	59	$400.00	$1200.00
Lint, Royce	55B	62	$ 1.50	$ 4.50	Mantle, Mickey	54B	65	$200.00	$580.00
Lipon, Johnny	51B	285	$12.00	$37.50	Mantle, Mickey	55B	202	$100.00	$330.00
Lipon, Johnny	52B	163	$ 3.00	$10.50	Mapes, Cliff	50B	218	$ 2.25	$ 9.00
Lipon, Johnny	53BC	123	$ 8.50	$30.00	Mapes, Cliff	51B	289	$12.00	$37.50
Littlefield, Dick	52B	209	$ 3.00	$10.50	Mapes, Cliff	52B	13	$ 3.25	$12.50
Littlefield, Dick	54B	213	$ 1.50	$ 4.50	Marchildon, Phil	49B	187	$16.00	$65.00
Littlefield, Dick	55B	200	$ 1.50	$ 4.50	Marion, Marty	48B	40	$ 8.50	$29.50
Litwhiler, Danny	49B	97	$ 3.50	$12.00	Marion, Marty	49B	54	$ 3.50	$13.00
Litwhiler, Danny	50B	198	$ 2.25	$ 9.00	Marion, Marty	50B	88	$ 3.00	$12.00
Litwhiler, Danny	51B	179	$ 4.00	$14.00	Marion, Marty	51B	34	$ 3.50	$12.00

Player	Year	No.	VG	EX/MT
Marion, Marty	52B	85	$ 3.25	$12.50
Marion, Marty	53BC	52	$ 6.00	$21.50
Marlowe, Dick	55B	91	$ 1.50	$ 4.50
Marrero, Conrado	51B	206	$ 4.00	$14.00
Marrero, Conrado	54B	200	$ 1.50	$ 4.50
Marshall, Willard	48B	13	$ 7.50	$32.00
Marshall, Willard	49B	48	$ 2.25	$ 9.00
Marshall, Willard	50B	73	$ 2.25	$ 9.00
Marshall, Willard	51B	98	$ 4.00	$14.00
Marshall, Willard	52B	97	$ 3.00	$10.50
Marshall, Willard	53BC	58	$ 6.00	$21.50
Marshall, Willard	54B	70	$ 1.50	$ 4.50
Marshall, Willard	55B	131	$ 1.50	$ 4.50
Martin, Babe	49B	167	$16.00	$65.00
Martin, Billy	53BC	118	$75.00	$195.00

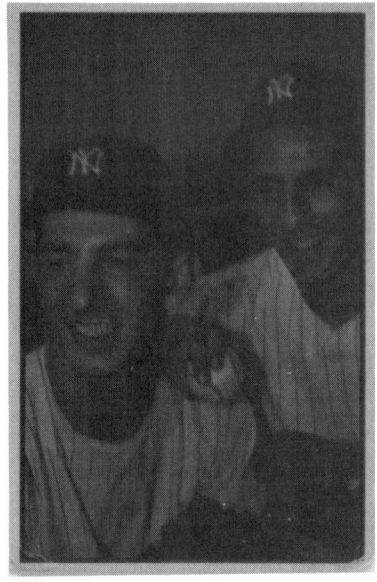

Player	Year	No.	VG	EX/MT
Martin, Billy	53BC	93	$72.50	$190.00
Martin, Billy	54B	145	$ 9.50	$40.00
Martin, Morris	53BW	53	$ 6.50	$21.50
Martin, Morris	54B	179	$ 1.50	$ 4.50
Masi, Phil	49B	153	$16.00	$65.00
Masi, Phil	50B	128	$ 2.25	$ 9.00
Masi, Phil	51B	160	$ 3.00	$ 8.00
Masterson, Walt	49B	157	$16.00	$65.00
Masterson, Walt	50B	153	$ 2.25	$ 9.00
Masterson, Walt	51B	307	$12.00	$37.50
Masterson, Walt	52B	205	$ 3.00	$10.50
Masterson, Walt	53BW	9	$ 6.50	$21.50
Mathews, Eddie	53BC	97	$30.00	$100.00
Mathews, Eddie	54B	64	$ 9.50	$32.00
Mathews, Eddie	55B	103	$ 6.00	$20.00
Mauch, Gene	51B	312	$10.00	$40.00
Maxwell, Charlie	55B	162	$ 1.50	$ 4.50
Mayo, Eddie	49B	75	$ 3.50	$12.00
Mayo, Jackie	49B	228	$16.00	$65.00
Mays, Willie	51B	305	$300.00	$1000.00
Mays, Willie	52B	218	$150.00	$500.00
Mays, Willie	54B	89	$60.00	$200.00
Mays, Willie	55B	184	$30.00	$110.00
McBride, Tom	49B	74	$ 3.50	$12.00
McCahan, Bill	48B	31	$ 3.00	$ 8.00
McCahan, Bill	49B	80	$ 3.50	$12.00

Player	Year	No.	VG	EX/MT
McCarthy, Johnny	49B	220	$16.00	$65.00
McCormick, Frank	49B	239	$18.00	$65.00
McCormick, Mike	49B	146	$16.00	$65.00
McCoskey, Barney	48B	25	$ 3.00	$ 8.00
McCosky, Barney	49B	203	$16.00	$65.00
McCosky, Barney	51B	84	$ 3.00	$ 8.00
McCullough, Clyde	49B	163	$16.00	$65.00
McCullough, Clyde	50B	124	$ 2.25	$ 9.00
McCullough, Clyde	51B	94	$ 3.00	$ 8.00
McCullough, Clyde	52B	99	$ 3.00	$10.50
McCullough, Clyde	55B	280	$ 3.50	$12.00
McDermott, Maurice	50B	97	$ 2.25	$ 9.00
McDermott, Maurice	51B	16	$ 3.00	$ 8.00
McDermott, "Maury"	52B	25	$ 3.25	$12.50
McDermott, Maury	53BC	35	$ 6.00	$21.50
McDermott, Maury	54B	56	$ 3.75	$15.00
McDermott, Maury	55B	165	$ 1.50	$ 4.50
McDonald, Jim	55B	77	$ 1.50	$ 4.50
McDougald, Gil	52B	33	$11.50	$40.00
McDougald, Gil	53BC	63	$10.00	$32.50
McDougald, Gil	54B	97	$ 2.75	$10.50
McDougald, Gil	55B	9	$ 3.50	$12.00
McKinley, W. F.	55B	226	$ 3.00	$12.00
McMillan, Roy	53BC	26	$ 6.00	$21.50
McMillan, Roy	54B	12	$ 1.50	$ 4.50
Mcmillan, Roy	52B	238	$ 4.00	$16.50
McQuinn, George	49B	232	$16.00	$65.00
Mele, Sam	49B	118	$ 3.00	$10.50
Mele, Sam	50B	52	$ 6.50	$22.00
Mele, Sam	51B	168	$ 3.00	$ 8.00
Mele, Sam	52B	15	$ 3.25	$12.50
Mele, Sam	54B	22	$ 1.50	$ 4.50
Mele, Sam	55B	147	$ 1.50	$ 4.50
Merriman, Lloyd	50B	173	$ 2.25	$ 9.00
Merriman, Lloyd	51B	72	$ 3.00	$ 8.00
Merriman, Lloyd	52B	78	$ 3.00	$10.50
Merriman, Lloyd	55B	135	$ 1.50	$ 4.50
Metkovich, George	51B	274	$ 9.50	$30.00
Metkovich, George	52B	108	$ 3.00	$10.50
Meyer, Billy	51B	272	$12.00	$37.50
Meyer, Billy	52B	155	$ 3.00	$10.50
Meyer, Russ	51B	75	$ 3.00	$ 8.00
Meyer, Russ	52B	220	$ 3.75	$14.50
Meyer, Russ	53BC	129	$ 8.50	$30.00
Meyer, Russ	54B	186	$ 1.50	$ 4.50
Meyer, Russ	55B	196	$ 1.50	$ 4.50
Michaels, Cass	49B	12	$ 3.50	$12.00
Michaels, Cass	50B	91	$ 2.25	$ 9.00
Michaels, Cass	51B	132	$ 3.00	$ 8.00
Michaels, Cass	52B	36	$ 3.25	$12.50
Michaels, Cass	53BC	130	$ 8.50	$30.00
Michaels, Cass	54B	150	$ 1.50	$ 4.50
Michaels, Cass	55B	85	$ 1.50	$ 4.50
Miggins, Larry	53BC	142	$ 8.50	$30.00
Miksis, Eddie	51B	117	$ 3.00	$ 8.00
Miksis, Eddie	52B	32	$ 3.25	$12.50
Miksis, Eddie	54B	61	$ 1.50	$ 4.50
Miksis, Eddie	55B	181	$ 1.50	$ 4.50
Miller, Bill	53BW	54	$ 6.50	$21.50
Miller, Bill	55B	245	$ 3.50	$12.00
Miller, Bob	50B	227	$ 2.25	$ 9.00
Miller, Bob	51B	220	$ 3.00	$ 8.00
Miller, Bob	55B	110	$ 1.50	$ 4.50
Miller, Stu	53BW	16	$ 6.50	$21.50
Miller, Stu	54B	158	$ 1.50	$ 4.50
Minner, Paul	52B	211	$ 3.00	$10.50
Minner, Paul	53BC	71	$ 6.00	$21.50
Minner, Paul	54B	13	$ 1.50	$ 4.50
Minoso, Orestes	52B	5	$ 9.00	$35.00
Minoso, Orestes "Minnie"	53BC	36	$ 5.50	$22.50
Minoso, Minnie	54B	38	$ 2.75	$ 9.50
Minoso, Minnie	55B	25	$ 1.75	$ 6.50
Miranda, Willie	55B	79	$ 1.50	$ 4.50
Mitchell, Dale	49B	43	$ 3.00	$12.00
Mitchell, Dale	50B	130	$ 3.00	$12.00

Player	Year	No.	VG	EX/MT	Player	Year	No.	VG	EX/MT
Mitchell, Dale	51B	5	$ 3.50	$12.00	Nixon, Willard	51B	270	$12.00	$37.50
Mitchell, Dale	52B	239	$ 3.75	$14.50	Nixon, Willard	53BW	2	$ 6.50	$22.00
Mitchell, Dale	53BC	119	$ 8.50	$30.00	Nixon, Willard	54B	114	$ 1.50	$ 4.50
Mitchell, Dale	54B	148	$ 1.50	$ 4.50	Nixon, Willard	55B	177	$ 1.50	$ 4.50
Mitchell, Dale	55B	314	$ 3.50	$12.00	Noble, Ray	51B	269	$12.00	$37.50
Mize, Johnny	48B	4	$20.00	$65.00	Noren, Irv	50B	247	$ 2.25	$ 9.00
Mize, Johnny	49B	85	$19.50	$60.00	Noren, Irv	51B	241	$ 4.00	$14.00
Mize, Johnny	50B	139	$17.00	$50.00	Noren, Irv	52B	63	$ 3.00	$10.50
Mize, Johnny	51B	50	$16.00	$50.00	Noren, Irv	53BW	45	$ 6.00	$24.50
Mize, Johnny	52B	145	$16.00	$50.00	Noren, Irv	55B	63	$ 1.75	$ 6.50
Mizell, Wilmer	53BW	15	$35.00	$100.00	Northey, Ron	49B	79	$ 3.50	$12.00
Mizell, Wilmer	53BW	22	$ 6.50	$21.50	Northey, Ron	50B	81	$ 2.25	$ 9.00
Moore, Terry	49B	174	$16.00	$65.00	Northey, Ron	51B	70	$ 4.00	$14.00
Morgan, Bobby	50B	222	$ 2.25	$ 9.00	Nuxhall, Joe	53BC	90	$ 6.00	$24.50
Morgan, Bobby	53BC	135	$ 8.50	$30.00	Nuxhall, Joe	54B	76	$ 1.75	$ 6.50
Morgan, Bobby	55B	81	$ 1.50	$ 4.50	Nuxhall, Joe	55B	194	$ 1.75	$ 6.50
Morgan, Tom	52B	109	$ 3.00	$10.50	O'Connell, Danny	51B	93	$ 4.00	$14.00
Morgan, Tom	55B	100	$ 1.50	$ 4.50	O'Connell, Danny	54B	160	$ 1.50	$ 4.50
Moryn, Walt	55B	261	$ 3.50	$12.00	O'Connell, Danny	55B	44	$ 1.50	$ 4.50
Moses, Wally	51B	261	$ 9.00	$25.00	O'Neill, Steve	51B	201	$ 4.00	$14.00
Moses, Wally	53BC	95	$ 6.00	$21.50	Ostermueller, Fritz	49B	227	$16.00	$65.00
Moses, Wally	55B	294	$ 3.50	$12.00	Overmire, Frank	51B	280	$12.00	$37.50
Moss, John "Lester"	50B	251	$ 2.25	$ 9.00	Owen, Mickey	50B	78	$ 2.25	$ 9.00
Moss, Les	51B	210	$ 3.00	$ 8.00	Owen, Mickey	51B	174	$ 4.00	$14.00
Moss, Les	54B	181	$ 1.50	$ 4.50	Pafko, Andy	49B	63	$ 2.25	$ 9.00
Mossi, Don	55B	259	$ 2.25	$ 9.00	Pafko, Andy	50B	60	$ 6.50	$22.00
Moulder, Glen	49B	159	$16.00	$65.00	Pafko, Andy	51B	103	$ 4.00	$14.00
Mrozinski, Ron	55B	287	$ 3.50	$12.00	Pafko, Andy	52B	204	$ 3.25	$12.50
Mueller, Don	50B	221	$ 2.25	$ 9.00	Pafko, Andy	53BW	57	$ 5.50	$27.50
Mueller, Don	51B	268	$12.00	$37.50	Pafko, Andy	54B	112	$ 1.50	$ 4.50
Mueller, Don	52B	18	$ 3.25	$12.50	Pafko, Andy	55B	12	$ 1.50	$ 4.50
Mueller, Don	53BC	74	$ 6.00	$21.50	Page, Joe	48B	29	$ 9.00	$30.00
Mueller, Don	54B	73	$ 1.50	$ 4.50	Page, Joe	49B	82	$ 4.25	$14.00
Mueller, Ray	51B	313	$12.00	$37.50	Page, Joe	50B	12	$ 9.50	$38.00
Mullin, Pat	49B	56	$ 2.25	$ 9.00	Page, Joe	51B	217	$ 3.50	$12.00
Mullin, Pat	50B	135	$ 2.25	$ 9.00	Paige, Satchell	49B	224	$300.00	$950.00
Mullin, Pat	51B	106	$ 3.00	$ 8.00	Palica, Erv	51B	189	$ 4.00	$14.00
Mullin, Pat	52B	183	$ 3.00	$10.50	Palica, Erv	55B	195	$ 1.75	$ 6.50
Mullin, Pat	53BW	4	$ 6.50	$21.50	Papai, Al	50B	245	$ 2.25	$ 9.00
Mullin, Pat	54B	151	$ 1.50	$ 4.50	Paparella, J. A.	55B	235	$ 3.00	$12.00
Muncrief, Bob	49B	221	$16.00	$65.00	Parnell, Mel	50B	1	$20.00	$195.00
Munger, George	49B	40	$ 2.25	$ 9.00	Parnell, Mel	52B	241	$ 3.75	$14.50
Munger, George	50B	89	$ 2.25	$ 9.00	Parnell, Mel	53BC	66	$ 6.00	$21.50
Munger, George "Red"	51B	11	$ 3.00	$ 8.00	Partee, Roy	49B	149	$16.00	$65.00
Munger, Red	52B	243	$ 3.75	$14.50	Peck, Hall	49B	182	$16.00	$65.00
Murray, Ray	52B	118	$ 3.00	$10.50	Pellagrini, Eddie	49B	172	$16.00	$65.00
Murray, Ray	53BW	6	$ 6.50	$21.50	Pellagrini, Eddie	51B	292	$12.00	$37.50
Murray, Ray	54B	83	$ 1.50	$ 4.50	Perkowski, Harry	52B	202	$ 3.00	$10.50
Murtaugh, Danny	49B	124	$ 4.25	$14.00	Perkowski, Harry	53BC	87	$ 6.00	$21.50
Murtaugh, Danny	50B	203	$ 3.00	$12.00	Perkowski, Harry	54B	44	$ 1.50	$ 4.50
Murtaugh, Danny	51B	273	$10.00	$35.00	Pesky, Johnny	49B	86	$ 3.50	$12.00
Musial, Stan	48B	36	$120.00	$500.00	Pesky, Johnny	50B	137	$ 3.00	$12.00
Musial, Stan	49B	24	$95.00	$350.00	Pesky, Johnny	51B	15	$ 3.50	$12.00
Musial, Stan	52B	196	$100.00	$355.00	Pesky, Johnny	52B	45	$ 3.00	$10.50
Musial, Stan	53BC	32	$95.00	$350.00	Pesky, Johnny	53BC	134	$ 7.50	$25.00
Napp, Larry	55B	250	$ 3.00	$12.00	Pesky, Johnny	54B	135	$ 1.75	$ 6.50
Naragon, Hal	55B	129	$ 1.50	$ 4.50	Pesky, Johnny	55B	241	$ 3.50	$12.00
Narleski, Ray	55B	96	$ 1.50	$ 4.50	Peterson, Kent	51B	215	$ 4.00	$14.00
Neal, Charles	55B	278	$ 3.00	$12.00	Philley, Dave	49B	44	$ 2.25	$ 9.00
Newcombe, Don	50B	23	$22.00	$65.00	Philley, Dave	50B	127	$ 2.25	$ 9.00
Newcombe, Don	51B	6	$ 6.75	$25.00	Philley, Dave	51B	297	$12.00	$37.50
Newcombe, Don	52B	128	$ 5.25	$17.75	Philley, Dave	54B	163	$ 3.50	$12.00
Newcombe, Don	54B	154	$ 4.75	$17.50	Phillips, John M.	55B	228	$ 3.50	$12.00
Newcombe, Don	55B	143	$ 2.50	$12.00	Pierce, Billy	51B	196	$ 3.50	$13.00
Niarhos, Gus	49B	181	$16.00	$65.00	Pierce, Billy	52B	54	$ 3.00	$10.50
Niarhos, Gus	50B	154	$ 2.25	$ 9.00	Pierce, Billy	53BC	73	$ 6.00	$21.50
Niarhos, Gus	51B	124	$ 3.00	$ 8.00	Pierce, Billy	54B	102	$ 1.75	$ 6.50
Niarhos, Gus	52B	129	$ 3.00	$10.50	Pierce, Billy	55B	214	$ 1.75	$ 6.25
Nichols, Chet	52B	120	$ 3.00	$10.50	Pieretti, Marino	49B	217	$16.00	$65.00
Nichols, Chet	55B	72	$ 1.50	$ 4.50	Pieretti, Marino	50B	181	$ 2.25	$ 9.00
Nicholson, Bill	49B	76	$ 3.50	$12.00	Piersall, Jim	51B	306	$11.75	$45.00
Nicholson, Bill	50B	228	$ 2.25	$ 9.00	Piersall, Jim	52B	189	$ 3.00	$10.50
Nicholson, Bill	51B	113	$ 3.00	$ 8.00	Piersall, Jim	53BW	36	$ 9.00	$35.00
Nicholson, Bill	53BW	14	$ 6.50	$21.50	Piersall, Jim	54B	66	$30.00	$95.00
Nieman, Bob	55B	145	$ 1.50	$ 4.50	Piersall, Jim	54B	210	$ 2.25	$ 9.00

Player	Year	No.	VG	EX/MT	Player	Year	No.	VG	EX/MT
Piersall, Jim	55B	16	$ 1.75	$ 6.50	Rice, Del	53BC	53	$ 6.00	$21.50
Pillette, Duane	51B	316	$12.00	$37.50	Rice, Del	54B	30	$ 1.50	$ 4.50
Pillette, Duane	53BW	59	$ 6.50	$21.50	Rice, Del	55B	106	$ 1.50	$ 4.50
Pillette, Duane	54B	133	$ 1.50	$ 4.50	Rice, Hal	51B	300	$12.00	$37.50
Pillette, Duane	55B	244	$ 3.50	$12.00	Rice, Hal	54B	219	$ 1.50	$ 4.50
Pinelli, R. A. "Babe"	55B	307	$ 3.00	$12.00	Rice, Hal	55B	52	$ 1.50	$ 4.50
Platt, Mizell	49B	89	$ 3.50	$12.00	Richards, Paul	51B	195	$ 3.50	$13.00
Poat, Ray	48B	42	$ 6.00	$17.50	Richards, Paul	52B	93	$ 3.25	$12.50
Podbielan, Clarence "Bud"	53BW	21	$ 6.50	$21.50	Richards, Paul	53BC	39	$ 6.00	$21.50
Podres, John	55B	97	$ 1.75	$ 6.50	Richards, Paul	55B	225	$ 2.25	$ 9.00
Poholsky, Tom	55B	76	$ 1.50	$ 4.50	Richmond, Don	51B	264	$12.00	$37.50
Pollet, Howie	49B	95	$ 3.50	$12.00	Ridzik, Steve	53BW	48	$ 6.50	$21.50
Pollet, Howie	50B	72	$ 6.50	$22.00	Ridzik, Steve	54B	223	$ 1.50	$ 4.50
Pollet, Howie	51B	263	$12.00	$37.50	Ridzik, Steve	55B	111	$ 1.50	$ 4.50
Pollet, Howie	52B	83	$ 3.00	$10.50	Rigney, Bill	48B	32	$ 4.00	$14.00
Pope, Dave	55B	198	$ 1.50	$ 4.50	Rigney, Bill	49B	170	$16.00	$65.00
Porterfield, Bob	49B	3	$ 3.50	$12.00	Rigney, Bill	50B	117	$ 2.25	$ 9.00
Porterfield, Bob	50B	216	$ 2.25	$ 9.00					
Porterfield, Bob	52B	194	$ 3.00	$10.50					
Porterfield, Bob	53BC	22	$ 6.00	$21.50					
Porterfield, Bob	54B	24	$ 1.50	$ 4.50					
Porterfield, Bob	55B	104	$ 1.50	$ 4.50					
Post, Wally	55B	32	$ 1.00	$ 4.50					
Pramesa, Johnny	51B	324	$19.00	$95.00					
Pramesa, Johnny	52B	247	$ 3.75	$14.50					
Presko, Joe	52B	62	$ 3.00	$10.50					
Presko, Joe	54B	190	$ 1.50	$ 4.50					
Priddy, Jerry	49B	4	$ 3.50	$12.00					
Priddy, Jerry (Gerry)	50B	212	$ 2.25	$ 9.00					
Priddy, Jerry	51B	71	$ 4.00	$14.00					
Priddy, Jerry	52B	139	$ 3.00	$10.50					
Queen, Mel	51B	309	$12.00	$37.50					
Queen, Mel	52B	171	$ 3.00	$10.50					
Quinn, Frank	51B	276	$12.00	$37.50					
Raffensberger, Ken	49B	176	$16.00	$65.00					
Raffensberger, Ken	51B	48	$ 4.00	$14.00					
Raffensberger, Ken	52B	55	$ 3.00	$10.50					
Raffensberger, Ken	53BC	106	$ 6.00	$21.50					
Raffensberger, Ken	54B	92	$ 1.50	$ 4.50					
Ramazotti, Bob	51B	247	$ 4.00	$14.00					
Ramazotti, Bob	53BW	41	$ 6.50	$21.50					
Ramsdell, Willard	51B	251	$ 4.00	$14.00					
Ramsdell, Willard	52B	22	$ 3.25	$12.50					
Raschi, Vic	49B	35	$ 6.50	$21.50					
Raschi, Vic	50B	100	$ 6.50	$21.50					
Raschi, Vic	51B	25	$ 3.75	$15.00					
Raschi, Vic	52B	37	$ 4.25	$14.00					
Raschi, Vic	53BC	27	$ 6.00	$21.50					
Raschi, Vic	54B	33	$ 1.75	$ 7.50					
Raschi, Vic	55B	185	$ 1.75	$ 6.50					
Reese, Harold "Pee Wee"	49B	36	$35.00	$120.00	Rigney, Bill	51B	125	$ 4.00	$14.00
Reese, Pee Wee	50B	21	$45.00	$130.00	Rigney, Bill	53BW	3	$ 6.50	$22.00
Reese, Pee Wee	51B	80	$24.00	$100.00	Rizzuto, Phil	48B	8	$45.00	$160.00
Reese, Pee Wee	52B	8	$35.00	$100.00	Rizzuto, Phil	49B	98	$20.00	$80.00
Reese, Pee Wee	53BC	33	$65.00	$190.00	Rizzuto, Phil	50B	11	$22.50	$85.00
Reese, Pee Wee	54B	58	$15.00	$60.00	Rizzuto, Phil	51B	26	$21.00	$75.00
Reese, Pee Wee	55B	37	$14.00	$52.00	Rizzuto, Phil	52B	52	$21.00	$75.00
Regalado, Rudy	55B	142	$ 1.50	$ 4.50	Rizzuto, Phil	53BC	93	$72.50	$190.00
Reiser, Pete	48B	7	$ 7.00	$32.00	Rizzuto, Phil	53BC	9	$23.00	$80.00
Reiser, Pete	49B	185	$22.50	$85.00	Rizzuto, Phil	54B	1	$16.00	$100.00
Reiser, Pete	50B	193	$ 3.00	$12.00	Rizzuto, Phil	55B	10	$26.00	$70.00
Reiser, Pete	51B	238	$ 3.50	$12.00	Roberts, Robin	49B	46	$35.00	$120.00
Repulski, Rip	54B	46	$ 1.50	$ 4.50	Roberts, Robin	50B	32	$30.00	$85.00
Repulski, Rip	55B	205	$ 1.50	$ 4.50	Roberts, Robin	51B	3	$14.50	$50.00
Restelli, Dino	50B	123	$ 2.25	$ 9.00	Roberts, Robin	52B	4	$12.50	$39.00
Reynolds, Allie	48B	14	$ 7.00	$25.00	Roberts, Robin	53BC	65	$14.50	$50.00
Reynolds, Allie	49B	114	$ 6.00	$22.00	Roberts, Robin	54B	95	$ 7.50	$18.00
Reynolds, Allie	50B	138	$ 6.00	$22.00	Roberts, Robin	55B	171	$ 7.00	$18.00
Reynolds, Allie	51B	109	$ 4.00	$16.00	Robertson, Al	54B	211	$ 1.50	$ 4.50
Reynolds, Allie	53BC	68	$ 7.00	$27.50	Robertson, Jim	55B	5	$ 1.50	$ 4.50
Reynolds, Allie	54B	113	$ 3.00	$ 9.00	Robertson, Sherry	50B	161	$ 2.25	$ 9.00
Reynolds, Allie	55B	201	$ 3.00	$ 9.00	Robertson, Sherry	51B	95	$ 4.00	$14.00
Rice, Del	50B	125	$ 2.25	$ 9.00	Robinson, Aaron	49B	133	$ 3.00	$10.50
Rice, Del	51B	156	$ 4.00	$14.00	Robinson, Aaron	50B	95	$ 2.25	$ 9.00
Rice, Del	52B	107	$ 3.00	$10.50					

BILL RIGNEY

Player	Year	No.	VG	EX/MT	Player	Year	No.	VG	EX/MT
Robinson, Aaron	51B	142	$ 4.00	$14.00	Scheffing, Bob	50B	168	$ 2.25	$ 9.00
Robinson, Eddie	50B	18	$ 6.50	$22.00	Scheib, Carl	49B	25	$ 3.50	$12.00
Robinson, Eddie	51B	88	$ 4.00	$14.00	Scheib, Carl	50B	213	$ 2.25	$ 9.00
Robinson, Eddie	52B	77	$ 3.00	$10.50	Scheib, Carl	51B	83	$ 4.00	$14.00
Robinson, Eddie	53BW	20	$ 6.50	$21.50	Scheib, Carl	52B	46	$ 3.00	$10.50
Robinson, Eddie	54B	193	$ 1.75	$ 6.50	Scheib, Carl	53BC	150	$ 8.50	$30.00
Robinson, Eddie	55B	153	$ 1.50	$ 4.50	Scheib, Carl	54B	67	$ 1.50	$ 4.50
Robinson, Jackie	49B	50	$180.00	$555.00	Schmees, George	52B	245	$ 3.75	$14.50
Robinson, Jackie	50B	22	$150.00	$475.00	Schmitz, Johnny	49B	52	$ 2.25	$ 9.00
Rodriquez, Hector	53BC	98	$ 6.00	$21.50	Schmitz, Johnny	50B	24	$ 6.50	$22.00
Roe, Elwin "Preacher"	49B	162	$30.00	$100.00	Schmitz, Johnny	51B	69	$ 4.00	$14.00
Roe, Preacher	50B	167	$ 7.50	$28.50	Schmitz, Johnny	52B	224	$ 3.75	$14.50
Roe, Preacher	51B	118	$ 7.50	$28.00	Schmitz, Johnny	55B	105	$ 1.50	$ 4.50
Roe, Preacher	52B	168	$ 5.50	$19.00	Schoendienst, Al "Red"	48B	38	$15.00	$48.00
Roe, Preacher	53BW	26	$12.00	$45.00	Schoendienst, Red	49B	111	$12.75	$42.50
Roe, Preacher	54B	218	$ 3.25	$12.00	Schoendienst, Red	50B	71	$12.50	$40.00
Roe, Preacher	55B	216	$ 1.75	$ 6.25	Schoendienst, Red	51B	10	$12.50	$40.00
Rogovin, Saul	52B	165	$ 3.00	$10.50	Schoendienst, Red	52B	30	$ 9.00	$30.00
Rogovin, Saul	53BC	75	$ 6.00	$21.50	Schoendienst, Red	53BC	101	$11.00	$37.50
Rogovin, Saul	54B	140	$ 1.75	$ 6.50	Schoendienst, Red	54B	110	$ 6.00	$17.50
Rojek, Stan	49B	135	$ 3.00	$10.50	Schoendienst, Red	55B	29	$ 6.00	$17.50
Rojek, Stan	50B	86	$ 2.25	$ 9.00	Schroll, Albert B.	55B	319	$ 3.50	$12.00
Rojek, Stan	51B	166	$ 4.00	$14.00	Schultz, Bob	54B	59	$ 1.50	$ 4.50
Rojek, Stan	52B	137	$ 3.00	$10.50	Secory, Frank E.	55B	286	$ 3.00	$12.00
Rolfe, Red	51B	319	$10.00	$35.00	Seminick, Andy	49B	30	$ 3.50	$12.00
Rommel, Edwin A.	55B	239	$ 3.00	$12.00	Seminick, Andy	50B	121	$ 2.25	$ 9.00
Rosar, Buddy	48B	10	$ 4.00	$14.00	Seminick, Andy	51B	51	$ 4.00	$14.00
Rosar, Buddy "Warren"	49B	138	$ 3.00	$10.50	Seminick, Andy	53BW	7	$ 6.50	$21.50
Rosar, Warren	50B	136	$ 2.25	$ 9.00	Seminick, Andy	54B	172	$ 1.50	$ 4.50
Rosar, Warren	51B	236	$ 4.00	$14.00	Seminick, Andy	55B	93	$ 1.50	$ 4.50
Rosen, Al "Flip"	50B	232	$10.00	$39.00	Serena, Bill	50B	230	$ 2.25	$ 9.00
Rosen, Al "Flip"	51B	187	$ 6.50	$20.00	Serena, Bill	51B	246	$ 4.00	$14.00
Rosen, Al "Flip"	52B	151	$ 5.25	$17.75	Serena, Bill	53BC	122	$ 8.50	$30.00
Rosen, Al "Flip"	53BC	8	$12.50	$35.00	Serena, Bill	54B	93	$ 1.50	$ 4.50
Rotblatt, Marv	51B	303	$12.00	$37.50	Serena, Bill	55B	233	$ 3.50	$12.00
Rowe, Schoolboy	49B	216	$15.00	$65.00	Sewell, Luke	51B	322	$ 9.50	$30.00
Roy, Norman	51B	278	$12.00	$37.50	Sewell, Luke	52B	94	$ 3.00	$10.50
Runge, Ed	55B	277	$ 3.00	$12.00	Sewell, Rip	49B	234	$16.00	$65.00
Runnels, Pete	53BC	139	$ 8.50	$30.00	Shantz, Billy	55B	139	$ 1.75	$ 6.50
Runnels, Pete	55B	255	$ 2.25	$ 9.00	Shantz, Billy "Wilmer"	55B	175	$ 1.50	$ 4.50
Rush, Bob	50B	61	$ 6.50	$22.00	Shantz, Bobby	50B	234	$ 4.25	$14.00
Rush, Bob	51B	212	$ 4.00	$14.00	Shantz (Schantz), Bobby	51B	227	$ 3.50	$13.00
Rush, Bob	53BC	110	$ 6.00	$21.50	Shantz, Bobby	53BC	11	$ 3.75	$14.75
Rush, Bob	54B	77	$ 1.50	$ 4.50	Shantz, Bobby	54B	19	$ 1.75	$ 6.50
Rush, Bob	55B	182	$ 1.50	$ 4.50	Shantz, Bobby	55B	139	$ 1.75	$ 6.50
Russell, Jim	49B	235	$16.00	$65.00	Shantz, Bobby	55B	140	$ 1.75	$ 6.50
Russell, Jimmy	50B	223	$ 2.25	$ 9.00	Shea, Frank	48B	26	$ 9.00	$29.00
Ryan, Connie	51B	216	$ 4.00	$14.00	Shea, Frank	49B	49	$ 2.25	$ 9.00
Ryan, Connie	52B	164	$ 3.00	$10.50	Shea, Frank	50B	155	$ 2.75	$11.00
Ryan, Connie	53BC	131	$ 8.50	$30.00	Shea, Frank	52B	230	$ 3.75	$14.50
Saffell, Tom	51B	130	$ 4.00	$14.00	Shea, Frank	53BC	141	$ 8.50	$30.00
Sain, Johnny	48B	12	$ 9.00	$35.00	Shea, Frank	54B	104	$ 1.50	$ 4.50
Sain, Johnny	49B	47	$ 5.50	$17.00	Shea, Frank	55B	207	$ 1.50	$ 4.50
Sain, Johnny	51B	314	$14.00	$42.00	Shuba, George	53BC	145	$ 8.50	$30.00
Sain, Johnny	53BW	25	$14.00	$45.00	Shuba, George	54B	202	$ 1.75	$ 6.50
Salkeld, Bill	49B	88	$ 3.50	$12.00	Shuba, George	55B	66	$ 1.75	$ 6.50
Salkeld, Bill	50B	237	$ 2.25	$ 9.00	Sievers, Roy	50B	16	$ 9.00	$36.00
Sanford, Fred	49B	236	$16.00	$65.00	Sievers, Roy	51B	67	$ 3.50	$12.00
Sanford, Fred	50B	156	$ 2.75	$11.00	Silvera, Charlie	52B	197	$ 3.25	$12.50
Sanford, Fred	51B	145	$ 4.00	$14.00	Silvestri, Ken	51B	256	$12.00	$37.50
Sarni, Bill	55B	30	$ 1.50	$ 4.50	Silvestri, Ken	52B	200	$ 3.00	$10.50
Sauer, Hank	48B	45	$ 4.50	$15.00	Simmons, Curt	49B	14	$ 3.00	$15.00
Sauer, Hank	49B	5	$ 2.25	$ 9.00	Simmons, Curt	50B	68	$ 6.50	$22.00
Sauer, Hank	50B	25	$ 7.00	$32.00	Simmons, Curt	51B	111	$ 3.50	$13.00
Sauer, Hank	51B	22	$ 3.50	$12.00	Simmons, Curt	52B	184	$ 3.25	$12.50
Sauer, Hank	53BC	50	$ 6.00	$21.50	Simmons, Curt	53BC	64	$ 6.00	$21.50
Sauer, Hank	53BC	48	$ 6.00	$21.50	Simmons, Curt	54B	79	$ 1.75	$ 6.50
Savage, Bob	49B	204	$16.00	$65.00	Simmons, Curt	55B	64	$ 1.75	$ 6.50
Sawyer, Eddie	50B	225	$ 2.25	$ 9.00	Simpson, Harry	52B	223	$ 3.75	$14.50
Sawyer, Eddie	51B	184	$ 4.00	$14.00	Simpson, Harry	53BC	86	$ 6.00	$21.50
Scarborough, Ray	49B	140	$ 3.00	$10.50	Singleton, Bert	49B	147	$16.00	$65.00
Scarborough, Rae (Ray)	50B	108	$ 2.25	$ 9.00	Sisler, Dick	49B	205	$16.00	$65.00
Scarborough, Ray	51B	39	$ 4.00	$14.00	Sisler, Dick	50B	119	$ 2.25	$ 9.00
Scarborough, Ray	52B	140	$ 3.00	$10.50	Sisler, Dick	51B	52	$ 4.00	$14.00
Scheffing, Bob	49B	83	$ 3.50	$12.00	Sisler, Dick	52B	127	$ 3.00	$10.50

BOWMAN

Player	Year	No.	VG	EX/MT	Player	Year	No.	VG	EX/MT
Sisler, Dick	53BW	10	$ 6.50	$21.50	Spahn, Warren	50B	19	$35.00	$130.00
Sisti, Sibby	49B	201	$16.00	$65.00	Spahn, Warren	51B	134	$22.00	$85.00
Sisti, Sibby	50B	164	$ 2.25	$ 9.00	Spahn, Warren	52B	156	$20.00	$80.00
Sisti, Sibby	51B	170	$ 4.00	$14.00	Spahn, Warren	53BC	99	$35.00	$125.00
Sisti, Sibby	52B	100	$ 3.00	$10.50	Spence, Stan	49B	102	$ 3.50	$12.00
Skowron, Bill	55B	160	$ 1.00	$ 7.00	Spencer, Daryl	54B	185	$ 1.50	$ 4.50
Slaughter, Enos	48B	17	$18.00	$60.00	St. Clair, Ebba	53BW	34	$ 6.50	$21.50
Slaughter, Enos	49B	65	$17.50	$58.00	St. Claire, Ebba	52B	172	$ 3.00	$10.50
Slaughter, Enos	50B	35	$17.00	$55.00	St. Claire, Ebba	54B	128	$ 1.50	$ 4.50
					Staley, Gerry	51B	121	$ 4.00	$14.00
					Staley, Gerry	52B	50	$ 3.00	$10.50
					Staley, Gerry	53BC	17	$ 6.00	$21.50
					Staley, Gerry	54B	14	$ 1.50	$ 4.50
					Staley, Gerry	55B	155	$ 1.50	$ 4.50
					Stallcup, Virgil	49B	81	$ 3.50	$12.00
					Stallcup, Virgil "Red"	50B	116	$ 2.25	$ 9.00
					Stallcup, Virgil	51B	108	$ 4.00	$14.00
					Stallcup, Virgil 'Red'	52B	6	$ 3.25	$12.50
					Stanky, Ed	49B	104	$ 4.25	$14.00
					Stanky, Eddie	50B	29	$ 6.00	$24.50
					Stanky, Ed	51B	13	$ 3.50	$12.00
					Stanky, Eddie	52B	160	$ 3.25	$12.50
					Stanky, Eddie	53BC	49	$ 6.00	$21.50
					Stanky, Eddie	55B	238	$ 3.50	$12.00
					Starr, Dick	50B	191	$ 2.25	$ 9.00
					Starr, Dick	51B	137	$ 4.00	$14.00
					Stengel, Casey	50B	217	$25.00	$100.00
					Stengel, Casey	51B	181	$22.00	$80.00
					Stengel, Casey	52B	217	$25.00	$100.00
					Stengel, Casey	53BW	39	$80.00	$240.00
					Stephens, Vern	49B	71	$ 2.25	$ 9.00
					Stephens, Vern	50B	2	$ 6.50	$22.00
					Stephens, Vern	51B	92	$ 4.00	$14.00
					Stephens, Vern	52B	9	$ 3.25	$12.50
					Stephens, Vern	55B	109	$ 1.50	$ 4.50
					Stevens, Ed	49B	93	$ 3.50	$12.00
					Stevens, John W.	55B	258	$ 3.00	$12.00
					Stewart, Eddie	49B	173	$16.00	$65.00
					Stewart, Eddie	50B	143	$ 2.25	$ 9.00
					Stewart, Eddie	51B	159	$ 4.00	$14.00
					Stewart, Eddie	52B	185	$ 3.00	$10.50
					Stirnweiss, George	48B	35	$ 4.00	$14.00
					Stirnweiss, George "Snuffy"	49B	165	$16.00	$65.00
					Stirnweiss, George "Snuffy"	50B	249	$ 2.25	$ 9.00
Slaughter, Enos	51B	58	$12.00	$35.00	Stirnweiss, Snuffy	51B	21	$ 4.00	$14.00
Slaughter, Enos	52B	232	$15.00	$45.00	Strickland, George	52B	207	$ 3.00	$10.50
Slaughter, Enos	53BC	81	$15.00	$45.00	Strickland, George	54B	36	$ 1.50	$ 4.50
Slaughter, Enos	54B	62	$ 6.00	$17.50	Strickland, George	55B	192	$ 1.50	$ 4.50
Slaughter, Enos	55B	60	$ 4.50	$15.00	Stringer, Lou	49B	183	$16.00	$65.00
Smalley, Roy	50B	115	$ 2.25	$ 9.00	Stringer, Lou	50B	187	$ 2.25	$ 9.00
Smalley, Roy	51B	44	$ 4.00	$14.00	Stuart, Marlin	52B	147	$ 4.00	$18.00
Smalley, Roy	52B	64	$ 3.00	$10.50	Stuart, Marlin	53BC	120	$ 8.50	$30.00
Smalley, Roy	53BW	56	$ 6.50	$21.50	Suder, Pete	50B	140	$ 2.25	$ 9.00
Smalley, Roy	54B	109	$ 1.50	$ 4.50	Suder, Pete	51B	154	$ 4.00	$14.00
Smalley, Roy	55B	252	$ 3.50	$12.00	Suder, Pete	52B	179	$ 3.00	$10.50
Smith, Al	55B	20	$ 1.50	$ 4.50	Suder, Pete	53BW	8	$ 6.50	$21.50
Smith, Dick	55B	288	$ 3.50	$12.00	Suder, Pete	54B	99	$ 1.50	$ 4.50
Smith, Frank	52B	186	$ 3.00	$10.50	Suder, Pete	55B	6	$ 1.50	$ 4.50
Smith, Frank	54B	188	$ 1.50	$ 4.50	Sukeforth, Clyde	52B	227	$ 3.75	$14.50
Snider, Duke	49B	226	$250.00	$850.00	Sullivan, Frank	55B	15	$ 1.50	$ 4.50
Snider, Duke	50B	77	$60.00	$190.00	Summers, William R.	55B	317	$ 3.00	$12.00
Snider, Duke	51B	32	$50.00	$150.00	Surkont, Max	52B	12	$ 3.25	$12.50
Snider, Duke	52B	116	$45.00	$150.00	Surkont, Max	53BC	156	$ 8.50	$30.00
Snider, Duke	53BC	117	$155.00	$520.00	Surkont, Max	54B	75	$ 1.50	$ 4.50
Snider, Duke	54B	170	$30.00	$95.00	Surkont, Max	55B	83	$ 1.50	$ 4.50
Snyder, Jerry	52B	246	$ 3.75	$14.50	Susce, Jr., George	55B	320	$ 8.00	$35.00
Snyder, Jerry	54B	216	$ 1.50	$ 4.50	Swift, Bob	49B	148	$16.00	$65.00
Snyder, Jerry	55B	74	$ 1.50	$ 4.50	Swift, Bob	50B	149	$ 2.25	$ 9.00
Soar, Hank	55B	279	$ 3.00	$12.00	Swift, Bob	51B	214	$ 4.00	$14.00
Souchock, Steve	52B	235	$ 3.75	$14.50	Swift, Bob	52B	131	$ 3.00	$10.50
Souchock, Steve	53BC	91	$ 6.00	$21.50	Talbot, Bob	55B	137	$ 1.50	$ 4.50
Souchock, Steve	54B	103	$ 1.50	$ 4.50	Tappe, Elvin	55B	51	$ 1.50	$ 4.50
Southworth, Billy	51B	207	$ 4.00	$14.00	Taylor, Zack	51B	315	$12.00	$37.50
Spahn, Warren	48B	18	$60.00	$175.00	Tebbetts, Birdie	51B	257	$12.00	$37.50
Spahn, Warren	49B	33	$22.00	$95.00	Tebbetts, George "Birdie"	52B	124	$ 3.00	$10.50

ENOS SLAUGHTER

Player	Year	No.	VG	EX/MT	Player	Year	No.	VG	EX/MT
Tebbetts, Birdie	55B	232	$ 3.50	$12.00	Waitkus, Eddie	51B	28	$ 4.00	$14.00
Temple, Johnny	55B	31	$ 1.00	$ 4.50	Waitkus, Eddie	52B	92	$ 3.00	$10.50
Terwilliger, Wayne	50B	114	$ 2.25	$ 9.00	Waitkus, Eddie	55B	4	$ 1.50	$ 4.50
Terwilliger, Wayne	51B	175	$ 4.00	$14.00	Wakefield, Dick	49B	91	$ 3.50	$12.00
Thomas, Frank	54B	155	$ 1.75	$ 6.50	Walker, Harry	49B	130	$ 3.00	$10.50
Thomas, Frank	55B	58	$ 1.50	$ 4.50	Walker, Harry	50B	180	$ 3.00	$12.00
Thomas, Keith	53BW	62	$ 6.50	$21.50	Walls, Lee	55B	82	$ 1.50	$ 4.50
Thompson, Henry	50B	174	$ 2.25	$ 9.00	Ward, Preston	50B	231	$ 2.25	$ 9.00
Thompson, Henry	51B	89	$ 4.00	$14.00	Ward, Preston	54B	139	$ 1.75	$ 6.50
Thompson, Henry	52B	249	$ 3.75	$14.50	Ward, Preston	55B	27	$ 1.50	$ 4.50
Thompson, Henry	54B	217	$ 1.75	$ 6.50	Warneke, Lonnie	55B	299	$ 3.00	$12.00
Thompson, Henry "Hank"	55B	94	$ 1.75	$ 6.50	Wehmeier, Herman	48B	46	$ 6.00	$17.50
Thompson, Jocko	49B	161	$16.00	$65.00	Wehmeier, Herman	49B	51	$ 2.25	$ 9.00
Thompson, John	50B	120	$ 2.25	$ 9.00	Wehmeier, Herman	50B	27	$ 6.50	$22.00
Thompson, John "Jocko"	51B	294	$10.00	$35.00	Wehmeier, Herman	51B	144	$ 4.00	$14.00
Thomson, Bobby	48B	47	$15.00	$45.00	Wehmeier, Herman	52B	150	$ 3.00	$10.50
Thomson, Bobby	49B	18	$ 5.00	$18.00	Wehmeier, Herman	53BC	23	$ 6.00	$21.50
Thomson, Bobby	50B	28	$ 9.50	$29.50	Werle, Bill	50B	87	$ 2.25	$ 9.00
Thomson, Bobby	51B	126	$ 6.50	$20.00	Werle, Bill	51B	64	$ 4.00	$14.00
Thomson, Bobby	52B	2	$ 6.25	$19.75	Werle, Bill	52B	248	$ 3.75	$14.50
Thomson, Bobby	54B	201	$ 1.75	$ 6.50	Wertz, Vic	49B	164	$16.00	$65.00
Thomson, Bobby	55B	102	$ 1.75	$ 6.50	Wertz, Vic	50B	9	$ 6.50	$22.00
Tipton, Joe	49B	103	$ 3.50	$12.00	Wertz, Vic	51B	176	$ 3.50	$12.00
Tipton, Joe	50B	159	$ 2.25	$ 9.00	Wertz, Vic	52B	39	$ 3.00	$10.50
Tipton, Joe	51B	82	$ 4.00	$14.00	Wertz, Vic	53BC	2	$ 4.50	$17.25
Tipton, Joe	53BW	13	$ 6.50	$21.50	Wertz, Vic	54B	21	$ 1.75	$ 6.50
Tipton, Joe	54B	180	$ 1.50	$ 4.50	Wertz, Vic	55B	40	$ 1.00	$ 4.50
Torgeson, Earl	49B	17	$ 3.50	$12.00	Westlake, Wally	49B	45	$ 2.25	$ 9.00
Torgeson, Earl	50B	163	$ 2.25	$ 9.00	Westlake, Wally	50B	69	$ 6.50	$22.00
Torgeson, Earl	51B	99	$ 4.00	$14.00	Westrum, Wes	51B	161	$ 4.00	$14.00
Torgeson, Earl	52B	72	$ 3.00	$10.50	Westrum, Wes	52B	74	$ 3.00	$10.50
Torgeson, Earl	54B	63	$ 1.50	$ 4.50	Westrum, Wes	54B	25	$ 1.50	$ 4.50
Torgeson, Earl	55B	210	$ 1.50	$ 4.50	Westrum, Wes	55B	141	$ 1.50	$ 4.50
Tresh, Mike	49B	166	$16.00	$65.00	White, Hal	51B	320	$12.00	$37.50
Trinkle, Ken	49B	193	$16.00	$65.00	White, Sammy	53BC	41	$ 6.00	$21.50
Trout, Dizzy	49B	208	$19.00	$85.00	White, Sammy	54B	34	$ 1.75	$ 6.50
Trout, Paul "Dizzy"	50B	134	$ 3.00	$12.00	White, Sammy	55B	47	$ 1.50	$ 4.50
Trucks, Virgil	49B	219	$16.00	$65.00	Whitman, Dick	51B	221	$ 4.00	$14.00
Trucks, Virgil	50B	96	$ 2.25	$ 9.00	Widmar, Al	51B	281	$12.00	$37.50
Trucks, Virgil	51B	104	$ 4.00	$14.00	Wight, Bill	50B	38	$ 6.50	$22.00
Trucks, Virgil	53BW	17	$ 6.50	$22.00	Wight, Bill	51B	164	$ 4.00	$14.00
Trucks, Virgil	54B	198	$ 1.75	$ 6.50	Wight, Bill	52B	117	$ 3.00	$10.50
Trucks, Virgil	55B	26	$ 1.75	$ 6.50	Wight, Bill	53BC	100	$ 6.00	$21.50
Tucker, Thurman	51B	222	$ 4.00	$14.00	Wight, Bill	55B	312	$ 3.50	$12.00
Tuttle, Bill	55B	35	$ 1.50	$ 4.50	Wilber, Del	52B	225	$ 3.75	$14.50
Umont, Frank	55B	305	$ 3.00	$12.00	Wilber, Del	53BW	24	$ 6.50	$21.50
Umphlett, Tom	54B	88	$ 1.50	$ 4.50	Wilber, Del	54B	178	$ 1.50	$ 4.50
Umphlett, Tom	55B	45	$ 1.50	$ 4.50	Wilhelm, Hoyt	53BW	28	$28.00	$85.00
Usher, Bob	51B	286	$12.00	$37.50	Wilhelm, Hoyt	54B	57	$ 7.50	$22.00
Valo, Elmer	49B	66	$ 2.25	$ 9.00	Wilhelm, Hoyt	55B	1	$14.00	$90.00
Valo, Elmer	50B	49	$ 0.50	$22.00	Wilks, Ted	40B	137	$ 3.00	$10.50
Valo, Elmer	52B	206	$ 3.00	$10.50	Wilks, Ted	51B	193	$ 4.00	$14.00
VanderMeer, Johnny	49B	128	$ 3.00	$10.50	Wilks, Ted	52B	138	$ 3.00	$10.50
VanderMeer, Johnny	50B	79	$ 3.50	$12.00	Williams, Davey	52B	178	$ 3.00	$10.50
VanderMeer, Johnny	51B	223	$ 3.50	$13.00	Williams, Davey	53BC	1	$14.00	$80.00
Verban, Emil	48B	28	$ 6.50	$27.00	Williams, Davey	54B	9	$ 1.50	$ 4.50
Verban, Emil	49B	38	$ 2.25	$ 9.00	Williams, Davey	55B	138	$ 1.50	$ 4.50
Vernon, Mickey	49B	94	$ 6.00	$21.50	Williams, Ted	50B	98	$130.00	$450.00
Vernon, Mickey	50B	132	$ 3.00	$12.00	Williams, Ted	51B	165	$115.00	$400.00
Vernon, Mickey	51B	65	$ 3.50	$12.00	Williams, Ted	54B	66	$700.00	$2200.00
Vernon, Mickey	52B	87	$ 3.25	$12.50	Wilson, Archie	52B	210	$ 3.00	$10.50
Vernon, Mickey	53BC	159	$ 7.75	$25.00	Wilson, Jim	53BC	37	$ 6.00	$21.50
Vernon, Mickey	54B	152	$ 1.75	$ 6.50	Wilson, Jim	54B	16	$ 1.50	$ 4.50
Vernon, Mickey "James"	55B	46	$ 1.00	$ 4.50	Wilson, Jim	55B	253	$ 3.50	$12.00
Vico, George	49B	122	$ 3.00	$10.50	Wood, Ken	50B	190	$ 2.25	$ 9.00
Vico, George	50B	150	$ 2.25	$ 9.00	Wood, Ken	51B	209	$ 4.00	$14.00
Virdon, Bill	55B	296	$ 6.00	$24.50	Wood, Ken	53BC	109	$ 6.00	$21.50
Vollmer, Clyde	50B	53	$ 6.50	$22.00	Woodling, Gene	51B	219	$ 3.50	$13.00
Vollmer, Clyde	51B	91	$ 4.00	$14.00	Woodling, Gene	52B	177	$ 3.25	$12.50
Vollmer, Clyde	52B	57	$ 3.00	$10.50	Woodling, Gene	53BW	31	$ 9.00	$36.00
Vollmer, Clyde	53BC	152	$ 8.50	$30.00	Woodling, Gene	54B	209	$ 1.75	$ 6.50
Vollmer, Clyde	54B	136	$ 1.50	$ 4.50	Wooten, Earl	49B	189	$16.00	$65.00
Vollmer, Clyde	55B	13	$ 1.50	$ 4.50	Wright, Taft	49B	96	$ 3.50	$12.00
Waitkus, Eddie	49B	142	$ 3.00	$10.50	Wright, Tommy	51B	271	$12.00	$37.50
Waitkus, Eddie	50B	30	$ 6.50	$22.00	Wynn, Early	49B	110	$25.00	$90.00

BOWMAN

Player	Year	No.	VG	EX/MT	Player	Year	No.	VG	EX/MT
Wynn, Early	50B	148	$12.00	$42.00	Yost, Eddie	54B	72	$ 1.50	$ 4.50
Wynn, Early	51B	78	$11.00	$37.50	Yost, Eddie	55B	73	$ 1.50	$ 4.50
Wynn, Early	52B	142	$ 7.50	$30.00	Young, Babe	49B	240	$27.00	$100.00
Wynn, Early	53BC	146	$25.00	$85.00	Young, Bobby	52B	193	$ 3.00	$10.50
Wynn, Early	54B	164	$ 7.00	$21.00	Young, Bobby	54B	149	$ 1.50	$ 4.50
Wynn, Early	55B	38	$ 5.25	$15.00	Yvars, Sal	54B	78	$ 1.50	$ 4.50
Wyrostek, Johnny	48B	44	$ 6.00	$17.50	Zarilla, Al	49B	156	$16.00	$65.00
Wyrostek, Johnny	49B	37	$ 2.25	$ 9.00	Zarilla, Al	50B	45	$ 6.50	$22.00
Wyrostek, Johnny	50B	197	$ 2.25	$ 9.00	Zarilla, Al	51B	35	$ 4.00	$14.00
Wyrostek, Johnny	51B	107	$ 4.00	$14.00	Zarilla, Al	52B	113	$ 3.00	$10.50
Wyrostek, Johnny	52B	42	$ 3.00	$10.50	Zernial, Gus	50B	4	$ 9.00	$36.00
Wyrostek, Johnny	53BW	35	$ 6.50	$21.50	Zernial, Gus	51B	262	$ 9.00	$35.00
Wyrostek, Johnny	55B	237	$ 3.50	$12.00	Zernial, Gus	52B	82	$ 3.00	$10.50
Wyse, Hank	51B	192	$ 4.00	$14.00	Zernial, Gus	53BC	13	$ 6.00	$21.50
Yost, Eddie	49B	32	$ 3.50	$12.00	Zimmer, Don	55B	65	$ 3.50	$12.00
Yost, Eddie	50B	162	$ 3.00	$12.00	Zoldak, Sam	49B	78	$ 3.50	$12.00
Yost, Eddie	51B	41	$ 4.00	$14.00	Zoldak, Sam	50B	182	$ 2.25	$ 9.00
Yost, Eddie	52B	31	$ 3.25	$12.50	Zoldak, Sam	51B	114	$ 4.00	$14.00
Yost, Eddie	53BC	116	$ 9.00	$36.00	Zuverink, George	55B	92	$ 1.50	$ 4.50

1989 BOWMAN

Player	Year	No.	VG	EX/MT	Player	Year	No.	VG	EX/MT
Abbott, Jim	89B	39	$ .01	$1.75	Assenmacher, Paul	89B	265	$ .01	$ .05
Agosto, Juan	89B	321	$ .01	$ .05	August, Don	89B	130	$ .01	$ .05
Aguayo, Luis	89B	88	$ .01	$ .05	Avery, Steve	89B	268	$ .01	$ .75
Aldrete, Mike	89B	368	$ .01	$ .05	Backman, Wally	89B	159	$ .01	$ .05
Alexander, Doyle	89B	94	$ .01	$ .05	Baines, Harold	89B	72	$ .01	$ .10
Allanson, Andy	89B	83	$ .01	$ .05	Ballard, Jeff	89B	7	$ .01	$ .05
Alomar, Roberto	89B	458	$ .01	$ .50	Bankhead, Scott	89B	203	$ .01	$ .05
Alomar, Sandy	89B	258	$ .01	$ .05	Bannister, Floyd	89B	112	$ .01	$ .05
					Barfield, Jesse	89B	257	$ .01	$ .15
					Barrett, Marty	89B	28	$ .01	$ .05
					Bautista, Jose	89B	3	$ .01	$ .05
					Bedrosian, Steve	89B	395	$ .01	$ .10
					Belcher, Tim	89B	336	$ .01	$ .20
					Bell, Buddy	89B	229	$ .01	$ .10
					Bell, George	89B	256	$ .01	$ .15
					Bell, Juan	89B	11	$ .01	$ .25
					Bene, Bill	89B	340	$ .01	$ .15
					Benedict, Bruce	89B	271	$ .01	$ .05
					Benes, Andy	89B	448	$ .01	$ .85
					Benzinger, Todd	89B	312	$ .01	$ .05
					Berenguer, Juan	89B	152	$ .01	$ .05
					Berroa, Geronimo	89B	279	$ .01	$ .10
					Berryhill, Damon	89B	288	$ .01	$ .20
					Birkbeck, Mike	89B	132	$ .01	$ .05
					Bittiger, Jeff	89B	60	$ .01	$ .05
					Black, Bud	89B	82	$ .01	$ .05
					Blyleven, Bert	89B	41	$ .01	$ .15
					Bockus, Randy	89B	96	$ .01	$ .05
					Boddicker, Mike	89B	21	$ .01	$ .05
					Boggs, Wade	89B	32	$ .01	$ .35
					Bonds, Barry	89B	426	$ .01	$ .20
					Bonilla, Bobby	89B	422	$ .01	$ .15
					Boone, Bob	89B	119	$ .01	$ .05
					Bosio, Chris	89B	134	$ .01	$ .05
					Cerutti, John	89B	247	$ .01	$ .05
					Checklist, 1 - 121	89B	481	$ .01	$ .05
					Checklist, 122 - 242	89B	482	$ .01	$ .05
					Checklist, 243 - 363	89B	483	$ .01	$ .05
					Checklist, 364 - 484	89B	484	$ .01	$ .05
					Clancy, Jim	89B	324	$ .01	$ .05
					Clark, Jack	89B	456	$ .01	$ .05
					Clark, Jerald	89B	462	$ .01	$ .05
					Clark, Will	89B	476	$ .01	$ .75
					Clayton, Royce	89B	472	$ .01	$ .05
					Clemens, Roger	89B	26	$ .01	$ .30
					Clements, Pat	89B	452	$ .01	$ .05
					Coffman, Kevin	89B	282	$ .01	$ .05
					Coleman, Vince	89B	443	$ .01	$ .15
					Coles, Darnell	89B	217	$ .01	$ .05
Alomar, Jr., Sandy	89B	454	$ .01	$ .85	Combs, Pat	89B	398	$ .01	$ .75
Andersen, Larry	89B	325	$ .01	$ .05					
Anderson, Allan	89B	149	$ .01	$ .05					
Anderson, Brady	89B	18	$ .01	$ .25					
Ansley, Willie	89B	332	$ .05	$ .25					
Ard, Johnny	89B	153	$ .01	$ .05					
Armas, Tony	89B	51	$ .01	$ .05					
Ashby, Alan	89B	327	$ .01	$ .05					

Player	Year	No.	VG	EX/MT	Player	Year	No.	VG	EX/MT
Cone, David	89B	375	$ .01	$ .15	Gruber, Kelly	89B	251	$ .01	$ .05
Crim, Chuck	89B	136	$ .01	$ .05	Gubicza, Mark	89B	117	$ .01	$ .05
Daniels, Kal	89B	314	$ .01	$ .15	Guerrero, Pedro	89B	440	$ .01	$ .15
Darling, Ron	89B	372	$ .01	$ .15	Guillen, Ozzie	89B	64	$ .01	$ .05
Davis, Alvin	89B	215	$ .01	$ .05	Gwynn, Tony	89B	461	$ .01	$ .15
Davis, Chili	89B	50	$ .01	$ .05	Hall, Drew	89B	221	$ .01	$ .05
Davis, Eric	89B	316	$ .01	$ .25	Hanson, Erik	89B	206	$ .01	$ .25
Davis, Glenn	89B	331	$ .01	$ .15	Harkey, Mike	89B	286	$ .01	$ .20
Davis, Jody	89B	270	$ .01	$ .05	Harnisch, Pete	89B	4	$ .01	$ .05
Davis, Mark	89B	447	$ .01	$ .05	Harper, Brian	89B	155	$ .01	$ .05
Davis, Mike	89B	352	$ .01	$ .05	Harvey, Bryan	89B	40	$ .01	$ .05
Davis, Storm	89B	192	$ .01	$ .05	Hassey, Ron	89B	194	$ .01	$ .05
Dawson, Andre	89B	298	$ .01	$ .15	Hatcher, Mickey	89B	347	$ .01	$ .05
Dayley, Ken	89B	428	$ .01	$ .05	Hawkins, Andy	89B	166	$ .01	$ .05
Deer, Rob	89B	146	$ .01	$ .10	Hayes, Von	89B	406	$ .01	$ .15
DeLeon, Jose	89B	431	$ .01	$ .05	Heinkel, Don	89B	427	$ .01	$ .05
Dempsey, Rick	89B	343	$ .01	$ .05	Henderson, Dave	89B	200	$ .01	$ .05
Deshaies, Jim	89B	320	$ .01	$ .05	Henderson, Rickey	89B	181	$ .01	$ .25
Diaz, Bo	89B	307	$ .01	$ .05	Henke, Tom	89B	246	$ .01	$ .05
Dibble, Rob	89B	305	$ .01	$ .35	Henneman, Mike	89B	98	$ .01	$ .05
DiPino, Frank	89B	434	$ .01	$ .05	Hernandez, Keith	89B	385	$ .01	$ .10
Dopson, John	89B	24	$ .01	$ .05	Herr, Tom	89B	403	$ .01	$ .05
Doran, Bill	89B	329	$ .01	$ .05	Hershiser, Orel	89B	341	$ .01	$ .20
Downing, Brian	89B	53	$ .01	$ .05	Higuera, Teddy	89B	129	$ .01	$ .05
Downs, Kelly	89B	465	$ .01	$ .05	Hillegas, Shawn	89B	58	$ .01	$ .05
Drabek, Doug	89B	416	$ .01	$ .05	Holman, Brian	89B	357	$ .01	$ .05
Drew, Cameron	89B	334	$ .01	$ .20	Holton, Brian	89B	2	$ .01	$ .05
Dunston, Shawon	89B	294	$ .01	$ .15	Honeycutt, Rick	89B	187	$ .01	$ .05
DuVall, Brad	89B	430	$ .01	$ .05	Horton, Ricky	89B	338	$ .01	$ .05
Eckersley, Dennis	89B	190	$ .01	$ .05	Hough, Charlie	89B	224	$ .01	$ .05
Elster, Kevin	89B	383	$ .01	$ .05	Howell, Jack	89B	48	$ .01	$ .05
Ericks, John	89B	433	$ .01	$ .25	Howell, Jay	89B	335	$ .01	$ .05
Esasky, Nick	89B	31	$ .01	$ .05	Howell, Ken	89B	394	$ .01	$ .05
Espy, Cecil	89B	236	$ .01	$ .05	Hrbek, Kent	89B	157	$ .01	$ .10
Evans, Darrell	89B	275	$ .01	$ .15	Hubbard, Glenn	89B	199	$ .01	$ .05
Evans, Dwight	89B	35	$ .01	$ .05	Hudler, Rex	89B	364	$ .01	$ .05
Fariss, Monty	89B	233	$ .01	$ .05	Hurst, Bruce	89B	451	$ .01	$ .05
Farr, Steve	89B	114	$ .01	$ .05	Incaviglia, Pete	89B	238	$ .01	$ .15
Farrell, John	89B	74	$ .01	$ .05	Jackson, Bo	89B	126	$ .01	$1.00
Fernandez, Sid	89B	377	$ .01	$ .05	Jackson, Danny	89B	304	$ .01	$ .05
Fernandez, Tony	89B	254	$ .01	$ .15	Jackson, Mike	89B	207	$ .01	$ .05
Finley, Chuck	89B	37	$ .01	$ .05	Jacoby, Brook	89B	86	$ .01	$ .05
Finley, Steve	89B	15	$ .01	$ .30	James, Chris	89B	404	$ .01	$ .05
Fischer, Tom	89B	20	$ .01	$ .05	James, Dion	89B	277	$ .01	$ .05
Fisher, Brian	89B	415	$ .01	$ .05	Jefferies, Gregg	89B	381	$ .01	$1.00
Fisk, Carlton	89B	62	$ .01	$ .10	Jefferson, Stan	89B	180	$ .01	$ .05
Flanagan, Mike	89B	241	$ .01	$ .05	Jones, Doug	89B	78	$ .01	$ .05
Flannery, Tim	89B	457	$ .01	$ .05	Jones, Jimmy	89B	169	$ .01	$ .05
Fletcher, Scott	89B	230	$ .01	$ .05	Jones, Ron	89B	407	$ .01	$ .25
Ford, Curt	89B	408	$ .01	$ .05	Jones, Tim	89B	439	$ .01	$ .05
Franco, John	89B	301	$ .01	$ .15	Jones, Tracy	89B	479	$ .01	$ .05
Franco, Julio	89B	228	$ .01	$ .15	Jordan, Ricky	89B	401	$ .01	$ .95
Gaetti, Gary	89B	158	$ .01	$ .05	Joyner, Wally	89B	47	$ .01	$ .15
Gagne, Greg	89B	161	$ .01	$ .05	Kelly, Roberto	89B	183	$ .01	$ .05
Galarraga, Andres	89B	365	$ .01	$ .15	Kennedy, Terry	89B	470	$ .01	$ .05
Gallagher, Dave	89B	71	$ .01	$ .20	Key, Jimmy	89B	243	$ .01	$ .15
Gant, Ron	89B	274	$ .01	$ .15	Kilgus, Paul	89B	285	$ .01	$ .05
Gantner, Jim	89B	141	$ .01	$ .05	Kipper, Bob	89B	414	$ .01	$ .05
Gardner, Wes	89B	23	$ .01	$ .05	Kittle, Ron	89B	69	$ .01	$ .10
Garrelts, Scott	89B	467	$ .01	$ .05	Kruk, John	89B	460	$ .01	$ .10
Gedman, Rich	89B	27	$ .01	$ .05	Kunkel, Jeff	89B	231	$ .01	$ .05
Gibson, Kirk	89B	351	$ .01	$ .15	Lake, Steve	89B	399	$ .01	$ .05
Gibson, Paul	89B	99	$ .01	$ .05	Langston, Mark	89B	205	$ .01	$ .15
Gladden, Danny	89B	163	$ .01	$ .05	Lansford, Carney	89B	198	$ .01	$ .05
Glavine, Tom	89B	267	$ .01	$ .05	LaPoint, Dave	89B	165	$ .01	$ .05
Gooden, Doc	89B	376	$ .01	$ .25	Larkin, Barry	89B	311	$ .01	$ .35
Gordon, Tom	89B	115	$ .01	$1.00	Larkin, Gene	89B	160	$ .01	$ .05
Gott, Jim	89B	411	$ .01	$ .05	Laudner, Tim	89B	154	$ .01	$ .05
Grace, Mark	89B	291	$ .01	$2.25	LaValliere, Mike	89B	417	$ .01	$ .05
Greenwell, Mike	89B	34	$ .01	$ .50	Law, Vance	89B	293	$ .01	$ .05
Griffey, Ken	89B	259	$ .01	$ .15	Lawless, Tom	89B	255	$ .01	$ .05
Griffey, Jr., Ken	89B	220	$ .01	$4.00	Leach, Rick	89B	234	$ .01	$ .05
Griffin, Alfredo	89B	345	$ .01	$ .05	Leary, Tim	89B	339	$ .01	$ .05
Griffin, Ty	89B	289	$ .01	$ .50	Lefferts, Craig	89B	464	$ .01	$ .05
Gross, Kevin	89B	355	$ .01	$ .05	Leibrandt, Charlie	89B	116	$ .01	$ .05

Player	Year	No.	VG	EX/MT	Player	Year	No.	VG	EX/MT
Leiter, Al	89B	170	$ .01	$ .15	Miller, Keith	89B	380	$ .01	$ .05
Lemon, Chet	89B	108	$ .01	$ .05	Milligan, Randy	89B	10	$ .01	$ .05
Leonard, Jeffrey	89B	218	$ .01	$ .05	Mitchell, Kevin	89B	474	$ .01	$ .30
Lewis, Mark	89B	87	$ .01	$ .25	Molitor, Paul	89B	140	$ .01	$ .10
Lilliquist, Derek	89B	264	$ .01	$ .20	Montgomery, Jeff	89B	113	$ .01	$ .05
Lind, Jose	89B	421	$ .01	$ .05	Moore, Mike	89B	189	$ .01	$ .05
Long, Bill	89B	56	$ .01	$ .05	Moreland, Keith	89B	109	$ .01	$ .05
Lyons, Steve	89B	63	$ .01	$ .05	Morris, Jack	89B	93	$ .01	$ .05
Macfarlane, Mike	89B	118	$ .01	$ .05	Moyer, Jamie	89B	223	$ .01	$ .05
Maddux, Greg	89B	284	$ .01	$ .10	Mulliniks, Rance	89B	250	$ .01	$ .05
Maddux, Mike	89B	391	$ .01	$ .05	Murphy, Dale	89B	276	$ .01	$ .20
Magadan, Dave	89B	384	$ .01	$ .05	Murphy, Rob	89B	22	$ .01	$ .05
Magrane, Joe	89B	432	$ .01	$ .10	Murray, Eddie	89B	346	$ .01	$ .15
Mahler, Rick	89B	302	$ .01	$ .05	Musselman, Jeff	89B	240	$ .01	$ .05
Maldonado, Candy	89B	478	$ .01	$ .05	Myers, Randy	89B	374	$ .01	$ .05
Manahan, Austin	89B	420	$ .01	$ .05	Nagy, Charles	89B	73	$ .01	$ .20
Manrique, Fred	89B	66	$ .01	$ .05	Nelson, Gene	89B	185	$ .01	$ .05
					Newman, Al	89B	156	$ .01	$ .05
					Niedenfuer, Tom	89B	204	$ .01	$ .05
					Nieves, Juan	89B	131	$ .01	$ .05
					Nixon, Donell	89B	477	$ .01	$ .05
					Nixon, Otis	89B	366	$ .01	$ .05
					Nokes, Matt	89B	101	$ .01	$ .10
					O'Brien, Pete	89B	84	$ .01	$ .05
					O'Neill, Paul	89B	313	$ .01	$ .15
					Oberkfell, Ken	89B	418	$ .01	$ .05
					Oester, Ron	89B	310	$ .01	$ .05
					Ojeda, Bob	89B	371	$ .01	$ .05
					Olson, Gregg	89B	6	$ .01	$ .65
					Oquendo, Jose	89B	438	$ .01	$ .05
					Orossco, Jesse	89B	81	$ .01	$ .05
					Owen, Spike	89B	363	$ .01	$ .05
					Pagliarulo, Mike	89B	175	$ .01	$ .05
					Palmeiro, Rafael	89B	237	$ .01	$ .15
					Parker, Dave	89B	202	$ .01	$ .15
					Parrett, Jeff	89B	390	$ .01	$ .05
					Parrish, Lance	89B	45	$ .01	$ .05
					Pasqua, Dan	89B	67	$ .01	$ .05
					Pedrique, Al	89B	104	$ .01	$ .05
					Pena, Tony	89B	435	$ .01	$ .10
					Pendleton, Terry	89B	437	$ .01	$ .05
					Peraza, Oswald	89B	1	$ .01	$ .10
					Perez, Melido	89B	59	$ .01	$ .15
					Perez, Pascual	89B	354	$ .01	$ .15
					Perry, Gerald	89B	273	$ .01	$ .05
					Phelps, Ken	89B	177	$ .01	$ .05
					Plesac, Dan	89B	133	$ .01	$ .05
					Plunk, Eric	89B	191	$ .01	$ .05
					Portugal, Mark	89B	318	$ .01	$ .05
					Presley, Jim	89B	214	$ .01	$ .05
					Proctor, Dave	89B	378	$ .01	$ .05

Player	Year	No.	VG	EX/MT	Player	Year	No.	VG	EX/MT
Manwaring, Kirt	89B	469	$ .01	$ .05	Puckett, Kirby	89B	162	$ .01	$ .45
Marshall, Mike	89B	350	$ .01	$ .05	Puleo, Charlie	89B	263	$ .01	$ .05
Martinez, Carmelo	89B	459	$ .01	$ .05	Quinones, Rey	89B	213	$ .01	$ .05
Martinez, Dave	89B	370	$ .01	$ .05	Quirk, Jamie	89B	173	$ .01	$ .05
Martinez, Denny	89B	359	$ .01	$ .05	Raines, Rock	89B	369	$ .01	$ .15
Martinez, Edgar	89B	216	$ .01	$ .05	Ramirez, Rafael	89B	330	$ .01	$ .05
Martinez, Tino	89B	211	$ .01	$ .75	Randolph, Willie	89B	344	$ .01	$ .05
Mattingly, Don	89B	176	$ .01	$ .90	Rasmussen, Dennis	89B	450	$ .01	$ .05
McCaskill, Kirk	89B	38	$ .01	$ .05	Rawley, Shane	89B	151	$ .01	$ .05
McClendon, Lloyd	89B	287	$ .01	$ .05	Ray, Johnny	89B	49	$ .01	$ .05
McClure, Bob	89B	43	$ .01	$ .05	Reardon, Jeff	89B	148	$ .01	$ .05
McCullers, Lance	89B	168	$ .01	$ .05	Redus, Gary	89B	425	$ .01	$ .05
McDowell, Jack	89B	61	$ .01	$ .05	Reed, Jody	89B	30	$ .01	$ .05
McDowell, Oddibe	89B	90	$ .01	$ .05	Renteria, Rich	89B	212	$ .01	$ .05
McGaffigan, Andy	89B	356	$ .01	$ .05	Reuschel, Rick	89B	466	$ .01	$ .05
McGee, Willie	89B	442	$ .01	$ .05	Reuss, Jerry	89B	57	$ .01	$ .05
McGriff, Fred	89B	253	$ .01	$ .20	Reynolds, Craig	89B	328	$ .01	$ .05
McGwire, Mark	89B	197	$ .01	$ .55	Reynolds, Harold	89B	210	$ .01	$ .05
McReynolds, Kevin	89B	388	$ .01	$ .10	Rhoden, Rick	89B	323	$ .01	$ .05
McWilliams, Larry	89B	397	$ .01	$ .05	Rice, Jim	89B	33	$ .01	$ .10
Medvin, Scott	89B	412	$ .01	$ .05	Righetti, Dave	89B	167	$ .01	$ .05
Melvin, Bob	89B	8	$ .01	$ .01	Rijo, Jose	89B	300	$ .01	$ .15
Meyer, Brian	89B	319	$ .01	$ .05	Riles, Ernie	89B	475	$ .01	$ .05
Meyer, Joey	89B	138	$ .01	$ .05	Ripken, Billy	89B	12	$ .01	$ .05

Player	Year	No.	VG	EX/MT	Player	Year	No.	VG	EX/MT
Ripken, Cal	89B	9	$ .01	$ .15	Sutcliffe, Rick	89B	281	$ .01	$ .10
Ripken, Sr., Cal	89B	260	$ .01	$ .05	Sveum, Dale	89B	139	$ .01	$ .05
Rivera, Luis	89B	29	$ .01	$ .05	Swindell, Greg	89B	76	$ .01	$ .10
Robinson, Don	89B	463	$ .01	$ .05	Tabler, Pat	89B	125	$ .01	$ .05
Robinson, Jeff	89B	97	$ .01	$ .05	Tanana, Frank	89B	92	$ .01	$ .05
Robinson, Jeff	89B	410	$ .01	$ .05	Tartabull, Danny	89B	128	$ .01	$ .10
Robinson, Ron	89B	303	$ .01	$ .05	Tejada, Wil	89B	468	$ .01	$ .05
Royer, Stan	89B	195	$ .01	$ .05	Templeton, Garry	89B	455	$ .01	$ .05
Ruffin, Bruce	89B	393	$ .01	$ .05	Terrell, Walt	89B	445	$ .01	$ .05
Russell, Jeff	89B	226	$ .01	$ .05	Teufel, Tim	89B	382	$ .01	$ .05
Ryan, Nolan	89B	225	$ .01	$ .60	Thigpen, Bobby	89B	55	$ .01	$ .05
Saberhagen, Bret	89B	111	$ .01	$ .15	Thomas, Andres	89B	272	$ .01	$ .05
Sabo, Chris	89B	309	$ .01	$ .50	Thompson, Milt	89B	441	$ .01	$ .05
Samuel, Juan	89B	405	$ .01	$ .05	Thompson, Robby	89B	473	$ .01	$ .05
Sanchez, Alex	89B	245	$ .01	$ .05	Thon, Dickie	89B	400	$ .01	$ .05
Sandberg, Ryne	89B	290	$ .01	$ .25	Toliver, Fred	89B	147	$ .01	$ .05
Santana, Rafael	89B	174	$ .01	$ .05	Traber, Jim	89B	13	$ .01	$ .05
Santiago, Benny	89B	453	$ .01	$ .15	Trammell, Alan	89B	105	$ .01	$ .15
Santovenia, Nelson	89B	361	$ .01	$ .15	Trevino, Alex	89B	326	$ .01	$ .05
Sax, Steve	89B	178	$ .01	$ .05	Trillo, Manny	89B	308	$ .01	$ .05
Schmidt, Dave	89B	5	$ .01	$ .05	Uribe, Jose	89B	471	$ .01	$ .05
Schmidt, Mike	89B	402	$ .01	$ .35	Valenzuela, Fernando	89B	337	$ .01	$ .10
Schofield, Dick	89B	46	$ .01	$ .05	Valle, Dave	89B	208	$ .01	$ .05
Schroeder, Bill	89B	44	$ .01	$ .05	Van Slyke, Andy	89B	424	$ .01	$ .15
Scioscia, Mike	89B	342	$ .01	$ .05	Ventura, Robin	89B	65	$ .01	$ .85
Scott, Mike	89B	322	$ .01	$ .05	Viola, Frank	89B	150	$ .01	$ .15
Searcy, Steve	89B	95	$ .01	$ .20	Wainhouse, Dave	89B	358	$ .01	$ .05
Seitzer, Kevin	89B	123	$ .01	$ .15	Walk, Bob	89B	409	$ .01	$ .05
Sellers, Jeff	89B	299	$ .01	$ .05	Walker, Hugh	89B	127	$ .01	$ .05
Sharperson, Mike	89B	348	$ .01	$ .05	Walker, Mike	89B	77	$ .01	$ .05
Sheets, Larry	89B	16	$ .01	$ .05	Wallach, Tim	89B	362	$ .01	$ .05
Sheffield, Gary	89B	142	$ .01	$1.00	Walton, Jerome	89B	295	$ .01	$3.00
Shelby, John	89B	349	$ .01	$ .05	Washington, Claudell	89B	52	$ .01	$ .05
Sheridan, Pat	89B	107	$ .01	$ .05	Webster, Mitch	89B	296	$ .01	$ .05
Show, Eric	89B	446	$ .01	$ .05	Wegman, Bill	89B	135	$ .01	$ .05
Sierra, Ruben	89B	235	$ .01	$ .30	Weiss, Walt	89B	196	$ .01	$ .25
Slaught, Don	89B	172	$ .01	$ .05	Welch, Bob	89B	186	$ .01	$ .05
Smiley, John	89B	413	$ .01	$ .15	Whitaker, Lou	89B	103	$ .01	$ .10
Smith, Bryn	89B	353	$ .01	$ .05	White, Devon	89B	54	$ .01	$ .15
Smith, Dave	89B	317	$ .01	$ .05	White, Frank	89B	122	$ .01	$ .05
Smith, Dwight	89B	297	$ .01	$ .50	Whitehurst, Wally	89B	373	$ .01	$ .25
Smith, Lee	89B	19	$ .01	$ .05	Whitson, Eddie	89B	449	$ .01	$ .05
Smith, Lonnie	89B	278	$ .01	$ .05	Whitt, Ernie	89B	248	$ .01	$ .05
Smith, Ozzie	89B	436	$ .01	$ .15	Wickander, Kevin	89B	75	$ .01	$ .05
Smith, Pete	89B	269	$ .01	$ .25	Wilkerson, Curt	89B	292	$ .01	$ .05
Smith, Zane	89B	262	$ .01	$ .10	Williams, Frank	89B	100	$ .01	$ .05
Smoltz, John	89B	266	$ .01	$ .45	Williams, Mitch	89B	283	$ .01	$ .05
Snyder, Cory	89B	89	$ .01	$ .10	Wilson, Glenn	89B	423	$ .01	$ .05
Sprague, Ed	89B	252	$ .01	$ .15	Wilson, Mookie	89B	386	$ .01	$ .05
Stanicek, Pete	89B	14	$ .01	$ .05	Wilson, Steve	89B	280	$ .01	$ .05
Stanley, Bob	89B	25	$ .01	$ .05	Wilson, Willie	89B	124	$ .01	$ .10
Steinbach, Terry	89B	193	$ .01	$ .05	Winfield, Dave	89B	179	$ .01	$ .15
Stewart, Dave	89B	188	$ .01	$ .25	Witt, Bobby	89B	222	$ .01	$ .05
Stieb, Dave	89B	239	$ .01	$ .05	Witt, Mike	89B	42	$ .01	$ .05
Stillwell, Kurt	89B	120	$ .01	$ .05	Worrell, Todd	89B	429	$ .01	$ .10
Stottlemyre, Mel	89B	261	$ .01	$ .15	Yett, Rich	89B	79	$ .01	$ .05
Stottlemyre, Todd	89B	242	$ .01	$ .05	Youmans, Floyd	89B	396	$ .01	$ .10
Stottlemyre, Jr., Mel	89B	110	$ .01	$ .05	Young, Curt	89B	184	$ .01	$ .05
Strawberry, Darryl	89B	387	$ .01	$ .35	Young, Gerald	89B	333	$ .01	$ .05
Sundberg, Jim	89B	227	$ .01	$ .05	Youngblood, Joel	89B	315	$ .01	$ .05
Surhoff, B. J.	89B	137	$ .01	$ .10	Yount, Robin	89B	144	$ .01	$ .25

DONRUSS-LEAF INC. 1981-1990

Donruss baseball cards first made their appearance on the collecting scene in 1981. At first they contained bubble gum in the wax packs; but in 1982, after being sued successfully by Topps, a puzzle piece was included in each pack instead of bubble gum. Donruss was prolific, at best, and over produced the cards for collectors' demands. This condition carried over into 1982; and today both of these sets are priced cheaper than the 1983-1987 sets! As in most collecting fields, age does not equal value. Scarcity and demand are more important; and demand is the prime factor!

Donruss began producing factory collated sets in 1984, and these factory sets are commanding premium prices above those sets that are hand assembled. Although other companies also have produced factory sets, only Donruss seals the sets in cellophane wrappers to protect the cards from being handled.

All Donruss cards are 2½" x 3½" and in full color.

1981 - 600 cards plus 5 unnumbered checklists w/white border w/Donruss logo '81 (copyright 1981 Donruss back upper right)

1982 - 653 cards plus 7 unnumbered checklists w/white border w/Donruss logo '82 (copyright 1982 Donruss back upper right

1983 - 653 cards plus 7 unnumbered checklists w/white border w/Donruss logo '83 (copyright 1982 Donruss back upper right)

1984 - 651 cards plus 7 unnumbered checklists and 2 cards (A & B) w/white border w/ Donruss logo '84 (copyright 1983 Donruss back upper right)

1985 - 653 cards plus 7 unnumbered checklists w/black border w/five red stripes on sides, w/Donruss logo '85 (copyright 1984 Donruss back upper right)

1986 - 653 cards plus 7 unnumbered checklists w/blue border w/thin black stripes, w/ Donruss '86 (copyright 1985 Leaf-Donruss back upper right)

1987 - 660 cards w/black border with brown baseball filled strip inside yellow bands on each side, w/Donruss '87 (copyright 1986 Leaf, Inc. back upper right)

1988 - 660 cards plus 26BC cards w/blue border with black and red shadings, w/Donruss '88 (copyright 1987 Leaf, Inc. back upper right)

1989 - 660 cards plus 26BC cards w/black stripped side borders and multi-colored top and bottoms w/Donruss '89 (copyright 1988 Leaf, Inc. back upper right)

1990 - 716 cards plus 26BC cards w/red borders with Donruss '90 on top left and orange backs (copyright 1989 Leaf, Inc. back upper left)

Several abbreviations are used in the Donruss section that need some explanation:

DBC - There are twenty-six DONRUSS BONUS CARDS, one player (MVP) from each team, in the 1988 and 1989 sets. These cards (BC1-BC26) are randomly distributed in the wax, rack and cello packs.

DK - Beginning with the 1983 set, the first twenty-six cards of the Donruss sets were designated DIAMOND KINGS. These cards feature the art of Dick Perez of Perez-Steele Galleries.

DR - Donruss issues a fifty-six card set of DONRUSS ROOKIES at the end of the year. This was started in 1986.

DRR - Beginning with the 1984 set, a group of twenty top rookies are designated DONRUSS RATED ROOKIES on the cards following the Diamond King cards.

DTR - Donruss issued a fifty-six traded set beginning in 1989.

D#A & D#B refer to bonus cards numbered with A and B in the wax packs of 1984.

DBB - DONRUSS BASEBALL'S BEST-A 336 card set first issued in 1988.

DAS - Donruss All-Star card first issued in 1990 sets.

There are many unnumbered checklists in the early Donruss sets. Since there are no numbers on the cards themselves, they are numbered as **"0"** in the listing of cards.

The listing for each card shown appears immediately following the photograph.

Player	Year	No.	VG	EX/MT	Player	Year	No.	VG	EX/MT
Aaron, Hank	86DK	602	$ .03	$ .25	Allen, Neil	81D	276	$ .01	$ .05
Aase, Don	81D	411	$ .01	$ .05	Allen, Neil	82D	506	$ .01	$ .05
Aase, Don	82D	267	$ .01	$ .05	Allen, Neil	83D	98	$ .01	$ .05
Aase, Don	83D	38	$ .01	$ .05	Allen, Neil	84D	109	$ .03	$ .10
Aase, Don	85D	255	$ .01	$ .08	Allen, Neil	85D	205	$ .01	$ .08
Aase, Don	86D	392	$ .01	$ .06	Allen, Neil	86D	610	$ .01	$ .06
Aase, Don	87D	231	$ .01	$ .04	Allen, Neil	87D	507	$ .01	$ .04
Abbott, Glenn	81D	47	$ .01	$ .05	Allen, Neil	88D	597	$ .01	$ .05
Abbott, Glenn	82D	302	$ .01	$ .05	Allen, Neil	89D	196	$ .01	$ .04
Abbott, Jim	89DBB	171	$ .01	$1.00	Allenson, Gary	81D	455	$ .01	$ .05
Abbott, Jim	89DR	16	$ .01	$1.50	Allenson, Gary	82D	386	$ .01	$ .05
Abbott, Jim	90D	108	$ .01	$1.00	Allenson, Gary	83D	30	$ .01	$ .05
Abner, Shawn	88DBB	21	$ .01	$ .15	Allenson, Gary	84D	335	$ .03	$ .10
Abner, Shawn	88DR	5	$ .01	$ .15	Allred, Beau	90D	691	$ .01	$ .35
Abner, Shawn	88DRR	33	$ .05	$ .25	Almon, Bill	82D	637	$ .01	$ .05
Abner, Shawn	89D	323	$ .01	$ .10	Almon, Bill	83D	356	$ .01	$ .05
Abrego, Johnny	86DRR	32	$ .01	$ .06	Almon, Bill	84D	467	$ .03	$ .10
Acker, Jim	84D	146	$ .03	$ .10	Almon, Bill	85D	589	$ .01	$ .08
Acker, Jim	86D	363	$ .01	$ .06	Almon, Bill	86D	479	$ .01	$ .06
Acker, Jim	87D	659	$ .01	$ .04	Almon, Bill	87D	326	$ .01	$ .04
Acker, Jim	90D	558	$ .01	$ .03	Almon, Bill	88D	487	$ .01	$ .05
Adams, Glenn	81D	566	$ .01	$ .05	Alomar, Jr., Sandy	89DR	21	$ .01	$ .50
Adams, Glenn	82D	431	$ .01	$ .05	Alomar, Jr., Sandy	89DRR	28	$ .15	$1.00
Adams, Rick	84D	85	$ .03	$ .10	Alomar, Jr., Sandy	90DRR	30	$ .01	$ .25
Adduci, Jim	87D	495	$ .01	$ .04	Alomar, Roberto	88DBB	42	$ .05	$ .25
Agosto, Juan	84D	208	$ .03	$ .10	Alomar, Roberto	88DR	35	$ .10	$ .60
Agosto, Juan	85D	526	$ .01	$ .08	Alomar, Roberto	88DRR	34	$ .15	$1.25
Agosto, Juan	86D	488	$ .01	$ .06	Alomar, Roberto	89D	246	$ .05	$ .25
Agosto, Juan	89D	354	$ .01	$ .04	Alomar, Roberto	89DBB	21	$ .01	$ .15
Agosto, Juan	90D	477	$ .01	$ .03	Alomar, Roberto	90D	111	$ .01	$ .10
Aguayo, Luis	82D	622	$ .01	$ .05	Alou, Felipe	82D	650	$ .01	$ .05
Aguayo, Luis	83D	546	$ .01	$ .05	Alston, Dell	81D	322	$ .01	$ .05
Aguayo, Luis	85D	503	$ .01	$ .08	Altobelli, Joe	84D	88	$ .03	$ .10
Aguayo, Luis	86D	503	$ .01	$ .06	Alvarez, Jose	89D	405	$ .01	$ .10
Aguayo, Luis	88D	185	$ .01	$ .05	Alvarez, Jose	90D	389	$ .01	$ .03
Aguayo, Luis	89D	551	$ .01	$ .04	Amalfitano, Joe	81D	522	$ .01	$ .05
Aguilera, Rick	86D	441	$ .08	$ .35	Andersen (son), Larry	82D	428	$ .01	$ .05
Aguilera, Rick	87D	620	$ .01	$ .04	Andersen, Larry	83D	181	$ .01	$ .05
Aguilera, Rick	88D	446	$ .01	$ .05	Andersen, Larry	85D	570	$ .01	$ .08
Aguilera, Rick	89D	526	$ .01	$ .04	Andersen, Larry	86D	355	$ .01	$ .06
Aguilera, Rick	89DBB	265	$ .01	$ .04	Andersen, Larry	87D	640	$ .01	$ .04
Aguilera, Rick	90D	391	$ .01	$ .03	Andersen, Larry	89D	359	$ .01	$ .04
Aikens, Willie	81D	220	$ .01	$ .05	Andersen, Larry	90D	359	$ .01	$ .03
Aikens, Willie	82D	412	$ .01	$ .05	Anderson, Allan	86DR	3	$ .05	$ .35
Aikens, Willie	83D	212	$ .01	$ .05	Anderson, Allan	87D	368	$ .05	$ .35
Aikens, Willie	84D	155	$ .03	$ .10	Anderson, Allan	89D	419	$ .01	$ .10
Ainge, Danny	81D	569	$ .05	$ .30	Anderson, Allan	89DBB	270	$ .01	$ .04
Ainge, Danny	82D	638	$ .05	$ .30	Anderson, Allan	90D	64	$ .01	$ .03
Aldrete, Mike	87D	450	$ .03	$ .25	Anderson, Brady	88DR	14	$ .05	$ .35
Aldrete, Mike	88D	362	$ .01	$ .15	Anderson, Brady	89D	519	$ .05	$ .35
Aldrete, Mike	88DBB	191	$ .01	$ .05	Anderson, Brady	90D	638	$ .01	$ .03
Aldrete, Mike	89D	140	$ .01	$ .04	Anderson, Bud	84D	590	$ .03	$ .10
Aldrete, Mike	89DTR	25	$ .01	$ .05	Anderson, Dave	84D	642	$ .05	$ .25
Aldrich, Jay	88D	460	$ .01	$ .05	Anderson, Dave	85D	275	$ .01	$ .08
Alexander, Doyle	81D	448	$ .02	$ .15	Anderson, Dave	88D	475	$ .01	$ .05
Alexander, Doyle	82D	96	$ .01	$ .05	Anderson, Dave	89D	434	$ .01	$ .04
Alexander, Doyle	83D	451	$ .01	$ .05	Anderson, Dave	90D	486	$ .01	$ .03
Alexander, Doyle	84D	439	$ .03	$ .10	Anderson, Jim	81D	165	$ .01	$ .05
Alexander, Doyle	85D	561	$ .01	$ .08	Anderson, Jim	82D	181	$ .01	$ .05
Alexander, Doyle	86D	390	$ .01	$ .06	Anderson, Kent	90D	490	$ .01	$ .03
Alexander, Doyle	87D	657	$ .01	$ .04	Anderson, Larry	88D	332	$ .01	$ .05
Alexander, Doyle	88D	584	$ .01	$ .05	Anderson, Sparky	81D	370	$ .01	$ .05
Alexander, Doyle	88DBB	13	$ .01	$ .05	Anderson, Sparky	82D	29	$ .05	$ .20
Alexander, Doyle	89D	178	$ .01	$ .04	Anderson, Sparky	83D	533	$ .03	$ .20
Alexander, Doyle	89DBB	125	$ .01	$ .04	Andujar, Joaquin	81D	381	$ .01	$ .05
Alexander, Doyle	90D	62	$ .01	$ .03	Andujar, Joaquin	82D	607	$ .01	$ .05
Alexander, Gary	81D	200	$ .01	$ .05	Andujar, Joaquin	83D	316	$ .01	$ .05
Alicea, Luis	88DR	52	$ .01	$ .15	Andujar, Joaquin	84D	181	$ .03	$ .10
Alicea, Luis	89D	466	$ .01	$ .10	Andujar, Joaquin	85D	449	$ .01	$ .08
Allanson, Andy	86DR	43	$ .02	$ .09	Andujar, Joaquin	85DK	13	$ .03	$ .10
Allanson, Andy	87D	95	$ .01	$ .04	Andujar, Joaquin	86D	231	$ .01	$ .06
Allanson, Andy	88D	465	$ .01	$ .05	Andujar, Joaquin	87D	548	$ .01	$ .04
Allanson, Andy	88DBB	5	$ .01	$ .05	Anthony, Eric	90DRR	34	$ .01	$2.50
Allanson, Andy	89D	138	$ .01	$ .04	Aponte, Luis	83D	109	$ .01	$ .05
Allen, Jamie	84D	267	$ .03	$ .10	Aponte, Luis	84D	371	$ .03	$ .10

Player	Year	No.	VG	EX/MT
Aquino, Luis	87D	655	$ .01	$ .04
Aquino, Luis	89D	534	$ .01	$ .04
Aquino, Luis	90D	179	$ .01	$ .03
Armas, Tony	81D	239	$ .01	$ .05
Armas, Tony	82D	365	$ .01	$ .05
Armas, Tony	83D	71	$ .01	$ .05
Armas, Tony	84D	294	$ .03	$ .10
Armas, Tony	85D	249	$ .01	$ .08
Armas, Tony	86D	127	$ .01	$ .06
Armas, Tony	86DK	5	$ .01	$ .06
Armas, Tony	87D	498	$ .01	$ .04
Armas, Tony	89D	580	$ .01	$ .04
Armas, Tony	90D	525	$ .01	$ .03
Armstrong, Jack	89D	493	$ .15	$ .75
Armstrong, Jack	90D	544	$ .01	$ .25
Armstrong, Mike	84D	217	$ .03	$ .10

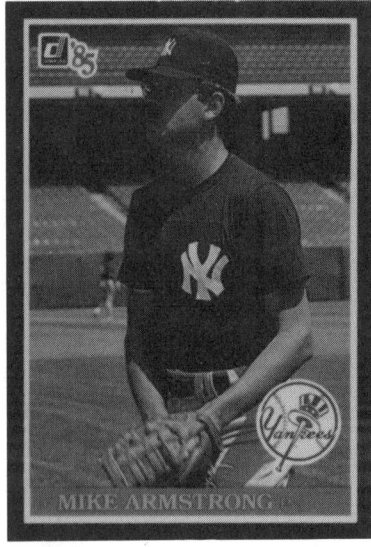

Player	Year	No.	VG	EX/MT
Armstrong, Mike	85D	602	$ .01	$ .08
Arroyo, Fernando	82D	177	$ .01	$ .05
Asadoor, Randy	87D	574	$ .05	$ .20
Ashby, Alan	81D	259	$ .01	$ .05
Ashby, Alan	82D	317	$ .01	$ .05
Ashby, Alan	83D	144	$ .01	$ .05
Ashby, Alan	84D	539	$ .03	$ .10
Ashby, Alan	85D	283	$ .01	$ .08
Ashby, Alan	86D	405	$ .01	$ .06
Ashby, Alan	87D	332	$ .01	$ .04
Ashby, Alan	88D	163	$ .01	$ .05
Ashby, Alan	88DBB	8	$ .01	$ .05
Ashby, Alan	89D	88	$ .01	$ .04
Asselstine, Brian	81D	186	$ .01	$ .05
Asselstine, Brian	82D	184	$ .01	$ .05
Assenmacher, Paul	86DR	28	$ .03	$ .15
Assenmacher, Paul	87D	290	$ .01	$ .15
Assenmacher, Paul	89D	357	$ .01	$ .04
Assenmacher, Paul	90D	459	$ .01	$ .03
Atherton, Keith	84D	497	$ .03	$ .10
Atherton, Keith	85D	340	$ .01	$ .08
Atherton, Keith	87D	272	$ .01	$ .04
Atherton, Keith	88D	318	$ .01	$ .05
Atherton, Keith	89D	273	$ .01	$ .04
August, Don	88D	602	$ .01	$ .15
August, Don	89D	410	$ .01	$ .04
August, Don	90D	617	$ .01	$ .03

Player	Year	No.	VG	EX/MT
Augustine, Jerry	81D	445	$ .01	$ .05
Augustine, Jerry	82D	332	$ .01	$ .05
Avery, Steve	90DRR	39	$ .01	$ .25
Ayala, Benny	81D	236	$ .01	$ .05
Ayala, Benny	82D	581	$ .01	$ .05
Ayala, Benny	83D	331	$ .01	$ .05
Ayala, Benny	84D	270	$ .03	$ .10
Babcock, Bob	82D	565	$ .01	$ .05
Babitt, Shooty	82D	556	$ .01	$ .05
Backman, Wally	83D	618	$ .03	$ .20
Backman, Wally	85D	319	$ .01	$ .08
Backman, Wally	86D	238	$ .01	$ .06
Backman, Wally	87D	316	$ .01	$ .04
Backman, Wally	88D	241	$ .01	$ .05
Backman, Wally	89D	383	$ .01	$ .04
Backman, Wally	89DBB	186	$ .01	$ .04
Backman, Wally	89DTR	10	$ .01	$ .05
Backman, Wally	90D	155	$ .01	$ .03
Bahnsen, Stan	81D	452	$ .01	$ .05
Bahnsen, Stan	82D	392	$ .01	$ .05
Bailes, Scott	86DR	25	$ .03	$ .25
Bailes, Scott	87D	227	$ .01	$ .04
Bailes, Scott	88D	104	$ .01	$ .05
Bailes, Scott	89D	202	$ .01	$ .04
Bailes, Scott	90D	468	$ .01	$ .03
Bailey, Howard	84D	212	$ .03	$ .10
Bailey, Mark	85D	450	$ .01	$ .08
Bailey, Mark	86D	354	$ .01	$ .06
Bailey, Mark	87D	235	$ .01	$ .04
Bailor, Bob	81D	389	$ .01	$ .05
Bailor, Bob	82D	308	$ .01	$ .05
Bailor, Bob	83D	506	$ .01	$ .05
Bailor, Bob	84D	595	$ .03	$ .10
Bailor, Bob	85D	397	$ .01	$ .08
Baines, Harold	82D	568	$ .05	$1.00
Baines, Harold	83D	143	$ .05	$ .30
Baines, Harold	84D	58	$ .04	$ .25
Baines, Harold	85D	58	$ .03	$ .20
Baines, Harold	86D	180	$ .02	$ .15
Baines, Harold	86DK	13	$ .01	$ .06
Baines, Harold	87D	429	$ .05	$ .20
Baines, Harold	88D	211	$ .01	$ .05
Baines, Harold	88DBB	11	$ .01	$ .05
Baines, Harold	89D	148	$ .01	$ .04
Baines, Harold	89DBB	81	$ .01	$ .10
Baines, Harold	90D	402	$ .01	$ .10
Baines, Harold	90DAS	660	$ .01	$ .10
Bair, Doug	81D	64	$ .01	$ .05
Bair, Doug	83D	372	$ .01	$ .05
Bair, Doug	84D	369	$ .03	$ .10
Bair, Doug	85D	369	$ .01	$ .08
Baker, Dusty	81D	179	$ .01	$ .10
Baker, Dusty	82D	336	$ .01	$ .05
Baker, Dusty	83D	462	$ .01	$ .05
Baker, Dusty	84D	226	$ .03	$ .10
Baker, Dusty	85D	445	$ .01	$ .08
Baker, Dusty	86D	467	$ .01	$ .06
Balboni, Steve	83D	73	$ .01	$ .05
Balboni, Steve	85D	419	$ .01	$ .08
Balboni, Steve	86D	222	$ .01	$ .06
Balboni, Steve	87D	102	$ .01	$ .04
Balboni, Steve	88D	424	$ .01	$ .05
Balboni, Steve	89D	143	$ .01	$ .04
Balboni, Steve	89DBB	188	$ .01	$ .04
Balboni, Steve	89DTR	48	$ .01	$ .05
Balboni, Steve	90D	315	$ .01	$ .03
Ballard, Jeff	88D	520	$ .01	$ .35
Ballard, Jeff	89D	495	$ .01	$ 04
Ballard, Jeff	89DBB	30	$ .01	$ .04
Ballard, Jeff	90D	51	$ .01	$ .03
Baller, Jay	86D	613	$ .01	$ .06
Bando, Chris	82D	551	$ .01	$ .05
Bando, Chris	83D	33	$ .01	$ .05
Bando, Chris	84D	224	$ .03	$ .10
Bando, Chris	85D	520	$ .01	$ .08

Player	Year	No.	VG	EX/MT	Player	Year	No.	VG	EX/MT
Bando, Chris	86D	373	$ .01	$ .06	Baylor, Don	82D	493	$ .03	$ .20
Bando, Chris	87D	501	$ .01	$ .04	Baylor, Don	83D	493	$ .03	$ .15
Bando, Chris	88D	95	$ .01	$ .05	Baylor, Don	84D	152	$ .03	$ .10
Bando, Sal	81D	84	$ .02	$ .15	Baylor, Don	85D	173	$ .03	$ .20
Bando, Sal	82D	592	$ .01	$ .05	Baylor, Don	86D	347	$ .01	$ .06
Bankhead, Scott	86DR	36	$ .02	$ .15	Baylor, Don	87D	339	$ .01	$ .04
Bankhead, Scott	88D	70	$ .01	$ .05	Beane, Billy	86D	647	$ .01	$ .06
Bankhead, Scott	89D	463	$ .01	$ .04	Beard, Dave	83D	113	$ .01	$ .05
Bankhead, Scott	89DBB	219	$ .01	$ .04	Beard, Dave	84D	218	$ .03	$ .10
Bankhead, Scott	90D	261	$ .01	$ .03	Beattie, Jim	81D	166	$ .01	$ .05
Bannister, Alan	82D	159	$ .01	$ .05	Beattie, Jim	82D	478	$ .01	$ .05
Bannister, Alan	83D	285	$ .01	$ .05	Beattie, Jim	83D	176	$ .01	$ .05
Bannister, Alan	84D	154	$ .03	$ .10	Beattie, Jim	84D	191	$ .03	$ .10
Bannister, Alan	86D	525	$ .01	$ .06	Beattie, Jim	85D	313	$ .01	$ .08
Bannister, Floyd	81D	286	$ .01	$ .05	Beattie, Jim	86D	196	$ .01	$ .06
Bannister, Floyd	82D	100	$ .01	$ .05	Beckwith, Joe	84D	337	$ .03	$ .10
Bannister, Floyd	83D	50	$ .01	$ .05	Beckwith, Joe	85D	541	$ .01	$ .08
Bannister, Floyd	83DK	21	$ .01	$ .05	Bedrosian, Steve	82D	401	$ .15	$ .95
Bannister, Floyd	84D	366	$ .03	$ .10	Bedrosian, Steve	83D	173	$ .03	$ .25
Bannister, Floyd	85D	379	$ .01	$ .08	Bedrosian, Steve	84D	565	$ .05	$ .30
Bannister, Floyd	86D	244	$ .01	$ .06	Bedrosian, Steve	85D	628	$ .03	$ .15
Bannister, Floyd	87D	211	$ .01	$ .04	Bedrosian, Steve	86D	199	$ .02	$ .15
Bannister, Floyd	88D	383	$ .01	$ .05	Bedrosian, Steve	87D	185	$ .02	$ .15
Bannister, Floyd	88DBB	7	$ .01	$ .05	Bedrosian, Steve	88D	62	$ .01	$ .05
Bannister, Floyd	89D	262	$ .01	$ .04	Bedrosian, Steve	88DBB	16	$ .01	$ .10
Barfield, Jesse	83D	595	$ .05	$1.00	Bedrosian, Steve	89D	75	$ .01	$ .10
Barfield, Jesse	84D	193	$ .15	$ .40	Bedrosian, Steve	89DBB	303	$ .01	$ .04
Barfield, Jesse	85D	195	$ .08	$ .25	Bedrosian, Steve	89DK	24	$ .01	$ .15
Barfield, Jesse	86D	193	$ .03	$ .25	Bedrosian, Steve	90D	295	$ .01	$ .03
Barfield, Jesse	87D	121	$ .01	$ .15	Behenna, Rick	84D	346	$ .05	$ .25
Barfield, Jesse	88D	442	$ .01	$ .15	Belanger, Mark	81D	472	$ .02	$ .15
Barfield, Jesse	88DBB	216	$ .01	$ .10	Belanger, Mark	83D	514	$ .01	$ .05
Barfield, Jesse	89D	425	$ .01	$ .04	Belcher, Tim	88D	587	$ .01	$ .50
Barfield, Jesse	89DBB	132	$ .01	$ .04	Belcher, Tim	88DBB	10	$ .01	$ .15
Barfield, Jesse	90D	74	$ .01	$ .03	Belcher, Tim	88DR	28	$ .01	$ .25
Barker, Len	81D	320	$ .01	$ .05	Belcher, Tim	89D	203	$ .01	$ .04
Barker, Len	82D	137	$ .01	$ .05	Belcher, Tim	89DBB	234	$ .01	$ .04
Barker, Len	82DK	6	$ .01	$ .05	Belcher, Tim	90D	79	$ .01	$ .03
Barker, Len	83D	111	$ .01	$ .05	Bell, Buddy	81D	145	$ .03	$ .20
Barker, Len	84D	443	$ .03	$ .10	Bell, Buddy	82D	368	$ .03	$ .20
Barker, Len	85D	165	$ .01	$ .08	Bell, Buddy	82DK	23	$ .03	$ .20
Barker, Len	86D	409	$ .01	$ .06	Bell, Buddy	83D	215	$ .03	$ .20
Barnes, Richard	84D	608	$ .03	$ .10	Bell, Buddy	84D	56	$ .08	$ .25
Barnes, Skeeter	85D	530	$ .01	$ .08	Bell, Buddy	85D	56	$ .03	$ .20
Barojas, Salome	83D	67	$ .01	$ .05	Bell, Buddy	86D	447	$ .05	$ .20
Barojas, Salome	84D	570	$ .03	$ .10	Bell, Buddy	87D	556	$ .01	$ .15
Barojas, Salome	85D	605	$ .01	$ .08	Bell, Buddy	88D	206	$ .01	$ .15
Barr, Jim	81D	412	$ .01	$ .05	Bell, Eric	87DR	2	$ .01	$ .07
Barr, Jim	83D	398	$ .01	$ .05	Bell, Eric	87DRR	39	$ .10	$ .35
Barr, Jim	84D	79	$ .03	$ .10	Bell, Eric	88D	125	$ .01	$ .05
Barrett, Marty	85D	127	$ .03	$ .25	Bell, George (Jorge)	82D	54	$1.50	$6.00
Barrett, Marty	86D	294	$ .01	$ .06	Bell, George	84D	73	$ .50	$1.50
Barrett, Marty	87D	523	$ .01	$ .04	Bell, George	85D	146	$ .25	$ .75
Barrett, Marty	88D	276	$ .01	$ .05	Bell, George	86D	71	$ .15	$ .40
Barrett, Marty	88DBB	9	$ .01	$ .05	Bell, George	86DK	4	$ .08	$ .25
Barrett, Marty	89D	184	$ .01	$ .04	Bell, George	87D	271	$ .05	$ .25
Barrett, Marty	89DBB	252	$ .01	$ .04	Bell, George	88D	656	$ .05	$ .20
Barrett, Marty	90D	240	$ .01	$ .03	Bell, George	88DBB	31	$ .01	$ .10
Bass, Kevin	84D	450	$ .03	$ .10	Bell, George	88DBC	19	$ .15	$ .50
Bass, Kevin	85D	136	$ .01	$ .08	Bell, George	89D	149	$ .01	$ .10
Bass, Kevin	86D	548	$ .01	$ .06	Bell, George	89DBB	272	$ .01	$ .10
Bass, Kevin	87D	410	$ .01	$ .04	Bell, George	90D	206	$ .01	$ .10
Bass, Kevin	88D	286	$ .01	$ .05	Bell, George	90DBC	13	$ .01	$ .10
Bass, Kevin	88DBB	38	$ .01	$ .05	Bell, Jay	88D	637	$ .05	$ .20
Bass, Kevin	89D	325	$ .01	$ .04	Bell, Jay	88DBB	61	$ .01	$ .05
Bass, Kevin	90D	589	$ .01	$ .03	Bell, Jay	89D	350	$ .01	$ .10
Bass, Randy	82D	439	$ .01	$ .05	Bell, Jay	90D	488	$ .01	$ .03
Bathe, Bill	86DR	41	$ .02	$ .09	Bell, Kevin	81D	39	$ .01	$ .05
Bathe, Bill	87D	281	$ .01	$ .04	Belle, Joey	90D	390	$ .01	$ .50
Bathe, Bill	90D	680	$ .01	$ .03	Belliard, Rafael	87D	538	$ .01	$ .04
Baumgarten, Ross	81D	41	$ .01	$ .05	Belliard, Rafael	90D	252	$ .01	$ .03
Baumgarten, Ross	82D	104	$ .01	$ .05	Bench, Johnny	81D	182	$ .15	$1.00
Bautista, Jose	88DR	41	$ .01	$ .05	Bench, Johnny	81D	62	$ .10	$1.00
Bautista, Jose	89D	451	$ .01	$ .10	Bench, Johnny	82D	400	$ .15	$1.25
Baylor, Don	81D	413	$ .03	$ .20	Bench, Johnny	82D	628	$ .15	$ .75

DONRUSS

Player	Year	No.	VG	EX/MT
Bench, Johnny	83D	500	$ .10	$ .75
Bench, Johnny	83DK	22	$ .10	$ .50
Bench, Johnny	84D#B	0	$1.50	$8.00
Benedict, Bruce	81D	208	$ .01	$ .05
Benedict, Bruce	82D	375	$ .01	$ .05
Benedict, Bruce	83D	299	$ .01	$ .05
Benedict, Bruce	84D	409	$ .03	$ .10
Benedict, Bruce	85D	261	$ .01	$ .08
Benedict, Bruce	85D	263	$ .01	$ .08
Benedict, Bruce	86D	554	$ .01	$ .06
Benedict, Bruce	87D	448	$ .01	$ .04
Benedict, Bruce	89D	475	$ .01	$ .04
Benes, Andy	90DRR	41	$ .01	$ .50
Beniquez, Juan	81D	518	$ .01	$ .05
Beniquez, Juan	82D	587	$ .01	$ .05
Beniquez, Juan	83D	640	$ .01	$ .05
Beniquez, Juan	84D	207	$ .03	$ .10
Beniquez, Juan	85D	573	$ .01	$ .08
Beniquez, Juan	86D	352	$ .01	$ .06
Beniquez, Juan	87D	371	$ .01	$ .04
Benzinger, Todd	87DR	30	$ .20	$ .60
Benzinger, Todd	88D	297	$ .05	$ .35
Benzinger, Todd	89D	358	$ .01	$ .15
Benzinger, Todd	89DBB	174	$ .01	$ .10
Benzinger, Todd	89DTR	47	$ .05	$ .20
Benzinger, Todd	90D	257	$ .01	$ .03
Berenguer, Juan	82D	580	$ .01	$ .05
Berenguer, Juan	84D	125	$ .03	$ .10
Berenguer, Juan	85D	272	$ .01	$ .08
Berenguer, Juan	87D	616	$ .01	$ .04
Berenguer, Juan	88D	395	$ .01	$ .05
Berenguer, Juan	89D	81	$ .01	$ .04
Berenguer, Juan	89DBB	46	$ .01	$ .04
Berenguer, Juan	90D	301	$ .01	$ .03
Berenyi, Bruce	83D	103	$ .01	$ .05
Berenyi, Bruce	84D	487	$ .03	$ .10
Berenyi, Bruce	85D	625	$ .01	$ .08
Bergman, Dave	81D	139	$ .01	$ .05
Bergman, Dave	82D	146	$ .01	$ .05
Bergman, Dave	83D	550	$ .01	$ .05
Bergman, Dave	84D	624	$ .03	$ .10
Bergman, Dave	85D	537	$ .01	$ .08
Bergman, Dave	86D	471	$ .01	$ .06
Bergman, Dave	87D	420	$ .01	$ .04
Bergman, Dave	88D	373	$ .01	$ .05
Bergman, Dave	89D	389	$ .01	$ .04
Bergman, Dave	90D	445	$ .01	$ .03
Bernard, Dwight	83D	28	$ .01	$ .05
Bernazard, Tony	81D	449	$ .01	$ .05
Bernazard, Tony	82D	143	$ .01	$ .05
Bernazard, Tony	83D	482	$ .01	$ .05
Bernazard, Tony	84D	240	$ .03	$ .10
Bernazard, Tony	85D	102	$ .01	$ .08
Bernazard, Tony	86D	520	$ .01	$ .06
Bernazard, Tony	87D	377	$ .01	$ .04
Bernazard, Tony	88D	344	$ .01	$ .05
Berra, Dale	81D	253	$ .01	$ .05
Berra, Dale	82D	250	$ .01	$ .05
Berra, Dale	83D	185	$ .01	$ .05
Berra, Dale	84D	430	$ .03	$ .10
Berra, Dale	85D	444	$ .01	$ .08
Berra, Dale	86D	295	$ .01	$ .06
Berra, Yogi	81D	351	$ .05	$ .30
Berra, Yogi	82D	387	$ .03	$ .20
Berroa, Geronimo	88D	659	$ .05	$ .40
Berroa, Geronimo	89DR	19	$ .01	$ .10
Berroa, Geronimo	90D	104	$ .01	$ .03
Berryhill, Damon	88D	639	$ .05	$ .50
Berryhill, Damon	88DBB	261	$ .01	$ .25
Berryhill, Damon	88DR	31	$ .01	$ .30
Berryhill, Damon	89D	275	$ .01	$ .10
Berryhill, Damon	89DBB	116	$ .01	$ .10
Berryhill, Damon	90D	167	$ .01	$ .10
Best, Karl	86D	511	$ .01	$ .06
Best, Karl	87D	198	$ .01	$ .04
Bevacqua, Kurt	84D	80	$ .03	$ .10
Bevacqua, Kurt	85D	647	$ .01	$ .08
Bevacqua, Kurt	86D	528	$ .01	$ .06
Biancalana, Buddy	86D	605	$ .01	$ .06
Biancalana, Buddy	87D	527	$ .01	$ .04
Bibby, Jim	81D	134	$ .01	$ .05
Bibby, Jim	82D	171	$ .01	$ .05
Bichette, Dante	89D	634	$ .01	$ .25
Bichette, Dante	89DR	29	$ .01	$ .10
Bielecki, Mike	85DRR	28	$ .25	$1.00
Bielecki, Mike	87D	415	$ .01	$ .04
Bielecki, Mike	88D	484	$ .01	$ .05
Bielecki, Mike	89D	512	$ .01	$ .04
Bielecki, Mike	89DBB	194	$ .01	$ .04
Bielecki, Mike	90D	373	$ .01	$ .03
Bielecki, Mike	90DK	9	$ .01	$ .10
Biggio, Craig	89D	561	$ .01	$ .50
Biggio, Craig	89DBB	176	$ .01	$ .15
Biggio, Craig	90D	306	$ .01	$ .10
Biittner, Larry	81D	515	$ .01	$ .05
Biittner, Larry	82D	43	$ .01	$ .05
Biittner, Larry	83D	440	$ .01	$ .05
Biittner, Larry	84D	342	$ .03	$ .10
Bilardello, Dann	85D	243	$ .01	$ .08
Billardello, Dann	84D	408	$ .03	$ .10
Bird, Doug	82D	504	$ .01	$ .05
Bird, Doug	83D	48	$ .01	$ .05
Birkbeck, Mike	87DR	19	$ .01	$ .20
Birkbeck, Mike	87DRR	33	$ .05	$ .25
Birkbeck, Mike	88D	49	$ .01	$ .05
Birkbeck, Mike	89D	501	$ .01	$ .04
Birtsas, Tim	86D	462	$ .01	$ .06
Birtsas, Tim	90D	493	$ .01	$ .10
Black, Bud	83D	322	$ .10	$ .35
Black, Bud	84D	130	$ .03	$ .10
Black, Bud	85D	100	$ .01	$ .08
Black, Bud	86D	374	$ .01	$ .06
Black, Bud	87D	404	$ .01	$ .04
Black, Bud	88D	301	$ .01	$ .05
Black, Bud	89D	556	$ .01	$ .04
Black, Bud	90D	556	$ .01	$ .03
Blackwell, Tim	81D	559	$ .01	$ .05
Blackwell, Tim	82D	99	$ .01	$ .05
Blackwell, Tim	83D	214	$ .01	$ .05
Blankenship, Kevin	89D	658	$ .01	$ .04
Blankenship, Lance	89D	621	$ .01	$ .25
Blauser, Jeff	88D	513	$ .01	$ .30
Blauser, Jeff	89D	592	$ .01	$ .04
Blauser, Jeff	90D	271	$ .01	$ .03
Blowers, Mike	90D	656	$ .01	$ .10
Blue, Vida	81D	433	$ .02	$ .15
Blue, Vida	82D	222	$ .01	$ .05
Blue, Vida	82DK	4	$ .01	$ .05
Blue, Vida	83D	34	$ .01	$ .05
Blue, Vida	83D	648	$ .01	$ .15
Blue, Vida	86D	509	$ .01	$ .06
Blue, Vida	87D	362	$ .01	$ .04
Blyleven, Bert	81D	135	$ .05	$ .30
Blyleven, Bert	82D	111	$ .02	$ .15
Blyleven, Bert	83D	589	$ .02	$ .15
Blyleven, Bert	84D	129	$ .10	$ .35
Blyleven, Bert	85D	224	$ .03	$ .25
Blyleven, Bert	85DK	4	$ .01	$ .08
Blyleven, Bert	86D	649	$ .05	$ .20
Blyleven, Bert	87D	71	$ .01	$ .04
Blyleven, Bert	88D	71	$ .01	$ .05
Blyleven, Bert	88DBB	18	$ .01	$ .05
Blyleven, Bert	89D	119	$ .01	$ .04
Blyleven, Bert	89DBB	3	$ .01	$ .04
Blyleven, Bert	89DTR	35	$ .01	$ .15
Blyleven, Bert	90D	331	$ .01	$ .03
Bochte, Bruce	81D	403	$ .01	$ .05
Bochte, Bruce	82D	505	$ .01	$ .05
Bochte, Bruce	83D	127	$ .01	$ .05
Bochte, Bruce	85D	253	$ .01	$ .08

Player	Year	No.	VG	EX/MT	Player	Year	No.	VG	EX/MT
Bochte, Bruce	86D	400	$ .01	$ .06	Boone, Bob	90D	326	$ .01	$ .03
Bochy, Bruce	81D	20	$ .01	$ .05	Boone, Danny	82D	187	$ .01	$ .05
Bochy, Bruce	85D	505	$ .01	$ .08	Borders, Pat	88DR	12	$ .01	$ .15
Bochy, Bruce	86D	551	$ .01	$ .06	Borders, Pat	89D	560	$ .01	$ .15
Bochy, Bruce	87D	311	$ .01	$ .04					
Boddicker, Mike	84D	123	$ .04	$ .25					
Boddicker, Mike	85D	291	$ .01	$ .08					
Boddicker, Mike	86D	47	$ .01	$ .06					
Boddicker, Mike	86DK	8	$ .01	$ .06					
Boddicker, Mike	87D	125	$ .01	$ .04					
Boddicker, Mike	88D	89	$ .01	$ .05					
Boddicker, Mike	89D	612	$ .01	$ .04					
Boddicker, Mike	89DBB	297	$ .01	$ .04					
Boddicker, Mike	90D	280	$ .01	$ .03					
Boever, Joe	89D	168	$ .01	$ .04					
Boever, Joe	90D	357	$ .01	$ .03					
Boggs, Tommy	81D	597	$ .01	$ .05					
Boggs, Tommy	82D	249	$ .01	$ .05					
Boggs, Tommy	83D	349	$ .01	$ .05					
Boggs, Wade	83D	586	$5.00	$18.00					
Boggs, Wade	84D	151	$3.50	$12.00					
Boggs, Wade	84DK	26	$1.00	$4.00					
Boggs, Wade	85D	172	$1.50	$5.00					
Boggs, Wade	86D	371	$1.00	$2.50					
Boggs, Wade	87D	252	$ .50	$1.50					
Boggs, Wade	88D	153	$ .35	$1.00					
Boggs, Wade	88DBB	65	$ .10	$ .50					
Boggs, Wade	88DBC	7	$ .35	$ .50					
Boggs, Wade	89D	68	$ .10	$ .50					
Boggs, Wade	89DBB	140	$ .01	$ .35					
Boggs, Wade	90D	68	$ .01	$ .25	Borders, Pat	90D	560	$ .01	$ .03
Boggs, Wade	90DAS	712	$ .01	$ .20	Bordi, Rich	85D	289	$ .01	$ .08
Bogner, Terry	83D	520	$ .01	$ .05	Bordi, Rich	86D	518	$ .01	$ .06
Bolton, Tom	89D	539	$ .01	$ .04	Bordi, Rich	87D	213	$ .01	$ .04
Bomback, Mark	82D	559	$ .01	$ .05	Borgmann, Glenn	81D	159	$ .01	$ .05
Bonds, Barry	86DR	11	$ .35	$2.00	Bosetti, Rick	81D	152	$ .01	$ .05
Bonds, Barry	87D	361	$ .25	$2.00	Bosetti, Rick	82D	626	$ .01	$ .05
Bonds, Barry	88D	326	$ .10	$ .25	Bosio, Chris	87D	478	$ .05	$ .35
Bonds, Barry	88DBB	17	$ .01	$ .15	Bosio, Chris	87DR	20	$ .01	$ .07
Bonds, Barry	89D	92	$ .01	$ .10	Bosio, Chris	88D	117	$ .01	$ .05
Bonds, Barry	89DBB	73	$ .01	$ .10	Bosio, Chris	89D	412	$ .01	$ .04
Bonds, Barry	90D	126	$ .01	$ .10	Bosio, Chris	89DBB	109	$ .01	$ .04
Bonds, Bobby	81D	71	$ .01	$ .05	Bosio, Chris	90D	57	$ .01	$ .03
Bonilla, Bobby	86DR	30	$ .35	$2.50	Bosio, Chris	90DK	20	$ .01	$ .10
Bonilla, Bobby	87D	558	$ .35	$2.00	Bosley, Thad	81D	162	$ .01	$ .05
Bonilla, Bobby	88D	238	$ .10	$ .50	Bosley, Thad	85D	388	$ .01	$ .08
Bonilla, Bobby	88DBB	33	$ .01	$ .10	Bosley, Thad	86D	483	$ .01	$ .06
Bonilla, Bobby	89D	151	$ .01	$ .15	Bosley, Thad	87D	191	$ .01	$ .04
Bonilla, Bobby	89DBB	33	$ .01	$ .20	Bosley, Thad	88D	348	$ .01	$ .05
Bonilla, Bobby	89DK	2	$ .01	$ .05	Boston, Daryl	85DRR	33	$ .08	$ .25
Bonilla, Bobby	90D	290	$ .01	$ .20	Boston, Daryl	86D	86	$ .01	$ .06
Bonilla, Bobby	90DBC	16	$ .01	$ .10	Boston, Daryl	87D	137	$ .01	$ .04
Bonilla, Juan	82D	220	$ .01	$ .05	Boston, Daryl	89D	455	$ .01	$ .04
Bonilla, Juan	83D	346	$ .01	$ .05	Bowa, Larry	81D	142	$ .03	$ .20
Bonilla, Juan	84D	234	$ .03	$ .10	Bowa, Larry	82D	63	$ .02	$ .15
Bonnell, Barry	81D	272	$ .01	$ .05	Bowa, Larry	83D	435	$ .01	$ .05
Bonnell, Barry	82D	432	$ .01	$ .05	Bowa, Larry	84D	239	$ .04	$ .25
Bonnell, Barry	83D	430	$ .01	$ .05	Bowa, Larry	85D	361	$ .03	$ .20
Bonnell, Barry	84D	559	$ .03	$ .10	Boyd, Dennis	84D	457	$ .20	$ .75
Bonnell, Barry	85D	191	$ .01	$ .08	Boyd, Dennis "Oil Can"	85D	151	$ .01	$ .10
Bonner, Bob	82D	610	$ .01	$ .05	Boyd, Oil Can	86D	50	$ .02	$ .15
Booker, Greg	88D	311	$ .01	$ .05	Boyd, Oil Can	87D	51	$ .01	$ .04
Boone, Bob	81D	262	$ .01	$ .05	Boyd, Oil Can	88D	462	$ .01	$ .05
Boone, Bob	82D	471	$ .01	$ .05	Boyd, Oil Can	89D	476	$ .01	$ .04
Boone, Bob	83D	192	$ .01	$ .05	Boyd, Oil Can	90D	633	$ .01	$ .03
Boone, Bob	84D	158	$ .03	$ .10	Bradford, Larry	81D	584	$ .01	$ .05
Boone, Bob	85D	230	$ .01	$ .08	Bradford, Larry	82D	553	$ .01	$ .05
Boone, Bob	86D	230	$ .01	$ .06	Bradley, Phil	85D	631	$ .35	$1.00
Boone, Bob	86DK	17	$ .01	$ .06	Bradley, Phil	86D	191	$ .08	$ .25
Boone, Bob	87D	233	$ .01	$ .04					
Boone, Bob	88D	305	$ .01	$ .05					
Boone, Bob	88DBB	3	$ .01	$ .05					
Boone, Bob	89D	170	$ .01	$ .04					
Boone, Bob	89DBB	263	$ .01	$ .04					
Boone, Bob	89DTR	5	$ .01	$ .05					

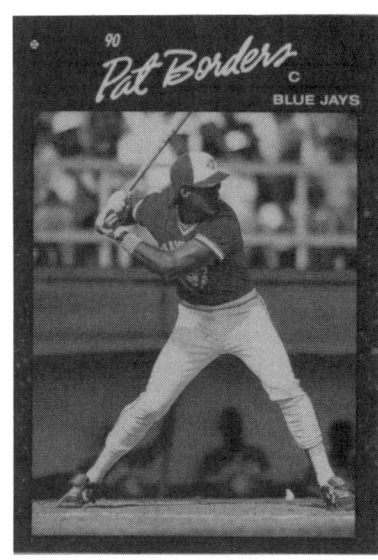

Player	Year	No.	VG	EX/MT
Bradley, Phil	86DK	22	$ .05	$ .20
Bradley, Phil	87D	270	$ .01	$ .04
Bradley, Phil	88D	243	$ .01	$ .05
Bradley, Phil	88DBB	47	$ .01	$ .05
Bradley, Phil	89D	369	$ .01	$ .04
Bradley, Phil	89DBB	198	$ .01	$ .04
Bradley, Phil	89DTR	41	$ .01	$ .05
Bradley, Phil	90D	259	$ .01	$ .03
Bradley, Scott	85DRR	37	$ .05	$ .25
Bradley, Scott	86D	396	$ .01	$ .06
Bradley, Scott	87D	440	$ .01	$ .04
Bradley, Scott	88D	147	$ .01	$ .05
Bradley, Scott	88DBB	24	$ .01	$ .05
Bradley, Scott	89D	261	$ .01	$ .04
Bradley, Scott	90D	581	$ .01	$ .03
Braggs, Glenn	87D	337	$ .08	$ .50
Braggs, Glenn	88D	240	$ .01	$ .05
Braggs, Glenn	88DBB	15	$ .01	$ .05
Braggs, Glenn	89D	103	$ .01	$ .04
Braggs, Glenn	89DBB	277	$ .01	$ .04
Braggs, Glenn	90D	264	$ .01	$ .03
Brantley, Jeff	89DR	41	$ .01	$ .10
Brantley, Jeff	90D	466	$ .01	$ .03
Brantley, Mickey	87D	656	$ .01	$ .15
Brantley, Mickey	87DR	27	$ .01	$ .07
Brantley, Mickey	88D	610	$ .01	$ .15
Brantley, Mickey	88DBB	80	$ .01	$ .05
Brantley, Mickey	89D	212	$ .01	$ .04
Braun, Steve	82D	418	$ .01	$ .05
Braun, Steve	86D	534	$ .01	$ .06
Bream, Sid	85D	470	$ .08	$ .35
Bream, Sid	86D	566	$ .01	$ .06
Bream, Sid	87D	79	$ .01	$ .04
Bream, Sid	88D	188	$ .01	$ .05
Bream, Sid	88DBB	45	$ .01	$ .05
Bream, Sid	89D	252	$ .01	$ .04
Bream, Sid	89DBB	89	$ .01	$ .04
Bream, Sid	90D	329	$ .01	$ .03
Breining, Fred	82D	186	$ .01	$ .05
Breining, Fred	83D	503	$ .01	$ .05
Breining, Fred	84D	387	$ .03	$ .10
Brenly, Bob	82D	574	$ .03	$ .20
Brenly, Bob	83D	377	$ .01	$ .05
Brenly, Bob	84D	616	$ .03	$ .10
Brenly, Bob	85D	187	$ .01	$ .08
Brenly, Bob	85DK	26	$ .03	$ .10
Brenly, Bob	86D	323	$ .01	$ .06
Brenly, Bob	87D	485	$ .01	$ .04
Brenly, Bob	88D	189	$ .01	$ .05
Brenly, Bob	89D	453	$ .01	$ .04
Brennan, Tom	84D	102	$ .03	$ .10
Brennan, William	89D	589	$ .01	$ .04
Brett, George	81D	100	$ .20	$1.00
Brett, George	81D	491	$ .10	$ .75
Brett, George	81D	537	$ .35	$1.25
Brett, George	82D	34	$ .10	$1.00
Brett, George	82DK	15	$ .15	$ .75
Brett, George	83D	338	$ .10	$1.00
Brett, George	84D	53	$ .50	$1.50
Brett, George	85D	53	$ .25	$ .75
Brett, George	86D	53	$ .15	$ .50
Brett, George	87D	54	$ .10	$ .35
Brett, George	87DK	15	$ .10	$ .35
Brett, George	88D	102	$ .10	$ .35
Brett, George	88DBB	39	$ .05	$ .25
Brett, George	89D	204	$ .05	$ .25
Brett, George	89DBB	7	$ .01	$ .25
Brett, George	89DBC	7	$ .05	$ .30
Brett, George	90D	144	$ .01	$ .25
Brett, Ken	82D	364	$ .01	$ .05
Brewer, Tony	85DRR	31	$ .01	$ .08
Briley, Greg	90D	463	$ .01	$ .20
Bristol, Dave	81D	436	$ .01	$ .05
Brock, Greg	83D	579	$ .10	$ .50
Brock, Greg	84D	296	$ .03	$ .10

Player	Year	No.	VG	EX/MT
Brock, Greg	86D	296	$ .01	$ .06
Brock, Greg	88D	337	$ .01	$ .05
Brock, Greg	88DBB	71	$ .01	$ .05
Brock, Greg	89D	57	$ .01	$ .04
Brock, Greg	89DBB	239	$ .01	$ .04
Brock, Greg	90D	293	$ .01	$ .03
Brookens, Tom	81D	6	$ .01	$ .05
Brookens, Tom	82D	202	$ .01	$ .05
Brookens, Tom	83D	454	$ .01	$ .05
Brookens, Tom	84D	578	$ .03	$ .10
Brookens, Tom	85D	593	$ .01	$ .08
Brookens, Tom	86D	537	$ .01	$ .06
Brookens, Tom	87D	296	$ .01	$ .04
Brookens, Tom	88D	107	$ .01	$ .05
Brookens, Tom	89D	508	$ .01	$ .04
Brookens, Tom	89DTR	53	$ .01	$ .05
Brooks, Hubie	82D	476	$ .15	$ .65
Brooks, Hubie	83D	49	$ .01	$ .05
Brooks, Hubie	84D	607	$ .03	$ .10
Brooks, Hubie	85D	197	$ .01	$ .08
Brooks, Hubie	86D	55	$ .01	$ .06
Brooks, Hubie	87D	88	$ .01	$ .04
Brooks, Hubie	87DK	17	$ .01	$ .04
Brooks, Hubie	88D	468	$ .01	$ .05
Brooks, Hubie	88DBB	12	$ .01	$ .05
Brooks, Hubie	89D	220	$ .01	$ .04
Brooks, Hubie	89DBB	292	$ .01	$ .04
Brooks, Hubie	90D	130	$ .01	$ .03
Bross, Terry	90D	502	$ .01	$ .10
Brouhard, Mark	82D	154	$ .01	$ .05
Brouhard, Mark	83D	532	$ .01	$ .05
Brouhard, Mark	84D	211	$ .03	$ .10
Brouhard, Mark	85D	149	$ .01	$ .08
Brower, Bob	87D	651	$ .05	$ .20
Brower, Bob	87DR	49	$ .01	$ .07
Brower, Bob	88D	346	$ .01	$ .05
Brower, Bob	89D	411	$ .01	$ .04
Brown, Bobby	81D	469	$ .01	$ .05
Brown, Bobby	82D	552	$ .01	$ .05

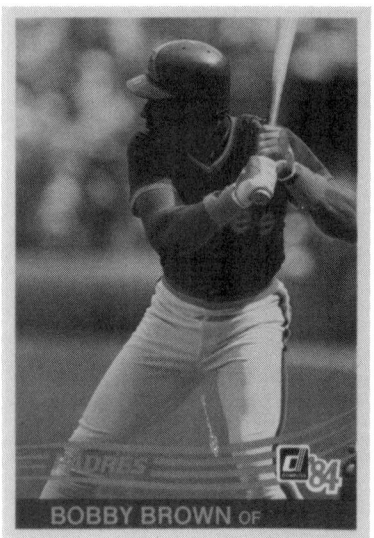

BOBBY BROWN OF

Player	Year	No.	VG	EX/MT
Brown, Bobby	84D	478	$ .03	$ .10
Brown, Bobby	85D	383	$ .01	$ .08
Brown, Chris	86D	553	$ .05	$ .25
Brown, Chris	87D	80	$ .01	$ .04

Player	Year	No.	VG	EX/MT	Player	Year	No.	VG	EX/MT
Brown, Chris	87DK	11	$ .05	$ .20	Buice, DeWayne	87DR	6	$ .01	$ .07
Brown, Chris	88D	483	$ .01	$ .05	Buice, DeWayne	88D	58	$ .01	$ .05
Brown, Chris	88DBB	77	$ .01	$ .05	Bulling, Terry	82D	612	$ .01	$ .05
Brown, Chris	89D	183	$ .01	$ .04	Bulling, Terry	83D	226	$ .01	$ .05
Brown, Chris	89DTR	9	$ .01	$ .05	Bumbry, Al	81D	355	$ .01	$ .05
Brown, Darrell	85D	558	$ .01	$ .08	Bumbry, Al	82D	153	$ .01	$ .05
Brown, Keith	89D	115	$ .01	$ .04	Bumbry, Al	83D	383	$ .01	$ .05
Brown, Kevin	87D	627	$ .15	$ 1.00	Bumbry, Al	84D	210	$ .03	$ .10
Brown, Kevin	89D	613	$ .01	$ .25	Bumbry, Al	85D	350	$ .01	$ .08
Brown, Kevin	89DBB	256	$ .01	$ .04	Burgmeier, Tom	81D	97	$ .01	$ .05
Brown, Kevin	89DR	44	$ .01	$ .10	Burgmeier, Tom	82D	361	$ .01	$ .05
Brown, Kevin	90D	343	$ .01	$ .03	Burgmeier, Tom	83D	235	$ .01	$ .05
Brown, Mike C.	84DRR	42	$ .03	$ .10	Burgmeier, Tom	84D	522	$ .03	$ .10
Brown, Mike C.	85D	207	$ .01	$ .08	Burgmeier, Tom	85D	400	$ .01	$ .08
Brown, Mike C.	86D	642	$ .01	$ .06	Burke, Tim	86D	421	$ .05	$ .25
Brown, Mike C.	87D	168	$ .01	$ .04	Burke, Tim	87D	222	$ .01	$ .04
Brown, Mike G.	84D	517	$ .03	$ .10	Burke, Tim	88D	98	$ .01	$ .05
Brown, Mike G.	87D	563	$ .01	$ .04	Burke, Tim	88DBB	34	$ .01	$ .05
Browne, Jerry	87DR	29	$ .01	$ .25	Burke, Tim	89D	274	$ .01	$ .04
Browne, Jerry	87DRR	41	$ .05	$ .50	Burke, Tim	89DBB	180	$ .01	$ .04
Browne, Jerry	88D	408	$ .01	$ .05	Burke, Tim	90D	334	$ .01	$ .03
Browne, Jerry	89D	529	$ .01	$ .04	Burks, Ellis	87DR	5	$ .50	$2.50
Browne, Jerry	89DBB	280	$ .01	$ .04	Burks, Ellis	88D	174	$ .50	$1.50
Browne, Jerry	89DTR	44	$ .01	$ .05	Burks, Ellis	88DBB	121	$ .15	$ .50
Browne, Jerry	90D	138	$ .01	$ .03	Burks, Ellis	89D	303	$ .15	$ .30
Browning, Tom	85D	634	$ .30	$1.75	Burks, Ellis	89DBB	9	$ .01	$ .20
Browning, Tom	86D	384	$ .10	$ .40	Burks, Ellis	90D	228	$ .01	$ .20
Browning, Tom	87D	63	$ .01	$ .15	Burks, Ellis	90DK	23	$ .01	$ .20
Browning, Tom	88D	63	$ .01	$ .10	Burleson, Rick	81D	454	$ .01	$ .05
Browning, Tom	89D	71	$ .01	$ .10	Burleson, Rick	82D	342	$ .01	$ .05
Browning, Tom	89DBB	62	$ .01	$ .04	Burleson, Rick	83D	318	$ .01	$ .05
Browning, Tom	90D	308	$ .01	$ .03	Burns, Britt	81D	279	$ .01	$ .05
Brumley, Mike	88D	609	$ .01	$ .15	Burns, Britt	82D	230	$ .01	$ .05
Brumley, Mike	89D	302	$ .01	$ .04	Burns, Britt	83D	193	$ .01	$ .05
Brumley, Mike	89DR	39	$ .01	$ .10	Burns, Britt	83DK	23	$ .01	$ .05
Brumley, Mike	90D	533	$ .01	$ .03	Burns, Britt	84D	424	$ .03	$ .10
Brummer, Glenn	83D	418	$ .01	$ .05	Burns, Britt	85D	257	$ .01	$ .08
Brummer, Glenn	84D	138	$ .03	$ .10	Burns, Britt	86D	58	$ .01	$ .06
Brummer, Glenn	85D	290	$ .01	$ .08	Burns, Todd	89D	564	$ .01	$ .25
Brunansky, Tom	83D	555	$ .10	$ .75	Burns, Todd	90D	446	$ .01	$ .03
Brunansky, Tom	84D	242	$ .10	$ .35	Burris, Ray	81D	524	$ .01	$ .05
Brunansky, Tom	85D	364	$ .08	$ .25	Burris, Ray	82D	414	$ .01	$ .05
Brunansky, Tom	86D	192	$ .05	$ .20	Burris, Ray	83D	36	$ .01	$ .05
Brunansky, Tom	86DK	24	$ .05	$ .20	Burris, Ray	84D	331	$ .03	$ .10
Brunansky, Tom	87D	194	$ .01	$ .04	Burris, Ray	85D	218	$ .01	$ .08
Brunansky, Tom	88D	245	$ .05	$ .20	Burris, Ray	86D	107	$ .01	$ .06
Brunansky, Tom	88DBB	19	$ .01	$ .05	Burroughs, Jeff	81D	66	$ .01	$ .05
Brunansky, Tom	89D	112	$ .01	$ .04	Burroughs, Jeff	82D	379	$ .01	$ .05
Brunansky, Tom	89DBB	187	$ .01	$ .04	Burroughs, Jeff	83D	323	$ .01	$ .05
Brunansky, Tom	90D	399	$ .01	$ .03	Burroughs, Jeff	84D	156	$ .03	$ .10
Brusstar, Warren	84D	442	$ .03	$ .10	Burroughs, Jeff	85D	542	$ .01	$ .08
Brusstar, Warren	85D	533	$ .01	$ .08	Bush, Randy	84D	513	$ .05	$ .25
Brusstar, Warren	86D	555	$ .01	$ .06	Bush, Randy	85D	633	$ .01	$ .08
Bryant, Ralph	87D	587	$ .01	$ .04	Bush, Randy	87D	441	$ .01	$ .04
Buckner, Bill	81D	482	$ .02	$ .15	Bush, Randy	88D	272	$ .01	$ .05
Buckner, Bill	82D	403	$ .01	$ .05	Bush, Randy	89D	537	$ .01	$ .04
Buckner, Bill	83D	99	$ .02	$ .15	Bush, Randy	89DBB	214	$ .01	$ .04
Buckner, Bill	83DK	14	$ .02	$ .10	Bush, Randy	90D	199	$ .01	$ .03
Buckner, Bill	84D	117	$ .03	$ .10	Buskey, Tom	81D	270	$ .01	$ .05
Buckner, Bill	85D	416	$ .03	$ .20	Butcher, John	83D	37	$ .01	$ .05
Buckner, Bill	86D	151	$ .02	$ .15	Butcher, John	84D	220	$ .03	$ .10
Buckner, Bill	87D	462	$ .01	$ .04	Butcher, John	85D	314	$ .01	$ .08
Buckner, Bill	88D	456	$ .01	$ .15	Butcher, John	86D	120	$ .01	$ .06
Buckner, Bill	90D	474	$ .01	$ .03	Butera, Sal	81D	530	$ .01	$ .05
Buechele, Steve	86D	544	$ .01	$ .20	Butera, Sal	82D	532	$ .01	$ .05
Buechele, Steve	87D	180	$ .01	$ .04	Butler, Brett	82D	275	$ .10	$ .75
Buechele, Steve	88D	224	$ .01	$ .05	Butler, Brett	83D	636	$ .01	$ .10
Buechele, Steve	89D	174	$ .01	$ .04	Butler, Brett	84D	141	$ .03	$ .10
Buechele, Steve	89DBB	223	$ .01	$ .04	Butler, Brett	85D	216	$ .01	$ .08
Buechele, Steve	90D	107	$ .01	$ .03	Butler, Brett	86D	102	$ .01	$ .06
Buhner, Jay	88D	545	$ .10	$ .45	Butler, Brett	86DK	12	$ .01	$ .06
Buhner, Jay	88DR	11	$ .01	$ .20	Butler, Brett	87D	219	$ .01	$ .04
Buhner, Jay	89D	581	$ .01	$ .15	Butler, Brett	88D	279	$ .01	$ .05
Buhner, Jay	89DBB	136	$ .01	$ .04	Butler, Brett	88DBB	23	$ .01	$ .05
Buhner, Jay	90D	448	$ .01	$ .03	Butler, Brett	89D	217	$ .01	$ .04

DONRUSS

Player	Year	No.	VG	EX/MT	Player	Year	No.	VG	EX/MT
Butler, Brett	89DBB	274	$.01	$.04	Candiotti, Tom	88D	377	$.01	$.05
Butler, Brett	90D	249	$.01	$.03	Candiotti, Tom	88DBB	112	$.01	$.05
Byers, Randall	88D	605	$.01	$.15	Candiotti, Tom	89D	256	$.01	$.04
Bystrom, Martin	83D	93	$.01	$.05	Candiotti, Tom	89DBB	117	$.01	$.04
Bystrom, Marty	82D	93	$.01	$.05	Candiotti, Tom	90D	256	$.01	$.03
Bystrom, Marty	84D	259	$.03	$.10	Cangelosi, John	86DR	51	$.02	$.09
Bystrom, Marty	86D	591	$.01	$.06	Cangelosi, John	87D	162	$.01	$.04
Cabell, Enos	81D	138	$.01	$.05	Cangelosi, John	88D	435	$.01	$.05
Cabell, Enos	82D	272	$.01	$.05	Cangelosi, John	90D	565	$.01	$.03
Cabell, Enos	83D	202	$.01	$.05	Canseco, Jose	86DR	22	$1.50	$12.50
Cabell, Enos	84D	456	$.03	$.10	Canseco, Jose	86DRR	39	$10.00	$90.00
Cabell, Enos	85D	110	$.01	$.08	Canseco, Jose	87D	97	$1.50	$10.00
Cabell, Enos	86D	418	$.01	$.06	Canseco, Jose	87DK	6	$.50	$3.00
Cabrera, Francisco	90D	646	$.01	$.25	Canseco, Jose	88D	302	$.50	$2.00
Cadaret, Greg	88D	528	$.01	$.15	Canseco, Jose	88DBB	22	$.25	$1.00
Cadaret, Greg	89D	479	$.01	$.04	Canseco, Jose	89D	643	$.10	$.50
Cadaret, Greg	90D	545	$.01	$.03	Canseco, Jose	89D	91	$.25	$1.00
Calderon, Ivan	86D	435	$.15	$.75	Canseco, Jose	89DBB	57	$.01	$.50
Calderon, Ivan	88D	182	$.03	$.25	Canseco, Jose	89DBC	5	$.05	$.60
Calderon, Ivan	88DBB	25	$.01	$.05	Canseco, Jose	90D	125	$.01	$.40
Calderon, Ivan	88DBC	5	$.05	$.20	Capel, Mike	88DR	46	$.01	$.05
Calderon, Ivan	88DK	25	$.01	$.05	Capilla, Doug	81D	587	$.01	$.05
Calderon, Ivan	89D	371	$.01	$.04	Carew, Rod	81D	169	$.15	$.75
Calderon, Ivan	89DBB	193	$.01	$.04	Carew, Rod	81D	49	$.10	$.75
Calderon, Ivan	90D	294	$.01	$.03	Carew, Rod	81D	537	$.35	$1.25
Caldwell, Mike	81D	86	$.01	$.05	Carew, Rod	82D	216	$.10	$.50
Caldwell, Mike	82D	330	$.01	$.05	Carew, Rod	82DK	8	$.08	$.50
Caldwell, Mike	83D	154	$.01	$.05	Carew, Rod	83D	90	$.01	$.45
Caldwell, Mike	84D	237	$.03	$.10	Carew, Rod	84D	352	$.25	$1.00
Caldwell, Mike	85D	490	$.01	$.08	Carew, Rod	85D	85	$.15	$.50
Calhoun, Jeff	86D	426	$.01	$.06	Carew, Rod	86D	280	$.10	$.35
Calhoun, Jeff	87D	578	$.01	$.04	Carlton, Steve	81D	33	$.08	$.75
Calhoun, Jeff	88D	509	$.01	$.05	Carlton, Steve	81D	481	$.05	$.50
Camacho, Ernie	85D	129	$.01	$.08	Carlton, Steve	82D	42	$.10	$.75
Camacho, Ernie	87D	350	$.01	$.04	Carlton, Steve	83D	219	$.07	$.45
Cambell, Bill	83D	504	$.01	$.05	Carlton, Steve	83DK	16	$.05	$.40
Caminiti, Ken	88D	308	$.03	$.25	Carlton, Steve	84D	111	$.20	$1.00
Caminiti, Ken	89D	542	$.01	$.10	Carlton, Steve	85D	305	$.15	$.50
Caminiti, Ken	89DBB	262	$.01	$.04	Carlton, Steve	86D	183	$.08	$.25
Caminiti, Ken	90D	424	$.01	$.03	Carlton, Steve	87D	617	$.08	$.25
Camp, Rick	81D	197	$.01	$.05	Carman, Don	86D	427	$.05	$.15
Camp, Rick	82D	223	$.01	$.05	Carman, Don	87D	432	$.01	$.15
Camp, Rick	83D	149	$.01	$.05	Carman, Don	88D	385	$.01	$.05
Camp, Rick	84D	165	$.03	$.10	Carman, Don	88DBB	72	$.01	$.05
Camp, Rick	85D	409	$.01	$.08	Carman, Don	89D	396	$.01	$.04
Camp, Rick	86D	385	$.01	$.06	Carman, Don	90D	604	$.01	$.03
Campaneris, Bert	81D	50	$.01	$.05	Carpenter, Cris	88DR	50	$.05	$.30
Campaneris, Bert	82D	593	$.01	$.05	Carpenter, Cris	89DR	40	$.01	$.25
Campbell, Bill	82D	487	$.01	$.05	Carpenter, Cris	89DRR	39	$.05	$.30
Campbell, Bill	84D	555	$.03	$.10	Carpenter, Cris	90D	634	$.01	$.20
Campbell, Bill	85D	163	$.01	$.08	Carreon, Mark	89DR	18	$.01	$.10
Campbell, Bill	86D	571	$.01	$.06	Carreon, Mark	90D	454	$.01	$.03
Campbell, Mike	88DBB	163	$.01	$.05	Carter, Gary	81D	90	$.10	$.50
Campbell, Mike	88DR	2	$.01	$.15	Carter, Gary	82D	114	$.10	$.50
Campbell, Mike	88DRR	30	$.05	$.20	Carter, Gary	82DK	2	$.10	$.45
Campbell, Mike	89D	497	$.01	$.04	Carter, Gary	83D	340	$.07	$.60
Campusano, Sil	88DR	42	$.01	$.25	Carter, Gary	84D	55	$.20	$.60
Campusano, Sil	89D	584	$.01	$.15	Carter, Gary	85D	55	$.15	$.40
Canale, George	90D	699	$.01	$.10	Carter, Gary	86D	68	$.08	$.25
Candaele, Casey	87D	549	$.01	$.04	Carter, Gary	87D	69	$.08	$.25
Candaele, Casey	87DR	33	$.01	$.07	Carter, Gary	88D	199	$.03	$.25
Candaele, Casey	88D	179	$.01	$.05	Carter, Gary	88DBB	14	$.01	$.15
Candaele, Casey	88DBB	68	$.01	$.05	Carter, Gary	89D	53	$.01	$.04
Candelaria, John	81D	374	$.03	$.20	Carter, Gary	89DBB	182	$.01	$.10
Candelaria, John	82D	297	$.02	$.15	Carter, Gary	90D	147	$.01	$.03
Candelaria, John	83D	549	$.02	$.15	Carter, Joe	84DRR	41	$3.00	$15.00
Candelaria, John	84D	357	$.03	$.10	Carter, Joe	85D	616	$.50	$2.50
Candelaria, John	85D	430	$.01	$.08	Carter, Joe	86D	224	$.10	$.50
Candelaria, John	86D	499	$.01	$.06	Carter, Joe	87D	156	$.01	$.50
Candelaria, John	87D	551	$.01	$.04	Carter, Joe	88D	254	$.05	$.20
Candelaria, John	88D	608	$.01	$.15	Carter, Joe	88DBB	56	$.01	$.15
Candelaria, John	88DBB	20	$.01	$.05	Carter, Joe	88DBC	9	$.01	$.25
Candelaria, John	89D	192	$.01	$.04	Carter, Joe	89D	83	$.01	$.15
Candiotti, Tom	84D	393	$.10	$.50	Carter, Joe	89DBB	56	$.01	$.10
Candiotti, Tom	87D	342	$.01	$.04	Carter, Joe	89DBC	3	$.01	$.15

Player	Year	No.	VG	EX/MT
Carter, Joe	90D	114	$ .01	$ .03
Carter, Steve	89DR	8	$ .01	$ .10
Cary, Chuck	87D	461	$ .01	$ .15
Cary, Chuck	90D	429	$ .01	$ .03
Cash, Dave	81D	121	$ .01	$ .05
Castillo, Bobby	81D	298	$ .01	$ .05
Castillo, Bobby	82D	236	$ .01	$ .05
Castillo, Bobby	83D	102	$ .01	$ .05
Castillo, Bobby	84D	436	$ .03	$ .10
Castillo, Carmen	85D	590	$ .01	$ .08
Castillo, Carmen	86D	460	$ .01	$ .06
Castillo, Carmen	87D	588	$ .01	$ .04
Castillo, Carmen	88D	403	$ .01	$ .05

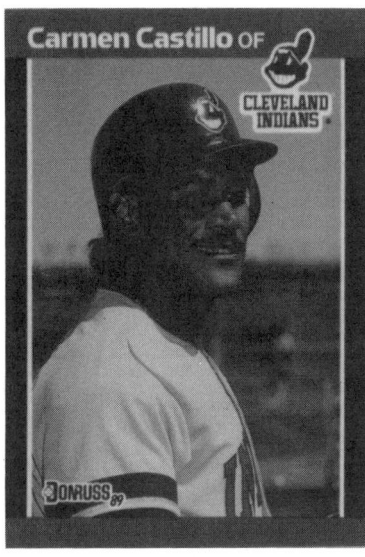

Player	Year	No.	VG	EX/MT
Castillo, Carmen	89D	374	$ .01	$ .04
Castillo, Carmen	90D	554	$ .01	$ .03
Castillo, Juan	87D	249	$ .01	$ .04
Castillo, Juan	88D	363	$ .01	$ .05
Castillo, Juan	89D	530	$ .01	$ .04
Castillo, Manny	83D	253	$ .01	$ .05
Castillo, Marty	84D	247	$ .03	$ .10
Castillo, Marty	85D	394	$ .01	$ .08
Castillo, Tony	89DR	12	$ .01	$ .10
Castillo, Tony	90D	592	$ .01	$ .03
Castino, John	81D	488	$ .01	$ .05
Castino, John	82D	256	$ .01	$ .05
Castino, John	83D	303	$ .01	$ .05
Castino, John	84D	120	$ .03	$ .10
Castino, John	84DK	4	$ .03	$ .10
Castro, Bill	81D	578	$ .01	$ .05
Caudill, Bill	81D	586	$ .01	$ .05
Caudill, Bill	82D	426	$ .01	$ .05
Caudill, Bill	83D	302	$ .01	$ .05
Caudill, Bill	84D	118	$ .03	$ .10
Caudill, Bill	85D	96	$ .01	$ .08
Caudill, Bill	86D	317	$ .01	$ .06
Cecena, Jose	88DR	6	$ .01	$ .05
Cedeno, Cesar	81D	263	$ .01	$ .05
Cedeno, Cesar	82D	118	$ .02	$ .15
Cedeno, Cesar	83D	43	$ .01	$ .05
Cedeno, Cesar	84D	306	$ .03	$ .10
Cedeno, Cesar	85D	447	$ .01	$ .08
Cedeno, Cesar	86D	648	$ .01	$ .06
Cerone, Rick	81D	346	$ .01	$ .05

Player	Year	No.	VG	EX/MT
Cerone, Rick	82D	199	$ .01	$ .05
Cerone, Rick	83D	577	$ .01	$ .05
Cerone, Rick	84D	492	$ .03	$ .10
Cerone, Rick	85D	274	$ .01	$ .08
Cerone, Rick	86D	310	$ .01	$ .06
Cerone, Rick	88D	351	$ .01	$ .05
Cerone, Rick	89D	398	$ .01	$ .04
Cerone, Rick	89DBB	308	$ .01	$ .04
Cerone, Rick	90D	305	$ .01	$ .03
Cerutti, John	86DR	20	$ .10	$ .25
Cerutti, John	87D	442	$ .05	$ .25
Cerutti, John	88D	321	$ .01	$ .05
Cerutti, John	89D	467	$ .01	$ .04
Cerutti, John	90D	645	$ .01	$ .03
Cey, Ron	81D	296	$ .02	$ .15
Cey, Ron	82D	210	$ .01	$ .05
Cey, Ron	83D	84	$ .01	$ .05
Cey, Ron	84D	361	$ .03	$ .10
Cey, Ron	85D	320	$ .01	$ .08
Cey, Ron	86D	198	$ .01	$ .06
Chadwick, Ray	87D	505	$ .01	$ .04
Chalk, Dave	81D	101	$ .01	$ .05
Chalk, Dave	82D	590	$ .01	$ .05
Chambers, Al	83D	649	$ .01	$ .05
Chambers, Al	85D	389	$ .01	$ .08
Chambliss, Chris	81D	219	$ .01	$ .05
Chambliss, Chris	82D	47	$ .01	$ .05
Chambliss, Chris	83D	123	$ .01	$ .05
Chambliss, Chris	84D	537	$ .03	$ .10
Chambliss, Chris	85D	287	$ .01	$ .08
Chambliss, Chris	86D	618	$ .01	$ .06
Chapman, Kelvin	85D	626	$ .01	$ .08
Charboneau, Joe	81D	82	$ .02	$ .15
Charboneau, Joe	82D	363	$ .01	$ .05
Charlton, Norm	89D	544	$ .01	$ .25
Charlton, Norm	90D	426	$ .01	$ .03
Checklist #1, Cards(1-120)	81D	0	$ .02	$ .15
Checklist #1, Cards(27-130)	82D	0	$ .02	$ .15
Checklist #1, Cards(27-130)	83D	0	$ .01	$ .15
Checklist #1, Cards(27-130)	84D	0	$ .03	$ .10
Checklist #1, Cards(27-130)	85D	0	$ .01	$ .08
Checklist #1, Cards(27-130)	86D	0	$ .02	$ .15
Checklist #1, Cards(28-133)	87D	100	$ .01	$ .04
Checklist #1, Cards(28-137)	88D	100	$ .01	$ .05
Checklist #2, Cards(121-240)	81D	0	$ .02	$ .15
Checklist #2, Cards(131-234)	82D	0	$ .02	$ .15
Checklist #2, Cards(131-234)	83D	0	$ .01	$ .15
Checklist #2, Cards(131-234)	84D	0	$ .03	$ .10
Checklist #2, Cards(131-234)	85D	0	$ .01	$ .08
Checklist #2, Cards(131-234)	86D	0	$ .01	$ .06
Checklist #2, Cards(134-239)	87D	200	$ .01	$ .04
Checklist #2, Cards(138-247)	88D	200	$ .01	$ .05
Checklist #3, Cards(235-338)	82D	0	$ .02	$ .15
Checklist #3, Cards(235-338)	83D	0	$ .01	$ .15
Checklist #3, Cards(235-338)	84D	0	$ .03	$ .10
Checklist #3, Cards(235-338)	85D	0	$ .09	$ .06
Checklist #3, Cards(235-338)	86D	0	$ .01	$ .06
Checklist #3, Cards(240-345)	87D	300	$ .01	$ .04
Checklist #3, Cards(241-360)	81D	0	$ .02	$ .15
Checklist #3, Cards(248-357)	88D	300	$ .01	$ .05
Checklist #4, Cards(339-442)	82D	0	$ .02	$ .15
Checklist #4, Cards(339-442)	83D	0	$ .01	$ .15
Checklist #4, Cards(339-442)	84D	0	$ .03	$ .10
Checklist #4, Cards(339-442)	85D	0	$ .01	$ .08
Checklist #4, Cards(339-442)	86D	0	$ .01	$ .06
Checklist #4, Cards(346-451)	87D	400	$ .01	$ .04
Checklist #4, Cards(358-467)	88D	400	$ .01	$ .05
Checklist #4, Cards(361-480)	81D	0	$ .02	$ .15
Checklist #5, Cards(443-544)	82D	0	$ .02	$ .15
Checklist #5, Cards(443-546)	83D	0	$ .01	$ .15
Checklist #5, Cards(443-546)	84D	0	$ .03	$ .10
Checklist #5, Cards(443-546)	85D	0	$ .01	$ .08
Checklist #5, Cards(443-546)	86D	0	$ .01	$ .06
Checklist #5, Cards(452-557)	87D	500	$ .01	$ .04
Checklist #5, Cards(468-577)	88D	500	$ .01	$ .05

Player	Year	No.	VG	EX/MT	Player	Year	No.	VG	EX/MT
Checklist #5, Cards(481-600)	81D	0	$ .02	$ .15	Christensen, John	86D	360	$ .01	$ .06
Checklist #6, Cards(545-653)	82D	0	$ .02	$ .15	Christenson, Larry	82D	219	$ .01	$ .05
Checklist #6, Cards(547-651)	84D	0	$ .03	$ .10	Christenson, Larry	83D	345	$ .01	$ .05
Checklist #6, Cards(547-653)	83D	0	$ .01	$ .15	Christiansen, Clay	85D	396	$ .01	$ .08
Checklist #6, Cards(547-653)	85D	0	$ .01	$ .08	Citarella, Ralph	85D	504	$ .01	$ .08
Checklist #6, Cards(547-653)	86D	0	$ .01	$ .06	Clancy, JIm	86D	268	$ .01	$ .06
Checklist #6, Cards(558-660)	87D	600	$ .01	$ .04	Clancy, Jim	82D	227	$ .01	$ .05
Checklist #6, Cards(578/BC-26)	88D	600	$ .01	$ .15	Clancy, Jim	83D	101	$ .01	$ .05
Checklist DK, Cards(1-26)	82D	0	$ .05	$ .30	Clancy, Jim	84D	119	$ .03	$ .10
Checklist DK, Cards(1-26)	83D	0	$ .05	$ .30	Clancy, Jim	84DK	19	$ .03	$ .10
Checklist DK, Cards(1-26)	84D	0	$ .05	$ .30	Clancy, Jim	85D	439	$ .01	$ .08
Checklist DK, Cards(1-26)	85D	0	$ .05	$ .20	Clancy, Jim	87D	639	$ .01	$ .04
Checklist DK, Cards(1-26)	86D	0	$ .01	$ .06	Clancy, Jim	88D	74	$ .01	$ .05
Checklist DK, Cards(1-26)	87D	27	$ .01	$ .04	Clancy, Jim	88DBB	48	$ .01	$ .05
Checklist DK, Cards(1-26)	88D	27	$ .01	$ .05	Clancy, Jim	89D	268	$ .01	$ .04
Checklist DK, Cards(1-26)	89D	27	$ .01	$ .05	Clancy, Jim	89DBB	206	$ .01	$ .04
Checklist, Cards(1-112)	89DBB	300	$ .01	$ .04	Clancy, Jim	89DTR	32	$ .01	$ .05
Checklist, Cards(1-26)	90DK	27	$ .01	$ .03	Clancy, Jim	90D	69	$ .01	$ .03
Checklist, Cards(1-56)	86DR	56	$ .02	$ .15	Clark, Bobby	81D	572	$ .01	$ .05
Checklist, Cards(1-56)	87DR	56	$ .01	$ .15	Clark, Bobby	82D	318	$ .01	$ .05
Checklist, Cards(1-56)	88DR	56	$ .01	$ .05	Clark, Bobby	83D	444	$ .01	$ .05
Checklist, Cards(1-56)	89DR	56	$ .01	$ .10	Clark, Bobby	84D	524	$ .03	$ .10
Checklist, Cards(1-56)	89DTR	56	$ .01	$ .05	Clark, Bobby	85D	481	$ .01	$ .08
Checklist, Cards(113-224)	89DBB	329	$ .01	$ .04	Clark, Bryan	82D	596	$ .01	$ .05
Checklist, Cards(130-231)	90D	200	$ .01	$ .03	Clark, Bryan	83D	603	$ .01	$ .05
Checklist, Cards(138-247)	89D	200	$ .01	$ .04	Clark, Bryan	84D	562	$ .03	$ .10
Checklist, Cards(225-336)	89DBB	332	$ .01	$ .04	Clark, Dave	87D	623	$ .08	$ .30
Checklist, Cards(232-333)	90D	300	$ .01	$ .03	Clark, Dave	88D	473	$ .03	$ .25
Checklist, Cards(248-357)	89D	300	$ .01	$ .04	Clark, Dave	89D	585	$ .01	$ .04
Checklist, Cards(28-129)	90D	100	$ .01	$ .03	Clark, Dave	90D	492	$ .01	$ .03
Checklist, Cards(28-137)	89D	100	$ .01	$ .04	Clark, Jack	81D	315	$ .05	$ .30
Checklist, Cards(334-435)	90D	400	$ .01	$ .03	Clark, Jack	82D	46	$ .05	$ .30
Checklist, Cards(358-467)	89D	400	$ .01	$ .04	Clark, Jack	83D	222	$ .05	$ .20
Checklist, Cards(436-537)	90D	500	$ .01	$ .03	Clark, Jack	84D	65	$ .10	$ .35
Checklist, Cards(468-577)	89D	500	$ .01	$ .04	Clark, Jack	84DK	7	$ .10	$ .35
Checklist, Cards(538-639)	90D	600	$ .01	$ .03	Clark, Jack	85D	65	$ .05	$ .30
Checklist, Cards(578-660)	89D	600	$ .01	$ .04	Clark, Jack	86D	168	$ .08	$ .25
Checklist, Cards(640-720)	90D	700	$ .01	$ .03	Clark, Jack	87D	111	$ .05	$ .20
Chicken, San Diego	82D	531	$ .25	$1.00	Clark, Jack	88D	183	$ .05	$ .20
					Clark, Jack	88DBB	49	$ .01	$ .10
					Clark, Jack	88DK	15	$ .05	$ .20
					Clark, Jack	89D	311	$ .01	$ .10
					Clark, Jack	89DBB	98	$ .01	$ .10
					Clark, Jack	89DTR	2	$ .01	$ .15
					Clark, Jack	90D	128	$ .01	$ .03
					Clark, Jerald	89D	599	$ .01	$ .25
					Clark, Jerald	90D	593	$ .01	$ .03
					Clark, Jerry	89D	607	$ .01	$ .04
					Clark, Will	86DR	32	$3.00	$15.00
					Clark, Will	87D	66	$2.75	$12.00
					Clark, Will	88D	204	$ .45	$1.50
					Clark, Will	88DBB	79	$ .15	$ .75
					Clark, Will	88DBC	24	$ .15	$ .75
					Clark, Will	88DK	21	$ .10	$ .45
					Clark, Will	89D	249	$ .15	$ .75
					Clark, Will	89DBB	23	$ .01	$1.00
					Clark, Will	89DBC	22	$ .05	$ .50
					Clark, Will	90D	230	$ .01	$ .75
					Clark, Will	90DAS	707	$ .01	$ .50
					Clary, Marty	86DRR	36	$ .01	$ .06
					Clary, Marty	90D	381	$ .01	$ .03
					Clear, Mark	81D	291	$ .01	$ .05
					Clear, Mark	82D	452	$ .01	$ .05
					Clear, Mark	83D	361	$ .01	$ .05
					Clear, Mark	84D	611	$ .03	$ .10
					Clear, Mark	85D	538	$ .01	$ .08
					Clear, Mark	86D	493	$ .01	$ .06
					Clear, Mark	87D	355	$ .01	$ .04
					Clear, Mark	88D	372	$ .01	$ .05
					Clear, Mark	89D	528	$ .01	$ .04
					Clemens, Roger	85D	273	$4.25	$13.00
Chicken, San Diego	83D	645	$ .10	$ .35	Clemens, Roger	86D	172	$1.35	$4.00
Chicken, San Diego	84D	651	$ .10	$ .35	Clemens, Roger	87D	276	$ .70	$2.00
Chiffer, Floyd	83D	44	$ .01	$ .05	Clemens, Roger	87DK	2	$ .20	$ .60
Childress, Rocky	88D	554	$ .01	$ .05	Clemens, Roger	88D	51	$ .10	$ .50

Player	Year	No.	VG	EX/MT	Player	Year	No.	VG	EX/MT
Clemens, Roger	88DBB	57	$ .10	$ .35	Cooper, Cecil	81D	83	$ .03	$ .20
Clemens, Roger	89D	280	$ .01	$ .25	Cooper, Cecil	82D	258	$ .05	$ .20
Clemens, Roger	89DBB	65	$ .01	$ .35	Cooper, Cecil	83D	106	$ .03	$ .20
Clemens, Roger	90D	184	$ .01	$ .15	Cooper, Cecil	84D	351	$ .03	$ .10
Clemente, Roberto	87D	612	$ .03	$ .25	Cooper, Cecil	85D	170	$ .03	$ .20
Clements, Pat	86D	600	$ .01	$ .06	Cooper, Cecil	86D	170	$ .01	$ .06
Clements, Pat	87D	390	$ .01	$ .04	Cooper, Cecil	86DK	7	$ .05	$ .20
Clements, Pat	88D	52	$ .01	$ .05	Cooper, Cecil	87D	363	$ .01	$ .04
Cleveland, Reggie	81D	206	$ .01	$ .05	Cora, Joey	90D	538	$ .01	$ .03
Cleveland, Reggie	82D	456	$ .01	$ .05	Corbett, Doug	81D	546	$ .01	$ .05
Cliburn, Stew	89D	462	$ .01	$ .04	Corbett, Doug	82D	53	$ .01	$ .05
Cliburn, Stu	86D	301	$ .01	$ .06	Corbett, Doug	85D	474	$ .01	$ .08
Cliburn, Stu	87D	530	$ .01	$ .04	Corbett, Doug	87D	333	$ .01	$ .04
Clutterbuck, Bryan	87D	397	$ .01	$ .04	Corbett, Sherman	89D	407	$ .01	$ .10
Cobb, Ty	83D	653	$ .05	$ .20	Corcoran, Tim	81D	367	$ .01	$ .05
Cocanower, Jaime	85D	455	$ .01	$ .08	Corcoran, Tim	85D	381	$ .01	$ .08
Cocanower, Jaime	86D	393	$ .01	$ .06	Corcoran, Tim	86D	381	$ .01	$ .06
Codiroli, Chris	84D	345	$ .03	$ .10	Corrales, Pat	83D	626	$ .01	$ .05
Codiroli, Chris	85D	462	$ .01	$ .08	Correa, Ed	86DR	4	$ .01	$ .15
Codiroli, Chris	86D	278	$ .01	$ .06	Correa, Ed	87D	57	$ .01	$ .04
Codiroli, Chris	87D	226	$ .01	$ .04	Correa, Ed	88D	57	$ .01	$ .05
Coffman, Kevin	88DR	49	$ .01	$ .05	Corsi, Jim	90D	422	$ .01	$ .03
Coleman, Vince	86D	181	$ .70	$2.00	Costello, John	89D	518	$ .01	$ .04
Coleman, Vince	86D	651	$ .03	$ .25	Costello, John	90D	555	$ .01	$ .03
Coleman, Vince	87D	263	$ .03	$ .25	Cotto, Henry	85D	411	$ .01	$ .15
Coleman, Vince	88D	293	$ .05	$ .20	Cotto, Henry	88DBB	51	$ .01	$ .05
Coleman, Vince	88DBB	44	$ .01	$ .10	Cotto, Henry	89D	109	$ .01	$ .04
Coleman, Vince	89D	181	$ .01	$ .10	Cotto, Henry	90D	644	$ .01	$ .03
Coleman, Vince	89DBB	19	$ .01	$ .15	Cowens, Al	81D	369	$ .01	$ .05
Coleman, Vince	89DK	19	$ .01	$ .05	Cowens, Al	82D	207	$ .01	$ .05
Coleman, Vince	90D	279	$ .01	$ .10	Cowens, Al	83D	554	$ .01	$ .05
Coles, Darnell	84D	630	$ .04	$ .50	Cowens, Al	84D	511	$ .03	$ .10
Coles, Darnell	85D	118	$ .01	$ .08	Cowens, Al	85D	196	$ .01	$ .08
Coles, Darnell	86D	557	$ .01	$ .06	Cowens, Al	86D	389	$ .01	$ .06
Coles, Darnell	87D	230	$ .01	$ .04	Cowley, Joe	85D	613	$ .01	$ .08
Coles, Darnell	88D	572	$ .01	$ .05	Cowley, Joe	86D	608	$ .01	$ .06
Coles, Darnell	88DBB	185	$ .01	$ .05	Cowley, Joe	87D	552	$ .01	$ .04
Coles, Darnell	89D	566	$ .01	$ .04	Cox, Bobby	81D	426	$ .01	$ .05
Coles, Darnell	90D	212	$ .01	$ .03	Cox, Danny	84D	449	$ .15	$ .50
Collins, Dave	81D	185	$ .01	$ .05	Cox, Danny	85D	571	$ .01	$ .08
Collins, Dave	82D	169	$ .01	$ .05	Cox, Danny	86D	382	$ .01	$ .06
Collins, Dave	83D	234	$ .01	$ .05	Cox, Danny	87D	553	$ .01	$ .04
Collins, Dave	84D	650	$ .03	$ .10	Cox, Danny	88D	60	$ .01	$ .05
Collins, Dave	85D	241	$ .01	$ .08	Cox, Danny	88DBB	75	$ .01	$ .05
Collins, Dave	86D	218	$ .01	$ .06	Cox, Danny	89D	348	$ .01	$ .04
Collins, Dave	87D	215	$ .01	$ .04	Cox, Jeff	81D	230	$ .01	$ .05
Combs, Pat	90DRR	44	$ .01	$ .25	Cox, Larry	81D	285	$ .01	$ .05
Comer, Steve	82D	341	$ .01	$ .05	Cox, Ted	81D	283	$ .01	$ .05
Comer, Steve	83D	163	$ .01	$ .05	Craig, Rodney	81D	288	$ .01	$ .05
Concepcion, Dave	81D	181	$ .03	$ .20	Craig, Rodney	83D	515	$ .01	$ .05
Concepcion, Dave	82D	421	$ .05	$ .30	Crandall, Del	84D	632	$ .03	$ .10
Concepcion, Dave	83D	148	$ .03	$ .20	Crawford, Steve	82D	564	$ .01	$ .05
Concepcion, Dave	84D	121	$ .03	$ .10	Crawford, Steve	85D	395	$ .01	$ .08
Concepcion, Dave	84DK	2	$ .10	$ .35	Crawford, Steve	86D	416	$ .01	$ .06
Concepcion, Dave	85D	155	$ .01	$ .08	Crawford, Steve	87D	399	$ .01	$ .04
Concepcion, Dave	85D	203	$ .03	$ .20	Creel, Keith	83D	574	$ .01	$ .05
Concepcion, Dave	86D	243	$ .05	$ .20	Crews, Tim	88D	464	$ .01	$ .05
Concepcion, Dave	88D	329	$ .01	$ .05	Crews, Tim	88DR	20	$ .01	$ .05
Concepcion, Onix	83D	516	$ .01	$ .05	Crews, Tim	89D	486	$ .01	$ .04
Concepcion, Onix	84D	95	$ .03	$ .10	Crews, Tim	90D	550	$ .01	$ .03
Concepcion, Onix	86D	252	$ .01	$ .06	Crim, Chuck	87DR	18	$ .01	$ .07
Cone, David	87D	502	$ .35	$3.00	Crim, Chuck	88D	355	$ .01	$ .05
Cone, David	87DR	35	$ .15	$1.00	Crim, Chuck	89D	617	$ .01	$ .04
Cone, David	88D	653	$ .01	$ .60	Crim, Chuck	89DBB	127	$ .01	$ .04
Cone, David	88DBB	40	$ .05	$ .25	Crim, Chuck	90D	221	$ .01	$ .03
Cone, David	89D	388	$ .05	$ .25	Cromartie, Warren	81D	332	$ .01	$ .05
Cone, David	89DBB	96	$ .01	$ .10	Cromartie, Warren	82D	340	$ .01	$ .05
Cone, David	89DK	9	$ .05	$ .25	Cromartie, Warren	83D	466	$ .01	$ .05
Cone, David	90D	265	$ .01	$ .03	Crowley, Terry	81D	507	$ .01	$ .05
Conroy, Tim	84D	340	$ .03	$ .10	Crowley, Terry	82D	383	$ .01	$ .05
Conroy, Tim	85D	156	$ .01	$ .08	Crowley, Terry	83D	457	$ .01	$ .05
Cook, Dennis	89D	646	$ .01	$ .25	Cruz, Hector	82D	57	$ .01	$ .05
Cook, Dennis	89DBB	327	$ .01	$ .04	Cruz, Jose	81D	383	$ .01	$ .05
Cook, Dennis	90D	193	$ .01	$ .03	Cruz, Jose	82D	244	$ .01	$ .05
Coolbaugh, Scott	90DRR	43	$ .01	$ .50	Cruz, Jose	83D	41	$ .01	$ .05

Player	Year	No.	VG	EX/MT	Player	Year	No.	VG	EX/MT
Cruz, Jose	84D	182	$ .03	$ .10	Davis, Butch	84D	277	$ .03	$ .10
Cruz, Jose	85D	304	$ .01	$ .08	Davis, Charles "Chili"	83D	348	$ .01	$ .25
Cruz, Jose	85DK	20	$ .03	$ .10	Davis, Chili	84D	114	$ .03	$ .10
Cruz, Jose	86D	60	$ .01	$ .06	Davis, Chili	85D	480	$ .01	$ .08
Cruz, Jose	87D	85	$ .01	$ .04	Davis, Chili	86D	65	$ .01	$ .06
Cruz, Julio	81D	163	$ .01	$ .05	Davis, Chili	86DK	6	$ .01	$ .06
Cruz, Julio	82D	50	$ .01	$ .05	Davis, Chili	87D	268	$ .01	$ .04
Cruz, Julio	83D	379	$ .01	$ .05	Davis, Chili	88D	313	$ .01	$ .05
Cruz, Julio	84D	379	$ .03	$ .10	Davis, Chili	89D	449	$ .01	$ .04
Cruz, Julio	85D	452	$ .01	$ .08	Davis, Chili	89DBB	115	$ .01	$ .04
Cruz, Julio	86D	257	$ .01	$ .06	Davis, Chili	90D	136	$ .01	$ .03
Cruz, Todd	83D	505	$ .01	$ .05	Davis, Chili	90DBC	20	$ .01	$ .03
Cruz, Todd	84D	148	$ .03	$ .10	Davis, Dick	81D	528	$ .01	$ .05
Cruz, Victor	81D	321	$ .01	$ .05	Davis, Dick	82D	147	$ .01	$ .05
Cubbage, Mike	81D	492	$ .01	$ .05	Davis, Dick	83D	647	$ .01	$ .05
Cummings, Steve	90D	698	$ .01	$ .10	Davis, Eric	85D	325	$6.00	$20.00
Curtis, John	83D	170	$ .01	$ .05	Davis, Eric	86D	164	$1.50	$4.00
Daniels, Kal	86DRR	27	$1.50	$3.50	Davis, Eric	87D	265	$ .70	$1.50
Daniels, Kal	87D	142	$ .40	$ .75	Davis, Eric	87DK	22	$ .25	$ 1.00
Daniels, Kal	88D	289	$ .01	$ .25	Davis, Eric	88D	369	$ .10	$ .50
Daniels, Kal	88DBB	6	$ .01	$ .15	Davis, Eric	88DBB	62	$ .05	$ .25
Daniels, Kal	88DK	14	$ .10	$ .25	Davis, Eric	88DBC	2	$ .35	$ .35
Daniels, Kal	89D	198	$ .01	$ .10	Davis, Eric	89D	80	$ .05	$ .35
Daniels, Kal	89DBB	118	$ .01	$ .04	Davis, Eric	89DBB	6	$ .01	$ .35
Daniels, Kal	89DBC	18	$ .01	$ .20	Davis, Eric	90D	232	$ .01	$ .15
Daniels, Kal	90D	432	$ .01	$ .03	Davis, Eric	90DAS	695	$ .01	$ .15
Darling, Ron	84DRR	30	$2.00	$6.00	Davis, Eric	90DBC	23	$ .01	$ .20
Darling, Ron	85D	434	$ .15	$ .75	Davis, Glenn	86D	380	$ .50	$3.50
Darling, Ron	86D	563	$ .08	$ .25	Davis, Glenn	87D	61	$ .05	$ .60
Darling, Ron	87D	192	$ .05	$ .20	Davis, Glenn	88D	184	$ .05	$ .20
Darling, Ron	88D	76	$ .01	$ .15	Davis, Glenn	88DBB	64	$ .01	$ .10
Darling, Ron	88DBB	41	$ .01	$ .15	Davis, Glenn	89D	236	$ .01	$ .10
Darling, Ron	88DK	6	$ .03	$ .25	Davis, Glenn	89DBB	8	$ .01	$ .10
Darling, Ron	89D	171	$ .01	$ .10	Davis, Glenn	89DK	25	$ .01	$ .15
Darling, Ron	89DBB	41	$ .01	$ .04	Davis, Glenn	90D	118	$ .01	$ .03
Darling, Ron	90D	289	$ .01	$ .03	Davis, Glenn	90DBC	21	$ .01	$ .03
Darwin, Danny	81D	147	$ .01	$ .05	Davis, Jerry	85D	162	$ .01	$ .08
Darwin, Danny	82D	321	$ .01	$ .05	Davis, Jerry	86D	429	$ .01	$ .06
Darwin, Danny	83D	289	$ .01	$ .05	Davis, Jody	82D	225	$ .05	$ .30
Darwin, Danny	84D	544	$ .03	$ .10	Davis, Jody	83D	183	$ .01	$ .05
Darwin, Danny	85D	98	$ .01	$ .08	Davis, Jody	84D	433	$ .03	$ .10
Darwin, Danny	86D	149	$ .01	$ .06	Davis, Jody	85D	76	$ .01	$ .08
Darwin, Danny	87D	508	$ .01	$ .04	Davis, Jody	86D	289	$ .01	$ .06
Darwin, Danny	88D	358	$ .01	$ .05	Davis, Jody	87D	269	$ .01	$ .04
Darwin, Danny	89D	390	$ .01	$ .04	Davis, Jody	88D	119	$ .01	$ .05
Darwin, Danny	90D	561	$ .01	$ .03	Davis, Jody	89D	650	$ .01	$ .04
Dascenzo, Doug	89D	491	$ .01	$ .25	Davis, Jody	89DBB	58	$ .01	$ .04
Dauer, Rich	81D	232	$ .01	$ .05	Davis, Joel	86D	623	$ .01	$ .06
Dauer, Rich	82D	257	$ .01	$ .05	Davis, Joel	87D	124	$ .01	$ .04
Dauer, Rich	83D	455	$ .01	$ .05	Davis, John	88D	594	$ .05	$ .20
Dauer, Rich	84D	350	$ .03	$ .10	Davis, John	88DR	48	$ .01	$ .05
Dauer, Rich	85D	106	$ .01	$ .08	Davis, Mark	84D	201	$ .50	$1.75
Daugherty, Jack	90D	461	$ .01	$ .03	Davis, Mark	85D	553	$ .05	$ .25
Daulton, Darren	86D	477	$ .01	$ .15	Davis, Mark	86D	265	$ .01	$ .15
Daulton, Darren	87D	262	$ .01	$ .04	Davis, Mark	87D	313	$ .01	$ .15
Daulton, Darren	88D	309	$ .01	$ .05	Davis, Mark	88D	64	$ .01	$ .15
Daulton, Darren	89D	549	$ .01	$ .04	Davis, Mark	88DBB	98	$ .01	$ .05
Daulton, Darren	89DBB	128	$ .01	$ .04	Davis, Mark	89D	65	$ .01	$ .04
Daulton, Darren	90D	194	$ .01	$ .03	Davis, Mark	89DBB	133	$ .01	$ .10
David, Andre	87D	519	$ .01	$ .04	Davis, Mark	90D	302	$ .01	$ .03
Davidson, Mark	87DR	22	$ .01	$ .07	Davis, Mike	86DK	14	$ .01	$ .06
Davidson, Mark	88D	519	$ .01	$ .05	Davis, Mike	81D	470	$ .05	$ .20
Davis, Alvin	85D	69	$ .40	$3.50	Davis, Mike	84D	298	$ .03	$ .10
Davis, Alvin	85DK	18	$ .10	$ .45	Davis, Mike	85D	223	$ .01	$ .08
Davis, Alvin	86D	69	$ .08	$ .25	Davis, Mike	86D	96	$ .01	$ .06
Davis, Alvin	87D	75	$ .01	$ .15	Davis, Mike	87D	133	$ .01	$ .04
Davis, Alvin	88D	193	$ .01	$ .15	Davis, Mike	88D	281	$ .01	$ .05
Davis, Alvin	88DBB	107	$ .01	$ .10	Davis, Mike	88DBB	36	$ .01	$ .05
Davis, Alvin	88DBC	25	$ .10	$ .25	Davis, Mike	89D	316	$ .01	$ .04
Davis, Alvin	89D	345	$ .01	$ .04	Davis, Mike	90D	552	$ .01	$ .03
Davis, Alvin	89DBB	24	$ .01	$ .10	Davis, Ron	81D	467	$ .01	$ .05
Davis, Alvin	89DBC	25	$ .01	$ .10	Davis, Ron	82D	451	$ .01	$ .05
Davis, Alvin	90D	109	$ .01	$ .10	Davis, Ron	83D	228	$ .01	$ .05
Davis, Alvin	90DBC	9	$ .01	$ .10	Davis, Ron	84D	269	$ .03	$ .10
Davis, Bob	81D	30	$ .01	$ .05	Davis, Ron	85D	120	$ .01	$ .08

Player	Year	No.	VG	EX/MT	Player	Year	No.	VG	EX/MT
Davis, Ron	86D	364	$ .01	$ .06	DeLeon, Jose	87D	457	$ .01	$ .04
Davis, Ron	87D	438	$ .01	$ .04	DeLeon, Jose	88D	59	$ .01	$ .05
Davis, Storm	83D	619	$ .15	$ .65	DeLeon, Jose	89D	437	$ .01	$ .04
Davis, Storm	84D	585	$ .03	$ .10	DeLeon, Jose	90D	536	$ .01	$ .03
Davis, Storm	85D	454	$ .01	$ .08	DeLeon, Luis	82D	588	$ .01	$ .05
Davis, Storm	86D	169	$ .01	$ .06	DeLeon, Luis	83D	296	$ .01	$ .05
Davis, Storm	87D	273	$ .01	$ .04	DeLeon, Luis	84D	162	$ .03	$ .10
Davis, Storm	88D	595	$ .01	$ .05	DeLeon, Luis	85D	406	$ .01	$ .08
Davis, Storm	89D	210	$ .01	$ .04	Dempsey, Rick	81D	113	$ .01	$ .05
Davis, Storm	90D	479	$ .01	$ .03	Dempsey, Rick	82D	77	$ .01	$ .05
Davis, Tommy	82D	648	$ .01	$ .05	Dempsey, Rick	83D	329	$ .01	$ .05
Dawley, Bill	84D	328	$ .03	$ .10	Dempsey, Rick	84D	413	$ .03	$ .10
Dawley, Bill	85D	354	$ .01	$ .08	Dempsey, Rick	85D	332	$ .01	$ .08
Dawley, Bill	86D	283	$ .01	$ .06	Dempsey, Rick	86D	106	$ .01	$ .06
Dawley, Bill	87D	628	$ .01	$ .04	Dempsey, Rick	87D	294	$ .01	$ .04
Dawley, Bill	88D	331	$ .01	$ .05	Dempsey, Rick	89D	432	$ .01	$ .04
Dawson, Andre	81D	212	$ .06	$ .40	Dempsey, Rick	90D	557	$ .01	$ .03
Dawson, Andre	82D	88	$ .10	$ .45	Denny, John	82D	572	$ .01	$ .05
Dawson, Andre	83D	518	$ .10	$ .40	Denny, John	83D	237	$ .02	$ .15
Dawson, Andre	84D	97	$ .20	$ .60	Denny, John	84D	407	$ .03	$ .10
Dawson, Andre	85D	421	$ .08	$ .25	Denny, John	85D	111	$ .01	$ .08
Dawson, Andre	86D	87	$ .08	$ .25	Denny, John	86D	204	$ .01	$ .06
Dawson, Andre	86DK	25	$ .03	$ .25	Denny, John	87D	329	$ .01	$ .04
Dawson, Andre	87D	458	$ .15	$ .50	Dent, Bucky	81D	465	$ .01	$ .05
Dawson, Andre	88D	269	$ .05	$ .20	Dent, Bucky	82D	209	$ .01	$ .05
Dawson, Andre	88DBB	225	$ .01	$ .15	Dent, Bucky	84D	300	$ .03	$ .10
Dawson, Andre	88DBC	10	$ .05	$ .25	Dernier, Bob	83D	189	$ .01	$ .05
Dawson, Andre	88DK	9	$ .03	$ .25	Dernier, Bob	84D	541	$ .03	$ .10
Dawson, Andre	89D	167	$ .01	$ .10	Dernier, Bob	85D	510	$ .01	$ .08
Dawson, Andre	89DBB	4	$ .01	$ .10	Dernier, Bob	86D	266	$ .01	$ .06
Dawson, Andre	89DBC	8	$ .01	$ .10	Dernier, Bob	87D	146	$ .01	$ .04
Dawson, Andre	90D	223	$ .01	$ .03	Dernier, Bob	88D	392	$ .01	$ .05
Dayett, Brian	84DRR	45	$ .03	$ .10	Dernier, Bob	89D	430	$ .01	$ .04
Dayett, Brian	85D	152	$ .01	$ .08	DeSa, Joe	86D	546	$ .01	$ .06
Dayett, Brian	88D	416	$ .01	$ .05	Deshaies, Jim	86DR	34	$ .15	$ .50
Dayley, Ken	82D	501	$ .03	$ .20	Deshaies, Jim	87D	184	$ .08	$ .35
Dayley, Ken	83D	375	$ .01	$ .05	Deshaies, Jim	88D	85	$ .01	$ .05
Dayley, Ken	84D	199	$ .03	$ .10	Deshaies, Jim	88DBB	94	$ .01	$ .05
Dayley, Ken	86D	303	$ .01	$ .06	Deshaies, Jim	89D	241	$ .01	$ .04
Dayley, Ken	87D	357	$ .01	$ .04					
Dayley, Ken	88D	357	$ .01	$ .05					
Dayley, Ken	89D	299	$ .01	$ .04					
Dayley, Ken	89DBB	268	$ .01	$ .04					
Dayley, Ken	90D	281	$ .01	$ .03					
De Los Santos, Luis	89D	562	$ .01	$ .15					
De Los Santos, Luis	89DR	33	$ .01	$ .10					
DeCinces, Doug	81D	352	$ .01	$ .05					
DeCinces, Doug	82D	279	$ .01	$ .05					
DeCinces, Doug	83D	216	$ .01	$ .05					
DeCinces, Doug	84D	230	$ .03	$ .10					
DeCinces, Doug	85D	179	$ .01	$ .08					
DeCinces, Doug	85DK	2	$ .01	$ .08					
DeCinces, Doug	86D	57	$ .01	$ .06					
DeCinces, Doug	87D	356	$ .01	$ .04					
Dedmon, Jeff	85D	554	$ .01	$ .08					
Dedmon, Jeff	86D	443	$ .01	$ .06					
Dedmon, Jeff	87D	314	$ .01	$ .04					
Dedmon, Jeff	88D	325	$ .01	$ .05					
Deer, Rob	87D	274	$ .05	$ .20					
Deer, Rob	88D	274	$ .01	$ .05					
Deer, Rob	88DBB	109	$ .01	$ .05					
Deer, Rob	89D	173	$ .01	$ .04					
Deer, Rob	90D	55	$ .01	$ .03					
Deer, Ron	89DBB	71	$ .01	$ .04					
DeJesus, Ivan	81D	483	$ .01	$ .05					
DeJesus, Ivan	82D	48	$ .01	$ .05					
DeJesus, Ivan	82DK	14	$ .01	$ .05					
DeJesus, Ivan	83D	399	$ .01	$ .05					
DeJesus, Ivan	84D	427	$ .03	$ .10					
DeJesus, Ivan	85D	204	$ .01	$ .08					
DeJesus, Ivan	86D	449	$ .01	$ .06					
DeJesus, Jose	89D	558	$ .01	$ .04	Deshaies, Jim	89DBB	120	$ .01	$ .04
DeLeon, Jose	84D	628	$ .10	$ .60	Deshaies, Jim	90D	187	$ .01	$ .03
DeLeon, Jose	85D	308	$ .01	$ .08	Deshaies, Jim	90DK	7	$ .01	$ .10
DeLeon, Jose	86D	235	$ .01	$ .06	Deshields, Delino	90DRR	42	$ .01	$ .50

Player	Year	No.	VG	EX/MT
Devereaux, Mike	88D	546	$ .05	$ .30
Devereaux, Mike	89D	603	$ .01	$ .15
Devereaux, Mike	89DBB	326	$ .01	$ .04
Devereaux, Mike	89DR	51	$ .01	$ .10
Devereaux, Mike	89DTR	30	$ .01	$ .05
Devereaux, Mike	90D	282	$ .01	$ .03
Diaz, Bo	81D	517	$ .01	$ .05
Diaz, Bo	82D	263	$ .02	$ .15
Diaz, Bo	83D	147	$ .01	$ .05
Diaz, Bo	84D	137	$ .03	$ .10
Diaz, Bo	86D	530	$ .01	$ .06
Diaz, Bo	87D	246	$ .01	$ .04
Diaz, Bo	88D	186	$ .01	$ .05
Diaz, Bo	88DBB	110	$ .01	$ .05
Diaz, Bo	89D	242	$ .01	$ .04
Diaz, Bo	89DBB	293	$ .01	$ .04
Diaz, Bo	90D	139	$ .01	$ .03
Diaz, Carlos	83D	562	$ .01	$ .05
Diaz, Carlos	84D	600	$ .03	$ .10

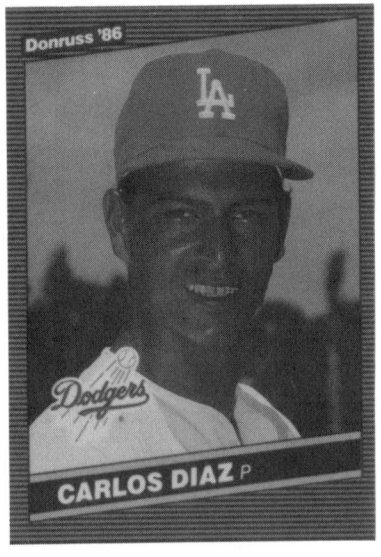

CARLOS DIAZ P

Player	Year	No.	VG	EX/MT
Diaz, Carlos	86D	348	$ .01	$ .06
Diaz, Mike	87D	267	$ .01	$ .04
Diaz, Mike	88D	267	$ .01	$ .05
Diaz, Mike	89D	655	$ .01	$ .04
Dibble, Rob	89D	426	$ .05	$ .50
Dibble, Rob	89DBB	334	$ .01	$ .25
Dibble, Rob	90D	189	$ .01	$ .25
Dillard, Steve	81D	502	$ .01	$ .05
Dillard, Steve	82D	174	$ .01	$ .05
Dilone, Miguel	81D	441	$ .01	$ .05
Dilone, Miguel	82D	515	$ .01	$ .05
Dilone, Miguel	83D	85	$ .01	$ .05
Dilone, Miguel	85D	453	$ .01	$ .08
DiPino, Frank	84D	502	$ .03	$ .10
DiPino, Frank	85D	232	$ .01	$ .08
DiPino, Frank	86D	304	$ .01	$ .06
DiPino, Frank	87D	416	$ .01	$ .04
DiPino, Frank	88D	570	$ .01	$ .05
DiPino, Frank	88DBB	205	$ .01	$ .05
DiPino, Frank	89D	393	$ .01	$ .04
DiPino, Frank	90D	518	$ .01	$ .03
Distefano, Benny	85D	166	$ .01	$ .08
Distefano, Benny	86D	78	$ .01	$ .06

Player	Year	No.	VG	EX/MT
Distefano, Benny	87D	514	$ .01	$ .04
Dixon, Ken	85D	270	$ .01	$ .08
Dixon, Ken	86D	148	$ .01	$ .06
Dixon, Ken	87D	171	$ .01	$ .04
Dixon, Ken	88D	48	$ .01	$ .05
Dodson, Pat	87DRR	44	$ .03	$ .25
Donohue, Tom	81D	51	$ .01	$ .05
Dopson, John	88DR	43	$ .01	$ .25
Dopson, John	89D	392	$ .01	$ .10
Dopson, John	89DBB	177	$ .01	$ .04
Dopson, John	89DTR	7	$ .01	$ .05
Dopson, John	90D	162	$ .01	$ .03
Doran, Bill	84D	580	$ .35	$1.00
Doran, Bill	85D	84	$ .03	$ .20
Doran, Bill	86D	110	$ .01	$ .06
Doran, Bill	86DK	10	$ .01	$ .06
Doran, Bill	87D	286	$ .01	$ .04
Doran, Bill	88D	235	$ .01	$ .15
Doran, Bill	88DBB	120	$ .01	$ .05
Doran, Bill	89D	306	$ .01	$ .04
Doran, Bill	89DBB	38	$ .01	$ .04
Doran, Bill	90D	236	$ .01	$ .03
Dotson, Rich	81D	280	$ .05	$ .35
Dotson, Rich	82D	356	$ .01	$ .05
Dotson, Rich	83D	319	$ .01	$ .05
Dotson, Rich	84D	180	$ .03	$ .10
Dotson, Rich	85D	302	$ .01	$ .08
Dotson, Rich	85DK	3	$ .01	$ .08
Dotson, Rich	86D	160	$ .01	$ .06
Dotson, Rich	87D	383	$ .01	$ .04
Dotson, Rich	88DBB	52	$ .01	$ .05
Dotson, Rich	89D	277	$ .01	$ .04
Dotson, Richard	88D	124	$ .01	$ .05
Downing, Brian	81D	410	$ .01	$ .05
Downing, Brian	82D	115	$ .01	$ .05
Downing, Brian	83D	367	$ .01	$ .05
Downing, Brian	84D	423	$ .03	$ .10
Downing, Brian	85D	158	$ .01	$ .08
Downing, Brian	86D	108	$ .01	$ .06
Downing, Brian	87D	86	$ .01	$ .04
Downing, Brian	88D	258	$ .01	$ .05
Downing, Brian	88DBB	27	$ .01	$ .05
Downing, Brian	89D	254	$ .01	$ .04
Downing, Brian	89DBB	321	$ .01	$ .04
Downing, Brian	90D	352	$ .01	$ .03
Downing, Brian	90DK	10	$ .01	$ .10
Downs, Kelly	87D	573	$ .01	$ .15
Downs, Kelly	88D	145	$ .01	$ .05
Downs, Kelly	88DBB	106	$ .01	$ .05
Downs, Kelly	89D	367	$ .01	$ .04
Downs, Kelly	89DBB	247	$ .01	$ .04
Downs, Kelly	90D	177	$ .01	$ .03
Drabek, Doug	86DR	31	$ .02	$ .09
Drabek, Doug	87D	251	$ .03	$ .25
Drabek, Doug	88D	79	$ .01	$ .05
Drabek, Doug	88DBB	73	$ .01	$ .05
Drabek, Doug	89D	211	$ .01	$ .04
Drabek, Doug	89DBB	17	$ .01	$ .04
Drabek, Doug	90D	92	$ .01	$ .03
Drago, Dick	81D	336	$ .01	$ .05
Dravecky, Dave	84D	551	$ .15	$ .70
Dravecky, Dave	84DK	8	$ .04	$ .25
Dravecky, Dave	85D	112	$ .01	$ .08
Dravecky, Dave	86D	162	$ .01	$ .06
Dravecky, Dave	87D	187	$ .01	$ .04
Dravecky, Dave	88D	485	$ .01	$ .05
Dravecky, Dave	88DBB	135	$ .01	$ .05
Dressler, Rob	81D	406	$ .01	$ .05
Drew, Cameron	89DRR	30	$ .05	$ .25
Driessen, Dan	81D	301	$ .01	$ .05
Driessen, Dan	82D	248	$ .01	$ .05
Driessen, Dan	83D	274	$ .01	$ .05
Driessen, Dan	84D	243	$ .03	$ .10
Driessen, Dan	85D	619	$ .01	$ .08
Driessen, Dan	86D	641	$ .01	$ .06

Player	Year	No.	VG	EX/MT	Player	Year	No.	VG	EX/MT
Drummond, Tim	90D	510	$ .01	$ .10	Eckersley, Dennis	89DBB	134	$ .01	$ .10
Drumright, Keith	82D	616	$ .01	$ .05	Eckersley, Dennis	90D	210	$ .01	$ .03
Dubois, Brian	90DRR	38	$ .01	$ .25	Edwards, Dave	81D	595	$ .01	$ .05
Dunbar, Tommy	84DRR	28	$ .03	$ .10	Edwards, Dave	82D	247	$ .01	$ .05
Dunbar, Tommy	85D	159	$ .01	$ .08	Edwards, Dave	83D	565	$ .01	$ .05
Dunbar, Tommy	86D	221	$ .01	$ .06	Edwards, Marshall	83D	406	$ .01	$ .05
Duncan, Mariano	86D	128	$ .05	$ .35	Edwards, Marshall	84D	490	$ .03	$ .10
Duncan, Mariano	87D	253	$ .01	$ .15	Edwards, Mike	81D	497	$ .01	$ .05
Duncan, Mariano	88D	155	$ .01	$ .05	Eichelberger, Juan	82D	422	$ .01	$ .05
Duncan, Mariano	90D	684	$ .01	$ .10	Eichelberger, Juan	83D	422	$ .01	$ .05
Dunne, Mike	87DR	38	$ .10	$ .30	Eichelberger, Juan	84D	398	$ .03	$ .10
Dunne, Mike	88D	390	$ .01	$ .15	Eichhorn, Mark	86DR	13	$ .15	$ .50
Dunne, Mike	88DBB	89	$ .01	$ .05	Eichhorn, Mark	87D	321	$ .03	$ .25
Dunne, Mike	89D	269	$ .01	$ .04	Eichhorn, Mark	88D	121	$ .01	$ .05
Dunston, Shawon	85DRR	39	$ .50	$3.00	Eiland, Dave	89D	481	$ .01	$ .10
Dunston, Shawon	86D	311	$ .10	$ .50	Eisenreich, Jim	88D	343	$ .01	$ .05
Dunston, Shawon	87D	119	$ .01	$ .25	Eisenreich, Jim	89DBB	306	$ .01	$ .04
Dunston, Shawon	88D	146	$ .01	$ .15	Eisenreich, Jim	90D	238	$ .01	$ .03
Dunston, Shawon	88DBB	37	$ .01	$ .05	Elia, Lee	83D	614	$ .01	$ .05
Dunston, Shawon	89D	137	$ .01	$ .04	Ellis, John	81D	26	$ .01	$ .05
Dunston, Shawon	89DBB	93	$ .01	$ .04	Ellis, John	82D	642	$ .01	$ .05
Dunston, Shawon	90D	49	$ .01	$ .03	Ellsworth, Steve	88DR	54	$ .01	$ .05
Durham, Leon	81D	427	$ .01	$ .05	Elster, Kevin	87D	635	$ .20	$ .75
Durham, Leon	82D	151	$ .01	$ .05	Elster, Kevin	88DBB	70	$ .01	$ .05
Durham, Leon	83D	477	$ .01	$ .05	Elster, Kevin	88DR	34	$ .01	$ .20
Durham, Leon	84D	67	$ .03	$ .10	Elster, Kevin	88DRR	37	$ .07	$ .30
Durham, Leon	84DK	5	$ .01	$ .10	Elster, Kevin	89D	289	$ .01	$ .04
Durham, Leon	85D	189	$ .01	$ .08	Elster, Kevin	89DBB	97	$ .01	$ .04
Durham, Leon	86D	320	$ .01	$ .06	Elster, Kevin	90D	152	$ .01	$ .03
Durham, Leon	87D	242	$ .01	$ .04	Engel, Steve	86D	510	$ .01	$ .06
Durham, Leon	88D	191	$ .01	$ .05	Engle, Dave	82D	102	$ .01	$ .05
Dwyer, Jim	81D	577	$ .01	$ .05	Engle, Dave	84D	598	$ .03	$ .10
Dwyer, Jim	82D	611	$ .01	$ .05	Engle, Dave	85D	72	$ .01	$ .08
Dwyer, Jim	83D	583	$ .01	$ .05	Engle, Dave	86D	438	$ .01	$ .06
Dwyer, Jim	84D	454	$ .03	$ .10	Engle, Ralph	83D	646	$ .01	$ .05
Dwyer, Jim	86D	413	$ .01	$ .06	Erickson, Roger	81D	549	$ .01	$ .05
Dwyer, Jim	87D	418	$ .01	$ .04	Erickson, Roger	82D	303	$ .01	$ .05
Dwyer, Jim	88D	459	$ .01	$ .05	Esasky, Nick	84D	602	$ .50	$3.50
Dwyer, Jim	89DBB	311	$ .01	$ .04	Esasky, Nick	85D	121	$ .01	$ .25
Dwyer, Jim	90D	484	$ .01	$ .03	Esasky, Nick	86D	286	$ .01	$ .06
Dybzinski, Jerry	81D	438	$ .01	$ .05	Esasky, Nick	87D	166	$ .01	$ .04
Dybzinski, Jerry	82D	647	$ .01	$ .05	Esasky, Nick	88D	413	$ .01	$ .05
Dybzinski, Jerry	83D	576	$ .01	$ .05	Esasky, Nick	88DBB	118	$ .01	$ .05
Dybzinski, Jerry	84D	160	$ .03	$ .10	Esasky, Nick	89D	189	$ .01	$ .04
Dyer, Duffy	81D	7	$ .01	$ .05	Esasky, Nick	89DBB	284	$ .01	$ .04
Dyer, Mike	90D	642	$ .01	$ .10	Esasky, Nick	89DTR	18	$ .01	$ .10
Dykstra, Lenny	86D	482	$ .25	$4.50	Esasky, Nick	90D	303	$ .01	$ .03
Dykstra, Lenny	87D	611	$ .05	$ .75	Escarrega, Ernesto	83D	291	$ .01	$ .05
Dykstra, Lenny	88D	364	$ .01	$ .35	Espino, Juan	84D	92	$ .03	$ .10
Dykstra, Lenny	88DBB	264	$ .01	$ .10	Espinoza, Alvaro	89DBB	161	$ .01	$ .04
Dykstra, Lenny	89D	353	$ .01	$ .10	Espinoza, Alvaro	90D	245	$ .01	$ .03
Dykstra, Lenny	89DBB	159	$ .01	$ .10	Espy, Cecil	88DR	9	$ .01	$ .15
Dykstra, Lenny	90D	313	$ .01	$ .10	Espy, Cecil	89D	292	$ .01	$ .15
Earl, Scottie	85D	491	$ .01	$ .08	Espy, Cecil	89DBB	335	$ .01	$ .04
Easler, Mike	81D	256	$ .01	$ .05	Espy, Cecil	90D	260	$ .01	$ .03
Easler, Mike	82D	221	$ .01	$ .05	Essian, Jim	81D	503	$ .01	$ .05
Easler, Mike	83D	221	$ .01	$ .05	Essian, Jim	82D	369	$ .01	$ .05
Easler, Mike	84D	444	$ .03	$ .10	Essian, Jim	83D	478	$ .01	$ .05
Easler, Mike	85D	213	$ .01	$ .08	Essian, Jim	84D	629	$ .03	$ .10
Easler, Mike	86D	395	$ .01	$ .06	Eufemia, Frank	86D	513	$ .01	$ .06
Easler, Mike	87D	277	$ .01	$ .04	Evans, Barry	82D	271	$ .01	$ .05
Easterly, Jamie	82D	623	$ .01	$ .05	Evans, Darrell	81D	192	$ .03	$ .20
Easterly, Jamie	83D	280	$ .01	$ .05	Evans, Darrell	82D	398	$ .03	$ .20
Easterly, Jamie	86D	582	$ .01	$ .06	Evans, Darrell	83D	251	$ .02	$ .15
Eave, Gary	90D	713	$ .01	$ .10	Evans, Darrell	84D	431	$ .04	$ .25
Eckersley, Dennis	81D	96	$ .05	$ .30	Evans, Darrell	85D	227	$ .03	$ .10
Eckersley, Dennis	82D	30	$ .05	$ .35	Evans, Darrell	86D	369	$ .01	$ .06
Eckersley, Dennis	83D	487	$ .01	$ .25	Evans, Darrell	87D	398	$ .01	$ .04
Eckersley, Dennis	84D	639	$ .04	$ .25	Evans, Darrell	88D	250	$ .01	$ .05
Eckersley, Dennis	85D	442	$ .01	$ .08	Evans, Darrell	88DBB	35	$ .01	$ .05
Eckersley, Dennis	86D	239	$ .01	$ .06	Evans, Darrell	89D	533	$ .01	$ .04
Eckersley, Dennis	87D	365	$ .01	$ .04	Evans, Dwight	81D	458	$ .05	$ .20
Eckersley, Dennis	88D	349	$ .01	$ .05	Evans, Dwight	82D	109	$ .02	$ .15
Eckersley, Dennis	88DBB	43	$ .01	$ .05	Evans, Dwight	82DK	7	$ .02	$ .15
Eckersley, Dennis	89D	67	$ .01	$ .04	Evans, Dwight	83D	452	$ .03	$ .20

DONRUSS

Player	Year	No.	VG	EX/MT	Player	Year	No.	VG	EX/MT
Evans, Dwight	84D	395	$ .08	$ .25	Filson, Pete	86D	436	$ .01	$ .06
Evans, Dwight	85D	294	$ .03	$ .20	Fimple, Jack	84D	372	$ .03	$ .10
Evans, Dwight	86D	249	$ .03	$ .25	Fingers, Rollie	81D	2	$ .05	$ .30
Evans, Dwight	87D	129	$ .01	$ .04	Fingers, Rollie	82D	28	$ .05	$ .20
Evans, Dwight	88D	216	$ .01	$ .15	Fingers, Rollie	83D	78	$ .03	$ .20
Evans, Dwight	88DBB	84	$ .01	$ .05	Fingers, Rollie	83DK	2	$ .02	$ .15
Evans, Dwight	88DK	16	$ .01	$ .15	Fingers, Rollie	84D#A	0	$1.00	$3.00
Evans, Dwight	89D	240	$ .01	$ .04	Fingers, Rollie	85D	292	$ .03	$ .25
Evans, Dwight	89DBB	121	$ .01	$ .04	Fingers, Rollie	86D	229	$ .05	$ .20
Evans, Dwight	90D	122	$ .01	$ .03	Finley, Chuck	87D	407	$ .01	$ .50
Fahey, Bill	81D	361	$ .01	$ .05	Finley, Chuck	88D	530	$ .01	$ .10
Fahey, Bill	83D	281	$ .01	$ .05	Finley, Chuck	89D	226	$ .01	$ .10
Falcone, Pete	81D	395	$ .01	$ .05	Finley, Chuck	89DBB	333	$ .01	$ .04
Falcone, Pete	82D	380	$ .01	$ .05	Finley, Chuck	90D	344	$ .01	$ .03
Falcone, Pete	83D	182	$ .01	$ .05	Finley, Steve	89DR	47	$ .01	$ .25
Falcone, Pete	84D	385	$ .03	$ .10	Finley, Steve	90D	215	$ .01	$ .15
Fanning, Jim	82D	492	$ .01	$ .05	Fischlin, Mike	83D	489	$ .01	$ .05
Farmer, Ed	81D	40	$ .01	$ .05	Fischlin, Mike	85D	495	$ .01	$ .08
Farmer, Ed	82D	482	$ .01	$ .05	Fishel, John	89D	443	$ .01	$ .10
Farmer, Ed	83D	471	$ .01	$ .05	Fisher, Brian	86D	492	$ .08	$ .25
Farr, Steve	85D	653	$ .01	$ .25	Fisher, Brian	87D	340	$ .01	$ .04
Farr, Steve	86D	588	$ .01	$ .06	Fisher, Brian	88D	415	$ .01	$ .05
Farr, Steve	87D	301	$ .01	$ .04	Fisher, Brian	88DBB	101	$ .01	$ .05
Farr, Steve	88D	378	$ .01	$ .05	Fisher, Brian	89D	126	$ .01	$ .04
Farr, Steve	89D	356	$ .01	$ .04	Fisk, Carlton	81D	335	$ .10	$ .40
Farr, Steve	89DBB	151	$ .01	$ .04	Fisk, Carlton	82D	495	$ .10	$ .40
Farr, Steve	90D	356	$ .01	$ .03	Fisk, Carlton	82DK	20	$ .03	$ .20
Farrell, John	88DBB	117	$ .01	$ .25	Fisk, Carlton	83D	104	$ .10	$ .35
Farrell, John	88DRR	42	$ .01	$ .35	Fisk, Carlton	84D	302	$ .10	$ .50
Farrell, John	89D	320	$ .01	$ .10	Fisk, Carlton	85D	208	$ .03	$ .20
Farrell, John	89DBB	285	$ .01	$ .25	Fisk, Carlton	86D	366	$ .03	$ .25
Farrell, John	90D	233	$ .01	$ .25	Fisk, Carlton	87D	247	$ .01	$ .15
Felder, Mike	86D	634	$ .03	$ .25	Fisk, Carlton	88D	260	$ .01	$ .05
Felder, Mike	87D	295	$ .01	$ .04	Fisk, Carlton	88DBB	67	$ .01	$ .05
Felder, Mike	88D	397	$ .01	$ .05	Fisk, Carlton	89D	101	$ .01	$ .04
Felder, Mike	90D	609	$ .01	$ .03	Fisk, Carlton	89DBB	11	$ .01	$ .10
Felix, Junior	89DBB	199	$ .01	$ .40	Fisk, Carlton	89DK	7	$ .01	$ .05
Felix, Junior	89DR	55	$ .01	$1.50	Fisk, Carlton	90D	58	$ .01	$ .10
Felix, Junior	90D	70	$ .01	$ .40	Fisk, Carlton	90DBC	19	$ .01	$ .10
Felton, Terry	83D	354	$ .01	$ .05	Fitzgerald, Mike	84D	482	$ .03	$ .10
Ferguson, Joe	81D	177	$ .01	$ .05	Fitzgerald, Mike	85D	238	$ .01	$ .08
Ferguson, Joe	83D	604	$ .01	$ .05	Fitzgerald, Mike	86D	97	$ .01	$ .06
Fermin, Felix	88D	144	$ .01	$ .05	Fitzgerald, Mike	87D	345	$ .01	$ .04
Fermin, Felix	89D	565	$ .01	$ .04	Fitzgerald, Mike	88D	159	$ .01	$ .05
Fermin, Felix	89DBB	229	$ .01	$ .04	Fitzgerald, Mike	89D	456	$ .01	$ .04
Fermin, Felix	89DTR	33	$ .01	$ .05	Fitzgerald, Mike	90D	392	$ .01	$ .03
Fermin, Felix	90D	191	$ .01	$ .03	Flanagan, Mike	81D	234	$ .01	$ .05
Fernandez, Sid	84DRR	44	$1.50	$7.00	Flanagan, Mike	82D	329	$ .01	$ .05
Fernandez, Sid	85D	563	$ .15	$ .60	Flanagan, Mike	83D	105	$ .01	$ .05
Fernandez, Sid	86D	625	$ .05	$ .20	Flanagan, Mike	84D	169	$ .03	$ .10
Fernandez, Sid	87D	323	$ .01	$ .15	Flanagan, Mike	85D	88	$ .01	$ .08
Fernandez, Sid	88D	118	$ .01	$ .10	Flanagan, Mike	86D	576	$ .01	$ .06
Fernandez, Sid	89D	471	$ .01	$ .10	Flanagan, Mike	87D	459	$ .01	$ .04
Fernandez, Sid	90D	572	$ .01	$ .03	Flanagan, Mike	88D	636	$ .01	$ .05
Fernandez, Tony	84DRR	32	$2.00	$7.50	Flanagan, Mike	89D	324	$ .01	$ .04
Fernandez, Tony	85D	390	$ .10	$ .60	Flanagan, Mike	89DBB	316	$ .01	$ .04
Fernandez, Tony	86D	119	$ .02	$ .25	Flanagan, Mike	90D	324	$ .01	$ .03
Fernandez, Tony	87D	72	$ .05	$ .20	Flannery, Tim	82D	61	$ .01	$ .05
Fernandez, Tony	88D	319	$ .01	$ .15	Flannery, Tim	83D	472	$ .01	$ .05
Fernandez, Tony	88DBB	87	$ .01	$ .05	Flannery, Tim	84D	202	$ .03	$ .10
Fernandez, Tony	88DK	12	$ .01	$ .15	Flannery, Tim	85D	551	$ .01	$ .08
Fernandez, Tony	89D	206	$ .01	$ .04	Flannery, Tim	86D	383	$ .01	$ .06
Fernandez, Tony	89DBB	48	$ .01	$ .04	Flannery, Tim	87D	287	$ .01	$ .04
Fernandez, Tony	90D	149	$ .01	$ .03	Flannery, Tim	88D	328	$ .01	$ .05
Fetters, Mike	90DRR	35	$ .01	$ .10	Flannery, Tim	89D	364	$ .01	$ .04
Fidrych, Mark	81D	8	$ .01	$ .05	Fletcher, Scott	82D	554	$ .01	$ .25
Fielder, Cecil	86D	512	$ .50	$10.00	Fletcher, Scott	84D	452	$ .03	$ .10
Fielder, Cecil	88D	565	$ .10	$1.00	Fletcher, Scott	85D	330	$ .01	$ .08
Fielder, Cecil	89D	442	$ .10	$ .50	Fletcher, Scott	86D	282	$ .01	$ .06
Fields, Bruce	87DRR	47	$ .01	$ .04	Fletcher, Scott	87D	304	$ .01	$ .04
Figueroa, Jesus	81D	556	$ .01	$ .05	Fletcher, Scott	88D	180	$ .01	$ .05
Filer, Tom	86D	439	$ .01	$ .06	Fletcher, Scott	88DBB	32	$ .01	$ .05
Filer, Tom	90D	687	$ .01	$ .03	Fletcher, Scott	88DK	11	$ .01	$ .05
Filson, Pete	84D	194	$ .03	$ .10	Fletcher, Scott	89D	142	$ .01	$ .04
Filson, Pete	85D	607	$ .01	$ .08	Fletcher, Scott	89DBB	167	$ .01	$ .04

Player	Year	No.	VG	EX/MT	Player	Year	No.	VG	EX/MT
Fletcher, Scott	90D	455	$ .01	$ .03	Forsch, Bob	89D	118	$ .01	$ .04
Flynn, Doug	81D	394	$ .01	$ .05	Forsch, Ken	81D	141	$ .01	$ .05
					Forsch, Ken	82D	393	$ .01	$ .05
					Forsch, Ken	83D	164	$ .01	$ .05
					Forsch, Ken	84D	280	$ .03	$ .10
					Forster, Terry	82D	362	$ .01	$ .05
					Forster, Terry	83D	453	$ .01	$ .05
					Forster, Terry	86D	432	$ .01	$ .06
					Fossas, Tony	90D	457	$ .01	$ .03
					Foster, George	81D	65	$ .05	$ .20
					Foster, George	82D	274	$ .05	$ .20
					Foster, George	83D	427	$ .03	$ .20
					Foster, George	83DK	6	$ .05	$ .20
					Foster, George	84D	312	$ .08	$ .25
					Foster, George	85D	603	$ .03	$ .10
					Foster, George	86D	116	$ .02	$ .15
					Fowlkes, Alan	83D	46	$ .01	$ .05
					Franco, John	85D	164	$ .25	$2.00
					Franco, John	86D	487	$ .03	$ .30
					Franco, John	87D	289	$ .01	$ .10
					Franco, John	88D	123	$ .01	$ .05
					Franco, John	88DBB	54	$ .01	$ .10
					Franco, John	89D	233	$ .01	$ .10
					Franco, John	89DBB	166	$ .01	$ .10
					Franco, John	90D	124	$ .01	$ .10
					Franco, John	90DK	14	$ .01	$ .10
					Franco, Julio	83D	525	$1.00	$4.50
					Franco, Julio	84D	216	$ .08	$1.00
					Franco, Julio	85D	94	$ .10	$ .50
					Franco, Julio	86D	216	$ .05	$ .25
					Franco, Julio	87D	131	$ .01	$ .15
					Franco, Julio	88D	156	$ .01	$ .05
					Franco, Julio	88DBB	168	$ .01	$ .05
					Franco, Julio	88DK	10	$ .01	$ .05
Flynn, Doug	82D	427	$ .01	$ .05	Franco, Julio	89D	310	$ .01	$ .04
Flynn, Doug	83D	240	$ .01	$ .05	Franco, Julio	89DBB	32	$ .01	$ .10
Flynn, Doug	84D	254	$ .03	$ .10	Franco, Julio	89DTR	31	$ .01	$ .15
Flynn, Doug	85D	463	$ .01	$ .08	Franco, Julio	90D	142	$ .01	$ .10
Foley, Marvis	81D	399	$ .01	$ .05	Franco, Julio	90DAS	701	$ .01	$ .10
Foley, Marvis	83D	652	$ .01	$ .05	Franco, Julio	90DBC	14	$ .01	$ .10
Foley, Marvis	85D	500	$ .01	$ .08	Francona, Terry	82D	627	$ .01	$ .05
Foley, Tom	84D	81	$ .03	$ .10	Francona, Terry	83D	592	$ .01	$ .05
Foley, Tom	85D	569	$ .01	$ .08	Francona, Terry	84D	463	$ .03	$ .10
Foley, Tom	86D	549	$ .01	$ .06	Francona, Terry	85D	132	$ .01	$ .08
Foley, Tom	87D	504	$ .01	$ .04	Francona, Terry	86D	401	$ .01	$ .06
Foley, Tom	88D	303	$ .01	$ .05	Fraser, Will	87DR	9	$ .01	$ .07
Foley, Tom	89D	342	$ .01	$ .04	Fraser, Will	87DRR	40	$ .01	$ .04
Foley, Tom	89DBB	314	$ .01	$ .04	Fraser, Willie	88D	135	$ .01	$ .05
Foley, Tom	90D	274	$ .01	$ .03	Fraser, Willie	89D	567	$ .01	$ .04
Foli, Tim	81D	13	$ .01	$ .05	Fraser, Willie	90D	587	$ .01	$ .03
Foli, Tim	82D	376	$ .01	$ .05	Frazier, George	81D	310	$ .01	$ .05
Foli, Tim	83D	342	$ .01	$ .05	Frazier, George	82D	584	$ .01	$ .05
Foli, Tim	84D	474	$ .03	$ .10	Frazier, George	83D	535	$ .01	$ .05
Fontenot, Ray	84D	370	$ .03	$ .10	Frazier, George	84D	591	$ .03	$ .10
Fontenot, Ray	85D	248	$ .01	$ .08	Frazier, George	85D	167	$ .01	$ .08
Fontenot, Ray	86D	361	$ .01	$ .06	Frazier, George	86D	411	$ .01	$ .06
Foote, Barry	81D	558	$ .01	$ .05	Frazier, George	87D	564	$ .01	$ .04
Foote, Barry	82D	83	$ .01	$ .05	Frazier, George	88D	443	$ .01	$ .05
Ford, Curt	87D	454	$ .01	$ .04	Freeman, Marvin	87D	576	$ .01	$ .15
Ford, Curt	88D	417	$ .01	$ .05	Freeman, Marvin	89D	631	$ .01	$ .04
Ford, Curt	90D	694	$ .01	$ .03	Fregosi, Jim	81D	414	$ .01	$ .05
Ford, Dan	81D	54	$ .01	$ .05	Frey, Jim	81D	464	$ .01	$ .05
Ford, Dan	82D	468	$ .01	$ .05	Frobel, Doug	84DRR	38	$ .03	$ .10
Ford, Dan	83D	509	$ .01	$ .05	Frohwirth, Todd	88DR	3	$ .01	$ .05
Ford, Dan	84D	367	$ .03	$ .10	Frohwirth, Todd	89D	587	$ .01	$ .04
Ford, Dan	85D	489	$ .01	$ .08	Frohwirth, Todd	90D	631	$ .01	$ .03
Ford, Dave	81D	552	$ .01	$ .05	Frost, Dave	81D	52	$ .01	$ .05
Ford, Dave	82D	597	$ .01	$ .05	Frost, Dave	82D	290	$ .01	$ .05
Forsch, Bob	81D	69	$ .01	$ .05	Fryman, Woodie	81D	331	$ .01	$ .05
Forsch, Bob	82D	91	$ .01	$ .05	Fryman, Woodie	82D	68	$ .01	$ .05
Forsch, Bob	83D	64	$ .01	$ .05	Fryman, Woodie	83D	162	$ .01	$ .05
Forsch, Bob	84D	168	$ .03	$ .10	Fuentes, Mike	84DRR	40	$ .03	$ .10
Forsch, Bob	86D	353	$ .01	$ .06	Fulgham, John	81D	70	$ .01	$ .05
Forsch, Bob	87D	540	$ .01	$ .04	Funderburk, Mark	86D	630	$ .01	$ .06
Forsch, Bob	88D	111	$ .01	$ .05	Gaetti, Gary	83D	53	$ .50	$3.00

DOUG FLYNN 2b/ss — Mets

DONRUSS

Player	Year	No.	VG	EX/MT	Player	Year	No.	VG	EX/MT
Gaetti, Gary	84D	314	$ .15	$ .90	Garcia, Damaso	83D	54	$ .01	$ .05
Gaetti, Gary	85D	242	$ .03	$ .35	Garcia, Damaso	84D	241	$ .03	$ .10
Gaetti, Gary	86D	314	$ .03	$ .25	Garcia, Damaso	85D	315	$ .01	$ .08
Gaetti, Gary	87D	122	$ .01	$ .04	Garcia, Damaso	86D	241	$ .01	$ .06
Gaetti, Gary	88D	194	$ .01	$ .15	Garcia, Damaso	87D	614	$ .01	$ .04
Gaetti, Gary	88DBB	46	$ .01	$ .05	Garcia, Damaso	88D	414	$ .01	$ .05
Gaetti, Gary	88DK	19	$ .01	$ .05	Garcia, Dave	81D	442	$ .01	$ .05
Gaetti, Gary	89D	64	$ .01	$ .10	Garcia, Dave	82D	337	$ .01	$ .05
Gaetti, Gary	89DBB	102	$ .01	$ .04	Garcia, Kiko	81D	514	$ .01	$ .05
Gaetti, Gary	90D	151	$ .01	$ .03	Garcia, Kiko	82D	470	$ .01	$ .05
Gaff, Brent	83D	553	$ .01	$ .05	Garcia, Kiko	83D	569	$ .01	$ .05
Gagne, Greg	84DRR	39	$ .10	$ .50	Garcia, Kiko	84D	545	$ .03	$ .10
Gagne, Greg	86D	558	$ .01	$ .10	Garcia, Miguel	89D	622	$ .01	$ .04
Gagne, Greg	87D	395	$ .01	$ .04	Gardenhire, Ron	82D	649	$ .01	$ .05
Gagne, Greg	88D	441	$ .01	$ .05	Gardenhire, Ron	83D	175	$ .01	$ .05
Gagne, Greg	88DBB	74	$ .01	$ .05	Gardenhire, Ron	85D	360	$ .01	$ .08
Gagne, Greg	89D	318	$ .01	$ .04	Gardner, Billy	82D	591	$ .01	$ .05
Gagne, Greg	89DBB	158	$ .01	$ .04	Gardner, Mark	90DRR	40	$ .01	$ .10
Gagne, Greg	90D	237	$ .01	$ .03	Gardner, Wes	88D	634	$ .01	$ .15
Gainey, Ty	86DRR	31	$ .01	$ .06	Gardner, Wes	89D	541	$ .01	$ .04
Gainey, Ty	87D	533	$ .01	$ .04	Gardner, Wes	90D	541	$ .01	$ .03
Gainey, Ty	88D	578	$ .01	$ .05	Garland, Wayne	81D	440	$ .01	$ .05
Galarraga, Andres	86DR	7	$ .15	$1.00	Garland, Wayne	82D	489	$ .01	$ .05
Galarraga, Andres	86DRR	33	$1.00	$4.00	Garner, Phil	81D	372	$ .01	$ .05
Galarraga, Andres	87D	303	$ .01	$ .50	Garner, Phil	82D	544	$ .01	$ .05
Galarraga, Andres	88D	282	$ .01	$ .15	Garner, Phil	83D	270	$ .01	$ .05
Galarraga, Andres	88DBB	90	$ .01	$ .15	Garner, Phil	84D	354	$ .03	$ .10
Galarraga, Andres	89D	130	$ .01	$ .10	Garner, Phil	85D	161	$ .01	$ .08
Galarraga, Andres	89DBB	12	$ .01	$ .10	Garner, Phil	86D	527	$ .01	$ .06
Galarraga, Andres	89DBC	16	$ .01	$ .10	Garner, Phil	87D	358	$ .01	$ .04
Galarraga, Andres	89DK	14	$ .01	$ .05	Garrelts, Scott	84D	646	$ .15	$1.00
Galarraga, Andres	90D	97	$ .01	$ .03	Garrelts, Scott	86D	309	$ .01	$ .06
Gale, Rich	81D	462	$ .01	$ .05	Garrelts, Scott	87D	116	$ .01	$ .04
Gale, Rich	82D	138	$ .01	$ .05	Garrelts, Scott	88D	80	$ .01	$ .05
Gale, Rich	83D	172	$ .01	$ .05	Garrelts, Scott	88DBB	162	$ .01	$ .05
Gale, Rich	84D	140	$ .03	$ .10	Garrelts, Scott	89D	295	$ .01	$ .04
Gallagher, Dave	88DR	7	$ .05	$ .35	Garrelts, Scott	89DBB	218	$ .01	$ .04
Gallagher, Dave	89D	384	$ .01	$ .25	Garrelts, Scott	90D	217	$ .01	$ .03
Gallagher, Dave	89DBB	67	$ .01	$ .04	Garvey, Steve	81D	176	$ .12	$ .75
Gallagher, Dave	90D	219	$ .01	$ .03					
Gallego, Mike	86D	156	$ .01	$ .06					
Gallego, Mike	88D	379	$ .01	$ .05					
Gallego, Mike	89D	422	$ .01	$ .04					
Gallego, Mike	90D	361	$ .01	$ .03					
Gamble, Oscar	81D	229	$ .01	$ .05					
Gamble, Oscar	82D	360	$ .01	$ .05					
Gamble, Oscar	83D	461	$ .01	$ .05					
Gant, Ron	88D	654	$ .05	$ .55					
Gant, Ron	88DBB	2	$ .01	$ .15					
Gant, Ron	88DR	47	$ .01	$ .15					
Gant, Ron	89D	50	$ .01	$ .10					
Gant, Ron	90D	475	$ .01	$ .03					
Gantner, Jim	81D	204	$ .01	$ .05					
Gantner, Jim	82D	406	$ .01	$ .05					
Gantner, Jim	83D	232	$ .01	$ .05					
Gantner, Jim	84D	115	$ .03	$ .10					
Gantner, Jim	85D	229	$ .01	$ .08					
Gantner, Jim	86D	115	$ .01	$ .06					
Gantner, Jim	87D	172	$ .01	$ .04					
Gantner, Jim	88D	214	$ .01	$ .05					
Gantner, Jim	88DBB	53	$ .01	$ .05					
Gantner, Jim	89D	264	$ .01	$ .04					
Gantner, Jim	89DBB	295	$ .01	$ .04					
Gantner, Jim	90D	291	$ .01	$ .03					
Garber, Gene	81D	77	$ .01	$ .05					
Garber, Gene	82D	123	$ .01	$ .05					
Garber, Gene	83D	223	$ .01	$ .05					
Garber, Gene	84D	287	$ .03	$ .10					
Garber, Gene	87D	414	$ .01	$ .04					
Garber, Gene	88D	618	$ .01	$ .15					
Garber, Gene	88DBB	63	$ .01	$ .05	STEVE GARVEY FIRST BASE				
Garbey, Barbaro	85D	456	$ .01	$ .08					
Garbey, Barbaro	86D	349	$ .01	$ .06	Garvey, Steve	81D	56	$ .08	$ .75
Garcia, Damaso	81D	269	$ .01	$ .10	Garvey, Steve	82D	84	$ .10	$ .75
Garcia, Damaso	82D	479	$ .01	$ .05	Garvey, Steve	82DK	3	$ .06	$ .50
					Garvey, Steve	83D	488	$ .08	$ .40

Player	Year	No.	VG	EX/MT	Player	Year	No.	VG	EX/MT
Garvey, Steve	84D	63	$ .20	$ .60	Gonzales, Julio	82D	645	$ .01	$ .05
Garvey, Steve	85D	307	$ .15	$ .40	Gonzales, R. C.	89D	377	$ .01	$ .04
Garvey, Steve	86D	63	$ .15	$ .50	Gonzales, Rene	88D	582	$ .01	$ .05
Garvey, Steve	87D	81	$ .08	$ .25	Gonzales, Rene	90D	401	$ .01	$ .03
Garvin, Jerry	81D	150	$ .01	$ .05	Gonzalez, Denny	85D	600	$ .01	$ .08
Garvin, Jerry	82D	430	$ .01	$ .05	Gonzalez, Denny	86D	410	$ .02	$ .04
Garvin, Jerry	83D	227	$ .01	$ .05	Gonzalez, German	89D	590	$ .01	$ .04
Gates, Mike	83D	114	$ .01	$ .05	Gonzalez, German	89DR	24	$ .01	$ .10
Gedman, Rich	82D	512	$ .10	$ .40	Gonzalez, Jose	87D	525	$ .01	$ .25
Gedman, Rich	83D	156	$ .01	$ .05	Gonzalez, Jose	88D	341	$ .01	$ .05
Gedman, Rich	84D	579	$ .03	$ .10	Gonzalez, Jose	89DBB	260	$ .01	$ .04
Gedman, Rich	85D	457	$ .01	$ .08	Gonzalez, Jose	90D	314	$ .01	$ .03
Gedman, Rich	86D	273	$ .01	$ .06	Gonzalez, Juan	90DRR	33	$ .01	$ .45
Gedman, Rich	87D	153	$ .01	$ .04	Gooden, Dwight	85D	190	$3.50	$14.00
Gedman, Rich	88D	129	$ .01	$ .05	Gooden, Dwight	86D	75	$ .80	$3.00
Gedman, Rich	88DBB	140	$ .01	$ .05	Gooden, Dwight	86DK	26	$ .25	$ .75
Gedman, Rich	89D	162	$ .01	$ .04	Gooden, Dwight	87D	199	$ .15	$1.75
Gedman, Rich	90D	346	$ .01	$ .03	Gooden, Dwight	88D	69	$ .10	$ .50
Gehrig, Lou	85D	635	$ .03	$ .25	Gooden, Dwight	88DBB	96	$ .05	$ .25
Geisel, Dave	82D	633	$ .01	$ .05	Gooden, Dwight	89D	270	$ .01	$ .25
Geisel, Dave	84D	645	$ .03	$ .10	Gooden, Dwight	89DBB	14	$ .01	$ .25
Gerber, Craig	86D	545	$ .01	$ .06	Gooden, Dwight	90D	171	$ .01	$ .15
Geren, Bob	89DR	11	$ .01	$ .25	Goodwin, Danny	81D	494	$ .01	$ .05
Geren, Bob	90D	395	$ .01	$ .10	Goodwin, Danny	82D	305	$ .01	$ .05
Gerhart, Ken	87DR	24	$ .01	$ .07	Gordon, Tom	89DBB	287	$ .01	$ .35
Gerhart, Ken	87DRR	30	$ .10	$ .30	Gordon, Tom	89DR	4	$ .01	$1.00
Gerhart, Ken	88D	213	$ .01	$ .15	Gordon, Tom	89DRR	45	$ .25	$1.50
Geronimo, Cesar	81D	305	$ .01	$ .05	Gordon, Tom	90D	297	$ .01	$ .25
Geronimo, Cesar	82D	322	$ .01	$ .05	Goryl, John	81D	527	$ .01	$ .05
Geronimo, Cesar	83D	448	$ .01	$ .05	Gossage, Goose	84D	396	$ .08	$ .25
Geronimo, Cesar	84D	252	$ .03	$ .10	Gossage, Goose	85D	185	$ .08	$ .25
Geurrero, Pedro	89D	418	$ .01	$ .10	Gossage, Goose	86D	185	$ .03	$ .25
Giamatti, Bart	90D	716	$ .01	$1.50	Gossage, Goose	86DK	2	$ .05	$ .20
Gibbons, John	85D	116	$ .01	$ .08	Gossage, Goose	90D	678	$ .01	$ .03
Gibbons, John	87D	626	$ .01	$ .04	Gossage, Goose "Rich"	87D	483	$ .01	$ .04
Gibson, Bob	84D	246	$ .03	$ .10	Gossage, Goose "Rich"	88DBB	26	$ .01	$ .05
Gibson, Bob	85D	393	$ .01	$ .08	Gossage, Rich	81D	347	$ .05	$ .20
Gibson, Bob	86D	271	$ .01	$ .06	Gossage, Rich	82D	283	$ .03	$ .20
Gibson, Kirk	82D	407	$ .50	$1.50	Gossage, Rich	83D	157	$ .03	$ .20
Gibson, Kirk	83D	459	$ .05	$ .30	Gossage, Rich	88D	434	$ .01	$ .15
Gibson, Kirk	84D	593	$ .15	$ .75	Gossage, Rich	89D	158	$ .01	$ .04
Gibson, Kirk	85D	471	$ .08	$ .25	Gott, Jim	83D	353	$ .01	$ .25
Gibson, Kirk	86D	125	$ .08	$ .25	Gott, Jim	84D	268	$ .03	$ .10
Gibson, Kirk	86DK	1	$ .03	$ .25	Gott, Jim	85D	632	$ .01	$ .08
Gibson, Kirk	87D	50	$ .05	$ .20	Gott, Jim	86D	358	$ .01	$ .06
Gibson, Kirk	88D	275	$ .05	$ .20	Gott, Jim	88D	606	$ .01	$ .15
Gibson, Kirk	88DBB	66	$ .05	$ .20	Gott, Jim	88DBB	213	$ .01	$ .05
Gibson, Kirk	89D	132	$ .01	$ .10	Gott, Jim	89D	362	$ .01	$ .04
Gibson, Kirk	89DBB	10	$ .01	$ .10	Gott, Jim	90D	605	$ .01	$ .03
Gibson, Kirk	89DK	15	$ .01	$ .15	Gozzo, Mauro	90D	655	$ .01	$ .10
Gibson, Kirk	90D	368	$ .01	$ .03	Grace, Mark	88DBB	4	$ .15	$2.00
Gibson, Paul	88DR	19	$ .01	$ .05	Grace, Mark	88DR	1	$ .25	$5.50
Gibson, Paul	89D	445	$ .01	$ .04	Grace, Mark	88DRR	40	$1.00	$4.00
Gibson, Paul	90D	657	$ .01	$ .03	Grace, Mark	89D	255	$ .25	$1.50
Giles, Brian	84D	563	$ .03	$ .10	Grace, Mark	89DK	17	$ .15	$ .75
Girardi, Joe	89DR	23	$ .01	$ .25	Grace, Mark	90D	577	$ .01	$ .25
Girardi, Joe	90D	404	$ .01	$ .10	Graham, Dan	82D	455	$ .01	$ .05
Gladden, Dan	85D	567	$ .10	$ .45	Grant, Mark	85D	601	$ .01	$ .08
Gladden, Dan	86D	187	$ .01	$ .06	Grant, Mark	87D	644	$ .01	$ .04
Gladden, Dan	87D	189	$ .01	$ .04	Grant, Mark	88D	511	$ .01	$ .05
Gladden, Dan	88D	491	$ .01	$ .05	Grant, Mark	88DBB	133	$ .01	$ .05
Gladden, Dan	88DBB	130	$ .01	$ .05	Grant, Mark	90D	441	$ .01	$ .03
Gladden, Dan	89D	391	$ .01	$ .04	Gray, Gary	83D	637	$ .01	$ .05
Gladden, Dan	89DBB	298	$ .01	$ .04	Green, Dallas	81D	415	$ .01	$ .05
Gladden, Dan	90D	182	$ .01	$ .03	Green, David	83D	166	$ .01	$ .05
Gladden, Dan	90DK	22	$ .01	$ .10	Green, David	84D	425	$ .03	$ .10
Glavine, Tom	88D	644	$ .05	$ .35	Green, David	84D	625	$ .01	$ .25
Glavine, Tom	89D	381	$ .01	$ .04	Green, David	85D	303	$ .01	$ .08
Glavine, Tom	89DBB	2	$ .01	$ .04	Green, David	86D	114	$ .01	$ .06
Glavine, Tom	90D	145	$ .01	$ .03	Greene, Tommy	90D	576	$ .01	$ .30
Gleaton, Jerry	88D	547	$ .01	$ .05	Greenwell, Mike	87D	585	$2.50	$9.00
Gleaton, Jerry Don	89D	444	$ .01	$ .04	Greenwell, Mike	87DR	4	$ .80	$3.00
Glynn, Ed	83D	537	$ .01	$ .05	Greenwell, Mike	88D	339	$ .25	$1.25
Goltz, Dave	82D	604	$ .01	$ .05	Greenwell, Mike	88DBB	177	$ .25	$1.00
Gomez, Luis	81D	88	$ .01	$ .05	Greenwell, Mike	89D	186	$ .10	$ .50

DONRUSS

Player	Year	No.	VG	EX/MT	Player	Year	No.	VG	EX/MT
Greenwell, Mike	89DBB	28	$ .01	$ .25	Grubb, John	83D	341	$ .01	$ .05
Greenwell, Mike	89DBC	13	$ .01	$ .25	Grubb, John	84D	90	$ .03	$ .10
Greenwell, Mike	89DK	1	$ .10	$ .50	Grubb, John	85D	578	$ .01	$ .08
Greenwell, Mike	90D	66	$ .01	$ .20	Grubb, John	86D	615	$ .01	$ .06
Greenwell, Mike	90DBC	17	$ .01	$ .10	Grubb, John	87D	476	$ .01	$ .04
Gregg, Tommy	88D	203	$ .03	$ .30	Gruber, Kelly	86DR	16	$ .25	$2.00
Gregg, Tommy	89D	121	$ .01	$ .04	Gruber, Kelly	87D	444	$ .15	$1.50
Gregg, Tommy	89DBB	170	$ .01	$ .04	Gruber, Kelly	88D	244	$ .01	$ .25
Gregg, Tommy	90D	239	$ .01	$ .03	Gruber, Kelly	88DBB	255	$ .01	$ .15
Grich, Bobby	81D	289	$ .01	$ .05	Gruber, Kelly	89D	113	$ .01	$ .25
Grich, Bobby	82D	90	$ .01	$ .05	Gruber, Kelly	89DBB	31	$ .01	$ .15
Grich, Bobby	83D	468	$ .01	$ .05	Gruber, Kelly	90D	113	$ .01	$ .15
Grich, Bobby	84D	179	$ .03	$ .10	Gruber, Kelly	90DK	12	$ .01	$ .10
Grich, Bobby	85D	280	$ .01	$ .08	Guante, Cecilio	84D	78	$ .03	$ .10
Grich, Bobby	86D	207	$ .01	$ .06	Guante, Cecilio	85D	357	$ .01	$ .08
Grich, Bobby	87D	456	$ .01	$ .04	Guante, Cecilio	86D	142	$ .01	$ .06
Griffey, Jr., Ken	89DBB	192	$ .01	$3.00	Guante, Cecilio	87D	238	$ .01	$ .04
Griffey, Jr., Ken	89DR	3	$ .01	$6.00	Guante, Cecilio	89D	260	$ .01	$ .04
Griffey, Jr., Ken	89DRR	33	$1.50	$8.00	Guante, Cecilio	90D	403	$ .01	$ .03
Griffey, Jr., Ken	90D	365	$ .01	$2.00	Guante, Matt	83D	423	$ .01	$ .05
Griffey, Jr., Ken	90DK	4	$ .01	$1.00	Gubicza, Mark	85D	344	$ .25	$2.00
Griffey, Ken	81D	184	$ .03	$ .25	Gubicza, Mark	86D	583	$ .01	$ .15
Griffey, Ken	82D	634	$ .03	$ .20	Gubicza, Mark	87D	466	$ .01	$ .04
Griffey, Ken	83D	486	$ .01	$ .05	Gubicza, Mark	88D	54	$ .01	$ .05
Griffey, Ken	84D	613	$ .04	$ .25	Gubicza, Mark	88DBB	95	$ .01	$ .05
Griffey, Ken	85D	347	$ .03	$ .20	Gubicza, Mark	89D	179	$ .01	$ .04
Griffey, Ken	86D	126	$ .01	$ .06	Gubicza, Mark	89DBB	119	$ .01	$ .04
Griffey, Ken	87D	513	$ .01	$ .04	Gubicza, Mark	90D	204	$ .01	$ .03
Griffey, Ken	88D	202	$ .01	$ .15	Guerrero, Pedro	82D	136	$ .10	$ .55
Griffey, Ken	88DBB	141	$ .01	$ .10	Guerrero, Pedro	83D	110	$ .05	$ .30
Griffey, Ken	90D	469	$ .01	$ .03	Guerrero, Pedro	84D	174	$ .15	$ .50
Griffin, Alfredo	81D	149	$ .01	$ .05	Guerrero, Pedro	84DK	24	$ .08	$ .25
Griffin, Alfredo	82D	101	$ .01	$ .05	Guerrero, Pedro	85D	174	$ .08	$ .25
Griffin, Alfredo	83D	180	$ .01	$ .05	Guerrero, Pedro	86D	174	$ .08	$ .25
Griffin, Alfredo	84D	605	$ .03	$ .10	Guerrero, Pedro	87D	53	$ .03	$ .25
Griffin, Alfredo	85D	73	$ .01	$ .08	Guerrero, Pedro	88D	278	$ .01	$ .05
Griffin, Alfredo	86D	101	$ .01	$ .06	Guerrero, Pedro	88DBB	122	$ .01	$ .10
Griffin, Alfredo	87D	256	$ .01	$ .04	Guerrero, Pedro	88DBC	16	$ .05	$ .25
Griffin, Alfredo	88D	226	$ .01	$ .05	Guerrero, Pedro	89DBB	75	$ .01	$ .10
Griffin, Alfredo	88DBB	92	$ .01	$ .05	Guerrero, Pedro	90D	63	$ .01	$ .03
Griffin, Alfredo	89D	79	$ .01	$ .04	Guerrero, Pedro	90DAS	674	$ .01	$ .03
Griffin, Alfredo	89DBB	178	$ .01	$ .04	Guerrero, Pedro	90DBC	6	$ .01	$ .03
Griffin, Alfredo	90D	195	$ .01	$ .03	Guetterman, Lee	87D	322	$ .01	$ .15
Griffin, Mike	82D	533	$ .01	$ .05	Guetterman, Lee	88D	270	$ .01	$ .05
Griffin, Mike	88D	494	$ .01	$ .05	Guetterman, Lee	89DBB	108	$ .01	$ .04
Griffin, Tom	81D	75	$ .01	$ .05	Guetterman, Lee	90D	127	$ .01	$ .03
Griffin, Tom	82D	474	$ .01	$ .05	Guidry, Ron	81D	227	$ .05	$ .20
Grissom, Marquis	90DRR	36	$ .01	$ .75	Guidry, Ron	82D	548	$ .03	$ .20
Gross, Greg	81D	598	$ .01	$ .05	Guidry, Ron	82D	558	$ .03	$ .20
Gross, Greg	82D	371	$ .01	$ .05	Guidry, Ron	83D	31	$ .03	$ .20
Gross, Greg	83D	441	$ .01	$ .05	Guidry, Ron	83DK	17	$ .05	$ .20
Gross, Greg	84D	285	$ .03	$ .10	Guidry, Ron	84D	173	$ .04	$ .25
Gross, Greg	85D	407	$ .01	$ .08	Guidry, Ron	85D	214	$ .03	$ .20
Gross, Greg	86D	163	$ .01	$ .06	Guidry, Ron	86D	103	$ .03	$ .25
Gross, Greg	87D	385	$ .01	$ .04	Guidry, Ron	87D	93	$ .05	$ .20
Gross, Greg	88D	412	$ .01	$ .05	Guidry, Ron	88D	175	$ .01	$ .15
Gross, Kevin	84D	381	$ .04	$ .30	Guillen, Ozzie	86D	208	$ .15	$ .75
Gross, Kevin	85D	477	$ .01	$ .08	Guillen, Ozzie	87D	87	$ .01	$ .04
Gross, Kevin	86D	529	$ .01	$ .06	Guillen, Ozzie	88D	137	$ .01	$ .05
Gross, Kevin	87D	236	$ .01	$ .04	Guillen, Ozzie	88DBB	81	$ .01	$ .05
Gross, Kevin	88D	113	$ .01	$ .05	Guillen, Ozzie	89D	176	$ .01	$ .04
Gross, Kevin	88DBB	103	$ .01	$ .05	Guillen, Ozzie	89DBB	137	$ .01	$ .04
Gross, Kevin	89D	194	$ .01	$ .04	Guillen, Ozzie	89DBC	23	$ .01	$ .10
Gross, Kevin	89DBB	202	$ .01	$ .04	Guillen, Ozzie	90D	135	$ .01	$ .03
Gross, Kevin	89DBC	12	$ .01	$ .10	Guillen, Ozzie	90DK	15	$ .01	$ .10
Gross, Kevin	89DTR	3	$ .01	$ .05	Gulden, Brad	85D	365	$ .01	$ .08
Gross, Kevin	90D	248	$ .01	$ .03	Gullickson, Bill	81D	91	$ .05	$ .30
Gross, Wayne	81D	237	$ .01	$ .05	Gullickson, Bill	82D	162	$ .01	$ .05
Gross, Wayne	82D	139	$ .01	$ .05	Gullickson, Bill	83D	288	$ .01	$ .05
Gross, Wayne	83D	591	$ .01	$ .05	Gullickson, Bill	84D	401	$ .03	$ .10
Gross, Wayne	84D	375	$ .03	$ .10	Gullickson, Bill	85D	97	$ .01	$ .08
Gross, Wayne	85D	228	$ .01	$ .08	Gullickson, Bill	86D	331	$ .01	$ .06
Gross, Wayne	86D	535	$ .01	$ .06	Gullickson, Bill	87D	369	$ .01	$ .04
Grubb, John	81D	148	$ .01	$ .05	Gullickson, Bill	88D	586	$ .01	$ .05
Grubb, John	82D	467	$ .01	$ .05	Gulliver, Glenn	83D	131	$ .01	$ .05

Player	Year	No.	VG	EX/MT	Player	Year	No.	VG	EX/MT
Gura, Larry	81D	461	$ .01	$ .05	Hammaker, Atlee	89D	414	$ .01	$ .04
Gura, Larry	82D	338	$ .01	$ .05	Hammaker, Atlee	90D	532	$ .01	$ .03
Gura, Larry	83D	160	$ .01	$ .05	Hancock. Garry	82D	608	$ .01	$ .05
Gura, Larry	84D	100	$ .03	$ .10	Hanna, Preston	81D	523	$ .01	$ .05
Gura, Larry	85D	217	$ .01	$ .08	Hanson, Eric	89DR	49	$ .01	$ .10
Guthrie, Mark	90D	622	$ .01	$ .10	Hanson, Erik	89DBB	320	$ .01	$ .10
Gutierrez, Jackie	85D	335	$ .01	$ .08	Hanson, Erik	89DRR	32	$ .01	$ .35
Gutierrez, Jackie	86D	335	$ .01	$ .06	Hanson, Erik	90D	345	$ .01	$ .10
Gutierrez, Jackie	87D	601	$ .01	$ .04	Hargrove, Mike	81D	78	$ .01	$ .05
Guzman, Jose	86DR	24	$ .02	$ .09	Hargrove, Mike	82D	389	$ .01	$ .05
Guzman, Jose	86DRR	30	$ .01	$ .25	Hargrove, Mike	83D	450	$ .01	$ .05
Guzman, Jose	87D	101	$ .01	$ .04	Hargrove, Mike	84D	495	$ .03	$ .10
Guzman, Jose	88D	136	$ .01	$ .05	Hargrove, Mike	85D	398	$ .01	$ .08
Guzman, Jose	88DBB	88	$ .01	$ .05	Hargrove, Mike	86D	590	$ .01	$ .06
Guzman, Jose	89D	284	$ .01	$ .04	Harkey, Mike	89DRR	43	$ .05	$ .30
Gwosdz, Doug	84D	383	$ .03	$ .10	Harkey, Mike	90D	522	$ .01	$ .03
Gwynn, Tony	83D	598	$2.50	$12.50	Harnisch, Pete	89DRR	44	$ .01	$ .04
Gwynn, Tony	84D	324	$ .80	$5.00	Harnisch, Pete	90D	596	$ .01	$ .03
Gwynn, Tony	85D	63	$ .25	$1.50	Harper, Brian	84D	142	$ .05	$ .35
Gwynn, Tony	85DK	25	$ .15	$ .50	Harper, Brian	85D	566	$ .01	$ .08
Gwynn, Tony	86D	112	$ .15	$ .75	Harper, Brian	86D	547	$ .01	$ .06
Gwynn, Tony	87D	64	$ .15	$ .50	Harper, Brian	89D	641	$ .01	$ .04
Gwynn, Tony	88D	164	$ .10	$ .35	Harper, Brian	90D	355	$ .01	$ .03
Gwynn, Tony	88DBB	154	$ .05	$ .25	Harper, Terry	83D	607	$ .01	$ .05
Gwynn, Tony	88DBC	6	$ .15	$ .50	Harper, Terry	86D	627	$ .01	$ .06
Gwynn, Tony	89D	128	$ .01	$ .20	Harrah, Toby	81D	318	$ .01	$ .05
Gwynn, Tony	89DBB	42	$ .01	$ .15	Harrah, Toby	82D	72	$ .01	$ .05
Gwynn, Tony	89DBC	20	$ .01	$ .20	Harrah, Toby	83D	337	$ .01	$ .05
Gwynn, Tony	89DK	6	$ .05	$ .35	Harrah, Toby	83DK	13	$ .01	$ .05
Gwynn, Tony	90D	86	$ .01	$ .20	Harrah, Toby	84D	251	$ .03	$ .10
Gwynn, Tony	90DAS	705	$ .01	$ .10	Harrah, Toby	86D	159	$ .01	$ .06
Gwynn, Tony	90DBC	4	$ .01	$ .10	Harrah, Toby	87D	408	$ .01	$ .04
Haas, Moose	81D	85	$ .01	$ .05	Harris, Gene	89DBB	325	$ .01	$ .04
Haas, Moose	82D	206	$ .01	$ .05	Harris, Gene	90D	247	$ .01	$ .03
Haas, Moose	83D	204	$ .01	$ .05	Harris, Greg	83D	295	$ .01	$ .05
Haas, Moose	84D	368	$ .03	$ .10	Harris, Greg	86D	465	$ .01	$ .06
Haas, Moose	85D	473	$ .01	$ .08	Harris, Greg	87D	382	$ .01	$ .04
Haas, Moose	86D	237	$ .01	$ .06	Harris, Greg	88D	427	$ .01	$ .05
Haas, Moose	87D	528	$ .01	$ .04	Harris, Greg	89D	548	$ .01	$ .04
Habyan, John	86DRR	45	$ .05	$ .15	Harris, Greg	89DR	46	$ .01	$ .10
Habyan, John	87D	494	$ .01	$ .04					
Habyan, John	88D	354	$ .01	$ .05					
Haddix, Harvey	82D	651	$ .01	$ .05					
Hairston, Jerry	83D	616	$ .01	$ .05					
Hairston, Jerry	84D	86	$ .03	$ .10					
Hairston, Jerry	85D	135	$ .01	$ .08					
Hairston, Jerry	86D	424	$ .01	$ .06					
Hairston, Jerry	87D	285	$ .01	$ .04					
Hairston, Jerry	88D	285	$ .01	$ .05					
Hale, Chip	90D	690	$ .01	$ .10					
Halicki, Ed	81D	53	$ .01	$ .05					
Hall, Albert	88D	290	$ .01	$ .05					
Hall, Albert	88DBB	253	$ .01	$ .05					
Hall, Drew	87D	594	$ .01	$ .04					
Hall, Drew	89D	522	$ .01	$ .04					
Hall, Mel	83D	126	$ .05	$ .40					
Hall, Mel	84D	411	$ .03	$ .10					
Hall, Mel	85D	338	$ .01	$ .08					
Hall, Mel	86D	276	$ .01	$ .06					
Hall, Mel	87D	473	$ .01	$ .04					
Hall, Mel	88D	342	$ .01	$ .05					
Hall, Mel	88DBB	173	$ .01	$ .05					
Hall, Mel	89D	73	$ .01	$ .04					
Hall, Mel	89DTR	36	$ .01	$ .05					
Hall, Mel	90D	598	$ .01	$ .03					
Hamilton, Jeff	87D	464	$ .08	$ .25					
Hamilton, Jeff	88D	525	$ .01	$ .05					
Hamilton, Jeff	89D	550	$ .01	$ .04					
Hamilton, Jeff	89DBB	290	$ .01	$ .04					
Hamilton, Jeff	90D	321	$ .01	$ .03					
Hammaker, Atlee	83D	298	$ .01	$ .05					
Hammaker, Atlee	84D	236	$ .03	$ .10					
Hammaker, Atlee	85D	509	$ .01	$ .08	Harris, Greg	89DRR	34	$ .01	$ .04
Hammaker, Atlee	86D	445	$ .01	$ .06	Harris, Greg	90D	582	$ .01	$ .03
Hammaker, Atlee	88D	450	$ .01	$ .05	Harris, Greg	90D	65	$ .01	$ .03

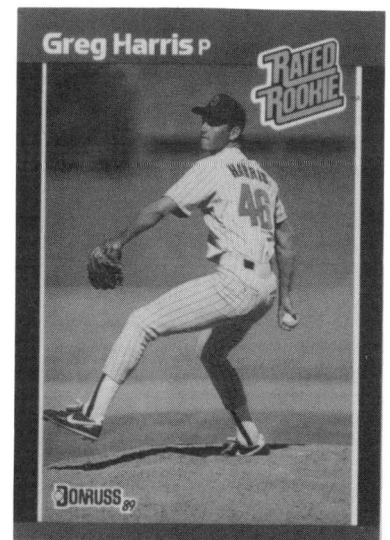

Greg Harris P — RATED ROOKIE — DONRUSS 89

DONRUSS

Player	Year	No.	VG	EX/MT	Player	Year	No.	VG	EX/MT
Harris, John	82D	444	$ .01	$ .05	Heath, Mike	86D	253	$ .01	$ .06
Harris, Lenny	90D	434	$ .01	$ .03	Heath, Mike	87D	496	$ .01	$ .04
Harvey, Bryan	88DR	53	$ .05	$ .25					
Harvey, Bryan	89D	525	$ .01	$ .15					
Harvey, Bryan	89DBB	317	$ .01	$ .04					
Harvey, Bryan	90D	372	$ .01	$ .03					
Hassey, Ron	81D	80	$ .01	$ .05					
Hassey, Ron	82D	463	$ .01	$ .05					
Hassey, Ron	83D	159	$ .01	$ .05					
Hassey, Ron	84D	460	$ .03	$ .10					
Hassey, Ron	86D	370	$ .01	$ .06					
Hassey, Ron	87D	532	$ .01	$ .04					
Hassey, Ron	88D	580	$ .01	$ .05					
Hassey, Ron	89D	361	$ .01	$ .04					
Hassey, Ron	90D	450	$ .01	$ .03					
Hassler, Andy	81D	581	$ .01	$ .05					
Hassler, Andy	82D	519	$ .01	$ .05					
Hassler, Andy	83D	290	$ .01	$ .05					
Hassler, Andy	84D	255	$ .03	$ .10					
Hatcher, Billy	85DRR	41	$ .20	$ .60					
Hatcher, Billy	86D	433	$ .02	$ .15					
Hatcher, Billy	87D	481	$ .01	$ .04					
Hatcher, Billy	88D	261	$ .01	$ .05					
Hatcher, Billy	88DBB	150	$ .01	$ .05					
Hatcher, Billy	88DK	23	$ .01	$ .05					
Hatcher, Billy	89D	187	$ .01	$ .04					
Hatcher, Billy	89DBB	150	$ .01	$ .04					
Hatcher, Billy	90D	616	$ .01	$ .03					
Hatcher, Mickey	81D	526	$ .01	$ .05					
Hatcher, Mickey	82D	480	$ .01	$ .05					
Hatcher, Mickey	83D	615	$ .01	$ .05					
Hatcher, Mickey	84D	147	$ .03	$ .10					
Hatcher, Mickey	85D	194	$ .01	$ .08	Mike Heath c				
Hatcher, Mickey	86D	269	$ .01	$ .06					
Hatcher, Mickey	87D	491	$ .01	$ .04	Heath, Mike	88D	338	$ .01	$ .05
Hatcher, Mickey	88D	299	$ .01	$ .05	Heath, Mike	88DBB	69	$ .01	$ .05
Hatcher, Mickey	89D	346	$ .01	$ .04	Heath, Mike	89D	271	$ .01	$ .04
Hatcher, Mickey	90D	439	$ .01	$ .03	Heath, Mike	89DBB	147	$ .01	$ .04
Hausman, Tom	81D	396	$ .01	$ .05	Heath, Mike	90D	209	$ .01	$ .03
Hausman, Tom	82D	301	$ .01	$ .05	Heathcock, Jeff	86D	182	$ .01	$ .06
Havens, Brad	82D	382	$ .01	$ .05	Heaton, Neal	84D	373	$ .10	$ .50
Havens, Brad	83D	480	$ .01	$ .05	Heaton, Neal	85D	373	$ .01	$ .08
Havens, Brad	86D	599	$ .01	$ .06	Heaton, Neal	86D	338	$ .01	$ .06
Hawkins, Andy	85D	528	$ .01	$ .25	Heaton, Neal	87D	615	$ .01	$ .04
Hawkins, Andy	86D	284	$ .01	$ .06	Heaton, Neal	88D	134	$ .01	$ .05
Hawkins, Andy	87D	264	$ .01	$ .04	Heaton, Neal	88DBB	124	$ .01	$ .05
Hawkins, Andy	89D	583	$ .01	$ .04	Heaton, Neal	89D	224	$ .01	$ .04
Hawkins, Andy	89DBB	52	$ .01	$ .04	Heaton, Neal	90D	658	$ .01	$ .03
Hawkins, Andy	89DTR	52	$ .01	$ .05	Heaverlo, Dave	81D	407	$ .01	$ .05
Hawkins, Andy	90D	159	$ .01	$ .03	Hebner, Richie	81D	125	$ .01	$ .05
Hayes, Charlie	90D	548	$ .01	$ .10	Hebner, Richie	82D	328	$ .01	$ .05
Hayes, Von	82D	237	$ .12	$1.00	Hebner, Richie	85D	564	$ .01	$ .08
Hayes, Von	83D	324	$ .03	$ .35	Heep, Danny	83D	443	$ .01	$ .05
Hayes, Von	84D	477	$ .04	$ .25	Heep, Danny	84D	434	$ .03	$ .10
Hayes, Von	85D	326	$ .01	$ .20	Heep, Danny	85D	556	$ .01	$ .08
Hayes, Von	86D	305	$ .01	$ .06	Heep, Danny	86D	556	$ .01	$ .06
Hayes, Von	87D	113	$ .01	$ .04	Heep, Danny	87D	649	$ .01	$ .04
Hayes, Von	87DK	12	$ .01	$ .04	Heep, Danny	89D	368	$ .01	$ .04
Hayes, Von	88D	207	$ .01	$ .05	Heep, Danny	90D	358	$ .01	$ .03
Hayes, Von	88DBB	128	$ .01	$ .15	Heimueller, Gorman	84D	131	$ .03	$ .10
Hayes, Von	89DBB	47	$ .01	$ .04	Henderson, Dave	84D	557	$ .05	$ .40
Hayes, Von	90D	278	$ .01	$ .03	Henderson, Dave	86D	318	$ .01	$ .06
Hayes, Von	90DBC	25	$ .01	$ .03	Henderson, Dave	87D	622	$ .01	$ .04
Hayes, Von Frances	89D	160	$ .01	$ .04	Henderson, Dave	89D	450	$ .01	$ .04
Hayward, Ray	87D	632	$ .01	$ .04	Henderson, Dave	89DBB	190	$ .01	$ .04
Hayward, Ray	89D	521	$ .01	$ .04	Henderson, Dave	89DK	20	$ .01	$ .05
Hearn, Ed	86DR	54	$ .02	$ .09	Henderson, Dave	90D	243	$ .01	$ .03
Hearn, Ed	87D	446	$ .01	$ .04	Henderson, Rickey	81D	119	$1.00	$4.00
Hearn, Ed	89D	297	$ .01	$ .04	Henderson, Rickey	82D	113	$ .15	$2.00
Hearron, Jeff	87D	490	$ .01	$ .04	Henderson, Rickey	83D	35	$ .10	$1.75
Heath, Mike	81D	120	$ .01	$ .05	Henderson, Rickey	83DK	11	$ .10	$1.00
Heath, Mike	82D	413	$ .01	$ .05	Henderson, Rickey	84D	54	$ .75	$3.25
Heath, Mike	83D	517	$ .01	$ .05	Henderson, Rickey	85D	176	$ .25	$1.50
Heath, Mike	84D	223	$ .03	$ .10	Henderson, Rickey	86D	51	$ .10	$ .75
Heath, Mike	85D	298	$ .01	$ .08	Henderson, Rickey	87D	228	$ .05	$ .50

Player	Year	No.	VG	EX/MT	Player	Year	No.	VG	EX/MT
Henderson, Rickey	88D	277	$ .10	$ .30	Herr, Tommy	88D	208	$ .01	$ .05
Henderson, Rickey	88DBB	76	$ .05	$ .25	Herr, Tommy	89D	301	$ .01	$ .04
Henderson, Rickey	89D	245	$ .05	$ .25	Herr, Tommy	89DBB	72	$ .01	$ .04
Henderson, Rickey	89DBB	78	$ .01	$ .25	Herr, Tommy	89DTR	4	$ .01	$ .05
Henderson, Rickey	90D	304	$ .01	$ .20	Herr, Tommy	90D	75	$ .01	$ .03
Henderson, Steve	81D	157	$ .01	$ .05	Herr, Tommy	90DK	21	$ .01	$ .10
Henderson, Steve	82D	183	$ .01	$ .05	Hershiser, Orel	85D	581	$ .70	$10.00
Henderson, Steve	83D	252	$ .01	$ .05	Hershiser, Orel	86D	226	$ .10	$2.00
Henderson, Steve	84D	389	$ .03	$ .10	Hershiser, Orel	86DK	18	$ .08	$ .40
Henderson, Steve	85D	145	$ .01	$ .08	Hershiser, Orel	87D	106	$ .05	$ .30
Henderson, Steve	86D	375	$ .01	$ .06	Hershiser, Orel	88D	94	$ .05	$ .20
Hendrick, George	81D	430	$ .01	$ .05	Hershiser, Orel	88DBB	148	$ .05	$ .25
Hendrick, George	82D	40	$ .01	$ .05	Hershiser, Orel	89D	197	$ .05	$ .25
Hendrick, George	82DK	9	$ .01	$ .05	Hershiser, Orel	89D	648	$ .05	$ .25
Hendrick, George	83D	404	$ .01	$ .05	Hershiser, Orel	89DBB	225	$ .01	$ .10
Hendrick, George	84D	475	$ .03	$ .10	Hershiser, Orel	89DBC	4	$ .01	$ .20
Hendrick, George	85D	181	$ .01	$ .08	Hershiser, Orel	90D	197	$ .01	$ .10
Hendrick, George	88D	479	$ .01	$ .05	Hershiser, Orel	90DBC	5	$ .01	$ .10
Hengel, Dave	88D	629	$ .05	$ .30	Herzog, Whitey	82D	190	$ .02	$ .15
Henke, Tom	84D	134	$ .25	$1.00	Herzog, Whitey	83D	530	$ .01	$ .05
Henke, Tom	85D	403	$ .01	$ .08	Hesketh, Joe	85D	157	$ .03	$ .20
Henke, Tom	86D	437	$ .01	$ .06	Hesketh, Joe	86D	341	$ .01	$ .06
Henke, Tom	87D	197	$ .01	$ .04	Hesketh, Joe	87D	134	$ .01	$ .04
Henke, Tom	88D	490	$ .01	$ .05	Hesketh, Joe	88D	504	$ .01	$ .05
Henke, Tom	88DBB	104	$ .01	$ .05	Hesketh, Joe	89D	460	$ .01	$ .04
Henke, Tom	89D	385	$ .01	$ .04	Hesketh, Joe	90D	511	$ .01	$ .03
Henke, Tom	89DBB	301	$ .01	$ .04	Hetzel, Eric	89D	660	$ .01	$ .10
Henke, Tom	90D	349	$ .01	$ .03	Hetzel, Eric	90D	539	$ .01	$ .03
Henneman, Mike	87DR	32	$ .10	$ .35	Hibbard, Greg	90D	384	$ .01	$ .15
Henneman, Mike	88D	420	$ .03	$ .25	Hickey, Kevin	82D	631	$ .01	$ .05
Henneman, Mike	88DBB	91	$ .01	$ .05	Hickey, Kevin	83D	445	$ .01	$ .05
Henneman, Mike	89D	327	$ .01	$ .04	Hickey, Kevin	84D	135	$ .03	$ .10
Henneman, Mike	89DBB	237	$ .01	$ .04	Hickey, Kevin	90D	583	$ .01	$ .03
Henneman, Mike	90D	296	$ .01	$ .03	Higuera, Ted	86D	351	$ .50	$1.50
Henry, Dwayne	86D	603	$ .01	$ .06	Higuera, Ted	87D	49	$ .05	$ .20
Henry, Dwayne	87D	637	$ .01	$ .04	Higuera, Ted	87DK	16	$ .05	$ .20
Hernandez, Guillermo	89D	62	$ .01	$ .04	Higuera, Ted	88DBB	127	$ .01	$ .05
Hernandez, Guillermo	90D	610	$ .01	$ .03	Higuera, Ted	89D	175	$ .01	$ .04
Hernandez, Keith	81D	67	$ .10	$ .50	Higuera, Ted	89DBB	183	$ .01	$ .04
Hernandez, Keith	82D	278	$ .08	$ .40	Higuera, Ted	90D	339	$ .01	$ .03
Hernandez, Keith	83D	152	$ .05	$ .20	Higuera, Teddy	88D	90	$ .03	$ .25
Hernandez, Keith	83DK	20	$ .05	$ .30	Hill, Donnie	84D	96	$ .03	$ .10
Hernandez, Keith	84D	238	$ .15	$ .50	Hill, Donnie	85D	375	$ .01	$ .08
Hernandez, Keith	85D	68	$ .10	$ .35	Hill, Donnie	86D	340	$ .01	$ .06
Hernandez, Keith	86D	190	$ .03	$ .25	Hill, Donnie	87D	405	$ .01	$ .04
Hernandez, Keith	87D	76	$ .03	$ .25	Hill, Donnie	88D	87	$ .01	$ .05
Hernandez, Keith	88D	316	$ .05	$ .20	Hill, Glenallen	87D	561	$ .08	$1.00
Hernandez, Keith	88DBB	152	$ .01	$ .10	Hill, Glenallen	90D	627	$ .01	$ .10
Hernandez, Keith	89D	117	$ .01	$ .10	Hill, Ken	89D	536	$ .01	$ .04
Hernandez, Keith	89DBB	208	$ .01	$ .10	Hill, Ken	89DBB	304	$ .01	$ .04
Hernandez, Keith	90D	388	$ .01	$ .10	Hill, Ken	89DR	31	$ .01	$ .10
Hernandez, Manny	88D	481	$ .01	$ .05	Hill, Ken	90D	397	$ .01	$ .03
Hernandez, Willie	81D	589	$ .01	$ .15	Hill, Marc	83D	230	$ .01	$ .05
Hernandez, Willie	83D	174	$ .04	$ .30	Hill, Marc	84D	330	$ .03	$ .10
Hernandez, Willie	84D	163	$ .20	$ .50	Hill, Marc	85D	160	$ .01	$ .08
Hernandez, Willie	85D	212	$ .03	$ .20	Hillegas, Shawn	88DRR	35	$ .01	$ .05
Hernandez, Willie	86D	227	$ .01	$ .06	Hillegas, Shawn	89D	503	$ .01	$ .04
Hernandez, Willie	87D	522	$ .01	$ .04	Hillegas, Shawn	90D	619	$ .01	$ .03
Hernandez, Willie	88D	398	$ .01	$ .05	Hinzo, Tommy	88D	526	$ .01	$ .05
Hernandez, Willie	88DBB	125	$ .01	$ .05	Hisle, Larry	81D	87	$ .01	$ .05
Hernandez, Xavier	90D	682	$ .01	$ .10	Hisle, Larry	82D	358	$ .01	$ .05
Herndon, Larry	81D	196	$ .01	$ .05	Hobson, Butch	81D	542	$ .01	$ .05
Herndon, Larry	82D	172	$ .01	$ .05	Hobson, Butch	82D	577	$ .01	$ .05
Herndon, Larry	83D	585	$ .01	$ .05	Hodges, Ron	83D	476	$ .01	$ .05
Herndon, Larry	84D	349	$ .03	$ .10	Hodges, Ron	84D	603	$ .03	$ .10
Herndon, Larry	85D	150	$ .01	$ .08	Hoffman, Glenn	81D	95	$ .01	$ .05
Herndon, Larry	86D	593	$ .01	$ .06	Hoffman, Glenn	82D	460	$ .01	$ .05
Herndon, Larry	88D	353	$ .01	$ .05	Hoffman, Glenn	83D	282	$ .01	$ .05
Herr, Tom	81D	68	$ .01	$ .05	Hoffman, Glenn	84D	606	$ .03	$ .10
Herr, Tom	82D	530	$ .01	$ .05	Hoffman, Glenn	86D	457	$ .01	$ .06
Herr, Tom	83D	217	$ .01	$ .05	Hoffman, Glenn	90D	407	$ .01	$ .03
Herr, Tom	84D	596	$ .03	$ .10	Hoffman, Guy	88D	452	$ .01	$ .05
Herr, Tom	85D	425	$ .01	$ .08	Holland, Al	82D	377	$ .01	$ .05
Herr, Tommy	86D	83	$ .01	$ .06	Holland, Al	83D	146	$ .01	$ .05
Herr, Tommy	87D	140	$ .01	$ .04	Holland, Al	84D	204	$ .03	$ .10

DONRUSS

Player	Year	No.	VG	EX/MT	Player	Year	No.	VG	EX/MT
Holland, Al	85D	427	$ .01	$ .08	Howell, Jack	89DBB	307	$ .01	$ .04
Holland, Al	86D	573	$ .01	$ .06	Howell, Jack	90D	254	$ .01	$ .03
Holman, Brian	89D	511	$ .01	$ .15	Howell, Jay	83D	587	$ .01	$ .05
Holman, Brian	90D	143	$ .01	$ .03	Howell, Jay	85D	103	$ .01	$ .08
Holman, Scott	83D	224	$ .01	$ .05	Howell, Jay	86D	223	$ .01	$ .06
Holton, Brian	87D	598	$ .01	$ .15	Howell, Jay	87D	503	$ .01	$ .04
Holton, Brian	87DR	54	$ .01	$ .07	Howell, Jay	88D	55	$ .01	$ .05
Holton, Brian	88D	402	$ .01	$ .05	Howell, Jay	89D	610	$ .01	$ .04
Holton, Brian	89D	439	$ .01	$ .04	Howell, Jay	89DBB	36	$ .01	$ .04
Holton, Brian	89DTR	20	$ .01	$ .05	Howell, Jay	90D	203	$ .01	$ .03
Holton, Brian	90D	635	$ .01	$ .03	Howell, Ken	85D	592	$ .01	$ .15
Honeycutt, Rick	81D	46	$ .01	$ .05	Howell, Ken	86D	275	$ .01	$ .06
Honeycutt, Rick	82D	494	$ .01	$ .05	Howell, Ken	87D	229	$ .01	$ .04
Honeycutt, Rick	83D	415	$ .01	$ .05	Howell, Ken	88D	130	$ .01	$ .05
Honeycutt, Rick	84D	494	$ .03	$ .10	Howell, Ken	89DBB	184	$ .01	$ .05
Honeycutt, Rick	85D	215	$ .01	$ .08	Howell, Ken	90D	430	$ .01	$ .03
Honeycutt, Rick	86D	372	$ .01	$ .06	Howell, Roy	81D	392	$ .01	$ .05
Honeycutt, Rick	87D	402	$ .01	$ .04	Howell, Roy	82D	204	$ .01	$ .05
Honeycutt, Rick	88D	590	$ .01	$ .05	Howell, Roy	83D	358	$ .01	$ .05
Honeycutt, Rick	88DBB	211	$ .01	$ .05	Howell, Roy	85D	577	$ .01	$ .08
Honeycutt, Rick	89D	328	$ .01	$ .04	Howser, Dick	83D	590	$ .01	$ .05
Honeycutt, Rick	89DBB	313	$ .01	$ .04	Hoyt, LaMarr	81D	160	$ .05	$ .20
Honeycutt, Rick	90D	386	$ .01	$ .03	Hoyt, LaMarr	82D	117	$ .01	$ .05
Hood, Don	83D	390	$ .01	$ .05	Hoyt, LaMarr	83D	632	$ .03	$ .20
Hooton, Burt	81D	541	$ .01	$ .05	Hoyt, LaMarr	84D	488	$ .03	$ .10
Hooton, Burt	82D	32	$ .01	$ .05	Hoyt, LaMarr	85D	86	$ .01	$ .08
Hooton, Burt	83D	32	$ .01	$ .05	Hoyt, LaMarr	86D	139	$ .01	$ .06
Hooton, Burt	84D	459	$ .03	$ .10	Hoyt, LaMarr	87D	434	$ .01	$ .04
Hooton, Burt	85D	104	$ .01	$ .08	Hrabosky, Al	81D	550	$ .01	$ .05
Hooton, Burt	86D	300	$ .01	$ .06	Hrabosky, Al	82D	97	$ .01	$ .05
Horn, Sam	88D	498	$ .05	$ .25	Hrabosky, Al	83D	475	$ .01	$ .05
Horner, Bob	81D	99	$ .05	$ .20	Hrbek, Kent	82D	557	$ .50	$3.00
Horner, Bob	82D	173	$ .05	$ .30	Hrbek, Kent	83D	179	$ .06	$ .50
Horner, Bob	83D	58	$ .05	$ .30	Hrbek, Kent	83DK	19	$ .05	$ .40
Horner, Bob	84D	535	$ .08	$ .25	Hrbek, Kent	84D	70	$ .15	$ .65
Horner, Bob	84DK	14	$ .10	$ .35	Hrbek, Kent	85D	70	$ .10	$ .35
Horner, Bob	85D	77	$ .03	$ .25	Hrbek, Kent	86D	70	$ .08	$ .25
Horner, Bob	86D	188	$ .03	$ .25	Hrbek, Kent	87D	73	$ .05	$ .20
Horner, Bob	87D	389	$ .05	$ .20	Hrbek, Kent	88D	320	$ .01	$ .15
Horton, Ricky	85D	83	$ .01	$ .25	Hrbek, Kent	88DBB	102	$ .01	$ .05
Horton, Ricky	86D	138	$ .01	$ .06	Hrbek, Kent	89D	199	$ .01	$ .10
Horton, Ricky	87D	234	$ .01	$ .04	Hrbek, Kent	89DBB	18	$ .01	$ .10
Horton, Ricky	88D	430	$ .01	$ .05	Hrbek, Kent	90D	81	$ .01	$ .03
Horton, Ricky	89D	582	$ .01	$ .04	Hubbard, Glenn	81D	459	$ .01	$ .05
Horton, Ricky	90D	666	$ .01	$ .03	Hubbard, Glenn	82D	436	$ .01	$ .05
Hostetler, Dave	83D	89	$ .01	$ .05	Hubbard, Glenn	83D	184	$ .01	$ .05
Hostetler, Dave	84D	159	$ .03	$ .10	Hubbard, Glenn	84D	432	$ .03	$ .10
Hough, Charlie	82D	447	$ .01	$ .05	Hubbard, Glenn	85D	199	$ .01	$ .08
Hough, Charlie	83D	69	$ .01	$ .05	Hubbard, Glenn	86D	141	$ .01	$ .06
Hough, Charlie	84D	638	$ .03	$ .10	Hubbard, Glenn	87D	634	$ .01	$ .04
Hough, Charlie	85D	422	$ .01	$ .08	Hubbard, Glenn	88D	314	$ .01	$ .05
Hough, Charlie	86D	342	$ .01	$ .06	Hubbard, Glenn	88DK	22	$ .01	$ .05
Hough, Charlie	87D	470	$ .01	$ .04	Hubbard, Glenn	89D	568	$ .01	$ .04
Hough, Charlie	87DK	7	$ .01	$ .04	Hudler, Rex	85D	469	$ .01	$ .08
Hough, Charlie	88D	99	$ .01	$ .05	Hudler, Rex	89D	452	$ .01	$ .04
Hough, Charlie	88DBB	256	$ .01	$ .05	Hudler, Rex	90D	366	$ .01	$ .03
Hough, Charlie	89D	165	$ .01	$ .04	Hudson, Charles	89D	514	$ .01	$ .04
Hough, Charlie	90D	411	$ .01	$ .03	Hudson, Charles	89DTR	50	$ .01	$ .05
Houk, Ralph	82D	282	$ .01	$ .05	Hudson, Charlie	84D	448	$ .01	$ .25
Householder, Paul	81D	303	$ .01	$ .05	Hudson, Charlie	85D	355	$ .01	$ .08
Householder, Paul	82D	314	$ .01	$ .05	Hudson, Charlie	86D	622	$ .01	$ .06
Householder, Paul	83D	566	$ .01	$ .05	Hudson, Charlie	87D	630	$ .01	$ .04
Householder, Paul	86D	414	$ .01	$ .06	Hudson, Charlie	88D	374	$ .01	$ .05
Howe, Art	81D	258	$ .01	$ .05	Hughes, Keith	88D	643	$ .01	$ .15
Howe, Art	82D	92	$ .01	$ .05	Huismann, Mark	84D	339	$ .03	$ .10
Howe, Art	83D	396	$ .01	$ .05	Huismann, Mark	85D	583	$ .01	$ .08
Howe, Steve	81D	511	$ .02	$ .15	Hulett, Tim	85D	645	$ .01	$ .08
Howe, Steve	82D	158	$ .01	$ .05	Hulett, Tim	86D	404	$ .01	$ .06
Howe, Steve	83D	630	$ .01	$ .05	Hulett, Tim	87D	260	$ .01	$ .04
Howe, Steve	88D	593	$ .01	$ .05	Hume, Tom	82D	229	$ .01	$ .05
Howell, Jack	86D	524	$ .08	$ .50	Hume, Tom	83D	229	$ .01	$ .05
Howell, Jack	87D	305	$ .01	$ .04	Hume, Tom	84D	550	$ .03	$ .10
Howell, Jack	88D	333	$ .01	$ .05	Hume, Tom	85D	408	$ .01	$ .08
Howell, Jack	88DBB	59	$ .01	$ .05	Hume, Tom	86D	365	$ .01	$ .06
Howell, Jack	89D	288	$ .01	$ .04	Hunt, Randy	87D	625	$ .01	$ .04

Player	Year	No.	VG	EX/MT
Hurdle, Clint	81D	224	$ .01	$ .05
Hurdle, Clint	82D	516	$ .01	$ .05
Hurdle, Clint	86D	434	$ .01	$ .06
Hurst, Bruce	83D	134	$ .03	$ .40
Hurst, Bruce	84D	213	$ .03	$ .15
Hurst, Bruce	85D	493	$ .01	$ .08
Hurst, Bruce	86D	517	$ .01	$ .06
Hurst, Bruce	88D	252	$ .01	$ .05
Hurst, Bruce	88DBB	233	$ .01	$ .15
Hurst, Bruce	89D	423	$ .01	$ .04
Hurst, Bruce	89DBB	77	$ .01	$ .04
Hurst, Bruce	89DTR	45	$ .01	$ .15
Hurst, Bruce	90D	183	$ .01	$ .03
Hurst, Brust	87D	174	$ .01	$ .04
Huson, Jeff	Ford	693	$ .01	$ .10
Hutton, Tommy	81D	93	$ .01	$ .05
Incaviglia, Pete	86DR	23	$ .80	$1.00
Incaviglia, Pete	87D	224	$ .50	$ .75
Incaviglia, Pete	88D	304	$ .10	$ .25
Incaviglia, Pete	88DBB	55	$ .01	$ .10
Incaviglia, Pete	89D	56	$ .01	$ .10
Incaviglia, Pete	89DBB	144	$ .01	$ .10

PETE INCAVIGLIA

Player	Year	No.	VG	EX/MT
Incaviglia, Pete	89DK	3	$ .01	$ .05
Incaviglia, Pete	90D	48	$ .01	$ .10
Infante, Alexis	89DR	30	$ .01	$ .10
Innis, Jeff	90D	408	$ .01	$ .03
Iorg, Dane	81D	311	$ .01	$ .05
Iorg, Dane	82D	166	$ .01	$ .05
Iorg, Dane	83D	469	$ .01	$ .05
Iorg, Dane	84D	571	$ .03	$ .10
Iorg, Dane	85D	252	$ .01	$ .08
Iorg, Garth	82D	353	$ .01	$ .05
Iorg, Garth	83D	306	$ .01	$ .05
Iorg, Garth	84D	561	$ .03	$ .10
Iorg, Garth	85D	363	$ .01	$ .08
Iorg, Garth	86D	640	$ .01	$ .06
Iorg, Garth	87D	394	$ .01	$ .04
Iorg, Garth	88D	444	$ .01	$ .05
Ivie, Mike	81D	312	$ .01	$ .05
Ivie, Mike	82D	396	$ .01	$ .05
Ivie, Mike	83D	485	$ .01	$ .05
Jackson, Bo	86DR	38	$3.00	$13.50
Jackson, Bo	87DR	14	$1.00	$5.00

Player	Year	No.	VG	EX/MT
Jackson, Bo	87DRR	35	$2.00	$10.00
Jackson, Bo	88D	220	$ .15	$ 2.00
Jackson, Bo	88DBB	119	$ .15	$ .75
Jackson, Bo	89D	208	$ .10	$ .75
Jackson, Bo	89DBB	169	$ .01	$1.00
Jackson, Bo	90D	61	$ .01	$ .75
Jackson, Bo	90DAS	650	$ .01	$ .50
Jackson, Bo	90DBC	1	$ .01	$ .50
Jackson, Bo	90DK	1	$ .01	$ .50
Jackson, Chuck	87DR	55	$ .01	$ .07
Jackson, Danny	84D	461	$ .40	$2.25
Jackson, Danny	85D	374	$ .05	$ .50
Jackson, Danny	86D	95	$ .02	$ .15
Jackson, Danny	87D	157	$ .01	$ .10
Jackson, Danny	88D	132	$ .01	$ .10
Jackson, Danny	88DBB	166	$ .01	$ .10
Jackson, Danny	89D	124	$ .01	$ .10
Jackson, Danny	89DBB	54	$ .01	$ .10
Jackson, Danny	90D	80	$ .01	$ .10
Jackson, Darrell	81D	547	$ .01	$ .05
Jackson, Darrell	82D	179	$ .01	$ .05
Jackson, Darrin	88DR	45	$ .01	$ .15
Jackson, Darrin	90D	641	$ .01	$ .03
Jackson, Grant	81D	15	$ .01	$ .05
Jackson, Grant	82D	518	$ .01	$ .05
Jackson, Mike	87DR	36	$ .01	$ .07
Jackson, Mike	88D	139	$ .01	$ .15
Jackson, Mike	89D	652	$ .01	$ .04
Jackson, Reggie	81D	228	$ .20	$1.00
Jackson, Reggie	81D	348	$ .20	$1.00
Jackson, Reggie	81D	468	$ .15	$1.00
Jackson, Reggie	82D	535	$ .15	$ .65
Jackson, Reggie	82D	575	$ .10	$ .50
Jackson, Reggie	83D	115	$ .15	$ .60
Jackson, Reggie	83DK	3	$ .10	$ .50
Jackson, Reggie	84D	57	$ .30	$1.50
Jackson, Reggie	85D	57	$ .20	$ .60
Jackson, Reggie	86D	377	$ .15	$ .50
Jackson, Reggie	87D	210	$ .15	$ .40
Jackson, Ron	81D	489	$ .01	$ .05
Jackson, Ron	82D	602	$ .01	$ .05
Jackson, Ron	83D	639	$ .05	$ .30
Jackson, Ron	84D	133	$ .03	$ .10
Jackson, Roy Lee	81D	36	$ .01	$ .05
Jackson, Roy Lee	82D	541	$ .01	$ .05
Jackson, Roy Lee	83D	479	$ .01	$ .05
Jackson, Roy Lee	84D	195	$ .03	$ .10
Jackson, Roy Lee	85D	606	$ .01	$ .08
Jacoby, Brook	84D	542	$ .20	$1.00
Jacoby, Brook	85D	154	$ .08	$ 25
Jacoby, Brook	86D	154	$ .02	$ .15
Jacoby, Brook	87D	104	$ .01	$ .04
Jacoby, Brook	87DK	8	$ .01	$ .04
Jacoby, Brook	88D	131	$ .01	$ .05
Jacoby, Brook	88DBB	229	$ .01	$ .05
Jacoby, Brook	89D	114	$ .01	$ .04
Jacoby, Brook	89DBB	61	$ .01	$ .04
Jacoby, Brook	90D	83	$ .01	$ .03
James, Bob	84D	87	$ .03	$ .10
James, Bob	85D	279	$ .01	$ .08
James, Bob	86D	379	$ .01	$ .06
James, Bob	87D	493	$ .01	$ .04
James, Bob	88D	507	$ .01	$ .05
James, Chris	87DRR	42	$ .15	$ .85
James, Chris	88D	453	$ .01	$ .10
James, Chris	88DBB	159	$ .01	$ .05
James, Chris	89D	312	$ .01	$ .04
James, Chris	89DBB	266	$ .01	$ .04
James, Chris	90D	323	$ .01	$ .03
James, Dion	84DRR	31	$ .05	$ .50
James, Dion	85D	211	$ .03	$ .15
James, Dion	86D	89	$ .03	$ .15
James, Dion	88D	190	$ .01	$ .05
James, Dion	88DBB	29	$ .01	$ .05
James, Dion	89D	340	$ .01	$ .04

DONRUSS

Player	Year	No.	VG	EX/MT	Player	Year	No.	VG	EX/MT
James, Dion	89DBB	253	$ .01	$ .04	Johnson, Cliff	81D	484	$ .01	$ .05
James, Dion	90D	428	$ .01	$ .03	Johnson, Cliff	82D	339	$ .01	$ .05
Javier, Stan	86D	584	$ .05	$ .25	Johnson, Cliff	83D	601	$ .01	$ .05
Javier, Stan	87D	590	$ .01	$ .04	Johnson, Cliff	84D	512	$ .03	$ .10
Javier, Stan	88DBB	155	$ .01	$ .05	Johnson, Cliff	85D	512	$ .01	$ .08
Javier, Stan	89D	185	$ .01	$ .04	Johnson, Cliff	86D	639	$ .01	$ .06
Javier, Stan	90D	568	$ .01	$ .03	Johnson, Cliff	87D	645	$ .01	$ .04
Jeffcoat, Mike	84DRR	43	$ .03	$ .10	Johnson, Dave	90D	702	$ .01	$ .03
Jeffcoat, Mike	85D	251	$ .01	$ .08	Johnson, Howard	83D	328	$2.00	$10.00
Jeffcoat, Mike	90D	521	$ .01	$ .03	Johnson, Howard	85D	247	$ .25	$ 2.00
Jefferies, Gregg	88D	657	$1.00	$3.50	Johnson, Howard	86D	312	$ .05	$ .50
Jefferies, Gregg	89DBB	152	$ .01	$ .35	Johnson, Howard	87D	646	$ .03	$ .25
Jefferies, Gregg	89DR	2	$ .01	$ .50	Johnson, Howard	88D	569	$ .01	$ .15
Jefferies, Gregg	89DRR	35	$ .35	$1.50	Johnson, Howard	88DBB	97	$ .05	$ .25
Jefferies, Gregg	90D	270	$ .01	$ .30	Johnson, Howard	89D	235	$ .05	$ .15
Jefferson, Stan	87D	642	$ .03	$ .25	Johnson, Howard	89DBB	126	$ .01	$ .10
Jefferson, Stan	87DR	43	$ .01	$ .07	Johnson, Howard	90D	99	$ .01	$ .10
Jefferson, Stan	88D	187	$ .01	$ .05	Johnson, Howard	90DAS	654	$ .01	$ .20
Jeltz, Steve	85DRR	44	$ .01	$ .08	Johnson, Howard	90DBC	2	$ .01	$ .10
Jeltz, Steve	87D	359	$ .01	$ .04	Johnson, Howard	90DK	18	$ .01	$ .20
Jeltz, Steve	88D	576	$ .01	$ .05	Johnson, Joe	86D	624	$ .01	$ .06
Jeltz, Steve	89D	431	$ .01	$ .04	Johnson, Joe	87D	650	$ .01	$ .04
Jeltz, Steve	89DBB	271	$ .01	$ .04	Johnson, John Henry	82D	550	$ .01	$ .05
Jeltz, Steve	90D	133	$ .01	$ .03	Johnson, John Henry	84D	91	$ .03	$ .10
Jenkins, Fergie (Ferguson)	81D	146	$ .03	$ .20	Johnson, Lamar	81D	38	$ .01	$ .05
Jenkins, Fergie	82D	643	$ .03	$ .20	Johnson, Lamar	82D	269	$ .01	$ .05
Jenkins, Fergie	83D	300	$ .03	$ .20	Johnson, Lamar	83D	142	$ .01	$ .05
Jenkins, Fergie	84D	189	$ .04	$ .25	Johnson, Lance	88DRR	31	$ .10	$ .25
Jennings, Doug	88DR	13	$ .01	$ .35	Johnson, Lance	89D	606	$ .01	$ .04
Jennings, Doug	89D	505	$ .01	$ .25	Johnson, Lance	90D	573	$ .01	$ .03
Jimenez, Houston	85D	269	$ .01	$ .08	Johnson, Randy	83D	305	$ .01	$ .05
John, Tommy	81D	107	$ .05	$ .20	Johnson, Randy	84D	321	$ .03	$ .10
John, Tommy	82D	409	$ .03	$ .20	Johnson, Randy	85D	531	$ .01	$ .08
John, Tommy	82D	558	$ .03	$ .20	Johnson, Randy	89DBB	80	$ .01	$ .10
John, Tommy	83D	570	$ .03	$ .20	Johnson, Randy	89DR	43	$ .01	$ .10
John, Tommy	84D	301	$ .08	$ .25	Johnson, Randy	89DRR	42	$ .01	$ .25
John, Tommy	85D	423	$ .03	$ .25	Johnson, Randy	90D	379	$ .01	$ .03
John, Tommy	88D	401	$ .01	$ .15	Johnson, Roy	83D	492	$ .01	$ .05
John, Tommy	88DBB	220	$ .01	$ .05	Johnson, Wallace	89D	484	$ .01	$ .04
John, Tommy	88DK	17	$ .01	$ .15	Johnson, Wallace	90D	570	$ .01	$ .03
					Johnstone, Jay	81D	300	$ .01	$ .05
					Johnstone, Jay	82D	262	$ .01	$ .05
					Johnstone, Jay	83D	561	$ .01	$ .05
					Johnstone, Jay	84D	540	$ .03	$ .10
					Jones, Al	85D	404	$ .01	$ .08
					Jones, Barry	87D	602	$ .03	$ .25
					Jones, Barry	89D	647	$ .01	$ .04
					Jones, Bobby	85D	134	$ .01	$ .08
					Jones, Doug	88D	588	$ .01	$ .35
					Jones, Doug	89D	438	$ .01	$ .10
					Jones, Doug	89DBB	173	$ .01	$ .04
					Jones, Doug	90D	320	$ .01	$ .03
					Jones, Jeff	82D	213	$ .01	$ .05
					Jones, Jeff	83D	651	$ .01	$ .05
					Jones, Jeff	84D	262	$ .03	$ .10
					Jones, Jimmy	87D	557	$ .01	$ .25
					Jones, Jimmy	88D	141	$ .01	$ .05
					Jones, Jimmy	88DBB	189	$ .01	$ .05
					Jones, Jimmy	89D	247	$ .01	$ .04
					Jones, Jimmy	89DBB	217	$ .01	$ .04
					Jones, Lynn	82D	542	$ .01	$ .05
					Jones, Lynn	86D	466	$ .01	$ .06
					Jones, Mike	85D	640	$ .01	$ .08
					Jones, Mike	86D	419	$ .01	$ .06
					Jones, Odell	84D	256	$ .03	$ .10
					Jones, Odell	85D	525	$ .01	$ .08
					Jones, Odell	87D	582	$ .01	$ .04
					Jones, Randy	81D	122	$ .01	$ .05
					Jones, Ron	89DR	42	$ .01	$ .10
					Jones, Ron	89DRR	40	$ .01	$ .10
					Jones, Ron	90D	487	$ .01	$ .03
					Jones, Ruppert	81D	349	$ .01	$ .05
					Jones, Ruppert	82D	346	$ .01	$ .05
					Jones, Ruppert	83D	373	$ .01	$ .05

Player	Year	No.	VG	EX/MT	Player	Year	No.	VG	EX/MT
Johnson, Anthony	83D	629	$ .01	$ .05	Jones, Ruppert	84D	261	$ .03	$ .10
Johnson, Bob	83D	494	$ .01	$ .05					
Johnson, Bob	84D	500	$ .03	$ .10					

Player	Year	No.	VG	EX/MT	Player	Year	No.	VG	EX/MT
Jones, Ruppert	85D	612	$ .01	$ .08	Keough, Matt	83D	239	$ .01	$ .05
Jones, Ruppert	86D	423	$ .01	$ .06	Keough, Matt	84D	627	$ .03	$ .10
Jones, Ruppert	87D	428	$ .01	$ .04	Kepshire, Kurt	85D	382	$ .01	$ .08
Jones, Tim	89D	555	$ .01	$ .10	Kepshire, Kurt	86D	504	$ .01	$ .06
Jones, Tim	89DR	28	$ .01	$ .10	Kerfeld, Charlie	86DR	6	$ .13	$ .15
Jones, Tim	90D	686	$ .01	$ .03	Kerfeld, Charlie	87D	209	$ .01	$ .04
Jones, Tracy	86DR	2	$ .10	$ .40	Kern, Jim	81D	27	$ .01	$ .05
Jones, Tracy	87D	413	$ .01	$ .10	Kern, Jim	82D	89	$ .01	$ .05
Jones, Tracy	88D	310	$ .01	$ .10	Kern, Jim	83D	355	$ .01	$ .05
Jones, Tracy	88DBB	174	$ .01	$ .05	Key, Jimmy	85D	559	$ .35	$1.50
Jones, Tracy	89D	574	$ .01	$ .04	Key, Jimmy	86D	561	$ .05	$ .20
Jones, Tracy	90D	636	$ .01	$ .03	Key, Jimmy	87D	244	$ .01	$ .04
Jordan, Ricky	89D	624	$ .40	$1.25	Key, Jimmy	88D	72	$ .01	$ .15
Jordan, Ricky	89DBB	103	$ .01	$ .20	Key, Jimmy	88DBB	143	$ .01	$ .05
Jordan, Ricky	90D	76	$ .01	$ .20	Key, Jimmy	89D	188	$ .01	$ .04
Jordan, Scott	89D	609	$ .01	$ .04	Key, Jimmy	89DBB	87	$ .01	$ .04
Jorgensen, Mike	81D	274	$ .01	$ .05	Key, Jimmy	90D	231	$ .01	$ .03
Jorgensen, Mike	82D	224	$ .01	$ .05	Khalifa, Sam	86D	308	$ .01	$ .06
Jose, Felix	89DRR	38	$ .10	$ .50	Kiefer, Steve	85DRR	35	$ .01	$ .08
Jose, Felix	90D	564	$ .01	$ .25	Kiefer, Steve	86D	420	$ .01	$ .06
Joyner, Wally	86DR	1	$ .50	$4.00	Kiefer, Steve	88D	542	$ .01	$ .05
Joyner, Wally	87D	135	$ .50	$1.75	Kilgus, Paul	88D	469	$ .01	$ .05
Joyner, Wally	87DK	1	$ .15	$1.00	Kilgus, Paul	88DBB	111	$ .01	$ .05
Joyner, Wally	88D	110	$ .15	$ .50	Kilgus, Paul	89D	283	$ .01	$ .04
Joyner, Wally	88DBB	115	$ .05	$ .25	Kilgus, Paul	89DBB	149	$ .01	$ .04
Joyner, Wally	88DBC	13	$ .05	$ .35	Kilgus, Paul	89DTR	42	$ .01	$ .15
Joyner, Wally	89DBB	139	$ .01	$ .15	Kilgus, Paul	90D	276	$ .01	$ .03
Joyner, Wally	89DBC	21	$ .01	$ .20	King, Eric	86DR	27	$ .05	$ .25
Joyner, Wally	90D	94	$ .01	$ .10	King, Eric	87D	250	$ .08	$ .25
Jurak, Ed	84D	127	$ .03	$ .10	King, Eric	88D	50	$ .01	$ .05
Jurak, Ed	85D	579	$ .01	$ .08	King, Eric	89D	535	$ .01	$ .04
Justice, Dave	90D	704	$ .01	$ .10	King, Eric	89DBB	235	$ .01	$ .04
Kaat, Jim	81D	536	$ .02	$ .25	King, Eric	89DTR	37	$ .01	$ .05
Kaat, Jim	82D	217	$ .05	$ .30	King, Eric	90D	337	$ .01	$ .03
Kaat, Jim	83D	343	$ .03	$ .20	King, Jeff	90D	480	$ .01	$ .03
Karkovice, Ron	87D	334	$ .01	$ .04	Kingery, Mike	87D	424	$ .01	$ .15
Karkovice, Ron	90D	413	$ .01	$ .03	Kingery, Mike	88D	322	$ .01	$ .05
Kaufman, Curt	85D	524	$ .01	$ .08	Kingery, Mike	90D	601	$ .01	$ .03
Kearney, Bob	83D	539	$ .01	$ .05	Kingman, Brian	81D	360	$ .01	$ .05
Kearney, Bob	84D	462	$ .03	$ .10	Kingman, Brian	82D	87	$ .01	$ .05
Kearney, Bob	85D	362	$ .01	$ .08	Kingman, Dave	81D	553	$ .03	$ .20
Kearney, Bob	86D	74	$ .01	$ .06	Kingman, Dave	82D	182	$ .02	$ .15
Kearney, Bob	87D	445	$ .01	$ .04	Kingman, Dave	82DK	17	$ .03	$ .20
Keeton, Rickey	82D	618	$ .01	$ .05	Kingman, Dave	83D	301	$ .01	$ .05
Kelleher, Mick	81D	513	$ .01	$ .05	Kingman, Dave	84D	360	$ .03	$ .10
Kelleher, Mick	82D	601	$ .01	$ .05	Kingman, Dave	85D	54	$ .03	$ .10
Kelly, Pat	81D	600	$ .02	$ .15	Kingman, Dave	86D	54	$ .01	$ .06
Kelly, Roberto	88D	635	$ .25	$1.25	Kingman, Dave	87D	425	$ .01	$ .04
Kelly, Roberto	88DR	16	$ .01	$ .50	Kinney, Dennis	81D	363	$ .01	$ .05
Kelly, Roberto	89D	433	$ .01	$ .15	Kipper, Bob	86DR	46	$ .02	$ .09
Kelly, Roberto	89DBB	270	$ .01	$ .20	Kipper, Bob	86DRR	44	$ .01	$ .06
Kelly, Roberto	90D	192	$ .01	$ .10	Kipper, Bob	87D	572	$ .01	$ .04
Kemp, Steve	81D	249	$ .01	$ .05	Kipper, Bob	88D	115	$ .01	$ .05
Kemp, Steve	82D	594	$ .01	$ .05	Kipper, Bob	89D	409	$ .01	$ .04
Kemp, Steve	83D	269	$ .01	$ .05	Kipper, Bob	90D	362	$ .01	$ .03
Kemp, Steve	84D	469	$ .03	$ .10	Kison, Bruce	82D	66	$ .01	$ .05
Kemp, Steve	85D	225	$ .01	$ .08	Kison, Bruce	83D	267	$ .01	$ .05
Kemp, Steve	86D	200	$ .01	$ .06	Kison, Bruce	84D	499	$ .03	$ .10
Kennedy, Junior	81D	424	$ .01	$ .05	Kison, Bruce	85D	377	$ .01	$ .08
Kennedy, Junior	82D	188	$ .01	$ .05	Kison, Bruce	86D	616	$ .01	$ .06
Kennedy, Junior	83D	529	$ .01	$ .05	Kittle, Ron	84D	244	$ .04	$ .25
Kennedy, Terry	81D	428	$ .01	$ .05	Kittle, Ron	84DK	18	$ .04	$ .25
Kennedy, Terry	82D	121	$ .01	$ .05	Kittle, Ron	85D	180	$ .01	$ .20
Kennedy, Terry	83D	220	$ .01	$ .05	Kittle, Ron	86D	526	$ .01	$ .06
Kennedy, Terry	83DK	26	$ .01	$ .05	Kittle, Ron	87D	351	$ .01	$ .04
Kennedy, Terry	84D	112	$ .03	$ .10	Kittle, Ron	88D	422	$ .01	$ .05
Kennedy, Terry	85D	429	$ .01	$ .08	Kittle, Ron	89D	428	$ .01	$ .04
Kennedy, Terry	86D	356	$ .01	$ .06	Kittle, Ron	89DBB	249	$ .01	$ .04
Kennedy, Terry	87D	205	$ .01	$ .04	Kittle, Ron	89DTR	51	$ .01	$ .15
Kennedy, Terry	88D	150	$ .01	$ .05	Kittle, Ron	90D	148	$ .01	$ .03
Kennedy, Terry	88DBB	30	$ .01	$ .05	Klutts, Mickey	81D	110	$ .01	$ .05
Kennedy, Terry	89D	141	$ .01	$ .04	Klutts, Mickey	83D	465	$ .01	$ .05
Kennedy, Terry	90D	602	$ .01	$ .03	Knapp, Chris	81D	173	$ .01	$ .05
Keough, Matt	81D	358	$ .01	$ .05	Knepper, Bob	81D	194	$ .01	$ .05
Keough, Matt	82D	71	$ .01	$ .05	Knepper, Bob	82D	41	$ .01	$ .05

Player	Year	No.	VG	EX/MT	Player	Year	No.	VG	EX/MT
Knepper, Bob	84D	572	$ .03	$ .10	Lachmann, Rene	82D	600	$ .01	$ .05
Knepper, Bob	85D	476	$ .01	$ .08	LaCock, Pete	81D	344	$ .01	$ .05
Knepper, Bob	86D	161	$ .01	$ .06	LaCorte, Frank	81D	143	$ .01	$ .05
Knepper, Bob	87D	112	$ .01	$ .04	LaCorte, Frank	82D	270	$ .01	$ .05
Knepper, Bob	88D	138	$ .01	$ .05	LaCorte, Frank	83D	218	$ .01	$ .05
Knepper, Bob	88DBB	176	$ .01	$ .05	LaCorte, Frank	84D	283	$ .03	$ .10
Knepper, Bob	89D	123	$ .01	$ .04	LaCoss, Mlke	83D	344	$ .01	$ .05
Knepper, Bob	90D	485	$ .01	$ .03	LaCoss, Mike	81D	183	$ .01	$ .05
Knepper, Robert	83D	92	$ .01	$ .05	LaCoss, Mike	82D	440	$ .01	$ .05
Knicely, Alan	83D	620	$ .01	$ .05	LaCoss, Mike	84D	206	$ .03	$ .10
Knight, Ray	81D	61	$ .01	$ .05	LaCoss, Mike	85D	405	$ .01	$ .08
Knight, Ray	82D	374	$ .01	$ .05	LaCoss, Mike	87D	636	$ .01	$ .04
Knight, Ray	83D	522	$ .01	$ .05	LaCoss, Mike	88D	436	$ .01	$ .05
Knight, Ray	84D	232	$ .03	$ .10	LaCoss, Mike	89D	602	$ .01	$ .04
Knight, Ray	84DK	12	$ .08	$ .25	LaCoss, Mike	90D	652	$ .01	$ .03
Knight, Ray	85D	617	$ .01	$ .08	Lacy, Lee	81D	376	$ .01	$ .05
Knight, Ray	86D	597	$ .08	$ .25	Lacy, Lee	82D	276	$ .01	$ .05
Knight, Ray	87D	586	$ .01	$ .04	Lacy, Lee	83D	276	$ .01	$ .05
Knight, Ray	88D	108	$ .01	$ .05	Lacy, Lee	84D	479	$ .03	$ .10
Knudson, Mark	88D	495	$ .01	$ .05	Lacy, Lee	85D	508	$ .01	$ .08
Knudson, Mark	90D	575	$ .01	$ .03	Lacy, Lee	86D	228	$ .01	$ .06
Komminsk, Brad	84DRR	36	$ .03	$ .10	Lacy, Lee	87D	336	$ .01	$ .04
Komminsk, Brad	85D	321	$ .01	$ .08	Ladd, Pete	84D	124	$ .03	$ .10
Komminsk, Brad	88D	583	$ .01	$ .05	Ladd, Pete	87D	660	$ .01	$ .15
Komminsk, Brad	90D	350	$ .01	$ .03	Ladd, Peter	85D	271	$ .01	$ .08
Koosman, Jerry	81D	531	$ .02	$ .15	LaFrancois, Roger	83D	534	$ .01	$ .05
Koosman, Jerry	82D	603	$ .02	$ .15	Laga, Mike	84D	491	$ .03	$ .10
Koosman, Jerry	83D	39	$ .02	$ .15	Laga, Mike	86D	578	$ .01	$ .06
Koosman, Jerry	84D	501	$ .03	$ .10	Laga, Mike	87D	293	$ .01	$ .04
Koosman, Jerry	85D	233	$ .03	$ .20	Lahti, Jeff	84D	327	$ .03	$ .10
Koosman, Jerry	86DK	23	$ .05	$ .20	Lahti, Jeff	86D	475	$ .01	$ .06
Kramer, Randy	89D	480	$ .01	$ .04	Lahti, Jeff	87D	577	$ .01	$ .04
Kramer, Randy	89DBB	213	$ .01	$ .04	Lake, Steve	84D	198	$ .03	$ .10
Kramer, Randy	89DR	48	$ .01	$ .10	Lake, Steve	87D	604	$ .01	$ .04
Kramer, Randy	90D	409	$ .01	$ .03	Lake, Steve	88D	510	$ .01	$ .05
Kravec, Ken	82D	378	$ .01	$ .05	Lake, Steve	90D	431	$ .01	$ .03
Krenchicki, Wayne	83D	314	$ .01	$ .05	Lamp, Dennis	81D	573	$ .01	$ .05
Krenchicki, Wayne	84D	334	$ .03	$ .10	Lamp, Dennis	82D	619	$ .01	$ .05
Krenchicki, Wayne	85D	140	$ .01	$ .08	Lamp, Dennis	83D	165	$ .01	$ .05
Krenchicki, Wayne	86D	140	$ .01	$ .06	Lamp, Dennis	84D	526	$ .03	$ .10
Krenchicki, Wayne	87D	406	$ .01	$ .04	Lamp, Dennis	85D	119	$ .01	$ .08
Kreuter, Chad	89D	579	$ .01	$ .15	Lamp, Dennis	86D	626	$ .01	$ .06
Kreuter, Chad	90D	520	$ .01	$ .03	Lamp, Dennis	89D	633	$ .01	$ .04
Krueger, Bill	85D	467	$ .01	$ .08	Lamp, Dennis	90D	423	$ .01	$ .03
Krueger, Bill	86D	298	$ .01	$ .06	Lampkin, Tom	89D	639	$ .01	$ .04
Kruk, John	86DR	42	$ .15	$ .50	Lancaster, Les	87DR	10	$ .01	$ .25
Kruk, John	87D	328	$ .05	$ .25	Lancaster, Les	88DBB	172	$ .01	$ .05
Kruk, John	88D	205	$ .01	$ .10	Lancaster, Les	89D	341	$ .01	$ .04
Kruk, John	88DBB	245	$ .01	$ .05	Lancaster, Les	90D	628	$ .01	$ .03
Kruk, John	89D	86	$ .01	$ .04	Lancaster, Lester	88D	561	$ .01	$ .20
Kruk, John	89DBB	240	$ .01	$ .04	Landestoy, Rafael	81D	19	$ .01	$ .05
Kruk, John	90D	160	$ .01	$ .03	Landreaux, Ken	81D	565	$ .01	$ .05
Krukow, Mike	82D	351	$ .01	$ .05	Landreaux, Ken	82D	388	$ .01	$ .05
Krukow, Mike	83D	119	$ .01	$ .05	Landreaux, Ken	83D	236	$ .01	$ .05
Krukow, Mike	84D	509	$ .03	$ .10	Landreaux, Ken	84D	470	$ .03	$ .10
Krukow, Mike	85D	630	$ .01	$ .08	Landreaux, Ken	85D	494	$ .01	$ .08
Krukow, Mike	86D	143	$ .01	$ .06	Landreaux, Ken	86D	470	$ .01	$ .06
Krukow, Mike	87D	609	$ .01	$ .04	Landreaux, Ken	87D	352	$ .01	$ .04
Krukow, Mike	88D	116	$ .01	$ .05	Landrum, Bill	90D	668	$ .01	$ .03
Krukow, Mike	88DBB	50	$ .01	$ .05	Landrum, Tito	82D	292	$ .01	$ .05
Krukow, Mike	89D	258	$ .01	$ .04	Landrum, Tito	83D	498	$ .01	$ .05
Krukow, Mike	89DBB	135	$ .01	$ .04	Landrum, Tito	85D	168	$ .01	$ .08
Kuenn, Harvey	82D	578	$ .01	$ .05	Landrum, Tito	86D	425	$ .01	$ .06
Kuenn, Harvey	83D	608	$ .01	$ .05	Landrum, Tito	87D	386	$ .01	$ .04
Kuiper, Duane	81D	319	$ .01	$ .05	Langford, Rick	81D	238	$ .01	$ .05
Kuiper, Duane	82D	198	$ .01	$ .05	Langford, Rick	82D	161	$ .01	$ .05
Kuiper, Duane	84D	553	$ .03	$ .10	Langford, Rick	83D	365	$ .01	$ .05
Kunkel, Jeff	85D	587	$ .01	$ .08	Langston, Mark	85D	557	$1.00	$7.50
Kunkel, Jeff	89D	496	$ .01	$ .04	Langston, Mark	86D	118	$ .15	$ .75
Kunkel, Jeff	90D	496	$ .01	$ .03	Langston, Mark	87D	568	$ .05	$ .35
Kuntz, Rusty	81D	282	$ .01	$ .05	Langston, Mark	88D	317	$ .01	$ .15
Kuntz, Rusty	85D	516	$ .01	$ .08	Langston, Mark	88DBB	136	$ .01	$ .10
Kutcher, Randy	87D	547	$ .01	$ .04	Langston, Mark	88DK	20	$ .01	$ .10
Kutzler, Jerry	90D	503	$ .01	$ .03	Langston, Mark	89D	227	$ .01	$ .15
Lacey, Bob	81D	240	$ .01	$ .05	Langston, Mark	89DBB	68	$ .01	$ .10

Player	Year	No.	VG	EX/MT	Player	Year	No.	VG	EX/MT
Langston, Mark	90D	338	$ .01	$ .03	Law, Vance	83D	117	$ .01	$ .05
Lansford, Carney	81D	409	$ .01	$ .25	Law, Vance	84D	546	$ .03	$ .10
Lansford, Carney	82D	82	$ .01	$ .25	Law, Vance	85D	122	$ .01	$ .08
Lansford, Carney	83D	408	$ .01	$ .20	Law, Vance	86D	132	$ .01	$ .06
Lansford, Carney	84D	176	$ .03	$ .10	Law, Vance	87D	212	$ .01	$ .04
Lansford, Carney	85D	345	$ .01	$ .08	Law, Vance	88D	212	$ .01	$ .05
Lansford, Carney	85DK	8	$ .03	$ .10	Law, Vance	88DBB	60	$ .01	$ .05
Lansford, Carney	86D	131	$ .01	$ .06	Law, Vance	89D	276	$ .01	$ .04
Lansford, Carney	87D	158	$ .01	$ .04	Law, Vance	90D	629	$ .01	$ .03
Lansford, Carney	88D	178	$ .01	$ .05	Lawless, Tom	83D	400	$ .01	$ .05
Lansford, Carney	88DBB	246	$ .01	$ .05	Lawless, Tom	90D	681	$ .01	$ .03
Lansford, Carney	89D	243	$ .10	$ .04	Lazorko, Jack	86D	628	$ .01	$ .06
Lansford, Carney	89DBB	22	$ .01	$ .04	Lazorko, Jack	88D	160	$ .01	$ .05
Lansford, Carney	90D	95	$ .01	$ .03	Lea, Charlie	82D	320	$ .01	$ .05
LaPoint, Dave	83D	544	$ .01	$ .40	Lea, Charlie	83D	414	$ .01	$ .05
LaPoint, Dave	84D	290	$ .03	$ .10	Lea, Charlie	84D	376	$ .03	$ .10
LaPoint, Dave	85D	138	$ .01	$ .08	Lea, Charlie	85D	177	$ .01	$ .08
LaPoint, Dave	86D	387	$ .01	$ .06	Lea, Charlie	85DK	21	$ .03	$ .10
LaPoint, Dave	87D	607	$ .01	$ .04	Lea, Charlie	86D	376	$ .01	$ .06
LaPoint, Dave	88D	552	$ .01	$ .05	Lea, Charlie	89D	473	$ .01	$ .04
LaPoint, Dave	88DBB	123	$ .01	$ .05	Leach, Rick	82D	583	$ .01	$ .05
LaPoint, Dave	89D	488	$ .01	$ .04	Leach, Rick	83D	81	$ .01	$ .05
LaPoint, Dave	89DBB	244	$ .01	$ .04					
LaPoint, Dave	89DTR	27	$ .01	$ .05					
LaPoint, Dave	90D	72	$ .01	$ .03					
Larkin, Barry	87D	492	$1.00	$4.00					
Larkin, Barry	88D	492	$ .15	$ .75					
Larkin, Barry	88DBB	222	$ .05	$ .25					
Larkin, Barry	89D	257	$ .05	$ .25					
Larkin, Barry	89DBB	110	$ .01	$ .15					
Larkin, Barry	90D	71	$ .01	$ .10					
Larkin, Gene	87DR	23	$ .10	$ .50					
Larkin, Gene	88D	564	$ .01	$ .25					
Larkin, Gene	88DBB	158	$ .01	$ .05					
Larkin, Gene	89D	355	$ .01	$ .04					
Larkin, Gene	90D	436	$ .01	$ .03					
Laroche, Dave	82D	569	$ .01	$ .05					
Larussa, Tony	81D	402	$ .01	$ .05					
Larussa, Tony	82D	319	$ .01	$ .05					
Larussa, Tony	83D	571	$ .01	$ .05					
Laskey, Bill	83D	424	$ .01	$ .05					
Laskey, Bill	84D	358	$ .03	$ .10					
Laskey, Bill	85D	387	$ .01	$ .08					
Laskey, Bill	86D	585	$ .01	$ .06					
LaSorda, Tom	81D	420	$ .01	$ .05					
LaSorda, Tom	82D	110	$ .05	$ .20					
LaSorda, Tom	83D	136	$ .02	$ .15					
Laudner, Tim	82D	549	$ .01	$ .25					
Laudner, Tim	83D	177	$ .01	$ .05					
Laudner, Tim	85D	652	$ .01	$ .08					
Laudner, Tim	86D	391	$ .01	$ .06					
Laudner, Tim	87D	320	$ .01	$ .04					
Laudner, Tim	88D	631	$ .01	$ .15					
Laudner, Tim	89D	615	$ .01	$ .04					
Laudner, Tim	90D	419	$ .01	$ .03					
LaValliere, Mike	88DBB	129	$ .01	$ .05	Leach, Rick	87D	567	$ .01	$ .04
LaValliere, Mike	89D	244	$ .01	$ .04	Leach, Rick	88D	518	$ .01	$ .05
LaValliere, Mike	89DBB	201	$ .01	$ .04	Leach, Rick	89D	638	$ .01	$ .04
LaValliere, Mike	90D	211	$ .01	$ .03	Leach, Rick	90D	613	$ .01	$ .03
Lavalliere, Mike	86DR	35	$ .05	$ .25	Leach, Terry	83D	634	$ .01	$ .25
Lavalliere, Mike	87D	331	$ .04	$ .20	Leach, Terry	88D	603	$ .01	$ .15
Lavalliere, Mike	88D	312	$ .01	$ .05	Leach, Terry	89D	502	$ .01	$ .04
Lavelle, Gary	81D	314	$ .01	$ .05	Leach, Terry	90D	534	$ .01	$ .03
Lavelle, Gary	82D	60	$ .01	$ .05	Leal, Luis	82D	255	$ .01	$ .05
Lavelle, Gary	83D	60	$ .01	$ .05	Leal, Luis	83D	129	$ .01	$ .05
Lavelle, Gary	84D	573	$ .03	$ .10	Leal, Luis	84D	485	$ .03	$ .10
Lavelle, Gary	85D	265	$ .01	$ .08	Leal, Luis	85D	317	$ .01	$ .08
Lavelle, Gary	86D	621	$ .01	$ .06	Leal, Luis	86D	315	$ .01	$ .06
Law, Rudy	81D	180	$ .01	$ .05	Leary, Tim	86D	577	$ .05	$ .35
Law, Rudy	83D	521	$ .01	$ .05	Leary, Tim	87D	232	$ .01	$ .04
Law, Rudy	84D	257	$ .03	$ .10	Leary, Tim	89D	552	$ .01	$ .04
Law, Rudy	85D	244	$ .01	$ .08	Leary, Tim	89DBB	309	$ .01	$ .04
Law, Rudy	86D	632	$ .01	$ .06	Leary, Tim	90D	670	$ .01	$ .03
Law, Rudy	87D	343	$ .01	$ .04	Lee, Bill	81D	211	$ .01	$ .05
Law, Vance	82D	582	$ .03	$ .20	Lee, Bill	82D	194	$ .01	$ .05
					Lee, Manny	87D	518	$ .01	$ .04

RICK LEACH DH

Player	Year	No.	VG	EX/MT	Player	Year	No.	VG	EX/MT
Lee, Manny	88D	650	$ .01	$ .15	Lerch, Randy	82D	595	$ .01	$ .05
Lee, Manny	89D	504	$ .01	$ .04	Lerch, Randy	85D	309	$ .01	$ .08
Lee, Manny	90D	620	$ .01	$ .03					
Leeper, Dave	86D	461	$ .01	$ .06					
Lefebvre, Joe	81D	571	$ .01	$ .05					
Lefebvre, Joe	82D	373	$ .01	$ .05					
Lefebvre, Joe	83D	523	$ .01	$ .05					
Lefebvre, Joe	84D	82	$ .03	$ .10					
Lefebvre, Joe	85D	285	$ .01	$ .08					
Lefferts, Craig	84D	388	$ .10	$ .50					
Lefferts, Craig	85D	261	$ .01	$ .08					
Lefferts, Craig	86D	307	$ .01	$ .06					
Lefferts, Craig	87D	387	$ .01	$ .04					
Lefferts, Craig	88D	515	$ .01	$ .05					
Lefferts, Craig	89D	59	$ .01	$ .04					
Lefferts, Craig	90D	376	$ .01	$ .03					
LeFlore, Ron	81D	576	$ .01	$ .05					
LeFlore, Ron	82D	165	$ .01	$ .05					
LeFlore, Ron	83D	543	$ .01	$ .05					
Leibrandt, Charlie	81D	421	$ .10	$ .50					
Leibrandt, Charlie	83D	421	$ .01	$ .05					
Leibrandt, Charlie	85D	399	$ .01	$ .08					
Leibrandt, Charlie	86D	297	$ .01	$ .06					
Leibrandt, Charlie	87D	220	$ .01	$ .04					
Leibrandt, Charlie	88D	157	$ .01	$ .05					
Leibrandt, Charlie	88DBB	151	$ .01	$ .05					
Leibrandt, Charlie	89D	89	$ .01	$ .04					
Leibrandt, Charlie	89DBB	231	$ .01	$ .04					
Leibrandt, Charlie	90D	208	$ .01	$ .03					
Leiper, Dave	87D	472	$ .01	$ .04					
Leiper, Dave	88D	557	$ .01	$ .05					
Leiper, Dave	89D	465	$ .01	$ .04					
Leiter, Al	88DBB	132	$ .01	$ .10					
Leiter, Al	88DR	27	$ .05	$ .25	Lesley, Brad	83D	547	$ .01	$ .05
Leiter, Al	88DRR	43	$ .15	$ .50	Lezcano, Carlos	81D	521	$ .01	$ .05
Leiter, Al	89D	315	$ .01	$ .10	Lezcano, Sixto	81D	207	$ .01	$ .05
Leiter, Al	90D	543	$ .01	$ .03	Lezcano, Sixto	82D	64	$ .01	$ .05
Lemanczyk, Dave	81D	292	$ .01	$ .05	Lezcano, Sixto	83D	499	$ .01	$ .05
Lemaster, Johnnie	81D	432	$ .01	$ .05	Lezcano, Sixto	85D	529	$ .01	$ .08
Lemaster, Johnnie	82D	524	$ .01	$ .05	Lilliquist, Derek	89D	653	$ .05	$ .35
Lemaster, Johnnie	83D	125	$ .01	$ .05	Lilliquist, Derek	89DBB	226	$ .01	$ .15
Lemaster, Johnnie	84D	649	$ .03	$ .10	Lilliquist, Derek	89DR	54	$ .01	$ .25
Lemaster, Johnnie	85D	114	$ .01	$ .08	Lilliquist, Derek	90D	286	$ .01	$ .15
Lemke, Mark	89D	523	$ .01	$ .04	Lillis, Bob	84D	84	$ .03	$ .10
Lemke, Mark	90D	624	$ .01	$ .03	Linares, Rufino	82D	310	$ .01	$ .05
Lemon, Bob	82D	635	$ .03	$ .20	Linares, Rufino	83D	275	$ .01	$ .05
Lemon, Chet	81D	281	$ .01	$ .05	Lind, Jose	88DBB	145	$ .01	$ .30
Lemon, Chet	82D	291	$ .01	$ .05	Lind, Jose	88DRR	38	$ .01	$ .35
Lemon, Chet	83D	511	$ .01	$ .05	Lind, Jose	89D	290	$ .01	$ .10
Lemon, Chet	84D	171	$ .03	$ .10	Lind, Jose	89DBB	101	$ .01	$ .04
Lemon, Chet	85D	90	$ .01	$ .08	Lind, Jose	90D	172	$ .01	$ .03
Lemon, Chet	86D	90	$ .01	$ .06	Lindeman, Jim	87DR	41	$ .01	$ .07
Lemon, Chet	87D	353	$ .01	$ .04	Lindeman, Jim	87DRR	37	$ .01	$ .04
Lemon, Chet	88D	215	$ .01	$ .05	Lindeman, Jim	88D	540	$ .01	$ .05
Lemon, Chet	88DBB	147	$ .01	$ .05	Lindeman, Jim	88DRR	32	$ .01	$ .25
Lemon, Chet	89D	209	$ .01	$ .04	Liriano, Nelson	89D	627	$ .01	$ .04
Lemon, Chet	89DBB	69	$ .01	$ .04	Liriano, Nelson	89DBB	160	$ .01	$ .04
Lemon, Chet	90D	60	$ .01	$ .03	Liriano, Nelson	90D	267	$ .01	$ .03
Lentine, Jim	81D	250	$ .01	$ .05	Littell, Mark	81D	580	$ .01	$ .05
Leonard, Dennis	81D	102	$ .01	$ .05	Littell, Mark	82D	442	$ .01	$ .05
Leonard, Dennis	82D	264	$ .01	$ .25	Little, Bryan	84D	157	$ .03	$ .10
Leonard, Dennis	83D	412	$ .01	$ .05	Little, Bryan	86D	452	$ .01	$ .06
Leonard, Jeff	81D	264	$ .01	$ .05	Littlefield, John	81D	309	$ .01	$ .05
Leonard, Jeff	82D	438	$ .02	$ .15	Littlefield, John	82D	145	$ .01	$ .05
Leonard, Jeff	83D	474	$ .01	$ .05	Littlejohn, Dennis	81D	313	$ .01	$ .05
Leonard, Jeff	84D	567	$ .03	$ .10	Litton, Greg	90D	453	$ .01	$ .25
Leonard, Jeff	85D	358	$ .01	$ .08	Lockwood, Skip	81D	217	$ .01	$ .05
Leonard, Jeff	86D	79	$ .01	$ .06	Lollar, Tim	86D	620	$ .01	$ .06
Leonard, Jeff	87D	391	$ .01	$ .04	Lollar, Tim	83D	61	$ .01	$ .05
Leonard, Jeffrey	88D	327	$ .01	$ .05	Lollar, Tim	84D	284	$ .03	$ .10
Leonard, Jeffrey	89D	457	$ .01	$ .04	Lollar, Tim	85D	324	$ .01	$ .08
Leonard, Jeffrey	89DBB	107	$ .01	$ .04	Loman, Doug	85DRR	46	$ .01	$ .08
Leonard, Jeffrey	89DTR	1	$ .01	$ .15	Litton, Greg	90D	453	$ .01	$ .25
Leonard, Jeffrey	90D	93	$ .01	$ .03	Lombardi, Phil	87D	401	$ .01	$ .04
Lerch, Randy	81D	574	$ .01	$ .05	Lombardozzi, Steve	86D	598	$ .01	$ .06

BRAD LESLEY

Player	Year	No.	VG	EX/MT	Player	Year	No.	VG	EX/MT
Lombardozzi, Steve	86DR	18	$ .02	$ .09	Lyons, Steve	87D	409	$ .01	$ .04
Lombardozzi, Steve	87D	318	$ .01	$ .04	Lyons, Steve	88D	532	$ .01	$ .05
Lombardozzi, Steve	88D	196	$ .01	$ .05	Lyons, Steve	89D	253	$ .01	$ .04
Lombardozzi, Steve	89D	554	$ .01	$ .04	Lyons, Steve	90D	651	$ .01	$ .03
Lombardozzi, Steve	90D	688	$ .01	$ .03	Lysander, Rick	84D	560	$ .03	$ .10
Long, Bill	87DR	48	$ .01	$ .07	Lysander, Rick	85D	560	$ .01	$ .08
Long, Bill	88D	306	$ .01	$ .05	Macfarlane, Mike	88DR	55	$ .01	$ .15
Long, Bill	89D	573	$ .01	$ .04	Macfarlane, Mike	89D	416	$ .01	$ .15
Lopes, Davey	81D	416	$ .02	$ .15	Macfarlane, Mike	90D	498	$ .01	$ .03
Lopes, Davey	82D	327	$ .01	$ .05	Macha, Ken	81D	540	$ .01	$ .05
Lopes, Davey	83D	339	$ .01	$ .05	Machado, Julio	90DRR	47	$ .01	$ .25
Lopes, Davey	84D	400	$ .03	$ .10	Mack, Shane	87DR	42	$ .05	$ .25
Lopes, Davey	85D	604	$ .01	$ .08	Mack, Shane	88D	411	$ .01	$ .05
Lopes, Davey	86D	388	$ .01	$ .06	Mack, Shane	89D	538	$ .01	$ .04
Lopes, Davey	86DK	9	$ .01	$ .06	Mackanin, Pete	82D	354	$ .01	$ .05
Lopes, Davey	87D	455	$ .01	$ .04	Macko, Steve	81D	535	$ .01	$ .05
Lopez, Aurelio	82D	359	$ .01	$ .05	Madden, Mike	84D	161	$ .03	$ .10
Lopez, Aurelio	84D	516	$ .03	$ .10	Maddox, Elliott	81D	397	$ .01	$ .05
Lopez, Aurelio	85D	349	$ .01	$ .08	Maddox, Garry	81D	55	$ .01	$ .05
Lopez, Aurelio	86D	293	$ .01	$ .06	Maddox, Garry	82D	315	$ .01	$ .05
Lopez, Aurelio	87D	629	$ .01	$ .04	Maddox, Garry	83D	63	$ .01	$ .05
Lovullo, Torey	89DR	17	$ .01	$ .10	Maddox, Garry	84D	305	$ .03	$ .10
Lowenstein, John	81D	235	$ .01	$ .05	Maddox, Garry	85D	137	$ .01	$ .08
Lowenstein, John	82D	599	$ .01	$ .05	Maddox, Garry	86D	407	$ .01	$ .06
Lowenstein, John	83D	153	$ .01	$ .05	Maddux, Greg	87DR	52	$ .05	$ .50
Lowenstein, John	84D	228	$ .03	$ .10	Maddux, Greg	87DRR	36	$ .15	$1.50
Lowenstein, John	85D	245	$ .01	$ .08	Maddux, Greg	88D	539	$ .05	$ .25
Lowry, Dwight	87D	338	$ .01	$ .04	Maddux, Greg	88DBB	82	$ .01	$ .05
Loynd, Mike	87D	506	$ .08	$ .25	Maddux, Greg	89D	373	$ .01	$ .04
Loynd, Mike	88D	550	$ .01	$ .05	Maddux, Greg	89DBB	37	$ .01	$ .04
Lozado, Willie	85D	595	$ .01	$ .08	Maddux, Greg	90D	158	$ .01	$ .03
Lubratich, Steve	84D	377	$ .03	$ .10	Maddux, Mike	87D	535	$ .03	$ .25
Lucas, Gary	81D	243	$ .01	$ .05	Maddux, Mike	89D	487	$ .01	$ .04
Lucas, Gary	82D	296	$ .01	$ .05	Maddux, Mike	90D	312	$ .01	$ .03
Lucas, Gary	83D	187	$ .01	$ .05	Madlock, Bill	81D	252	$ .05	$ .30
Lucas, Gary	84D	307	$ .03	$ .10	Madlock, Bill	82D	653	$ .03	$ .20
Lucas, Gary	85D	498	$ .01	$ .08	Madlock, Bill	83D	311	$ .02	$ .15
Lucas, Gary	86D	453	$ .01	$ .06	Madlock, Bill	84D	113	$ .04	$ .25
Lucas, Gary	87D	618	$ .01	$ .04	Madlock, Bill	84DK	20	$ .08	$ .25
Lucas, Gary	88D	579	$ .01	$ .05	Madlock, Bill	85D	200	$ .03	$ .10
Luecken, Rick	90D	562	$ .01	$ .10	Madlock, Bill	86D	617	$ .02	$ .15
Lugo, Urbano	86D	329	$ .01	$ .06	Madlock, Bill	87D	155	$ .01	$ .04
Lum, Mike	82D	300	$ .01	$ .05	Madlock, Bill	88D	496	$ .01	$ .05
Lusader, Scott	88D	615	$ .03	$ .25	Madrid, Alex	89D	604	$ .01	$ .04
Lusader, Scott	90D	696	$ .01	$ .03	Magadan, Dave	87D	575	$ .15	$ .75
Luzinski, Greg	81D	175	$ .03	$ .20	Magadan, Dave	87DR	34	$ .10	$ .50
Luzinski, Greg	82D	193	$ .02	$ .15	Magadan, Dave	88D	323	$ .01	$ .10
Luzinski, Greg	83D	395	$ .01	$ .05	Magadan, Dave	89D	408	$ .01	$ .04
Luzinski, Greg	84D	122	$ .03	$ .10	Magadan, Dave	89DBB	264	$ .01	$ .04
Luzinski, Greg	85D	546	$ .01	$ .08	Magadan, Dave	90D	383	$ .01	$ .03
Lyle, Sparky	81D	284	$ .02	$ .15	Magrane, Joe	87DR	40	$ .15	$1.00
Lyle, Sparky	82D	189	$ .01	$ .05	Magrane, Joe	88D	140	$ .10	$ .65
Lynch, Ed	82D	641	$ .01	$ .05	Magrane, Joe	88DBB	100	$ .01	$ .15
Lynch, Ed	83D	308	$ .01	$ .05	Magrane, Joe	89D	201	$ .01	$ .10
Lynch, Ed	84D	75	$ .03	$ .10	Magrane, Joe	89DBB	131	$ .01	$ .04
Lynch, Ed	85D	623	$ .01	$ .08	Magrane, Joe	90D	163	$ .01	$ .03
Lynch, Ed	86D	631	$ .01	$ .06	Magrane, Joe	90DK	13	$ .01	$ .10
Lynch, Ed	87D	516	$ .01	$ .04	Magrann, Tom	90D	374	$ .01	$ .10
Lynch, Ed	88D	77	$ .01	$ .05	Mahler, Rick	82D	349	$ .03	$ .20
Lynn, Fred	81D	218	$ .05	$ .20	Mahler, Rick	83D	527	$ .01	$ .05
Lynn, Fred	82D	367	$ .05	$ .20	Mahler, Rick	85D	385	$ .01	$ .08
Lynn, Fred	83D	241	$ .03	$ .20	Mahler, Rick	86D	77	$ .01	$ .06
Lynn, Fred	84D	108	$ .05	$ .25	Mahler, Rick	86DK	21	$ .01	$ .06
Lynn, Fred	84DK	17	$ .08	$ .25	Mahler, Rick	87D	190	$ .01	$ .04
Lynn, Fred	85D	133	$ .03	$ .20	Mahler, Rick	88D	389	$ .01	$ .05
Lynn, Fred	86D	245	$ .05	$ .20	Mahler, Rick	88DBB	114	$ .01	$ .05
Lynn, Fred	87D	108	$ .01	$ .25	Mahler, Rick	89D*	222	$ .01	$ .04
Lynn, Fred	87DK	9	$ .05	$ .20	Mahler, Rick	89DBB	286	$ .01	$ .04
Lynn, Fred	88D	248	$ .01	$ .05	Mahler, Rick	89DTR	24	$ .01	$ .15
Lynn, Fred	89D	563	$ .01	$ .10	Mahler, Rick	90D	375	$ .01	$ .05
Lyons, Barry	88D	619	$ .05	$ .20	Maldonado, Candy	83D	262	$ .05	$ .50
Lyons, Barry	89D	572	$ .01	$ .04	Maldonado, Candy	84D	93	$ .05	$ .35
Lyons, Barry	90D	526	$ .01	$ .03	Maldonado, Candy	85D	250	$ .01	$ .08
Lyons, Steve	85DRR	29	$ .01	$ .08	Maldonado, Candy	87D	327	$ .01	$ .04
Lyons, Steve	86D	579	$ .01	$ .06	Maldonado, Candy	88D	391	$ .05	$ .20

Player	Year	No.	VG	EX/MT	Player	Year	No.	VG	EX/MT
Maldonado, Candy	88DBB	247	$ .01	$ .05	Martinez, Ramon	89D	464	$ .05	$ .35
Maldonado, Candy	89D	177	$ .01	$ .04	Martinez, Ramon	89DR	45	$ .01	$ .25
Maldonado, Candy	90D	611	$ .01	$ .03	Martinez, Ramon	90D	685	$ .01	$ .20
Mann, Kelly	90DRR	46	$ .01	$ .20	Martinez, Silvio	81D	429	$ .01	$ .05
Manning, Rick	81D	202	$ .01	$ .05	Martinez, Silvio	82D	469	$ .01	$ .05
Manning, Rick	82D	85	$ .01	$ .05	Martinez, Tippy	81D	354	$ .01	$ .05
Manning, Rick	83D	198	$ .01	$ .05	Martinez, Tippy	82D	205	$ .01	$ .05
Manning, Rick	84D	170	$ .03	$ .10	Martinez, Tippy	83D	357	$ .01	$ .05
Manning, Rick	85D	237	$ .01	$ .08	Martinez, Tippy	84D	472	$ .03	$ .10
Manning, Rick	86D	368	$ .01	$ .06	Martinez, Tippy	85D	210	$ .01	$ .08
Manning, Rick	87D	521	$ .01	$ .04	Martinez, Tippy	86D	514	$ .01	$ .06
Manning, Rick	88D	486	$ .01	$ .05	Martz, Randy	82D	126	$ .01	$ .05
Manrique, Fred	88D	493	$ .01	$ .05	Martz, Randy	83D	151	$ .01	$ .05
Manrique, Fred	89D	489	$ .01	$ .04	Marzano, John	88D	421	$ .10	$ .35
Manrique, Fred	90D	165	$ .01	$ .25	Mason, Mike	85D	281	$ .01	$ .08
Manwaring, Kirt	88DRR	39	$ .01	$ .25	Mason, Mike	86D	422	$ .01	$ .06
Manwaring, Kirt	89D	494	$ .01	$ .04	Mason, Mike	87D	284	$ .01	$ .04
Manwaring, Kirt	89DBB	330	$ .01	$ .04	Mason, Roger	86D	633	$ .01	$ .06
Manwaring, Kirt	90D	59	$ .01	$ .03	Mason, Roger	87D	204	$ .01	$ .04
Marshall, Mike	82D	562	$ .15	$1.00	Mata, Vic	85D	629	$ .01	$ .08
Marshall, Mike	83D	362	$ .01	$ .25	Mathews, Greg	86DR	26	$ .10	$ .35
Marshall, Mike	84D	348	$ .03	$ .10	Mathews, Greg	87D	208	$ .03	$ .25
Marshall, Mike	85D	296	$ .01	$ .08	Mathews, Greg	88D	84	$ .01	$ .05
Marshall, Mike	85DK	12	$ .03	$ .10	Mathews, Greg	89D	281	$ .01	$ .04
Marshall, Mike	86D	52	$ .01	$ .06	Matlack, Jon	81D	266	$ .01	$ .05
Marshall, Mike	87D	176	$ .01	$ .04	Matlack, Jon	82D	215	$ .01	$ .05
Marshall, Mike	88D	229	$ .01	$ .05	Matlack, Jon	83D	195	$ .01	$ .05
Marshall, Mike	88DBB	178	$ .01	$ .05	Matlack, Jon	84D	378	$ .03	$ .10
Marshall, Mike	89D	110	$ .01	$ .04	Matthews, Gary	81D	306	$ .02	$ .15
Marshall, Mike	89DBB	204	$ .01	$ .04	Matthews, Gary	82D	441	$ .01	$ .05
Marshall, Mike	90D	84	$ .01	$ .03	Matthews, Gary	83D	420	$ .01	$ .05
Martin, Billy	81D	479	$ .05	$ .20	Matthews, Gary	84D	233	$ .03	$ .10
Martin, Billy	82D	491	$ .03	$ .20	Matthews, Gary	85D	239	$ .01	$ .08
Martin, Billy	83D	575	$ .02	$ .15	Matthews, Gary	86D	76	$ .01	$ .06
Martin, Jerry	81D	555	$ .01	$ .05	Mattick, Bobby	81D	570	$ .01	$ .05
Martin, Jerry	82D	298	$ .01	$ .05	Mattingly, Don	84D	248	$15.00	$75.00
Martin, Jerry	83D	138	$ .01	$ .05	Mattingly, Don	85D	295	$5.00	$15.00
Martin, John	82D	343	$ .01	$ .05	Mattingly, Don	85D	651	$1.00	$5.00
Martin, John	83D	617	$ .01	$ .05	Mattingly, Don	85DK	7	$1.50	$5.00
Martin, Renie	81D	103	$ .01	$ .05	Mattingly, Don	86D	173	$1.75	$5.00
Martin, Renie	82D	238	$ .01	$ .05	Mattingly, Don	87D	52	$1.00	$2.50
Martin, Renie	83D	272	$ .01	$ .05	Mattingly, Don	88D	217	$ .40	$1.50
Martin, Renie	84D	445	$ .03	$ .10	Mattingly, Don	88DBB	1	$ .25	$1.00
Martinez, Alfredo	81D	172	$ .01	$ .05	Mattingly, Don	88DBC	21	$ .30	$ .50
Martinez, Buck	81D	444	$ .01	$ .05	Mattingly, Don	89D	74	$ .25	$ .75
Martinez, Buck	82D	561	$ .01	$ .05	Mattingly, Don	89DBB	1	$ .01	$1.00
Martinez, Buck	83D	178	$ .01	$ .05	Mattingly, Don	89DK	26	$ .10	$ .75
Martinez, Buck	84D	612	$ .03	$ .10	Mattingly, Don	90D	190	$ .01	$ .50
Martinez, Carlos	89DR	14	$ .01	$ .20	Matula, Rick	81D	317	$ .01	$ .05
Martinez, Carlos	90D	531	$ .01	$ .15	Matuszek, Len	84D	549	$ .03	$ .10
Martinez, Carmelo	84D	623	$ .05	$ .30	Matuszek, Len	85D	259	$ .01	$ .08
Martinez, Carmelo	85D	478	$ .01	$ .08	Matuszek, Len	86D	494	$ .01	$ .06
Martinez, Carmelo	86D	324	$ .01	$ .06	Matuszek, Len	87D	423	$ .01	$ .04
Martinez, Carmelo	88D	287	$ .01	$ .05	Mauch, Gene	82D	141	$ .01	$ .05
Martinez, Carmelo	89D	601	$ .01	$ .04	May, Lee	82D	570	$ .01	$ .05
Martinez, Carmelo	90D	482	$ .01	$ .03	May, Lee	83D	538	$ .01	$ .05
Martinez, Dave	87D	488	$ .10	$ .40	May, Milt	81D	193	$ .01	$ .05
Martinez, Dave	88D	438	$ .03	$ .25	May, Milt	82D	503	$ .01	$ .05
Martinez, Dave	88DBB	149	$ .01	$ .05	May, Milt	83D	312	$ .01	$ .05
Martinez, Dave	89D	102	$ .01	$ .04	May, Milt	84D	386	$ .03	$ .10
Martinez, Dave	90D	452	$ .01	$ .03	May, Milt	85D	410	$ .01	$ .08
Martinez, Dennis	81D	533	$ .01	$ .05	May, Rudy	82D	325	$ .01	$ .05
Martinez, Dennis	82D	79	$ .01	$ .05	May, Rudy	83D	135	$ .01	$ .05
Martinez, Dennis	83D	231	$ .01	$ .05	May, Rudy	84D	626	$ .03	$ .10
Martinez, Dennis	84D	633	$ .03	$ .10	May, Scott	89D	636	$ .01	$ .04
Martinez, Dennis	85D	514	$ .01	$ .08	Mayberry, John	81D	29	$ .01	$ .05
Martinez, Dennis	86D	454	$ .01	$ .06	Mayberry, John	82D	306	$ .01	$ .05
Martinez, Dennis	88D	549	$ .01	$ .05	Mayberry, John	82DK	25	$ .01	$ .05
Martinez, Dennis	88DBB	146	$ .01	$ .05	Mazzilli, Lee	81D	34	$ .01	$ .05
Martinez, Dennis	89D	106	$ .01	$ .04	Mazzilli, Lee	82D	49	$ .01	$ .05
Martinez, Dennis	89DBB	90	$ .01	$ .04	Mazzilli, Lee	83D	638	$ .01	$ .05
Martinez, Dennis	90D	156	$ .01	$ .03	Mazzilli, Lee	84D	166	$ .03	$ .10
Martinez, Edgar	88DR	36	$ .05	$ .25	Mazzilli, Lee	85D	386	$ .01	$ .08
Martinez, Edgar	89D	645	$ .01	$ .04	Mazzilli, Lee	86D	288	$ .01	$ .06
Martinez, Edgar	89DR	15	$ .01	$ .10	Mazzilli, Lee	87D	562	$ .01	$ .04

Player	Year	No.	VG	EX/MT	Player	Year	No.	VG	EX/MT
Mazzilli, Lee	88D	614	$ .01	$ .15	McGregor, Scott	82D	331	$ .01	$ .05
Mazzilli, Lee	88DBB	209	$ .01	$ .05	McGregor, Scott	83D	483	$ .01	$ .05
Mazzilli, Lee	90D	584	$ .01	$ .03	McGregor, Scott	84D	594	$ .03	$ .10
McBride, Bake	81D	404	$ .03	$ .20	McGregor, Scott	85D	413	$ .01	$ .08
McBride, Bake	82D	497	$ .01	$ .05	McGregor, Scott	86D	291	$ .01	$ .06
McCaskill, Kirk	86D	474	$ .10	$ .50	McGregor, Scott	87D	520	$ .01	$ .04
McCaskill, Kirk	87D	381	$ .01	$ .15	McGriff, Fred	86DRR	28	$3.00	$15.00
McCaskill, Kirk	88D	381	$ .01	$ .05	McGriff, Fred	87D	621	$ .25	$3.00
McCaskill, Kirk	88DBB	83	$ .01	$ .05	McGriff, Fred	87DR	31	$ .25	$2.50
McCaskill, Kirk	89D	136	$ .01	$ .04	McGriff, Fred	88D	195	$ .15	$ .60
McCaskill, Kirk	89DBB	83	$ .01	$ .04	McGriff, Fred	88DBB	160	$ .05	$ .25
McCaskill, Kirk	90D	170	$ .01	$ .03	McGriff, Fred	89D	70	$ .01	$ .15
McCatty, Steve	81D	478	$ .01	$ .05	McGriff, Fred	89DBB	104	$ .01	$ .20
McCatty, Steve	82D	35	$ .01	$ .05	McGriff, Fred	89DBC	19	$ .01	$ .15
McCatty, Steve	83D	491	$ .01	$ .05	McGriff, Fred	89DK	16	$ .01	$ .15
McCatty, Steve	84D	420	$ .03	$ .10	McGriff, Fred	90D	188	$ .01	$ .15
McCatty, Steve	85D	497	$ .01	$ .08	McGriff, Terry	87D	512	$ .01	$ .15
McClendon, Lloyd	89D	595	$ .01	$ .15	McGriff, Terry	88D	556	$ .01	$ .05
McClendon, Lloyd	89DBB	228	$ .01	$ .04	McGwire, Mark	87DR	1	$ .70	$3.50
McClendon, Lloyd	90D	341	$ .01	$ .03	McGwire, Mark	87DRR	46	$2.65	$8.00
McClure, Bob	81D	510	$ .01	$ .05	McGwire, Mark	88D	256	$ .60	$1.00
McClure, Bob	83D	582	$ .01	$ .05	McGwire, Mark	88DBB	169	$ .15	$ .50
McClure, Bob	84D	359	$ .03	$ .10	McGwire, Mark	88DBC	23	$ .25	$ .50
McClure, Bob	85D	536	$ .01	$ .08	McGwire, Mark	88DK	1	$ .25	$ .50
McClure, Bob	90D	470	$ .01	$ .03	McGwire, Mark	89D	95	$ .15	$ .50
McClure, Rob	88D	529	$ .01	$ .05	McGwire, Mark	89DBB	43	$ .01	$ .25
McCullers, Lance	86DRR	41	$ .01	$ .40	McGwire, Mark	90D	185	$ .01	$ .25
McCullers, Lance	87D	237	$ .01	$ .04	McGwire, Mark	90DAS	697	$ .01	$ .15
McCullers, Lance	88D	451	$ .01	$ .05	McKay, Dave	81D	350	$ .01	$ .05
McCullers, Lance	88DBB	210	$ .01	$ .05	McKay, Dave	82D	391	$ .01	$ .05
McCullers, Lance	89D	129	$ .01	$ .04	McKay, Dave	83D	213	$ .01	$ .05
McCullers, Lance	89DBB	220	$ .01	$ .04	McKeon, Joel	86DR	55	$ .02	$ .09
McCullers, Lance	89DTR	13	$ .01	$ .05	McLaughlin, Byron	81D	287	$ .01	$ .05
McCullers, Lance	90D	433	$ .01	$ .03	McLaughlin, Joey	81D	271	$ .01	$ .05
McDonald, Ben	90DRR	32	$ .01	$2.50	McLaughlin, Joey	82D	507	$ .01	$ .05
McDowell, Jack	88DR	40	$ .01	$ .15					
McDowell, Jack	88DRR	47	$ .10	$ .30					
McDowell, Jack	89D	531	$ .01	$ .10					
McDowell, Oddibe	86D	56	$ .05	$ .25					
McDowell, Oddibe	87D	161	$ .01	$ .04					
McDowell, Oddibe	88D	382	$ .01	$ .05					
McDowell, Oddibe	89D	378	$ .01	$ .04					
McDowell, Oddibe	89DTR	49	$ .01	$ .15					
McDowell, Oddibe	90D	340	$ .01	$ .03					
McDowell, Roger	86D	629	$ .15	$ .50					
McDowell, Roger	87D	241	$ .01	$ .15					
McDowell, Roger	88D	651	$ .01	$ .15					
McDowell, Roger	88DBB	126	$ .01	$ .05					
McDowell, Roger	89D	265	$ .01	$ .04					
McDowell, Roger	89DBB	16	$ .01	$ .04					
McDowell, Roger	90D	251	$ .01	$ .03					
McGaffigan, Andy	84D	309	$ .03	$ .10					
McGaffigan, Andy	85D	646	$ .01	$ .08					
McGaffigan, Andy	87D	380	$ .01	$ .04					
McGaffigan, Andy	88D	380	$ .01	$ .05					
McGaffigan, Andy	89D	338	$ .01	$ .04					
McGaffigan, Andy	90D	574	$ .01	$ .03					
McGee, Willie	83D	190	$ .30	$1.50					
McGee, Willie	84D	353	$ .10	$ .50					
McGee, Willie	84D	625	$ .01	$ .25					
McGee, Willie	85D	475	$ .10	$ .35					
McGee, Willie	86D	109	$ .05	$ .20					
McGee, Willie	86D	651	$ .03	$ .25					
McGee, Willie	86DK	3	$ .05	$ .20					
McGee, Willie	87D	84	$ .01	$ .15	McLaughlin, Joey	83D	255	$ .01	$ .05
McGee, Willie	88D	307	$ .01	$ .05	McLaughlin, Joey	84D	617	$ .03	$ .10
McGee, Willie	88DBB	131	$ .01	$ .15	McLemore, Mark	86DRR	35	$ .02	$ .15
McGee, Willie	89D	161	$ .01	$ .04	McLemore, Mark	87D	479	$ .01	$ .04
McGee, Willie	90D	632	$ .01	$ .03	McLemore, Mark	87DR	7	$ .01	$ .07
McGlothen, Lynn	81D	562	$ .01	$ .05	McLemore, Mark	88D	181	$ .01	$ .05
McGraw, Tug	81D	273	$ .02	$ .15	McLemore, Mark	88DBB	251	$ .01	$ .05
McGraw, Tug	82D	420	$ .01	$ .05	McLemore, Mark	89D	94	$ .01	$ .04
McGraw, Tug	83D	371	$ .02	$ .15					
McGraw, Tug	84D	547	$ .03	$ .10					
McGregor, Scott	81D	114	$ .01	$ .05					

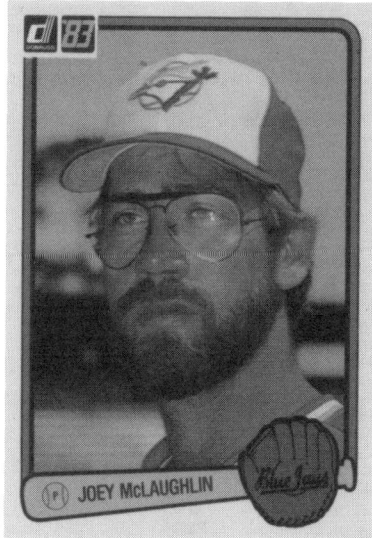

JOEY McLAUGHLIN

DONRUSS

Player	Year	No.	VG	EX/MT
McMurtry, Craig	84D	599	$ .03	$ .10
McMurtry, Craig	85D	188	$ .03	$ .10
McMurtry, Craig	89D	520	$ .01	$ .04
McNamara, John	82D	526	$ .01	$ .05
McRae, Hal	81D	463	$ .02	$ .15
McRae, Hal	82D	196	$ .01	$ .05
McRae, Hal	83D	238	$ .01	$ .05
McRae, Hal	84D	297	$ .03	$ .10
McRae, Hal	84DK	11	$ .08	$ .25
McRae, Hal	85D	588	$ .01	$ .08
McRae, Hal	86D	521	$ .01	$ .06
McRae, Hal	87D	471	$ .01	$ .04
McReynolds, Kevin	84DRR	34	$2.75	$11.00
McReynolds, Kevin	85D	139	$ .25	$1.25
McReynolds, Kevin	86D	80	$ .10	$ .45
McReynolds, Kevin	87D	451	$ .01	$ .25
McReynolds, Kevin	87DK	14	$ .01	$ .25
McReynolds, Kevin	88D	617	$ .01	$ .15
McReynolds, Kevin	88DBB	153	$ .01	$ .15
McReynolds, Kevin	89D	99	$ .01	$ .10
McReynolds, Kevin	89DBB	70	$ .01	$ .10
McReynolds, Kevin	90D	218	$ .01	$ .10
McWilliams, Larry	82D	527	$ .01	$ .05
McWilliams, Larry	83D	45	$ .01	$ .05
McWilliams, Larry	84D	566	$ .03	$ .10
McWilliams, Larry	85D	78	$ .01	$ .08
McWilliams, Larry	86D	264	$ .01	$ .06
McWilliams, Larry	89D	516	$ .01	$ .04
McWilliams, Larry	90D	709	$ .01	$ .03
Meacham, Bobby	84D	336	$ .03	$ .10
Meacham, Bobby	85D	126	$ .01	$ .08
Meacham, Bobby	86D	638	$ .01	$ .06
Meacham, Bobby	88D	616	$ .01	$ .15
Meads, Dave	87DR	46	$ .01	$ .07
Meads, Dave	89D	424	$ .01	$ .04
Meads, David	88D	455	$ .01	$ .05
Medich, Doc	81D	386	$ .01	$ .05
Medich, Doc	82D	142	$ .01	$ .05
Medina, Luis	89DR	20	$ .01	$ .25
Medina, Luis	89DRR	36	$ .05	$ .35
Medvin, Scott	89D	597	$ .01	$ .04
Meier, Dave	85D	147	$ .01	$ .08
Mejias, Sam	82D	295	$ .01	$ .05
Melendez, Francisco	89D	611	$ .01	$ .25
Melvin, Bob	86D	456	$ .01	$ .06
Melvin, Bob	87D	239	$ .01	$ .04
Melvin, Bob	88D	638	$ .01	$ .15
Melvin, Bob	90D	451	$ .01	$ .03
Mendoza, Mario	81D	45	$ .01	$ .05
Mendoza, Mario	82D	394	$ .01	$ .05
Mercado, Orlando	84D	318	$ .03	$ .10
Mercker, Kent	90DRR	31	$ .01	$ .25
Meridith, Ron	86D	533	$ .01	$ .06
Merullo, Matt	89DR	50	$ .01	$ .10
Mesa, Jose	88D	601	$ .01	$ .15
Meulens, Hensley	89D	547	$ .15	$ .60
Meyer, Brian	89D	640	$ 01	$ .04
Meyer, Brian	90D	648	$ .01	$ .03
Meyer, Dan	81D	43	$ .01	$ .05
Meyer, Dan	82D	176	$ .01	$ .05
Meyer, Dan	83D	413	$ .01	$ .05
Meyer, Joey	87D	460	$ .10	$ .30
Meyer, Joey	88DBB	239	$ .01	$ .05
Meyer, Joey	88DR	38	$ .01	$ .15
Meyer, Joey	88DRR	36	$ .01	$ .25
Meyer, Joey	89D	339	$ .01	$ .04
Michael, Gene	81D	500	$ .01	$ .05
Mielke, Gary	90D	679	$ .01	$ .10
Milacki, Bob	89D	651	$ .01	$ .30
Milacki, Bob	89DBB	254	$ .01	$ .10
Milacki, Bob	89DR	22	$ .01	$ .10
Milacki, Bob	90D	333	$ .01	$ .10
Milbourne, Larry	81D	486	$ .01	$ .05
Milbourne, Larry	82D	614	$ .01	$ .05
Milbourne, Larry	83D	411	$ .01	$ .05

Player	Year	No.	VG	EX/MT
Miller, Darrell	85D	644	$ .01	$ .08
Miller, Darrell	88D	551	$ .01	$ .05
Miller, Eddie	82D	425	$ .01	$ .05
Miller, Keith	88D	562	$ .03	$ .20
Miller, Keith	89D	623	$ .01	$ .04
Miller, Keith	90D	507	$ .01	$ .03
Miller, Mike	84D	493	$ .03	$ .10
Miller, Rick	81D	294	$ .01	$ .05
Miller, Rick	82D	334	$ .01	$ .05
Miller, Rick	83D	82	$ .01	$ .05
Miller, Rick	85D	517	$ .01	$ .08
Milligan, Randy	88DR	32	$ .01	$ .05
Milligan, Randy	90D	519	$ .01	$ .03
Mills, Brad	83D	366	$ .01	$ .05
Milner, Eddie	83D	169	$ .01	$ .05
Milner, Eddie	84D	365	$ .03	$ .10
Milner, Eddie	85D	428	$ .01	$ .08
Milner, Eddie	86D	325	$ .01	$ .06
Milner, Eddie	87D	433	$ .01	$ .04
Milner, John	81D	377	$ .01	$ .05
Milner, John	82D	266	$ .01	$ .05
Minton, Greg	81D	579	$ .01	$ .05
Minton, Greg	82D	348	$ .01	$ .05
Minton, Greg	83D	186	$ .01	$ .05
Minton, Greg	84D	187	$ .03	$ .10
Minton, Greg	85D	143	$ .01	$ .08
Minton, Greg	86D	480	$ .01	$ .06
Minton, Greg	88D	505	$ .01	$ .05
Minton, Greg	89D	490	$ .01	$ .04
Minton, Greg	89DBB	283	$ .01	$ .04

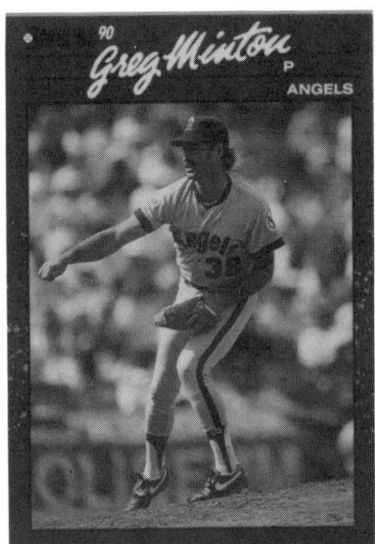

Player	Year	No.	VG	EX/MT
Minton, Greg	90D	116	$ .01	$ .03
Mirabella, Paul	81D	151	$ .01	$ .05
Mirabella, Paul	82D	629	$ .01	$ .05
Mirabella, Paul	83D	541	$ .01	$ .05
Mirabella, Paul	89D	654	$ .01	$ .04
Mitchell, Charlie	85DRR	40	$ .01	$ .08
Mitchell, John	87DR	37	$ .01	$ .07
Mitchell, Kevin	86DR	17	$1.00	$7.50
Mitchell, Kevin	87D	599	$ .75	$5.50
Mitchell, Kevin	88D	66	$ .10	$ .50
Mitchell, Kevin	89D	485	$ .05	$ .35
Mitchell, Kevin	89DBB	281	$ .01	$ .35
Mitchell, Kevin	90D	98	$ .01	$ .30

Player	Year	No.	VG	EX/MT	Player	Year	No.	VG	EX/MT
Mitchell, Kevin	90DAS	715	$ .01	$ .20	Moore, Mike	89DTR	21	$ .01	$ .05
Mitchell, Kevin	90DBC	11	$ .01	$ .20	Moore, Mike	90D	214	$ .01	$ .03
Mitchell, Kevin	90DK	11	$ .01	$ .35	Morales, Jerry	82D	309	$ .01	$ .05
Mitchell, Paul	81D	205	$ .01	$ .05	Morales, Jose	81D	495	$ .01	$ .05
Mizerock, John	84D	380	$ .03	$ .10	Morales, Jose	82D	203	$ .01	$ .05
Mizerock, John	86D	502	$ .01	$ .06	Morales, Jose	84D	275	$ .05	$ .30
Mizerock, John	87D	653	$ .01	$ .04	Moreland, Keith	81D	382	$ .05	$ .30
Mmahat, Kevin	90D	481	$ .01	$ .10	Moreland, Keith	82D	119	$ .01	$ .05
Moffitt, Randy	81D	195	$ .01	$ .05	Moreland, Keith	83D	309	$ .01	$ .05
Moffitt, Randy	83D	545	$ .01	$ .05	Moreland, Keith	84D	483	$ .03	$ .10
Moffitt, Randy	84D	390	$ .03	$ .10	Moreland, Keith	85D	117	$ .01	$ .08
Mohorcic, Dale	87D	531	$ .05	$ .20	Moreland, Keith	86D	167	$ .01	$ .06
Mohorcic, Dale	88D	470	$ .01	$ .05	Moreland, Keith	87D	169	$ .01	$ .04
Mohorcic, Dale	88DBB	144	$ .01	$ .05	Moreland, Keith	87DK	24	$ .01	$ .04
Mohorcic, Dale	89D	630	$ .01	$ .04	Moreland, Keith	88D	201	$ .01	$ .05
Molinaro, Bobby	82D	417	$ .01	$ .05	Moreland, Keith	88DBB	266	$ .01	$ .05
Molinaro, Bobby	83D	596	$ .01	$ .05	Moreland, Keith	89D	111	$ .01	$ .04
Molitor, Paul	81D	203	$ .03	$ .20	Moreland, Keith	89DBB	203	$ .01	$ .04
Molitor, Paul	82D	78	$ .02	$ .15	Moreno, Omar	81D	17	$ .01	$ .05
Molitor, Paul	83D	484	$ .03	$ .20	Moreno, Omar	82D	347	$ .01	$ .05
Molitor, Paul	84D	107	$ .04	$ .25	Moreno, Omar	83D	347	$ .01	$ .05
Molitor, Paul	85D	359	$ .03	$ .20	Moreno, Omar	84D	637	$ .03	$ .10
Molitor, Paul	86D	124	$ .01	$ .06	Moreno, Omar	85D	591	$ .01	$ .08
Molitor, Paul	87D	117	$ .01	$ .04	Morgan, Joe	81D	18	$ .10	$ .50
Molitor, Paul	88D	249	$ .01	$ .05	Morgan, Joe	82D	312	$ .05	$ .50
Molitor, Paul	88DBB	165	$ .01	$ .05	Morgan, Joe	83D	438	$ .05	$ .30
Molitor, Paul	88DBC	3	$ .05	$ .20	Morgan, Joe	83D	648	$ .01	$ .15
Molitor, Paul	88DK	7	$ .01	$ .15	Morgan, Joe	83DK	24	$ .05	$ .50
Molitor, Paul	89D	291	$ 01	$ 04	Morgan, Joe	84D	355	$ .10	$ .50
Molitor, Paul	89DBB	15	$ .01	$ .10	Morgan, Joe	85D	584	$ .08	$ .50
Molitor, Paul	89DBC	9	$ .01	$ .10	Morgan, Mike	83D	108	$ .01	$ .05
Molitor, Paul	90D	103	$ .01	$ .03	Morgan, Mike	87D	366	$ .01	$ .04
Molitor, Paul	90DBC	15	$ .01	$ .03	Morgan, Mike	88D	120	$ .01	$ .05
Monday, Rick	81D	60	$ .01	$ .05	Morgan, Mike	88DBB	86	$ .01	$ .05
Monday, Rick	82D	514	$ .01	$ .05	Morgan, Mike	89D	164	$ .01	$ .04
Monday, Rick	83D	643	$ .01	$ .05	Morgan, Mike	89DBB	122	$ .01	$ .04
Money, Don	81D	443	$ .01	$ .05	Morgan, Mike	90D	132	$ .01	$ .03
Money, Don	82D	384	$ .01	$ .05	Morman, Russ	87D	306	$ .08	$ .25
Money, Don	83D	132	$ .01	$ .05	Morris, Hal	89D	545	$ .01	$ .15
Monge, Sid	81D	81	$ .01	$ .05	Morris, Hal	90D	514	$ .01	$ .03
Monge, Sid	82D	620	$ .01	$ .05	Morris, Jack	81D	127	$ .05	$. 25
Monge, Sid	83D	245	$ .01	$ .05	Morris, Jack	82D	107	$ .03	$ .25
Monge, Sid	84D	139	$ .03	$ .10	Morris, Jack	83D	107	$ .03	$ .25
Montefusco, John	81D	434	$ .01	$ .05	Morris, Jack	83DK	5	$ .01	$ .15
Montefusco, John	83D	313	$ .01	$ .05	Morris, Jack	84D	415	$ .08	$ .25
Montefusco, John	84D	126	$ .03	$ .10	Morris, Jack	85D	415	$ .08	$ .25
Montefusco, John	85D	580	$ .01	$ .08	Morris, Jack	86D	105	$ .07	$ .25
Monteleone, Rich	90D	462	$ .01	$ .03	Morris, Jack	87D	173	$ .05	$ .20
Montgomery, Jeff	89D	440	$ .01	$ .15	Morris, Jack	87DK	13	$ .05	$ .20
Montgomery, Jeff	89DBB	319	$ .01	$ .04	Morris, Jack	88D	127	$ .05	$ .20
Montgomery, Jeff	90D	380	$ .01	$ .03	Morris, Jack	00D	480	$ .01	$ .05
Mooneyham, Bill	86DR	50	$ .02	$ .09	Morris, Jack	88DBB	181	$ .01	$ .05
Mooneyham, Bill	87D	302	$ .01	$ .04	Morris, Jack	89D	234	$ .01	$ .04
Moore, Charlie	81D	324	$ .01	$ .05	Morris, Jack	90D	639	$ .01	$ .10
Moore, Charlie	82D	280	$ .01	$ .05	Morris, John	85DRR	32	$ .01	$ .08
Moore, Charlie	83D	206	$ .01	$ .05	Morris, John	87D	480	$ .01	$ .04
Moore, Charlie	84D	292	$ .03	$ .10	Morris, John	90D	516	$ .01	$ .03
Moore, Charlie	85D	351	$ .01	$ .08	Morrison, Jim	81D	158	$ .01	$ .05
Moore, Charlie	86D	246	$ .01	$ .06	Morrison, Jim	82D	395	$ .01	$ .05
Moore, Charlie	87D	372	$ .01	$ .04	Morrison, Jim	83D	150	$ .01	$ .05
Moore, Donnie	85D	650	$ .01	$ .08	Morrison, Jim	84D	322	$ .03	$ .10
Moore, Donnie	86D	255	$ .01	$ .06	Morrison, Jim	85D	532	$ .01	$ .08
Moore, Donnie	87D	110	$ .01	$ .04	Morrison, Jim	86D	386	$ .01	$ .06
Moore, Donnie	88D	621	$ .01	$ .15	Morrison, Jim	87D	484	$ .01	$ .04
Moore, Kelvin	82D	534	$ .01	$ .05	Morrison, Jim	88D	543	$ .01	$ .05
Moore, Kelvin	83D	87	$ .01	$ .05	Moseby, Lloyd	82D	129	$ .10	$ .45
Moore, Mike	83D	428	$ .01	$1.25	Moseby, Lloyd	83D	556	$ .01	$ .05
Moore, Mike	84D	634	$ .05	$ .35	Moseby, Lloyd	84D	363	$ .03	$ .10
Moore, Mike	85D	440	$ .01	$ .08	Moseby, Lloyd	85D	437	$ .03	$ .10
Moore, Mike	86D	240	$ .01	$ .06	Moseby, Lloyd	87D	74	$ .01	$ .04
Moore, Mike	87D	70	$ .01	$ .04	Moseby, Lloyd	87DK	21	$ .01	$ .04
Moore, Mike	88D	75	$ .01	$ .05	Moseby, Lloyd	88D	367	$ .01	$ .05
Moore, Mike	88DBB	192	$ .01	$ .05	Moseby, Lloyd	88DBB	199	$ .01	$ .05
Moore, Mike	89D	448	$ .01	$ .04	Moseby, Lloyd	89D	231	$ .01	$ .04
Moore, Mike	89DBB	246	$ .01	$ .04	Moseby, Lloyd	90D	504	$ .01	$ .03

DONRUSS

Player	Year	No.	VG	EX/MT	Player	Year	No.	VG	EX/MT
Moseby, Llyod	86D	73	$ .01	$ .06	Murray, Dale	83D	381	$ .01	$ .05
Moses, John	84D	74	$ .03	$ .10	Murray, Dale	84D	577	$ .03	$ .10
Moses, John	87D	393	$ .01	$ .04	Murray, Eddie	81D	112	$ .20	$1.00
Moses, John	88D	440	$ .01	$ .05	Murray, Eddie	82D	483	$ .10	$ .75
Moses, John	89D	626	$ .01	$ .04	Murray, Eddie	83D	405	$ .10	$ .50
Moses, John	90D	590	$ .01	$ .03	Murray, Eddie	84D	47	$ .25	$1.00
Moskau, Paul	82D	355	$ .01	$ .05	Murray, Eddie	84DK	22	$ .25	$ .75
Mota, Manny	81D	299	$ .02	$ .15	Murray, Eddie	85D	47	$ .15	$1.00
Motley, Darryl	82D	390	$ .01	$ .05	Murray, Eddie	86D	88	$ .10	$ .35
Motley, Darryl	84D	344	$ .03	$ .10	Murray, Eddie	87D	48	$ .05	$ .20
Motley, Darryl	85D	461	$ .01	$ .08	Murray, Eddie	88D	231	$ .10	$ .25
Motley, Darryl	86D	217	$ .01	$ .06	Murray, Eddie	88DBB	142	$ .01	$ .15
Moyer, Jamie	87D	315	$ .08	$ .30	Murray, Eddie	89D	96	$ .01	$ .10
Moyer, Jamie	88D	169	$ .01	$ .05	Murray, Eddie	89DBB	92	$ .01	$ .15
Moyer, Jamie	88DBB	228	$ .01	$ .05	Murray, Eddie	89DTR	12	$ .01	$ .15
Moyer, Jamie	89D	157	$ .01	$ .04	Murray, Eddie	90D	77	$ .01	$ .10
Moyer, Jamie	89DTR	39	$ .01	$ .05	Musial, Stan	88D	641	$ .05	$ .20
Moyer, Jamie	90D	378	$ .01	$ .03	Musselman, Jeff	87D	591	$ .03	$ .30
Mulholland, Terry	87D	515	$ .01	$ .04	Musselman, Jeff	87DR	53	$ .01	$ .07
Mulholland, Terry	90D	515	$ .01	$ .03	Musselman, Jeff	88D	630	$ .01	$ .15
Mulliniks, Rance	81D	504	$ .01	$ .05	Musselman, Jeff	89D	656	$ .01	$ .04
Mulliniks, Rance	82D	630	$ .01	$ .05	Musselman, Jeff	90D	623	$ .01	$ .03
Mulliniks, Rance	83D	432	$ .01	$ .05	Myers, Greg	88D	624	$ .05	$ .20
Mulliniks, Rance	84D	584	$ .03	$ .10	Myers, Greg	90D	706	$ .01	$ .03
Mulliniks, Rance	85D	485	$ .01	$ .08	Myers, Randy	87DRR	29	$ .15	$ .75
Mulliniks, Rance	86D	606	$ .01	$ .06	Myers, Randy	88D	620	$ .01	$ .15
Mulliniks, Rance	87D	319	$ .01	$ .04	Myers, Randy	88DBB	265	$ .01	$ .15
Mulliniks, Rance	88D	197	$ .01	$ .05	Myers, Randy	89D	336	$ .01	$ .10
Mulliniks, Rance	89D	87	$ .01	$ .04	Myers, Randy	89DBB	153	$ .01	$ .10
Mulliniks, Rance	90D	607	$ .01	$ .03	Myers, Randy	90D	336	$ .01	$ .10
Mumphrey, Jerry	81D	124	$ .01	$ .05	Narron, Jerry	81D	405	$ .01	$ .05
Mumphrey, Jerry	82D	261	$ .01	$ .05	Narron, Jerry	82D	433	$ .01	$ .05
Mumphrey, Jerry	83D	360	$ .01	$ .05	Narron, Jerry	85D	643	$ .01	$ .08
Mumphrey, Jerry	84D	426	$ .03	$ .10	Narron, Jerry	86D	451	$ .01	$ .06
Mumphrey, Jerry	85D	206	$ .01	$ .08	Narron, Jerry	87D	603	$ .01	$ .04
Mumphrey, Jerry	86D	84	$ .01	$ .06	Navarro, Jaime	90D	640	$ .01	$ .10
Mumphrey, Jerry	87D	324	$ .01	$ .04	Nelson, Gene	82D	513	$ .01	$ .05
Mumphrey, Jerry	88D	447	$ .01	$ .05	Nelson, Gene	83D	55	$ .01	$ .05
Mura, Steve	81D	362	$ .01	$ .05	Nelson, Gene	85D	615	$ .01	$ .08
Mura, Steve	82D	523	$ .01	$ .05	Nelson, Gene	86D	501	$ .01	$ .06
Mura, Steve	83D	292	$ .01	$ .05	Nelson, Gene	87D	580	$ .01	$ .04
Murcer, Bobby	81D	111	$ .01	$ .05	Nelson, Gene	88D	133	$ .01	$ .05
Murcer, Bobby	82D	486	$ .01	$ .05	Nelson, Gene	89D	540	$ .01	$ .04
Murcer, Bobby	83D	261	$ .01	$ .05	Nelson, Gene	90D	540	$ .01	$ .03
Murphy, Dale	81D	437	$ .20	$1.25	Nelson, Ricky	84D	636	$ .03	$ .10
Murphy, Dale	82D	299	$ .25	$1.25	Nelson, Rob	87D	595	$ .01	$ .04
Murphy, Dale	83D	47	$ .15	$1.00	Nelson, Rob	88D	574	$ .01	$ .05
Murphy, Dale	83DK	12	$ .12	$ .60	Nettles, Graig	81D	105	$ .05	$ .20
Murphy, Dale	84D	66	$ .50	$1.50	Nettles, Graig	82D	335	$ .03	$ .20
Murphy, Dale	85D	66	$ .20	$ .60	Nettles, Graig	83D	83	$ .03	$ .20
Murphy, Dale	86D	66	$ .15	$ .50	Nettles, Graig	84D	518	$ .04	$ .25
Murphy, Dale	87D	78	$ .10	$ .35	Nettles, Graig	85D	234	$ .03	$ .20
Murphy, Dale	87DK	3	$ .10	$ .35	Nettles, Graig	86D	478	$ .05	$ .20
Murphy, Dale	88D	78	$ .10	$ .25	Newell, Tom	88D	604	$ .01	$ .15
Murphy, Dale	88DBB	113	$ .01	$ .15	Newman, Al	86DR	9	$ .02	$ .09
Murphy, Dale	88DBC	14	$ .01	$ .25	Newman, Al	87D	426	$ .01	$ .04
Murphy, Dale	89D	104	$ .01	$ .10	Newman, Al	88D	645	$ .01	$ .15
Murphy, Dale	89DBB	29	$ .01	$ .10	Newman, Al	89D	436	$ .01	$ .04
Murphy, Dale	90D	168	$ .01	$ .10	Newman, Al	90D	506	$ .01	$ .03
Murphy, Dwayne	81D	359	$ .01	$ .05	Newman, Jeff	81D	477	$ .01	$ .05
Murphy, Dwayne	82D	239	$ .01	$ .05	Newman, Jeff	82D	517	$ .01	$ .05
Murphy, Dwayne	83D	161	$ .01	$ .05	Newman, Jeff	83D	635	$ .01	$ .05
Murphy, Dwayne	84D	101	$ .03	$ .10	Newman, Jeff	84D	249	$ .03	$ .10
Murphy, Dwayne	84DK	3	$ .03	$ .15	Nezelek, Andy	89D	616	$ .01	$ .25
Murphy, Dwayne	85D	420	$ .01	$ .05	Nezelek, Andy	90D	523	$ .01	$ .03
Murphy, Dwayne	86D	176	$ .01	$ .06	Nichols, Carl	88D	477	$ .01	$ .05
Murphy, Dwayne	87D	379	$ .01	$ .04	Nichols, Carl	88DR	39	$ .01	$ .05
Murphy, Dwayne	88D	405	$ .01	$ .05	Nichols, Reid	82D	632	$ .01	$ .05
Murphy, Rob	87D	452	$ .05	$ .20	Nichols, Reid	83D	460	$ .01	$ .05
Murphy, Rob	88D	82	$ .01	$ .05	Nichols, Reid	84D	614	$ .03	$ .10
Murphy, Rob	88DBB	230	$ .01	$ .05	Nichols, Reid	85D	636	$ .01	$ .08
Murphy, Rob	89D	139	$ .01	$ .04	Nichols, Reid	86D	574	$ .01	$ .06
Murphy, Rob	89DBB	196	$ .01	$ .04	Nichols, Rod	89D	649	$ .01	$ .04
Murphy, Rob	89DTR	15	$ .01	$ .10	Nichols, Rod	90D	546	$ .01	$ .03
Murphy, Rob	90D	186	$ .01	$ .03	Nicosia, Steve	81D	373	$ .01	$ .05

Player	Year	No.	VG	EX/MT
Nicosia, Steve	82D	45	$ .01	$ .05
Nicosia, Steve	83D	528	$ .01	$ .05
Niedenfuer, Tom	83D	536	$ .01	$ .05
Niedenfuer, Tom	84D	128	$ .03	$ .10
Niedenfuer, Tom	85D	153	$ .01	$ .08
Niedenfuer, Tom	86D	397	$ .01	$ .06
Niedenfuer, Tom	87D	218	$ .01	$ .04
Niedenfuer, Tom	88D	294	$ .01	$ .05
Niedenfuer, Tom	89D	282	$ .01	$ .04
Niedenfuer, Tom	89DTR	54	$ .01	$ .05
Niekro, Joe	81D	380	$ .03	$ .20
Niekro, Joe	82D	167	$ .02	$ .10
Niekro, Joe	83D	470	$ .01	$ .05
Niekro, Joe	83D	613	$ .05	$ .30
Niekro, Joe	83DK	10	$ .02	$ .15
Niekro, Joe	84D	110	$ .03	$ .10
Niekro, Joe	86D	601	$ .01	$ .06
Niekro, Joe	86D	645	$ .03	$ .25
Niekro, Joe	87D	217	$ .01	$ .04
Niekro, Phil	81D	328	$ .05	$ .30
Niekro, Phil	82D	475	$ .05	$ .30
Niekro, Phil	82DK	10	$ .05	$ .20
Niekro, Phil	83D	613	$ .05	$ .30
Niekro, Phil	83D	97	$ .06	$ .30
Niekro, Phil	84D	188	$ .15	$ .40
Niekro, Phil	85D	182	$ .01	$ .08
Niekro, Phil	85D	458	$ .08	$ .25
Niekro, Phil	86D	580	$ .08	$ .25
Niekro, Phil	86D	645	$ .03	$ .25
Niekro, Phil	87D	465	$ .08	$ .20
Nielsen, Scott	87D	597	$ .01	$ .15
Niemann, Randy	82D	473	$ .01	$ .05
Nieto, Tom	85D	596	$ .01	$ .08
Nieto, Tom	86D	327	$ .01	$ .06
Nieto, Tom	88D	612	$ .01	$ .15
Nieves, Juan	86DR	12	$ .06	$ .35
Nieves, Juan	86DRR	40	$ .06	$ .30
Nieves, Juan	87D	90	$ .05	$ .20
Nieves, Juan	88D	126	$ .01	$ .05
Nieves, Juan	89D	575	$ .01	$ .04
Nipper, Al	85D	614	$ .03	$ .20
Nipper, Al	86D	538	$ .01	$ .06
Nipper, Al	87D	297	$ .01	$ .04
Nipper, Al	88D	523	$ .01	$ .05
Nipper, Al	88DBB	250	$ .01	$ .05
Nipper, Al	89D	394	$ .01	$ .04
Nixon, Donell	90D	571	$ .01	$ .03
Nixon, Otis	90D	456	$ .01	$ .03
Noce, Paul	87DR	51	$ .01	$ .07
Noce, Paul	88D	315	$ .01	$ .05
Nokes, Matt	87DR	12	$ .10	$ .55
Nokes, Matt	88D	152	$ .10	$ .50
Nokes, Matt	88DBB	237	$ .01	$ .05
Nokes, Matt	89D	116	$ .01	$ .04
Nokes, Matt	89DBB	181	$ .01	$ .04
Nokes, Matt	90D	178	$ .01	$ .03
Nolan, Joe	81D	302	$ .01	$ .05
Nolan, Joe	82D	62	$ .01	$ .05
Nolan, Joe	83D	79	$ .01	$ .05
Nolan, Joe	84D	489	$ .03	$ .10
Nolan, Joe	85D	594	$ .01	$ .08
Noles, Dick	81D	568	$ .01	$ .05
Noles, Dickie	83D	426	$ .01	$ .05
Noles, Dickie	84D	266	$ .03	$ .10
Noles, Dickie	86D	587	$ .01	$ .06
Nolte, Eric	88D	534	$ .01	$ .05
Nordhagen, Wayne	81D	401	$ .01	$ .05
Nordhagen, Wayne	82D	67	$ .01	$ .05
Norman, Fred	81D	92	$ .01	$ .05
Norman, Nelson	81D	509	$ .01	$ .05
Norris, Jim	81D	388	$ .01	$ .05
Norris, Mike	81D	118	$ .01	$ .05
Norris, Mike	82D	197	$ .01	$ .05
Norris, Mike	82DK	19	$ .01	$ .05
Norris, Mike	83D	139	$ .01	$ .05

Player	Year	No.	VG	EX/MT
North, Bill	81D	76	$ .01	$ .05
Norwood, Willie	81D	516	$ .01	$ .05

ED NUNEZ P

Player	Year	No.	VG	EX/MT
Nunez, Ed	84D	435	$ .01	$ .20
Nunez, Ed	85D	484	$ .01	$ .08
Nunez, Ed	86D	145	$ .01	$ .06
Nunez, Ed	87D	243	$ .01	$ .04
Nunez, Ed	88D	445	$ .01	$ .05
Nunez, Edwin	90D	563	$ .01	$ .03
Nunez, Jose	88D	611	$ .01	$ .15
Nunez, Jose	90D	467	$ .01	$ .03
O'Berry, Mike	82D	538	$ .01	$ .05
O'Brien, Charlie	90D	410	$ .01	$ .03
O'Brien, Pete	89DBB	5	$ .01	$ .04
O'Brien, Pete	90D	202	$ .01	$ .03
O'Brien, Pete	90DK	24	$ .01	$ .10
O'Brien, Pete	84D	281	$ .35	$1.50
O'Brien, Pete	85D	178	$ .03	$ .20
O'Brien, Pete	86D	99	$ .02	$ .15
O'Brien, Pete	87D	259	$ .01	$ .04
O'Brien, Pete	88D	284	$ .01	$ .05
O'Brien, Pete	88DBB	167	$ .01	$ .05
O'Brien, Pete	89D	107	$ .01	$ .04
O'Brien, Pete	89DTR	16	$ .01	$ .05
O'Connor, Jack	82D	539	$ .01	$ .05
O'Connor, Jack	83D	51	$ .01	$ .05
O'Malley, Tom	83D	96	$ .01	$ .05
O'Malley, Tom	84D	601	$ .03	$ .10
O'Neal, Randy	86D	394	$ .01	$ .06
O'Neal, Randy	87D	584	$ .01	$ .04
O'Neill, Paul	89DBB	230	$ .01	$ .10
O'Neill, Paul	90D	198	$ .01	$ .10
O'Neill, Paul	86DRR	37	$ .15	$1.50
O'Neill, Paul	88D	433	$ .03	$ .15
O'Neill, Paul	89D	360	$ .01	$ .15
Oberkfell, Ken	81D	583	$ .01	$ .05
Oberkfell, Ken	82D	404	$ .01	$ .05
Oberkfell, Ken	83D	246	$ .01	$ .05
Oberkfell, Ken	84D	504	$ .03	$ .10
Oberkfell, Ken	85D	432	$ .01	$ .08
Oberkfell, Ken	86D	531	$ .01	$ .06
Oberkfell, Ken	87D	437	$ .01	$ .04
Oberkfell, Ken	88D	67	$ .01	$ .05
Oberkfell, Ken	88DBB	226	$ .01	$ .05

Player	Year	No.	VG	EX/MT	Player	Year	No.	VG	EX/MT
Oberkfell, Ken	89D	506	$ .01	$ .04	Orsulak, Joe	89DBB	310	$ .01	$ .04
Oberkfell, Ken	90D	494	$ .01	$ .03	Orsulak, Joe	90D	287	$ .01	$ .03
Oelkers, Bryan	84D	486	$ .03	$ .10	Orta, Jorge	81D	439	$ .01	$ .05
Oelkers, Bryan	87D	596	$ .01	$ .04	Orta, Jorge	82D	211	$ .01	$ .05
Oester, Ron	81D	423	$ .01	$ .05	Orta, Jorge	83D	388	$ .01	$ .05
Oester, Ron	82D	500	$ .01	$ .05	Orta, Jorge	84D	317	$ .03	$ .10
Oester, Ron	83D	526	$ .01	$ .05	Orta, Jorge	85D	130	$ .01	$ .08
Oester, Ron	84D	62	$ .03	$ .10	Orta, Jorge	86D	339	$ .01	$ .06
Oester, Ron	85D	81	$ .01	$ .08	Orta, Jorge	87D	348	$ .01	$ .04
Oester, Ron	86D	81	$ .01	$ .06	Ortiz, Junior	84D	319	$ .03	$ .10
Oester, Ron	87D	206	$ .01	$ .04	Ortiz, Junior	86D	508	$ .01	$ .06
Oester, Ron	88D	246	$ .01	$ .05	Ortiz, Junior	87D	449	$ .01	$ .04
Oester, Ron	89D	553	$ .01	$ .04	Ortiz, Junior	88D	168	$ .01	$ .05
Oester, Ron	90D	317	$ .01	$ .03	Ortiz, Junior	89D	387	$ .01	$ .04
Office, Rowland	81D	213	$ .01	$ .05	Ortiz, Junior	89DBB	269	$ .01	$ .04
Oglivie, Ben	81D	446	$ .01	$ .05	Otis, Amos	81D	104	$ .01	$ .05
Oglivie, Ben	82D	484	$ .01	$ .05	Otis, Amos	82D	70	$ .01	$ .05
Oglivie, Ben	83D	384	$ .01	$ .05	Otis, Amos	83D	364	$ .01	$ .05
Oglivie, Ben	84D	229	$ .03	$ .10	Ott, Ed	81D	133	$ .02	$ .06
Oglivie, Ben	85D	333	$ .01	$ .08	Ott, Ed	82D	192	$ .01	$ .05
Oglivie, Ben	86D	333	$ .01	$ .06	Owchinko, Bob	81D	563	$ .01	$ .05
Oglivie, Ben	87D	419	$ .01	$ .04	Owchinko, Bob	82D	287	$ .01	$ .05
Ojeda, Bob	82D	540	$ .10	$ .50	Owchinko, Bob	83D	265	$ .01	$ .05
Ojeda, Bob	83D	260	$ .01	$ .05	Owchinko, Bob	85D	506	$ .01	$ .08
Ojeda, Bob	84D	538	$ .03	$ .10	Owen, Dave	85D	483	$ .01	$ .08
Ojeda, Bob	85D	371	$ .01	$ .08	Owen, Spike	84D	313	$ .10	$ .40
Ojeda, Bob	86D	636	$ .01	$ .06	Owen, Spike	85D	435	$ .01	$ .08
Ojeda, Bob	87D	364	$ .01	$ .04	Owen, Spike	86D	362	$ .01	$ .06
Ojeda, Bob	88D	632	$ .01	$ .15	Owen, Spike	87D	633	$ .01	$ .04
Ojeda, Bob	88DBB	238	$ .01	$ .05	Owen, Spike	88D	544	$ .01	$ .05
Ojeda, Bob	89D	218	$ .01	$ .04	Owen, Spike	89D	593	$ .01	$ .04
Ojeda, Bob	89DBB	209	$ .01	$ .04	Owen, Spike	89DBB	236	$ .01	$ .04
Ojeda, Bob	90D	117	$ .01	$ .03	Owen, Spike	89DTR	14	$ .01	$ .05
Olerud, John	90D	711	$ .01	$3.00	Owen, Spike	90D	102	$ .01	$ .03
Olin, Steve	90D	438	$ .01	$ .10	Pacella, John	83D	130	$ .01	$ .05
Oliver, Al	81D	387	$ .03	$ .20	Pacillo, Pat	88D	536	$ .01	$ .05
Oliver, Al	82D	116	$ .02	$ .15	Paciorek, Tom	81D	408	$ .01	$ .05
Oliver, Al	83D	140	$ .03	$ .20	Paciorek, Tom	82D	253	$ .01	$ .05
Oliver, Al	84D	177	$ .08	$ .25	Paciorek, Tom	83D	243	$ .01	$ .05
Oliver, Al	84DK	9	$ .08	$ .25	Paciorek, Tom	84D	282	$ .03	$ .10
Oliver, Al	85D	598	$ .03	$ .10	Paciorek, Tom	85D	488	$ .01	$ .08
Oliver, Al	86D	485	$ .01	$ .06	Page, Mitchell	81D	480	$ .01	$ .05
Oliver, Joe	90D	586	$ .01	$ .40	Pagliarulo, Mike	85D	539	$ .40	$1.25
Oliveras, Francisco	89DR	9	$ .01	$ .10	Pagliarulo, Mike	86D	152	$ .03	$ .25
Olson, Gregg	89DBB	322	$ .01	$ .25	Pagliarulo, Mike	87D	298	$ .01	$ .15
Olson, Gregg	89DR	35	$ .01	$ .50	Pagliarulo, Mike	88D	105	$ .01	$ .15
Olson, Gregg	89DRR	46	$ .05	$1.25	Pagliarulo, Mike	88DBB	105	$ .01	$ .10
Olson, Gregg	90D	377	$ .01	$ .20	Pagliarulo, Mike	89D	127	$ .01	$ .04
Olwine, Ed	87D	560	$ .01	$ .04	Pagliarulo, Mike	90D	364	$ .01	$ .03
Ontiveros, Steve	86D	589	$ .01	$ .06	Pagnozzi, Tom	88D	577	$ .01	$ .05
Ontiveros, Steve	87D	221	$ .01	$ .04	Pagnozzi, Tom	89D	399	$ .01	$ .04
Ontiveros, Steve	88D	467	$ .01	$ .05	Pagnozzi, Tom	90D	591	$ .01	$ .03
Ontiveros, Steve	89D	596	$ .01	$ .04	Palacios, Vicente	88DRR	45	$ .10	$ .35
Ontiveros, Steve	89DTR	11	$ .01	$ .05	Pall, Donn	89DR	7	$ .01	$ .10
Oquendo, Jose	84D	643	$ .15	$1.00	Pall, Donn	90D	606	$ .01	$ .03
Oquendo, Jose	87D	510	$ .01	$ .04	Palmeiro, Rafael	87DR	47	$ .25	$ .85
Oquendo, Jose	88D	234	$ .01	$ .05	Palmeiro, Rafael	87DRR	43	$ .45	$2.25
Oquendo, Jose	89D	319	$ .01	$ .04	Palmeiro, Rafael	88D	324	$ .01	$ .25
Oquendo, Jose	89DBB	100	$ .01	$ .04	Palmeiro, Rafael	88DBB	93	$ .10	$ .35
Oquendo, Jose	90D	161	$ .01	$ .03	Palmeiro, Rafael	89D	49	$ .05	$ .25
Orosco, Jesse	82D	646	$ .03	$ .20	Palmeiro, Rafael	89DBB	88	$ .01	$ .10
Orosco, Jesse	83D	434	$ .01	$ .05	Palmeiro, Rafael	89DTR	6	$ .15	$ .50
Orosco, Jesse	84D	197	$ .03	$ .10	Palmeiro, Rafael	90D	225	$ .01	$ .05
Orosco, Jesse	85D	75	$ .01	$ .08	Palmer, Dave	81D	451	$ .01	$ .05
Orosco, Jesse	85DK	22	$ .03	$ .20	Palmer, Dave	83D	68	$ .01	$ .05
Orosco, Jesse	86D	646	$ .01	$ .06	Palmer, Dave	85D	341	$ .01	$ .08
Orosco, Jesse	87D	439	$ .01	$ .04	Palmer, David	86D	254	$ .01	$ .06
Orosco, Jesse	88D	192	$ .01	$ .05	Palmer, David	87D	325	$ .01	$ .04
Orosco, Jesse	88DBB	234	$ .01	$ .05	Palmer, David	88D	266	$ .01	$ .05
Orosco, Jesse	89D	228	$ .01	$ .04	Palmer, David	89D	133	$ .01	$ .04
Orosco, Jesse	89DTR	26	$ .01	$ .05	Palmer, Dean	90D	529	$ .01	$ .40
Orosco, Jesse	90D	154	$ .01	$ .03	Palmer, Jim	81D	353	$ .10	$ .75
Orsulak, Joe	86D	444	$ .01	$ .06	Palmer, Jim	81D	473	$ .10	$ .75
Orsulak, Joe	87D	291	$ .01	$ .04	Palmer, Jim	82D	231	$ .05	$ .75
Orsulak, Joe	89D	287	$ .01	$ .04	Palmer, Jim	83D	77	$ .05	$ .75

Player	Year	No.	VG	EX/MT
Palmer, Jim	83DK	4	$ .05	$ .50
Palmer, Jim	84D	576	$ .15	$1.25
Pankovits, Jim	85D	502	$ .01	$ .08
Pankovits, Jim	86D	450	$ .01	$ .06
Pankovits, Jim	87D	605	$ .01	$ .04
Papi, Stan	81D	246	$ .01	$ .05
Papi, Stan	82D	333	$ .01	$ .05
Pardo, Al	86D	489	$ .01	$ .06
Paredes, Johhny	88DR	29	$ .01	$ .05
Paredes, Johhny	89D	570	$ .01	$ .04

Mark Parent c

Player	Year	No.	VG	EX/MT
Parent, Mark	88DR	8	$ .01	$ .15
Parent, Mark	89D	420	$ .01	$ .15
Parent, Mark	90D	229	$ .01	$ .03
Paris, Kelly	84D	384	$ .03	$ .10
Parker, Clay	89DBB	164	$ .01	$ .04
Parker, Clay	89DR	52	$ .01	$ .10
Parker, Clay	90D	363	$ .01	$ .03
Parker, Dave	81D	136	$ .05	$ .30
Parker, Dave	82D	06	$ .05	$ .30
Parker, Dave	82DK	12	$ .05	$ .30
Parker, Dave	83D	473	$ .05	$ .30
Parker, Dave	84D	288	$ .08	$ .25
Parker, Dave	85D	62	$ .05	$ .30
Parker, Dave	86D	203	$ .03	$ .25
Parker, Dave	87D	388	$ .05	$ .20
Parker, Dave	88D	388	$ .01	$ .15
Parker, Dave	88DBB	190	$ .01	$ .05
Parker, Dave	89D	150	$ .01	$ .04
Parker, Dave	89DBB	336	$ .01	$ .10
Parker, Dave	90D	328	$ .01	$ .03
Parrett, Jeff	88D	406	$ .01	$ .15
Parrett, Jeff	89D	334	$ .01	$ .04
Parrett, Jeff	89DBB	296	$ .01	$ .04
Parrett, Jeff	89DTR	55	$ .01	$ .05
Parrett, Jeff	90D	369	$ .01	$ .03
Parrish, Lance	81D	366	$ .05	$ .30
Parrish, Lance	82D	281	$ .03	$ .20
Parrish, Lance	83D	407	$ .03	$ .20
Parrish, Lance	84D	49	$ .10	$ .35
Parrish, Lance	84DK	15	$ .10	$ .35
Parrish, Lance	85D	49	$ .03	$ .25
Parrish, Lance	86D	334	$ .05	$ .20
Parrish, Lance	87D	91	$ .05	$ .20

Player	Year	No.	VG	EX/MT
Parrish, Lance	88D	359	$ .01	$ .05
Parrish, Lance	88DBB	184	$ .01	$ .05
Parrish, Lance	89D	278	$ .01	$ .04
Parrish, Lance	89DBB	59	$ .01	$ .04
Parrish, Lance	90D	213	$ .01	$ .03
Parrish, Larry	81D	89	$ .01	$ .05
Parrish, Larry	82D	466	$ .01	$ .05
Parrish, Larry	83D	467	$ .01	$ .05
Parrish, Larry	84D	422	$ .03	$ .10
Parrish, Larry	84DK	21	$ .08	$ .25
Parrish, Larry	85D	300	$ .01	$ .08
Parrish, Larry	86D	178	$ .01	$ .06
Parrish, Larry	87D	469	$ .01	$ .04
Parrish, Larry	88D	347	$ .01	$ .05
Parrott, Mike	82D	226	$ .01	$ .05
Pashnick, Larry	83D	233	$ .01	$ .05
Pashnick, Larry	84D	394	$ .03	$ .10
Pasqua, Dan	85D	637	$ .15	$ .50
Pasqua, Dan	86D	417	$ .05	$ .20
Pasqua, Dan	87D	474	$ .05	$ .20
Pasqua, Dan	88D	463	$ .01	$ .05
Pasqua, Dan	88DBB	137	$ .01	$ .05
Pasqua, Dan	89D	294	$ .01	$ .04
Pasqua, Dan	89DBB	123	$ .01	$ .04
Pasqua, Dan	90D	176	$ .01	$ .03
Pastore, Frank	82D	122	$ .01	$ .05
Pastore, Frank	83D	62	$ .01	$ .05
Pastore, Frank	84D	164	$ .03	$ .10
Pastore, Frank	85D	550	$ .01	$ .08
Pate, Bob	81D	545	$ .01	$ .05
Patek, Fred	81D	170	$ .01	$ .05
Patek, Fred	82D	241	$ .01	$ .05
Patterson, Ken	89DR	37	$ .01	$ .10
Patterson, Ken	90D	371	$ .01	$ .03
Pattin, Marty	81D	343	$ .01	$ .05
Pawlowski, John	88D	457	$ .01	$ .05
Pecota, Bill	88D	466	$ .01	$ .05
Pedrique, Al	88D	361	$ .01	$ .05
Pena, Alejandro	84D	250	$ .03	$ .50
Pena, Alejandro	85D	337	$ .03	$ .10
Pena, Alejandro	88D	598	$ .01	$ .05
Pena, Alejandro	89D	557	$ .01	$ .04
Pena, Alejandro	90D	664	$ .01	$ .03
Pena, Hipolito	89D	598	$ .01	$ .04
Pena, Tony	82D	124	$ .10	$ .50
Pena, Tony	83D	59	$ .02	$ .15
Pena, Tony	84D	186	$ .04	$ .25
Pena, Tony	85D	64	$ .05	$ .20
Pena, Tony	85DK	24	$ .03	$ .10
Pena, Tony	86D	64	$ .05	$ .20
Pena, Tony	87D	115	$ .01	$ .04
Pena, Tony	88D	170	$ .01	$ .05
Pena, Tony	88DBB	156	$ .01	$ .05
Pena, Tony	89D	163	$ .01	$ .04
Pena, Tony	89DBB	299	$ .01	$ .04
Pena, Tony	90D	181	$ .01	$ .03
Pendleton, Jeff	85D	534	$ .15	$ .75
Pendleton, Terry	86D	205	$ .01	$ .06
Pendleton, Terry	87D	183	$ .01	$ .15
Pendleton, Terry	88D	454	$ .01	$ .05
Pendleton, Terry	88DBB	187	$ .01	$ .05
Pendleton, Terry	89D	230	$ .01	$ .04
Pendleton, Terry	89DBB	156	$ .01	$ .04
Pendleton, Terry	90D	299	$ .01	$ .03
Peraza, Oswald	89D	524	$ .01	$ .15
Perconte, Jack	83D	463	$ .01	$ .05
Perconte, Jack	85D	74	$ .01	$ .08
Perez, Melido	88D	589	$ .05	$ .20
Perez, Melido	88DBB	179	$ .01	$ .15
Perez, Melido	88DR	21	$ .01	$ .15
Perez, Melido	89D	58	$ .01	$ .15
Perez, Melido	89DBB	179	$ .01	$ .04
Perez, Melido	90D	101	$ .01	$ .03
Perez, Pascual	83D	557	$ .05	$ .25
Perez, Pascual	84D	507	$ .05	$ .35

Player	Year	No.	VG	EX/MT
Perez, Pascual	85D	507	$ .01	$ .08
Perez, Pascual	88D	591	$ .01	$ .05
Perez, Pascual	88DBB	236	$ .01	$ .05
Perez, Pascual	89D	248	$ .01	$ .04
Perez, Pascual	89DBB	302	$ .01	$ .04
Perez, Pascual	90D	342	$ .01	$ .03
Perez, Tony	81D	334	$ .05	$ .30
Perez, Tony	82D	408	$ .05	$ .30
Perez, Tony	83D	578	$ .03	$ .20
Perez, Tony	84D	503	$ .10	$ .35
Perez, Tony	86D	428	$ .03	$ .25
Perez, Tony	86DK	15	$ .05	$ .20
Perkins, Broderick	81D	525	$ .01	$ .05
Perkins, Broderick	82D	397	$ .01	$ .05
Perkins, Broderick	83D	121	$ .01	$ .05
Perkins, Broderick	84D	276	$ .03	$ .10
Perry, Gaylord	81D	471	$ .05	$ .30
Perry, Gaylord	82D	543	$ .05	$ .30
Perry, Gaylord	83D	307	$ .03	$ .20
Perry, Gaylord	84D#A	0	$1.00	$3.00
Perry, Gerald	84D	263	$ .25	$1.50

GERALD PERRY 1B-OF

Player	Year	No.	VG	EX/MT
Perry, Gerald	85D	443	$ .05	$ .25
Perry, Gerald	86D	165	$ .01	$ .06
Perry, Gerald	88D	437	$ .01	$ .05
Perry, Gerald	88DBB	58	$ .01	$ .05
Perry, Gerald	89D	239	$ .01	$ .04
Perry, Gerald	89DBB	291	$ .01	$ .04
Perry, Gerald	89DBC	24	$ .01	$ .10
Perry, Gerald	89DK	22	$ .01	$ .05
Perry, Gerald	90D	153	$ .01	$ .03
Perry, Pat	86D	596	$ .01	$ .06
Perry, Pat	87D	430	$ .01	$ .04
Perry, Pat	88D	626	$ .01	$ .15
Perry, Pat	89D	404	$ .01	$ .05
Peterek, Jeff	90D	530	$ .01	$ .10
Peters, Rick	81D	10	$ .01	$ .05
Peters, Rick	82D	155	$ .01	$ .05
Peters, Steve	88DR	22	$ .01	$ .05
Peterson, Adam	89D	619	$ .01	$ .10
Petralli, Geno	83D	623	$ .01	$ .05
Petralli, Geno	87D	619	$ .01	$ .04
Petralli, Geno	88D	506	$ .01	$ .05
Petralli, Geno	89D	343	$ .01	$ .04

Player	Year	No.	VG	EX/MT
Petralli, Geno	89DBB	312	$ .01	$ .04
Petralli, Geno	90D	56	$ .01	$ .03
Petry, Dan	81D	128	$ .01	$ .05
Petry, Dan	82D	133	$ .01	$ .05
Petry, Dan	83D	359	$ .01	$ .05
Petry, Dan	84D	105	$ .03	$ .10
Petry, Dan	85D	334	$ .01	$ .08
Petry, Dan	86D	212	$ .01	$ .06
Petry, Dan	87D	373	$ .01	$ .04
Petry, Dan	88D	476	$ .01	$ .05
Petry, Dan	88DBB	139	$ .01	$ .05
Petry, Dan	89D	344	$ .01	$ .04
Pettis, Gary	84D	647	$ .04	$ .50
Pettis, Gary	85D	499	$ .01	$ .08
Pettis, Gary	86D	158	$ .01	$ .06
Pettis, Gary	87D	160	$ .01	$ .04
Pettis, Gary	88D	210	$ .01	$ .05
Pettis, Gary	88DBB	203	$ .05	$ .25
Pettis, Gary	89D	60	$ .01	$ .04
Pettis, Gary	90D	661	$ .01	$ .03
Phelps, Ken	85D	318	$ .05	$ .35
Phelps, Ken	87D	317	$ .01	$ .04
Phelps, Ken	88D	489	$ .01	$ .05
Phelps, Ken	88DBB	248	$ .01	$ .05
Phelps, Ken	89D	363	$ .01	$ .04
Phelps, Ken	89DBB	276	$ .01	$ .04
Phelps, Ken	90D	675	$ .01	$ .03
Phillips, Mike	81D	188	$ .01	$ .05
Phillips, Tony	84D	278	$ .03	$ .10
Phillips, Tony	85D	101	$ .01	$ .08
Phillips, Tony	86D	542	$ .01	$ .06
Phillips, Tony	87D	103	$ .01	$ .04
Phillips, Tony	88D	221	$ .01	$ .05
Phillips, Tony	89DBB	211	$ .01	$ .04
Phillips, Tony	90D	91	$ .01	$ .03
Picciolo, Rob	81D	357	$ .01	$ .05
Picciolo, Rob	82D	465	$ .01	$ .05
Picciolo, Rob	83D	456	$ .01	$ .05
Picciolo, Rob	84D	455	$ .03	$ .10
Picciolo, Rob	86D	497	$ .01	$ .06
Pico, Jeff	89D	513	$ .01	$ .10
Pico, Jeff	90D	585	$ .01	$ .03
Piniella, Lou	81D	109	$ .03	$ .20
Piniella, Lou	82D	135	$ .03	$ .20
Piniella, Lou	83D	335	$ .01	$ .05
Piniella, Lou	84D	274	$ .04	$ .15
Pinson, Vada	82D	445	$ .03	$ .20
Pittaro, Chris	86D	150	$ .01	$ .06
Pittman, Joe	82D	218	$ .01	$ .05
Pittman, Joe	83D	247	$ .01	$ .05
Plesac, Dan	86DR	14	$ .05	$ .30
Plesac, Dan	87D	214	$ .03	$ .25
Plesac, Dan	88D	109	$ .01	$ .05
Plesac, Dan	88DBB	221	$ .01	$ .05
Plesac, Dan	89D	382	$ .01	$ .04
Plesac, Dan	89DBB	165	$ .01	$ .04
Plesac, Dan	90D	175	$ .01	$ .03
Plunk, Eric	86DR	40	$ .05	$ .25
Plunk, Eric	87D	178	$ .01	$ .04
Plunk, Eric	88D	503	$ .01	$ .05
Plunk, Eric	88DBB	267	$ .01	$ .05
Plunk, Eric	89D	125	$ .01	$ .04
Plunk, Eric	89DBB	49	$ .01	$ .04
Plunk, Eric	90D	196	$ .01	$ .03
Pocoroba, Biff	83D	436	$ .01	$ .05
Pocoroba, Biff	84D	77	$ .03	$ .10
Podres, Johnny	82D	566	$ .01	$ .05
Polidor, Gus	87D	579	$ .01	$ .04
Polidor, Gus	88D	356	$ .01	$ .05
Polidor, Gus	90D	412	$ .01	$ .03
Polonia, Luis	87DR	25	$ .10	$ .35
Polonia, Luis	88D	425	$ .04	$ .20
Polonia, Luis	89D	386	$ .01	$ .04
Polonia, Luis	90D	547	$ .01	$ .03
Ponce, Carlos	86D	595	$ .01	$ .06

Player	Year	No.	VG	EX/MT	Player	Year	No.	VG	EX/MT
Porter, Chuck	84D	333	$ .03	$ .10	Puhl, Terry	89DBB	294	$ .01	$ .04
Porter, Chuck	85D	115	$ .01	$ .08	Puhl, Terry	90D	354	$ .01	$ .03
Porter, Darrell	81D	505	$ .01	$ .05	Pujols, Luis	81D	379	$ .01	$ .05
Porter, Darrell	82D	498	$ .03	$ .20	Pujols, Luis	82D	576	$ .01	$ .05
Porter, Darrell	83D	278	$ .01	$ .05	Pujols, Luis	83D	642	$ .01	$ .05
Porter, Darrell	84D	303	$ .03	$ .10	Puleo, Charlie	83D	128	$ .01	$ .05
Porter, Darrell	85D	353	$ .01	$ .08	Puleo, Charlie	84D	530	$ .03	$ .10
Porter, Darrell	86D	290	$ .01	$ .06	Puleo, Charlie	88D	537	$ .01	$ .05
Porter, Darrell	87D	593	$ .01	$ .04	Puleo, Charlie	89D	286	$ .01	$ .04
Portugal, Mark	86DR	44	$ .01	$ .25	Pulido, Alfonso	85DRR	34	$ .01	$ .08
Portugal, Mark	87D	566	$ .01	$ .25	Putnam, Pat	81D	265	$ .01	$ .05
Portugal, Mark	90D	542	$ .01	$ .03	Putnam, Pat	82D	520	$ .01	$ .05
Powell, Dennis	86D	250	$ .01	$ .06	Putnam, Pat	84D	145	$ .03	$ .10
Powell, Dennis	87D	499	$ .01	$ .04	Pyznarski, Tim	87D	654	$ .01	$ .04
Powell, Hosken	81D	567	$ .01	$ .05	Quinones (nez), Rey	86DR	48	$ .02	$ .09
Powell, Hosken	82D	228	$ .01	$ .05	Quinones (nez), Rey	87D	638	$ .01	$ .04
Powell, Hosken	83D	644	$ .01	$ .05	Quinones, Luis	88D	365	$ .01	$ .05
Power, Ted	84D	447	$ .03	$ .10	Quinones, Luis	90D	595	$ .01	$ .03
Power, Ted	85D	286	$ .01	$ .08	Quinones, Rey	88D	198	$ .01	$ .04
Power, Ted	86D	408	$ .01	$ .06	Quinones, Rey	89D	330	$ .01	$ .04
Power, Ted	87D	536	$ .01	$ .04	Quinones, Rey	89DBB	185	$ .01	$ .04
Power, Ted	88D	142	$ .01	$ .05	Quintana, Carlos	89DRR	37	$ .05	$ .35
Power, Ted	89D	153	$ .01	$ .04	Quintana, Carlos	90D	517	$ .01	$ .10
Power, Ted	90D	653	$ .01	$ .03	Quirk, Jamie	81D	341	$ .01	$ .05
Presley, Jim	85D	240	$ .30	$1.00	Quirk, Jamie	82D	212	$ .01	$ .05
Presley, Jim	86D	313	$ .01	$ .15	Quirk, Jamie	88D	404	$ .01	$ .05
Presley, Jim	87D	120	$ .01	$ .10	Quisenberry, Dan	81D	222	$ .05	$ .30
Presley, Jim	87DK	23	$ .01	$ .04	Quisenberry, Dan	82D	112	$ .02	$ .15
Presley, Jim	88D	366	$ .01	$ .15	Quisenberry, Dan	83D	70	$ .02	$ .15
Presley, Jim	88DBB	219	$ .01	$ .05	Quisenberry, Dan	84D	583	$ .08	$ .25
Presley, Jim	89D	379	$ .01	$ .04	Quisenberry, Dan	85D	95	$ .03	$ .20
Presley, Jim	89DBB	331	$ .01	$ .04	Quisenberry, Dan	85DK	6	$ .05	$ .20
Presley, Jim	90D	497	$ .01	$ .03	Quisenberry, Dan	86D	541	$ .05	$ .20
Price, Joe	82D	481	$ .01	$ .05	Quisenberry, Dan	87D	177	$ .01	$ .04
Price, Joe	83D	481	$ .01	$ .05	Quisenberry, Dan	88D	471	$ .01	$ .15
Price, Joe	84D	506	$ .03	$ .10	Quisenberry, Dan	90D	437	$ .01	$ .03
Price, Joe	85D	627	$ .01	$ .08	Rabb, John	84D	143	$ .03	$ .10
Price, Joe	86D	506	$ .01	$ .06	Rabb, John	85D	236	$ .01	$ .08
Price, Joe	88D	655	$ .01	$ .15	Rader, Dave	81D	512	$ .01	$ .05
Price, Joe	89D	376	$ .01	$ .04	Raines, Tim	81D	538	$1.00	$5.00
Prince, Tom	88D	538	$ .01	$ .05	Raines, Tim	82D	214	$ .20	$1.00
Prince, Tom	89D	527	$ .01	$ .04	Raines, Tim	83D	540	$ .15	$ .60
Proly, Mike	81D	596	$ .01	$ .05	Raines, Tim	84D	299	$ .25	$ .75
Proly, Mike	82D	345	$ .01	$ .05	Raines, Tim	85D	299	$ .15	$ .60
Proly, Mike	83D	225	$ .01	$ .05	Raines, Tim	86D	177	$ .08	$ .30
Proly, Mike	84D	320	$ .03	$ .10	Raines, Tim	87D	56	$ .08	$ .25
Pryor, Greg	81D	278	$ .01	$ .05	Raines, Tim	88D	345	$ .03	$ .25
Pryor, Greg	82D	521	$ .01	$ .05	Raines, Tim	88DBB	180	$ .01	$ .15
Pryor, Greg	83D	264	$ .01	$ .05	Raines, Tim	88DBC	18	$ .05	$ .25
Pryor, Greg	84D	374	$ .03	$ .10	Raines, Tim	88DK	2	$ .10	$ .25
Pryor, Greg	85D	277	$ .01	$ .08	Raines, Tim	89D	97	$ .01	$ .10
Pryor, Greg	86D	344	$ .01	$ .06	Raines, Tim	89DBB	258	$ .01	$ .15
Pryor, Greg	87D	378	$ .01	$ .04	Raines, Tim	90D	216	$ .01	$ .10
Puckett, Kirby	85D	438	$4.50	$22.50	Raines, Tim	90DBC	7	$ .01	$ .10
Puckett, Kirby	86D	72	$ .50	$4.00	Rainey, Chuck	83D	334	$ .01	$ .05
Puckett, Kirby	87D	149	$ .25	$1.50	Rainey, Chuck	84D	76	$ .03	$ .10
Puckett, Kirby	87DK	19	$ .10	$ .35	Rainey, Chuck	85D	618	$ .01	$ .08
Puckett, Kirby	88D	368	$ .01	$ .25	Rajsich, Dave	81D	267	$ .01	$ .05
Puckett, Kirby	88DBB	186	$ .10	$ .35	Rajsich, Gary	83D	599	$ .01	$ .05
Puckett, Kirby	88DBC	15	$ .01	$ .25	Ramirez, Allan	84D	332	$ .03	$ .10
Puckett, Kirby	89D	182	$ .01	$ .25	Ramirez, Mario	86D	568	$ .01	$ .06
Puckett, Kirby	89DBB	130	$ .01	$ .25	Ramirez, Rafael	82D	546	$ .01	$ .05
Puckett, Kirby	89DBC	1	$ .05	$ .30	Ramirez, Rafael	83D	310	$ .01	$ .05
Puckett, Kirby	90D	269	$ .01	$ .25	Ramirez, Rafael	84D	589	$ .03	$ .10
Puckett, Kirby	90DAS	683	$ .01	$ .15	Ramirez, Rafael	85D	141	$ .01	$ .08
Puckett, Kirby	90DBC	8	$ .01	$ .15	Ramirez, Rafael	86D	263	$ .01	$ .06
Puhl, Terry	81D	24	$ .01	$ .05	Ramirez, Rafael	87D	202	$ .01	$ .04
Puhl, Terry	82D	370	$ .01	$ .05	Ramirez, Rafael	88D	448	$ .01	$ .05
Puhl, Terry	83D	167	$ .01	$ .05	Ramirez, Rafael	89D	509	$ .01	$ .04
Puhl, Terry	84D	476	$ .03	$ .10	Ramirez, Rafael	89DBB	64	$ .01	$ .04
Puhl, Terry	85D	426	$ .01	$ .08	Ramirez, Rafael	90D	241	$ .01	$ .03
Puhl, Terry	86D	206	$ .01	$ .06	Ramos, Bobby	84D	209	$ .03	$ .10
Puhl, Terry	87D	431	$ .01	$ .04	Ramos, Domingo	84D	440	$ .03	$ .10
Puhl, Terry	88D	533	$ .01	$ .05	Ramos, Domingo	88D	622	$ .01	$ .15
Puhl, Terry	89D	472	$ .01	$ .04	Ramos, Domingo	90D	491	$ .01	$ .03

Player	Year	No.	VG	EX/MT	Player	Year	No.	VG	EX/MT
Ramsey, Mike	82D	316	$ .01	$ .05	Redus, Gary	84D	184	$ .03	$ .25
Ramsey, Mike	83D	568	$ .01	$ .05	Redus, Gary	85D	306	$ .01	$ .08
Ramsey, Mike	84D	382	$ .03	$ .10	Redus, Gary	86D	306	$ .01	$ .06
Randle, Lenny	81D	485	$ .01	$ .05	Redus, Gary·	87D	288	$ .01	$ .04
Randle, Lenny	82D	307	$ .01	$ .05	Redus, Gary	88D	370	$ .01	$ .05
Randolph, Willie	81D	345	$ .01	$ .05	Redus, Gary	89D	605	$ .01	$ .04
Randolph, Willie	82D	461	$ .01	$ .05	Redus, Gary	90D	597	$ .01	$ .03
Randolph, Willie	83D	283	$ .01	$ .05	Reed, Jeff	85DRR	30	$ .01	$ .08
Randolph, Willie	84D	417	$ .03	$ .10	Reed, Jeff	88D	88	$ .01	$ .05
Randolph, Willie	85D	92	$ .01	$ .08	Reed, Jeff	89D	469	$ .01	$ .04
Randolph, Willie	86D	92	$ .01	$ .06	Reed, Jeff	90D	351	$ .01	$ .03
Randolph, Willie	86DK	16	$ .01	$ .06	Reed, Jerry	88D	517	$ .01	$ .05
Randolph, Willie	87D	154	$ .01	$ .04	Reed, Jerry	89D	657	$ .01	$ .04
Randolph, Willie	88D	228	$ .01	$ .05	Reed, Jerry	90D	614	$ .01	$ .03
Randolph, Willie	88DBB	108	$ .01	$ .05	Reed, Jody	88DBB	196	$ .01	$ .50
Randolph, Willie	89D	395	$ .01	$ .04	Reed, Jody	88DR	44	$ .05	$ .25
Randolph, Willie	89DBB	148	$ .01	$ .04	Reed, Jody	88DRR	41	$ .05	$ .35
Randolph, Willie	89DTR	8	$ .01	$ .15	Reed, Jody	89D	305	$ .01	$ .04
Randolph, Willie	90D	250	$ .01	$ .03	Reed, Jody	89DBB	289	$ .01	$ .04
Randolph, Willie	90DK	19	$ .01	$ .10	Reed, Jody	90D	398	$ .01	$ .03
Rasmussen, Dennis	84D	446	$ .15	$ .50	Reed, Rick	90D	527	$ .01	$ .10
Rasmussen, Dennis	85D	518	$ .01	$ .08	Reed, Ron	81D	44	$ .01	$ .05
Rasmussen, Dennis	86D	336	$ .01	$ .06	Reed, Ron	82D	399	$ .01	$ .05
Rasmussen, Dennis	87D	175	$ .01	$ .04	Reed, Ron	83D	567	$ .01	$ .05
Rasmussen, Dennis	88D	575	$ .01	$ .15	Reed, Ron	84D	529	$ .03	$ .10
Rasmussen, Dennis	89D	559	$ .01	$ .04	Reed, Ron	85D	282	$ .01	$ .08
Rasmussen, Dennis	90D	420	$ .01	$ .10	Reitz, Ken	81D	307	$ .01	$ .05
Rasmussen, Eric	81D	123	$ .01	$ .05	Reitz, Ken	82D	277	$ .01	$ .05
Rawley, Shane	81D	167	$ .01	$ .05	Remmerswaal, Win	81D	98	$ .01	$ .05
Rawley, Shane	82D	352	$ .01	$ .05	Remy, Jerry	81D	215	$ .01	$ .05
Rawley, Shane	83D	513	$ .01	$ .05	Remy, Jerry	82D	156	$ .01	$ .05
Rawley, Shane	84D	295	$ .03	$ .10	Remy, Jerry	83D	74	$ .01	$ .05
Rawley, Shane	85D	599	$ .01	$ .08	Remy, Jerry	84D	172	$ .03	$ .10
Rawley, Shane	86D	233	$ .01	$ .06	Renko, Steve	81D	337	$ .01	$ .05
Rawley, Shane	87D	83	$ .01	$ .04	Renko, Steve	82D	38	$ .01	$ .05
Rawley, Shane	88D	83	$ .01	$ .05	Renko, Steve	83D	393	$ .01	$ .05
Rawley, Shane	88DBB	240	$ .01	$ .05	Reuschel, Rick	81D	561	$ .02	$ .20
Rawley, Shane	88DK	13	$ .01	$ .05	Reuschel, Rick	82D	157	$ .01	$ .10
Rawley, Shane	89D	251	$ .01	$ .04	Reuschel, Rick	86D	532	$ .01	$ .10
Rawley, Shane	90D	537	$ .01	$ .03	Reuschel, Rick	87D	188	$ .01	$ .15
Ray, Johnny	82D	528	$ .15	$ .75	Reuschel, Rick	88D	613	$ .01	$ .15
Ray, Johnny	83D	437	$ .03	$ .20	Reuschel, Rick	88DBB	218	$ .01	$ .05
Ray, Johnny	84D	308	$ .03	$ .20	Reuschel, Rick	89D	335	$ .01	$ .04
Ray, Johnny	85D	186	$ .01	$ .10	Reuschel, Rick	89DBB	162	$ .01	$ .04
Ray, Johnny	86D	186	$ .05	$ .20	Reuschel, Rick	89DK	11	$ .01	$ .05
Ray, Johnny	86DK	19	$ .01	$ .06	Reuschel, Rick	90D	112	$ .01	$ .03
Ray, Johnny	87D	144	$ .01	$ .04	Reuschel, Rick	90DAS	663	$ .01	$ .03
Ray, Johnny	88D	428	$ .01	$ .05	Reuss, Jerry	81D	417	$ .01	$ .05
Ray, Johnny	88DBB	171	$ .01	$ .05	Reuss, Jerry	82D	284	$ .01	$ .05
Ray, Johnny	89D	331	$ .01	$ .04	Reuss, Jerry	83D	158	$ .01	$ .05
Ray, Johnny	89DBB	195	$ .01	$ .04	Reuss, Jerry	84D	418	$ .03	$ .10
Ray, Johnny	89DK	12	$ .01	$ .05	Reuss, Jerry	85D	226	$ .01	$ .08
Ray, Johnny	90D	234	$ .01	$ .03	Reuss, Jerry	86D	104	$ .02	$ .15
Rayford, Floyd	85D	576	$ .01	$ .08	Reuss, Jerry	89D	413	$ .01	$ .04
Rayford, Floyd	86D	332	$ .01	$ .06	Reuss, Jerry	89DBB	305	$ .01	$ .04
Ready, Randy	86D	481	$ .01	$ .06	Reuss, Jerry	90D	528	$ .01	$ .03
Ready, Randy	88D	264	$ .01	$ .05	Revering, Dave	81D	117	$ .01	$ .05
Ready, Randy	89D	365	$ .01	$ .04	Revering, Dave	82D	234	$ .01	$ .05
Ready, Randy	89DBB	215	$ .01	$ .04	Reyes, Gilberto	86D	581	$ .01	$ .06
Ready, Randy	90D	396	$ .01	$ .03	Reynolds, Craig	81D	378	$ .01	$ .05
Reardon, Jeff	81D	156	$ .25	$1.00	Reynolds, Craig	82D	344	$ .01	$ .05
Reardon, Jeff	82D	547	$ .01	$ .25	Reynolds, Craig	83D	317	$ .01	$ .05
Reardon, Jeff	83D	194	$ .01	$ .05	Reynolds, Craig	84D	405	$ .03	$ .10
Reardon, Jeff	84D	279	$ .03	$ .10	Reynolds, Craig	85D	328	$ .01	$ .08
Reardon, Jeff	85D	331	$ .01	$ .08	Reynolds, Craig	86D	232	$ .01	$ .06
Reardon, Jeff	86D	209	$ .01	$ .06	Reynolds, Craig	87D	384	$ .01	$ .04
Reardon, Jeff	87D	98	$ .01	$ .04	Reynolds, Craig	88D	209	$ .01	$ .05
Reardon, Jeff	88D	122	$ .01	$ .05	Reynolds, Craig	89D	477	$ .01	$ .04
Reardon, Jeff	88DBB	242	$ .01	$ .05	Reynolds, Harold	86D	484	$ .05	$ .65
Reardon, Jeff	89D	155	$ .01	$ .04	Reynolds, Harold	87D	489	$ .01	$ .10
Reardon, Jeff	89DBB	242	$ .01	$ .04	Reynolds, Harold	88D	563	$ .01	$ .05
Reardon, Jeff	90D	119	$ .01	$ .03	Reynolds, Harold	89D	93	$ .01	$ .04
Redfern, Pete	81D	548	$ .01	$ .05	Reynolds, Harold	89DBB	51	$ .01	$ .04
Redfern, Pete	82D	51	$ .01	$ .05	Reynolds, Harold	89DK	21	$ .01	$ .05
Redfern, Pete	83D	256	$ .01	$ .05	Reynolds, Harold	90D	227	$ .01	$ .03

Player	Year	No.	VG	EX/MT
Reynolds, R. J.	89DBB	257	$ .01	$ .04
Reynolds, R. J.	90D	447	$ .01	$ .03
Reynolds, R.J.	85D	128	$ .08	$ .25
Reynolds, R.J.	86D	552	$ .01	$ .06
Reynolds, R.J.	87D	65	$ .01	$ .04
Reynolds, R.J.	88D	65	$ .01	$ .05
Reynolds, R.J.	88DBB	201	$ .01	$ .05
Reynolds, R.J.	89D	134	$ .01	$ .04
Rhoden, Rick	82D	423	$ .01	$ .05
Rhoden, Rick	83D	250	$ .01	$ .05
Rhoden, Rick	84D	552	$ .03	$ .10
Rhoden, Rick	85D	552	$ .01	$ .08
Rhoden, Rick	86D	166	$ .01	$ .06
Rhoden, Rick	87D	435	$ .01	$ .04
Rhoden, Rick	87DK	10	$ .01	$ .04
Rhoden, Rick	88D	128	$ .01	$ .05
Rhoden, Rick	88DBB	161	$ .01	$ .05
Rhoden, Rick	89D	429	$ .01	$ .04
Rhoden, Rick	89DTR	40	$ .01	$ .10
Rice, Jim	81D	338	$ .10	$ .35
Rice, Jim	82D	200	$ .10	$ .40
Rice, Jim	83D	208	$ .05	$ .30
Rice, Jim	84D	50	$ .10	$ .40
Rice, Jim	85D	50	$ .15	$ .50
Rice, Jim	85DK	15	$ .15	$ .50
Rice, Jim	86D	213	$ .03	$ .25
Rice, Jim	87D	92	$ .03	$ .25
Rice, Jim	88D	399	$ .04	$ .20
Rice, Jim	88DBB	28	$ .01	$ .15
Rice, Jim	89D	122	$ .01	$ .15
Richard, J.R.	81D	140	$ .02	$ .15
Richards, Gene	81D	4	$ .01	$ .05
Richards, Gene	82D	499	$ .01	$ .05
Richards, Gene	83D	271	$ .01	$ .05
Richards, Gene	84D	429	$ .03	$ .10
Richardt, Mike	83D	368	$ .01	$ .05
Righetti, Dave	82D	73	$ .30	$1.75
Righetti, Dave	83D	199	$ .05	$ .25
Righetti, Dave	84D	103	$ .08	$ .25
Righetti, Dave	84DK	10	$ .08	$ .25
Righetti, Dave	85D	336	$ .03	$ .20
Righetti, Dave	86D	214	$ .01	$ .06
Righetti, Dave	87D	128	$ .01	$ .04
Righetti, Dave	88D	93	$ .01	$ .15
Righetti, Dave	88DBB	164	$ .01	$ .05
Righetti, Dave	89D	78	$ .01	$ .04
Righetti, Dave	89DBB	76	$ .01	$ .04
Righetti, Dave	90D	311	$ .01	$ .03
Rijo, Jose	85D	492	$ .20	$ .75
Rijo, Jose	86D	522	$ .05	$ .25
Rijo, Jose	87D	55	$ .04	$ .20
Rijo, Jose	88D	548	$ .01	$ .15
Rijo, Jose	89D	375	$ .01	$ .04
Rijo, Jose	89DBB	278	$ .01	$ .04
Rijo, Jose	90D	115	$ .01	$ .03
Riles, Ernest	87D	151	$ .01	$ .04
Riles, Ernest	88D	478	$ .01	$ .05
Riles, Ernest	89D	625	$ .01	$ .04
Riles, Ernest	89DBB	50	$ .01	$ .04
Riles, Ernest	90D	131	$ .01	$ .03
Riles, Ernset	86D	359	$ .03	$ .25
Riley, George	81D	588	$ .01	$ .05
Ripken, Billy	87DR	16	$ .15	$ .50
Ripken, Billy	88D	336	$ .06	$ .30
Ripken, Billy	88D	625	$ .05	$ .30
Ripken, Billy	88DBB	254	$ .01	$ .10
Ripken, Billy	89D	259	$ .01	$ .04
Ripken, Billy	89DBB	318	$ .01	$ .04
Ripken, Billy	90D	164	$ .01	$ .03
Ripken, Cal	89DBB	142	$ .01	$ .10
Ripken, Cal	90D	96	$ .01	$ .10
Ripken, Cal	90DAS	676	$ .01	$ .10
Ripken, Cal	90DBC	18	$ .01	$ .10
Ripken, Jr., Cal	82D	405	$1.50	$10.00
Ripken, Jr., Cal	83D	279	$ .25	$1.50

Player	Year	No.	VG	EX/MT
Ripken, Jr., Cal	84D	106	$ .40	$2.25
Ripken, Jr., Cal	85D	169	$ .15	$ .75
Ripken, Jr., Cal	85DK	14	$ .15	$ .50
Ripken, Jr., Cal	86D	210	$ .15	$ .50
Ripken, Jr., Cal	87D	89	$ .08	$ .25
Ripken, Jr., Cal	88D	171	$ .03	$ .25
Ripken, Jr., Cal	88D	625	$ .05	$ .30
Ripken, Jr., Cal	88DBB	198	$ .05	$ .25
Ripken, Jr., Cal	88DBC	1	$ .05	$ .25
Ripken, Jr., Cal	88DK	26	$ .10	$ .25
Ripken, Jr., Cal	89D	51	$ .04	$ .20
Ripken, Jr., Cal	89DBC	15	$ .01	$ .20
Ripken, Sr., Cal	82D	579	$ .03	$ .20
Ripken, Sr., Cal	88D	625	$ .05	$ .30
Ripley, Allen	82D	125	$ .01	$ .05
Ripley, Allen	83D	57	$ .01	$ .05
Ritchie, Wally	88D	555	$ .01	$ .05
Ritz, Kevin	90D	415	$ .01	$ .10
Rivera, Bombo	81D	593	$ .01	$ .05
Rivera, German	85D	638	$ .01	$ .08
Rivera, Luis	89D	578	$ .01	$ .04
Rivera, Luis	90D	421	$ .01	$ .03

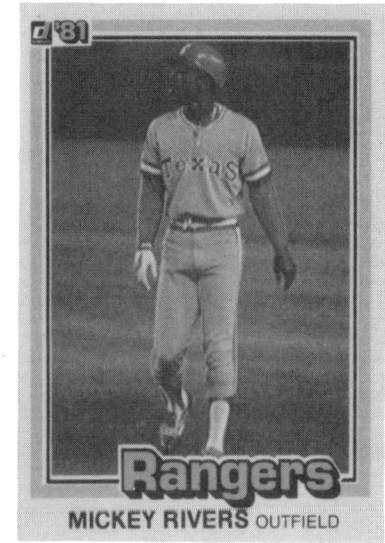

MICKEY RIVERS OUTFIELD

Player	Year	No.	VG	EX/MT
Rivers, Mickey	81D	496	$ .02	$ .15
Rivers, Mickey	82D	242	$ .02	$ .15
Rivers, Mickey	83D	394	$ .01	$ .05
Rivers, Mickey	84D	465	$ .03	$ .10
Rivers, Mickey	85D	465	$ .01	$ .08
Robbins, Bruce	81D	129	$ .01	$ .05
Roberge, Bert	83D	496	$ .01	$ .05
Roberge, Bert	86D	575	$ .01	$ .06
Roberts, Bip	90D	347	$ .01	$ .03
Roberts, Dave	81D	490	$ .01	$ .05
Roberts, Dave	81D	501	$ .01	$ .05
Roberts, Dave	82D	625	$ .01	$ .05
Roberts, Dave	83D	273	$ .01	$ .05
Roberts, Leon	81D	48	$ .01	$ .05
Roberts, Leon	82D	415	$ .01	$ .05
Roberts, Leon	84D	399	$ .03	$ .10
Roberts, Leon (Bip)	86DR	33	$ .01	$ .25
Roberts, Leon (Bip)	87D	114	$ .01	$ .15
Robertson, Andre	83D	387	$ .01	$ .05
Robertson, Andre	84D	347	$ .03	$ .10
Robertson, Andre	86D	469	$ .01	$ .06

Player	Year	No.	VG	EX/MT	Player	Year	No.	VG	EX/MT
Robidoux, Billy	86D	515	$ .05	$ .20	Roenicke, Gary	85D	123	$ .01	$ .08
Robidoux, Billy	87D	240	$ .01	$ .04	Roenicke, Gary	86D	472	$ .01	$ .06
Robinson, Bill	81D	137	$ .01	$ .05	Roenicke, Ron	83D	327	$ .01	$ .05
					Roenicke, Ron	84D	392	$ .03	$ .10
					Roenicke, Ron	84D	484	$ .03	$ .10
					Roenicke, Ron	87D	412	$ .01	$ .04
					Rogers, Kenny	89DBB	315	$ .01	$ .15
					Rogers, Kenny	89DR	13	$ .01	$ .25
					Rogers, Kenny	90D	283	$ .01	$ .10
					Rogers, Steve	81D	330	$ .01	$ .05
					Rogers, Steve	82D	36	$ .01	$ .05
					Rogers, Steve	83D	320	$ .01	$ .05
					Rogers, Steve	83DK	18	$ .01	$ .05
					Rogers, Steve	84D	219	$ .03	$ .10
					Rogers, Steve	85D	219	$ .01	$ .08
					Romanick, Ron	85D	451	$ .01	$ .08
					Romanick, Ron	86D	85	$ .01	$ .06
					Romero, Ed	82D	536	$ .01	$ .05
					Romero, Ed	83D	584	$ .01	$ .05
					Romero, Ed	84D	89	$ .03	$ .10
					Romero, Ed	85D	515	$ .01	$ .08
					Romero, Ed	86D	455	$ .01	$ .06
					Romero, Ed	87D	606	$ .01	$ .04
					Romero, Ed	88D	623	$ .01	$ .15
					Romero, Ramon	86D	495	$ .01	$ .06
					Romine, Kevin	90D	476	$ .01	$ .03
					Romo, Enrique	81D	255	$ .01	$ .05
					Romo, Enrique	82D	59	$ .01	$ .05
					Roof, Phil	82D	615	$ .01	$ .05
					Roomes, Rolando	89D	577	$ .05	$ .45
					Roomes, Rolando	90D	360	$ .01	$ .03
					Rose, Pete	81D	131	$ .25	$1.00
					Rose, Pete	81D	251	$ .25	$1.25
					Rose, Pete	81D	371	$ .25	$1.25
					Rose, Pete	82D	168	$ .25	$1.25
Robinson, Bill	82D	402	$ .01	$ .05	Rose, Pete	82D	585	$ .15	$1.25
Robinson, Don	81D	375	$ .01	$ .05	Rose, Pete	82DK	1	$ .25	$1.25
Robinson, Don	83D	171	$ .01	$ .05	Rose, Pete	83D	42	$ .25	$1.00
Robinson, Don	84D	532	$ .03	$ .10	Rose, Pete	84D	61	$ .80	$2.50
Robinson, Don	85D	262	$ .01	$ .08	Rose, Pete	85D	254	$ .40	$1.25
Robinson, Don	85D	264	$ .01	$ .08	Rose, Pete	85D	641	$ .50	$1.50
Robinson, Don	86D	357	$ .01	$ .06	Rose, Pete	86D	62	$ .15	$ .75
Robinson, Don	87D	608	$ .01	$ .04	Rose, Pete	86D	644	$ .05	$ .35
Robinson, Don	88D	573	$ .01	$ .05	Rose, Pete	86DK	653	$ .35	$1.00
Robinson, Don	89D	571	$ .01	$ .04	Rose, Pete	87D	186	$ .20	$ .60
Robinson, Don	89DBB	191	$ .01	$ .04	Rosello, Dave	81D	79	$ .01	$ .05
Robinson, Don	90D	258	$ .01	$ .03	Rosello, Dave	82D	617	$ .01	$ .05
Robinson, Frank	82D	424	$ .03	$ .20	Rosenberg, Steve	89D	219	$ .01	$ .04
Robinson, Frank	83D	564	$ .02	$ .15	Rosenberg, Steve	90D	253	$ .01	$ .03
Robinson, Frank	83D	648	$ .01	$ .15	Rowdon, Wade	85D	642	$ .01	$ .08
Robinson, Jeff D.	85D	201	$ .01	$ .25	Royster, Jerry	81D	339	$ .01	$ .05
Robinson, Jeff D.	87D	559	$ .01	$ .04	Royster, Jerry	82D	555	$ .01	$ .05
Robinson, Jeff D.	88D	558	$ .01	$ .05	Royster, Jerry	83D	425	$ .01	$ .05
Robinson, Jeff D.	88DBB	241	$ .01	$ .05	Royster, Jerry	84D	531	$ .03	$ .10
Robinson, Jeff D.	89D	370	$ .01	$ .04	Royster, Jerry	86D	446	$ .01	$ .06
Robinson, Jeff D.	89DBB	129	$ .01	$ .04	Royster, Jerry	87D	534	$ .01	$ .04
Robinson, Jeff D.	90D	134	$ .01	$ .03	Royster, Jerry	88D	660	$ .01	$ .15
Robinson, Jeff M.	87DR	13	$ .01	$ .45	Rozema, Dave	81D	9	$ .01	$ .05
Robinson, Jeff M.	88D	296	$ .01	$ .35	Rozema, Dave	82D	259	$ .01	$ .05
Robinson, Jeff M.	89D	470	$ .01	$ .04	Rozema, Dave	83D	133	$ .01	$ .05
Robinson, Jeff M.	89DK	18	$ .01	$ .05	Rozema, Dave	84D	272	$ .03	$ .10
Robinson, Jeff M.	90D	417	$ .01	$ .03	Rozema, Dave	85D	125	$ .01	$ .08
Robinson, Ron	85D	649	$ .08	$ .25	Rozema, Dave	86D	343	$ .01	$ .06
Robinson, Ron	86D	121	$ .01	$ .06	Rucker, Dave	83D	641	$ .01	$ .05
Robinson, Ron	87D	310	$ .01	$ .04	Rucker, Dave	84D	260	$ .03	$ .10
Robinson, Ron	88D	166	$ .01	$ .05	Rucker, Dave	85D	260	$ .01	$ .08
Robinson, Ron	89D	308	$ .01	$ .04	Rucker, Dave	86D	448	$ .01	$ .06
Robinson, Ron	90D	553	$ .01	$ .03	Rudi, Joe	81D	174	$ .01	$ .05
Rodgers, Bob	81D	327	$ .01	$ .05	Rudi, Joe	82D	586	$ .01	$ .05
Rodgers, Bob	82D	232	$ .01	$ .05	Rudi, Joe	83D	287	$ .01	$ .05
Rodriguez, Aurelio	83D	369	$ .01	$ .05	Ruffin, Bruce	87D	555	$ .08	$ .25
Rodriguez, Vic	85D	535	$ .01	$ .08	Ruffin, Bruce	88D	165	$ .01	$ .15
Roenicke, Gary	81D	116	$ .01	$ .05	Ruffin, Bruce	89D	515	$ .01	$ .04
Roenicke, Gary	82D	509	$ .01	$ .05	Ruhle, Vern	81D	261	$ .01	$ .05
Roenicke, Gary	83D	27	$ .01	$ .05	Ruhle, Vern	82D	293	$ .01	$ .05

Pirates — BILL ROBINSON of

Player	Year	No.	VG	EX/MT	Player	Year	No.	VG	EX/MT
Ruhle, Vern	83D	627	$ .01	$ .05	Salazar, Luis	90D	513	$ .01	$ .03
Ruhle, Vern	84D	564	$ .03	$ .10	Sambito, Joe	81D	21	$ .01	$ .05
Ruhle, Vern	85D	380	$ .01	$ .08	Sambito, Joe	82D	65	$ .01	$ .05
Runnells, Tom	86D	569	$ .01	$ .06	Sambito, Joe	83D	244	$ .01	$ .05
Russell, Bill	81D	57	$ .01	$ .05	Sambito, Joe	85D	572	$ .01	$ .08
Russell, Bill	82D	453	$ .01	$ .05	Sambito, Joe	87D	421	$ .01	$ .04
Russell, Bill	83D	210	$ .01	$ .05	Sample, Billy	81D	268	$ .01	$ .05
Russell, Bill	84D	587	$ .03	$ .10	Sample, Billy	82D	69	$ .01	$ .05
Russell, Bill	85D	93	$ .01	$ .08	Sample, Billy	83D	242	$ .01	$ .05
Russell, Bill	86D	153	$ .01	$ .06	Sample, Billy	84D	403	$ .03	$ .10
Russell, Jeff	84D	569	$ .05	$ .75	Sample, Billy	85D	464	$ .01	$ .08
Russell, Jeff	85D	487	$ .01	$ .08	Sample, Billy	86D	539	$ .01	$ .06
Russell, Jeff	86D	586	$ .01	$ .06	Sample, Billy	87D	143	$ .01	$ .04
Russell, Jeff	87D	550	$ .01	$ .04	Samuel, Juan	85D	183	$ .30	$1.50
Russell, Jeff	88D	531	$ .01	$ .05	Samuel, Juan	85DK	23	$ .10	$ .50
Russell, Jeff	89D	403	$ .01	$ .04	Samuel, Juan	86D	326	$ .03	$ .25
Russell, Jeff	89DBB	200	$ .01	$ .04	Samuel, Juan	87D	165	$ .01	$ .04
Russell, Jeff	90D	284	$ .01	$ .03	Samuel, Juan	88D	288	$ .05	$ .20
Russell, John	85D	648	$ .01	$ .08	Samuel, Juan	88DBB	215	$ .01	$ .05
Russell, John	86D	82	$ .01	$ .06	Samuel, Juan	89D	76	$ .01	$ .04
Russell, John	87D	207	$ .01	$ .04	Samuel, Juan	89DBB	238	$ .01	$ .04
Russell, John	90D	458	$ .01	$ .03	Samuel, Juan	90D	53	$ .01	$ .03
Ruthven, Dick	81D	153	$ .01	$ .05	Sanchez, Alejandro	85DRR	43	$ .01	$ .08
Ruthven, Dick	82D	525	$ .01	$ .05	Sanchez, Alejandro	86D	415	$ .01	$ .06
Ruthven, Dick	83D	497	$ .01	$ .05	Sanchez, Alex	89DRR	47	$ .01	$ .25
Ruthven, Dick	84D	510	$ .03	$ .10	Sanchez, Alex	90DRR	45	$ .01	$ .10
Ruthven, Dick	86D	564	$ .01	$ .06	Sanchez, Israel	89D	474	$ .01	$ .10
Ryal, Mark	87D	583	$ .01	$ .04	Sanchez, Luis	83D	519	$ .01	$ .05
Ryan, Nolan	81D	260	$ .30	$2.50	Sanchez, Luis	84D	597	$ .03	$ .10
Ryan, Nolan	82D	419	$ .15	$2.00	Sanchez, Luis	85D	352	$ .01	$ .08
Ryan, Nolan	82DK	13	$ .15	$1.00	Sanchez, Orlando	82D	636	$ .01	$ .05
Ryan, Nolan	83D	118	$ .15	$2.25	Sandberg, Ryne	83D	277	$2.50	$11.00
Ryan, Nolan	84D	60	$1.00	$4.00	Sandberg, Ryne	84D	311	$1.00	$4.00
Ryan, Nolan	85D	60	$ .35	$2.25	Sandberg, Ryne	85D	67	$ .10	$1.25
Ryan, Nolan	86D	258	$ .15	$1.25	Sandberg, Ryne	85DK	1	$ .15	$ .60
Ryan, Nolan	87D	138	$ .15	$ .75	Sandberg, Ryne	86D	67	$ .08	$ .50
Ryan, Nolan	88D	61	$ .10	$ .50	Sandberg, Ryne	87D	77	$ .08	$ .25
Ryan, Nolan	88DBB	232	$ .10	$ .35	Sandberg, Ryne	88D	242	$ .01	$ .15
Ryan, Nolan	89D	154	$ .10	$ .35	Sandberg, Ryne	88DBB	116	$ .01	$ .05
Ryan, Nolan	89DBB	55	$ .01	$ .50	Sandberg, Ryne	89D	105	$ .01	$ .10
Ryan, Nolan	89DTR	19	$ .01	$ .25	Sandberg, Ryne	89DBB	26	$ .01	$ .15
Ryan, Nolan	90D	166	$ .10	$ .50	Sandberg, Ryne	90D	105	$ .01	$ .10
Ryan, Nolan	90DAS	659	$ .01	$1.00	Sandberg, Ryne	90DAS	692	$ .01	$ .10
Ryan, Nolan	90DK	665	$ .01	$1.00	Sandberg, Ryne	90DBC	10	$ .01	$ .10
Saberhagen, Bret	85D	222	$1.35	$8.50	Sanders, Deion	89DR	6	$ .01	$1.00
Saberhagen, Bret	86D	100	$ .15	$1.25	Sanders, Deion	90D	427	$ .01	$ .50
Saberhagen, Bret	86DK	11	$ .08	$ .25	Sanderson, Scott	81D	450	$ .01	$ .05
Saberhagen, Bret	87D	132	$ .08	$ .35	Sanderson, Scott	82D	288	$ .01	$ .05
Saberhagen, Bret	88D	96	$ .05	$ .20	Sanderson, Scott	83D	446	$ .01	$ .05
Saberhagen, Bret	88DBB	231	$ .01	$ .10	Sanderson, Scott	84D	341	$ .03	$ .10
Saberhagen, Bret	00D	144	$ .01	$ .10	Sanderson, Scott	85D	266	$ .01	$ .08
Saberhagen, Bret	89DBB	95	$ .01	$ .15	Sanderson, Scott	86D	442	$ .01	$ .06
Saberhagen, Bret	90D	89	$ .01	$ .10	Sanderson, Scott	87D	447	$ .01	$ .04
Sabo, Chris	88DR	30	$ .45	$1.75	Sanderson, Scott	88D	646	$ .01	$ .15
Sabo, Chris	89D	317	$ .25	$1.25	Sanderson, Scott	89D	629	$ .01	$ .04
Sabo, Chris	89DBB	222	$ .01	$ .20	Sanderson, Scott	90D	647	$ .01	$ .03
Sabo, Chris	89DK	4	$ .15	$ .50	Sanguillen, Manny	81D	14	$ .01	$ .05
Sabo, Chris	90D	242	$ .01	$ .15	Santana, Rafael	85D	610	$ .03	$ .10
Sadek, Mike	81D	498	$ .01	$ .05	Santana, Rafael	86D	319	$ .01	$ .06
Sakata, Lenn	81D	499	$ .01	$ .05	Santana, Rafael	87D	569	$ .01	$ .04
Sakata, Lenn	82D	644	$ .01	$ .05	Santana, Rafael	88D	633	$ .01	$ .15
Sakata, Lenn	83D	205	$ .01	$ .05	Santana, Rafael	89D	309	$ .01	$ .04
Sakata, Lenn	84D	620	$ .03	$ .10	Santiago, Benito	87DR	44	$ .15	$ .60
Salas, Mark	85D	547	$ .01	$ .08	Santiago, Benito	87DRR	31	$ .50	$2.25
Salas, Mark	86D	316	$ .01	$ .06	Santiago, Benito	88D	114	$ .05	$ .35
Salazar, Angel	84DRR	33	$ .03	$ .10	Santiago, Benito	88DK	3	$ .10	$ .25
Salazar, Angel	85D	523	$ .01	$ .08	Santiago, Benito	89D	205	$ .01	$ .10
Salazar, Angel	87D	624	$ .01	$ .04	Santiago, Benito	90D	465	$ .01	$ .03
Salazar, Angel	88D	502	$ .01	$ .05	Santiago, Benito	90DAS	708	$ .01	$ .03
Salazar, Luis	82D	472	$ .01	$ .05	Santovenia, Nelson	89D	366	$ .01	$ .25
Salazar, Luis	83D	548	$ .01	$ .05	Santovenia, Nelson	89DBB	146	$ .01	$ .04
Salazar, Luis	84D	356	$ .03	$ .10	Santovenia, Nelson	90D	224	$ .01	$ .03
Salazar, Luis	85D	568	$ .01	$ .08	Sarimento, Manny	83D	502	$ .01	$ .05
Salazar, Luis	86D	302	$ .01	$ .06	Sarmiento, Manny	84D	200	$ .03	$ .10
Salazar, Luis	89D	352	$ .01	$ .04	Sasser, Mackey	88DR	51	$ .01	$ .05

DONRUSS

Player	Year	No.	VG	EX/MT	Player	Year	No.	VG	EX/MT
Sasser, Mackey	88DRR	28	$ .01	$ .25	Schooler, Mike	90D	330	$ .01	$ .03
Sasser, Mackey	89D	454	$ .01	$ .04	Schroeder, Bill	84D	515	$ .03	$ .10
Sasser, Mackey	90D	471	$ .01	$ .03	Schroeder, Bill	85D	124	$ .01	$ .08
Saucier, Kevin	82D	485	$ .01	$ .05	Schroeder, Bill	86D	211	$ .01	$ .06
Savage, Jack	89D	618	$ .01	$ .10	Schroeder, Bill	87D	486	$ .01	$ .04
Sax, Dave	84D	519	$ .03	$ .10	Schroeder, Bill	88D	419	$ .01	$ .05
Sax, Dave	87D	647	$ .01	$ .04					
Sax, Steve	82D	624	$ .50	$3.00					
Sax, Steve	83D	336	$ .06	$ .50					
Sax, Steve	84D	104	$ .04	$ .40					
Sax, Steve	85D	418	$ .03	$ .35					
Sax, Steve	86D	540	$ .02	$ .15					
Sax, Steve	87D	278	$ .01	$ .15					
Sax, Steve	87DK	26	$ .01	$ .04					
Sax, Steve	88D	176	$ .01	$ .05					
Sax, Steve	88DBB	204	$ .01	$ .05					
Sax, Steve	89D	84	$ .01	$ .15					
Sax, Steve	89DBB	20	$ .01	$ .10					
Sax, Steve	89DTR	23	$ .05	$1.25					
Sax, Steve	90D	78	$ .01	$ .10					
Sax, Steve	90DBC	22	$ .01	$ .03					
Sax, Steve	90DK	2	$ .01	$ .10					
Schatzeder, Dan	81D	248	$ .01	$ .05					
Schatzeder, Dan	82D	385	$ .01	$ .05					
Schatzeder, Dan	84D	132	$ .03	$ .10					
Schatzeder, Dan	85D	543	$ .01	$ .08					
Schatzeder, Dan	87D	482	$ .01	$ .04					
Schatzeder, Dan	90D	594	$ .01	$ .03					
Scherrer, Bill	84D	203	$ .03	$ .10					
Scherrer, Bill	86D	516	$ .01	$ .06					
Schilling, Curt	89D	635	$ .01	$ .04					
Schilling, Curt	90D	667	$ .01	$ .03					
Schiraldi, Calvin	85DRR	38	$ .05	$ .25					
Schiraldi, Calvin	86D	652	$ .01	$ .06					
Schiraldi, Calvin	87D	641	$ .01	$ .04					
Schiraldi, Calvin	88D	375	$ .01	$ .05					
Schiraldi, Calvin	88DBB	194	$ .01	$ .05					
Schiraldi, Calvin	89D	285	$ .01	$ .04					
Schiraldi, Calvin	89DBB	82	$ .01	$ .04	Schroeder, Bill	89D	644	$ .01	$ .04
Schiraldi, Calvin	90D	672	$ .01	$ .03	Schroeder, Bill	90D	567	$ .01	$ .03
Schmidt, Dave	83D	321	$ .01	$ .15	Schrom, Ken	84D	72	$ .03	$ .10
Schmidt, Dave	84D	586	$ .03	$ .10	Schrom, Ken	85D	486	$ .01	$ .08
Schmidt, Dave	85D	586	$ .01	$ .08	Schrom, Ken	86D	635	$ .01	$ .06
Schmidt, Dave	86D	378	$ .01	$ .06	Schrom, Ken	87D	403	$ .01	$ .04
Schmidt, Dave	87D	182	$ .01	$ .04	Schrom, Ken	88D	501	$ .01	$ .05
Schmidt, Dave	89D	215	$ .01	$ .04	Schu, Rick	85D	448	$ .03	$ .10
Schmidt, Dave	89DK	13	$ .01	$ .05	Schu, Rick	86D	570	$ .01	$ .06
Schmidt, Dave	90D	524	$ .01	$ .03	Schu, Rick	87D	509	$ .01	$ .04
Schmidt, Mike	81D	11	$ .40	$2.00	Schu, Rick	88D	432	$ .01	$ .05
Schmidt, Mike	81D	590	$ .10	$1.25	Schu, Rick	89D	406	$ .01	$ .04
Schmidt, Mike	82D	294	$ .15	$1.25	Schu, Rick	90D	599	$ .01	$ .03
Schmidt, Mike	82D	585	$ .15	$1.25	Schulze, Don	85D	639	$ .01	$ .08
Schmidt, Mike	83D	168	$ .10	$1.75	Scioscia, Mike	82D	598	$ .01	$ .25
Schmidt, Mike	84D	183	$ .40	$3.50	Scioscia, Mike	83D	75	$ .01	$ .05
Schmidt, Mike	84DK	23	$ .25	$1.25	Scioscia, Mike	85D	459	$ .01	$ .08
Schmidt, Mike	85D	61	$ .25	$1.75	Scioscia, Mike	86D	93	$ .01	$ .06
Schmidt, Mike	86D	61	$ .20	$ .75	Scioscia, Mike	87D	130	$ .01	$ .04
Schmidt, Mike	87D	139	$ .15	$ .60	Scioscia, Mike	88D	106	$ .01	$ .05
Schmidt, Mike	88D	330	$ .10	$ .40	Scioscia, Mike	88DBB	260	$ .01	$ .05
Schmidt, Mike	88D	371	$ .01	$ .35	Scioscia, Mike	89D	77	$ .01	$ .04
Schmidt, Mike	88DBC	4	$ .05	$ .30	Scioscia, Mike	89DBB	66	$ .01	$ .04
Schmidt, Mike	89D	193	$ .05	$ .25	Scioscia, Mike	90D	316	$ .01	$ .03
Schmidt, Mike	90D	643	$ .01	$ .35	Sconiers, Daryl	83D	141	$ .01	$ .05
Schoendienst, Red	81D	431	$ .01	$ .15	Sconiers, Daryl	84D	451	$ .03	$ .10
Schofield, Dick	84DRR	35	$ .10	$ .60	Sconiers, Daryl	85D	620	$ .01	$ .08
Schofield, Dick	85D	329	$ .01	$ .08	Scott, Donnie	85D	544	$ .01	$ .08
Schofield, Dick	86D	133	$ .01	$ .06	Scott, Mike	81D	37	$ .20	$1.00
Schofield, Dick	87D	283	$ .01	$ .04	Scott, Mike	82D	128	$ .10	$ .50
Schofield, Dick	88D	108	$ .01	$ .04	Scott, Mike	84D	136	$ .10	$ .50
Schofield, Dick	88D	233	$ .01	$ .05	Scott, Mike	85D	258	$ .03	$ .25
Schofield, Dick	88DBB	195	$ .01	$ .05	Scott, Mike	86D	476	$ .10	$ .35
Schofield, Dick	89DBB	251	$ .01	$ .04	Scott, Mike	87D	163	$ .05	$ .20
Schofield, Dick	90D	288	$ .01	$ .03	Scott, Mike	87DK	18	$ .01	$ .04
Schooler, Mike	89D	637	$ .01	$ .35	Scott, Mike	88D	112	$ .01	$ .05
Schooler, Mike	89DBB	275	$ .01	$ .04	Scott, Mike	88DBB	206	$ .05	$ .25

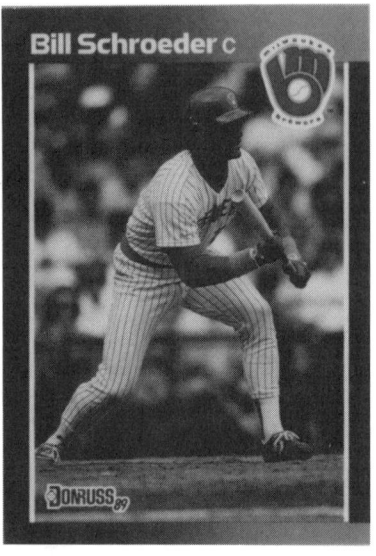

Bill Schroeder c

Player	Year	No.	VG	EX/MT
Scott, Mike	88DBC	12	$ .10	$ .25
Scott, Mike	89D	69	$ .05	$ .25

Player	Year	No.	VG	EX/MT
Scott, Mike	89DBB	94	$ .01	$ .10
Scott, Mike	89DBC	2	$ .01	$ .15
Scott, Mike	90D	207	$ .01	$ .10
Scott, Rodney	81D	209	$ .01	$ .05
Scott, Rodney	82D	240	$ .01	$ .05
Scott, Tony	82D	522	$ .01	$ .05
Scott, Tony	83D	293	$ .01	$ .05
Scott, Tony	84D	527	$ .03	$ .10
Scott, Tony (Anthony)	81D	191	$ .01	$ .05
Scudder, Scott	90D	435	$ .01	$ .20
Scurry, Rod	82D	185	$ .01	$ .05
Scurry, Rod	83D	376	$ .01	$ .05
Scurry, Rod	84D	235	$ .03	$ .10
Scurry, Rod	85D	142	$ .01	$ .08
Scurry, Rod	87D	374	$ .01	$ .04
Searage, Ray	86D	536	$ .01	$ .06
Searage, Ray	88D	420	$ .01	$ .05
Searage, Ray	90D	649	$ .01	$ .03
Searcy, Steve	89DRR	29	$ .05	$ .25
Seaver, Tom	81D	422	$ .15	$ .75
Seaver, Tom	81D	425	$ .15	$ .75
Seaver, Tom	82D	148	$ .12	$ .60
Seaver, Tom	82D	628	$ .15	$ .75
Seaver, Tom	82DK	16	$ .10	$ .50
Seaver, Tom	83D	122	$ .15	$ .65
Seaver, Tom	84D	116	$ .20	$1.00
Seaver, Tom	85D	424	$ .35	$1.00
Seaver, Tom	86D	609	$ .15	$ .40
Seaver, Tom	87D	375	$ .08	$ .25
Sebra, Bob	87D	468	$ .01	$ .04
Sebra, Bob	88D	458	$ .01	$ .05
Seitzer, Kevin	87DR	15	$ .25	$1.25
Seitzer, Kevin	88D	280	$ .10	$ .75
Seitzer, Kevin	88DBB	175	$ .05	$ .25
Seitzer, Kevin	88DBC	17	$ .05	$ .30
Seitzer, Kevin	89D	238	$ .01	$ .15
Seitzer, Kevin	89DBB	207	$ .01	$ .10
Seitzer, Kevin	89DK	10	$ .01	$ .15
Seitzer, Kevin	90D	85	$ .01	$ .10
Sellers, Jeff	86DR	29	$ .02	$ .09
Sellers, Jeff	87D	544	$ .01	$ .15

Player	Year	No.	VG	EX/MT
Sellers, Jeff	88D	585	$ .01	$ .05
Sellers, Jeff	89D	517	$ .01	$ .04
Senteney, Steven	83D	52	$ .01	$ .05
Serna, Paul	82D	567	$ .01	$ .05
Sexton, Jimmy	83D	449	$ .01	$ .05
Sharperson, Mike	87D	565	$ .01	$ .04
Sharperson, Mike	90D	603	$ .01	$ .03
Sheets, Larry	85DRR	36	$ .10	$ .60
Sheets, Larry	86D	350	$ .02	$ .15
Sheets, Larry	87D	248	$ .01	$ .04
Sheets, Larry	88D	273	$ .01	$ .05
Sheets, Larry	89D	333	$ .01	$ .04
Sheets, Larry	90D	495	$ .01	$ .03
Sheffield, Gary	89DBB	113	$ .01	$ .50
Sheffield, Gary	89DR	1	$ .01	$1.00
Sheffield, Gary	89DRR	31	$ .35	$1.00
Sheffield, Gary	90D	501	$ .01	$ .50
Shelby, John	84D	291	$ .04	$ .35
Shelby, John	85D	472	$ .01	$ .08
Shelby, John	86D	643	$ .01	$ .06
Shelby, John	87D	354	$ .01	$ .04
Shelby, John	88D	352	$ .01	$ .05
Shelby, John	89D	314	$ .01	$ .04
Sheridan, Pat	84D	588	$ .01	$ .25
Sheridan, Pat	85D	339	$ .01	$ .08
Sheridan, Pat	86D	155	$ .01	$ .06
Sheridan, Pat	88D	522	$ .01	$ .05
Sheridan, Pat	89D	417	$ .01	$ .04
Sheridan, Pat	90D	367	$ .01	$ .03
Shines, Razor	85D	401	$ .01	$ .08
Shipanoff, Dave	86DRR	34	$ .01	$ .06
Shirley, Bob	81D	242	$ .01	$ .05
Shirley, Bob	82D	120	$ .01	$ .05
Shirley, Bob	84D	214	$ .03	$ .10
Shirley, Bob	85D	370	$ .01	$ .08
Shirley, Bob	86D	458	$ .01	$ .06
Shirley, Bob	87D	463	$ .01	$ .04
Show, Eric	83D	439	$ .05	$ .35
Show, Eric	84D	406	$ .03	$ .10
Show, Eric	85D	202	$ .01	$ .08
Show, Eric	86D	234	$ .01	$ .06
Show, Eric	87D	164	$ .01	$ .04
Show, Eric	88D	387	$ .01	$ .05
Show, Eric	89D	482	$ .01	$ .04
Show, Eric	90D	559	$ .01	$ .03
Sierra, Ruben	86DR	52	$2.00	$8.00
Sierra, Ruben	87D	346	$ .75	$5.50
Sierra, Ruben	88D	223	$ .15	$ .60
Sierra, Ruben	88DBB	200	$ .01	$ .25
Sierra, Ruben	88DBC	26	$ .10	$ .25
Sierra, Ruben	89D	48	$ .01	$ .30
Sierra, Ruben	89DBB	111	$ .01	$ .25
Sierra, Ruben	89DBC	26	$ .01	$ .30
Sierra, Ruben	90D	174	$ .01	$ .15
Sierra, Ruben	90DAS	673	$ .01	$ .10
Sierra, Ruben	90DK	3	$ .01	$ .25
Simmons, Nelson	86D	272	$ .01	$ .06
Simmons, Ted	81D	308	$ .03	$ .20
Simmons, Ted	82D	106	$ .02	$ .15
Simmons, Ted	83D	332	$ .01	$ .05
Simmons, Ted	84D	473	$ .08	$ .25
Simmons, Ted	85D	414	$ .03	$ .20
Simmons, Ted	86D	292	$ .05	$ .20
Simmons, Ted	87D	537	$ .01	$ .04
Simmons, Ted	88D	560	$ .01	$ .05
Simpson, Joe	81D	168	$ .01	$ .05
Simpson, Joe	82D	55	$ .01	$ .05
Simpson, Joe	84D	496	$ .03	$ .10
Sinatro, Matt	82D	149	$ .01	$ .05
Sinatro, Matt	83D	622	$ .01	$ .05
Singleton, Ken	81D	115	$ .02	$ .15
Singleton, Ken	82DK	24	$ .01	$ .05
Singleton, Ken	83D	257	$ .01	$ .05
Singleton, Ken	84D	610	$ .03	$ .10
Singleton, ken	82D	105	$ .01	$ .05

DONRUSS

Player	Year	No.	VG	EX/MT	Player	Year	No.	VG	EX/MT
Sisk, Doug	84D	615	$ .03	$ .10	Smith, Lee	85D	311	$ .01	$ .08
Sisk, Doug	85D	441	$ .01	$ .08	Smith, Lee	86D	144	$ .01	$ .06
Sisk, Doug	88D	642	$ .01	$ .15	Smith, Lee	87D	292	$ .01	$ .04
Skinner, Joel	84DRR	27	$ .03	$ .10	Smith, Lee	88D	292	$ .01	$ .05
Skinner, Joel	85D	574	$ .01	$ .08	Smith, Lee	88DBB	252	$ .01	$ .05
Skinner, Joel	86D	330	$ .01	$ .06	Smith, Lee	89D	66	$ .01	$ .04
Skinner, Joel	87D	545	$ .01	$ .04	Smith, Lee	89DBB	84	$ .01	$ .04
Skinner, Joel	88D	474	$ .01	$ .05	Smith, Lee	90D	110	$ .01	$ .03
Skinner, Joel	89D	427	$ .01	$ .04	Smith, Lonnie	81D	295	$ .10	$ .60
Skinner, Joel	89DBB	224	$ .01	$ .04	Smith, Lonnie	82D	606	$ .01	$ .25
Skinner, Joel	89DTR	22	$ .01	$ .05	Smith, Lonnie	83D	91	$ .07	$ .35
Skinner, Joel	90D	73	$ .01	$ .03	Smith, Lonnie	84D	231	$ .03	$ .25
Slaton, Jim	86D	402	$ .01	$ .06	Smith, Lonnie	84D	625	$ .01	$ .25
Slaton, Jim	81D	447	$ .01	$ .05	Smith, Lonnie	85D	231	$ .01	$ .10
Slaton, Jim	82D	80	$ .01	$ .05	Smith, Lonnie	86D	399	$ .01	$ .06
Slaton, Jim	83D	330	$ .01	$ .05	Smith, Lonnie	87D	225	$ .01	$ .04
Slaton, Jim	85D	545	$ .01	$ .08	Smith, Lonnie	88D	527	$ .01	$ .05
Slaught, Don	83D	196	$ .10	$ .40	Smith, Lonnie	89DBB	114	$ .01	$ .04
Slaught, Don	84D	419	$ .03	$ .10	Smith, Lonnie	90D	222	$ .01	$ .03
Slaught, Don	85D	496	$ .01	$ .08	Smith, Ozzie	81D	1	$ .25	$1.00
Slaught, Don	86D	281	$ .01	$ .06	Smith, Ozzie	82D	94	$ .10	$ .45
Slaught, Don	87D	136	$ .01	$ .04	Smith, Ozzie	82DK	21	$ .03	$ .20
Slaught, Don	88DBB	188	$ .01	$ .05	Smith, Ozzie	83D	120	$ .10	$ .40
Slaught, Don	89D	190	$ .01	$ .04	Smith, Ozzie	84D	59	$ .10	$ .65
Slaught, Don	89DBB	105	$ .01	$ .04	Smith, Ozzie	84D	625	$ .01	$ .25
Slaught, Don	90D	277	$ .01	$ .03	Smith, Ozzie	85D	59	$ .03	$ .25
Slayton, Jim	84D	481	$ .03	$ .10	Smith, Ozzie	86D	59	$ .05	$ .20
Smalley, Roy	81D	487	$ .01	$ .05	Smith, Ozzie	87D	60	$ .01	$ .15
Smalley, Roy	82D	573	$ .01	$ .05	Smith, Ozzie	87DK	5	$ .05	$ .20
Smalley, Roy	82DK	22	$ .01	$ .05	Smith, Ozzie	88D	263	$ .01	$ .05
Smalley, Roy	83D	209	$ .01	$ .05	Smith, Ozzie	88DBB	243	$ .01	$ .15
Smalley, Roy	84D	225	$ .03	$ .10	Smith, Ozzie	88DBC	22	$ .10	$ .25
Smalley, Roy	85D	622	$ .01	$ .08	Smith, Ozzie	89D	63	$ .01	$ .04
Smalley, Roy	86D	486	$ .01	$ .06	Smith, Ozzie	89DBB	44	$ .01	$ .25
Smalley, Roy	87D	443	$ .01	$ .04	Smith, Ozzie	89DBC	14	$ .01	$ .10
Smalley, Roy	88D	566	$ .01	$ .05	Smith, Ozzie	90D	201	$ .01	$ .10
Smiley, John	87DR	39	$ .03	$ .45	Smith, Ozzie	90DAS	710	$ .01	$ .10
Smiley, John	88D	449	$ .05	$ .35	Smith, Pete	88D	571	$ .01	$ .15
Smiley, John	88DBB	257	$ .01	$ .05	Smith, Pete	88DBB	197	$ .01	$ .05
Smiley, John	89D	329	$ .01	$ .04	Smith, Pete	88DR	10	$ .01	$ .05
Smiley, John	89DBB	157	$ .01	$ .10	Smith, Pete	89D	263	$ .01	$ .04
Smiley, John	90D	54	$ .01	$ .10	Smith, Pete	90D	499	$ .01	$ .03
Smiley, John	90DK	17	$ .01	$ .10	Smith, Reggie	81D	59	$ .01	$ .05
Smith, Bryn	83D	88	$ .05	$ .35	Smith, Reggie	82D	488	$ .01	$ .05
Smith, Bryn	84D	453	$ .03	$ .40	Smith, Reggie	83D	611	$ .01	$ .05
Smith, Bryn	85D	209	$ .01	$ .08	Smith, Roy	85D	611	$ .01	$ .08
Smith, Bryn	86D	299	$ .01	$ .06	Smith, Roy	86D	468	$ .01	$ .06
Smith, Bryn	87D	159	$ .01	$ .04	Smith, Roy	90D	273	$ .01	$ .03
Smith, Bryn	88D	335	$ .01	$ .05	Smith, Zane	86D	565	$ .01	$ .25
Smith, Bryn	88DBB	202	$ .01	$ .05	Smith, Zane	87D	167	$ .01	$ .04
Smith, Bryn	89D	216	$ .01	$ .04	Smith, Zane	88D	167	$ .01	$ .05
Smith, Bryn	89DBB	124	$ .01	$ .04	Smith, Zane	88DBB	170	$ .01	$ .05
Smith, Bryn	90D	106	$ .01	$ .03	Smith, Zane	89D	499	$ .01	$ .04
Smith, Bryn	90DK	25	$ .01	$ .10	Smith, Zane	90D	460	$ .01	$ .03
Smith, Chris	84DRR	46	$ .03	$ .10	Smithson, Mike	84D	221	$ .03	$ .10
Smith, Dave	81D	23	$ .10	$ .40	Smithson, Mike	85D	316	$ .01	$ .08
Smith, Dave	82D	191	$ .01	$ .05	Smithson, Mike	86D	147	$ .01	$ .06
Smith, Dave	83D	370	$ .01	$ .05	Smithson, Mike	87D	245	$ .01	$ .04
Smith, Dave	84D	548	$ .03	$ .10	Smithson, Mike	89D	628	$ .01	$ .04
Smith, Dave	85D	548	$ .01	$ .08	Smithson, Mike	90D	464	$ .01	$ .03
Smith, Dave	86D	328	$ .01	$ .06	Smoltz, John	89D	642	$ .05	$ .50
Smith, Dave	87D	308	$ .01	$ .04	Smoltz, John	89DBB	85	$ .01	$ .10
Smith, Dave	88D	410	$ .01	$ .05	Smoltz, John	90D	121	$ .01	$ .10
Smith, Dave	88DBB	262	$ .01	$ .05	Smoltz, John	90DBC	12	$ .01	$ .10
Smith, Dave	89D	272	$ .01	$ .04	Smoltz, John	90DK	8	$ .01	$ .20
Smith, Dave	89DBB	232	$ .01	$ .04	Snell, Nate	86D	367	$ .01	$ .06
Smith, Dave	90D	88	$ .01	$ .03	Snell, Nate	87D	396	$ .01	$ .04
Smith, Dwight	89DBB	205	$ .01	$1.00	Snider, Duke	84D	648	$ .04	$ .15
Smith, Dwight	89DR	32	$ .01	$2.00	Snider, Van	89D	586	$ .01	$ .10
Smith, Dwight	90D	393	$ .01	$ .75	Snyder, Cory	86DR	15	$ .25	$1.25
Smith, Jimmy	83D	402	$ .01	$ .05	Snyder, Cory	86DRR	29	$ .50	$2.50
Smith, Keith	81D	539	$ .01	$ .05	Snyder, Cory	87D	526	$ .25	$ .75
Smith, Lee	82D	252	$ .15	$ .75	Snyder, Cory	88D	350	$ .01	$ .15
Smith, Lee	83D	403	$ .01	$ .10	Snyder, Cory	88DBB	224	$ .01	$ .15
Smith, Lee	84D	289	$ .03	$ .10	Snyder, Cory	89D	191	$ .01	$ .10

Player	Year	No.	VG	EX/MT	Player	Year	No.	VG	EX/MT
Snyder, Cory	89DBB	168	$ .01	$ .04	Stanley, Fred	82D	449	$ .01	$ .05
Snyder, Cory	89DK	8	$ .01	$ .05	Stanley, Fred	83D	197	$ .01	$ .05
Snyder, Cory	90D	272	$ .01	$ .03	Stanley, Mike	87D	592	$ .01	$ .04
Soderholm, Eric	81D	106	$ .01	$ .05	Stanley, Mike	87DR	28	$ .01	$ .07
Soff, Ray	87D	631	$ .01	$ .04	Stanley, Mike	88D	259	$ .01	$ .05
Sofield, Rick	81D	592	$ .01	$ .05	Stanley, Mike	88DBB	223	$ .01	$ .05
Solomon, Eddie	81D	16	$ .01	$ .05	Stanley, Mike	89D	166	$ .01	$ .04
Solomon, Eddie	82D	437	$ .01	$ .05	Stanley, Mike	90D	579	$ .01	$ .03
Sorensen, Lary	81D	325	$ .01	$ .05	Stanton, Mike	82D	285	$ .01	$ .05
Sorensen, Lary	82D	246	$ .01	$ .05	Stanton, Mike	83D	433	$ .01	$ .05
Sorensen, Lary	83D	363	$ .01	$ .05	Stanton, Mike	85D	562	$ .01	$ .08
Sorensen, Lary	84D	635	$ .03	$ .10	Stanton, Mike	90D	508	$ .01	$ .25
Sorensen, Lary	85D	131	$ .01	$ .08	Stapleton, Dave	81D	544	$ .02	$ .15
Sorrento, Paul	90D	626	$ .01	$ .10	Stapleton, Dave	82D	208	$ .01	$ .05
Sosa, Elias	81D	599	$ .01	$ .05	Stapleton, Dave	83D	200	$ .01	$ .05
Sosa, Elias	82D	446	$ .01	$ .05	Stapleton, Dave	84D	273	$ .03	$ .10
Sosa, Elias	83D	259	$ .01	$ .05	Stapleton, Dave	88D	521	$ .01	$ .05
Sosa, Sammy	89DBB	324	$ .01	$ .25	Stapleton, Dave	88DR	4	$ .01	$ .05
Sosa, Sammy	90D	489	$ .01	$ .25	Stargell, Willie	81D	12	$ .06	$ .30
Soto, Mario	81D	63	$ .03	$ .20	Stargell, Willie	81D	132	$ .06	$ .30
Soto, Mario	82D	103	$ .01	$ .05	Stargell, Willie	82D	639	$ .05	$ .30
Soto, Mario	83D	248	$ .02	$ .15	Stargell, Willie	83D	610	$ .10	$ .50
Soto, Mario	84D	428	$ .03	$ .10	Stargell, Willie	83DK	8	$ .05	$ .30
Soto, Mario	85D	184	$ .03	$ .10	Staub, Rusty	82D	56	$ .02	$ .15
Soto, Mario	85DK	19	$ .03	$ .10					
Soto, Mario	86D	184	$ .01	$ .06					
Soto, Mario	87D	82	$ .01	$ .04					
Spahn, Warren	89D	588	$ .01	$ .04					
Speck, Cliff	87D	571	$ .01	$ .04					
Speier, Chris	81D	329	$ .01	$ .05					
Speier, Chris	82D	366	$ .01	$ .05					
Speier, Chris	83D	266	$ .01	$ .05					
Speier, Chris	84D	523	$ .03	$ .10					
Speier, Chris	87D	392	$ .01	$ .04					
Speier, Chris	88D	239	$ .01	$ .05					
Speier, Chris	89D	532	$ .01	$ .04					
Spencer, Jim	81D	226	$ .01	$ .05					
Spencer, Jim	82D	265	$ .01	$ .05					
Spiers, Bill	89DR	5	$ .01	$ .25					
Spiers, Bill	90D	382	$ .01	$ .10					
Spillner, Dan	82D	411	$ .01	$ .05					
Spillner, Dan	83D	137	$ .01	$ .05					
Spillner, Dan	84D	582	$ .03	$ .10					
Spillner, Dan	86D	122	$ .01	$ .06					
Spilman, Harry	81D	304	$ .01	$ .05					
Spilman, Harry	83D	65	$ .01	$ .05					
Spilman, Harry	84D	258	$ .03	$ .10					
Spilman, Harry	88D	607	$ .01	$ .15					
Splittorff, Paul	81D	342	$ .01	$ .05					
Splittorff, Paul	82D	464	$ .01	$ .05					
Splittorff, Paul	83D	286	$ .01	$ .05					
Splittorff, Paul	84D	521	$ .03	$ .10					
Squires, Mike	81D	398	$ .01	$ .05					
Squires, Mike	82D	39	$ .01	$ .05					
Squires, Mike	83D	495	$ .01	$ .05					
Squires, Mike	84D	404	$ .03	$ .10					
Squires, Mike	85D	501	$ .01	$ .08	Staub, Rusty	83D	350	$ .01	$ .05
St. Claire, Randy	85D	575	$ .01	$ .08	Staub, Rusty	84D	554	$ .08	$ .25
St. Claire, Randy	86D	463	$ .01	$ .06	Staub, Rusty	84DK	6	$ .08	$ .25
St. Claire, Randy	88D	426	$ .01	$ .05	Stearns, John	81D	35	$ .01	$ .05
Stanhouse, Don	81D	557	$ .01	$ .05	Stearns, John	82D	434	$ .01	$ .05
Stanicek, Pete	88D	541	$ .03	$ .25	Stearns, John	83D	380	$ .01	$ .05
Stanicek, Pete	88DR	15	$ .01	$ .15	Steels, James	87DR	50	$ .01	$ .07
Stanicek, Pete	89D	169	$ .01	$ .04	Steels, James	88D	360	$ .01	$ .05
Stanley, Bob	81D	456	$ .01	$ .05	Stefero, John	84D	622	$ .03	$ .10
Stanley, Bob	82D	134	$ .01	$ .05	Stefero, John	87D	541	$ .01	$ .04
Stanley, Bob	83D	386	$ .01	$ .05	Steib, Dave	82D	52	$ .03	$ .20
Stanley, Bob	84D	644	$ .03	$ .10	Steib, Dave	87D	195	$ .01	$ .15
Stanley, Bob	85D	91	$ .01	$ .08	Stein, Bill	81D	543	$ .01	$ .05
Stanley, Bob	86D	91	$ .01	$ .06	Stein, Bill	82D	37	$ .01	$ .05
Stanley, Bob	87D	216	$ .01	$ .04	Stein, Bill	83D	594	$ .01	$ .05
Stanley, Bob	88D	92	$ .01	$ .05	Stein, Bill	85D	621	$ .01	$ .08
Stanley, Bob	89D	421	$ .01	$ .04	Stein, Bill	86D	403	$ .01	$ .06
Stanley, Bob	89DBB	233	$ .01	$ .04	Steinbach, Terry	87DR	26	$ .05	$ .45
Stanley, Fred	81D	585	$ .01	$ .05	Steinbach, Terry	87DRR	34	$ .25	$1.25

RUSTY STAUB

DONRUSS

Player	Year	No.	VG	EX/MT	Player	Year	No.	VG	EX/MT
Steinbach, Terry	88D	158	$ .03	$ .25	Strawberry, Darryl	84D	68	$8.00	$33.50
Steinbach, Terry	88DBB	78	$ .01	$ .05					
Steinbach, Terry	89D	267	$ .01	$ .04					
Steinbach, Terry	89DBB	323	$ .01	$ .10					
Steinbach, Terry	90D	268	$ .01	$ .10					
Steinback, Terry	90DAS	637	$ .01	$ .10					
Stenhouse, Mike	84DRR	29	$ .01	$ .25					
Stenhouse, Mike	85D	376	$ .01	$ .08					
Stennett, Rennie	81D	72	$ .01	$ .05					
Stennett, Rennie	82D	563	$ .01	$ .05					
Stephans, Russ	85DRR	42	$ .01	$ .08					
Stephenson, Phil	89DR	36	$ .01	$ .10					
Stevens, Lee	90D	449	$ .01	$ .15					
Stewart, Dave	82D	410	$1.00	$4.25					
Stewart, Dave	83D	588	$ .15	$ .75					
Stewart, Dave	84D	343	$ .15	$ .75					
Stewart, Dave	85D	343	$ .01	$ .08					
Stewart, Dave	86D	619	$ .05	$ .35					
Stewart, Dave	87D	648	$ .01	$ .25					
Stewart, Dave	88D	472	$ .01	$ .15					
Stewart, Dave	88DBB	99	$ .01	$ .05					
Stewart, Dave	89D	214	$ .01	$ .04					
Stewart, Dave	89DBB	99	$ .01	$ .20					
Stewart, Dave	90D	150	$ .01	$ .10					
Stewart, Dave	90DAS	703	$ .01	$ .10					
Stewart, Dave	90DBC	3	$ .01	$ .10					
Stewart, Dave	90DK	6	$ .01	$ .10					
Stewart, Sammy	81D	474	$ .01	$ .05					
Stewart, Sammy	82D	457	$ .01	$ .05					
Stewart, Sammy	83D	203	$ .01	$ .05					
Stewart, Sammy	84D	514	$ .03	$ .10					
Stewart, Sammy	85D	148	$ .01	$ .08					
Stewart, Sammy	86D	270	$ .01	$ .06	Strawberry, Darryl	85D	312	$1.00	$4.50
Stewart, Sammy	87D	658	$ .01	$ .04	Strawberry, Darryl	86D	197	$ .40	$3.00
Stewart, Sammy	88D	596	$ .01	$ .05	Strawberry, Darryl	87D	118	$ .25	$ .75
Stieb, Dave	81D	582	$ .10	$ .40	Strawberry, Darryl	87DK	4	$ .10	$ .35
Stieb, Dave	83D	507	$ .03	$ .15	Strawberry, Darryl	88D	439	$ .15	$ .50
Stieb, Dave	83DK	9	$ .02	$ .15	Strawberry, Darryl	88DBB	182	$ .10	$ .35
Stieb, Dave	84D	71	$ .04	$ .25	Strawberry, Darryl	88DBC	20	$ .15	$ .40
Stieb, Dave	85D	193	$ .03	$ .20	Strawberry, Darryl	89D	147	$ .05	$ .35
Stieb, Dave	86D	146	$ .05	$ .20	Strawberry, Darryl	89DBB	40	$ .01	$ .25
Stieb, Dave	88D	148	$ .01	$ .05	Strawberry, Darryl	89DBC	6	$ .01	$ .25
Stieb, Dave	89D	349	$ .01	$ .04	Strawberry, Darryl	90D	235	$ .01	$ .25
Stieb, Dave	89DBB	143	$ .01	$ .04	Stubbs, Franklin	85D	348	$ .07	$ .25
Stieb, Dave	90D	87	$ .01	$ .03	Stubbs, Franklin	86D	592	$ .05	$ .20
Stillwell, Kurt	87D	123	$ .10	$ .50	Stubbs, Franklin	87D	299	$ .01	$ .04
Stillwell, Kurt	88D	265	$ .01	$ .05	Stubbs, Franklin	88D	218	$ .01	$ .05
Stillwell, Kurt	88DBB	207	$ .01	$ .05	Stubbs, Franklin	89D	321	$ .01	$ .04
Stillwell, Kurt	89D	322	$ .01	$ .04	Stubbs, Franklin	90D	615	$ .01	$ .03
Stillwell, Kurt	89DBB	63	$ .01	$ .04	Stuper, John	83D	621	$ .01	$ .05
Stillwell, Kurt	90D	120	$ .01	$ .03	Stuper, John	84D	412	$ .03	$ .10
Stoddard, Bob	84D	619	$ .03	$ .10	Sularz, Guy	83D	605	$ .01	$ .05
Stoddard, Tim	81D	475	$ .01	$ .05	Sullivan, Marc	86D	614	$ .01	$ .06
Stoddard, Tim	82D	131	$ .01	$ .05	Sullivan, Marc	87D	643	$ .01	$ .04
Stoddard, Tim	83D	581	$ .01	$ .05	Summers, Champ	81D	130	$ .01	$ .05
Stoddard, Tim	84D	245	$ .03	$ .10	Summers, Champ	82D	81	$ .01	$ .05
Stoddard, Tim	85D	144	$ .01	$ .08	Sundberg, Jim	81D	385	$ .01	$ .05
Stoddard, Tim	86D	406	$ .01	$ .06	Sundberg, Jim	82D	268	$ .01	$ .05
Stoddard, Tim	87D	497	$ .01	$ .04	Sundberg, Jim	83D	609	$ .01	$ .05
Stoddard, Tim	88D	497	$ .01	$ .05	Sundberg, Jim	83DK	7	$ .02	$ .15
Stone, Jeff	85D	624	$ .03	$ .20	Sundberg, Jim	84D	178	$ .03	$ .10
Stone, Jeff	86D	259	$ .01	$ .06	Sundberg, Jim	85D	89	$ .01	$ .08
Stone, Jeff	87D	309	$ .01	$ .04	Sundberg, Jim	86D	277	$ .01	$ .06
Stone, Jeff	88D	482	$ .01	$ .05	Sundberg, Jim	87D	280	$ .01	$ .04
Stone, Steve	81D	476	$ .01	$ .05	Sundberg, Jim	88D	488	$ .01	$ .05
Stone, Steve	81D	591	$ .02	$ .15	Surhoff, B. J.	89DBB	221	$ .01	$ .04
Stone, Steve	82D	357	$ .01	$ .05	Surhoff, B. J.	90D	173	$ .01	$ .03
Stottlemyre, Todd	88D	658	$ .05	$ .40	Surhoff, B.J.	87DR	17	$ .10	$ .30
Stottlemyre, Todd	88DR	37	$ .01	$ .15	Surhoff, B.J.	87DRR	28	$ .15	$ .50
Stottlemyre, Todd	89D	620	$ .01	$ .10	Surhoff, B.J.	88D	172	$ .01	$ .15
Stottlemyre, Todd	90D	669	$ .01	$ .03	Surhoff, B.J.	89D	221	$ .01	$ .04
Strain, Joe	81D	73	$ .01	$ .05	Surhoff, Rick	86DRR	42	$ .01	$ .06
Straker, Les	87DR	21	$ .01	$ .07	Sutcliffe, Rick	81D	418	$ .03	$ .20
Straker, Les	88D	73	$ .01	$ .05	Sutcliffe, Rick	83D	72	$ .03	$ .20
Strange, Doug	90D	535	$ .01	$ .10					

DARRYL STRAWBERRY OF

Player	Year	No.	VG	EX/MT	Player	Year	No.	VG	EX/MT
Sutcliffe, Rick	84D	338	$ .10	$ .35	Tanner, Chuck	83D	124	$ .01	$ .05
Sutcliffe, Rick	85D	433	$ .03	$ .10	Tapani, Kevin	90D	473	$ .01	$ .10
Sutcliffe, Rick	86D	189	$ .05	$ .20	Tartabull, Danny	85DRR	27	$2.00	$5.50
Sutcliffe, Rick	87D	68	$ .01	$ .04	Tartabull, Danny	86DR	45	$ .10	$ .75
Sutcliffe, Rick	88D	68	$ .01	$ .05	Tartabull, Danny	86DRR	38	$ .15	$1.00
Sutcliffe, Rick	88DBB	138	$ .01	$ .05	Tartabull, Danny	87D	147	$ .15	$ .50
Sutcliffe, Rick	89D	223	$ .01	$ .04	Tartabull, Danny	88D	177	$ .03	$ .25
Sutcliffe, Rick	89DBB	138	$ .01	$ .04	Tartabull, Danny	88DK	5	$ .01	$ .15
Sutcliffe, Rick	90D	157	$ .01	$ .03	Tartabull, Danny	89D	61	$ .01	$ .10
Sutherland, Leo	81D	42	$ .01	$ .05	Tartabull, Danny	89DBB	39	$ .01	$ .04
Sutter, Bruce	81D	560	$ .03	$ .20	Tartabull, Danny	90D	322	$ .01	$ .03
Sutter, Bruce	82D	372	$ .03	$ .20	Taveras, Frank	81D	154	$ .01	$ .05
Sutter, Bruce	83D	40	$ .01	$ .15	Taveras, Frank	82D	98	$ .01	$ .05
Sutter, Bruce	84D	534	$ .01	$ .20	Tejada, Wilfredo	87D	529	$ .01	$ .04
Sutter, Bruce	84DK	13	$ .08	$ .25	Tekulve, Kent	81D	254	$ .01	$ .05
Sutter, Bruce	85D	109	$ .03	$ .20	Tekulve, Kent	82D	311	$ .01	$ .05
Sutter, Bruce	86D	321	$ .01	$ .06	Tekulve, Kent	83D	297	$ .01	$ .05
Sutter, Bruce	89D	458	$ .01	$ .04	Tekulve, Kent	84D	410	$ .03	$ .10
Sutton, Don	81D	58	$ .05	$ .30	Tekulve, Kent	85D	479	$ .01	$ .08
Sutton, Don	82D	443	$ .05	$ .30	Tekulve, Kent	86D	111	$ .01	$ .06
Sutton, Don	83D	531	$ .10	$ .50	Tekulve, Kent	87D	453	$ .01	$ .04
Sutton, Don	84D	414	$ .10	$ .45	Tekulve, Kent	88D	535	$ .01	$ .05
Sutton, Don	85D	107	$ .05	$ .30	Tellmann, Tom	84D	149	$ .03	$ .10
Sutton, Don	85DK	16	$ .08	$ .25	Tellmann, Tom	85D	246	$ .01	$ .08
Sutton, Don	86D	611	$ .08	$ .25	Templeton, Garry	81D	187	$ .01	$ .05
Sutton, Don	87D	181	$ .03	$ .25	Templeton, Garry	82D	545	$ .01	$ .05
Sutton, Don	88D	407	$ .01	$ .15	Templeton, Garry	83D	145	$ .01	$ .05
Sveum, Dale	86DR	37	$ .10	$ .35	Templeton, Garry	84D	185	$ .03	$ .10
Sveum, Dale	87D	542	$ .08	$ .25	Templeton, Garry	85D	356	$ .01	$ .08
Sveum, Dale	88D	232	$ .01	$ .15	Templeton, Garry	86D	202	$ .01	$ .06
Sveum, Dale	89D	146	$ .01	$ .04	Templeton, Garry	87D	141	$ .01	$ .04
Swaggerty, Bill	85D	392	$ .01	$ .08	Templeton, Garry	88D	649	$ .05	$ .20
Swaggerty, Bill	86D	594	$ .01	$ .06	Templeton, Garry	89D	483	$ .01	$ .04
Swan, Craig	81D	155	$ .01	$ .05	Templeton, Garry	89DBB	154	$ .01	$ .04
Swan, Craig	82D	589	$ .01	$ .05	Templeton, Garry	90D	246	$ .01	$ .03
Swan, Craig	83D	254	$ .01	$ .05	Tenace, Gene	81D	241	$ .01	$ .05
Swan, Craig	84D	441	$ .03	$ .10	Tenace, Gene	82D	152	$ .01	$ .05
Sweet, Rick	83D	352	$ .01	$ .05	Tenace, Gene	83D	442	$ .01	$ .05
Sweet, Rick	84D	196	$ .03	$ .10	Tenace, Gene	84D	264	$ .03	$ .10
Swift, Bill	87D	517	$ .01	$ .04	Terrell, Walt	84D	640	$ .10	$ .50
Swift, Billy	86D	562	$ .01	$ .06	Terrell, Walt	85D	597	$ .01	$ .08
Swift, Billy	90D	566	$ .01	$ .03	Terrell, Walt	86D	247	$ .01	$ .06
Swindell, Greg	87DRR	32	$ .50	$1.50	Terrell, Walt	87D	275	$ .01	$ .04
Swindell, Greg	88D	227	$ .01	$ .25	Terrell, Walt	88D	91	$ .01	$ .05
Swindell, Greg	89D	232	$ .01	$ .10	Terrell, Walt	89D	296	$ .01	$ .04
Swindell, Greg	89DBB	112	$ .01	$ .10	Terrell, Walt	89DBB	245	$ .01	$ .04
Swindell, Greg	90D	310	$ .01	$ .10	Terrell, Walt	89DTR	28	$ .01	$ .05
Swindell, Greg	90DBC	24	$ .01	$ .10	Terrell, Walt	90D	309	$ .01	$ .03
Swisher, Steve	83D	633	$ .01	$ .05	Terry, Scott	88D	647	$ .01	$ .15
Sykes, Bob	82D	640	$ .01	$ .05	Terry, Scott	09D	397	$ .01	$ .04
Tabler, Pat	82D	529	$ .03	$ .30	Terry, Scott	90D	418	$ .01	$ .03
Tabler, Pat	83D	552	$ .01	$ .05	Tettleton, Mickey	86D	345	$ .01	$ .45
Tabler, Pat	84D	536	$ .03	$ .10	Tettleton, Mickey	87D	349	$ .01	$ .15
Tabler, Pat	85D	460	$ .01	$ .08	Tettleton, Mickey	88D	103	$ .01	$ .05
Tabler, Pat	86D	129	$ .01	$ .06	Tettleton, Mickey	89D	401	$ .01	$ .04
Tabler, Pat	87D	254	$ .01	$ .04	Tettleton, Mickey	89DBB	86	$ .01	$ .10
Tabler, Pat	88D	219	$ .01	$ .05	Tettleton, Mickey	90D	169	$ .01	$ .10
Tabler, Pat	89D	326	$ .01	$ .04	Tettleton, Mickey	90DK	5	$ .01	$ .10
Tabler, Pat	90D	444	$ .01	$ .03	Teufel, Tim	84DRR	37	$ .10	$ .45
Tamargo, John	81D	210	$ .01	$ .05	Teufel, Tim	85D	192	$ .01	$ .08
Tanana, Frank	81D	171	$ .01	$ .05	Teufel, Tim	86D	242	$ .01	$ .06
Tanana, Frank	82D	326	$ .01	$ .05	Teufel, Tim	87D	581	$ .01	$ .04
Tanana, Frank	83D	447	$ .01	$ .05	Teufel, Tim	88D	648	$ .01	$ .15
Tanana, Frank	84D	98	$ .03	$ .10	Teufel, Tim	89D	507	$ .01	$ .04
Tanana, Frank	85D	220	$ .01	$ .08	Teufel, Tim	90D	618	$ .01	$ .03
Tanana, Frank	85DK	9	$ .03	$ .10	Tewksbury, Bob	86DR	8	$ .10	$ .25
Tanana, Frank	86D	491	$ .01	$ .06	Tewksbury, Bob	87D	422	$ .01	$ .04
Tanana, Frank	87D	152	$ .01	$ .04	Tewksbury, Bob	90D	714	$ .01	$ .03
Tanana, Frank	88D	461	$ .01	$ .05	Thigpen, Bobby	87D	370	$ .05	$ .20
Tanana, Frank	88DBB	259	$ .01	$ .05	Thigpen, Bobby	88D	247	$ .01	$ .05
Tanana, Frank	89D	90	$ .01	$ .04	Thigpen, Bobby	88DBB	235	$ .01	$ .05
Tanana, Frank	89DBB	91	$ .01	$ .04	Thigpen, Bobby	89D	266	$ .01	$ .04
Tanana, Frank	90D	180	$ .01	$ .03	Thigpen, Bobby	89DBB	25	$ .01	$ .04
Tanner, Chuck	81D	257	$ .01	$ .05	Thigpen, Bobby	90D	266	$ .01	$ .03
Tanner, Chuck	82D	150	$ .01	$ .05	Thomas, Andres	86DR	10	$ .10	$ .25

DONRUSS

Player	Year	No.	VG	EX/MT	Player	Year	No.	VG	EX/MT
Thomas, Andres	87D	266	$ .03	$ .25	Tolleson, Wayne	83D	573	$ .01	$ .25
Thomas, Andres	88D	627	$ .01	$ .15	Tolleson, Wayne	84D	464	$ .03	$ .10
Thomas, Andres	89D	576	$ .01	$ .04	Tolleson, Wayne	85D	378	$ .01	$ .08
Thomas, Andres	89DBB	197	$ .01	$ .04	Tolleson, Wayne	86D	134	$ .01	$ .06
Thomas, Andres	90D	263	$ .01	$ .03	Tolleson, Wayne	87D	524	$ .01	$ .04
Thomas, Derrel	81D	419	$ .01	$ .05	Tolleson, Wayne	88D	154	$ .01	$ .05
Thomas, Derrel	82D	537	$ .01	$ .05	Tolleson, Wayne	89D	659	$ .01	$ .04
Thomas, Derrel	84D	397	$ .03	$ .10	Torre, Joe	81D	506	$ .01	$ .05
Thomas, Gorman	81D	326	$ .01	$ .05	Torre, Joe	83D	628	$ .01	$ .05
Thomas, Gorman	82D	132	$ .01	$ .05	Torrez, Mike	81D	216	$ .01	$ .05
Thomas, Gorman	82DK	26	$ .01	$ .05	Torrez, Mike	82D	235	$ .01	$ .05
Thomas, Gorman	83D	510	$ .01	$ .05	Torrez, Mike	83D	512	$ .01	$ .05
Thomas, Gorman	84D	574	$ .03	$ .10	Torrez, Mike	84D	556	$ .03	$ .10
Thomas, Gorman	86D	440	$ .01	$ .06	Traber, Jim	85DRR	45	$ .15	$ .40
Thomasson, Gary	81D	534	$ .01	$ .05	Traber, Jim	87D	477	$ .01	$ .04
Thompson, Jason	81D	293	$ .01	$ .05	Traber, Jim	90D	569	$ .01	$ .03
Thompson, Jason	82D	502	$ .01	$ .05	Tracy, Jim	81D	520	$ .01	$ .05
Thompson, Jason	83D	95	$ .01	$ .05	Trammell, Alan	81D	5	$ .10	$ .50
Thompson, Jason	84D	64	$ .03	$ .10	Trammell, Alan	82D	76	$ .10	$ .45
Thompson, Jason	85D	322	$ .01	$ .08	Trammell, Alan	82DK	5	$ .10	$ .40
Thompson, Jason	86D	322	$ .01	$ .06	Trammell, Alan	83D	207	$ .10	$ .50
Thompson, Milt	86D	507	$ .15	$ .50	Trammell, Alan	84D	293	$ .15	$ .60
Thompson, Milt	87D	330	$ .01	$ .04	Trammell, Alan	85D	171	$ .08	$ .25
Thompson, Milt	88D	236	$ .01	$ .15	Trammell, Alan	86D	171	$ .10	$ .35
Thompson, Milt	89D	313	$ .01	$ .04	Trammell, Alan	87D	127	$ .01	$ .15
Thompson, Milt	89DBB	212	$ .01	$ .04	Trammell, Alan	88D	230	$ .01	$ .05
Thompson, Milt	89DTR	43	$ .01	$ .05	Trammell, Alan	88DBC	11	$ .10	$ .35
Thompson, Milt	90D	82	$ .01	$ .03	Trammell, Alan	88DK	4	$ .01	$ .15
Thompson, Rob	86DR	39	$ .15	$ .50	Trammell, Alan	89D	180	$ .01	$ .15
Thompson, Rob	87D	145	$ .08	$ .25	Trammell, Alan	89DBB	13	$ .01	$ .10
Thompson, Rob	88D	268	$ .01	$ .05	Trammell, Alan	89DBC	17	$ .01	$ .20
Thompson, Rob	89D	98	$ .01	$ .04	Trammell, Alan	90D	90	$ .01	$ .10
Thompson, Robby	89DBB	79	$ .01	$ .04	Trammell, Alan	90DBC	26	$ .01	$ .10
Thompson, Robby	90D	140	$ .01	$ .03	Trautwein, John	88DR	24	$ .01	$ .05
Thompson, Scot	81D	519	$ .01	$ .05	Travers, Bill	81D	508	$ .01	$ .05
Thompson, Scot	83D	378	$ .01	$ .05	Treadway, Jeff	88DR	17	$ .01	$ .15
Thompson, Scot	84D	167	$ .03	$ .10	Treadway, Jeff	88DRR	29	$ .05	$ .30
Thon, Dickie	81D	290	$ .01	$ .05	Treadway, Jeff	89D	351	$ .01	$ .15
Thon, Dickie	83D	191	$ .01	$ .05	Treadway, Jeff	89DBB	141	$ .01	$ .04
Thon, Dickie	84D	304	$ .03	$ .10	Treadway, Jeff	90D	50	$ .01	$ .03
Thon, Dickie	86D	572	$ .01	$ .06	Trevino, Alex	82D	350	$ .01	$ .05
Thon, Dickie	87D	261	$ .01	$ .04	Trevino, Alex	83D	374	$ .01	$ .05
Thon, Dickie	89D	441	$ .01	$ .04	Trevino, Alex	84D	286	$ .03	$ .10
Thon, Dickie	90D	549	$ .01	$ .03	Trevino, Alex	85D	565	$ .01	$ .08
Thornton, Andre	81D	198	$ .01	$ .05	Trevino, Alex	87D	546	$ .01	$ .04
Thornton, Andre	82D	324	$ .01	$ .05	Trevino, Alex	88D	376	$ .01	$ .05
Thornton, Andre	83D	211	$ .01	$ .05	Trevino, Alex	90D	443	$ .01	$ .03
Thornton, Andre	84DK	25	$ .03	$ .10	Trillo, Manny	81D	22	$ .01	$ .05
Thornton, Andre	85D	468	$ .01	$ .08	Trillo, Manny	82D	245	$ .01	$ .05
Thornton, Andre	86D	251	$ .01	$ .06	Trillo, Manny	83D	294	$ .01	$ .05
Thornton, Andre	87D	279	$ .01	$ .04	Trillo, Manny	84D	575	$ .03	$ .10
Thornton, Andy	84D	94	$ .03	$ .10	Trillo, Manny	85D	431	$ .01	$ .08
Thurman, Gary	88DR	33	$ .01	$ .15	Trillo, Manny	86D	201	$ .01	$ .06
Thurman, Gary	88DRR	44	$ .01	$ .15	Trillo, Manny	87D	570	$ .01	$ .04
Thurman, Gary	89D	498	$ .01	$ .10	Trillo, Manny	88D	516	$ .01	$ .05
Thurman, Gary	90D	416	$ .01	$ .03	Trillo, Manny	89D	608	$ .01	$ .04
Thurmond, Mark	84D	505	$ .03	$ .10	Trout, Steve	81D	400	$ .01	$ .05
Thurmond, Mark	85D	284	$ .01	$ .08	Trout, Steve	82D	243	$ .01	$ .05
Thurmond, Mark	86D	261	$ .01	$ .06	Trout, Steve	83D	417	$ .01	$ .05
Thurmond, Mark	87D	543	$ .01	$ .04	Trout, Steve	84D	533	$ .03	$ .10
Thurmond, Mark	88D	599	$ .01	$ .05	Trout, Steve	85D	198	$ .01	$ .08
Thurmond, Mark	90D	612	$ .01	$ .03	Trout, Steve	86D	117	$ .01	$ .06
Tiant, Luis	81D	231	$ .03	$ .20	Trout, Steve	87D	201	$ .01	$ .04
Tiant, Luis	83D	542	$ .01	$ .05	Trout, Steve	88D	524	$ .01	$ .05
Tibbs, Jay	85D	262	$ .01	$ .08	Trujillo, Mike	87D	613	$ .01	$ .04
Tibbs, Jay	86D	262	$ .01	$ .06	Tudor, John	81D	457	$ .25	$1.00
Tibbs, Jay	87D	282	$ .01	$ .04	Tudor, John	82D	260	$ .03	$ .20
Tidrow, Dick	81D	551	$ .01	$ .05	Tudor, John	83D	563	$ .01	$ .05
Tidrow, Dick	82D	477	$ .01	$ .05	Tudor, John	84D	416	$ .03	$ .10
Tobik, Dave	82D	511	$ .01	$ .05	Tudor, John	85D	235	$ .03	$ .10
Tobik, Dave	83D	385	$ .01	$ .05	Tudor, John	86D	260	$ .01	$ .06
Todd, Jackson	81D	31	$ .01	$ .05	Tudor, John	87D	170	$ .01	$ .04
Todd, Jackson	82D	178	$ .01	$ .05	Tudor, John	88D	553	$ .01	$ .05
Toliver, Fred	86D	612	$ .01	$ .06	Tudor, John	88DBB	212	$ .01	$ .15
Toliver, Fred	89D	510	$ .01	$ .04	Tudor, John	89D	195	$ .01	$ .04

Player	Year	No.	VG	EX/MT
Tunnell, Lee	84D	592	$ .03	$ .10
Tunnell, Lee	85D	288	$ .01	$ .08
Turner, Jerry	81D	244	$ .01	$ .05
Turner, Jerry	82D	609	$ .01	$ .05
Tyson, Mike	82D	435	$ .01	$ .05
Ujdur, Jerry	83D	600	$ .01	$ .05
Ullger, Scott	84D	438	$ .03	$ .10
Underwood, Pat	81D	368	$ .01	$ .05
Underwood, Pat	83D	29	$ .01	$ .05
Underwood, Tom	81D	108	$ .01	$ .05
Underwood, Tom	82D	323	$ .01	$ .05
Underwood, Tom	83D	391	$ .01	$ .05
Underwood, Tom	84D	253	$ .03	$ .10
Unser, Del	81D	164	$ .01	$ .05
Unser, Del	82D	273	$ .01	$ .05
Upshaw, Willie	82D	652	$ .01	$ .05
Upshaw, Willie	83D	558	$ .01	$ .05
Upshaw, Willie	84D	315	$ .03	$ .10
Upshaw, Willie	85D	71	$ .01	$ .08
Upshaw, Willie	85DK	10	$ .03	$ .10
Upshaw, Willie	86D	195	$ .01	$ .06
Upshaw, Willie	87D	367	$ .01	$ .04
Upshaw, Willie	88D	271	$ .01	$ .05
Upshaw, Willie	89D	492	$ .01	$ .04
Uribe, Jose	86D	236	$ .05	$ .20
Uribe, Jose	87D	436	$ .01	$ .04
Uribe, Jose	88D	559	$ .01	$ .05
Uribe, Jose	89D	131	$ .01	$ .04
Uribe, Jose	89DBB	106	$ .01	$ .04
Uribe, Jose	90D	335	$ .01	$ .03
Urrea, John	81D	190	$ .01	$ .05
Urrea, John	82D	313	$ .01	$ .05
Vail, Mike	81D	554	$ .01	$ .05
Vail, Mike	83D	597	$ .01	$ .05
Valdez, Julio	82D	560	$ .01	$ .05
Valdez, Sergio	90D	405	$ .01	$ .10
Valentine, Ellis	82D	605	$ .01	$ .05
Valenzuela, Fernando	82D	462	$ .25	$1.25
Valenzuela, Fernando	83D	284	$ .10	$ .50
Valenzuela, Fernando	83DK	1	$ .10	$ .50
Valenzuela, Fernando	88D	53	$ .03	$ .25
Valenzuela, Fernando	89D	250	$ .01	$ .10
Valenzuela, Fernando	90D	625	$ .01	$ .10
Valle, Dave	87D	610	$ .01	$ .04
Valle, Dave	88D	393	$ .01	$ .05
Valle, Dave	89D	614	$ .01	$ .04
Valle, Dave	89DBB	248	$ .01	$ .04
Valle, Dave	90D	129	$ .01	$ .03
Van Gorder, Dave	83D	188	$ .01	$ .05
Van Gorder, Dave	85D	384	$ .01	$ .08
Van Gorder, Dave	86D	550	$ .01	$ .06
Van Slyke, Andy	84D	83	$ .75	$4.00
Van Slyke, Andy	85D	327	$ .15	$ .75
Van Slyke, Andy	86D	412	$ .01	$ .25
Van Slyke, Andy	87D	417	$ .01	$ .15
Van Slyke, Andy	88D	291	$ .01	$ .05
Van Slyke, Andy	88DBB	157	$ .01	$ .15
Van Slyke, Andy	88DBC	8	$ .10	$ .25
Van Slyke, Andy	88DK	18	$ .01	$ .05
Van Slyke, Andy	89D	54	$ .03	$ .15
Van Slyke, Andy	89DBB	45	$ .01	$ .04
Van Slyke, Andy	89DBC	10	$ .01	$ .10
Van Slyke, Andy	90D	244	$ .01	$ .03
Vande Berg, Ed	83D	100	$ .01	$ .05
Vande Berg, Ed	84D	604	$ .03	$ .10
Vande Berg, Ed	85D	511	$ .01	$ .08
Vande Berg, Ed	86D	637	$ .01	$ .06
Vande Berg, Ed	87D	376	$ .01	$ .04
Vaughn, DeWayne	88DR	25	$ .01	$ .15
Vaughn, Greg	90DRR	37	$ .01	$1.25
Vega, Jesus	83D	650	$ .01	$ .05
Velarde, Randy	90D	630	$ .01	$ .03
Velez, Otto	81D	391	$ .01	$ .05
Velez, Otto	82D	304	$ .01	$ .05
Venable, Max	84D	323	$ .03	$ .10
Venable, Max	86D	650	$ .01	$ .06
Ventura, Robin	90DRR	28	$ .01	$ .50
Verhoeven, John	81D	564	$ .01	$ .05
Veryzer, Tom	81D	199	$ .01	$ .05
Veryzer, Tom	82D	450	$ .01	$ .05
Viola, Frank	83D	382	$1.00	$4.00
Viola, Frank	84D	364	$ .50	$2.00
Viola, Frank	85D	436	$ .15	$ .50
Viola, Frank	85DK	17	$ .05	$ .25
Viola, Frank	86D	194	$ .05	$ .25
Viola, Frank	87D	196	$ .08	$ .25
Viola, Frank	88D	149	$ .01	$ .15
Viola, Frank	88DBB	214	$ .05	$ .20
Viola, Frank	89D	237	$ .01	$ .10
Viola, Frank	89DBB	74	$ .01	$ .25
Viola, Frank	89DK	23	$ .01	$ .15
Viola, Frank	90D	353	$ .01	$ .20
Virdon, Bill	81D	384	$ .01	$ .05
Virdon, Bill	82D	144	$ .01	$ .05
Virgil, Ozzie	83D	606	$ .01	$ .05
Virgil, Ozzie	84D	326	$ .03	$ .10
Virgil, Ozzie	85D	82	$ .01	$ .08
Virgil, Ozzie	86D	137	$ .01	$ .06
Virgil, Ozzie	87D	67	$ .01	$ .04
Virgil, Ozzie	88D	143	$ .01	$ .05
Virgil, Ozzie	88DBB	85	$ .01	$ .05
Virgil, Ozzie	89D	145	$ .01	$ .04
Vizquel, Omar	89DBB	163	$ .01	$ .04
Vizquel, Omar	89DR	53	$ .01	$ .10
Vizquel, Omar	90D	483	$ .01	$ .03
Von Ohlen, Dave	84D	205	$ .03	$ .10
Von Ohlen, Dave	85D	412	$ .01	$ .08
Vuckovich, Pete	81D	189	$ .01	$ .05
Vuckovich, Pete	82D	458	$ .03	$ .20
Vuckovich, Pete	83D	80	$ .01	$ .05
Vuckovich, Pete	86D	473	$ .01	$ .06
Vukovich, George	83D	315	$ .01	$ .05
Vukovich, George	84D	468	$ .03	$ .10
Vukovich, George	85D	276	$ .01	$ .08
Vukovich, George	86D	346	$ .01	$ .06

Player	Year	No.	VG	EX/MT
Valenzuela, Fernando	84D	52	$ .20	$ .60
Valenzuela, Fernando	85D	52	$ .10	$ .35
Valenzuela, Fernando	86D	215	$ .10	$ .35
Valenzuela, Fernando	87D	94	$ .08	$ .25

Player	Year	No.	VG	EX/MT
Waddel, Tom	85D	582	$ .01	$ .08
Waddel, Tom	86D	94	$ .01	$ .06
Wagner, Mark	81D	126	$ .01	$ .05
Wagner, Mark	82D	163	$ .01	$ .05
Wagner, Mark	83D	268	$ .01	$ .05
Waits, Rick	81D	201	$ .01	$ .05
Waits, Rick	82D	33	$ .01	$ .05
Waits, Rick	83D	263	$ .01	$ .05
Waits, Rick	85D	368	$ .01	$ .08
Walewander, Jim	89D	415	$ .01	$ .04
Walk, Bob	81D	393	$ .01	$ .25
Walk, Bob	83D	401	$ .01	$ .05
Walk, Bob	86D	430	$ .01	$ .06
Walk, Bob	87D	203	$ .01	$ .04
Walk, Bob	88D	514	$ .01	$ .05
Walk, Bob	89D	172	$ .01	$ .04
Walk, Bob	89DBB	145	$ .01	$ .04
Walk, Bob	90D	370	$ .01	$ .03
Walker, Chico	87D	539	$ .01	$ .04
Walker, Duane	83D	624	$ .01	$ .05
Walker, Duane	84D	325	$ .03	$ .10
Walker, Duane	85D	608	$ .01	$ .08
Walker, Duane	86D	500	$ .01	$ .06
Walker, Greg	84D	609	$ .05	$ .55
Walker, Greg	85D	366	$ .01	$ .08
Walker, Greg	87D	59	$ .01	$ .04
Walker, Greg	87DK	25	$ .01	$ .04
Walker, Greg	88D	162	$ .01	$ .05
Walker, Greg	88DBB	193	$ .01	$ .05
Walker, Greg	89D	135	$ .01	$ .04
Walker, Larry	90D	578	$ .01	$ .25
Wallach, Tim	82D	140	$ .20	$1.00
Wallach, Tim	83D	392	$ .01	$ .20
Wallach, Tim	84D	421	$ .01	$ .25
Wallach, Tim	85D	87	$ .03	$ .20
Wallach, Tim	86D	219	$ .02	$ .15
Wallach, Tim	87D	179	$ .01	$ .04
Wallach, Tim	88D	222	$ .01	$ .05
Wallach, Tim	88DBB	258	$ .01	$ .05
Wallach, Tim	89D	156	$ .01	$ .04
Wallach, Tim	89DBB	34	$ .01	$ .04
Wallach, Tim	90D	220	$ .01	$ .03
Walling, Dennis	81D	144	$ .01	$ .05
Walling, Denny	82D	496	$ .01	$ .05
Walling, Denny	83D	419	$ .01	$ .05
Walling, Denny	84D	641	$ .04	$ .25
Walling, Denny	85D	527	$ .01	$ .08
Walling, Denny	86D	136	$ .01	$ .06
Walling, Denny	87D	554	$ .01	$ .04
Walling, Denny	88D	384	$ .01	$ .05
Walling, Denny	89D	279	$ .01	$ .04
Walling, Denny	90D	677	$ .01	$ .03
Walter, Gene	86DR	47	$ .02	$ .09
Walter, Gene	87D	511	$ .01	$ .04
Walton, Jerome	89DBB	172	$ .01	$1.00
Walton, Jerome	89DR	26	$ .01	$3.00
Walton, Jerome	90D	285	$ .01	$1.00
Ward, Duane	87DRR	45	$ .01	$ .25
Ward, Duane	88D	567	$ .01	$ .05
Ward, Duane	89D	543	$ .01	$ .04
Ward, Duane	89DBB	216	$ .01	$ .04
Ward, Duane	90D	307	$ .01	$ .03
Ward, Gary	81D	594	$ .01	$ .05
Ward, Gary	82D	571	$ .01	$ .05
Ward, Gary	83D	429	$ .01	$ .05
Ward, Gary	84D	192	$ .03	$ .10
Ward, Gary	85D	342	$ .01	$ .08
Ward, Gary	86D	98	$ .01	$ .06
Ward, Gary	86DK	20	$ .01	$ .06
Ward, Gary	87D	427	$ .01	$ .04
Ward, Gary	88D	251	$ .01	$ .05
Ward, Gary	90D	621	$ .01	$ .03
Warren, Mike	84D	631	$ .03	$ .10
Warren, Mike	85D	278	$ .01	$ .08
Washington, Claudell	82D	58	$ .01	$ .05

Player	Year	No.	VG	EX/MT
Washington, Claudell	83D	249	$ .01	$ .05
Washington, Claudell	84D	310	$ .03	$ .10
Washington, Claudell	85D	310	$ .01	$ .08
Washington, Claudell	85DK	11	$ .03	$ .10
Washington, Claudell	86D	287	$ .01	$ .06

Claudell Washington OF

Player	Year	No.	VG	EX/MT
Washington, Claudell	88D	340	$ .01	$ .05
Washington, Claudell	88DBB	217	$ .01	$ .05
Washington, Claudell	89D	72	$ .01	$ .04
Washington, Claudell	89DBB	227	$ .01	$ .04
Washington, Claudell	89DTR	46	$ .01	$ .05
Washington, Claudell	90D	52	$ .01	$ .03
Washington, Ron	83D	431	$ .01	$ .05
Washington, Ron	84D	391	$ .03	$ .10
Washington, Ron	85D	391	$ .01	$ .08
Washington, Ron	86D	560	$ .01	$ .06
Washington, Ron	89D	468	$ .01	$ .04
Washington, U L	81D	460	$ .01	$ .05
Washington, U.L.	82D	160	$ .01	$ .05
Washington, U.L.	83D	490	$ .01	$ .05
Washington, U.L.	84D	543	$ .03	$ .10
Washington, U.L.	85D	521	$ .01	$ .08
Washington, U.L.	86D	498	$ .01	$ .06
Wathan, John	81D	221	$ .01	$ .05
Wathan, John	82D	86	$ .01	$ .05
Wathan, John	83D	86	$ .01	$ .05
Wathan, John	84D	466	$ .03	$ .10
Wathan, John	85D	466	$ .01	$ .08
Wathan, John	86D	496	$ .01	$ .06
Watson, Bob	81D	225	$ .01	$ .05
Watson, Bob	82D	108	$ .01	$ .05
Watson, Bob	83D	551	$ .01	$ .05
Wayne, Gary	89DR	27	$ .01	$ .10
Wayne, Gary	90D	318	$ .01	$ .03
Weaver, Earl	81D	356	$ .01	$ .05
Weaver, Earl	82D	27	$ .02	$ .15
Webster, Mitch	86D	523	$ .08	$ .25
Webster, Mitch	87D	335	$ .01	$ .04
Webster, Mitch	88D	257	$ .01	$ .05
Webster, Mitch	89D	459	$ .01	$ .04
Webster, Mitch	89DBB	261	$ .01	$ .04
Webster, Mitch	90D	137	$ .01	$ .03
Wegman, Bill	86D	490	$ .01	$ .06
Wegman, Bill	87D	109	$ .01	$ .04

Player	Year	No.	VG	EX/MT	Player	Year	No.	VG	EX/MT
Wegman, Bill	88D	151	$ .01	$ .05	Whitfield, Terry	85D	540	$ .01	$ .08
Wegman, Bill	89D	293	$ .01	$ .04	Whitfield, Terry	86D	337	$ .01	$ .06
Weiss, Walt	88DR	18	$ .25	$1.25	Whitson, Ed	81D	74	$ .01	$ .05
Weiss, Walt	89D	446	$ .05	$ .35	Whitson, Ed	82D	251	$ .01	$ .05
Weiss, Walt	89DBB	155	$ .01	$ .10	Whitson, Ed	83D	389	$ .01	$ .05
Weiss, Walt	90D	67	$ .01	$ .10	Whitson, Ed	84D	528	$ .03	$ .10
Welch, Bob	81D	178	$ .03	$ .20	Whitson, Ed	85D	446	$ .01	$ .08
Welch, Bob	82D	75	$ .01	$ .10	Whitson, Ed	86D	225	$ .01	$ .06
Welch, Bob	83D	410	$ .01	$ .05	Whitson, Ed	87D	360	$ .01	$ .04
Welch, Bob	84D	153	$ .03	$ .10	Whitson, Ed	88D	81	$ .01	$ .05
Welch, Bob	85D	372	$ .01	$ .08	Whitson, Ed	89D	229	$ .01	$ .04
Welch, Bob	86D	459	$ .01	$ .06	Whitson, Ed	89DBB	210	$ .01	$ .10
Welch, Bob	87D	475	$ .01	$ .04	Whitson, Ed	90D	205	$ .01	$ .10
Welch, Bob	88D	253	$ .01	$ .05	Whitson, Ed	90DK	26	$ .01	$ .10
Welch, Bob	88DBB	134	$ .01	$ .05	Whitt, Ernie	81D	390	$ .01	$ .05
Welch, Bob	88DK	24	$ .01	$ .05	Whitt, Ernie	82D	381	$ .01	$ .05
Welch, Bob	89D	332	$ .01	$ .04	Whitt, Ernie	83D	304	$ .01	$ .05
Welch, Bob	89DBB	267	$ .01	$ .04	Whitt, Ernie	84D	437	$ .03	$ .10
Welch, Bob	90D	332	$ .01	$ .03	Whitt, Ernie	85D	268	$ .01	$ .08
Wellman, Brad	84D	265	$ .03	$ .10	Whitt, Ernie	86D	559	$ .01	$ .06
Wellman, Brad	86D	431	$ .01	$ .06	Whitt, Ernie	87D	148	$ .01	$ .04
Wellman, Brad	89D	380	$ .01	$ .04	Whitt, Ernie	88D	394	$ .01	$ .05
Wells, David	88D	640	$ .01	$ .30	Whitt, Ernie	89D	591	$ .01	$ .04
Wells, David	88DR	26	$ .01	$ .05	Whitt, Ernie	89DBB	255	$ .01	$ .04
Wells, David	89D	307	$ .01	$ .04	Whitt, Ernie	90D	385	$ .01	$ .03
Wells, David	89DBB	328	$ .01	$ .04	Wiggins, Alan	83D	397	$ .01	$ .05
Wells, David	90D	425	$ .01	$ .03	Wiggins, Alan	84D	568	$ .03	$ .10
Welsh, Chris	82D	44	$ .01	$ .05	Wiggins, Alan	85D	80	$ .01	$ .08
Welsh, Chris	83D	94	$ .01	$ .05	Wiggins, Alan	86D	607	$ .01	$ .06
Welsh, Chris	84D	498	$ .03	$ .10	Wilcox, Milt	81D	247	$ .01	$ .05
Welsh, Chris	86D	464	$ .01	$ .06	Wilcox, Milt	82D	233	$ .01	$ .05
Werner, Don	83D	593	$ .01	$ .05	Wilcox, Milt	83D	155	$ .01	$ .05
Werth, Dennis	81D	466	$ .01	$ .05	Wilcox, Milt	84D	471	$ .03	$ .10
West, Dave	89DRR	41	$ .05	$ .35	Wilcox, Milt	85D	105	$ .01	$ .08
West, Dave	90D	387	$ .01	$ .03	Wilfong, Rob	81D	493	$ .01	$ .05
Wetteland, John	90D	671	$ .01	$ .25	Wilfong, Rob	82D	130	$ .01	$ .05
Whisenton, Larry	83D	501	$ .01	$ .05	Wilfong, Rob	83D	612	$ .01	$ .05
Whitaker, Lou	81D	365	$ .05	$ .40	Wilfong, Rob	84D	329	$ .03	$ .10
Whitaker, Lou	82D	454	$ .03	$ .20	Wilfong, Rob	85D	402	$ .01	$ .08
Whitaker, Lou	83D	333	$ .03	$ .20	Wilfong, Rob	87D	258	$ .01	$ .04
Whitaker, Lou	84D	227	$ .10	$ .45	Wilkerson, Curt	84D	99	$ .03	$ .10
Whitaker, Lou	85D	293	$ .03	$ .25	Wilkerson, Curt	85D	99	$ .01	$ .08
Whitaker, Lou	85DK	5	$ .03	$ .25	Wilkerson, Curt	90D	608	$ .01	$ .03
Whitaker, Lou	86D	49	$ .03	$ .25	Wilkerson, Curtis	86D	256	$ .01	$ .06
Whitaker, Lou	87D	107	$ .05	$ .20	Wilkerson, Curtis	87D	223	$ .01	$ .04
Whitaker, Lou	88D	173	$ .01	$ .05	Wilkerson, Curtis	88D	592	$ .01	$ .05
Whitaker, Lou	89D	298	$ .01	$ .15	Wilkerson, Curtis	89D	402	$ .01	$ .04
Whitaker, Lou	89DBB	35	$ .01	$ .10	Wilkerson, Curtis	89DTR	34	$ .01	$ .05
Whitaker, Lou	90D	298	$ .01	$ .10	Wilkinson, Bill	88D	568	$ .01	$ .05
Whitaker, Lou	90DK	16	$ .01	$ .10	Willard, Gerry "Jerry"	84D	520	$ .03	$ .10
White, Devon	87/DR	8	$ .15	$ .50	Willard, Jerry	85D	346	$ .01	$ .08
White, Devon	87DRR	38	$ .50	$1.25	Willard, Jerry	86D	398	$ .01	$ .06
White, Devon	88D	283	$ .03	$ .25	Willard, Jerry	87D	467	$ .01	$ .04
White, Devon	88DBB	227	$ .01	$ .15	Williams, Al	82D	429	$ .01	$ .05
White, Devon	88DK	8	$ .01	$ .15	Williams, Al	83D	508	$ .01	$ .05
White, Devon	89D	213	$ .01	$ .10	Williams, Al	84D	316	$ .03	$ .10
White, Devon	89DBB	27	$ .01	$ .10	Williams, Bernie	90D	689	$ .01	$ .30
White, Devon	90D	226	$ .01	$ .10	Williams, Dick	81D	453	$ .01	$ .05
White, Frank	81D	340	$ .01	$ .05	Williams, Dick	83D	625	$ .01	$ .05
White, Frank	82D	286	$ .01	$ .05	Williams, Eddie	88DRR	46	$ .10	$ .30
White, Frank	83D	464	$ .01	$ .05	Williams, Eddie	89DTR	29	$ .01	$ .05
White, Frank	84D	222	$ .03	$ .10	Williams, Frank	85D	323	$ .03	$ .25
White, Frank	85D	175	$ .01	$ .08	Williams, Frank	88D	512	$ .01	$ .05
White, Frank	86D	130	$ .01	$ .06	Williams, Frank	89D	478	$ .01	$ .04
White, Frank	87D	255	$ .01	$ .04	Williams, Frank	89DBB	259	$ .01	$ .04
White, Frank	88D	225	$ .01	$ .05	Williams, Frank	90D	327	$ .01	$ .03
White, Frank	89D	85	$ .01	$ .04	Williams, Ken	87DR	11	$ .01	$ .25
White, Frank	89DBB	175	$ .01	$ .04	Williams, Ken	88D	334	$ .03	$ .25
White, Frank	90D	262	$ .01	$ .03	Williams, Ken	88DBB	249	$ .01	$ .05
White, Jerry	81D	333	$ .01	$ .05	Williams, Ken	89D	337	$ .01	$ .04
White, Jerry	82D	621	$ .01	$ .05	Williams, Ken	89DTR	17	$ .01	$ .05
White, Jerry	83D	602	$ .01	$ .05	Williams, Matt	87DR	45	$ .75	$3.50
Whitehouse, Len	84D	558	$ .03	$ .10	Williams, Matt	88D	628	$ .15	$1.00
Whitehouse, Len	85D	513	$ .01	$ .08	Williams, Matt	89D	594	$ .01	$ .25
Whitfield, Terry	81D	435	$ .01	$ .05	Williams, Matt	90D	348	$ .01	$ .10

DONRUSS

Player	Year	No.	VG	EX/MT
Williams, Mitch	86DR	19	$ .10	$ .65
Williams, Mitch	87D	347	$ .03	$ .45
Williams, Mitch	88D	161	$ .01	$ .15
Williams, Mitch	89D	225	$ .01	$ .04
Williams, Mitch	89DBB	60	$ .01	$ .04
Williams, Mitch	89DTR	38	$ .01	$ .05
Williams, Mitch	90D	275	$ .01	$ .03
Williams, Reggie	86DR	5	$ .02	$ .09
Williams, Reggie	87D	341	$ .01	$ .04
Williamson, Mark	87DR	3	$ .01	$ .07
Williamson, Mark	88D	418	$ .01	$ .05
Williamson, Mark	90D	406	$ .01	$ .03
Wills, Bump	81D	25	$ .01	$ .05
Wills, Bump	82D	289	$ .01	$ .05
Wills, Bump	83D	351	$ .01	$ .05
Wilson, Glenn	83D	580	$ .06	$ .35
Wilson, Glenn	84D	618	$ .03	$ .10
Wilson, Glenn	85D	609	$ .01	$ .08
Wilson, Glenn	86D	285	$ .01	$ .06
Wilson, Glenn	87D	62	$ .01	$ .04
Wilson, Glenn	88D	262	$ .01	$ .05
Wilson, Glenn	89D	447	$ .01	$ .04
Wilson, Glenn	89DBB	241	$ .01	$ .04
Wilson, Glenn	90D	472	$ .01	$ .03
Wilson, Mookie	81D	575	$ .08	$ .50
Wilson, Mookie	82D	175	$ .01	$ .10
Wilson, Mookie	83D	56	$ .01	$ .10
Wilson, Mookie	84D	190	$ .03	$ .10
Wilson, Mookie	85D	482	$ .01	$ .08
Wilson, Mookie	86D	604	$ .01	$ .06
Wilson, Mookie	88D	652	$ .01	$ .15
Wilson, Mookie	88DBB	208	$ .01	$ .05
Wilson, Mookie	89D	152	$ .01	$ .04
Wilson, Mookie	90D	442	$ .01	$ .03
Wilson, Steve	89DBB	250	$ .01	$ .04
Wilson, Steve	89DR	10	$ .01	$ .10
Wilson, Steve	90D	394	$ .01	$ .03
Wilson, Trevor	90D	414	$ .01	$ .03
Wilson, Willie	81D	223	$ .01	$ .15
Wilson, Willie	82D	448	$ .03	$ .20
Wilson, Willie	83D	112	$ .03	$ .20
Wilson, Willie	83DK	15	$ .03	$ .20
Wilson, Willie	84D	175	$ .04	$ .25
Wilson, Willie	85D	297	$ .01	$ .08
Wilson, Willie	86D	175	$ .01	$ .06
Wilson, Willie	87D	487	$ .01	$ .04
Wilson, Willie	87D	96	$ .01	$ .04
Wilson, Willie	88D	255	$ .01	$ .05
Wilson, Willie	88DBB	263	$ .01	$ .05
Wilson, Willie	89D	120	$ .01	$ .04
Wilson, Willie	90D	440	$ .01	$ .03
Wine, Robbie	88D	508	$ .01	$ .05
Winfield, Dave	81D	364	$ .10	$ .75
Winfield, Dave	82D	31	$ .10	$ .50
Winfield, Dave	82D	575	$ .10	$ .50
Winfield, Dave	82DK	18	$ .10	$ .45
Winfield, Dave	83D	409	$ .10	$ .45
Winfield, Dave	84D	51	$ .20	$1.00
Winfield, Dave	85D	51	$ .10	$ .35
Winfield, Dave	85D	651	$1.00	$5.00
Winfield, Dave	86D	248	$ .08	$ .25
Winfield, Dave	87D	105	$ .10	$ .35
Winfield, Dave	87DK	20	$ .10	$ .35
Winfield, Dave	88D	298	$ .05	$ .20
Winfield, Dave	88DBB	244	$ .01	$ .15
Winfield, Dave	89D	159	$ .01	$ .10
Winfield, Dave	89DBC	11	$ .01	$ .10
Winfield, Dave	90D	551	$ .01	$ .15
Winn, Jim	87D	312	$ .01	$ .04
Winn, Jim	88D	409	$ .01	$ .05
Winningham, Herm	86D	279	$ .02	$ .15
Winningham, Herm	88D	581	$ .01	$ .05
Winningham, Herm	89D	435	$ .01	$ .04
Winningham, Herm	90D	478	$ .01	$ .03
Wise, Rick	81D	3	$ .01	$ .05

Player	Year	No.	VG	EX/MT
Wise, Rick	82D	170	$ .01	$ .05
Witt, Bobby	86DR	49	$ .15	$ .50
Witt, Bobby	87D	99	$ .08	$ .25
Witt, Bobby	88D	101	$ .01	$ .05
Witt, Bobby	89D	461	$ .01	$ .04
Witt, Bobby	89DBB	279	$ .01	$ .04
Witt, Bobby	90D	292	$ .01	$ .03
Witt, Mike	82D	416	$ .25	$1.00
Witt, Mike	83D	416	$ .03	$ .20
Witt, Mike	85D	108	$ .01	$ .08
Witt, Mike	86D	179	$ .01	$ .06
Witt, Mike	87D	58	$ .05	$ .20
Witt, Mike	88D	86	$ .01	$ .05
Witt, Mike	89D	372	$ .01	$ .04

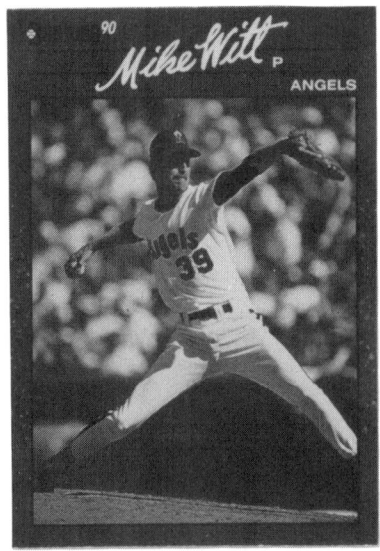

Player	Year	No.	VG	EX/MT
Witt, Mike	90D	580	$ .01	$ .03
Wlaker, Greg	86D	135	$ .05	$ .20
Wockenfuss, John	81D	245	$ .01	$ .05
Wockenfuss, John	82D	459	$ .01	$ .05
Wockenfuss, John	83D	76	$ .01	$ .05
Wockenfuss, John	84D	150	$ .03	$ .10
Wockenfuss, John	85D	549	$ .01	$ .08
Wohlford, Jim	81D	316	$ .01	$ .05
Wohlford, Jim	83D	524	$ .01	$ .05
Wohlford, Jim	85D	585	$ .01	$ .08
Wohlford, Jim	86D	157	$ .01	$ .06
Wojna, Ed	86D	505	$ .01	$ .06
Wojna, Ed	87D	589	$ .01	$ .04
Woodard, Mike	86DRR	46	$ .01	$ .06
Woods, Al	81D	32	$ .01	$ .05
Woods, Al	82D	180	$ .01	$ .05
Woods, Gary	83D	631	$ .01	$ .05
Woods, Gary	84D	144	$ .03	$ .10
Woods, Gary	85D	555	$ .01	$ .08
Woodson, Tracy	88D	499	$ .01	$ .05
Woodward, Rob	86DR	53	$ .02	$ .09
Woodward, Rob	87D	652	$ .01	$ .04
Worrell, Todd	86DR	21	$ .15	$ .50
Worrell, Todd	86DRR	43	$ .30	$1.00
Worrell, Todd	87D	307	$ .05	$ .20
Worrell, Todd	88D	386	$ .01	$ .15
Worrell, Todd	89D	82	$ .01	$ .04
Worrell, Todd	89DBB	243	$ .01	$ .04
Worrell, Todd	90D	319	$ .01	$ .03

Player	Year	No.	VG	EX/MT	Player	Year	No.	VG	EX/MT
Wortham, Rich	81D	161	$ .01	$ .05	Young, Curt	90D	505	$ .01	$ .03
Worthington, Craig	88DR	23	$ .05	$1.00	Young, Gerald	88D	431	$ .05	$ .40
Worthington, Craig	89D	569	$ .01	$ .50	Young, Gerald	89D	207	$ .01	$ .04
Worthington, Craig	89DBB	282	$ .01	$ .10	Young, Gerald	89DBB	288	$ .01	$ .04
Worthington, Craig	89DR	25	$ .01	$ .25	Young, Gerald	90D	325	$ .01	$ .03
Worthington, Craig	90D	141	$ .01	$ .03	Young, Matt	84D	362	$ .03	$ .10
Wright, George	83D	116	$ .01	$ .05	Young, Matt	84DK	16	$ .03	$ .10
Wright, George	84D	525	$ .03	$ .10	Young, Matt	85D	267	$ .01	$ .08
Wright, George	85D	256	$ .01	$ .08	Young, Matt	86D	267	$ .01	$ .06
Wright, George	86D	220	$ .01	$ .06	Young, Matt	87D	193	$ .01	$ .04
Wright, Jim	82D	490	$ .01	$ .05	Young, Matt	88D	423	$ .01	$ .05
Wrona, Rick	89DR	38	$ .01	$ .25	Young, Mike	85D	367	$ .03	$ .20
Wrona, Rick	90D	512	$ .01	$ .15	Young, Mike	84D	621	$ .10	$ .35
Wynegar, Butch	81D	529	$ .01	$ .05	Young, Mike	86D	123	$ .01	$ .06
Wynegar, Butch	82D	508	$ .01	$ .05	Young, Mike	87D	150	$ .01	$ .04
Wynegar, Butch	83D	325	$ .01	$ .05	Young, Mike	88D	396	$ .01	$ .05
Wynegar, Butch	84D	458	$ .03	$ .10	Young, Mike	89D	632	$ .01	$ .04
Wynegar, Butch	85D	417	$ .01	$ .08	Youngblood, Joel	81D	277	$ .01	$ .05
Wynegar, Butch	86D	274	$ .01	$ .06	Youngblood, Joel	82D	613	$ .01	$ .05
Wynne, Marvell	84D	508	$ .03	$ .10	Youngblood, Joel	83D	572	$ .01	$ .05
Wynne, Marvell	85D	113	$ .01	$ .08	Youngblood, Joel	84D	480	$ .03	$ .10
Wynne, Marvell	86D	113	$ .01	$ .06	Youngblood, Joel	85D	79	$ .01	$ .08
Wynne, Marvell	87D	411	$ .01	$ .04	Youngblood, Joel	86D	567	$ .01	$ .06
Wynne, Marvell	88D	237	$ .01	$ .05	Yount, Robin	81D	323	$ .15	$1.75
Wynne, Marvell	89D	347	$ .01	$ .04	Yount, Robin	82D	510	$ .15	$1.25
Wynne, Marvell	89DBB	189	$ .01	$ .04	Yount, Robin	83D	258	$ .10	$1.00
Wynne, Marvell	90D	255	$ .01	$ .03	Yount, Robin	84D	48	$ .50	$2.00
Yastrzemski, Carl	81D	214	$ .25	$1.00	Yount, Robin	84DK	1	$ .35	$1.25
Yastrzemski, Carl	81D	94	$ .25	$1.50	Yount, Robin	85D	48	$ .10	$1.00
Yastrzemski, Carl	82D	74	$ .15	$1.50	Yount, Robin	86D	48	$ .10	$ .75
Yastrzemski, Carl	83D	326	$ .15	$1.00	Yount, Robin	87D	126	$ .08	$ .40
Yastrzemski, Carl	83DK	25	$ .15	$1.00	Yount, Robin	88D	295	$ .05	$ .20
Yastrzemski, Carl	84D#B	0	$1.50	$8.00	Yount, Robin	88DBB	183	$ .01	$ .15
Yastrzemski, Carl	90D	588	$ .01	$ .10	Yount, Robin	89D	55	$ .03	$ .15
Yeager, Steve	81D	297	$ .02	$ .15	Yount, Robin	89DBB	53	$ .01	$ .20
Yeager, Steve	82D	201	$ .01	$ .05	Yount, Robin	89DK	5	$ .01	$ .10
Yeager, Steve	83D	201	$ .01	$ .05	Yount, Robin	90D	146	$ .01	$ .10
Yeager, Steve	84D	581	$ .03	$ .10	Zachry, Pat	81D	275	$ .01	$ .05
Yeager, Steve	85D	519	$ .01	$ .08	Zachry, Pat	82D	254	$ .01	$ .05
Yeager, Steve	86D	519	$ .01	$ .06	Zachry, Pat	83D	560	$ .01	$ .05
Yelding, Eric	89DR	34	$ .01	$ .10	Zachry, Pat	84D	215	$ .03	$ .10
Yelding, Eric	90D	123	$ .01	$ .03	Zahn, Geoff	82D	164	$ .01	$ .05
Yett, Rich	89D	546	$ .01	$ .04	Zahn, Geoff	83D	66	$ .01	$ .05
Yett, Rich	90D	509	$ .01	$ .03	Zahn, Geoff	84D	402	$ .03	$ .10
Yost, Ned	83D	458	$ .01	$ .05	Zahn, Geoff	85D	301	$ .01	$ .08
Yost, Ned	84D	271	$ .03	$ .10	Zahn, Geoff (Jeff)	81D	532	$ .01	$ .05
Yost, Ned	85D	221	$ .01	$ .08	Zavaras, Clint	90D	662	$ .01	$ .10
Youmans, Floyd	86D	543	$ .20	$ .60	Zeile, Todd	90DRR	29	$ .01	$2.00
Youmans, Floyd	87D	257	$ .01	$ .15	Zimmer, Don	82D	195	$ .01	$ .05
Youmans, Floyd	88D	56	$ .01	$ .15	Zisk, Richie	81D	28	$ .01	$ .05
Young, Curt	85D	522	$ .15	$ .50	Zisk, Richie	82D	127	$ .01	$ .05
Young, Curt	87D	344	$ .01	$ .04	Zisk, Richie	82DK	11	$ .01	$ .05
Young, Curt	88D	97	$ .01	$ .05	Zisk, Richie	83D	559	$ .01	$ .05
Young, Curt	89D	304	$ .01	$ .04	Zisk, Richie	84D	69	$ .03	$ .10

FLEER CORPORATION 1981-1990

The Fleer Company issued a baseball card set in 1981 to compete with Topps and the newly released Donruss cards. Fleer also issued these cards in wax packs with bubble gum, but was forced to issue the cards without bubble gum in 1982 as Topps was able to stop the bubble gum format through a lawsuit. Fleer has chosen to issue their wax packs packages with a peel off sticker since 1982.

Fleer made the same mistake as Donruss the first few years. They over produced their product and glutted the market. Today, the 1981 and 1982 sets are priced less than any of the subsequent sets. They sell for about the current price of the 1989 sets.

Fleer began issuing factory sets in 1984. Unlike Donruss, the sets are not in numerical order. Beginning in 1988, Fleer attached a factory seal to the box to show if it has been opened or not. This is a significant breakthrough in my way of thinking. Now an unopened factory set can be believed!

All Fleer cards are 2½" x 3½" and in full color.

1981 - 660 cards w/white border and player's team in baseball on left (Fleer found on back to right of card number but no date on card)

1982 - 660 cards w/white border and player's name, team and position in oval design (Fleer name found under card's number on the back but no date on card)

1983 - 660 cards w/beige border (copyright 1983 Fleer above statistical information on back)

1984 - 660 cards w/white border and blue stripes inside border top and bottom (copyright 1984 Fleer above statistical information on back)

1985 - 660 cards w/grey border and Fleer in white at lower right (copyright 1985 Fleer on back above statistical information)

1986 - 660 cards w/dark blue border w/Fleer in white on top right (copyright 1986 Fleer on back bottom)

1987 - 660 cards w/sky blue and white border w/Fleer in white on colored strip at bottom (copyright 1987 Fleer top right on back)

1988 - 660 cards w/white border w/blue and red stripes and Fleer in blue box at bottom right (copyright 1988 Fleer on back above statistical breakdown)

1989 - 660 cards w/grey border w/white vertical stripes and Fleer in black print on lower right (copyright 1989 Fleer on back lower left side)

1990 - 660 cards w/white borders; player encircled by a colored banner and Fleer '90 in upper left corner (copyright 1990 Fleer Corp. on back at bottom)

Abbreviations used in the Fleer section include the following:

F - Fleer used for all cards in this section

FPD - Player of decade ten card subset issued in 1990 with one card per year of Fleer's first ten years back in the baseball card business.

FU - Update card issued at end of year in sets of 132 since 1984.

The listing for each card shown appears immediately following the photograph.

Player	Year	No.	VG	EX/MT	Player	Year	No.	VG	EX/MT
Aase, Don	81F	286	$ .01	$ .04	Allen, Klm	81F	612	$ .01	$ .04
Aase, Don	82F	450	$ .01	$ .04	Allen, Neil	81F	322	$ .01	$ .04
Aase, Don	83F	76	$ .01	$ .04	Allen, Neil	82F	520	$ .01	$ .04
Aase, Don	85F	293	$ .01	$ .05	Allen, Neil	83F	536	$ .01	$ .04
Aase, Don	85FU	1	$ .01	$ .10	Allen, Neil	84F	318	$ .01	$ .06
Aase, Don	86F	268	$ .01	$ .05	Allen, Neil	85F	219	$ .01	$ .05
Aase, Don	87F	461	$ .01	$ .04	Allen, Neil	86F	98	$ .01	$ .05
Aase, Don	87F	627	$ .01	$ .10	Allen, Neil	86FU	3	$ .01	$ .05
Aase, Don	88F	553	$ .01	$ .04	Allen, Neil	87F	484	$ .01	$ .04
Aase, Don	89FU	100	$ .01	$ .05	Allen, Neil	89F	250	$ .01	$ .05
Aase, Don	90F	196	$ .01	$ .03	Allen, Rod	89F	397	$ .01	$ .05
Abbott, Glenn	81F	615	$ .01	$ .04	Allenson, Gary	82F	287	$ .01	$ .04
Abbott, Glenn	82F	502	$ .01	$ .04	Allenson, Gary	83F	177	$ .01	$ .04
Abbott, Glenn	84F	74	$ .01	$ .06	Allenson, Gary	84F	388	$ .01	$ .06
Abbott, Jim	89FU	11	$ .01	$3.00	Allenson, Gary	85F	148	$ .01	$ .05
Abbott, Jim	90F	125	$ .01	$1.00	Almon, Bill	81F	332	$ .01	$ .04
Abner, Shawn	88F	576	$ .01	$ .20	Almon, Bill	82F	335	$ .01	$ .04
Acker, Jim	84F	145	$ .03	$ .10	Almon, Bill	83F	228	$ .01	$ .04
Acker, Jim	85F	96	$ .01	$ .05	Almon, Bill	84F	436	$ .01	$ .06
Acker, Jim	86F	50	$ .01	$ .05	Almon, Bill	85F	414	$ .01	$ .05
Acker, Jim	87F	509	$ .01	$ .04	Almon, Bill	85FU	2	$ .01	$ .05
Acker, Jim	88F	531	$ .01	$ .04	Almon, Bill	86F	602	$ .01	$ .05
Adams, Glenn	81F	562	$ .01	$ .04	Almon, Bill	87F	601	$ .01	$ .04
Adams, Glenn	82F	545	$ .01	$ .04	Alomar, Jr., Sandy	89F	300	$ .25	$1.50
Adduci, Jim	89F	176	$ .01	$ .05	Alomar, Jr., Sandy	89F	630	$ .01	$ .25
Agosto, Juan	84F	50	$ .01	$ .06	Alomar, Jr., Sandy	90F	150	$ .01	$ .30
Agosto, Juan	85F	506	$ .01	$ .05	Alomar, Roberto	88FU	122	$ .05	$1.25
Agosto, Juan	86F	197	$ .01	$ .05	Alomar, Roberto	89F	299	$ .05	$ .50
Agosto, Juan	88F	437	$ .01	$ .04	Alomar, Roberto	89F	630	$ .01	$ .25
Agosto, Juan	89F	348	$ .01	$ .05	Alomar, Roberto	90F	149	$ .01	$ .10
Agosto, Juan	90F	220	$ .01	$ .03	Alou, Moises	90F	650	$ .01	$ .35
Aguayo, Luis	82F	238	$ .01	$ .04	Altamirano, Porfirio	83F	153	$ .01	$ .04
Aguayo, Luis	86F	433	$ .01	$ .05	Altobelli, Joe	84F	643	$ .01	$ .06
Aguayo, Luis	87F	169	$ .01	$ .04	Alvarez, Jose	88FU	70	$ .01	$ .15
Aguayo, Luis	88F	297	$ .01	$ .04	Alvarez, Jose	89F	585	$ .01	$ .15
Aguayo, Luis	89F	249	$ .01	$ .05	Alvarez, Jose	90F	574	$ .01	$ .03
Aguilera, Rick	86F	74	$ .06	$ .35	Andersen, Larry	83F	470	$ .01	$ .04
Aguilera, Rick	87F	1	$ .01	$ .10	Andersen, Larry	85F	244	$ .01	$ .05
Aguilera, Rick	88F	127	$ .01	$ .04	Andersen, Larry	86F	434	$ .01	$ .05
Aguilera, Rick	89F	27	$ .01	$ .05	Andersen, Larry	87F	49	$ .01	$ .04
Aguilera, Rick	90F	365	$ .01	$ .03					
Aikens, Willie	81F	43	$ .01	$ .04					
Aikens, Willie	82F	404	$ .01	$ .04					
Aikens, Willie	83F	104	$ .01	$ .04					
Aikens, Willie	84F	341	$ .01	$ .06					
Aikens, Willie	84FU	1	$ .04	$ .25					
Aikens, Willie	85F	97	$ .01	$ .05					
Ainge, Dan	81F	418	$ .05	$ .30					
Ainge, Danny	82F	608	$ .01	$ .10					
Aldrete, Mike	86FU	1	$ .05	$ .30					
Aldrete, Mike	87F	264	$ .06	$ .25					
Aldrete, Mike	88F	76	$ .01	$ .10					
Aldrete, Mike	89F	323	$ .01	$ .05					
Aldrete, Mike	89FU	95	$ .01	$ .05					
Aldrich, Jay	88F	155	$ .01	$ .10					
Alexander, Doyle	81F	255	$ .01	$ .10					
Alexander, Doyle	82F	383	$ .01	$ .10					
Alexander, Doyle	84F	146	$ .01	$ .06					
Alexander, Doyle	85F	98	$ .01	$ .05					
Alexander, Doyle	86F	51	$ .01	$ .05					
Alexander, Doyle	87F	510	$ .01	$ .04					
Alexander, Doyle	88F	51	$ .01	$ .04					
Alexander, Doyle	89F	128	$ .01	$ .05					
Alexander, Doyle	90F	599	$ .01	$ .03					
Alexander, Gary	81F	398	$ .01	$ .04					
Alexander, Gary	82F	475	$ .01	$ .04					
Alicea, Luis	88FU	116	$ .01	$ .15					
Alicea, Luis	89F	443	$ .01	$ .15					
All-Star Game, Cleveland	82F	628	$ .01	$ .04					
Allanson, Andy	86FU	2	$ .04	$ .25					
Allanson, Andy	87F	241	$ .01	$ .10					
Allanson, Andy	88FU	21	$ .01	$ .05					
Allanson, Andy	89F	396	$ .01	$ .05	Andersen, Larry	88F	438	$ .01	$ .04
Allanson, Andy	90F	483	$ .01	$ .03	Andersen, Larry	89F	349	$ .01	$ .05
Allen, Jamie	84F	604	$ .01	$ .06	Andersen, Larry	90F	221	$ .01	$ .03

FLEER

Player	Year	No.	VG	EX/MT	Player	Year	No.	VG	EX/MT
Anderson, Allan	87F	533	$ .01	$ .40	Armas, Tony	90F	126	$ .01	$ .03
Anderson, Allan	88FU	41	$ .01	$ .15	Armstrong, Jack	90F	412	$ .01	$ .50
Anderson, Allan	89F	102	$ .01	$ .15	Armstrong, Mike	81F	503	$ .01	$ .04
Anderson, Allan	90F	366	$ .01	$ .03	Armstrong, Mike	83F	105	$ .01	$ .04
Anderson, Brady	89F	606	$ .01	$ .30	Armstrong, Mike	84F	342	$ .01	$ .06
Anderson, Brady	90F	172	$ .01	$ .03	Armstrong, Mike	85F	120	$ .01	$ .05
Anderson, Dave	84F	533	$ .01	$ .06	Arnsberg, Brad	88F	202	$ .01	$ .15
Anderson, Dave	85F	366	$ .01	$ .05	Arroyo, Fernando	82F	546	$ .01	$ .04
Anderson, Dave	86F	123	$ .01	$ .05	Asadoor, Randy	87F	650	$ .04	$ .25
Anderson, Dave	87F	436	$ .01	$ .04	Ashby, Alan	81F	64	$ .01	$ .04
Anderson, Dave	88F	508	$ .01	$ .04	Ashby, Alan	82F	212	$ .01	$ .04
Anderson, Dave	89F	53	$ .01	$ .05	Ashby, Alan	83F	445	$ .01	$ .04
Anderson, Jim	81F	598	$ .01	$ .04	Ashby, Alan	84F	220	$ .01	$ .06
Anderson, Jim	82F	503	$ .01	$ .04	Ashby, Alan	85F	343	$ .01	$ .05
Anderson, Rick	87F	2	$ .01	$ .04	Ashby, Alan	86F	292	$ .01	$ .05
Anderson, Sparky	81F	460	$ .01	$ .10	Ashby, Alan	87F	50	$ .01	$ .04
Anderson, Sparky	85F	628	$ .01	$ .05	Ashby, Alan	88F	439	$ .01	$ .04
Andujar, Joaquin	81F	63	$ .01	$ .10	Ashby, Alan	89F	350	$ .01	$ .05
Andujar, Joaquin	82F	110	$ .01	$ .10	Asselstine, Brian	81F	256	$ .01	$ .04
Andujar, Joaquin	83F	1	$ .01	$ .10	Asselstine, Brian	82F	428	$ .01	$ .04
Andujar, Joaquin	84F	319	$ .03	$ .10	Assenmacher, Paul	86FU	5	$ .04	$ .25
Andujar, Joaquin	85F	220	$ .01	$ .05	Assenmacher, Paul	87F	511	$ .01	$ .04
Andujar, Joaquin	86F	26	$ .01	$ .10	Assenmacher, Paul	88F	532	$ .01	$ .04
Andujar, Joaquin	86FU	4	$ .01	$ .05	Assenmacher, Paul	89F	586	$ .01	$ .05
Andujar, Joaquin	87F	385	$ .01	$ .04	Assenmacher, Paul	90F	25	$ .01	$ .03
Anthony, Eric	90F	222	$ .01	$2.00	Atherton, Keith	84F	437	$ .01	$ .06
Aponte, Luis	83F	178	$ .01	$ .04	Atherton, Keith	85F	415	$ .01	$ .05
Aponte, Luis	84F	389	$ .01	$ .06	Atherton, Keith	86F	410	$ .01	$ .05
Aponte, Luis	84FU	2	$ .01	$ .10	Atherton, Keith	87F	534	$ .01	$ .04
Aponte, Luis	85F	437	$ .01	$ .05	Atherton, Keith	88F	1	$ .01	$ .04
Appier, Kevin	89FU	35	$ .01	$ .25	Atherton, Keith	89F	103	$ .01	$ .05
Appier, Kevin	90F	100	$ .01	$ .15	Atherton, Keith	89FU	24	$ .01	$ .05
Aquino, Luis	89F	275	$ .01	$ .05	August, Don	88FU	37	$ .01	$ .25
Aquino, Luis	90F	101	$ .01	$ .03	August, Don	89F	177	$ .01	$ .10
Armas, Tony	81F	575	$ .01	$ .10	Augustine, Jerry	82F	133	$ .01	$ .04
Armas, Tony	82F	85	$ .01	$ .10	Augustine, Jerry	83F	26	$ .01	$ .04
Armas, Tony	83F	513	$ .03	$ .20	Augustine, Jerry	84F	194	$ .01	$ .06
Armas, Tony	84F	390	$ .01	$ .06	Ault, Doug	81F	424	$ .01	$ .04
Armas, Tony	85F	149	$ .01	$ .05	Aviles, Ramon	81F	23	$ .01	$ .04
Armas, Tony	86F	339	$ .01	$ .05	Aviles, Ramon	82F	239	$ .01	$ .04
					Ayala, Benny	81F	185	$ .01	$ .04
					Ayala, Benny	82F	157	$ .01	$ .04
					Ayala, Benny	83F	52	$ .01	$ .04
					Babbitt, Shooty	82F	86	$ .01	$ .04
					Backman, Wally	81F	336	$ .10	$ .50
					Backman, Wally	83F	537	$ .01	$ .04
					Backman, Wally	85F	72	$ .01	$ .05
					Backman, Wally	86F	75	$ .01	$ .05
					Backman, Wally	87F	3	$ .01	$ .04
					Backman, Wally	88F	128	$ .01	$ .04
					Backman, Wally	89F	28	$ .01	$ .05
					Backman, Wally	89FU	43	$ .01	$ .05
					Backman, Wally	90F	367	$ .01	$ .03
					Bahnsen, Stan	81F	156	$ .01	$ .04
					Bahnsen, Stan	82F	183	$ .01	$ .04
					Bailes, Scott	86FU	6	$ .04	$ .25
					Bailes, Scott	87F	242	$ .01	$ .10
					Bailes, Scott	88F	600	$ .01	$ .04
					Bailes, Scott	89F	398	$ .01	$ .05
					Bailes, Scott	90F	484	$ .01	$ .03
					Bailey, Howard	84F	75	$ .01	$ .06
					Bailey, Mark	84FU	3	$ .06	$ .35
					Bailey, Mark	85F	344	$ .01	$ .05
					Bailey, Mark	86F	293	$ .01	$ .05
					Bailor, Bob	81F	409	$ .01	$ .04
					Bailor, Bob	82F	521	$ .01	$ .04
					Bailor, Bob	83F	538	$ .01	$ .04
					Bailor, Bob	84F	580	$ .01	$ .06
					Bailor, Bob	84FU	4	$ .01	$ .10
					Bailor, Bob	85F	367	$ .01	$ .05
					Bailor, Bob	86F	124	$ .01	$ .05
					Baines, Harold	81F	346	$ .25	$2.00
Armas, Tony	87F	26	$ .01	$ .04	Baines, Harold	82F	336	$ .04	$ .35
Armas, Tony	88F	484	$ .01	$ .04	Baines, Harold	83F	229	$ .03	$ .20
Armas, Tony	89F	467	$ .01	$ .05	Baines, Harold	84F	51	$ .03	$ .20

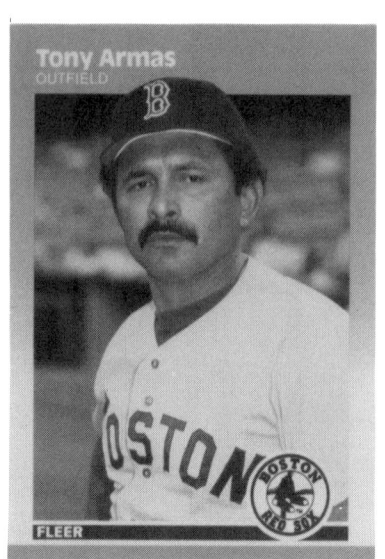

Tony Armas
OUTFIELD

Player	Year	No.	VG	EX/MT	Player	Year	No.	VG	EX/MT
Baines, Harold	85F	507	$ .04	$ .25	Barker, Len	81F	408	$ .01	$ .04
Baines, Harold	86F	198	$ .01	$ .10	Barker, Len	82F	360	$ .01	$ .04
Baines, Harold	87F	485	$ .03	$ .20	Barker, Len	82F	639	$ .01	$ .04
Baines, Harold	87F	643	$ .01	$ .04	Barker, Len	83F	402	$ .01	$ .04
Baines, Harold	88F	391	$ .01	$ .10	Barker, Len	83F	642	$ .01	$ .04
Baines, Harold	89F	491	$ .01	$ .05	Barker, Len	84F	170	$ .01	$ .06
Baines, Harold	90F	290	$ .01	$ .03	Barker, Len	85F	318	$ .01	$ .05
Bair, Doug	81F	213	$ .01	$ .04	Barker, Len	86F	507	$ .01	$ .05
Bair, Doug	83F	2	$ .01	$ .04	Barojas, Salome	83F	230	$ .01	$ .04
Bair, Doug	84F	76	$ .01	$ .06	Barojas, Salome	84F	53	$ .01	$ .06
Bair, Doug	85F	1	$ .01	$ .10	Barojas, Salome	85F	482	$ .01	$ .05
Bair, Doug	87F	386	$ .01	$ .04	Barr, Jim	81F	287	$ .01	$ .04
Baker, Chuck	81F	500	$ .01	$ .04	Barr, Jim	83F	252	$ .01	$ .04
Baker, Chuck	82F	561	$ .01	$ .04	Barr, Jim	84F	365	$ .01	$ .06
Baker, Doug	90F	368	$ .01	$ .10	Barrett, Marty	84FU	8	$ .50	$4.00
Baker, Dusty	81F	115	$ .01	$ .10	Barrett, Marty	85F	150	$ .05	$ .25
Baker, Dusty	82F	1	$ .01	$ .10	Barrett, Marty	86F	340	$ .01	$ .05
Baker, Dusty	83F	201	$ .01	$ .04	Barrett, Marty	87F	27	$ .01	$ .10
Baker, Dusty	84F	96	$ .01	$ .06	Barrett, Marty	88F	343	$ .01	$ .04
Baker, Dusty	84FU	5	$ .06	$ .35	Barrett, Marty	89F	78	$ .01	$ .05
Baker, Dusty	85F	602	$ .01	$ .05	Barrett, Marty	90F	266	$ .01	$ .03
Baker, Dusty	85FU	3	$ .01	$ .10	Barrios, Francisco	81F	352	$ .01	$ .04
Baker, Dusty	86F	411	$ .01	$ .05	Bass, Kevin	84F	221	$ .04	$ .25
Baker, Dusty	87F	387	$ .01	$ .04	Bass, Kevin	85F	345	$ .01	$ .10
Balboni, Steve	84FU	6	$ .06	$ .35	Bass, Kevin	86F	294	$ .01	$ .10
Balboni, Steve	85F	196	$ .01	$ .05	Bass, Kevin	87F	51	$ .01	$ .10
Balboni, Steve	86F	1	$ .01	$ .10	Bass, Kevin	88F	440	$ .01	$ .04
Balboni, Steve	87F	362	$ .01	$ .04	Bass, Kevin	89F	351	$ .01	$ .05
Balboni, Steve	88F	251	$ .01	$ .04	Bass, Kevin	90F	223	$ .01	$ .03
Balboni, Steve	89F	538	$ .01	$ .05	Bass, Randy	82F	566	$ .01	$ .04
Balboni, Steve	89FU	45	$ .01	$ .05	Bathe, Bill	86FU	9	$ .01	$ .05
Balboni, Steve	90F	436	$ .01	$ .03	Baumgarten, Ross	82F	337	$ .01	$ .04
Ballard, Jeff	88F	554	$ .01	$ .10	Baumgarten, Ross	83F	302	$ .01	$ .04
Ballard, Jeff	89F	607	$ .01	$ .05	Bautista, Jose	88FU	1	$ .01	$ .15
Ballard, Jeff	90F	173	$ .01	$ .03	Bautista, Jose	89F	608	$ .01	$ .15
Baller, Jay	86FU	7	$ .01	$ .05	Baylor, Don	81F	271	$ .03	$ .20
Bando, Chris	83F	400	$ .01	$ .04	Baylor, Don	82F	451	$ .01	$ .10
Bando, Chris	84F	534	$ .01	$ .06	Baylor, Don	83F	77	$ .01	$ .10
Bando, Chris	85F	438	$ .01	$ .05	Baylor, Don	84F	119	$ .03	$ .10
Bando, Chris	86F	579	$ .01	$ .05	Baylor, Don	85F	121	$ .03	$ .20
Bando, Chris	87F	243	$ .01	$ .04	Baylor, Don	86F	631	$ .04	$ .25
Bando, Chris	88F	601	$ .01	$ .04	Baylor, Don	86F	99	$ .01	$ .10
Bando, Sal	81F	510	$ .01	$ .04	Baylor, Don	86FU	10	$ .01	$ .10
Bando, Sal	82F	134	$ .01	$ .04	Baylor, Don	87F	28	$ .01	$ .10
Bankhead, Scott	86FU	8	$ .03	$ .20	Baylor, Don	88F	2	$ .01	$ .10
Bankhead, Scott	87F	363	$ .05	$ .25	Baylor, Don	89F	1	$ .01	$ .05
Bankhead, Scott	87FU	1	$ .01	$ .05	Beane, Billy	86FU	11	$ .01	$ .05
Bankhead, Scott	88F	368	$ .01	$ .04	Beane, Billy	87F	535	$ .01	$ .04
Bankhead, Scott	89F	539	$ .01	$ .05	Beard, Dave	82F	87	$ .01	$ .04
Bankhead, Scott	90F	505	$ .01	$ .03	Beard, Dave	83F	514	$ .01	$ .04
Bannister, Alan	82F	359	$ .01	$ .04	Beard, Dave	84F	438	$ .01	$ .06
Bannister, Alan	83F	401	$ .01	$ .04	Beard, Dave	84FU	9	$ .01	$ .10
Bannister, Alan	84F	535	$ .01	$ .06	Beard, Dave	85F	483	$ .01	$ .05
Bannister, Alan	85F	555	$ .01	$ .05	Beattie, Jim	83F	472	$ .01	$ .04
Bannister, Alan	86F	556	$ .01	$ .05	Beattie, Jim	84F	605	$ .01	$ .06
Bannister, Floyd	81F	599	$ .01	$ .04	Beattie, Jim	85F	484	$ .01	$ .05
Bannister, Floyd	82F	504	$ .01	$ .04	Beatty, Blaine	90F	197	$ .01	$ .10
Bannister, Floyd	83F	471	$ .01	$ .04	Beckwith, Joe	83F	202	$ .01	$ .04
Bannister, Floyd	84F	52	$ .01	$ .06	Beckwith, Joe	84F	97	$ .01	$ .06
Bannister, Floyd	85F	508	$ .01	$ .05	Beckwith, Joe	84FU	10	$ .01	$ .10
Bannister, Floyd	86F	199	$ .01	$ .05	Beckwith, Joe	85F	197	$ .01	$ .05
Bannister, Floyd	87F	486	$ .01	$ .04	Beckwith, Joe	86F	2	$ .01	$ .05
Bannister, Floyd	88F	392	$ .01	$ .04	Bedrosian, Steve	83F	129	$ .05	$ .30
Bannister, Floyd	89F	276	$ .01	$ .05	Bedrosian, Steve	84F	171	$ .03	$ .10
Bannister, Steve	84FU	7	$ .01	$ .10	Bedrosian, Steve	85F	319	$ .01	$ .10
Barfield, Jesse	83F	424	$ .10	$ .80	Bedrosian, Steve	86F	508	$ .01	$ .10
Barfield, Jesse	84F	147	$ .05	$ .30	Bedrosian, Steve	86FU	12	$ .01	$ .10
Barfield, Jesse	85F	99	$ .04	$ .25	Bedrosian, Steve	87F	170	$ .01	$ .10
Barfield, Jesse	86F	52	$ .04	$ .25	Bedrosian, Steve	88F	298	$ .01	$ .04
Barfield, Jesse	87F	219	$ .04	$ .25	Bedrosian, Steve	88F	627	$ .01	$ .10
Barfield, Jesse	87F	643	$ .01	$ .04	Bedrosian, Steve	89F	562	$ .01	$ .05
Barfield, Jesse	88F	102	$ .01	$ .10	Bedrosian, Steve	90F	50	$ .01	$ .03
Barfield, Jesse	89F	225	$ .01	$ .05	Belanger, Mark	81F	175	$ .01	$ .04
Barfield, Jesse	89FU	46	$ .01	$ .10	Belanger, Mark	82F	158	$ .01	$ .04
Barfield, Jesse	90F	437	$ .01	$ .03	Belcher, Tim	88F	509	$ .01	$ .50

FLEER

Player	Year	No.	VG	EX/MT	Player	Year	No.	VG	EX/MT
Belcher, Tim	89F	54	$ .01	$ .05	Berenyi, Bruce	85F	73	$ .01	$ .05
Belcher, Tim	90F	389	$ .01	$ .03	Bergman, Dave	81F	76	$ .01	$ .04
Bell, Buddy	81F	625	$ .03	$ .20	Bergman, Dave	83F	253	$ .01	$ .04
Bell, Buddy	82F	313	$ .03	$ .20	Bergman, Dave	84F	366	$ .01	$ .06
Bell, Buddy	83F	562	$ .03	$ .20	Bergman, Dave	84FU	11	$ .01	$ .10
Bell, Buddy	83F	632	$ .03	$ .20	Bergman, Dave	85F	3	$ .01	$ .05
Bell, Buddy	84F	413	$ .03	$ .20	Bergman, Dave	86F	222	$ .01	$ .05
Bell, Buddy	85F	556	$ .03	$ .20	Bergman, Dave	87F	144	$ .01	$ .04
Bell, Buddy	86F	172	$ .01	$ .10	Bergman, Dave	88F	52	$ .01	$ .04
Bell, Buddy	87F	193	$ .01	$ .10	Bergman, Dave	89F	129	$ .01	$ .05
Bell, Buddy	88F	227	$ .01	$ .10	Bergman, Dave	90F	600	$ .01	$ .03
Bell, Buddy	89F	352	$ .01	$ .05	Bernard, Dwight	83F	27	$ .01	$ .04
Bell, Eric	87FU	2	$ .01	$ .10	Bernazard, Tony	81F	168	$ .01	$ .04
Bell, Eric	88F	555	$ .01	$ .04	Bernazard, Tony	82F	338	$ .01	$ .04
Bell, George	84F	148	$ .20	$1.00	Bernazard, Tony	83F	231	$ .01	$ .04
Bell, George	85F	100	$ .10	$ .50	Bernazard, Tony	84F	606	$ .01	$ .06
Bell, George	86F	53	$ .06	$ .35	Bernazard, Tony	84FU	12	$ .04	$ .25
Bell, George	87F	220	$ .05	$ .30	Bernazard, Tony	85F	439	$ .01	$ .05
Bell, George	88F	103	$ .01	$ .25	Bernazard, Tony	86F	580	$ .01	$ .05
Bell, George	88F	623	$ .01	$ .04	Bernazard, Tony	87F	244	$ .01	$ .04
Bell, George	89F	226	$ .01	$ .10	Bernazard, Tony	88F	275	$ .01	$ .04
Bell, George	90F	76	$ .01	$ .03	Berra, Dale	81F	369	$ .01	$ .04
Bell, George	90FPD	628	$ .01	$ .15	Berra, Dale	82F	476	$ .01	$ .04
Bell, George (Jorge)	82F	609	$1.20	$6.00	Berra, Dale	83F	303	$ .01	$ .04
Bell, Jay	88F	602	$ .01	$ .15	Berra, Dale	84F	245	$ .01	$ .06
Bell, Jay	90F	459	$ .01	$ .03	Berra, Dale	85F	461	$ .01	$ .05
Bell, Kevin	81F	343	$ .01	$ .04	Berra, Dale	85FU	4	$ .01	$ .05
Belle, Joey	89FU	25	$ .01	$1.25	Berra, Dale	86F	100	$ .01	$ .05
Belle, Joey	90F	485	$ .01	$ .50	Berroa, Geronimo	89FU	72	$ .01	$ .10
Belliard, Rafael	87F	602	$ .01	$ .04	Berroa, Geronimo	90F	575	$ .01	$ .03
Belliard, Rafael	88F	321	$ .01	$ .04	Berryhill, Damon	88F	642	$ .01	$1.00
Belliard, Rafael	89F	201	$ .01	$ .05	Berryhill, Damon	88FU	75	$ .01	$ .30
Belliard, Rafael	90F	460	$ .01	$ .03	Berryhill, Damon	89F	418	$ .01	$ .10
Bench, Johnny	81F	196	$ .12	$1.00	Berryhill, Damon	90F	26	$ .01	$ .03
Bench, Johnny	82F	57	$ .10	$1.00	Best, Karl	85FU	5	$ .03	$ .20
Bench, Johnny	82F	634	$ .01	$ .30	Best, Karl	86F	459	$ .01	$ .05
Bench, Johnny	83F	584	$ .10	$1.00	Best, Karl	87F	579	$ .01	$ .04
Bench, Johnny	84F	462	$ .08	$1.00	Bevacqua, Kurt	81F	382	$ .01	$ .04
Bench, Johnny	84F	640	$ .10	$ .50	Bevacqua, Kurt	82F	477	$ .01	$ .04
Benedict, Bruce	81F	248	$ .01	$ .04	Bevacqua, Kurt	83F	352	$ .01	$ .04
Benedict, Bruce	82F	429	$ .01	$ .04	Bevacqua, Kurt	84F	294	$ .01	$ .06
Benedict, Bruce	83F	130	$ .01	$ .04	Bevacqua, Kurt	85F	26	$ .01	$ .05
Benedict, Bruce	84F	172	$ .01	$ .06	Bevacqua, Kurt	86F	315	$ .01	$ .05
Benedict, Bruce	85F	320	$ .01	$ .05	Biancalana, Buddy	86F	3	$ .01	$ .05
Benedict, Bruce	86F	509	$ .01	$ .05	Biancalana, Buddy	87F	364	$ .01	$ .04
Benedict, Bruce	87F	512	$ .01	$ .04	Bibby, Jim	81F	370	$ .01	$ .04
Benedict, Bruce	89F	587	$ .01	$ .05	Bibby, Jim	82F	478	$ .01	$ .04
Benes, Andy	90F	151	$ .01	$ .75	Bibby, Jim	84F	246	$ .01	$ .06
Beniquez, Juan	81F	596	$ .01	$ .04	Bichette, Dante	89F	468	$ .01	$ .15
Beniquez, Juan	82F	452	$ .01	$ .04	Bichette, Dante	90F	127	$ .01	$ .03
Beniquez, Juan	83F	78	$ .01	$ .04	Bielecki, Mike	85F	650	$ .05	$1.00
Beniquez, Juan	84F	508	$ .01	$ .06	Bielecki, Mike	86F	603	$ .01	$ .05
Beniquez, Juan	85F	294	$ .01	$ .05	Bielecki, Mike	87F	603	$ .01	$ .04
Beniquez, Juan	86F	148	$ .01	$ .05	Bielecki, Mike	89F	419	$ .01	$ .05
Beniquez, Juan	86FU	13	$ .01	$ .05	Bielecki, Mike	90F	27	$ .01	$ .03
Beniquez, Juan	87F	462	$ .01	$ .04	Biggio, Craig	88F	89	$ .01	$1.25
Beniquez, Juan	87FU	3	$ .01	$ .05	Biggio, Craig	89F	353	$ .01	$ .75
Beniquez, Juan	88F	104	$ .01	$ .04	Biggio, Craig	90F	224	$ .01	$ .15
Benjamin, Mike	90F	51	$ .01	$ .25	Biittner, Larry	81F	314	$ .01	$ .04
Benzinger, Todd	88F	344	$ .15	$ .75	Biittner, Larry	82F	59	$ .01	$ .04
Benzinger, Todd	88F	630	$ .10	$ .75	Biittner, Larry	83F	586	$ .01	$ .04
Benzinger, Todd	89F	79	$ .01	$ .15	Biittner, Larry	84F	414	$ .01	$ .06
Benzinger, Todd	89FU	83	$ .01	$ .05	Bilardello, Dann	84F	464	$ .01	$ .06
Benzinger, Todd	90F	413	$ .01	$ .03	Bilardello, Dann	87F	313	$ .01	$ .04
Berenguer, Juan	84F	77	$ .01	$ .06	Bird, Doug	81F	106	$ .01	$ .04
Berenguer, Juan	85F	2	$ .01	$ .05	Bird, Doug	82F	586	$ .01	$ .04
Berenguer, Juan	86F	221	$ .01	$ .05	Bird, Doug	83F	490	$ .01	$ .04
Berenguer, Juan	87F	265	$ .01	$ .04	Bird, Doug	84F	391	$ .01	$ .06
Berenguer, Juan	87FU	4	$ .01	$ .05	Birkbeck, Mike	87FU	5	$ .01	$ .05
Berenguer, Juan	88F	3	$ .01	$ .04	Birkbeck, Mike	89F	178	$ .01	$ .05
Berenguer, Juan	89F	104	$ .01	$ .05	Birtsas, Tim	85FU	6	$ .03	$ .20
Berenguer, Juan	90F	369	$ .01	$ .03	Birtsas, Tim	86F	412	$ .01	$ .10
Berenyi, Bruce	82F	58	$ .01	$ .04	Birtsas, Tim	88FU	82	$ .01	$ .05
Berenyi, Bruce	83F	585	$ .01	$ .04	Birtsas, Tim	89F	152	$ .01	$ .05
Berenyi, Bruce	84F	463	$ .01	$ .06	Birtsas, Tim	90F	414	$ .01	$ .03

Player	Year	No.	VG	EX/MT	Player	Year	No.	VG	EX/MT
Black, Bud	83F	107	$ .03	$ .20	Bomback, Mark	81F	323	$ .01	$ .04
Black, Bud	83F	644	$ .01	$ .04	Bomback, Mark	82F	610	$ .01	$ .04
Black, Bud	84F	343	$ .01	$ .06	Bonds, Barry	86FU	14	$ .25	$2.00
Black, Bud	85F	198	$ .01	$ .05	Bonds, Barry	87F	604	$ .25	$2.75
Black, Bud	86F	4	$ .01	$ .05	Bonds, Barry	88F	322	$ .10	$ .50
Black, Bud	87F	365	$ .01	$ .04	Bonds, Barry	89F	202	$ .01	$ .15
Black, Bud	88F	252	$ .01	$ .04	Bonds, Barry	90F	461	$ .01	$ .03
Black, Bud	90F	486	$ .01	$ .03	Bonds, Bobby	81F	548	$ .01	$ .10
Blackwell, Tim	81F	304	$ .01	$ .04	Bonds, Bobby	82F	588	$ .01	$ .04
Blackwell, Tim	82F	587	$ .01	$ .04	Bonham, Bill	81F	215	$ .01	$ .04
Blankenship, Kevin	90F	28	$ .01	$ .03	Bonilla, Bobby	86FU	15	$ .50	$2.50
Blankenship, Lance	89F	2	$ .01	$ .20	Bonilla, Bobby	87F	605	$ .75	$3.75
Blankenship, Lance	90F	1	$ .01	$ .03	Bonilla, Bobby	88F	323	$ .10	$ .60
Blauser, Jeff	88F	533	$ .01	$ .30	Bonilla, Bobby	89F	203	$ .01	$ .10
Blauser, Jeff	89F	588	$ .01	$ .05	Bonilla, Bobby	89F	637	$ .01	$ .35
Blauser, Jeff	90F	576	$ .01	$ .03	Bonilla, Bobby	90F	462	$ .01	$ .03
Blocker, Terry	89F	589	$ .01	$ .05	Bonilla, Juan	82F	567	$ .01	$ .04
Blowers, Mike	90F	438	$ .01	$ .25	Bonilla, Juan	83F	353	$ .01	$ .04
Blue, Vida	81F	432	$ .01	$ .10	Bonilla, Juan	84F	295	$ .01	$ .06
Blue, Vida	82F	384	$ .01	$ .10	Bonilla, Juan	87F	464	$ .01	$ .04
Blue, Vida	83F	106	$ .01	$ .04	Bonnell, Barry	81F	413	$ .01	$ .04
Blue, Vida	83F	643	$ .01	$ .04	Bonnell, Barry	82F	611	$ .01	$ .04
Blue, Vida	85FU	7	$ .03	$ .20	Bonnell, Barry	83F	425	$ .01	$ .04
Blue, Vida	86F	533	$ .01	$ .05	Bonnell, Barry	84F	149	$ .01	$ .06
Blue, Vida	87F	266	$ .01	$ .04	Bonnell, Barry	84FU	14	$ .01	$ .10
Blyleven, Bert	81F	383	$ .03	$ .20	Bonnell, Barry	85F	485	$ .01	$ .05
Blyleven, Bert	82F	361	$ .01	$ .25	Bonnell, Barry	86F	460	$ .01	$ .05
Blyleven, Bert	84F	536	$ .03	$ .10	Bonner, Bob	83F	53	$ .01	$ .04
Blyleven, Bert	85F	440	$ .01	$ .10	Booker, Greg	85F	27	$ .01	$ .10
Blyleven, Bert	86F	386	$ .01	$ .10	Booker, Greg	88F	577	$ .01	$ .04
Blyleven, Bert	87F	536	$ .01	$ .10	Booker, Rod	87FU	7	$ .01	$ .15
Blyleven, Bert	88F	4	$ .01	$ .10	Boone, Bob	81F	4	$ .01	$ .04
Blyleven, Bert	89F	105	$ .01	$ .10	Boone, Bob	82F	240	$ .01	$ .04
Blyleven, Bert	89FU	12	$ .01	$ .10	Boone, Bob	83F	79	$ .01	$ .04
Blyleven, Bert	90F	128	$ .01	$ .10	Boone, Bob	84F	509	$ .01	$ .06
Bobbicker, Mike	86F	269	$ .01	$ .10	Boone, Bob	84F	637	$ .01	$ .06
Bochte, Bruce	81F	600	$ .01	$ .04	Boone, Bob	85F	295	$ .01	$ .05
Bochte, Bruce	82F	505	$ .01	$ .04					
Bochte, Bruce	83F	473	$ .01	$ .04					
Bochte, Bruce	84FU	13	$ .01	$ .10					
Bochte, Bruce	85F	416	$ .01	$ .05					
Bochte, Bruce	86F	413	$ .01	$ .05					
Bochte, Bruce	87F	388	$ .01	$ .04					
Bochy, Bruce	81F	69	$ .01	$ .04					
Bochy, Bruce	87F	411	$ .01	$ .04					
Bockus, Randy	87FU	6	$ .01	$ .05					
Bockus, Randy	88FU	127	$ .01	$ .05					
Boddicker, Mike	84F	1	$ .03	$ .10					
Boddicker, Mike	84F	645	$ .01	$ .06					
Boddicker, Mike	85F	170	$ .01	$ .05					
Boddicker, Mike	87F	463	$ .01	$ .04					
Boddicker, Mike	88F	556	$ .01	$ .04					
Boddicker, Mike	88FU	5	$ .01	$ .05					
Boddicker, Mike	89F	80	$ .01	$ .05					
Boddicker, Mike	90F	267	$ .01	$ .03					
Boever, Joe	88F	534	$ .01	$ .10					
Boever, Joe	90F	577	$ .01	$ .03					
Boggs, Tommy	81F	261	$ .01	$ .04					
Boggs, Tommy	82F	430	$ .01	$ .04					
Boggs, Tommy	83F	131	$ .01	$ .04					
Boggs, Wade	83F	179	$4.00	$18.00					
Boggs, Wade	84F	392	$1.50	$ 7.00					
Boggs, Wade	84F	630	$ .10	$ .50					
Boggs, Wade	85F	151	$ .75	$4.00					
Boggs, Wade	86F	341	$ .50	$2.00					
Boggs, Wade	86F	634	$ .10	$ .50					
Boggs, Wade	86F	639	$ .30	$1.50					
Boggs, Wade	87F	29	$ .25	$1.50	Boone, Bob	86F	149	$ .01	$ .05
Boggs, Wade	87F	637	$ .06	$ .35	Boone, Bob	87F	73	$ .01	$ .04
Boggs, Wade	88F	345	$ .05	$ .50	Boone, Bob	88F	485	$ .01	$ .05
Boggs, Wade	89F	633	$ .05	$ .35	Boone, Bob	89F	469	$ .01	$ .05
Boggs, Wade	89F	81	$ .05	$ .50	Boone, Bob	89FU	36	$ .01	$ .05
Boggs, Wade	90F	268	$ .01	$ .35	Boone, Bob	90F	102	$ .01	$ .03
Boggs, Wade	90F	632	$ .01	$ .03					
Bolton, Tom	88F	346	$ .01	$ .10					

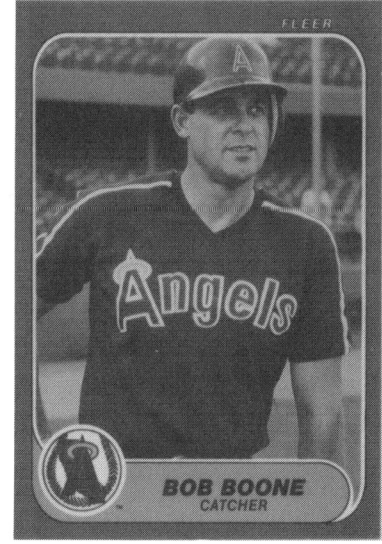

BOB BOONE
CATCHER

FLEER

Player	Year	No.	VG	EX/MT	Player	Year	No.	VG	EX/MT
Boone, Danny	82F	568	$ .01	$ .04	Bradley, Phil	88F	369	$ .01	$ .10
Borders, Pat	88FU	65	$ .01	$ .25	Bradley, Phil	88FU	107	$ .01	$ .05
Borders, Pat	89F	227	$ .01	$ .10	Bradley, Phil	89F	563	$ .01	$ .05
Borders, Pat	90F	77	$ .01	$ .03	Bradley, Phil	89FU	1	$ .01	$ .05
Bordi, Rich	85F	49	$ .01	$ .05	Bradley, Phil	90F	174	$ .01	$ .03
Bordi, Rich	85FU	8	$ .01	$ .05	Bradley, Scott	87F	580	$ .01	$ .04
Bordi, Rich	86F	101	$ .01	$ .05	Bradley, Scott	88F	370	$ .01	$ .04
Bordi, Rich	86FU	16	$ .01	$ .05	Bradley, Scott	89F	540	$ .01	$ .05
Bordi, Rich	87F	465	$ .01	$ .04	Bradley, Scott	90F	506	$ .01	$ .03
Bosetti, Rick	82F	88	$ .01	$ .04	Braggs, Glenn	87F	339	$ .05	$ .60
Bosio, Chris	87F	338	$ .01	$ .45	Braggs, Glenn	88F	157	$ .01	$ .10
Bosio, Chris	88F	156	$ .01	$ .10	Braggs, Glenn	89F	180	$ .01	$ .05
Bosio, Chris	89F	179	$ .01	$ .05	Braggs, Glenn	90F	317	$ .01	$ .03
Bosio, Chris	90F	316	$ .01	$ .03	Brantley, Jeff	89FU	127	$ .01	$ .15
Bosley, Thad	81F	353	$ .01	$ .04	Brantley, Jeff	90F	52	$ .01	$ .10
Bosley, Thad	86F	361	$ .01	$ .05	Brantley, Mickey	86F	651	$ .01	$ .25
Bosley, Thad	87F	555	$ .01	$ .04	Brantley, Mickey	87F	582	$ .01	$ .04
Bosley, Thad	87FU	8	$ .01	$ .05	Brantley, Mickey	88F	371	$ .01	$ .04
Bosley, Thad	88F	253	$ .01	$ .04	Brantley, Mickey	89F	541	$ .01	$ .05
Boston, Daryl	85FU	9	$ .01	$ .05	Braun, Steve	81F	427	$ .01	$ .04
Boston, Daryl	87F	487	$ .01	$ .04	Braun, Steve	82F	111	$ .01	$ .04
Boston, Daryl	88F	393	$ .01	$ .04	Braun, Steve	83F	3	$ .01	$ .04
Boston, Daryl	89F	492	$ .01	$ .05	Braun, Steve	84F	320	$ .01	$ .06
Bowa, Larry	81F	2	$ .01	$ .10	Braun, Steve	85F	221	$ .01	$ .05
Bowa, Larry	81F	645	$ .20	$1.50	Braun, Steve	86F	27	$ .01	$ .05
Bowa, Larry	82F	241	$ .01	$ .10	Bream, Sid	86F	604	$ .01	$ .05
Bowa, Larry	83F	491	$ .01	$ .10	Bream, Sid	87F	606	$ .01	$ .04
Bowa, Larry	84F	486	$ .01	$ .10	Bream, Sid	88F	324	$ .01	$ .04
Bowa, Larry	85F	50	$ .01	$ .10	Bream, Sid	89F	204	$ .01	$ .05
Bower, Bob	89F	514	$ .01	$ .05	Bream, Sid	90F	463	$ .01	$ .03
					Breining, Fred	82F	385	$ .01	$ .04
					Breining, Fred	83F	254	$ .01	$ .04
					Breining, Fred	84F	367	$ .01	$ .06
					Breining, Fred	84FU	16	$ .01	$ .10
					Breining, Fred	85F	392	$ .01	$ .05
					Brenly, Bob	83F	255	$ .01	$ .04
					Brenly, Bob	84F	368	$ .01	$ .06
					Brenly, Bob	85F	603	$ .01	$ .05
					Brenly, Bob	86F	534	$ .01	$ .05
					Brenly, Bob	87F	267	$ .01	$ .04
					Brenly, Bob	88F	77	$ .01	$ .04
					Brennan, Tom	83F	403	$ .01	$ .04
					Brennan, Tom	84F	537	$ .01	$ .06
					Brett, George	81F	28	$ .13	$1.00
					Brett, George	81F	655	$ .20	$1.00
					Brett, George	82F	405	$ .12	$ .75
					Brett, George	83F	108	$ .10	$ .75
					Brett, George	84F	344	$ .10	$1.25
					Brett, George	84F	638	$ .01	$ .25
					Brett, George	85F	199	$ .10	$ .50
					Brett, George	86F	5	$ .08	$ .40
					Brett, George	86F	634	$ .10	$ .50
					Brett, George	87F	366	$ .06	$ .35
					Brett, George	88F	254	$ .01	$ .30
					Brett, George	89F	277	$ .01	$ .25
					Brett, George	90F	103	$ .01	$ .10
					Brett, George	90FPD	621	$ .01	$ .25
					Brett, Ken	82F	406	$ .01	$ .04
					Briley, Greg	89FU	57	$ .01	$ .75
					Briley, Greg	90F	507	$ .01	$ .25
					Brock, Greg	83F	203	$ .08	$ .40
					Brock, Greg	84F	98	$ .01	$ .06

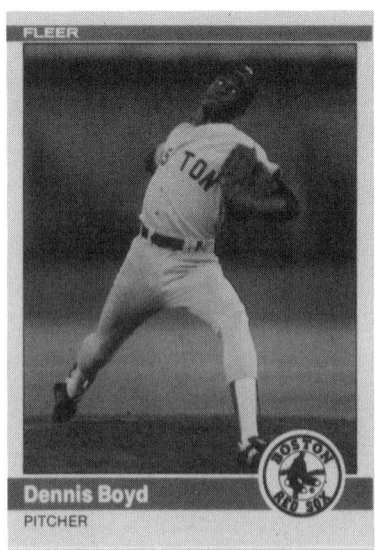

Dennis Boyd
PITCHER

Player	Year	No.	VG	EX/MT	Player	Year	No.	VG	EX/MT
Boyd, Dennis 'Oil Can'	84F	393	$ .07	$ .50	Brock, Greg	85F	368	$ .01	$ .05
Boyd, Dennis	85F	152	$ .03	$ .20	Brock, Greg	86F	125	$ .01	$ .05
Boyd, Dennis	86F	342	$ .01	$ .05	Brock, Greg	87F	437	$ .01	$ .04
Boyd, Dennis	87F	30	$ .01	$ .04	Brock, Greg	87FU	9	$ .01	$ .05
Boyd, Dennis	88F	347	$ .01	$ .04	Brock, Greg	88F	158	$ .01	$ .04
Boyd, "Oil Can"	89F	82	$ .01	$ .05	Brock, Greg	89F	181	$ .01	$ .05
Bradford, Larry	81F	265	$ .01	$ .04	Brock, Greg	90F	318	$ .01	$ .03
Bradford, Larry	82F	431	$ .01	$ .04	Brohamer, Jack	81F	393	$ .01	$ .04
Bradley, Mark	84F	581	$ .01	$ .06	Brookens, Tom	81F	473	$ .01	$ .04
Bradley, Phil	84FU	15	$ .25	$3.00	Brookens, Tom	82F	263	$ .01	$ .04
Bradley, Phil	85F	486	$ .05	$1.00	Brookens, Tom	83F	327	$ .01	$ .04
Bradley, Phil	86F	461	$ .03	$ .20	Brookens, Tom	84F	78	$ .01	$ .06
Bradley, Phil	87F	581	$ .01	$ .10	Brookens, Tom	85F	4	$ .01	$ .05

Player	Year	No.	VG	EX/MT	Player	Year	No.	VG	EX/MT
Brookens, Tom	86F	223	$ .01	$ .05	Bryant, Ralph	87F	649	$ .04	$ .25
Brookens, Tom	87F	145	$ .01	$ .04	Bryant, Ralph	87FU	13	$ .01	$ .05
Brookens, Tom	88F	53	$ .01	$ .04	Bryant, Ralph	88F	510	$ .01	$ .04
Brookens, Tom	89F	132	$ .01	$ .15	Buckner, Bill	81F	292	$ .01	$ .10
Brookens, Tom	90F	439	$ .01	$ .03	Buckner, Bill	82F	589	$ .01	$ .10
Brooks, Hubie	82F	522	$ .15	$ .75	Buckner, Bill	83F	492	$ .01	$ .10
Brooks, Hubie	83F	539	$ .01	$ .10	Buckner, Bill	84F	488	$ .01	$ .06
Brooks, Hubie	84F	582	$ .03	$ .10	Buckner, Bill	84FU	18	$ .06	$ .35
Brooks, Hubie	85F	74	$ .01	$ .10	Buckner, Bill	85F	153	$ .01	$ .05
Brooks, Hubie	85FU	10	$ .04	$ .25	Buckner, Bill	86F	343	$ .01	$ .10
Brooks, Hubie	86F	244	$ .01	$ .10	Buckner, Bill	87F	31	$ .01	$ .04
Brooks, Hubie	87F	314	$ .01	$ .10	Buckner, Bill	88F	486	$ .01	$ .04
Brooks, Hubie	88F	179	$ .01	$ .10	Buckner, Bill	89F	278	$ .01	$ .05
Brooks, Hubie	89F	371	$ .01	$ .05	Buechele, Steve	86F	558	$ .04	$ .25
Brooks, Hubie	90F	341	$ .01	$ .03	Buechele, Steve	87F	121	$ .01	$ .04
Brouhard, Mark	82F	135	$ .01	$ .04	Buechele, Steve	88F	463	$ .01	$ .04
Brouhard, Mark	83F	28	$ .01	$ .04	Buechele, Steve	89F	515	$ .01	$ .05
Brouhard, Mark	84F	195	$ .01	$ .06	Buechele, Steve	90F	292	$ .01	$ .03
Brouhard, Mark	85F	576	$ .01	$ .05	Buhner, Jay	89F	542	$ .01	$ .05
Brower, Bob	87FU	10	$ .03	$ .20	Buhner, Jay	90F	508	$ .01	$ .03
Brower, Bob	88F	461	$ .01	$ .04	Buice, DeWayne	87FU	14	$ .01	$ .05
Brown, Bobby	81F	95	$ .01	$ .04	Buice, DeWayne	88F	487	$ .01	$ .04
Brown, Bobby	82F	30	$ .01	$ .04	Bulling, Terry	83F	630	$ .01	$ .10
Brown, Bobby	84F	296	$ .01	$ .06	Bullock, Eric	89F	106	$ .01	$ .05
Brown, Bobby	85F	28	$ .01	$ .05	Bumbry, Al	81F	172	$ .01	$ .04
Brown, Chris	85FU	11	$ .25	$1.25	Bumbry, Al	82F	159	$ .01	$ .04
Brown, Chris	86F	535	$ .11	$ .55	Bumbry, Al	83F	54	$ .01	$ .04
Brown, Chris	87F	268	$ .03	$ .20	Bumbry, Al	84F	2	$ .01	$ .06
Brown, Chris	87FU	11	$ .03	$ .20	Bumbry, Al	85F	171	$ .01	$ .05
Brown, Chris	88F	578	$ .01	$ .10	Bumbry, Al	85FU	13	$ .01	$ .05
Brown, Chris	89F	301	$ .01	$ .05	Bumbry, Al	86F	316	$ .01	$ .05
Brown, Darrell	84F	556	$ .01	$ .06	Burgmeier, Tom	82F	288	$ .01	$ .04
Brown, Darrell	85F	270	$ .01	$ .05	Burgmeier, Tom	83F	180	$ .01	$ .04
Brown, Keith	89F	154	$ .01	$ .15	Burgmeier, Tom	84F	439	$ .01	$ .06
Brown, Kevin	89F	641	$ .01	$ .25	Burgmeier, Tom	85F	417	$ .01	$ .05
Brown, Kevin	89FU	63	$ .01	$ .10	Burke, Tim	85FU	14	$ .05	$ .35
Brown, Kevin	90F	291	$ .01	$ .03	Burke, Tim	86F	245	$ .05	$ .30
Brown, Marty	89F	645	$ .05	$ .35	Burke, Tim	87F	315	$ .01	$ .04
Brown, Mike	84F	394	$ .01	$ .06	Burke, Tim	88F	180	$ .01	$ .04
Brown, Mike	84FU	17	$ .01	$ .10	Burke, Tim	89F	372	$ .01	$ .05
Brown, Mike	85F	296	$ .01	$ .05	Burke, Tim	90F	342	$ .01	$ .03
Brown, Mike	86F	605	$ .01	$ .05	Burkett, John	88F	651	$ .01	$ .35
Brown, Mike	87F	583	$ .01	$ .04	Burks, Ellis	87FU	15	$ .50	$2.50
Brown, Mike	87F	607	$ .01	$ .04	Burks, Ellis	88F	348	$ .50	$1.75
Brown, Scott	82F	60	$ .01	$ .04	Burks, Ellis	88F	630	$ .10	$ .75
Browne, Jerry	87F	647	$ .01	$ .45	Burks, Ellis	89F	83	$ .05	$ .35
Browne, Jerry	87FU	12	$ .01	$ .05	Burks, Ellis	90F	269	$ .01	$ .15
Browne, Jerry	88F	462	$ .01	$ .04	Burleson, Rick	81F	225	$ .01	$ .04
Browne, Jerry	89FU	26	$ .01	$ .10	Burleson, Rick	82F	453	$ .01	$ .04
Browne, Jerry	90F	487	$ .01	$ .03	Burleson, Rick	83F	00	$ .01	$ .04
Browning, Tom	85FU	12	$ .40	$1.25	Burleson, Rick	84F	510	$ .01	$ .06
Browning, Tom	86F	173	$ .25	$ .75	Burleson, Rick	87F	74	$ .01	$ .04
Browning, Tom	87F	194	$ .05	$ .25	Burmeier, Tom	81F	228	$ .01	$ .04
Browning, Tom	88F	228	$ .01	$ .15	Burns, Britt	81F	342	$ .04	$ .25
Browning, Tom	89F	153	$ .01	$ .10	Burns, Britt	82F	339	$ .01	$ .04
Browning, Tom	89F	629	$ .01	$ .10	Burns, Britt	83F	232	$ .01	$ .04
Browning, Tom	90F	415	$ .01	$ .10	Burns, Britt	84F	54	$ .01	$ .06
Brumley, Mike	89F	302	$ .01	$ .05	Burns, Britt	85F	509	$ .01	$ .05
Brumley, Mike	89FU	30	$ .01	$ .05	Burns, Britt	86F	200	$ .01	$ .05
Brummer, Glenn	83F	4	$ .01	$ .04	Burns, Todd	88FU	52	$ .01	$ .35
Brummer, Glenn	84F	321	$ .01	$ .06	Burns, Todd	89F	3	$ .01	$ .35
Brummer, Glenn	86F	557	$ .01	$ .05	Burns, Todd	90F	2	$ .01	$ .03
Brunansky, Tom	83F	607	$ .01	$ .75	Burnside, Sheldon	81F	220	$ .01	$ .04
Brunansky, Tom	84F	557	$ .09	$ .45	Burris, Ray	81F	328	$ .01	$ .04
Brunansky, Tom	85F	271	$ .03	$ .20	Burris, Ray	82F	184	$ .01	$ .04
Brunansky, Tom	86F	387	$ .01	$ .10	Burris, Ray	83F	277	$ .01	$ .04
Brunansky, Tom	87F	537	$ .01	$ .04	Burris, Ray	84F	270	$ .01	$ .06
Brunansky, Tom	88F	5	$ .01	$ .10	Burris, Ray	84FU	19	$ .01	$ .10
Brunansky, Tom	88FU	117	$ .01	$ .15	Burris, Ray	85F	418	$ .01	$ .05
Brunansky, Tom	89F	444	$ .01	$ .10	Burris, Ray	85FU	15	$ .01	$ .05
Brunansky, Tom	90F	242	$ .01	$ .03	Burris, Ray	86F	482	$ .01	$ .05
Brusstar, Warren	82F	242	$ .01	$ .04	Burroughs, Jeff	81F	245	$ .01	$ .04
Brusstar, Warren	84F	487	$ .01	$ .06	Burroughs, Jeff	82F	506	$ .01	$ .04
Brusstar, Warren	85F	51	$ .01	$ .05	Burroughs, Jeff	83F	515	$ .01	$ .04
Brusstar, Warren	86F	362	$ .01	$ .05	Burroughs, Jeff	84F	440	$ .01	$ .06

FLEER

Player	Year	No.	VG	EX/MT	Player	Year	No.	VG	EX/MT
Burroughs, Jeff	85FU	16	$ .01	$ .05	Campbell, Bill	81F	240	$ .01	$ .04
Burroughs, Jeff	86F	54	$ .01	$ .05	Campbell, Bill	82F	289	$ .01	$ .04
Busby, Steve	81F	33	$ .01	$ .04	Campbell, Bill	83F	493	$ .01	$ .04
Bush, Randy	84F	558	$ .01	$ .06	Campbell, Bill	84F	489	$ .01	$ .06
Bush, Randy	85F	272	$ .01	$ .05	Campbell, Bill	84FU	23	$ .01	$ .10
Bush, Randy	86F	388	$ .01	$ .05	Campbell, Bill	85F	245	$ .01	$ .05
Bush, Randy	87F	538	$ .01	$ .04	Campbell, Bill	85FU	19	$ .01	$ .05
Bush, Randy	88F	6	$ .01	$ .04	Campbell, Bill	86F	28	$ .01	$ .05
Bush, Randy	89F	107	$ .01	$ .05	Campbell, Bill	86FU	17	$ .01	$ .05
Bush, Randy	90F	370	$ .01	$ .03	Campbell, Bill	87F	146	$ .01	$ .04
Butcher, John	81F	635	$ .01	$ .04	Campbell, Jim	89F	646	$ .01	$ .20
Butcher, John	83F	563	$ .01	$ .04	Campbell, Mike	88F	372	$ .01	$ .20
Butcher, John	84F	415	$ .01	$ .06	Campbell, Mike	89F	543	$ .01	$ .05
Butcher, John	84FU	20	$ .01	$ .10	Campusano, Sil	88FU	66	$ .01	$ .25
Butcher, John	85F	273	$ .01	$ .05	Canale, George	90F	641	$ .01	$ .03
Butcher, John	86F	389	$ .01	$ .05	Candaele, Casey	87FU	16	$ .03	$ .20
Butcher, John	87F	245	$ .01	$ .04	Candaele, Casey	88F	181	$ .01	$ .04
Butera, Sal	81F	570	$ .01	$ .04	Candelaria, John	81F	375	$ .01	$ .10
Butera, Sal	82F	548	$ .01	$ .04	Candelaria, John	82F	479	$ .01	$ .04
Butera, Sal	87F	195	$ .01	$ .04	Candelaria, John	83F	304	$ .01	$ .04
Butler, Brett	83F	132	$ .05	$ .35	Candelaria, John	84F	247	$ .01	$ .06
Butler, Brett	84F	173	$ .03	$ .10	Candelaria, John	85F	462	$ .01	$ .05
Butler, Brett	84FU	21	$ .07	$ .50	Candelaria, John	86F	150	$ .01	$ .05
Butler, Brett	85F	441	$ .01	$ .05	Candelaria, John	87F	75	$ .01	$ .04
Butler, Brett	86F	581	$ .01	$ .05	Candelaria, John	88FU	46	$ .01	$ .05
Butler, Brett	87F	246	$ .01	$ .04	Candelaria, John	89F	251	$ .01	$ .05
Butler, Brett	88F	603	$ .01	$ .04	Candiotti, Tom	84F	197	$ .10	$ .40
Butler, Brett	88FU	128	$ .01	$ .05	Candiotti, Tom	86FU	18	$ .01	$ .05
Butler, Brett	89F	324	$ .01	$ .05	Candiotti, Tom	87F	248	$ .01	$ .04
Butler, Brett	90F	53	$ .01	$ .03	Candiotti, Tom	88F	604	$ .01	$ .04
Byers, Randell	88F	653	$ .01	$ .25	Candiotti, Tom	89F	399	$ .01	$ .05
Bystrom, Marty	83F	154	$ .01	$ .04	Candiotti, Tom	90F	488	$ .01	$ .03
Bystrom, Marty	84F	24	$ .01	$ .06	Cangelosi, John	86FU	19	$ .04	$ .25
Bystrom, Marty	85F	122	$ .01	$ .05	Cangelosi, John	87F	489	$ .01	$ .10
Bystrom, Marty	86F	102	$ .01	$ .05	Cangelosi, John	88F	325	$ .01	$ .04
Cabell, Enos	81F	58	$ .01	$ .04	Canseco, Jose	86F	649	$10.00	$40.00
Cabell, Enos	82F	386	$ .01	$ .04	Canseco, Jose	86FU	20	$2.25	$12.00
Cabell, Enos	83F	328	$ .01	$ .04	Canseco, Jose	87F	389	$1.00	$10.00
Cabell, Enos	84F	79	$ .01	$ .06	Canseco, Jose	87F	625	$ .10	$ .75
Cabell, Enos	84FU	22	$ .01	$ .10	Canseco, Jose	87F	628	$ .30	$1.50
Cabell, Enos	85F	346	$ .01	$ .05	Canseco, Jose	87F	633	$ .25	$ .75
Cabell, Enos	86F	126	$ .01	$ .05	Canseco, Jose	88F	276	$ .50	$2.50
Cabell, Enos	87F	438	$ .01	$ .04	Canseco, Jose	88F	624	$ .10	$1.00
Cabrera, Francisco	89FU	68	$ .01	$ .35	Canseco, Jose	89F	5	$ .10	$1.50
Cadaret, Greg	89F	4	$ .01	$ .05	Canseco, Jose	89F	628	$ .05	$ .50
Caderet, Greg	90F	440	$ .01	$ .03	Canseco, Jose	89F	634	$ .01	$ .35
Calderon, Ivan	85FU	17	$ .15	$ .75	Canseco, Jose	90F	3	$ .01	$1.00
Calderon, Ivan	86F	462	$ .10	$ .50	Canseco, Jose	90FPD	629	$ .01	$ .35
Calderon, Ivan	87F	488	$ .01	$ .10	Capel, Mike	89F	643	$ .01	$ .20
Calderon, Ivan	88F	394	$ .01	$ .04	Capilla, Doug	81F	309	$ .01	$ .04
Calderon, Ivan	89F	493	$ .01	$ .05	Cappuzzello, George	82F	264	$ .01	$ .04
Calderon, Ivan	90F	529	$ .01	$ .03	Capra, Nick	89F	279	$ .01	$ .05
Caldwell, Mike	81F	512	$ .01	$ .04	Carew, Rod	81F	268	$ .10	$ .75
Caldwell, Mike	82F	136	$ .01	$ .04	Carew, Rod	82F	455	$ .07	$ .50
Caldwell, Mike	83F	29	$ .01	$ .04	Carew, Rod	83F	81	$ .09	$ .45
Caldwell, Mike	84F	196	$ .01	$ .06	Carew, Rod	84F	511	$ .09	$ .45
Caldwell, Mike	85F	577	$ .01	$ .05	Carew, Rod	84F	629	$ .04	$ .25
Calhoun, Jeff	85FU	18	$ .01	$ .05	Carew, Rod	85F	297	$ .07	$ .50
Calhoun, Jeff	86F	295	$ .01	$ .05	Carew, Rod	86F	151	$ .05	$ .30
Calhoun, Jeff	87F	52	$ .01	$ .04	Carew, Rod	86F	629	$ .04	$ .25
Calhoun, Jeff	88F	299	$ .01	$ .04	Carlton, Steve	81F	6	$ .09	$ .45
Camacho, Ernie	85F	442	$ .01	$ .05	Carlton, Steve	81F	660	$ .15	$ .75
Camacho, Ernie	86F	582	$ .01	$ .05	Carlton, Steve	82F	243	$ .08	$ .40
Camacho, Ernie	87F	247	$ .01	$ .04	Carlton, Steve	82F	632	$ .04	$ .25
Caminiti, Ken	88F	441	$ .01	$ .25	Carlton, Steve	82F	641	$ .05	$ .30
Caminiti, Ken	90F	225	$ .01	$ .03	Carlton, Steve	83F	155	$ .06	$ .35
Camp, Rick	81F	246	$ .01	$ .04	Carlton, Steve	84F	25	$ .07	$ .50
Camp, Rick	82F	432	$ .01	$ .04	Carlton, Steve	84F	642	$ .03	$ .20
Camp, Rick	83F	133	$ .01	$ .04	Carlton, Steve	85F	246	$ .05	$ .30
Camp, Rick	84F	174	$ .01	$ .06	Carlton, Steve	86F	435	$ .05	$ .30
Camp, Rick	85F	321	$ .01	$ .05	Carlton, Steve	87F	490	$ .05	$ .30
Camp, Rick	86F	510	$ .01	$ .05	Carlton, Steve	87F	635	$ .03	$ .20
Campaneris, Bert	81F	280	$ .01	$ .04	Carlton, Steve	87FU	17	$ .04	$ .25
Campaneris, Bert	82F	454	$ .01	$ .04	Carlton, Steve	88F	7	$ .01	$ .20
Campaneris, Bert	84F	120	$ .01	$ .06	Carman, Don	85FU	20	$ .05	$ .25

Player	Year	No.	VG	EX/MT	Player	Year	No.	VG	EX/MT
Carman, Don	86F	436	$ .04	$ .25	Cecena, Jose	88FU	62	$ .01	$ .15
Carman, Don	87F	171	$ .01	$ .04	Cecena, Jose	89F	516	$ .01	$ .15
Carman, Don	88F	300	$ .01	$ .04	Cedeno, Cesar	81F	59	$ .01	$ .10
Carman, Don	89F	564	$ .01	$ .05	Cedeno, Cesar	82F	213	$ .01	$ .04
Carman, Don	90F	552	$ .01	$ .03	Cedeno, Cesar	83F	587	$ .01	$ .10
Carpenter, Cris	89FU	117	$ .01	$ .20	Cedeno, Cesar	84F	465	$ .01	$ .06
Carpenter, Cris	90F	243	$ .01	$ .10	Cedeno, Cesar	85F	531	$ .01	$ .05
Carreon, Mark	88F	129	$ .10	$ .35	Cedeno, Cesar	86F	29	$ .01	$ .05
Carreon, Mark	89F	29	$ .01	$ .05	Cerone, Rick	81F	83	$ .01	$ .04
Carreon, Mark	90F	198	$ .01	$ .10	Cerone, Rick	82F	31	$ .01	$ .04
Carter, Gary	81F	142	$ .09	$ .50	Cerone, Rick	83F	376	$ .01	$ .04
Carter, Gary	82F	185	$ .07	$ .50	Cerone, Rick	84F	121	$ .01	$ .06
Carter, Gary	82F	635	$ .04	$ .25	Cerone, Rick	85F	123	$ .01	$ .05
Carter, Gary	82F	638	$ .04	$ .25	Cerone, Rick	85FU	24	$ .01	$ .05
Carter, Gary	83F	278	$ .05	$ .30	Cerone, Rick	86F	511	$ .01	$ .05
Carter, Gary	83F	637	$ .01	$ .10	Cerone, Rick	86FU	23	$ .01	$ .05
Carter, Gary	83F	638	$ .03	$ .20	Cerone, Rick	87F	340	$ .01	$ .04
Carter, Gary	84F	271	$ .07	$ .50	Cerone, Rick	88F	203	$ .01	$ .04
Carter, Gary	85F	393	$ .05	$ .30	Cerone, Rick	88FU	6	$ .01	$ .05
Carter, Gary	85F	631	$ .05	$ .30	Cerone, Rick	89F	84	$ .01	$ .05
Carter, Gary	85F	632	$ .01	$ .10	Cerone, Rick	90F	270	$ .01	$ .03
Carter, Gary	85FU	21	$ .10	$ .50	Cerutti, John	86FU	24	$ .05	$ .30
Carter, Gary	86F	76	$ .05	$ .30	Cerutti, John	87F	222	$ .04	$ .25
Carter, Gary	87F	4	$ .05	$ .30	Cerutti, John	88F	105	$ .01	$ .10
Carter, Gary	87F	629	$ .10	$ .50	Cerutti, John	89F	228	$ .01	$ .10
Carter, Gary	87F	634	$ .05	$ .30	Cerutti, John	90F	78	$ .01	$ .03
Carter, Gary	88F	130	$ .01	$ .15	Cey, Ron	81F	126	$ .03	$ .20
Carter, Gary	88F	636	$ .01	$ .15	Cey, Ron	82F	3	$ .01	$ .10
Carter, Gary	89F	30	$ .01	$ .15	Cey, Ron	83F	204	$ .01	$ .10
Carter, Gary	90F	199	$ .01	$ .10	Cey, Ron	84F	490	$ .01	$ .06
Carter, Joe	85F	443	$ .50	$3.00	Cey, Ron	85F	52	$ .01	$ .05
Carter, Joe	86F	583	$ .10	$ .50	Cey, Ron	86F	363	$ .01	$ .10
Carter, Joe	87F	249	$ .01	$ .10	Cey, Ron	87F	556	$ .01	$ .04
Carter, Joe	88F	605	$ .01	$ .04	Chalk, Dave	81F	35	$ .01	$ .04
Carter, Joe	89F	400	$ .01	$ .15	Chalk, Dave	82F	407	$ .01	$ .04
Carter, Joe	90F	489	$ .01	$ .15	Chambliss, Chris	81F	252	$ .01	$ .04
Cary, Chuck	86FU	21	$ .01	$ .10	Chambliss, Chris	82F	433	$ .01	$ .04
Cary, Chuck	87F	147	$ .01	$ .05	Chambliss, Chris	83F	134	$ .01	$ .04
Cash, Dave	81F	492	$ .01	$ .04					
Castillo, Bobby	83F	608	$ .01	$ .04					
Castillo, Bobby	84F	559	$ .01	$ .06					
Castillo, Bobby	85F	274	$ .01	$ .05					
Castillo, Bobby	85FU	22	$ .01	$ .05					
Castillo, Bobby	86F	127	$ .01	$ .05					
Castillo, Carmelo	83F	404	$ .01	$ .04					
Castillo, Carmelo	85F	444	$ .01	$ .05					
Castillo, Carmelo	87F	250	$ .01	$ .04					
Castillo, Carmelo	88F	606	$ .01	$ .04					
Castillo, Carmelo "Carmen"	86F	584	$ .01	$ .05					
Castillo, Carmen	89F	401	$ .01	$ .05					
Castillo, Carmen	90F	371	$ .01	$ .03					
Castillo, Juan	86FU	22	$ .01	$ .05					
Castillo, Juan	87FU	18	$ .01	$ .05					
Castillo, Juan	88F	159	$ .01	$ .04					
Castillo, Manny	83F	474	$ .01	$ .04					
Castillo, Manny	84F	607	$ .01	$ .06					
Castillo, Marty	82F	265	$ .01	$ .04					
Castillo, Marty	85F	5	$ .01	$ .05					
Castillo, Robert	81F	137	$ .01	$ .04					
Castillo, Robert	82F	2	$ .01	$ .04					
Castino, John	81F	554	$ .01	$ .04					
Castino, John	82F	549	$ .01	$ .04					
Castino, John	83F	609	$ .01	$ .04					
Castino, John	84F	560	$ .01	$ .06					
Castro, Bill	81F	517	$ .01	$ .04					
Castro, Bill	83F	109	$ .01	$ .04					
Caudill, Bill	81F	306	$ .01	$ .04					
Caudill, Bill	82F	590	$ .01	$ .04					
Caudill, Bill	83F	475	$ .01	$ .04					
Caudill, Bill	84F	608	$ .01	$ .06					
Caudill, Bill	84FU	24	$ .01	$ .10	Chambliss, Chris	84F	175	$ .01	$ .06
Caudill, Bill	85F	419	$ .01	$ .05	Chambliss, Chris	85F	322	$ .01	$ .05
Caudill, Bill	85FU	23	$ .01	$ .05	Chambliss, Chris	86F	512	$ .01	$ .05
Caudill, Bill	86F	55	$ .01	$ .05	Chambliss, Chris	87F	513	$ .01	$ .04
Caudill, Bill	87F	221	$ .01	$ .04	Chapman, Kelvin	85F	75	$ .01	$ .05

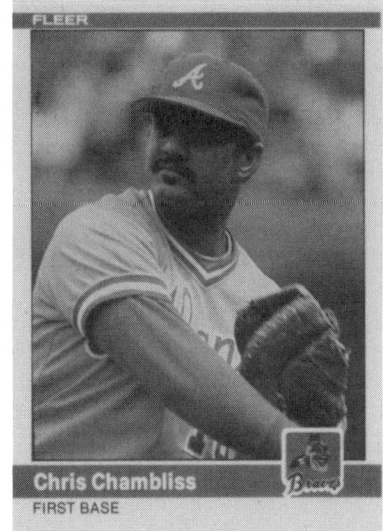

Chris Chambliss
FIRST BASE

Player	Year	No.	VG	EX/MT
Charboneau, Joe	81F	397	$.01	$.10
Charboneau, Joe	82F	362	$.01	$.04
Charland, Colin	90F	640	$.01	$.03
Charlton, Norm	89F	155	$.01	$.15
Charlton, Norm	90F	416	$.01	$.10
Checklist Team Cards(628-60)	82F	660	$.02	$.15
Checklist, A's(436-461)	84F	651	$.01	$.06
Checklist, Angels(508-532)	84F	654	$.01	$.06
Checklist, Astros(220-244)	84F	656	$.01	$.06
Checklist, Blue Jays(145-169)	84F	653	$.01	$.06
Checklist, Braves(170-193)	84F	654	$.01	$.06
Checklist, Brewers(194-219)	84F	655	$.01	$.06
Checklist, Cardinals(318-340)	84F	660	$.03	$.10
Checklist, Cards(1-101)	88F	654	$.01	$.04
Checklist, Cards(1-101)	89F	654	$.01	$.05
Checklist, Cards(1-132)	84FU	132	$.04	$.25
Checklist, Cards(1-132)	85FU	132	$.01	$.10
Checklist, Cards(1-132)	86FU	132	$.01	$.10
Checklist, Cards(1-132)	87FU	132	$.01	$.10
Checklist, Cards(1-132)	88FU	132	$.01	$.05
Checklist, Cards(1-132)	89FU	132	$.01	$.10
Checklist, Cards(1-50)	81F	641	$.01	$.10
Checklist, Cards(1-51)	83F	647	$.01	$.04
Checklist, Cards(1-56)	82F	647	$.01	$.10
Checklist, Cards(1-95)	85F	654	$.01	$.05
Checklist, Cards(1-95)	87F	654	$.01	$.04
Checklist, Cards(1-97)	86F	654	$.01	$.05
Checklist, Cards(1-99)	90F	654	$.01	$.03
Checklist, Cards(100-195)	90F	655	$.01	$.03
Checklist, Cards(102-200)	89F	655	$.01	$.05
Checklist, Cards(102-201)	88F	655	$.01	$.04
Checklist, Cards(104-152)	83F	649	$.01	$.04
Checklist, Cards(110-156)	82F	649	$.01	$.10
Checklist, Cards(110-168)	81F	643	$.01	$.10
Checklist, Cards(153-200)	83F	650	$.01	$.04
Checklist, Cards(157-211)	83F	650	$.01	$.10
Checklist, Cards(169-220)	81F	644	$.01	$.10
Checklist, Cards(193-288)	87F	656	$.01	$.04
Checklist, Cards(196-289)	90F	656	$.01	$.03
Checklist, Cards(196-292)	85F	656	$.01	$.05
Checklist, Cards(197-291)	86F	656	$.01	$.05
Checklist, Cards(201-251)	83F	651	$.01	$.04
Checklist, Cards(201-298)	89F	656	$.01	$.05

CHECKLIST

MINNESOTA TWINS
- 102 Allan Anderson
- 103 Keith Atherton
- 104 Juan Berenguer
- 105 Bert Blyleven
- 106 Eric Bullock
- 107 Randy Bush
- 108 John Christensen
- 109 Mark Davidson
- 110 Gary Gaetti
- 111 Greg Gagne
- 112 Dan Gladden
- 113 German Gonzalez
- 114 Brian Harper
- 115 Tom Herr
- 116 Kent Hrbek
- 117 Gene Larkin
- 118 Tim Laudner
- 119 Charlie Lea
- 120 Steve Lombardozzi
- 121 John Moses
- 122 Al Newman
- 123 Mark Portugal
- 124 Kirby Puckett
- 125 Jeff Reardon
- 126 Fred Toliver
- 127 Frank Viola

DETROIT TIGERS
- 128 Doyle Alexander
- 129 Dave Bergman
- 130 Tom Brookens
- 131 Paul Gibson
- 132 Mike Heath
- 133 Don Heinkel
- 134 Mike Henneman
- 135 Guillermo Hernandez
- 136 Eric King
- 137 Chet Lemon
- 138 Fred Lynn
- 139 Jack Morris
- 140 Matt Nokes
- 141 Gary Pettis
- 142 Ted Power
- 143 Jeff M. Robinson
- 144 Luis Salazar
- 145 Steve Searcy
- 146 Pat Sheridan
- 147 Frank Tanana
- 148 Alan Trammell
- 149 Walt Terrell
- 150 Jim Walewander
- 151 Lou Whitaker

FLEER

Player	Year	No.	VG	EX/MT
Checklist, Cards(202-296)	88F	656	$.01	$.04
Checklist, Cards(212-262)	82F	651	$.01	$.10
Checklist, Cards(221-267)	81F	646	$.01	$.04
Checklist, Cards(252-301)	83F	652	$.01	$.04
Checklist, Cards(263-312)	82F	652	$.01	$.10
Checklist, Cards(268-315)	81F	647	$.01	$.04
Checklist, Cards(289-384)	87F	657	$.01	$.04
Checklist, Cards(290-388)	90F	657	$.01	$.03
Checklist, Cards(292-385)	86F	657	$.01	$.05
Checklist, Cards(293-391)	85F	657	$.01	$.05
Checklist, Cards(297-390)	88F	657	$.01	$.04
Checklist, Cards(299-395)	89F	657	$.01	$.05
Checklist, Cards(302-351)	83F	653	$.01	$.04
Checklist, Cards(313-358)	82F	653	$.01	$.10
Checklist, Cards(316-359)	81F	648	$.01	$.04
Checklist, Cards(352-399)	83F	654	$.01	$.04
Checklist, Cards(359-403)	82F	654	$.01	$.10
Checklist, Cards(360-408)	81F	649	$.01	$.04
Checklist, Cards(385-483)	87F	658	$.01	$.04
Checklist, Cards(386-481)	86F	658	$.01	$.05
Checklist, Cards(389-482)	90F	658	$.01	$.03
Checklist, Cards(391-483)	88F	658	$.01	$.04
Checklist, Cards(392-481)	85F	658	$.01	$.05
Checklist, Cards(396-490)	89F	658	$.01	$.05
Checklist, Cards(400-444)	83F	655	$.01	$.04
Checklist, Cards(404-449)	82F	655	$.01	$.10
Checklist, Cards(409-458)	81F	651	$.01	$.04
Checklist, Cards(445-489)	83F	656	$.01	$.04
Checklist, Cards(450-501)	82F	656	$.01	$.10
Checklist, Cards(459-506)	81F	652	$.01	$.10
Checklist, Cards(482-575)	85F	659	$.01	$.05
Checklist, Cards(482-578)	86F	659	$.01	$.05
Checklist, Cards(483-573)	90F	659	$.01	$.03
Checklist, Cards(484-532)	87F	659	$.01	$.04
Checklist, Cards(484-575)	88F	659	$.01	$.04
Checklist, Cards(490-535)	83F	657	$.01	$.04
Checklist, Cards(491-584)	89F	659	$.01	$.05
Checklist, Cards(502-544)	82F	657	$.01	$.10
Checklist, Cards(507-550)	81F	654	$.01	$.10
Checklist, Cards(51-109)	81F	642	$.01	$.10
Checklist, Cards(52-110)	83F	648	$.01	$.04
Checklist, Cards(536-583)	83F	658	$.01	$.04
Checklist, Cards(545-585)	82F	658	$.01	$.10
Checklist, Cards(551-593)	81F	656	$.01	$.04
Checklist, Cards(57-109)	82F	648	$.01	$.10
Checklist, Cards(574-660)	90F	660	$.01	$.03
Checklist, Cards(576-660)	85F	660	$.01	$.10
Checklist, Cards(576-660)	88F	660	$.01	$.04
Checklist, Cards(579-660)	86F	660	$.01	$.10
Checklist, Cards(579-660)	87F	660	$.01	$.10
Checklist, Cards(584-628)	83F	659	$.01	$.04
Checklist, Cards(585-660)	89F	660	$.01	$.05
Checklist, Cards(586-627)	82F	659	$.01	$.10
Checklist, Cards(594-637)	81F	658	$.01	$.04
Checklist, Cards(626-646)	84F	659	$.01	$.06
Checklist, Cards(629-656)	83F	660	$.01	$.10
Checklist, Cards(96-192)	87F	655	$.01	$.04
Checklist, Cards(96-195)	85F	655	$.01	$.05
Checklist, Cards(98-196)	86F	655	$.01	$.05
Checklist, Cubs(486-507)	84F	653	$.01	$.06
Checklist, Dodgers(96-118)	84F	651	$.01	$.06
Checklist, Expos(270-293)	84F	658	$.01	$.06
Checklist, Giants(365-387)	84F	648	$.01	$.06
Checklist, Indians(533-555)	84F	655	$.01	$.06
Checklist, Mariners(604-625)	84F	658	$.01	$.06
Checklist, Mets(580-603)	84F	657	$.01	$.06
Checklist, Orioles(1-23)	84F	647	$.01	$.06
Checklist, Padres(294-317)	84F	659	$.01	$.06
Checklist, Phillies(24-49)	84F	648	$.01	$.06
Checklist, Pirates(245-269)	84F	657	$.01	$.06
Checklist, Rangers(413-435)	84F	650	$.01	$.06
Checklist, Red Sox(388-412)	84F	649	$.01	$.06
Checklist, Reds(462-485)	84F	652	$.01	$.06
Checklist, Royals(341-364)	84F	647	$.01	$.06
Checklist, Teams(1-660)	84F	660	$.03	$.10

Player	Year	No.	VG	EX/MT
Checklist, Tigers(74-95)	84F	650	$.01	$.06
Checklist, Twins(556-579)	84F	656	$.01	$.06
Checklist, White Sox(50-73)	84F	649	$.01	$.06
Checklist, Yankees(119-144)	84F	652	$.01	$.06
Checklist-Team Cards(640-60)	81F	659	$.01	$.10
Chiffer, Floyd	83F	354	$.01	$.04
Childress, Rocky	88F	442	$.01	$.10
Christensen, John	89F	108	$.01	$.05
Christenson, Larry	81F	8	$.01	$.04
Christenson, Larry	82F	244	$.01	$.04
Christenson, Larry	83F	156	$.01	$.04
Clancy, Jim	81F	412	$.01	$.04
Clancy, Jim	82F	612	$.01	$.04
Clancy, Jim	83F	426	$.01	$.04
Clancy, Jim	84F	150	$.01	$.06
Clancy, Jim	85F	101	$.01	$.05
Clancy, Jim	86F	56	$.01	$.05
Clancy, Jim	87F	223	$.01	$.04
Clancy, Jim	88F	106	$.01	$.04
Clancy, Jim	89F	229	$.01	$.05
Clancy, Jim	89FU	88	$.01	$.05
Clancy, Jim	90F	226	$.01	$.03
Clark, Bob	82F	456	$.01	$.04
Clark, Bobby	83F	82	$.01	$.04
Clark, Bobby	84F	512	$.01	$.06
Clark, Bobby	84FU	25	$.01	$.10
Clark, Bobby	85F	578	$.01	$.05
Clark, Bryan	82F	507	$.01	$.04
Clark, Bryan	83F	476	$.01	$.04
Clark, Bryan	84F	609	$.01	$.06
Clark, Bryan	84FU	26	$.01	$.10
Clark, Dave	87F	644	$.50	$2.25
Clark, Dave	89F	402	$.01	$.05
Clark, Dave	90F	490	$.01	$.03
Clark, Jack	81F	433	$.04	$.25
Clark, Jack	82F	387	$.04	$.25
Clark, Jack	83F	256	$.04	$.25
Clark, Jack	84F	369	$.04	$.25
Clark, Jack	85F	604	$.05	$.30
Clark, Jack	85FU	25	$.06	$.35
Clark, Jack	86F	30	$.04	$.25
Clark, Jack	87F	289	$.04	$.25
Clark, Jack	88F	26	$.01	$.15
Clark, Jack	88FU	47	$.01	$.15
Clark, Jack	89F	252	$.01	$.10
Clark, Jack	89FU	123	$.01	$.10
Clark, Jack	90F	152	$.01	$.03
Clark, Jerald	89F	642	$.01	$.25
Clark, Terry	89F	470	$.01	$.05
Clark, Will	86FU	25	$1.50	$15.00
Clark, Will	87F	269	$2.50	$35.00
Clark, Will	88F	78	$.50	$4.50
Clark, Will	89F	325	$.05	$1.00
Clark, Will	89F	631	$.05	$.40
Clark, Will	89F	632	$.05	$.40
Clark, Will	90F	54	$.01	$.50
Clark, Will	90F	637	$.01	$.03
Clark, Will	90FPD	630	$.01	$.35
Clary, Martin	90F	578	$.01	$.03
Clary, Marty	88F	535	$.01	$.04
Clay, Danny	88FU	108	$.01	$.05
Clay, Ken	81F	633	$.01	$.04
Clay, Ken	82F	508	$.01	$.04
Clear, Mark	82F	290	$.01	$.04
Clear, Mark	83F	181	$.01	$.04
Clear, Mark	83F	629	$.04	$.25
Clear, Mark	84F	395	$.01	$.06
Clear, Mark	85F	154	$.01	$.05
Clear, Mark	86F	344	$.01	$.05
Clear, Mark	86FU	26	$.01	$.05
Clear, Mark	87F	341	$.01	$.04
Clear, Mark	88F	160	$.01	$.04
Clear, Mark	89F	182	$.01	$.05
Clemens, Roger	84FU	27	$20.00	$85.00
Clemens, Roger	85F	155	$3.00	$11.00
Clemens, Roger	86F	345	$.60	$3.00
Clemens, Roger	87F	32	$.10	$1.50
Clemens, Roger	87F	634	$.05	$.30
Clemens, Roger	87F	640	$.10	$.50
Clemens, Roger	88F	349	$.10	$.50
Clemens, Roger	89F	85	$.05	$.40
Clemens, Roger	90F	271	$.01	$.10
Clemens, Roger	90FPD	627	$.01	$.20
Clements, Pat	85FU	26	$.05	$.15
Clements, Pat	86F	606	$.03	$.20
Clements, Pat	87F	608	$.01	$.04
Clements, Pat	88F	204	$.01	$.04
Clements, Pat	90F	153	$.01	$.03
Cleveland, Reggie	81F	523	$.01	$.04
Cleveland, Reggie	82F	137	$.01	$.04
Cliburn, Stew	89F	471	$.01	$.05
Cliburn, Stewart	85FU	27	$.01	$.05
Cliburn, Stewart	86F	152	$.01	$.05
Clutterbuck, Bryan	87F	342	$.01	$.04
Cocanower, Jaime	84FU	28	$.01	$.10
Cocanower, Jaime	85F	579	$.01	$.05
Cocanower, Jaime	86F	483	$.01	$.05
Codiroli, Chris	84F	441	$.01	$.06
Codiroli, Chris	85F	420	$.01	$.05
Codiroli, Chris	86F	414	$.01	$.05
Codiroli, Chris	87F	390	$.01	$.04
Coffman, Kevin	88F	536	$.01	$.10
Cole, Alex	90F	244	$.01	$.10
Coleman, Vince	85FU	28	$1.50	$4.00
Coleman, Vince	86F	31	$.65	$2.00
Coleman, Vince	86F	636	$.01	$.25
Coleman, Vince	86F	637	$.01	$.25
Coleman, Vince	87F	290	$.05	$.40
Coleman, Vince	88F	27	$.01	$.10
Coleman, Vince	88F	634	$.01	$.10
Coleman, Vince	89F	445	$.01	$.10
Coleman, Vince	90F	245	$.01	$.03
Coles, Darnell	86FU	27	$.01	$.05
Coles, Darnell	87F	148	$.01	$.04
Coles, Darnell	89F	544	$.01	$.05
Coles, Darnell	90F	509	$.01	$.03
Collins, Dave	81F	201	$.01	$.04
Collins, Dave	82F	61	$.01	$.04
Collins, Dave	83F	377	$.01	$.04
Collins, Dave	84F	151	$.01	$.06
Collins, Dave	85F	102	$.01	$.05
Collins, Dave	85FU	29	$.01	$.05
Collins, Dave	86F	415	$.01	$.05
Collins, Dave	86FU	28	$.01	$.05
Collins, Dave	87F	149	$.01	$.04
Combe, Geoff	82F	62	$.01	$.04
Combs, Pat	90F	553	$.01	$.50
Comer, Steve	82F	314	$.01	$.04
Comer, Steve	83F	564	$.01	$.04
Comstock, Keith	88F	579	$.01	$.10
Comstock, Keith	90F	510	$.01	$.03
Concepcion, Dave	81F	197	$.03	$.20
Concepcion, Dave	82F	63	$.03	$.20
Concepcion, Dave	82F	630	$.01	$.04
Concepcion, Dave	83F	588	$.01	$.04
Concepcion, Dave	83F	631	$.01	$.10
Concepcion, Dave	84F	466	$.01	$.06
Concepcion, Dave	85F	532	$.01	$.10
Concepcion, Dave	86F	174	$.01	$.10
Concepcion, Dave	87F	196	$.01	$.10
Concepcion, Dave	88F	229	$.01	$.04
Concepcion, Dave	89F	156	$.01	$.05
Concepcion, Onix	83F	110	$.01	$.04
Concepcion, Onix	84F	345	$.01	$.06
Concepcion, Onix	85F	200	$.01	$.05
Concepcion, Onix	86F	6	$.01	$.05
Cone, David	88F	131	$.25	$1.25
Cone, David	89F	31	$.01	$.30
Cone, David	89F	636	$.01	$.15
Cone, David	90F	200	$.01	$.03

Player	Year	No.	VG	EX/MT	Player	Year	No.	VG	EX/MT
Connally, Fritz	85FU	30	$ .01	$ .05	Cotto, Henry	88F	205	$ .01	$ .04
Conroy, Tim	84F	442	$ .01	$ .06	Cotto, Henry	88FU	58	$ .01	$ .05
Conroy, Tim	85F	421	$ .01	$ .05	Cotto, Henry	89F	545	$ .01	$ .05
Conroy, Tim	86FU	29	$ .01	$ .05	Cotto, Henry	90F	511	$ .01	$ .03
Conroy, Tim	87F	291	$ .01	$ .04	Cowens, Al	81F	471	$ .01	$ .04
Cook, Dennis	89F	652	$ .01	$ .45	Cowens, Al	82F	266	$ .01	$ .04
Cook, Dennis	89FU	104	$ .01	$ .05	Cowens, Al	83F	477	$ .01	$ .04
Cook, Dennis	90F	554	$ .01	$ .10	Cowens, Al	84F	610	$ .01	$ .06
Cook, Mike	89F	472	$ .01	$ .05	Cowens, Al	85F	487	$ .01	$ .05
					Cowens, Al	86F	463	$ .01	$ .05
					Cowley, Joe	85F	124	$ .01	$ .05
					Cowley, Joe	86F	103	$ .01	$ .05
					Cowley, Joe	86FU	31	$ .01	$ .05
					Cowley, Joe	87F	491	$ .01	$ .04
					Cox, Bob	81F	247	$ .01	$ .04
					Cox, Danny	85F	222	$ .03	$ .20
					Cox, Danny	86F	32	$ .01	$ .10
					Cox, Danny	87F	292	$ .01	$ .04
					Cox, Danny	88F	28	$ .01	$ .10
					Cox, Danny	89F	447	$ .01	$ .05
					Cox, Larry	81F	604	$ .01	$ .04
					Cox, Ted	81F	602	$ .01	$ .04
					Craig, Rodney	81F	597	$ .01	$ .04
					Crawford, Steve	82F	291	$ .01	$ .04
					Crawford, Steve	85F	156	$ .01	$ .05
					Crawford, Steve	86F	346	$ .01	$ .05
					Crawford, Steve	87F	33	$ .01	$ .04
					Crawford, Steve	88F	350	$ .01	$ .04
					Creel, Keith	84F	346	$ .01	$ .06
					Crews, Tim	88F	511	$ .01	$ .10
					Crews, Tim	90F	390	$ .01	$ .03
					Crim, Chuck	87FU	19	$ .01	$ .10
					Crim, Chuck	88F	162	$ .01	$ .10
					Crim, Chuck	89F	183	$ .01	$ .05
					Crim, Chuck	90F	319	$ .01	$ .03
					Cromartie, Warren	81F	144	$ .01	$ .04
					Cromartie, Warren	83F	279	$ .01	$ .04
					Cromartie, Warren	84F	272	$ .01	$ .06
					Cromartie, Wayne	82F	186	$ .01	$ .04
					Crowley, Terry	81F	190	$ .01	$ .04
					Crowley, Terry	82F	160	$ .01	$ .04
Coolbaugh, Scott	90F	293	$ .01	$ .35	Crowley, Terry	83F	55	$ .01	$ .04
Cooper, Cecil	81F	639	$ .01	$ .10	Cruz, Hector	81F	206	$ .01	$ .04
Cooper, Cecil	82F	138	$ .01	$ .10	Cruz, Hector	82F	591	$ .01	$ .04
Cooper, Cecil	83F	30	$ .01	$ .10	Cruz, Jose	81F	60	$ .01	$ .10
Cooper, Cecil	84F	198	$ .01	$ .10	Cruz, Jose	82F	214	$ .01	$ .10
Cooper, Cecil	85F	580	$ .03	$ .20	Cruz, Jose	83F	446	$ .01	$ .10
Cooper, Cecil	86F	484	$ .01	$ .10	Cruz, Jose	84F	222	$ .01	$ .10
Cooper, Cecil	87F	343	$ .01	$ .10	Cruz, Jose	85F	347	$ .01	$ .10
Cooper, Cecil	88F	161	$ .01	$ .10	Cruz, Jose	86F	201	$ .01	$ .10
Cooper, Don	82F	550	$ .01	$ .04	Cruz, Jose	86F	296	$ .01	$ .10
Cora, Joey	88F	580	$ .01	$ .10	Cruz, Jose	87F	53	$ .01	$ .10
Cora, Joey	90F	154	$ .01	$ .10	Cruz, Jose	88F	443	$ .01	$ .04
Corbett, Doug	81F	555	$ .01	$ .04	Cruz, Julio	81F	601	$ .01	$ .04
Corbett, Doug	82F	551	$ .01	$ .04	Cruz, Julio	82F	509	$ .01	$ .04
Corbett, Doug	83F	83	$ .01	$ .04	Cruz, Julio	83F	478	$ .01	$ .04
Corbett, Doug	85F	298	$ .01	$ .05	Cruz, Julio	84F	55	$ .01	$ .06
Corbett, Doug	87F	76	$ .01	$ .04	Cruz, Julio	85F	510	$ .01	$ .05
Corbett, Sherman	88FU	11	$ .01	$ .10	Cruz, Julio	87F	492	$ .01	$ .04
Corbett, Sherman	89F	473	$ .01	$ .05	Cruz, Todd	81F	341	$ .01	$ .04
Corcoran, Tim	81F	479	$ .01	$ .04	Cruz, Todd	83F	479	$ .01	$ .04
Corcoran, Tim	85F	247	$ .01	$ .05	Cruz, Todd	84F	3	$ .01	$ .06
Corcoran, Tim	86F	437	$ .01	$ .05	Cruz, Todd	85F	172	$ .01	$ .05
Corey, Mark	81F	193	$ .01	$ .04	Cruz, Victor	81F	407	$ .01	$ .04
Corrales, Pat	81F	623	$ .01	$ .04	Cruz, Victor	82F	480	$ .01	$ .04
Correa, Ed	86FU	30	$ .04	$ .25	Cubbage, Mike	81F	566	$ .01	$ .04
Correa, Ed	87F	122	$ .04	$ .25	Cubbage, Mike	82F	523	$ .01	$ .04
Correa, Ed	88F	464	$ .01	$ .04	Cubs, Chicago	85F	642	$ .01	$ .05
Corsi, Jim	89F	649	$ .01	$ .25	Curry, Steve	89F	86	$ .01	$ .15
Corsi, Jim	90F	4	$ .01	$ .03	Curtis, John	81F	491	$ .01	$ .04
Costello, John	88FU	118	$ .01	$ .15	Curtis, John	82F	569	$ .01	$ .04
Costello, John	89F	446	$ .01	$ .15	Curtis, John	83F	84	$ .01	$ .04
Costello, John	90F	246	$ .01	$ .03	Curtis, John	84F	513	$ .01	$ .06
Cotto, Henry	85F	53	$ .01	$ .10	D'Acquisto, John	81F	163	$ .01	$ .04
Cotto, Henry	85FU	31	$ .01	$ .05	D'Acquisto, John	83F	516	$ .01	$ .04

FLEER'90

Scott Coolbaugh   THIRD BASE

FLEER

Player	Year	No.	VG	EX/MT	Player	Year	No.	VG	EX/MT
Daniels, Kal	86F	646	$1.00	$4.50	Davis, Jody	82F	592	$ .07	$ .50
Daniels, Kal	87F	197	$ .17	$ .85	Davis, Jody	83F	494	$ .01	$ .10
Daniels, Kal	88F	230	$ .01	$ .20	Davis, Jody	84F	491	$ .01	$ .06
Daniels, Kal	89F	157	$ .01	$ .20	Davis, Jody	85F	54	$ .01	$ .05
Darling, Ron	84FU	29	$2.00	$9.00	Davis, Jody	86F	364	$ .01	$ .10
Darling, Ron	85F	76	$ .15	$1.25	Davis, Jody	87F	557	$ .01	$ .10
Darling, Ron	86F	77	$ .01	$ .20	Davis, Jody	88F	414	$ .01	$ .04
Darling, Ron	87F	5	$ .03	$ .20	Davis, Jody	89F	421	$ .01	$ .05
Darling, Ron	88F	132	$ .01	$ .10	Davis, Jody	90F	579	$ .01	$ .03
Darling, Ron	89F	32	$ .01	$ .05	Davis, Joel	86F	202	$ .01	$ .10
Darling, Ron	90F	201	$ .01	$ .03	Davis, John	88F	255	$ .01	$ .15
Darwin, Danny	81F	632	$ .01	$ .04	Davis, John	88FU	15	$ .01	$ .05
Darwin, Danny	82F	315	$ .01	$ .04	Davis, Mark	84F	371	$ .01	$ .06
Darwin, Danny	83F	565	$ .01	$ .04	Davis, Mark	85F	606	$ .01	$ .05
Darwin, Danny	84F	416	$ .01	$ .06	Davis, Mark	86F	537	$ .01	$ .05
Darwin, Danny	85F	557	$ .01	$ .05	Davis, Mark	87F	271	$ .01	$ .04
Darwin, Danny	85FU	32	$ .03	$ .20	Davis, Mark	87FU	21	$ .01	$ .05
Darwin, Danny	86F	485	$ .01	$ .05	Davis, Mark	88F	581	$ .01	$ .04
Darwin, Danny	87F	54	$ .01	$ .04	Davis, Mark	89F	303	$ .01	$ .05
Darwin, Danny	88F	444	$ .01	$ .04	Davis, Mark	89F	635	$ .01	$ .15
Darwin, Danny	89F	354	$ .01	$ .05	Davis, Mark	89FU	18	$ .01	$ .05
Darwin, Danny	90F	227	$ .01	$ .03	Davis, Mark	90F	155	$ .01	$ .03
Dascenzo, Doug	89F	420	$ .01	$ .10	Davis, Mark	90F	631	$ .01	$ .03
Dauer, Rich	81F	182	$ .01	$ .04	Davis, Mike	81F	586	$ .04	$ .25
Dauer, Rich	82F	161	$ .01	$ .04	Davis, Mike	84F	443	$ .01	$1.00
Dauer, Rich	83F	57	$ .01	$ .04	Davis, Mike	85F	422	$ .01	$ .10
Dauer, Rich	84F	4	$ .01	$ .06	Davis, Mike	86F	416	$ .01	$ .05
Dauer, Rich	85F	173	$ .01	$ .05	Davis, Mike	87F	391	$ .01	$ .04
Dauer, Rich	86F	270	$ .01	$ .05	Davis, Mike	88F	277	$ .01	$ .04
Daugherty, Jack	90F	294	$ .01	$ .10	Davis, Mike	89F	55	$ .01	$ .05
Daulton, Darren	85FU	33	$ .01	$ .05	Davis, Mike	90F	391	$ .01	$ .03
Daulton, Darren	86F	438	$ .03	$ .20	Davis, Ron	81F	86	$ .01	$ .04
Daulton, Darren	87F	172	$ .01	$ .04	Davis, Ron	82F	32	$ .01	$ .04
Daulton, Darren	90F	555	$ .01	$ .03	Davis, Ron	83F	610	$ .01	$ .04
Davalillo, Vic	81F	132	$ .01	$ .04	Davis, Ron	84F	561	$ .01	$ .04
Davidson, Mark	87FU	20	$ .04	$ .25	Davis, Ron	85F	275	$ .01	$ .05
Davidson, Mark	88F	8	$ .01	$ .10	Davis, Ron	86F	390	$ .01	$ .05
Davidson, Mark	89F	109	$ .01	$ .05	Davis, Ron	87F	558	$ .01	$ .04
Davis, Alvin	84FU	30	$3.00	$10.00	Davis, Storm	83F	56	$ .01	$ .60
Davis, Alvin	85F	488	$ .75	$3.00	Davis, Storm	84F	5	$ .03	$ .15
Davis, Alvin	86F	464	$ .03	$ .20	Davis, Storm	85F	174	$ .01	$ .10
Davis, Alvin	87F	584	$ .01	$ .04	Davis, Storm	86F	271	$ .01	$ .05
Davis, Alvin	88F	373	$ .01	$ .10	Davis, Storm	87F	466	$ .01	$ .04
Davis, Alvin	89F	546	$ .01	$ .10	Davis, Storm	87FU	22	$ .01	$ .05
Davis, Alvin	90F	512	$ .01	$ .03	Davis, Storm	88F	278	$ .01	$ .04
Davis, Bob	81F	428	$ .01	$ .04	Davis, Storm	89F	6	$ .01	$ .05
Davis, Chili	83F	257	$ .03	$ .20	Davis, Storm	90F	5	$ .01	$ .10
Davis, Chili	84F	370	$ .03	$ .10	Dawley, Bill	84F	223	$ .01	$ .06
Davis, Chili	85F	605	$ .01	$ .10	Dawley, Bill	85F	348	$ .01	$ .05
Davis, Chili	86F	536	$ .01	$ .10	Dawley, Bill	86F	298	$ .01	$ .05
Davis, Chili	87F	270	$ .01	$ .10	Dawley, Bill	86FU	32	$ .01	$ .05
Davis, Chili	88F	79	$ .01	$ .10	Dawley, Bill	87F	493	$ .01	$ .04
Davis, Chili	88FU	12	$ .01	$ .05	Dawley, Bill	87FU	23	$ .01	$ .05
Davis, Chili	89F	474	$ .01	$ .05	Dawley, Bill	88F	29	$ .01	$ .04
Davis, Chili	90F	129	$ .01	$ .03	Dawson, Andre	81F	145	$ .05	$ .30
Davis, Dick	81F	527	$ .01	$ .04	Dawson, Andre	82F	187	$ .10	$ .45
Davis, Dick	82F	245	$ .01	$ .04	Dawson, Andre	83F	280	$ .05	$ .30
Davis, Dick	83F	305	$ .01	$ .04	Dawson, Andre	84F	273	$ .07	$ .50
Davis, Eric	85F	533	$3.50	$16.00	Dawson, Andre	85F	394	$ .06	$ .35
Davis, Eric	86F	175	$ .80	$3.00	Dawson, Andre	86F	246	$ .05	$ .30
Davis, Eric	87F	198	$ .45	$1.50	Dawson, Andre	87F	316	$ .04	$ .25
Davis, Eric	88F	231	$ .25	$ .75	Dawson, Andre	87FU	24	$ .06	$ .35
Davis, Eric	88F	637	$ .10	$ .50	Dawson, Andre	88F	415	$ .01	$ .20
Davis, Eric	89F	158	$ .05	$ .40	Dawson, Andre	89F	422	$ .01	$ .10
Davis, Eric	89F	639	$ .01	$ .25	Dawson, Andre	90F	29	$ .01	$ .10
Davis, Eric	90F	417	$ .01	$ .15	Dayett, Brian	85F	125	$ .01	$ .05
Davis, Glenn	85F	652	$2.00	$10.00	Dayett, Brian	85FU	35	$ .01	$ .05
Davis, Glenn	86F	297	$ .25	$1.50	Dayett, Brian	87FU	25	$ .01	$ .05
Davis, Glenn	87F	55	$ .05	$ .30	Dayett, Brian	88F	416	$ .01	$ .04
Davis, Glenn	87F	636	$ .03	$ .20	Dayley, Ken	83F	135	$ .01	$ .04
Davis, Glenn	88F	445	$ .01	$ .15	Dayley, Ken	84F	176	$ .01	$ .06
Davis, Glenn	89F	355	$ .01	$ .15	Dayley, Ken	86F	33	$ .01	$ .05
Davis, Glenn	90F	228	$ .01	$ .10	Dayley, Ken	87F	293	$ .01	$ .04
Davis, Jerry	85FU	34	$ .01	$ .05	Dayley, Ken	88F	30	$ .01	$ .04
Davis, Jerry	86F	317	$ .01	$ .05	Dayley, Ken	89F	448	$ .01	$ .05

FLEER

Player	Year	No.	VG	EX/MT	Player	Year	No.	VG	EX/MT
Dayley, Ken	90F	247	$ .01	$ .03	Deshaies, Jim	88F	446	$ .01	$ .04
De Los Santos, Luis	89F	646	$ .01	$ .20	Deshaies, Jim	89F	356	$ .01	$ .05
De Los Santos, Luis	89FU	37	$ .01	$ .10	Deshaies, Jim	90F	229	$ .01	$ .03
De Los Santos, Luis	90F	105	$ .01	$ .10	Deshields, Delino	90F	653	$ .01	$1.50
DeCinces, Doug	81F	173	$ .01	$ .10	Devereaux, Mike	88F	512	$ .01	$ .35
DeCinces, Doug	81F	195	$ .01	$ .10	Devereaux, Mike	89F	56	$ .01	$ .15
DeCinces, Doug	82F	162	$ .01	$ .10	Devereaux, Mike	89FU	2	$ .01	$ .05
DeCinces, Doug	83F	85	$ .01	$ .04	Devereaux, Mike	90F	175	$ .01	$ .03
DeCinces, Doug	84F	514	$ .01	$ .06	Diaz, Bo	81F	404	$ .03	$ .20
DeCinces, Doug	85F	299	$ .01	$ .05	Diaz, Bo	82F	364	$ .01	$ .10
DeCinces, Doug	86F	153	$ .01	$ .05	Diaz, Bo	82F	639	$ .01	$ .10
DeCinces, Doug	87F	77	$ .01	$ .04	Diaz, Bo	83F	160	$ .01	$ .10
DeCinces, Doug	88F	31	$ .01	$ .04	Diaz, Bo	83F	637	$ .01	$ .10
Dedmon, Jeff	85F	323	$ .01	$ .05	Diaz, Bo	84F	29	$ .03	$ .10
Dedmon, Jeff	86F	513	$ .01	$ .05	Diaz, Bo	85F	250	$ .01	$ .10
Dedmon, Jeff	87F	514	$ .01	$ .04	Diaz, Bo	86F	176	$ .01	$ .05
Dedmon, Jeff	88F	537	$ .01	$ .04	Diaz, Bo	87F	200	$ .01	$ .04
Deer, Rob	85F	648	$ .25	$1.50	Diaz, Bo	88F	232	$ .01	$ .04
Deer, Rob	86F	538	$ .01	$ .10	Diaz, Bo	89F	159	$ .01	$ .05
Deer, Rob	86FU	33	$ .04	$ .25	Diaz, Carlos	83F	540	$ .01	$ .04
Deer, Rob	87F	344	$ .01	$ .10	Diaz, Carlos	84F	583	$ .01	$ .06
Deer, Rob	88F	163	$ .01	$ .10	Diaz, Carlos	84FU	32	$ .01	$ .10
Deer, Rob	89F	184	$ .01	$ .05	Diaz, Carlos	85F	369	$ .01	$ .05
Deer, Rob	90F	320	$ .01	$ .03	Diaz, Carlos	86F	128	$ .01	$ .05
DeJesus, Ivan	81F	297	$ .01	$ .04	Diaz, Mario	88F	649	$ .01	$ .25
DeJesus, Ivan	82F	593	$ .01	$ .04	Diaz, Marion	88FU	59	$ .01	$ .15
DeJesus, Ivan	83F	157	$ .01	$ .04	Diaz, Marion	89F	547	$ .01	$ .05
DeJesus, Ivan	84F	26	$ .01	$ .06	Diaz, Mike	87F	609	$ .05	$ .30
DeJesus, Ivan	85F	248	$ .01	$ .05	Diaz, Mike	88F	326	$ .01	$ .04
DeJesus, Ivan	86F	34	$ .01	$ .05	Diaz, Mike	89F	494	$ .01	$ .05
DeJesus, Jose	89F	280	$ .01	$ .05	Dibble, Rob	88FU	83	$ .01	$1.00
DeJesus, Jose	90F	104	$ .01	$ .03	Dibble, Rob	89F	160	$ .01	$ .50
DeLeon, Jose	84F	248	$ .01	$ .50	Dibble, Rob	90F	418	$ .01	$ .20
DeLeon, Jose	85F	463	$ .01	$ .05	Dillard, Steve	81F	298	$ .01	$ .04
DeLeon, Jose	86F	607	$ .01	$ .05	Dillard, Steve	82F	594	$ .01	$ .04
DeLeon, Jose	87F	494	$ .01	$ .04	Dilone, Miguel	81F	391	$ .01	$ .04
DeLeon, Jose	88F	395	$ .01	$ .04	Dilone, Miguel	82F	365	$ .01	$ .04
DeLeon, Jose	88FU	119	$ .01	$ .05	Dilone, Miguel	83F	405	$ .01	$ .04
DeLeon, Jose	89F	449	$ .01	$ .05	Dilone, Miguel	85F	395	$ .01	$ .05
DeLeon, Jose	90F	248	$ .01	$ .03	DiPino, Frank	84F	224	$ .01	$ .06
DeLeon, Luis	83F	355	$ .01	$ .04	DiPino, Frank	85F	349	$ .01	$ .05
DeLeon, Luis	84F	297	$ .01	$ .06	DiPino, Frank	86F	299	$ .01	$ .05
DeLeon, Luis	85F	29	$ .01	$ .05	DiPino, Frank	87F	560	$ .01	$ .04
DeLeon, Luis	86F	318	$ .01	$ .05	DiPino, Frank	88F	418	$ .01	$ .04
Dempsey, Rick	81F	177	$ .01	$ .10	DiPino, Frank	89F	423	$ .01	$ .05
Dempsey, Rick	82F	163	$ .01	$ .04	DiPino, Frank	89FU	118	$ .01	$ .05
Dempsey, Rick	83F	58	$ .01	$ .04	DiPino, Frank	90F	249	$ .01	$ .03
Dempsey, Rick	84F	6	$ .03	$ .10	Distefano, Benny	89F	205	$ .01	$ .05
Dempsey, Rick	85F	175	$ .01	$ .05	Distefano, Benny	90F	464	$ .01	$ .03
Dempsey, Rick	86F	272	$ .01	$ .05	Dixon, Ken	85FU	36	$ .03	$ .20
Dempsey, Rick	87F	467	$ .01	$ .04	Dixon, Ken	86F	273	$ .01	$ .05
Dempsey, Rick	87FU	26	$ .01	$ .05	Dixon, Ken	87F	468	$ .01	$ .04
Dempsey, Rick	90F	392	$ .01	$ .03	Dixon, Ken	88F	557	$ .01	$ .04
Denny, John	82F	363	$ .01	$ .04	Donohue, Tom	81F	281	$ .01	$ .04
Denny, John	83F	158	$ .01	$ .10	Dopson, John	88FU	99	$ .01	$ .25
Denny, John	84F	27	$ .03	$ .10	Dopson, John	89F	373	$ .01	$ .25
Denny, John	85F	249	$ .01	$ .05	Dopson, John	89FU	8	$ .01	$ .15
Denny, John	86F	439	$ .01	$ .05	Dopson, John	90F	272	$ .01	$ .03
Denny, John	86FU	34	$ .01	$ .05	Doran, Bill	84F	225	$ .06	$1.00
Denny, John	87F	199	$ .01	$ .04	Doran, Bill	85F	350	$ .01	$ .20
Dent, Bucky	81F	80	$ .01	$ .04	Doran, Bill	86F	300	$ .01	$ .10
Dent, Bucky	82F	33	$ .01	$ .04	Doran, Bill	87F	57	$ .01	$ .10
Dent, Bucky	82F	629	$ .01	$ .04	Doran, Bill	88F	447	$ .01	$ .04
Dent, Bucky	83F	566	$ .01	$ .04	Doran, Bill	89F	357	$ .01	$ .05
Dent, Bucky	84F	417	$ .01	$ .06	Doran, Bill	90F	230	$ .01	$ .03
Dernier, Bob	83F	159	$ .01	$ .04	Dorsett, Brian	88F	607	$ .01	$ .15
Dernier, Bob	84F	28	$ .01	$ .06	Dotson, Richard	81F	356	$ .04	$ .25
Dernier, Bob	84FU	31	$ .01	$ .10	Dotson, Richard	82F	340	$ .01	$ .10
Dernier, Bob	85F	55	$ .01	$ .05	Dotson, Richard	83F	233	$ .01	$ .04
Dernier, Bob	86F	365	$ .01	$ .05	Dotson, Richard	84F	56	$ .01	$ .06
Dernier, Bob	87F	559	$ .01	$ .04	Dotson, Richard	85F	511	$ .01	$ .05
Dernier, Bob	88F	417	$ .01	$ .04	Dotson, Richard	86F	203	$ .01	$ .05
Dernier, Bob	89F	565	$ .01	$ .05	Dotson, Richard	87F	495	$ .01	$ .04
Deshaies, Jim	86FU	35	$ .06	$ .35	Dotson, Richard	88F	396	$ .01	$ .04
Deshaies, Jim	87F	56	$ .05	$ .30	Dotson, Richard	88FU	48	$ .01	$ .05

Player	Year	No.	VG	EX/MT
Dotson, Richard	89F	253	$ .01	$ .05
Dowell, Ken	87FU	27	$ .01	$ .05
Downing, Brian	81F	282	$ .01	$ .04

Brian Downing
ANGELS • CATCHER

Player	Year	No.	VG	EX/MT
Downing, Brian	82F	457	$ .01	$ .04
Downing, Brian	83F	86	$ .01	$ .04
Downing, Brian	84F	515	$ .01	$ .06
Downing, Brian	85F	300	$ .01	$ .05
Downing, Brian	86F	154	$ .01	$ .05
Downing, Brian	87F	78	$ .01	$ .04
Downing, Brian	88F	488	$ .01	$ .04
Downing, Brian	89F	475	$ .01	$ .05
Downing, Brian	90F	130	$ .01	$ .03
Downs, Kelly	87F	272	$ .04	$ .25
Downs, Kelly	88F	80	$ .01	$ .10
Downs, Kelly	89F	326	$ .01	$ .05
Downs, Kelly	90F	55	$ .01	$ .03
Doyle, Brian	81F	104	$ .01	$ .04
Drabek, Doug	86FU	36	$ .05	$ .35
Drabek, Doug	87F	96	$ .10	$ .50
Drabek, Doug	88F	327	$ .01	$ .15
Drabek, Doug	89F	206	$ .01	$ .05
Drabek, Doug	90F	465	$ .01	$ .03
Drago, Dick	81F	239	$ .01	$ .04
Drago, Dick	82F	510	$ .01	$ .04
Dravecky, Dave	83F	356	$ .06	$1.25
Dravecky, Dave	84F	298	$ .03	$ .25
Dravecky, Dave	85F	30	$ .01	$ .05
Dravecky, Dave	86F	319	$ .01	$ .05
Dravecky, Dave	87F	412	$ .01	$ .04
Dravecky, Dave	87FU	28	$ .01	$ .05
Dravecky, Dave	88F	81	$ .01	$ .04
Dravecky, Dave	89F	327	$ .01	$ .05
Drees, Tom	90F	644	$ .01	$ .03
Drew, Cameron	89F	640	$ .01	$ .20
Driessen, Dan	81F	205	$ .01	$ .10
Driessen, Dan	82F	630	$ .01	$ .04
Driessen, Dan	82F	64	$ .01	$ .04
Driessen, Dan	83F	589	$ .01	$ .04
Driessen, Dan	84F	467	$ .01	$ .06
Driessen, Dan	85F	396	$ .01	$ .05
Driessen, Dan	86F	539	$ .01	$ .05
Drumright, Keith	82F	89	$ .01	$ .04
Dubois, Brian	90F	601	$ .01	$ .15

Player	Year	No.	VG	EX/MT
Ducey, Rob	88F	107	$ .01	$ .25
Dunbar, Tommy	85FU	37	$ .01	$ .05
Duncan, Mariano	85FU	38	$ .10	$ .75
Duncan, Mariano	86F	129	$ .10	$ .40
Duncan, Mariano	87F	439	$ .01	$ .04
Duncan, Mariano	88F	513	$ .01	$ .04
Dunne, Mike	87FU	29	$ .10	$ .50
Dunne, Mike	88F	328	$ .01	$ .25
Dunne, Mike	89F	207	$ .01	$ .05
Dunston, Shawon	85F	649	$ 1.00	$3.50
Dunston, Shawon	86F	366	$ .03	$ .20
Dunston, Shawon	87F	561	$ .05	$ .30
Dunston, Shawon	88F	419	$ .01	$ .10
Dunston, Shawon	89F	424	$ .01	$ .05
Dunston, Shawon	90F	30	$ .01	$ .15
Durham, Leon	81F	540	$ .01	$ .10
Durham, Leon	82F	595	$ .01	$ .05
Durham, Leon	83F	495	$ .01	$ .10
Durham, Leon	84F	492	$ .01	$ .05
Durham, Leon	85F	56	$ .01	$ .05
Durham, Leon	86F	367	$ .01	$ .05
Durham, Leon	87F	562	$ .01	$ .05
Durham, Leon	88F	420	$ .01	$ .05
Dwyer, Jim	81F	235	$ .01	$ .04
Dwyer, Jim	82F	164	$ .01	$ .04
Dwyer, Jim	83F	59	$ .01	$ .04
Dwyer, Jim	84F	7	$ .01	$ .06
Dwyer, Jim	85F	176	$ .01	$ .05
Dwyer, Jim	86F	274	$ .01	$ .05
Dwyer, Jim	88F	558	$ .01	$ .04
Dwyer, Kim	87F	469	$ .01	$ .04
Dybzinski, Jerry	81F	399	$ .01	$ .04
Dybzinski, Jerry	82F	366	$ .01	$ .04
Dybzinski, Jerry	83F	406	$ .01	$ .04
Dybzinski, Jerry	84F	57	$ .01	$ .06
Dybzinski, Jerry	85F	512	$ .01	$ .05
Dyer, Mike	90F	372	$ .01	$ .10
Dykstra, Len	86F	78	$ .01	$5.00
Dykstra, Len	87F	6	$ .03	$ .75
Dykstra, Len	88F	133	$ .01	$ .25
Dykstra, Len	89F	33	$ .01	$ .10
Dykstra, Lenny	89FU	105	$ .01	$ .10
Dykstra, Lenny	90F	556	$ .01	$ .10
Easler, Mike	81F	372	$ .01	$ .04
Easler, Mike	82F	481	$ .01	$ .04
Easler, Mike	83F	306	$ .01	$ .04
Easler, Mike	84F	249	$ .01	$ .06
Easler, Mike	84FU	33	$ .01	$ .10
Easler, Mike	85F	157	$ .01	$ .05
Easler, Mike	86F	347	$ .01	$ .05
Easler, Mike	86FU	37	$ .01	$ .05
Easler, Mike	87F	97	$ .01	$ .04
Easler, Mike	88F	206	$ .01	$ .04
Easterly, Jamie	82F	139	$ .01	$ .04
Easterly, Jamie	83F	31	$ .01	$ .04
Easterly, Jamie	84F	538	$ .01	$ .06
Easterly, Jamie	85F	445	$ .01	$ .05
Easterly, Jamie	86F	585	$ .01	$ .05
Eastwick, Rawly	82F	596	$ .01	$ .04
Eckersley, Dennis	81F	226	$ .01	$ .25
Eckersley, Dennis	82F	292	$ .01	$ .25
Eckersley, Dennis	83F	182	$ .01	$ .25
Eckersley, Dennis	83F	629	$ .04	$ .25
Eckersley, Dennis	84F	396	$ .01	$ .06
Eckersley, Dennis	84FU	34	$ .04	$ .55
Eckersley, Dennis	85F	57	$ .01	$ .05
Eckersley, Dennis	86F	368	$ .01	$ .05
Eckersley, Dennis	87F	563	$ .01	$ .04
Eckersley, Dennis	87FU	30	$ .01	$ .05
Eckersley, Dennis	88F	279	$ .01	$ .04
Eckersley, Dennis	89F	7	$ .01	$ .05
Eckersley, Dennis	90F	6	$ .01	$ .03
Edelen, Joe	82F	65	$ .01	$ .04
Edler, Dave	81F	610	$ .01	$ .04
Edwards, Dave	81F	568	$ .01	$ .04

FLEER

Player	Year	No.	VG	EX/MT	Player	Year	No.	VG	EX/MT
Edwards, Dave	83F	357	$ .01	$ .04	Faedo, Lenny	84F	563	$ .01	$ .06
Edwards, Marshall	82F	140	$ .01	$ .04	Fahey, Bill	81F	490	$ .01	$ .04
Edwards, Marshall	83F	32	$ .01	$ .04	Falcone, Pete	81F	327	$ .01	$ .04
Edwards, Wayne	90F	652	$ .01	$ .03	Falcone, Pete	82F	524	$ .01	$ .04
Eichelberger, Juan	82F	570	$ .01	$ .04	Falcone, Pete	83F	541	$ .01	$ .04
Eichelberger, Juan	83F	358	$ .01	$ .04	Falcone, Pete	84F	177	$ .01	$ .06
Eichelberger, Juan	84F	539	$ .01	$ .06	Fallon, Bob	85FU	39	$ .01	$ .05
Eichhorn, Mark	86FU	38	$ .05	$ .30	Farmer, Ed	81F	339	$ .01	$ .04
Eichhorn, Mark	87F	224	$ .05	$ .20	Farmer, Ed	82F	342	$ .01	$ .04
Eichhorn, Mark	88F	108	$ .01	$ .10	Farmer, Ed	83F	161	$ .01	$ .04
Eichhorn, Mark	89F	230	$ .01	$ .05	Farr, Steve	85F	446	$ .01	$ .05
Eichhorn, Mark	90F	580	$ .01	$ .03	Farr, Steve	86F	7	$ .01	$ .05
Eisenreich, Jim	89FU	38	$ .01	$ .05	Farr, Steve	87F	367	$ .01	$ .04
Eisenreich, Jim	90F	106	$ .01	$ .03	Farr, Steve	88F	256	$ .01	$ .04
Ellis, John	82F	316	$ .01	$ .04	Farr, Steve	89F	281	$ .01	$ .05
Elster, Kevin	87F	7	$ .05	$ .50	Farr, Steve	90F	107	$ .01	$ .03
Elster, Kevin	88FU	104	$ .01	$ .15	Farrell, John	88F	608	$ .01	$ .30
Elster, Kevin	89F	34	$ .01	$ .05	Farrell, John	89F	403	$ .01	$ .10
Elster, Kevin	90F	202	$ .01	$ .03	Farrell, John	90F	491	$ .01	$ .03
Engle, Dave	82F	552	$ .01	$ .04	Felder, Mike	88F	164	$ .01	$ .04
Engle, Dave	84F	562	$ .01	$ .06	Felder, Mike	90F	321	$ .01	$ .03
Engle, Dave	85F	276	$ .01	$ .05	Felix, Junior	89FU	69	$ .01	$ 1.00
Engle, Dave	86F	391	$ .01	$ .05	Felix, Junior	90F	79	$ .01	$ .75
Engle, Dave	86FU	39	$ .01	$ .05	Felton, Terry	83F	612	$ .01	$ .04
Eppard, Jim	88F	645	$ .10	$ .40	Ferguson, Joe	81F	124	$ .01	$ .04
Eppard, Jim	88FU	13	$ .01	$ .05	Ferguson, Joe	83F	87	$ .01	$ .04
Eppard, Jim	89F	476	$ .01	$ .05	Fermin, Felix	88F	643	$ .01	$ .25
Erickson, Roger	81F	561	$ .01	$ .04	Fermin, Felix	89F	208	$ .01	$ .05
Erickson, Roger	82F	553	$ .01	$ .04	Fermin, Felix	89FU	27	$ .01	$ .05
Erickson, Roger	83F	378	$ .01	$ .04	Fermin, Felix	90F	492	$ .01	$ .03
Esasky, Nick	84F	468	$ .50	$ 2.00	Fernandez, Sid	85F	77	$ .15	$ .90
Esasky, Nick	85F	534	$ .01	$ .20	Fernandez, Sid	86F	79	$ .01	$ .20
Esasky, Nick	86F	177	$ .01	$ .05	Fernandez, Sid	87F	629	$ .10	$ .50
Esasky, Nick	87F	201	$ .01	$ .04	Fernandez, Sid	87F	8	$ .03	$ .20
Esasky, Nick	88F	233	$ .01	$ .04	Fernandez, Sid	88F	134	$ .01	$ .10
Esasky, Nick	89F	161	$ .01	$ .05	Fernandez, Sid	89F	35	$ .01	$ .05
Esasky, Nick	89FU	9	$ .01	$ .05	Fernandez, Sid	90F	203	$ .01	$ .03
Esasky, Nick	90F	273	$ .01	$ .03	Fernandez, Tony	84F	152	$ .70	$ 5.00
Escarrega, Ernesto	83F	234	$ .01	$ .04	Fernandez, Tony	85F	103	$ .10	$ .50
Espinosa, Nino	81F	20	$ .01	$ .04	Fernandez, Tony	86F	57	$ .03	$ .20
Espinoza, Alvaro	89FU	47	$ .01	$ .25	Fernandez, Tony	87F	225	$ .01	$ .10
Espinoza, Alvaro	90F	441	$ .01	$ .15	Fernandez, Tony	88F	109	$ .01	$ .10
Espy, Cecil	88F	465	$ .01	$ .25	Fernandez, Tony	88F	635	$ .01	$ .10
Espy, Cecil	89F	517	$ .01	$ .05	Fernandez, Tony	89F	231	$ .01	$ .05
Espy, Cecil	90F	295	$ .01	$ .03	Fernandez, Tony	90F	634	$ .01	$ .03
Essian, Jim	81F	593	$ .01	$ .04	Fernandez, Tony	90F	80	$ .01	$ .10
Essian, Jim	82F	341	$ .01	$ .04	Fetters, Mike	90F	131	$ .01	$ .15
Essian, Jim	84F	540	$ .01	$ .06	Fidrych, Mark	81F	462	$ .01	$ .04
Essian, Jim	84FU	35	$ .01	$ .10	Fielder, Cecil	86F	653	$ 1.25	$ 12.50
Essian, Jim	85F	423	$ .01	$ .05	Fielder, Cecil	87FU	31	$ .01	$ 2.00
Eufemia, Frank	86F	392	$ .01	$ .05	Fielder, Cecil	88F	110	$ .01	$ 1.00
Evans, Barry	81F	499	$ .01	$ .04	Fielder, Cecil	89F	232	$ .01	$ .50
Evans, Barry	82F	571	$ .01	$ .04	Figueroa, Ed	81F	624	$ .01	$ .04
Evans, Darrell	81F	436	$ .01	$ .10	Filer, Tom	86F	58	$ .01	$ .05
Evans, Darrell	82F	388	$ .01	$ .10	Filer, Tom	89F	185	$ .01	$ .05
Evans, Darrell	83F	258	$ .01	$ .10	Filer, Tom	90F	322	$ .01	$ .03
Evans, Darrell	84F	372	$ .03	$ .10	Filson, Pete	84F	564	$ .01	$ .06
Evans, Darrell	84FU	36	$ .03	$ .20	Filson, Pete	85F	277	$ .01	$ .05
Evans, Darrell	85F	6	$ .01	$ .10	Filson, Pete	86F	393	$ .01	$ .05
Evans, Darrell	86F	224	$ .01	$ .10	Fimple, Jack	84F	99	$ .01	$ .06
Evans, Darrell	87F	150	$ .01	$ .10	Fingers, Rollie	81F	485	$ .04	$ .25
Evans, Darrell	88F	54	$ .01	$ .10	Fingers, Rollie	82F	141	$ .03	$ .20
Evans, Darrell	90F	581	$ .01	$ .03	Fingers, Rollie	82F	644	$ .01	$ .10
Evans, Dwight	81F	232	$ .03	$ .20	Fingers, Rollie	83F	33	$ .03	$ .20
Evans, Dwight	82F	293	$ .03	$ .20	Fingers, Rollie	84F	199	$ .01	$ .20
Evans, Dwight	82F	642	$ .01	$ .04	Fingers, Rollie	85F	581	$ .03	$ .20
Evans, Dwight	83F	183	$ .01	$ .10	Fingers, Rollie	86F	486	$ .01	$ .10
Evans, Dwight	84F	397	$ .03	$ .10	Finley, Chuck	87F	79	$ .25	$ 1.25
Evans, Dwight	85F	158	$ .03	$ .20	Finley, Chuck	88F	489	$ .01	$ .20
Evans, Dwight	86F	348	$ .01	$ .10	Finley, Chuck	89F	477	$ .01	$ .10
Evans, Dwight	87F	34	$ .01	$ .10	Finley, Chuck	90F	132	$ .01	$ .10
Evans, Dwight	88F	351	$ .01	$ .10	Finley, Steve	89FU	3	$ .01	$ .30
Evans, Dwight	89F	87	$ .01	$ .05	Finley, Steve	90F	176	$ .01	$ .20
Evans, Dwight	90F	274	$ .01	$ .03	Fireovid, Steve	87F	653	$ .01	$ .04
Faedo, Lenny	83F	611	$ .01	$ .04	Fischlin, Mike	83F	407	$ .01	$ .04

Player	Year	No.	VG	EX/MT
Fischlin, Mike	84F	541	$ .01	$ .06
Fischlin, Mike	85F	447	$ .01	$ .05
Fischlin, Mike	86FU	40	$ .01	$ .05
Fischlin, Mike	87F	98	$ .01	$ .04
Fishel, John	88FU	88	$ .01	$ .15
Fishel, John	89F	358	$ .01	$ .10
Fisher, Brian	85FU	40	$ .01	$ .05
Fisher, Brian	86F	104	$ .01	$ .25
Fisher, Brian	87F	99	$ .01	$ .04
Fisher, Brian	87FU	32	$ .01	$ .05
Fisher, Brian	88F	329	$ .01	$ .04
Fisher, Brian	89F	209	$ .01	$ .05
Fisk, Carlton	81F	224	$ .04	$ .25
Fisk, Carlton	82F	343	$ .03	$ .20
Fisk, Carlton	82F	632	$ .04	$ .25
Fisk, Carlton	83F	235	$ .03	$ .20
Fisk, Carlton	83F	638	$ .31	$ .15
Fisk, Carlton	84F	58	$ .03	$ .20
Fisk, Carlton	85F	513	$ .03	$ .20
Fisk, Carlton	86F	204	$ .01	$ .10
Fisk, Carlton	86F	643	$ .01	$ .10
Fisk, Carlton	87F	496	$ .01	$ .10
Fisk, Carlton	88F	397	$ .01	$ .10
Fisk, Carlton	89F	495	$ .01	$ .10
Fisk, Carlton	90F	530	$ .01	$ .03
Fitzgerald, Mike	84FU	37	$ .03	$ .20
Fitzgerald, Mike	85F	78	$ .01	$ .05
Fitzgerald, Mike	85FU	41	$ .01	$ .05
Fitzgerald, Mike	86F	247	$ .01	$ .05
Fitzgerald, Mike	87F	317	$ .01	$ .04
Fitzgerald, Mike	88F	182	$ .01	$ .04
Fitzgerald, Mike	89F	374	$ .01	$ .05
Fitzgerald, Mike	90F	343	$ .01	$ .03
Flanagan, Mike	81F	171	$ .01	$ .10
Flanagan, Mike	82F	165	$ .01	$ .04
Flanagan, Mike	83F	60	$ .01	$ .04
Flanagan, Mike	84F	8	$ .03	$ .10
Flanagan, Mike	85F	177	$ .01	$ .05
Flanagan, Mike	86F	275	$ .01	$ .05
Flanagan, Mike	87F	470	$ .01	$ .04
Flanagan, Mike	88FU	67	$ .01	$ .05
Flanagan, Mike	89F	233	$ .01	$ .05
Flanagan, Mike	90F	81	$ .01	$ .03
Flannery, Tim	81F	493	$ .01	$ .04
Flannery, Tim	82F	572	$ .01	$ .04
Flannery, Tim	83F	359	$ .01	$ .04
Flannery, Tim	84F	299	$ .01	$ .06
Flannery, Tim	85F	31	$ .01	$ .05
Flannery, Tim	86F	320	$ .01	$ .05
Flannery, Tim	87F	413	$ .01	$ .04
Flannery, Tim	88F	582	$ .01	$ .04
Fletcher, Scott	84F	59	$ .03	$ .10
Fletcher, Scott	85F	514	$ .01	$ .05
Fletcher, Scott	86F	205	$ .01	$ .05
Fletcher, Scott	86FU	41	$ .01	$ .05
Fletcher, Scott	87F	123	$ .01	$ .04
Fletcher, Scott	88F	466	$ .01	$ .04
Fletcher, Scott	89F	518	$ .01	$ .05
Fletcher, Scott	90F	531	$ .01	$ .03
Flynn, Doug	81F	330	$ .01	$ .04
Flynn, Doug	82F	525	$ .01	$ .04
Flynn, Doug	83F	282	$ .01	$ .04
Flynn, Doug	84F	274	$ .01	$ .06
Flynn, Doug	85F	397	$ .01	$ .05
Foley, Tom	85F	535	$ .01	$ .05
Foley, Tom	86F	440	$ .01	$ .05
Foley, Tom	87F	318	$ .01	$ .04
Foley, Tom	88F	183	$ .01	$ .04
Foley, Tom	89F	375	$ .01	$ .05
Foley, Tom	90F	344	$ .01	$ .03
Foli, Tim	81F	379	$ .01	$ .04
Foli, Tim	82F	482	$ .01	$ .04
Foli, Tim	83F	88	$ .01	$ .04
Foli, Tim	84F	516	$ .01	$ .06
Foli, Tim	84FU	38	$ .01	$ .10

Player	Year	No.	VG	EX/MT
Foli, Tim	85F	126	$ .01	$ .05
Fontenot, Ray	84F	122	$ .01	$ .06
Fontenot, Ray	85F	127	$ .01	$ .05
Fontenot, Ray	85FU	42	$ .01	$ .05
Fontenot, Ray	86F	369	$ .01	$ .05
Foote, Barry	81F	313	$ .01	$ .04
Foote, Barry	82F	34	$ .01	$ .04
Ford, Curt	86F	648	$ .05	$ .30
Ford, Curt	87F	294	$ .01	$ .04
Ford, Curt	88F	32	$ .01	$ .04
Ford, Curt	89F	450	$ .01	$ .05
Ford, Curt	90F	557	$ .01	$ .03
Ford, Dan	81F	273	$ .01	$ .04
Ford, Dan	82F	458	$ .01	$ .04
Ford, Dan	83F	61	$ .01	$ .04
Ford, Dan	84F	9	$ .01	$ .06
Ford, Dan	85F	178	$ .01	$ .05

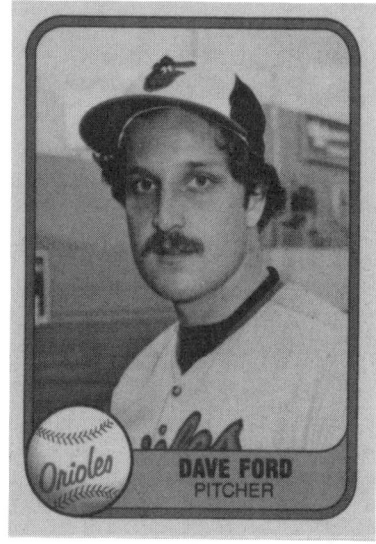

DAVE FORD
PITCHER

Player	Year	No.	VG	EX/MT
Ford, Dave	81F	192	$ .01	$ .04
Ford, Dave	82F	166	$ .01	$ .04
Forsch, Bob	81F	537	$ .01	$ .04
Forsch, Bob	82F	112	$ .01	$ .04
Forsch, Bob	83F	5	$ .01	$ .04
Forsch, Bob	84F	322	$ .01	$ .06
Forsch, Bob	84F	639	$ .01	$ .06
Forsch, Bob	85F	223	$ .01	$ .05
Forsch, Bob	86F	35	$ .01	$ .05
Forsch, Bob	87F	295	$ .01	$ .04
Forsch, Bob	88F	33	$ .01	$ .04
Forsch, Bob	90F	231	$ .01	$ .03
Forsch, Ken	81F	52	$ .01	$ .04
Forsch, Ken	82F	459	$ .01	$ .04
Forsch, Ken	83F	89	$ .01	$ .04
Forsch, Ken	84F	517	$ .01	$ .06
Forsch, Ken	85F	301	$ .01	$ .05
Forsch, Ken	86F	155	$ .01	$ .05
Forster, Terry	81F	119	$ .01	$ .04
Forster, Terry	82F	4	$ .01	$ .04
Forster, Terry	83F	205	$ .01	$ .04
Forster, Terry	84F	178	$ .01	$ .06
Forster, Terry	85F	324	$ .01	$ .05
Forster, Terry	86F	514	$ .01	$ .05
Forster, Terry	86FU	42	$ .01	$ .05
Forster, Terry	87F	80	$ .01	$ .04

Player	Year	No.	VG	EX/MT

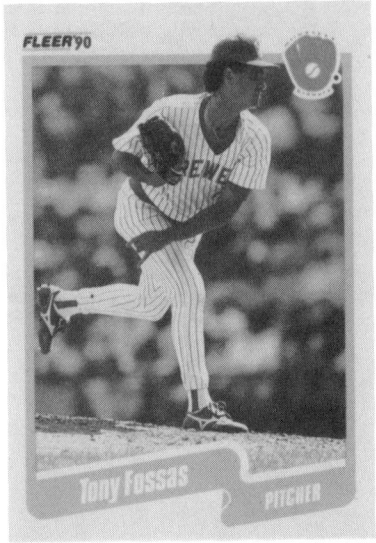

FLEER 90

Tony Fossas — PITCHER

Player	Year	No.	VG	EX/MT
Fossas, Tony	90F	323	$ .01	$ .10
Foster, George	81F	202	$ .05	$ .30
Foster, George	81F	216	$ .05	$ .30
Foster, George	82F	630	$ .01	$ .10
Foster, George	82F	66	$ .04	$ .25
Foster, George	83F	542	$ .03	$ .20
Foster, George	84F	584	$ .03	$ .20
Foster, George	85F	79	$ .03	$ .20
Foster, George	86F	80	$ .01	$ .15
Fowlkes, Alan	83F	259	$ .01	$ .04
Franco, John	84FU	39	$1.50	$6.00
Franco, John	85F	536	$ .25	$1.50
Franco, John	86F	178	$ .01	$ .15
Franco, John	87F	202	$ .01	$ .10
Franco, John	87F	631	$ .01	$ .10
Franco, John	88F	234	$ .01	$ .10
Franco, John	88F	627	$ .01	$ .10
Franco, John	89F	162	$ .01	$ .10
Franco, John	90F	419	$ .01	$ .10
Franco, Julio	84F	542	$ .25	$1.75
Franco, Julio	85F	448	$ .01	$ .20
Franco, Julio	86F	586	$ .01	$ .25
Franco, Julio	87F	251	$ .01	$ .10
Franco, Julio	88F	609	$ .01	$ .10
Franco, Julio	89F	404	$ .01	$ .05
Franco, Julio	89FU	64	$ .01	$ .10
Franco, Julio	90F	296	$ .01	$ .03
Francona, Terry	82F	188	$ .03	$ .20
Francona, Terry	83F	281	$ .01	$ .04
Francona, Terry	84F	275	$ .01	$ .06
Francona, Terry	85F	398	$ .01	$ .05
Francona, Terry	86F	248	$ .01	$ .05
Francona, Terry	86FU	43	$ .01	$ .05
Francona, Terry	87F	564	$ .01	$ .04
Fraser, Willie	87F	646	$ .40	$1.25
Fraser, Willie	87FU	33	$ .01	$ .05
Fraser, Willie	88F	490	$ .01	$ .04
Fraser, Willie	89F	478	$ .01	$ .05
Fraser, Willie	90F	133	$ .01	$ .03
Frazier, George	82F	35	$ .01	$ .04
Frazier, George	83F	379	$ .01	$ .04
Frazier, George	84F	123	$ .01	$ .06
Frazier, George	84FU	40	$ .01	$ .10
Frazier, George	85F	58	$ .01	$ .05
Frazier, George	86F	370	$ .01	$ .05
Frazier, George	87F	539	$ .01	$ .04
Frazier, George	88F	9	$ .01	$ .04
Freeman, Marvin	87F	651	$ .10	$ .40
Freeman, Marvin	89F	566	$ .01	$ .05
Fregosi, Jim	81F	274	$ .01	$ .04
Frey, Steve	90F	649	$ .01	$ .03
Frias, Pepe	81F	134	$ .01	$ .04
Frobel, Doug	85F	464	$ .01	$ .05
Frohwirth, Todd	88F	301	$ .01	$ .15
Frohwirth, Todd	89F	567	$ .01	$ .05
Frost, Dave	81F	275	$ .01	$ .04
Frost, Dave	82F	460	$ .01	$ .04
Frost, Dave	83F	111	$ .01	$ .04
Fryman, Woodie	81F	159	$ .01	$ .04
Fryman, Woodie	82F	189	$ .01	$ .04
Fryman, Woodie	83F	283	$ .01	$ .04
Funderburk, Mark	86F	652	$ .01	$ .10
Gaetti, Gary	83F	613	$ .50	$3.50
Gaetti, Gary	84F	565	$ .25	$ .75
Gaetti, Gary	85F	278	$ .05	$ .30
Gaetti, Gary	86F	394	$ .01	$ .10
Gaetti, Gary	87F	540	$ .01	$ .10
Gaetti, Gary	88F	10	$ .01	$ .10
Gaetti, Gary	89F	110	$ .01	$ .10
Gaetti, Gary	90F	373	$ .01	$ .03
Gaff, Brent	85F	80	$ .01	$ .05
Gagne, Greg	85FU	43	$ .10	$ .30
Gagne, Greg	86F	395	$ .01	$ .10
Gagne, Greg	87F	541	$ .01	$ .04
Gagne, Greg	88F	11	$ .01	$ .04
Gagne, Greg	89F	111	$ .01	$ .05
Gagne, Greg	90F	374	$ .01	$ .03
Gainey, Ty	88F	448	$ .01	$ .04
Galarraga, Andres	86F	647	$1.00	$3.00
Galarraga, Andres	86FU	44	$ .30	$1.00
Galarraga, Andres	87F	319	$ .15	$ .50
Galarraga, Andres	88F	184	$ .10	$ .25
Galarraga, Andres	89F	376	$ .01	$ .15
Galarraga, Andres	89F	638	$ .01	$ .05
Galarraga, Andres	90F	345	$ .01	$ .10
Gale, Rich	81F	40	$ .01	$ .04
Gale, Rich	82F	408	$ .01	$ .04
Gale, Rich	83F	260	$ .01	$ .04
Gale, Rich	84F	469	$ .01	$ .06
Gale, Rich	84FU	41	$ .01	$ .10
Gallagher, Dave	88FU	16	$ .01	$ .25
Gallagher, Dave	89F	496	$ .01	$ .15
Gallagher, Dave	90F	532	$ .01	$ .03
Gallego, Mike	89F	8	$ .01	$ .05
Gallego, Mike	90F	7	$ .01	$ .03
Gamble, Oscar	81F	98	$ .01	$ .04
Gamble, Oscar	82F	36	$ .01	$ .04
Gamble, Oscar	83F	380	$ .01	$ .04
Gamble, Oscar	84F	124	$ .01	$ .06
Gamble, Oscar	85FU	44	$ .01	$ .05
Gant, Ron	88F	538	$ .01	$ .65
Gant, Ron	89F	590	$ .01	$ .10
Gant, Ron	90F	582	$ .01	$ .03
Gantner, Jim	81F	522	$ .01	$ .04
Gantner, Jim	82F	142	$ .01	$ .04
Gantner, Jim	83F	34	$ .01	$ .04
Gantner, Jim	84F	200	$ .01	$ .06
Gantner, Jim	85F	582	$ .01	$ .05
Gantner, Jim	86F	487	$ .01	$ .05
Gantner, Jim	87F	345	$ .01	$ .04
Gantner, Jim	88F	165	$ .01	$ .04
Gantner, Jim	89F	186	$ .01	$ .05
Gantner, Jim	90F	324	$ .01	$ .03
Garber, Gene	81F	249	$ .01	$ .04
Garber, Gene	82F	434	$ .01	$ .04
Garber, Gene	83F	136	$ .01	$ .04
Garber, Gene	84F	179	$ .01	$ .06
Garber, Gene	85F	325	$ .01	$ .05
Garber, Gene	86F	515	$ .01	$ .05

Player	Year	No.	VG	EX/MT	Player	Year	No.	VG	EX/MT
Garber, Gene	87F	515	$ .01	$ .04	Gibson, Kirk	82F	267	$ .15	$ .75
Garber, Gene	88F	257	$ .01	$ .04	Gibson, Kirk	83F	329	$ .10	$ .40
Garbey, Barbaro	84FU	42	$ .01	$ .10	Gibson, Kirk	84F	80	$ .05	$ .30
Garbey, Barbaro	85F	7	$ .01	$ .05	Gibson, Kirk	85F	8	$ .05	$ .30
Garbey, Barbaro	86F	225	$ .01	$ .10	Gibson, Kirk	86F	226	$ .04	$ .25
Garcia, Damaso	81F	415	$ .03	$ .20	Gibson, Kirk	87F	151	$ .03	$ .20
Garcia, Damaso	82F	613	$ .01	$ .04	Gibson, Kirk	88F	55	$ .01	$ .10
Garcia, Damaso	83F	427	$ .01	$ .04	Gibson, Kirk	88FU	93	$ .01	$ .15
Garcia, Damaso	84F	153	$ .01	$ .06	Gibson, Kirk	89F	57	$ .01	$ .15
Garcia, Damaso	85F	104	$ .01	$ .05	Gibson, Kirk	90F	393	$ .01	$ .03
Garcia, Damaso	86F	59	$ .01	$ .05	Gibson, Paul	88FU	26	$ .01	$ .15
Garcia, Damaso	87F	226	$ .01	$ .04	Gibson, Paul	89F	131	$ .01	$ .05
Garcia, Damaso	90F	346	$ .01	$ .03	Gibson, Paul	90F	602	$ .01	$ .03
Garcia, Kiko	81F	191	$ .01	$ .04	Gideon, Brett	88F	330	$ .01	$ .15
Garcia, Kiko	82F	215	$ .01	$ .04	Giles, Brian	83F	544	$ .01	$ .04
Garcia, Kiko	83F	447	$ .01	$ .04	Giles, Brian	84F	585	$ .01	$ .06
Garcia, Kiko	84F	30	$ .01	$ .06	Girardi, Joe	89F	644	$ .01	$ .60
Garcia, Miguel	89F	647	$ .01	$ .20	Girardi, Joe	90F	31	$ .01	$ .10
Gardenhire, Ron	83F	543	$ .01	$ .04	Gladden, Dan	85F	607	$ .05	$ .50
Gardenhire, Ron	85F	81	$ .01	$ .05	Gladden, Dan	86F	541	$ .01	$ .05
Gardner, Mark	90F	646	$ .01	$ .03	Gladden, Dan	87F	274	$ .01	$ .04
Gardner, Wes	88F	352	$ .01	$ .10	Gladden, Dan	87FU	36	$ .01	$ .05
Gardner, Wes	89F	88	$ .01	$ .05	Gladden, Dan	88F	12	$ .01	$ .04
Gardner, Wes	90F	275	$ .01	$ .03	Gladden, Dan	89F	112	$ .01	$ .05
Garland, Wayne	81F	394	$ .01	$ .04	Gladden, Dan	90F	375	$ .01	$ .03
Garland, Wayne	82F	367	$ .01	$ .04	Glavine, Tom	88F	539	$ .01	$ .40
Garner, Phil	81F	364	$ .01	$ .04	Glavine, Tom	89F	591	$ .01	$ .05
Garner, Phil	82F	216	$ .01	$ .04	Glavine, Tom	90F	583	$ .01	$ .03
Garner, Phil	83F	448	$ .01	$ .04	Gleaton, Jerry	88F	258	$ .01	$ .04
Garner, Phil	84F	226	$ .01	$ .06	Gleaton, Jerry	89F	282	$ .01	$ .05
Garner, Phil	85F	351	$ .01	$ .05	Glynn, Ed	83F	408	$ .01	$ .04
Garner, Phil	86F	301	$ .01	$ .05	Goltz, Dave	81F	127	$ .01	$ .04
Garner, Phil	87F	58	$ .01	$ .04	Goltz, Dave	82F	6	$ .01	$ .04
Garrelts, Scott	86F	540	$ .01	$ .05	Goltz, Dave	83F	90	$ .01	$ .04
Garrelts, Scott	87F	273	$ .01	$ .04	Gomez, Luis	81F	253	$ .01	$ .04
Garrelts, Scott	88F	82	$ .01	$ .04	Gonzales, Rene	88F	560	$ .01	$ .15
Garrelts, Scott	89F	328	$ .01	$ .05	Gonzalez, Denny	86F	608	$ .01	$ .05
Garrelts, Scott	90F	56	$ .01	$ .03	Gonzalez, German	89F	113	$ .01	$ .15
Garvey, Steve	81F	110	$ .08	$ .75	Gonzalez, German	90F	376	$ .01	$ .03
Garvey, Steve	81F	606	$ .07	$ .75	Gonzalez, Jose	87F	649	$ .04	$ .25
Garvey, Steve	82F	5	$ .07	$ .50	Gonzalez, Jose	90F	394	$ .01	$ .03
Garvey, Steve	83F	206	$ .06	$ .35	Gonzalez, Juan	90F	297	$ .01	$ .50
Garvey, Steve	84F	300	$ .07	$ .50	Gonzalez, Julio	81F	73	$ .01	$ .04
Garvey, Steve	84F	628	$ .04	$ .25	Gonzalez, Orlando	81F	585	$ .01	$ .04
Garvey, Steve	85F	32	$ .05	$ .30	Gooden, Dwight	84FU	43	$15.00	$75.00
Garvey, Steve	85F	631	$ .05	$ .30	Gooden, Dwight	85F	634	$ .20	$1.00
Garvey, Steve	85F	633	$ .01	$ .10	Gooden, Dwight	85F	82	$3.00	$12.00
Garvey, Steve	86F	321	$ .05	$ .30	Gooden, Dwight	86F	626	$ .06	$ .35
Garvey, Steve	86F	640	$ .04	$ .25	Gooden, Dwight	86F	638	$ .15	$ .75
Garvey, Steve	87F	414	$ .04	$ .25	Gooden, Dwight	86F	641	$ .05	$ .30
Garvin, Jerry	81F	429	$ .01	$ .04	Gooden, Dwight	86F	81	$ .50	$2.00
Garvin, Jerry	82F	614	$ .01	$ .04	Gooden, Dwight	87F	629	$ .10	$ .50
Garvin, Jerry	83F	428	$ .01	$ .04	Gooden, Dwight	87F	640	$ .10	$ .50
Gedman, Rich	82F	294	$ .06	$ .35	Gooden, Dwight	87F	9	$ .35	$1.25
Gedman, Rich	83F	184	$ .01	$ .10	Gooden, Dwight	88F	135	$ .10	$ .90
Gedman, Rich	84F	398	$ .03	$ .10	Gooden, Dwight	89F	36	$ .01	$ .30
Gedman, Rich	85F	159	$ .01	$ .05	Gooden, Dwight	89F	635	$ .01	$ .15
Gedman, Rich	86F	349	$ .01	$ .10	Gooden, Dwight	90F	204	$ .01	$ .10
Gedman, Rich	86F	643	$ .01	$ .10	Goodwin, Danny	82F	554	$ .01	$ .04
Gedman, Rich	87F	35	$ .01	$ .04	Gordon, Don	89F	405	$ .01	$ .05
Gedman, Rich	88F	353	$ .01	$ .04	Gordon, Tom	89F	284	$ .05	$2.00
Gedman, Rich	89F	89	$ .01	$ .05	Gordon, Tom	90F	108	$ .01	$ .50
Gedman, Rich	90F	276	$ .01	$ .03	Gorman, Tom	85F	83	$ .01	$ .05
Geisel, Dave	84F	154	$ .01	$ .06	Gorman, Tom	86F	82	$ .01	$ .05
Gerber, Craig	86F	156	$ .01	$ .05	Gossage, Goose	82F	37	$ .04	$ .25
Geren, Bob	89FU	48	$ .01	$ .35	Gossage, Goose	83F	381	$ .03	$ .20
Geren, Bob	90F	442	$ .01	$ .10	Gossage, Goose	84F	125	$ .03	$ .20
Gerhart, Ken	87FU	34	$ .04	$ .25	Gossage, Goose	84FU	44	$ .12	$ .60
Gerhart, Ken	88F	559	$ .01	$ .04	Gossage, Goose	85F	33	$ .03	$ .20
Gerhart, Ken	89F	609	$ .01	$ .05	Gossage, Goose	85F	633	$ .01	$ .10
Geronimo, Cesar	82F	409	$ .01	$ .04	Gossage, Goose	86F	322	$ .03	$ .20
Geronimo, Cesar	83F	112	$ .01	$ .04	Gossage, Goose	87F	415	$ .01	$ .10
Gibson, Bob	84F	201	$ .01	$ .06	Gossage, Goose	88F	583	$ .01	$ .10
Gibson, Bob	86F	488	$ .01	$ .05	Gossage, Goose	88FU	76	$ .01	$ .05
Gibson, Kirk	81F	481	$1.00	$3.00	Gossage, Goose	89F	425	$ .01	$ .05

FLEER

Player	Year	No.	VG	EX/MT	Player	Year	No.	VG	EX/MT
Gossage, Goose 'Rich'	81F	89	$ .03	$ .25	Grissom, Marquis	90F	347	$ .01	$ .35
Gott, Jim	84F	155	$ .01	$ .25	Gross, Greg	81F	18	$ .01	$ .04
Gott, Jim	85F	105	$ .01	$ .05	Gross, Greg	82F	246	$ .01	$ .04
Gott, Jim	85FU	45	$ .01	$ .05	Gross, Greg	83F	162	$ .01	$ .04
Gott, Jim	86F	542	$ .01	$ .05	Gross, Greg	84F	31	$ .01	$ .06
Gott, Jim	87FU	35	$ .01	$ .05	Gross, Greg	85F	251	$ .01	$ .05
Gott, Jim	88FU	112	$ .01	$ .05	Gross, Greg	86F	441	$ .01	$ .05
Gott, Jim	89F	210	$ .01	$ .05	Gross, Greg	87F	173	$ .01	$ .04
Gott, Jim	90F	466	$ .01	$ .03	Gross, Greg	88F	302	$ .01	$ .04
Gozzo, Mauro	90F	82	$ .01	$ .25	Gross, Greg	89F	568	$ .01	$ .05
Grace, Mark	88F	641	$2.00	$12.50	Gross, Kevin	84F	32	$ .04	$ .25
Grace, Mark	88FU	77	$ .25	$5.50	Gross, Kevin	85F	252	$ .01	$ .05
Grace, Mark	89F	426	$ .10	$2.00	Gross, Kevin	86F	442	$ .01	$ .05
Grace, Mark	90F	32	$ .01	$ .35	Gross, Kevin	87F	174	$ .01	$ .04
Graham, Dan	81F	189	$ .01	$ .04	Gross, Kevin	88F	303	$ .01	$ .04
Graham, Dan	82F	167	$ .01	$ .04	Gross, Kevin	89F	569	$ .01	$ .05
Grant, Mark	88F	584	$ .01	$ .04	Gross, Kevin	89FU	96	$ .01	$ .05
Grant, Mark	89F	304	$ .01	$ .05	Gross, Kevin	90F	348	$ .01	$ .03
Grant, Mark	90F	156	$ .01	$ .03	Gross, Wayne	81F	587	$ .01	$ .04
Gray, Gary	81F	402	$ .01	$ .04	Gross, Wayne	82F	90	$ .01	$ .04
Gray, Gary	82F	511	$ .01	$ .04	Gross, Wayne	83F	517	$ .01	$ .04
Gray, Gary	83F	480	$ .01	$ .04	Gross, Wayne	84F	444	$ .01	$ .06
Green, David	83F	6	$ .01	$ .04	Gross, Wayne	84FU	45	$ .01	$ .10
Green, David	84F	323	$ .01	$ .06	Gross, Wayne	85F	179	$ .01	$ .05
Green, David	85F	224	$ .01	$ .05	Gross, Wayne	86F	276	$ .01	$ .05
Green, David	85FU	46	$ .01	$ .05	Grubb, John	81F	631	$ .01	$ .04
Green, David	86F	543	$ .01	$ .05	Grubb, John	82F	317	$ .01	$ .04
Green, David	88F	34	$ .01	$ .04	Grubb, John	83F	567	$ .01	$ .04
Greene, Tommy	90F	584	$ .01	$ .25	Grubb, John	84F	81	$ .01	$ .06
Greenwell, Mike	87FU	37	$ .75	$4.00	Grubb, John	85F	9	$ .01	$ .05
Greenwell, Mike	88F	354	$ .75	$2.50	Grubb, John	86F	227	$ .01	$ .05
Greenwell, Mike	88F	630	$ .10	$ .75	Grubb, John	87F	152	$ .01	$ .04
Greenwell, Mike	89F	90	$ .01	$1.25	Gruber, Kelly	85F	645	$ .75	$3.50
Greenwell, Mike	90F	277	$ .01	$ .25	Gruber, Kelly	87F	227	$ .10	$ .50
Greenwell, Mike	90F	632	$ .01	$ .03	Gruber, Kelly	88F	111	$ .10	$ .35
Gregg, Tommy	88FU	113	.01	.30	Gruber, Kelly	89F	234	$ .01	$ .25
Gregg, Tommy	89F	592	$ .01	$ .05	Gruber, Kelly	90F	83	$ .01	$ .03
Gregg, Tommy	90F	585	$ .01	$ .03	Guante, Cecilio	84F	250	$ .01	$ .06
Grich, Bobby	81F	269	$ .01	$ .04	Guante, Cecilio	85F	465	$ .01	$ .05
Grich, Bobby	82F	461	$ .01	$ .04	Guante, Cecilio	86F	609	$ .01	$ .05
Grich, Bobby	83F	91	$ .01	$ .04	Guante, Cecilio	87F	610	$ .01	$ .04
Grich, Bobby	84F	518	$ .01	$ .06	Guante, Cecilio	87FU	38	$ .01	$ .05
Grich, Bobby	85F	302	$ .01	$ .05	Guante, Cecilio	89F	519	$ .01	$ .05
Grich, Bobby	86F	157	$ .01	$ .05	Guante, Cecilio	90F	298	$ .01	$ .03
Grich, Bobby	87F	81	$ .01	$ .04	Gubicza, Mark	84FU	46	$1.00	$6.00
Griffey, Jr., Ken	89F	548	$1.00	$9.00	Gubicza, Mark	85F	201	$ .25	$1.50
Griffey, Jr., Ken	90F	513	$ .01	$2.00	Gubicza, Mark	86F	8	$ .01	$ .15
Griffey, Ken	81F	199	$ .01	$ .10	Gubicza, Mark	87F	368	$ .01	$ .04
Griffey, Ken	82F	67	$ .01	$ .10	Gubicza, Mark	88F	259	$ .01	$ .04
Griffey, Ken	83F	382	$ .01	$ .10	Gubicza, Mark	89F	283	$ .01	$ .10
Griffey, Ken	84F	126	$ .03	$ .10	Gubicza, Mark	90F	109	$ .01	$ .15
Griffey, Ken	85F	128	$ .01	$ .10	Gubicza, Mark	90F	633	$ .01	$ .03
Griffey, Ken	86F	105	$ .01	$ .10	Guerrero, Mario	81F	591	$ .01	$ .04
Griffey, Ken	87F	516	$ .01	$ .04	Guerrero, Pedro	82F	7	$ .10	$ .50
Griffey, Ken	88F	540	$ .01	$ .04	Guerrero, Pedro	83F	207	$ .05	$ .30
Griffey, Ken	89FU	84	$ .01	$ .10	Guerrero, Pedro	84F	100	$ .05	$ .30
Griffey, Ken	90F	420	$ .01	$ .05	Guerrero, Pedro	85F	370	$ .01	$ .30
Griffin, Alfredo	81F	430	$ .01	$ .04	Guerrero, Pedro	86F	130	$ .04	$ .25
Griffin, Alfredo	82F	615	$ .01	$ .04	Guerrero, Pedro	87F	440	$ .01	$ .10
Griffin, Alfredo	83F	429	$ .01	$ .04	Guerrero, Pedro	88F	514	$ .01	$ .10
Griffin, Alfredo	84F	156	$ .01	$ .06	Guerrero, Pedro	88F	623	$ .01	$ .04
Griffin, Alfredo	85F	106	$ .01	$ .05	Guerrero, Pedro	89F	451	$ .01	$ .05
Griffin, Alfredo	85FU	47	$ .01	$ .05	Guerrero, Pedro	90F	250	$ .01	$ .10
Griffin, Alfredo	86F	417	$ .01	$ .05	Guetterman, Lee	86FU	45	$ .05	$ .30
Griffin, Alfredo	87F	392	$ .01	$ .04	Guetterman, Lee	87F	585	$ .03	$ .20
Griffin, Alfredo	88F	280	$ .01	$ .04	Guetterman, Lee	88F	374	$ .01	$ .04
Griffin, Alfredo	88FU	94	$ .01	$ .05	Guetterman, Lee	90F	443	$ .01	$ .03
Griffin, Alfredo	89F	58	$ .01	$ .05	Guidry, Ron	81F	88	$ .04	$ .25
Griffin, Alfredo	90F	395	$ .01	$ .03	Guidry, Ron	82F	38	$ .04	$ .25
Griffin, Mike	81F	107	$ .01	$ .04	Guidry, Ron	83F	383	$ .01	$ .15
Griffin, Mike	88F	561	$ .01	$ .04	Guidry, Ron	84F	127	$ .03	$ .15
Griffin, Tom	81F	456	$ .01	$ .04	Guidry, Ron	85F	129	$ .03	$ .15
Griffin, Tom	82F	389	$ .01	$ .04	Guidry, Ron	86F	106	$ .01	$ .10
Grimsley, Jason	90F	653	$ .01	$1.50	Guidry, Ron	87F	100	$ .03	$ .10
Grimsley, Ross	81F	406	$ .01	$ .04	Guidry, Ron	88F	207	$ .01	$ .10

Player	Year	No.	VG	EX/MT
Guillen, Ozzie	85FU	48	$ .25	$1.25
Guillen, Ozzie	86F	206	$ .15	$ .65
Guillen, Ozzie	87F	497	$ .01	$ .10
Guillen, Ozzie	88F	398	$ .01	$ .04
Guillen, Ozzie	89F	497	$ .01	$ .05
Guillen, Ozzie	90F	533	$ .01	$ .03
Gulden, Brad	85F	537	$ .01	$ .05
Gullickson, Bill	81F	150	$ .06	$ .35

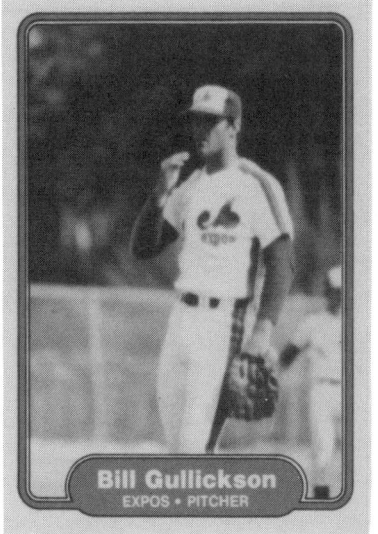

Bill Gullickson
EXPOS • PITCHER

Player	Year	No.	VG	EX/MT
Gullickson, Bill	82F	190	$ .01	$ .10
Gullickson, Bill	83F	284	$ .01	$ .04
Gullickson, Bill	84F	276	$ .03	$ .10
Gullickson, Bill	85F	399	$ .01	$ .05
Gullickson, Bill	86F	249	$ .01	$ .05
Gullickson, Bill	86FU	46	$ .01	$ .05
Gullickson, Bill	87F	203	$ .01	$ .04
Gullickson, Bill	88F	208	$ .01	$ .04
Gulliver, Glenn	83F	62	$ .01	$ .04
Gumpert, Dave	87F	565	$ .01	$ .04
Gura, Larry	81F	38	$ .01	$ .04
Gura, Larry	82F	410	$ .01	$ .04
Gura, Larry	83F	113	$ .01	$ .04
Gura, Larry	84F	347	$ .01	$ .06
Gura, Larry	85F	202	$ .01	$ .05
Gutierrez, Jackie	84FU	47	$ .01	$ .10
Gutierrez, Jackie	85F	160	$ .01	$ .05
Gutierrez, Jackie	86F	350	$ .01	$ .05
Gutierrez, Jackie	86FU	47	$ .01	$ .05
Gutierrez, Jackie	87F	471	$ .01	$ .04
Guzman, Jose	86F	559	$ .04	$ .30
Guzman, Jose	87F	124	$ .01	$ .04
Guzman, Jose	88F	467	$ .01	$ .04
Guzman, Jose	89F	520	$ .01	$ .05
Gwynn, Chris	88F	647	$ .01	$ .30
Gwynn, Chris	89F	59	$ .01	$ .10
Gwynn, Tony	83F	360	$2.00	$11.00
Gwynn, Tony	84F	301	$ .75	$3.00
Gwynn, Tony	85F	34	$ .25	$1.50
Gwynn, Tony	86F	323	$ .06	$ .75
Gwynn, Tony	87F	416	$ .01	$ .50
Gwynn, Tony	88F	585	$ .01	$ .25
Gwynn, Tony	88F	631	$ .01	$ .10
Gwynn, Tony	88F	634	$ .01	$ .10
Gwynn, Tony	89F	305	$ .01	$ .25
Gwynn, Tony	90F	157	$ .01	$ .10

Player	Year	No.	VG	EX/MT
Haas, Moose	81F	516	$ .01	$ .04
Haas, Moose	82F	143	$ .01	$ .04
Haas, Moose	83F	35	$ .01	$ .04
Haas, Moose	84F	202	$ .01	$ .06
Haas, Moose	85F	583	$ .01	$ .05
Haas, Moose	86F	489	$ .01	$ .05
Haas, Moose	86FU	48	$ .01	$ .05
Haas, Moose	87F	393	$ .01	$ .04
Hairston, Jerry	83F	236	$ .01	$ .04
Hairston, Jerry	84F	60	$ .01	$ .06
Hairston, Jerry	85F	515	$ .01	$ .05
Hairston, Jerry	86F	207	$ .01	$ .05
Hairston, Jerry	87F	498	$ .01	$ .04
Hall, Albert	85F	326	$ .01	$ .05
Hall, Albert	87FU	39	$ .01	$ .05
Hall, Albert	88F	541	$ .01	$ .04
Hall, Albert	89F	593	$ .01	$ .05
Hall, Drew	89F	643	$ .01	$ .20
Hall, Drew	90F	299	$ .01	$ .03
Hall, Grady	89F	650	$ .01	$ .20
Hall, Mel	84F	493	$ .03	$ .10
Hall, Mel	85F	449	$ .01	$ .05
Hall, Mel	86F	587	$ .01	$ .05
Hall, Mel	87F	252	$ .01	$ .04
Hall, Mel	88F	610	$ .01	$ .04
Hall, Mel	89F	406	$ .01	$ .05
Hall, Mel	89FU	49	$ .01	$ .05
Hall, Mel	90F	444	$ .01	$ .03
Hamilton, Darryl	88FU	38	$ .01	$ .15
Hamilton, Darryl	89F	187	$ .01	$ .15
Hamilton, Darryl	90F	325	$ .01	$ .03
Hamilton, Jeff	88F	515	$ .01	$ .04
Hamilton, Jeff	89F	60	$ .01	$ .05
Hamilton, Jeff	90F	396	$ .01	$ .03
Hammaker, Atlee	83F	261	$ .01	$ .04
Hammaker, Atlee	84F	373	$ .01	$ .06
Hammaker, Atlee	85F	608	$ .01	$ .05
Hammaker, Atlee	86F	544	$ .01	$ .05
Hammaker, Atlee	87FU	40	$ .01	$ .05
Hammaker, Atlee	88F	83	$ .01	$ .04
Hammaker, Atlee	89F	329	$ .01	$ .05
Hammaker, Atlee	90F	57	$ .01	$ .03
Hammond, Chris	90F	421	$ .01	$ .10
Hammond, Steve	83F	114	$ .01	$ .04
Hancock, Garry	81F	229	$ .01	$ .04
Hancock, Garry	82F	295	$ .01	$ .04
Hancock, Garry	84F	445	$ .01	$ .06
Hanna, Preston	81F	264	$ .01	$ .04
Hanna, Preston	82F	435	$ .01	$ .04
Hansen, Dave	00F	642	$ .01	$ .25
Hanson, Erik	89F	549	$ .01	$ .35
Hanson, Erik	90F	514	$ .01	$ .10
Hargesheimer, Alan	81F	457	$ .01	$ .04
Hargrove, Mike	81F	387	$ .01	$ .04
Hargrove, Mike	82F	368	$ .01	$ .04
Hargrove, Mike	83F	409	$ .01	$ .04
Hargrove, Mike	84F	543	$ .01	$ .06
Hargrove, Mike	85F	450	$ .01	$ .05
Hargrove, Mike	86F	588	$ .01	$ .05
Harkey, Mike	89F	427	$ .01	$ .35
Harkey, Mike	90F	33	$ .01	$ .10
Harlow, Larry	81F	289	$ .01	$ .04
Harlow, Larry	82F	462	$ .01	$ .04
Harnisch, Pete	90F	177	$ .01	$ .10
Harper, Brian	85F	466	$ .01	$ .05
Harper, Brian	86F	36	$ .01	$ .05
Harper, Brian	88FU	42	$ .01	$ .05
Harper, Brian	89F	114	$ .01	$ .05
Harper, Brian	90F	377	$ .01	$ .03
Harper, Terry	83F	137	$ .01	$ .04
Harper, Terry	84F	180	$ .01	$ .06
Harper, Terry	85F	327	$ .01	$ .05
Harper, Terry	86F	516	$ .01	$ .05
Harper, Terry	87F	517	$ .01	$ .04
Harper, Terry	88F	331	$ .01	$ .04

FLEER

Player	Year	No.	VG	EX/MT
Harrah, Toby	81F	389	$ .01	$ .04
Harrah, Toby	82F	369	$ .01	$ .04
Harrah, Toby	83F	410	$ .01	$ .04
Harrah, Toby	83F	635	$ .01	$ .04
Harrah, Toby	84F	544	$ .01	$ .06
Harrah, Toby	84FU	48	$ .01	$ .10
Harrah, Toby	85F	130	$ .01	$ .05
Harrah, Toby	85FU	49	$ .01	$ .05
Harrah, Toby	86F	560	$ .01	$ .05
Harrah, Toby	87F	125	$ .01	$ .04
Harris, Gene	89FU	58	$ .01	$ .15
Harris, Gene	90F	515	$ .01	$ .03
Harris, Greg	83F	590	$ .01	$ .04
Harris, Greg	85F	35	$ .01	$ .05
Harris, Greg	86F	561	$ .01	$ .05
Harris, Greg	87F	126	$ .01	$ .04
Harris, Greg	88F	468	$ .01	$ .04
Harris, Greg	88FU	109	$ .01	$ .05
Harris, Greg W.	89F	306	$ .01	$ .05
Harris, Greg	89F	570	$ .01	$ .05
Harris, Greg	90F	158	$ .01	$ .10
Harris, John	82F	463	$ .01	$ .04
Harris, Lenny	89F	645	$ .05	$ .35
Harris, Lenny	90F	397	$ .01	$ .10
Hartley, Mike	90F	651	$ .01	$ .03
Harvey, Bryan	88FU	14	$ .01	$ .25
Harvey, Bryan	89F	479	$ .01	$ .25
Harvey, Bryan	90F	134	$ .01	$ .03
Hassey, Ron	81F	405	$ .01	$ .04
Hassey, Ron	82F	370	$ .01	$ .04
Hassey, Ron	83F	411	$ .01	$ .04
Hassey, Ron	83F	642	$ .01	$ .04
Hassey, Ron	84F	545	$ .01	$ .06
Hassey, Ron	84FU	49	$ .01	$ .10
Hassey, Ron	85FU	50	$ .01	$ .05
Hassey, Ron	86F	107	$ .01	$ .05
Hassey, Ron	87F	499	$ .01	$ .04

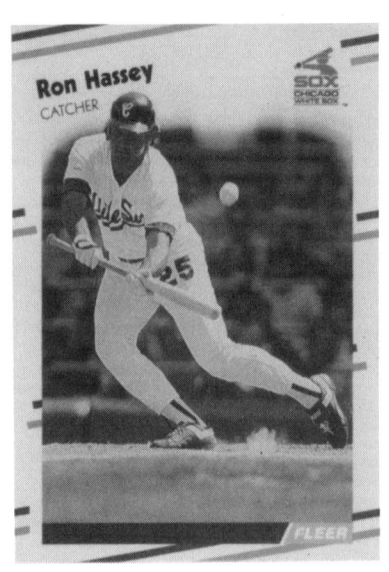

Ron Hassey
CATCHER

Player	Year	No.	VG	EX/MT
Hassey, Ron	88F	399	$ .01	$ .04
Hassey, Ron	89F	9	$ .01	$ .05
Hassey, Ron	90F	8	$ .01	$ .03
Hassler, Andy	81F	290	$ .01	$ .04
Hassler, Andy	82F	464	$ .01	$ .04
Hassler, Andy	83F	92	$ .01	$ .04

Player	Year	No.	VG	EX/MT
Hassler, Andy	84F	519	$ .01	$ .06
Hatcher, Billy 'Bill'	85F	649	$1.00	$3.50
Hatcher, Billy	86F	371	$ .03	$ .20
Hatcher, Billy	86FU	49	$ .01	$ .05
Hatcher, Billy	87F	59	$ .01	$ .04
Hatcher, Billy	88F	449	$ .01	$ .04
Hatcher, Billy	89F	359	$ .01	$ .05
Hatcher, Billy	90F	467	$ .01	$ .03
Hatcher, Mickey	81F	135	$ .01	$ .04
Hatcher, Mickey	83F	614	$ .01	$ .04
Hatcher, Mickey	84F	566	$ .01	$ .06
Hatcher, Mickey	85F	279	$ .01	$ .05
Hatcher, Mickey	86F	396	$ .01	$ .05
Hatcher, Mickey	87F	542	$ .01	$ .04
Hatcher, Mickey	87FU	41	$ .01	$ .05
Hatcher, Mickey	88F	516	$ .01	$ .04
Hatcher, Mickey	90F	398	$ .01	$ .03
Hausman, Tom	81F	333	$ .01	$ .04
Hausman, Tom	82F	526	$ .01	$ .04
Havens, Brad	83F	615	$ .01	$ .04
Havens, Brad	87F	472	$ .01	$ .04
Havens, Brad	88F	517	$ .01	$ .04
Havens, Brad	89F	408	$ .01	$ .05
Hawkins, Andy	84F	302	$ .03	$ .50
Hawkins, Andy	85F	36	$ .01	$ .10
Hawkins, Andy	86F	324	$ .01	$ .05
Hawkins, Andy	87F	417	$ .01	$ .04
Hawkins, Andy	88F	586	$ .01	$ .04
Hawkins, Andy	89F	307	$ .01	$ .05
Hawkins, Andy	89FU	50	$ .01	$ .05
Hawkins, Andy	90F	445	$ .01	$ .03
Hayban, John	88F	562	$ .01	$ .04
Hayes, Ben	83F	591	$ .01	$ .04
Hayes, Ben	84F	470	$ .01	$ .06
Hayes, Charlie	89F	330	$ .01	$ .35
Hayes, Charlie	89FU	106	$ .01	$ .10
Hayes, Charlie	90F	558	$ .01	$ .10
Hayes, Von	82F	371	$ .15	$ .75
Hayes, Von	83F	412	$ .03	$ .20
Hayes, Von	84F	33	$ .03	$ .20
Hayes, Von	85F	253	$ .03	$ .20
Hayes, Von	86F	443	$ .01	$ .10
Hayes, Von	87F	175	$ .01	$ .10
Hayes, Von	88F	304	$ .01	$ .10
Hayes, Von	89F	571	$ .01	$ .05
Hayes, Von	90F	559	$ .01	$ .03
Hayward, Ray	88FU	63	$ .01	$ .05
Hayward, Ray	89F	521	$ .01	$ .05
Hearn, Ed	87F	10	$ .01	$ .10
Heath, Mike	81F	583	$ .01	$ .04
Heath, Mike	82F	91	$ .01	$ .04
Heath, Mike	83F	518	$ .01	$ .04
Heath, Mike	84F	446	$ .01	$ .06
Heath, Mike	85F	424	$ .01	$ .05
Heath, Mike	86F	418	$ .01	$ .05
Heath, Mike	86FU	50	$ .01	$ .05
Heath, Mike	87FU	42	$ .01	$ .05
Heath, Mike	88F	56	$ .01	$ .04
Heath, Mike	89F	130	$ .01	$ .15
Heath, Mike	90F	603	$ .01	$ .03
Heathcock, Jeff	86F	302	$ .01	$ .05
Heathcock, Jeff	88F	450	$ .01	$ .04
Heaton, Neal	84F	546	$ .04	$ .25
Heaton, Neal	85F	451	$ .01	$ .05
Heaton, Neal	86F	589	$ .01	$ .05
Heaton, Neal	87F	543	$ .01	$ .04
Heaton, Neal	87FU	43	$ .01	$ .05
Heaton, Neal	88F	185	$ .01	$ .04
Heaton, Neal	89F	377	$ .01	$ .05
Heaton, Neal	89FU	113	$ .01	$ .05
Heaton, Neal	90F	468	$ .01	$ .03
Heaverlo, Dave	81F	594	$ .01	$ .04
Hebner, Richie	81F	474	$ .01	$ .04
Hebner, Richie	82F	268	$ .01	$ .04
Hebner, Richie	83F	307	$ .01	$ .04

Player	Year	No.	VG	EX/MT	Player	Year	No.	VG	EX/MT
Hebner, Richie	84F	251	$ .01	$ .06	Hernandez, Keith	87F	12	$ .05	$ .30
Hebner, Richie	84FU	50	$ .01	$ .10	Hernandez, Keith	87F	629	$ .10	$ .50
Hebner, Richie	85F	59	$ .01	$ .05	Hernandez, Keith	87F	637	$ .06	$ .35
Heep, Danny	81F	72	$ .01	$ .20	Hernandez, Keith	88F	136	$ .01	$ .20
Heep, Danny	82F	217	$ .01	$ .04	Hernandez, Keith	88F	639	$ .01	$ .15
Heep, Danny	83F	449	$ .01	$ .04	Hernandez, Keith	89F	37	$ .01	$ .15
Heep, Danny	84F	586	$ .01	$ .06	Hernandez, Keith	90F	205	$ .01	$ .10
Heep, Danny	85F	84	$ .01	$ .05	Hernandez, Willie	81F	310	$ .03	$ .20
Heep, Danny	86F	83	$ .01	$ .05	Hernandez, Willie	83F	497	$ .01	$ .10
Heep, Danny	87F	11	$ .01	$ .04	Hernandez, Willie	84F	34	$ .03	$ .10
Heep, Danny	89F	61	$ .01	$ .05	Hernandez, Willie	84FU	51	$ .10	$ .50
Heep, Danny	90F	278	$ .01	$ .03	Hernandez, Willie	85F	10	$ .01	$ .10
Heinkel, Don	88FU	27	$ .01	$ .15	Hernandez, Willie	86F	228	$ .01	$ .10
Heinkel, Don	89F	133	$ .01	$ .15	Hernandez, Willie	87F	153	$ .01	$ .04
Hemond, Scott	90F	646	$ .01	$ .03	Hernandez, Willie	88F	58	$ .01	$ .04
Henderson, Dave	83F	481	$ .01	$ .04	Herndon, Larry	81F	451	$ .01	$ .04
Henderson, Dave	84F	611	$ .01	$ .06	Herndon, Larry	82F	390	$ .01	$ .04
Henderson, Dave	85F	489	$ .01	$ .05	Herndon, Larry	83F	330	$ .01	$ .04
Henderson, Dave	86F	465	$ .01	$ .05	Herndon, Larry	84F	82	$ .01	$ .06
Henderson, Dave	87F	36	$ .01	$ .04	Herndon, Larry	85F	11	$ .01	$ .05
Henderson, Dave	88F	84	$ .01	$ .04	Herndon, Larry	86F	229	$ .01	$ .05
Henderson, Dave	88FU	53	$ .01	$ .05	Herndon, Larry	87F	154	$ .01	$ .04
Henderson, Dave	89F	10	$ .01	$ .05	Herndon, Larry	88F	59	$ .01	$ .04
Henderson, Dave	90F	9	$ .01	$ .03	Herr, Tom	81F	550	$ .01	$ .10
Henderson, Rickey	81F	351	$ .50	$8.00	Herr, Tom	82F	115	$ .01	$ .04
Henderson, Rickey	81F	574	$ .75	$12.00	Herr, Tom	83F	9	$ .01	$ .04
Henderson, Rickey	82F	92	$ .25	$3.00	Herr, Tom	84F	325	$ .01	$ .06
Henderson, Rickey	82F	643	$ .05	$ .50	Herr, Tom	85F	226	$ .01	$ .05
Henderson, Rickey	83F	519	$ .10	$1.50	Herr, Tom	86F	37	$ .01	$ .05
Henderson, Rickey	83F	639	$ .05	$ .50	Herr, Tom	87F	296	$ .01	$ .04
Henderson, Rickey	83F	646	$ .06	$ .50	Herr, Tom	88F	35	$ .01	$ .04
Henderson, Rickey	84F	447	$ .50	$2.27	Herr, Tom	88FU	43	$ .01	$ .05
Henderson, Rickey	85F	425	$ .07	$1.00	Herr, Tom	89F	115	$ .01	$ .05
Henderson, Rickey	85F	629	$ .05	$ .50	Herr, Tom	90F	560	$ .01	$ .03
Henderson, Rickey	85FU	51	$ .15	$2.25	Herr, Tommy	89FU	107	$ .01	$ .05
Henderson, Rickey	86F	108	$ .07	$ .50	Hershiser, Orel	85F	371	$2.00	$9.00
Henderson, Rickey	87F	101	$ .15	$ .75	Hershiser, Orel	86F	131	$ .25	$1.50
Henderson, Rickey	88F	209	$ .01	$ .25	Hershiser, Orel	87F	441	$ .05	$ .40
Henderson, Rickey	89F	254	$ .01	$ .25	Hershiser, Orel	88F	518	$ .01	$ .20
Henderson, Rickey	89FU	54	$ .01	$ .25	Hershiser, Orel	88F	632	$ .01	$ .10
Henderson, Rickey	90F	10	$ .01	$ .10	Hershiser, Orel	89F	62	$ .01	$ .25
Henderson, Steve	81F	321	$ .01	$ .04	Hershiser, Orel	90F	399	$ .01	$ .10
Henderson, Steve	82F	597	$ .01	$ .04	Hesketh, Joe	85F	652	$2.00	$10.00
Henderson, Steve	83F	496	$ .01	$ .04	Hesketh, Joe	86F	250	$ .01	$ .05
Henderson, Steve	84F	612	$ .01	$ .06	Hesketh, Joe	87F	320	$ .01	$ .04
Henderson, Steve	85F	490	$ .01	$ .05	Hesketh, Joe	89F	378	$ .01	$ .05
Henderson, Steve	85FU	52	$ .01	$ .05	Hesketh, Joe	90F	349	$ .01	$ .03
Henderson, Steve	86F	419	$ .01	$ .05	Hetzel, Eric	90F	279	$ .01	$ .10
Hendrick, George	81F	542	$ .01	$ .04	Hibbard, Greg	90F	534	$ .01	$ .10
Hendrick, George	82F	113	$ .01	$ .04	Hickey, Kevin	82F	344	$ .01	$ .04
Hendrick, George	83F	7	$ .01	$ .04	Hickey, Kevin	83F	237	$ .01	$ .04
Hendrick, George	84F	324	$ .01	$ .06	Hickey, Kevin	84F	61	$ .01	$ .06
Hendrick, George	85F	225	$ .01	$ .05	Hickey, Kevin	89FU	4	$ .01	$ .05
Hendrick, George	85FU	53	$ .01	$ .05	Hickey, Kevin	90F	178	$ .01	$ .03
Hendrick, George	86F	158	$ .01	$ .05	Higuera, Ted	86F	490	$ .20	$1.25
Hendrick, George	87F	82	$ .01	$ .04	Higuera, Ted	87F	346	$ .03	$ .20
Hengel, Dave	88F	375	$ .01	$ .20	Higuera, Ted	88F	166	$ .01	$ .10
Henke, Tom	86F	60	$ .01	$ .10	Higuera, Ted	89F	188	$ .01	$ .05
Henke, Tom	87F	228	$ .01	$ .04	Higuera, Ted	90F	326	$ .01	$ .03
Henke, Tom	88F	112	$ .01	$ .04	Higuera, Ted 'Teddy'	85FU	54	$ .40	$2.50
Henke, Tom	89F	235	$ .01	$ .05	Hill, Don 'Donnie'	84F	448	$ .01	$ .06
Henke, Tom	90F	84	$ .01	$ .03	Hill, Donnie	85F	426	$ .01	$ .05
Henneman, Mike	87FU	44	$ .05	$ .30	Hill, Donnie	86F	420	$ .01	$ .05
Henneman, Mike	88F	57	$ .01	$ .10	Hill, Donnie	87F	394	$ .01	$ .04
Henneman, Mike	89F	134	$ .01	$ .05	Hill, Donnie	88F	400	$ .01	$ .04
Henneman, Mike	90F	604	$ .01	$ .03	Hill, Ken	89F	652	$ .01	$ .45
Henry, Dwayne	86F	562	$ .01	$ .10	Hill, Ken	89FU	119	$ .01	$ .10
Hernandez, Guillermo	89F	135	$ .01	$ .05	Hill, Ken	90F	251	$ .01	$ .03
Hernandez, Guillermo	90F	605	$ .01	$ .03	Hill, Marc	84F	62	$ .01	$ .06
Hernandez, Keith	81F	545	$ .05	$ .30	Hill, Marc	85F	516	$ .01	$ .05
Hernandez, Keith	82F	114	$ .05	$ .30	Hillegas, Shawn	88F	519	$ .01	$ .15
Hernandez, Keith	83F	8	$ .05	$ .30	Hillegas, Shawn	89F	498	$ .01	$ .05
Hernandez, Keith	84F	587	$ .05	$ .30	Hillegas, Shawn	90F	535	$ .01	$ .03
Hernandez, Keith	85F	85	$ .05	$ .30	Hinzo, Tommy	88F	611	$ .01	$ .10
Hernandez, Keith	86F	84	$ .05	$ .30	Hisle, Larry	81F	509	$ .01	$ .04

FLEER

Player	Year	No.	VG	EX/MT	Player	Year	No.	VG	EX/MT
Hisle, Larry	82F	144	$ .01	$ .04	Hough, Charlie	85F	558	$ .01	$ .05
Hobson, Butch	81F	227	$ .01	$ .04	Hough, Charlie	86F	564	$ .01	$ .05
Hobson, Butch	82F	465	$ .01	$ .04	Hough, Charlie	87F	127	$ .01	$ .04
Hodge, Ed	84FU	52	$ .01	$ .10	Hough, Charlie	87F	641	$ .01	$ .04
Hodge, Ed	85F	280	$ .01	$ .05	Hough, Charlie	88F	469	$ .01	$ .04
Hodges, Ron	82F	527	$ .01	$ .04	Hough, Charlie	89F	522	$ .01	$ .05
Hodges, Ron	83F	545	$ .01	$ .04	Hough, Charlie	90F	300	$ .01	$ .03
Hodges, Ron	84F	588	$ .01	$ .06	Householder, Paul	81F	217	$ .01	$ .04
Hoffman, Glenn	81F	237	$ .01	$ .04	Householder, Paul	82F	68	$ .01	$ .04
Hoffman, Glenn	82F	296	$ .01	$ .04	Householder, Paul	83F	592	$ .01	$ .04
Hoffman, Glenn	83F	185	$ .01	$ .04	Householder, Paul	84F	471	$ .01	$ .06
Hoffman, Glenn	84F	399	$ .01	$ .06	Householder, Paul	86F	491	$ .01	$ .05
Hoffman, Glenn	86F	351	$ .01	$ .05	Howe, Art	81F	51	$ .01	$ .04
Hoffman, Guy	86FU	51	$ .01	$ .05	Howe, Art	82F	218	$ .01	$ .04
Hoffman, Guy	87F	566	$ .01	$ .04	Howe, Art	83F	450	$ .01	$ .04
Hoffman, Guy	87FU	45	$ .01	$ .05	Howe, Art	84F	227	$ .01	$ .06
Hoffman, Guy	88F	235	$ .01	$ .04	Howe, Art	84FU	54	$ .01	$ .10
Holland, Al	81F	445	$ .01	$ .10	Howe, Art	85F	228	$ .01	$ .05
Holland, Al	82F	391	$ .01	$ .04	Howe, Steve	81F	136	$ .01	$ .10
Holland, Al	83F	262	$ .01	$ .04	Howe, Steve	82F	9	$ .01	$ .04
Holland, Al	84F	35	$ .01	$ .06	Howe, Steve	83F	209	$ .01	$ .04
Holland, Al	85F	254	$ .01	$ .05	Howe, Steve	84F	103	$ .01	$ .06
Holland, Al	85F	637	$ .01	$ .05	Howell, Jack	87F	83	$ .01	$ .04
Holland, Al	85FU	55	$ .01	$ .05	Howell, Jack	88F	491	$ .01	$ .04
Holland, Al	86F	159	$ .01	$ .05	Howell, Jack	89F	480	$ .01	$ .05
Holman, Brian	88FU	100	$ .05	$ .40	Howell, Jack	90F	135	$ .01	$ .03
Holman, Brian	89F	379	$ .01	$ .25	Howell, Jay	84F	128	$ .01	$ .06
Holman, Brian	90F	516	$ .01	$ .10	Howell, Jay	85F	131	$ .01	$ .05
Holman, Scott	84F	589	$ .01	$ .06	Howell, Jay	85FU	57	$ .01	$ .10
Holman, Shawn	90F	606	$ .01	$ .10	Howell, Jay	86F	421	$ .01	$ .05
Holton, Brian	89F	63	$ .01	$ .05	Howell, Jay	87F	395	$ .01	$ .04
Holton, Brian	89FU	5	$ .01	$ .05	Howell, Jay	88F	282	$ .01	$ .04
Holton, Brian	90F	179	$ .01	$ .03	Howell, Jay	88FU	95	$ .01	$ .05
Honeycutt, Rick	82F	318	$ .01	$ .04	Howell, Jay	89F	64	$ .01	$ .05
Honeycutt, Rick	83F	568	$ .01	$ .04	Howell, Jay	90F	400	$ .01	$ .03
Honeycutt, Rick	84F	101	$ .01	$ .06	Howell, Ken	85F	374	$ .03	$ .20
Honeycutt, Rick	85F	372	$ .01	$ .05	Howell, Ken	86F	133	$ .01	$ .05
Honeycutt, Rick	86F	132	$ .01	$ .05	Howell, Ken	87F	443	$ .01	$ .04
Honeycutt, Rick	87F	442	$ .01	$ .04	Howell, Ken	88F	520	$ .01	$ .04
Honeycutt, Rick	88F	281	$ .01	$ .04	Howell, Ken	89FU	108	$ .01	$ .05
Honeycutt, Rick	89F	11	$ .01	$ .05	Howell, Ken	90F	561	$ .01	$ .03
Honeycutt, Rick	90F	11	$ .01	$ .03	Howell, Roy	81F	417	$ .01	$ .04
Hood, Don	81F	547	$ .01	$ .04	Howell, Roy	82F	145	$ .01	$ .04
Hood, Don	83F	115	$ .01	$ .04	Howell, Roy	83F	36	$ .01	$ .04
Hood, Don	84F	348	$ .01	$ .06	Howell, Roy	84F	203	$ .01	$ .06
Hooton, Burt	81F	113	$ .01	$ .04	Howitt, Dann	90F	644	$ .01	$ .03
Hooton, Burt	82F	8	$ .01	$ .04	Howser, Dick	81F	84	$ .03	$ .20
Hooton, Burt	83F	208	$ .01	$ .04	Hoyt, LaMarr	82F	345	$ .01	$ .04
Hooton, Burt	84F	102	$ .01	$ .06	Hoyt, LaMarr	83F	238	$ .01	$ .04
Hooton, Burt	85F	373	$ .01	$ .05	Hoyt, LaMarr	84F	63	$ .03	$ .10
Hooton, Burt	85FU	56	$ .01	$ .10	Hoyt, LaMarr	85F	517	$ .01	$ .05
Hooton, Burt	86F	563	$ .01	$ .05	Hoyt, LaMarr	85FU	58	$ .01	$ .10
Horn, Sam	88F	355	$ .05	$ .25	Hoyt, LaMarr	86F	325	$ .01	$ .05
Horner, Bob	81F	244	$ .05	$ .30	Hoyt, LaMarr	87F	418	$ .01	$ .04
Horner, Bob	82F	436	$ .05	$ .30	Hrabosky, Al	81F	262	$ .01	$ .04
Horner, Bob	83F	138	$ .05	$ .30	Hrabosky, Al	82F	438	$ .01	$ .10
Horner, Bob	84F	181	$ .05	$ .30	Hrbek, Kent	83F	616	$ .25	$1.50
Horner, Bob	85F	328	$ .05	$ .30	Hrbek, Kent	83F	633	$ .03	$ .20
Horner, Bob	86F	517	$ .03	$ .20	Hrbek, Kent	84F	567	$ .06	$ .50
Horner, Bob	86F	635	$ .05	$ .30	Hrbek, Kent	85F	281	$ .05	$ .30
Horner, Bob	87F	518	$ .03	$ .20	Hrbek, Kent	86F	397	$ .03	$ .20
Horner, Bob	87F	632	$ .01	$ .04	Hrbek, Kent	87F	544	$ .03	$ .20
Horner, Bob	88FU	120	$ .01	$ .10	Hrbek, Kent	88F	13	$ .01	$ .10
Horner, Bob	89F	452	$ .01	$ .05	Hrbek, Kent	89F	116	$ .01	$ .10
Horton, Ricky	84FU	53	$ .12	$ .60	Hrbek, Kent	90F	378	$ .01	$ .03
Horton, Ricky	85F	227	$ .05	$ .30	Hubbard, Glenn	81F	260	$ .01	$ .04
Horton, Ricky	86F	38	$ .01	$ .05	Hubbard, Glenn	82F	437	$ .01	$ .04
Horton, Ricky	87F	297	$ .01	$ .04	Hubbard, Glenn	83F	139	$ .01	$ .04
Horton, Ricky	88F	36	$ .01	$ .04	Hubbard, Glenn	84F	182	$ .01	$ .06
Horton, Ricky	88FU	17	$ .01	$ .05	Hubbard, Glenn	85F	329	$ .01	$ .05
Hostetler, Dave	83F	569	$ .01	$ .04	Hubbard, Glenn	86F	518	$ .01	$ .05
Hostetler, Dave	84F	418	$ .01	$ .06	Hubbard, Glenn	87F	519	$ .01	$ .04
Hough, Charlie	82F	319	$ .01	$ .04	Hubbard, Glenn	88F	542	$ .01	$ .04
Hough, Charlie	83F	570	$ .01	$ .04	Hubbard, Glenn	89F	12	$ .01	$ .05
Hough, Charlie	84F	419	$ .01	$ .06	Hudler, Rex	88FU	101	$ .01	$ .05

Player	Year	No.	VG	EX/MT	Player	Year	No.	VG	EX/MT
Hudler, Rex	89F	380	$ .01	$ .05	Jackson, Danny	89F	163	$ .01	$ .15
Hudson, Charles	84F	36	$ .04	$ .25	Jackson, Danny	89F	636	$ .01	$ .15
Hudson, Charles	85F	255	$ .01	$ .05	Jackson, Danny	90F	422	$ .01	$ .10
Hudson, Charles	86F	444	$ .01	$ .05	Jackson, Darrell	81F	567	$ .01	$ .04
Hudson, Charles	87F	176	$ .01	$ .04	Jackson, Darrell	82F	555	$ .01	$ .04
Hudson, Charles	87FU	46	$ .01	$ .05	Jackson, Darrin	88F	641	$2.00	$12.50
Hudson, Charles	88F	210	$ .01	$ .04	Jackson, Darrin	88FU	78	$ .01	$ .05
Huff, Mike	90F	649	$ .01	$ .03	Jackson, Darrin	89F	428	$ .01	$ .05
Hughes, Keith	88F	305	$ .01	$ .15	Jackson, Darrin	90F	160	$ .01	$ .03
Huismann, Mark	85F	203	$ .01	$ .05	Jackson, Grant	81F	378	$ .01	$ .04
Huismann, Mark	87F	586	$ .01	$ .04	Jackson, Grant	82F	191	$ .01	$ .04
Hulett, Tim	85FU	59	$ .01	$ .10	Jackson, Mike	87FU	48	$ .03	$ .20
Hulett, Tim	86F	208	$ .01	$ .05	Jackson, Mike	88F	306	$ .01	$ .10
Hulett, Tim	87F	500	$ .01	$ .04	Jackson, Mike	88FU	60	$ .01	$ .05
Hume, Tom	81F	211	$ .01	$ .04	Jackson, Mike	89F	550	$ .01	$ .05
Hume, Tom	82F	69	$ .01	$ .04	Jackson, Mike	90F	517	$ .01	$ .03
Hume, Tom	83F	593	$ .01	$ .04	Jackson, Reggie	81F	650	$ .20	$1.00
Hume, Tom	84F	472	$ .01	$ .06					
Hume, Tom	85F	538	$ .01	$ .05					
Hume, Tom	86F	179	$ .01	$ .05					
Hume, Tom	86FU	52	$ .01	$ .05					
Hume, Tom	87F	177	$ .01	$ .04					
Hume, Tom	88F	236	$ .01	$ .04					
Hurdle, Clint	81F	45	$ .01	$ .04					
Hurdle, Clint	82F	411	$ .01	$ .04					
Hurdle, Clint	87F	298	$ .01	$ .04					
Hurst, Bruce	82F	297	$ .04	$ .25					
Hurst, Bruce	83F	186	$ .01	$ .10					
Hurst, Bruce	84F	400	$ .03	$ .10					
Hurst, Bruce	85F	161	$ .01	$ .05					
Hurst, Bruce	86F	352	$ .01	$ .10					
Hurst, Bruce	87F	37	$ .01	$ .10					
Hurst, Bruce	88F	356	$ .01	$ .04					
Hurst, Bruce	89F	91	$ .01	$ .05					
Hurst, Bruce	89FU	124	$ .01	$ .05					
Hurst, Bruce	90F	159	$ .01	$ .03					
Huson, Jeff	90F	350	$ .01	$ .10					
Hutton, Tommy	81F	164	$ .01	$ .04					
Incaviglia, Pete	86FU	53	$ .30	$1.50					
Incaviglia, Pete	87F	128	$ .25	$1.25					
Incaviglia, Pete	87F	625	$ .10	$ .75					
Incaviglia, Pete	88F	470	$ .01	$ .20					
Incaviglia, Pete	89F	523	$ .01	$ .10					
Incaviglia, Pete	90F	301	$ .01	$ .10					
Innis, Jeff	88FU	105	$ .01	$ .20					
Innis, Jeff	90F	206	$ .01	$ .10					
Iorg, Dane	81F	543	$ .01	$ .04					
Iorg, Dane	82F	116	$ .01	$ .04					
Iorg, Dane	83F	10	$ .01	$ .04					
Iorg, Dane	84F	326	$ .01	$ .06	Jackson, Reggie	81F	70	$ .12	$1.00
Iorg, Dane	84FU	55	$ .01	$ .10	Jackson, Reggie	82F	39	$ .08	$1.00
Iorg, Dane	85F	204	$ .01	$ .05	Jackson, Reggie	82F	646	$ .10	$ .50
Iorg, Dane	86F	9	$ .01	$ .05	Jackson, Reggie	83F	640	$ .04	$ .25
Iorg, Dane	86FU	54	$ .01	$ .05	Jackson, Reggie	83F	645	$ .06	$ .35
Iorg, Garth	81F	423	$ .01	$ .04	Jackson, Reggie	83F	93	$ .07	$ .75
Iorg, Garth	82F	616	$ .01	$ .04	Jackson, Reggie	84F	520	$ .09	$ .75
Iorg, Garth	83F	430	$ .01	$ .04	Jackson, Reggie	85F	303	$ .08	$ .50
Iorg, Garth	84F	157	$ .01	$ .06	Jackson, Reggie	85F	639	$ .07	$ .50
Iorg, Garth	85F	107	$ .01	$ .05	Jackson, Reggie	86F	160	$ .06	$ .35
Iorg, Garth	86F	61	$ .01	$ .05	Jackson, Reggie	87F	84	$ .05	$ .30
Iorg, Garth	87F	229	$ .01	$ .04	Jackson, Reggie	87FU	49	$ .07	$ .50
Iorg, Garth	88F	113	$ .01	$ .04	Jackson, Reggie	88F	283	$ .01	$ .25
Ivie, Mike	81F	435	$ .01	$ .04	Jackson, Ron	81F	557	$ .01	$ .04
Ivie, Mike	83F	331	$ .01	$ .04	Jackson, Ron	82F	269	$ .01	$ .04
Jackson, Bo	87F	369	$7.00	$22.50	Jackson, Ron	83F	94	$ .01	$ .04
Jackson, Bo	88F	260	$ 1.00	$3.75	Jackson, Ron	84F	521	$ .01	$ .06
Jackson, Bo	89F	285	$ .05	$1.00	Jackson, Roy Lee	83F	431	$ .01	$ .04
Jackson, Bo	90F	110	$ .01	$ .50	Jackson, Roy Lee	84F	158	$ .01	$ .06
Jackson, Bo	90F	635	$ .01	$ .25	Jackson, Roy Lee	85F	108	$ .01	$ .05
Jackson, Chuck	87FU	47	$ .03	$ .20	Jackson, Roy Lee	86F	326	$ .01	$ .05
Jackson, Danny	85F	205	$ .25	$1.00	Jackson, Roy Lee	87F	545	$ .01	$ .04
Jackson, Danny	86F	10	$ .05	$ .20	Jacoby, Brook	84FU	56	$ .25	$2.00
Jackson, Danny	87F	370	$ .01	$ .10	Jacoby, Brook	85F	452	$ .05	$ .30
Jackson, Danny	88F	261	$ .01	$ .10	Jacoby, Brook	86F	590	$ .01	$ .10
Jackson, Danny	88FU	84	$ .01	$ .15	Jacoby, Brook	87F	253	$ .01	$ .04

REGGIE JACKSON
OUTFIELD DH

FLEER

Player	Year	No.	VG	EX/MT	Player	Year	No.	VG	EX/MT
Jacoby, Brook	88F	612	$ .01	$ .04	Jenkins, Ferguson	83F	498	$ .01	$ .10
Jacoby, Brook	89F	407	$ .01	$ .05	Jenkins, Ferguson	84F	494	$ .03	$ .10
Jacoby, Brook	90F	493	$ .01	$ .03	Jenkins, Ferguson 'Fergie'	81F	622	$ .03	$ .20
James, Bob	84F	277	$ .03	$ .20	Jennings, Doug	88FU	54	$ .01	$ .25
James, Bob	85F	400	$ .01	$ .05	Jennings, Doug	89F	14	$ .01	$ .25
James, Bob	85FU	60	$ .01	$ .05	Jimenez, Cesar	88FU	72	$ .01	$ .05
James, Bob	86F	209	$ .01	$ .05	Jimenez, Houston	85F	282	$ .01	$ .05
James, Bob	87F	501	$ .01	$ .04	John, Tommy	81F	81	$ .03	$ .20
James, Bob	88F	401	$ .01	$ .04	John, Tommy	82F	40	$ .03	$ .20
James, Chris	86FU	55	$ .15	$ .60	John, Tommy	83F	95	$ .03	$ .20
James, Chris	87FU	50	$ .07	$ .25	John, Tommy	84F	522	$ .03	$ .20
James, Chris	88F	307	$ .01	$ .10	John, Tommy	85F	304	$ .03	$ .20
James, Chris	89F	572	$ .01	$ .05	John, Tommy	86F	422	$ .03	$ .20
James, Chris	90F	161	$ .01	$ .03	John, Tommy	86FU	57	$ .03	$ .20
James, Dion	84FU	57	$ .10	$ .50	John, Tommy	87F	102	$ .03	$ .20
James, Dion	85F	584	$ .04	$ .25	John, Tommy	88F	211	$ .01	$ .10
James, Dion	87FU	51	$ .01	$ .05	John, Tommy	89F	255	$ .01	$ .05
James, Dion	88F	543	$ .01	$ .04	Johnson, Bobby	84F	420	$ .01	$ .06
James, Dion	89F	594	$ .01	$ .05	Johnson, Cliff	81F	303	$ .01	$ .04
James, Dion	90F	494	$ .01	$ .03	Johnson, Cliff	82F	93	$ .01	$ .04
Javier, Stan	86FU	56	$ .01	$ .05	Johnson, Cliff	83F	520	$ .01	$ .04
Javier, Stan	87FU	52	$ .01	$ .05	Johnson, Cliff	84F	159	$ .01	$ .06
Javier, Stan	89F	13	$ .01	$ .05	Johnson, Cliff	85F	109	$ .01	$ .05
Javier, Stan	90F	12	$ .01	$ .03	Johnson, Cliff	85FU	61	$ .01	$ .05
Jeffcoat, Mike	84FU	58	$ .04	$ .25	Johnson, Cliff	86F	62	$ .01	$ .05
Jeffcoat, Mike	85F	453	$ .01	$ .05	Johnson, Cliff	87F	231	$ .01	$ .04
Jeffcoat, Mike	86F	545	$ .01	$ .05	Johnson, Howard	83F	332	$3.00	$10.00
Jeffcoat, Mike	89F	524	$ .01	$ .05	Johnson, Howard	85F	12	$ .10	$1.75
Jeffcoat, Mike	90F	302	$ .01	$ .03	Johnson, Howard	85FU	62	$ .25	$2.00
Jefferies, Gregg	88F	137	$ .75	$4.50	Johnson, Howard	86F	85	$ .05	$ .40
					Johnson, Howard	87F	13	$ .05	$ .25
					Johnson, Howard	88F	138	$ .05	$ .25
					Johnson, Howard	89F	39	$ .01	$ .15
					Johnson, Howard	90F	208	$ .01	$ .15
					Johnson, Howard	90F	639	$ .01	$ .10
					Johnson, Joe	86F	519	$ .01	$ .10
					Johnson, Joe	87F	230	$ .01	$ .04
					Johnson, John Henry	82F	321	$ .01	$ .04
					Johnson, John Henry	84F	401	$ .01	$ .06
					Johnson, John Henry	85F	162	$ .01	$ .05
					Johnson, John Henry	87F	347	$ .01	$ .04
					Johnson, Lamar	81F	350	$ .01	$ .04
					Johnson, Lamar	82F	346	$ .01	$ .04
					Johnson, Lamar	83F	571	$ .01	$ .04
					Johnson, Lance	88F	37	$ .01	$ .20
					Johnson, Lance	89F	499	$ .01	$ .05
					Johnson, Lance	90F	536	$ .01	$ .03
					Johnson, Randy	83F	617	$ .01	$ .04
					Johnson, Randy	84F	183	$ .01	$ .06
					Johnson, Randy	85F	330	$ .01	$ .05
					Johnson, Randy	89F	381	$ .01	$ .30
					Johnson, Randy	89FU	59	$ .01	$ .10
					Johnson, Randy	90F	518	$ .01	$ .10
					Johnson, Wallace	82F	192	$ .01	$ .04
					Johnson, Wallace	83F	285	$ .01	$ .04
					Johnson, Wallace	87F	321	$ .01	$ .04
					Johnson, Wallace	88F	186	$ .01	$ .04
					Johnson, Wallace	89F	382	$ .01	$ .05
					Johnson, Wallace	90F	351	$ .01	$ .03
					Johnstone, Jay	81F	128	$ .01	$ .04
					Johnstone, Jay	82F	10	$ .01	$ .04
					Johnstone, Jay	83F	499	$ .01	$ .04
					Johnstone, Jay	84F	495	$ .01	$ .06
Jefferies, Gregg	89F	38	$ .25	$1.50	Jones, Barry	87F	611	$ .01	$ .10
Jefferies, Gregg	90F	207	$ .01	$ .35	Jones, Barry	88FU	114	$ .01	$ .05
Jefferson, Jesse	81F	419	$ .01	$ .04	Jones, Barry	89F	500	$ .01	$ .05
Jefferson, Jesse	82F	466	$ .01	$ .04	Jones, Bobby	85F	559	$ .01	$ .05
Jefferson, Stan	87FU	53	$ .01	$ .25	Jones, Doug	88F	613	$ .01	$ .10
Jefferson, Stan	88F	587	$ .01	$ .04	Jones, Doug	89F	409	$ .01	$ .35
Jelks, Greg	88F	648	$ .01	$ .30	Jones, Doug	90F	495	$ .01	$ .03
Jeltz, Steve	85F	653	$ .03	$ .20	Jones, Jeff	82F	94	$ .01	$ .04
Jeltz, Steve	87F	178	$ .01	$ .04	Jones, Jimmy	87F	650	$ .04	$ .25
Jeltz, Steve	88F	308	$ .01	$ .04	Jones, Jimmy	87FU	54	$ .01	$ .05
Jeltz, Steve	89F	573	$ .01	$ .05	Jones, Jimmy	88F	588	$ .01	$ .04
Jeltz, Steve	90F	562	$ .01	$ .03	Jones, Jimmy	89F	308	$ .01	$ .05
Jenkins, Ferguson	82F	320	$ .03	$ .20					

GREGG JEFFERIES
THIRD BASE

FLEER

Player	Year	No.	VG	EX/MT
Jones, Lynn	82F	270	$ .01	$ .04
Jones, Lynn	83F	333	$ .01	$ .04
Jones, Lynn	86F	11	$ .01	$ .05
Jones, Mike	82F	412	$ .01	$ .04
Jones, Mike	86F	12	$ .01	$ .05
Jones, Odell	84F	421	$ .01	$ .06
Jones, Odell	85F	560	$ .01	$ .05
Jones, Odell	89F	189	$ .01	$ .05
Jones, Randy	81F	487	$ .01	$ .04
Jones, Randy	82F	528	$ .01	$ .04
Jones, Randy	83F	546	$ .01	$ .04
Jones, Ron	89F	574	$ .01	$ .45
Jones, Ron	90F	563	$ .01	$ .10
Jones, Ross	88F	262	$ .01	$ .10
Jones, Ruppert	81F	101	$ .01	$ .04
Jones, Ruppert	82F	573	$ .01	$ .04
Jones, Ruppert	83F	361	$ .01	$ .04
Jones, Ruppert	84F	303	$ .01	$ .06
Jones, Ruppert	84FU	59	$ .01	$ .10
Jones, Ruppert	85F	13	$ .04	$ .25
Jones, Ruppert	85FU	63	$ .01	$ .05
Jones, Ruppert	86F	161	$ .01	$ .05
Jones, Ruppert	87F	85	$ .01	$ .04
Jones, Ruppert	88F	492	$ .01	$ .04
Jones, Tim	89F	453	$ .01	$ .05
Jones, Tracy	86FU	58	$ .12	$ .60
Jones, Tracy	87F	651	$ .10	$ .40
Jones, Tracy	87FU	55	$ .05	$ .20
Jones, Tracy	88F	237	$ .01	$ .04
Jones, Tracy	89F	383	$ .01	$ .05
Jones, Tracy	89FU	31	$ .01	$ .05
Jones, Tracy	90F	607	$ .01	$ .03
Jordan, Ricky	88FU	110	$ .25	$2.75
Jordan, Ricky	89F	575	$ .01	$1.75
Jordan, Ricky	90F	564	$ .01	$ .30
Jorgensen, Mike	81F	324	$ .01	$ .04
Jorgensen, Mike	82F	529	$ .01	$ .04
Jorgensen, Mike	83F	547	$ .01	$ .04
Jorgensen, Mike	85F	229	$ .01	$ .05
Jose, Felix	89F	15	$ .01	$ .50
Jose, Felix	90F	13	$ .01	$ .15
Joyner, Wally	86FU	59	$ .50	$2.50
Joyner, Wally	87F	628	$ .30	$1.50
Joyner, Wally	87F	86	$ .25	$2.50
Joyner, Wally	88F	493	$ .10	$ .50
Joyner, Wally	88F	622	$ .01	$ .40
Joyner, Wally	89F	481	$ .01	$ .20
Joyner, Wally	90F	136	$ .01	$ .10
Jurak, Ed	84F	402	$ .01	$ .06
Justice, David	90F	586	$ .01	$ .15
Kaat, Jim	81F	536	$ .03	$ .20
Kaat, Jim	82F	117	$ .03	$ .20
Kaat, Jim	83F	11	$ .03	$ .20
Kaiser, Jeff	89F	410	$ .01	$ .05
Karkovice, Ron	87F	645	$ .03	$ .20
Kaufman, Curt	85F	305	$ .01	$ .05
Kearney, Bob	84F	449	$ .01	$ .06
Kearney, Bob	84FU	60	$ .01	$ .10
Kearney, Bob	85F	491	$ .01	$ .05
Kearney, Bob	86F	466	$ .01	$ .05
Kearney, Bob	87F	587	$ .01	$ .04
Keeton, Rickey	82F	146	$ .01	$ .04
Kelly, Pat	82F	372	$ .01	$ .04
Kelly, Roberto	88F	212	$ .25	$1.50
Kelly, Roberto	89F	256	$ .01	$ .25
Kelly, Roberto	90F	446	$ .01	$ .10
Kemp, Steve	81F	459	$ .01	$ .04
Kemp, Steve	82F	271	$ .01	$ .04
Kemp, Steve	83F	239	$ .01	$ .04
Kemp, Steve	84F	129	$ .01	$ .06
Kemp, Steve	85F	132	$ .01	$ .05
Kemp, Steve	85FU	64	$ .01	$ .05
Kemp, Steve	86F	610	$ .01	$ .05
Kennedy, Junior	82F	70	$ .01	$ .04
Kennedy, Junior	83F	500	$ .01	$ .04
Kennedy, Terry	81F	203	$ .01	$ .04
Kennedy, Terry	81F	541	$ .01	$ .04
Kennedy, Terry	82F	574	$ .01	$ .04
Kennedy, Terry	83F	362	$ .01	$ .04
Kennedy, Terry	84F	304	$ .01	$ .06
Kennedy, Terry	85F	37	$ .01	$ .05
Kennedy, Terry	86F	327	$ .01	$ .05
Kennedy, Terry	87F	419	$ .01	$ .04
Kennedy, Terry	87FU	56	$ .01	$ .05
Kennedy, Terry	88F	563	$ .01	$ .04
Kennedy, Terry	89F	610	$ .01	$ .05
Kennedy, Terry	89FU	128	$ .01	$ .05
Kennedy, Terry	90F	58	$ .01	$ .03
Keough, Matt	81F	588	$ .01	$ .04
Keough, Matt	82F	95	$ .01	$ .04
Keough, Matt	83F	521	$ .01	$ .04
Keough, Matt	84F	130	$ .01	$ .06
Kepshire, Kurt	85F	230	$ .01	$ .05
Kepshire, Kurt	86F	39	$ .01	$ .05
Kerfeld, Charlie	86F	303	$ .04	$ .25
Kerfeld, Charlie	87F	60	$ .01	$ .04
Kern, Jim	81F	618	$ .01	$ .04
Kern, Jim	82F	322	$ .01	$ .04
Kern, Jim	83F	240	$ .01	$ .04
Key, Jimmy	84FU	61	$1.00	$5.00
Key, Jimmy	85F	110	$ .25	$ .75
Key, Jimmy	86F	63	$ .03	$ .20
Key, Jimmy	86F	642	$ .01	$ .10
Key, Jimmy	87F	232	$ .01	$ .10
Key, Jimmy	88F	114	$ .01	$ .10
Key, Jimmy	89F	236	$ .01	$ .05
Key, Jimmy	90F	85	$ .01	$ .03
Khalifa, Sam	86F	611	$ .01	$ .05
Kiefer, Steve	85F	647	$1.00	$4.00
Kiefer, Steve	88F	167	$ .01	$ .04
Kilgus, Paul	88F	471	$ .01	$ .10
Kilgus, Paul	89F	525	$ .01	$ .05
Kilgus, Paul	89FU	76	$ .01	$ .05
Kilgus, Paul	90F	34	$ .01	$ .03
Kimm, Bruce	81F	355	$ .01	$ .04
King, Eric	87F	155	$ .03	$ .20
King, Eric	88F	60	$ .01	$ .10
King, Eric	89F	136	$ .01	$ .05
King, Eric	89FU	19	$ .01	$ .05
King, Eric	90F	537	$ .01	$ .03
King, Jeff	90F	469	$ .01	$ .10
King, Jeff	88F	653	$ .01	$ .25
King, Jeff	89FU	114	$ .01	$ .05
Kingery, Mike	87F	371	$ .03	$ .20
Kingery, Mike	87FU	57	$ .01	$ .05
Kingery, Mike	88F	376	$ .01	$ .04
Kingman, Brian	81F	579	$ .01	$ .04
Kingman, Brian	82F	96	$ .01	$ .04
Kingman, Brian	83F	522	$ .01	$ .04
Kingman, Dave	81F	291	$ .03	$ .20
Kingman, Dave	82F	530	$ .03	$ .20
Kingman, Dave	83F	548	$ .01	$ .10
Kingman, Dave	84F	590	$ .03	$ .10
Kingman, Dave	84FU	62	$ .08	$ .40
Kingman, Dave	85F	427	$ .01	$ .10
Kingman, Dave	86F	423	$ .01	$ .10
Kingman, Dave	87F	396	$ .01	$ .10
Kinney, Dennis	81F	505	$ .01	$ .04
Kinzer, Matt	90F	652	$ .01	$ .03
Kipper, Bob	86F	648	$ .05	$ .30
Kipper, Bob	87F	612	$ .01	$ .04
Kipper, Bob	88F	332	$ .01	$ .04
Kipper, Bob	89F	211	$ .01	$ .05
Kipper, Bob	90F	470	$ .01	$ .03
Kison, Bruce	81F	284	$ .01	$ .04
Kison, Bruce	82F	467	$ .01	$ .04
Kison, Bruce	83F	96	$ .01	$ .04
Kison, Bruce	84F	523	$ .01	$ .06
Kison, Bruce	85F	306	$ .01	$ .05
Kison, Bruce	85FU	65	$ .01	$ .05

FLEER

Player	Year	No.	VG	EX/MT
Kison, Bruce	86F	353	$ .01	$ .05
Kittle, Ron	83F	241	$ .05	$ .75
Kittle, Ron	84F	64	$ .03	$ .20
Kittle, Ron	85F	518	$ .01	$ .10
Kittle, Ron	86F	210	$ .01	$ .10
Kittle, Ron	87F	103	$ .01	$ .10
Kittle, Ron	88F	213	$ .01	$ .04
Kittle, Ron	89FU	20	$ .01	$ .05
Kittle, Ron	90F	538	$ .01	$ .03
Klutts, Mickey	81F	584	$ .01	$ .04
Klutts, Mickey	82F	97	$ .01	$ .04
Knepper, Bob	81F	447	$ .01	$ .10
Knepper, Bob	82F	219	$ .01	$ .04
Knepper, Bob	83F	451	$ .01	$ .04
Knepper, Bob	84F	228	$ .01	$ .06
Knepper, Bob	85F	352	$ .01	$ .05
Knepper, Bob	86F	304	$ .01	$ .05
Knepper, Bob	87F	61	$ .01	$ .04
Knepper, Bob	88F	451	$ .01	$ .04
Knepper, Bob	89F	360	$ .01	$ .05
Knicely, Alan	83F	452	$ .01	$ .04
Knicely, Alan	84F	473	$ .01	$ .06
Knight, Ray	81F	198	$ .01	$ .10
Knight, Ray	82F	71	$ .01	$ .10
Knight, Ray	83F	453	$ .01	$ .10
Knight, Ray	84F	229	$ .03	$ .10
Knight, Ray	85F	86	$ .01	$ .10
Knight, Ray	86F	86	$ .01	$ .05
Knight, Ray	87F	14	$ .01	$ .04
Knight, Ray	87FU	58	$ .01	$ .05
Knight, Ray	88F	564	$ .01	$ .04
Knight, Ray	88FU	28	$ .01	$ .05
Knudson, Mark	90F	327	$ .01	$ .03
Komminsk, Brad	84FU	63	$ .04	$ .25
Komminsk, Brad	85F	331	$ .01	$ .05
Komminsk, Brad	86F	520	$ .01	$ .05
Komminsk, Brad	89FU	28	$ .01	$ .05
Komminsk, Brad	90F	496	$ .01	$ .03
Koosman, Jerry	81F	552	$ .01	$ .10
Koosman, Jerry	82F	347	$ .01	$ .10
Koosman, Jerry	83F	242	$ .01	$ .10
Koosman, Jerry	84F	65	$ .01	$ .10
Koosman, Jerry	84FU	64	$ .03	$ .20
Koosman, Jerry	85F	256	$ .01	$ .10
Kramer, Randy	89F	647	$ .01	$ .20
Kramer, Randy	89FU	115	$ .01	$ .05
Kramer, Randy	90F	471	$ .01	$ .03
Krenchicki, Wayne	82F	168	$ .01	$ .04
Krenchicki, Wayne	83F	594	$ .01	$ .04
Krenchicki, Wayne	84F	83	$ .01	$ .06
Krenchicki, Wayne	84FU	65	$ .01	$ .10
Krenchicki, Wayne	85F	539	$ .01	$ .05
Krenchicki, Wayne	86F	180	$ .01	$ .05
Krenchicki, Wayne	86FU	60	$ .01	$ .05
Krenchicki, Wayne	87F	322	$ .01	$ .04
Kreuter, Chad	89F	526	$ .01	$ .15
Kreuter, Chad	90F	303	$ .01	$ .03
Krueger, Bill	84F	450	$ .01	$ .06
Krueger, Bill	85F	428	$ .01	$ .05
Krueger, Bill	86F	424	$ .01	$ .05
Krueger, Bill	90F	328	$ .01	$ .03
Kruk, John	86FU	61	$ .05	$ .50
Kruk, John	87F	420	$ .01	$ .40
Kruk, John	88F	589	$ .01	$ .10
Kruk, John	89F	309	$ .01	$ .05
Kruk, John	89FU	109	$ .01	$ .05
Kruk, John	90F	565	$ .01	$ .03
Krukow, Mike	81F	312	$ .01	$ .10
Krukow, Mike	82F	598	$ .01	$ .04
Krukow, Mike	83F	163	$ .01	$ .04
Krukow, Mike	84F	374	$ .01	$ .06
Krukow, Mike	85F	609	$ .01	$ .05
Krukow, Mike	86F	546	$ .01	$ .05
Krukow, Mike	87F	275	$ .01	$ .04
Krukow, Mike	87F	630	$ .01	$ .10

Player	Year	No.	VG	EX/MT
Krukow, Mike	88F	85	$ .01	$ .04
Krukow, Mike	89F	331	$ .01	$ .05
Kuiper, Duane	82F	373	$ .01	$ .04
Kuiper, Duane	83F	263	$ .01	$ .04
Kuiper, Duane	84F	375	$ .01	$ .06
Kuiper, Duane	85F	610	$ .01	$ .05
Kunkel, Jeff	85F	561	$ .01	$ .05
Kunkel, Jeff	89F	527	$ .01	$ .05
Kunkel, Jeff	90F	304	$ .01	$ .03
Kuntz, Rusty	82F	348	$ .01	$ .04
Kuntz, Rusty	84F	568	$ .01	$ .06
Kuntz, Rusty	84FU	66	$ .01	$ .10
Kuntz, Rusty	85F	14	$ .01	$ .05
Kutcher, Randy	87F	276	$ .01	$ .10
Lacey, Bob	81F	578	$ .01	$ .04

Player	Year	No.	VG	EX/MT
Lacey, Bob	85F	611	$ .01	$ .05
LaCock, Pete	81F	47	$ .01	$ .04
LaCorte, Frank	81F	55	$ .01	$ .04
LaCorte, Frank	82F	220	$ .01	$ .04
LaCorte, Frank	83F	454	$ .01	$ .04
LaCorte, Frank	84F	230	$ .01	$ .06
LaCorte, Frank	84FU	67	$ .01	$ .10
LaCoss, Mike	82F	72	$ .01	$ .04
LaCoss, Mike	83F	455	$ .01	$ .04
LaCoss, Mike	84F	231	$ .01	$ .06
LaCoss, Mike	85F	353	$ .01	$ .05
LaCoss, Mike	85FU	66	$ .01	$ .05
LaCoss, Mike	86FU	62	$ .01	$ .05
LaCoss, Mike	87F	277	$ .01	$ .04
LaCoss, Mike	88F	86	$ .01	$ .04
LaCoss, Mike	89FU	129	$ .01	$ .05
LaCoss, Mike	90F	59	$ .01	$ .03
Lacy, Lee	81F	374	$ .01	$ .04
Lacy, Lee	82F	483	$ .01	$ .04
Lacy, Lee	83F	308	$ .01	$ .04
Lacy, Lee	84F	252	$ .01	$ .06
Lacy, Lee	85F	467	$ .01	$ .05
Lacy, Lee	85FU	67	$ .01	$ .05
Lacy, Lee	86F	277	$ .01	$ .05
Lacy, Lee	87F	473	$ .01	$ .04
Lacy, Lee	88F	565	$ .01	$ .04
Ladd, Pete	83F	37	$ .01	$ .04
Ladd, Pete	84F	204	$ .01	$ .06

Player	Year	No.	VG	EX/MT	Player	Year	No.	VG	EX/MT
Ladd, Pete	85F	585	$ .01	$ .05	LaPoint, Dave	86F	547	$ .01	$ .05
Ladd, Pete	86F	492	$ .01	$ .05	LaPoint, Dave	86FU	64	$ .01	$ .05
Ladd, Pete	87F	588	$ .01	$ .04	LaPoint, Dave	87F	421	$ .01	$ .04
Ladd, Peter	86FU	63	$ .01	$ .05	LaPoint, Dave	88F	402	$ .01	$ .04
Lahti, Jeff	83F	12	$ .01	$ .04	LaPoint, Dave	89F	212	$ .01	$ .05
Lahti, Jeff	84F	327	$ .01	$ .06	Larkin, Barry	87F	204	$2.00	$7.50
Lahti, Jeff	85F	231	$ .01	$ .05	Larkin, Barry	88F	239	$ .25	$1.00
Lahti, Jeff	86F	40	$ .01	$ .05	Larkin, Barry	89F	164	$ .01	$ .25
Lahti, Jeff	87F	299	$ .01	$ .04	Larkin, Barry	90F	423	$ .01	$ .15
Lake, Steve	87F	300	$ .01	$ .04	Larkin, Gene	87FU	59	$ .04	$ .25
Lake, Steve	88F	38	$ .01	$ .04	Larkin, Gene	88F	14	$ .10	$ .40
Lake, Steve	89F	454	$ .01	$ .05	Larkin, Gene	89F	117	$ .01	$ .05
Lake, Steve	90F	566	$ .01	$ .03	Larkin, Gene	90F	379	$ .01	$ .03
Lamp, Dennis	81F	305	$ .01	$ .04	LaRoche, Dave	81F	285	$ .01	$ .04
Lamp, Dennis	82F	349	$ .01	$ .04	LaRoche, Dave	83F	384	$ .01	$ .04
Lamp, Dennis	83F	243	$ .01	$ .04	LaRussa, Tony	81F	344	$ .01	$ .04
Lamp, Dennis	84F	66	$ .01	$ .06	Laskey, Bill	83F	264	$ .01	$ .04
Lamp, Dennis	84FU	68	$ .01	$ .10	Laskey, Bill	84F	376	$ .01	$ .06
Lamp, Dennis	85F	111	$ .01	$ .05	Laskey, Bill	85F	612	$ .01	$ .05
Lamp, Dennis	86F	64	$ .01	$ .05	Laskey, Bill	86F	251	$ .01	$ .05
Lamp, Dennis	87F	233	$ .01	$ .04	Lasorda, Tom	81F	116	$ .01	$ .10
Lamp, Dennis	88F	284	$ .01	$ .04	Laudner, Tim	83F	618	$ .01	$ .04
Lamp, Dennis	89F	92	$ .01	$ .05	Laudner, Tim	84F	569	$ .01	$ .06
Lamp, Dennis	90F	280	$ .01	$ .03	Laudner, Tim	85F	283	$ .01	$ .05
Lancaster, Les	88F	421	$ .01	$ .15	Laudner, Tim	86F	398	$ .01	$ .05
Lancaster, Les	89F	429	$ .01	$ .05	Laudner, Tim	87F	546	$ .01	$ .04
Lancaster, Les	90F	35	$ .01	$ .03	Laudner, Tim	88F	15	$ .01	$ .04
Landestoy, Rafael	81F	70	$ .01	$ .04	Laudner, Tim	89F	118	$ .01	$ .05
Landestoy, Rafael	82F	73	$ .01	$ .04	Laudner, Tim	90F	380	$ .01	$ .03
Landestoy, Rafael	83F	595	$ .01	$ .04	LaValliere, Mike	86FU	65	$ .05	$ .50
Landreaux, Ken	81F	553	$ .01	$ .04	LaValliere, Mike	87F	302	$ .03	$ .20
Landreaux, Ken	82F	11	$ .01	$ .04	LaValliere, Mike	87FU	60	$ .01	$ .15
Landreaux, Ken	83F	210	$ .01	$ .04	LaValliere, Mike	88F	333	$ .01	$ .04
Landreaux, Ken	84F	104	$ .01	$ .06	LaValliere, Mike	89F	213	$ .01	$ .05
Landreaux, Ken	85F	375	$ .01	$ .05	LaValliere, Mike	90F	473	$ .01	$ .03
Landreaux, Ken	86F	134	$ .01	$ .05	Lavelle, Gary	81F	448	$ .01	$ .04
Landreaux, Ken	87F	444	$ .01	$ .04	Lavelle, Gary	82F	392	$ .01	$ .04
Landrum, Bill	88F	238	$ .01	$ .04	Lavelle, Gary	83F	265	$ .01	$ .04
Landrum, Bill	89FU	116	$ .01	$ .05	Lavelle, Gary	84F	377	$ .01	$ .06
Landrum, Bill	90F	472	$ .01	$ .03	Lavelle, Gary	85F	613	$ .01	$ .05
Landrum, Terry 'Tito'	81F	539	$ .01	$ .04	Lavelle, Gary	85FU	69	$ .01	$ .05
Landrum, Tito	82F	118	$ .01	$ .04	Lavelle, Gary	86F	65	$ .01	$ .05
Landrum, Tito	83F	13	$ .01	$ .04	Law, Rudy	81F	139	$ .01	$ .04
Landrum, Tito	84FU	69	$ .01	$ .10	Law, Rudy	83F	244	$ .01	$ .04
Landrum, Tito	85F	232	$ .01	$ .05	Law, Rudy	84F	67	$ .01	$ .06
Landrum, Tito	86F	41	$ .01	$ .05	Law, Rudy	85F	519	$ .01	$ .05
Landrum, Tito	87F	301	$ .01	$ .04	Law, Rudy	86F	211	$ .01	$ .05
Langford, Rick	81F	572	$ .01	$ .04	Law, Rudy	86FU	66	$ .01	$ .05
Langford, Rick	82F	98	$ .01	$ .04	Law, Rudy	87F	372	$ .01	$ .04
Langford, Rick	83F	523	$ .01	$ .04	Law, Vance	82F	484	$ .01	$ .04
Langford, Rick	84F	451	$ .01	$ .06	Law, Vance	83F	245	$ .01	$ .04
Langford, Hick	86F	425	$ .01	$ .05	Law, Vance	84F	68	$ .01	$ .06
Langston, Mark	84FU	70	$7.00	$25.00	Law, Vance	85F	520	$ .01	$ .05
Langston, Mark	85F	492	$ .50	$5.00	Law, Vance	85FU	70	$ .01	$ .05
Langston, Mark	86F	467	$ .01	$ .50	Law, Vance	86F	252	$ .01	$ .05
Langston, Mark	87F	589	$ .01	$ .20	Law, Vance	87F	323	$ .01	$ .04
Langston, Mark	88F	377	$ .01	$ .10	Law, Vance	88F	187	$ .01	$ .04
Langston, Mark	89F	551	$ .01	$ .10	Law, Vance	88FU	79	$ .01	$ .05
Langston, Mark	89FU	97	$ .01	$ .15	Law, Vance	89F	430	$ .01	$ .05
Langston, Mark	90F	352	$ .01	$ .10	Law, Vance	90F	36	$ .01	$ .03
Lansford, Carney	81F	270	$ .01	$ .10	Lazorko, Jack	87FU	61	$ .01	$ .05
Lansford, Carney	82F	298	$ .01	$ .10	Lazorko, Jack	88F	494	$ .01	$ .04
Lansford, Carney	83F	187	$ .01	$ .10	Lazorko, Jack	89F	482	$ .01	$ .05
Lansford, Carney	84F	452	$ .01	$ .06	Lea, Charlie	81F	165	$ .03	$ .20
Lansford, Carney	85F	429	$ .01	$ .05	Lea, Charlie	82F	193	$ .01	$ .04
Lansford, Carney	86F	426	$ .01	$ .05	Lea, Charlie	83F	286	$ .01	$ .04
Lansford, Carney	87F	397	$ .01	$ .04	Lea, Charlie	84F	278	$ .01	$ .06
Lansford, Carney	88F	285	$ .01	$ .04	Lea, Charlie	85F	401	$ .01	$ .05
Lansford, Carney	89F	16	$ .01	$ .05	Lea, Charlie	85F	632	$ .01	$ .10
Lansford, Carney	89F	633	$ .05	$ .35	Lea, Charlie	86F	253	$ .01	$ .05
Lansford, Carney	90F	14	$ .01	$ .35	Lea, Charlie	88FU	44	$ .01	$ .05
LaPoint, Dave	83F	14	$ .01	$ .40	Lea, Charlie	89F	119	$ .01	$ .05
LaPoint, Dave	84F	328	$ .01	$ .15	Leach, Rick	82F	272	$ .01	$ .04
LaPoint, Dave	85F	233	$ .01	$ .10	Leach, Rick	83F	334	$ .01	$ .04
LaPoint, Dave	85FU	68	$ .01	$ .05	Leach, Rick	84F	84	$ .01	$ .06

FLEER

Player	Year	No.	VG	EX/MT	Player	Year	No.	VG	EX/MT
Leach, Rick	84FU	71	$ .01	$ .10	Lentine, Jim	81F	476	$ .01	$ .04
Leach, Rick	85F	112	$ .01	$ .05	Leonard, Dennis	81F	42	$ .01	$ .04
Leach, Rick	87F	234	$ .01	$ .04	Leonard, Dennis	82F	413	$ .01	$ .04
Leach, Rick	87FU	63	$ .01	$ .05	Leonard, Dennis	83F	116	$ .01	$ .04
Leach, Rick	88F	115	$ .01	$ .04	Leonard, Dennis	84F	349	$ .01	$ .06
Leach, Rick	89F	237	$ .01	$ .05	Leonard, Dennis	86FU	67	$ .01	$ .05
Leach, Rick	90F	305	$ .01	$ .03	Leonard, Dennis	87F	374	$ .01	$ .04
Leach, Terry	86F	87	$ .01	$ .05	Leonard, Jeff	81F	67	$ .03	$ .20
Leach, Terry	87FU	62	$ .01	$ .05	Leonard, Jeff	84F	379	$ .03	$ .10
Leach, Terry	88F	139	$ .01	$ .04	Leonard, Jeff	85F	615	$ .03	$ .20
Leach, Terry	89F	40	$ .01	$ .05	Leonard, Jeff	86F	548	$ .01	$ .10
Leach, Terry	90F	111	$ .01	$ .03	Leonard, Jeff	87F	278	$ .01	$ .10
Leal, Luis	82F	617	$ .01	$ .04	Leonard, Jeff	88F	88	$ .01	$ .04
Leal, Luis	83F	432	$ .01	$ .04	Leonard, Jeff	88FU	39	$ .01	$ .05
Leal, Luis	84F	160	$ .01	$ .06	Leonard, Jeffrey	89F	190	$ .01	$ .05
Leal, Luis	85F	113	$ .01	$ .05	Leonard, Jeffrey	89FU	60	$ .01	$ .05
Leary, Tim	87F	348	$ .01	$ .04	Leonard, Jeffrey	90F	519	$ .01	$ .03
Leary, Tim	88F	521	$ .01	$ .04	Lerch, Randy	81F	25	$ .01	$ .04
Leary, Tim	89F	65	$ .01	$ .05	Lerch, Randy	82F	147	$ .01	$ .04
Leary, Tim	90F	424	$ .01	$ .03	Lerch, Randy	83F	287	$ .01	$ .04
Lee, Bill	81F	157	$ .01	$ .04	Lerch, Randy	84F	380	$ .01	$ .06
Lee, Bill	82F	194	$ .01	$ .04	Lerch, Randy	85F	616	$ .01	$ .05
Lee, Manny	85FU	71	$ .03	$ .20	Lezcano, Carlos	81F	307	$ .01	$ .04
Lee, Manny	88F	116	$ .01	$ .04	Lezcano, Sixto	81F	513	$ .01	$ .04
Lee, Manny	89F	238	$ .01	$ .05	Lezcano, Sixto	82F	119	$ .01	$ .04
Lee, Manny	90F	86	$ .01	$ .03	Lezcano, Sixto	83F	364	$ .01	$ .04
Lefebvre, Joe	81F	103	$ .01	$ .04	Lezcano, Sixto	84F	38	$ .01	$ .06
Lefebvre, Joe	82F	575	$ .01	$ .04	Lezcano, Sixto	85F	258	$ .01	$ .05
Lefebvre, Joe	83F	363	$ .01	$ .04	Lezcano, Sixto	85FU	72	$ .01	$ .05
Lefebvre, Joe	84F	37	$ .01	$ .06	Lilliquist, Derek	89FU	73	$ .01	$ .20
Lefebvre, Joe	85F	257	$ .01	$ .05	Lilliquist, Derek	90F	588	$ .01	$ .10
Lefferts, Craig	84F	496	$ .01	$ .06	Linares, Rufino	82F	439	$ .01	$ .04
Lefferts, Craig	84FU	72	$ .01	$ .10	Linares, Rufino	83F	140	$ .01	$ .04
Lefferts, Craig	85F	38	$ .01	$ .05	Lind, Jose	88F	334	$ .01	$ .20
Lefferts, Craig	86F	328	$ .01	$ .05	Lind, Jose	89F	214	$ .01	$ .10
Lefferts, Craig	87F	422	$ .01	$ .04	Lind, Jose	90F	474	$ .01	$ .03
Lefferts, Craig	87FU	64	$ .01	$ .05	Lindeman, Jim	87FU	65	$ .05	$ .30
Lefferts, Craig	88F	87	$ .01	$ .04	Lindeman, Jim	88F	39	$ .01	$ .10
Lefferts, Craig	90F	60	$ .01	$ .03	Lindsey, Bill	88F	403	$ .01	$ .10
LeFlore, Ron	81F	154	$ .01	$ .04	Liriano, Nelson	88F	117	$ .01	$ .30
LeFlore, Ron	82F	350	$ .01	$ .04	Liriano, Nelson	89F	239	$ .01	$ .05
LeFlore, Ron	83F	246	$ .01	$ .04	Liriano, Nelson	90F	87	$ .01	$ .03
Leibrandt, Charlie	81F	208	$ .05	$ .30	Littell, Mark	81F	544	$ .01	$ .04
Leibrandt, Charlie	82F	74	$ .01	$ .10	Littell, Mark	82F	120	$ .01	$ .04
Leibrandt, Charlie	83F	596	$ .01	$ .04	Little, Bryan	84F	279	$ .01	$ .06
Leibrandt, Charlie	85F	206	$ .01	$ .05	Little, Bryan	85F	402	$ .01	$ .05
Leibrandt, Charlie	86F	13	$ .01	$ .05	Little, Bryan	86F	212	$ .01	$ .05
Leibrandt, Charlie	87F	373	$ .01	$ .04	Little, Jeff	83F	619	$ .01	$ .04
Leibrandt, Charlie	88F	263	$ .01	$ .04	Littlefield, John	81F	535	$ .01	$ .04
Leibrandt, Charlie	89F	286	$ .01	$ .05	Littlefield, John	82F	576	$ .01	$ .04
Leibrandt, Charlie	90F	112	$ .01	$ .03	Littlejohn, Dennis	81F	455	$ .01	$ .04
Leifferts, Craig	89F	332	$ .01	$ .05	Litton, Greg	89FU	130	$ .01	$ .20
Leiper, Dave	88FU	123	$ .01	$ .05	Litton, Greg	90F	61	$ .01	$ .15
Leiper, Dave	89F	310	$ .01	$ .05	Lollar, Tim	81F	108	$ .01	$ .04
Leiper, David	87F	398	$ .01	$ .10	Lollar, Tim	83F	365	$ .01	$ .04
Leiter, Al	88FU	49	$ .01	$ .25	Lollar, Tim	84F	305	$ .01	$ .06
Leiter, Al	89F	257	$ .01	$ .10	Lollar, Tim	85F	39	$ .01	$ .05
Leiter, Al	89FU	70	$ .01	$ .10	Lollar, Tim	85FU	73	$ .01	$ .05
Leius, Scott	90F	647	$ .01	$ .03	Lollar, Tim	86F	354	$ .01	$ .05
LeMaster, Johnnie	81F	450	$ .01	$ .04	Lollar, Tim	87F	38	$ .01	$ .04
LeMaster, Johnnie	82F	393	$ .01	$ .04	Lombardi, Phil	87F	648	$ .10	$1.00
LeMaster, Johnnie	83F	266	$ .01	$ .04	Lombardozzi, Steve	86FU	68	$ .05	$ .30
LeMaster, Johnnie	84F	378	$ .01	$ .06	Lombardozzi, Steve	87F	547	$ .01	$ .04
LeMaster, Johnnie	85F	614	$ .01	$ .05	Lombardozzi, Steve	88F	16	$ .01	$ .04
Lemke, Mark	90F	587	$ .01	$ .03	Lombardozzi, Steve	89F	120	$ .01	$ .05
Lemon, Chet	81F	354	$ .01	$ .04	Long, Bill	87FU	66	$ .01	$ .10
Lemon, Chet	82F	351	$ .01	$ .04	Long, Bill	88F	404	$ .01	$ .15
Lemon, Chet	83F	335	$ .01	$ .04	Long, Bill	89F	501	$ .01	$ .05
Lemon, Chet	84F	85	$ .01	$ .06	Long, Bob	86F	468	$ .01	$ .05
Lemon, Chet	85F	15	$ .01	$ .05	Lopes, Davey	82F	12	$ .01	$ .10
Lemon, Chet	86F	230	$ .01	$ .05	Lopes, Davey	83F	524	$ .01	$ .10
Lemon, Chet	87F	156	$ .01	$ .04	Lopes, Davey	84F	453	$ .01	$ .06
Lemon, Chet	88F	61	$ .01	$ .04	Lopes, Davey	85F	60	$ .01	$ .05
Lemon, Chet	89F	137	$ .01	$ .05	Lopes, Davey	86F	372	$ .01	$ .05
Lemon, Chet	90F	608	$ .01	$ .03	Lopes, Davey	87F	62	$ .01	$ .04

Player	Year	No.	VG	EX/MT
Lopes, Davey 'Dave'	81F	114	$ .01	$ .10
Lopez, Aurelio	82F	273	$ .01	$ .04
Lopez, Aurelio	84F	86	$ .01	$ .06
Lopez, Aurelio	85F	16	$ .01	$ .05
Lopez, Aurelio	86F	231	$ .01	$ .05
Lopez, Aurelio	86FU	69	$ .01	$ .05
Lopez, Aurelio	87F	63	$ .01	$ .04
Lovelace, Vance	89F	651	$ .01	$ .20
Lovullo, Torey	89F	648	$ .01	$ .25
Lowenstein, John	81F	186	$ .01	$ .04
Lowenstein, John	82F	169	$ .01	$ .04
Lowenstein, John	83F	63	$ .01	$ .04
Lowenstein, John	84F	10	$ .01	$ .06
Lowenstein, John	85F	180	$ .01	$ .05
Lowry, Dwight	87F	157	$ .01	$ .04
Loynd, Mike	87FU	67	$ .01	$ .05
Loynd, Mike	88F	472	$ .01	$ .04
Lozado, Willie	85F	644	$ .01	$ .05
Lubratich, Steve	84F	524	$ .01	$ .06
Lucas, Gary	81F	502	$ .01	$ .04
Lucas, Gary	82F	577	$ .01	$ .04
Lucas, Gary	83F	366	$ .01	$ .04
Lucas, Gary	84F	306	$ .01	$ .06
Lucas, Gary	84FU	73	$ .01	$ .10
Lucas, Gary	85F	403	$ .01	$ .05
Lucas, Gary	86F	254	$ .01	$ .05
Lucas, Gary	87F	87	$ .01	$ .04
Lucas, Gary	88F	495	$ .01	$ .04
Luecken, Rick	90F	113	$ .01	$ .15
Lugo, Urbano	85FU	74	$ .01	$ .05
Lugo, Urbano	86F	162	$ .01	$ .05
Lum, Mike	81F	258	$ .01	$ .04
Lum, Mike	82F	599	$ .01	$ .04
Lusader, Scott	88F	62	$ .01	$ .15
Luzinski, Greg	81F	10	$ .01	$ .10
Luzinski, Greg	82F	352	$ .01	$ .10
Luzinski, Greg	83F	247	$ .01	$ .10

Greg Luzinski
DESIGNATED HITTER

Player	Year	No.	VG	EX/MT
Luzinski, Greg	84F	69	$ .01	$ .06
Luzinski, Greg	85F	521	$ .01	$ .05
Lyle, Sparky	81F	17	$ .01	$ .10
Lyle, Sparky	82F	247	$ .01	$ .10
Lynch, Ed	82F	531	$ .01	$ .04
Lynch, Ed	83F	549	$ .01	$ .04

Player	Year	No.	VG	EX/MT
Lynch, Ed	84F	591	$ .01	$ .06
Lynch, Ed	85F	87	$ .01	$ .05
Lynch, Ed	86F	88	$ .01	$ .05
Lynch, Ed	87F	567	$ .01	$ .04
Lynch, Ed	88F	422	$ .01	$ .04
Lynn, Fred	81F	223	$ .04	$ .25
Lynn, Fred	82F	468	$ .03	$ .20
Lynn, Fred	83F	97	$ .03	$ .20
Lynn, Fred	84F	525	$ .03	$ .20
Lynn, Fred	84F	626	$ .03	$ .10
Lynn, Fred	85F	307	$ .03	$ .20
Lynn, Fred	85FU	75	$ .05	$ .30
Lynn, Fred	86F	278	$ .03	$ .20
Lynn, Fred	87F	474	$ .03	$ .20
Lynn, Fred	88F	566	$ .01	$ .10
Lynn, Fred	89F	138	$ .01	$ .05
Lynn, Fred	90F	609	$ .01	$ .03
Lyons, Barry	88F	140	$ .01	$ .10
Lyons, Barry	89FU	101	$ .01	$ .05
Lyons, Barry	90F	209	$ .01	$ .03
Lyons, Steve	85FU	76	$ .01	$ .05
Lyons, Steve	86F	355	$ .01	$ .05
Lyons, Steve	87F	502	$ .01	$ .04
Lyons, Steve	88F	405	$ .01	$ .04
Lyons, Steve	89F	502	$ .01	$ .05
Lyons, Steve	90F	539	$ .01	$ .03
Lysander, Rick	84F	570	$ .01	$ .06
Lysander, Rick	85F	284	$ .04	$ .05
Lysander, Rick	86F	399	$ .01	$ .05
Maas, Kevin	90F	641	$ .01	$ .03
MacFarlane (f), Mike	88FU	31	$ .01	$ .15
Macfarlane, Mike	89F	287	$ .01	$ .20
Macfarlane, Mike	90F	114	$ .01	$ .03
Macha, Ken	81F	167	$ .01	$ .04
Macha, Ken	82F	618	$ .01	$ .04
Mack, Shane	88F	590	$ .01	$ .25
Mackanin, Pete	81F	565	$ .01	$ .04
Mackanin, Pete	82F	556	$ .01	$ .04
Madden, Mike	84F	232	$ .01	$ .06
Maddox, Elliott	81F	326	$ .01	$ .04
Maddox, Garry	81F	19	$ .01	$ .04
Maddox, Garry	82F	248	$ .01	$ .04
Maddox, Garry	83F	164	$ .01	$ .04
Maddox, Garry	84F	39	$ .01	$ .06
Maddox, Garry	85F	259	$ .01	$ .05
Maddox, Garry	86F	445	$ .01	$ .05
Maddux, Greg	87FU	68	$ .25	$1.00
Maddux, Greg	88F	423	$ .10	$ .50
Maddux, Greg	89F	431	$ .01	$ .05
Maddux, Greg	90F	37	$ .01	$ .10
Maddux, Mike	87F	179	$ .01	$ .04
Maddux, Mike	88F	309	$ .01	$ .04
Maddux, Mike	89F	576	$ .01	$ .05
Madlock, Bill	81F	381	$ .03	$ .20
Madlock, Bill	82F	485	$ .01	$ .10
Madlock, Bill	83F	309	$ .01	$ .10
Madlock, Bill	84F	253	$ .03	$ .10
Madlock, Bill	85F	468	$ .01	$ .10
Madlock, Bill	86F	135	$ .01	$ .10
Madlock, Bill	87F	445	$ .01	$ .10
Madlock, Bill	87FU	69	$ .01	$ .05
Madlock, Bill	88F	63	$ .01	$ .10
Magadan, Dave	87F	648	$ .10	$1.00
Magadan, Dave	87FU	70	$ .05	$ .25
Magadan, Dave	88F	141	$ .01	$ .10
Magadan, Dave	89F	41	$ .01	$ .05
Magadan, Dave	90F	210	$ .01	$ .03
Magrane, Joe	87FU	71	$ .15	$1.25
Magrane, Joe	88F	40	$ .10	$ .75
Magrane, Joe	89F	455	$ .01	$ .15
Magrane, Joe	90F	252	$ .01	$ .03
Mahler, Mickey	85FU	77	$ .01	$ .05
Mahler, Mickey	86FU	70	$ .01	$ .05
Mahler, Rick	82F	440	$ .04	$ .25

FLEER

Player	Year	No.	VG	EX/MT	Player	Year	No.	VG	EX/MT
Mahler, Rick	83F	141	$ .01	$ .04	Martinez, Dennis	82F	170	$ .01	$ .04
Mahler, Rick	85F	332	$ .01	$ .05	Martinez, Dennis	83F	64	$ .01	$ .04
Mahler, Rick	86F	521	$ .01	$ .05	Martinez, Dennis	84F	11	$ .01	$ .06
Mahler, Rick	87F	520	$ .01	$ .04	Martinez, Dennis	85F	181	$ .01	$ .05
Mahler, Rick	89F	595	$ .01	$ .05	Martinez, Dennis	86F	280	$ .01	$ .05
Mahler, Rick	89FU	85	$ .01	$ .05	Martinez, Dennis	87F	324	$ .01	$ .04
Mahler, Rick	90F	425	$ .01	$ .03	Martinez, Dennis	88F	188	$ .01	$ .04
Maldonado, Candy	83F	212	$ .10	$ .45	Martinez, Dennis	89F	385	$ .01	$ .05
Maldonado, Candy	85F	376	$ .01	$ .10	Martinez, Dennis	90F	354	$ .01	$ .03
Maldonado, Candy	86F	136	$ .01	$ .10	Martinez, Edgar	88F	378	$ .10	$ .45
Maldonado, Candy	86FU	71	$ .01	$ .05	Martinez, Edgar	89F	552	$ .01	$ .05
Maldonado, Candy	87F	279	$ .01	$ .10	Martinez, Edgar	90F	520	$ .01	$ .03
Maldonado, Candy	88F	89	$ .01	$ .04	Martinez, Ramon	89F	67	$ .05	$ .45
Maldonado, Candy	89F	333	$ .01	$ .05	Martinez, Ramon	90F	402	$ .01	$ .10
Maldonado, Candy	90F	62	$ .01	$ .03	Martinez, Silvio	81F	546	$ .01	$ .04
Mallicoat, Rob	88F	452	$ .01	$ .10	Martinez, Silvio	82F	122	$ .01	$ .04
Mann, Kelly	90F	642	$ .01	$ .25	Martinez, Tippy	81F	179	$ .01	$ .04
Manning, Rick	81F	403	$ .01	$ .04	Martinez, Tippy	82F	171	$ .01	$ .04
Manning, Rick	82F	374	$ .01	$ .04	Martinez, Tippy	83F	65	$ .01	$ .04
Manning, Rick	83F	413	$ .01	$ .04	Martinez, Tippy	84F	12	$ .01	$ .06
Manning, Rick	84F	205	$ .01	$ .06	Martinez, Tippy	84F	635	$ .01	$ .06
Manning, Rick	85F	586	$ .01	$ .05	Martinez, Tippy	85F	182	$ .01	$ .05
Manning, Rick	86F	493	$ .01	$ .05	Martinez, Tippy	86F	279	$ .01	$ .05
Manning, Rick	87F	349	$ .01	$ .04	Martz, Randy	81F	300	$ .01	$ .04
Manning, Rick	88F	168	$ .01	$ .04	Martz, Randy	82F	600	$ .01	$ .04
Manrique, Fred	87FU	72	$ .04	$ .25	Martz, Randy	83F	501	$ .01	$ .04
Manrique, Fred	88F	406	$ .01	$ .15	Marzano, John	88F	357	$ .05	$ .35
Manrique, Fred	89F	503	$ .01	$ .05	Mason, Mike	84FU	76	$ .06	$ .35
Manrique, Fred	90F	306	$ .01	$ .03	Mason, Mike	85F	562	$ .01	$ .05
Manto, Jeff	89FU	13	$ .01	$ .25	Mason, Mike	86F	565	$ .01	$ .05
Manto, Jeff	90F	137	$ .01	$ .15	Mason, Mike	87F	129	$ .01	$ .04
Manuel, Jerry	82F	195	$ .01	$ .04	Mason, Mike	87FU	73	$ .01	$ .05
Manwaring, Kirt	88F	651	$ .01	$ .35	Mason, Roger	86FU	72	$ .01	$ .05
Manwaring, Kirt	89F	334	$ .01	$ .05	Mason, Roger	87F	280	$ .01	$ .04
Manwaring, Kirt	90F	63	$ .01	$ .03	Mata, Vic	85F	644	$ .01	$ .05
Marshall, Mike	82F	13	$ .15	$1.25	Mathews, Greg	86FU	73	$ .05	$ .30
Marshall, Mike	82F	532	$ .01	$ .04	Mathews, Greg	87F	303	$ .04	$ .20
Marshall, Mike	83F	211	$ .03	$ .20	Mathews, Greg	88F	41	$ .01	$ .10
Marshall, Mike	84F	105	$ .03	$ .20	Mathews, Greg	89F	456	$ .01	$ .05
Marshall, Mike	85F	377	$ .01	$ .10	Mathis, Ron	85FU	78	$ .01	$ .05
Marshall, Mike	86F	137	$ .01	$ .10	Mathis, Ron	86F	305	$ .01	$ .05
Marshall, Mike	87F	446	$ .01	$ .10	Matlack, Jon	81F	621	$ .01	$ .04
Marshall, Mike	88F	522	$ .01	$ .04	Matlack, Jon	82F	323	$ .01	$ .04
Marshall, Mike	89F	66	$ .01	$ .05	Matlack, Jon	83F	572	$ .01	$ .04
Marshall, Mike	90F	401	$ .01	$ .03	Matlack, Jon	84F	422	$ .01	$ .06
Martin, Billy	81F	581	$ .01	$ .10	Matthews, Gary	81F	251	$ .01	$ .10
Martin, Jerry	81F	295	$ .01	$ .04	Matthews, Gary	82F	249	$ .01	$ .04
Martin, Jerry	82F	394	$ .01	$ .04	Matthews, Gary	83F	165	$ .01	$ .04
Martin, Jerry	83F	117	$ .01	$ .04	Matthews, Gary	84F	40	$ .01	$ .06
Martin, Jerry	84FU	74	$ .01	$ .10	Matthews, Gary	84FU	77	$ .04	$ .25
Martin, John	82F	121	$ .01	$ .04	Matthews, Gary	85F	61	$ .01	$ .05
Martin, Renie	81F	39	$ .01	$ .04	Matthews, Gary	86F	373	$ .01	$ .05
Martin, Renie	82F	414	$ .01	$ .04	Matthews, Gary	87F	568	$ .01	$ .04
Martin, Renie	83F	267	$ .01	$ .04	Mattick, Bob	81F	431	$ .01	$ .04
Martin, Renie	84F	381	$ .01	$ .06	Mattingly, Don	84F	131	$8.00	$40.00
Martinez, Alfredo	81F	288	$ .01	$ .04	Mattingly, Don	85F	133	$3.00	$12.00
Martinez, Buck	81F	526	$ .01	$ .04	Mattingly, Don	86F	109	$ .60	$4.00
Martinez, Buck	83F	433	$ .01	$ .04	Mattingly, Don	86F	627	$ .30	$1.50
Martinez, Buck	84F	161	$ .01	$ .06	Mattingly, Don	86F	639	$ .30	$1.50
Martinez, Buck	85F	114	$ .01	$ .05	Mattingly, Don	87F	104	$ .50	$2.50
Martinez, Buck	86F	66	$ .01	$ .05	Mattingly, Don	87F	638	$ .10	$1.00
Martinez, Buck	87F	235	$ .01	$ .04	Mattingly, Don	88F	214	$ .25	$1.50
Martinez, Carlos	90F	540	$ .01	$ .20	Mattingly, Don	89F	258	$ .10	$ .75
Martinez, Carmelo	84F	497	$ .04	$ .25	Mattingly, Don	90F	447	$ .01	$ .40
Martinez, Carmelo	84FU	75	$ .04	$ .25	Mattingly, Don	90F	638	$ .01	$ .10
Martinez, Carmelo	85F	40	$ .01	$ .05	Mattingly, Don	90FPD	626	$ .01	$ .35
Martinez, Carmelo	86F	329	$ .01	$ .05	Matula, Rick	81F	263	$ .01	$ .04
Martinez, Carmelo	87F	423	$ .01	$ .04	Matuszek, Len	84F	41	$ .01	$ .06
Martinez, Carmelo	88F	591	$ .01	$ .04	Matuszek, Len	85F	260	$ .01	$ .05
Martinez, Carmelo	89F	311	$ .01	$ .05	Matuszek, Len	85FU	79	$ .01	$ .05
Martinez, Carmelo	90F	162	$ .01	$ .03	Matuszek, Len	86F	138	$ .01	$ .05
Martinez, Dave	88F	424	$ .01	$ .04	Matuszek, Len	87F	447	$ .01	$ .04
Martinez, Dave	89F	384	$ .01	$ .05	May, Derrick	90F	645	$ .01	$ .03
Martinez, Dave	90F	353	$ .01	$ .03	May, Lee	81F	183	$ .01	$ .04
Martinez, Dennis	81F	180	$ .01	$ .04	May, Lee	82F	415	$ .01	$ .04

Player	Year	No.	VG	EX/MT	Player	Year	No.	VG	EX/MT
May, Lee	83F	118	$ .01	$ .04	McClure, Bob	85F	587	$ .01	$ .05
May, Milt	81F	442	$ .01	$ .04	McClure, Bob	86F	494	$ .01	$ .05
May, Milt	82F	395	$ .01	$ .04	McClure, Bob	87F	325	$ .01	$ .04
May, Milt	83F	268	$ .01	$ .04	McClure, Bob	88F	189	$ .01	$ .04
May, Milt	84F	254	$ .01	$ .06	McClure, Bob	89F	42	$ .01	$ .05
May, Rudy	81F	90	$ .01	$ .04	McClure, Bob	89FU	14	$ .01	$ .10
May, Rudy	82F	41	$ .01	$ .04	McClure, Bob	90F	139	$ .01	$ .03
May, Rudy	83F	385	$ .01	$ .04	McCovey, Willie	81F	434	$ .07	$ .50
Mayberry, John	81F	416	$ .01	$ .04	McCullers, Lance	86F	330	$ .04	$ .25
Mayberry, John	82F	619	$ .01	$ .04	McCullers, Lance	87F	424	$ .01	$ .04
Mayberry, John	83F	386	$ .01	$ .04	McCullers, Lance	88F	592	$ .01	$ .04
Mazzilli, Lee	81F	316	$ .01	$ .04	McCullers, Lance	89F	312	$ .01	$ .05
Mazzilli, Lee	82F	533	$ .01	$ .04	McCullers, Lance	90F	448	$ .01	$ .03
Mazzilli, Lee	83F	387	$ .01	$ .04	McDonald, Ben	90F	180	$ .01	$2.00
Mazzilli, Lee	84F	255	$ .01	$ .06	McDowell, Jack	88F	407	$ .01	$ .20
Mazzilli, Lee	85F	469	$ .01	$ .05	McDowell, Jack	89F	504	$ .01	$ .15
Mazzilli, Lee	86F	612	$ .01	$ .05	McDowell, Oddibe	85FU	80	$ .10	$ .70
Mazzilli, Lee	87F	15	$ .01	$ .04	McDowell, Oddibe	86F	566	$ .04	$ .20
Mazzilli, Lee	90F	88	$ .01	$ .03	McDowell, Oddibe	87F	130	$ .01	$ .10
McBride, Bake	81F	9	$ .01	$ .04	McDowell, Oddibe	88F	473	$ .01	$ .10
McBride, Bake	82F	250	$ .01	$ .04	McDowell, Oddibe	89F	528	$ .01	$ .05
McBride, Bake	83F	414	$ .01	$ .04	McDowell, Oddibe	90F	589	$ .01	$ .03
McBride, Bake	84F	547	$ .01	$ .06	McDowell, Roger	85FU	81	$ .15	$ .85
McCament, Randy	90F	64	$ .01	$ .10	McDowell, Roger	86F	89	$ .06	$ .35
McCarthy, Tom	90F	541	$ .01	$ .03	McDowell, Roger	87F	16	$ .01	$ .10
McCarver, Tim	81F	27	$ .01	$ .04	McDowell, Roger	88F	142	$ .01	$ .10
McCaskill, Kirk	86F	163	$ .06	$ .50	McDowell, Roger	89F	43	$ .01	$ .05
McCaskill, Kirk	87F	88	$ .01	$ .04	McDowell, Roger	89FU	110	$ .01	$ .05
McCaskill, Kirk	88F	496	$ .01	$ .04	McDowell, Roger	90F	567	$ .01	$ .03
McCaskill, Kirk	89F	483	$ .01	$ .05	McElroy, Chuck	90F	650	$ .01	$ .03
McCaskill, Kirk	90F	138	$ .01	$ .03	McGaffigan, Andy	84F	382	$ .01	$ .06
McCatty, Steve	81F	589	$ .01	$ .04	McGaffigan, Andy	84FU	78	$ .01	$ .10
McCatty, Steve	82F	99	$ .01	$ .04	McGaffigan, Andy	85F	540	$ .01	$ .05
McCatty, Steve	83F	525	$ .01	$ .04	McGaffigan, Andy	86F	181	$ .01	$ .05
McCatty, Steve	84F	454	$ .01	$ .06	McGaffigan, Andy	86FU	74	$ .01	$ .05
McCatty, Steve	85F	430	$ .01	$ .05	McGaffigan, Andy	87F	326	$ .01	$ .04
McCatty, Steve	86F	427	$ .01	$ .05	McGaffigan, Andy	88F	190	$ .01	$ .04
					McGaffigan, Andy	89F	386	$ .01	$ .05
					McGaffigan, Andy	90F	355	$ .01	$ .03
					McGee, Willie	83F	15	$ .20	$1.50
					McGee, Willie	84F	329	$ .05	$ .40
					McGee, Willie	85F	234	$ .05	$ .30
					McGee, Willie	86F	42	$ .01	$ .10
					McGee, Willie	86F	636	$ .01	$ .25
					McGee, Willie	87F	304	$ .01	$ .10
					McGee, Willie	88F	42	$ .01	$ .10
					McGee, Willie	89F	457	$ .01	$ .05
					McGee, Willie	90F	253	$ .01	$ .03
					McGlothen, Lynn	81F	302	$ .01	$ .04
					McGraw, Tug	81F	657	$ .10	$ .50
					McGraw, Tug	81F	7	$ .01	$ .04
					McGraw, Tug	82F	251	$ .01	$ .10
					McGraw, Tug	83F	166	$ .01	$ .10
					McGraw, Tug	84F	42	$ .03	$ .20
					McGraw, Tug	85F	261	$ .01	$ .10
					McGregor, Scott	81F	174	$ .01	$ .04
					McGregor, Scott	82F	172	$ .01	$ .04
					McGregor, Scott	83F	66	$ .01	$ .04
					McGregor, Scott	84F	13	$ .01	$ .06
					McGregor, Scott	84F	646	$ .01	$ .06
					McGregor, Scott	85F	183	$ .01	$ .05
					McGregor, Scott	86F	281	$ .01	$ .05
					McGregor, Scott	87F	475	$ .01	$ .04
					McGriff, Fred	87FU	75	$ .40	$2.50
					McGriff, Fred	88F	118	$ .25	$2.00
					McGriff, Fred	89F	240	$ .01	$ .30
					McGriff, Fred	90F	89	$ .01	$ .10
					McGriff, Terry	88F	240	$ .01	$ .10
					McGuire, Bill	89F	553	$ .01	$ .05

Lloyd McClendon
INFIELD
FLEER

Player	Year	No.	VG	EX/MT
McClendon, Lloyd	87FU	74	$ .04	$ .25
McClendon, Lloyd	89FU	77	$ .01	$ .10
McClendon, Lloyd	90F	88	$ .01	$ .03
McClure, Bob	81F	520	$ .01	$ .04
McClure, Bob	83F	38	$ .01	$ .04
McClure, Bob	84F	206	$ .01	$ .06

Player	Year	No.	VG	EX/MT
McGuire, Mark	87FU	76	$1.00	$3.25
McGwire, Mark	88F	286	$ .50	$2.50
McGwire, Mark	88F	624	$ .10	$1.00
McGwire, Mark	88F	629	$ .10	$ .75
McGwire, Mark	88F	633	$ .01	$ .35
McGwire, Mark	89F	17	$ .05	$ .75

Player	Year	No.	VG	EX/MT	Player	Year	No.	VG	EX/MT
McGwire, Mark	89F	634	$ .05	$ .35	Meyer, Dan	83F	527	$ .01	$ .04
McGwire, Mark	90F	15	$ .01	$ .25	Meyer, Dan	84F	455	$ .01	$ .06
McGwire, Mark	90F	638	$ .01	$ .10	Meyer, Joey	88F	645	$ .10	$ .40
McIntosh, Tim	90F	329	$ .01	$ .15	Meyer, Joey	88FU	40	$ .01	$ .15
McKay, Dave	81F	592	$ .01	$ .04	Meyer, Joey	89F	191	$ .01	$ .10
McKay, Dave	82F	100	$ .01	$ .04	Milacki, Bob	89F	649	$ .01	$ .25
McKay, Dave	83F	526	$ .01	$ .04	Milacki, Bob	89FU	6	$ .01	$ .20
McKeon, Joel	86FU	75	$ .01	$ .05	Milacki, Bob	90F	182	$ .01	$ .03
McKeon, Joel	87F	503	$ .01	$ .10	Milbourne, Larry	81F	611	$ .01	$ .04
McLaughlin, Joey	81F	420	$ .01	$ .04	Milbourne, Larry	82F	42	$ .01	$ .04
McLaughlin, Joey	82F	620	$ .01	$ .04	Milbourne, Larry	83F	415	$ .01	$ .04
McLaughlin, Joey	83F	434	$ .01	$ .04	Milbourne, Larry	85F	493	$ .01	$ .05
McLaughlin, Joey	84F	162	$ .01	$ .06	Miller, Darrell	88F	498	$ .01	$ .04
McLaughlin, Joey	84FU	79	$ .01	$ .10	Miller, Dyar	82F	534	$ .01	$ .04
McLemore, Mark	86F	650	$ .03	$ .20					
McLemore, Mark	87FU	77	$ .01	$ .05					
McLemore, Mark	88F	497	$ .01	$ .04					
McLemore, Mark	89F	484	$ .01	$ .05					
McMurtry, Craig	84F	184	$ .01	$ .06					
McMurtry, Craig	85F	333	$ .01	$ .05					
McRae, Hal	81F	41	$ .01	$ .10					
McRae, Hal	82F	416	$ .01	$ .10					
McRae, Hal	83F	119	$ .01	$ .10					
McRae, Hal	84F	350	$ .03	$ .10					
McRae, Hal	85F	207	$ .01	$ .05					
McRae, Hal	86F	14	$ .01	$ .05					
McRae, Hal	87F	375	$ .01	$ .04					
McReynolds, Kevin	84F	307	$1.50	$6.50					
McReynolds, Kevin	85F	41	$ .25	$1.25					
McReynolds, Kevin	86F	331	$ .05	$ .30					
McReynolds, Kevin	87F	425	$ .05	$ .25					
McReynolds, Kevin	87FU	78	$ .03	$ .20					
McReynolds, Kevin	88F	143	$ .01	$ .10					
McReynolds, Kevin	89F	44	$ .01	$ .15					
McReynolds, Kevin	90F	211	$ .01	$ .10					
McWilliams, Larry	81F	267	$ .01	$ .04					
McWilliams, Larry	83F	310	$ .01	$ .04					
McWilliams, Larry	84F	256	$ .01	$ .06					
McWilliams, Larry	85F	470	$ .01	$ .05					
McWilliams, Larry	86F	613	$ .01	$ .05					
McWilliams, Larry	87F	613	$ .01	$ .04					
McWilliams, Larry	89F	458	$ .01	$ .05					
Meacham, Bobby	85F	134	$ .01	$ .05					
Meacham, Bobby	86F	110	$ .01	$ .05					
Meacham, Bobby	87F	105	$ .01	$ .04					
Meacham, Bobby	88F	215	$ .01	$ .04					
Meadows, Louie	88FU	92	$ .01	$ .15	Miller, Ed	82F	441	$ .01	$ .04
Meadows, Louie	89F	361	$ .01	$ .15	Miller, Keith	88F	144	$ .01	$ .10
Meads, Dave	87FU	79	$ .01	$ .05	Miller, Keith	89F	45	$ .01	$ .05
Meads, Dave	88F	453	$ .01	$ .05	Miller, Rick	81F	279	$ .01	$ .04
Meads, Dave	89F	362	$ .01	$ .05	Miller, Rick	82F	299	$ .01	$ .04
Medich, Doc	81F	627	$ .01	$ .04	Miller, Rick	83F	188	$ .01	$ .04
Medich, Doc	82F	324	$ .01	$ .04	Miller, Rick	84F	403	$ .01	$ .06
Medich, Doc	83F	39	$ .01	$ .04	Miller, Rick	85F	163	$ .01	$ .05
Medina, Luis	89F	411	$ .05	$ .35	Milligan, Randy	88FU	115	$ .01	$ .30
Meier, Dave	85F	285	$ .01	$ .05	Milligan, Randy	89FU	7	$ .01	$ .05
Meier, Dave	86F	400	$ .01	$ .05	Milligan, Randy	90F	183	$ .01	$ .03
Mejias, Sam	81F	219	$ .01	$ .04	Mills, Brad	82F	196	$ .01	$ .04
Mejias, Sam	82F	75	$ .01	$ .04	Mills, Brad	83F	288	$ .01	$ .04
Melvin, Bob	87F	281	$ .01	$ .04	Milner, Eddie	83F	597	$ .01	$ .10
Melvin, Bob	88F	91	$ .01	$ .04	Milner, Eddie	84F	474	$ .01	$ .06
Melvin, Bob	89F	335	$ .01	$ .05	Milner, Eddie	85F	541	$ .01	$ .05
Melvin, Bob	90F	181	$ .01	$ .03	Milner, Eddie	86F	182	$ .01	$ .05
Mendoza, Mario	81F	613	$ .01	$ .04	Milner, Eddie	87F	205	$ .01	$ .04
Mendoza, Mario	82F	325	$ .01	$ .04	Milner, Eddie	88F	90	$ .01	$ .04
Mercado, Orlando	84F	613	$ .01	$ .06	Milner, John	81F	386	$ .01	$ .04
Mercker, Kent	90F	590	$ .01	$ .50	Milner, John	82F	197	$ .01	$ .04
Meredith, Ron	86F	374	$ .01	$ .05	Milner, John	83F	311	$ .01	$ .04
Merullo, Matt	89FU	21	$ .01	$ .15	Minton, Greg	81F	449	$ .01	$ .04
Merullo, Matt	90F	542	$ .01	$ .10	Minton, Greg	82F	396	$ .01	$ .04
Meulens, Hensley	89FU	51	$ .01	$ .35	Minton, Greg	83F	269	$ .01	$ .04
Meulens, Hensley	90F	449	$ .01	$ .15	Minton, Greg	84F	383	$ .01	$ .06
Meyer, Brian	90F	232	$ .01	$ .03	Minton, Greg	85F	617	$ .01	$ .05
Meyer, Dan	81F	603	$ .01	$ .04	Minton, Greg	86F	549	$ .01	$ .05
Meyer, Dan	82F	512	$ .01	$ .04	Minton, Greg	87F	282	$ .01	$ .04

Ed Miller
BRAVES • OUTFIELD

Player	Year	No.	VG	EX/MT	Player	Year	No.	VG	EX/MT
Minton, Greg	87FU	80	$ .01	$ .05	Moore, Donnie	85F	334	$ .01	$ .05
Minton, Greg	88F	499	$ .01	$ .04	Moore, Donnie	85FU	82	$ .01	$ .05
Minton, Greg	89F	485	$ .01	$ .05	Moore, Donnie	86F	164	$ .01	$ .05
Minton, Greg	90F	140	$ .01	$ .03	Moore, Donnie	87F	89	$ .01	$ .04
Mirabella, Paul	83F	573	$ .01	$ .04	Moore, Donnie	88F	500	$ .01	$ .04
Mirabella, Paul	85F	494	$ .01	$ .05	Moore, Mike	83F	482	$ .25	$ 1.25
Mirabella, Paul	89F	192	$ .01	$ .05	Moore, Mike	84F	614	$ .01	$ .06
Mitchell, Bob	83F	620	$ .01	$ .04	Moore, Mike	85F	495	$ .01	$ .05
Mitchell, Bobby	82F	14	$ .01	$ .04	Moore, Mike	86F	469	$ .01	$ .05
Mitchell, Bobby	84F	571	$ .01	$ .06	Moore, Mike	87F	590	$ .01	$ .04
Mitchell, John	87FU	81	$ .04	$ .25	Moore, Mike	88F	379	$ .01	$ .04
Mitchell, John	88F	145	$ .01	$ .20	Moore, Mike	89F	554	$ .01	$ .05
Mitchell, Kevin	86FU	76	$1.50	$7.00	Moore, Mike	89FU	55	$ .01	$ .05
Mitchell, Kevin	87F	17	$1.25	$8.00	Moore, Mike	90F	16	$ .01	$ .03
Mitchell, Kevin	87FU	82	$ .35	$2.00	Morales, Jerry	81F	338	$ .01	$ .04
Mitchell, Kevin	88F	92	$ .15	$1.50	Morales, Jerry	82F	601	$ .01	$ .04
Mitchell, Kevin	89F	336	$ .05	$ .50	Morales, Jerry	83F	502	$ .01	$ .04
Mitchell, Kevin	90F	637	$ .01	$ .03	Morales, Jerry	84F	498	$ .01	$ .06
Mitchell, Kevin	90F	65	$ .01	$ .25	Morales, Jose	81F	571	$ .01	$ .04
Moffitt, Randy	81F	446	$ .01	$ .04	Morales, Jose	82F	173	$ .01	$ .04
Moffitt, Randy	83F	456	$ .01	$ .04	Morales, Jose	84F	107	$ .01	$ .06
Moffitt, Randy	84F	163	$ .01	$ .06	Moreland, Keith	81F	13	$ .06	$ .35
Mohorcic, Dale	87F	131	$ .04	$ .25	Moreland, Keith	82F	252	$ .01	$ .10
Mohorcic, Dale	88F	474	$ .01	$ .04	Moreland, Keith	83F	503	$ .01	$ .04
Mohorcic, Dale	89F	259	$ .01	$ .05	Moreland, Keith	84F	499	$ .01	$ .06
Mohoric, Dale	90F	450	$ .01	$ .03	Moreland, Keith	85F	62	$ .01	$ .05
Molinaro, Bob	81F	340	$ .01	$ .04	Moreland, Keith	86F	375	$ .01	$ .05
Molinaro, Bob	82F	353	$ .01	$ .04	Moreland, Keith	87F	569	$ .01	$ .04
Molinaro, Bob	83F	167	$ .01	$ .04	Moreland, Keith	88F	425	$ .01	$ .04
Molitor, Paul	81F	515	$ .03	$ .20	Moreland, Keith	88FU	124	$ .01	$ .05
Molitor, Paul	82F	148	$ .03	$ .20	Moreland, Keith	89F	313	$ .01	$ .05
Molitor, Paul	83F	40	$ .03	$ .20	Moreno, Angel	82F	469	$ .01	$ .04
Molitor, Paul	84F	207	$ .03	$ .20	Moreno, Omar	81F	361	$ .01	$ .04
Molitor, Paul	85F	588	$ .03	$ .20	Moreno, Omar	82F	487	$ .01	$ .04
Molitor, Paul	86F	495	$ .03	$ .20	Moreno, Omar	83F	312	$ .01	$ .04
Molitor, Paul	87F	350	$ .01	$ .10	Moreno, Omar	84F	133	$ .01	$ .06
Molitor, Paul	88F	169	$ .01	$ .10	Moreno, Omar	85F	136	$ .01	$ .05
Molitor, Paul	89F	193	$ .01	$ .10	Moreno, Omar	86F	15	$ .01	$ .05
Molitor, Paul	90F	330	$ .01	$ .03	Moreno, Omar	86FU	78	$ .01	$ .05
Monday, Rick	81F	122	$ .01	$ .04	Moreno, Omar	87F	521	$ .01	$ .04
Monday, Rick	82F	15	$ .01	$ .04	Morgan, Joe	81F	78	$ .06	$ .50
Monday, Rick	83F	213	$ .01	$ .04	Morgan, Joe	82F	397	$ .05	$ .50
Monday, Rick	84F	106	$ .01	$ .06	Morgan, Joe	83F	270	$ .05	$ .50
Money, Don	81F	524	$ .01	$ .04	Morgan, Joe	84F	43	$ .05	$ .50
Money, Don	82F	149	$ .01	$ .04	Morgan, Joe	84F	636	$ .10	$ .50
Money, Don	83F	41	$ .01	$ .04	Morgan, Joe	84FU	80	$ .40	$3.00
Money, Don	84F	208	$ .01	$ .06	Morgan, Joe	85F	431	$ .01	$ .25
Monge, Sid	81F	395	$ .01	$ .04	Morgan, Mike	83F	388	$ .01	$ .04
Monge, Sid	82F	375	$ .01	$ .04	Morgan, Mike	87F	591	$ .01	$ .04
Monge, Sid	83F	168	$ .01	$ .04	Morgan, Mike	88F	380	$ .01	$ .04
Monge, Sid	84F	308	$ .01	$ .06	Morgan, Mike	88FU	91	$ .01	$ .05
Monge, Sid	85F	17	$ .01	$ .05	Morgan, Mike	90F	403	$ .01	$ .03
Montanez, Willy	82F	486	$ .01	$ .04	Morman, Russ	87F	645	$ .03	$ .20
Montanez, Willy 'Willie'	81F	506	$ .01	$ .04	Morris, Hal	89F	260	$ .01	$ .05
Montefusco, John	81F	439	$ .01	$ .04	Morris, Jack	81F	475	$ .04	$ .25
Montefusco, John	82F	442	$ .01	$ .04	Morris, Jack	82F	274	$ .04	$ .25
Montefusco, John	83F	367	$ .01	$ .04	Morris, Jack	83F	336	$ .04	$ .25
Montefusco, John	84F	132	$ .01	$ .06	Morris, Jack	84F	87	$ .04	$ .25
Montefusco, John	85F	135	$ .01	$ .05	Morris, Jack	85F	18	$ .04	$ .25
Montefusco, John	86F	111	$ .01	$ .05	Morris, Jack	85F	643	$ .01	$ .15
Monteleone, Rich	90F	648	$ .01	$ .03	Morris, Jack	86F	232	$ .03	$ .20
Montgomery, Jeff	88F	642	$ .01	$1.00	Morris, Jack	87F	158	$ .03	$ .20
Montgomery, Jeff	88FU	32	$ .01	$ .15	Morris, Jack	88F	626	$ .01	$ .04
Montgomery, Jeff	89F	288	$ .01	$ .15	Morris, Jack	88F	64	$ .01	$ .10
Montgomery, Jeff	90F	115	$ .01	$ .03	Morris, Jack	89F	139	$ .01	$ .10
Mooneyham, Bill	86FU	77	$ .01	$ .05	Morris, Jack	90F	610	$ .01	$ .03
Mooneyham, Bill	87F	399	$ .01	$ .04	Morris, John	87FU	83	$ .01	$ .05
Moore, Charlie	81F	521	$ .01	$ .04	Morris, John	88F	43	$ .01	$ .04
Moore, Charlie	82F	150	$ .01	$ .04	Morris, John	90F	254	$ .01	$ .03
Moore, Charlie	83F	42	$ .01	$ .04	Morrison, Jim	81F	357	$ .01	$ .04
Moore, Charlie	84F	209	$ .01	$ .06	Morrison, Jim	82F	354	$ .01	$ .04
Moore, Charlie	85F	589	$ .01	$ .05	Morrison, Jim	83F	313	$ .01	$ .04
Moore, Charlie	86F	496	$ .01*	$ .05	Morrison, Jim	84F	257	$ .01	$ .06
Moore, Charlie	87F	351	$ .01	$ .04	Morrison, Jim	85F	471	$ .01	$ .05
Moore, Donnie	84F	185	$ .01	$ .06	Morrison, Jim	86F	614	$ .01	$ .05

FLEER

Player	Year	No.	VG	EX/MT	Player	Year	No.	VG	EX/MT
Morrison, Jim	87F	614	$ .01	$ .04	Mumphrey, Jerry	82F	43	$ .01	$ .04
Morrison, Jim	88F	65	$ .01	$ .04	Mumphrey, Jerry	83F	389	$ .01	$ .04
Moseby, Lloyd	81F	421	$ .13	$ .75	Mumphrey, Jerry	84F	233	$ .01	$ .06
Moseby, Lloyd	82F	621	$ .01	$ .10	Mumphrey, Jerry	85F	354	$ .01	$ .05
					Mumphrey, Jerry	86F	306	$ .01	$ .05
					Mumphrey, Jerry	86FU	79	$ .01	$ .05
					Mumphrey, Jerry	87F	571	$ .01	$ .04
					Mumphrey, Jerry	88F	427	$ .01	$ .04
					Mura, Steve	81F	496	$ .01	$ .04
					Mura, Steve	82F	578	$ .01	$ .04
					Mura, Steve	83F	16	$ .01	$ .04
					Murcer, Bobby	81F	94	$ .01	$ .10
					Murcer, Bobby	82F	44	$ .01	$ .10
					Murcer, Bobby	83F	390	$ .01	$ .10
					Murphy, Dale	81F	243	$ .24	$1.20
					Murphy, Dale	82F	443	$ .25	$1.00
					Murphy, Dale	83F	142	$ .15	$1.00
					Murphy, Dale	84F	186	$ .13	$1.00
					Murphy, Dale	85F	335	$ .12	$ .60
					Murphy, Dale	86F	522	$ .07	$ .50
					Murphy, Dale	86F	635	$ .05	$ .30
					Murphy, Dale	86F	640	$ .04	$ .25
					Murphy, Dale	87F	522	$ .08	$ .40
					Murphy, Dale	88F	544	$ .01	$ .25
					Murphy, Dale	88F	639	$ .01	$ .15
					Murphy, Dale	89F	596	$ .01	$ .15
					Murphy, Dale	90F	591	$ .01	$ .05
					Murphy, Dale	90FPD	623	$ .01	$ .10
					Murphy, Dwayne	81F	590	$ .01	$ .04
					Murphy, Dwayne	82F	101	$ .01	$ .04
					Murphy, Dwayne	83F	528	$ .01	$ .04
					Murphy, Dwayne	84F	456	$ .01	$ .06
					Murphy, Dwayne	85F	432	$ .01	$ .05
					Murphy, Dwayne	86F	428	$ .01	$ .05
					Murphy, Dwayne	87F	400	$ .01	$ .04
					Murphy, Dwayne	88F	287	$ .01	$ .04
Moseby, Lloyd	83F	435	$ .01	$ .10	Murphy, Dwayne	90F	569	$ .01	$ .03
Moseby, Lloyd	84F	164	$ .03	$ .10	Murphy, Rob	87F	206	$ .05	$ .30
Moseby, Lloyd	85F	115	$ .03	$ .20	Murphy, Rob	88F	241	$ .01	$ .04
Moseby, Lloyd	85F	636	$ .01	$ .10	Murphy, Rob	89F	165	$ .01	$ .05
Moseby, Lloyd	86F	67	$ .01	$ .10	Murphy, Rob	89FU	10	$ .01	$ .05
Moseby, Lloyd	87F	236	$ .01	$ .04	Murphy, Rob	90F	281	$ .01	$ .03
Moseby, Lloyd	88F	119	$ .01	$ .10	Murray, Dale	83F	437	$ .01	$ .04
Moseby, Lloyd	89F	241	$ .01	$ .05	Murray, Dale	84F	134	$ .01	$ .06
Moseby, Lloyd	90F	90	$ .01	$ .03	Murray, Dale	85F	137	$ .01	$ .05
Moses, John	87F	592	$ .01	$ .04	Murray, Eddie	81F	184	$ .13	$1.00
Moses, John	88F	381	$ .01	$ .04	Murray, Eddie	82F	174	$ .10	$ .60
Moses, John	88FU	45	$ .01	$ .05	Murray, Eddie	83F	67	$ .10	$ .60
Moses, John	89F	121	$ .01	$ .05	Murray, Eddie	84F	14	$ .10	$ .60
Moses, John	90F	381	$ .01	$ .03	Murray, Eddie	85F	184	$ .10	$ .50
Moskau, Paul	81F	207	$ .01	$ .04	Murray, Eddie	86F	282	$ .06	$ .35
Moskau, Paul	82F	76	$ .01	$ .04	Murray, Eddie	87F	476	$ .05	$ .30
Mota, Manny	81F	141	$ .01	$ .04	Murray, Eddie	87F	636	$ .03	$ .20
Motley, Darryl	82F	417	$ .01	$ .04	Murray, Eddie	88F	567	$ .01	$ .15
Motley, Darryl	84FU	81	$ .01	$ .10	Murray, Eddie	89F	611	$ .01	$ .15
Motley, Darryl	85F	208	$ .01	$ .05	Murray, Eddie	89FU	92	$ .01	$ .15
Motley, Darryl	86F	16	$ .01	$ .05	Murray, Eddie	90F	404	$ .01	$ .10
Moyer, Jamie	87F	570	$ .01	$ .10	Murray, Rich	81F	452	$ .01	$ .04
Moyer, Jamie	88F	426	$ .01	$ .04	Musselman, Jeff	87FU	84	$ .04	$ .25
Moyer, Jamie	89F	432	$ .01	$ .05	Musselman, Jeff	88F	121	$ .01	$ .04
Moyer, Jamie	89FU	65	$ .01	$ .05	Musselman, Jeff	89F	243	$ .01	$ .05
Moyer, Jamie	90F	307	$ .01	$ .03	Musselman, Jeff	90F	212	$ .01	$ .03
Mulholland, Terry	89FU	111	$ .01	$ .05	Musselman, Ron	85FU	83	$ .01	$ .05
Mulholland, Terry	90F	568	$ .01	$ .03	Myers, Greg	88F	644	$ .01	$ .30
Mulliniks, Rance	81F	48	$ .01	$ .04	Myers, Randy	87FU	85	$ .01	$ .60
Mulliniks, Rance	82F	418	$ .01	$ .04	Myers, Randy	88F	146	$ .01	$ .35
Mulliniks, Rance	83F	436	$ .01	$ .04	Myers, Randy	89F	46	$ .01	$ .15
Mulliniks, Rance	84F	165	$ .01	$ .06	Myers, Randy	90F	213	$ .01	$ .03
Mulliniks, Rance	85F	116	$ .01	$ .05	Nahorodny, Bill	81F	254	$ .01	$ .04
Mulliniks, Rance	86F	68	$ .01	$ .05	Nahorodny, Bill	83F	416	$ .01	$ .04
Mulliniks, Rance	87F	237	$ .01	$ .04	Narron, Jerry	82F	513	$ .01	$ .04
Mulliniks, Rance	88F	120	$ .01	$ .04	Navarro, Jaime	89FU	39	$ .01	$ .35
Mulliniks, Rance	89F	242	$ .01	$ .05	Navarro, Jaime	90F	331	$ .01	$ .20
Mulliniks, Rance	90F	91	$ .01	$ .03	Nelson, Gene	82F	45	$ .01	$ .25
Mumphrey, Jerry	81F	494	$ .01	$ .04	Nelson, Gene	85F	522	$ .01	$ .05

FLEER

Lloyd Moseby
OUTFIELD

Player	Year	No.	VG	EX/MT	Player	Year	No.	VG	EX/MT
Nelson, Gene	86F	213	$ .01	$ .05	Nieves, Juan	88F	170	$ .01	$ .10
Nelson, Gene	87F	504	$ .01	$ .04	Nipper, Al	85F	165	$ .04	$ .25
Nelson, Gene	87FU	86	$ .01	$ .05	Nipper, Al	86F	356	$ .01	$ .05
Nelson, Gene	88F	288	$ .01	$ .04	Nipper, Al	87F	39	$ .01	$ .04
Nelson, Gene	89F	18	$ .01	$ .05	Nipper, Al	88F	358	$ .01	$ .04
Nelson, Gene	90F	17	$ .01	$ .03	Nipper, Al	89F	433	$ .01	$ .05
Nelson, Ricky	84F	615	$ .01	$ .06	Nixon, Donell	88F	382	$ .01	$ .15
Nelson, Rob	87F	653	$ .01	$ .04	Nixon, Donell	88FU	129	$ .01	$ .05
Nettles, Graig	81F	87	$ .09	$ .45	Nixon, Donell	89F	337	$ .01	$ .05
Nettles, Graig	82F	46	$ .03	$ .20	Nixon, Donell	90F	66	$ .01	$ .03
Nettles, Graig	83F	391	$ .01	$ .20	Nixon, Otis	86F	591	$ .01	$ .10
Nettles, Graig	84F	135	$ .03	$ .20	Nixon, Otis	87F	255	$ .01	$ .04
Nettles, Graig	84FU	82	$ .15	$1.25	Nixon, Otis	89F	387	$ .01	$ .05
Nettles, Graig	85F	42	$ .03	$ .20	Nixon, Otis	90F	356	$ .01	$ .03
Nettles, Graig	86F	332	$ .01	$ .10	Noca, Paul	88F	428	$ .01	$ .10
Nettles, Graig	87F	426	$ .01	$ .10	Nokes, Matt	87FU	90	$ .25	$ .50
Newell, Tom	88F	648	$ .01	$ .30	Nokes, Matt	88F	638	$ .01	$ .30
Newman, Al	86FU	80	$ .01	$ .05	Nokes, Matt	88F	66	$ .10	$ .50
Newman, Al	87F	327	$ .01	$ .04	Nokes, Matt	89F	140	$ .01	$ .10
Newman, Al	88F	17	$ .01	$ .04	Nokes, Matt	90F	611	$ .01	$ .03
Newman, Al	89F	122	$ .01	$ .05	Nolan, Joe	81F	212	$ .01	$ .04
Newman, Al	90F	382	$ .01	$ .03	Nolan, Joe	82F	77	$ .01	$ .04
Newman, Jeff	81F	577	$ .01	$ .04	Nolan, Joe	83F	68	$ .01	$ .04
Newman, Jeff	82F	102	$ .01	$ .04	Nolan, Joe	84F	15	$ .01	$ .06
Newman, Jeff	83F	529	$ .01	$ .04	Nolan, Joe	85F	185	$ .01	$ .05
Newman, Jeff	84F	404	$ .01	$ .06	Noles, Dickie	81F	12	$ .01	$ .04
Nichols, Carl	89F	612	$ .01	$ .15	Noles, Dickie	82F	253	$ .01	$ .04
Nichols, Reid	82F	300	$ .01	$ .04	Noles, Dickie	83F	504	$ .01	$ .04
Nichols, Reid	83F	189	$ .01	$ .04	Noles, Dickie	84F	500	$ .01	$ .06
Nichols, Reid	84F	405	$ .01	$ .06	Noles, Dickie	86F	567	$ .01	$ .05
Nichols, Reid	85F	164	$ .01	$ .05	Noles, Dickie	87F	256	$ .01	$ .04
Nichols, Reid	86F	214	$ .01	$ .05	Noles, Dickie	87FU	91	$ .01	$ .05
Nichols, Reid	87FU	89	$ .01	$ .05	Nolte, Eric	88F	593	$ .01	$ .15
Nichols, Reid	88F	191	$ .01	$ .04	Nordhagen, Wayne	81F	348	$ .01	$ .04
Nichols, Rod	90F	497	$ .01	$ .03	Nordhagen, Wayne	82F	355	$ .01	$ .04
Nicosia, Steve	81F	371	$ .01	$ .04	Nordhagen, Wayne	83F	438	$ .01	$ .04
Nicosia, Steve	82F	488	$ .01	$ .04	Norman, Dan	81F	337	$ .01	$ .04
Nicosia, Steve	83F	314	$ .01	$ .04	Norman, Dan	83F	289	$ .01	$ .04
Nicosia, Steve	85F	618	$ .01	$ .05	Norman, Fred	81F	158	$ .01	$ .04
Niedenfuer, Tom	82F	16	$ .05	$ .30	Norris, Jim	81F	634	$ .01	$ .04
Niedenfuer, Tom	83F	214	$ .01	$ .04	Norris, Mike	81F	573	$ .01	$ .04
Niedenfuer, Tom	84F	108	$ .01	$ .06	Norris, Mike	82F	103	$ .01	$ .04
Niedenfuer, Tom	85F	378	$ .01	$ .05	Norris, Mike	83F	530	$ .01	$ .04
Niedenfuer, Tom	86F	139	$ .01	$ .05	Norris, Mike	84F	457	$ .01	$ .06
Niedenfuer, Tom	87F	448	$ .01	$ .04	North, Bill	81F	441	$ .01	$ .04
Niedenfuer, Tom	88F	568	$ .01	$ .04	Nunez, Edwin	85F	496	$ .01	$ .05
Niedenfuer, Tom	89F	613	$ .01	$ .05	Nunez, Edwin	86F	470	$ .01	$ .05
Niekro, Joe	81F	54	$ .01	$ .10	Nunez, Edwin	87FU	92	$ .01	$ .05
Niekro, Joe	82F	221	$ .01	$ .10	Nunez, Edwin	88F	383	$ .01	$ .04
Niekro, Joe	83F	457	$ .01	$ .10	Nunez, Jose	87FU	93	$ .01	$ .10
Niekro, Joe	84F	234	$ .03	$ .10	Nunez, Jose	88F	122	$ .01	$ .15
Niekro, Joe	85F	355	$ .01	$ .10	O'Berry, Mike	82F	78	$ .01	$ .04
Niekro, Joe	87F	106	$ .01	$ .10	O'Brien, Charlie	90F	332	$ .01	$ .03
Niekro, Joe	87FU	87	$ .01	$ .10	O'Brien, Charlie	89F	194	$ .01	$ .05
Niekro, Joe	88F	18	$ .01	$ .10	O'Brien, Pete	89FU	29	$ .01	$ .05
Niekro, Phil	81F	242	$ .05	$ .30	O'Brien, Pete	90F	498	$ .01	$ .03
Niekro, Phil	82F	444	$ .05	$ .30	O'Brien, Pete	84F	423	$ .20	$1.25
Niekro, Phil	83F	143	$ .04	$ .25	O'Brien, Pete	85F	563	$ .03	$ .20
Niekro, Phil	84F	187	$ .04	$ .25	O'Brien, Pete	86F	568	$ .05	$ .20
Niekro, Phil	84FU	83	$ .30	$2.50	O'Brien, Pete	87F	132	$ .01	$ .10
Niekro, Phil	85F	138	$ .04	$ .25	O'Brien, Pete	88F	475	$ .01	$ .04
Niekro, Phil	86F	112	$ .03	$ .20	O'Brien, Pete	89F	529	$ .01	$ .05
Niekro, Phil	86F	630	$ .04	$ .25	O'Connor, Jack	82F	557	$ .01	$ .04
Niekro, Phil	86FU	81	$ .05	$ .30	O'Connor, Jack	83F	621	$ .01	$ .04
Niekro, Phil	87F	254	$ .03	$ .20	O'Malley, Tom	83F	271	$ .01	$ .04
Niekro, Phil	87F	626	$ .01	$ .10	O'Malley, Tom	84F	384	$ .01	$ .06
Nielson, Scott	89F	261	$ .01	$ .05	O'Malley, Tom	87F	477	$ .01	$ .04
Niemann, Randy	81F	77	$ .01	$ .04	O'Neal, Randy	85F	645	$ .75	$3.00
Niemann, Randy	86FU	82	$ .01	$ .05	O'Neal, Randy	86F	233	$ .01	$ .05
Niemann, Randy	87F	18	$ .01	$ .04	O'Neal, Randy	87F	159	$ .01	$ .04
Nieto, Tom	85F	235	$ .01	$ .05	O'Neill, Paul	90F	427	$ .01	$ .10
Nieto, Tom	86F	43	$ .01	$ .05	O'Neill, Paul	86F	646	$1.00	$4.50
Nieto, Tom	87FU	88	$ .01	$ .05	O'Neill, Paul	87FU	94	$ .05	$ .25
Nieves, Juan	86FU	83	$ .05	$ .30	O'Neill, Paul	88FU	85	$ .01	$ .15
Nieves, Juan	87F	352	$ .01	$ .10	O'Neill, Paul	89F	166	$ .01	$ .15

FLEER

Player	Year	No.	VG	EX/MT	Player	Year	No.	VG	EX/MT
Oates, Johnny	81F	99	$ .01	$ .04	Orsulak, Joe	88FU	2	$ .01	$ .05
Oates, Johnny	82F	47	$ .01	$ .04	Orsulak, Joe	89F	614	$ .01	$ .05
Oberkfell, Ken	81F	532	$ .01	$ .04	Orsulak, Joe	90F	185	$ .01	$ .03
Oberkfell, Ken	82F	123	$ .01	$ .04	Orta, Jorge	81F	388	$ .01	$ .04
Oberkfell, Ken	83F	17	$ .01	$ .04	Orta, Jorge	82F	376	$ .01	$ .04
Oberkfell, Ken	84F	330	$ .01	$ .06	Orta, Jorge	83F	215	$ .01	$ .04
Oberkfell, Ken	84FU	84	$ .01	$ .10	Orta, Jorge	84F	166	$ .01	$ .06
Oberkfell, Ken	85F	336	$ .01	$ .05	Orta, Jorge	84FU	86	$ .01	$ .10
Oberkfell, Ken	86F	523	$ .01	$ .05	Orta, Jorge	85F	209	$ .01	$ .05
Oberkfell, Ken	87F	523	$ .01	$ .04	Orta, Jorge	86F	17	$ .01	$ .05
Oberkfell, Ken	88F	545	$ .01	$ .04	Orta, Jorge	87F	376	$ .01	$ .04
Oberkfell, Ken	90F	67	$ .01	$ .03	Ortiz, Junior	84F	594	$ .01	$ .06
Oelkers, Bryan	87F	257	$ .01	$ .04	Ortiz, Junior	87F	616	$ .01	$ .04
Oester, Ron	81F	218	$ .01	$ .04	Ortiz, Junior	88F	335	$ .01	$ .04
Oester, Ron	82F	79	$ .01	$ .04	Ortiz, Junior	89F	215	$ .01	$ .05
Oester, Ron	83F	598	$ .01	$ .04	Ortiz, Junior	90F	475	$ .01	$ .03
Oester, Ron	84F	475	$ .01	$ .06	Orton, John	90F	647	$ .01	$ .03
Oester, Ron	85F	542	$ .01	$ .05	Otis, Amos	81F	32	$ .01	$ .10
Oester, Ron	86F	183	$ .01	$ .05	Otis, Amos	81F	483	$ .05	$ .30
Oester, Ron	87F	207	$ .01	$ .04	Otis, Amos	82F	419	$ .01	$ .04
Oester, Ron	88F	242	$ .01	$ .04	Otis, Amos	83F	120	$ .01	$ .04
Office, Rowland	81F	147	$ .01	$ .04	Otis, Amos	84F	351	$ .03	$ .10
Office, Rowland	82F	198	$ .01	$ .04	Otis, Amos	84FU	87	$ .01	$ .10
Oglivie, Ben	81F	508	$ .01	$ .04	Ott, Ed	81F	365	$ .01	$ .04
Oglivie, Ben	82F	151	$ .01	$ .04	Ott, Ed	82F	470	$ .01	$ .04
Oglivie, Ben	83F	43	$ .01	$ .04	Ott, Ed	83F	98	$ .01	$ .04
Oglivie, Ben	83F	640	$ .04	$ .25	Dave Otto	88F	652	$ .30	$1.25
Oglivie, Ben	84F	210	$ .01	$ .06	Owchinko, Bob	82F	104	$ .01	$ .04
Oglivie, Ben	85F	590	$ .01	$ .05	Owchinko, Bob	83F	531	$ .01	$ .04
Oglivie, Ben	86F	497	$ .01	$ .05	Owchinko, Bob	84FU	88	$ .01	$ .10
Oglivie, Ben	87F	353	$ .01	$ .04	Owchinko, Bob	85F	543	$ .01	$ .05
Ojeda, Bob	82F	301	$ .15	$ .75	Owen, Spike	84F	616	$ .10	$ .45
Ojeda, Bob	83F	190	$ .01	$ .10	Owen, Spike	85F	497	$ .01	$ .05
Ojeda, Bob	84F	406	$ .01	$ .06	Owen, Spike	86F	471	$ .01	$ .05
Ojeda, Bob	85F	166	$ .01	$ .05	Owen, Spike	87F	40	$ .01	$ .04
Ojeda, Bob	86F	357	$ .01	$ .05	Owen, Spike	88F	359	$ .01	$ .04
Ojeda, Bob	86FU	84	$ .01	$ .05	Owen, Spike	89F	93	$ .01	$ .05
Ojeda, Bob	87F	19	$ .01	$ .04	Owen, Spike	89FU	98	$ .01	$ .05
Ojeda, Bob	88F	147	$ .01	$ .10	Owen, Spike	90F	357	$ .01	$ .03
Ojeda, Bob	89F	47	$ .01	$ .05	Owens, Paul	84F	643	$ .01	$ .06
Ojeda, Bob	90F	214	$ .01	$ .03	Ownbey, Rick	83F	551	$ .01	$ .04
Olin, Steve	90F	499	$ .01	$ .10	Ownbey, Rick	86FU	85	$ .01	$ .05
Oliver, Al	81F	626	$ .01	$ .10	Pacella, John	83F	622	$ .01	$ .04
Oliver, Al	82F	326	$ .01	$ .10	Paciorek, Jim	87FU	95	$ .01	$ .05
Oliver, Al	83F	290	$ .01	$ .10	Paciorek, Tom	81F	614	$ .01	$ .04
Oliver, Al	84F	280	$ .03	$ .10	Paciorek, Tom	82F	514	$ .01	$ .04
Oliver, Al	84F	632	$ .01	$ .06	Paciorek, Tom	83F	248	$ .01	$ .04
Oliver, Al	84FU	85	$ .08	$ .40	Paciorek, Tom	84F	70	$ .01	$ .06
Oliver, Al	85F	262	$ .01	$ .10	Paciorek, Tom	85F	523	$ .01	$ .05
Oliver, Al	85FU	84	$ .03	$ .20	Paciorek, Tom	86F	91	$ .01	$ .05
Oliver, Al	86F	69	$ .01	$ .10	Paciorek, Tom	86FU	86	$ .01	$ .05
Oliver, Joe	90F	426	$ .01	$ .25	Paciorek, Tom	87F	133	$ .01	$ .04
Olson, Gregg	90F	184	$ .01	$ .25	Page, Mitchell	81F	580	$ .01	$ .04
Olwine, Ed	87F	524	$ .01	$ .10	Page, Mitchell	82F	105	$ .01	$ .04
Ontiveros, Steve	86F	429	$ .03	$ .20	Pagliarulo, Mike	85F	139	$ .25	$1.00
Ontiveros, Steve	87F	401	$ .01	$ .04	Pagliarulo, Mike	86F	113	$ .04	$ .25
Ontiveros, Steve	88F	289	$ .01	$ .04	Pagliarulo, Mike	87F	107	$ .01	$ .10
Oquendo, Jose	84F	592	$ .03	$ .65	Pagliarulo, Mike	88F	216	$ .01	$ .10
Oquendo, Jose	85F	88	$ .01	$ .10	Pagliarulo, Mike	89F	262	$ .01	$ .05
Oquendo, Jose	87F	305	$ .01	$ .04	Pagliarulo, Mike	90F	163	$ .01	$ .03
Oquendo, Jose	88F	44	$ .01	$ .04	Palacios, Robert	89F	648	$ .01	$ .25
Oquendo, Jose	89F	459	$ .01	$ .05	Palacios, Vicente	88F	336	$ .01	$ .15
Oquendo, Jose	90F	255	$ .01	$ .03	Palacios, Vicente	89F	216	$ .01	$ .05
Orosco, Jesse	83F	550	$ .01	$ .10	Pall, Donn	89F	505	$ .01	$ .05
Orosco, Jesse	84F	593	$ .01	$ .06	Pall, Donn	90F	543	$ .01	$ .03
Orosco, Jesse	85F	89	$ .01	$ .05	Palmeiro, Rafael	88F	429	$ .25	$ .50
Orosco, Jesse	86F	90	$ .01	$ .05	Palmeiro, Rafael	89F	434	$ .01	$ .15
Orosco, Jesse	87F	20	$ .01	$ .04	Palmeiro, Rafael	89F	631	$ .05	$ .40
Orosco, Jesse	88F	148	$ .01	$ .04	Palmeiro, Rafael	89FU	66	$ .01	$ .10
Orosco, Jesse	88FU	96	$ .01	$ .05	Palmeiro, Rafael	90F	308	$ .01	$ .03
Orosco, Jesse	89F	68	$ .01	$ .05	Palmer, Dave 'David'	81F	160	$ .01	$ .04
Orosco, Jesse	90F	500	$ .01	$ .03	Palmer, David	82F	199	$ .01	$ .04
Orsulak, Joe	85FU	85	$ .03	$ .20	Palmer, David	83F	291	$ .01	$ .04
Orsulak, Joe	86F	615	$ .01	$ .10	Palmer, David	85F	404	$ .01	$ .15
Orsulak, Joe	87F	615	$ .01	$ .04	Palmer, David	85F	643	$ .01	$ .10

Player	Year	No.	VG	EX/MT	Player	Year	No.	VG	EX/MT
Palmer, David	86F	255	$ .01	$ .05	Parrish, Lance	82F	276	$ .04	$ .25
Palmer, David	86FU	87	$ .01	$ .05	Parrish, Lance	83F	337	$ .04	$ .25
Palmer, David	87F	525	$ .01	$ .04	Parrish, Lance	84F	637	$ .01	$ .06
Palmer, David	88F	546	$ .01	$ .04	Parrish, Lance	84F	88	$ .03	$ .20
Palmer, David	88FU	111	$ .01	$ .05	Parrish, Lance	85F	19	$ .04	$ .20
Palmer, David	89F	577	$ .01	$ .05	Parrish, Lance	86F	234	$ .03	$ .20
Palmer, Jim	81F	169	$ .06	$1.00	Parrish, Lance	87F	160	$ .03	$ .20
Palmer, Jim	82F	175	$ .05	$ .75	Parrish, Lance	87FU	96	$ .01	$ .05
Palmer, Jim	83F	69	$ .05	$ .75	Parrish, Lance	88F	310	$ .01	$ .10
Palmer, Jim	84F	16	$ .05	$1.00	Parrish, Lance	89F	578	$ .01	$ .05
Pankovits, Jim	86F	307	$ .01	$ .05	Parrish, Lance	89FU	15	$ .01	$ .05
Pankovits, Jim	87F	64	$ .01	$ .04	Parrish, Lance	90F	141	$ .01	$ .10
Pankovits, Jim	89F	363	$ .01	$ .05	Parrish, Larry	81F	146	$ .01	$ .10
Papi, Stan	81F	480	$ .01	$ .10	Parrish, Larry	82F	200	$ .01	$ .10
Papi, Stan	82F	280	$ .01	$ .04	Parrish, Larry	83F	574	$ .01	$ .04
Paredes, Johnny	89F	388	$ .01	$ .10	Parrish, Larry	84F	424	$ .01	$ .06
Parent, Mark	88FU	125	$ .01	$ .15	Parrish, Larry	85F	564	$ .01	$ .05
Parent, Mark	89FU	125	$ .01	$ .05	Parrish, Larry	86F	569	$ .01	$ .05
Parent, Mark	90F	164	$ .01	$ .03	Parrish, Larry	87F	134	$ .01	$ .04
					Parrish, Larry	88F	476	$ .01	$ .04
					Parrish, Larry	88FU	7	$ .01	$ .05
					Parrish, Larry	89F	94	$ .01	$ .05
					Parsons, Casey	82F	515	$ .01	$ .04
					Pashnick, Larry	83F	338	$ .01	$ .04
					Pasqua, Dan	85FU	86	$ .10	$ .50
					Pasqua, Dan	86F	114	$ .03	$ .20
					Pasqua, Dan	87F	108	$ .01	$ .10
					Pasqua, Dan	88F	217	$ .01	$ .10
					Pasqua, Dan	88FU	18	$ .01	$ .05
					Pasqua, Dan	89F	507	$ .01	$ .05
					Pasqua, Dan	90F	544	$ .01	$ .03
					Pastore, Frank	81F	204	$ .01	$ .04
					Pastore, Frank	82F	80	$ .01	$ .04
					Pastore, Frank	83F	599	$ .01	$ .04
					Pastore, Frank	84F	477	$ .01	$ .06
					Pastore, Frank	85F	545	$ .01	$ .05
					Pastore, Frank	86F	185	$ .01	$ .05
					Patek, Fred	81F	283	$ .01	$ .04
					Patek, Fred	82F	471	$ .01	$ .04
					Patterson, Bob	88F	337	$ .01	$ .10
					Patterson, Ken	89F	508	$ .01	$ .05
					Patterson, Ken	90F	545	$ .01	$ .10
					Patterson, Reggie	86F	376	$ .01	$ .05
					Pattin, Marty	81F	37	$ .01	$ .04
					Paxton, Mike	81F	401	$ .01	$ .04
					Pecota, Bill	87FU	97	$ .04	$ .25
					Pecota, Bill	88F	264	$ .01	$ .15
					Pecota, Bill	89F	289	$ .01	$ .05
					Pedrique, Al	88F	338	$ .01	$ .15
					Pena, Alejandro	84F	100	$ .03	$ .10

Kelly Paris
INFIELD

Player	Year	No.	VG	EX/MT	Player	Year	No.	VG	EX/MT
Paris, Kelly	84F	476	$ .01	$ .06	Pena, Alejandro	85F	379	$ .01	$ .05
Paris, Kelly	89F	506	$ .01	$ .05	Pena, Alejandro	86F	140	$ .01	$ .05
Parker, Clay	88F	649	$ .01	$ .25	Pena, Alejandro	87F	449	$ .01	$ .04
Parker, Clay	90F	451	$ .01	$ .03	Pena, Alejandro	88FU	97	$ .01	$ .05
Parker, Dave	81F	360	$ .07	$ .50	Pena, Alejandro	89F	69	$ .01	$ .05
Parker, Dave	82F	489	$ .05	$ .30	Pena, Aljandro	90F	405	$ .01	$ .03
Parker, Dave	82F	638	$ .05	$ .30	Pena, Hipolito	89F	263	$ .01	$ .10
Parker, Dave	83F	315	$ .05	$ .30	Pena, Tony	82F	490	$ .05	$ .30
Parker, Dave	84F	258	$ .04	$ .25	Pena, Tony	83F	316	$ .04	$ .20
Parker, Dave	84FU	89	$ .25	$1.00	Pena, Tony	84F	259	$ .03	$ .20
Parker, Dave	85F	544	$ .05	$ .30	Pena, Tony	85F	472	$ .01	$ .10
Parker, Dave	86F	184	$ .04	$ .25	Pena, Tony	86F	616	$ .01	$ .10
Parker, Dave	86F	640	$ .04	$ .25	Pena, Tony	87F	617	$ .01	$ .10
Parker, Dave	87F	208	$ .03	$ .20	Pena, Tony	87FU	98	$ .01	$ .05
Parker, Dave	87F	639	$ .01	$ .10	Pena, Tony	88F	45	$ .01	$ .10
Parker, Dave	88F	243	$ .01	$ .15	Pena, Tony	89F	460	$ .01	$ .05
Parker, Dave	88FU	55	$ .01	$ .05	Pena, Tony	90F	256	$ .01	$ .03
Parker, Dave	89F	19	$ .01	$ .05	Pendleton, Terry	85F	236	$ .10	$ .50
Parker, Dave	90F	18	$ .01	$ .10	Pendleton, Terry	86F	44	$ .01	$ .05
Parrett, Jeff	86FU	88	$ .05	$ .30	Pendleton, Terry	87F	306	$ .01	$ .04
Parrett, Jeff	88FU	102	$ .01	$ .15	Pendleton, Terry	88F	46	$ .01	$ .04
Parrett, Jeff	89F	389	$ .01	$ .15	Pendleton, Terry	89F	461	$ .01	$ .05
Parrett, Jeff	89FU	112	$ .01	$ .05	Pendleton, Terry	90F	257	$ .01	$ .03
Parrett, Jeff	90F	570	$ .01	$ .03	Peraza, Oswaldo	89F	615	$ .01	$ .15
Parrish, Lance	81F	467	$ .04	$ .25	Perconte, Jack	83F	417	$ .01	$ .04

FLEER

Player	Year	No.	VG	EX/MT	Player	Year	No.	VG	EX/MT
Perconte, Jack	84FU	90	$ .01	$ .10	Pettis, Gary	88FU	29	$ .01	$ .05
Perconte, Jack	85F	498	$ .01	$ .05	Pettis, Gary	89F	141	$ .01	$ .05
Perconte, Jack	86F	472	$ .01	$ .05	Pettis, Gary	90F	612	$ .01	$ .03
Perez, Melido	88F	265	$ .01	$ .30	Phelps, Ken	82F	420	$ .04	$ .25
Perez, Melido	88FU	19	$ .01	$ .15	Phelps, Ken	85F	499	$ .01	$ .05
Perez, Melido	89F	509	$ .01	$ .15	Phelps, Ken	87F	593	$ .01	$ .04
Perez, Melido	90F	546	$ .01	$ .03	Phelps, Ken	88F	384	$ .01	$ .04
Perez, Pascual	82F	491	$ .05	$ .30	Phelps, Ken	89F	264	$ .01	$ .05
Perez, Pascual	83F	144	$ .01	$ .04	Phillips, Mike	81F	538	$ .01	$ .04
Perez, Pascual	84F	188	$ .01	$ .06	Phillips, Mike	82F	201	$ .01	$ .04
Perez, Pascual	86F	524	$ .01	$ .05	Phillips, Tony	84F	459	$ .01	$ .06
Perez, Pascual	88F	192	$ .01	$ .04	Phillips, Tony	85F	433	$ .01	$ .05
Perez, Pascual	89F	390	$ .01	$ .05	Phillips, Tony	86F	430	$ .01	$ .05
Perez, Pascual	90F	358	$ .01	$ .03	Phillips, Tony	87F	402	$ .01	$ .04
Perez, Tony	81F	241	$ .05	$ .30	Phillips, Tony	88F	290	$ .01	$ .04
Perez, Tony	82F	302	$ .04	$ .25	Phillips, Tony	89FU	56	$ .01	$ .05
Perez, Tony	83F	191	$ .04	$ .25	Phillips, Tony	90F	19	$ .01	$ .03
Perez, Tony	84F	44	$ .04	$ .25	Picciolo, Rob	81F	582	$ .01	$ .04
Perez, Tony	84F	636	$ .10	$ .50	Picciolo, Rob	82F	106	$ .01	$ .04
Perez, Tony	84FU	91	$ .10	$1.50	Pico, Jeff	88FU	80	$ .01	$ .15
Perez, Tony	85F	546	$ .03	$ .20	Pico, Jeff	89F	436	$ .01	$ .15
Perez, Tony	86F	186	$ .03	$ .20	Pico, Jeff	90F	39	$ .01	$ .03
Perez, Tony	87F	209	$ .03	$ .20	Piniella, Lou	81F	85	$ .01	$ .10
Perezchica, Tony	89F	338	$ .01	$ .05	Piniella, Lou	82F	48	$ .01	$ .10
Perkins, Broderick	81F	498	$ .01	$ .04	Piniella, Lou	83F	392	$ .01	$ .10
Perkins, Broderick	82F	579	$ .01	$ .04	Piniella, Lou	84F	136	$ .01	$ .06
Perkins, Broderick	83F	368	$ .01	$ .04	Pittaro, Chris	85FU	87	$ .01	$ .05
Perkins, Broderick	84F	548	$ .01	$ .06	Pittman, Joe	82F	222	$ .01	$ .04
Perlman, Jon	88F	93	$ .01	$ .10	Pittman, Joe	83F	369	$ .01	$ .04
Perlman, Jon	88FU	22	$ .01	$ .05	Plesac, Dan	86FU	90	$ .05	$ .30
Perry, Gaylord	81F	91	$ .04	$ .25	Plesac, Dan	87F	354	$ .06	$ .50
Perry, Gaylord	82F	445	$ .05	$ .30	Plesac, Dan	88F	171	$ .01	$ .10
Perry, Gaylord	83F	483	$ .03	$ .20	Plesac, Dan	88F	625	$ .01	$ .04
Perry, Gaylord	83F	630	$ .01	$ .10	Plesac, Dan	89F	195	$ .01	$ .05
Perry, Gaylord	84F	352	$ .03	$ .20	Plesac, Dan	90F	334	$ .01	$ .03
Perry, Gaylord	84F	638	$ .01	$ .25	Plunk, Eric	86F	649	$10.00	$40.00
Perry, Gaylord	84F	641	$ .01	$ .10	Plunk, Eric	87F	403	$ .01	$ .04
Perry, Gerald	84FU	92	$ .25	$1.50	Plunk, Eric	88F	291	$ .01	$ .04
Perry, Gerald	85F	338	$ .01	$ .10	Plunk, Eric	89F	20	$ .01	$ .05
Perry, Gerald	86F	525	$ .01	$ .05	Plunk, Eric	90F	452	$ .01	$ .03
Perry, Gerald	88F	547	$ .01	$ .04	Pocoroba, Biff	81F	257	$ .01	$ .04
Perry, Gerald	89F	597	$ .01	$ .05	Pocoroba, Biff	82F	446	$ .01	$ .04
Perry, Gerald	89F	638	$ .01	$ .05	Pocoroba, Biff	83F	145	$ .01	$ .04
Perry, Gerald	90F	592	$ .01	$ .03	Pocoroba, Biff	84F	189	$ .01	$ .06
Perry, Pat	86FU	89	$ .01	$ .10	Polidor, Gus	86F	650	$ .03	$ .20
Perry, Pat	87F	307	$ .01	$ .04	Polidor, Gus	88F	501	$ .01	$ .04
Perry, Pat	88F	244	$ .01	$ .04	Polonia, Luis	87FU	99	$ .06	$ .35
Perry, Pat	89F	435	$ .01	$ .05	Polonia, Luis	88F	292	$ .01	$ .15
Peterek, Jeff	90F	333	$ .01	$ .10	Polonia, Luis	89F	21	$ .01	$ .05
Peters, Rick	81F	470	$ .01	$ .04	Porter, Chuck	84F	211	$ .01	$ .06
Peters, Rick	82F	277	$ .01	$ .04	Porter, Chuck	85F	591	$ .01	$ .05
Peters, Ricky	84F	458	$ .01	$ .06	Porter, Darrell	81F	36	$ .01	$ .04
Peters, Steve	89F	462	$ .01	$ .05	Porter, Darrell	82F	124	$ .01	$ .04
Peterson, Adam	88F	646	$ .01	$ .20	Porter, Darrell	83F	18	$ .01	$ .04
Petralli, Gene	83F	439	$ .01	$ .15	Porter, Darrell	84F	331	$ .01	$ .06
Petralli, Geno	87F	135	$ .01	$ .04	Porter, Darrell	85F	237	$ .01	$ .05
Petralli, Geno	88F	477	$ .01	$ .04	Porter, Darrell	85F	337	$ .01	$ .05
Petralli, Geno	89F	530	$ .01	$ .05	Porter, Darrell	86F	45	$ .01	$ .05
Petralli, Geno	90F	309	$ .01	$ .03	Porter, Darrell	86FU	91	$ .01	$ .05
Petry, Dan	81F	468	$ .01	$ .10	Porter, Darrell	87F	136	$ .01	$ .04
Petry, Dan	82F	278	$ .01	$ .10	Portugal, Mark	87F	548	$ .01	$ .04
Petry, Dan	83F	339	$ .01	$ .10	Portugal, Mark	89F	123	$ .01	$ .05
Petry, Dan	84F	89	$ .01	$ .06	Pounders, Brad	89F	642	$ .01	$ .25
Petry, Dan	85F	20	$ .01	$ .05	Powell, Dennis	87F	450	$ .01	$ .04
Petry, Dan	86F	235	$ .01	$ .10	Powell, Dennis	89FU	61	$ .01	$ .05
Petry, Dan	87F	161	$ .01	$ .04	Powell, Dennis	90F	521	$ .01	$ .03
Petry, Dan	88F	67	$ .01	$ .04	Powell, Hosken	81F	559	$ .01	$ .04
Petry, Dan	89F	486	$ .01	$ .05	Powell, Hosken	82F	558	$ .01	$ .04
Petry, Dan	90F	142	$ .01	$ .03	Powell, Hosken	83F	440	$ .01	$ .04
Pettini, Joe	81F	453	$ .01	$ .04	Power, Ted	82F	17	$ .05	$ .30
Pettini, Joe	82F	398	$ .01	$ .04	Power, Ted	84F	478	$ .01	$ .06
Pettis, Gary	84F	526	$ .07	$ .50	Power, Ted	85F	547	$ .01	$ .05
Pettis, Gary	85F	308	$ .01	$ .05	Power, Ted	86F	187	$ .01	$ .05
Pettis, Gary	86F	165	$ .01	$ .05	Power, Ted	87F	210	$ .01	$ .04
Pettis, Gary	87F	90	$ .01	$ .04	Power, Ted	88F	245	$ .01	$ .04

Player	Year	No.	VG	EX/MT
Power, Ted	88FU	33	$ .01	$ .05
Power, Ted	89F	142	$ .01	$ .05
Power, Ted	90F	258	$ .01	$ .03
Presley, Jim	85F	500	$ .15	$ .75
Presley, Jim	86F	473	$ .04	$ .25
Presley, Jim	87F	594	$ .01	$ .10
Presley, Jim	88F	385	$ .01	$ .10
Presley, Jim	89F	555	$ .01	$ .05
Presley, Jim	90F	522	$ .01	$ .03
Price, Joe	81F	210	$ .01	$ .04
Price, Joe	82F	81	$ .01	$ .04
Price, Joe	83F	600	$ .01	$ .04
Price, Joe	84F	479	$ .01	$ .06
Price, Joe	85F	548	$ .01	$ .05
Price, Joe	86F	188	$ .01	$ .05
Price, Joe	87F	211	$ .01	$ .04
Price, Joe	89F	339	$ .01	$ .05
Price, Joe	90F	282	$ .01	$ .03
Prince, Tom	89F	217	$ .01	$ .05
Proly, Mike	81F	358	$ .01	$ .04
Proly, Mike	82F	254	$ .01	$ .04
Proly, Mike	83F	505	$ .01	$ .04
Proly, Mike	84F	501	$ .01	$ .06
Pryor, Greg	81F	359	$ .01	$ .04
Pryor, Greg	82F	356	$ .01	$ .04
Pryor, Greg	83F	121	$ .01	$ .04
Pryor, Greg	84F	353	$ .01	$ .06
Pryor, Greg	85F	210	$ .01	$ .05
Puckett, Kirby	84FU	93	$15.00	$110.00
Puckett, Kirby	85F	286	$5.00	$18.00
Puckett, Kirby	86F	401	$1.00	$4.00
Puckett, Kirby	87F	549	$ .50	$2.00
Puckett, Kirby	87F	633	$ .25	$ .75
Puckett, Kirby	88F	19	$ .01	$ .50
Puckett, Kirby	88F	638	$ .25	$ .75
Puckett, Kirby	89F	124	$ .01	$ .35
Puckett, Kirby	89F	639	$ .01	$ .25
Puckett, Kirby	90F	383	$ .01	$ .25

HUMAN DYNAMOS — KIRBY PUCKETT / BO JACKSON

Player	Year	No.	VG	EX/MT
Puckett, Kirby	90F	635	$ .01	$ .03
Puhl, Terry	81F	62	$ .01	$ .04
Puhl, Terry	82F	223	$ .01	$ .04
Puhl, Terry	83F	458	$ .01	$ .04
Puhl, Terry	84F	235	$ .01	$ .06

Player	Year	No.	VG	EX/MT
Puhl, Terry	85F	356	$ .01	$ .05
Puhl, Terry	86F	308	$ .01	$ .05
Puhl, Terry	87F	65	$ .01	$ .04
Puhl, Terry	88FU	90	$ .01	$ .05
Puhl, Terry	89F	364	$ .01	$ .05
Puhl, Terry	90F	233	$ .01	$ .03
Pujols, Luis	81F	68	$ .01	$ .04
Pujols, Luis	82F	224	$ .01	$ .04
Pujols, Luis	83F	459	$ .01	$ .04
Pujols, Luis	84F	236	$ .01	$ .06
Puleo, Charlie	83F	552	$ .01	$ .04
Puleo, Charlie	84F	480	$ .01	$ .06
Puleo, Charlie	88F	548	$ .01	$ .04
Puleo, Charlie	89F	598	$ .01	$ .05
Putnam, Pat	81F	630	$ .01	$ .04
Putnam, Pat	82F	327	$ .01	$ .04
Putnam, Pat	84F	617	$ .01	$ .06
Putnam, Pat	85F	287	$ .01	$ .05
Quinones (z), Rey	86FU	93	$ .05	$ .30
Quinones, Luis	86FU	92	$ .01	$ .05
Quinones, Luis	90F	428	$ .01	$ .03
Quinones, Rey	87F	595	$ .04	$ .25
Quinones, Rey	88F	386	$ .01	$ .04
Quinones, Rey	89F	556	$ .01	$ .05
Quintana, Carlos	89F	95	$ .01	$ .35
Quintana, Carlos	90F	283	$ .01	$ .10
Quirk, Jamie	81F	50	$ .01	$ .04
Quirk, Jamie	82F	421	$ .01	$ .04
Quirk, Jamie	84F	332	$ .01	$ .06
Quirk, Jamie	87F	377	$ .01	$ .04
Quirk, Jamie	88F	266	$ .01	$ .04
Quirk, Jamie	89F	290	$ .01	$ .05
Quisenberry, Dan	81F	31	$ .03	$ .20
Quisenberry, Dan	82F	422	$ .03	$ .20
Quisenberry, Dan	83F	122	$ .03	$ .20
Quisenberry, Dan	84F	354	$ .03	$ .20
Quisenberry, Dan	84F	635	$ .01	$ .06
Quisenberry, Dan	85F	211	$ .03	$ .20
Quisenberry, Dan	86F	18	$ .03	$ .20
Quisenberry, Dan	87F	378	$ .01	$ .10
Quisenberry, Dan	88F	267	$ .01	$ .10
Quisenberry, Dan	89FU	120	$ .01	$ .05
Quisenberry, Dan	90F	259	$ .01	$ .03
Raines, Tim	82F	202	$ .15	$ .75
Raines, Tim	83F	292	$ .05	$ .30
Raines, Tim	84F	281	$ .06	$ .35
Raines, Tim	84F	631	$ .04	$ .25
Raines, Tim	85F	405	$ .06	$ .35
Raines, Tim	86F	256	$ .05	$ .30
Raines, Tim	86F	632	$ .05	$ .30
Raines, Tim	87F	328	$ .05	$ .30
Raines, Tim	87F	642	$ .01	$ .04
Raines, Tim	88F	193	$ .01	$ .15
Raines, Tim	88F	631	$ .01	$ .10
Raines, Tim	89F	391	$ .01	$ .15
Raines, Tim	90F	359	$ .01	$ .03
Rainey, Chuck	82F	303	$ .01	$ .04
Rainey, Chuck	83F	192	$ .01	$ .04
Rainey, Chuck	84F	502	$ .01	$ .06
Rajsich, Gary	83F	553	$ .01	$ .04
Ramirez, Mario	84F	309	$ .01	$ .06
Ramirez, Rafael	81F	266	$ .04	$ .25
Ramirez, Rafael	82F	447	$ .01	$ .04
Ramirez, Rafael	83F	146	$ .01	$ .04
Ramirez, Rafael	84F	190	$ .01	$ .06
Ramirez, Rafael	85F	339	$ .01	$ .05
Ramirez, Rafael	86F	526	$ .01	$ .05
Ramirez, Rafael	87F	526	$ .01	$ .04
Ramirez, Rafael	88FU	91	$ .01	$ .05
Ramirez, Rafael	89F	365	$ .01	$ .05
Ramirez, Rafael	90F	234	$ .01	$ .03
Ramos, Bobby	82F	203	$ .01	$ .04
Ramos, Bobby	84F	282	$ .01	$ .06
Ramos, Bobby 'Roberto'	81F	162	$ .01	$ .04
Ramos, Domingo	88FU	23	$ .01	$ .05

Player	Year	No.	VG	EX/MT	Player	Year	No.	VG	EX/MT
Ramsey, Mike	81F	549	$ .01	$ .04	Ray, Johnny	87F	618	$ .01	$ .10
Ramsey, Mike	82F	125	$ .01	$ .04	Ray, Johnny	88F	502	$ .01	$ .10
					Ray, Johnny	89F	487	$ .01	$ .05
					Ray, Johnny	90F	143	$ .01	$ .03
					Rayford, Floyd	84F	334	$ .01	$ .06
					Rayford, Floyd	84FU	95	$ .01	$ .10
					Rayford, Floyd	85F	186	$ .01	$ .05
					Rayford, Floyd	86F	283	$ .01	$ .05
					Ready, Randy	85F	592	$ .03	$ .20
					Ready, Randy	86F	498	$ .01	$ .05
					Ready, Randy	87FU	100	$ .01	$ .05
					Ready, Randy	88F	594	$ .01	$ .04
					Ready, Randy	89F	315	$ .01	$ .15
					Ready, Randy	90F	571	$ .01	$ .03
					Reardon, Jeff	81F	335	$ .10	$1.25
					Reardon, Jeff	82F	204	$ .03	$ .20
					Reardon, Jeff	83F	293	$ .01	$ .10
					Reardon, Jeff	84F	283	$ .01	$ .10
					Reardon, Jeff	85F	407	$ .01	$ .10
					Reardon, Jeff	86F	257	$ .01	$ .10
					Reardon, Jeff	87F	329	$ .01	$ .10
					Reardon, Jeff	87FU	101	$ .01	$ .10
					Reardon, Jeff	88F	20	$ .01	$ .10
					Reardon, Jeff	89F	125	$ .01	$ .05
					Reardon, Jeff	90F	385	$ .01	$ .03
					Redfern, Pete	81F	560	$ .01	$ .04
					Redfern, Pete	82F	559	$ .01	$ .04
					Redfern, Pete	83F	623	$ .01	$ .04
					Redus, Gary	84F	481	$ .04	$ .25
					Redus, Gary	85F	549	$ .01	$ .05
					Redus, Gary	86F	189	$ .01	$ .05
					Redus, Gary	86FU	94	$ .01	$ .05
					Redus, Gary	87F	181	$ .01	$ .04
					Redus, Gary	87FU	102	$ .01	$ .05
Ramsey, Mike	83F	19	$ .01	$ .04	Redus, Gary	88F	408	$ .01	$ .04
Ramsey, Mike	84F	333	$ .01	$ .06	Redus, Gary	89F	218	$ .01	$ .05
Ramsey, Mike	85F	406	$ .01	$ .05	Redus, Gary	90F	476	$ .01	$ .03
Randle, Lenny	81F	301	$ .01	$ .04	Reed, Jeff	86FU	95	$ .01	$ .05
Randle, Lenny	82F	516	$ .01	$ .04	Reed, Jeff	87F	550	$ .01	$ .04
Randolph, Willie	81F	109	$ .01	$ .10	Reed, Jeff	88F	194	$ .01	$ .04
Randolph, Willie	82F	49	$ .01	$ .04	Reed, Jeff	89F	167	$ .01	$ .05
Randolph, Willie	83F	393	$ .01	$ .04	Reed, Jeff	90F	429	$ .01	$ .05
Randolph, Willie	84F	137	$ .01	$ .06	Reed, Jerry	86F	592	$ .01	$ .05
Randolph, Willie	85F	140	$ .01	$ .05	Reed, Jerry	88F	387	$ .01	$ .04
Randolph, Willie	86F	115	$ .01	$ .05	Reed, Jerry	89F	557	$ .01	$ .05
Randolph, Willie	87F	109	$ .01	$ .04	Reed, Jerry	90F	523	$ .01	$ .03
Randolph, Willie	88F	218	$ .01	$ .04	Reed, Jody	89F	96	$ .01	$ .05
Randolph, Willie	89F	265	$ .01	$ .05	Reed, Jody	90F	284	$ .01	$ .03
Randolph, Willie	89FU	93	$ .01	$ .05	Reed, Joey	88F	360	$ .01	$ .25
Randolph, Willie	90F	406	$ .01	$ .03	Reed, Rick	90F	477	$ .01	$ .10
Rasmussen, Dennis	85F	141	$ .03	$ .20	Reed, Ron	81F	11	$ .01	$ .04
Rasmussen, Dennis	87F	110	$ .01	$ .04	Reed, Ron	82F	255	$ .01	$ .04
Rasmussen, Dennis	88F	246	$ .01	$ .04	Reed, Ron	83F	169	$ .01	$ .04
Rasmussen, Dennis	88FU	126	$ .01	$ .05	Reed, Ron	84F	45	$ .01	$ .06
Rasmussen, Dennis	89F	314	$ .01	$ .05	Reed, Ron	84FU	96	$ .04	$ .25
Rasmussen, Dennis	90F	165	$ .01	$ .03	Reed, Ron	85F	524	$ .01	$ .05
Rasmussen, Eric	81F	497	$ .01	$ .04	Reid, Jessie	88F	643	$ .01	$ .25
Rau, Doug	81F	133	$ .01	$ .04	Reimer, Kevin	89F	641	$ .01	$ .05
Rawley, Shane	82F	517	$ .01	$ .10	Reimer, Kevin	90F	310	$ .01	$ .10
Rawley, Shane	83F	394	$ .01	$ .04	Reitz, Ken	81F	530	$ .01	$ .04
Rawley, Shane	84F	138	$ .01	$ .06	Reitz, Ken	82F	602	$ .01	$ .04
Rawley, Shane	84FU	94	$ .06	$ .35	Remy, Jerry	81F	238	$ .01	$ .04
Rawley, Shane	85F	263	$ .01	$ .05	Remy, Jerry	82F	304	$ .01	$ .04
Rawley, Shane	86F	446	$ .01	$ .05	Remy, Jerry	83F	193	$ .01	$ .04
Rawley, Shane	86F	456	$ .01	$ .05	Remy, Jerry	84F	407	$ .01	$ .06
Rawley, Shane	87F	180	$ .01	$ .04	Remy, Jerry	85F	167	$ .01	$ .05
Rawley, Shane	88F	311	$ .01	$ .04	Renko, Steve	81F	231	$ .01	$ .04
Rawley, Shane	89F	579	$ .01	$ .05	Renko, Steve	82F	472	$ .01	$ .04
Rawley, Shane	89FU	44	$ .01	$ .05	Renko, Steve	83F	99	$ .01	$ .04
Rawley, Shane	90F	384	$ .01	$ .03	Renko, Steve	84F	355	$ .01	$ .06
Ray, Johnny	82F	492	$ .15	$ .75	Reuschel, Rick	81F	293	$ .01	$ .10
Ray, Johnny	83F	317	$ .01	$ .10	Reuschel, Rick	82F	50	$ .01	$ .04
Ray, Johnny	84F	260	$ .03	$ .10	Reuschel, Rick	85F	63	$ .01	$ .05
Ray, Johnny	85F	473	$ .01	$ .10	Reuschel, Rick	85FU	88	$ .01	$ .05
Ray, Johnny	86F	617	$ .01	$ .10	Reuschel, Rick	86F	618	$ .01	$ .05

Mike Ramsey
SECOND BASE

Player	Year	No.	VG	EX/MT	Player	Year	No.	VG	EX/MT
Reuschel, Rick	87F	619	$ .01	$ .04	Righetti, Dave	87F	111	$ .01	$ .10
Reuschel, Rick	88F	94	$ .01	$ .10	Righetti, Dave	87F	627	$ .01	$ .10
Reuschel, Rick	89F	340	$ .01	$ .05	Righetti, Dave	88F	220	$ .01	$ .10
Reuschel, Rick	90F	68	$ .01	$ .03	Righetti, Dave	88F	625	$ .01	$ .04
Reuss, Jerry	81F	118	$ .01	$ .10	Righetti, Dave	89F	267	$ .01	$ .05
Reuss, Jerry	82F	18	$ .01	$ .04	Righetti, Dave	90F	453	$ .01	$ .03
Reuss, Jerry	83F	216	$ .01	$ .04	Rijo, Jose	84FU	99	$ .50	$2.50
Reuss, Jerry	84F	110	$ .01	$ .06	Rijo, Jose	85F	143	$ .10	$ .50
Reuss, Jerry	85F	380	$ .01	$ .05	Rijo, Jose	86F	431	$ .05	$ .25
Reuss, Jerry	86F	141	$ .01	$ .05	Rijo, Jose	87F	404	$ .01	$ .10
Reuss, Jerry	87F	451	$ .01	$ .04	Rijo, Jose	88FU	86	$ .01	$ .15
Reuss, Jerry	89F	510	$ .01	$ .05	Rijo, Jose	89F	168	$ .01	$ .10
Reuss, Jerry	90F	335	$ .01	$ .03	Rijo, Jose	90F	430	$ .01	$ .15
Revering, Dave	81F	576	$ .01	$ .04	Riles, Earnest	88FU	130	$ .01	$ .05
Revering, Dave	82F	51	$ .01	$ .04	Riles, Earnest	89F	341	$ .01	$ .05
Revering, Dave	83F	484	$ .01	$ .04	Riles, Earnie	86F	499	$ .04	$ .25
Reynolds, Craig	81F	74	$ .01	$ .04	Riles, Earnie	87F	355	$ .01	$ .04
Reynolds, Craig	82F	225	$ .01	$ .04	Riles, Earnie	88F	172	$ .01	$ .04
Reynolds, Craig	83F	460	$ .01	$ .04	Riles, Earnie "Earnest"	85FU	89	$ .05	$ .30
Reynolds, Craig	84F	237	$ .01	$ .06	Riles, Ernest	90F	69	$ .01	$ .03
Reynolds, Craig	85F	357	$ .01	$ .05	Ripken, Bill	89F	616	$ .01	$ .50
Reynolds, Craig	86F	309	$ .01	$ .05	Ripken, Bill	90F	186	$ .01	$ .03
Reynolds, Craig	87F	66	$ .01	$ .04	Ripken, Bill (obscene bat)	89F	616	$5.00	$15.00
Reynolds, Craig	88F	454	$ .01	$ .04	Ripken, Billy	88F	569	$ .01	$ .30
Reynolds, Craig	89F	366	$ .01	$ .05	Ripken, Billy	88F	640	$ .01	$ .10
Reynolds, Harold	87F	596	$ .01	$ .04	Ripken, Jr., Cal	82F	176	$3.00	$12.00
Reynolds, Harold	88F	388	$ .01	$ .04	Ripken, Jr., Cal	83F	70	$ .50	$1.75
Reynolds, Harold	89F	558	$ .01	$ .05	Ripken, Jr., Cal	84F	17	$ .10	$1.00
Reynolds, Harold	90F	524	$ .01	$ .03	Ripken, Jr., Cal	85F	187	$ .10	$ .75
Reynolds, R. J.	84FU	97	$ .25	$1.00	Ripken, Jr., Cal	85F	625	$ .05	$ .30
Reynolds, R. J.	85F	381	$ .05	$ .30	Ripken, Jr., Cal	85F	641	$ .03	$ .25
Reynolds, R. J.	86F	619	$ .01	$ .05	Ripken, Jr., Cal	86F	284	$ .06	$ .35
Reynolds, R. J.	87F	620	$ .01	$ .04	Ripken, Jr., Cal	86F	633	$ .04	$ .25
Reynolds, R. J.	88F	339	$ .01	$ .04	Ripken, Jr., Cal	87F	478	$ .05	$ .30
Reynolds, R. J.	89F	219	$ .01	$ .05	Ripken, Jr., Cal	88F	570	$ .01	$ .25
Reynolds, R.J.	90F	478	$ .01	$ .03	Ripken, Jr., Cal	88F	635	$ .01	$ .10
Reynolds, Ronn	86F	92	$ .01	$ .05	Ripken, Jr., Cal	88F	640	$ .01	$ .10
Rhoden, Rick	81F	377	$ .01	$ .10	Ripken, Jr., Cal	89F	617	$ .01	$ .15
Rhoden, Rick	82F	493	$ .01	$ .04	Ripken, Jr., Cal	90F	187	$ .01	$ .15
Rhoden, Rick	83F	318	$ .01	$ .04	Ripken, Jr., Cal	90F	634	$ .01	$ .03
Rhoden, Rick	84F	261	$ .01	$ .06	Ripken, Jr., Cal	90FPD	624	$ .01	$ .15
Rhoden, Rick	85F	474	$ .01	$ .05	Ripken, Sr., Cal	85F	641	$ .03	$ .25
Rhoden, Rick	86F	620	$ .01	$ .05	Ripley, Allen	81F	454	$ .01	$ .04
Rhoden, Rick	87F	621	$ .01	$ .04	Ripley, Allen	82F	399	$ .01	$ .04
Rhoden, Rick	87FU	103	$ .01	$ .05	Ripley, Allen	83F	506	$ .01	$ .04
Rhoden, Rick	88F	219	$ .01	$ .10	Ritchie, Wally	87FU	104	$ .01	$ .05
Rhoden, Rick	89F	266	$ .01	$ .05	Ritchie, Wally	88F	312	$ .01	$ .10
Rhoden, Rick	89FU	89	$ .01	$ .05	Ritz, Kevin	90F	613	$ .01	$ .15
Rhoden, Rick	90F	235	$ .01	$ .03	Rivera, Bombo	81F	556	$ .01	$ .04
Rice, Jim	81F	222	$ .08	$ .40	Rivera, German	85F	382	$ .01	$ .05
Rice, Jim	82F	305	$ .05	$ .30	Rivera, Luis	87F	330	$ .01	$ .04
Rice, Jim	83F	194	$ .05	$ .30	Rivera, Luis	89F	392	$ .01	$ .05
Rice, Jim	84F	408	$ .05	$ .30	Rivera, Luis	90F	285	$ .01	$ .03
Rice, Jim	85F	168	$ .06	$ .35	Rivers, Mickey	81F	617	$ .01	$ .04
Rice, Jim	86F	358	$ .06	$ .35	Rivers, Mickey	82F	328	$ .01	$ .04
Rice, Jim	87F	41	$ .05	$ .30	Rivers, Mickey	83F	576	$ .01	$ .04
Rice, Jim	87F	633	$ .25	$ .75	Rivers, Mickey	84F	425	$ .01	$ .06
Rice, Jim	88F	361	$ .01	$ .15	Rivers, Mickey	85F	565	$ .01	$ .05
Rice, Jim	89F	97	$ .01	$ .10	Robbins, Bruce	81F	477	$ .01	$ .04
Richard, J. R.	81F	56	$ .01	$ .10	Roberge, Bert	83F	461	$ .01	$ .04
Richard, J. R.	82F	226	$ .01	$ .10	Roberge, Bert	85F	525	$ .01	$ .05
Richards, Gene	81F	486	$ .01	$ .04	Roberge, Bert	86F	258	$ .01	$ .05
Richards, Gene	82F	580	$ .01	$ .04	Roberts, Bip	86FU	96	$ .01	$ .25
Richards, Gene	83F	370	$ .01	$ .04	Roberts, Bip	87F	427	$ .01	$ .04
Richards, Gene	84F	310	$ .01	$ .06	Roberts, Bip	89FU	126	$ .01	$ .05
Richards, Gene	84FU	98	$ .01	$ .10	Roberts, Bip	90F	166	$ .01	$ .03
Richards, Gene	85F	619	$ .01	$ .05	Roberts, Dave	81F	607	$ .01	$ .04
Richardt, Mike	83F	575	$ .01	$ .04	Roberts, Dave	81F	636	$ .01	$ .04
Rick, Dempsey	84F	644	$ .01	$ .06	Roberts, Dave	82F	227	$ .01	$ .04
Righetti, Dave	82F	52	$ .35	$1.75	Roberts, Leon	81F	608	$ .01	$ .04
Righetti, Dave	83F	395	$ .03	$ .20	Roberts, Leon	82F	329	$ .01	$ .04
Righetti, Dave	84F	139	$ .03	$ .20	Roberts, Leon	84F	356	$ .01	$ .06
Righetti, Dave	84F	639	$ .01	$ .06	Robertson, Andre	83F	396	$ .01	$ .04
Righetti, Dave	85F	142	$ .03	$ .20	Robertson, Andre	84F	140	$ .01	$ .06
Righetti, Dave	86F	116	$ .01	$ .15	Robertson, Andre	85F	144	$ .01	$ .05

FLEER

Player	Year	No.	VG	EX/MT	Player	Year	No.	VG	EX/MT
Robertson, Andre	86F	117	$.01	$.05	Roof, Gene	83F	20	$.01	$.04
Robidoux, Billy Joe	86F	652	$.01	$.10	Rooker, Jim	81F	368	$.01	$.04
Robidoux, Billy Joe	86FU	97	$.01	$.05	Roomes, Rolando	89F	644	$.01	$.60
Robidoux, Billy Joe	87F	356	$.01	$.04	Roomes, Rolando	89FU	86	$.01	$.15
Robinson, Bill	81F	373	$.01	$.04	Roomes, Rolando	90F	432	$.01	$.03
Robinson, Bill	82F	494	$.01	$.04	Rose, Bobby	90F	651	$.01	$.03
Robinson, Don	81F	366	$.01	$.04	Rose, Jr, Pete	82F	640	$.30	$2.50
Robinson, Don	82F	495	$.01	$.04	Rose, Pete	81F	1	$.25	$2.00
Robinson, Don	83F	319	$.01	$.04	Rose, Pete	81F	645	$.20	$1.50
Robinson, Don	84F	262	$.01	$.06	Rose, Pete	82F	256	$.10	$1.00
Robinson, Don	85F	475	$.01	$.05	Rose, Pete	82F	640	$.30	$2.50
Robinson, Don	86F	621	$.01	$.05	Rose, Pete	83F	171	$.20	$1.00
Robinson, Don	87F	622	$.01	$.04	Rose, Pete	83F	634	$.10	$.50
Robinson, Don	88F	95	$.01	$.04	Rose, Pete	84F	46	$.20	$1.00
Robinson, Don	89F	342	$.01	$.05	Rose, Pete	84F	636	$.10	$.50
Robinson, Don	90F	70	$.01	$.03	Rose, Pete	84FU	102	$5.00	$15.00
Robinson, Jeff D.	84FU	100	$.10	$.75	Rose, Pete	85F	550	$.20	$1.00
Robinson, Jeff D.	85F	620	$.05	$.30	Rose, Pete	85F	640	$.10	$.50
Robinson, Jeff D.	87F	283	$.01	$.04	Rose, Pete	86F	191	$.12	$.60
Robinson, Jeff D.	89F	220	$.01	$.05	Rose, Pete	86F	628	$.10	$.50
Robinson, Jeff D.	90F	479	$.01	$.03	Rose, Pete	86F	638	$.15	$.75
Robinson, Jeff M.	87FU	105	$.05	$.30	Rose, Pete	87F	213	$.10	$.50
Robinson, Jeff M.	88F	68	$.10	$.50	Rosello, Dave	82F	377	$.01	$.04
Robinson, Jeff M.	89F	143	$.01	$.05	Rosenberg, Steve	89FU	22	$.01	$.05
Robinson, Jeff M.	90F	614	$.01	$.03	Rosenberg, Steve	90F	547	$.01	$.03
Robinson, Ron	83F	170	$.01	$.04	Rowdon, Wade	88F	430	$.01	$.04
Robinson, Ron	85F	650	$.05	$1.00	Royster, Jerry	81F	250	$.01	$.04
Robinson, Ron	86F	190	$.01	$.05	Royster, Jerry	82F	448	$.01	$.04
Robinson, Ron	87F	212	$.01	$.04	Royster, Jerry	83F	147	$.01	$.04
Robinson, Ron	88F	247	$.01	$.04	Royster, Jerry	84F	191	$.01	$.06
Robinson, Ron	89F	169	$.01	$.05	Royster, Jerry	85F	340	$.01	$.05
Robinson, Ron	90F	431	$.01	$.03	Royster, Jerry	85FU	90	$.01	$.05
Rochford, Mike	89F	650	$.01	$.20	Royster, Jerry	86F	333	$.01	$.05
Rodriguez, Rick	88FU	24	$.01	$.05	Royster, Jerry	87F	428	$.01	$.04
Rodriguez, Aurelio	81F	105	$.01	$.04	Royster, Jerry	88F	221	$.01	$.04
Rodriguez, Aurelio	82F	53	$.01	$.04	Rozema, Dave	81F	464	$.01	$.04
Rodriguez, Aurelio	83F	249	$.01	$.04	Rozema, Dave	83F	340	$.01	$.04
Rodriguez, Rick	88F	293	$.01	$.15	Rozema, Dave	84F	90	$.01	$.06
Roenicke, Gary	81F	187	$.01	$.04	Rozema, Dave	85F	21	$.01	$.05
Roenicke, Gary	83F	71	$.01	$.04	Rozema, Dave	85FU	91	$.01	$.05
Roenicke, Gary	84F	18	$.01	$.06	Rozema, Dave	86F	570	$.01	$.05
Roenicke, Gary	85F	188	$.01	$.05	Rozema, Dave 'David'	82F	279	$.01	$.04
Roenicke, Gary	86F	285	$.01	$.05	Rucker, Dave	83F	341	$.01	$.04
Roenicke, Gary	86FU	98	$.01	$.05	Rucker, Dave	85F	238	$.01	$.05
Roenicke, Gary	87F	112	$.01	$.04	Rucker, Dave	85FU	92	$.01	$.05
Roenicke, Ron	82F	177	$.01	$.04	Rucker, Dave	86F	447	$.01	$.05
Roenicke, Ron	82F	19	$.01	$.04	Rudi, Joe	81F	272	$.01	$.04
Roenicke, Ron	83F	217	$.01	$.04	Rudi, Joe	82F	306	$.01	$.04
Roenicke, Ron	84F	618	$.01	$.06	Rudi, Joe	83F	532	$.01	$.04
Roenicke, Ron	86FU	99	$.01	$.05	Ruffin, Bruce	87F	183	$.01	$.04
Roenicke, Ron	87F	182	$.01	$.04	Ruffin, Bruce	88F	313	$.01	$.10
Roesler, Mike	90F	645	$.01	$.03	Ruffin, Bruce	89F	581	$.01	$.05
Rogers, Kenny	90F	311	$.01	$.20	Ruffin, Bruce	90F	572	$.01	$.03
Rogers, Steve	81F	143	$.01	$.04	Ruhle, Vern	81F	53	$.01	$.04
Rogers, Steve	82F	205	$.01	$.04	Ruhle, Vern	82F	228	$.01	$.04
Rogers, Steve	83F	294	$.01	$.04	Ruhle, Vern	83F	462	$.01	$.04
Rogers, Steve	84F	284	$.01	$.06	Ruhle, Vern	84F	238	$.01	$.06
Rogers, Steve	85F	408	$.01	$.05	Ruhle, Vern	85F	358	$.01	$.05
Roman, Jose	85F	646	$.01	$.10	Ruhle, Vern	85FU	93	$.01	$.05
Romanick, Ron	84FU	101	$.05	$.25	Ruhle, Vern	86F	593	$.01	$.05
Romanick, Ron	85F	309	$.01	$.05	Ruhle, Vern	87F	91	$.01	$.04
Romanick, Ron	86F	166	$.01	$.05	Runge, Paul	88FU	71	$.01	$.05
Romero, Ed	83F	44	$.01	$.04	Russell, Bill	81F	117	$.01	$.04
Romero, Ed	84F	212	$.01	$.06	Russell, Bill	82F	20	$.01	$.04
Romero, Ed	85F	593	$.01	$.05	Russell, Bill	83F	219	$.01	$.04
Romero, Ed	86F	500	$.01	$.05	Russell, Bill	84F	111	$.01	$.06
Romero, Ed	87F	42	$.01	$.04	Russell, Bill	85F	383	$.01	$.05
Romero, Ed	88F	362	$.01	$.04	Russell, Bill	86F	142	$.01	$.05
Romine, Kevin	88F	363	$.01	$.04	Russell, Bill	87F	452	$.01	$.04
Romine, Kevin	89F	98	$.01	$.20	Russell, Jeff	85F	551	$.01	$.05
Romine, Kevin	90F	286	$.01	$.03	Russell, Jeff	87F	137	$.01	$.04
Romo, Enrique	81F	385	$.01	$.04	Russell, Jeff	88F	478	$.01	$.04
Romo, Enrique	82F	496	$.01	$.04	Russell, Jeff	89F	531	$.01	$.05
Romo, Enrique	83F	320	$.01	$.04	Russell, Jeff	90F	312	$.01	$.03
Romo, Vincente	83F	218	$.01	$.04	Russell, Jeff	90F	633	$.01	$.03

Player	Year	No.	VG	EX/MT	Player	Year	No.	VG	EX/MT
Russell, John	85F	653	$ .03	$ .20	Samuel, Juan	84F	47	$ .50	$3.00
Russell, John	86F	448	$ .01	$ .05	Samuel, Juan	85F	264	$ .06	$ .40
Russell, John	86F	458	$ .01	$ .05	Samuel, Juan	85F	634	$ .20	$1.00
Russell, John	87F	184	$ .01	$ .04	Samuel, Juan	86F	449	$ .01	$ .10
Ruthven, Dick	81F	16	$ .01	$ .04	Samuel, Juan	87F	185	$ .01	$ .10
Ruthven, Dick	82F	257	$ .01	$ .04	Samuel, Juan	88F	314	$ .01	$ .10
Ruthven, Dick	83F	172	$ .01	$ .04	Samuel, Juan	89F	580	$ .01	$ .05
Ruthven, Dick	84F	503	$ .01	$ .06	Samuel, Juan	89FU	102	$ .01	$ .10
Ruthven, Dick	85F	64	$ .01	$ .05	Samuel, Juan	90F	215	$ .01	$ .03
Ruthven, Dick	86F	377	$ .01	$ .05	Samuels, Juan	87F	642	$ .01	$ .04
Ryal, Mark	88F	503	$ .01	$ .04	Samuels, Roger	88FU	131	$ .01	$ .05
Ryan, Nolan	81F	57	$ .45	$2.25	Sanchez, Alejandro "Alex"	85F	648	$ .25	$1.50
Ryan, Nolan	82F	229	$ .40	$2.00	Sanchez, Alex	85FU	98	$ .01	$ .05
Ryan, Nolan	83F	463	$ .50	$1.75	Sanchez, Alex	86F	236	$ .01	$ .05
Ryan, Nolan	84F	239	$ .75	$3.00					
Ryan, Nolan	85F	359	$ .07	$1.00					
Ryan, Nolan	86F	310	$ .25	$1.75					
Ryan, Nolan	87F	67	$ .05	$1.00					
Ryan, Nolan	88F	455	$ .01	$ .65					
Ryan, Nolan	89F	368	$ .05	$ .35					
Ryan, Nolan	89FU	67	$ .01	$1.50					
Ryan, Nolan	90F	313	$ .01	$ .35					
Ryan, Nolan	90F	636	$ .01	$ .03					
Saberhagen, Bret	84FU	103	$7.00	$37.00					
Saberhagen, Bret	85F	212	$1.00	$8.00					
Saberhagen, Bret	86F	19	$ .08	$1.00					
Saberhagen, Bret	87F	379	$ .04	$ .35					
Saberhagen, Bret	88F	268	$ .01	$ .25					
Saberhagen, Bret	88F	626	$ .01	$ .04					
Saberhagen, Bret	89F	291	$ .01	$ .15					
Saberhagen, Bret	90F	116	$ .01	$ .03					
Sabo, Chris	88FU	87	$ .25	$1.50					
Sabo, Chris	89F	170	$ .01	$1.00					
Sabo, Chris	89F	637	$ .01	$ 35					
Sabo, Chris	90F	433	$ .01	$ .15					
Sakata, Lenn	81F	194	$ .01	$ .04					
Sakata, Lenn	82F	178	$ .01	$ .04					
Sakata, Lenn	83F	72	$ .01	$ .04					
Sakata, Lenn	84F	19	$ .01	$ .06					
Sakata, Lenn	85F	189	$ .01	$ .05					
Salas, Mark	85FU	94	$ .04	$ .25					
Salas, Mark	86F	402	$ .01	$ .05					
Salas, Mark	87F	551	$ .01	$ .04					
Salas, Mark	87FU	106	$ .01	$ .05					
Salas, Mark	89F	511	$ .01	$ .05	Sanchez, Alex	89FU	71	$ .01	$ .25
Salazar, Angel	86FU	100	$ .01	$ .05	Sanchez, Alex	90F	92	$ .01	$ .10
Salazar, Angel	87F	380	$ .01	$ .04	Sanchez, Israel	88FU	34	$ .01	$ .15
Salazar, Angel	88F	269	$ .01	$ .04	Sanchez, Luis	83F	100	$ .01	$ .04
Salazar, Luis	81F	501	$ .01	$ .04	Sanchez, Luis	84F	527	$ .01	$ .06
Salazar, Luis	82F	581	$ .01	$ .04	Sanchez, Luis	85F	310	$ .01	$ .06
Salazar, Luis	83F	371	$ .01	$ .04	Sanchez, Orlando	82F	126	$ .01	$ .04
Salazar, Luis	84F	311	$ .01	$ .06	Sandberg, Ryne	83F	507	$2.00	$10.00
Salazar, Luis	85F	43	$ .01	$ .05	Sandberg, Ryne	84F	504	$ .75	$3.00
Salazar, Luis	85FU	95	$ .01	$ .05	Sandberg, Ryne	85F	630	$ .05	$ .60
Salazar, Luis	86F	215	$ .01	$ .05	Sandberg, Ryne	85F	65	$ .05	$ .30
Salazar, Luis	88F	595	$ .01	$ .04	Sandberg, Ryne	86F	378	$ .05	$ .35
Salazar, Luis	88FU	30	$ .01	$ .05	Sandberg, Ryne	87F	572	$ .04	$ .25
Salazar, Luis	89F	144	$ .01	$ .05	Sandberg, Ryne	87F	639	$ .01	$ .10
Sambito, Joe	81F	65	$ .01	$ .04	Sandberg, Ryne	88F	431	$ .01	$ .25
Sambito, Joe	82F	230	$ .01	$ .04	Sandberg, Ryne	88F	628	$ .01	$ .04
Sambito, Joe	83F	464	$ .01	$ .04	Sandberg, Ryne	89F	437	$ .01	$ .15
Sambito, Joe	85F	360	$ .01	$ .05	Sandberg, Ryne	90F	40	$ .01	$ .10
Sambito, Joe	85FU	96	$ .01	$ .05	Sandberg, Ryne	90F	639	$ .01	$ .03
Sambito, Joe	86FU	101	$ .01	$ .05	Sandberg, Ryne	90FPD	625	$ .01	$ .15
Sambito, Joe	87F	43	$ .01	$ .04	Sanders, Deion	89FU	53	$ .01	$1.25
Sambito, Joe	88F	364	$ .01	$ .04	Sanders, Deion	90F	454	$ .01	$ .40
Sample, Billy	81F	637	$ .01	$ .04	Sanderson, Scott	81F	166	$ .01	$ .04
Sample, Billy	82F	330	$ .01	$ .04	Sanderson, Scott	82F	206	$ .01	$ .04
Sample, Billy	83F	577	$ .01	$ .04	Sanderson, Scott	83F	295	$ .01	$ .04
Sample, Billy	84F	426	$ .01	$ .06	Sanderson, Scott	84F	285	$ .01	$ .06
Sample, Billy	85F	566	$ .01	$ .05	Sanderson, Scott	84FU	104	$ .01	$ .05
Sample, Billy	85FU	97	$ .01	$ .05	Sanderson, Scott	85F	66	$ .01	$ .05
Sample, Billy	86F	118	$ .01	$ .05	Sanderson, Scott	86F	379	$ .01	$ .05
Sample, Billy	86FU	102	$ .01	$ .05					
Sample, Billy	87F	527	$ .01	$ .04					

ALEX SANCHEZ
PITCHER
FLEER

Player	Year	No.	VG	EX/MT	Player	Year	No.	VG	EX/MT
Sanderson, Scott	87F	573	$ .01	$ .04	Schmidt, Mike	85F	627	$ .06	$ .35
Sanderson, Scott	88F	432	$ .01	$ .04	Schmidt, Mike	85F	630	$ .10	$ .50
Sanderson, Scott	89FU	78	$ .01	$ .05	Schmidt, Mike	86F	450	$ .01	$ .75
Sanderson, Scott	90F	41	$ .01	$ .03	Schmidt, Mike	87F	187	$ .06	$ .75
Sanguillen, Manny	81F	376	$ .01	$ .04	Schmidt, Mike	88F	315	$ .01	$ .45
Santana, Rafael	85F	90	$ .03	$ .20	Schmidt, Mike	88F	636	$ .01	$ .15
Santana, Rafael	86F	93	$ .01	$ .05	Schmidt, Mike	89F	582	$ .01	$ .25
Santana, Rafael	87F	21	$ .01	$ .04	Schmidt, Mike	89FU	131	$ .01	$1.50
Santana, Rafael	88F	149	$ .01	$ .04	Schofield, Dick	84FU	105	$ .01	$ .10
Santana, Rafael	88FU	50	$ .01	$ .05	Schofield, Dick	85F	311	$ .01	$ .05
Santana, Rafael	89F	268	$ .01	$ .05	Schofield, Dick	86F	167	$ .01	$ .05
Santiago, Benito	86F	644	$1.25	$5.00	Schofield, Dick	87F	92	$ .01	$ .04
Santiago, Benito	87F	429	$ .35	$1.25	Schofield, Dick	88F	504	$ .01	$ .10
Santiago, Benito	88F	596	$ .01	$ .50	Schofield, Dick	89F	488	$ .01	$ .05
Santiago, Benito	89F	316	$ .01	$ .25	Schofield, Dick	90F	144	$ .01	$ .03
Santiago, Benito	90F	167	$ .01	$ .03	Schooler, Mike	89F	559	$ .01	$ .35
Santovenia, Nelson	88FU	103	$ .01	$ .30	Schooler, Mike	90F	525	$ .01	$ .03
Santovenia, Nelson	89F	393	$ .01	$ .15	Schroeder, Bill	85F	594	$ .01	$ .05
Santovenia, Nelson	90F	360	$ .01	$ .03	Schroeder, Bill	86F	501	$ .01	$ .05
Sarmiento, Manny	83F	321	$ .01	$ .04	Schroeder, Bill	87F	357	$ .01	$ .04
Sarmiento, Manny	84F	263	$ .01	$ .06	Schroeder, Bill	88F	173	$ .01	$ .04
Sasser, Mackey	88FU	106	$ .01	$ .05	Schrom, Ken	81F	425	$ .03	$ .20
Sasser, Mackey	89F	48	$ .01	$ .05	Schrom, Ken	84F	572	$ .01	$ .06
Sasser, Mackey	90F	216	$ .01	$ .03	Schrom, Ken	85F	288	$ .01	$ .05
Saucier, Kevin	81F	24	$ .01	$ .04	Schrom, Ken	86F	403	$ .01	$ .05
Saucier, Kevin	82F	275	$ .01	$ .04	Schrom, Ken	86FU	104	$ .01	$ .05
Savage, Jack	88F	650	$ .01	$ .25	Schrom, Ken	87F	258	$ .01	$ .04
Sax, Steve	82F	21	$ .35	$2.00	Schrom, Ken	88F	614	$ .01	$ .04
Sax, Steve	83F	220	$ .10	$ .60	Schu, Rick	85FU	100	$ .04	$ .25
Sax, Steve	84F	112	$ .06	$ .35	Schu, Rick	86F	451	$ .01	$ .05
Sax, Steve	84F	633	$ .01	$ .06	Schu, Rick	87F	188	$ .01	$ .04
Sax, Steve	85F	384	$ .03	$ .20	Schu, Rick	88F	316	$ .01	$ .04
Sax, Steve	86F	143	$ .01	$ .10	Schu, Rick	89F	619	$ .01	$ .05
Sax, Steve	87F	453	$ .01	$ .10	Schulze, Don	85F	454	$ .01	$ .05
Sax, Steve	88F	523	$ .01	$ .10	Schulze, Don	87F	259	$ .01	$ .04
Sax, Steve	89F	70	$ .01	$ .15	Schwabe, Mike	89FU	32	$ .01	$ .20
Sax, Steve	89FU	52	$ .01	$ .10	Scioscia, Mike	81F	131	$ .06	$ .60
Sax, Steve	90F	455	$ .01	$ .03	Scioscia, Mike	82F	22	$ .01	$ .10
Schatzader, Dan	88F	21	$ .01	$ .04	Scioscia, Mike	83F	221	$ .01	$ .04
Schatzeder, Dan	81F	482	$ .01	$ .04	Scioscia, Mike	84F	113	$ .01	$ .06
Schatzeder, Dan	82F	281	$ .01	$ .04	Scioscia, Mike	85F	385	$ .01	$ .05
Schatzeder, Dan	83F	296	$ .01	$ .04	Scioscia, Mike	86F	144	$ .01	$ .05
Schatzeder, Dan	84F	286	$ .01	$ .06	Scioscia, Mike	87F	454	$ .01	$ .04
Schatzeder, Dan	85F	409	$ .01	$ .05	Scioscia, Mike	88F	524	$ .01	$ .04
Schatzeder, Dan	86F	259	$ .01	$ .05	Scioscia, Mike	89F	71	$ .01	$ .05
Schatzeder, Dan	87F	186	$ .01	$ .04	Scioscia, Mike	90F	407	$ .01	$ .03
Schatzeder, Dan	89FU	90	$ .01	$ .05	Sconiers, Daryl	84F	528	$ .01	$ .06
Schatzeder, Dan	90F	236	$ .01	$ .03	Sconiers, Daryl	85F	312	$ .01	$ .05
Scherrer, Bill	84F	482	$ .01	$ .06	Sconiers, Daryl	86F	168	$ .01	$ .05
Scherrer, Bill	85F	22	$ .01	$ .05	Scott, Donnie	85F	568	$ .01	$ .05
Scherrer, Bill	86F	237	$ .01	$ .05	Scott, Donnie	86F	474	$ .01	$ .05
Schiraldi, Calvin	85FU	99	$ .04	$ .25	Scott, Mike	82F	535	$ .15	$1.00
Schiraldi, Calvin	87F	44	$ .01	$ .04	Scott, Mike	83F	554	$ .05	$ .30
Schiraldi, Calvin	88F	365	$ .01	$ .04	Scott, Mike	84F	240	$ .05	$ .30
Schiraldi, Calvin	89F	438	$ .01	$ .05	Scott, Mike	85F	361	$ .05	$ .30
Schiraldi, Calvin	90F	168	$ .01	$ .03	Scott, Mike	86F	311	$ .03	$ .20
Schmidt, Dave	83F	578	$ .01	$ .10	Scott, Mike	87F	630	$ .01	$ .10
Schmidt, Dave	84F	427	$ .01	$ .06	Scott, Mike	87F	68	$ .03	$ .20
Schmidt, Dave	85F	567	$ .01	$ .05	Scott, Mike	88F	456	$ .01	$ .10
Schmidt, Dave	86F	571	$ .01	$ .05	Scott, Mike	88F	632	$ .01	$ .10
Schmidt, Dave	86FU	103	$ .01	$ .05	Scott, Mike	89F	367	$ .01	$ .05
Schmidt, Dave	87F	505	$ .01	$ .04	Scott, Mike	90F	237	$ .01	$ .03
Schmidt, Dave	87FU	107	$ .01	$ .05	Scott, Mike	90F	636	$ .01	$ .03
Schmidt, Dave	88F	571	$ .01	$ .04	Scott, Rodney	81F	155	$ .01	$ .04
Schmidt, Dave	89F	618	$ .01	$ .05	Scott, Rodney	82F	207	$ .01	$ .04
Schmidt, Dave	90F	188	$ .01	$ .03	Scott, Tony	81F	531	$ .01	$ .04
Schmidt, Mike	81F	5	$ .12	$1.00	Scott, Tony	82F	231	$ .01	$ .04
Schmidt, Mike	81F	640	$ .10	$2.00	Scott, Tony	83F	465	$ .01	$ .04
Schmidt, Mike	81F	645	$ .20	$1.50	Scott, Tony	84F	241	$ .01	$ .06
Schmidt, Mike	82F	258	$ .12	$1.00	Scudder, Scott	89FU	87	$ .01	$ .35
Schmidt, Mike	82F	637	$ .06	$ .50	Scudder, Scott	90F	434	$ .01	$ .15
Schmidt, Mike	82F	641	$ .05	$ .50	Scurry, Rod	81F	380	$ .01	$ .04
Schmidt, Mike	83F	173	$ .25	$1.50	Scurry, Rod	83F	322	$ .01	$ .04
Schmidt, Mike	84F	48	$ .03	$2.00	Scurry, Rod	84F	264	$ .01	$ .06
Schmidt, Mike	85F	265	$ .10	$1.00	Scurry, Rod	85F	476	$ .01	$ .05

Player	Year	No.	VG	EX/MT	Player	Year	No.	VG	EX/MT
Scurry, Rod	87F	113	$ .01	$ .04	Sheffield, Gary	90F	336	$ .01	$ .35
Scurry, Ron	82F	497	$ .01	$ .04	Shelby, John	84F	20	$ .04	$ .25
Seanez, Rudy	90F	640	$ .01	$ .03	Shelby, John	85F	190	$ .01	$ .05
Searage, Ray	85F	595	$ .01	$ .05	Shelby, John	86F	287	$ .01	$ .05
Searage, Ray	86F	502	$ .01	$ .05	Shelby, John	87F	480	$ .01	$ .04
Searage, Ray	87F	506	$ .01	$ .04	Shelby, John	87FU	109	$ .01	$ .05
Searage, Ray	88F	409	$ .01	$ .04	Shelby, John	88F	526	$ .01	$ .04
Searage, Ray	89FU	94	$ .01	$ .05	Shelby, John	89F	73	$ .01	$ .05
Searage, Ray	90F	408	$ .01	$ .03	Shepherd, Ron	85FU	102	$ .01	$ .05
Searcy, Steve	89F	145	$ .01	$ .25	Sheridan, Pat	84F	357	$ .03	$ .10
Searcy, Steve	90F	615	$ .01	$ .03	Sheridan, Pat	85F	213	$ .01	$ .05
Seaver, Tom	81F	200	$ .12	$ .75	Sheridan, Pat	86F	20	$ .01	$ .05
Seaver, Tom	82F	634	$ .06	$ .35	Sheridan, Pat	87F	162	$ .01	$ .04
Seaver, Tom	82F	645	$ .05	$ .30	Sheridan, Pat	88F	69	$ .01	$ .04
Seaver, Tom	82F	82	$ .10	$ .75	Sheridan, Pat	89F	146	$ .01	$ .05
Seaver, Tom	83F	601	$ .08	$ .75	Sheridan, Pat	90F	71	$ .01	$ .03
					Shields, Steve	86F	527	$ .01	$ .05
					Shields, Steve	89F	269	$ .01	$ .05
					Shipanoff, Dave	86F	452	$ .01	$ .05
					Shirley, Bob	81F	495	$ .01	$ .04
					Shirley, Bob	82F	127	$ .01	$ .04
					Shirley, Bob	83F	602	$ .01	$ .04
					Shirley, Bob	84F	141	$ .01	$ .06
					Shirley, Bob	85F	145	$ .01	$ .05
					Shirley, Bob	86F	119	$ .01	$ .05
					Shirley, Bob	87F	114	$ .01	$ .04
					Show, Eric	83F	372	$ .01	$ .10
					Show, Eric	84F	312	$ .01	$ .06
					Show, Eric	85F	44	$ .01	$ .05
					Show, Eric	86F	334	$ .01	$ .05
					Show, Eric	87F	430	$ .01	$ .04
					Show, Eric	88F	597	$ .01	$ .04
					Show, Eric	89F	317	$ .01	$ .05
					Show, Eric	90F	169	$ .01	$ .03
					Sierra, Candy	89F	171	$ .01	$ .15
					Sierra, Ruben	86FU	105	$1.50	$7.50
					Sierra, Ruben	87F	138	$2.75	$11.00
					Sierra, Ruben	88F	479	$ .10	$1.25
					Sierra, Ruben	89F	532	$ .01	$ .30
					Sierra, Ruben	90F	314	$ .01	$ .15
					Simmons, Nelson	85FU	103	$ .01	$ .05
					Simmons, Nelson	86F	238	$ .01	$ .05
					Simmons, Ted	81F	528	$ .01	$ .10
					Simmons, Ted	82F	152	$ .01	$ .10
					Simmons, Ted	83F	45	$ .01	$ .10
					Simmons, Ted	84F	213	$ .03	$ .10
					Simmons, Ted	85F	596	$ .01	$ .10
					Simmons, Ted	86F	503	$ .01	$ .10
Seaver, Tom	84F	595	$ .06	$1.00	Simmons, Ted	86FU	106	$ .01	$ .10
Seaver, Tom	84FU	106	$1.40	$7.00	Simmons, Ted	87F	528	$ .01	$ .10
Seaver, Tom	85F	526	$ .06	$ .35	Simmons, Ted	88F	549	$ .01	$ .10
Seaver, Tom	86F	216	$ .06	$ .35	Simmons, Ted	89F	599	$ .01	$ .05
Seaver, Tom	86F	630	$ .04	$ .25	Simmons, Todd	88F	650	$ .01	$ .25
Seaver, Tom	87F	45	$ .05	$ .30	Simmons, Todd	89F	318	$ .01	$ .05
Sebra, Bob	87F	331	$ .01	$ .04	Simpson, Joe	81F	616	$ .01	$ .04
Sebra, Bob	88F	195	$ .01	$ .04	Simpson, Joe	82F	518	$ .01	$ .04
Segura, Jose	88FU	20	$ .01	$ .15	Simpson, Joe	83F	485	$ .01	$ .04
Seitzer, Kevin	87F	652	$1.50	$5.00	Simpson, Joe	84F	358	$ .01	$ .06
Seitzer, Kevin	87FU	108	$ .25	$1.00	Singleton, Ken	81F	188	$ .01	$ .10
Seitzer, Kevin	88F	270	$ .15	$ .75	Singleton, Ken	82F	179	$ .01	$ .10
Seitzer, Kevin	89F	292	$ .01	$ .25	Singleton, Ken	83F	73	$ .01	$ .04
Seitzer, Kevin	90F	117	$ .01	$ .03	Singleton, Ken	84F	21	$ .01	$ .06
Sellers, Jeff	87F	46	$ .01	$ .10	Singleton, Ken	85F	191	$ .01	$ .05
Sellers, Jeff	88F	366	$ .01	$ .04	Sisk, Doug	84F	596	$ .01	$ .06
Service, Scott	89F	653	$ .01	$ .20	Sisk, Doug	85F	91	$ .01	$ .05
Sexton, Jimmy	83F	533	$ .01	$ .04	Sisk, Doug	86F	94	$ .01	$ .05
Sharperson, Mike	88F	525	$ .01	$ .04	Sisk, Doug	87F	22	$ .01	$ .04
Sharperson, Mike	89F	72	$ .01	$ .05	Sisk, Doug	88F	150	$ .01	$ .04
Sheets, Larry	85FU	101	$ .05	$ .45	Sisk, Doug	88FU	3	$ .01	$ .05
Sheets, Larry	86F	286	$ .06	$ .35	Sisk, Doug	89F	621	$ .01	$ .05
Sheets, Larry	87F	479	$ .01	$ .04	Skinner, Joel	85F	646	$ .01	$ .10
Sheets, Larry	88F	572	$ .01	$ .04	Skinner, Joel	87F	115	$ .01	$ .04
Sheets, Larry	89F	620	$ .01	$ .05	Skinner, Joel	89F	270	$ .01	$ .05
Sheets, Larry	90F	189	$ .01	$ .03	Skinner, Joel	90F	501	$ .01	$ .03
Sheffield, Gary	89F	196	$ .25	$1.50	Slaton, Jim	81F	518	$ .01	$ .04

Tom Seaver
PITCHER

Player	Year	No.	VG	EX/MT
Slaton, Jim	82F	153	$ .01	$ .04
Slaton, Jim	83F	46	$ .01	$ .04
Slaton, Jim	84F	214	$ .01	$ .06
Slaton, Jim	84FU	107	$ .01	$ .10
Slaton, Jim	85F	313	$ .01	$ .05
Slaton, Jim	86F	169	$ .01	$ .05
Slaton, Jim	87F	163	$ .01	$ .04
Slaught, Don	83F	123	$ .01	$ .15
Slaught, Don	84F	359	$ .01	$ .06
Slaught, Don	85F	214	$ .01	$ .05
Slaught, Don	85FU	104	$ .01	$ .05
Slaught, Don	86F	572	$ .01	$ .05
Slaught, Don	87F	139	$ .01	$ .04
Slaught, Don	88FU	51	$ .01	$ .05
Slaught, Don	89F	271	$ .01	$ .05
Slaught, Don	90F	456	$ .01	$ .03
Smalley, Roy	81F	551	$ .01	$ .04
Smalley, Roy	82F	560	$ .01	$ .04
Smalley, Roy	83F	397	$ .01	$ .04
Smalley, Roy	84F	142	$ .01	$ .06
Smalley, Roy	85F	527	$ .01	$ .05
Smalley, Roy	85FU	105	$ .01	$ .05
Smalley, Roy	86F	404	$ .01	$ .05
Smalley, Roy	87F	552	$ .01	$ .04
Smalley, Roy	88F	22	$ .01	$ .04
Smiley, John	87FU	110	$ .04	$ .45
Smiley, John	88F	340	$ .01	$ .35

JOHN SMILEY
PITCHER

Player	Year	No.	VG	EX/MT
Smiley, John	89F	221	$ .01	$ .10
Smiley, John	90F	480	$ .01	$ .03
Smith, Billy	82F	400	$ .01	$ .04
Smith, Bryn	83F	297	$ .01	$ .04
Smith, Bryn	84F	287	$ .01	$ .06
Smith, Bryn	85F	410	$ .01	$ .05
Smith, Bryn	86F	260	$ .01	$ .05
Smith, Bryn	87F	332	$ .01	$ .04
Smith, Bryn	88F	196	$ .01	$ .04
Smith, Bryn	89F	394	$ .01	$ .05
Smith, Bryn	90F	361	$ .01	$ .03
Smith, Dave	81F	71	$ .05	$ .30
Smith, Dave	82F	232	$ .01	$ .10
Smith, Dave	83F	466	$ .01	$ .04
Smith, Dave	84F	242	$ .01	$ .06
Smith, Dave	85F	362	$ .01	$ .05

Player	Year	No.	VG	EX/MT
Smith, Dave	86F	312	$ .01	$ .05
Smith, Dave	87F	69	$ .01	$ .04
Smith, Dave	88F	457	$ .01	$ .04
Smith, Dave	89F	369	$ .01	$ .05
Smith, Dave	90F	238	$ .01	$ .03
Smith, Dwight	89FU	79	$ .01	$1.50
Smith, Dwight	90F	42	$ .01	$ .60
Smith, Greg	90F	643	$ .01	$ .03
Smith, Jim	83F	323	$ .01	$ .04
Smith, Keith	81F	534	$ .01	$ .04
Smith, Ken	83F	148	$ .01	$ .04
Smith, Lee	82F	603	$ .15	$ .75
Smith, Lee	83F	508	$ .03	$ .20
Smith, Lee	84F	505	$ .01	$ .10
Smith, Lee	85F	67	$ .01	$ .10
Smith, Lee	86F	380	$ .01	$ .10
Smith, Lee	87F	574	$ .01	$ .04
Smith, Lee	88F	433	$ .01	$ .04
Smith, Lee	88FU	8	$ .01	$ .05
Smith, Lee	89F	99	$ .01	$ .05
Smith, Lee	90F	287	$ .01	$ .03
Smith, Lonnie	81F	15	$ .01	$ .04
Smith, Lonnie	82F	259	$ .01	$ .04
Smith, Lonnie	82F	641	$ .05	$ .30
Smith, Lonnie	83F	21	$ .01	$ .04
Smith, Lonnie	83F	636	$ .01	$ .04
Smith, Lonnie	84F	335	$ .01	$ .06
Smith, Lonnie	85F	239	$ .01	$ .05
Smith, Lonnie	85FU	106	$ .01	$ .05
Smith, Lonnie	86F	21	$ .01	$ .05
Smith, Lonnie	87F	381	$ .01	$ .04
Smith, Lonnie	89FU	74	$ .01	$ .05
Smith, Lonnie	90F	593	$ .01	$ .03
Smith, Ozzie	81F	488	$ .04	$ .25
Smith, Ozzie	82F	582	$ .10	$ .45
Smith, Ozzie	83F	22	$ .10	$ .45
Smith, Ozzie	83F	636	$ .01	$ .04
Smith, Ozzie	84F	336	$ .10	$ .50
Smith, Ozzie	85F	240	$ .05	$ .30
Smith, Ozzie	85F	631	$ .05	$ .30
Smith, Ozzie	86F	46	$ .04	$ .25
Smith, Ozzie	87F	308	$ .01	$ .10
Smith, Ozzie	88F	47	$ .01	$ .10
Smith, Ozzie	88F	628	$ .01	$ .04
Smith, Ozzie	89F	463	$ .01	$ .05
Smith, Ozzie	90F	260	$ .01	$ .05
Smith, Pete	88FU	73	$ .01	$ .15
Smith, Pete	89F	600	$ .01	$ .05
Smith, Pete	90F	594	$ .01	$ .03
Smith, Peter	88F	647	$ .01	$ .30
Smith, Ray	84F	573	$ .01	$ .06
Smith, Reggie	81F	111	$ .01	$ .10
Smith, Reggie	82F	23	$ .01	$ .04
Smith, Reggie	83F	272	$ .01	$ .04
Smith, Roy	85F	455	$ .01	$ .05
Smith, Roy	90F	386	$ .01	$ .10
Smith, Zane	85F	651	$ .08	$ .40
Smith, Zane	86F	528	$ .01	$ .10
Smith, Zane	87F	529	$ .01	$ .10
Smith, Zane	88F	550	$ .01	$ .04
Smith, Zane	89F	601	$ .01	$ .05
Smith, Zane	89FU	99	$ .01	$ .05
Smith, Zane	90F	362	$ .01	$ .03
Smithson, Mike	84F	428	$ .01	$ .06
Smithson, Mike	84FU	108	$ .01	$ .10
Smithson, Mike	85F	289	$ .01	$ .05
Smithson, Mike	86F	405	$ .01	$ .05
Smithson, Mike	87F	553	$ .01	$ .04
Smithson, Mike	88F	23	$ .01	$ .04
Smithson, Mike	88FU	9	$ .01	$ .05
Smithson, Mike	89F	100	$ .01	$ .05
Smithson, Mike	90F	288	$ .01	$ .03
Smoltz, John	88FU	74	$ .05	$1.50
Smoltz, John	89F	602	$ .01	$ .55
Smoltz, John	90F	595	$ .01	$ .15

Player	Year	No.	VG	EX/MT	Player	Year	No.	VG	EX/MT
Snell, Nate	85FU	107	$ .01	$ .05	St. Claire, Randy	87FU	113	$ .01	$ .05
Snell, Nate	86F	288	$ .01	$ .05	St. Claire, Randy	88F	197	$ .01	$ .04
Snell, Nate	87F	481	$ .01	$ .04	Stanhouse, Don	81F	121	$ .01	$ .04
Snell, Nate	88F	70	$ .01	$ .04	Stanicek, Pete	88F	573	$ .01	$ .15
Snider, Van	89F	172	$ .01	$ .15	Stanicek, Pete	89F	622	$ .01	$ .05
Snyder, Cory	86F	653	$1.25	$12.50	Stanicek, Steve	88F	174	$ .01	$ .20
Snyder, Cory	87F	260	$ .12	$ .60	Stanley, Bob	81F	234	$ .01	$ .04
Snyder, Cory	88F	615	$ .01	$ .10	Stanley, Bob	82F	307	$ .01	$ .04
Snyder, Cory	88F	622	$ .01	$ .40	Stanley, Bob	83F	195	$ .01	$ .04
Snyder, Cory	89F	412	$ .01	$ .10	Stanley, Bob	84F	409	$ .01	$ .06
Snyder, Cory	90F	502	$ .01	$ .03	Stanley, Bob	85F	169	$ .01	$ .05
Soderholm, Eric	81F	92	$ .01	$ .04	Stanley, Bob	86F	359	$ .01	$ .05
Soff, Ray	87F	309	$ .01	$ .04	Stanley, Bob	87F	47	$ .01	$ .04
Sofield, Rick	81F	563	$ .01	$ .04	Stanley, Bob	88F	367	$ .01	$ .04
Solano, Julio	85F	363	$ .01	$ .05	Stanley, Bob	89F	101	$ .01	$ .05
Solomon, Eddie	81F	384	$ .01	$ .04	Stanley, Bob	90F	289	$ .01	$ .03
Solomon, Eddie	82F	498	$ .01	$ .04	Stanley, Fred	81F	100	$ .01	$ .04
Sorensen, Lary	81F	519	$ .01	$ .04	Stanley, Fred	82F	108	$ .01	$ .04
Sorensen, Lary	83F	418	$ .01	$ .04	Stanley, Fred	83F	534	$ .01	$ .04
Sorensen, Lary	84F	549	$ .01	$ .06	Stanley, Mike	87F	647	$ .01	$ .45
Sorensen, Lary	85F	434	$ .01	$ .05	Stanley, Mike	88F	480	$ .01	$ .04
Sorensen, Lary	85FU	108	$ .01	$ .05	Stanley, Mike	89F	533	$ .01	$ .05
Sorensen, Lary	86F	381	$ .01	$ .05	Stanton, Mike	81F	400	$ .01	$ .04
Sorensen, Lary	87FU	111	$ .01	$ .05	Stanton, Mike	82F	379	$ .01	$ .04
Sorensen, Lary	82F	128	$ .01	$ .04	Stanton, Mike	83F	486	$ .01	$ .04
Sorenson, Lary	84FU	109	$ .01	$ .10	Stanton, Mike	84F	619	$ .01	$ .06
Sosa, Elias	81F	151	$ .01	$ .04	Stanton, Mike	85F	501	$ .01	$ .05
Sosa, Elias	82F	208	$ .01	$ .04	Stanton, Mike	90F	596	$ .01	$ .15
Sosa, Elias	83F	342	$ .01	$ .04	Stapleton, Dave	81F	236	$ .01	$ .04
Sosa, Elias	84F	313	$ .01	$ .06	Stapleton, Dave	82F	308	$ .01	$ .04
Sosa, Sammy	90F	548	$ .01	$ .35	Stapleton, Dave	83F	196	$ .01	$ .04
Soto, Mario	81F	214	$ .05	$ .30	Stapleton, Dave	84F	410	$ .01	$ .06
Soto, Mario	82F	83	$ .03	$ .20	Stargell, Willie	81F	363	$ .07	$ .50
Soto, Mario	83F	603	$ .03	$ .20	Stargell, Willie	82F	499	$ .05	$ .30
Soto, Mario	84F	483	$ .01	$ .06	Stargell, Willie	83F	324	$ .05	$ .30
Soto, Mario	85F	552	$ .01	$ .05	Stargell, Willie	83F	634	$ .10	$ .50
Soto, Mario	86F	192	$ .01	$ .05	Staub, Rusty	81F	629	$ .01	$ .10
Soto, Mario	87F	214	$ .01	$ .04	Staub, Rusty	82F	536	$ .01	$ .10
Speier, Chris	81F	153	$ .01	$ .04	Staub, Rusty	83F	555	$ .01	$ .10
Speier, Chris	82F	209	$ .01	$ .04	Staub, Rusty	84F	597	$ .01	$ .10
Speier, Chris	83F	298	$ .01	$ .04	Staub, Rusty	85F	92	$ .01	$ .10
Speier, Chris	84F	288	$ .01	$ .06	Staub, Rusty	86F	95	$ .01	$ .10
Speier, Chris	85FU	109	$ .01	$ .05	Stearns, John	81F	317	$ .01	$ .04
Speier, Chris	86F	382	$ .01	$ .05	Stearns, John	82F	537	$ .01	$ .04
Speier, Chris	87F	575	$ .01	$ .04	Stearns, John	83F	556	$ .01	$ .04
Speier, Chris	87FU	112	$ .01	$ .05	Stearns, John	84F	598	$ .01	$ .06
Speier, Chris	88F	96	$ .01	$ .04	Steels, Jim	88FU	64	$ .01	$ .05
Speier, Chris	89F	343	$ .01	$ .05	Stefero, John	87F	652	$1.50	$5.00
Speier, Chris	90F	72	$ .01	$ .03	Stein, Bill	81F	605	$ .01	$ .04
Spencer, Jim	81F	96	$ .01	$ .04	Stein, Bill	82F	331	$ .01	$ .04
Spencer, Jim	82F	107	$ .01	$ .04	Stein, Bill	83F	579	$ .01	$ .04
Spiers, Bill	89FU	40	$ .01	$ .35	Stein, Bill	84F	429	$ .01	$ .06
Spiers, Bill	90F	337	$ .01	$ .15	Steinbach, Terry	87F	405	$ .10	$1.00
Spikes, Charlie	81F	259	$ .01	$ .04	Steinbach, Terry	88F	294	$ .05	$ .20
Spillner, Dan	81F	392	$ .01	$ .04	Steinbach, Terry	89F	22	$ .01	$ .10
Spillner, Dan	83F	419	$ .01	$ .04	Steinbach, Terry	89F	634	$ .05	$ .35
Spillner, Dan	84F	550	$ .01	$ .06	Steinbach, Terry	90F	20	$ .01	$ .03
Spillner, Dan	85F	528	$ .01	$ .05	Stenhouse, Mike	85F	411	$ .01	$ .05
Spillner, Dan	86F	217	$ .01	$ .05	Stenhouse, Mike	85FU	110	$ .01	$ .05
Spillner, Dave	82F	378	$ .01	$ .04	Stenhouse, Mike	86F	406	$ .01	$ .05
Spilman, Harry	81F	209	$ .01	$ .04	Stennett, Rennie	81F	438	$ .01	$ .04
Spilman, Harry	82F	233	$ .01	$ .04	Stennett, Rennie	82F	401	$ .01	$ .04
Spilman, Harry	83F	467	$ .01	$ .04	Stevens, Lee	89FU	16	$ .01	$ .35
Spilman, Harry	87F	284	$ .01	$ .04	Stevens, Lee	90F	145	$ .01	$ .25
Spilman, Harry	88F	97	$ .01	$ .04	Stewart, Dave	82F	24	$1.00	$4.00
Splittorff, Paul	81F	30	$ .01	$ .04	Stewart, Dave	83F	222	$ .10	$ .60
Splittorff, Paul	82F	423	$ .01	$ .04	Stewart, Dave	84F	430	$ .01	$ .50
Splittorff, Paul	83F	124	$ .01	$ .04	Stewart, Dave	85F	569	$ .10	$ .50
Splittorff, Paul	84F	360	$ .01	$ .06	Stewart, Dave	86F	453	$ .05	$ .30
Squires, Mike	81F	349	$ .01	$ .04	Stewart, Dave	87F	406	$ .05	$ .30
Squires, Mike	82F	357	$ .01	$ .04	Stewart, Dave	88F	295	$ .01	$ .10
Squires, Mike	83F	250	$ .01	$ .04	Stewart, Dave	89F	23	$ .01	$ .10
Squires, Mike	84F	71	$ .01	$ .06	Stewart, Dave	90F	21	$ .01	$ .03
Squires, Mike	85F	529	$ .01	$ .05	Stewart, Sammy	81F	181	$ .01	$ .04
St. Claire, Randy	86F	261	$ .01	$ .05	Stewart, Sammy	82F	180	$ .01	$ .04

FLEER

Player	Year	No.	VG	EX/MT	Player	Year	No.	VG	EX/MT
Stewart, Sammy	83F	74	$ .01	$ .04	Stone, Steve	82F	182	$ .01	$ .04
Stewart, Sammy	84F	22	$ .01	$ .06	Stottlemyre, Todd	88FU	68	$ .01	$ .30
Stewart, Sammy	85F	192	$ .01	$ .05	Stottlemyre, Todd	89F	245	$ .01	$ .25
Stewart, Sammy	86F	289	$ .01	$ .05	Stottlemyre, Todd	90F	94	$ .01	$ .03
Stewart, Sammy	86FU	107	$ .01	$ .05	Strain, Joe	81F	458	$ .01	$ .04
Stewart, Sammy	87F	48	$ .01	$ .04	Straker, Les	88F	24	$ .01	$ .10
Stewart, Sammy	88F	616	$ .01	$ .04	Strawberry, Darryl	84F	599	$4.00	$25.00
Stieb, Dave	81F	414	$ .04	$ .25	Strawberry, Darryl	85F	631	$ .05	$ .30
Stieb, Dave	82F	622	$ .01	$ .10	Strawberry, Darryl	85F	93	$1.00	$4.00
Stieb, Dave	83F	441	$ .01	$ .10	Strawberry, Darryl	86F	632	$ .05	$ .30
Stieb, Dave	84F	167	$ .01	$ .10	Strawberry, Darryl	86F	96	$ .50	$2.00
Stieb, Dave	85F	117	$ .01	$ .10	Strawberry, Darryl	87F	23	$ .07	$ .80
Stieb, Dave	86F	642	$ .01	$ .10	Strawberry, Darryl	87F	629	$ .10	$ .50
Stieb, Dave	86F	70	$ .01	$ .10	Strawberry, Darryl	87F	638	$ .10	$1.00
Stieb, Dave	87F	238	$ .01	$ .10	Strawberry, Darryl	88F	151	$ .01	$ .35
Stieb, Dave	88F	123	$ .01	$ .10	Strawberry, Darryl	88F	637	$ .10	$ .50
Stieb, Dave	89F	244	$ .01	$ .05	Strawberry, Darryl	89F	49	$ .05	$ .30
Stieb, Dave	90F	93	$ .01	$ .03	Strawberry, Darryl	89F	632	$ .05	$ .40
Stillwell, Kurt	86FU	108	$ .08	$ .40	Strawberry, Darryl	90F	217	$ .01	$ .15
Stillwell, Kurt	87F	215	$ .10	$ .75	Stubbs, Franklin	85F	386	$ .10	$ .50
Stillwell, Kurt	88F	248	$ .01	$ .10	Stubbs, Franklin	87F	455	$ .01	$ .04
Stillwell, Kurt	88FU	35	$ .01	$ .15	Stubbs, Franklin	88F	527	$ .01	$ .04
Stillwell, Kurt	89F	293	$ .01	$ .05	Stubbs, Franklin	89F	74	$ .01	$ .05
Stillwell, Kurt	90F	118	$ .01	$ .03	Stuper, John	83F	23	$ .01	$ .04
Stoddard, Bob	84F	620	$ .01	$ .06	Stuper, John	84F	337	$ .01	$ .06
Stoddard, Bob	85F	502	$ .01	$ .05	Stuper, John	85FU	112	$ .01	$ .05
Stoddard, Bob	87F	431	$ .01	$ .04	Stuper, John	86F	193	$ .01	$ .05
Stoddard, Tim	81F	176	$ .01	$ .04	Sularz, Guy	83F	273	$ .01	$ .04
Stoddard, Tim	82F	181	$ .01	$ .04	Summers, Champ	81F	466	$ .01	$ .04
Stoddard, Tim	83F	75	$ .01	$ .04	Summers, Champ	82F	282	$ .01	$ .04
Stoddard, Tim	84F	23	$ .01	$ .06	Summers, Champ	83F	274	$ .01	$ .04
Stoddard, Tim	84FU	110	$ .01	$ .10	Summers, Champ	84FU	112	$ .01	$ .10
Stoddard, Tim	85F	68	$ .01	$ .05	Sundberg, Jim	81F	619	$ .01	$ .04
Stoddard, Tim	85FU	111	$ .01	$ .05	Sundberg, Jim	82F	332	$ .01	$ .10
Stoddard, Tim	86F	335	$ .01	$ .05	Sundberg, Jim	83F	580	$ .01	$ .04
Stoddard, Tim	87F	116	$ .01	$ .04	Sundberg, Jim	84F	431	$ .01	$ .06
Stoddard, Tim	88F	222	$ .01	$ .04	Sundberg, Jim	84FU	113	$ .04	$ .25
Stone, Jeff	84FU	111	$ .10	$ .50	Sundberg, Jim	85F	597	$ .01	$ .05
					Sundberg, Jim	85FU	113	$ .03	$ .20
					Sundberg, Jim	86F	22	$ .01	$ .05
					Sundberg, Jim	87F	382	$ .01	$ .04
					Sundberg, Jim	87FU	114	$ .01	$ .05
					Sundberg, Jim	88F	434	$ .01	$ .04
					Surhoff, B. J.	87FU	115	$ .15	$ .75
					Surhoff, B. J.	88F	175	$ .01	$ .20
					Surhoff, B. J.	89F	197	$ .01	$ .05
					Surhoff, B. J.	90F	338	$ .01	$ .03
					Sutcliffe, Rick	81F	125	$ .04	$ .25
					Sutcliffe, Rick	82F	25	$ .03	$ .20
					Sutcliffe, Rick	83F	420	$ .01	$ .10
					Sutcliffe, Rick	84F	551	$ .03	$ .10
					Sutcliffe, Rick	84FU	114	$ .13	$ .65
					Sutcliffe, Rick	85F	69	$ .01	$ .10
					Sutcliffe, Rick	86F	383	$ .01	$ .10
					Sutcliffe, Rick	87F	576	$ .01	$ .10
					Sutcliffe, Rick	88F	435	$ .01	$ .10
					Sutcliffe, Rick	89F	439	$ .01	$ .10
					Sutcliffe, Rick	90F	43	$ .01	$ .03
					Sutter, Bruce	81F	294	$ .04	$ .25
					Sutter, Bruce	82F	129	$ .01	$ .10
					Sutter, Bruce	82F	631	$ .01	$ .04
					Sutter, Bruce	83F	24	$ .01	$ .10
					Sutter, Bruce	84F	338	$ .03	$ .10
					Sutter, Bruce	85F	241	$ .01	$ .10
					Sutter, Bruce	85FU	114	$ .04	$ .25
					Sutter, Bruce	86F	529	$ .01	$ .10
					Sutter, Bruce	87F	530	$ .01	$ .10
					Sutter, Bruce	89F	603	$ .01	$ .05
					Sutton, Don	81F	112	$ .05	$ .30
					Sutton, Don	82F	234	$ .05	$ .30
					Sutton, Don	83F	47	$ .04	$ .25
					Sutton, Don	84F	215	$ .04	$ .25
					Sutton, Don	85F	598	$ .04	$ .25
					Sutton, Don	85FU	115	$ .06	$ .50
					Sutton, Don	86F	170	$ .03	$ .20

JEFF STONE
OUTFIELD
FLEER

Player	Year	No.	VG	EX/MT
Stone, Jeff	85F	266	$ .03	$ .20
Stone, Jeff	86F	454	$ .01	$ .05
Stone, Jeff	87F	189	$ .01	$ .04
Stone, Jeff	88F	317	$ .01	$ .04
Stone, Steve	81F	170	$ .01	$ .04

Player	Year	No.	VG	EX/MT	Player	Year	No.	VG	EX/MT
Sutton, Don	87F	626	$ .01	$ .10	Tellmann, Tom	85F	599	$ .01	$ .05
Sutton, Don	87F	93	$ .01	$ .10	Templeton, Garry	81F	529	$ .01	$ .10
Sutton, Don	88F	505	$ .01	$ .04	Templeton, Garry	82F	131	$ .01	$ .10
Sveum, Dale	86FU	109	$ .10	$ .50	Templeton, Garry	83F	373	$ .01	$ .10
Sveum, Dale	87F	358	$ .06	$ .35	Templeton, Garry	84F	314	$ .03	$ .10
Sveum, Dale	88F	176	$ .01	$ .10	Templeton, Garry	85F	45	$ .01	$ .10
Sveum, Dale	89F	198	$ .01	$ .05	Templeton, Garry	86F	336	$ .01	$ .05
Swaggerty, Bill	85F	193	$ .01	$ .05	Templeton, Garry	87F	432	$ .01	$ .04
Swan, Craig	81F	319	$ .01	$ .04	Templeton, Garry	88F	598	$ .01	$ .04
Swan, Craig	82F	538	$ .01	$ .04	Templeton, Garry	89F	319	$ .01	$ .05
Swan, Craig	83F	557	$ .01	$ .04	Templeton, Garry	90F	170	$ .01	$ .03
Swan, Craig	84F	600	$ .01	$ .06	Tenace, Gene	81F	489	$ .01	$ .04
Swan, Craig	84FU	115	$ .01	$ .10	Tenace, Gene	82F	132	$ .01	$ .04
Sweet, Rick	83F	487	$ .01	$ .04	Tenace, Gene	83F	25	$ .01	$ .04
Sweet, Rick	84F	621	$ .01	$ .06	Tenace, Gene	84F	266	$ .01	$ .06
Swift, Bill	86F	475	$ .01	$ .05	Terrell, Walt	84F	601	$ .06	$ .35
Swift, Bill	87F	597	$ .01	$ .04	Terrell, Walt	85F	94	$ .01	$ .05
Swift, Bill	88FU	61	$ .01	$ .05	Terrell, Walt	85FU	118	$ .01	$ .05
Swift, Bill	89F	560	$ .01	$ .05	Terrell, Walt	86F	240	$ .01	$ .05
Swift, Bill	90F	526	$ .01	$ .03	Terrell, Walt	87F	165	$ .01	$ .04
Swindell, Greg	87F	644	$ .50	$2.25	Terrell, Walt	88F	72	$ .01	$ .04
Swindell, Greg	87FU	116	$ .15	$ .50	Terrell, Walt	89F	149	$ .01	$ .05
Swindell, Greg	88F	617	$ .01	$ .10	Terrell, Walt	90F	457	$ .01	$ .03
Swindell, Greg	89F	413	$ .01	$ .15	Terry, Scott	88FU	121	$ .01	$ .15
Swindell, Greg	90F	503	$ .01	$ .03	Terry, Scott	89F	464	$ .01	$ .05
Sykes, Bob	81F	533	$ .01	$ .04	Terry, Scott	90F	261	$ .01	$ .03
Sykes, Bob	82F	130	$ .01	$ .04	Tettleton, Mickey	85FU	119	$ .10	$1.00
Tabler, Pat	83F	509	$ .03	$ .20	Tettleton, Mickey	86F	432	$ .10	$ .75
Tabler, Pat	84F	552	$ .01	$ .10	Tettleton, Mickey	87F	407	$ .01	$ .04
Tabler, Pat	85F	456	$ .01	$ .10	Tettleton, Mickey	89F	623	$ .01	$ .05
Tabler, Pat	86F	594	$ .01	$ .05	Tettleton, Mickey	90F	190	$ .01	$ .03
Tabler, Pat	87F	261	$ .01	$ .04	Teufel, Tim	84F	574	$ .06	$ .35
Tabler, Pat	88F	618	$ .01	$ .04	Teufel, Tim	85F	290	$ .01	$ .05
Tabler, Pat	88F	633	$ .01	$ .35	Teufel, Tim	86F	407	$ .01	$ .05
Tabler, Pat	88FU	36	$ .01	$ .05	Teufel, Tim	86FU	110	$ .01	$ .05
Tabler, Pat	89F	294	$ .01	$ .05	Teufel, Tim	87F	24	$ .01	$ .04
Tabler, Pat	90F	119	$ .01	$ .03	Teufel, Tim	88F	152	$ .01	$ .04
Tabor, Greg	88F	644	$ .01	$ .30	Teufel, Tim	89F	50	$ .01	$ .05
Tamargo, John	81F	152	$ .01	$ .04	Teufel, Tim	90F	218	$ .01	$ .03
Tanana, Frank	81F	276	$ .01	$ .04	Tewksbury, Bob	86FU	111	$ .05	$ .30
Tanana, Frank	82F	309	$ .01	$ .04	Tewksbury, Bob	87F	117	$ .03	$ .20
Tanana, Frank	83F	581	$ .01	$ .04	Thigpen, Bobby	87F	507	$ .03	$ .20
Tanana, Frank	84F	432	$ .01	$ .06	Thigpen, Bobby	88F	410	$ .01	$ .04
Tanana, Frank	85F	570	$ .01	$ .05	Thigpen, Bobby	89F	512	$ .01	$ .05
Tanana, Frank	86F	239	$ .01	$ .05	Thigpen, Bobby	90F	549	$ .01	$ .03
Tanana, Frank	87F	164	$ .01	$ .04	Thomas, Andres	86FU	112	$ .04	$ .25
Tanana, Frank	88F	71	$ .01	$ .04	Thomas, Andres	87F	531	$ .03	$ .20
Tanana, Frank	89F	147	$ .01	$ .05	Thomas, Andres	88F	551	$ .01	$ .04
Tanana, Frank	90F	616	$ .01	$ .03	Thomas, Andres	89F	604	$ .01	$ .05
Tanner, Bruce	85FU	116	$ .01	$ .05	Thomas, Andres	90F	597	$ .01	$ .03
Tanner, Bruce	86F	218	$ .01	$ .10	Thomas, Derrel	81F	123	$ .01	$ .04
Tanner, Chuck	81F	367	$ .01	$ .04	Thomas, Derrel	82F	26	$ .01	$ .04
Tartabull, Danny	85F	647	$1.00	$4.00	Thomas, Derrel	83F	223	$ .01	$ .04
Tartabull, Danny	86F	476	$ .25	$ .50	Thomas, Derrel	84F	114	$ .01	$ .06
Tartabull, Danny	87F	598	$ .15	$ .50	Thomas, Derrel	84FU	116	$ .01	$ .10
Tartabull, Danny	87FU	117	$ .06	$ .35	Thomas, Derrel	85F	314	$ .01	$ .05
Tartabull, Danny	88F	271	$ .05	$ .25	Thomas, Gorman	81F	507	$ .01	$ .10
Tartabull, Danny	89F	295	$ .01	$ .15	Thomas, Gorman	82F	154	$ .01	$ .10
Tartabull, Danny	90F	120	$ .01	$ .03	Thomas, Gorman	83F	48	$ .01	$ .10
Tate, Stu	90F	643	$ .01	$ .03	Thomas, Gorman	84F	553	$ .01	$ .06
Taveras, Frank	81F	320	$ .01	$ .04	Thomas, Gorman	84FU	117	$ .06	$ .35
Taveras, Frank	82F	539	$ .01	$ .04	Thomas, Gorman	85F	503	$ .01	$ .05
Taylor, Dorn	87FU	118	$ .01	$ .05	Thomas, Gorman	86F	477	$ .01	$ .10
Taylor, Terry	89F	651	$ .01	$ .20	Thomas, Gorman	87F	359	$ .01	$ .04
Tekulve, Kent	81F	362	$ .01	$ .10	Thomas, Roy	84F	622	$ .01	$ .06
Tekulve, Kent	82F	500	$ .01	$ .04	Thomas, Roy	86F	478	$ .01	$ .05
Tekulve, Kent	84F	265	$ .01	$ .06	Thomasson, Gary	81F	138	$ .01	$ .04
Tekulve, Kent	85F	477	$ .01	$ .05	Thompson, Jason	81F	278	$ .01	$ .04
Tekulve, Kent	85FU	117	$ .01	$ .05	Thompson, Jason	82F	501	$ .01	$ .04
Tekulve, Kent	86F	455	$ .01	$ .05	Thompson, Jason	83F	325	$ .01	$ .04
Tekulve, Kent	87F	190	$ .01	$ .04	Thompson, Jason	84F	267	$ .01	$ .06
Tekulve, Kent	88F	318	$ .01	$ .04	Thompson, Jason	85F	478	$ .01	$ .05
Tekulve, Kent	89F	583	$ .01	$ .05	Thompson, Jason	86F	622	$ .01	$ .05
Tekulve, kent	83F	326	$ .01	$ .04	Thompson, Jason	86FU	113	$ .01	$ .05
Tellmann, Tom	84F	216	$ .01	$ .06	Thompson, Milt	86F	530	$ .06	$ .35

Player	Year	No.	VG	EX/MT	Player	Year	No.	VG	EX/MT
Thompson, Milt	86FU	114	$ .01	$ .10	Thurmond, Mark	90F	191	$ .01	$ .03
Thompson, Milt	87F	191	$ .01	$ .10	Tiant, Luis	81F	82	$ .01	$ .10
Thompson, Milt	88F	319	$ .01	$ .04	Tibbs, Jay	85F	553	$ .03	$ .20
Thompson, Milt	89F	584	$ .01	$ .05	Tibbs, Jay	86F	194	$ .01	$ .05
Thompson, Milt	89FU	121	$ .01	$ .05	Tibbs, Jay	86FU	116	$ .01	$ .05
					Tibbs, Jay	87F	333	$ .01	$ .04
					Tibbs, Jay	89F	624	$ .01	$ .05
					Tibbs, Jay	90F	192	$ .01	$ .03
					Tidrow, Dick	81F	299	$ .01	$ .04
					Tidrow, Dick	82F	604	$ .01	$ .04
					Tidrow, Dick	83F	510	$ .01	$ .04
					Tidrow, Dick	84F	72	$ .01	$ .06
					Tingley, Ron	89F	414	$ .01	$ .05
					Tobik, Dave	83F	343	$ .01	$ .04
					Tobik, Dave	84F	433	$ .01	$ .06
					Todd, Jackson	82F	623	$ .01	$ .04
					Toliver, Fred	86F	647	$1.00	$3.00
					Toliver, Fred	86FU	117	$ .01	$ .05
					Toliver, Fred	89F	126	$ .01	$ .05
					Tolleson, Wayne	84F	434	$ .01	$ .06
					Tolleson, Wayne	85F	571	$ .01	$ .05
					Tolleson, Wayne	86F	573	$ .01	$ .05
					Tolleson, Wayne	86FU	118	$ .01	$ .05
					Tolleson, Wayne	87F	118	$ .01	$ .04
					Tolleson, Wayne	88F	223	$ .01	$ .04
					Torre, Joe	81F	325	$ .01	$ .10
					Torrez, Mike	81F	233	$ .01	$ .04
					Torrez, Mike	82F	310	$ .01	$ .04
					Torrez, Mike	83F	197	$ .01	$ .04
					Torrez, Mike	84F	602	$ .01	$ .06
					Traber, Jim	87F	482	$ .01	$ .04
					Traber, Jim	89F	625	$ .01	$ .05
					Traber, Jim	90F	193	$ .01	$ .03
					Tracy, Jim	81F	308	$ .01	$ .04
					Tracy, Jim	82F	605	$ .01	$ .04
					Trammell, Alan	81F	461	$ .10	$ .50
					Trammell, Alan	82F	283	$ .05	$ .35
Thompson, Milt	90F	262	$ .01	$ .03	Trammell, Alan	83F	344	$ .05	$ .30
Thompson, Rich	85FU	120	$ .01	$ .05	Trammell, Alan	84F	91	$ .05	$ .30
Thompson, Rich	86F	595	$ .01	$ .05	Trammell, Alan	85F	23	$ .05	$ .30
Thompson, Rob	87F	285	$ .06	$ .40	Trammell, Alan	86F	241	$ .05	$ .30
Thompson, Rob	88F	98	$ .01	$ .10	Trammell, Alan	86F	633	$ .04	$ .25
Thompson, Rob 'Robby'	86FU	115	$ .06	$ .40	Trammell, Alan	87F	167	$ .03	$ .20
Thompson, Robby	89F	344	$ .01	$ .05	Trammell, Alan	88F	635	$ .01	$ .10
Thompson, Robby	90F	73	$ .01	$ .03	Trammell, Alan	88F	74	$ .01	$ .10
Thompson, Scot	85F	621	$ .01	$ .05	Trammell, Alan	89F	148	$ .01	$ .15
Thompson, Scott	81F	296	$ .01	$ .04	Trammell, Alan	90F	617	$ .01	$ .10
Thompson, Scott	86F	262	$ .01	$ .05	Trautwein, John	88FU	10	$ .01	$ .10
Thon, Dickie	81F	277	$ .01	$ .04	Travers, Billy	81F	514	$ .01	$ .04
Thon, Dickie	82F	235	$ .01	$ .04	Travers, Billy	81F	525	$ .01	$ .04
Thon, Dickie	83F	468	$ .01	$ .04	Treadway, Jeff	88F	249	$ .01	$ .30
Thon, Dickie	84F	243	$ .01	$ .06	Treadway, Jeff	89F	173	$ .01	$ .15
Thon, Dickie	84F	634	$ .01	$ .06	Treadway, Jeff	89FU	75	$ .01	$ .05
Thon, Dickie	85F	364	$ .01	$ .05	Treadway, Jeff	90F	598	$ .01	$ .03
Thon, Dickie	86F	313	$ .01	$ .05	Trevino, Alex	81F	318	$ .01	$ .04
Thon, Dickie	87F	70	$ .01	$ .04	Trevino, Alex	82F	540	$ .01	$ .04
Thon, Dickie	89F	320	$ .01	$ .05	Trevino, Alex	83F	604	$ .01	$ .04
Thon, Dickie	90F	573	$ .01	$ .03	Trevino, Alex	84F	484	$ .01	$ .06
Thornton, Andre	82F	380	$ .01	$ .10	Trevino, Alex	84FU	118	$ .01	$ .10
Thornton, Andre	83F	421	$ .01	$ .10	Trevino, Alex	85F	341	$ .01	$ .05
Thornton, Andre	83F	635	$ .01	$ .04	Trevino, Alex	85FU	122	$ .01	$ .05
Thornton, Andre	84F	554	$ .03	$ .10	Trevino, Alex	86F	550	$ .01	$ .05
Thornton, Andre	85F	457	$ .01	$ .05	Trevino, Alex	86FU	119	$ .01	$ .05
Thornton, Andre	86F	596	$ .01	$ .05	Trevino, Alex	87F	456	$ .01	$ .04
Thornton, Andre	87F	262	$ .01	$ .04	Trevino, Alex	90F	239	$ .01	$ .03
Thornton, Louis	85FU	121	$ .01	$ .05	Trillo, Manny	81F	3	$ .01	$ .04
Thornton, Louis	86F	71	$ .01	$ .10	Trillo, Manny	82F	260	$ .01	$ .04
Thurman, Gary	88F	272	$ .01	$ .20	Trillo, Manny	83F	174	$ .01	$ .04
Thurman, Gary	89F	296	$ .01	$ .10	Trillo, Manny	83F	631	$ .01	$ .10
Thurman, Gary	90F	121	$ .01	$ .03	Trillo, Manny	84F	289	$ .01	$ .06
Thurmond, Mark	84F	315	$ .03	$ .10	Trillo, Manny	84F	627	$ .01	$ .06
Thurmond, Mark	85F	46	$ .01	$ .05	Trillo, Manny	84FU	119	$ .01	$ .10
Thurmond, Mark	86F	337	$ .01	$ .05	Trillo, Manny	85F	622	$ .01	$ .05
Thurmond, Mark	87F	166	$ .01	$ .04	Trillo, Manny	86F	551	$ .01	$ .05
Thurmond, Mark	88F	73	$ .01	$ .04	Trillo, Manny	86FU	120	$ .01	$ .05

FLEER'90

Milt Thompson   OUTFIELD

FLEER

Player	Year	No.	VG	EX/MT	Player	Year	No.	VG	EX/MT
Trillo, Manny	87F	577	$.01	$.04	Valenzuela, Fernando	83F	224	$.05	$.30
Trillo, Manny	88F	436	$.01	$.04	Valenzuela, Fernando	84F	115	$.01	$.06
Trillo, Manny	89F	440	$.01	$.05	Valenzuela, Fernando	85F	387	$.06	$.35
Trout, Steve	81F	345	$.01	$.04	Valenzuela, Fernando	86F	145	$.05	$.30
Trout, Steve	82F	358	$.01	$.04	Valenzuela, Fernando	86F	641	$.05	$.30
Trout, Steve	83F	251	$.01	$.04	Valenzuela, Fernando	87F	457	$.05	$.30
Trout, Steve	84F	506	$.01	$.06	Valenzuela, Fernando	87F	631	$.01	$.10
Trout, Steve	85F	70	$.01	$.05	Valenzuela, Fernando	88F	528	$.01	$.20
Trout, Steve	86F	384	$.01	$.05	Valenzuela, Fernando	89F	76	$.01	$.15
Trout, Steve	87F	578	$.01	$.04	Valenzuela, Fernando	90F	409	$.01	$.03
Trujillo, Mike	86F	360	$.01	$.05	Valenzuela, Fernando	90FPD	622	$.01	$.15
Tudor, John	82F	311	$.10	$.50	Valle, Dave	85FU	125	$.01	$.05
Tudor, John	83F	198	$.01	$.10	Valle, Dave	88F	389	$.01	$.04
Tudor, John	84F	411	$.03	$.10	Valle, Dave	89F	561	$.01	$.05
Tudor, John	84FU	120	$.05	$.30	Valle, David	90F	527	$.01	$.03
Tudor, John	85F	479	$.01	$.10	Van Gorder, David	86F	195	$.01	$.05
Tudor, John	85FU	123	$.04	$.25	Van Slyke, Andy	84F	339	$.75	$3.00
Tudor, John	86F	47	$.01	$.10	Van Slyke, Andy	85F	242	$.03	$.50
Tudor, John	87F	310	$.01	$.10	Van Slyke, Andy	86F	48	$.01	$.20
Tudor, John	88F	48	$.01	$.10	Van Slyke, Andy	87F	311	$.01	$.10
Tudor, John	89F	75	$.01	$.05	Van Slyke, Andy	87FU	121	$.01	$.05
Tunnell, Lee	84F	268	$.01	$.06	Van Slyke, Andy	88F	341	$.01	$.04
Tunnell, Lee	85F	480	$.01	$.05	Van Slyke, Andy	89F	222	$.01	$.05
Tunnell, Lee	85F	638	$.01	$.05	Van Slyke, Andy	90F	481	$.01	$.03
Tunnell, Lee	86F	623	$.01	$.05	Vande Berg, Ed	83F	488	$.01	$.04
Tunnell, Lee	87FU	119	$.01	$.05	Vande Berg, Ed	84F	623	$.01	$.06
Tunnell, Lee	88F	49	$.01	$.04	Vande Berg, Ed	85F	504	$.01	$.05
Turner, Jerry	81F	504	$.01	$.04	Vande Berg, Ed	86F	479	$.01	$.05
Turner, Jerry	83F	345	$.01	$.04	Vande Berg, Ed	86FU	121	$.01	$.05
Turner, Shane	89F	653	$.01	$.20	Vande Berg, Ed	87F	458	$.01	$.04
Twitty, Jeff	81F	49	$.01	$.04	Vande Berg, Ed	87FU	120	$.01	$.05
Tyson, Mike	81F	315	$.01	$.04	Vande Berg, Ed	88F	619	$.01	$.04
Tyson, Mike	82F	606	$.01	$.04	Vande Berg, Ed	89F	534	$.01	$.05
Ujdur, Jerry	83F	346	$.01	$.04	Varsho, Gary	88FU	81	$.01	$.15
Underwood, Pat	81F	469	$.01	$.04	Varsho, Gary	89F	441	$.01	$.15
Underwood, Pat	83F	347	$.01	$.04	Vaughn, Greg	89FU	41	$.01	$2.75
Underwood, Tom	81F	97	$.01	$.04	Vaughn, Greg	90F	339	$.01	$1.25
Underwood, Tom	82F	109	$.01	$.04	Vega, Jesus	83F	624	$.01	$.04
Underwood, Tom	83F	535	$.01	$.04	Velarde, Randy	88F	646	$.01	$.20
Underwood, Tom	84F	460	$.01	$.06	Velez, Otto	81F	410	$.01	$.04
Underwood, Tom	84FU	121	$.01	$.10	Velez, Otto	82F	625	$.01	$.04
Underwood, Tom	85F	194	$.01	$.05	Venable, Max	81F	443	$.01	$.04
Unser, Del	81F	26	$.01	$.04	Venable, Max	83F	275	$.01	$.04
Unser, Del	82F	261	$.01	$.04	Venable, Max	84F	385	$.01	$.06
Upshaw, Willie	82F	624	$.01	$.04	Venable, Max	86F	196	$.01	$.05
Upshaw, Willie	83F	442	$.01	$.04	Venable, Max	87F	216	$.01	$.04
Upshaw, Willie	84F	168	$.01	$.06	Ventura, Robin	89FU	23	$.01	$1.50
Upshaw, Willie	85F	118	$.01	$.05	Ventura, Robin	90F	550	$.01	$.50
Upshaw, Willie	85F	635	$.01	$.10	Veres, Randy	89FU	42	$.01	$.15
Upshaw, Willie	86F	72	$.01	$.05	Verhoeven, John	82F	547	$.01	$.04
Upshaw, Willie	87F	230	$.01	$.04	Veryzer, Tom	81F	390	$.01	$.04
Upshaw, Willie	88F	124	$.01	$.04	Veryzer, Tom	82F	381	$.01	$.04
Upshaw, Willie	88FU	25	$.01	$.05	Veryzer, Tom	83F	559	$.01	$.04
Upshaw, Willie	89F	415	$.01	$.05	Viola, Frank	83F	625	$.75	$4.00
Uribe, Jose	85FU	124	$.05	$.30	Viola, Frank	84F	575	$.25	$1.25
Uribe, Jose	86F	552	$.01	$.20	Viola, Frank	85F	291	$.15	$.50
Uribe, Jose	87F	286	$.01	$.04	Viola, Frank	86F	408	$.10	$.40
Uribe, Jose	88F	99	$.01	$.04	Viola, Frank	87F	554	$.05	$.20
Uribe, Jose	89F	345	$.01	$.05	Viola, Frank	88F	25	$.01	$.10
Uribe, Jose	90F	74	$.01	$.03	Viola, Frank	89F	127	$.01	$.15
Urrea, John	82F	583	$.01	$.04	Viola, Frank	90F	219	$.01	$.15
Vail, Mike	81F	311	$.01	$.04	Virdon, Bill	81F	61	$.01	$.04
Vail, Mike	82F	84	$.01	$.04	Virgil, Ozzie	83F	175	$.01	$.04
Vail, Mike	83F	605	$.01	$.04	Virgil, Ozzie	84F	49	$.01	$.06
Vail, Mike	84F	290	$.01	$.06	Virgil, Ozzie	85F	267	$.01	$.05
Vail, Mike	84FU	122	$.01	$.10	Virgil, Ozzie	86FU	122	$.01	$.05
Valdez, Julio	83F	199	$.01	$.04	Virgil, Ozzie	87F	532	$.01	$.04
Valentine, Ellis	81F	148	$.01	$.04	Virgil, Ozzie	88F	552	$.01	$.04
Valentine, Ellis	82F	541	$.01	$.04	Virgil, Ozzie	89F	605	$.01	$.05
Valentine, Ellis	83F	558	$.01	$.04	Vizcaino, Jose	90F	410	$.01	$.25
Valentine, Ellis	84F	529	$.01	$.04	Vizquel, Omar	89FU	62	$.01	$.25
Valenzuela, Fernando	81F	140	$.80	$4.25	Vizquel, Omar	90F	528	$.01	$.10
Valenzuela, Fernando	82F	27	$.07	$.60	Von Ohlen, Dave	84F	340	$.01	$.06
Valenzuela, Fernando	82F	635	$.04	$.25	Von Ohlen, Dave	85F	243	$.01	$.05
Valenzuela, Fernando	82F	636	$.04	$.25	Von Ohlen, Dave	85FU	126	$.01	$.05

165

Player	Year	No.	VG	EX/MT	Player	Year	No.	VG	EX/MT
Von Ohlen, Dave	86F	597	$ .01	$ .05	Ward, Duane	90F	95	$ .01	$ .03
Von Ohlen, Dave	87F	408	$ .01	$ .04	Ward, Gary	82F	562	$ .01	$ .04
Vuckovich, Pete	82F	156	$ .01	$ .04	Ward, Gary	83F	627	$ .01	$ .04
Vuckovich, Pete	83F	49	$ .01	$ .04	Ward, Gary	84F	576	$ .01	$ .06
Vuckovich, Pete	84F	217	$ .01	$ .06	Ward, Gary	84FU	124	$ .04	$ .25
Vuckovich, Pete	86F	504	$ .01	$ .05	Ward, Gary	85F	572	$ .01	$ .05
Vukovich, George	81F	21	$ .01	$ .04	Ward, Gary	86F	575	$ .01	$ .05
Vukovich, George	82F	262	$ .01	$ .04	Ward, Gary	87F	140	$ .01	$ .04
Vukovich, George	83F	176	$ .01	$ .04	Ward, Gary	87FU	122	$ .01	$ .05
Vukovich, George	84F	555	$ .01	$ .06	Ward, Gary	88F	224	$ .01	$ .04
Vukovich, George	85F	458	$ .01	$ .05					
Vukovich, George	86F	598	$ .01	$ .05					
Vukovich, John	81F	22	$ .01	$ .04					
Waddell, Tom	84FU	123	$ .05	$ .30					
Waddell, Tom	85F	459	$ .01	$ .05					
Waddell, Tom	86F	599	$ .01	$ .05					
Wagner, Mark	81F	478	$ .01	$ .04					
Wagner, Mark	82F	333	$ .01	$ .04					
Wagner, Mark	83F	582	$ .01	$ .04					
Waits, Rick	81F	396	$ .01	$ .04					
Waits, Rick	82F	382	$ .01	$ .04					
Waits, Rick	83F	422	$ .01	$ .04					
Waits, Rick	85F	600	$ .01	$ .05					
Waits, Rick	86F	505	$ .01	$ .05					
Walewander, Jim	89F	150	$ .01	$ .05					
Walk, Bob	81F	14	$ .01	$ .04					
Walk, Bob	83F	149	$ .01	$ .04					
Walk, Bob	87F	623	$ .01	$ .04					
Walk, Bob	88F	342	$ .01	$ .04					
Walk, Bob	89F	223	$ .01	$ .05					
Walk, Bob	90F	482	$ .01	$ .03					
Walker, Duane	83F	606	$ .01	$ .04					
Walker, Duane	84F	485	$ .01	$ .06					
Walker, Duane	85F	554	$ .01	$ .05					
Walker, Duane	86F	574	$ .01	$ .05					
Walker, Greg	84F	73	$ .10	$ .50					
Walker, Greg	85F	530	$ .01	$ .05					
Walker, Greg	86F	219	$ .01	$ .10					
Walker, Greg	87F	508	$ .01	$ .04					
Walker, Greg	88F	411	$ .01	$ .04					
Walker, Greg	90F	551	$ .01	$ .03					
Walker, Larry	90F	363	$ .01	$ .35					
Walker, Tony	86FU	123	$ .01	$ .05	Ward, Gary	89F	273	$ .01	$ .05
Walker, Tony	87F	71	$ .01	$ .10	Ward, Gary	89FU	33	$ .01	$ .05
Wallach, Tim	82F	210	$ .25	$1.00	Ward, Gary	90F	618	$ .01	$ .03
Wallach, Tim	83F	299	$ .05	$ .25	Wardle, Curt	85FU	127	$ .01	$ .05
Wallach, Tim	84F	291	$ .03	$ .20	Wardle, Curt	86F	600	$ .01	$ .05
Wallach, Tim	85F	412	$ .03	$ .20	Warren, Mike	84F	461	$ .01	$ .06
Wallach, Tim	86F	263	$ .01	$ .10	Warren, Mike	84F	639	$ .01	$ .06
Wallach, Tim	87F	334	$ .01	$ .10	Warren, Mike	85F	435	$ .01	$ .05
Wallach, Tim	88F	198	$ .01	$ .10	Washington, Claudell	81F	329	$ .01	$ .04
Wallach, Tim	89F	395	$ .01	$ .05	Washington, Claudell	82F	449	$ .01	$ .04
Wallach, Tim	90F	364	$ .01	$ .03	Washington, Claudell	83F	150	$ .01	$ .04
Waller, Ty	82F	607	$ .01	$ .04	Washington, Claudell	84F	192	$ .01	$ .06
Walling, Denny	81F	66	$ .01	$ .04	Washington, Claudell	85F	342	$ .01	$ .05
Walling, Denny	82F	236	$ .01	$ .04	Washington, Claudell	86F	531	$ .01	$ .05
Walling, Denny	83F	469	$ .01	$ .04	Washington, Claudell	87F	119	$ .01	$ .04
Walling, Denny	84F	244	$ .01	$ .06	Washington, Claudell	88F	225	$ .01	$ .04
Walling, Denny	85F	365	$ .01	$ .05	Washington, Claudell	89F	272	$ .01	$ .05
Walling, Denny	86F	314	$ .01	$ .05	Washington, Claudell	89FU	17	$ .01	$ .05
Walling, Denny	87F	72	$ .01	$ .04	Washington, Claudell	90F	146	$ .01	$ .03
Walling, Denny	88F	458	$ .01	$ .04	Washington, Ron	83F	626	$ .01	$ .04
Walling, Denny	89F	465	$ .01	$ .05	Washington, Ron	84F	577	$ .01	$ .06
Walling, Denny	90F	263	$ .01	$ .03	Washington, Ron	85F	292	$ .01	$ .05
Walter, Gene	86F	644	$1.25	$5.00	Washington, Ron	86F	409	$ .01	$ .05
Walter, Gene	86FU	124	$ .01	$ .05	Washington, Ron	89F	416	$ .01	$ .05
Walter, Gene	87F	433	$ .01	$ .04	Washington, U. L.	81F	34	$ .01	$ .04
Walter, Gene	88F	153	$ .01	$ .04	Washington, U. L.	82F	424	$ .01	$ .04
Walton, Jerome	89FU	80	$ .01	$4.00	Washington, U. L.	83F	125	$ .01	$ .04
Walton, Jerome	90F	44	$ .01	$1.50	Washington, U. L.	84F	361	$ .01	$ .06
Walton, Reggie	81F	609	$ .01	$ .04	Washington, U. L.	85F	215	$ .01	$ .05
Ward, Colin	86F	645	$ .01	$ .10	Washington, U. L.	85FU	128	$ .01	$ .05
Ward, Duane	86FU	125	$ .04	$ .25	Washington, U. L.	86F	264	$ .01	$ .05
Ward, Duane	88F	125	$ .01	$ .04	Wasinger, Mark	88F	100	$ .01	$ .15
Ward, Duane	89F	246	$ .01	$ .05	Wathan, John	81F	46	$ .01	$ .04

GARY WARD
OUTFIELD

FLEER

Player	Year	No.	VG	EX/MT	Player	Year	No.	VG	EX/MT
Wathan, John	82F	425	$ .01	$ .04	White, Frank	87F	383	$ .01	$ .04
Wathan, John	83F	126	$ .01	$ .04	White, Frank	88F	273	$ .01	$ .04
Wathan, John	84F	362	$ .01	$ .06	White, Frank	89F	297	$ .01	$ .05
Wathan, John	85F	216	$ .01	$ .05	White, Frank	90F	122	$ .01	$ .03
Wathan, John	86F	23	$ .01	$ .05	White, Jerry	81F	161	$ .01	$ .04
Watson, Bob	81F	93	$ .01	$ .04	White, Jerry	82F	211	$ .01	$ .04
Watson, Bob	82F	54	$ .01	$ .04	White, Jerry	83F	300	$ .01	$ .04
Watson, Bob	83F	151	$ .01	$ .04	Whitehouse, Len	84F	578	$ .01	$ .06
Watson, Bob	84F	193	$ .01	$ .06	Whitehurst, Wally	89FU	103	$ .01	$ .20
Wayne, Gary	90F	387	$ .01	$ .10	Whitfield, Terry	81F	437	$ .01	$ .04
Weaver, Earl	81F	178	$ .01	$ .04	Whitfield, Terry	84FU	125	$ .01	$ .10
Webster, Mich	90F	45	$ .01	$ .03	Whitfield, Terry	85F	389	$ .01	$ .05
Webster, Mitch	86F	265	$ .05	$ .25	Whitfield, Terry	86F	147	$ .01	$ .05
Webster, Mitch	87F	335	$ .01	$ .04	Whitson, Ed	81F	444	$ .01	$ .04
Webster, Mitch	88F	199	$ .01	$ .04	Whitson, Ed	82F	402	$ .01	$ .04
Webster, Mitch	89F	442	$ .01	$ .05	Whitson, Ed	84F	316	$ .01	$ .06
Wegman, Bill	87F	360	$ .01	$ .04	Whitson, Ed	85F	47	$ .01	$ .05
Wegman, Bill	88F	177	$ .01	$ .04	Whitson, Ed	85FU	129	$ .01	$ .05
Wegman, Bill	89F	199	$ .01	$ .05	Whitson, Ed	86F	120	$ .01	$ .05
Wehrmeister, Dave	86F	220	$ .01	$ .05	Whitson, Ed	87F	434	$ .01	$ .04
Weiss, Gary	81F	130	$ .01	$ .04	Whitson, Ed	88F	599	$ .01	$ .04
Weiss, Walt	88F	652	$ .30	$1.25	Whitson, Ed	89F	321	$ .01	$ .05
Weiss, Walt	88FU	56	$ .10	$ .75	Whitson, Ed	90F	171	$ .01	$ .03
Weiss, Walt	89F	24	$ .01	$ .25	Whitson, Eddie	83F	423	$ .01	$ .04
Weiss, Walt	90F	22	$ .01	$ .10	Whitt, Ernie	81F	411	$ .01	$ .04
Welch, Bob	81F	120	$ .03	$ .20	Whitt, Ernie	82F	626	$ .01	$ .04
Welch, Bob	82F	28	$ .01	$ .10	Whitt, Ernie	83F	443	$ .01	$ .04
Welch, Bob	83F	225	$ .01	$ .04	Whitt, Ernie	84F	169	$ .01	$ .06
Welch, Bob	84F	116	$ .01	$ .06	Whitt, Ernie	85F	119	$ .01	$ .05
Welch, Bob	85F	388	$ .01	$ .05	Whitt, Ernie	86F	73	$ .01	$ .05
Welch, Bob	86F	146	$ .01	$ .05	Whitt, Ernie	87F	240	$ .01	$ .04
Welch, Bob	87F	459	$ .01	$ .04	Whitt, Ernie	88F	126	$ .01	$ .04
Welch, Bob	88F	529	$ .01	$ .04	Whitt, Ernie	89F	248	$ .01	$ .05
Welch, Bob	88FU	57	$ .01	$ .05	Whitt, Ernie	90F	97	$ .01	$ .03
Welch, Bob	89F	25	$ .01	$ .05	Wiggins, Alan	83F	375	$ .01	$ .10
Welch, Bob	90F	23	$ .01	$ .10	Wiggins, Alan	84F	317	$ .01	$ .06
Wellman, Brad	84F	386	$ .01	$ .06	Wiggins, Alan	85F	48	$ .01	$ .05
Wellman, Brad	85F	623	$ .01	$ .05	Wiggins, Alan	86F	290	$ .01	$ .05
Wellman, Brad	86F	553	$ .01	$ .05	Wiggins, Alan	87FU	124	$ .01	$ .05
Wells, David	88FU	69	$ .01	$ .05	Wilcox, Milt	81F	465	$ .01	$ .04
Wells, David	89F	247	$ .01	$ .05	Wilcox, Milt	82F	285	$ .01	$ .04
Wells, David	90F	96	$ .01	$ .03	Wilcox, Milt	83F	349	$ .01	$ .04
Welsh, Chris	82F	584	$ .01	$ .04	Wilcox, Milt	84F	93	$ .01	$ .06
Welsh, Chris	83F	374	$ .01	$ .04	Wilcox, Milt	85F	25	$ .01	$ .05
Welsh, Chris	84F	292	$ .01	$ .06	Wilcox, Milt	86F	243	$ .01	$ .05
Welsh, Chris	86F	576	$ .01	$ .05	Wilfong, Bob	81F	569	$ .01	$ .04
Welsh, Chris	87F	217	$ .01	$ .04	Wilfong, Rob	82F	563	$ .01	$ .04
Werth, Dennis	81F	102	$ .01	$ .04	Wilfong, Rob	83F	101	$ .01	$ .04
Werth, Dennis	82F	55	$ .01	$ .04	Wilfong, Rob	84F	530	$ .01	$ .06
West, Dave	89F	51	$ .05	$ .50	Wilfong, Rob	85F	315	$ .01	$ .05
West, Dave	00F	300	$ .01	$ .20	Wiltong, Rob	87F	94	$ .01	$ .04
Wetteland, John	90F	411	$ .01	$ .25	Wilkerson, Curt	90F	46	$ .01	$ .03
Whisenton, Larry	83F	152	$ .01	$ .04	Wilkerson, Curtis	84FU	126	$ .01	$ .10
Whitaker, Lou	81F	463	$ .05	$ .30	Wilkerson, Curtis	85F	573	$ .01	$ .05
Whitaker, Lou	82F	284	$ .05	$ .25	Wilkerson, Curtis	86F	577	$ .01	$ .05
Whitaker, Lou	83F	348	$ .03	$ .20	Wilkerson, Curtis	87F	141	$ .01	$ .04
Whitaker, Lou	84F	92	$ .03	$ .20	Wilkerson, Curtis	88F	481	$ .01	$ .04
Whitaker, Lou	85F	24	$ .03	$ .20	Wilkerson, Curtis	89F	535	$ .01	$ .05
Whitaker, Lou	86F	242	$ .03	$ .20	Wilkins, Dean	90F	47	$ .01	$ .15
Whitaker, Lou	87F	168	$ .01	$ .10	Wilkinson, Bill	87FU	125	$ .01	$ .10
Whitaker, Lou	88F	75	$ .01	$ .10	Wilkinson, Bill	88F	390	$ .01	$ .10
Whitaker, Lou	89F	151	$ .01	$ .10	Willard, Jerry	85F	460	$ .01	$ .05
Whitaker, Lou	90F	619	$ .01	$ .10	Willard, Jerry	86F	601	$ .01	$ .05
White, Devon	87F	646	$ .25	$1.25	Willard, Jerry	86FU	126	$ .01	$ .05
White, Devon	87FU	123	$ .11	$ .55	Willard, Jerry	87F	409	$ .01	$ .04
White, Devon	88F	506	$ .01	$ .20	Williams, Al	82F	564	$ .01	$ .04
White, Devon	89F	489	$ .01	$ .15	Williams, Al	83F	628	$ .01	$ .04
White, Devon	90F	147	$ .01	$ .03	Williams, Al	84F	579	$ .01	$ .06
White, Frank	81F	44	$ .01	$ .10	Williams, Dana	90F	648	$ .01	$ .03
White, Frank	82F	426	$ .01	$ .10	Williams, Dick	81F	149	$ .01	$ .10
White, Frank	82F	629	$ .01	$ .04	Williams, Eddie	88F	620	$ .01	$ .20
White, Frank	83F	127	$ .01	$ .04	Williams, Frank	84FU	127	$ .06	$ .35
White, Frank	84F	363	$ .01	$ .06	Williams, Frank	85F	624	$ .04	$ .25
White, Frank	85F	217	$ .01	$ .05	Williams, Frank	86F	554	$ .01	$ .05
White, Frank	86F	24	$ .01	$ .05	Williams, Frank	87F	287	$ .01	$ .04

FLEER

Player	Year	No.	VG	EX/MT	Player	Year	No.	VG	EX/MT
Williams, Frank	87FU	127	$ .01	$ .05	Wilson, Mookie	85F	95	$ .01	$ .05
Williams, Frank	88F	250	$ .01	$ .04	Wilson, Mookie	86F	97	$ .01	$ .05
Williams, Frank	89F	174	$ .01	$ .05	Wilson, Mookie	87F	25	$ .01	$ .04
Williams, Frank	89FU	34	$ .01	$ .05	Wilson, Mookie	88F	154	$ .01	$ .04
Williams, Frank	90F	620	$ .01	$ .03	Wilson, Mookie	89F	52	$ .01	$ .05
Williams, Ken 'Kenny'	87FU	128	$ .05	$ .30	Wilson, Mookie	90F	99	$ .01	$ .03
Williams, Ken	88F	412	$ .01	$ .20	Wilson, Steve	89F	640	$ .01	$ .20
Williams, Matt	87FU	129	$ .06	$2.50	Wilson, Steve	89FU	82	$ .01	$ .10
Williams, Matt	88F	101	$ .50	$2.50	Wilson, Steve	90F	49	$ .01	$ .10
Williams, Matt	89F	346	$ .01	$ .25	Wilson, Trevor	89F	347	$ .01	$ .05
Williams, Matt	90F	75	$ .01	$ .15	Wilson, Willie	81F	29	$ .03	$ .20
Williams, Mitch	86FU	127	$ .05	$ .60	Wilson, Willie	81F	653	$ .01	$ .10
Williams, Mitch	87F	142	$ .03	$ .55	Wilson, Willie	82F	427	$ .03	$ .20
Williams, Mitch	88F	482	$ .01	$ .10	Wilson, Willie	83F	128	$ .01	$ .10
Williams, Mitch	89F	536	$ .01	$ .10	Wilson, Willie	84F	364	$ .01	$ .10
Williams, Mitch	89FU	81	$ .01	$ .15	Wilson, Willie	85F	218	$ .01	$ .10
Williams, Mitch	90F	48	$ .01	$ .03	Wilson, Willie	86F	25	$ .01	$ .10
Williams, Mitch	90F	631	$ .01	$ .03	Wilson, Willie	87F	384	$ .04	$ .10
Williams, Reggie	86FU	128	$ .03	$ .20	Wilson, Willie	88F	274	$ .01	$ .10
Williams, Reggie	87F	460	$ .01	$ .04	Wilson, Willie	89F	298	$ .01	$ .05
Williamson, Mark	88F	574	$ .01	$ .10	Wilson, Willie	90F	123	$ .01	$ .03
Williamson, Mark	89F	626	$ .01	$ .05	Wine, Robbie	88F	459	$ .01	$ .15
Williamson, Mark	90F	194	$ .01	$ .03	Winfield, Dave	81F	484	$ .06	$ .75
Willis, Carl	87F	218	$ .01	$ .04	Winfield, Dave	82F	56	$ .09	$ .75
Willis, Mike	81F	426	$ .01	$ .04	Winfield, Dave	82F	646	$ .10	$ .50
Wills, Bump	81F	628	$ .01	$ .04	Winfield, Dave	83F	398	$ .06	$ .40
Wills, Bump	82F	334	$ .01	$ .04	Winfield, Dave	83F	633	$ .03	$ .20
Wills, Bump	83F	511	$ .01	$ .04	Winfield, Dave	84F	143	$ .06	$ .75
Wills, Frank	86F	480	$ .01	$ .05	Winfield, Dave	85F	146	$ .01	$ .25
Wills, Frank	90F	98	$ .01	$ .10	Winfield, Dave	85F	629	$ .05	$ .50
Wills, Maury	81F	595	$ .01	$ .04	Winfield, Dave	86F	121	$ .05	$ .30
Wilson, Glenn	83F	350	$ .08	$ .40	Winfield, Dave	87F	120	$ .05	$ .30
Wilson, Glenn	84F	94	$ .03	$ .20	Winfield, Dave	88F	226	$ .01	$ .20
Wilson, Glenn	84FU	128	$ .06	$ .35	Winfield, Dave	89F	274	$ .01	$ .15
					Winfield, Dave	90F	458	$ .01	$ .15
					Winn, Jim	86F	624	$ .01	$ .05
					Winn, Jim	87F	624	$ .01	$ .04
					Winn, Jim	87FU	126	$ .01	$ .05
					Winn, Jim	88F	413	$ .01	$ .04
					Winningham, Herm	85FU	130	$ .04	$ .25
					Winningham, Herm	86F	266	$ .01	$ .10
					Winningham, Herm	87FU	130	$ .01	$ .05
					Winningham, Herm	88F	200	$ .01	$ .04
					Winningham, Herm	89F	175	$ .01	$ .05
					Winningham, Herm	90F	435	$ .01	$ .03
					Winters, Matt	90F	124	$ .01	$ .15
					Wise, Rick	82F	585	$ .01	$ .04
					Witt, Bobby	86FU	129	$ .06	$ .50
					Witt, Bobby	87F	143	$ .05	$ .40
					Witt, Bobby	88F	483	$ .01	$ .04
					Witt, Bobby	89F	537	$ .01	$ .05
					Witt, Bobby	90F	315	$ .01	$ .15
					Witt, Mike	82F	473	$ .12	$1.00
					Witt, Mike	83F	102	$ .05	$ .25
					Witt, Mike	84F	531	$ .04	$ .25
					Witt, Mike	85F	316	$ .01	$ .10
					Witt, Mike	85F	643	$ .01	$ .15
					Witt, Mike	86F	171	$ .01	$ .10
					Witt, Mike	87F	641	$ .01	$ .04
					Witt, Mike	87F	95	$ .01	$ .10
					Witt, Mike	88F	507	$ .01	$ .04
					Witt, Mike	88F	626	$ .01	$ .04
					Witt, Mike	89F	490	$ .01	$ .05
					Witt, Mike	90F	148	$ .01	$ .03
					Wockenfuss, John	81F	472	$ .01	$ .04
					Wockenfuss, John	82F	286	$ .01	$ .04
Wilson, Glenn	85F	268	$ .01	$ .05	Wockenfuss, John	83F	351	$ .01	$ .04
Wilson, Glenn	86F	457	$ .01	$ .05	Wockenfuss, John	84F	95	$ .01	$ .06
Wilson, Glenn	87F	192	$ .01	$ .10	Wockenfuss, John	84FU	129	$ .01	$ .10
Wilson, Glenn	88F	320	$ .01	$ .04	Wockenfuss, John	85F	269	$ .01	$ .05
Wilson, Glenn	89F	224	$ .01	$ .05	Wohlford, Jim	81F	440	$ .01	$ .04
Wilson, Glenn	90F	240	$ .01	$ .03	Wohlford, Jim	82F	403	$ .01	$ .04
Wilson, Mookie	82F	542	$ .01	$ .10	Wohlford, Jim	83F	276	$ .01	$ .04
Wilson, Mookie	83F	560	$ .01	$ .10	Wohlford, Jim	84F	293	$ .01	$ .06
Wilson, Mookie	84F	603	$ .01	$ .06	Wohlford, Jim	85F	413	$ .01	$ .05

GLENN WILSON
OUTFIELD

FLEER

Player	Year	No.	VG	EX/MT	Player	Year	No.	VG	EX/MT
Wohlford, Jim	87F	336	$ .01	$ .04	Yost, Ned	84F	218	$ .01	$ .06
Wojna, Ed	86F	338	$ .01	$ .10	Yost, Ned	84FU	130	$ .01	$ .10
Woodard, Mike	86F	645	$ .01	$ .10	Yost, Ned	85F	575	$ .01	$ .05
Woodard, Mike	89F	513	$ .01	$ .05	Youmans, Floyd	86F	267	$ .10	$ .50
Woods, Al	81F	422	$ .01	$ .04	Youmans, Floyd	87F	337	$ .01	$ .10
Woods, Al	82F	627	$ .01	$ .04	Youmans, Floyd	88F	201	$ .01	$ .10
Woods, Al	83F	444	$ .01	$ .04	Young, Curt	85F	436	$ .08	$ .40
Woods, Gary	81F	75	$ .01	$ .04	Young, Curt	87F	410	$ .01	$ .04
Woods, Gary	82F	237	$ .01	$ .04	Young, Curt	88F	296	$ .01	$ .04
Woods, Gary	83F	512	$ .01	$ .04	Young, Curt	89F	26	$ .01	$ .05
Woods, Gary	84F	507	$ .01	$ .06	Young, Curt	90F	24	$ .01	$ .03
Woods, Gary	85F	71	$ .01	$ .05	Young, Gerald	88F	460	$ .01	$ .25
Woods, Gary	86F	385	$ .01	$ .05	Young, Gerald	89F	370	$ .01	$ .05
Woodson, Tracy	88FU	98	$ .01	$ .05	Young, Gerald	90F	241	$ .01	$ .03
Woodson, Tracy	89F	77	$ .01	$ .05	Young, Matt	84F	624	$ .03	$ .20
Woodward, Rob	86F	651	$ .01	$ .25	Young, Matt	85F	505	$ .01	$ .05
Worrell, Todd	86F	49	$ .15	$ .75	Young, Matt	86F	481	$ .01	$ .05
Worrell, Todd	87F	312	$ .04	$ .25	Young, Matt	87F	600	$ .01	$ .04
Worrell, Todd	88F	50	$ .01	$ .10	Young, Matt	87FU	131	$ .01	$ .05
Worrell, Todd	89F	466	$ .01	$ .05	Young, Matt	88F	530	$ .01	$ .25
Worrell, Todd	90F	264	$ .01	$ .03	Young, Mike	84FU	131	$ .05	$ .25
Wortham, Richard	81F	347	$ .01	$ .04	Young, Mike	85F	195	$ .03	$ .20
Worthington, Craig	88FU	4	$ .01	$ .60	Young, Mike	86F	291	$ .01	$ .05
Worthington, Craig	89F	627	$ .01	$ .45	Young, Mike	87F	483	$ .01	$ .04
Worthington, Craig	90F	195	$ .01	$ .10	Young, Mike	88F	575	$ .01	$ .04
Wright, George	83F	583	$ .01	$ .04	Youngblood, Joel	81F	331	$ .01	$ .04
Wright, George	84F	435	$ .01	$ .06	Youngblood, Joel	82F	543	$ .01	$ .04
Wright, George	85F	574	$ .01	$ .05	Youngblood, Joel	83F	301	$ .01	$ .04
Wright, George	86F	578	$ .01	$ .05	Youngblood, Joel	83F	641	$ .01	$ .04
Wright, Ricky	83F	226	$ .01	$ .04	Youngblood, Joel	84F	387	$ .01	$ .06
Wynegar, Butch	81F	558	$ .01	$ .04	Youngblood, Joel	86F	555	$ .01	$ .05
Wynegar, Butch	82F	565	$ .01	$ .04	Youngblood, Joel	87F	288	$ .01	$ .04
Wynegar, Butch	83F	399	$ .01	$ .04	Yount, Robin	81F	511	$ .15	$1.25
Wynegar, Butch	84F	144	$ .01	$ .06	Yount, Robin	82F	155	$ .15	$1.25
Wynegar, Butch	85F	147	$ .01	$ .05	Yount, Robin	83F	51	$ .10	$1.00
Wynegar, Butch	86F	122	$ .01	$ .05	Yount, Robin	83F	632	$ .03	$ .20
Wynne, Marvell	84F	269	$ .01	$ .06	Yount, Robin	84F	219	$ .25	$1.25
Wynne, Marvell	85F	481	$ .01	$ .05	Yount, Robin	85F	601	$ .05	$ .80
Wynne, Marvell	86F	625	$ .01	$ .05	Yount, Robin	86F	506	$ .05	$ .30
Wynne, Marvell	86FU	130	$ .01	$ .05	Yount, Robin	87F	361	$ .05	$ .30
Wynne, Marvell	87F	435	$ .01	$ .04	Yount, Robin	88F	178	$ .01	$ .15
Wynne, Marvell	89F	322	$ .01	$ .05	Yount, Robin	89F	200	$ .01	$ .15
Yastrzemski, Carl	81F	221	$ .20	$1.25	Yount, Robin	90F	340	$ .01	$ .10
Yastrzemski, Carl	81F	638	$ .12	$1.00	Zachry, Pat	81F	334	$ .01	$ .04
Yastrzemski, Carl	82F	312	$ .13	$1.00	Zachry, Pat	82F	544	$ .01	$ .04
Yastrzemski, Carl	82F	633	$ .06	$ .35	Zachry, Pat	83F	561	$ .01	$ .04
Yastrzemski, Carl	83F	200	$ .12	$ .75	Zachry, Pat	84F	118	$ .01	$ .06
Yastrzemski, Carl	83F	629	$ .05	$ .25	Zachry, Pat	85F	391	$ .01	$ .05
Yastrzemski, Carl	84F	412	$ .25	$1.00	Zahn, Geoff	81F	564	$ .01	$ .04
Yastrzemski, Carl	84F	640	$ .10	$ .50	Zahn, Geoff	82F	474	$ .01	$ .04
Yeager, Steve	81F	129	$ .01	$ .04	Zahn, Geoff	83F	103	$ .01	$ .04
Yeager, Steve	82F	29	$ .01	$ .04	Zahn, Geoff	84F	532	$ .01	$ .06
Yeager, Steve	83F	227	$ .01	$ .04	Zahn, Geoff	85F	317	$ .01	$ .05
Yeager, Steve	84F	117	$ .01	$ .06	Zeile, Todd	89FU	122	$ .01	$3.25
Yeager, Steve	85F	390	$ .01	$ .05	Zeile, Todd	90F	265	$ .01	$2.00
Yeager, Steve	86FU	131	$ .01	$ .05	Zimmer, Don	81F	230	$ .01	$ .04
Yeager, Steve	87F	599	$ .01	$ .04	Zisk, Richie	81F	620	$ .01	$ .04
Yett, Rich	85FU	131	$ .01	$ .10	Zisk, Richie	82F	519	$ .01	$ .04
Yett, Rich	87F	263	$ .01	$ .04	Zisk, Richie	83F	489	$ .01	$ .04
Yett, Rich	88F	621	$ .01	$ .04	Zisk, Richie	84F	625	$ .01	$ .06
Yett, Rich	89F	417	$ .01	$ .05	Zuvella, Paul	85F	651	$ .08	$ .40
Yett, Rich	90F	504	$ .01	$ .03	Zuvella, Paul	86F	532	$ .01	$ .05
Yost, Ned	83F	50	$ .01	$ .04					

MAJOR LEAGUE MARKETING (SCORE/SPORTFLICS) 1986-1990

In 1986 a new concept of "Magic Motion" cards called Sportflics was introduced by Major League Marketing. Each card had three poses of a single player or several players on the same card. Although there were only 200 cards in the 1986 set, it takes 361 listings to complete the set. One card has 12 players; ten have 6 players; fifty have 3 players, and the other 139 have three poses of the same player.

The idea was a novel one. Three dimensional cards had been successful for Kellogg's in cereal boxes, so why not over the counter.

Three pictures are on each card until 1990 when only two pictures are used. It is certainly easier to see these images than the previous years.

On a good note the Score sets produced by Major League Marketing are colorful with lots of action shots. The reverse of the cards feature a color close-up portrait photo of the player.

The Score Traded sets first issued in 1988 containing 110 cards caught many dealers unaware of demand for new updated sets. Many dealers were ordering the Topps sets with the Olympic Baseball Team cards instead of Score Updates. This first set of Score Traded cards has proven to be in short supply.

Both Score and Sportflics cards measure 2½" x 3½".

1988SC - Score set of 660 cards w/six different colored borders (blue, green, gold, purple, red and yellow) Score logo on front lower right corner (copyright 1988 Score on back lower right)

1988SCTR - Score set of 110 cards of rookies and traded players with same format as regular cards except orange borders and numbers ending in T.

1989SC - Score set of 660 cards w/white borders w/six different colored inside borders (green, light blue, purple, orange, red, dark blue). Score logo on front upper right corner (copyright 1989 Score on back lower left)

1989SCTR - Score set of 110 cards of rookies and traded players with same format as regular cards except mint green inside border and numbers ending in T.

1990SC Score set of 704 cards with four different colored borders(red, blue, green and white) whose color scheme is carried onto the back. Score logo on front upper left corner (copyright 1990 Score on back right center)

1986SP - Sportflics set of 200 cards w/white border (copyright 1986 Sportflics on back lower right)

1987SP - Sportflics set of 200 cards w/red border, small color photo on back in upper left corner (copyright 1986 or 1987 Sportflics on back lower right)

1988SP - Sportflics set of 225 cards w/red border, large color photo on back leftside (copyright 1987 Sportflics on back bottom of card)

1989SP - Sportflics set of 225 cards w/white border w/orange/purple inside borders (copyright 1989 Sportflics on back bottom of card)

1990SP -Sportflics set of 225 cards with orange, yellow, black and white borders (Copyright 1990 Sportflics on back bottom of card)

There are only four abbreviations used in this section:
SC - Score cards
SP - Sportflics cards
SCTR - Score traded cards
SCDT - Score "Dream Team"
SPR - Sportflics Rookie cards

The listing for each card shown appears immediately following the photograph.

Player	Year	No.	VG	EX/MT
Aase, Don	88SC	518	$ .01	$ .04
Aase, Don	89SC	524	$ .01	$ .04
Aase, Don	90SC	377	$ .01	$ .04
Abbott, Jim	89SCTR	88	$ .01	$2.25
Abbott, Jim	90SC	330	$ .01	$ .75
Abbott, Kyle	90SC	673	$ .01	$ .20
Abner, Shawn	88SC	626	$ .05	$ .25
Abner, Shawn	89SC	411	$ .01	$ .10
Abner, Shawn	90SC	352	$ .01	$ .04
Acker, Jim	88SC	576	$ .01	$ .04
Adduci, Jim	89SC	587	$ .01	$ .04
Agosto, Juan	88SC	558	$ .01	$ .04
Agosto, Juan	89SC	283	$ .01	$ .04
Agosto, Juan	90SC	284	$ .01	$ .04
Aguayo, Luis	88SC	499	$ .01	$ .04
Aguayo, Luis	89SC	436	$ .01	$ .04
Aguilera, Rick	88SC	521	$ .01	$ .04
Aguilera, Rick	89SC	327	$ .01	$ .04
Aguilera, Rick	90SC	519	$ .01	$ .04
Akerfelds, Darrel	88SC	632	$ .01	$ .04
Aldrete, Mike	88SC	556	$ .01	$ .04
Aldrete, Mike	89SC	82	$ .01	$ .04
Aldrete, Mike	89SCTR	68	$ .01	$ .05
Aldrete, Mike	90SC	220	$ .01	$ .04
Aldrich, Jay	88SC	578	$ .01	$ .04
Alexander, Doyle	88SC	610	$ .01	$ .04
Alexander, Doyle	89SC	129	$ .01	$ .04
Alexander, Doyle	90SC	237	$ .01	$ .04
Alicea, Luis	88SCTR	98	$ .01	$ .10
Alicea, Luis	89SC	231	$ .01	$ .15
Allanson, Andy	88SC	586	$ .01	$ .04
Allanson, Andy	89SC	46	$ .01	$ .04
Allanson, Andy	90SC	452	$ .01	$ .04
Allen, Neil	89SC	375	$ .01	$ .04
Alomar, Jr., Sandy	90SC	577	$ .01	$ .35
Alomar, Roberto	88SCTR	105	$ .05	$6.00
Alomar, Roberto	89SC	232	$ .01	$ .75
Alomar, Roberto	90SC	12	$ .01	$ .25
Alomar, Sandy	89SC	630	$ .01	$ .75
Alou, Moises	90SC	592	$ .01	$ .50
Alvarez, Jose	90SC	148	$ .01	$ .04
Andersen, Larry	88SC	133	$ .01	$ .04
Andersen, Larry	89SC	523	$ .01	$ .04
Andersen, Larry	90SC	282	$ .01	$ .04
Anderson, Allan	89SC	394	$ .01	$ .15
Anderson, Allan	90SC	292	$ .01	$ .04
Anderson, Brady	88SCTR	70	$ .01	$ .50
Anderson, Brady	89SC	563	$ .01	$ .25
Anderson, Brady	90SC	33	$ .01	$ .04
Anderson, Dave	88SC	166	$ .01	$ .04
Anderson, Dave	89SC	478	$ .01	$ .04
Anderson, Dave	90SC	238	$ .01	$ .04
Anderson, Kent	90SC	412	$ .01	$ .04
Anderson, Rick	89SC	441	$ .01	$ .04
Andujar, Joaquin	88SC	193	$ .01	$ .04
Andujar, Joaquin	89SC	472	$ .01	$ .04
Anthony, Eric	90SC	584	$ .01	$1.50
Appier, Kevin	90SC	625	$ .01	$ .10
Aquino, Luis	90SC	432	$ .01	$ .04
Armas, Tony	88SC	487	$ .01	$ .04
Armas, Tony	89SC	182	$ .01	$ .04
Armas, Tony	90SC	378	$ .01	$ .04
Armstrong, Jack	88SCTR	78	$ .01	$8.00
Armstrong, Jack	89SC	462	$ .01	$1.00
Ashby, Alan	88SC	73	$ .01	$ .04
Ashby, Alan	89SC	366	$ .01	$ .04
Assenmacher, Paul	89SC	373	$ .01	$ .04
Atherton, Keith	88SC	613	$ .01	$ .04
Atherton, Keith	89SC	381	$ .01	$ .04
August, Don	88SCTR	104	$ .01	$ .15
August, Don	89SC	419	$ .01	$ .10
August, Don	90SC	144	$ .01	$ .04
Austin, Pat	90SC	626	$ .01	$ .04
Backman, Wally	88SC	303	$ .01	$ .04
Backman, Wally	89SC	315	$ .01	$ .04

Player	Year	No.	VG	EX/MT
Backman, Wally	89SCTR	34	$ .01	$ .05
Backman, Wally	90SC	281	$ .01	$ .04
Bailes, Scott	89SC	424	$ .01	$ .04

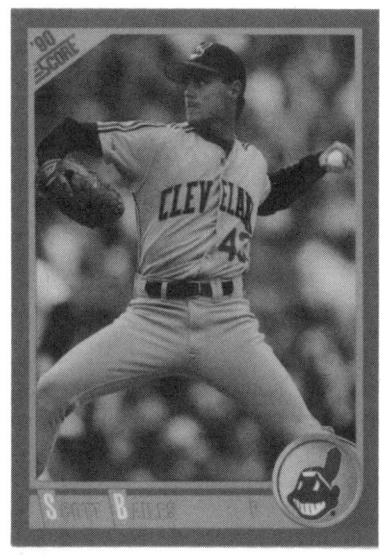

Player	Year	No.	VG	EX/MT
Bailes, Scott	90SC	218	$ .01	$ .04
Baines, Harold	88SC	590	$ .01	$ .04
Baines, Harold	89SC	128	$ .01	$ .04
Baines, Harold	89SCTR	62	$ .01	$ .10
Baines, Harold	90SC	470	$ .01	$ .04
Bair, Doug	90SC	517	$ .01	$ .04
Balboni, Steve	88SC	273	$ .01	$ .04
Balboni, Steve	88SCTR	46	$ .01	$ .05
Balboni, Steve	89SC	353	$ .01	$ .04
Balboni, Steve	89SCTR	27	$ .01	$ .05
Balboni, Steve	90SC	327	$ .01	$ .04
Ballard, Jeff	89SC	551	$ .01	$ .15
Ballard, Jeff	90SC	349	$ .01	$ .04
Bando, Chris	88SC	172	$ .01	$ .04
Bankhead, Scott	88SC	238	$ .01	$ .04
Bankhead, Scott	89SC	341	$ .01	$ .04
Bankhead, Scott	90SC	555	$ .01	$ .04
Bannister, Floyd	88SC	622	$ .01	$ .04
Bannister, Floyd	88SCTR	63	$ .01	$ .05
Bannister, Floyd	89SC	249	$ .01	$ .04
Barfield, Jesse	88SC	8	$ .01	$ .10
Barfield, Jesse	89SC	160	$ .01	$ .10
Barfield, Jesse	89SCTR	22	$ .01	$ .10
Barfield, Jesse	90SC	222	$ .01	$ .10
Barrett, Marty	88SC	155	$ .01	$ .04
Barrett, Marty	89SC	63	$ .01	$ .04
Barrett, Marty	90SC	15	$ .01	$ .04
Barrett, Tom	90SC	633	$ .01	$ .04
Bass, Kevin	88SC	33	$ .01	$ .04
Bass, Kevin	89SC	226	$ .01	$ .04
Bass, Kevin	90SC	279	$ .01	$ .04
Bates, Billy	90SC	608	$ .01	$ .04
Bautista, Jose	89SC	573	$ .01	$ .15
Baylor, Don	88SC	250	$ .01	$ .04
Baylor, Don	88SCTR	55	$ .01	$ .10
Baylor, Don	89SC	205	$ .01	$ .04
Beatty, Blaine	90SC	632	$ .01	$ .15
Bedrosian, Steve	88SC	161	$ .01	$ .10
Bedrosian, Steve	88SC	656	$ .01	$ .04
Bedrosian, Steve	89SC	260	$ .01	$ .04

SCORE

Player	Year	No.	VG	EX/MT	Player	Year	No.	VG	EX/MT
Bedrosian, Steve	89SCTR	49	$ .01	$ .10	Boggs, Wade	89SC	654	$ .01	$ .40
Bedrosian, Steve	90SC	379	$ .01	$ .04	Boggs, Wade	90SC	245	$ .01	$ .20
Belcher, Tim	88SCTR	101	$ .01	$ .25	Boggs, Wade	90SC	704	$ .01	$ .10
Belcher, Tim	89SC	418	$ .01	$ .15	Boggs, Wade	90SCDT	683	$ .01	$ .15
Belcher, Tim	90SC	126	$ .01	$ .10	Bolton, Tom	89SC	531	$ .01	$ .04
Belinda, Stan	90SC	634	$ .01	$ .04	Bonds, Barry	88SC	265	$ .04	$ .25
Bell, Buddy	88SC	99	$ .01	$ .10	Bonds, Barry	89SC	127	$ .01	$ .15
Bell, Buddy	89SC	610	$ .01	$ .04	Bonds, Barry	90SC	4	$ .01	$ .10
Bell, Eric	88SC	101	$ .01	$ .04	Bonilla, Bobby	88SC	116	$ .04	$ .25
Bell, George	88SC	540	$ .01	$ .10	Bonilla, Bobby	89SC	195	$ .01	$ .10
Bell, George	89SC	347	$ .01	$ .04	Bonilla, Bobby	90SC	170	$ .01	$ .15
Bell, George	90SC	286	$ .01	$ .10	Booker, Greg	88SC	447	$ .01	$ .04
Bell, Jay	89SC	352	$ .01	$ .04	Booker, Greg	89SC	417	$ .01	$ .04
Bell, Jay	90SC	563	$ .01	$ .04	Boone, Bob	88SC	63	$ .01	$ .04
Bell, Juan	90SC	603	$ .01	$ .15	Boone, Bob	89SC	233	$ .01	$ .04
Belle, Joey	89SCTR	106	$ .01	$1.25	Boone, Bob	89SCTR	74	$ .01	$ .05
Belle, Joey	90SC	508	$ .01	$ .50	Boone, Bob	90SC	60	$ .01	$ .04
Belliard, Rafael	88SC	453	$ .01	$ .04	Borders, Pat	88SCTR	99	$ .01	$ .35
Belliard, Rafael	89SC	379	$ .01	$ .04	Borders, Pat	89SC	198	$ .01	$ .15
Belliard, Rafael	90SC	520	$ .01	$ .04	Borders, Pat	90SC	288	$ .01	$ .04
Benedict, Bruce	88SC	423	$ .01	$ .04	Bosio, Chris	88SC	38	$ .01	$ .04
Benedict, Bruce	89SC	502	$ .01	$ .04	Bosio, Chris	89SC	243	$ .01	$ .04
Benes, Andy	90SC	578	$ .01	$ .50	Bosio, Chris	90SC	283	$ .01	$ .04
Benzinger, Todd	88SC	546	$ .05	$ .35	Boston Red Sox, A. L. Wins	89SC	660	$ .01	$ .04
Benzinger, Todd	89SC	371	$ .01	$ .04	Boston, Daryl	88SC	582	$ .01	$ .04
Benzinger, Todd	89SCTR	15	$ .01	$ .10	Boston, Daryl	89SC	443	$ .01	$ .04
Benzinger, Todd	90SC	65	$ .01	$ .04	Boston, Daryl	90SC	213	$ .01	$ .04
Berenguer, Juan	89SC	414	$ .01	$ .04	Boyd, Dennis	88SC	121	$ .01	$ .04
Berenguer, Juan	90SC	223	$ .01	$ .04	Boyd, Dennis	89SC	238	$ .01	$ .04
Bergman, Dave	88SC	217	$ .01	$ .04	Boyd, Dennis	90SC	137	$ .01	$ .04
Bergman, Dave	89SC	469	$ .01	$ .04	Bradley, Phil	88SC	66	$ .01	$ .10
Bergman, Dave	90SC	254	$ .01	$ .04	Bradley, Phil	88SCTR	34	$ .01	$ .05
Bernazard, Tony	88SC	604	$ .01	$ .04	Bradley, Phil	89SC	79	$ .01	$ .04
Berroa, Geronimo	89SC	632	$ .01	$ .10	Bradley, Phil	89SCTR	44	$ .01	$ .05
Berroa, Geronimo	90SC	151	$ .01	$ .04	Bradley, Phil	90SC	24	$ .01	$ .04
Berryhill, Damon	88SCTR	82	$ .01	$ .45	Bradley, Scott	88SC	151	$ .01	$ .04
Berryhill, Damon	89SC	336	$ .01	$ .10	Bradley, Scott	89SC	324	$ .01	$ .04
Berryhill, Damon	90SC	163	$ .01	$ .10	Bradley, Scott	90SC	228	$ .01	$ .04
Biancalana, Buddy	88SC	383	$ .01	$ .04	Braggs, Glenn	88SC	59	$ .01	$ .04
Bielecki, Mike	88SC	611	$ .01	$ .04	Braggs, Glenn	89SC	147	$ .01	$ .04
Bielecki, Mike	90SC	484	$ .01	$ .04	Braggs, Glenn	90SC	105	$ .01	$ .04
Biggio, Craig	88SCTR	103	$ .01	$2.25	Brantley, Jeff	89SCTR	101	$ .01	$ .20
Biggio, Craig	89SC	237	$ .01	$ .50	Brantley, Jeff	90SC	371	$ .01	$ .10
Biggio, Craig	90SC	275	$ .01	$ .10	Brantley, Mickey	89SC	89	$ .01	$ .04
Birkbeck, Mike	88SC	369	$ .01	$ .04	Bream, Sid	88SC	260	$ .01	$ .04
Birkbeck, Mike	89SC	596	$ .01	$ .04	Bream, Sid	89SC	48	$ .01	$ .04
Birtsas, Tim	89SC	454	$ .01	$ .04	Bream, Sid	90SC	423	$ .01	$ .04
Birtsas, Tim	90SC	408	$ .01	$ .04	Brenly, Bob	88SC	134	$ .01	$ .04
Bittiger, Jeff	88SCTR	66	$ .01	$ .15	Brenly, Bob	89SC	395	$ .01	$ .04
Bittiger, Jeff	89SC	512	$ .01	$ .15	Brennan, Bill	89SC	622	$ .01	$ .04
Black, Bud	88SC	313	$ .01	$ .04	Brett, George	88SC	11	$ .05	$ .25
Black, Bud	88SCTR	11	$ .01	$ .05	Brett, George	89SC	75	$ .01	$ .20
Black, Bud	89SC	404	$ .01	$ .04	Brett, George	90SC	140	$ .01	$ .15
Black, Bud	90SC	197	$ .01	$ .04	Briley, Greg	88SCTR	74	$ .01	$2.00
Blankenship, Kevin	90SC	646	$ .01	$ .04	Briley, Greg	90SC	303	$ .01	$ .20
Blankenship, Lance	89SC	641	$ .01	$ .25	Brock, Greg	88SC	234	$ .01	$ .04
Blankenship, Lance	90SC	536	$ .01	$ .04	Brock, Greg	89SC	307	$ .01	$ .04
Blauser, Jeff	88SC	562	$ .01	$ .04	Brock, Greg	90SC	485	$ .01	$ .04
Blauser, Jeff	89SC	589	$ .01	$ .04	Brookens, Tom	88SC	233	$ .01	$ .04
Blauser, Jeff	90SC	178	$ .01	$ .04	Brookens, Tom	89SC	269	$ .01	$ .04
Blocker, Terry	89SC	605	$ .01	$ .04	Brookens, Tom	89SCTR	73	$ .01	$ .05
Blosser, Greg	90SC	681	$ .01	$ .20	Brookens, Tom	90SC	297	$ .01	$ .04
Blowers, Mike	90SC	624	$ .01	$ .25	Brooks, Hubie	88SC	305	$ .01	$ .04
Blyleven, Bert	88SC	90	$ .01	$ .10	Brooks, Hubie	89SC	53	$ .01	$ .04
Blyleven, Bert	89SC	215	$ .01	$ .10	Brooks, Hubie	90SC	299	$ .01	$ .04
Blyleven, Bert	89SCTR	17	$ .01	$ .10	Brower, Bob	88SC	236	$ .01	$ .04
Blyleven, Bert	90SC	180	$ .01	$ .05	Brower, Bob	89SC	344	$ .01	$ .04
Bochy, Bruce	88SC	469	$ .01	$ .04	Brown, Chris	88SC	363	$ .01	$ .04
Boddicker, Mike	88SC	67	$ .01	$ .10	Brown, Chris	89SC	369	$ .01	$ .04
Boddicker, Mike	89SC	549	$ .01	$ .04	Brown, Kevin	89SCTR	89	$ .01	$ .15
Boddicker, Mike	90SC	31	$ .01	$ .04	Brown, Kevin	90SC	210	$ .01	$ .04
Boever, Joe	88SC	542	$ .01	$ .04	Browne, Jerry	88SC	278	$ .01	$ .04
Boever, Joe	90SC	81	$ .01	$ .04	Browne, Jerry	90SC	52	$ .01	$ .04
Boggs, Wade	88SC	2	$ .15	$ .75	Browning, Tom	88SC	132	$ .01	$ .15
Boggs, Wade	89SC	175	$ .05	$ .40	Browning, Tom	89SC	554	$ .01	$ .10

Player	Year	No.	VG	EX/MT
Browning, Tom	89SC	658	$ .01	$ .10
Browning, Tom	90SC	165	$ .01	$ .10
Brunansky, Tom	88SC	194	$ .01	$ .04
Brunansky, Tom	88SCTR	5	$ .01	$ .10
Brunansky, Tom	89SC	184	$ .01	$ .04
Brunansky, Tom	90SC	72	$ .01	$ .04
Bryant, Scott	90SC	667	$ .01	$ .04
Buckner, Bill	88SC	591	$ .01	$ .04
Buckner, Bill	88SCTR	36	$ .01	$ .05
Buckner, Bill	89SC	214	$ .01	$ .04
Buckner, Bill	90SC	396	$ .01	$ .04
Buechele, Steve	88SC	306	$ .01	$ .04
Buechele, Steve	89SC	368	$ .01	$ .04
Buechele, Steve	90SC	221	$ .01	$ .04
Buhner, Jay	88SCTR	95	$ .01	$ .35
Buhner, Jay	89SC	530	$ .01	$ .20
Buhner, Jay	90SC	521	$ .01	$ .04
Buice, DeWayne	88SC	376	$ .01	$ .04
Buice, DeWayne	89SC	153	$ .01	$ .04
Burke, Tim	88SC	187	$ .01	$ .04
Burke, Tim	89SC	228	$ .01	$ .04
Burke, Tim	90SC	127	$ .01	$ .04
Burks, Ellis	88SC	472	$ .25	$1.00
Burks, Ellis	89SC	9	$ .01	$ .35
Burks, Ellis	90SC	340	$ .01	$ .15
Burns, Todd	88SCTR	106	$ .01	$ .35
Burns, Todd	89SC	465	$ .01	$ .25
Burns, Todd	90SC	64	$ .01	$ .04
Bush, Randy	88SC	292	$ .01	$ .04
Bush, Randy	89SC	212	$ .01	$ .04
Bush, Randy	90SC	278	$ .01	$ .04
Butera, Sal	88SC	361	$ .01	$ .04
Butler, Brett	88SC	122	$ .01	$ .04
Butler, Brett	88SCTR	3	$ .01	$ .05
Butler, Brett	89SC	216	$ .01	$ .04
Butler, Brett	90SC	236	$ .01	$ .04
Cadaret, Greg	89SC	340	$ .01	$ .04
Cadaret, Greg	89SCTR	69	$ .01	$ .05
Calderon, Ivan	88SC	607	$ .01	$ .04
Calderon, Ivan	89SC	331	$ .01	$ .04
Calderon, Ivan	90SC	94	$ .01	$ .04
Caminiti, Ken	88SC	164	$ .01	$ .15
Caminiti, Ken	90SC	76	$ .01	$ .04
Campbell, Mike	89SC	568	$ .01	$ .15
Campusano, Sil	88SCTR	93	$ .01	$ .15
Campusano, Sil	89SC	473	$ .01	$ .15
Canale, George	90SC	656	$ .01	$ .15
Candaele, Casey	88SC	97	$ .01	$ .04
Candelaria, John	88SC	293	$ .01	$ .04
Candelaria, John	88SCTR	40	$ .01	$ .10
Candelaria, John	093C	246	$ .01	$ .04
Candiotti, Tom	88SC	595	$ .01	$ .04
Candiotti, Tom	89SC	239	$ .01	$ .04
Candiotti, Tom	90SC	269	$ .01	$ .04
Cangelosi, John	88SC	418	$ .01	$ .04
Cangelosi, John	89SC	601	$ .01	$ .04
Cangelosi, John	90SC	367	$ .01	$ .04
Canseco, Jose	88SC	45	$ .20	$1.50
Canseco, Jose	89SC	1	$ .15	$1.00
Canseco, Jose	89SC	655	$ .01	$ .50
Canseco, Jose	90SC	375	$ .01	$ .50
Carman, Don	88SC	401	$ .01	$ .04
Carman, Don	89SC	222	$ .01	$ .04
Carpenter, Cris	89SCTR	81	$ .01	$ .15
Carreon, Mark	89SCTR	108	$ .01	$ .05
Carreon, Mark	90SC	363	$ .01	$ .04
Carter, Gary	88SC	325	$ .01	$ .04
Carter, Gary	89SC	240	$ .01	$ .04
Carter, Gary	90SC	416	$ .01	$ .04
Carter, Joe	88SC	80	$ .01	$ .15
Carter, Joe	89SC	213	$ .01	$ .10
Carter, Joe	90SC	319	$ .01	$ .15
Cary, Chuck	90SC	393	$ .01	$ .04
Casillo, Juan	88SC	429	$ .01	$ .04
Castillo, Carmelo	89SCTR	23	$ .01	$ .05

Player	Year	No.	VG	EX/MT
Castillo, Carmelo	90SC	123	$ .01	$ .04
Castillo, Carmen	88SC	581	$ .01	$ .04
Castillo, Carmen	89SC	497	$ .01	$ .04
Cerone, Rick	88SC	486	$ .01	$ .04
Cerone, Rick	88SCTR	21	$ .01	$ .05
Cerone, Rick	89SC	396	$ .01	$ .04
Cerone, Rick	90SC	139	$ .01	$ .04
Cerutti, John	88SC	98	$ .01	$ .10
Cerutti, John	89SC	304	$ .01	$ .04
Cerutti, John	90SC	429	$ .01	$ .04
Charlton, Norm	89SC	646	$ .01	$ .15
Charlton, Norm	90SC	248	$ .01	$ .10
Christensen, John	88SC	419	$ .01	$ .04
Clancy, Jim	88SC	530	$ .01	$ .04
Clancy, Jim	89SC	538	$ .01	$ .04
Clancy, Jim	89SCTR	42	$ .01	$ .05
Clancy, Jim	90SC	424	$ .01	$ .04
Clark, Dave	88SC	633	$ .01	$ .04
Clark, Dave	90SC	141	$ .01	$ .04
Clark, Jack	88SC	100	$ .04	$ .15
Clark, Jack	88SC	650	$ .10	$ .50
Clark, Jack	88SCTR	1	$ .01	$ .20
Clark, Jack	89SC	25	$ .01	$ .10
Clark, Jack	89SCTR	3	$ .01	$ .10
Clark, Jack	90SC	20	$ .01	$ .04
Clark, Jerald	89SC	644	$ .01	$ .04
Clark, Jerald	90SC	660	$ .01	$ .04
Clark, Terry	89SC	566	$ .01	$ .04
Clark, Will	88SC	78	$ .25	$1.00
Clark, Will	89SC	450	$ .10	$ .60
Clark, Will	90SC	300	$ .01	$ .50
Clark, Will	90SC	699	$ .01	$ .35
Clark, Will	90SCDT	684	$ .01	$ .25
Clear, Mark	88SC	446	$ .01	$ .04
Clear, Mark	89SC	430	$ .01	$ .04
Clemens, Roger	88SC	110	$ .10	$ .50
Clemens, Roger	89SC	350	$ .05	$ .40
Clemens, Roger	90SC	310	$ .01	$ .15
Clements, Pat	88SC	389	$ .01	$ .04
Cliburn, Stewart	89SC	445	$ .01	$ .04

Player	Year	No.	VG	EX/MT
Coleman, Paul	90SC	662	$ .01	$ .25
Coleman, Vince	88SC	652	$ .01	$ .10
Coleman, Vince	88SC	68	$ .04	$ .15

SCORE

Player	Year	No.	VG	EX/MT
Coleman, Vince	89SC	155	$ .01	$ .10
Coleman, Vince	90SC	260	$ .01	$ .04
Coles, Darnell	88SC	554	$ .01	$ .04
Coles, Darnell	89SC	83	$ .01	$ .04
Coles, Darnell	90SC	62	$ .01	$ .04
Collins, Dave	88SC	371	$ .01	$ .04
Collins, Dave	89SC	267	$ .01	$ .04
Combs, Pat	90SC	623	$ .01	$ .35
Comstock, Keith	88SC	438	$ .01	$ .04
Concepcion, Dave	88SC	210	$ .01	$ .04
Concepcion, Dave	89SC	166	$ .01	$ .04
Cone, David	88SC	49	$ .15	$1.00
Cone, David	89SC	221	$ .01	$ .25
Cone, David	90SC	430	$ .01	$ .10
Conroy, Tim	88SC	384	$ .01	$ .04
Cook, Dennis	90SC	545	$ .01	$ .04
Coolbaugh, Scott	90SC	612	$ .01	$ .35
Cooper, Cecil	88SC	169	$ .01	$ .04
Cooper, Scott	90SC	651	$ .01	$ .04
Cora, Joey	88SC	420	$ .01	$ .04

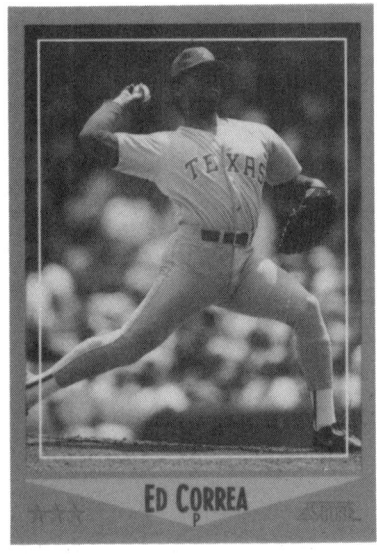

ED CORREA
P

Player	Year	No.	VG	EX/MT
Correa, Ed	88SC	523	$ .01	$ .04
Corsi, Jim	90SC	553	$ .01	$ .04
Costello, John	88SCTR	107	$ .01	$ .25
Costello, John	89SC	534	$ .01	$ .15
Costello, John	90SC	347	$ .01	$ .04
Cotto, Henry	88SC	368	$ .01	$ .04
Cotto, Henry	88SCTR	48	$ .01	$ .05
Cotto, Henry	89SC	209	$ .01	$ .04
Cotto, Henry	90SC	161	$ .01	$ .04
Cox, Danny	88SC	415	$ .01	$ .04
Cox, Danny	89SC	613	$ .01	$ .04
Crawford, Steve	88SC	289	$ .01	$ .04
Crews, Tim	88SC	641	$ .01	$ .04
Crews, Tim	89SC	505	$ .01	$ .04
Crews, Tim	90SC	164	$ .01	$ .04
Crim, Chuck	88SC	402	$ .01	$ .04
Crim, Chuck	89SC	272	$ .01	$ .04
Crim, Chuck	90SC	108	$ .01	$ .04
Cruz, Jose	88SC	28	$ .01	$ .04
Cunningham, Earl	90SC	670	$ .01	$ .50
Curry, Steve	88SCTR	81	$ .01	$ .15
Cuyler, Milt	90SC	583	$ .01	$ .04
Daniels, Kal	88SC	86	$ .05	$ .15

Player	Year	No.	VG	EX/MT
Daniels, Kal	89SC	7	$ .01	$ .10
Daniels, Kal	89SCTR	48	$ .01	$ .05
Daniels, Kal	90SC	490	$ .01	$ .04
Darling, Ron	88SC	141	$ .01	$ .10
Darling, Ron	89SC	180	$ .01	$ .04
Darling, Ron	90SC	446	$ .01	$ .04
Darwin, Danny	88SC	184	$ .01	$ .04
Darwin, Danny	89SC	553	$ .01	$ .04
Darwin, Danny	90SC	402	$ .01	$ .04
Dascenzo, Doug	89SC	621	$ .01	$ .20
Daugherty, Jack	90SC	564	$ .01	$ .04
Daulton, Darren	88SC	473	$ .01	$ .04
Daulton, Darren	89SC	413	$ .01	$ .04
Daulton, Darren	90SC	389	$ .01	$ .04
Davidson, Mark	88SC	570	$ .01	$ .04
Davidson, Mark	89SC	107	$ .01	$ .04
Davis, Alvin	88SC	83	$ .01	$ .10
Davis, Alvin	89SC	51	$ .01	$ .10
Davis, Alvin	90SC	205	$ .01	$ .04
Davis, Chili	88SC	605	$ .01	$ .04
Davis, Chili	88SCTR	28	$ .01	$ .05
Davis, Chili	89SC	54	$ .01	$ .04
Davis, Chili	90SC	326	$ .01	$ .04
Davis, Eric	88SC	10	$ .15	$ .50
Davis, Eric	88SC	649	$ .05	$ .25
Davis, Eric	89SC	109	$ .01	$ .25
Davis, Eric	90SC	185	$ .01	$ .20
Davis, Glenn	88SC	460	$ .01	$ .10
Davis, Glenn	89SC	164	$ .01	$ .10
Davis, Glenn	90SC	272	$ .01	$ .10
Davis, Jody	88SC	551	$ .01	$ .04
Davis, Jody	89SC	173	$ .01	$ .04
Davis, Jody	89SCTR	64	$ .01	$ .05
Davis, Jody	90SC	328	$ .01	$ .04
Davis, John	88SC	636	$ .01	$ .04
Davis, John	89SC	608	$ .01	$ .04
Davis, Mark	88SC	391	$ .01	$ .04
Davis, Mark	89SC	490	$ .01	$ .04
Davis, Mark	90SC	259	$ .01	$ .04
Davis, Mike	88SC	211	$ .01	$ .04
Davis, Mike	88SCTR	53	$ .01	$ .05
Davis, Mike	89SC	376	$ .01	$ .04
Davis, Mike	90SC	437	$ .01	$ .04
Davis, Steve	90SC	187	$ .01	$ .10
Davis, Storm	89SC	248	$ .01	$ .04
Davis, Storm	90SC	266	$ .01	$ .04
Dawley, Bill	88SC	328	$ .01	$ .04
Dawson, Andre	88SC	4	$ .01	$ .10
Dawson, Andre	89SC	2	$ .01	$ .10
Dawson, Andre	90SC	265	$ .01	$ .10
Dayett, Brian	88SC	205	$ .01	$ .04
Dayley, Ken	88SC	517	$ .01	$ .04
Dayley, Ken	90SC	556	$ .01	$ .04
De Los Santos, Luis	89SC	648	$ .01	$ .04
De Los Santos, Luis	90SC	659	$ .01	$ .10
DeCinces, Doug	88SC	239	$ .01	$ .04
Dedmon, Jeff	88SC	498	$ .01	$ .04
Deer, Rob	88SC	95	$ .01	$ .04
Deer, Rob	89SC	72	$ .01	$ .04
Deer, Rob	90SC	390	$ .01	$ .04
DeJesus, Jose	90SC	587	$ .01	$ .04
DeLeon, Jose	88SC	508	$ .01	$ .04
DeLeon, Jose	88SCTR	7	$ .01	$ .05
DeLeon, Jose	89SC	115	$ .01	$ .04
DeLeon, Jose	90SC	309	$ .01	$ .04
Dempsey, Rick	88SC	262	$ .01	$ .04
Dempsey, Rick	88SCTR	32	$ .01	$ .05
Dempsey, Rick	89SC	556	$ .01	$ .04
Dempsey, Rick	90SC	414	$ .01	$ .04
Dernier, Bob	88SC	451	$ .01	$ .04
Dernier, Bob	88SCTR	45	$ .01	$ .05
Dernier, Bob	89SC	357	$ .01	$ .04
Deshaies, Jim	88SC	354	$ .01	$ .04
Deshaies, Jim	89SC	546	$ .01	$ .04
Deshaies, Jim	90SC	154	$ .01	$ .04

Player	Year	No.	VG	EX/MT	Player	Year	No.	VG	EX/MT
DeShields, Delino	90SC	645	$ .01	$1.25	Eppard, Jim	89SC	607	$ .01	$ .10
Destrade, Orestes	88SCTR	110	$ .01	$ .10	Esasky, Nick	88SC	163	$ .01	$ .04
Devereaux, Mike	88SC	637	$ .04	$ .25	Esasky, Nick	89SC	64	$ .01	$ .04
Devereaux, Mike	90SC	232	$ .01	$ .04	Esasky, Nick	89SCTR	37	$ .01	$ .10
DeWillis, Jeff	88SC	583	$ .01	$ .04	Esasky, Nick	90SC	91	$ .01	$ .04
Diaz, Bo	88SC	206	$ .01	$ .04	Espinoza, Alvaro	90SC	101	$ .01	$ .10
Diaz, Bo	89SC	187	$ .01	$ .04	Espy, Cecil	88SCTR	73	$ .01	$ .20
Diaz, Bo	90SC	434	$ .01	$ .04	Espy, Cecil	89SC	401	$ .01	$ .15
Diaz, Mike	88SC	143	$ .01	$ .04	Espy, Cecil	90SC	69	$ .01	$ .10
Diaz, Mike	89SC	603	$ .01	$ .04	Evans, Darrell	88SC	75	$ .01	$ .04
Dibble, Rob	88SCTR	86	$ .01	$2.00	Evans, Darrell	89SC	171	$ .01	$ .04
Dibble, Rob	89SC	618	$ .01	$ .75	Evans, Darrell	89SCTR	65	$ .01	$ .10
Dibble, Rob	90SC	277	$ .01	$ .20	Evans, Darrell	90SC	302	$ .01	$ .04
DiPino, Frank	88SC	413	$ .01	$ .04	Evans, Dwight	88SC	65	$ .01	$ .10
DiPino, Frank	89SC	146	$ .01	$ .04	Evans, Dwight	89SC	193	$ .01	$ .10
DiPino, Frank	90SC	462	$ .01	$ .04	Evans, Dwight	90SC	3	$ .01	$ .05
Dixon, Ken	88SC	411	$ .01	$ .04	Farr, Steve	88SC	466	$ .01	$ .04
Dodson, Pat	88SC	352	$ .01	$ .04	Farr, Steve	89SC	183	$ .01	$ .04
Dopson, John	88SCTR	88	$ .01	$ .25	Farr, Steve	90SC	356	$ .01	$ .04
Dopson, John	89SC	466	$ .01	$ .15	Farrell, John	88SC	620	$ .01	$ .25
Dopson, John	89SCTR	40	$ .01	$ .05	Farrell, John	89SC	266	$ .01	$ .04
Dopson, John	90SC	331	$ .01	$ .04	Farrell, John	90SC	103	$ .01	$ .10
Doran, Bill	88SC	52	$ .01	$ .04	Felder, Mike	88SC	388	$ .01	$ .04
Doran, Bill	89SC	21	$ .01	$ .04	Felder, Mike	90SC	268	$ .01	$ .04
Doran, Bill	90SC	182	$ .01	$ .04	Felix, Junior	89SCTR	83	$ .01	$1.00
Dotson, Richard	88SC	480	$ .01	$ .04	Felix, Junior	90SC	258	$ .01	$ .50
Dotson, Richard	88SCTR	60	$ .01	$ .05	Fermin, Felix	89SC	620	$ .01	$ .04
Dotson, Richard	89SC	278	$ .01	$ .04	Fermin, Felix	89SCTR	78	$ .01	$ .05
Dotson, Richard	89SCTR	80	$ .01	$ .05	Fermin, Felix	90SC	256	$ .01	$ .04
Dotson, Richard	90SC	19	$ .01	$ .04	Fernandez, Sid	88SC	615	$ .01	$ .04
Downing, Brian	88SC	44	$ .01	$ .04	Fernandez, Sid	89SC	268	$ .01	$ .04
Downing, Brian	89SC	76	$ .01	$ .04	Fernandez, Sid	90SC	18	$ .01	$ .04
Downing, Brian	90SC	26	$ .01	$ .04	Fernandez, Tony	88SC	20	$ .01	$ .15
Downs, Kelly	88SC	27	$ .01	$ .04	Fernandez, Tony	88SC	651	$ .01	$ .10
Downs, Kelly	89SC	124	$ .01	$ .04	Fernandez, Tony	89SC	57	$ .01	$ .10
Downs, Kelly	90SC	534	$ .01	$ .04	Fernandez, Tony	90SC	89	$ .01	$ .10
Drabek, Doug	88SC	51	$ .01	$ .04	Fielder, Cecil	88SC	399	$ .01	$ .85
Drabek, Doug	89SC	117	$ .01	$ .04	Fielder, Cecil	89SC	120	$ .01	$ .75
Drabek, Doug	90SC	505	$ .01	$ .04	Finley, Chuck	89SC	503	$ .01	$ .04
Dravecky, Dave	88SC	564	$ .01	$ .10	Finley, Chuck	90SC	380	$ .01	$ .10
Dravecky, Dave	90SC	550	$ .01	$ .10	Finley, Steve	89SCTR	95	$ .01	$ .25
Drew, Cameron	89SC	643	$ .01	$ .04	Finley, Steve	90SC	339	$ .01	$ .15
Dubois, Brian	90SC	657	$ .01	$ .25	Fischer, Jeff	90SC	654	$ .01	$ .04
Ducey, Rob	88SC	629	$ .01	$ .15	Fisher, Brian	88SC	130	$ .01	$ .04
Duncan, Mariano	88SC	321	$ .01	$ .10	Fisher, Brian	89SC	24	$ .01	$ .04
Duncan, Mariano	90SC	506	$ .01	$ .10	Fisher, Brian	90SC	547	$ .01	$ .04
Dunne, Mike	88SC	432	$ .05	$ .20	Fisk, Carlton	88SC	592	$ .01	$ .04
Dunne, Mike	89SC	285	$ .01	$ .04	Fisk, Carlton	89SC	449	$ .01	$ .04
Dunston, Shawon	88SC	529	$ .01	$ .10	Fisk, Carlton	90SC	290	$ .01	$ .04
Dunston, Shawon	89SC	235	$ .01	$ .04	Fitzgerald, Mike	88SC	318	$ .01	$ .04
Dunston, Shawon	90SC	169	$ .01	$ .04	Fitzgerald, Mike	89SC	511	$ .01	$ .04
Durham, Leon	88SC	378	$ .01	$ .04	Fitzgerald, Mike	90SC	361	$ .01	$ .04
Dwyer, Jim	88SC	229	$ .01	$ .04	Flanagan, Mike	88SC	427	$ .01	$ .04
Dyer, Mike	90SC	571	$ .01	$ .04	Flanagan, Mike	89SC	475	$ .01	$ .04
Dykstra, Len	88SC	370	$ .01	$ .10	Flanagan, Mike	90SC	67	$ .01	$ .04
Dykstra, Lenny	89SC	84	$ .01	$ .10	Flannery, Tim	88SC	483	$ .01	$ .04
Dykstra, Lenny	89SCTR	28	$ .01	$ .10	Flannery, Tim	89SC	513	$ .01	$ .04
Dykstra, Lenny	90SC	427	$ .01	$ .10	Fletcher, Darrin	90SC	622	$ .01	$ .04
Easler, Mike	88SC	220	$ .01	$ .04	Fletcher, Scott	88SC	251	$ .01	$ .04
Eave, Gary	90SC	621	$ .01	$ .04	Fletcher, Scott	89SC	78	$ .01	$ .04
Eckersley, Dennis	88SC	104	$ .01	$ .04	Fletcher, Scott	89SCTR	47	$ .01	$ .05
Eckersley, Dennis	89SC	276	$ .01	$ .04	Fletcher, Scott	90SC	58	$ .01	$ .04
Eckersley, Dennis	90SC	315	$ .01	$ .04	Foley, Tom	88SC	159	$ .01	$ .04
Eichhorn, Mark	88SC	198	$ .01	$ .04	Foley, Tom	89SC	405	$ .01	$ .04
Eichhorn, Mark	89SC	152	$ .01	$ .04	Foley, Tom	90SC	32	$ .01	$ .04
Eiland, Dave	90SC	652	$ .01	$ .04	Ford, Curt	88SC	288	$ .01	$ .04
Eisenreich, Jim	88SC	456	$ .01	$ .04	Ford, Curt	90SC	183	$ .01	$ .04
Eisenreich, Jim	89SC	594	$ .01	$ .04	Forsch, Bob	88SC	264	$ .01	$ .04
Eisenreich, Jim	90SC	179	$ .01	$ .04	Forsch, Bob	89SC	525	$ .01	$ .04
Eldred, Cal	90SC	669	$ .01	$ .04	Forsch, Bob	90SC	219	$ .01	$ .04
Ellsworth, Steve	88SCTR	83	$ .01	$ .15	Fossas, Tony	90SC	567	$ .01	$ .04
Elster, Kevin	88SC	624	$ .05	$ .25	Franco, John	88SC	535	$ .01	$ .10
Elster, Kevin	89SC	130	$ .01	$ .10	Franco, John	89SC	575	$ .01	$ .10
Elster, Kevin	90SC	443	$ .01	$ .04	Franco, John	90SC	273	$ .01	$ .04
Engle, Dave	88SC	617	$ .01	$ .04	Franco, Julio	88SC	60	$ .01	$ .10

SCORE

Player	Year	No.	VG	EX/MT	Player	Year	No.	VG	EX/MT
Franco, Julio	89SC	11	$ .01	$ .10	Gordon, Don	89SC	547	$ .01	$ .04
Franco, Julio	89SCTR	35	$ .01	$ .10	Gordon, Tom	89SC	634	$ .15	$1.00
Franco, Julio	90SC	160	$ .01	$ .10	Gordon, Tom	90SC	472	$ .01	$ .50
Francona, Terry	88SC	297	$ .01	$ .04	Gossage, Goose	88SC	331	$ .01	$ .10
Francona, Terry	89SC	597	$ .01	$ .04	Gossage, Goose	89SC	223	$ .01	$ .04
Francona, Terry	90SC	216	$ .01	$ .04	Gott, Jim	88SC	320	$ .01	$ .04
Fraser, Willie	88SC	394	$ .01	$ .04	Gott, Jim	89SC	257	$ .01	$ .04
Fraser, Willie	89SC	157	$ .01	$ .04	Gott, Jim	90SC	515	$ .01	$ .04
Fraser, Willie	90SC	358	$ .01	$ .04	Gozzo, Goose	90SC	610	$ .01	$ .15
Frazier, Goerge	88SC	332	$ .01	$ .04	Grace, Mark	88SCTR	80	$ .25	$30.00
Frohwirth, Todd	89SC	647	$ .01	$ .15	Grace, Mark	89SC	362	$ .15	$2.00
Gaetti, Gary	88SC	62	$ .01	$ .10	Grace, Mark	90SC	150	$ .01	$1.00
Gaetti, Gary	89SC	8	$ .01	$ .10	Grant, Mark	89SC	349	$ .01	$ .04
Gaetti, Gary	90SC	145	$ .01	$ .04	Grant, Mark	90SC	466	$ .01	$ .04
Gagne, Greg	89SC	159	$ .01	$ .04	Green, Willie	90SC	682	$ .01	$ .04
Gagne, Greg	90SC	102	$ .01	$ .04	Greene, Tommy	90SC	640	$ .01	$ .20
Galarraga, Andres	88SC	19	$ .01	$ .20	Greenwell, Mike	88SC	175	$ .25	$1.50
Galarraga, Andres	89SC	144	$ .01	$ .15	Greenwell, Mike	89SC	659	$ .01	$ .25
Galarraga, Andres	90SC	25	$ .01	$ .10	Greenwell, Mike	89SC	66	$ .10	$ .60
Gallagher, Dave	88SCTR	89	$ .01	$ .25	Greenwell, Mike	90SC	345	$ .01	$ .25
Gallagher, Dave	89SC	455	$ .01	$ .25	Greg, Gagne	88SC	214	$ .01	$ .04
Gallagher, Dave	90SC	115	$ .01	$ .04	Gregg, Tommy	88SCTR	69	$ .01	$ .30
Gallego, Mike	88SC	428	$ .01	$ .04	Gregg, Tommy	90SC	78	$ .01	$ .10
Gallego, Mike	89SC	537	$ .01	$ .04	Griffey, Jr., Ken	89SCTR	100	$ .01	$6.00
Gallego, Mike	90SC	323	$ .01	$ .04	Griffey, Jr., Ken	90SC	560	$ .01	$2.00
Gant, Ron	88SC	647	$ .01	$ .40	Griffey, Sr., Ken	88SC	390	$ .01	$ .10
Gant, Ron	89SC	372	$ .01	$ .10	Griffey, Sr., Ken	89SC	609	$ .01	$ .10
Gantner, Jim	88SC	197	$ .01	$ .04	Griffey, Sr., Ken	90SC	338	$ .01	$ .04
Gantner, Jim	89SC	313	$ .01	$ .04	Griffin, Alfredo	88SC	88	$ .01	$ .04
Gantner, Jim	90SC	382	$ .01	$ .04	Griffin, Alfredo	88SCTR	37	$ .01	$ .05
Garber, Gene	88SC	565	$ .01	$ .04	Griffin, Alfredo	89SC	167	$ .01	$ .04
Gardner, Mark	90SC	639	$ .01	$ .04	Griffin, Alfredo	90SC	156	$ .01	$ .04
Gardner, Wes	89SC	412	$ .01	$ .04	Grimsley, Jason	90SC	649	$ .01	$ .04
Gardner, Wes	90SC	348	$ .01	$ .04	Grissom, Marquis	90SC	591	$ .01	$ .50
Garner, Phil	88SC	431	$ .01	$ .04	Gross, Greg	88SC	386	$ .01	$ .04
Garrelts, Scott	88SC	533	$ .01	$ .04	Gross, Greg	89SC	125	$ .01	$ .04
Garrelts, Scott	89SC	258	$ .01	$ .04	Gross, Kevin	88SC	468	$ .01	$ .04
Garrelts, Scott	90SC	246	$ .01	$ .04	Gross, Kevin	89SC	227	$ .01	$ .04
Garvey, Steve	88SC	225	$ .05	$ .25	Gross, Kevin	89SCTR	39	$ .01	$ .05
Gedman, Rich	88SC	241	$ .01	$ .04	Gross, Kevin	90SC	251	$ .01	$ .04
Gedman, Rich	89SC	345	$ .01	$ .04	Grubb, John	88SC	199	$ .01	$ .04
Gedman, Rich	90SC	173	$ .01	$ .04	Gruber, Kelly	88SC	422	$ .01	$ .04
Geren, Bob	89SCTR	93	$ .01	$ .25	Gruber, Kelly	89SC	194	$ .01	$ .04
Geren, Bob	90SC	464	$ .01	$ .10	Gruber, Kelly	90SC	425	$ .01	$ .04
Gerhart, Ken	88SC	58	$ .01	$ .10	Guante, Cecilio	89SC	439	$ .01	$ .04
Gerhart, Ken	89SC	506	$ .01	$ .04	Guante, Cecilio	90SC	438	$ .01	$ .04
Gibson, Kirk	88SC	525	$ .04	$ .20	Gubicza, Mark	88SC	516	$ .01	$ .04
Gibson, Kirk	88SCTR	10	$ .01	$ .15	Gubicza, Mark	89SC	291	$ .01	$ .04
Gibson, Kirk	89SC	210	$ .01	$ .15	Gubicza, Mark	90SC	121	$ .01	$ .04
Gibson, Kirk	90SC	487	$ .01	$ .04	Guerrero, Pedro	88SC	9	$ .01	$ .10
Gibson, Paul	89SC	595	$ .01	$ .04	Guerrero, Pedro	89SC	564	$ .01	$ .04
Gibson, Paul	90SC	261	$ .01	$ .04	Guerrero, Pedro	90SC	13	$ .01	$ .10
Girardi, Joe	89SCTR	84	$ .01	$ .30	Guetterman, Lee	88SC	323	$ .01	$ .04
Girardi, Joe	90SC	535	$ .01	$ .15	Guetterman, Lee	90SC	294	$ .01	$ .04
Gladden, Dan	88SC	324	$ .01	$ .04	Guidry, Ron	88SC	310	$ .01	$ .04
Gladden, Dan	89SC	62	$ .01	$ .04	Guidry, Ron	89SC	342	$ .01	$ .04
Gladden, Dan	90SC	61	$ .01	$ .04	Guillen, Ozzie	88SC	603	$ .01	$ .04
Glavine, Tom	88SC	638	$ .01	$ .25	Guillen, Ozzie	89SC	433	$ .01	$ .04
Glavine, Tom	89SC	442	$ .01	$ .04	Guillen, Ozzie	90SC	6	$ .01	$ .04
Glavine, Tom	90SC	481	$ .01	$ .04	Gullickson, Bill	88SC	585	$ .01	$ .04
Gleaton, Jerry Don	88SC	343	$ .01	$ .04	Guzman, Jose	88SC	322	$ .01	$ .04
Gleaton, Jerry Don	89SC	423	$ .01	$ .04	Guzman, Jose	89SC	143	$ .01	$ .04
Gohr, Greg	90SC	679	$ .01	$ .04	Gwynn, Chris	88SC	640	$ .04	$ .30
Gonzales, Rene	89SC	585	$ .01	$ .04	Gwynn, Tony	88SC	385	$ .04	$ .25
Gonzales, Rene	90SC	118	$ .01	$ .04	Gwynn, Tony	89SC	90	$ .01	$ .15
Gonzalez, German	90SC	133	$ .01	$ .04	Gwynn, Tony	90SC	255	$ .01	$ .15
Gonzalez, Jose	88SC	364	$ .01	$ .04	Gwynn, Tony	90SCDT	685	$ .01	$ .10
Gonzalez, Jose	90SC	368	$ .01	$ .04	Haas, Moose	88SC	177	$ .01	$ .04
Gonzalez, Juan	90SC	637	$ .01	$ .35	Habyan, John	88SC	353	$ .01	$ .04
Gooden, Dwight "Doc"	88SC	350	$ .10	$ .35	Hale, Chip	90SC	588	$ .01	$ .04
Gooden, Doc	89SC	200	$ .01	$ .25	Hall, Albert	88SC	148	$ .01	$ .04
Gooden, Doc	90SC	313	$ .01	$ .15	Hall, Albert	89SC	74	$ .01	$ .04
Goodwin, Tom	90SC	668	$ .01	$ .25	Hall, Drew	90SC	516	$ .01	$ .04
Goosage, Goose	88SCTR	14	$ .01	$ .10	Hall, Mel	88SC	441	$ .01	$ .04
Gordon, Don	88SCTR	92	$ .01	$ .15	Hall, Mel	89SC	17	$ .01	$ .04

Player	Year	No.	VG	EX/MT
Hall, Mel	89SCTR	54	$ .01	$ .05
Hall, Mel	90SC	383	$ .01	$ .04
Hamilton, Darryl	88SCTR	72	$ .01	$ .20
Hamilton, Jeff	89SC	570	$ .01	$ .04
Hamilton, Jeff	90SC	132	$ .01	$ .04
Hammaker, Atlee	88SC	528	$ .01	$ .04
Hammaker, Atlee	89SC	422	$ .01	$ .04
Hammaker, Atlee	90SC	231	$ .01	$ .04
Hammond, Chris	90SC	629	$ .01	$ .15
Hanson, Erik	90SC	530	$ .01	$ .04
Harkey, Mike	89SC	624	$ .01	$ .35
Harnisch, Pete	89SCTR	110	$ .01	$ .20
Harnisch, Pete	90SC	355	$ .01	$ .04
Harper, Brian	89SC	408	$ .01	$ .04
Harper, Brian	90SC	189	$ .01	$ .04
Harris, Donald	90SC	661	$ .01	$ .25
Harris, Gene	90SC	548	$ .01	$ .04
Harris, Greg	88SC	179	$ .01	$ .04
Harris, Greg	89SC	476	$ .01	$ .04
Harris, Greg	89SCTR	87	$ .01	$ .15
Harris, Greg	90SC	257	$ .01	$ .04

Player	Year	No.	VG	EX/MT
Harris, Lenny	90SC	23	$ .01	$ .04
Hartley, Mike	90SC	641	$ .01	$ .04
Harvey, Bryan	88SCTR	87	$ .01	$ .35
Harvey, Bryan	89SC	185	$ .01	$ .15
Harvey, Bryan	90SC	8	$ .01	$ .04
Hassey, Ron	88SCTR	33	$ .01	$ .05
Hassey, Ron	89SC	334	$ .01	$ .04
Hassey, Ron	90SC	168	$ .01	$ .04
Hatcher, Billy	88SC	505	$ .01	$ .04
Hatcher, Billy	89SC	61	$ .01	$ .04
Hatcher, Billy	90SC	562	$ .01	$ .04
Hatcher, Mickey	88SC	298	$ .01	$ .04
Hatcher, Mickey	89SC	332	$ .01	$ .04
Hatcher, Mickey	90SC	359	$ .01	$ .04
Hawkins, Andy	88SC	347	$ .01	$ .04
Hawkins, Andy	89SC	118	$ .01	$ .04
Hawkins, Andy	89SCTR	14	$ .01	$ .05
Hayes, Charlie	89SC	628	$ .01	$ .04
Hayes, Charlie	90SC	507	$ .01	$ .04
Hayes, Von	88SC	515	$ .01	$ .04
Hayes, Von	89SC	38	$ .01	$ .04
Hayes, Von	90SC	36	$ .01	$ .10

Player	Year	No.	VG	EX/MT
Hayward, Ray	88SCTR	67	$ .01	$ .05
Hayward, Ray	89SC	514	$ .01	$ .10
Hearn, Ed	88SC	569	$ .01	$ .04
Heath, Mike	88SC	156	$ .01	$ .04
Heath, Mike	89SC	131	$ .01	$ .04
Heath, Mike	90SC	172	$ .01	$ .04
Heaton, Neal	88SC	430	$ .01	$ .04
Heaton, Neal	89SC	253	$ .01	$ .04
Heep, Danny	88SC	417	$ .01	$ .04
Heep, Danny	89SC	343	$ .01	$ .04
Heep, Danny	89SCTR	57	$ .01	$ .05
Heep, Danny	90SC	113	$ .01	$ .04
Heinkel, Don	88SCTR	79	$ .01	$ .15
Heinkel, Don	89SC	168	$ .01	$ .10
Hemond, Scott	90SC	598	$ .01	$ .04
Henderson, Dave	88SC	228	$ .01	$ .04
Henderson, Dave	88SCTR	49	$ .01	$ .05
Henderson, Dave	89SC	533	$ .01	$ .04
Henderson, Dave	90SC	325	$ .01	$ .04
Henderson, Rickey	88SC	13	$ .05	$ .25
Henderson, Rickey	89SC	657	$ .01	$ .04
Henderson, Rickey	89SC	70	$ .01	$ .20
Henderson, Rickey	89SCTR	50	$ .01	$ .35
Henderson, Rickey	90SC	360	$ .01	$ .15
Henderson, Rickey	90SC	698	$ .01	$ .20
Henderson, Rickey	90SCDT	686	$ .01	$ .10
Henderson, Steve	88SC	547	$ .01	$ .04
Hendrick, George	88SC	308	$ .01	$ .04
Henke, Tom	88SC	57	$ .01	$ .04
Henke, Tom	89SC	318	$ .01	$ .04
Henke, Tom	90SC	157	$ .01	$ .04
Henneman, Mike	88SC	520	$ .01	$ .04
Henneman, Mike	89SC	293	$ .01	$ .04
Henneman, Mike	90SC	184	$ .01	$ .04
Hernandez, Guillermo	89SC	275	$ .01	$ .04
Hernandez, Guillermo	90SC	267	$ .01	$ .04
Hernandez, Keith	88SC	400	$ .04	$ .25
Hernandez, Keith	89SC	41	$ .01	$ .10
Hernandez, Keith	90SC	193	$ .01	$ .04
Hernandez, Willie	88SC	507	$ .01	$ .04
Herndon, Larry	88SC	138	$ .01	$ .04
Herndon, Larry	89SC	279	$ .01	$ .04
Herr, Tom	88SC	84	$ .01	$ .04
Herr, Tom	88SCTR	8	$ .01	$ .05
Herr, Tom	89SCTR	9	$ .01	$ .05
Herr, Tom	90SC	171	$ .01	$ .04
Herr, Tommy	89SC	191	$ .01	$ .04
Hershiser, Orel	88SC	470	$ .01	$ .15
Hershiser, Orel	89SC	370	$ .01	$ .15
Hershiser, Orel	89SC	653	$ .01	$ .15
Hershiser, Orel	90SC	50	$ .01	$ .10
Hesketh, Joe	89SC	498	$ .01	$ .04
Hesketh, Joe	90SC	483	$ .01	$ .04
Hetzel, Eric	90SC	543	$ .01	$ .04
Hibbard, Greg	90SC	369	$ .01	$ .04
Hickey, Kevin	90SC	214	$ .01	$ .04
Higuera, Teddy	88SC	280	$ .01	$ .04
Higuera, Teddy	89SC	132	$ .01	$ .04
Higuera, Teddy	90SC	305	$ .01	$ .04
Hill, Donnie	88SC	572	$ .01	$ .04
Hill, Donnie	89SC	583	$ .01	$ .04
Hill, Glenallen	90SC	601	$ .01	$ .25
Hill, Ken	89SCTR	98	$ .01	$ .20
Hill, Ken	90SC	233	$ .01	$ .04
Hillegas, Shawn	88SC	612	$ .01	$ .15
Hillegas, Shawn	89SC	488	$ .01	$ .04
Hillegas, Shawn	90SC	329	$ .01	$ .04
Hinzo, Tommy	88SC	567	$ .01	$ .04
Hoffman, Guy	88SC	609	$ .01	$ .04
Holman, Brian	90SC	387	$ .01	$ .04
Holman, Shawn	90SC	620	$ .01	$ .15
Holton, Brian	88SC	208	$ .01	$ .04
Holton, Brian	89SC	507	$ .01	$ .04
Holton, Brian	89SCTR	59	$ .01	$ .05
Holton, Brian	90SC	177	$ .01	$ .04

Player	Year	No.	VG	EX/MT	Player	Year	No.	VG	EX/MT
Honeycutt, Rick	88SC	87	$ .01	$ .04	Jackson, Bo	88SC	180	$ .10	$1.50
Honeycutt, Rick	89SC	416	$ .01	$ .04	Jackson, Bo	89SC	330	$ .05	$ .75
Honeycutt, Rick	90SC	317	$ .01	$ .04	Jackson, Bo	90SC	280	$ .01	$ .50
Horn, Sam	88SC	201	$ .01	$ .20	Jackson, Bo	90SC	566	$ .01	$ .35
Horner, Bob	89SC	68	$ .01	$ .04	Jackson, Bo	90SC	697	$ .01	$10.00
Horton, Rick	88SC	412	$ .01	$ .04	Jackson, Bo	90SCDT	687	$ .01	$ .35
Horton, Rick	88SCTR	24	$ .01	$ .05	Jackson, Chuck	88SC	222	$ .01	$ .04
Horton, Rick	89SC	145	$ .01	$ .04	Jackson, Chuck	89SC	584	$ .01	$ .04
Hosey, Steve	90SC	666	$ .01	$ .04	Jackson, Danny	88SC	398	$ .04	$ .20
Hough, Charlie	88SC	140	$ .01	$ .04	Jackson, Danny	88SCTR	2	$ .01	$ .20
Hough, Charlie	89SC	295	$ .01	$ .04	Jackson, Danny	89SC	555	$ .01	$ .10
Hough, Charlie	90SC	202	$ .01	$ .04	Jackson, Danny	90SC	289	$ .01	$ .04
Houston, Tyler	90SC	677	$ .01	$ .35	Jackson, Darrin	88SCTR	109	$ .01	$ .25
Howe, Steve	88SC	543	$ .01	$ .04	Jackson, Darrin	89SC	360	$ .01	$ .15
Howell, Jack	88SC	124	$ .01	$ .04	Jackson, Darrin	90SC	541	$ .01	$ .04
Howell, Jack	89SC	261	$ .01	$ .04	Jackson, Jeff	90SC	678	$ .01	$ .20
Howell, Jack	90SC	206	$ .01	$ .04	Jackson, Mike	88SC	144	$ .01	$ .04
Howell, Jay	88SC	522	$ .01	$ .04	Jackson, Mike	88SCTR	62	$ .01	$ .05
Howell, Jay	88SCTR	35	$ .01	$ .05	Jackson, Mike	89SC	398	$ .01	$ .04
Howell, Jay	89SC	378	$ .01	$ .04	Jackson, Mike	90SC	546	$ .01	$ .04
Howell, Jay	90SC	227	$ .01	$ .04	Jackson, Reggie #1	88SC	500	$ .04	$ .25
Howell, Ken	88SC	406	$ .01	$ .04	Jackson, Reggie #2	88SC	501	$ .04	$ .25
Hrbek, Kent	88SC	43	$ .01	$ .04	Jackson, Reggie #3	88SC	502	$ .04	$ .25
Hrbek, Kent	89SC	382	$ .01	$ .10	Jackson, Reggie #4	88SC	503	$ .04	$ .25
Hrbek, Kent	90SC	381	$ .01	$ .04	Jackson, Reggie #5	88SC	504	$ .04	$ .25
Hubbard, Glenn	88SC	111	$ .01	$ .04	Jacoby, Brook	88SC	39	$ .01	$ .10
Hubbard, Glenn	88SCTR	58	$ .01	$ .05	Jacoby, Brook	89SC	19	$ .01	$ .04
Hubbard, Glenn	89SC	34	$ .01	$ .04	Jacoby, Brook	90SC	56	$ .01	$ .04
Hudler, Rex	89SC	470	$ .01	$ .04	James, Chris	88SC	409	$ .01	$ .04
Hudler, Rex	90SC	287	$ .01	$ .04	James, Chris	89SC	202	$ .01	$ .04
Hudson, Charles	89SC	415	$ .01	$ .04	James, Chris	89SCTR	46	$ .01	$ .05
Huff, Mike	90SC	597	$ .01	$ .04	James, Chris	90SC	498	$ .01	$ .04
Hughes, Keith	88SC	635	$ .01	$ .04	James, Dion	88SC	395	$ .01	$ .04
Hume, Tom	88SC	494	$ .01	$ .04	James, Dion	89SC	163	$ .01	$ .04
Hurst, Bruce	88SC	380	$ .01	$ .04	James, Dion	89SCTR	51	$ .01	$ .05
Hurst, Bruce	89SC	325	$ .01	$ .04	James, Dion	90SC	514	$ .01	$ .04
Hurst, Bruce	89SCTR	19	$ .01	$ .10	Javier, Stan	88SC	367	$ .01	$ .04
Hurst, Bruce	90SC	270	$ .01	$ .04	Javier, Stan	89SC	322	$ .01	$ .04
Huson, Jeff	90SC	615	$ .01	$ .04	Javier, Stan	90SC	394	$ .01	$ .04
Incaviglia, Pete	88SC	485	$ .01	$ .15	Jeffcoat, Mike	90SC	158	$ .01	$ .04
Incaviglia, Pete	89SC	201	$ .01	$ .15	Jefferies, Gregg	88SC	645	$ .50	$2.50
					Jefferies, Gregg	89SC	600	$ .15	$1.00
					Jefferies, Gregg	90SC	468	$ .01	$ .35
					Jefferson, Stan	88SC	114	$ .01	$ .04
					Jefferson, Stan	89SC	519	$ .01	$ .04
					Jeltz, Steve	88SC	435	$ .01	$ .04
					Jeltz, Steve	89SC	355	$ .01	$ .04
					Jeltz, Steve	90SC	421	$ .01	$ .04
					Jennings, Doug	89SC	459	$ .01	$ .10
					John, Tommy	88SC	240	$ .01	$ .10
					John, Tommy	89SC	477	$ .01	$ .04
					Johnson, Dave	90SC	528	$ .01	$ .04
					Johnson, Howard	88SC	69	$ .01	$ .15
					Johnson, Howard	89SC	136	$ .01	$ .10
					Johnson, Howard	90SC	124	$ .01	$ .10
					Johnson, Lance	90SC	570	$ .01	$ .04
					Johnson, Randy	89SC	645	$ .01	$ .25
					Johnson, Randy	89SCTR	77	$ .01	$ .05
					Johnson, Randy	90SC	415	$ .01	$ .04
					Johnson, Wallace	88SC	433	$ .01	$ .04
					Johnson, Wallace	89SC	196	$ .01	$ .04
					Johnson, Wallace	90SC	479	$ .01	$ .04
					Jones, Barry	89SC	333	$ .01	$ .04
					Jones, Barry	90SC	152	$ .01	$ .04
					Jones, Doug	88SC	594	$ .01	$ .25
					Jones, Doug	89SC	387	$ .01	$ .04
					Jones, Doug	89SC	656	$ .01	$ .04
					Jones, Doug	90SC	130	$ .01	$ .04
					Jones, Jimmy	88SC	246	$ .01	$ .04
					Jones, Jimmy	89SC	294	$ .01	$ .04
					Jones, Keith "Kiki"	90SC	676	$ .01	$ .20
					Jones, Odell	89SC	579	$ .01	$ .04
					Jones, Ron	89SC	639	$ .01	$ .35
Incaviglia, Pete	90SC	93	$ .01	$ .10	Jones, Ron	90SC	364	$ .01	$ .04
Iorg, Garth	88SC	204	$ .01	$ .04	Jones, Ross	88SC	598	$ .01	$ .04

Player	Year	No.	VG	EX/MT	Player	Year	No.	VG	EX/MT
Jones, Ruppert	88SC	333	$ .01	$ .04	Lake, Steve	89SCTR	12	$ .01	$ .05
Jones, Tim	89SC	649	$ .01	$ .04	Lake, Steve	90SC	435	$ .01	$ .04
Jones, Tim	90SC	579	$ .01	$ .04	Lamp, Dennis	88SC	616	$ .01	$ .04
Jones, Tracy	88SC	326	$ .01	$ .04	Lamp, Dennis	88SCTR	6	$ .01	$ .05
Jones, Tracy	89SC	510	$ .01	$ .04	Lamp, Dennis	89SC	508	$ .01	$ .04
Jones, Tracy	89SCTR	43	$ .01	$ .05	Lamp, Dennis	90SC	471	$ .01	$ .04
Jones, Tracy	90SC	291	$ .01	$ .04	Lancaster, Les	88SC	602	$ .01	$ .10
Jordan, Ricky	88SCTR	68	$ .01	$3.50	Lancaster, Les	89SC	60	$ .01	$ .04
Jordan, Ricky	89SC	548	$ .15	$1.25	Lancaster, Les	90SC	413	$ .01	$ .04
Jordan, Ricky	90SC	16	$ .01	$ .20	Landreaux, Ken	88SC	247	$ .01	$ .04
Jorgensen, Terry	90SC	655	$ .01	$ .04	Landrum, Bill	90SC	456	$ .01	$ .04
Jose, Felix	89SC	629	$ .01	$ .25	Langston, Mark	88SC	30	$ .01	$ .10
Jose, Felix	90SC	321	$ .01	$ .15	Langston, Mark	89SC	161	$ .01	$ .10
Jose, Uribe	88SC	165	$ .01	$ .04	Langston, Mark	89SCTR	25	$ .01	$ .10
Joyner, Wally	88SC	7	$ .10	$ .30	Langston, Mark	90SC	401	$ .01	$ .10
Joyner, Wally	89SC	65	$ .01	$ .15	Langston, Mark	90SCDT	688	$ .01	$ .10
Joyner, Wally	90SC	120	$ .01	$ .10	Lansford, Carney	88SC	253	$ .01	$ .04
Justice, Dave	90SC	650	$ .01	$ .15	Lansford, Carney	89SC	179	$ .01	$ .04
Karkovice, Ron	88SC	374	$ .01	$ .04	Lansford, Carney	90SC	296	$ .01	$ .04
Karkovice, Ron	90SC	22	$ .01	$ .04	LaPoint, Dave	88SC	589	$ .01	$ .04
Kelly, Roberto	88SC	634	$ .10	$ .75	LaPoint, Dave	89SC	384	$ .01	$ .04
Kelly, Roberto	89SC	487	$ .01	$ .15	LaPoint, Dave	89SCTR	4	$ .01	$ .05
Kelly, Roberto	90SC	100	$ .01	$ .10	LaPoint, Dave	90SC	357	$ .01	$ .04
Kennedy, Terry	88SC	123	$ .01	$ .04	Larkin, Barry	88SC	72	$ .10	$ .75
Kennedy, Terry	89SC	123	$ .01	$ .04	Larkin, Barry	89SC	31	$ .01	$ .35
Kennedy, Terry	89SCTR	30	$ .01	$ .05	Larkin, Barry	90SC	155	$ .01	$ .15
Kennedy, Terry	90SC	7	$ .01	$ .04	Larkin, Barry	90SCDT	689	$ .01	$ .10
Kerfeld, Charlie	88SC	479	$ .01	$ .04	Larkin, Gene	88SC	276	$ .01	$ .10
Key, Jimmy	88SC	216	$ .01	$ .04	Larkin, Gene	89SC	280	$ .01	$ .04
Key, Jimmy	89SC	480	$ .01	$ .04	Larkin, Gene	90SC	276	$ .01	$ .04
Key, Jimmy	90SC	407	$ .01	$ .04	Laudner, Tim	88SC	153	$ .01	$ .04
Kiefer, Steve	88SC	630	$ .01	$ .04	Laudner, Tim	89SC	134	$ .01	$ .04
Kilgus, Paul	88SC	536	$ .01	$ .04	Laudner, Tim	90SC	318	$ .01	$ .04
Kilgus, Paul	89SC	271	$ .01	$ .04	LaValliere, Mike	88SC	421	$ .01	$ .04
King, Eric	88SC	471	$ .01	$ .04	LaValliere, Mike	89SC	33	$ .01	$ .04
King, Eric	89SC	471	$ .01	$ .04	LaValliere, Mike	90SC	116	$ .01	$ .04
King, Eric	89SCTR	26	$ .01	$ .05	Law, Vance	88SC	85	$ .01	$ .04
King, Eric	90SC	28	$ .01	$ .04	Law, Vance	88SCTR	16	$ .01	$ .05
King, Jeff	90SC	549	$ .01	$ .04	Law, Vance	89SC	102	$ .01	$ .04
Kingery, Mike	88SC	178	$ .01	$ .04	Law, Vance	90SC	73	$ .01	$ .04
Kinzer, Matt	90SC	628	$ .01	$ .04	Lazorko, Jack	88SC	437	$ .01	$ .04
Kipper, Bob	89SC	354	$ .01	$ .04	Lea, Charlie	89SC	501	$ .01	$ .04
Kittle, Ron	88SC	449	$ .01	$ .04	Leach, Rick	88SC	257	$ .01	$ .04
Kittle, Ron	88SCTR	44	$ .01	$ .05	Leach, Rick	89SC	540	$ .01	$ .04
Kittle, Ron	89SC	96	$ .01	$ .04	Leach, Rick	90SC	426	$ .01	$ .04
Kittle, Ron	90SC	529	$ .01	$ .04	Leach, Terry	88SC	203	$ .01	$ .04
Knepper, Bob	88SC	344	$ .01	$ .04	Leach, Terry	89SC	431	$ .01	$ .04
Knepper, Bob	89SC	273	$ .01	$ .04	Leach, Terry	89SCTR	24	$ .01	$ .05
Knight, Ray	88SC	96	$ .01	$ .04	Leach, Terry	90SC	502	$ .01	$ .04
Knight, Ray	88SCTR	17	$ .01	$ .05	Leary, Tim	88SC	224	$ .01	$ .04
Knight, Ray	89SC	135	$ .01	$ .04	Leary, Tim	89SC	429	$ .01	$ .04
Knoblauch, Chuck	90SC	672	$ .01	$ .04	Leary, Tim	89SCTR	52	$ .01	$ .05
Knudson, Mark	90SC	539	$ .01	$ .04	Leary, Tim	90SC	504	$ .01	$ .04
Komminsk, Brad	90SC	496	$ .01	$ .04	Lee, Manny	88SC	561	$ .01	$ .04
Kreuter, Chad	89SC	638	$ .01	$ .04	Lee, Manny	89SC	326	$ .01	$ .04
Kreuter, Chad	90SC	406	$ .01	$ .04	Lee, Manny	90SC	482	$ .01	$ .04
Krueger, Bill	90SC	366	$ .01	$ .04	Lefferts, Craig	88SC	553	$ .01	$ .04
Kruk, John	88SC	36	$ .01	$ .10	Lefferts, Craig	89SC	178	$ .01	$ .04
Kruk, John	89SC	148	$ .01	$ .04	Lefferts, Craig	90SC	209	$ .01	$ .04
Kruk, John	89SCTR	70	$ .01	$ .05	Leibrandt, Charlie	88SC	61	$ .01	$ .04
Kruk, John	90SC	467	$ .01	$ .04	Leibrandt, Charlie	89SC	133	$ .01	$ .04
Krukow, Mike	88SC	185	$ .01	$ .04	Leibrandt, Charlie	90SC	82	$ .01	$ .04
Krukow, Mike	89SC	190	$ .01	$ .04	Leiper, Dave	88SC	348	$ .01	$ .04
Krukow, Mike	90SC	215	$ .01	$ .04	Leiper, Dave	89SC	515	$ .01	$ .04
Kunkel, Jeff	88SC	407	$ .01	$ .04	Leiper, Dave	90SC	212	$ .01	$ .04
Kunkel, Jeff	89SC	484	$ .01	$ .04	Leiter, Al	88SCTR	97	$ .01	$ .25
Kunkel, Jeff	90SC	431	$ .01	$ .04	Leiter, Al	89SC	580	$ .01	$ .15
Kutcher, Randy	90SC	551	$ .01	$ .04	Lemke, Mark	90SC	593	$ .01	$ .04
LaCoss, Mike	88SC	465	$ .01	$ .04	Lemon, Chet	88SC	119	$ .01	$ .04
LaCoss, Mike	89SC	500	$ .01	$ .04	Lemon, Chet	89SC	44	$ .01	$ .04
LaCoss, Mike	90SC	253	$ .01	$ .04	Lemon, Chet	90SC	106	$ .01	$ .04
Lacy, Lee	88SC	173	$ .01	$ .04	Leonard, Jeff	89SC	557	$ .01	$ .04
Laga, Mike	89SC	536	$ .01	$ .04	Leonard, Jeffrey	88SC	580	$ .01	$ .04
Lake, Steve	88SC	596	$ .01	$ .04	Leonard, Jeffrey	89SCTR	7	$ .01	$ .05
Lake, Steve	89SC	363	$ .01	$ .04	Leonard, Jeffrey	90SC	98	$ .01	$ .04

SCORE

Player	Year	No.	VG	EX/MT	Player	Year	No.	VG	EX/MT
Lilliquist, Derek	89SC	631	$ .01	$ .30	Martinez, Ramon	90SC	461	$ .01	$ .15
Lilliquist, Derek	90SC	243	$ .01	$ .10	Martinez, Tino	90SC	596	$ .01	$ .25
Lind, Jose	88SC	597	$ .04	$ .25	Marzano, John	88SC	584	$ .05	$ .25
Lind, Jose	89SC	87	$ .01	$ .10	Mathews, Greg	88SC	226	$ .01	$ .04
Lind, Jose	90SC	83	$ .01	$ .10	Mathews, Greg	89SC	286	$ .01	$ .04
Lindeman, Jim	88SC	302	$ .01	$ .04	Mathews, Greg	90SC	537	$ .01	$ .04
Liriano, Nelson	88SC	621	$ .01	$ .04	Matthews, Gary	88SC	599	$ .01	$ .04
Liriano, Nelson	89SC	577	$ .01	$ .04	Mattingly, Don	88SC	1	$ .25	$1.00
Liriano, Nelson	90SC	77	$ .01	$ .04	Mattingly, Don	88SC	650	$ .10	$ .50
Litton, Greg	89SCTR	86	$ .01	$ .15	Mattingly, Don	88SC	658	$ .10	$ .50
Litton, Greg	90SC	497	$ .01	$ .04	Mattingly, Don	89SC	100	$ .10	$ .60
Lombardozzi, Steve	88SC	174	$ .01	$ .04	Mattingly, Don	90SC	1	$ .01	$ .50
Lombardozzi, Steve	89SC	421	$ .01	$ .04	Matuszek, Len	88SC	424	$ .01	$ .04
Long, Bill	88SC	539	$ .01	$ .04	Mayne, Brent	90SC	664	$ .01	$ .04
Long, Bill	89SC	351	$ .01	$ .04	Mazzilli, Lee	88SC	158	$ .01	$ .04
Long, Bill	90SC	526	$ .01	$ .04	Mazzilli, Lee	89SC	217	$ .01	$ .04
Lopes, Davey	88SC	489	$ .01	$ .04	Mazzilli, Lee	90SC	459	$ .01	$ .04
Loynd, Mike	88SC	491	$ .01	$ .04	McCament, Randy	90SC	580	$ .01	$ .04
Lusader, Scott	90SC	575	$ .01	$ .04	McCaskill, Kirk	88SC	552	$ .01	$ .04
Lynch, Ed	88SC	506	$ .01	$ .04	McCaskill, Kirk	89SC	181	$ .01	$ .04
Lynn, Fred	88SC	42	$ .01	$ .10	McCaskill, Kirk	90SC	217	$ .01	$ .04
Lynn, Fred	89SC	126	$ .01	$ .04	McClendon, Lloyd	89SC	521	$ .01	$ .04
Lynn, Fred	90SC	131	$ .01	$ .04	McClendon, Lloyd	90SC	176	$ .01	$ .04
Lyons, Barry	88SC	387	$ .01	$ .04	McClure, Bob	89SC	572	$ .01	$ .04
Lyons, Barry	89SC	456	$ .01	$ .04	McClure, Bob	89SCTR	58	$ .01	$ .05
Lyons, Barry	90SC	29	$ .01	$ .04	McClure, Bob	90SC	117	$ .01	$ .04
Lyons, Steve	89SC	388	$ .01	$ .04	McClure, Rob	88SC	381	$ .01	$ .04
Lyons, Steve	90SC	88	$ .01	$ .04	McCullers, Lance	88SC	150	$ .01	$ .04
Maas, Kevin	90SC	606	$ .01	$ .20	McCullers, Lance	89SC	158	$ .01	$ .04
Macfarlane, Mike	88SCTR	76	$ .01	$ .20	McCullers, Lance	89SCTR	63	$ .01	$ .05
Macfarlane, Mike	89SC	319	$ .01	$ .15	McCullers, Lance	90SC	186	$ .01	$ .04
Mack, Shane	88SC	414	$ .01	$ .04	McDonald, Ben	90SC	680	$ .01	$2.00
Mack, Shane	89SC	270	$ .01	$ .04	McDowell, Jack	88SCTR	85	$ .01	$ .25
Maddux, Greg	89SC	119	$ .01	$ .10	McDowell, Jack	89SC	289	$ .01	$ .15
Maddux, Greg	90SC	403	$ .01	$ .04	McDowell, Oddibe	88SC	215	$ .01	$ .04
Maddux, Mike	89SC	393	$ .01	$ .04	McDowell, Oddibe	89SC	59	$ .01	$ .04
Madlock, Bill	88SC	445	$ .01	$ .10	McDowell, Oddibe	89SCTR	72	$ .01	$ .05
Magadan, Dave	88SC	41	$ .01	$ .10	McDowell, Oddibe	90SC	476	$ .01	$ .04
Magadan, Dave	89SC	312	$ .01	$ .04	McDowell, Roger	88SC	188	$ .01	$ .04
Magadan, Dave	90SC	46	$ .01	$ .04	McDowell, Roger	89SC	281	$ .01	$ .04
Magrane, Joe	88SC	94	$ .04	$ .30	McDowell, Roger	89SCTR	53	$ .01	$ .05
Magrane, Joe	89SC	460	$ .01	$ .10	McDowell, Roger	90SC	445	$ .01	$ .04
Magrane, Joe	90SC	17	$ .01	$ .04	McGaffigan, Andy	88SC	366	$ .01	$ .04
Mahler, Rick	88SC	319	$ .01	$ .04	McGaffigan, Andy	89SC	138	$ .01	$ .04
Mahler, Rick	89SC	229	$ .01	$ .04	McGaffigan, Andy	90SC	224	$ .01	$ .04
Mahler, Rick	89SCTR	79	$ .01	$ .05	McGee, Willie	88SC	40	$ .01	$ .10
Mahler, Rick	90SC	87	$ .01	$ .04	McGee, Willie	89SC	88	$ .01	$ .04
Maldonado, Candy	88SC	54	$ .01	$ .04	McGee, Willie	90SC	374	$ .01	$ .04
Maldonado, Candy	89SC	47	$ .01	$ .04	McGregor, Scott	88SC	315	$ .01	$ .04
Maldonado, Candy	90SC	138	$ .01	$ .04	McGriff, Fred	88SC	107	$ .07	$1.00
Mann, Kelly	90SC	627	$ .01	$ .25	McGriff, Fred	89SC	6	$ .01	$ .30
Manning, Rick	88SC	593	$ .01	$ .04	McGriff, Fred	90SC	271	$ .01	$ .10
Manrique, Fred	88SC	139	$ .01	$ .04	McGriff, Terry	88SC	281	$ .01	$ .04
Manrique, Fred	89SC	457	$ .01	$ .04	McGwire, Mark	88SC	5	$ .25	$1.25
Manrique, Fred	90SC	166	$ .01	$ .04	McGwire, Mark	88SC	648	$ .15	$ .50
Manwaring, Kirt	88SC	627	$ .01	$ .04	McGwire, Mark	88SC	659	$ .10	$ .50
Manwaring, Kirt	89SC	619	$ .01	$ .04	McGwire, Mark	89SC	3	$ .10	$ .50
Manwaring, Kirt	90SC	146	$ .01	$ .04	McGwire, Mark	90SC	385	$ .01	$ .25
Marshall, Mike	88SC	135	$ .01	$ .10	McLemore, Mark	88SC	152	$ .01	$ .04
Marshall, Mike	89SC	186	$ .01	$ .04	McLemore, Mark	89SC	208	$ .01	$ .04
Marshall, Mike	90SC	384	$ .01	$ .04	McReynolds, Kevin	88SC	21	$ .01	$ .15
Martinez, Carlos	89SCTR	103	$ .01	$ .20	McReynolds, Kevin	89SC	93	$ .01	$ .15
Martinez, Carlos	90SC	314	$ .01	$ .04	McReynolds, Kevin	90SC	5	$ .01	$ .04
Martinez, Carmelo	88SC	181	$ .01	$ .04	McWilliams, Larry	88SCTR	23	$ .01	$ .05
Martinez, Carmelo	89SC	517	$ .01	$ .04	McWilliams, Larry	89SC	259	$ .01	$ .04
Martinez, Carmelo	90SC	114	$ .01	$ .04	Meacham, Bobby	88SC	137	$ .01	$ .04
Martinez, Dave	88SC	223	$ .01	$ .04	Meacham, Bobby	89SC	509	$ .01	$ .04
Martinez, Dave	89SC	77	$ .01	$ .04	Meads, Dave	88SC	243	$ .01	$ .04
Martinez, Dave	90SC	27	$ .01	$ .04	Meads, Dave	89SC	593	$ .01	$ .04
Martinez, Dennis	88SC	601	$ .01	$ .04	Medina, Luis	89SC	633	$ .01	$ .30
Martinez, Dennis	89SC	114	$ .01	$ .04	Melvin, Bob	88SC	477	$ .01	$ .04
Martinez, Dennis	90SC	47	$ .01	$ .04	Melvin, Bob	89SC	617	$ .01	$ .04
Martinez, Edgar	89SC	637	$ .01	$ .25	Melvin, Bob	89SCTR	61	$ .01	$ .05
Martinez, Edgar	90SC	324	$ .01	$ .20	Melvin, Bob	90SC	453	$ .01	$ .04
Martinez, Ramon	89SC	635	$ .01	$ .40	Merullo, Matt	90SC	605	$ .01	$ .04

Player	Year	No.	VG	EX/MT
Meyer, Joey	88SCTR	75	$ .01	$ .20
Meyer, Joey	89SC	374	$ .01	$ .15
Meyer, Joey	90SC	532	$ .01	$ .04
Mickey, Brantley	88SC	213	$ .01	$ .04
Mielke, Gary	90SC	574	$ .01	$ .04
Milacki, Bob	89SC	651	$ .01	$ .30
Milacki, Bob	90SC	239	$ .01	$ .04
Miller, Darrell	88SC	463	$ .01	$ .04
Miller, Darrell	89SC	499	$ .01	$ .04
Miller, Keith	88SC	639	$ .01	$ .04
Miller, Keith	89SC	464	$ .01	$ .04
Miller, Keith	90SC	559	$ .01	$ .04
Milligan, Randy	88SC	623	$ .04	$ .30
Milligan, Randy	90SC	252	$ .01	$ .04
Milner, Eddie	88SC	548	$ .01	$ .04
Minton, Greg	88SC	176	$ .01	$ .04
Minton, Greg	89SC	543	$ .01	$ .04
Minton, Greg	90SC	48	$ .01	$ .04
Mirabella, Paul	89SC	569	$ .01	$ .04
Mitchell, John	88SC	249	$ .01	$ .04
Mitchell, Kevin	88SC	481	$ .10	$ .50
Mitchell, Kevin	89SC	39	$ .01	$ .35
Mitchell, Kevin	90SC	343	$ .01	$ .25
Mmahat, Kevin	90SC	643	$ .01	$ .04
Mohorcic, Dale	88SC	452	$ .01	$ .04
Mohorcic, Dale	89SC	420	$ .01	$ .04
Mohoric, Dale	90SC	191	$ .01	$ .04
Molitor, Paul	88SC	340	$ .01	$ .04
Molitor, Paul	88SC	660	$ .01	$ .10
Molitor, Paul	89SC	565	$ .01	$ .04
Molitor, Paul	90SC	460	$ .01	$ .04
Monteleone, Rich	89SCTR	92	$ .01	$ .20
Monteleone, Rich	90SC	565	$ .01	$ .04
Montgomery, Jeff	88SC	497	$ .01	$ .30
Montgomery, Jeff	88SCTR	71	$ .01	$ .20
Montgomery, Jeff	89SC	367	$ .01	$ .10
Montgomery, Jeff	90SC	365	$ .01	$ .04
Moore, Charlie	88SC	444	$ .01	$ .04
Moore, Donnie	88SC	195	$ .01	$ .04
Moore, Donnie	89SC	535	$ .01	$ .04
Moore, Mike	88SC	464	$ .01	$ .04
Moore, Mike	89SC	274	$ .01	$ .04
Moore, Mike	89SCTR	5	$ .01	$ .05
Moore, Mike	90SC	190	$ .01	$ .04
Moreland, Keith	88SC	71	$ .01	$ .04
Moreland, Keith	88SCTR	9	$ .01	$ .05
Moreland, Keith	89SC	42	$ .01	$ .04
Moreland, Keith	89SCTR	29	$ .01	$ .05
Moreland, Keith	90SC	444	$ .01	$ .04
Morgan, Mike	88SC	295	$ .01	$ .04
Morgan, Mike	90SC	342	$ .01	$ .04
Morris, Hal	90SC	602	$ .01	$ .04
Morris, Jack	88SC	545	$ .01	$ .10
Morris, Jack	89SC	250	$ .01	$ .04
Morris, Jack	90SC	203	$ .01	$ .04
Morris, John	88SC	346	$ .01	$ .04
Morris, John	90SC	134	$ .01	$ .04
Morrison, Jim	88SC	272	$ .01	$ .04
Moseby, Lloyd	88SC	109	$ .01	$ .04
Moseby, Lloyd	89SC	12	$ .01	$ .04
Moseby, Lloyd	90SC	404	$ .01	$ .04
Moses, John	88SC	309	$ .01	$ .04
Moses, John	89SC	432	$ .01	$ .04
Moses, John	90SC	391	$ .01	$ .04
Moyer, Jamie	88SC	573	$ .01	$ .04
Moyer, Jamie	89SC	263	$ .01	$ .04
Moyer, Jamie	90SC	107	$ .01	$ .04
Muellens, Hensley	90SC	636	$ .01	$ .15
Mulholland, Terry	89SC	474	$ .01	$ .04
Mulholland, Terry	90SC	542	$ .01	$ .04
Mulliniks, Rance	88SC	235	$ .01	$ .04
Mulliniks, Rance	89SC	385	$ .01	$ .04
Mulliniks, Rance	90SC	204	$ .01	$ .04
Mumphrey, Jerry	88SC	467	$ .01	$ .04
Mumphrey, Jerry	89SC	288	$ .01	$ .04

Player	Year	No.	VG	EX/MT
Munoz, Mike	90SC	653	$ .01	$ .15
Murphy, Dale	88SC	450	$ .04	$ .25

Player	Year	No.	VG	EX/MT
Murphy, Dale	89SC	30	$ .01	$ .15
Murphy, Dale	90SC	66	$ .01	$ .10
Murphy, Dwayne	88SC	455	$ .01	$ .04
Murphy, Dwayne	89SC	545	$ .01	$ .04
Murphy, Rob	88SC	559	$ .01	$ .04
Murphy, Rob	89SC	141	$ .01	$ .04
Murphy, Rob	89SCTR	8	$ .01	$ .05
Murphy, Rob	90SC	181	$ .01	$ .04
Murray, Eddie	88SC	18	$ .04	$ .25
Murray, Eddie	89SC	94	$ .01	$ .10
Murray, Eddie	89SCTR	31	$ .01	$ .10
Murray, Eddie	90SC	80	$ .01	$ .10
Musselman, Jeff	88SC	478	$ .01	$ .04
Musselman, Jeff	89SC	558	$ .01	$ .04
Musselman, Jeff	90SC	525	$ .01	$ .04
Myers, Randy	88SC	336	$ .01	$ .04
Myers, Randy	89SC	306	$ .01	$ .04
Myers, Randy	90SC	351	$ .01	$ .10
Nagy, Charles	90SC	611	$ .01	$ .15
Navarro, Jaime	90SC	569	$ .01	$ .20
Nelson, Gene	88SC	588	$ .01	$ .04
Nelson, Gene	89SC	434	$ .01	$ .04
Nelson, Gene	90SC	441	$ .01	$ .04
Nettles, Craig	88SCTR	25	$ .01	$ .10
Nettles, Graig	88SC	440	$ .01	$ .04
Nettles, Graig	89SC	277	$ .01	$ .04
Newman, Al	88SC	252	$ .01	$ .04
Newman, Al	89SC	493	$ .01	$ .04
Newman, Al	90SC	128	$ .01	$ .04
Niedenfuer, Tom	88SC	261	$ .01	$ .04
Niedenfuer, Tom	89SC	252	$ .01	$ .04
Niekro, Joe	88SC	237	$ .01	$ .04
Niekro, Phil	88SC	555	$ .01	$ .10
Nieves, Juan	88SC	513	$ .01	$ .04
Nieves, Juan	88SC	655	$ .01	$ .04
Nieves, Juan	89SC	410	$ .01	$ .04
Nipper, Al	88SC	527	$ .01	$ .04
Nipper, Al	89SC	532	$ .01	$ .04
Nixon, Donell	88SC	436	$ .01	$ .04
Nixon, Donell	89SC	481	$ .01	$ .04
Nixon, Donell	90SC	538	$ .01	$ .04

SCORE

Player	Year	No.	VG	EX/MT	Player	Year	No.	VG	EX/MT
Nixon, Otis	89SC	451	$ .01	$ .04	Orosco, Jesse	89SC	356	$ .01	$ .04
Nixon, Otis	90SC	241	$ .01	$ .04	Orosco, Jesse	90SC	353	$ .01	$ .04
Noce, Paul	88SC	329	$ .01	$ .04	Orsulak, Joe	88SCTR	41	$ .01	$ .05
Nokes, Matt	88SC	15	$ .10	$ .40	Orsulak, Joe	89SC	247	$ .01	$ .04
Nokes, Matt	88SC	648	$ .15	$ .50	Orsulak, Joe	90SC	41	$ .01	$ .04
Nokes, Matt	89SC	23	$ .01	$ .04	Ortiz, Junior	88SC	404	$ .01	$ .04
Nokes, Matt	90SC	55	$ .01	$ .04	Ortiz, Junior	89SC	402	$ .01	$ .04
Nolte, Eric	88SC	568	$ .01	$ .04	Ortiz, Junior	90SC	143	$ .01	$ .04
Nosek, Randy	90SC	607	$ .01	$ .10	Orton, John	90SC	582	$ .01	$ .04
Nunez, Jose	88SC	312	$ .01	$ .04	Owen, Larry	88SC	230	$ .01	$ .04
O'Brien, Charlie	89SC	606	$ .01	$ .04	Owen, Spike	88SC	372	$ .01	$ .04
O'Brien, Pete	89SCTR	6	$ .01	$ .05	Owen, Spike	89SC	218	$ .01	$ .04
O'Brien, Pete	90SC	175	$ .01	$ .04	Owen, Spike	89SCTR	13	$ .01	$ .05
O'Brien, Pete	88SC	29	$ .01	$ .04	Owen, Spike	90SC	247	$ .01	$ .04
O'Brien, Pete	89SC	22	$ .01	$ .04	Paciorek, Tom	88SC	531	$ .01	$ .04
O'Connor, Jack	88SC	434	$ .01	$ .04	Pagliarulo, Mike	88SC	170	$ .01	$ .10
O'Malley, Tom	88SC	534	$ .01	$ .04	Pagliarulo, Mike	89SC	189	$ .01	$ .04
O'Neill, Paul	90SC	295	$ .01	$ .10	Pagliarulo, Mike	89SCTR	11	$ .01	$ .05
O'Neill, Paul	88SC	304	$ .01	$ .15	Pagliarulo, Mike	90SC	494	$ .01	$ .04
O'Neill, Paul	89SC	206	$ .01	$ .04	Pagnozzi, Tom	88SC	358	$ .01	$ .04
Oberkfell, Ken	88SC	245	$ .01	$ .04	Pagnozzi, Tom	89SC	483	$ .01	$ .15
Oberkfell, Ken	89SC	139	$ .01	$ .04	Palacios, Vicente	88SC	643	$ .01	$ .15
Oberkfell, Ken	90SC	422	$ .01	$ .04	Pall, Donn	89SCTR	102	$ .01	$ .05
Oester, Ron	88SC	183	$ .01	$ .04	Pall, Donn	90SC	304	$ .01	$ .04
Oester, Ron	89SC	615	$ .01	$ .04	Palmeiro, Rafael	88SC	186	$ .07	$ .40
Oester, Ron	90SC	59	$ .01	$ .04	Palmeiro, Rafael	89SC	199	$ .01	$ .15
Ojeda, Bob	88SC	563	$ .01	$ .04	Palmeiro, Rafael	89SCTR	1	$ .01	$ .05
Ojeda, Bob	89SC	116	$ .01	$ .04	Palmeiro, Rafael	90SC	405	$ .01	$ .04
Ojeda, Bob	90SC	53	$ .01	$ .04	Palmer, Dave	89SC	544	$ .01	$ .04
Olerud, John	90SC	589	$ .01	$2.50	Palmer, David	88SC	457	$ .01	$ .04
Olin, Steve	90SC	590	$ .01	$ .15	Palmer, Dean	90SC	594	$ .01	$ .15
Oliver, Joe	89SCTR	104	$ .01	$ .35	Pankovits, Jim	89SC	192	$ .01	$ .04
Oliver, Joe	90SC	576	$ .01	$ .35	Parent, Mark	89SC	576	$ .01	$ .15
Olson, Gregg	89SCTR	96	$ .01	$1.00	Parent, Mark	90SC	119	$ .01	$ .04
Olson, Gregg	90SC	63	$ .01	$ .30	Parker, Clay	89SCTR	94	$ .01	$ .15
Olwine, Ed	88SC	379	$ .01	$ .04	Parker, Clay	90SC	316	$ .01	$ .04
Ontiveros, Steve	88SC	511	$ .01	$ .04	Parker, Dave	88SC	17	$ .01	$ .15
Ontiveros, Steve	89SC	337	$ .01	$ .04	Parker, Dave	88SCTR	50	$ .01	$ .10
Oquendo, Jose	88SC	248	$ .01	$ .10	Parker, Dave	89SC	108	$ .01	$ .04
					Parker, Dave	90SC	135	$ .01	$ .10
					Parrett, Jeff	89SC	377	$ .01	$ .10
					Parrett, Jeff	89SCTR	33	$ .01	$ .05
					Parrish, Lance	88SC	131	$ .01	$ .10
					Parrish, Lance	89SC	95	$ .01	$ .04
					Parrish, Lance	89SCTR	36	$ .01	$ .10
					Parrish, Lance	90SC	35	$ .01	$ .04
					Parrish, Larry	88SC	191	$ .01	$ .04
					Parrish, Larry	88SCTR	65	$ .01	$ .05
					Parrish, Larry	89SC	495	$ .01	$ .04
					Pasqua, Dan	88SC	196	$ .01	$ .04
					Pasqua, Dan	88SCTR	56	$ .01	$ .05
					Pasqua, Dan	89SC	338	$ .01	$ .04
					Pasqua, Dan	90SC	306	$ .01	$ .04
					Patterson, Ken	89SCTR	97	$ .01	$ .05
					Patterson, Ken	90SC	207	$ .01	$ .04
					Paul, Kilgus	90SC	196	$ .01	$ .04
					Pawlowski, John	90SC	617	$ .01	$ .04
					Pecota, Bill	88SC	377	$ .01	$ .04
					Pecota, Bill	89SC	339	$ .01	$ .04
					Pedrique, Al	88SC	301	$ .01	$ .04
					Pedrique, Al	89SC	614	$ .01	$ .04
					Pena, Alejandro	89SC	389	$ .01	$ .04
					Pena, Alejandro	90SC	39	$ .01	$ .04
					Pena, Tony	88SC	48	$ .01	$ .04
					Pena, Tony	89SC	36	$ .01	$ .04
					Pena, Tony	90SC	122	$ .01	$ .04
					Pendleton, Terry	88SC	190	$ .01	$ .04
					Pendleton, Terry	89SC	137	$ .01	$ .04
					Pendleton, Terry	90SC	208	$ .01	$ .04
					Peraza, Oswald	88SCTR	77	$ .01	$ .15
					Peraza, Oswald	89SC	571	$ .01	$ .15
					Perez, Melido	88SCTR	108	$ .01	$ .30
					Perez, Melido	89SC	386	$ .01	$ .15
					Perez, Melido	90SC	311	$ .01	$ .04

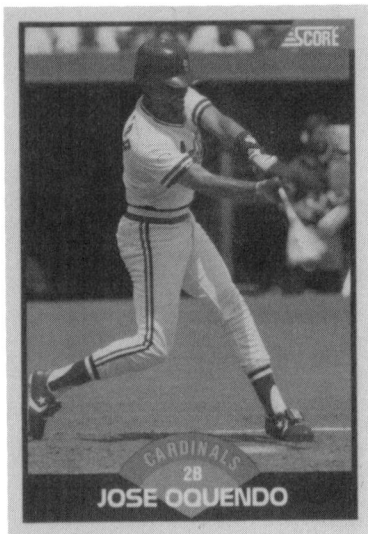

Player	Year	No.	VG	EX/MT
Oquendo, Jose	89SC	529	$ .01	$ .04
Oquendo, Jose	90SC	68	$ .01	$ .04
Orosco, Jesse	88SC	495	$ .01	$ .04
Orosco, Jesse	88SCTR	64	$ .01	$ .05

Perez, Pascual	88SC	459	$ .01	$ .04

Player	Year	No.	VG	EX/MT	Player	Year	No.	VG	EX/MT
Perez, Pascual	89SC	299	$ .01	$ .04	Ramirez, Rafael	88SCTR	12	$ .01	$ .05
Perez, Pascual	90SC	486	$ .01	$ .04	Ramirez, Rafael	89SC	113	$ .01	$ .04
Perlman, Jon	89SC	591	$ .01	$ .04	Ramirez, Rafael	90SC	42	$ .01	$ .04
Perry, Gerald	88SC	136	$ .01	$ .04	Ramos, Domingo	88SC	362	$ .01	$ .04
Perry, Gerald	89SC	101	$ .01	$ .04	Ramos, Domingo	90SC	489	$ .01	$ .04
Perry, Gerald	90SC	249	$ .01	$ .04	Ramsey, Mike	88SC	267	$ .01	$ .04
Perry, Pat	88SC	557	$ .01	$ .04	Randolph, Willie	88SC	266	$ .01	$ .04
Perry, Pat	89SC	364	$ .01	$ .04	Randolph, Willie	89SC	45	$ .01	$ .04
Perry, Pat	90SC	436	$ .01	$ .04	Randolph, Willie	89SCTR	41	$ .01	$ .10
Petralli, Geno	88SC	373	$ .01	$ .04	Randolph, Willie	90SC	395	$ .01	$ .04
Petralli, Geno	89SC	526	$ .01	$ .04	Rasmussen, Dennis	88SC	560	$ .01	$ .04
Petralli, Geno	90SC	153	$ .01	$ .04	Rasmussen, Dennis	89SC	562	$ .01	$ .04
Petry, Dan	88SC	461	$ .01	$ .04	Rasmussen, Dennis	90SC	129	$ .01	$ .04
Petry, Dan	88SCTR	26	$ .01	$ .05	Rawley, Shane	88SC	375	$ .01	$ .04
Petry, Dan	89SC	122	$ .01	$ .04	Rawley, Shane	89SC	170	$ .01	$ .04
Petry, Dan	90SC	211	$ .01	$ .04	Rawley, Shane	90SC	71	$ .01	$ .04
Pettis, Gary	88SC	255	$ .01	$ .04	Ray, Johnny	88SC	254	$ .01	$ .04
Pettis, Gary	88SCTR	38	$ .01	$ .05	Ray, Johnny	89SC	14	$ .01	$ .04
Pettis, Gary	89SC	26	$ .01	$ .04	Ray, Johnny	90SC	293	$ .01	$ .04
Pettis, Gary	90SC	136	$ .01	$ .04	Rayford, Floyd	88SC	359	$ .01	$ .04
Phelps, Ken	88SC	256	$ .01	$ .04	Ready, Randy	88SC	512	$ .01	$ .04
Phelps, Ken	89SC	242	$ .01	$ .04	Ready, Randy	89SC	426	$ .01	$ .04
Philips, Tony	90SC	84	$ .01	$ .04	Ready, Randy	89SCTR	60	$ .01	$ .05
Phillips, Tony	88SC	294	$ .01	$ .04	Ready, Randy	90SC	376	$ .01	$ .04
Phillips, Tony	89SC	156	$ .01	$ .04	Reardon, Jeff	88SC	91	$ .01	$ .04
Pico, Jeff	88SCTR	94	$ .01	$ .25	Reardon, Jeff	89SC	305	$ .01	$ .04
Pico, Jeff	89SC	13	$ .01	$ .10	Reardon, Jeff	90SC	522	$ .01	$ .04
Pico, Jeff	90SC	428	$ .01	$ .04	Redus, Gary	88SC	443	$ .01	$ .04
Plesac, Dan	88SC	77	$ .01	$ .04	Redus, Gary	89SC	177	$ .01	$ .04
Plesac, Dan	89SC	320	$ .01	$ .04	Redus, Gary	90SC	14	$ .01	$ .04
Plesac, Dan	90SC	86	$ .01	$ .04	Reed, Jeff	88SC	408	$ .01	$ .04
Plunk, Eric	88SC	614	$ .01	$ .04	Reed, Jeff	89SC	99	$ .01	$ .04
Plunk, Eric	89SC	392	$ .01	$ .04	Reed, Jeff	90SC	147	$ .01	$ .04
Polidor, Gus	88SC	341	$ .01	$ .04	Reed, Jerry	88SC	488	$ .01	$ .04
Polonia, Luis	88SC	64	$ .04	$ .25	Reed, Jerry	89SC	427	$ .01	$ .04
Polonia, Luis	89SC	380	$ .01	$ .10	Reed, Jerry	90SC	492	$ .01	$ .04
Polonia, Luis	89SCTR	38	$ .01	$ .05	Reed, Jody	88SC	625	$ .01	$ .25
Polonia, Luis	90SC	442	$ .01	$ .04	Reed, Jody	89SC	486	$ .01	$ .15
Porter, Darrell	88SC	537	$ .01	$ .04	Reed, Jody	90SC	11	$ .01	$ .04
Portugal, Mark	89SC	482	$ .01	$ .04	Reed, Rick	90SC	544	$ .01	$ .04
Portugal, Mark	90SC	552	$ .01	$ .04	Renteria, Rich	89SC	142	$ .01	$ .04
Powell, Dennis	90SC	308	$ .01	$ .04	Reuschel, Rick	88SC	519	$ .01	$ .04
Power, Ted	88SC	242	$ .01	$ .04	Reuschel, Rick	89SC	5	$ .01	$ .04
Power, Ted	89SC	348	$ .01	$ .04	Reuschel, Rick	90SC	465	$ .01	$ .04
Presley, Jim	88SC	46	$ .01	$ .10	Reuss, Jerry	88SC	270	$ .01	$ .04
Presley, Jim	89SC	73	$ .01	$ .04	Reuss, Jerry	88SCTR	61	$ .01	$ .05
Presley, Jim	90SC	34	$ .01	$ .04	Reuss, Jerry	89SC	489	$ .01	$ .04
Price, Joe	89SC	444	$ .01	$ .04	Reynolds, Craig	88SC	207	$ .01	$ .04
Prince, Tom	89SC	626	$ .01	$ .10	Reynolds, Craig	89SC	468	$ .01	$ .04
Puckett, Kirby	88SC	24	$ .04	$ .40	Reynolds, Harold	88SC	277	$ .01	$ .04
Puckett, Kirby	88SC	653	$ .01	$ .15	Reynolds, Harold	89SC	310	$ .01	$ .04
Puckett, Kirby	89SC	20	$ .01	$ .30	Reynolds, Harold	90SC	167	$ .01	$ .04
Puckett, Kirby	90SC	400	$ .01	$ .15	Reynolds, R. J.	88SC	34	$ .01	$ .04
Puckett, Kirby	90SCDT	690	$ .01	$ .15	Reynolds, R. J.	89SC	91	$ .01	$ .04
Puhl, Terry	88SC	282	$ .01	$ .04	Reynolds, R. J.	90SC	469	$ .01	$ .04
Puhl, Terry	89SC	567	$ .01	$ .04	Rhoden, Rick	88SC	74	$ .01	$ .04
Puhl, Terry	90SC	473	$ .01	$ .04	Rhoden, Rick	89SC	317	$ .01	$ .04
Puleo, Charlie	88SC	454	$ .01	$ .04	Rice, Jim	88SC	14	$ .01	$ .10
Puleo, Charlie	89SC	448	$ .01	$ .04	Rice, Jim	89SC	85	$ .01	$ .10
Quinones, Luis	90SC	499	$ .01	$ .04	Righetti, Dave	88SC	351	$ .01	$ .04
Quinones, Rey	88SC	192	$ .01	$ .04	Righetti, Dave	89SC	225	$ .01	$ .04
Quinones, Rey	89SC	361	$ .01	$ .04	Righetti, Dave	90SC	194	$ .01	$ .04
Quintana, Carlos	89SC	623	$ .01	$ .25	Rijo, Jose	88SC	392	$ .01	$ .15
Quintana, Carlos	90SC	658	$ .01	$ .10	Rijo, Jose	88SCTR	27	$ .01	$ .15
Quirk, Jamie	88SC	577	$ .01	$ .04	Rijo, Jose	89SC	552	$ .01	$ .15
Quirk, Jamie	89SC	461	$ .01	$ .04	Rijo, Jose	90SC	511	$ .01	$ .04
Quisenberry, Dan	88SC	290	$ .01	$ .04	Riles, Ernest	88SC	349	$ .01	$ .04
Quisenberry, Dan	88SCTR	18	$ .01	$ .05	Riles, Ernest	88SCTR	57	$ .01	$ .05
Quisenberry, Dan	89SC	520	$ .01	$ .04	Riles, Ernest	89SC	458	$ .01	$ .04
Quisenberry, Dan	90SC	475	$ .01	$ .04	Riles, Ernest	90SC	447	$ .01	$ .04
Raines, Tim	88SC	3	$ .04	$ .25	Ripken, Bill	88SC	200	$ .05	$ .25
Raines, Tim	88SC	649	$ .05	$ .25	Ripken, Bill	89SC	18	$ .01	$ .04
Raines, Tim	89SC	40	$ .01	$ .15	Ripken, Bill	90SC	174	$ .01	$ .04
Raines, Tim	90SC	409	$ .01	$ .04	Ripken, Jr., Cal	88SC	550	$ .04	$ .20
Ramirez, Rafael	88SC	426	$ .01	$ .04	Ripken, Jr., Cal	88SC	651	$ .01	$ .10

SCORE

Player	Year	No.	VG	EX/MT	Player	Year	No.	VG	EX/MT
Ripken, Jr., Cal	89SC	15	$ .01	$ .10	Santiago, Benny	89SC	4	$ .01	$ .15
Ripken, Jr., Cal	90SC	2	$ .01	$ .15	Santiago, Benny	90SC	454	$ .01	$ .04
Ritchie, Wally	88SC	526	$ .01	$ .04	Santovenia, Nelson	88SCTR	96	$ .01	$ .35
Ritz, Kevin	90SC	572	$ .01	$ .04	Santovenia, Nelson	89SC	346	$ .01	$ .15
Rivera, Luis	89SC	169	$ .01	$ .04	Santovenia, Nelson	90SC	451	$ .01	$ .04
Roberts, Bip	90SC	51	$ .01	$ .04	Sasser, Mackey	88SC	642	$ .01	$ .04
Robidoux, Billy Jo	88SC	334	$ .01	$ .04	Sasser, Mackey	88SCTR	30	$ .01	$ .05
Robinson, Don	88SC	618	$ .01	$ .04	Sasser, Mackey	89SC	303	$ .01	$ .04
Robinson, Don	89SC	440	$ .01	$ .04	Sasser, Mackey	90SC	510	$ .01	$ .04
Robinson, Don	90SC	112	$ .01	$ .04	Sax, Steve	88SC	35	$ .01	$ .10
Robinson, Jeff (Detroit)	88SC	549	$ .05	$ .30	Sax, Steve	89SC	69	$ .01	$ .10
Robinson, Jeff(Detroit)	89SC	284	$ .01	$ .04	Sax, Steve	89SCTR	20	$ .01	$ .10
Robinson, Jeff(Detroit)	90SC	333	$ .01	$ .04	Sax, Steve	90SC	125	$ .01	$ .10
Robinson, Jeff (Pirates)	88SC	439	$ .01	$ .04	Schatzeder, Dan	90SC	418	$ .01	$ .04
Robinson, Jeff(Pirates)	89SC	309	$ .01	$ .04	Schilling, Curt	90SC	581	$ .01	$ .04
Robinson, Ron	88SC	476	$ .01	$ .04	Schiraldi, Calvin	88SC	218	$ .01	$ .04
Robinson, Ron	89SC	559	$ .01	$ .04	Schiraldi, Calvin	88SCTR	39	$ .01	$ .05
Robinson, Ron	90SC	495	$ .01	$ .04	Schiraldi, Calvin	89SC	321	$ .01	$ .04
Roenicke, Gary	88SC	482	$ .01	$ .04	Schmidt, Dave	88SC	103	$ .01	$ .04
Roenicke, Ron	88SC	566	$ .01	$ .04	Schmidt, Dave	89SC	292	$ .01	$ .04
Roesler, Mike	90SC	648	$ .01	$ .04	Schmidt, Dave	90SC	30	$ .01	$ .04
Rogers, Kenny	89SCTR	107	$ .01	$ .25	Schmidt, Mike	88SC	16	$ .04	$ .30
Rogers, Kenny	90SC	301	$ .01	$ .15	Schmidt, Mike	88SC	657	$ .04	$ .15
Romero, Ed	88SC	259	$ .01	$ .04	Schmidt, Mike	89SC	149	$ .01	$ .25
Romine, Kevin	88SC	644	$ .01	$ .04	Schofield, Dick	88SC	274	$ .01	$ .04
Romine, Kevin	89SC	541	$ .01	$ .04	Schofield, Dick	89SC	16	$ .01	$ .04
Romine, Kevin	90SC	458	$ .01	$ .04	Schofield, Dick	90SC	44	$ .01	$ .04
Roomes, Rolando	89SCTR	109	$ .01	$ .30	Schooler, Mike	88SCTR	91	$ .01	$ .35
Roomes, Rolando	90SC	417	$ .01	$ .10	Schooler, Mike	89SC	528	$ .01	$ .25
Rose, Bobby	90SC	604	$ .01	$ .25	Schooler, Mike	90SC	149	$ .01	$ .04
Rosenberg, Steve	90SC	523	$ .01	$ .04	Schroeder, Bill	88SC	311	$ .01	$ .04
Ruffin, Bruce	88SC	492	$ .01	$ .04	Schroeder, Bill	90SC	362	$ .01	$ .04
Ruffin, Bruce	89SC	328	$ .01	$ .04	Schrom, Ken	88SC	574	$ .01	$ .04
Russell, Jeff	88SC	514	$ .01	$ .04	Schu, Rick	88SC	448	$ .01	$ .04
Russell, Jeff	89SC	438	$ .01	$ .04	Schu, Rick	89SC	452	$ .01	$ .04
Russell, Jeff	90SC	263	$ .01	$ .04	Scioscia, Mike	88SC	53	$ .01	$ .04
Ryan, Nolan	88SC	575	$ .01	$ .75	Scioscia, Mike	89SC	121	$ .01	$ .04
Ryan, Nolan	89SC	300	$ .01	$ .50	Scioscia, Mike	90SC	398	$ .01	$ .04
Ryan, Nolan	89SCTR	2	$ .01	$1.20	Scott, Mike	88SC	335	$ .01	$ .04
Ryan, Nolan	90SC	250	$ .01	$ .35	Scott, Mike	89SC	550	$ .01	$ .04
Ryan, Nolan	90SC	696	$ .01	$ .35	Scott, Mike	90SC	40	$ .01	$ .04
Saberhagen, Bret	88SC	89	$ .05	$ .15	Scott, Mike	90SCDT	692	$ .01	$ .10
Saberhagen, Bret	89SC	251	$ .01	$ .10	Scudder, Scott	89SCTR	99	$ .01	$ .35
Saberhagen, Bret	90SC	195	$ .01	$ .10	Scudder, Scott	90SC	518	$ .01	$ .15
Sabo, Chris	88SCTR	100	$ .25	$5.00	Scurry, Rod	89SC	516	$ .01	$ .04
Sabo, Chris	89SC	104	$ .15	$1.00	Searcy, Steve	89SC	627	$ .01	$ .20
Sabo, Chris	90SC	70	$ .01	$ .35	Sebra, Bob	88SC	337	$ .01	$ .04
Salas, Mark	88SC	232	$ .01	$ .04	Seitzer, Kevin	88SC	6	$ .25	$ .50
Salas, Mark	88SCTR	52	$ .01	$ .05	Seitzer, Kevin	89SC	55	$ .01	$ .15
Salas, Mark	89SC	542	$ .01	$ .04	Seitzer, Kevin	90SC	199	$ .01	$ .04
Salazar, Angel	88SC	330	$ .01	$ .04	Sellers, Jeff	88SC	541	$ .01	$ .04
Salazar, Angel	89SC	527	$ .01	$ .04	Sellers, Jeff	89SC	491	$ .01	$ .04
Salazar, Luis	88SC	284	$ .01	$ .04	Sharperson, Mike	89SC	602	$ .01	$ .04
Salazar, Luis	88SCTR	13	$ .01	$ .05	Sheets, Larry	88SC	219	$ .01	$ .04
Salazar, Luis	89SC	316	$ .01	$ .04	Sheets, Larry	89SC	81	$ .01	$ .04
Salazar, Luis	90SC	92	$ .01	$ .04	Sheets, Larry	90SC	111	$ .01	$ .04
Salkeld, Roger	90SC	674	$ .01	$ .25	Sheffield, Gary	89SC	625	$ .25	$1.50
Sambito, Joe	88SC	314	$ .01	$ .04	Sheffield, Gary	90SC	97	$ .01	$ .30
Samuel, Juan	88SC	32	$ .01	$ .04	Shelby, John	88SC	286	$ .01	$ .10
Samuel, Juan	89SC	255	$ .01	$ .04	Shelby, John	89SC	103	$ .01	$ .04
Samuel, Juan	89SCTR	21	$ .01	$ .05	Sheridan, Pat	88SC	171	$ .01	$ .04
Samuel, Juan	90SC	198	$ .01	$ .04	Sheridan, Pat	89SC	204	$ .01	$ .04
Sandberg, Ryne	88SC	26	$ .01	$ .15	Sheridan, Pat	89SCTR	71	$ .01	$ .05
Sandberg, Ryne	89SC	35	$ .01	$ .15	Sheridan, Pat	90SC	509	$ .01	$ .04
Sandberg, Ryne	90SC	561	$ .01	$ .10	Shields, Steve	88SC	396	$ .01	$ .04
Sandberg, Ryne	90SC	90	$ .01	$ .10	Shields, Steve	88SCTR	47	$ .01	$ .05
Sandberg, Ryne	90SCDT	691	$ .01	$ .10	Shields, Steve	89SC	578	$ .01	$ .04
Sanders, Deion	90SC	586	$ .01	$ .50	Show, Eric	88SC	338	$ .01	$ .04
Sanderson, Scott	88SC	544	$ .01	$ .04	Show, Eric	89SC	254	$ .01	$ .04
Sanderson, Scott	90SC	488	$ .01	$ .04	Show, Eric	90SC	493	$ .01	$ .04
Santana, Rafael	88SC	316	$ .01	$ .04	Sierra, Ruben	88SC	113	$ .05	$ .50
Santana, Rafael	88SCTR	54	$ .01	$ .05	Sierra, Ruben	89SC	43	$ .01	$ .20
Santana, Rafael	89SC	296	$ .01	$ .04	Sierra, Ruben	90SC	420	$ .01	$ .20
Santiago, Benny	88SC	25	$ .08	$ .50	Simmons, Ted	88SC	285	$ .01	$ .04
Santiago, Benny	88SC	654	$ .04	$ .25	Simmons, Ted	89SC	611	$ .01	$ .04

Player	Year	No.	VG	EX/MT
Sisk, Doug	88SC	227	$ .01	$ .04
Sisk, Doug	89SC	264	$ .01	$ .04
Skalski, Joe	90SC	618	$ .01	$ .04
Skinner, Joel	88SC	532	$ .01	$ .04
Skinner, Joel	89SC	447	$ .01	$ .04
Skinner, Joel	89SCTR	76	$ .01	$ .05
Slaught, Don	88SC	268	$ .01	$ .04
Slaught, Don	88SCTR	19	$ .01	$ .05
Slaught, Don	89SC	561	$ .01	$ .04
Slaught, Don	90SC	79	$ .01	$ .04
Smalley, Roy	88SC	606	$ .01	$ .04
Smiley, John	88SC	287	$ .05	$ .30
Smiley, John	89SC	409	$ .01	$ .10
Smiley, John	90SC	334	$ .01	$ .10
Smith, Bryn	88SC	356	$ .01	$ .04
Smith, Bryn	89SC	428	$ .01	$ .04
Smith, Bryn	90SC	419	$ .01	$ .04
Smith, Dave	88SC	365	$ .01	$2.00
Smith, Dave	89SC	245	$ .01	$ .04
Smith, Dave	90SC	45	$ .01	$ .04
Smith, Dwight	89SC	642	$ .01	$ .04
Smith, Dwight	90SC	240	$ .01	$ .35
Smith, Greg	90SC	614	$ .01	$ .04
Smith, Lee	88SC	31	$ .01	$ .04
Smith, Lee	88SCTR	20	$ .01	$ .10
Smith, Lee	89SC	150	$ .01	$ .04
Smith, Lee	90SC	37	$ .01	$ .04
Smith, Lonnie	88SC	263	$ .01	$ .04
Smith, Lonnie	90SC	399	$ .01	$ .04
Smith, Mike	90SC	635	$ .01	$ .04
Smith, Ozzie	88SC	12	$ .01	$ .10
Smith, Ozzie	89SC	80	$ .01	$ .10
Smith, Ozzie	90SC	285	$ .01	$ .04
Smith, Pete	88SCTR	84	$ .01	$ .05
Smith, Pete	89SC	207	$ .01	$ .04
Smith, Pete	90SC	225	$ .01	$ .04
Smith, Roy	90SC	568	$ .01	$ .04
Smith, Zane	88SC	410	$ .01	$ .04
Smith, Zane	89SC	492	$ .01	$ .04
Smith, Zane	89SCTR	56	$ .01	$ .05
Smith, Zane	90SC	477	$ .01	$ .04
Smithson, Mike	90SC	512	$ .01	$ .04
Smoltz, John	89SC	616	$ .01	$ .40
Smoltz, John	90SC	370	$ .01	$ .15
Snider, Van	89SC	640	$ .01	$ .15
Snyder, Cory	88SC	92	$ .01	$ .20
Snyder, Cory	89SC	52	$ .01	$ .15
Snyder, Cory	90SC	10	$ .01	$ .04
Sorrento, Paul	90SC	647	$ .01	$ .15
Sosa, Sammy	90SC	558	$ .01	$ .35
Soto, Mario	89SC	588	$ .01	$ .04
Speier, Chris	88SC	493	$ .01	$ .04
Speier, Chris	89SC	297	$ .01	$ .04
Spiers, Bill	89SCTR	82	$ .01	$ .25
Spiers, Bill	90SC	449	$ .01	$ .15
Spilman, Harry	88SC	619	$ .01	$ .04
St. Claire, Randy	88SC	397	$ .01	$ .04
Stanicek, Pete	88SC	628	$ .01	$ .04
Stanicek, Pete	89SC	236	$ .01	$ .04
Stanley, Bob	88SC	300	$ .01	$ .04
Stanley, Bob	89SC	383	$ .01	$ .04
Stanley, Mike	88SC	47	$ .01	$ .04
Stanley, Mike	89SC	241	$ .01	$ .04
Stanton, Mike	90SC	609	$ .01	$ .10
Stapleton, Dave	89SC	581	$ .01	$ .10
Steib, Dave	90SC	201	$ .01	$ .04
Steinbach, Terry	88SC	82	$ .01	$ .35
Steinbach, Terry	89SC	365	$ .01	$ .10
Steinbach, Terry	90SC	162	$ .01	$ .04
Steinbach, Terry	90SCDT	693	$ .01	$ .10
Stephenson, Phil	90SC	642	$ .01	$ .04
Stewart, Dave	88SC	458	$ .01	$ .35
Stewart, Dave	89SC	32	$ .01	$ .25
Stewart, Dave	90SC	410	$ .01	$ .10
Stieb, Dave	88SC	76	$ .01	$ .04
Stieb, Dave	89SC	197	$ .01	$ .04
Stillwell, Kurt	88SC	221	$ .01	$ .04
Stillwell, Kurt	88SCTR	4	$ .01	$ .05
Stillwell, Kurt	89SC	162	$ .01	$ .04
Stillwell, Kurt	90SC	96	$ .01	$ .04
Stoddard, Tim	88SC	258	$ .01	$ .04
Stottlemyre, Todd	88SCTR	90	$ .01	$ .35
Stottlemyre, Todd	89SC	453	$ .01	$ .15
Stottlemyre, Todd	90SC	554	$ .01	$ .04
Straker, Les	88SC	108	$ .01	$ .04
Straker, Les	89SC	244	$ .01	$ .04
Strawberry, Darryl	88SC	360	$ .06	$ .35
Strawberry, Darryl	89SC	10	$ .01	$ .25
Strawberry, Darryl	90SC	200	$ .01	$ .15
Stubbs, Franklin	88SC	147	$ .01	$ .04
Stubbs, Franklin	89SC	599	$ .01	$ .04
Stubbs, Franklin	90SC	478	$ .01	$ .04
Sullivan, Marc	88SC	271	$ .01	$ .04
Sundberg, Jim	88SC	244	$ .01	$ .04
Surhoff, B. J.	88SC	22	$ .01	$ .15
Surhoff, B. J.	89SC	154	$ .01	$ .10
Surhoff, B.J.	90SC	74	$ .01	$ .04
Sutcliffe, Rick	88SC	50	$ .01	$ .10
Sutcliffe, Rick	89SC	407	$ .01	$ .04
Sutcliffe, Rick	90SC	450	$ .01	$ .04
Sutter, Bruce	89SC	425	$ .01	$ .04
Sutton, Don	88SC	105	$ .01	$ .10
Sutton, Don	89SC	400	$ .01	$ .10
Sveum, Dale	88SC	120	$ .01	$ .04
Sveum, Dale	89SC	256	$ .01	$ .04
Swift, Bill	89SC	219	$ .01	$ .04
Swindell, Greg	88SC	154	$ .05	$ .40
Swindell, Greg	89SC	282	$ .01	$ .15
Swindell, Greg	90SC	230	$ .01	$ .10
Tabler, Pat	88SC	23	$ .01	$ .04
Tabler, Pat	88SCTR	22	$ .01	$ .05
Tabler, Pat	89SC	391	$ .01	$ .04
Tabler, Pat	90SC	242	$ .01	$ .04
Tanana, Frank	88SC	490	$ .01	$ .04
Tanana, Frank	89SC	112	$ .01	$ .04
Tanana, Frank	90SC	57	$ .01	$ .04

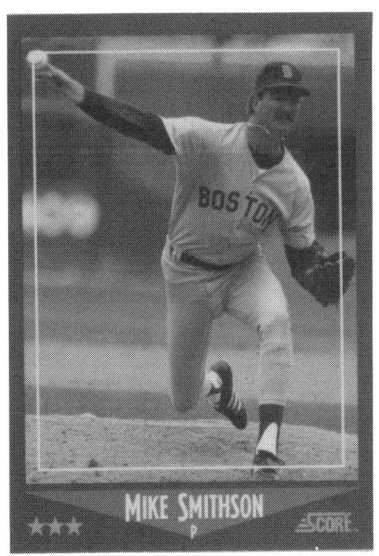

Player	Year	No.	VG	EX/MT
Smithson, Mike	88SCTR	59	$ .01	$ .05
Smithson, Mike	89SC	403	$ .01	$ .04

SCORE

Player	Year	No.	VG	EX/MT
Tartabull, Danny	88SC	106	$.01	$.15
Tartabull, Danny	89SC	105	$.01	$.15
Tartabull, Danny	90SC	244	$.01	$.04
Tekulve, Kent	88SC	425	$.01	$.04
Tekulve, Kent	89SC	287	$.01	$.04
Templeton, Garry	88SC	189	$.01	$.04
Templeton, Garry	89SC	176	$.01	$.04
Templeton, Garry	90SC	336	$.01	$.04
Terrell, Walt	88SC	538	$.01	$.04
Terrell, Walt	89SC	314	$.01	$.04
Terrell, Walt	89SCTR	75	$.01	$.05
Terrell, Walt	90SC	463	$.01	$.04
Terry, Scott	89SC	397	$.01	$.04
Terry, Scott	90SC	235	$.01	$.04
Tettleton, Mickey	88SC	269	$.01	$.04
Tettleton, Mickey	88SCTR	31	$.01	$.05
Tettleton, Mickey	89SC	358	$.01	$.04
Tettleton, Mickey	90SC	322	$.01	$.04
Teufel, Tim	88SC	128	$.01	$.04
Teufel, Tim	89SC	58	$.01	$.04
Teufel, Tim	90SC	501	$.01	$.04
Thigpen, Bobby	88SC	307	$.01	$.04
Thigpen, Bobby	89SC	399	$.01	$.04
Thigpen, Bobby	90SC	335	$.01	$.04
Thigpen, Bobby	90SCDT	694	$.01	$.10
Thomas, Andres	88SC	299	$.01	$.04
Thomas, Andres	89SC	406	$.01	$.04
Thomas, Andres	90SC	99	$.01	$.04
Thomas, Frank	90SC	663	$.01	$.25
Thompson, Milt	88SC	115	$.01	$.10
Thompson, Milt	89SC	92	$.01	$.04
Thompson, Milt	89SCTR	45	$.01	$.05
Thompson, Milt	90SC	49	$.01	$.04
Thompson, Robby	88SC	146	$.01	$.04
Thompson, Robby	89SC	172	$.01	$.04
Thompson, Robby	90SC	397	$.01	$.04
Thon, Dickie	88SCTR	29	$.01	$.05
Thon, Dickie	89SC	234	$.01	$.04
Thon, Dickie	89SCTR	55	$.01	$.05
Thon, Dickie	90SC	142	$.01	$.04
Thornton, Andre	88SC	231	$.01	$.04
Thurman, Gary	88SC	631	$.05	$.25
Thurmond, Mark	88SC	382	$.01	$.04
Thurmond, Mark	90SC	350	$.01	$.04
Tibbs, Jay	88SC	608	$.01	$.04
Tibbs, Jay	89SC	262	$.01	$.04
Tibbs, Jay	90SC	480	$.01	$.04
Toliver, Fred	89SC	479	$.01	$.04
Tolleson, Wayne	88SC	117	$.01	$.04
Tolleson, Wayne	90SC	386	$.01	$.04
Traber, Jim	89SC	590	$.01	$.04
Trammell, Alan	88SC	37	$.04	$.15
Trammell, Alan	88SC	651	$.01	$.10
Trammell, Alan	89SC	110	$.01	$.10
Trammell, Alan	90SC	9	$.01	$.10
Treadway, Jeff	88SC	646	$.05	$.25
Treadway, Jeff	89SC	86	$.01	$.10
Treadway, Jeff	89SCTR	18	$.01	$.05
Treadway, Jeff	90SC	95	$.01	$.04
Trevino, Alex	88SC	182	$.01	$.04
Trevino, Alex	89SC	574	$.01	$.04
Trillo, Manny	88SC	524	$.01	$.04
Trillo, Manny	89SC	446	$.01	$.04
Trout, Steve	88SC	342	$.01	$.04
Trout, Steve	89SC	522	$.01	$.04
Tudor, John	88SC	275	$.01	$.04
Tudor, John	89SC	560	$.01	$.04
Tunnell, Lee	88SC	587	$.01	$.04
Upshaw, Willie	88SC	279	$.01	$.04
Upshaw, Willie	88SCTR	42	$.01	$.05
Upshaw, Willie	89SC	188	$.01	$.04
Uribe, Jose	89SC	56	$.01	$.04
Uribe, Jose	90SC	455	$.01	$.04
Valenzuela, Fernando	88SC	600	$.01	$.10
Valenzuela, Fernando	89SC	437	$.01	$.10

Player	Year	No.	VG	EX/MT
Valenzuela, Fernando	90SC	54	$.01	$.04

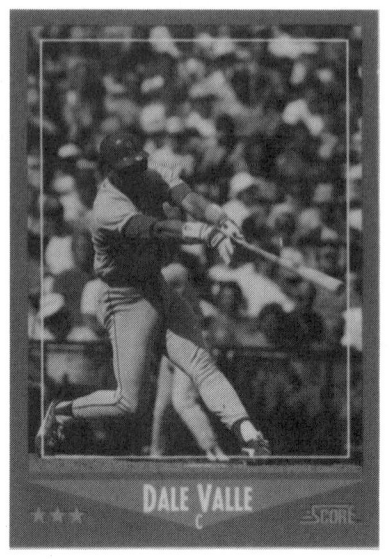

Player	Year	No.	VG	EX/MT
Valle, Dave	88SC	126	$.01	$.04
Valle, Dave	89SC	27	$.01	$.04
Valle, Dave	90SC	109	$.01	$.04
Van Slyke, Andy	88SC	416	$.01	$.04
Van Slyke, Andy	89SC	174	$.01	$.04
Van Slyke, Andy	90SC	440	$.01	$.10
Varsho, Gary	89SC	604	$.01	$.15
Vaughn, Greg	90SC	585	$.01	$1.00
Vaughn, Maurice	90SC	675	$.01	$.25
Velarde, Randy	90SC	524	$.01	$.04
Ventura, Robin	90SC	595	$.01	$.50
Viola, Frank	88SC	475	$.01	$.20
Viola, Frank	89SC	290	$.01	$.15
Viola, Frank	89SCTR	67	$.01	$.15
Viola, Frank	90SC	500	$.01	$.10
Virgil, Ozzie	88SC	129	$.01	$.04
Virgil, Ozzie	89SC	111	$.01	$.04
Vizcaino, Jose	90SC	613	$.01	$.10
Vizquel, Omar	89SCTR	105	$.01	$.20
Vizquel, Omar	90SC	264	$.01	$.04
Walewander, Jim	88SC	571	$.01	$.04
Walewander, Jim	89SC	311	$.01	$.04
Walk, Bob	88SC	162	$.01	$.04
Walk, Bob	89SC	224	$.01	$.04
Walk, Bob	90SC	21	$.01	$.04
Walker, Greg	88SC	93	$.01	$.04
Walker, Greg	89SC	37	$.01	$.04
Walker, Greg	90SC	354	$.01	$.04
Walker, Larry	90SC	631	$.01	$.25
Wallach, Tim	88SC	70	$.01	$.10
Wallach, Tim	89SC	220	$.01	$.04
Wallach, Tim	90SC	192	$.01	$.04
Walling, Dennis	88SC	145	$.01	$.04
Walling, Denny	89SC	49	$.01	$.04
Walton, Jerome	89SCTR	85	$.01	$4.00
Walton, Jerome	90SC	229	$.01	$1.25
Ward, Duane	89SC	359	$.01	$.04
Ward, Duane	90SC	439	$.01	$.04
Ward, Gary	88SC	157	$.01	$.04
Ward, Gary	89SC	435	$.01	$.04
Ward, Gary	90SC	513	$.01	$.04
Washington, Claudell	88SC	579	$.01	$.04

Player	Year	No.	VG	EX/MT	Player	Year	No.	VG	EX/MT
Washington, Claudell	89SC	211	$ .01	$ .04	Wilson, Mookie	88SC	474	$ .01	$ .04
Washington, Claudell	89SCTR	10	$ .01	$ .05	Wilson, Mookie	89SC	302	$ .01	$ .04
Washington, Claudell	90SC	298	$ .01	$ .04	Wilson, Mookie	89SCTR	16	$ .01	$ .05
Wasinger, Mark	88SC	283	$ .01	$ .04	Wilson, Mookie	90SC	448	$ .01	$ .04
Wayne, Gary	89SCTR	91	$ .01	$ .20	Wilson, Steve	90SC	531	$ .01	$ .04
Wayne, Gary	90SC	527	$ .01	$ .04	Wilson, Willie	88SC	102	$ .01	$ .04
Webster, Lenny	90SC	638	$ .01	$ .04	Wilson, Willie	89SC	28	$ .01	$ .04
Webster, Mitch	88SC	345	$ .01	$ .04	Wilson, Willie	90SC	104	$ .01	$ .04
Webster, Mitch	89SC	71	$ .01	$ .04	Wine, Jr., Robbie	88SC	496	$ .01	$ .04
Webster, Mitch	90SC	85	$ .01	$ .04	Winfield, Dave	88SC	55	$ .04	$ .20
Wegman, Bill	88SC	296	$ .01	$ .04	Winfield, Dave	89SC	50	$ .01	$ .15
Wegman, Bill	89SC	335	$ .01	$ .04	Winfield, Dave	90SC	307	$ .01	$ .10
Wegman, Bill	90SC	188	$ .01	$ .04	Winn, Jim	88SC	462	$ .01	$ .04
Weiss, Walt	88SCTR	102	$ .15	$1.50	Winningham, Herm	88SC	142	$ .01	$ .04
Weiss, Walt	89SC	165	$ .10	$ .50	Winningham, Herm	88SCTR	43	$ .01	$ .05
Weiss, Walt	90SC	110	$ .01	$ .10	Winningham, Herm	89SC	496	$ .01	$ .04
Welch, Bob	88SC	510	$ .01	$ .04	Winningham, Herm	90SC	38	$ .01	$ .04
Welch, Bob	88SCTR	15	$ .01	$ .10	Witt, Bob	88SC	149	$ .01	$ .10
Welch, Bob	89SC	308	$ .01	$ .04	Witt, Bobby	89SC	463	$ .01	$ .04
Welch, Bob	90SC	159	$ .01	$ .04	Witt, Bobby	90SC	457	$ .01	$ .04
Wellman, Brad	89SC	504	$ .01	$ .04	Witt, Mike	88SC	81	$ .01	$ .10
Wells, David	90SC	491	$ .01	$ .04	Witt, Mike	89SC	298	$ .01	$ .04
West, Dave	89SC	650	$ .10	$ .35	Witt, Mike	90SC	226	$ .01	$ .04
West, Dave	90SC	573	$ .01	$ .04	Woodson, Tracy	89SC	586	$ .01	$ .04
Weston, Mickey	90SC	616	$ .01	$ .04	Woodward, Rob	88SC	403	$ .01	$ .04
Wetherby, Jeff	90SC	540	$ .01	$ .04	World Series '89, Game 1&2	90SC	700	$ .01	$ .10
Wetteland, John	89SCTR	90	$ .01	$ .35	World Series '89, Game 3	90SC	702	$ .01	$ .10
Wetteland, John	90SC	388	$ .01	$ .15	World Series '89, Game 4	90SC	703	$ .01	$ .10
Whitaker, Lou	88SC	56	$ .01	$ .10	World Series '89, Lights Out	90SC	701	$ .01	$ .25
Whitaker, Lou	89SC	230	$ .01	$ .04	World Series, 1988	89SC	582	$ .01	$ .10
Whitaker, Lou	90SC	75	$ .01	$ .04	Worrell, Todd	88SC	202	$ .01	$ .04
White, Devon	88SC	212	$ .05	$ .25	Worrell, Todd	89SC	265	$ .01	$ .04
White, Devon	89SC	323	$ .01	$ .15	Worrell, Todd	90SC	392	$ .01	$ .04
White, Devon	90SC	312	$ .01	$ .04	Worthington, Craig	89SC	636	$ .01	$ .50
White, Frank	88SC	79	$ .01	$ .04	Worthington, Craig	90SC	234	$ .01	$ .10
White, Frank	89SC	390	$ .01	$ .04	Wrigley Field, 1st Nite Game	89SC	652	$ .01	$ .04
White, Frank	90SC	372	$ .01	$ .04	Wrona, Rick	90SC	557	$ .01	$ .10
Whited, Ed	90SC	644	$ .01	$ .04	Wynegar, Butch	88SC	355	$ .01	$ .04
Whitehurst, Wally	90SC	599	$ .01	$ .15	Wynegar, Butch	89SC	140	$ .01	$ .04
Whitson, Ed	88SC	167	$ .01	$ .04	Wynne, Marvell	88SC	209	$ .01	$ .04
Whitson, Ed	89SC	329	$ .01	$ .04	Wynne, Marvell	89SC	203	$ .01	$ .04
Whitson, Ed	90SC	373	$ .01	$ .04	Wynne, Marvell	90SC	337	$ .01	$ .04
Whitt, Ernie	88SC	168	$ .01	$ .04	Yelding, Eric	90SC	411	$ .01	$ .10
Whitt, Ernie	89SC	98	$ .01	$ .04	Yett, Rich	88SC	484	$ .01	$ .04
Whitt, Ernie	90SC	433	$ .01	$ .04	Yett, Rich	89SC	467	$ .01	$ .04
Wiggins, Alan	88SC	291	$ .01	$ .04	Yett, Rich	90SC	274	$ .01	$ .04
Wilkerson, Curt	88SC	127	$ .01	$ .04	Youmans, Floyd	88SC	327	$ .01	$ .04
Wilkerson, Curtis	89SC	518	$ .01	$ .04	Young, Curt	88SC	125	$ .01	$ .10
Wilkerson, Curtis	90SC	474	$ .01	$ .04	Young, Curt	89SC	29	$ .01	$ .04
Wilkins, Dean	90SC	630	$ .01	$ .04	Young, Curt	90SC	533	$ .01	$ .04
Williams, Bernie	90SC	610	$ .01	$ .35	Young, Gerald	88SC	442	$ .05	$ .25
Williams, Frank	88SC	317	$ .01	$ .04	Young, Gerald	89SC	97	$ .01	$ .04
Williams, Frank	89SC	485	$ .01	$ .04	Young, Gerald	90SC	43	$ .01	$ .04
Williams, Frank	90SC	341	$ .01	$ .04	Young, Matt	88SC	357	$ .01	$ .04
Williams, Ken	88SC	112	$ .04	$ .20	Young, Mike	88SC	393	$ .01	$ .04
Williams, Ken	89SC	67	$ .01	$ .04	Young, Mike	88SCTR	51	$ .01	$ .05
Williams, Matt	88SC	118	$ .01	$ .50	Young, Mike	89SC	494	$ .01	$ .04
Williams, Matt	89SC	612	$ .01	$ .15	Youngblood, Joel	88SC	509	$ .01	$ .04
Williams, Matt	90SC	503	$ .01	$ .10	Youngblood, Joel	89SC	539	$ .01	$ .04
Williams, Mitch	88SC	339	$ .01	$ .04	Youngblood, Joel	89SCTR	66	$ .01	$ .05
Williams, Mitch	89SC	301	$ .01	$ .04	Youngblood, Joel	90SC	344	$ .01	$ .04
Williams, Mitch	89SCTR	32	$ .01	$ .05	Yount, Robin	88SC	160	$ .05	$ .20
Williams, Mitch	90SC	262	$ .01	$ .04	Yount, Robin	89SC	151	$ .01	$ .15
Williams, Mitch	90SCDT	695	$ .01	$ .10	Yount, Robin	90SC	320	$ .01	$ .15
Williamson, Mark	89SC	592	$ .01	$ .10	Zeile, Todd	90SC	600	$ .01	$2.00
Williamson, Mark	90SC	332	$ .01	$ .04	Zinter, Alan	90SC	671	$ .01	$ .04
Wilson, Glenn	88SC	405	$ .01	$ .04	Zosky, Eddie	90SC	665	$ .01	$ .04
Wilson, Glenn	89SC	106	$ .01	$ .04	Zuvella, Paul	89SC	598	$ .01	$ .04
Wilson, Glenn	90SC	346	$ .01	$ .04					

SPORTFLICS

Player	Year	No.	VG	EX/MT	Player	Year	No.	VG	EX/MT
Aase, Don	87SP	165	$ .03	$ .10	Berroa, Geronimo	89SP	225	$ .10	$ .30
Aase, Don	87SP	194	$ .03	$ .10	Berryhill, Damon	89SP	216	$ .03	$ .10
Abbott, Jim	90SP	99	$ .03	$1.00	Berryhill, Damon	90SP	164	$ .03	$ .10
Abner, Shawn	88SP	223	$ .25	$ .45	Biancalana, Buddy	86SP	200	$ .03	$ .10
Aldrete, Mike	88SP	80	$ .03	$ .10	Biggio, Craig	90SP	22	$ .03	$ .30
Alexander, Doyle	86SP	133	$ .03	$ .10	Blauser, Jeff	87SPR	48	$ .03	$ .10
Alexander, Doyle	89SP	211	$ .03	$ .10	Blue, Vida	86SP	132	$ .03	$ .10
Alomar, Jr., Sandy	89SP	223	$ .50	$2.50	Blue, Vida	86SP	142	$ .03	$ .10
Alomar, Roberto	89SP	20	$ .03	$ .25	Blyleven, Bert	86SP	103	$ .03	$ .10
Alomar, Roberto	90SP	93	$ .03	$ .10	Blyleven, Bert	86SP	142	$ .03	$ .10
Anderson, Allan	89SP	220	$ .03	$ .10	Blyleven, Bert	86SP	64	$ .03	$ .10
Anderson, Allan	90SP	59	$ .03	$ .10	Blyleven, Bert	87SP	81	$ .03	$ .10
Andujar, Joaquin	86SP	101	$ .03	$ .10	Blyleven, Bert	88SP	92	$ .03	$ .10
Andujar, Joaquin	86SP	133	$ .03	$ .10	Blyleven, Bert	90SP	193	$ .03	$ .10
Andujar, Joaquin	86SP	185	$ .15	$ .60	Boddicker, Mike	86SP	104	$ .03	$ .10
Anthony, Eric	90SP	179	$ .03	$ .10	Boddicker, Mike	86SP	149	$ .03	$ .10
Armas, Tony	86SP	145	$ .03	$ .10	Boddicker, Mike	87SP	56	$ .03	$ .10
Armas, Tony	86SP	61	$ .10	$ .40	Boddicker, Mike	88SP	146	$ .03	$ .10
Asadoor, Randy	87SP	158	$ .65	$2.50	Boddicker, Mike	89SP	122	$ .03	$ .10
Ashby, Alan	88SP	219	$ .03	$ .10	Boggs, Wade	86SP	180	$ .20	$ .80
Assenmacher, Paul	86SPR	24	$ .03	$ .10	Boggs, Wade	86SP	183	$ .20	$ .80
August, Don	89SP	131	$ .03	$ .10	Boggs, Wade	86SP	184	$ .32	$ .75
Backman, Wally	87SP	124	$ .03	$ .10	Boggs, Wade	86SP	3	$ .50	$2.50
Bailes, Scott	86SPR	9	$ .03	$ .10	Boggs, Wade	86SP	75	$ .35	$1.50
Baines, Harold	86SP	52	$ .10	$ .40	Boggs, Wade	87SP	114	$ .12	$ .50
Baines, Harold	86SP	7	$ .03	$ .10	Boggs, Wade	87SP	197	$ .12	$ .50
Baines, Harold	87SP	153	$ .03	$ .10	Boggs, Wade	87SP	2	$ .35	$1.50
Baines, Harold	87SP	171	$ .03	$ .10	Boggs, Wade	88SP	50	$ .25	$1.00
Baines, Harold	88SP	33	$ .03	$ .10	Boggs, Wade	89SP	100	$ .15	$ .75
Baines, Harold	89SP	157	$ .03	$ .10	Boggs, Wade	89SP	221	$ .15	$1.25
Baines, Harold	90SP	125	$ .03	$ .10	Boggs, Wade	90SP	2	$ .03	$ .50
Balboni, Steve	86SP	186	$ .10	$ .40	Bonds, Barry	86SPR	13	$ .08	$ .75
Ballard, Jeff	90SP	123	$ .03	$ .10	Bonds, Barry	88SP	119	$ .03	$ .20
Bankhead, Scott	86SPR	39	$ .03	$ .10	Bonds, Barry	89SP	146	$ .03	$ .20
Bankhead, Scott	90SP	41	$ .03	$ .10	Bonds, Barry	90SP	143	$ .03	$ .20
Bannister, Floyd	89SP	154	$ .03	$ .10	Bonilla, Bobby	86SPR	26	$ .25	$1.00
Barfield, Jesse	86SP	76	$ .03	$ .10	Bonilla, Bobby	88SP	131	$ .15	$ .60
Barfield, Jesse	87SP	14	$ .03	$ .10					
Barfield, Jesse	87SP	153	$ .03	$ .10					
Barfield, Jesse	88SP	13	$ .03	$ .10					
Barfield, Jesse	89SP	9	$ .03	$ .10					
Barfield, Jesse	90SP	10	$ .03	$ .10					
Barrett, Marty	87SP	112	$ .03	$ .10					
Barrett, Marty	87SP	182	$ .03	$ .10					
Barrett, Marty	88SP	157	$ .03	$ .10					
Barrett, Marty	89SP	198	$ .03	$ .10					
Bass, Kevin	87SP	117	$ .03	$ .25					
Bass, Kevin	87SP	175	$ .03	$ .10					
Bass, Kevin	88SP	55	$ .03	$ .10					
Bass, Kevin	89SP	11	$ .03	$ .10					
Bass, Kevin	90SP	198	$ .03	$ .10					
Baylor, Don	86SP	57	$ .10	$ .40					
Baylor, Don	87SP	163	$ .03	$ .10					
Bedrosian, Steve	87SP	110	$ .03	$ .10					
Bedrosian, Steve	88SP	222	$ .15	$ .60					
Bedrosian, Steve	88SP	70	$ .03	$ .10					
Bedrosian, Steve	89SP	63	$ .03	$ .10					
Bedrosian, Steve	90SP	104	$ .03	$ .10	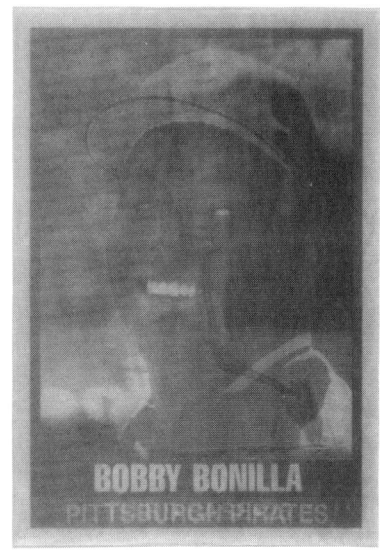				
Belcher, Tim	89SP	121	$ .03	$ .10					
Bell, Buddy	86SP	151	$ .03	$ .10					
Bell, Buddy	87SP	141	$ .03	$ .10					
Bell, Buddy	88SP	147	$ .03	$ .10					
Bell, Eric	87SPR	1	$ .03	$ .10					
Bell, George	86SP	102	$ .03	$ .10					
Bell, George	87SP	51	$ .10	$ .40					
Bell, George	87SP	80	$ .20	$ .80					
Bell, George	88SP	4	$ .05	$ .20					
Bell, George	89SP	25	$ .03	$ .15					
Bell, George	90SP	17	$ .03	$ .10					
Belle, Joey	90SP	159	$ .03	$ .50	Bonilla, Bobby	89SP	182	$ .03	$ .20
Benes, Andy	90SP	90	$ .03	$ .50	Bonilla, Bobby	90SP	195	$ .03	$ .20
Benzinger, Todd	87SPR	47	$ .10	$ .40	Boone, Bob	88SP	212	$ .03	$ .10
Benzinger, Todd	90SP	56	$ .03	$ .10	Boone, Bob	89SP	40	$ .03	$ .10
Bernazard, Tony	87SP	112	$ .03	$ .10	Boone, Bob	90SP	40	$ .03	$ .10
Bernazard, Tony	87SP	60	$ .03	$ .10	Borders, Pat	90SP	45	$ .03	$ .10

Player	Year	No.	VG	EX/MT	Player	Year	No.	VG	EX/MT
Bosio, Chris	87SPR	2	$ .03	$ .10	Candaele, Casey	88SP	140	$ .03	$ .10
Bosio, Chris	90SP	25	$ .03	$ .10	Candelaria, John	86SP	129	$ .03	$ .10
Boyd, Dennis	86SP	152	$ .03	$ .10	Candelaria, John	87SP	148	$ .03	$ .10
Boyd, Dennis	87SP	47	$ .03	$ .10	Candelaria, John	89SP	202	$ .03	$ .10
Bradley, Phil	86SP	77	$ .03	$ .10	Candiotti, Tom	88SP	37	$ .03	$ .10
Bradley, Phil	87SP	89	$ .03	$ .10	Candiotti, Tom	90SP	126	$ .03	$ .10
Bradley, Phil	88SP	93	$ .03	$ .10	Cangelosi, John	86SPR	31	$ .03	$ .10
Bradley, Phil	90SP	95	$ .03	$ .10	Cangelosi, John	87SP	157	$ .03	$ .10
Braggs, Glenn	86SPR	21	$ .03	$ .10	Canseco, Jose	86SP	178	$4.00	$18.00
Braggs, Glenn	89SP	29	$ .03	$ .10	Canseco, Jose	86SPR	11	$1.00	$4.50
Brantley, Mickey	86SPR	45	$ .03	$ .10	Canseco, Jose	87SP	80	$ .20	$ .80
Brantley, Mickey	89SP	6	$ .03	$ .10	Canseco, Jose	87SP	90	$ .60	$2.50
Bream, Sid	88SP	98	$ .03	$ .10	Canseco, Jose	88SP	201	$ .50	$1.50
Brett, George	86SP	1	$ .25	$1.00	Canseco, Jose	89SP	1	$ .25	$1.00
Brett, George	86SP	179	$ .20	$ .80	Canseco, Jose	89SP	221	$ .15	$1.25
Brett, George	86SP	180	$ .20	$ .80	Canseco, Jose	90SP	23	$ .03	$ .75
Brett, George	86SP	186	$ .10	$ .40	Carew, Rod	86SP	106	$ .12	$ .50
Brett, George	86SP	52	$ .10	$ .40	Carew, Rod	86SP	146	$ .03	$ .10
Brett, George	86SP	63	$ .10	$ .40	Carew, Rod	86SP	180	$ .20	$ .80
Brett, George	87SP	114	$ .12	$ .50	Carew, Rod	86SP	182	$ .20	$ .80
Brett, George	87SP	197	$ .12	$ .50	Carew, Rod	86SP	69	$ .15	$ .80
Brett, George	87SP	5	$ .20	$ .75	Carew, Rod	86SP	74	$ .03	$ .10
Brett, George	88SP	150	$ .12	$ .50	Carlton, Steve	86SP	27	$ .08	$ .50
Brett, George	89SP	64	$ .03	$ .25	Carlton, Steve	86SP	70	$ .08	$ .30
Brett, George	90SP	214	$ .03	$ .25	Carlton, Steve	87SP	200	$ .03	$ .10
Briley, Greg	90SP	43	$ .03	$ .25	Carman, Don	87SP	108	$ .03	$ .10
Brock, Greg	88SP	184	$ .03	$ .10	Carter, Gary	86SP	126	$ .03	$ .10
Brooks, Hubie	86SP	187	$ .03	$ .10	Carter, Gary	86SP	137	$ .03	$ .10
Brooks, Hubie	87SP	18	$ .03	$ .10	Carter, Gary	86SP	28	$ .08	$ .30
Brooks, Hubie	87SP	197	$ .12	$ .50	Carter, Gary	87SP	151	$ .03	$ .10
Brooks, Hubie	87SP	79	$ .03	$ .10	Carter, Gary	87SP	50	$ .03	$ .10
Brooks, Hubie	88SP	187	$ .03	$ .10	Carter, Gary	88SP	28	$ .05	$ .20
Brooks, Hubie	89SP	96	$ .03	$ .10	Carter, Gary	89SP	155	$ .03	$ .10
Brower, Bob	87SPR	3	$ .03	$ .10	Carter, Joe	87SP	176	$ .03	$ .40
Brown, Chris	86SP	78	$ .12	$ .50	Carter, Joe	88SP	5	$ .03	$ .30
Brown, Chris	87SP	115	$ .03	$ .30	Carter, Joe	89SP	104	$ .03	$ .30
Brown, Chris	87SP	13	$ .03	$ .10	Carter, Joe	90SP	120	$ .03	$ .10
Brown, Kevin	90SP	73	$ .03	$ .10	Cerutti, John	86SPR	36	$ .03	$ .25
Browne, Jerry	87SPR	4	$ .03	$ .10	Cerutti, John	90SP	86	$ .03	$ .10
Browne, Jerry	90SP	111	$ .03	$ .10	Cey, Ron	86SP	130	$ .18	$ .75
Browning, Tom	86SP	185	$ .15	$ .60	Clancy, Jim	87SP	189	$ .03	$ .10
Browning, Tom	86SP	79	$ .03	$ .30	Clancy, Jim	88SP	215	$ .03	$ .10
Browning, Tom	89SP	180	$ .03	$ .20	Clark, David	87SP	118	$ .45	$1.75
Browning, Tom	89SP	222	$ .05	$ .25	Clark, Jack	86SP	107	$ .03	$ .10
Browning, Tom	90SP	91	$ .03	$ .15	Clark, Jack	88SP	18	$ .03	$ .10
Brunansky, Tom	86SP	80	$ .03	$ .10	Clark, Jack	89SP	26	$ .03	$ .10
Brunansky, Tom	87SP	134	$ .03	$ .10	Clark, Jack	90SP	28	$ .03	$ .10
Brunansky, Tom	88SP	194	$ .03	$ .10	Clark, Jerald	89SP	179	$ .03	$ .20
Brunansky, Tom	89SP	161	$ .03	$ .10	Clark, Will	86SPR	6	$1.00	$4.50
Buckner, Bill	86SP	140	$ .03	$ .10	Clark, Will	87SP	195	$ .10	$ .40
Buckner, Bill	86SP	81	$ .03	$ .10	Clark, Will	87SP	95	$ .90	$2.50
Buckner, Bill	87SP	70	$ .03	$ .10	Clark, Will	88SP	9	$ .30	$1.50
Buhner, Jay	88SP	223	$ .25	$ .45	Clark, Will	89SP	170	$ .15	$1.25
Buhner, Jay	89SP	89	$ .03	$ .20	Clark, Will	90SP	5	$ .03	$1.00
Buice, DeWayne	87SPR	26	$ .03	$ .10	Clemens, Roger	87SP	10	$ .20	$ .80
Burke, Tim	89SP	73	$ .03	$ .10	Clemens, Roger	87SP	111	$ .12	$ .50
Burke, Tim	90SP	199	$ .03	$ .10	Clemens, Roger	87SP	159	$ .35	$1.50
Burks, Ellis	87SPR	5	$ .25	$1.00	Clemens, Roger	87SP	196	$ .08	$ .30
Burks, Ellis	88SP	144	$ .45	$1.50	Clemens, Roger	88SP	207	$ .12	$ .90
Burks, Ellis	89SP	191	$ .15	$ .75	Clemens, Roger	89SP	3	$ .10	$ .75
Burks, Ellis	90SP	80	$ .03	$ .35	Clemens, Roger	90SP	149	$ .03	$ .25
Burns, Britt	86SP	105	$ .03	$ .10	Cliburn, Stewart	86SP	177	$ .12	$ .50
Burns, Todd	89SP	87	$ .03	$ .20	Cochrane, Dave	87SP	158	$ .65	$2.50
Butler, Brett	86SP	26	$ .03	$ .10	Coleman, Vince	86SP	136	$ .25	$ .75
Butler, Brett	87SP	69	$ .03	$ .10	Coleman, Vince	86SP	176	$ .32	$1.00
Butler, Brett	88SP	153	$ .03	$ .10	Coleman, Vince	86SP	24	$ .50	$1.25
Butler, Brett	89SP	31	$ .03	$ .10	Coleman, Vince	87SP	152	$ .03	$ .10
Butler, Brett	90SP	136	$ .03	$ .10	Coleman, Vince	87SP	199	$ .25	$ .90
Calderon, Ivan	88SP	166	$ .03	$ .10	Coleman, Vince	87SP	65	$ .08	$ .30
Calderon, Ivan	90SP	167	$ .03	$ .10	Coleman, Vince	88SP	221	$ .10	$ .40
Caminiti, Ken	87SPR	37	$ .03	$ .10	Coleman, Vince	88SP	67	$ .05	$ .20
Caminiti, Ken	88SP	124	$ .03	$ .10	Coleman, Vince	89SP	113	$ .03	$ .10
Caminiti, Ken	90SP	209	$ .03	$ .10	Coleman, Vince	90SP	142	$ .03	$ .15
Candaele, Casey	87SP	158	$ .65	$2.50	Concepcion, Dave	86SP	131	$ .03	$ .10
Candaele, Casey	87SPR	6	$ .03	$ .10	Concepcion, Dave	86SP	153	$ .03	$ .10

SPORTFLICS

Player	Year	No.	VG	EX/MT	Player	Year	No.	VG	EX/MT
Concepcion, Dave	88SP	218	$ .03	$ .10	Denny, John	86SP	64	$ .03	$ .10
Cone, David	87SPR	39	$ .30	$1.00	Deshaies, Jim	86SPR	15	$ .05	$ .20
Cone, David	89SP	51	$ .03	$ .25	Deshaies, Jim	87SP	156	$ .03	$ .30
Cone, David	90SP	201	$ .03	$ .15	Deshaies, Jim	88SP	190	$ .03	$ .10
Coolbaugh, Scott	90SP	180	$ .03	$ .25	Deshaies, Jim	90SP	32	$ .03	$ .10
Cooper, Cecil	86SP	145	$ .03	$ .10	Devereaux, Mike	90SP	114	$ .03	$ .10
Cooper, Cecil	86SP	180	$ .20	$ .80	Diaz, Bo	88SP	117	$ .03	$ .10
Cooper, Cecil	86SP	29	$ .03	$ .10	Diaz, Mike	86SPR	50	$ .03	$ .10
Cooper, Cecil	87SP	169	$ .03	$ .10	Dodson, Pat	87SP	118	$ .45	$1.75
Correa, Edwin	86SPR	2	$ .03	$ .10	Doran, Bill	87SP	116	$ .03	$ .25
Cowley, Joe	87SP	196	$ .08	$ .30	Doran, Bill	87SP	162	$ .03	$ .10
Cox, Danny	86SP	108	$ .03	$ .10	Doran, Bill	88SP	48	$ .03	$ .10
Cox, Danny	88SP	84	$ .03	$ .10	Doran, Bill	89SP	57	$ .03	$ .10
Crews, Tim	88SP	224	$ .08	$ .30	Dotson, Rich	86SP	194	$ .03	$ .10
Cruz, Jose	86SP	30	$ .03	$ .10	Dotson, Richard	89SP	133	$ .03	$ .10
Cruz, Jose	87SP	152	$ .03	$ .10	Downing, Brian	86SP	154	$ .03	$ .10
Cruz, Jose	87SP	42	$ .03	$ .10	Downing, Brian	87SP	161	$ .03	$ .10
Daniels, Kal	86SPR	43	$ .30	$ .75	Downing, Brian	88SP	181	$ .03	$ .10
Daniels, Kal	88SP	112	$ .08	$ .30	Downing, Brian	89SP	117	$ .03	$ .10
Daniels, Kal	89SP	52	$ .03	$ .25	Downing, Brian	90SP	77	$ .03	$ .10
Darling, Ron	86SP	109	$ .03	$ .10	Downs, Kelly	88SP	203	$ .03	$ .10
Darling, Ron	87SP	53	$ .05	$ .20	Downs, Kelly	89SP	39	$ .03	$ .10
Darling, Ron	88SP	73	$ .03	$ .10	Drabek, Doug	89SP	27	$ .03	$ .10
Darling, Ron	89SP	32	$ .03	$ .10	Drew, Cameron	89SP	225	$ .10	$ .30
Darwin, Danny	90SP	83	$ .03	$ .10	Dunne, Mike	87SPR	40	$ .05	$ .25
Dascenzo, Doug	89SP	42	$ .03	$ .20	Dunne, Mike	88SP	171	$ .05	$ .20
Davis, Alvin	86SP	31	$ .08	$ .30	Dunston, Shawon	86SP	155	$ .03	$ .10
Davis, Alvin	86SP	74	$ .03	$ .10	Dunston, Shawon	87SP	79	$ .03	$ .10
Davis, Alvin	87SP	21	$ .03	$ .10	Dunston, Shawon	87SP	98	$ .03	$ .10
Davis, Alvin	88SP	52	$ .03	$ .10	Dunston, Shawon	88SP	163	$ .03	$ .10
Davis, Alvin	89SP	33	$ .03	$ .10	Dunston, Shawon	89SP	190	$ .03	$ .10
Davis, Alvin	90SP	112	$ .03	$ .10	Durham, Leon	86SP	111	$ .03	$ .10
Davis, Chili	86SP	82	$ .03	$ .10	Durham, Leon	87SP	185	$ .03	$ .10
Davis, Chili	87SP	45	$ .03	$ .10	Dykstra, Len	87SP	58	$ .05	$ .20
Davis, Chili	88SP	172	$ .03	$ .10	Dykstra, Len	88SP	106	$ .03	$ .10
Davis, Chili	89SP	129	$ .03	$ .10	Dykstra, Len	89SP	123	$ .03	$ .10
Davis, Chili	90SP	21	$ .03	$ .10	Dykstra, Len	90SP	156	$ .03	$ .10
Davis, Eric	87SP	155	$ .15	$ .70	Easler, Mike	87SP	92	$ .03	$ .10
Davis, Eric	87SP	199	$ .25	$ .90	Eckersley, Dennis	86SP	129	$ .03	$ .10
Davis, Eric	87SP	22	$ .32	$1.25	Eckersley, Dennis	89SP	101	$ .03	$ .10
Davis, Eric	88SP	10	$ .25	$ .90	Eckersley, Dennis	89SP	222	$ .05	$ .25
Davis, Eric	89SP	69	$ .10	$ .50	Eckersley, Dennis	90SP	170	$ .03	$ .10
Davis, Eric	90SP	97	$ .03	$ .35	Eichhorn, Mark	86SPR	38	$ .05	$ .20
Davis, Glenn	86SP	188	$ .10	$ .40	Eichhorn, Mark	87SP	194	$ .03	$ .10
Davis, Glenn	87SP	17	$ .08	$ .30	Eichhorn, Mark	88SP	210	$ .03	$ .10
Davis, Glenn	87SP	195	$ .10	$ .40	Eisenreich, Jim	90SP	166	$ .03	$ .10
Davis, Glenn	88SP	102	$ .03	$ .10	Elster, Kevin	89SP	71	$ .03	$ .10
Davis, Glenn	89SP	137	$ .03	$ .10	Elster, Kevin	90SP	118	$ .03	$ .10
Davis, Glenn	90SP	19	$ .03	$ .20	Esasky, Nick	90SP	72	$ .03	$ .10
Davis, Jody	87SP	170	$ .03	$ .10	Evans, Darrell	86SP	183	$ .20	$ .80
Davis, Jody	88SP	60	$ .03	$ .10	Evans, Darrell	86SP	189	$ .03	$ .10
Davis, Jody	89SP	187	$ .03	$ .10	Evans, Darrell	87SP	132	$ .03	$ .10
Davis, John	88SP	224	$ .08	$ .30	Evans, Darrell	88SP	188	$ .03	$ .10
Davis, Mark	89SP	74	$ .03	$ .10	Evans, Dwight	86SP	32	$ .03	$ .10
Davis, Mark	90SP	62	$ .03	$ .10	Evans, Dwight	87SP	128	$ .03	$ .10
Davis, Mike	86SP	83	$ .03	$ .10	Evans, Dwight	88SP	137	$ .03	$ .10
Davis, Mike	88SP	206	$ .03	$ .10	Evans, Dwight	89SP	204	$ .03	$ .10
Dawson, Andre	86SP	110	$ .03	$ .10	Evans, Dwight	90SP	217	$ .03	$ .10
Dawson, Andre	86SP	66	$ .03	$ .10	Farrell, John	88SP	132	$ .05	$ .20
Dawson, Andre	87SP	139	$ .03	$ .10	Farrell, John	89SP	37	$ .03	$ .10
Dawson, Andre	88SP	3	$ .08	$ .30	Felix, Junior	90SP	186	$ .03	$ .25
Dawson, Andre	89SP	95	$ .03	$ .20	Fernandez, Sid	87SP	63	$ .08	$ .30
Dawson, Andre	90SP	108	$ .03	$ .10	Fernandez, Sid	88SP	177	$ .03	$ .10
DeCinces, Doug	86SP	173	$ .03	$ .10	Fernandez, Sid	90SP	113	$ .03	$ .10
DeCinces, Doug	87SP	106	$ .03	$ .10	Fernandez, Tony	86SP	112	$ .03	$ .10
DeCinces, Doug	88SP	185	$ .03	$ .10	Fernandez, Tony	87SP	113	$ .03	$ .10
Deer, Rob	87SP	172	$ .03	$ .10	Fernandez, Tony	87SP	187	$ .03	$ .10
Deer, Rob	88SP	183	$ .03	$ .10	Fernandez, Tony	88SP	26	$ .03	$ .10
Deer, Rob	89SP	111	$ .03	$ .10	Fernandez, Tony	89SP	93	$ .03	$ .10
Deer, Rob	90SP	137	$ .03	$ .10	Fernandez, Tony	90SP	6	$ .03	$ .15
DeJesus, Jose	90SP	131	$ .03	$ .10	Fingers, Rollie	86SP	130	$ .18	$ .75
DeLeon, Jose	90SP	76	$ .03	$ .10	Fingers, Rollie	86SP	146	$ .03	$ .10
Dempsey, Rick	86SP	147	$ .03	$ .10	Fingers, Rollie	86SP	65	$ .03	$ .10
Denny, John	86SP	132	$ .03	$ .10	Finley, Chuck	90SP	172	$ .03	$ .10
Denny, John	86SP	134	$ .03	$ .10	Fisher, Brian	86SP	177	$ .12	$ .50

Player	Year	No.	VG	EX/MT
Fisk, Carlton	86SP	125	$ .03	$ .10
Fisk, Carlton	86SP	67	$ .08	$ .30
Fisk, Carlton	87SP	140	$ .03	$ .10
Fisk, Carlton	88SP	43	$ .03	$ .10
Fisk, Carlton	89SP	219	$ .03	$ .10
Fisk, Carlton	90SP	204	$ .03	$ .10
Flanagan, Mike	86SP	59	$ .03	$ .10
Fletcher, Scott	87SP	113	$ .03	$ .10
Fletcher, Scott	87SP	136	$ .03	$ .10

Player	Year	No.	VG	EX/MT
Fletcher, Scott	88SP	77	$ .03	$ .10
Fletcher, Scott	89SP	185	$ .03	$ .10
Fletcher, Scott	90SP	220	$ .03	$ .10
Forsch, Bob	86SP	129	$ .03	$ .10
Forsch, Bob	87SP	191	$ .03	$ .10
Forsch, Bob	88SP	199	$ .03	$ .10
Foster, George	86SP	126	$ .03	$ .10
Foster, George	86SP	131	$ .03	$ .10
Foster, George	86SP	139	$ .10	$ .40
Foster, George	86SP	68	$ .03	$ .30
Franco, John	86SP	156	$ .03	$ .30
Franco, John	87SP	192	$ .05	$ .25
Franco, John	88SP	195	$ .03	$ .15
Franco, John	89SP	176	$ .03	$ .20
Franco, John	90SP	138	$ .03	$ .10
Franco, Julio	86SP	33	$ .05	$ .25
Franco, Julio	87SP	84	$ .03	$ .20
Franco, Julio	88SP	58	$ .03	$ .20
Franco, Julio	89SP	149	$ .03	$ .20
Franco, Julio	90SP	158	$ .03	$ .10
Fraser, Willie	87SPR	27	$ .03	$ .10
Funderburk, Mark	86SP	178	$ 4.00	$18.00
Gaetti, Gary	87SP	114	$ .12	$ .50
Gaetti, Gary	87SP	64	$ .03	$ .10
Gaetti, Gary	88SP	154	$ .03	$ .10
Gaetti, Gary	89SP	48	$ .03	$ .10
Gaetti, Gary	90SP	51	$ .03	$ .10
Gainey, Ty	87SP	118	$ .45	$1.75
Galarraga, Andres	86SPR	27	$ .25	$ .75
Galarraga, Andres	88SP	182	$ .08	$ .30
Galarraga, Andres	89SP	139	$ .03	$ .10
Galarraga, Andres	90SP	148	$ .03	$ .10
Gallagher, Dave	89SP	88	$ .03	$ .20
Gallagher, Dave	90SP	105	$ .03	$ .10

Player	Year	No.	VG	EX/MT
Gant, Ron	89SP	28	$ .03	$ .25
Gantner, Jim	88SP	130	$ .03	$ .10
Garber, Gene	88SP	88	$ .03	$ .10
Garcia, Damaso	86SP	34	$ .03	$ .10
Garcia, Damaso	87SP	183	$ .03	$ .10
Garrelts, Scott	86SP	157	$ .03	$ .10
Garrelts, Scott	87SP	68	$ .03	$ .10
Garrelts, Scott	88SP	44	$ .03	$ .10
Garrelts, Scott	90SP	39	$ .03	$ .10
Garvey, Steve	86SP	137	$ .03	$ .10
Garvey, Steve	86SP	35	$ .08	$ .60
Garvey, Steve	86SP	51	$ .15	$ .60
Garvey, Steve	87SP	40	$ .10	$ .40
Gedman, Rich	86SP	84	$ .03	$ .10
Gedman, Rich	87SP	149	$ .03	$ .10
Gedman, Rich	87SP	154	$ .03	$ .10
Geren, Bob	90SP	205	$ .03	$ .10
Gerhart, Ken	87SPR	7	$ .03	$ .10
Gibson, Kirk	86SP	21	$ .15	$ .50
Gibson, Kirk	87SP	48	$ .10	$ .40
Gibson, Kirk	88SP	111	$ .08	$ .30
Gibson, Kirk	89SP	65	$ .03	$ .25
Gladden, Dan	90SP	190	$ .03	$ .10
Glavine, Tom	90SP	34	$ .03	$ .10
Gooden, Dwight	86SP	100	$ .32	$1.25
Gooden, Dwight	86SP	136	$ .25	$ .75
Gooden, Dwight	86SP	143	$ .20	$1.00
Gooden, Dwight	86SP	176	$ .32	$1.00
Gooden, Dwight	86SP	184	$ .32	$ .75
Gooden, Dwight	86SP	185	$ .15	$ .60
Gooden, Dwight	86SPR	47	$ .12	$ .50
Gooden, Dwight	87SP	100	$ .25	$ .90
Gooden, Dwight	87SP	120	$ .12	$ .50
Gooden, Dwight	87SP	159	$ .35	$1.50
Gooden, Dwight	88SP	200	$ .20	$ .80
Gooden, Dwight	89SP	140	$ .10	$ .40
Gooden, Doc	90SP	145	$ .03	$ .15
Gordon, Tom	90SP	30	$ .03	$ .50
Gossage, Goose	86SP	55	$ .03	$ .10
Gossage, Goose "Rich"	86SP	190	$ .03	$ .10
Gott, Jim	89SP	83	$ .03	$ .10
Gozzo, Goose	90SP	168	$ .03	$ .10
Grace, Mark	89SP	15	$ .25	$1.00
Grace, Mark	90SP	15	$ .03	$ .75
Greene, Tommy	90SP	224	$ .03	$ .15
Greenwell, Mike	86SP	178	$4.00	$18.00
Greenwell, Mike	87SPR	8	$ .50	$2.00
Greenwell, Mike	88SP	118	$ .50	$1.25
Greenwell, Mike	89SP	143	$ .15	$1.00
Greenwell, Mike	89SP	221	$ .15	$1.25
Grich, Bobby	87SP	184	$ .03	$ .10
Greenwell, Mike	90SP	50	$ .00	$ .50
Griffey, Jr., Ken	90SP	7	$ .03	$1.25
Griffey, Ken	88SP	178	$ .03	$ .10
Griffin, Alfredo	86SP	136	$ .25	$ .75
Griffin, Alfredo	87SP	164	$ .03	$ .10
Griffin, Alfredo	88SP	156	$ .03	$ .10
Grissom, Marquis	90SP	134	$ .03	$ .35
Gross, Kevin	89SP	213	$ .03	$ .10
Gruber, Kelly	89SP	163	$ .03	$ .10
Gruber, Kelly	90SP	57	$ .03	$ .10
Gubicza, Mark	89SP	102	$ .03	$ .10
Guerrero, Pedro	86SP	14	$ .05	$ .20
Guerrero, Pedro	86SP	148	$ .03	$ .30
Guerrero, Pedro	86SP	181	$ .20	$ .80
Guerrero, Pedro	87SP	27	$ .03	$ .10
Guerrero, Pedro	88SP	97	$ .03	$ .10
Guerrero, Pedro	90SP	66	$ .03	$ .10
Guetterman, Lee	88SP	45	$ .03	$ .10
Guidry, Ron	86SP	149	$ .03	$ .10
Guidry, Ron	86SP	179	$ .20	$ .80
Guidry, Ron	86SP	18	$ .03	$ .10
Guidry, Ron	86SP	185	$ .15	$ .60
Guidry, Ron	86SP	59	$ .03	$ .10
Guidry, Ron	87SP	83	$ .03	$ .10

SPORTFLICS

Player	Year	No.	VG	EX/MT	Player	Year	No.	VG	EX/MT
Guillen, Ozzie	86SP	176	$ .12	$1.00	Higuera, Teddy	87SP	11	$ .03	$ .25
Guillen, Ozzie	86SP	22	$ .03	$ .10	Higuera, Teddy	87SP	111	$ .12	$ .50
Guillen, Ozzie	87SP	186	$ .03	$ .10	Higuera, Teddy	88SP	20	$ .03	$ .10
Guillen, Ozzie	88SP	14	$ .03	$ .10	Higuera, Teddy	89SP	47	$ .03	$ .10
Guillen, Ozzie	89SP	85	$ .03	$ .10	Higuera, Teddy	90SP	44	$ .03	$ .10
Guillen, Ozzie	90SP	48	$ .03	$ .10	Hillegas, Shawn	87SPR	30	$ .03	$ .10
Gwynn, Tony	86SP	13	$ .10	$ .75	Horn, Sam	87SPR	38	$ .12	$ .20
Gwynn, Tony	86SP	140	$ .03	$ .10	Horn, Sam	88SP	114	$ .10	$ .20
Gwynn, Tony	86SP	181	$ .20	$ .80	Horner, Bob	86SP	115	$ .03	$ .10
Gwynn, Tony	87SP	117	$ .03	$ .25	Horner, Bob	86SP	66	$ .03	$ .10
Gwynn, Tony	87SP	197	$ .12	$ .50	Horner, Bob	87SP	196	$ .08	$ .30
Gwynn, Tony	87SP	31	$ .08	$ .30	Horner, Bob	87SP	73	$ .03	$ .10
Gwynn, Tony	88SP	16	$ .08	$ .30	Hough, Charlie	88SP	87	$ .03	$ .10
Gwynn, Tony	89SP	160	$ .03	$ .20	Hough, Charlie	89SP	92	$ .03	$ .10
Gwynn, Tony	90SP	98	$ .03	$ .25	Howell, Jay	86SP	192	$ .03	$ .10
Hale, Chip	90SP	223	$ .03	$ .10	Howell, Jay	88SP	86	$ .03	$ .10
Hall, Mel	87SP	180	$ .03	$ .10	Howell, Jay	90SP	78	$ .03	$ .10
Hall, Mel	88SP	189	$ .03	$ .10	Hoyt, LaMarr	86SP	193	$ .03	$ .10
Hall, Mel	89SP	144	$ .03	$ .10	Hoyt, LaMarr	86SP	59	$ .03	$ .10
Harkey, Mike	89SP	132	$ .05	$ .30					
Harper, Brian	90SP	121	$ .03	$ .10					
Harris, Greg	87SP	126	$ .03	$ .10					
Harvey, Bryan	89SP	130	$ .03	$ .20					
Harvey, Bryan	90SP	31	$ .03	$ .10					
Hatcher, Billy	88SP	63	$ .03	$ .10					
Hatcher, Billy	89SP	174	$ .03	$ .10					
Hawkins, Andy	86SP	191	$ .03	$ .10					
Hawkins, Andy	89SP	84	$ .03	$ .10					
Hayes, Charlie	90SP	36	$ .03	$ .10					
Hayes, Von	87SP	193	$ .03	$ .10					
Hayes, Von	88SP	62	$ .03	$ .10					
Hayes, Von	89SP	181	$ .03	$ .10					
Hayes, Von	90SP	147	$ .03	$ .10					
Heaton, Neal	88SP	81	$ .03	$ .10					
Henderson, Dave	89SP	127	$ .03	$ .10					
Henderson, Rickey	86SP	184	$ .32	$ .75					
Henderson, Rickey	86SP	6	$ .15	$1.00					
Henderson, Rickey	87SP	157	$ .03	$ .90					
Henderson, Rickey	87SP	159	$ .35	$1.50					
Henderson, Rickey	87SP	198	$ .08	$ .30					
Henderson, Rickey	87SP	4	$ .12	$ .50					
Henderson, Rickey	88SP	11	$ .08	$ .75					
Henderson, Rickey	89SP	145	$ .03	$ .60					
Henderson, Rickey	90SP	208	$ .03	$ .35					
Henke, Tom	88SP	65	$ .03	$ .10					
Henke, Tom	89SP	126	$ .03	$ .10					
Henke, Tom	90SP	42	$ .03	$ .10					
Henneman, Mike	87SPR	29	$ .03	$ .10					
Henneman, Mike	88SP	129	$ .03	$ .10					
Henneman, Mike	89SP	56	$ .03	$ .10					
Henneman, Mike	90SP	144	$ .03	$ .10					
Hernandez, Keith	86SP	127	$ .08	$ .30	Hrbek, Kent	86SP	36	$ .05	$ .20
Hernandez, Keith	86SP	15	$ .08	$ .30	Hrbek, Kent	87SP	15	$ .03	$ .10
Hernandez, Keith	86SP	179	$ .20	$ .80	Hrbek, Kent	88SP	95	$ .03	$ .10
Hernandez, Keith	86SP	181	$ .20	$ .80	Hrbek, Kent	89SP	188	$ .03	$ .10
Hernandez, Keith	86SP	62	$ .12	$ .50	Hrbek, Kent	90SP	203	$ .03	$ .10
Hernandez, Keith	87SP	133	$ .05	$ .20	Hurst, Bruce	87SP	38	$ .03	$ .10
Hernandez, Keith	87SP	195	$ .10	$ .40	Hurst, Bruce	88SP	197	$ .03	$ .10
Hernandez, Keith	88SP	31	$ .05	$ .20	Hurst, Bruce	89SP	175	$ .03	$ .10
Hernandez, Keith	89SP	60	$ .03	$ .20	Hurst, Bruce	90SP	47	$ .03	$ .10
Hernandez, Keith	90SP	106	$ .03	$ .10	Huson, Jeff	90SP	176	$ .03	$ .10
Hernandez, Willie	86SP	65	$ .03	$ .10	Incaviglia, Pete	86SPR	3	$ .20	$ .80
Hernandez, Willie	86SP	85	$ .03	$ .10	Incaviglia, Pete	87SP	37	$ .15	$ .60
Hernandez, Willie	87SP	105	$ .03	$ .10	Incaviglia, Pete	88SP	169	$ .08	$ .30
Herr, Tom	86SP	113	$ .03	$ .10	Incaviglia, Pete	89SP	112	$ .03	$ .10
Herr, Tom	88SP	141	$ .03	$ .10	Iorg, Dane	86SP	186	$ .10	$ .40
Herr, Tom	90SP	63	$ .03	$ .10	Jackson, Bo	86SPR	40	$ .60	$3.50
Hershiser, Orel	86SP	9	$ .15	$ .60	Jackson, Bo	87SP	190	$ .35	$2.00
Hershiser, Orel	87SP	43	$ .10	$ .40	Jackson, Bo	88SP	148	$ .15	$1.50
Hershiser, Orel	88SP	160	$ .10	$ .40	Jackson, Bo	89SP	70	$ .10	$1.25
Hershiser, Orel	89SP	222	$ .05	$ .25	Jackson, Bo	90SP	200	$ .03	$1.25
Hershiser, Orel	89SP	36	$ .03	$ .25	Jackson, Danny	86SP	186	$ .10	$ .40
Hershiser, Orel	90SP	197	$ .03	$ .15	Jackson, Danny	89SP	80	$ .03	$ .10
Hesketh, Joe	86SP	177	$ .12	$ .50	Jackson, Danny	90SP	89	$ .03	$ .10
Higuera, Teddy	86SP	114	$ .15	$ .60	Jackson, Mike	87SPR	33	$ .03	$ .10

Player	Year	No.	VG	EX/MT	Player	Year	No.	VG	EX/MT
Jackson, Reggie	86SP	147	$ .03	$ .10	Larkin, Barry	90SP	160	$ .03	$ .25
Jackson, Reggie	86SP	150	$ .03	$ .10	Larkin, Gene	87SPR	34	$ .03	$ .25
Jackson, Reggie	86SP	37	$ .20	$1.00	Larkin, Gene	88SP	107	$ .03	$ .10
Jackson, Reggie	86SP	57	$ .10	$ .40	Laudner, Tim	89SP	152	$ .03	$ .10
Jackson, Reggie	86SP	61	$ .10	$ .40	LaValliere, Mike	88SP	193	$ .03	$ .10
Jackson, Reggie	86SP	71	$ .03	$ .10	LaValliere, Mike	89SP	98	$ .03	$ .10
Jackson, Reggie	87SP	44	$ .10	$ .40	LaValliere, Mike	90SP	157	$ .03	$ .10
Jackson, Reggie	88SP	120	$ .05	$ .20	Law, Vance	88SP	41	$ .03	$ .10
Jacoby, Brook	87SP	109	$ .03	$ .10	Law, Vance	89SP	162	$ .03	$ .10
Jacoby, Brook	88SP	72	$ .03	$ .10	Leach, Terry	88SP	139	$ .03	$ .10
Jacoby, Brook	89SP	192	$ .03	$ .10	Leary, Tim	89SP	81	$ .03	$ .10
Jacoby, Brook	90SP	155	$ .03	$ .10	Lefferts, Craig	90SP	130	$ .03	$ .10
James, Bob	86SP	158	$ .03	$ .10	Leibrandt, Charlie	86SP	159	$ .03	$ .10
James, Dion	88SP	36	$ .03	$ .10	Leibrandt, Charlie	86SP	186	$ .10	$ .40
Jefferies, Gregg	89SP	223	$ .50	$2.50	Leibrandt, Charlie	88SP	21	$ .03	$ .10
Jefferies, Gregg	89SP	90	$ .50	$1.00	Lemon, Chet	89SP	171	$ .03	$ .10
Jefferies, Gregg	90SP	14	$ .03	$ .50	Leonard, Jeffrey	88SP	82	$ .03	$ .10
Jefferson, Stan	87SPR	9	$ .03	$ .10	Leonard, Jeffrey	90SP	20	$ .03	$ .10
John, Tommy	88SP	122	$ .05	$ .20	Lilliquist, Derek	90SP	24	$ .03	$ .10
Johnson, Howard	88SP	138	$ .05	$ .25	Lind, Jose	90SP	58	$ .03	$ .10
Johnson, Howard	90SP	109	$ .03	$ .25	Lind, Jose	89SP	62	$ .03	$ .10
Johnson, Randy	89SP	224	$ .15	$ .50	Lindeman, Jim	87SPR	43	$ .03	$ .10
Johnson, Randy	90SP	64	$ .03	$ .10	Lombardi, Phil	87SP	118	$ .45	$1.75
Jones, Doug	89SP	38	$ .03	$ .10	Lombardozzi, Steve	86SP	178	$4.00	$18.00
Jones, Doug	90SP	96	$ .03	$ .10	Lombardozzi, Steve	86SPR	17	$ .03	$ .10
Jones, Jimmy	87SPR	35	$ .03	$ .10	Lopes, Davey	86SP	144	$ .03	$ .10
Jones, Ron	89SP	178	$ .03	$ .20	Lopes, Davey	86SP	194	$ .03	$ .10
Jones, Ron	89SP	225	$ .10	$ .30	Lynn, Fred	86SP	137	$ .03	$ .10
Jones, Tracy	88SP	38	$ .03	$ .10	Lynn, Fred	86SP	150	$ .03	$ .10
Jordan, Ricky	89SP	44	$ .25	$1.00	Lynn, Fred	86SP	38	$ .05	$ .20
Jordan, Ricky	90SP	153	$ .03	$ .70	Lynn, Fred	86SP	63	$ .10	$ .40
Joyner, Wally	86SPR	7	$ .45	$2.00	Lynn, Fred	86SP	71	$ .03	$ .10
Joyner, Wally	87SP	26	$ .40	$1.00	Lynn, Fred	86SP	73	$ .12	$ .50
Joyner, Wally	87SP	75	$ .35	$1.00	Lynn, Fred	86SPR	46	$ .12	$ .50
Joyner, Wally	88SP	75	$ .15	$ .45	Lynn, Fred	87SP	198	$ .08	$ .30
Joyner, Wally	89SP	2	$ .03	$ .30	Lynn, Fred	87SP	49	$ .03	$ .10
Joyner, Wally	90SP	49	$ .03	$ .25	Lynn, Fred	88SP	23	$ .03	$ .10
Kelly, Roberto	90SP	184	$ .03	$ .25	Lynn, Fred	89SP	68	$ .03	$ .10
Kennedy, Terry	88SP	94	$ .03	$ .10	Mack, Shane	87SPR	31	$ .03	$ .10
Kerfeld, Charlie	86SPR	23	$ .03	$ .10	Maddux, Greg	89SP	108	$ .03	$ .10
Kerfeld, Charlie	87SP	146	$ .03	$ .10	Maddux, Greg	90SP	211	$ .03	$ .10
Key, Jimmy	88SP	116	$ .03	$ .10	Madlock, Bill	86SP	131	$ .03	$ .10
Key, Jimmy	89SP	167	$ .03	$ .10	Madlock, Bill	86SP	181	$ .20	$ .80
King, Eric	86SPR	42	$ .03	$ .10	Madlock, Bill	86SP	58	$ .20	$ .80
Kingery, Mike	86SPR	37	$ .03	$ .10	Madlock, Bill	86SP	88	$ .03	$ .10
Kingman, Dave	86SP	116	$ .03	$ .10	Madlock, Bill	87SP	130	$ .03	$ .10
Kingman, Dave	86SP	150	$ .03	$ .10	Madlock, Bill	88SP	123	$ .03	$ .10
Kingman, Dave	86SP	68	$ .03	$ .30	Magadan, Dave	87SPR	10	$ .12	$ .50
Kingman, Dave	87SP	178	$ .03	$ .10	Magadan, Dave	88SP	83	$ .05	$ .20
Kittle, Ron	86SP	67	$ .08	$ .30	Magadan, Dave	90SP	173	$ .03	$ .10
Kittle, Ron	86SP	86	$ .03	$ .10	Magrane, Joe	87SPR	11	$ .08	$ .30
Knepper, Bob	87SP	29	$ .03	$ .10	Magrane, Joe	88SP	128	$ .05	$ .20
Knight, Ray	87SP	88	$ .03	$ .10	Magrane, Joe	90SP	151	$ .03	$ .10
Knight, Ray	88SP	115	$ .03	$ .10	Maldonado, Candy	87SP	78	$ .03	$ .10
Koosman, Jerry	86SP	64	$ .03	$ .10	Maldonado, Candy	88SP	126	$ .03	$ .10
Kreuter, Chad	89SP	43	$ .03	$ .20	Marshall, Mike	86SP	89	$ .05	$ .20
Kruk, John	86SPR	1	$ .05	$ .20	Marshall, Mike	87SP	82	$ .03	$ .10
Kruk, John	87SP	61	$ .03	$ .10	Marshall, Mike	88SP	220	$ .03	$ .10
Kruk, John	88SP	64	$ .03	$ .10	Marshall, Mike	89SP	54	$ .03	$ .10
Kruk, John	89SP	184	$ .03	$ .10	Martinez, Carlos	90SP	213	$ .03	$ .10
Kruk, John	90SP	124	$ .03	$ .10	Martinez, Dennis	89SP	106	$ .03	$ .10
Krukow, Mike	87SP	62	$ .03	$ .10	Martinez, Dennis	90SP	53	$ .03	$ .10
Lacy, Lee	86SP	87	$ .03	$ .10	Martinez, Ramon	89SP	224	$ .15	$ .50
Lacy, Lee	87SP	86	$ .03	$ .10	Martinez, Ramon	90SP	68	$ .03	$ .25
Langston, Mark	87SP	102	$ .05	$ .25	Marzano, John	87SPR	49	$ .08	$ .30
Langston, Mark	88SP	46	$ .03	$ .10	Mathews, Greg	86SPR	41	$ .03	$ .10
Langston, Mark	89SP	159	$ .03	$ .10	Matthews, Gary	86SP	66	$ .03	$ .10
Langston, Mark	90SP	110	$ .03	$ .15	Mattingly, Don	86SP	176	$ .32	$1.00
Lansford, Carney	86SP	75	$ .35	$1.50	Mattingly, Don	86SP	179	$ .20	$ .80
Lansford, Carney	87SP	138	$ .03	$ .10	Mattingly, Don	86SP	180	$ .20	$ .80
Lansford, Carney	88SP	202	$ .03	$ .10	Mattingly, Don	86SP	183	$ .20	$ .80
Lansford, Carney	89SP	53	$ .03	$ .10	Mattingly, Don	86SP	184	$ .32	$ .75
Lansford, Carney	90SP	84	$ .03	$ .10	Mattingly, Don	86SP	2	$1.00	$4.00
Larkin, Barry	86SPR	34	$ .15	$1.50	Mattingly, Don	86SP	54	$ .25	$1.00
Larkin, Barry	89SP	136	$ .05	$ .35	Mattingly, Don	86SP	75	$ .35	$1.50

SPORTFLICS

Player	Year	No.	VG	EX/MT	Player	Year	No.	VG	EX/MT
Mattingly, Don	87SP	1	$ .75	$3.00	McReynolds, Kevin	87SP	155	$ .15	$ .70
Mattingly, Don	87SP	159	$ .35	$1.50	McReynolds, Kevin	88SP	56	$ .03	$ .40
Mattingly, Don	87SP	75	$ .35	$1.00	McReynolds, Kevin	89SP	97	$ .03	$ .30
Mattingly, Don	88SP	1	$ .65	$2.50	McReynolds, Kevin	90SP	127	$ .03	$ .10
Mattingly, Don	88SP	222	$ .15	$ .60	Meyer, Joey	89SP	135	$ .03	$ .10
Mattingly, Don	89SP	50	$ .25	$1.00	Milacki, Bob	89SP	224	$ .15	$ .50
Mattingly, Don	90SP	150	$ .03	$ .70	Miller, Keith	87SPR	50	$ .03	$ .10
Mays, Willie	86SPR	46	$ .12	$ .50	Miller, Keith	88SP	225	$ .15	$ .60
McCaskill, Kirk	87SP	127	$ .03	$ .10	Mitchell, Kevin	86SPR	49	$ .85	$2.50
McCaskill, Kirk	88SP	78	$ .03	$ .10	Mitchell, Kevin	87SP	144	$ .25	$1.00
McCaskill, Kirk	89SP	214	$ .03	$ .10	Mitchell, Kevin	89SP	142	$ .03	$ .40
McCaskill, Kirk	90SP	169	$ .03	$ .10	Mitchell, Kevin	90SP	1	$ .03	$ .50
McCullers, Lance	86SPR	8	$ .03	$ .10	Molitor, Paul	86SP	128	$ .03	$ .10
McCullers, Lance	88SP	85	$ .03	$ .10	Molitor, Paul	86SP	39	$ .03	$ .10
McCullers, Lance	89SP	76	$ .03	$ .10	Molitor, Paul	87SP	54	$ .03	$ .10
McDowell, Oddibe	86SP	160	$ .10	$ .40	Molitor, Paul	88SP	221	$ .10	$ .40
McDowell, Oddibe	87SP	131	$ .03	$ .10	Molitor, Paul	88SP	79	$ .03	$ .10
McDowell, Oddibe	88SP	175	$ .03	$ .10	Molitor, Paul	89SP	209	$ .03	$ .10
McDowell, Oddibe	90SP	207	$ .03	$ .10	Molitor, Paul	90SP	183	$ .03	$ .10
McDowell, Roger	86SP	161	$ .10	$ .40	Moore, Mike	86SP	162	$ .03	$ .10
McDowell, Roger	87SP	160	$ .03	$ .10	Moore, Mike	89SP	77	$ .03	$ .10
McDowell, Roger	88SP	42	$ .03	$ .10	Moore, Mike	90SP	185	$ .03	$ .10
McDowell, Roger	89SP	79	$ .03	$ .10	Moreland, Keith	86SP	90	$ .03	$ .10
McDowell, Roger	90SP	75	$ .03	$ .10	Moreland, Keith	87SP	122	$ .03	$ .10
McGee, Willie	86SP	176	$ .32	$1.00	Moreland, Keith	88SP	164	$ .03	$ .10
McGee, Willie	86SP	179	$ .20	$ .80	Moreland, Keith	89SP	141	$ .03	$ .10
McGee, Willie	86SP	183	$ .20	$ .80	Moreland, Keith	90SP	139	$ .03	$ .10
McGee, Willie	86SP	184	$ .32	$ .75	Morman, Russ	86SPR	33	$ .03	$ .10
					Morris, Jack	86SP	117	$ .03	$ .10
					Morris, Jack	86SP	141	$ .03	$ .40
					Morris, Jack	87SP	111	$ .12	$ .50
					Morris, Jack	87SP	87	$ .03	$ .10
					Morris, Jack	88SP	176	$ .05	$ .20
					Morris, Jack	89SP	5	$ .03	$ .15
					Morris, John	87SPR	42	$ .03	$ .10
					Moseby, Lloyd	87SP	96	$ .03	$ .10
					Moseby, Lloyd	88SP	74	$ .03	$ .10
					Motley, Darryl	86SP	186	$ .10	$ .40
					Murphy, Dale	86SP	179	$ .20	$ .80
					Murphy, Dale	86SP	183	$ .20	$ .80
					Murphy, Dale	86SP	5	$ .22	$ .90
					Murphy, Dale	86SP	62	$ .12	$ .50
					Murphy, Dale	87SP	155	$ .15	$ .70
					Murphy, Dale	87SP	159	$ .35	$1.50
					Murphy, Dale	87SP	3	$ .15	$ .60
					Murphy, Dale	88SP	170	$ .08	$ .30
					Murphy, Dale	89SP	110	$ .03	$ .25
					Murphy, Dale	90SP	189	$ .03	$ .15
					Murray, Eddie	86SP	145	$ .03	$ .10
					Murray, Eddie	86SP	4	$ .12	$ .75
					Murray, Eddie	86SP	73	$ .12	$ .50
					Murray, Eddie	86SPR	48	$ .12	$ .50
					Murray, Eddie	87SP	159	$ .35	$1.50
					Murray, Eddie	87SP	6	$ .10	$ .60
					Murray, Eddie	87SP	75	$ .15	$1.00
					Murray, Eddie	88SP	59	$ .05	$ .30
					Murray, Eddie	89SP	147	$ .03	$ .25
					Musselman, Jeff	87SPR	15	$ .03	$ .10
					Nettles, Graig	86SP	91	$ .03	$ .10
					Niekro, Phil	86SP	135	$ .08	$ .30

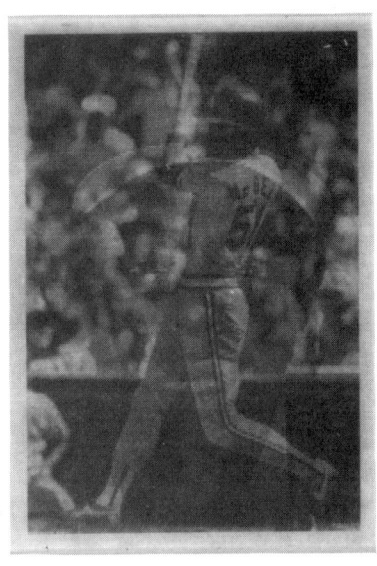

Player	Year	No.	VG	EX/MT	Player	Year	No.	VG	EX/MT
McGee, Willie	86SP	19	$ .03	$ .10	Niekro, Phil	86SP	163	$ .08	$ .30
McGee, Willie	87SP	74	$ .05	$ .20	Niekro, Phil	86SP	182	$ .20	$ .80
McGee, Willie	88SP	91	$ .03	$ .10	Niekro, Phil	86SP	53	$ .03	$ .10
McGee, Willie	89SP	206	$ .03	$ .10	Niekro, Phil	87SP	147	$ .05	$ .20
McGriff, Fred	87SPR	12	$ .25	$1.20	Nieves, Juan	86SPR	5	$ .03	$ .10
McGriff, Fred	88SP	168	$ .15	$ .50	Nieves, Juan	88SP	180	$ .05	$ .20
McGriff, Fred	89SP	14	$ .05	$ .30	Nieves, Juan	88SP	211	$ .03	$ .10
McGriff, Fred	90SP	13	$ .03	$ .25	Nokes, Matt	87SPR	16	$ .05	$ .25
McGwire, Mark	87SPR	13	$ .50	$1.75	Nokes, Matt	88SP	6	$ .05	$ .25
McGwire, Mark	88SP	100	$ .03	$1.00	Nokes, Matt	89SP	203	$ .03	$ .10
McGwire, Mark	88SP	221	$ .10	$ .40	O'Brien, Pete	87SP	52	$ .03	$ .10
McGwire, Mark	89SP	200	$ .15	$ .75	O'Brien, Pete	88SP	145	$ .03	$ .10
McGwire, Mark	90SP	141	$ .03	$ .50	O'Brien, Pete	89SP	8	$ .03	$ .10
McLemore, Mark	87SPR	14	$ .03	$ .10	O'Brien, Pete	90SP	92	$ .03	$ .10
McReynolds, Kevin	87SP	135	$ .05	$ .50	O'Neill, Paul	90SP	4	$ .03	$ .15

Player	Year	No.	VG	EX/MT	Player	Year	No.	VG	EX/MT
O'Neill, Paul	87SPR	17	$ .10	$ .40	Quisenberry, Dan	86SP	55	$ .03	$ .10
Oberkfell, Ken	88SP	165	$ .03	$ .10	Quisenberry, Dan	87SP	167	$ .03	$ .10
Ojeda, Bob	87SP	36	$ .03	$ .10	Quisenberry, Dan	88SP	76	$ .03	$ .10
Olin, Steve	90SP	178	$ .03	$ .10	Raines, Tim	86SP	11	$ .08	$ .50
Oliver, Al	86SP	126	$ .03	$ .10	Raines, Tim	86SP	127	$ .08	$ .30
Oliver, Al	86SP	140	$ .03	$ .10	Raines, Tim	86SP	144	$ .03	$ .10
Oliver, Al	86SP	164	$ .03	$ .10	Raines, Tim	87SP	152	$ .03	$ .10
Oliver, Joe	90SP	71	$ .03	$ .10	Raines, Tim	87SP	197	$ .12	$ .50
Olson, Gregg	90SP	215	$ .03	$ .35	Raines, Tim	87SP	199	$ .25	$ .90
Oquendo, Jose	90SP	85	$ .03	$ .10	Raines, Tim	87SP	34	$ .08	$ .30
Orosco, Jesse	88SP	89	$ .03	$ .10	Raines, Tim	88SP	2	$ .08	$ .30
Orosco, Jessie	87SP	76	$ .03	$ .10	Raines, Tim	89SP	150	$ .03	$ .20
Orsulak, Joe	86SP	177	$ .12	$ .50	Raines, Tim	90SP	69	$ .03	$ .10
Orsulak, Joe	90SP	38	$ .03	$ .10	Randolph, Willie	88SP	47	$ .03	$ .10
Orton, John	90SP	132	$ .03	$ .10	Randolph, Willie	90SP	175	$ .03	$ .10
Pagliarulo, Mike	87SP	55	$ .03	$ .10	Rasmussen, Dennis	87SP	71	$ .03	$ .10
Pagliarulo, Mike	88SP	121	$ .03	$ .10	Rasmussen, Dennis	89SP	212	$ .03	$ .10
Pagliarulo, Mike	89SP	153	$ .03	$ .10	Rawley, Shane	87SP	181	$ .03	$ .10
Palacios, Vicente	88SP	224	$ .08	$ .30	Rawley, Shane	88SP	51	$ .03	$ .10
Palmeiro, Rafael	87SP	158	$ .65	$2.50	Ray, Johnny	87SP	116	$ .03	$ .25
Palmeiro, Rafael	87SPR	32	$ .35	$ .60	Ray, Johnny	87SP	121	$ .03	$ .10
Palmeiro, Rafael	89SP	30	$ .03	$ .20	Ray, Johnny	88SP	186	$ .03	$ .10
Palmeiro, Rafael	90SP	9	$ .03	$ .10	Ray, Johnny	89SP	195	$ .03	$ .10
Palmer, Dean	90SP	225	$ .03	$ .15	Ray, Johnny	90SP	82	$ .03	$ .10
Parker, Dave	86SP	181	$ .20	$ .80	Reardon, Jeff	86SP	119	$ .03	$ .20
Parker, Dave	86SP	183	$ .20	$ .80	Reardon, Jeff	87SP	77	$ .03	$ .10
Parker, Dave	86SP	23	$ .05	$ .20	Reardon, Jeff	88SP	53	$ .03	$ .10
Parker, Dave	86SP	58	$ .20	$ .80	Reardon, Jeff	89SP	168	$ .03	$ .10
Parker, Dave	87SP	117	$ .03	$ .25	Reardon, Jeff	90SP	37	$ .03	$ .10
Parker, Dave	87SP	35	$ .03	$ .10	Reed, Jody	88SP	225	$ .15	$ .60
Parker, Dave	88SP	101	$ .03	$ .10	Reed, Jody	89SP	210	$ .03	$ .10
Parker, Dave	89SP	49	$ .03	$ .10	Reuschel, Rick	88SP	136	$ .03	$ .10
Parrish, Lance	86SP	92	$ .05	$ .20	Reuschel, Rick	89SP	72	$ .03	$ .10
Parrish, Lance	87SP	101	$ .03	$ .10	Reuschel, Rick	90SP	161	$ .03	$ .10
Parrish, Lance	87SP	154	$ .03	$ .10	Reuss, Jerry	86SP	53	$ .03	$ .10
Parrish, Lance	88SP	143	$ .03	$ .10	Reynolds, Harold	88SP	127	$ .03	$ .10
Parrish, Lance	89SP	59	$ .03	$ .10	Reynolds, Harold	89SP	165	$ .03	$ .10
Parrish, Larry	87SP	174	$ .03	$ .10	Reynolds, Harold	90SP	119	$ .03	$ .10
Parrish, Larry	88SP	49	$ .03	$ .10	Rhoden, Rick	87SP	129	$ .03	$ .10
Pasqua, Dan	87SP	143	$ .03	$ .10	Rhoden, Rick	88SP	104	$ .03	$ .10
Pena, Tony	86SP	165	$ .03	$ .10	Rice, Jim	86SP	139	$ .10	$ .40
Pena, Tony	87SP	151	$ .03	$ .10	Rice, Jim	86SP	146	$ .03	$ .10
Pena, Tony	87SP	93	$ .03	$ .10	Rice, Jim	86SP	17	$ .05	$ .40
Pena, Tony	88SP	142	$ .03	$ .10	Rice, Jim	86SP	52	$ .10	$ .40
Pendleton, Terry	88SP	159	$ .05	$ .25	Rice, Jim	86SP	61	$ .10	$ .40
Pendleton, Terry	89SP	99	$ .03	$ .10	Rice, Jim	87SP	80	$ .20	$ .80
Pendleton, Terry	90SP	174	$ .03	$ .10	Rice, Jim	87SP	97	$ .08	$ .30
Perez, Melido	89SP	118	$ .03	$ .10	Rice, Jim	88SP	158	$ .03	$ .10
Perez, Tony	86SP	138	$ .15	$ .60	Rice, Jim	89SP	173	$ .03	$ .10
Perry, Gerald	89SP	164	$ .03	$ .10	Righetti, Dave	86SP	141	$ .03	$ .50
Pettis, Gary	87SP	157	$ .03	$ .10	Righetti, Dave	86SP	41	$ .03	$ .30
Pettis, Gary	90SP	202	$ .03	$ .10	Righetti, Dave	86SP	72	$ .03	$ .10
Plesac, Dan	86SPR	10	$ .03	$ .10	Righetti, Dave	86SPR	48	$ .12	$ .50
Plesac, Dan	88SP	191	$ .03	$ .10	Righetti, Dave	87SP	119	$ .03	$ .10
Plesac, Dan	89SP	128	$ .03	$ .10	Righetti, Dave	87SP	194	$ .03	$ .10
Plesac, Dan	90SP	102	$ .03	$ .10	Righetti, Dave	87SP	57	$ .03	$ .10
Polonia, Luis	87SPR	18	$ .05	$ .20	Righetti, Dave	88SP	135	$ .03	$ .10
Polonia, Luis	88SP	71	$ .05	$ .20	Righetti, Dave	89SP	158	$ .03	$ .10
Polonia, Luis	89SP	133	$ .03	$ .10	Righetti, Dave	90SP	88	$ .03	$ .10
Porter, Darrell	86SP	148	$ .03	$ .25	Riles, Ernest	86SP	16	$ .03	$ .10
Power, Ted	86SP	166	$ .03	$ .10	Ripken, Bill	87SPR	28	$ .10	$ .40
Presley, Jim	86SP	40	$ .03	$ .25	Ripken, Bill	88SP	216	$ .08	$ .30
Presley, Jim	87SP	179	$ .03	$ .20	Ripken, Jr., Cal	86SP	128	$ .03	$ .10
Presley, Jim	88SP	54	$ .03	$ .10	Ripken, Jr., Cal	86SP	54	$ .25	$1.00
Presley, Jim	89SP	7	$ .03	$ .10	Ripken, Jr., Cal	86SP	57	$ .10	$ .40
Puckett, Kirby	86SP	93	$ .25	$1.25	Ripken, Jr., Cal	86SP	69	$ .15	$ .80
Puckett, Kirby	87SP	198	$ .08	$ .30	Ripken, Jr., Cal	86SP	73	$ .12	$ .50
Puckett, Kirby	87SP	7	$ .10	$ .90	Ripken, Jr., Cal	86SP	8	$ .15	$ .75
Puckett, Kirby	88SP	180	$ .05	$ .40	Ripken, Jr., Cal	86SPR	48	$ .12	$ .50
Puckett, Kirby	88SP	8	$ .05	$ .80	Ripken, Jr., Cal	87SP	113	$ .03	$ .10
Puckett, Kirby	89SP	156	$ .05	$ .65	Ripken, Jr., Cal	87SP	9	$ .08	$ .30
Puckett, Kirby	90SP	11	$ .08	$ .40	Ripken, Jr., Cal	88SP	152	$ .08	$ .30
Pyznarski, Tim	87SP	158	$ .65	$2.50	Ripken, Jr., Cal	89SP	66	$ .03	$ .20
Quisenberry, Dan	86SP	118	$ .03	$ .10	Ripken, Jr., Cal	90SP	100	$ .03	$ .25
Quisenberry, Dan	86SP	186	$ .10	$ .40	Ritz, Kevin	90SP	29	$ .03	$ .10

SPORTFLICS

Player	Year	No.	VG	EX/MT	Player	Year	No.	VG	EX/MT
Roberts, Bip	90SP	116	$ .03	$ .10	Schmidt, Mike	88SP	180	$ .05	$ .20
Robidoux, Billy "Joe"	86SP	178	$4.00	$18.00	Schmidt, Mike	88SP	35	$ .10	$1.00
Robidoux, Billy Jo	86SPR	28	$ .03	$ .10	Schmidt, Mike	89SP	21	$ .10	$1.00
Robinson, Don	88SP	90	$ .03	$ .10	Schooler, Mike	90SP	187	$ .03	$ .10
Robinson, Jeff	87SPR	46	$ .03	$ .10					
Robinson, Jeff	89SP	193	$ .03	$ .10					
Rogers, Kenny	90SP	216	$ .03	$ .10					
Rose, Pete	86SP	130	$ .18	$ .75					
Rose, Pete	86SP	138	$ .15	$ .60					
Rose, Pete	86SP	181	$ .20	$ .80					
Rose, Pete	86SP	182	$ .20	$ .80					
Rose, Pete	86SP	50	$ .40	$1.50					
Rose, Pete	86SP	51	$ .15	$ .60					
Rose, Pete	86SP	56	$ .20	$ .80					
Rose, Pete	86SP	58	$ .20	$ .80					
Rose, Pete	86SP	69	$ .15	$ .80					
Rose, Pete	86SPR	46	$ .12	$ .50					
Rose, Pete	87SP	25	$ .25	$1.00					
Ruffin, Bruce	86SPR	29	$ .03	$ .10					
Russell, Jeff	90SP	192	$ .03	$ .10					
Ryan, Nolan	86SP	141	$ .03	$ .50					
Ryan, Nolan	86SP	143	$ .20	$1.00					
Ryan, Nolan	86SP	182	$ .20	$ .80					
Ryan, Nolan	86SP	43	$ .15	$1.50					
Ryan, Nolan	87SP	125	$ .15	$1.25					
Ryan, Nolan	88SP	39	$ .15	$1.25					
Ryan, Nolan	89SP	115	$ .10	$1.00					
Ryan, Nolan	90SP	8	$ .03	$1.00					
Saberhagen, Bret	86SP	10	$ .10	$ .75					
Saberhagen, Bret	86SP	176	$ .32	$1.00					
Saberhagen, Bret	86SP	185	$ .15	$ .60					
Saberhagen, Bret	86SP	186	$ .10	$ .40					
Saberhagen, Bret	87SP	145	$ .08	$ .50					
Saberhagen, Bret	88SP	15	$ .05	$ .30					
Saberhagen, Bret	89SP	109	$ .03	$ .30					
Saberhagen, Bret	90SP	94	$ .03	$ .25					
Sabo, Chris	89SP	13	$ .25	$1.00	Schrom, Ken	87SP	107	$ .03	$ .10
Salas, Mark	86SP	177	$ .12	$ .50	Scioscia, Mike	86SP	167	$ .03	$ .10
Samuel, Juan	86SP	94	$ .05	$ .30	Scioscia, Mike	87SP	151	$ .03	$ .10
Samuel, Juan	87SP	123	$ .03	$ .10	Scioscia, Mike	87SP	67	$ .03	$ .10
Samuel, Juan	88SP	96	$ .03	$ .10	Scioscia, Mike	88SP	110	$ .03	$ .10
Samuel, Juan	89SP	17	$ .03	$ .15	Scioscia, Mike	89SP	138	$ .03	$ .10
Sandberg, Ryne	86SP	127	$ .08	$ .30	Scioscia, Mike	90SP	163	$ .03	$ .10
Sandberg, Ryne	86SP	20	$ .05	$ .75	Scott, Mike	86SP	195	$ .08	$ .30
Sandberg, Ryne	86SP	51	$ .15	$ .60	Scott, Mike	87SP	119	$ .03	$ .10
Sandberg, Ryne	87SP	116	$ .03	$ .25	Scott, Mike	87SP	120	$ .12	$ .50
Sandberg, Ryne	87SP	197	$ .12	$ .50	Scott, Mike	87SP	19	$ .03	$ .10
Sandberg, Ryne	87SP	8	$ .08	$ .50	Scott, Mike	88SP	66	$ .03	$ .10
Sandberg, Ryne	88SP	12	$ .05	$ .20	Scott, Mike	89SP	120	$ .03	$ .10
Sandberg, Ryne	89SP	201	$ .03	$ .10	Scott, Mike	90SP	55	$ .03	$ .10
Sandberg, Ryne	90SP	54	$ .03	$ .25	Seaver, Tom	86SP	134	$ .03	$ .10
Sanders, Deion	90SP	221	$ .03	$ .65	Seaver, Tom	86SP	135	$ .08	$ .30
Santiago, Benito "Benny"	87SP	118	$ .45	$1.75	Seaver, Tom	86SP	142	$ .03	$ .10
Santiago, Benny	87SPR	19	$ .15	$ .75	Seaver, Tom	86SP	182	$ .20	$ .80
Santiago, Benny	88SP	22	$ .15	$ .75	Seaver, Tom	86SP	25	$ .20	$ .75
Santiago, Benny	88SP	222	$ .15	$ .60	Seaver, Tom	86SP	60	$ .08	$ .30
Santiago, Benny	89SP	22	$ .03	$ .25	Seaver, Tom	86SP	67	$ .08	$ .30
Santiago, Benny	90SP	115	$ .03	$ .10	Seaver, Tom	86SP	70	$ .08	$ .30
Santovenia, Nelson	90SP	162	$ .03	$ .10	Seaver, Tom	86SPR	47	$ .12	$ .50
Sax, Steve	86SP	56	$ .20	$ .80	Seaver, Tom	87SP	28	$ .08	$ .30
Sax, Steve	86SP	95	$ .03	$ .10	Seitzer, Kevin	87SP	158	$ .65	$2.50
Sax, Steve	86SPR	48	$ .12	$ .50	Seitzer, Kevin	87SPR	20	$ .03	$1.25
Sax, Steve	87SP	12	$ .03	$ .10	Seitzer, Kevin	88SP	17	$ .30	$ .75
Sax, Steve	89SP	58	$ .03	$ .10	Seitzer, Kevin	89SP	55	$ .03	$ .25
Sax, Steve	90SP	12	$ .03	$ .10	Seitzer, Kevin	90SP	46	$ .03	$ .10
Schilling, Curt	90SP	133	$ .03	$ .10	Sheets, Larry	86SP	177	$ .12	$ .50
Schiraldi, Calvin	86SPR	44	$ .03	$ .10	Sheets, Larry	88SP	161	$ .03	$ .10
Schmidt, Mike	86SP	139	$ .10	$ .40	Sheffield, Gary	89SP	223	$ .50	$2.50
Schmidt, Mike	86SP	148	$ .03	$ .30	Sheffield, Gary	89SP	41	$ .50	$1.00
Schmidt, Mike	86SP	44	$ .25	$1.50	Sheffield, Gary	90SP	52	$ .03	$ .50
Schmidt, Mike	86SP	62	$ .12	$ .50	Sierra, Ruben	86SPR	16	$ .25	$2.50
Schmidt, Mike	86SP	68	$ .03	$ .30	Sierra, Ruben	88SP	113	$ .10	$ .75
Schmidt, Mike	87SP	115	$ .03	$ .30	Sierra, Ruben	89SP	189	$ .03	$ .25
Schmidt, Mike	87SP	156	$ .03	$ .30	Sierra, Ruben	90SP	188	$ .03	$ .50
Schmidt, Mike	87SP	30	$ .08	$1.00	Simmons, Ted	86SP	196	$ .03	$ .10

Player	Year	No.	VG	EX/MT
Slaught, Don	87SP	154	$ .03	$ .10
Slaught, Don	87SP	32	$ .03	$ .10
Slaught, Don	89SP	218	$ .03	$ .10
Smiley, John	87SPR	21	$ .10	$ .40
Smiley, John	90SP	191	$ .03	$ .10
Smith, Bryn	86SP	120	$ .03	$ .10
Smith, Dave	87SP	77	$ .03	$ .10
Smith, Dave	87SP	94	$ .03	$ .10
Smith, Dave	88SP	208	$ .03	$ .10
Smith, Dave	90SP	140	$ .03	$ .10
Smith, Dwight	90SP	152	$ .03	$ .50
Smith, Lee	86SP	45	$ .03	$ .10
Smith, Lee	86SP	55	$ .03	$ .10
Smith, Lee	87SP	104	$ .03	$ .10
Smith, Lee	88SP	179	$ .03	$ .10
Smith, Lee	89SP	148	$ .03	$ .10
Smith, Lonnie	86SP	186	$ .10	$ .40
Smith, Lonnie	90SP	65	$ .03	$ .10
Smith, Ozzie	86SP	121	$ .03	$ .10
Smith, Ozzie	87SP	142	$ .03	$ .10
Smith, Ozzie	87SP	79	$ .03	$ .10
Smith, Ozzie	88SP	68	$ .03	$ .10
Smith, Ozzie	89SP	105	$ .03	$ .10
Smith, Ozzie	90SP	16	$ .03	$ .10
Smith, Zane	88SP	134	$ .03	$ .10
Smoltz, John	90SP	61	$ .03	$ .25
Snider, Van	89SP	177	$ .03	$ .20
Snyder, Cory	86SPR	18	$ .15	$1.00
Snyder, Cory	87SP	24	$ .15	$ .60
Snyder, Cory	88SP	29	$ .05	$ .20
Snyder, Cory	89SP	196	$ .03	$ .10
Snyder, Cory	90SP	3	$ .03	$ .15
Sosa, Sammy	90SP	81	$ .03	$ .35
Soto, Mario	86SP	168	$ .03	$ .10
Spiers, Bill	90SP	206	$ .03	$ .25
Stanley, Bob	86SP	169	$ .03	$ .10
Stanley, Mike	87SPR	44	$ .08	$ .30
Staub, Rusty	86SP	138	$ .15	$ .60
Steinbach, Terry	87SP	118	$ .45	$1.75
Steinbach, Terry	87SPR	22	$ .05	$ .50
Steinbach, Terry	88SP	174	$ .03	$ .25
Steinbach, Terry	89SP	119	$ .03	$ .25
Steinback, Terry	90SP	33	$ .03	$ .10
Stewart, Dave	88SP	162	$ .03	$ .25
Stewart, Dave	89SP	23	$ .03	$ .25
Stewart, Dave	90SP	194	$ .03	$ .15
Stieb, Dave	86SP	96	$ .03	$ .10
Stieb, Dave	89SP	35	$ .03	$ .10
Stieb, Dave	90SP	26	$ .03	$ .10
Straker, Les	87SPR	45	$ .03	$ .10
Strawberry, Darryl	86SP	56	$ .20	$ .80
Strawberry, Darryl	86SP	97	$ .32	$1.25
Strawberry, Darryl	86SPR	48	$ .12	$ .50
Strawberry, Darryl	87SP	20	$ .20	$ .75
Strawberry, Darryl	88SP	155	$ .12	$ .50
Strawberry, Darryl	89SP	205	$ .10	$ .50
Strawberry, Darryl	90SP	146	$ .03	$ .35
Sundberg, Jim	86SP	186	$ .10	$ .40
Surhoff, B.J.	87SPR	23	$ .08	$ .30
Surhoff, B.J.	88SP	57	$ .05	$ .20
Surhoff, B.J.	89SP	208	$ .03	$ .10
Sutcliffe, Rick	86SP	134	$ .03	$ .10
Sutcliffe, Rick	86SP	149	$ .03	$ .10
Sutcliffe, Rick	86SP	46	$ .03	$ .10
Sutcliffe, Rick	86SP	60	$ .08	$ .30
Sutcliffe, Rick	86SP	70	$ .08	$ .30
Sutcliffe, Rick	86SP	72	$ .03	$ .10
Sutcliffe, Rick	88SP	27	$ .03	$ .10
Sutcliffe, Rick	89SP	217	$ .03	$ .10
Sutcliffe, Rick	90SP	181	$ .03	$ .10
Sutter, Bruce	86SP	47	$ .03	$ .10
Sutter, Bruce	86SP	65	$ .03	$ .10
Sutton, Don	86SP	135	$ .08	$ .30
Sutton, Don	86SP	175	$ .03	$ .10
Sutton, Don	87SP	156	$ .03	$ .30

Player	Year	No.	VG	EX/MT
Sutton, Don	87SP	99	$ .03	$ .10
Sutton, Don	88SP	213	$ .05	$ .20
Sveum, Dale	86SPR	4	$ .03	$ .10
Swindell, Greg	86SPR	30	$ .15	$ .60
Swindell, Greg	89SP	4	$ .03	$ .25
Tabler, Pat	87SP	66	$ .03	$ .10
Tabler, Pat	88SP	205	$ .03	$ .10
Tabler, Pat	89SP	172	$ .03	$ .10
Tabler, Pat	90SP	218	$ .03	$ .10
Tallman, Matt	86SP	182	$ .20	$ .80
Tanana, Frank	88SP	133	$ .03	$ .10
Tanana, Frank	89SP	103	$ .03	$ .10
Tartabull, Dan	86SP	178	$4.00	$18.00
Tartabull, Danny	86SPR	22	$ .10	$ .75
Tartabull, Danny	87SP	23	$ .10	$ .40
Tartabull, Danny	88SP	19	$ .05	$ .25
Tartabull, Danny	89SP	46	$ .03	$ .20
Tartabull, Danny	90SP	129	$ .03	$ .10
Templeton, Garry	86SP	170	$ .03	$ .10
Tettleton, Mickey	90SP	171	$ .03	$ .10
Thigpen, Bobby	89SP	207	$ .03	$ .10
Thigpen, Bobby	90SP	27	$ .03	$ .10
Thomas, Andres	86SPR	14	$ .03	$ .10
Thompson, Milt	88SP	173	$ .03	$ .10
Thompson, Milt	89SP	169	$ .03	$ .10
Thompson, Robby	86SPR	25	$ .08	$ .30
Thompson, Robby	87SP	46	$ .03	$ .10
Thompson, Robby	88SP	24	$ .03	$ .10
Thompson, Robby	89SP	78	$ .03	$ .10
Thompson, Robby	90SP	60	$ .03	$ .10
Thornton, Andre	86SP	171	$ .03	$ .10
Thurman, Gary	88SP	223	$ .25	$ .45
Traber, Jim	86SPR	32	$ .03	$ .10
Trammell, Alan	86SP	147	$ .03	$ .10
Trammell, Alan	86SP	172	$ .08	$ .30
Trammell, Alan	87SP	188	$ .03	$ .10
Trammell, Alan	88SP	25	$ .05	$ .20
Trammell, Alan	89SP	215	$ .05	$ .25
Trammell, Alan	90SP	154	$ .03	$ .10
Treadway, Jeff	88SP	225	$ .15	$ .60

Treadway, Jeff	89SP	107	$ .03	$ .25
Treadway, Jeff	90SP	219	$ .03	$ .10
Tudor, John	86SP	122	$ .03	$ .20

SPORTFLICS

Player	Year	No.	VG	EX/MT	Player	Year	No.	VG	EX/MT
Tudor, John	86SP	184	$ .32	$ .75	White, Devon	87SPR	24	$ .12	$ .50
Tudor, John	86SP	185	$ .15	$ .60	White, Devon	88SP	99	$ .05	$ .20
Tudor, John	87SP	173	$ .03	$ .10	White, Devon	89SP	16	$ .03	$ .20
Tudor, John	88SP	198	$ .03	$ .10	White, Devon	90SP	210	$ .03	$ .10
Tudor, John	89SP	86	$ .03	$ .10	White, Frank	86SP	186	$ .10	$ .40
Upshaw, Willie	86SP	98	$ .03	$ .10	White, Frank	87SP	168	$ .03	$ .10
Upshaw, Willie	88SP	214	$ .03	$ .10	White, Frank	88SP	149	$ .03	$ .10
Uribe, Jose	89SP	61	$ .03	$ .10	Whitson, Ed	90SP	212	$ .03	$ .10
Uribe, Jose	90SP	79	$ .03	$ .10	Williams, Ken	87SPR	41	$ .03	$ .10
Valenzuela, Fernando	86SP	12	$ .08	$ .30	Williams, Ken	88SP	69	$ .05	$ .20
Valenzuela, Fernando	86SP	132	$ .03	$ .10	Williams, Matt	87SPR	25	$ .05	$ .75
Valenzuela, Fernando	86SP	143	$ .20	$ .80	Williams, Matt	90SP	70	$ .03	$ .35
Valenzuela, Fernando	86SP	60	$ .08	$ .30	Williams, Mitch	86SPR	20	$ .03	$ .25
Valenzuela, Fernando	86SP	72	$ .03	$ .10	Williams, Mitch	89SP	151	$ .03	$ .10
Valenzuela, Fernando	86SPR	47	$ .12	$ .50	Williams, Mitch	90SP	196	$ .03	$ .10
Valenzuela, Fernando	87SP	119	$ .03	$ .10	Williams, Reggie	86SPR	19	$ .03	$ .10
Valenzuela, Fernando	87SP	120	$ .12	$ .50	Wilson, Glenn	87SP	166	$ .03	$ .10
Valenzuela, Fernando	87SP	150	$ .08	$ .30	Wilson, Glenn	88SP	204	$ .03	$ .10
Valenzuela, Fernando	88SP	40	$ .05	$ .20	Wilson, Glenn	89SP	12	$ .03	$ .10
Valenzuela, Fernando	89SP	124	$ .03	$ .10	Wilson, Mookie	90SP	128	$ .03	$ .10
Van Slyke, Andy	88SP	109	$ .03	$ .15	Wilson, Willie	86SP	124	$ .03	$ .10
Van Slyke, Andy	89SP	166	$ .03	$ .10	Wilson, Willie	86SP	128	$ .03	$ .10
Van Slyke, Andy	90SP	101	$ .03	$ .10	Wilson, Willie	86SP	144	$ .03	$ .10
Vaughn, Greg	90SP	135	$ .03	$1.00	Wilson, Willie	86SP	180	$ .20	$ .80
Ventura, Robin	90SP	222	$ .03	$ .50	Wilson, Willie	86SP	186	$ .10	$ .40
Viola, Frank	86SP	99	$ .03	$ .30	Wilson, Willie	87SP	85	$ .03	$ .10
Viola, Frank	88SP	196	$ .03	$ .30	Wilson, Willie	88SP	192	$ .03	$ .10
Viola, Frank	89SP	10	$ .03	$ .20	Wilson, Willie	89SP	186	$ .03	$ .10
Viola, Frank	90SP	122	$ .03	$ .20	Winfield, Dave	86SP	49	$ .15	$ .60
Virgil, Ozzie	88SP	217	$ .03	$ .10	Winfield, Dave	87SP	153	$ .03	$ .10
Virgil, Ozzie	89SP	94	$ .03	$ .10	Winfield, Dave	87SP	41	$ .10	$ .40
Walk, Bob	89SP	34	$ .03	$ .10	Winfield, Dave	88SP	7	$ .05	$ .20
Walker, Greg	86SP	174	$ .03	$ .10	Winfield, Dave	89SP	24	$ .03	$ .15
Walker, Greg	88SP	103	$ .03	$ .10	Winfield, Dave	90SP	87	$ .03	$ .15
Walker, Greg	89SP	19	$ .03	$ .10	Witt, Bobby	86SPR	12	$ .05	$ .20
Wallach, Tim	86SP	123	$ .03	$ .10	Witt, Bobby	87SP	39	$ .03	$ .10
Wallach, Tim	87SP	115	$ .03	$ .30	Witt, Bobby	89SP	82	$ .03	$ .10
Wallach, Tim	87SP	72	$ .03	$ .10	Witt, Mike	86SP	53	$ .03	$ .10
Wallach, Tim	88SP	151	$ .03	$ .10	Witt, Mike	87SP	59	$ .03	$ .10
Wallach, Tim	89SP	114	$ .03	$ .10	Witt, Mike	88SP	32	$ .03	$ .10
Wallach, Tim	90SP	182	$ .03	$ .10	Witt, Mike	89SP	197	$ .03	$ .10
Walton, Jerome	90SP	67	$ .03	$1.00	Worrell, Todd	86SPR	35	$ .10	$ .50
Ward, Duane	90SP	107	$ .03	$ .10	Worrell, Todd	87SP	33	$ .08	$ .30
Ward, Gary	86SP	197	$ .03	$ .10	Worrell, Todd	87SP	77	$ .03	$ .10
Ward, Gary	87SP	91	$ .03	$ .10	Worrell, Todd	88SP	61	$ .03	$ .10
Ward, Gary	88SP	125	$ .03	$ .10	Worrell, Todd	89SP	183	$ .03	$ .10
Washington, Claudell	89SP	75	$ .03	$ .10	Worrell, Todd	90SP	165	$ .03	$ .10
Webster, Mitch	87SP	177	$ .03	$ .10	Worthington, Craig	89SP	134	$ .05	$ .25
Webster, Mitch	88SP	105	$ .03	$ .10	Worthington, Craig	90SP	117	$ .03	$ .10
Webster, Mitch	89SP	67	$ .03	$ .10	Youmans, Floyd	87SP	103	$ .03	$ .10
Weiss, Walt	89SP	116	$ .05	$ .30	Youmans, Floyd	88SP	108	$ .03	$ .10
Weiss, Walt	90SP	74	$ .03	$ .25	Young, Curt	88SP	209	$ .03	$ .10
Welch, Bob	86SP	198	$ .03	$ .10	Young, Gerald	87SPR	36	$ .08	$ .30
Welch, Bob	88SP	167	$ .03	$ .10	Young, Gerald	89SP	125	$ .03	$ .10
Welch, Bob	89SP	91	$ .03	$ .10	Young, Mike	86SP	199	$ .03	$ .10
Welch, Bob	90SP	35	$ .03	$ .10	Yount, Robin	86SP	42	$ .10	$ .75
West, Dave	89SP	45	$ .10	$ .50	Yount, Robin	86SP	54	$ .25	$1.00
Whitaker, Lou	86SP	48	$ .05	$ .25	Yount, Robin	86SP	63	$ .10	$ .40
Whitaker, Lou	86SP	74	$ .03	$ .10	Yount, Robin	86SP	71	$ .03	$ .10
Whitaker, Lou	86SPR	48	$ .12	$ .50	Yount, Robin	87SP	16	$ .08	$ .75
Whitaker, Lou	87SP	112	$ .03	$ .10	Yount, Robin	88SP	34	$ .05	$ .75
Whitaker, Lou	87SP	137	$ .03	$ .10	Yount, Robin	89SP	199	$ .03	$ .50
Whitaker, Lou	88SP	30	$ .03	$ .10	Yount, Robin	90SP	18	$ .03	$ .35
Whitaker, Lou	89SP	18	$ .03	$ .15	Zeile, Todd	90SP	177	$ .03	$1.00
Whitaker, Lou	90SP	103	$ .03	$ .10					

TOPPS CHEWING GUM COMPANY, INC. 1951-1990

The billions of cards printed success story of the Topps Chewing Gum Company began in 1951 with two game baseball cards which had to be punched out of a perforated piece of cardboard. Those first cards had either blue or red backs and were for use in playing a baseball game. You also received a piece of candy for your penny investment.

Improving on those small cards, Topps produced a baseball card set in 1952 containing 407 cards, Topps was able to control the market after bankruptcy forced its competitor to cease making sets in 1955. Until 1981, there were few challenges to Topps and they prospered.

Refer to the color section beginning on page 4 to see a representative sample of each year of the Topps cards in color. A brief description of each set follows. **All cards from 1957 to 1988 are 2 ½" x 3 ½"** except for Topps Big Baseball cards which are 2⅝" x 3¾".

1951bb - 52 cards 2" x 2 ⅝" white border with blue and white back (no copyright or date)
1951rb - 52 cards 2" x 2 ⅝" white border with red and white back (no copyright or date)
1952 - 407 cards 2 ⅝" x 3 ¾" white border (Topps baseball in either red or black printing on back bottom and copyright T.C.G. on lower left)
1953 - 280 card numbers with 6 numbers not used (253,261,267,268,272,275) 2 ⅝" x 3¾" white border except for black or red name strip on bottom (copyright T.C.G. on back in lower left corner with Topps written in card numbered baseball)
1954 - 250 cards 2⅝" x 3 ¾" white border with black and white photo insert on front (copyright T.G.C. up right side from bottom with Topps written in card numbered baseball)
1955 - 210 card numbers with 4 numbers not used (175,186,203,209) 2 ⅝" x 3 ¾" white border horizontal card with color insert photo on front (copyright T.G.C. below birth date with Topps written in card numbered baseball)
1956 - 340 cards 2 ⅝" x 3 ¾" white border horizontal card with color insert photo on front (copyright T.G.C. up right border on back with Topps written in card numbered baseball)
1957 - 407 cards w/white borders(copyright T.G.C. up right border on back with Topps written in card numbered baseball)
1958 - 495 card numbers (#145 not used) w/white borders (copyright T.G.C. up right border on back and card number in hatted baseball)
1959 - 572 cards w/white borders and green and red or black and red printing on back (copyright T.G.C. up right side on back)
1960 - 572 cards w/white borders horizontal with black and white photo insert on front (copyright T.G.C. up right side on back)
1961 - 589 cards with 3 numbers not used (426,587,588) white border(copyright T.G.C. lower right corner on back with Topps written in card numbered baseball)
1962 - 598 cards w/brown wood grain effect borders (copyright T.G.C. above statistical record on back with Topps written in card numbered baseball)
1963 - 576 cards w/brightly colored name panel at bottom and black and white circular portrait also (copyright T.G.C. on lower back corner with Topps written above card number)
1964 - 587 cards w/white border but bold team name at top of card (copyright T.G.C. above rub-off quiz on back with Topps written in card numbered baseball)
1965 - 598 cards w/white border but pennant waving team name in lower left corner (copyright T.G.C. on back lower right corner with Topps written in card numbered baseball)

1966 - 598 cards w/white border and team name in upper left corner in diagonal strip (copyright T.G.C. on back lower right corner with Topps written in card numbered baseball)

1967 - 609 cards w/white borders and bold team name at bottom (copyright T.G.C. on back lower right corner and Topps written in card numbered baseball)

1968 - 598 cards with brown basket weave borders and team name in brightly colored circle (copyright T.G.C. on back lower right corner with Topps written in card numbered baseball)

1969 - 664 cards w/white border (copyright T.G.C. up right side on back with "T" in Topps encircling the card number)

1970 - 720 cards w/grey border (copyright T.G.C. up right side on back with Topps written in circle above card number)

1971 - 752 cards w/black border and player black and white photo on reverse (copyright T.G.C. up left side on back is only indication of Topps card)

1972 - 787 cards w/white border and arched effect with team name in that arch above the player (copyright T.G.C. on lower right corner on back)

1973 - 660 cards w/ white border and back in black bordered design (copyright T.G.C. at bottom on back)

1974 - 660 cards w/white border and pennant-like player name at bottom and team name at top (copyright T.G.C. at bottom on back.)

1975 - 660 cards w/bright colored borders of two colors depending upon team for the colors (copyright 1975 Topps Chewing Gum, Inc. on bottom back)

1976 - 660 cards w/white border plus 44 traded cards issued later with same number and "T" added to number (copyright 1976 Topps Chewing Gum, Inc. up right border on back)

1977 - 660 cards w/white borders (copyright 1977 Topps Chewing Gum, Inc. on bottom back)

1978 - 726 cards w/white borders (copyright 1978 Topps Chewing Gum, Inc. on lower right side of back)

1979 - 726 cards w/white border and Topps logo in baseball on front (copyright 1979 Topps Chewing Gum, Inc. on lower right corner of back)

1980 - 726 cards w/white border (copyright 1980 Topps Chewing Gum, Inc. lower left side on back)

1981 - 726 cards w/white border and Topps logo in baseball on front (copyright 1981 Topps Chewing Gum, Inc. on lower right side of back)

1982 - 792 cards w/white borders and Topps logo above team name on the front lower right side (copyright 1982 Topps Chewing Gum, Inc. on back lower right side)

1983 - 792 cards w/white borders and Topps logo in upper right corner on front (copyright 1983 Topps Chewing Gum, Inc. on bottom of back)

1984 - 792 cards w/white borders, team name vertically down left and Topps logo in upper right corner on front (copyright 1984 Topps Chewing Gum, Inc. up right side on back)

1985 - 792 cards w/white border and Topps logo in upper left corner on front (copyright 1985 Topps Chewing Gum, Inc. above "Baseball Trivia Quiz" on back)

1986 - 792 cards w/black border across the top and down the sides becoming white and Topps logo on upper right of front (Copyright 1986 Topps Chewing Gum, Inc. on bottom of back)

1987 - 792 cards w/brown wood grain effect similar to 1962 and Topps logo on lower left corner of front (copyright 1987 Topps Chewing Gum, Inc. on back above personal statistical information)

1988 - 792 cards w/white border and Topps logo in lower left corner on front (copyright 1988 Topps Chewing Gum, Inc. up the right side on back)

1989 - 792 cards w/ white border and Topps logo on the front in various locations (copyright 1989 on back in dark pink area inside black border at lower right.)

1990 - 792 cards w/multi-colored borders and Topps logo on front in various locations (copyright 1990 on mustard yellow back right side)

There are abbreviations used throughout the Topps section that need some explanation. All of the following will be found under the year section referring to the type of card that is listed:

T - Topps used for designation of all cards in section.

TAS - Topps All Star card of any given year.

TATL - Topps All Time Leader up to that time of issue.

TBB - Topps Big Baseball set first issued in 1988.

Tbb - Refers to 1951 Topps blue back cards only.

THL - Topps Highlights (usually refers to the previous year accomplishments).

TIA - Topps In Action (another way of including a star more than once).

TMVP - Topps Most Valuable Player.

TRB - Topps Record Breaker usually refers to previous year or lifetime accomplishments.

Trb - Refers to 1951 Topps red backs only.

TRH - Topps Record Holder.

TTB - Topps Turn Back The Clock refers to happenings of previous years usually in increments of five years.

TTR - Topps Traded cards usually numbered 1T-132T, with "T" omitted on the number listing and placed on the year. The Traded cards of 1981 continued the numbers of that year's set and are numbered 727-858.

TMLD - Topps Major League Debut card set of 152 cards of players first game appearance (first issued in 1989).

The listing for each card shown appears immediately following the photograph.

TOPPS

Player	Year	No.	VG	EX/MT
A's, Team	56T	236	$5.00	$15.00
A's, Team	57T	204	$2.10	$7.50
A's, Team	58T	174	$2.25	$5.50
A's, Team	59T	172	$1.65	$7.00
A's, Team	60T	413	$1.65	$7.00
A's, Team	61T	297	$ .60	$1.75
A's, Team	62T	384	$1.50	$3.75
A's, Team	63T	397	$ .75	$3.00
A's, Team	64T	151	$1.00	$3.75
A's, Team	65T	151	$ .50	$1.95
A's, Team	66T	492	$ .70	$4.00
A's, Team	67T	262	$ .70	$2.00
A's, Team	68T	554	$ .70	$2.00
A's, Team	70T	631	$ .80	$3.75
A's, Team	71T	624	$ .60	$1.75
A's, Team	72T	454	$ .60	$1.75
A's, Team	73T	500	$ .50	$1.95
A's, Team	74T	246	$ .35	$1.10
A's, Team Checklist	75T	561	$ .30	$1.00
A's, Team Checklist	76T	421	$ .30	$1.00
A's, Team Checklist	77T	74	$ .15	$ .50
A's, Team Checklist	78T	577	$ .05	$ .25
A's, Team Checklist	79T	328	$ .05	$ .25
A's, Team Checklist	80T	96	$ .05	$ .25
A's, Team Checklist	81T	671	$ .02	$ .20
A's, Team Leaders	86T	216	$ .01	$ .03
A's, Team Leaders	87T	456	$ .01	$ .03
A's, Team Leaders	88T	759	$ .01	$ .03
A's, Team Leaders	89T	639	$ .01	$ .04
Aaron, Hank	54T	128	$375.00	$1500.00
Aaron, Hank	55T	47	$60.00	$250.00
Aaron, Hank	56T	31	$50.00	$200.00
Aaron, Hank	57T	20	$75.00	$225.00
Aaron, Hank	58T	30	$40.00	$150.00
Aaron, Hank	58T	351	$7.00	$20.00
Aaron, Hank	58T	418	$35.00	$130.00
Aaron, Hank	58TAS	488	$7.00	$28.00
Aaron, Hank	59T	212	$7.00	$28.00
Aaron, Hank	59T	380	$25.00	$100.00
Aaron, Hank	59T	467	$5.00	$15.00
Aaron, Hank	59TAS	561	$22.50	$85.00
Aaron, Hank	60T	300	$25.00	$75.00
Aaron, Hank	60TAS	566	$20.00	$80.00
Aaron, Hank	61T	43	$1.50	$5.75
Aaron, Hank	61T	415	$25.00	$75.00
Aaron, Hank	61TAS	577	$40.00	$120.00
Aaron, Hank	61TMVP	484	$10.00	$30.00
Aaron, Hank	62T	320	$30.00	$90.00
Aaron, Hank	62TAS	394	$9.00	$30.00
Aaron, Hank	63T	1	$4.35	$22.00
Aaron, Hank	63T	3	$2.35	$9.00
Aaron, Hank	63T	242	$7.00	$20.00
Aaron, Hank	63T	390	$30.00	$90.00
Aaron, Hank	64T	7	$1.70	$5.00
Aaron, Hank	64T	9	$2.50	$7.50
Aaron, Hank	64T	11	$1.00	$4.00
Aaron, Hank	64T	300	$20.00	$65.00
Aaron, Hank	64T	423	$15.00	$45.00
Aaron, Hank	65T	2	$1.35	$4.00
Aaron, Hank	65T	170	$27.50	$87.50
Aaron, Hank	66T	215	$2.75	$9.50
Aaron, Hank	66T	500	$18.00	$65.00
Aaron, Hank	67T	242	$1.50	$3.75
Aaron, Hank	67T	244	$1.35	$4.00
Aaron, Hank	67T	250	$18.00	$70.00
Aaron, Hank	68T	3	$1.35	$4.00
Aaron, Hank	68T	5	$1.35	$4.00
Aaron, Hank	68T	110	$12.00	$45.00
Aaron, Hank	68TAS	370	$3.00	$9.00
Aaron, Hank	69T	100	$8.50	$42.50
Aaron, Hank	70T	65	$ .60	$1.75
Aaron, Hank	70T	500	$7.50	$30.00
Aaron, Hank	70TAS	462	$2.00	$8.00
Aaron, Hank	71T	400	$7.00	$22.00
Aaron, Hank	72T	87	$ .60	$2.00

Player	Year	No.	VG	EX/MT
Aaron, Hank	72T	89	$ .60	$2.00
Aaron, Hank	72T	299	$5.00	$20.00
Aaron, Hank	72TIA	300	$3.00	$9.00
Aaron, Hank	73T	1	$3.50	$12.50
Aaron, Hank	73T	100	$5.50	$17.00

THE ALL-TIME

HANK AARON

★★★★ 6,172

Player	Year	No.	VG	EX/MT
Aaron, Hank	73TATL	473	$ .60	$1.75
Aaron, Hank	74T	1	$3.50	$18.00
Aaron, Hank(1954-1957)	74T	2	$ .75	$3.00
Aaron, Hank(1958-1961)	74T	3	$ .75	$3.00
Aaron, Hank(1962-1965)	74T	4	$ .75	$3.00
Aaron, Hank(1966-1969)	74T	5	$ .75	$3.00
Aaron, Hank(1970-1973)	74T	6	$ .75	$3.00
Aaron, Hank	74TAS	332	$ .60	$1.75
Aaron, Hank	75T	195	$1.75	$5.00
Aaron, Hank	75T	660	$4.50	$17.50
Aaron, Hank	75THL	1	$3.50	$13.50
Aaron, Hank	76T	550	$3.50	$13.00
Aaron, Hank	76TRB	1	$2.50	$12.00
Aaron, Hank	79T	412	$ .15	$ .50
Aaron, Hank	79TRH	413	$ .20	$ .75
Aaron, Hank	89TTB	663	$ .01	$ .10
Aaron, Tommie	63T	46	$ .35	$1.10
Aaron, Tommie	64T	454	$ .50	$1.95
Aaron, Tommie	65T	567	$1.50	$3.75
Aaron, Tommie	68T	394	$ .15	$ .50
Aaron, Tommie	69T	128	$ .25	$ .85
Aaron, Tommie	70T	278	$ .25	$ .85
Aaron, Tommie	71T	717	$ .60	$1.75
Aase, Don	76T	597	$ .25	$ .65
Aase, Don	77T	472	$ .05	$ .15
Aase, Don	78T	12	$ .02	$ .10
Aase, Don	79T	368	$ .02	$ .10
Aase, Don	80T	239	$ .01	$ .07
Aase, Don	81T	601	$ .01	$ .07
Aase, Don	82T	199	$ .01	$ .06
Aase, Don	83T	599	$ .01	$ .06
Aase, Don	85T	86	$ .01	$ .04
Aase, Don	85TTR	1	$ .02	$ .10
Aase, Don	86T	288	$ .01	$ .03
Aase, Don	87T	766	$ .01	$ .03
Aase, Don	88T	467	$ .01	$ .03
Aase, Don	89TTR	1	$ .01	$ .05
Aase, Don	90T	301	$ .01	$ .03

Player	Year	No.	VG	EX/MT	Player	Year	No.	VG	EX/MT
Abarbanel, Mickey	68T	287	$ .25	$ .65	Adams, Bobby	58T	99	$1.00	$3.75
Abbott, Glenn	74T	602	$ .06	$ .25	Adams, Bobby	59T	249	$ .50	$1.95
Abbott, Glenn	75T	591	$ .06	$ .25	Adams, Glenn	76T	389	$ .05	$ .20
Abbott, Glenn	76T	322	$ .05	$ .20	Adams, Glenn	78T	497	$ .02	$ .10
Abbott, Glenn	77T	207	$ .05	$ .15	Adams, Glenn	79T	193	$ .02	$ .10
Abbott, Glenn	78T	31	$ .02	$ .10	Adams, Glenn	80T	604	$ .01	$ .07
Abbott, Glenn	79T	497	$ .02	$ .10	Adams, Glenn	81T	18	$ .01	$ .07
Abbott, Glenn	80T	166	$ .01	$ .07	Adams, Glenn	82T	519	$ .01	$ .06
Abbott, Glenn	81T	699	$ .01	$ .07	Adams, Glenn	83T	574	$ .01	$ .06
Abbott, Glenn	82T	336	$ .01	$ .06	Adams, Mike	74T	573	$ .06	$ .25
Abbott, Glenn	82T	571	$ .01	$ .06	Adams, Red	73T	569	$1.00	$3.75
Abbott, Glenn	84T	356	$ .01	$ .05	Adams, Red	74T	144	$ .50	$2.00
Abbott, Jim	88TTR	1	$1.00	$10.00	Adams, Ricky	84T	487	$ .01	$ .05
Abbott, Jim	89T	573	$ .25	$2.00	Adams, Ricky	86T	153	$ .01	$ .03
Abbott, Jim	89TBB	322	$ .01	$ .75	Adamson, Mike	69T	66	$ .25	$ .65
Abbott, Jim	89TMLD	1	$ .01	$ .50	Adamson, Mike	71T	362	$ .08	$ .20
Abbott, Jim	89TTR	2	$ .01	$1.50	Adcock, Joe	52T	347	$55.00	$160.00
Abbott, Jim	90T	675	$ .01	$ .50	Adcock, Joe	56T	320	$2.00	$6.00
Abbott, Kyle	90T	444	$ .01	$ .25	Adcock, Joe	57T	117	$1.35	$5.00
Aber, Al	53T	233	$11.00	$37.50	Adcock, Joe	58T	325	$ .45	$1.50
Aber, Al	54T	238	$2.10	$7.50	Adcock, Joe	58T	351	$7.00	$20.00
Aber, Al	56T	317	$1.80	$6.00	Adcock, Joe	59T	315	$ .60	$1.75
Aber, Al	57T	141	$ .95	$3.50	Adcock, Joe	60T	3	$ .50	$1.95
Abernathy, Ted	57T	293	$3.50	$13.00	Adcock, Joe	61T	245	$ .50	$2.00
Abernathy, Ted	59T	169	$ .50	$1.95	Adcock, Joe	62T	265	$ .50	$2.00
Abernathy, Ted	60T	334	$ .50	$1.95	Adcock, Joe	63T	170	$ .30	$1.00
Abernathy, Ted	64T	64	$ .25	$ .85	Adcock, Joe	67T	563	$6.00	$18.00
Abernathy, Ted	65T	332	$ .30	$1.00	Addis, Bob	52T	259	$11.50	$38.00
Abernathy, Ted	66T	2	$ .25	$ .85	Addis, Bob	53T	157	$3.75	$13.00
Abernathy, Ted	67T	597	$1.35	$4.00	Adduci, Jim	89T	338	$ .01	$ .04
Abernathy, Ted	68T	264	$ .25	$ .65	Adlesh, Dave	67T	51	$ .25	$ .65
Abernathy, Ted	69T	483	$ .25	$ .65	Adlesh, Dave	68T	576	$ .30	$1.00
Abernathy, Ted	70T	562	$ .25	$ .85	Adlesh, Dave	69T	341	$ .25	$ .65
Abernathy, Ted	71T	187	$ .10	$ .35	Agee, Tommie	65T	166	$ .50	$1.95
Abernathy, Ted	72T	519	$ .10	$ .35	Agee, Tommie	66T	164	$ .25	$ .85
Abernathy, Ted	73T	22	$ .06	$ .25	Agee, Tommie	67T	455	$ .25	$ .85
Abner, Shawn	85T	282	$ .10	$ .50	Agee, Tommie	68T	465	$ .30	$1.00
Abner, Shawn	90T	122	$ .01	$ .03	Agee, Tommie	69T	364	$ .25	$ .65
Abrams, Cal	52T	350	$39.00	$135.00	Agee, Tommie	70T	50	$ .10	$ .35
Abrams, Cal	53T	98	$3.75	$13.00	Agee, Tommie	71T	310	$ .10	$ .35
Acker, Jim	84T	359	$ .01	$ .05	Agee, Tommie	72T	245	$ .10	$ .35
Acker, Jim	85T	101	$ .01	$ .04	Agee, Tommie	73T	420	$ .10	$ .35
Acker, Jim	86T	569	$ .01	$ .03	Agee, Tommie	74T	630	$ .06	$ .25
Acker, Jim	87T	407	$ .01	$ .03	Agee, Tommie	74TTR	630	$ .06	$ .25
Acker, Jim	88T	678	$ .01	$ .03	Agganis, Harry	55T	152	$9.50	$50.00
Acker, Jim	89T	244	$ .01	$ .04	Agosto, Juan	84T	409	$ .01	$ .05
Acker, Jim	90T	728	$ .01	$ .03	Agosto, Juan	85T	351	$ .01	$ .04
Acker, Tom	57T	219	$ .95	$3.50	Agosto, Juan	86T	657	$ .01	$ .03
Acker, Tom	58T	149	$ .50	$2.00	Agosto, Juan	87T	277	$ .01	$ .03
Acker, Tom	59T	201	$ .50	$1.95	Agosto, Juan	88TTR	2	$ .01	$ .10
Acker, Tom	60T	274	$ .35	$1.10	Agosto, Juan	89T	559	$ .01	$ .04
Ackley, Fritz	64T	368	$ .25	$ .85	Agosto, Juan	90T	181	$ .01	$ .03
Ackley, Fritz	65T	477	$60.00	$250.00	Aguayo, Luis	82T	449	$ .01	$ .06
Acosta, Cy	73T	379	$ .06	$ .25	Aguayo, Luis	83T	252	$ .01	$ .06
Acosta, Cy	74T	22	$ .06	$ .25	Aguayo, Luis	85T	663	$ .01	$ .04
Acosta, Cy	75T	634	$ .06	$ .25	Aguayo, Luis	86T	69	$ .01	$ .03
Acosta, Ed	71T	343	$ .10	$ .35	Aguayo, Luis	87T	755	$ .01	$ .03
Acosta, Ed	72T	123	$ .10	$ .35	Aguayo, Luis	88T	356	$ .01	$ .03
Acosta, Ed	73T	244	$ .06	$ .25	Aguayo, Luis	88TBB	226	$ .01	$ .05
Adair, Jerry	61T	71	$ .30	$1.00	Aguayo, Luis	89T	561	$ .01	$ .04
Adair, Jerry	62T	449	$ .70	$2.10	Aguilera, Rick	86T	599	$ .03	$ .25
Adair, Jerry	63T	488	$2.50	$6.50	Aguilera, Rick	87T	103	$ .01	$ .03
Adair, Jerry	64T	22	$ .25	$ .85	Aguilera, Rick	88T	434	$ .01	$ .03
Adair, Jerry	65T	231	$ .30	$1.00	Aguilera, Rick	89T	257	$ .01	$ .04
Adair, Jerry	66T	533	$4.50	$15.00	Aguilera, Rick	90T	711	$ .01	$ .03
Adair, Jerry	67T	484	$ .50	$2.00	Aguirre, Hank	57T	96	$ .95	$3.50
Adair, Jerry	68T	346	$ .25	$ .65	Aguirre, Hank	58T	337	$ .50	$2.00
Adair, Jerry	69T	159	$ .25	$ .65	Aguirre, Hank	59T	36	$1.50	$3.75
Adair, Jerry	70T	525	$ .10	$ .35	Aguirre, Hank	60T	546	$2.00	$7.00
Adair, Jerry	73T	179	$ .25	$ .85	Aguirre, Hank	61T	324	$ .30	$1.00
Adams, Bobby	52T	249	$6.00	$19.00	Aguirre, Hank	62T	407	$ .70	$2.10
Adams, Bobby	53T	152	$3.75	$13.00	Aguirre, Hank	63T	6	$ .35	$1.10
Adams, Bobby	54T	123	$2.10	$7.50	Aguirre, Hank	63T	257	$ .10	$ .50
Adams, Bobby	55T	178	$4.25	$13.00	Aguirre, Hank	64T	39	$ .25	$ .85
Adams, Bobby	56T	287	$1.80	$6.00	Aguirre, Hank	65T	522	$ .50	$2.00

TOPPS

Player	Year	No.	VG	EX/MT	Player	Year	No.	VG	EX/MT
Aguirre, Hank	66T	113	$ .25	$ .85	Alexander, Matt	81T	68	$ .01	$ .07
Aguirre, Hank	67T	263	$ .25	$ .65	Alexander, Matt	82T	528	$ .01	$ .06
Aguirre, Hank	68T	553	$ .30	$1.00	Alfaro, Flavio	85T	391	$ .01	$ .04
Aguirre, Hank	69T	94	$ .25	$ .65	Alicea, Luis	88TTR	3	$ .01	$ .05
Aguirre, Hank	70T	699	$ .50	$2.00	Alicea, Luis	89T	588	$ .01	$ .15
Aguirre, Hank	73T	81	$ .25	$ .85	Allanson, Andy	86TTR	1	$ .03	$ .15
Aguirre, Hank	74T	354	$ .06	$ .25	Allanson, Andy	87T	436	$ .01	$ .10
Aikens, Willie	80T	368	$ .01	$ .07	Allanson, Andy	88T	728	$ .01	$ .03
Aikens, Willie	81T	524	$ .01	$ .07	Allanson, Andy	88TBB	231	$ .01	$ .05
Aikens, Willie	82T	35	$ .01	$ .06	Allanson, Andy	89T	283	$ .01	$ .04
Aikens, Willie	83T	136	$ .01	$ .06	Allanson, Andy	89TBB	311	$ .01	$ .05
Aikens, Willie	84T	685	$ .01	$ .05	Allanson, Andy	90T	514	$ .01	$ .03
Aikens, Willie	84TTR	1	$ .02	$ .10	Allard, Brian	80T	673	$ .01	$ .07
Aikens, Willie	85T	436	$ .01	$ .04	Allard, Brian	82T	283	$ .01	$ .06
Ainge, Danny	81TTR	727	$ .40	$1.50	Allen, Bernie	62T	596	$10.00	$30.00
Ainge, Danny	82T	125	$ .05	$ .25	Allen, Bernie	63T	427	$ .35	$1.20
Aker, Jack	66T	287	$ .25	$ .85	Allen, Bernie	64T	455	$ .40	$1.25
Aker, Jack	67T	110	$ .25	$ .65	Allen, Bernie	65T	237	$ .30	$1.00
Aker, Jack	68T	224	$ .25	$ .65	Allen, Bernie	66T	327	$ .25	$ .85
Aker, Jack	69T	612	$ .25	$ .85	Allen, Bernie	67T	118	$ .25	$ .65
Aker, Jack	70T	43	$ .10	$ .35	Allen, Bernie	68T	548	$ .30	$1.00
Aker, Jack	71T	593	$ .30	$1.00	Allen, Bernie	69T	27	$ .25	$ .65
Aker, Jack	72T	769	$ .70	$2.10	Allen, Bernie	70T	577	$ .25	$ .85
Aker, Jack	73T	262	$ .06	$ .25	Allen, Bernie	71T	427	$ .10	$ .35
Aker, Jack	74T	562	$ .06	$ .25	Allen, Bernie	72T	644	$ .25	$ .85
Akerfelds, Darrel	88T	82	$ .01	$ .05	Allen, Bernie	73T	293	$ .06	$ .25
Akins, Sid	85T	390	$ .01	$ .04	Allen, Bob	61T	452	$ .50	$2.00
Albury, Vic	72T	778	$ .60	$1.75	Allen, Bob	62T	543	$3.75	$11.00
Albury, Vic	74T	605	$ .30	$1.50	Allen, Bob	63T	266	$ .10	$ .50
Albury, Vic	75T	368	$ .06	$ .25	Allen, Bob	64T	209	$ .25	$ .85
Albury, Vic	76T	336	$ .05	$ .20	Allen, Bob	66T	538	$4.50	$15.00
Albury, Vic	77T	536	$ .05	$ .15	Allen, Bob	67T	24	$ .25	$ .65
Alcala, Santo	76T	589	$ .35	$1.10	Allen, Bob	68T	176	$ .25	$ .65
Alcala, Santo	77T	636	$ .05	$ .15	Allen, Hank	67T	569	$85.00	$310.00
Alcala, Santo	78T	321	$ .02	$ .10	Allen, Hank	68T	426	$ .25	$ .65
Alcaraz, Luis	69T	437	$ .25	$ .65	Allen, Hank	69T	623	$ .25	$ .85
Aldrete, Mike	87T	71	$ .25	$ .65	Allen, Hank	70T	14	$ .10	$ .35
Aldrete, Mike	88T	602	$ .01	$ .10	Allen, Jamie	84T	744	$ .01	$ .05
Aldrete, Mike	88TBB	119	$ .01	$ .05	Allen, Lloyd	71T	152	$ .10	$ .35
Aldrete, Mike	89T	158	$ .01	$ .04	Allen, Lloyd	72T	102	$ .10	$ .35
Aldrete, Mike	90T	589	$ .01	$ .03	Allen, Lloyd	73T	267	$ .06	$ .25
Aldrich, Jay	88T	616	$ .01	$ .03	Allen, Lloyd	74T	539	$ .06	$ .25
Alexander, Doyle	72T	579	$ .50	$1.95	Allen, Neil	80T	94	$ .03	$ .15
Alexander, Doyle	73T	109	$ .30	$1.00	Allen, Neil	81T	322	$ .01	$ .07
Alexander, Doyle	74T	282	$ .06	$ .25	Allen, Neil	82T	205	$ .01	$ .06
Alexander, Doyle	75T	491	$ .10	$ .35	Allen, Neil	83T	575	$ .01	$ .06
Alexander, Doyle	76T	638	$ .10	$ .35	Allen, Neil	83TTR	1	$ .02	$ .10
Alexander, Doyle	77T	254	$ .05	$ .15	Allen, Neil	84T	435	$ .01	$ .05
Alexander, Doyle	78T	146	$ .05	$ .20	Allen, Neil	85T	731	$ .01	$ .04
Alexander, Doyle	79T	442	$ .05	$ .20	Allen, Neil	86T	663	$ .01	$ .03
Alexander, Doyle	80T	67	$ .01	$ .07	Allen, Neil	86TTR	2	$ .02	$ .10
Alexander, Doyle	81T	708	$ .03	$ .15	Allen, Neil	87T	113	$ .01	$ .03
Alexander, Doyle	81TTR	728	$ .05	$ .20	Allen, Neil	88T	384	$ .01	$ .03
Alexander, Doyle	82T	364	$ .03	$ .15	Allen, Neil	89T	61	$ .01	$ .04
Alexander, Doyle	82TTR	1	$ .05	$ .20	Allen, Richie	64T	243	$3.00	$9.00
Alexander, Doyle	83T	512	$ .01	$ .06	Allen, Richie	65T	460	$4.00	$12.00
Alexander, Doyle	84T	677	$ .01	$ .05	Allen, Richie	66T	80	$ .80	$2.75
Alexander, Doyle	85T	218	$ .01	$ .04	Allen, Richie	67T	242	$1.50	$3.75
Alexander, Doyle	86T	196	$ .01	$ .03	Allen, Richie	67T	244	$1.35	$4.00
Alexander, Doyle	87T	686	$ .01	$ .03	Allen, Richie	67T	309	$ .60	$1.20
Alexander, Doyle	88T	492	$ .01	$ .03	Allen, Richie	67T	450	$1.00	$3.75
Alexander, Doyle	88TBB	34	$ .01	$ .05	Allen, Richie	68T	225	$ .50	$2.00
Alexander, Doyle	89T	77	$ .01	$ .04	Allen, Richie	69T	6	$ .80	$2.50
Alexander, Doyle	89TBB	182	$ .01	$ .05	Allen, Richie	69T	350	$ .35	$1.10
Alexander, Doyle	90T	748	$ .01	$ .03	Allen, Richie	70T	40	$ .35	$1.10
Alexander, Gary	77T	476	$20.00	$60.00	Allen, Richie	71T	650	$2.00	$7.00
Alexander, Gary	78T	624	$ .02	$ .10	Allen, Richie "Dick"	72T	240	$ .60	$1.75
Alexander, Gary	79T	332	$ .02	$ .10	Allen, Dick	73T	62	$ .50	$2.00
Alexander, Gary	80T	141	$ .01	$ .07	Allen, Dick	73T	63	$ .50	$2.00
Alexander, Gary	81T	416	$ .01	$ .07	Allen, Dick	73T	310	$ .25	$ .85
Alexander, Gary	81TTR	729	$ .02	$ .10	Allen, Dick	74T	70	$ .10	$ .35
Alexander, Gary	82T	11	$ .01	$ .06	Allen, Dick	74TAS	332	$ .60	$1.75
Alexander, Matt	76T	382	$ .05	$ .20	Allen, Dick	75T	210	$ .50	$2.00
Alexander, Matt	77T	644	$ .05	$ .15	Allen, Dick	75T	307	$ .30	$1.00
Alexander, Matt	78T	102	$ .02	$ .10	Allen, Dick	75T	400	$ .15	$ .50

Player	Year	No.	VG	EX/MT
Allen, Dick	76T	455	$ .10	$ .35
Allenson, Gary	80T	376	$ .01	$ .07
Allenson, Gary	81T	128	$ .01	$ .07
Allenson, Gary	82T	686	$ .01	$ .06
Allenson, Gary	83T	472	$ .01	$ .06
Allenson, Gary	84T	56	$ .01	$ .05
Allenson, Gary	85T	259	$ .01	$ .04
Alley, Gene	64T	509	$ .40	$1.25
Alley, Gene	65T	121	$ .25	$ .65
Alley, Gene	66T	336	$ .25	$ .85
Alley, Gene	67T	283	$ .25	$ .65
Alley, Gene	68T	53	$ .25	$ .65
Alley, Gene	68TAS	368	$ .25	$ .65
Alley, Gene	69T	436	$ .25	$ .65
Alley, Gene	70T	566	$ .25	$ .85
Alley, Gene	71T	416	$ .10	$ .35
Alley, Gene	72T	286	$ .10	$ .35
Alley, Gene	73T	635	$ .35	$1.10
Allie, Gair	54T	179	$2.10	$7.50
Allie, Gair	55T	59	$1.35	$5.00
Allietta, Bob	76T	623	$ .05	$ .20
Allison, Bob	59T	116	$1.35	$4.00
Allison, Bob	60T	320	$ .50	$1.95
Allison, Bob	61T	355	$ .30	$1.00
Allison, Bob	62T	180	$ .35	$1.10
Allison, Bob	63T	75	$ .30	$1.00
Allison, Bob	64T	10	$ .50	$2.00
Allison, Bob	64T	290	$ .35	$1.10
Allison, Bob	65T	180	$ .15	$ .50
Allison, Bob	66T	345	$ .25	$ .85
Allison, Bob	67T	194	$ .25	$ .65
Allison, Bob	67T	334	$1.50	$3.75
Allison, Bob	68T	335	$ .25	$ .85
Allison, Bob	69T	30	$ .15	$ .50
Allison, Bob	70T	635	$ .50	$2.00
Allred, Beau	89TMLD	2	$ .01	$ .25
Allred, Beau	90T	419	$ .01	$ .10
Almon, Bill	83T	362	$ .01	$ .06
Almon, Bill	83TTR	2	$ .02	$ .10
Almon, Bill	84T	241	$ .01	$ .05
Almon, Bill	85T	273	$ .01	$ .04
Almon, Bill	85T	607	$ .01	$ .04
Almon, Bill	85TTR	2	$ .02	$ .10
Almon, Bill	86T	48	$ .01	$ .03
Almon, Bill	87T	447	$ .01	$ .03
Almon, Bill	87TTR	1	$ .01	$ .07
Almon, Bill	88T	787	$ .01	$ .03
Almon, Billy	77T	490	$ .03	$ .12
Almon, Billy	78T	392	$ .02	$ .10
Almon, Billy	79T	616	$ .02	$ .10
Almon, Billy	80T	436	$ .01	$ .07
Almon, Billy	81T	163	$ .01	$ .07
Almon, Billy	81TTR	730	$ .02	$ .10
Almon, Billy "Bill"	82T	521	$ .01	$ .06
Aloma, Luis	52T	308	$11.50	$38.00
Aloma, Luis	54T	57	$4.75	$14.00
Alomar, Jr., Sandy	89T	648	$ .15	$1.00
Alomar, Jr., Sandy	90T	353	$ .01	$ .25
Alomar, Roberto	88TTR	4	$ .05	$1.00
Alomar, Roberto	89T	206	$ .01	$ .35
Alomar, Roberto	89TBB	102	$ .01	$ .10
Alomar, Roberto	90T	517	$ .01	$ .10
Alomar, Sandy	66T	428	$ .25	$ .85
Alomar, Sandy	67T	561	$6.00	$20.00
Alomar, Sandy	68T	541	$ .30	$1.00
Alomar, Sandy	69T	283	$ .25	$ .85
Alomar, Sandy	70T	29	$ .10	$ .35
Alomar, Sandy	71T	745	$ .70	$2.10
Alomar, Sandy	72T	253	$ .10	$ .35
Alomar, Sandy	73T	123	$ .06	$ .25
Alomar, Sandy	74T	347	$ .06	$ .25
Alomar, Sandy	75T	266	$ .06	$ .25
Alomar, Sandy	76T	629	$ .05	$ .20
Alomar, Sandy	77T	54	$ .05	$ .15
Alomar, Sandy	78T	533	$ .02	$ .10

Player	Year	No.	VG	EX/MT
Alomar, Sandy	79T	144	$ .02	$ .10
Alomar, Santos "Sandy"	65T	82	$ .25	$ .65
Alou, Felipe	59T	102	$2.00	$6.00
Alou, Felipe	60T	287	$ .50	$1.95
Alou, Felipe	61T	565	$6.00	$18.00
Alou, Felipe	62T	133	$ .35	$1.10
Alou, Felipe	63T	270	$ .10	$ .50
Alou, Felipe	64T	65	$ .30	$1.00
Alou, Felipe	65T	383	$ .30	$1.00
Alou, Felipe	66T	96	$ .15	$ .50
Alou, Felipe	67T	240	$ .35	$1.10
Alou, Felipe	67T	530	$ .70	$2.00
Alou, Felipe	68T	55	$ .25	$ .85
Alou, Felipe	69T	2	$1.35	$4.00
Alou, Felipe	69T	300	$ .30	$1.00
Alou, Felipe	70T	434	$ .25	$ .65
Alou, Felipe	71T	495	$ .10	$ .35
Alou, Felipe	72T	263	$ .10	$ .35
Alou, Felipe	73T	650	$ .50	$1.95
Alou, Felipe	74T	485	$ .06	$ .25
Alou, Felipe	74TTR	485	$ .06	$ .25
Alou, Jesus	64T	47	$ .30	$1.00
Alou, Jesus	65T	545	$1.50	$3.75
Alou, Jesus	66T	242	$ .25	$ .85
Alou, Jesus	67T	332	$ .25	$ .65
Alou, Jesus	68T	452	$ .25	$ .65
Alou, Jesus	69T	22	$ .25	$ .65
Alou, Jesus	70T	248	$ .10	$ .35
Alou, Jesus	71T	337	$ .10	$ .35
Alou, Jesus	72T	716	$ .70	$2.10

JESUS ALOU
HOUSTON ASTROS · OUTFIELD

Player	Year	No.	VG	EX/MT
Alou, Jesus	73T	93	$ .06	$ .25
Alou, Jesus	74T	654	$ .25	$ .85
Alou, Jesus	75T	253	$ .06	$ .25
Alou, Jesus	76T	468	$ .05	$ .20
Alou, Jesus	79T	107	$ .02	$ .10
Alou, Jesus	80T	593	$ .01	$ .07
Alou, Matty	61T	327	$1.50	$3.75
Alou, Matty	62T	413	$ .70	$2.00
Alou, Matty	63T	128	$ .10	$ .50
Alou, Matty	64T	204	$ .35	$1.10
Alou, Matty	65T	318	$ .30	$1.00
Alou, Matty	66T	94	$ .15	$ .50
Alou, Matty	67T	10	$ .25	$ .65

Player	Year	No.	VG	EX/MT
Alou, Matty	67T	240	$ .35	$1.10
Alou, Matty	68T	1	$2.50	$12.50
Alou, Matty	68T	270	$ .25	$ .85
Alou, Matty	69T	2	$1.35	$4.00
Alou, Matty	69T	490	$ .15	$ .50
Alou, Matty	70T	30	$ .25	$ .65
Alou, Matty	70TAS	460	$ .08	$ .50
Alou, Matty	71T	720	$1.00	$3.75
Alou, Matty	72T	395	$ .25	$ .65
Alou, Matty	73T	132	$ .25	$ .65
Alou, Matty	74T	430	$ .06	$ .25
Alston, Dell	78T	710	$ .15	$ .50
Alston, Dell	79T	54	$ .02	$ .10
Alston, Dell	80T	198	$ .01	$ .07
Alston, Walter	56T	8	$6.00	$20.00
Alston, Walter	58T	314	$8.00	$35.00
Alston, Walt	60T	212	$1.35	$4.00
Alston, Walt	61T	136	$1.00	$3.00
Alston, Walt	62T	217	$1.35	$4.00
Alston, Walt	63T	154	$ .80	$2.50
Alston, Walt	64T	101	$ .70	$2.00
Alston, Walt	65T	217	$ .70	$2.00
Alston, Walt	66T	116	$ .75	$2.00

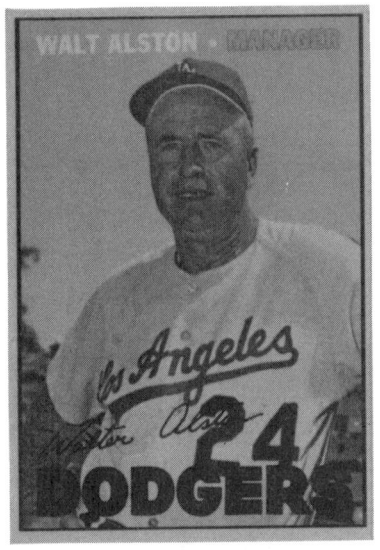

Player	Year	No.	VG	EX/MT
Alston, Walt	67T	294	$ .60	$1.75
Alston, Walt	68T	472	$ .70	$2.00
Alston, Walt	69T	24	$ .50	$1.95
Alston, Walt	70T	242	$ .50	$1.95
Alston, Walt	71T	567	$ .70	$2.00
Alston, Walt	72T	749	$ .90	$3.50
Alston, Walt	73T	569	$1.00	$3.75
Alston, Walt	74T	144	$ .50	$2.00
Altamirano, Porfirio	83T	432	$ .01	$ .06
Altamirano, Porfirio	84T	101	$ .01	$ .05
Altman, George	59T	512	$2.00	$7.00
Altman, George	60T	259	$ .35	$1.10
Altman, George	61T	551	$6.00	$18.00
Altman, George	62T	240	$ .35	$1.10
Altman, George	63T	357	$ .24	$ .60
Altman, George	64T	95	$ .25	$ .85
Altman, George	65T	528	$1.50	$3.75
Altman, George	66T	146	$ .25	$ .85
Altman, George	67T	87	$ .25	$ .65
Altobelli, Joe	78T	256	$ .02	$ .10

Player	Year	No.	VG	EX/MT
Altobelli, Joe	83TTR	3	$ .02	$ .10
Altobelli, Joe	84T	21	$ .01	$ .05
Altobelli, Joe	85T	574	$ .01	$ .04
Alusik, George	62T	261	$ .35	$1.10
Alusik, George	63T	51	$ .10	$ .50
Alusik, George	64T	431	$ .40	$1.25
Alvarado, Luis	70T	317	$ .25	$ .85
Alvarado, Luis	71T	489	$ .10	$ .35
Alvarado, Luis	72T	774	$ .70	$2.10
Alvarado, Luis	73T	627	$ .35	$1.10
Alvarado, Luis	74T	462	$ .06	$ .25
Alvarez, Jose	89T	253	$ .01	$ .10
Alvarez, Jose	90T	782	$ .01	$ .03
Alvarez, Ossie	59T	504	$ .50	$1.95
Alvarez, Rogelio	63T	158	$ .10	$ .50
Alvarez, Wilson	89TMLD	3	$ .01	$ .15
Alvis, Max	63T	228	$9.00	$35.00
Alvis, Max	64T	545	$1.50	$3.75
Alvis, Max	65T	185	$ .25	$ .65
Alvis, Max	66T	415	$ .25	$ .85
Alvis, Max	67T	520	$ .50	$2.00
Alvis, Max	68T	340	$ .25	$ .65
Alvis, Max	69T	145	$ .25	$ .65
Alvis, Max	70T	85	$ .10	$ .35
Alyea, Brant	66T	11	$ .25	$ .85
Alyea, Brant	69T	48	$ .25	$ .65
Alyea, Brant	70T	303	$ .10	$ .35
Alyea, Brant	71T	449	$ .10	$ .35
Alyea, Brant	72T	383	$ .10	$ .35
Amalfitano, Joe	55T	144	$1.35	$5.00
Amalfitano, Joe	60T	356	$ .45	$1.35
Amalfitano, Joe	61T	87	$ .30	$1.00
Amalfitano, Joe	62T	456	$ .70	$2.10
Amalfitano, Joe	63T	199	$ .10	$ .50
Amalfitano, Joe	64T	451	$ .40	$1.25
Amalfitano, Joe	65T	402	$ .30	$1.00
Amalfitano, Joe	73T	252	$ .25	$ .65
Amalfitano, Joe	74T	78	$ .06	$ .25
Amaro, Ruben	59T	178	$ .50	$1.95
Amaro, Ruben	61T	103	$ .30	$1.00
Amaro, Ruben	62T	284	$ .35	$1.10
Amaro, Ruben	63T	455	$2.50	$6.50
Amaro, Ruben	64T	432	$ .40	$1.25
Amaro, Ruben	65T	419	$ .30	$1.00
Amaro, Ruben	66T	186	$ .25	$ .85
Amaro, Ruben	67T	358	$ .25	$ .65
Amaro, Ruben	68T	138	$ .25	$ .65
Amaro, Ruben	69T	598	$ .25	$ .85
Amoros, Sandy	55T	75	$1.35	$5.00
Amoros, Sandy	56T	42	$1.25	$4.50
Amoros, Sandy	57T	201	$ .95	$3.50
Amoros, Sandy	58T	93	$1.00	$3.75
Amoros, Sandy	60T	531	$2.00	$7.00
Andersen, Larry	78T	703	$2.00	$7.00
Andersen, Larry	80T	665	$ .01	$ .07
Andersen, Larry	82T	52	$ .01	$ .06
Andersen, Larry	83T	234	$ .01	$ .06
Andersen, Larry	85T	428	$ .01	$ .04
Andersen, Larry	86T	183	$ .01	$ .03
Andersen, Larry	87T	503	$ .01	$ .03
Andersen, Larry	88T	342	$ .01	$ .03
Andersen, Larry	89T	24	$ .01	$ .04
Anderson, Allan	87T	336	$ .01	$ .03
Anderson, Allan	88T	101	$ .01	$ .03
Anderson, Allan	89T	672	$ .01	$ .04
Anderson, Allan	90T	71	$ .01	$ .10
Anderson, Bob	58T	209	$ .50	$2.00
Anderson, Bob	59T	447	$ .50	$1.95
Anderson, Bob	60T	412	$ .50	$1.95
Anderson, Bob	61T	283	$ .30	$1.00
Anderson, Bob	62T	557	$3.75	$11.00
Anderson, Bob	63T	379	$ .35	$1.20
Anderson, Brady	88TTR	5	$ .01	$ .20
Anderson, Brady	89T	757	$ .01	$ .25
Anderson, Brady	90T	598	$ .01	$ .03

Player	Year	No.	VG	EX/MT	Player	Year	No.	VG	EX/MT
Anderson, Bud	79T	712	$ .02	$ .10	Andujar, Joaquin	81TTR	731	$ .02	$ .10
Anderson, Bud	83T	367	$ .01	$ .06	Andujar, Joaquin	82T	533	$ .01	$ .06
Anderson, Bud	84T	497	$ .01	$ .05	Andujar, Joaquin	83T	228	$ .01	$ .06
Anderson, Craig	62T	593	$6.00	$18.00	Andujar, Joaquin	83T	561	$ .01	$ .06
Anderson, Craig	63T	59	$ .10	$ .50	Andujar, Joaquin	84T	785	$ .01	$ .05
Anderson, Dave	84T	376	$ .01	$ .05	Andujar, Joaquin	85T	655	$ .01	$ .04
Anderson, Dave	85T	654	$ .01	$ .04	Andujar, Joaquin	86T	150	$ .01	$ .03
Anderson, Dave	86T	758	$ .01	$ .03	Andujar, Joaquin	86TTR	3	$ .02	$ .10
Anderson, Dave	87T	73	$ .01	$ .03	Andujar, Joaquin	87T	775	$ .01	$ .03
Anderson, Dave	88T	456	$ .01	$ .03	Andujar, Joaquin	88T	47	$ .01	$ .03
Anderson, Dave	89T	117	$ .01	$ .04	Angelini, Norm	73T	616	$ .35	$1.10
Anderson, Dave	90T	248	$ .01	$ .03	Angels, Team	62T	132	$1.25	$4.50
Anderson, Dwain	72T	268	$ .10	$ .35	Angels, Team	63T	39	$ .50	$1.95
Anderson, Dwain	73T	241	$ .06	$ .25	Angels, Team	64T	213	$1.00	$3.00
Anderson, Harry	57T	404	$1.00	$3.75	Angels, Team	65T	293	$ .60	$1.75
Anderson, Harry	58T	171	$ .50	$2.00	Angels, Team	66T	131	$ .60	$1.75
Anderson, Harry	59T	85	$1.00	$3.75	Angels, Team	67T	327	$ .60	$1.75
Anderson, Harry	60T	285	$ .35	$1.10	Angels, Team	68T	252	$ .50	$2.00
Anderson, Harry	61T	76	$ .30	$1.00	Angels, Team	70T	522	$ .35	$1.10
Anderson, Jim	79T	703	$ .02	$ .10	Angels, Team	71T	442	$ .35	$1.10
Anderson, Jim	80T	183	$ .01	$ .07	Angels, Team	72T	71	$ .15	$ .50
Anderson, Jim	81T	613	$ .01	$ .07	Angels, Team	73T	243	$ .30	$1.00
Anderson, Jim	82T	497	$ .01	$ .06	Angels, Team	74T	114	$ .15	$ .50
Anderson, Jim	84T	353	$ .01	$ .05	Angels, Team Checklist	75T	236	$ .30	$1.00
Anderson, John	62T	266	$ .35	$1.10	Angels, Team Checklist	76T	304	$ .30	$1.00
Anderson, Kent	89TMLD	4	$ .01	$ .15	Angels, Team Checklist	77T	34	$ .15	$ .50
Anderson, Kent	89TTR	3	$ .01	$ .15	Angels, Team Checklist	78T	214	$ .07	$ .30
Anderson, Kent	90T	16	$ .01	$ .03	Angels, Team Checklist	79T	424	$ .08	$ .30
Anderson, Larry	76T	593	$ .10	$ .35	Angels, Team Checklist	80T	214	$ .05	$ .25
Anderson, Larry	77T	487	$ .03	$ .12	Angels, Team Checklist	81T	663	$ .02	$ .20
Anderson, Mike	72T	14	$ .10	$ .35	Angels, Team Leaders	86T	486	$ .01	$ .03
Anderson, Mike	73T	147	$ .06	$ .25	Angels, Team Leaders	87T	556	$ .01	$ .03
Anderson, Mike	74T	619	$ .06	$ .25	Angels, Team Leaders	88T	381	$ .01	$ .03
Anderson, Mike	75T	118	$ .06	$ .25	Angels, Team Leaders	89T	51	$ .01	$ .04
Anderson, Mike	76T	527	$ .05	$ .20	Ansley, Willie	89T	607	$ .01	$ .15
Anderson, Mike	76TTR	527	$ .05	$ .20	Anthony, Eric	89TMLD	5	$ .01	$1.00
Anderson, Mike	77T	72	$ .05	$ .15	Anthony, Eric	90T	608	$ .01	$1.50
Anderson, Mike	78T	714	$ .02	$ .10	Antonelli, John	52T	140	$6.00	$18.00
Anderson, Mike	79T	102	$ .02	$ .10	Antonelli, John	53T	106	$3.75	$13.00
Anderson, Mike	80T	317	$ .01	$ .07	Antonelli, Johnny	54T	119	$2.00	$7.00
Anderson, Rick	81T	282	$ .01	$ .07	Antonelli, Johnny	56T	138	$1.25	$3.50
Anderson, Rick	87T	594	$ .01	$ .03	Antonelli, Johnny	57T	105	$ .95	$3.50
Anderson, Sparky (George)	59T	338	$4.00	$12.00	Antonelli, Johnny	58T	152	$ .65	$2.00
Anderson, Sparky (George)	60T	34	$ .60	$1.75	Antonelli, Johnny	59T	377	$ .30	$1.25
Anderson, Sparky	70T	181	$ .50	$2.00	Antonelli, Johnny	60T	80	$ .35	$1.10
Anderson, Sparky	71T	688	$1.35	$4.00	Antonelli, Johnny	60TAS	572	$4.00	$20.00
Anderson, Sparky	72T	358	$ .25	$ .85	Antonelli, Johnny	61T	115	$ .30	$1.00
Anderson, Sparky	73T	296	$ .15	$ .50	Antonello, Bill	53T	272	$11.00	$37.50
Anderson, Sparky	74T	326	$ .15	$ .50	Aparicio, Luis	56T	292	$25.00	$85.00
Anderson, Sparky	78T	401	$ .05	$ .20	Aparicio, Luis	57T	7	$6.00	$15.00
Anderson, Sparky	83T	CCC	$ .01	$ .06	Aparicio, Luis	58T	85	$3.50	$10.00
Anderson, Sparky	84T	259	$ .01	$ .05	Aparicio, Luis	58TAS	483	$1.40	$6.00
Anderson, Sparky	85T	307	$ .01	$ .04	Aparicio, Luis	59T	310	$4.50	$13.00
Anderson, Sparky	86T	411	$ .01	$ .03	Aparicio, Luis	59T	408	$ .60	$1.80
Anderson, Sparky	87T	218	$ .01	$ .03	Aparicio, Luis	59TAS	560	$4.00	$12.00
Anderson, Sparky	88T	14	$ .01	$ .03	Aparicio, Luis	60T	240	$2.35	$7.00
Anderson, Sparky	89T	193	$ .01	$ .04	Aparicio, Luis	60TAS	559	$3.00	$9.50
Anderson, Sparky	90T	609	$ .01	$ .03	Aparicio, Luis	61T	440	$2.25	$6.50
Andrews, Mike	67T	314	$1.35	$4.00	Aparicio, Luis	61TAS	574	$8.50	$32.50
Andrews, Mike	68T	502	$ .30	$1.00	Aparicio, Luis	62T	325	$2.75	$8.00
Andrews, Mike	69T	52	$ .25	$ .65	Aparicio, Luis	62TAS	469	$3.00	$15.00
Andrews, Mike	70T	406	$ .10	$ .35	Aparicio, Luis	63T	205	$1.35	$4.00
Andrews, Mike	71T	191	$ .10	$ .35	Aparicio, Luis	64T	540	$2.50	$7.50
Andrews, Mike	72T	361	$ .10	$ .35	Aparicio, Luis	65T	410	$1.50	$4.50
Andrews, Mike	73T	42	$ .06	$ .25	Aparicio, Luis	66T	90	$1.25	$3.50
Andrews, Rob	76T	568	$ .05	$ .20	Aparicio, Luis	67T	60	$1.25	$3.50
Andrews, Rob	77T	209	$ .05	$ .15	Aparicio, Luis	68T	310	$1.35	$4.00
Andrews, Rob	78T	461	$ .02	$ .10	Aparicio, Luis	69T	75	$ .25	$ .65
Andrews, Rob	79T	34	$ .02	$ .10	Aparicio, Luis	70T	315	$1.35	$4.00
Andrews, Rob	80T	279	$ .01	$ .07	Aparicio, Luis	71T	740	$3.00	11.00
Andujar, Joaquin	77T	67	$ .15	$ .50	Aparicio, Luis	72T	313	$1.00	$4.00
Andujar, Joaquin	78T	158	$ .03	$ .15	Aparicio, Luis	72TIA	314	$ .50	$2.00
Andujar, Joaquin	79T	471	$ .05	$ .20	Aparicio, Luis	73T	165	$ .95	$3.50
Andujar, Joaquin	80T	617	$ .02	$ .10	Aparicio, Luis	74T	61	$1.00	$4.00
Andujar, Joaquin	81T	329	$ .01	$ .07	Apodaca, Bob	74T	608	$ .06	$ .25

TOPPS

Player	Year	No.	VG	EX/MT
Apodaca, Bob	75T	659	$ .06	$ .25
Apodaca, Bob	76T	16	$ .05	$ .20
Apodaca, Bob	77T	225	$ .10	$ .35
Apodaca, Bob	78T	592	$ .02	$ .10
Apodaca, Bob	79T	197	$ .02	$ .10
Apodaca, Bob	80T	633	$ .01	$ .07
Aponte, Luis	83T	577	$ .01	$ .06
Aponte, Luis	84T	187	$ .01	$ .05
Aponte, Luis	84TTR	2	$ .02	$ .10
Appier, Kevin	89TMLD	6	$ .01	$ .15
Appier, Kevin	90T	167	$ .01	$ .10
Appling, Luke	60T	461	$1.25	$4.50
Aquino, Luis	87T	301	$ .01	$ .03
Aquino, Luis	89T	266	$ .01	$ .04
Aquino, Luis	90T	707	$ .01	$ .03
Archer, Jim	61T	552	$5.00	$15.00
Archer, Jim	62T	433	$ .70	$2.10
Arcia, Jose	68T	258	$ .25	$ .65
Arcia, Jose	69T	473	$ .25	$ .65
Arcia, Jose	70T	587	$ .25	$ .85
Arcia, Jose	71T	134	$ .10	$ .35
Arcia, Jose	73T	466	$ .06	$ .25
Arft, Hank	52T	284	$14.00	$45.00
Arias, Rodolfo	59T	537	$2.00	$7.00
Arlin, Steve	72T	78	$ .10	$ .35
Arlin, Steve	73T	294	$ .06	$ .25
Arlin, Steve	74T	406	$ .06	$ .25
Arlin, Steve	75T	159	$ .06	$ .25
Armas, Tony	77T	492	$ .25	$ .80
Armas, Tony	78T	298	$ .05	$ .20
Armas, Tony	79T	507	$ .05	$ .20
Armas, Tony	80T	391	$ .02	$ .10
Armas, Tony	81T	629	$ .01	$ .07
Armas, Tony	82T	60	$ .01	$ .06
Armas, Tony	82T	162	$ .05	$ .25
Armas, Tony	83T	435	$ .01	$ .06
Armas, Tony	83TRB	1	$ .01	$ .10
Armas, Tony	83TTR	4	$ .02	$ .10
Armas, Tony	84T	105	$ .01	$ .05
Armas, Tony	85T	785	$ .01	$ .04
Armas, Tony	85TAS	707	$ .01	$ .04
Armas, Tony	86T	255	$ .01	$ .03
Armas, Tony	87T	535	$ .01	$ .03
Armas, Tony	88T	761	$ .01	$ .03
Armas, Tony	89T	332	$ .01	$ .04
Armas, Tony	89TBB	99	$ .01	$ .05
Armas, Tony	90T	603	$ .01	$ .03
Armbrister, Ed	72T	524	$ .10	$ .35
Armbrister, Ed	74T	601	$ .35	$1.10
Armbrister, Ed	75T	622	$2.25	$11.00
Armbrister, Ed	76T	652	$ .05	$ .20
Armbrister, Ed	77T	203	$ .05	$ .15
Armbrister, Ed	78T	556	$ .02	$ .10
Armstrong, Jack	88TTR	6	$ .20	$1.25
Armstrong, Jack	89T	317	$ .01	$ .50
Armstrong, Jack	90T	642	$ .01	$ .25
Armstrong, Mike	82T	731	$ .01	$ .06
Armstrong, Mike	83T	219	$ .01	$ .06
Armstrong, Mike	84T	417	$ .01	$ .05
Armstrong, Mike	84TTR	3	$ .02	$ .10
Armstrong, Mike	85T	612	$ .01	$ .04
Arndt, Larry	89TMLD	7	$ .01	$ .15
Arnold, Chris	72T	232	$ .10	$ .35
Arnold, Chris	73T	584	$ .35	$1.10
Arnold, Chris	74T	432	$ .06	$ .50
Arnold, Chris	77T	591	$ .05	$ .25
Arnsberg, Brad	88T	159	$ .01	$ .20
Arrigo, Gerry	64T	516	$ .40	$1.25
Arrigo, Gerry	65T	39	$ .25	$ .65
Arrigo, Gerry	66T	357	$ .25	$ .85
Arrigo, Gerry	67T	488	$ .50	$2.00
Arrigo, Gerry	68T	302	$ .25	$ .65
Arrigo, Gerry	69T	213	$ .25	$ .65
Arrigo, Gerry	70T	274	$ .10	$ .35
Arroyo, Fernando	76T	614	$ .05	$ .20
Arroyo, Fernando	78T	607	$ .02	$ .10
Arroyo, Fernando	81T	408	$ .01	$ .07
Arroyo, Fernando	82T	18	$ .01	$ .06
Arroyo, Fernando	82T	396	$ .01	$ .06
Arroyo, Luis	56T	64	$1.35	$4.00
Arroyo, Luis	57T	394	$1.00	$3.75
Arroyo, Luis	61T	142	$ .30	$1.00
Arroyo, Luis	62T	455	$1.00	$3.75
Arroyo, Luis	63T	569	$1.35	$4.00
Ashburn, Richie	51Tbb	3	$17.50	$70.00
Ashburn, Richie	52T	216	$17.50	$70.00
Ashburn, Richie	54T	45	$12.00	$30.00
Ashburn, Richie	56T	120	$5.50	$25.00
Ashburn, Richie	57T	70	$3.60	$12.50
Ashburn, Richie	58T	230	$3.00	$9.00
Ashburn, Richie	59T	300	$3.00	$9.00
Ashburn, Richie	59T	317	$4.00	$16.00
Ashburn, Richie	60T	305	$2.00	$8.00
Ashburn, Richie	61T	88	$1.35	$4.00
Ashburn, Richie	62T	213	$2.10	$6.25
Ashburn, Richie	63T	135	$2.00	$8.00
Ashby, Alan	76T	209	$ .06	$ .25
Ashby, Alan	77T	564	$ .05	$ .15
Ashby, Alan	78T	319	$ .02	$ .10
Ashby, Alan	79T	36	$ .02	$ .10
Ashby, Alan	80T	187	$ .01	$ .07
Ashby, Alan	81T	696	$ .01	$ .07
Ashby, Alan	82T	433	$ .01	$ .06
Ashby, Alan	83T	774	$ .01	$ .06
Ashby, Alan	84T	217	$ .01	$ .05
Ashby, Alan	85T	564	$ .01	$ .04
Ashby, Alan	86T	331	$ .01	$ .03
Ashby, Alan	87T	112	$ .01	$ .03
Ashby, Alan	88T	48	$ .01	$ .03
Ashby, Alan	89T	492	$ .01	$ .04
Ashford, Tucker	78T	116	$ .02	$ .10
Ashford, Tucker	79T	247	$ .02	$ .10
Ashford, Tucker	84T	492	$ .01	$ .05
Aspromonte, Bob	60T	547	$2.00	$7.00
Aspromonte, Bob	61T	396	$ .50	$2.00
Aspromonte, Bob	62T	248	$ .35	$1.10
Aspromonte, Bob	63T	45	$ .10	$ .50
Aspromonte, Bob	64T	467	$ .40	$1.25
Aspromonte, Bob	65T	175	$ .25	$ .65
Aspromonte, Bob	66T	273	$ .50	$2.00
Aspromonte, Bob	66T	352	$ .25	$ .85
Aspromonte, Bob	67T	274	$ .25	$ .65
Aspromonte, Bob	68T	95	$ .25	$ .65
Aspromonte, Bob	69T	542	$ .25	$ .85
Aspromonte, Bob	70T	529	$ .10	$ .35
Aspromonte, Bob	71T	469	$ .10	$ .35
Aspromonte, Bob	72T	659	$ .70	$2.10
Aspromonte, Ken	58T	405	$ .50	$2.00
Aspromonte, Ken	59T	424	$ .50	$1.95
Aspromonte, Ken	60T	114	$ .35	$1.10
Aspromonte, Ken	61T	176	$ .30	$1.00
Aspromonte, Ken	62T	563	$3.75	$11.00
Aspromonte, Ken	63T	464	$2.50	$6.50
Aspromonte, Ken	64T	252	$ .25	$ .85
Aspromonte, Ken	72T	784	$ .70	$2.10
Aspromonte, Ken	73T	449	$ .25	$ .65
Aspromonte, Ken	74T	521	$ .06	$ .25
Asselstine, Brian	77T	479	$ .03	$ .12
Asselstine, Brian	78T	372	$ .02	$ .10
Asselstine, Brian	79T	529	$ .02	$ .10
Asselstine, Brian	81T	64	$ .01	$ .07
Asselstine, Brian	82T	214	$ .01	$ .06
Assenmacher, Paul	86TTR	4	$ .02	$ .10
Assenmacher, Paul	87T	132	$ .01	$ .03
Assenmacher, Paul	88T	266	$ .01	$ .03
Assenmacher, Paul	89T	454	$ .01	$ .04
Assenmacher, Paul	90T	644	$ .01	$ .03
Astros, Team	70T	448	$ .35	$1.10
Astros, Team	71T	722	$1.35	$4.00
Astros, Team	72T	282	$ .30	$1.00

Player	Year	No.	VG	EX/MT	Player	Year	No.	VG	EX/MT
Astros, Team	73T	158	$ .30	$1.00	Award, Cy Young	72T	623	$ .35	$1.10
Astros, Team	74T	154	$ .25	$ .85	Award, Minor L.P. of Yr.	72T	624	$ .35	$1.10
Astros, Team Checklist	75T	487	$ .15	$ .50	Award, MVP	72T	622	$ .35	$1.10
Astros, Team Checklist	76T	147	$ .15	$ .50	Award, Rookie of Year	72T	625	$ .35	$1.10
Astros, Team Checklist	77T	327	$ .15	$ .50	Ayala, Benny	75T	619	$ .06	$ .25
Astros, Team Checklist	78T	112	$ .06	$ .30	Ayala, Benny	80T	262	$ .01	$ .07
Astros, Team Checklist	79T	381	$ .05	$ .25	Ayala, Benny	81T	101	$ .01	$ .07
Astros, Team Checklist	80T	82	$ .05	$ .25	Ayala, Benny	82T	331	$ .01	$ .06
Astros, Team Checklist	81T	678	$ .02	$ .20					
Astros, Team Leaders	86T	186	$ .01	$ .03					
Astros, Team Leaders	87T	531	$ .01	$ .03					
Astros, Team Leaders	88T	291	$ .01	$ .03					
Astros, Team Leaders	89T	579	$ .01	$ .04					
Astroth, Joe	52T	290	$14.00	$45.00					
Astroth, Joe	53T	103	$3.75	$13.00					
Astroth, Joe	56T	106	$1.25	$4.50					
Atherton, Keith	84T	529	$ .01	$ .05					
Atherton, Keith	85T	166	$ .01	$ .04					
Atherton, Keith	86T	353	$ .01	$ .03					
Atherton, Keith	87T	52	$ .01	$ .03					
Atherton, Keith	88T	451	$ .01	$ .03					
Atherton, Keith	89T	698	$ .01	$ .04					
Atherton, Keith	89TTR	4	$ .01	$ .05					
Atkinson, Bill	78T	43	$ .02	$ .10					
Atkinson, Bill	80T	415	$ .01	$ .07					
Atwell, Toby	52T	356	$39.00	$135.00					
Atwell, Toby	53T	23	$3.75	$13.00					
Atwell, Toby	56T	232	$2.50	$8.00					
Auerbach, Rick	72T	153	$ .10	$ .35					
Auerbach, Rick	73T	427	$ .06	$ .25					
Auerbach, Rick	74T	289	$ .06	$ .25					
Auerbach, Rick	75T	588	$ .06	$ .25					
Auerbach, Rick	76T	622	$ .05	$ .20					
Auerbach, Rick	78T	646	$ .02	$ .10					
Auerbach, Rick	79T	174	$ .02	$ .10					
Auerbach, Rick	80T	354	$ .01	$ .07					
Auerbach, Rick	82T	72	$ .01	$ .06					
August, Don	85T	392	$ .05	$ .40					
August, Don	88TTR	7	$ .01	$ .10					
August, Don	89T	696	$ .01	$ .10					
August, Don	89TBB	33	$ .01	$ .05	Ayala, Benny	83T	59	$ .01	$ .06
August, Don	90T	192	$ .01	$ .03	Ayala, Benny	84T	443	$ .01	$ .05
Augustine, Dave	74T	598	$1.00	$4.00	Ayala, Benny	85T	624	$ .01	$ .04
Augustine, Dave	75T	616	$8.50	$27.50	Ayala, Benny	85TTR	3	$ .02	$ .10
Augustine, Jerry	77T	577	$ .05	$ .15	Azcue, Joe	62T	417	$ .70	$2.10
Augustine, Jerry	78T	133	$ .02	$ .10	Azcue, Joe	63T	501	$2.50	$6.50
Augustine, Jerry	79T	357	$ .02	$ .10	Azcue, Joe	64T	199	$ .25	$ .85
Augustine, Jerry	80T	243	$ .01	$ .07	Azcue, Joe	65T	514	$ .50	$2.00
Augustine, Jerry	81T	596	$ .01	$ .07	Azcue, Joe	66T	452	$ .70	$2.10
Augustine, Jerry	82T	46	$ .01	$ .06	Azcue, Joe	67T	336	$ .25	$ .65
Augustine, Jerry	83T	424	$ .01	$ .06	Azcue, Joe	68T	443	$ .25	$ .65
Augustine, Jerry	84T	658	$ .01	$ .05	Azcue, Joe	69T	176	$ .25	$ .65
Ault, Doug	77T	477	$ .05	$ .15	Azcue, Joe "Jose"	70T	294	$ .10	$ .35
Ault, Doug	78T	267	$ .02	$ .10	Azcue, Jose	71T	657	$ .70	$2.10
Ault, Doug	79T	392	$ .02	$ .10	Babcock, Bob	81T	41	$ .01	$ .07
Aust, Dennis	66T	179	$ .25	$ .85	Babcock, Bob	82T	567	$ .01	$ .06
Austin, Rick	71T	41	$ .10	$ .35	Babitt, Shooty	82T	578	$ .01	$ .06
Austin, Rick	76T	269	$ .05	$ .20	Backman, Wally	83T	444	$ .01	$ .06
Averill, Earl	59T	301	$ .50	$1.95	Backman, Wally	85T	677	$ .01	$ .04
Averill, Earl	60T	39	$ .35	$1.10	Backman, Wally	86T	191	$ .01	$ .03
Averill, Earl	61T	358	$ .30	$1.00	Backman, Wally	87T	48	$ .01	$ .03
Averill, Earl	62T	452	$ .70	$2.10	Backman, Wally	88T	333	$ .01	$ .03
Averill, Earl	63T	139	$ .10	$ .50	Backman, Wally	89T	508	$ .01	$ .04
Avery, Steve	89T	784	$ .10	$1.00	Backman, Wally	89TBB	300	$ .01	$ .05
Avila, Bobby	52T	257	$11.50	$38.00	Backman, Wally	89TTR	5	$ .01	$ .05
Avila, Bobby	56T	132	$1.25	$4.50	Backman, Wally	90T	218	$ .01	$ .03
Avila, Bobby	57T	195	$ .95	$3.50	Bacsik, Mike	77T	103	$ .05	$ .15
Avila, Bobby	58T	276	$ .50	$2.00	Bacsik, Mike	80T	453	$ .01	$ .07
Avila, Bobby	59T	363	$ .50	$1.95	Baez, Jose	78T	311	$ .02	$ .10
Avila, Bobby	60T	90	$ .35	$1.10	Bahnsen, Stan	67T	93	$ .70	$2.00
Aviles, Ramon	80T	682	$ .01	$ .07	Bahnsen, Stan	68T	214	$ .35	$1.10
Aviles, Ramon	81T	644	$ .01	$ .07	Bahnsen, Stan	69T	380	$ .25	$ .65
Aviles, Ramon	82T	152	$ .01	$ .06	Bahnsen, Stan	70T	568	$ .25	$ .85
Award, Babe Ruth	72T	626	$ .50	$2.00	Bahnsen, Stan	71T	184	$ .10	$ .35
Award, Commissioners	72T	621	$ .35	$1.10	Bahnsen, Stan	72T	662	$ .70	$2.10

BENNY
AYALA
OUTFIELD
ORIOLES

Player	Year	No.	VG	EX/MT
Bahnsen, Stan	73T	20	$ .06	$ .25
Bahnsen, Stan	74T	254	$ .06	$ .25
Bahnsen, Stan	75T	161	$ .06	$ .25
Bahnsen, Stan	76T	534	$ .05	$ .20
Bahnsen, Stan	77T	383	$ .05	$ .15
Bahnsen, Stan	78T	97	$ .02	$ .10
Bahnsen, Stan	79T	468	$ .02	$ .10
Bahnsen, Stan	80T	653	$ .01	$ .07
Bahnsen, Stan	81T	267	$ .01	$ .07
Bahnsen, Stan	82T	131	$ .01	$ .06
Bailes, Scott	86TTR	5	$ .05	$ .20
Bailes, Scott	87T	585	$ .01	$ .10
Bailes, Scott	88T	107	$ .01	$ .03
Bailes, Scott	89T	339	$ .01	$ .04
Bailes, Scott	90T	784	$ .01	$ .03
Bailey, Bob	63T	228	$9.00	$35.00
Bailey, Bob	64T	91	$ .25	$ .85
Bailey, Bob	65T	412	$ .30	$1.00
Bailey, Bob	66T	485	$ .70	$2.10
Bailey, Bob	67T	32	$ .25	$ .65
Bailey, Bob	68T	580	$ .30	$1.00
Bailey, Bob	69T	399	$ .25	$ .65
Bailey, Bob	70T	293	$ .10	$ .35
Bailey, Bob	71T	157	$ .10	$ .35

Player	Year	No.	VG	EX/MT
Bailey, Bob	72T	493	$ .10	$ .35
Bailey, Bob	72T	526	$ .25	$ .85
Bailey, Bob	73T	505	$ .06	$ .25
Bailey, Bob	74T	97	$ .06	$ .25
Bailey, Bob	75T	365	$ .06	$ .25
Bailey, Bob	76T	338	$ .05	$ .20
Bailey, Bob	76TTR	338	$ .05	$ .20
Bailey, Bob	77T	221	$ .05	$ .15
Bailey, Bob	78T	457	$ .02	$ .10
Bailey, Bob	79T	549	$ .02	$ .10
Bailey, Ed	53T	206	$3.75	$13.00
Bailey, Ed	54T	184	$2.10	$7.50
Bailey, Ed	55T	69	$1.35	$5.00
Bailey, Ed	57T	128	$ .95	$3.50
Bailey, Ed	58T	330	$ .50	$2.00
Bailey, Ed	58T	386	$2.00	$6.00
Bailey, Ed	58TAS	490	$ .70	$2.25
Bailey, Ed	59T	210	$ .50	$1.95
Bailey, Ed	60T	411	$ .50	$1.95

Player	Year	No.	VG	EX/MT
Bailey, Ed	61T	418	$ .40	$1.50
Bailey, Ed	62T	459	$ .70	$2.10
Bailey, Ed	63T	368	$ .24	$ .60
Bailey, Ed	64T	437	$ .30	$ .75
Bailey, Ed	65T	559	$1.50	$3.75
Bailey, Ed	66T	246	$ .15	$ .35
Bailey, Howard	82T	261	$ .01	$ .06
Bailey, Howard	84T	284	$ .01	$ .05
Bailey, Mark	85T	64	$ .07	$ .04
Bailey, Mark	86T	432	$ .01	$ .03
Bailey, Mark	87T	197	$ .01	$ .03
Bailey, Mark	88TBB	248	$ .01	$ .05
Bailor, Bob	77T	474	$ .05	$ .15
Bailor, Bob	78T	196	$ .02	$ .09
Bailor, Bob	79T	492	$ .02	$ .08
Bailor, Bob	80T	581	$ .02	$ .07
Bailor, Bob	81T	297	$ .02	$ .07
Bailor, Bob	81TTR	732	$ .02	$ .10
Bailor, Bob	82T	79	$ .01	$ .06
Bailor, Bob	83T	343	$ .01	$ .06
Bailor, Bob	84T	654	$ .01	$ .05
Bailor, Bob	84TTR	4	$ .02	$ .10
Bailor, Bob	85T	728	$ .01	$ .04
Bailor, Bob	86T	522	$ .01	$ .03
Baines, Harold	81T	347	$ .95	$3.50
Baines, Harold	82T	684	$ .10	$1.00
Baines, Harold	83T	177	$ .03	$ .35
Baines, Harold	84T	434	$ .02	$ .25
Baines, Harold	85T	249	$ .01	$ .20
Baines, Harold	85T	275	$ .01	$ .10
Baines, Harold	86T	755	$ .02	$ .15
Baines, Harold	87T	772	$ .01	$ .10
Baines, Harold	88T	35	$ .01	$ .10
Baines, Harold	88TBB	224	$ .01	$ .05
Baines, Harold	89T	585	$ .01	$ .04
Baines, Harold	89TBB	266	$ .01	$ .05
Baines, Harold	90T	345	$ .01	$ .03
Bair, Doug	78T	353	$ .02	$ .10
Bair, Doug	79T	126	$ .02	$ .10
Bair, Doug	80T	449	$ .01	$ .07
Bair, Doug	81T	73	$ .01	$ .07
Bair, Doug	82T	262	$ .01	$ .06
Bair, Doug	83T	627	$ .01	$ .06
Bair, Doug	83TTR	5	$ .02	$ .10
Bair, Doug	84T	536	$ .01	$ .05
Bair, Doug	85T	744	$ .01	$ .04
Bakenhaster, Dave	64T	479	$ .40	$1.25
Baker, Chuck	79T	456	$ .02	$ .10
Baker, Chuck	82T	253	$ .01	$ .06
Baker, Del	54T	133	$2.10	$7.50
Baker, Del	60T	456	$1.25	$4.50
Baker, Doug	85T	269	$ .01	$ .04
Baker, Dusty	71T	709	$7.00	$22.50
Baker, Dusty	72T	764	$ .95	$3.50
Baker, Dusty	73T	215	$ .25	$ .65
Baker, Dusty	74T	320	$ .25	$ .85
Baker, Dusty	75T	33	$ .06	$ .25
Baker, Dusty	76T	28	$ .07	$ .25
Baker, Dusty	76TTR	28	$ .07	$ .25
Baker, Dusty	77T	146	$ .05	$ .15
Baker, Dusty	78T	668	$ .05	$ .25
Baker, Dusty	79T	562	$ .05	$ .20
Baker, Dusty	80T	255	$ .01	$ .07
Baker, Dusty	81T	495	$ .01	$ .07
Baker, Dusty	82T	311	$ .01	$ .06
Baker, Dusty	82T	375	$ .01	$ .06
Baker, Dusty	83T	220	$ .01	$ .06
Baker, Dusty	84T	40	$ .01	$ .05
Baker, Dusty	84TTR	5	$ .05	$ .20
Baker, Dusty	85T	165	$ .01	$ .04
Baker, Dusty	85TTR	4	$ .02	$ .10
Baker, Dusty	86T	645	$ .01	$ .03
Baker, Dusty	87T	565	$ .01	$ .03
Baker, Floyd	52T	292	$14.00	$45.00
Baker, Frank	70T	704	$ .50	$2.00

Player	Year	No.	VG	EX/MT	Player	Year	No.	VG	EX/MT
Baker, Frank	71T	213	$ .10	$ .35	Bane, Ed	74T	592	$ .06	$ .25
Baker, Frank	71T	689	$ .70	$2.10	Bane, Ed	77T	486	$ .05	$ .15
Baker, Frank	72T	409	$ .10	$ .35	Baney, Dick	70T	88	$ .10	$ .35
Baker, Frank	74T	411	$ .06	$ .25	Baney, Dick	74T	608	$ .06	$ .25
Baker, Gene	56T	142	$1.25	$4.50	Bankhead, Scott	85T	393	$ .05	$ .75
Baker, Gene	57T	176	$ .95	$3.50	Bankhead, Scott	87T	508	$ .01	$ .10
Baker, Gene	58T	358	$ .50	$2.00	Bankhead, Scott	87TTR	2	$ .01	$ .07
Baker, Gene	59T	238	$ .50	$1.95	Bankhead, Scott	88T	738	$ .01	$ .03
Baker, Gene	60T	539	$2.00	$7.00	Bankhead, Scott	89T	79	$ .01	$ .04
Baker, Gene	61T	339	$ .30	$1.00	Bankhead, Scott	90T	213	$ .01	$ .03
Baker, Steve	83TTR	6	$ .02	$ .10	Banks, Ernie	54T	94	$150.00	$475.00
Balaz, John	76T	539	$ .05	$ .20	Banks, Ernie	55T	28	$35.00	$125.00
Balboni, Steve	82T	83	$ .15	$ .50	Banks, Ernie	56T	15	$21.00	$65.00
Balboni, Steve	83T	8	$ .10	$ .50	Banks, Ernie	57T	55	$20.00	$60.00
Balboni, Steve	84T	782	$ .01	$ .05	Banks, Ernie	58T	310	$15.00	$45.00
Balboni, Steve	84TTR	6	$ .05	$ .25	Banks, Ernie	58TAS	482	$3.50	$9.50
Balboni, Steve	85T	486	$ .01	$ .04	Banks, Ernie	59T	147	$3.50	$10.00
Balboni, Steve	86T	164	$ .01	$ .03	Banks, Ernie	59T	350	$20.00	$80.00
Balboni, Steve	87T	240	$ .01	$ .03	Banks, Ernie	59T	469	$2.00	$7.00
Balboni, Steve	88T	638	$ .01	$ .03	Banks, Ernie	59TAS	559	$10.00	$30.00
Balboni, Steve	89T	336	$ .01	$ .04	Banks, Ernie	60T	10	$6.50	$23.50
Balboni, Steve	89TTR	6	$ .01	$ .05	Banks, Ernie	60TAS	560	$7.00	$22.00
Balboni, Steve	90T	716	$ .01	$ .03	Banks, Ernie	61T	43	$1.50	$5.75
Baldschun, Jack	62T	46	$ .35	$1.10	Banks, Ernie	61T	350	$7.00	$25.00
Baldschun, Jack	63T	341	$ .35	$1.20	Banks, Ernie	61TAS	575	$20.00	$65.00
Baldschun, Jack	64T	520	$ .40	$1.25	Banks, Ernie	61TMVP	485	$3.75	$12.00
Baldschun, Jack	65T	555	$1.50	$3.75	Banks, Ernie	62T	25	$7.50	$20.00
Baldschun, Jack	66T	272	$ .25	$ .85	Banks, Ernie	63T	3	$2.35	$9.00
Baldschun, Jack	67T	114	$ .25	$ .65	Banks, Ernie	63T	242	$7.00	$20.00
Baldschun, Jack	70T	284	$ .10	$ .35	Banks, Ernie	63T	380	$9.50	$30.00
Baldwin, Dave	68T	231	$ .25	$ .65	Banks, Ernie	64T	55	$$5.50	$23.00
Baldwin, Dave	69T	132	$ .25	$ .65	Banks, Ernie	65T	510	$10.00	$40.00
Baldwin, Dave	70T	613	$ .25	$ .85	Banks, Ernie	66T	110	$4.00	$13.00
Baldwin, Dave	71T	48	$ .10	$ .35	Banks, Ernie	67T	215	$4.00	$13.00
Baldwin, Reggie	80T	678	$ .01	$ .07	Banks, Ernie	68T	355	$2.50	$8.50
Baldwin, Rick	76T	372	$ .05	$ .20	Banks, Ernie	69T	6	$ .80	$2.50
Baldwin, Rick	77T	587	$ .05	$ .15	Banks, Ernie	69T	20	$3.00	$9.00
Bales, Wes	67T	51	$ .25	$ .65	Banks, Ernie	70T	630	$6.00	$18.00
Ballard, Jeff	88T	782	$ .01	$ .35	Banks, Ernie	71T	525	$5.00	$15.00
Ballard, Jeff	89T	69	$ .01	$ .10	Banks, Ernie	73T	81	$ .25	$ .85
Ballard, Jeff	90T	296	$ .01	$ .03	Banks, Ernie	75T	196	$ .30	$1.00
Ballard, Jeff	90TAS	394	$ .01	$ .03	Banks, Ernie	75T	197	$ .30	$1.00
Baller, Jay	88T	717	$ .01	$ .03	Banks, George	63T	564	$1.50	$3.75
Bamberger, George	59T	529	$3.00	$9.00	Banks, George	64T	223	$ .25	$ .85
Bamberger, George	73T	136	$ .15	$ .50	Banks, George	65T	348	$ .30	$1.00
Bamberger, George	74T	306	$ .15	$ .50	Banks, George	66T	488	$ .70	$2.10
Bamberger, George	83T	246	$ .01	$ .06	Bannister, Alan	77T	559	$ .05	$ .15
Bamberger, George	85TTR	5	$ .02	$ .10	Bannister, Alan	78T	213	$ .02	$ .10
Bamberger, George	86T	21	$ .01	$ .03	Bannister, Alan	79T	134	$ .02	$ .10
Bamberger, George	87T	468	$ .01	$ .03	Bannister, Alan	80T	608	$ .01	$ .07
Bando, Chris	81T	451	$ .01	$ .07	Bannister, Alan	81T	032	$ .01	$ .07
Bando, Chris	82T	141	$ .50	$1.50	Bannister, Alan	82T	287	$ .01	$ .06
Bando, Chris	83T	227	$ .01	$ .06	Bannister, Alan	83T	348	$ .01	$ .06
Bando, Chris	84T	431	$ .01	$ .05	Bannister, Alan	84T	478	$ .01	$ .05
Bando, Chris	85T	14	$ .01	$ .04	Bannister, Alan	84TTR	7	$ .02	$ .10
Bando, Chris	86T	594	$ .01	$ .03	Bannister, Alan	85T	76	$ .01	$ .04
Bando, Chris	87T	322	$ .01	$ .03	Bannister, Alan	86T	784	$ .01	$ .03
Bando, Chris	88T	604	$ .01	$ .03	Bannister, Floyd	78T	39	$ .25	$1.00
Bando, Sal	67T	33	$ .50	$2.00	Bannister, Floyd	79T	306	$ .02	$ .10
Bando, Sal	68T	146	$ .30	$1.00	Bannister, Floyd	80T	699	$ .01	$ .07
Bando, Sal	69T	371	$ .25	$ .85	Bannister, Floyd	81T	166	$ .01	$ .07
Bando, Sal	69T	556	$ .30	$1.00	Bannister, Floyd	82T	468	$ .01	$ .06
Bando, Sal	70T	120	$ .25	$ .65	Bannister, Floyd	83T	545	$ .01	$ .06
Bando, Sal	71T	285	$ .25	$ .85	Bannister, Floyd	83T	706	$ .01	$ .10
Bando, Sal	72T	348	$ .10	$ .35	Bannister, Floyd	83TTR	7	$ .02	$ .10
Bando, Sal	72T	650	$ .35	$1.10	Bannister, Floyd	84T	280	$ .01	$ .05
Bando, Sal	73T	155	$ .15	$ .50	Bannister, Floyd	85T	274	$ .01	$ .04
Bando, Sal	74T	103	$ .06	$ .25	Bannister, Floyd	85T	725	$ .01	$ .04
Bando, Sal	75T	380	$ .10	$ .35	Bannister, Floyd	86T	64	$ .01	$ .03
Bando, Sal	76T	90	$ .05	$ .20	Bannister, Floyd	87T	737	$ .01	$ .03
Bando, Sal	77T	498	$ .05	$ .15	Bannister, Floyd	88T	357	$ .01	$ .03
Bando, Sal	78T	265	$ .02	$ .10	Bannister, Floyd	88TBB	174	$ .01	$ .05
Bando, Sal	79T	550	$ .02	$ .10	Bannister, Floyd	88TTR	8	$ .01	$ .05
Bando, Sal	80T	715	$ .01	$ .07	Bannister, Floyd	89T	638	$ .01	$ .04
Bando, Sal	81T	623	$ .01	$ .07	Bannister, Floyd	90T	116	$ .01	$ .03

Player	Year	No.	VG	EX/MT	Player	Year	No.	VG	EX/MT
Barber, Steve	60T	514	$2.00	$7.00	Barrett, Marty	84T	683	$ .25	$1.25
Barber, Steve	61T	125	$ .30	$1.00	Barrett, Marty	85T	298	$ .01	$ .04
Barber, Steve	62T	57	$ .50	$1.95	Barrett, Marty	86T	734	$ .01	$ .03
Barber, Steve	62T	355	$ .35	$1.10	Barrett, Marty	87T	39	$ .01	$ .03
Barber, Steve	63T	12	$ .25	$ .85	Barrett, Marty	88T	525	$ .01	$ .03
Barber, Steve	64T	450	$ .40	$1.25	Barrett, Marty	88TBB	54	$ .01	$ .05
Barber, Steve	65T	113	$ .25	$ .65	Barrett, Marty	89T	155	$ .01	$ .04
Barber, Steve	66T	477	$ .70	$2.10	Barrett, Marty	89TBB	278	$ .01	$ .05
Barber, Steve	67T	82	$ .25	$ .65	Barrett, Marty	90T	355	$ .01	$ .03
Barber, Steve	68T	316	$ .25	$ .65	Barrett, Tommy	89T	653	$ .01	$ .10
Barber, Steve	69T	233	$ .25	$ .85	Barrett, Tommy	89TBB	177	$ .01	$ .05
Barber, Steve	70T	224	$ .10	$ .35	Barrios, Francisco	77T	222	$ .05	$ .15
Barber, Steve	72T	333	$ .10	$ .35	Barrios, Francisco	78T	552	$ .02	$ .10
Barber, Steve	73T	36	$ .06	$ .25	Barrios, Francisco	79T	386	$ .02	$ .10
Barber, Steve	74T	631	$ .06	$ .25	Barrios, Francisco	80T	107	$ .01	$ .07
Barberie, Bret	88TTR	9	$ .01	$ .35	Bartirome, Tony	52T	332	$39.00	$135.00
Barberie, Bret	89TBB	19	$ .01	$ .05	Bartirome, Tony	53T	71	$3.75	$13.00
Barbieri, Jim	67T	76	$ .25	$ .65	Barton, Bob	66T	511	$ .70	$2.10
Barclay, Curt	57T	361	$1.00	$3.75	Barton, Bob	67T	462	$ .50	$2.00
Barclay, Curt	58T	21	$1.00	$3.75	Barton, Bob	68T	351	$ .25	$ .65
Barclay, Curt	59T	307	$ .50	$1.95	Barton, Bob	69T	41	$ .25	$ .65
Bare, Ray	76T	507	$ .05	$ .20	Barton, Bob	70T	352	$ .10	$ .35
Bare, Ray	77T	43	$ .05	$ .15	Barton, Bob	71T	589	$ .30	$1.00
Barfield, Jesse	82T	203	$ .70	$3.50	Barton, Bob	72T	39	$ .10	$ .35
Barfield, Jesse	82TTR	2	$ .50	$2.25	Barton, Bob	72TIA	40	$ .10	$ .35
Barfield, Jesse	83T	257	$ .15	$ .75	Barton, Bob	73T	626	$ .35	$1.10
Barfield, Jesse	84T	488	$ .06	$ .30	Basgall, Monty	52T	12	$14.00	$45.00
Barfield, Jesse	85T	24	$ .04	$ .20	Basgall, Monty	73T	569	$1.00	$3.75
Barfield, Jesse	86T	593	$ .01	$ .10	Basgall, Monty	74T	144	$ .50	$2.00
Barfield, Jesse	87T	655	$ .01	$ .10	Bass, Kevin	79T	708	$ .35	$1.10
Barfield, Jesse	88T	140	$ .01	$ .10	Bass, Kevin	84T	538	$ .01	$ .05
Barfield, Jesse	88TBB	92	$ .05	$ .25	Bass, Kevin	85T	326	$ .01	$ .04
Barfield, Jesse	89T	325	$ .01	$ .10	Bass, Kevin	86T	458	$ .01	$ .03
Barfield, Jesse	89TTR	7	$ .01	$ .10	Bass, Kevin	87T	85	$ .01	$ .03
Barfield, Jesse	90T	740	$ .01	$ .03	Bass, Kevin	88T	175	$ .01	$ .03
Barfield, John	89TMLD	8	$ .01	$ .15	Bass, Kevin	88TBB	77	$ .01	$ .05
Bargar, Greg	84T	474	$ .01	$ .05					
Barker, Len	77T	489	$ .25	$ .65					
Barker, Len	78T	634	$ .02	$ .10					
Barker, Len	79T	94	$ .02	$ .10					
Barker, Len	80T	227	$ .01	$ .07					
Barker, Len	81T	6	$ .02	$ .10					
Barker, Len	81T	432	$ .01	$ .07					
Barker, Len	82T	166	$ .03	$ .15					
Barker, Len	82T	360	$ .01	$ .06					
Barker, Len	83T	120	$ .01	$ .06					
Barker, Len	84T	614	$ .01	$ .05					
Barker, Len	85T	557	$ .01	$ .04					
Barker, Len	86T	24	$ .01	$ .03					
Barker, Ray	61T	428	$ .50	$2.00					
Barker, Ray	65T	546	$1.50	$3.75					
Barker, Ray	66T	323	$ .25	$ .85					
Barker, Ray	67T	583	$5.00	$18.00					
Barkley, Jeff	86T	567	$ .01	$ .03					
Barlow, Mike	78T	429	$ .02	$ .10					
Barlow, Mike	80T	312	$ .01	$ .07					
Barlow, Mike	81T	77	$ .01	$ .07					
Barnes, Frank	60T	538	$2.00	$7.00					
Barnowski, Ed	66T	442	$ .25	$ .85					
Barnowski, Ed	67T	507	$ .50	$2.00					
Barr, Jim	72T	232	$ .10	$ .35					
Barr, Jim	73T	387	$ .06	$ .25					
Barr, Jim	74T	233	$ .06	$ .25					
Barr, Jim	75T	107	$ .06	$ .25					
Barr, Jim	76T	308	$ .05	$ .20					
Barr, Jim	77T	609	$ .05	$ .15					
Barr, Jim	78T	62	$ .02	$ .10					
Barr, Jim	79T	461	$ .02	$ .10					
Barr, Jim	80T	529	$ .01	$ .07	Bass, Kevin	89T	646	$ .01	$ .04
Barr, Jim	81T	717	$ .01	$ .07	Bass, Kevin	89TBB	187	$ .01	$ .05
Barr, Jim	83T	133	$ .01	$ .06	Bass, Kevin	90T	281	$ .01	$ .03
Barr, Jim	84T	282	$ .01	$ .05	Bass, Norm	62T	122	$ .35	$1.10
Barr, Steve	76T	595	$ .05	$ .20	Bass, Norm	63T	461	$2.50	$6.50
Barragan, Cuno	63T	557	$1.50	$3.75	Bass, Randy	79T	707	$ .02	$ .10
Barragon, Cuno	62T	66	$ .35	$1.10	Bass, Randy	82T	307	$ .01	$ .06

KEVIN BASS

Player	Year	No.	VG	EX/MT	Player	Year	No.	VG	EX/MT
Bateman, John	63T	386	$ .50	$1.95	Baxes, Mike	59T	381	$ .50	$1.95
Bateman, John	64T	142	$ .25	$ .85	Baylor, Don	71T	709	$7.00	$22.50
Bateman, John	65T	433	$ .30	$1.00	Baylor, Don	72T	474	$ .50	$2.35
Bateman, John	66T	86	$ .25	$ .85	Baylor, Don	73T	384	$ .30	$1.50
Bateman, John	67T	231	$ .25	$ .65	Baylor, Don	74T	187	$ .25	$ .85
Bateman, John	68T	592	$ .30	$1.00	Baylor, Don	75T	382	$ .25	$ .85
Bateman, John	69T	138	$ .25	$ .65	Baylor, Don	76T	125	$ .10	$ .35
Bateman, John	70T	417	$ .10	$ .35	Baylor, Don	77T	462	$ .25	$ .65
Bateman, John	71T	628	$ .30	$1.00	Baylor, Don	78T	48	$ .05	$ .25
Bateman, John	72T	5	$ .10	$ .35	Baylor, Don	79T	635	$ .15	$ .50
Bates, Billy	89TMLD	9	$ .01	$ .35	Baylor, Don	80T	203	$ .08	$ .30
Batiste, Kevin	89TMLD	10	$ .01	$ .15	Baylor, Don	80T	285	$ .05	$ .20
Battey, Earl	57T	401	$1.00	$3.75	Baylor, Don	81T	580	$ .03	$ .15
Battey, Earl	58T	364	$ .50	$2.00	Baylor, Don	82T	415	$ .03	$ .15
Battey, Earl	59T	114	$ .50	$1.95	Baylor, Don	83T	105	$ .01	$ .10
Battey, Earl	60T	328	$ .50	$1.95	Baylor, Don	83TTR	8	$ .05	$ .25
Battey, Earl	61T	315	$ .30	$1.00	Baylor, Don	84T	335	$ .02	$ .10
Battey, Earl	61TAS	582	$6.00	$18.00	Baylor, Don	84T	486	$ .01	$ .05
Battey, Earl	62T	371	$ .70	$2.10	Baylor, Don	85T	70	$ .01	$ .10
Battey, Earl	63T	306	$ .50	$1.95	Baylor, Don	86T	765	$ .01	$ .03
Battey, Earl	63T	410	$ .35	$1.20	Baylor, Don	86TTR	6	$ .03	$ .15
Battey, Earl	64T	90	$ .25	$ .85	Baylor, Don	87T	230	$ .01	$ .03
Battey, Earl	65T	490	$ .50	$2.00	Baylor, Don	88T	545	$ .01	$ .03
Battey, Earl	66T	240	$ .25	$ .85	Baylor, Don	88TBB	162	$ .01	$ .10
Battey, Earl	67T	15	$ .25	$ .65	Baylor, Don	88TTR	11	$ .01	$ .05
Batton, Chris	77T	475	$ .05	$ .15	Baylor, Don	89T	673	$ .01	$ .05
Batts, Matt	52T	230	$6.00	$19.00	Beall, Bob	79T	222	$ .02	$ .10
Batts, Matt	54T	88	$2.10	$7.50	Beamon, Charley	59T	192	$ .50	$1.95
Bauer, Hank	51Trb	24	$2.50	$10.00	Beamon, Charlie	80T	672	$ .01	$ .07
Bauer, Hank	52T	215	$13.00	$38.00	Beane, Billy	87T	114	$ .01	$ .03
Bauer, Hank	54T	130	$7.00	$21.00	Bean(e), Billy	88T	267	$ .01	$ .03
Bauer, Hank	55T	166	$8.50	$27.50	Beard, Dave	81T	96	$ .01	$ .07
Bauer, Hank	56T	177	$3.50	$12.50	Beard, Dave	83T	102	$ .01	$ .06
Bauer, Hank	57T	240	$3.00	$9.00	Beard, Dave	84T	513	$ .01	$ .05
Bauer, Hank	58T	9	$1.20	$4.00	Beard, Dave	84TTR	8	$ .02	$ .10
Bauer, Hank	59T	240	$1.35	$4.00	Beard, Dave	85T	232	$ .01	$ .04
Bauer, Hank	60T	262	$ .60	$1.75	Beard, Mike	76T	53	$ .05	$ .20
Bauer, Hank	61T	119	$ .35	$1.10	Beard, Ted	52T	150	$6.00	$19.00
Bauer, Hank	61T	398	$ .60	$1.75	Beardon, Gene	52T	229	$6.00	$19.00
Bauer, Hank	62T	127	$ .50	$2.00	Beare, Gary	78T	516	$ .02	$ .10
Bauer, Hank	62T	463	$1.00	$3.75	Bearnarth, Larry	63T	386	$ .50	$1.95
Bauer, Hank	64T	178	$ .25	$ .85	Bearnarth, Larry	64T	527	$1.50	$3.75
Bauer, Hank	65T	323	$ .30	$1.00	Bearnarth, Larry	65T	258	$ .30	$1.00
Bauer, Hank	66T	229	$ .15	$ .50	Bearnarth, Larry	66T	464	$ .70	$2.10
Bauer, Hank	67T	1	$5.00	$15.00	Beattie, Jim	79T	179	$ .02	$ .10
Bauer, Hank	67T	534	$3.00	$9.00	Beattie, Jim	80T	334	$ .01	$ .07
Bauer, Hank	68T	513	$ .50	$2.00	Beattie, Jim	81T	443	$ .01	$ .07
Bauer, Hank	69T	124	$ .25	$ .85	Beattie, Jim	82T	22	$ .01	$ .06
Baumann, Frank	58T	167	$ .50	$2.00	Beattie, Jim	83T	675	$ .01	$ .06
Baumann, Frank	59T	161	$ .50	$1.95	Beattie, Jim	83T	711	$ .01	$ .06
Baumann, Frank	60T	306	$ .60	$1.05	Beattie, Jim	84T	288	$ .01	$ .05
Baumann, Frank	61T	46	$ .50	$2.00	Beattie, Jim	85T	505	$ .01	$ .04
Baumann, Frank	61T	550	$6.00	$18.00	Beattie, Jim	86T	729	$ .01	$ .03
Baumann, Frank	62T	161	$ .35	$1.10	Beattie, Jim	87T	117	$ .01	$ .03
Baumann, Frank	63T	381	$ .35	$1.20	Beatty, Blaine	89TMLD	11	$ .01	$ .25
Baumann, Frank	64T	453	$ .40	$1.25	Beauchamp, Jim	64T	492	$ .40	$1.25
Baumann, Frank	65T	161	$ .25	$ .65	Beauchamp, Jim	65T	409	$ .30	$1.00
Baumer, Jim	61T	292	$ .30	$1.00	Beauchamp, Jim	66T	84	$ .25	$ .85
Baumgarten, Ross	79T	704	$ .02	$ .10	Beauchamp, Jim	67T	307	$ .25	$ .65
Baumgarten, Ross	80T	138	$ .01	$ .07	Beauchamp, Jim	69T	613	$ .25	$ .85
Baumgarten, Ross	81T	398	$ .01	$ .07	Beauchamp, Jim	71T	322	$ .10	$ .35
Baumgarten, Ross	82T	563	$ .01	$ .06	Beauchamp, Jim	72T	594	$ .25	$ .85
Baumgarten, Ross	82TTR	3	$ .02	$ .10	Beauchamp, Jim	73T	137	$ .06	$ .25
Baumgarten, Ross	83T	97	$ .01	$ .06	Beauchamp, Jim	74T	424	$ .06	$ .25
Baumholtz, Frank	52T	225	$6.00	$19.00	Beck, Rich	66T	234	$1.50	$5.00
Baumholtz, Frank	54T	60	$4.75	$14.00	Becker, Joe	60T	463	$ .85	$2.25
Baumholtz, Frank	55T	172	$3.25	$9.00	Beckert, Glenn	65T	549	$2.00	$5.00
Baumholtz, Frank	56T	274	$1.80	$6.00	Beckert, Glenn	66T	232	$ .25	$ .85
Bauta, Ed	62T	344	$ .35	$1.10	Beckert, Glenn	67T	296	$ .25	$ .65
Bauta, Ed	63T	336	$ .35	$1.20	Beckert, Glenn	68T	101	$ .25	$ .65
Bautista, Jose	88TTR	10	$ .01	$ .10	Beckert, Glenn	69T	171	$ .25	$ .65
Bautista, Jose	89T	469	$ .01	$ .10	Beckert, Glenn	70T	480	$ .10	$ .35
Baxes, Jim	59T	547	$2.00	$7.00	Beckert, Glenn	71T	390	$ .10	$ .35
Baxes, Jim	60T	318	$ .50	$1.95	Beckert, Glenn	72T	45	$ .10	$ .35
Baxes, Mike	58T	302	$ .50	$2.00	Beckert, Glenn	72T	85	$ .30	$1.00

TOPPS

Player	Year	No.	VG	EX/MT
Beckert, Glenn	72TIA	46	$ .10	$ .35
Beckert, Glenn	73T	440	$ .25	$ .65
Beckert, Glenn	74T	241	$ .06	$ .25
Beckert, Glenn	75T	484	$ .06	$ .25
Beckwith, Joe	80T	679	$ .01	$ .07
Beckwith, Joe	81T	231	$ .01	$ .07
Beckwith, Joe	84T	454	$ .01	$ .05
Beckwith, Joe	84TTR	9	$ .02	$ .10
Beckwith, Joe	85T	77	$ .01	$ .04
Beckwith, Joe	86T	562	$ .01	$ .03
Becquer, Julio	58T	458	$ .50	$1.95
Becquer, Julio	59T	93	$1.00	$3.75
Becquer, Julio	60T	271	$ .35	$1.10
Becquer, Julio	61T	329	$ .30	$1.00
Bedell, Howie	61T	353	$ .30	$1.00
Bedell, Howie	62T	76	$ .35	$1.10
Bedrosian, Steve	82T	502	$ .50	$2.00
Bedrosian, Steve	82TTR	4	$ .60	$1.75
Bedrosian, Steve	83T	157	$ .01	$ .06
Bedrosian, Steve	84T	365	$ .01	$ .05
Bedrosian, Steve	85T	25	$ .01	$ .04
Bedrosian, Steve	86T	648	$ .01	$ .03
Bedrosian, Steve	86TTR	7	$ .02	$ .10
Bedrosian, Steve	87T	736	$ .03	$ .15
Bedrosian, Steve	88T	440	$ .01	$ .03
Bedrosian, Steve	88TAS	407	$ .01	$ .03
Bedrosian, Steve	88TBB	23	$ .01	$ .05
Bedrosian, Steve	89T	20	$ .01	$ .04
Bedrosian, Steve	89TBB	137	$ .01	$ .10
Bedrosian, Steve	89TTR	8	$ .01	$ .05
Bedrosian, Steve	90T	310	$ .01	$ .03
Beene, Fred	70T	121	$ .10	$ .35
Beene, Fred	73T	573	$ .35	$1.10
Beene, Fred	74T	274	$ .06	$ .25
Beene, Fred	75T	181	$ .06	$ .25
Behney, Mel	72T	524	$ .10	$ .35
Behney, Mel	73T	602	$ .35	$1.10
Belanger, Mark	67T	558	$6.50	$24.00
Belanger, Mark	68T	118	$ .25	$ .85
Belanger, Mark	69T	299	$ .25	$ .85
Belanger, Mark	70T	615	$ .35	$1.10
Belanger, Mark	71T	99	$ .10	$ .35
Belanger, Mark	72T	456	$ .25	$ .65
Belanger, Mark	73T	253	$ .06	$ .25
Belanger, Mark	74T	329	$ .06	$ .25
Belanger, Mark	75T	74	$ .06	$ .25
Belanger, Mark	76T	505	$ .05	$ .20
Belanger, Mark	77T	135	$ .05	$ .15
Belanger, Mark	78T	315	$ .02	$ .10
Belanger, Mark	79T	65	$ .02	$ .10
Belanger, Mark	80T	425	$ .02	$ .10
Belanger, Mark	81T	641	$ .02	$ .10
Belanger, Mark	82T	776	$ .02	$ .10
Belanger, Mark	82TTR	5	$ .05	$ .20
Belanger, Mark	83T	273	$ .01	$ .06
Belcher, Tim	85T	281	$ .10	$1.50
Belcher, Tim	88TTR	12	$ .01	$ .05
Belcher, Tim	89T	456	$ .01	$ .04
Belcher, Tim	89TBB	145	$ .01	$ .05
Belcher, Tim	90T	173	$ .01	$ .03
Belinda, Stan	89TMLD	12	$ .01	$ .15
Belinda, Stan	90T	354	$ .01	$ .10
Belinsky, Bo	62T	592	$13.00	$40.00
Belinsky, Bo	63T	33	$ .50	$2.00
Belinsky, Bo	64T	315	$ .35	$1.10
Belinsky, Bo	65T	225	$ .35	$1.10
Belinsky, Bo	66T	506	$ .60	$1.75
Belinsky, Bo	67T	447	$ .35	$1.10
Belinsky, Bo	69T	366	$ .15	$ .50
Bell, Buddy	73T	31	$1.65	$5.00
Bell, Buddy	74T	257	$ .50	$1.95
Bell, Buddy	75T	38	$ .35	$1.10
Bell, Buddy	76T	66	$ .25	$ .85
Bell, Buddy	76T	358	$ .15	$ .50
Bell, Buddy	77T	590	$ .15	$ .50
Bell, Buddy	78T	280	$ .25	$ .65
Bell, Buddy	79T	690	$ .05	$ .20
Bell, Buddy	80T	190	$ .25	$ .65
Bell, Buddy	81T	475	$ .05	$ .20
Bell, Buddy	82T	50	$ .03	$ .15
Bell, Buddy	83T	330	$ .01	$ .15
Bell, Buddy	83T	412	$ .01	$ .06
Bell, Buddy	84T	37	$ .01	$ .05
Bell, Buddy	84T	665	$ .03	$ .15
Bell, Buddy	85T	131	$ .01	$ .10
Bell, Buddy	85T	745	$ .01	$ .10
Bell, Buddy	86T	285	$ .01	$ .10
Bell, Buddy	87T	545	$ .01	$ .03
Bell, Buddy	88T	130	$ .01	$ .10
Bell, Buddy	88TTR	13	$ .01	$ .05
Bell, Buddy	89T	461	$ .01	$ .04
Bell, Buddy	89TBB	270	$ .01	$ .05
Bell, Eric	87TTR	3	$ .05	$ .25
Bell, Eric	88T	383	$ .01	$ .03
Bell, Gary	59T	327	$ .50	$1.95
Bell, Gary	60T	441	$ .60	$1.75
Bell, Gary	61T	274	$ .30	$1.00
Bell, Gary	62T	273	$ .35	$1.10
Bell, Gary	63T	129	$ .25	$ .85
Bell, Gary	64T	234	$ .25	$ .85
Bell, Gary	65T	424	$ .30	$1.00
Bell, Gary	66T	525	$4.50	$15.00
Bell, Gary	67T	479	$ .50	$2.00
Bell, Gary	68T	43	$ .25	$ .65
Bell, Gary	69T	377	$ .25	$ .65
Bell, George (Jorge)	82T	254	$2.25	$9.00
Bell, George (Jorge)	84T	278	$ .35	$1.50
Bell, George (Jorge)	85T	698	$ .10	$ .50
Bell, George (Jorge)	86T	338	$ .04	$ .35
Bell, George	86TAS	718	$ .02	$ .15
Bell, George	87T	681	$ .25	$ .85
Bell, George	87TAS	612	$ .01	$ .10
Bell, George	88T	590	$ .01	$ .20
Bell, George	88TAS	390	$ .01	$ .10
Bell, George	88TBB	15	$ .01	$ .15
Bell, George	89T	50	$ .01	$ .04
Bell, George	89TBB	318	$ .01	$ .10
Bell, George	89TRB	1	$ .01	$ .04
Bell, George	90T	170	$ .01	$ .03
Bell, Dave (Gus)	51Trb	17	$2.00	$7.00
Bell, Gus	52T	170	$7.00	$20.00
Bell, Gus	53T	118	$4.50	$15.00
Bell, Gus	56T	162	$2.50	$8.00
Bell, Gus	57T	180	$1.35	$5.00
Bell, Gus	58T	75	$ .70	$2.25
Bell, Gus	59T	365	$ .60	$1.75
Bell, Gus	60T	235	$ .60	$1.75
Bell, Gus	60T	352	$ .90	$3.50
Bell, Gus	61T	25	$1.35	$4.00
Bell, Gus	61T	215	$ .30	$1.00
Bell, Gus	62T	408	$1.00	$3.75
Bell, Gus	63T	547	$1.50	$3.75
Bell, Gus	64T	534	$1.50	$3.75
Bell, Gus	76T	66	$ .25	$ .85
Bell, Gus	85T	131	$ .01	$ .10
Bell, Gus	88T	637	$ .01	$ .15
Bell, Jay	89T	144	$ .01	$ .04
Bell, Jay	90T	523	$ .01	$ .03
Bell, Jerry	72T	162	$ .25	$ .75
Bell, Jerry	73T	92	$ .06	$ .25
Bell, Jerry	74T	261	$ .06	$ .25
Bell, Juan	89TMLD	13	$ .01	$ .25
Bell, Juan	90T	724	$ .01	$ .15
Bell, Kevin	77T	83	$ .05	$ .15
Bell, Kevin	78T	463	$ .02	$ .10
Bell, Kevin	79T	662	$ .02	$ .10
Bell, Kevin	80T	379	$ .01	$ .07
Bella, Zeke	59T	254	$ .50	$1.95
Belle, Joey	89TMLD	14	$ .01	$ .50
Belle, Joey	90T	283	$ .01	$ .50

Player	Year	No.	VG	EX/MT
Belliard, Rafael	87T	541	$ .01	$ .10
Belliard, Rafael	88T	221	$ .01	$ .03
Belliard, Rafael	88TBB	175	$ .01	$ .05
Belliard, Rafael	89T	723	$ .01	$ .04
Belliard, Rafael	89TBB	196	$ .01	$ .05
Belliard, Rafael	90T	143	$ .01	$ .03
Belloir, Rob	77T	312	$ .05	$ .15
Belloir, Rob	78T	681	$ .02	$ .10
Bench, Johnny	68T	247	$90.00	$325.00
Bench, Johnny	69T	95	$30.00	$125.00
Bench, Johnny	69TAS	430	$3.00	$10.00
Bench, Johnny	70T	660	$40.00	$130.00
Bench, Johnny	70TAS	464	$2.00	$7.50
Bench, Johnny	71T	64	$ .60	$1.75
Bench, Johnny	71T	66	$ .60	$1.75
Bench, Johnny	71T	250	$8.00	$30.00
Bench, Johnny	72T	433	$8.00	$30.00
Bench, Johnny	72TIA	434	$3.00	$12.50
Bench, Johnny	73T	62	$ .50	$2.00
Bench, Johnny	73T	63	$ .50	$2.00
Bench, Johnny	73T	380	$6.00	$17.50
Bench, Johnny	74T	10	$3.00	$10.00
Bench, Johnny	74TAS	331	$1.50	$5.00
Bench, Johnny	75T	208	$ .45	$1.75
Bench, Johnny	75T	210	$ .50	$2.00
Bench, Johnny	75T	260	$2.50	$9.00
Bench, Johnny	75T	308	$ .30	$1.00
Bench, Johnny	76T	195	$ .30	$1.00
Bench, Johnny	76T	300	$3.00	$9.00
Bench, Johnny	77T	70	$1.50	$6.50
Bench, Johnny	78T	700	$1.25	$5.00
Bench, Johnny	79T	200	$ .50	$2.50
Bench, Johnny	80T	100	$ .95	$3.50
Bench, Johnny	81T	600	$ .35	$1.30
Bench, Johnny	81TRB	201	$ .10	$ .50
Bench, Johnny	82T	400	$ .35	$1.30
Bench, Johnny	82TIA	401	$ .12	$ .50
Bench, Johnny	83T	60	$ .25	$1.00
Bench, Johnny	83T	61	$ .05	$ .25
Bench, Johnny	84T	6	$ .10	$ .50
Bench, Johnny	90TTB	664	$ .01	$ .03
Bene, Bill	89T	84	$ .01	$ .25
Benedict, Bruce	79T	715	$ .05	$ .20
Benedict, Bruce	80T	675	$ .01	$ .07
Benedict, Bruce	81T	108	$ .01	$ .07
Benedict, Bruce	82T	424	$ .01	$ .06
Benedict, Bruce	83T	521	$ .01	$ .06
Benedict, Bruce	84T	255	$ .01	$ .05
Benedict, Bruce	85T	335	$ .01	$ .04
Benedict, Bruce	86T	78	$ .01	$ .03
Benedict, Bruce	87T	186	$ .01	$ .03
Benedict, Bruce	88T	652	$ .01	$ .03
Benedict, Bruce	89T	778	$ .01	$ .04
Benedict, Bruce	89TBB	83	$ .01	$ .05
Benedict, Bruce	90T	583	$ .01	$ .03
Benes, Andy	88TTR	14	$ .25	$3.50
Benes, Andy	89T	437	$ .05	$1.25
Benes, Andy	89TBB	114	$ .01	$ .35
Benes, Andy	89TMLD	15	$ .01	$ .60
Benes, Andy	90T	193	$ .01	$ .35
Beniquez, Juan	74T	647	$ .15	$ .50
Beniquez, Juan	75T	601	$ .06	$ .25
Beniquez, Juan	76T	496	$ .05	$ .20
Beniquez, Juan	77T	81	$ .05	$ .15
Beniquez, Juan	78T	238	$ .02	$ .10
Beniquez, Juan	79T	478	$ .02	$ .10
Beniquez, Juan	80T	114	$ .01	$ .07
Beniquez, Juan	81T	306	$ .01	$ .07
Beniquez, Juan	81TTR	733	$ .02	$ .10
Beniquez, Juan	82T	572	$ .01	$ .06
Beniquez, Juan	83T	678	$ .01	$ .06
Beniquez, Juan	84T	53	$ .01	$ .05
Beniquez, Juan	85T	226	$ .01	$ .04
Beniquez, Juan	86T	325	$ .01	$ .03
Beniquez, Juan	86TTR	8	$ .02	$ .10

Player	Year	No.	VG	EX/MT
Beniquez, Juan	87T	688	$ .01	$ .03
Beniquez, Juan	87TTR	4	$ .01	$ .07
Beniquez, Juan	88T	541	$ .01	$ .03
Benjamin, Mike	89TMLD	16	$ .01	$ .15
Bennett, Dave	64T	561	$1.35	$4.00
Bennett, Dave	65T	521	$ .50	$2.00
Bennett, Dennis	63T	56	$ .25	$ .85
Bennett, Dennis	64T	396	$ .40	$1.25
Bennett, Dennis	65T	147	$ .25	$ .65
Bennett, Dennis	66T	491	$ .70	$2.10
Bennett, Dennis	67T	206	$ .25	$ .65
Benson, Vern	53T	205	$3.75	$13.00
Benson, Vern	73T	497	$ .25	$ .65
Benson, Vern	74T	236	$ .06	$ .25
Benton, Al	52T	374	$39.00	$135.00
Benzinger, Todd	88T	96	$ .10	$ .60
Benzinger, Todd	89T	493	$ .01	$ .10
Benzinger, Todd	89TTR	9	$ .01	$ .05
Benzinger, Todd	90T	712	$ .01	$ .03
Berardino, Johnny	52T	253	$15.00	$40.00
Berberet, Lou	56T	329	$1.80	$6.00
Berberet, Lou	57T	315	$3.50	$13.00
Berberet, Lou	58T	383	$ .50	$2.00
Berberet, Lou	59T	96	$1.00	$3.75
Berberet, Lou	60T	6	$ .35	$1.10
Berenguer, Juan	79T	721	$ .05	$ .20
Berenguer, Juan	81T	259	$ .50	$1.50
Berenguer, Juan	82T	437	$ .01	$ .06
Berenguer, Juan	84T	174	$ .01	$ .05
Berenguer, Juan	85T	672	$ .01	$ .04
Berenguer, Juan	86T	47	$ .01	$ .03
Berenguer, Juan	86TTR	9	$ .02	$ .10
Berenguer, Juan	87T	303	$ .01	$ .03
Berenguer, Juan	87TTR	5	$ .01	$ .07
Berenguer, Juan	88T	526	$ .01	$ .03
Berenguer, Juan	88TBB	222	$ .01	$ .05

Player	Year	No.	VG	EX/MT
Berenguer, Juan	89T	294	$ .01	$ .04
Berenguer, Juan	89TBB	117	$ .01	$ .05
Berenguer, Juan	90T	709	$ .01	$ .03
Berenyi, Bruce	81T	606	$ .01	$ .07
Berenyi, Bruce	82T	459	$ .01	$ .06
Berenyi, Bruce	83T	139	$ .01	$ .06
Berenyi, Bruce	84T	297	$ .01	$ .05

TOPPS

Player	Year	No.	VG	EX/MT	Player	Year	No.	VG	EX/MT
Berenyi, Bruce	84TTR	10	$ .02	$ .10	Berroa, Geronimo	89TBB	297	$ .01	$ .10
Berenyi, Bruce	85T	27	$ .01	$ .04	Berroa, Geronimo	89TMLD	17	$ .01	$ .10
Berenyi, Bruce	86T	339	$ .01	$ .03	Berroa, Geronimo	89TTR	10	$ .01	$ .15
Berenyi, Bruce	87T	582	$ .01	$ .03	Berroa, Geronimo	90T	617	$ .01	$ .03
Bergman, Dave	78T	705	$ .02	$ .10	Berry, Ken	65T	368	$ .30	$1.00
Bergman, Dave	79T	697	$ .02	$ .10	Berry, Ken	66T	127	$ .25	$ .85
Bergman, Dave	81T	253	$ .01	$ .07	Berry, Ken	67T	67	$ .25	$ .65
Bergman, Dave	81TTR	734	$ .02	$ .10	Berry, Ken	68T	485	$ .30	$1.00
Bergman, Dave	82T	498	$ .01	$ .06	Berry, Ken	69T	494	$ .25	$ .65
Bergman, Dave	83T	32	$ .01	$ .06	Berry, Ken	70T	239	$ .10	$ .35
Bergman, Dave	84T	522	$ .01	$ .05	Berry, Ken	71T	466	$ .10	$ .35
Bergman, Dave	84TTR	11	$ .02	$ .10	Berry, Ken	72T	379	$ .10	$ .35
Bergman, Dave	85T	368	$ .01	$ .04	Berry, Ken	73T	445	$ .06	$ .25
Bergman, Dave	86T	101	$ .01	$ .03	Berry, Ken	74T	163	$ .06	$ .25
Bergman, Dave	87T	700	$ .01	$ .03	Berry, Ken	75T	432	$ .06	$ .25
Bergman, Dave	88T	289	$ .01	$ .03	Berryhill, Damon	88TTR	15	$ .01	$ .25
Bergman, Dave	89T	631	$ .01	$ .04	Berryhill, Damon	89T	543	$ .01	$ .10
Bergman, Dave	90T	77	$ .01	$ .03	Berryhill, Damon	89TBB	60	$ .01	$ .10
Beringer, Carroll	73T	486	$ .25	$ .85	Berryhill, Damon	90T	362	$ .01	$ .03
Beringer, Carroll	74T	119	$ .06	$ .25	Bertaina, Frank	65T	396	$ .30	$1.00
Bernard, Dwight	79T	721	$ .05	$ .20	Bertaina, Frank	66T	579	$4.50	$15.00
Bernard, Dwight	83T	244	$ .01	$ .06	Bertaina, Frank	68T	131	$ .25	$ .65
Bernazard, Tony	80T	680	$ .05	$ .20	Bertaina, Frank	69T	554	$ .25	$ .85
Bernazard, Tony	81T	413	$ .01	$ .07	Bertaina, Frank	70T	638	$ .50	$2.00
Bernazard, Tony	81TTR	735	$ .02	$ .10	Bertaina, Frank	71T	422	$ .10	$ .35
Bernazard, Tony	82T	206	$ .01	$ .06	Bertell, Dick	61T	441	$ .50	$2.00
Bernazard, Tony	83T	698	$ .01	$ .06	Bertell, Dick	63T	287	$ .35	$1.20
Bernazard, Tony	83TTR	9	$ .02	$ .10	Bertell, Dick	64T	424	$ .40	$1.25
Bernazard, Tony	84T	41	$ .01	$ .05	Bertell, Dick	65T	27	$ .25	$ .65
Bernazard, Tony	84TTR	12	$ .02	$ .10	Bertell, Dick	66T	587	$4.50	$15.00
Bernazard, Tony	85T	533	$ .01	$ .04	Bertoia, Reno	54T	131	$2.10	$7.50
Bernazard, Tony	86T	354	$ .01	$ .03	Bertoia, Reno	55T	94	$1.35	$5.00
Bernazard, Tony	87T	758	$ .01	$ .03	Bertoia, Reno	57T	390	$1.00	$3.75
Bernazard, Tony	87TAS	607	$ .01	$ .03	Bertoia, Reno	58T	232	$ .50	$2.00
Bernazard, Tony	88T	122	$ .01	$ .03	Bertoia, Reno	59T	84	$1.00	$3.75
Bernhardt, Juan	77T	494	$ .12	$ .40	Bertoia, Reno	60T	297	$ .50	$1.95
Bernhardt, Juan	78T	698	$ .02	$ .10	Bertoia, Reno	61T	392	$ .50	$2.00
Bernhardt, Juan	79T	366	$ .02	$ .10	Bessent, Don	56T	184	$2.50	$8.00
Bernier, Carlos	53T	243	$11.00	$37.50	Bessent, Don	57T	178	$ .95	$3.50
Berra, Dale	79T	723	$ .05	$ .20	Bessent, Don	58T	401	$ .50	$2.00
Berra, Dale	80T	292	$ .01	$ .07	Bessent, Don	59T	71	$1.00	$3.75
Berra, Dale	81T	147	$ .01	$ .07	Best, Karl	86T	61	$ .01	$ .03
Berra, Dale	82T	588	$ .01	$ .06	Best, Karl	87T	439	$ .01	$ .03
Berra, Dale	83T	433	$ .01	$ .06	Beswick, Jim	79T	725	$ .02	$ .10
Berra, Dale	84T	18	$ .01	$ .05	Bethke, Jim	65T	533	$3.00	$12.00
Berra, Dale	85T	132	$ .01	$ .10	Bevacqua, Kurt	72T	193	$ .10	$ .35
Berra, Dale	85T	305	$ .01	$ .04	Bevacqua, Kurt	74T	454	$ .06	$ .25
Berra, Dale	85TTR	6	$ .02	$ .10	Bevacqua, Kurt	74TTR	454	$ .06	$ .25
Berra, Dale	86T	692	$ .01	$ .03	Bevacqua, Kurt	76T	427	$ .05	$ .20
Berra, Larry "Yogi"	51Trb	1	$35.00	$125.00	Bevacqua, Kurt	76T	564	$ .10	$ .35
Berra, Yogi	52T	191	$120.00	$600.00	Bevacqua, Kurt	77T	317	$ .05	$ .15
Berra, Yogi	53T	104	$60.00	$180.00	Bevacqua, Kurt	78T	725	$ .02	$ .10
Berra, Yogi	54T	50	$65.00	$200.00	Bevacqua, Kurt	79T	44	$ .02	$ .10
Berra, Yogi	55T	198	$90.00	$275.00	Bevacqua, Kurt	80T	584	$ .01	$ .07
Berra, Yogi	56T	110	$35.00	$130.00	Bevacqua, Kurt	81T	118	$ .01	$ .07
Berra, Yogi	57T	2	$35.00	$135.00	Bevacqua, Kurt	82T	267	$ .01	$ .06
Berra, Yogi	57T	407	$100.00	$350.00	Bevacqua, Kurt	82TTR	6	$ .02	$ .10
Berra, Yogi	58T	370	$22.50	$77.50	Bevacqua, Kurt	83T	674	$ .01	$ .06
Berra, Yogi	59T	180	$20.00	$77.50	Bevacqua, Kurt	84T	346	$ .01	$ .05
Berra, Yogi	60T	480	$15.00	$60.00	Bevacqua, Kurt	85T	478	$ .01	$ .04
Berra, Yogi	61T	425	$15.00	$45.00	Bevacqua, Kurt	86T	789	$ .01	$ .03
Berra, Yogi	61TMVP	472	$6.00	$25.00	Bevan, Hal	61T	456	$ .50	$2.00
Berra, Yogi	62T	360	$15.00	$47.50	Biancalana, Buddy	85T	387	$ .01	$ .04
Berra, Yogi	63T	340	$15.00	$60.00	Biancalana, Buddy	86T	99	$ .01	$ .03
Berra, Yogi	64T	21	$10.00	$30.00	Biancalana, Buddy	87T	554	$ .01	$ .03
Berra, Yogi	65T	470	$22.50	$70.00	Bibby, Jim	72T	316	$ .10	$ .35
Berra, Yogi	73T	257	$ .50	$2.00	Bibby, Jim	74T	11	$ .06	$ .25
Berra, Yogi	74T	179	$ .50	$2.00	Bibby, Jim	75T	155	$ .06	$ .25
Berra, Yogi	75T	189	$ .50	$2.00	Bibby, Jim	76T	324	$ .05	$ .20
Berra, Yogi	75T	192	$ .50	$2.00	Bibby, Jim	77T	501	$ .05	$ .15
Berra, Yogi	75T	193	$ .50	$2.00	Bibby, Jim	78T	636	$ .02	$ .10
Berra, Yogi	84TTR	13	$ .25	$ .65	Bibby, Jim	79T	92	$ .02	$ .10
Berra, Yogi	85T	132	$ .01	$ .10	Bibby, Jim	80T	229	$ .01	$ .07
Berra, Yogi	85T	155	$ .01	$ .10	Bibby, Jim	81T	430	$ .01	$ .07
Berres, Ray	60T	458	$ .95	$3.50	Bibby, Jim	82T	170	$ .01	$ .06

Player	Year	No.	VG	EX/MT	Player	Year	No.	VG	EX/MT
Bibby, Jim	83T	355	$ .01	$ .06	Birkbeck, Mike	88T	692	$ .01	$ .03
Bibby, Jim	84T	566	$ .01	$ .05	Birkbeck, Mike	89T	491	$ .01	$ .04
Bichette, Dante	89T	761	$ .01	$ .10	Birrer, Babe	56T	84	$1.25	$4.50
Bichette, Dante	90T	43	$ .01	$ .03					
Bickford, Vern	52T	252	$11.50	$38.00					
Bickford, Vern	53T	161	$3.75	$13.00					
Bielecki, Mike	86TTR	10	$ .02	$ .10					
Bielecki, Mike	87T	394	$ .01	$ .03					
Bielecki, Mike	88T	436	$ .01	$ .03					
Bielecki, Mike	89T	668	$ .01	$ .04					
Bielecki, Mike	90T	114	$ .01	$ .03					
Biercevicz, Greg	79T	712	$ .02	$ .10					
Biercevicz, Greg	81T	282	$ .01	$ .07					
Biggio, Craig	89T	49	$ .10	$ .75					
Biggio, Craig	90T	157	$ .01	$ .15					
Biggio, Craig	90TAS	404	$ .01	$ .10					
Biittner, Larry	72T	122	$ .10	$ .35					
Biittner, Larry	73T	249	$ .06	$ .25					
Biittner, Larry	75T	543	$ .06	$ .25					
Biittner, Larry	76T	238	$ .05	$ .20					
Biittner, Larry	77T	64	$ .05	$ .15					
Biittner, Larry	78T	346	$ .02	$ .10					
Biittner, Larry	79T	433	$ .02	$ .10					
Biittner, Larry	80T	639	$ .01	$ .07					
Biittner, Larry	81T	718	$ .01	$ .07					
Biittner, Larry	81TTR	736	$ .02	$ .10					
Biittner, Larry	82T	159	$ .01	$ .06					
Biittner, Larry	83T	527	$ .01	$ .06					
Biittner, Larry	83TTR	10	$ .02	$ .10					
Biittner, Larry	84T	283	$ .01	$ .05					
Bilardello, Dann	83TTR	11	$ .02	$ .10					
Bilardello, Dann	84T	424	$ .01	$ .05					
Bilardello, Dann	85T	28	$ .01	$ .04					
Bilardello, Dann	86T	253	$ .01	$ .03					
Bilardello, Dann	87T	577	$ .01	$ .03					
Bilardello, Dann	90T	682	$ .01	$ .03	Birtsas, Tim	88T	501	$ .01	$ .03
Bilko, Steve	52T	287	$14.00	$45.00	Birtsas, Tim	89T	103	$ .01	$ .04
Bilko, Steve	54T	116	$2.10	$7.50	Birtsas, Tim	90T	687	$ .01	$ .03
Bilko, Steve	55T	93	$1.35	$5.00	Bishop, Charlie	53T	186	$3.75	$13.00
Bilko, Steve	58T	346	$ .50	$2.00	Bishop, Charlie	55T	96	$1.35	$5.00
Bilko, Steve	59T	43	$1.00	$3.75	Bittiger, Jeff	89T	209	$ .01	$ .04
Bilko, Steve	60T	396	$ .50	$1.95	Bjorkman, George	84T	116	$ .01	$ .05
Bilko, Steve	61T	184	$ .30	$1.00	Black, Bud	83T	238	$ .01	$ .10
Bilko, Steve	62T	422	$ .70	$2.10	Black, Bud	84T	26	$ .01	$ .05
Billingham, Jack	68T	228	$ .25	$ .85	Black, Bud	85T	412	$ .01	$ .04
Billingham, Jack	69T	92	$ .25	$ .65	Black, Bud	86T	697	$ .01	$ .03
Billingham, Jack	70T	701	$ .50	$2.00	Black, Bud	87T	669	$ .01	$ .03
Billingham, Jack	71T	162	$ .10	$ .35	Black, Bud	88T	301	$ .01	$ .03
Billingham, Jack	72T	542	$ .25	$ .85	Black, Bud	88TTR	16	$ .01	$ .05
Billingham, Jack	73T	89	$ .06	$ .25	Black, Bud	89T	500	$ .01	$ .04
Billingham, Jack	74T	158	$ .06	$ .25	Black, Bud	90T	144	$ .01	$ .03
Billingham, Jack	75T	235	$ .06	$ .25	Black, Joe	52T	321	$65.00	$200.00
Billingham, Jack	76T	155	$ .05	$ .20	Black, Joe	53T	81	$12.00	$45.00
Billingham, Jack	77T	512	$ .05	$ .15	Black, Joe	54T	98	$4.75	$22.00
Billingham, Jack	78T	47	$ .02	$ .10	Black, Joe	55T	156	$8.00	$25.00
Billingham, Jack	79T	388	$ .02	$ .10	Black, Joe	56T	178	$5.00	$25.00
Billingham, Jack	80T	603	$ .01	$ .07	Blackburn, Ron	58T	459	$ .50	$1.95
Billings, Dick	71T	729	$ .70	$2.10	Blackburn, Ron	59T	401	$ .50	$1.95
Billings, Dick	72T	148	$ .10	$ .35	Blackburn, Ron	60T	209	$ .35	$1.10
Billings, Dick	73T	94	$ .06	$ .25	Blackwell, Ewell	52T	344	$55.00	$160.00
Billings, Dick	74T	466	$ .06	$ .25	Blackwell, Ewell	53T	31	$6.00	$18.00
Bird, Doug	74T	17	$ .06	$ .25	Blackwell, Tim	78T	449	$ .02	$ .10
Bird, Doug	75T	364	$ .06	$ .25	Blackwell, Tim	80T	153	$ .01	$ .07
Bird, Doug	76T	96	$ .05	$ .20	Blackwell, Tim	81T	553	$ .01	$ .07
Bird, Doug	77T	556	$ .05	$ .15	Blackwell, Tim	82T	374	$ .01	$ .06
Bird, Doug	78T	183	$ .02	$ .10	Blackwell, Tim	82TTR	7	$ .02	$ .10
Bird, Doug	79T	664	$ .02	$ .10	Blackwell, Tim	83T	57	$ .01	$ .06
Bird, Doug	80T	421	$ .01	$ .07	Blades, Ray	54T	243	$2.10	$7.50
Bird, Doug	81T	516	$ .01	$ .07	Bladt, Rich	74T	601	$ .35	$1.10
Bird, Doug	81TTR	737	$ .02	$ .10	Blair, Dennis	75T	521	$ .06	$ .25
Bird, Doug	82T	273	$ .01	$ .06	Blair, Dennis	76T	642	$ .05	$ .20
Bird, Doug	83T	759	$ .01	$ .06	Blair, Dennis	77T	593	$ .05	$ .15
Bird, Doug	83TTR	12	$ .02	$ .10	Blair, Dennis	78T	466	$ .02	$ .10
Bird, Doug	84T	82	$ .01	$ .05	Blair, Paul	65T	473	$2.25	$10.00
Birkbeck, Mike	87T	229	$ .01	$ .03	Blair, Paul	66T	48	$ .25	$ .85

Player	Year	No.	VG	EX/MT
Blair, Paul	67T	319	$ .25	$ .65

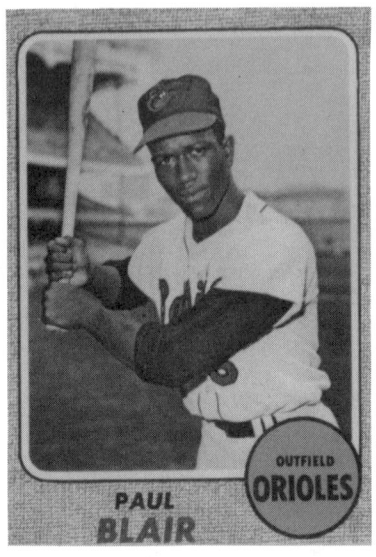

PAUL BLAIR — OUTFIELD — ORIOLES

Player	Year	No.	VG	EX/MT
Blair, Paul	68T	135	$ .25	$ .65
Blair, Paul	69T	506	$ .25	$ .65
Blair, Paul	70T	285	$ .10	$ .35
Blair, Paul	71T	53	$ .10	$ .35
Blair, Paul	72T	660	$ .60	$1.75
Blair, Paul	73T	528	$ .10	$ .35
Blair, Paul	74T	92	$ .06	$ .25
Blair, Paul	75T	275	$ .06	$ .25
Blair, Paul	76T	473	$ .05	$ .20
Blair, Paul	77T	313	$ .05	$ .15
Blair, Paul	78T	114	$ .02	$ .10
Blair, Paul	79T	582	$ .02	$ .10
Blair, Paul	80T	281	$ .01	$ .07
Blake, Ed	52T	144	$6.00	$19.00
Blanchard, John	59T	117	$ .50	$1.95
Blanchard, John	60T	283	$ .35	$1.10
Blanchard, John	61T	104	$ .30	$1.00
Blanchard, John	62T	93	$ .50	$2.00
Blanchard, John	63T	555	$1.35	$4.00
Blanchard, John	64T	118	$ .25	$ .85
Blanchard, John	65T	388	$ .35	$1.10
Blanchard, John	66T	268	$ .25	$ .85
Blanco, Gil	65T	566	$1.50	$3.75
Blanco, Gil	67T	303	$ .25	$ .65
Blankenship, Lance	90T	132	$ .01	$ .03
Blanks, Larvell	73T	609	$ .95	$3.50
Blanks, Larvell	75T	394	$ .06	$ .25
Blanks, Larvell	76T	127	$ .05	$ .20
Blanks, Larvell	77T	441	$ .05	$ .15
Blanks, Larvell	78T	61	$ .02	$ .10
Blanks, Larvell	79T	307	$ .02	$ .10
Blanks, Larvell	80T	656	$ .01	$ .07
Blasingame, Don	56T	309	$1.80	$6.00
Blasingame, Don	57T	47	$ .95	$3.50
Blasingame, Don	58T	199	$ .50	$2.00
Blasingame, Don	59T	491	$ .50	$1.95
Blasingame, Don	60T	397	$ .50	$1.95
Blasingame, Don	61T	294	$ .30	$1.00
Blasingame, Don	62T	103	$ .35	$1.10
Blasingame, Don	63T	518	$1.50	$3.75
Blasingame, Don	64T	327	$ .25	$ .85
Blasingame, Don	65T	21	$ .25	$ .65

Player	Year	No.	VG	EX/MT
Blasingame, Wade	65T	44	$ .25	$ .65
Blasingame, Wade	66T	355	$ .25	$ .85
Blasingame, Wade	67T	119	$ .25	$ .65
Blasingame, Wade	68T	507	$ .30	$1.00
Blasingame, Wade	69T	308	$ .25	$ .85
Blasingame, Wade	71T	79	$ .10	$ .35
Blasingame, Wade	72T	581	$ .50	$2.00
Blass, Steve	65T	232	$ .30	$1.00
Blass, Steve	66T	344	$ .25	$ .85
Blass, Steve	67T	562	$1.35	$4.00
Blass, Steve	68T	499	$ .30	$1.00
Blass, Steve	69T	104	$ .25	$ .65
Blass, Steve	70T	396	$ .10	$ .35
Blass, Steve	71T	143	$ .10	$ .35
Blass, Steve	72T	320	$ .10	$ .35
Blass, Steve	73T	95	$ .06	$ .25
Blass, Steve	74T	595	$ .06	$ .25
Blateric, Steve	73T	616	$ .35	$1.10
Blauser, Jeff	89T	83	$ .01	$ .10
Blauser, Jeff	89TBB	317	$ .01	$ .05
Blauser, Jeff	90T	251	$ .01	$ .03
Blaylock, Bob	59T	211	$ .50	$1.95
Blaylock, Gary	59T	539	$2.00	$7.00
Blaylock, Marv	57T	224	$ .95	$3.50
Blefary, Curt	65T	49	$ .50	$2.00
Blefary, Curt	66T	460	$ .70	$2.10
Blefary, Curt	67T	180	$ .25	$ .65
Blefary, Curt	67T	521	$ .60	$1.75
Blefary, Curt	68T	312	$ .25	$ .65
Blefary, Curt	69T	458	$ .25	$ .65
Blefary, Curt	70T	297	$ .10	$ .35
Blefary, Curt	71T	131	$ .10	$ .35
Blefary, Curt	72T	691	$ .70	$2.10
Blefary, Curt	72TIA	692	$ .70	$2.10
Blocker, Terry	89T	76	$ .01	$ .15
Blomberg, Ron	72T	203	$ .10	$ .35
Blomberg, Ron	73T	462	$ .06	$ .25
Blomberg, Ron	74T	117	$ .06	$ .25
Blomberg, Ron	75T	68	$ .06	$ .25
Blomberg, Ron	76T	354	$ .05	$ .20
Blomberg, Ron	77T	543	$ .05	$ .15
Blomberg, Ron	78T	506	$ .02	$ .10
Blomberg, Ron	79T	42	$ .02	$ .10
Blomberg, Ron	88TTB	663	$ .01	$ .03
Bloomfield, Bud	64T	532	$1.50	$3.75
Blowers, Mike	89TMLD	18	$ .01	$ .25
Blue Jays, Team Checklist	77T	113	$ .05	$ .15
Blue Jays, Team Checklist	78T	626	$ .02	$ .10
Blue Jays, Team Checklist	79T	282	$ .05	$ .25
Blue Jays, Team Checklist	80T	577	$ .05	$ .25
Blue Jays, Team Checklist	81T	674	$ .02	$ .20
Blue Jays, Team Leaders	86T	96	$ .01	$ .03
Blue Jays, Team Leaders	87T	106	$ .01	$ .03
Blue Jays, Team Leaders	88T	729	$ .01	$ .03
Blue Jays, Team Leaders	89T	201	$ .01	$ .04
Blue, Vida	70T	21	$1.00	$3.00
Blue, Vida	71T	544	$ .85	$2.25
Blue, Vida	72T	92	$ .65	$2.25
Blue, Vida	72T	94	$ .40	$1.50
Blue, Vida	72T	96	$ .40	$1.50
Blue, Vida	72T	169	$ .20	$ .70
Blue, Vida	72TIA	170	$ .25	$ .85
Blue, Vida	73T	430	$ .25	$ .85
Blue, Vida	74T	290	$ .25	$ .85
Blue, Vida	75T	209	$ .25	$ .65
Blue, Vida	75T	510	$ .25	$ .65
Blue, Vida	76T	140	$ .10	$ .35
Blue, Vida	76T	200	$ .35	$1.10
Blue, Vida	77T	230	$ .25	$ .65
Blue, Vida	78T	680	$ .05	$ .25
Blue, Vida	79T	110	$ .05	$ .20
Blue, Vida	80T	30	$ .05	$ .20
Blue, Vida	81T	310	$ .01	$ .07
Blue, Vida	82T	430	$ .01	$ .06
Blue, Vida	82T	576	$ .01	$ .06

Player	Year	No.	VG	EX/MT	Player	Year	No.	VG	EX/MT
Blue, Vida	82TIA	431	$ .01	$ .06	Boddicker, Mike	89T	71	$ .01	$ .04
Blue, Vida	82TTR	8	$ .05	$ .20	Boddicker, Mike	89TBB	296	$ .01	$ .05
Blue, Vida	83T	471	$ .01	$ .06	Boddicker, Mike	90T	652	$ .01	$ .03
Blue, Vida	83T	570	$ .01	$ .06	Boehmer, Len	69T	519	$ .25	$ .85
Blue, Vida	86T	770	$ .01	$ .03	Boever, Joe	88T	627	$ .01	$ .03
Blue, Vida	87T	260	$ .01	$ .03	Boever, Joe	89T	586	$ .01	$ .04
Blyleven, Bert	71T	26	$15.00	$45.00	Boever, Joe	90T	410	$ .01	$ .03
Blyleven, Bert	72T	515	$2.00	$6.00	Boggs, Tommy	77T	328	$ .05	$ .15
Blyleven, Bert	73T	199	$1.00	$3.00	Boggs, Tommy	78T	518	$ .02	$ .10
Blyleven, Bert	74T	98	$ .50	$1.50	Boggs, Tommy	79T	384	$ .02	$ .10
Blyleven, Bert	75T	30	$ .50	$1.50	Boggs, Tommy	81T	132	$ .01	$ .07
Blyleven, Bert	76T	204	$ .15	$ .50	Boggs, Tommy	82T	61	$ .01	$ .06
Blyleven, Bert	76T	235	$ .35	$1.20	Boggs, Tommy	83T	649	$ .01	$ .06
Blyleven, Bert	77T	630	$ .15	$ .50	Boggs, Wade	83T	498	$9.00	$33.00
Blyleven, Bert	78T	131	$ .06	$ .30	Boggs, Wade	84T	30	$2.00	$7.50
Blyleven, Bert	79T	308	$ .06	$ .30	Boggs, Wade	84T	131	$ .08	$ .35
Blyleven, Bert	80T	457	$ .25	$ .65	Boggs, Wade	84T	786	$ .06	$ .30
Blyleven, Bert	81T	554	$ .05	$ .25	Boggs, Wade	85T	350	$1.35	$5.00
Blyleven, Bert	81TTR	738	$ .25	$1.00	Boggs, Wade	86T	510	$ .35	$2.00
Blyleven, Bert	82T	559	$ .01	$ .06	Boggs, Wade	87T	150	$ .50	$1.95
Blyleven, Bert	82T	685	$ .05	$ .25	Boggs, Wade	87TAS	608	$ .25	$ .65
Blyleven, Bert	83T	280	$ .03	$ .15	Boggs, Wade	88T	200	$ .10	$ .65
Blyleven, Bert	84T	716	$ .01	$ .05	Boggs, Wade	88TAS	388	$ .01	$ .30
Blyleven, Bert	84T	789	$ .04	$ .20	Boggs, Wade	88TBB	32	$ .10	$ .50
Blyleven, Bert	85T	355	$ .01	$ .10	Boggs, Wade	89T	600	$ .05	$ .25
Blyleven, Bert	86T	445	$ .01	$ .10	Boggs, Wade	89TAS	399	$ .01	$ .15
Blyleven, Bert	87T	25	$ .01	$ .10	Boggs, Wade	89TBB	241	$ .01	$ .35
Blyleven, Bert	88T	295	$ .01	$ .10	Boggs, Wade	89TRB	2	$ .01	$ .15
Blyleven, Bert	88TBB	180	$ .01	$ .05	Boggs, Wade	90T	760	$ .01	$ .20
Blyleven, Bert	89T	555	$ .01	$ .04	Boggs, Wade	90TAS	387	$ .01	$ .15
Blyleven, Bert	89TTR	11	$ .01	$ .10	Bohammer, Jack	74T	586	$ .06	$ .25
Blyleven, Bert	90T	130	$ .01	$ .10	Boisclair, Bruce	77T	399	$ .05	$ .15
Blyzka, Mike	54T	152	$2.10	$7.50	Boisclair, Bruce	78T	277	$ .02	$ .10
Bobb, Randy	70T	429	$ .10	$ .35	Boisclair, Bruce	79T	148	$ .02	$ .10
Bobb, Randy	71T	83	$ .10	$ .35	Boisclair, Bruce	80T	654	$ .01	$ .07
Boccabella, John	64T	192	$ .25	$ .85	Boitano, Danny	80T	668	$ .01	$ .07
Boccabella, John	66T	482	$ .70	$2.10	Bokelmann, Dick	53T	204	$3.75	$13.00
Boccabella, John	67T	578	$1.35	$4.00	Boles, Carl	63T	428	$ .35	$1.20
Boccabella, John	68T	542	$ .30	$1.00	Bolger, Jim	55T	179	$4.25	$13.00
Boccabella, John	69T	466	$ .25	$ .65	Bolger, Jim	57T	289	$3.50	$13.00
Boccabella, John	70T	19	$ .10	$ .35	Bolger, Jim	58T	201	$ .50	$2.00
Boccabella, John	71T	452	$ .10	$ .35	Bolger, Jim	59T	29	$1.00	$3.75
Boccabella, John	72T	159	$ .10	$ .35	Bolin, Bobby	61T	449	$ .50	$2.00
Boccabella, John	73T	592	$ .35	$1.10	Bolin, Bobby	62T	329	$ .35	$1.10
Boccabella, John	74T	253	$ .06	$ .25	Bolin, Bobby	63T	106	$ .25	$ .85
Boccabella, John	75T	553	$ .06	$ .25	Bolin, Bobby	64T	374	$ .40	$1.25
Bochte, Bruce	75T	392	$ .06	$ .25	Bolin, Bobby	65T	341	$ .30	$1.00
Bochte, Bruce	76T	637	$ .05	$ .20	Bolin, Bobby	66T	61	$ .25	$ .85
Bochte, Bruce	77T	68	$ .05	$ .15	Bolin, Bobby	67T	252	$ .25	$ .65
Bochte, Bruce	78T	537	$ .02	$ .10	Bolin, Bobby	68T	169	$ .25	$ .65
Bochte, Bruce	79T	443	$ .02	$ .10	Bolin, Bobby	69T	8	$ .50	$2.00
Bochte, Bruce	80T	143	$ .01	$ .07	Bolin, Bobby	69T	505	$ .25	$ .65
Bochte, Bruce	81T	723	$ .01	$ .07	Bolin, Bobby	70T	574	$ .25	$ .85
Bochte, Bruce	82T	224	$ .01	$ .06	Bolin, Bobby	71T	446	$ .10	$ .35
Bochte, Bruce	83T	28	$ .01	$ .06	Bolin, Bobby	72T	266	$ .10	$ .35
Bochte, Bruce	83T	711	$ .01	$ .06	Bolin, Bobby	73T	541	$ .35	$1.10
Bochte, Bruce	85T	632	$ .01	$ .04	Bolin, Bobby	74T	427	$ .06	$ .25
Bochte, Bruce	86T	378	$ .01	$ .03	Bolling, Frank	57T	325	$3.50	$13.00
Bochte, Bruce	87T	496	$ .01	$ .03	Bolling, Frank	58T	95	$1.00	$3.75
Bochy, Bruce	79T	718	$ .02	$ .10	Bolling, Frank	59T	280	$ .50	$1.95
Bochy, Bruce	80T	289	$ .01	$ .07	Bolling, Frank	60T	482	$ .60	$1.75
Bochy, Bruce	84T	571	$ .01	$ .05	Bolling, Frank	61T	335	$ .30	$1.00
Bochy, Bruce	85T	324	$ .01	$ .04	Bolling, Frank	62T	130	$ .35	$1.10
Bochy, Bruce	86T	608	$ .01	$ .03	Bolling, Frank	62T	211	$ .50	$2.00
Bochy, Bruce	87T	428	$ .01	$ .03	Bolling, Frank	63T	570	$1.50	$3.75
Bochy, Bruce	88T	31	$ .01	$ .03	Bolling, Frank	64T	115	$ .25	$ .85
Bockus, Randy	89T	733	$ .01	$ .04	Bolling, Frank	65T	269	$ .30	$1.00
Boddicker, Mike	81T	399	$ .35	$1.10	Bolling, Milt	53T	280	$30.00	$300.00
Boddicker, Mike	84T	191	$ .03	$ .15	Bolling, Milt	54T	82	$2.10	$7.50
Boddicker, Mike	84T	426	$ .01	$ .05	Bolling, Milt	55T	91	$1.35	$5.00
Boddicker, Mike	85T	225	$ .01	$ .04	Bolling, Milt	56T	315	$1.80	$6.00
Boddicker, Mike	85TAS	709	$ .01	$ .04	Bolling, Milt	57T	131	$ .95	$3.50
Boddicker, Mike	86T	575	$ .01	$ .10	Bolling, Milt	58T	188	$ .50	$2.00
Boddicker, Mike	87T	455	$ .01	$ .15	Bollo, Greg	65T	541	$1.50	$3.75
Boddicker, Mike	88T	725	$ .01	$ .03	Bollo, Greg	66T	301	$ .25	$ .85

Player	Year	No.	VG	EX/MT	Player	Year	No.	VG	EX/MT
Bollweg, Don	52T	128	$6.00	$18.00	Booker, Greg	87TTR	6	$ .01	$ .07
Bolton, Tom	88T	442	$ .01	$ .03	Booker, Greg	88T	727	$ .01	$ .03
Bolton, Tom	89T	269	$ .01	$ .04	Booker, Greg	89T	319	$ .01	$ .04
Bomback, Mark	81T	567	$ .01	$ .07	Booker, Greg	89TBB	194	$ .01	$ .05
Bomback, Mark	81TTR	739	$ .02	$ .10	Booker, Jim	76T	243	$ .05	$ .20
Bomback, Mark	82T	707	$ .01	$ .06	Booker, Rod	88T	483	$ .01	$ .03
Bond, Walt	60T	552	$2.00	$7.00	Booker, Rod	89TBB	256	$ .01	$ .05
Bond, Walt	61T	334	$ .30	$1.00	Boone, Bob	73T	613	$9.00	$35.00
Bond, Walt	63T	493	$2.50	$6.50	Boone, Bob	74T	131	$ .75	$3.00
Bond, Walt	64T	339	$ .25	$ .85					
Bond, Walt	65T	109	$ .25	$ .65					
Bond, Walt	66T	431	$ .25	$ .85					
Bond, Walt	67T	224	$ .25	$ .65					
Bonds, Barry	86TTR	11	$ .35	$1.50					
Bonds, Barry	87T	320	$ .35	$1.25					
Bonds, Barry	88T	450	$ .01	$ .25					
Bonds, Barry	88TBB	89	$ .01	$ .15					
Bonds, Barry	89T	620	$ .01	$ .04					
Bonds, Barry	89TBB	5	$ .01	$ .10					
Bonds, Barry	90T	220	$ .01	$ .10					
Bonds, Bobby	69T	630	$1.50	$5.25					
Bonds, Bobby	70T	425	$ .50	$1.50					
Bonds, Bobby	71T	295	$ .40	$1.25					
Bonds, Bobby	72T	711	$1.35	$4.50					
Bonds, Bobby	72TIA	712	$ .60	$1.75					
Bonds, Bobby	73T	145	$ .12	$ .40					
Bonds, Bobby	74T	30	$ .12	$ .40					
Bonds, Bobby	75T	55	$ .25	$ .85					
Bonds, Bobby	76T	380	$ .10	$ .35					
Bonds, Bobby	76TRB	2	$ .05	$ .20					
Bonds, Bobby	76TTR	380	$ .06	$ .25					
Bonds, Bobby	77T	570	$ .10	$ .35					
Bonds, Bobby	78T	150	$ .05	$ .25					
Bonds, Bobby	79T	285	$ .05	$ .20					
Bonds, Bobby	80T	410	$ .02	$ .10					
Bonds, Bobby	81T	635	$ .05	$ .20					
Bonds, Bobby	81TTR	740	$ .08	$ .30					
Bonds, Bobby	82T	580	$ .01	$ .15					
Bonham, Bill	72T	29	$ .10	$ .35					
Bonham, Bill	73T	328	$ .06	$ .25					
Bonham, Bill	74T	528	$ .06	$ .25					
Bonham, Bill	75T	85	$ .06	$ .25	Boone, Bob	75T	351	$ .45	$1.35
Bonham, Bill	76T	151	$ .05	$ .20	Boone, Bob	76T	67	$ .08	$ .30
Bonham, Bill	77T	446	$ .05	$ .15	Boone, Bob	76T	318	$ .25	$ .85
Bonham, Bill	78T	276	$ .02	$ .10	Boone, Bob	77T	545	$ .25	$ .75
Bonham, Bill	79T	354	$ .02	$ .10	Boone, Bob	78T	161	$ .02	$ .25
Bonham, Bill	80T	47	$ .01	$ .07	Boone, Bob	79T	90	$ .02	$ .25
Bonham, Bill	81T	712	$ .01	$ .07	Boone, Bob	80T	470	$ .01	$ .20
Bonikowski, Joe	62T	592	$13.00	$40.00	Boone, Bob	81T	290	$ .01	$ .20
Bonilla, Bobby	86TTR	12	$ .35	$1.50	Boone, Bob	82T	615	$ .01	$ .15
Bonilla, Bobby	87T	184	$ .50	$1.50	Boone, Bob	82T	616	$ .01	$ .15
Bonilla, Bobby	88T	681	$ .01	$ .25	Boone, Bob	82TTR	9	$ .05	$ .20
Bonilla, Bobby	88TBB	25	$ .01	$ .25	Boone, Bob	83T	765	$ .01	$ .10
Bonilla, Bobby	89T	440	$ .01	$ .25	Boone, Bob	84T	520	$ .01	$ .10
Bonilla, Bobby	89TAS	388	$ .01	$ .10	Boone, Bob	85T	133	$ .01	$ .10
Bonilla, Bobby	89TBB	159	$ .01	$ .20	Boone, Bob	85T	348	$ .01	$ .04
Bonilla, Bobby	90T	273	$ .01	$ .20	Boone, Bob	86T	62	$ .01	$ .03
Bonilla, Juan	82T	464	$ .01	$ .06	Boone, Bob	87T	166	$ .01	$ .03
Bonilla, Juan	83T	563	$ .01	$ .06	Boone, Bob	88T	498	$ .01	$ .03
Bonilla, Juan	84T	168	$ .01	$ .05	Boone, Bob	88TBB	30	$ .01	$ .05
Bonilla, Juan	86TTR	13	$ .02	$ .10	Boone, Bob	89T	243	$ .01	$ .04
Bonilla, Juan	87T	668	$ .01	$ .03	Boone, Bob	89TAS	404	$ .01	$ .04
Bonnell, Barry	78T	242	$ .02	$ .10	Boone, Bob	89TBB	269	$ .01	$ .10
Bonnell, Barry	79T	496	$ .02	$ .10	Boone, Bob	89TTR	12	$ .01	$ .05
Bonnell, Barry	80T	632	$ .01	$ .07	Boone, Bob	90T	671	$ .01	$ .03
Bonnell, Barry	81T	558	$ .01	$ .07	Boone, Danny	82T	407	$ .01	$ .06
Bonnell, Barry	82T	99	$ .01	$ .06	Boone, Ray	51Trb	23	$1.35	$4.00
Bonnell, Barry	83T	766	$ .01	$ .06	Boone, Ray	52T	55	$14.00	$45.00
Bonnell, Barry	84T	302	$ .01	$ .05	Boone, Ray	53T	25	$3.75	$13.00
Bonnell, Barry	84TTR	15	$ .95	$3.50	Boone, Ray	54T	77	$1.75	$7.00
Bonnell, Barry	85T	423	$ .01	$ .04	Boone, Ray	55T	65	$1.35	$5.00
Bonnell, Barry	86T	119	$ .01	$ .03	Boone, Ray	56T	6	$1.25	$4.50
Bonner, Bob	82T	21	$3.25	$12.50	Boone, Ray	57T	102	$ .95	$3.50
Booker, Greg	85T	262	$ .01	$ .04	Boone, Ray	58T	185	$ .50	$2.00
Booker, Greg	86T	429	$ .01	$ .03	Boone, Ray	59T	252	$ .50	$1.95

PHILLIES

Catcher

BOB BOONE

Player	Year	No.	VG	EX/MT	Player	Year	No.	VG	EX/MT
Boone, Ray	60T	281	$ .35	$1.10	Bosley, Thad	84T	657	$ .01	$ .05
Boone, Ray	76T	67	$ .08	$ .30	Bosley, Thad	85T	432	$ .01	$ .04
Boone, Ray	85T	133	$ .01	$ .10	Bosley, Thad	86T	512	$ .01	$ .03
Boozer, John	63T	29	$ .35	$1.10	Bosley, Thad	87T	58	$ .01	$ .03
Boozer, John	64T	16	$ .25	$ .85	Bosley, Thad	87TTR	7	$ .01	$ .07
Boozer, John	65T	184	$ .25	$ .65	Bosley, Thad	88T	247	$ .01	$ .03
Boozer, John	66T	324	$ .25	$ .85	Bosman, Dick	67T	459	$1.50	$5.50
Boozer, John	68T	173	$ .25	$ .65	Bosman, Dick	68T	442	$ .25	$ .65
Boozer, John	69T	599	$ .25	$ .85	Bosman, Dick	69T	607	$ .25	$ .85
Borbon, Pedro	70T	358	$ .25	$ .65	Bosman, Dick	70T	68	$ .50	$2.00
Borbon, Pedro	71T	613	$ .35	$1.10	Bosman, Dick	70T	175	$ .35	$1.10
Borbon, Pedro	73T	492	$ .06	$ .25	Bosman, Dick	71T	60	$ .10	$ .35
Borbon, Pedro	74T	410	$ .06	$ .25	Bosman, Dick	72T	365	$ .10	$ .35
Borbon, Pedro	75T	157	$ .06	$ .25	Bosman, Dick	73T	640	$ .35	$1.10
Borbon, Pedro	76T	77	$ .05	$ .20	Bosman, Dick	74T	465	$ .06	$ .25
Borbon, Pedro	77T	581	$ .05	$ .15	Bosman, Dick	75T	354	$ .06	$ .25
Borbon, Pedro	78T	220	$ .02	$ .10	Bosman, Dick	75THL	7	$ .25	$ .85
Borbon, Pedro	79T	326	$ .02	$ .10	Bosman, Dick	76T	298	$ .05	$ .20
Borbon, Pedro	80T	627	$ .01	$ .07	Bosman, Dick	77T	101	$ .05	$ .15
Borders, Pat	88TTR	17	$ .01	$ .15	Bostock, Lyman	76T	263	$ .06	$ .25
Borders, Pat	89T	693	$ .01	$ .10	Bostock, Lyman	77T	531	$ .05	$ .15
Borders, Pat	90T	191	$ .01	$ .03	Bostock, Lyman	78T	655	$ .02	$ .10
Bordi, Rich	82T	531	$ .01	$ .06	Boston, Daryl	85TTR	8	$ .03	$ .15
Bordi, Rich	85T	357	$ .01	$ .04	Boston, Daryl	86T	139	$ .01	$ .03
Bordi, Rich	85TTR	7	$ .02	$ .10	Boston, Daryl	87T	482	$ .01	$ .03
Bordi, Rich	86T	94	$ .01	$ .03	Boston, Daryl	88T	739	$ .01	$ .03
Bordi, Rich	86TTR	14	$ .02	$ .10	Boston, Daryl	89T	633	$ .01	$ .04
Bordi, Rich	87T	638	$ .01	$ .03	Boston, Daryl	90T	524	$ .01	$ .03
Borgmann, Glenn	73T	284	$ .06	$ .25	Boswell, Dave	67T	575	$6.00	$20.00
Borgmann, Glenn	74T	547	$ .06	$ .25	Boswell, Dave	68T	322	$ .25	$ .65
Borgmann, Glenn	75T	127	$ .06	$ .25	Boswell, Dave	69T	459	$ .25	$ .65
Borgmann, Glenn	76T	498	$ .05	$ .20	Boswell, Dave	70T	70	$ .50	$2.00
Borgmann, Glenn	77T	87	$ .05	$ .15	Boswell, Dave	70T	325	$ .10	$ .35
Borgmann, Glenn	78T	307	$ .02	$ .10	Boswell, Dave	71T	675	$ .70	$2.10
Borgmann, Glenn	79T	431	$ .02	$ .10	Boswell, Ken	69T	402	$ .25	$ .65
Borgmann, Glenn	80T	634	$ .01	$ .07	Boswell, Ken	70T	214	$ .10	$ .35
Borgmann, Glenn	81T	716	$ .01	$ .07	Boswell, Ken	71T	492	$ .10	$ .35
Boris, Paul	83T	266	$ .01	$ .06	Boswell, Ken	72T	305	$ .10	$ .35
Bork, Frank	65T	592	$1.50	$3.75	Boswell, Ken	72TIA	306	$ .10	$ .35
Bork, Frank	66T	123	$ .25	$ .85	Boswell, Ken	73T	87	$ .06	$ .25
Borkowski, Bob	52T	328	$39.00	$135.00	Boswell, Ken	74T	645	$ .06	$ .25
Borkowski, Bob	53T	7	$3.75	$13.00	Boswell, Ken	75T	479	$ .06	$ .25
Borkowski, Bob	54T	138	$2.10	$7.50	Boswell, Ken	76T	379	$ .05	$ .20
Borkowski, Bob	55T	74	$1.35	$5.00	Boswell, Ken	77T	429	$ .05	$ .15
Borland, Tom	60T	117	$ .35	$1.10	Botting, Ralph	80T	663	$ .05	$ .20
Borland, Tom	61T	419	$ .50	$2.00	Botting, Ralph	81T	214	$ .01	$ .07
Boros, Steve	58T	81	$1.00	$3.75	Bouchee, Ed	57T	314	$3.50	$13.00
Boros, Steve	59T	331	$ .50	$1.95	Bouchee, Ed	59T	39	$1.00	$3.75
Boros, Steve	61T	348	$ .30	$1.00	Bouchee, Ed	60T	347	$ .50	$1.95
Boros, Steve	62T	62	$ .35	$1.10	Bouchee, Ed	61T	196	$ .30	$1.00
Boros, Steve	62T	72	$ .35	$1.10	Bouchee, Ed	62T	497	$ .50	$ .25
Boros, Steve	63T	532	$1.50	$3.75	Bouldin, Carl	63T	496	$2.50	$6.50
Boros, Steve	64T	131	$ .25	$ .85	Bouldin, Carl	64T	518	$ .40	$1.25
Boros, Steve	65T	102	$ .25	$ .65	Bourjos, Chris	81T	502	$ .01	$ .07
Boros, Steve	83TTR	13	$ .02	$ .10	Bourque, Pat	73T	605	$ .50	$2.00
Boros, Steve	84T	531	$ .01	$ .05	Bourque, Pat	74T	141	$ .06	$ .25
Boros, Steve	86TTR	15	$ .02	$ .10	Bourque, Pat	75T	502	$ .06	$ .25
Boros, Steve	87T	143	$ .01	$ .03	Bouton, Jim	62T	592	$13.00	$40.00
Bosch, Don	68T	572	$ .30	$1.00	Bouton, Jim	63T	401	$ .50	$4.00
Bosch, Don	69T	578	$ .25	$ .85	Bouton, Jim	64T	4	$1.50	$6.00
Bosch, Don	70T	527	$ .10	$ .35	Bouton, Jim	64T	219	$ .50	$2.00
Bosetti, Rick	78T	710	$ .15	$ .50	Bouton, Jim	64T	470	$ .50	$1.95
Bosetti, Rick	79T	542	$ .02	$ .10	Bouton, Jim	65T	30	$ .50	$2.00
Bosetti, Rick	80T	277	$ .01	$ .07	Bouton, Jim	66T	276	$ .35	$1.10
Bosetti, Rick	81T	46	$ .01	$ .07	Bouton, Jim	67T	393	$1.00	$3.00
Bosetti, Rick	81TTR	741	$ .02	$ .10	Bouton, Jim	68T	562	$ .50	$2.00
Bosetti, Rick	82T	392	$ .01	$ .06	Bowa, Larry	70T	539	$1.35	$4.00
Bosio, Chris	87T	448	$ .01	$ .10	Bowa, Larry	71T	233	$ .50	$2.00
Bosio, Chris	88T	137	$ .01	$ .03	Bowa, Larry	72T	520	$ .15	$ .75
Bosio, Chris	89T	311	$ .01	$ .04	Bowa, Larry	73T	119	$ .15	$ .50
Bosio, Chris	90T	597	$ .01	$ .03	Bowa, Larry	74T	255	$ .25	$ .85
Bosley, Thad	78T	619	$ .02	$ .10	Bowa, Larry	75T	420	$ .25	$ .85
Bosley, Thad	79T	127	$ .02	$ .10	Bowa, Larry	76T	145	$ .06	$ .25
Bosley, Thad	80T	412	$ .01	$ .07	Bowa, Larry	77T	310	$ .05	$ .15
Bosley, Thad	82T	350	$ .01	$ .06	Bowa, Larry	78T	90	$ .05	$ .25

Player	Year	No.	VG	EX/MT	Player	Year	No.	VG	EX/MT
Bowa, Larry	79T	210	$ .05	$ .20	Boyer, Cletis	57T	121	$2.00	$6.00
Bowa, Larry	80T	630	$ .02	$ .10	Boyer, Cletis	59T	251	$ .70	$2.00
Bowa, Larry	81T	120	$ .03	$ .15	Boyer, Cletis	60T	109	$ .60	$1.75
Bowa, Larry	82T	515	$ .03	$ .15	Boyer, Cletis	61T	19	$ .50	$1.95
Bowa, Larry	82TIA	516	$ .01	$ .06	Boyer, Cletis, "Clete"	62T	163	$ .50	$2.00
Bowa, Larry	82TTR	10	$ .05	$ .20	Boyer, Clete	62T	490	$ .70	$2.00
Bowa, Larry	83T	305	$ .01	$ .06	Boyer, Clete	63T	361	$ .50	$1.95
Bowa, Larry	84T	705	$ .02	$ .10	Boyer, Clete	64T	69	$ .35	$1.10
Bowa, Larry	84T	757	$ .01	$ .05	Boyer, Clete	65T	475	$ .70	$2.00
Bowa, Larry	85T	484	$ .01	$ .10	Boyer, Clete	66T	9	$ .50	$1.95
Bowa, Larry	87TTR	8	$ .02	$ .12	Boyer, Clete	67T	328	$ .25	$ .65
Bowa, Larry	88T	284	$ .01	$ .03	Boyer, Clete	68T	550	$ .35	$1.10
Bowens, Sam	64T	201	$ .25	$ .85	Boyer, Clete	69T	489	$ .25	$ .85
Bowens, Sam	65T	188	$ .25	$ .65	Boyer, Clete	70T	206	$ .10	$ .35
Bowens, Sam	66T	412	$ .25	$ .85	Boyer, Clete	71T	374	$ .10	$ .35
Bowens, Sam	67T	491	$ .50	$2.00	Boyer, Cloyd	52T	280	$11.50	$38.00
Bowens, Sam	68T	82	$ .25	$ .65	Boyer, Cloyd	53T	60	$3.75	$13.00
Bowman, Bob	57T	332	$3.50	$13.00	Boyer, Ken	55T	125	$7.50	$22.50
Bowman, Bob	58T	415	$ .50	$2.00	Boyer, Ken	56T	14	$2.25	$7.50
Bowman, Bob	59T	221	$ .50	$1.95	Boyer, Ken	57T	122	$ .60	$2.50
Bowman, Ernie	62T	231	$ .35	$1.10	Boyer, Ken	58T	350	$ .55	$1.75
Bowman, Ernie	63T	61	$ .25	$ .85	Boyer, Ken	59T	325	$ .60	$1.75
Bowman, Ernie	66T	302	$ .25	$ .85	Boyer, Ken	59TAS	557	$3.00	$9.00
Bowsfield, Ted	59T	236	$ .50	$1.95	Boyer, Ken	60T	160	$8.00	$35.00
Bowsfield, Ted	60T	382	$ .50	$1.95	Boyer, Ken	60T	485	$ .95	$3.50
Bowsfield, Ted	61T	216	$ .30	$1.00	Boyer, Ken	61T	43	$1.50	$5.75
Bowsfield, Ted	62T	369	$ .35	$1.10	Boyer, Ken	61T	375	$ .70	$2.00
Bowsfield, Ted	63T	339	$ .35	$1.20	Boyer, Ken	61TAS	573	$6.00	$17.50
Bowsfield, Ted	64T	447	$ .40	$1.25	Boyer, Ken	62T	52	$ .60	$1.75
Boyd, Bob	53T	257	$11.00	$37.50	Boyer, Ken	62T	370	$ .60	$1.75
Boyd, Bob	54T	113	$2.10	$7.50	Boyer, Ken	62TAS	392	$1.00	$3.75
Boyd, Bob	57T	26	$ .95	$3.50	Boyer, Ken	63T	375	$ .50	$1.95
					Boyer, Ken	64T	11	$1.00	$4.00
					Boyer, Ken	64T	160	$1.25	$4.50
					Boyer, Ken	65T	6	$ .95	$3.50
					Boyer, Ken	65T	100	$ .15	$ .50
					Boyer, Ken	66T	385	$ .50	$1.95
					Boyer, Ken	67T	105	$ .50	$2.00
					Boyer, Ken	68T	259	$ .25	$ .85
					Boyer, Ken	69T	379	$ .15	$ .50
					Boyer, Ken	75T	202	$ .35	$1.10
					Boyland, Dorian	80T	683	$ .01	$ .07
					Brabender, Gene	66T	579	$4.50	$15.00
					Brabender, Gene	67T	22	$ .25	$ .65
					Brabender, Gene	68T	163	$ .25	$ .65
					Brabender, Gene	69T	393	$ .25	$ .65
					Brabender, Gene	70T	289	$ .10	$ .35
					Brabender, Gene	71T	666	$ .70	$2.10
					Bradford, Buddy	68T	142	$ .25	$ .65
					Bradford, Buddy	69T	97	$ .25	$ .65
					Bradford, Buddy	70T	299	$ .10	$ .35
					Bradford, Buddy	71T	552	$ .30	$1.00
					Bradford, Buddy	74T	357	$ .06	$ .25
					Bradford, Buddy	75T	504	$ .06	$ .25
					Bradford, Buddy	76T	451	$ .05	$ .20
					Bradford, Larry	80T	675	$ .01	$ .07
					Bradford, Larry	81T	542	$ .01	$ .07
					Bradford, Larry	82T	271	$ .01	$ .06
					Bradley, Mark	84T	316	$ .01	$ .05
					Bradley, Phil	84TTR	14	$ .15	$ .75
					Bradley, Phil	85T	449	$ .15	$ .75
					Bradley, Phil	86T	305	$ .01	$ .10
					Bradley, Phil	87T	525	$ .01	$ .10
					Bradley, Phil	88T	55	$ .01	$ .10
					Bradley, Phil	88TTR	18	$ .01	$ .05
Boyd, Bob	58T	279	$ .50	$2.00	Bradley, Phil	89T	608	$ .01	$ .04
Boyd, Bob	59T	82	$1.00	$3.75	Bradley, Phil	89TTR	13	$ .01	$ .05
Boyd, Bob	60T	207	$ .35	$1.10	Bradley, Phil	90T	163	$ .01	$ .03
Boyd, Bob	61T	199	$ .30	$1.00	Bradley, Scott	86T	481	$ .01	$ .03
Boyd, Dennis	85T	116	$ .05	$ .25	Bradley, Scott	87T	376	$ .01	$ .10
Boyd, Dennis	86T	605	$ .01	$ .03	Bradley, Scott	88T	762	$ .01	$ .03
Boyd, Dennis	87T	285	$ .01	$ .03	Bradley, Scott	89T	279	$ .01	$ .04
Boyd, Dennis	88T	704	$ .01	$ .03	Bradley, Scott	90T	593	$ .01	$ .03
Boyd, Dennis	89T	326	$ .01	$ .04	Bradley, Tom	71T	588	$ .30	$1.00
Boyd, Dennis	90T	544	$ .01	$ .03	Bradley, Tom	72T	248	$ .10	$ .35
Boyd, Gary	70T	7	$ .10	$ .35					

Bob Boyd

1st BASE   BALTIMORE ORIOLES

Player	Year	No.	VG	EX/MT	Player	Year	No.	VG	EX/MT
Bradley, Tom	73T	336	$ .06	$ .25	Braves, Team	67T	477	$1.35	$4.00
Bradley, Tom	74T	455	$ .06	$ .25	Braves, Team	68T	221	$ .50	$2.00
Bradley, Tom	75T	179	$ .06	$ .25	Braves, Team	70T	472	$ .35	$1.10
Bradley, Tom	76T	644	$ .05	$ .20	Braves, Team	71T	652	$1.50	$3.75
Brady, Brian	89TMLD	19	$ .01	$ .15	Braves, Team	72T	21	$ .15	$ .50
Brady, Jim	56T	126	$1.25	$4.50	Braves, Team	73T	521	$ .30	$1.00
Bragan, Bobby	60T	463	$ .85	$2.25	Braves, Team	74T	483	$ .15	$ .50
Bragan, Bobby	63T	73	$ .25	$ .85	Braves, Team Checklist	77T	442	$ .15	$ .50
Bragan, Bobby	64T	506	$ .40	$1.25	Braves, Team Checklist	75T	589	$ .15	$ .50
Bragan, Bobby	65T	346	$ .30	$1.00	Braves, Team Checklist	76T	631	$ .30	$1.00
Bragan, Bobby	66T	476	$ .70	$2.10	Braves, Team Checklist	78T	551	$ .05	$ .25
Braggs, Glenn	87T	622	$ .10	$ .35	Braves, Team Checklist	79T	302	$ .05	$ .25
Braggs, Glenn	88T	263	$ .01	$ .03	Braves, Team Checklist	80T	192	$ .05	$ .25
Braggs, Glenn	89T	718	$ .01	$ .04	Braves, Team Checklist	81T	675	$ .02	$ .20
Braggs, Glenn	89TBB	204	$ .01	$ .05	Braves, Team Leaders	86T	456	$ .01	$ .10
Braggs, Glenn	90T	88	$ .01	$ .03	Braves, Team Leaders	87T	31	$ .01	$ .03
Branca, Ralph	51Tbb	20	$8.00	$30.00	Braves, Team Leaders	88T	549	$ .01	$ .03
Branca, Ralph	52T	274	$20.00	$75.00	Braves, Team Leaders	89T	171	$ .01	$ .04
Brand, Ron	64T	326	$ .25	$ .85	Bravo, Angel	70T	283	$ .10	$ .35
Brand, Ron	65T	212	$ .30	$1.00	Bravo, Angel	71T	538	$ .30	$1.00
Brand, Ron	66T	394	$ .25	$ .85	Brazle, Al	52T	228	$6.00	$19.00
Brand, Ron	68T	317	$ .25	$ .65	Bream, Sid	85T	253	$ .01	$ .10
Brand, Ron	69T	549	$ .25	$ .85	Bream, Sid	86T	589	$ .01	$ .03
Brand, Ron	70T	221	$ .10	$ .35	Bream, Sid	87T	35	$ .01	$ .03
Brand, Ron	71T	304	$ .10	$ .35	Bream, Sid	88T	478	$ .01	$ .03
Brand, Ron	72T	773	$ .70	$2.10	Bream, Sid	88TBB	205	$ .01	$ .05
Brandon, Darrell	66T	456	$ .70	$2.10	Bream, Sid	89T	126	$ .01	$ .04
Brandon, Darrell	67T	117	$ .25	$ .65	Bream, Sid	89TBB	106	$ .01	$ .05
Brandon, Darrell	68T	26	$ .25	$ .65	Bream, Sid	90T	622	$ .01	$ .03
Brandon, Darrell	69T	301	$ .25	$ .85	Breazeale, Jim	73T	33	$ .06	$ .25
Brandon, Darrell	72T	283	$ .10	$ .35	Brecheen, Harry	51Tbb	28	$5.50	$17.00
Brandon, Darrell	73T	326	$ .06	$ .25	Brecheen, Harry	52T	263	$14.00	$40.00
Brandt, Jackie	59T	297	$ .50	$1.95	Brecheen, Harry	54T	203	$2.00	$7.00
Brandt, Jackie	60T	53	$ .35	$1.10	Brecheen, Harry	55T	113	$1.35	$5.00
Brandt, Jackie	61T	515	$ .50	$2.00	Brecheen, Harry	56T	229	$3.00	$9.00
Brandt, Jackie	62T	165	$ .35	$1.10	Brecheen, Harry	60T	455	$ .95	$3.50
Brandt, Jackie	63T	65	$ .25	$ .85	Breeden, Danny	69T	536	$ .25	$ .85
Brandt, Jackie	64T	399	$ .40	$1.25	Breeden, Danny	70T	36	$ .25	$ .85
Brandt, Jackie	65T	33	$ .25	$ .65	Breeden, Hal	72T	684	$ .70	$2.10
Brandt, Jackie	66T	383	$ .25	$ .85	Breeden, Hal	73T	173	$ .06	$ .25
Brandt, Jackie	67T	142	$ .25	$ .65	Breeden, Hal	74T	297	$ .06	$ .25
Branson, Jeff	88TTR	19	$ .01	$ .30	Breeden, Hal	75T	341	$ .06	$ .25
Branson, Jeff	89TBB	69	$ .01	$ .05	Breeding, Marv	60T	525	$2.00	$7.00
Brantley, Jeff	89TTR	14	$ .01	$ .15	Breeding, Marv	61T	321	$ .30	$1.00
Brantley, Jeff	90T	703	$ .01	$ .10	Breeding, Marv	62T	6	$ .35	$1.10
Brantley, Mickey	87T	347	$ .01	$ .03	Breeding, Marv	63T	149	$ .25	$ .85
Brantley, Mickey	88T	687	$ .01	$ .03	Breining, Fred	82T	144	$ .01	$ .06
Brantley, Mickey	89T	568	$ .01	$ .04	Breining, Fred	83T	747	$ .01	$ .06
Brantley, Mickey	89TBB	38	$ .01	$ .05	Breining, Fred	84T	428	$ .01	$ .05
Braun, John	65T	82	$ .25	$ .65	Breining, Fred	84TTR	16	$ .02	$ .10
Braun, Steve	72T	244	$ .10	$ .35	Breining, Fred	85T	30	$ .01	$ .04
Braun, Steve	73T	16	$ .06	$ .25	Brenly, Bob	82T	171	$ .50	$1.50
Braun, Steve	74T	321	$ .06	$ .25	Brenly, Bob	83T	494	$ .01	$ .06
Braun, Steve	75T	273	$ .06	$ .25	Brenly, Bob	84T	378	$ .01	$ .05
Braun, Steve	76T	183	$ .05	$ .20	Brenly, Bob	85T	215	$ .01	$ .04
Braun, Steve	77T	606	$ .05	$ .15	Brenly, Bob	86T	625	$ .01	$ .03
Braun, Steve	78T	422	$ .02	$ .10	Brenly, Bob	87T	125	$ .01	$ .03
Braun, Steve	79T	502	$ .02	$ .10	Brenly, Bob	88T	703	$ .01	$ .03
Braun, Steve	80T	9	$ .01	$ .07	Brenly, Bob	88TBB	143	$ .01	$ .05
Braun, Steve	82T	316	$ .01	$ .06	Brenly, Bob	89T	52	$ .01	$ .04
Braun, Steve	83T	734	$ .01	$ .06	Brennan, Tom	81T	451	$ .01	$ .07
Braun, Steve	84T	227	$ .01	$ .05	Brennan, Tom	82T	141	$ .15	$ .75
Braun, Steve	85T	152	$ .01	$ .04	Brennan, Tom	83T	524	$ .01	$ .06
Braun, Steve	86T	631	$ .01	$ .03	Brennan, Tom	84T	662	$ .01	$ .05
Braves, Team	56T	95	$3.25	$9.50	Bressoud, Eddie	58T	263	$ .50	$2.00
Braves, Team	57T	114	$3.00	$8.00	Bressoud, Eddie	59T	19	$1.00	$3.75
Braves, Team	58T	377	$2.00	$7.00	Bressoud, Eddie	60T	253	$ .35	$1.10
Braves, Team	59T	419	$2.50	$9.50	Bressoud, Eddie	61T	203	$ .30	$1.00
Braves, Team	60T	381	$2.00	$8.00	Bressoud, Eddie	62T	504	$ .70	$2.10
Braves, Team	61T	463	$1.35	$5.00	Bressoud, Eddie	63T	188	$ .25	$ .85
Braves, Team	62T	158	$ .75	$2.00	Bressoud, Eddie	64T	352	$ .25	$ .85
Braves, Team	63T	503	$3.25	$9.50	Bressoud, Eddie	65T	525	$1.50	$3.75
Braves, Team	64T	132	$1.00	$3.75	Bressoud, Eddie	66T	516	$ .70	$2.10
Braves, Team	65T	426	$ .60	$1.95	Bressoud, Eddie	67T	121	$ .25	$ .65
Braves, Team	66T	326	$ .45	$1.75	Brett, George	75T	228	$25.00	$90.00

Player	Year	No.	VG	EX/MT	Player	Year	No.	VG	EX/MT
Brett, George	76T	19	$7.50	$25.00	Brett, Ken	82T	397	$ .01	$ .06
Brett, George	77T	1	$1.00	$4.00	Brewer, Jim	61T	317	$ .30	$1.00
Brett, George	77T	580	$2.75	$11.00	Brewer, Jim	62T	191	$ .35	$1.10
Brett, George	77T	631	$ .50	$2.00	Brewer, Jim	63T	309	$ .35	$1.20
Brett, George	77TRB	231	$ .50	$2.00	Brewer, Jim	64T	553	$1.50	$3.75
Brett, George	78T	100	$1.95	$6.00	Brewer, Jim	65T	416	$ .30	$1.00
Brett, George	79T	330	$ .95	$3.00	Brewer, Jim	66T	158	$ .25	$ .85
					Brewer, Jim	67T	31	$ .25	$ .65
					Brewer, Jim	68T	298	$ .25	$ .65
					Brewer, Jim	69T	241	$ .25	$ .85
					Brewer, Jim	70T	571	$ .25	$ .85
					Brewer, Jim	71T	549	$ .30	$1.00
					Brewer, Jim	72T	151	$ .10	$ .35
					Brewer, Jim	73T	126	$ .06	$ .25
					Brewer, Jim	74T	189	$ .06	$ .25
					Brewer, Jim	75T	163	$ .06	$ .25
					Brewer, Jim	76T	459	$ .05	$ .20
					Brewer, Tom	55T	83	$1.35	$5.00
					Brewer, Tom	56T	34	$1.25	$4.50
					Brewer, Tom	57T	112	$ .95	$3.50
					Brewer, Tom	58T	220	$ .50	$2.00
					Brewer, Tom	59T	55	$1.00	$3.75
					Brewer, Tom	59T	346	$ .50	$1.95
					Brewer, Tom	60T	439	$ .50	$1.95
					Brewer, Tom	61T	434	$ .50	$2.00
					Brewers, Team	71T	698	$1.35	$4.00
					Brewers, Team	72T	106	$ .20	$ .80
					Brewers, Team	73T	127	$ .20	$ .80
					Brewers, Team	74T	314	$ .20	$ .80
					Brewers, Team Checklist	75T	384	$ .25	$ .85
					Brewers, Team Checklist	76T	606	$ .30	$1.00
					Brewers, Team Checklist	77T	51	$ .15	$ .50
					Brewers, Team Checklist	78T	328	$ .05	$ .25
					Brewers, Team Checklist	79T	577	$ .05	$ .25
					Brewers, Team Checklist	80T	659	$ .05	$ .25
					Brewers, Team Checklist	81T	668	$ .02	$ .20
					Brewers, Team Leaders	86T	426	$ .01	$ .03
					Brewers, Team Leaders	87T	56	$ .01	$ .03
					Brewers, Team Leaders	88T	639	$ .01	$ .03
					Brewers, Team Leaders	89T	759	$ .01	$ .04
Brett, George	80T	450	$ .75	$3.00	Brickell, Fritz	61T	333	$ .30	$1.00
Brett, George	81T	1	$ .15	$ .90	Brideweser, Jim	57T	382	$1.00	$3.75
Brett, George	81T	700	$ .45	$1.75	Bridges, Rocky	52T	239	$6.00	$18.00
Brett, George	82T	96	$ .05	$ .25	Bridges, Rocky	56T	324	$1.80	$6.00
Brett, George	82T	200	$ .30	$1.50	Bridges, Rocky	57T	294	$3.50	$13.00
Brett, George	82TAS	549	$ .10	$ .50	Bridges, Rocky	58T	274	$ .50	$2.00
Brett, George	82TIA	201	$ .15	$ .65	Bridges, Rocky	59T	318	$ .50	$1.95
Brett, George	83T	600	$ .15	$1.00	Bridges, Rocky	60T	22	$ .35	$1.10
Brett, George	83TAS	388	$ .10	$ .50	Bridges, Rocky	61T	508	$ .50	$2.00
Brett, George	84T	500	$ .15	$ .75	Briggs, Dan	77T	592	$ .05	$ .15
Brett, George	84T	710	$ .04	$ .20	Briggs, Dan	79T	77	$ .02	$ .10
Brett, George	84TAS	399	$ .06	$ .30	Briggs, Dan	80T	352	$ .01	$ .07
Brett, George	85T	100	$ .10	$ .50	Briggs, Dan	82T	102	$ .01	$ .06
Brett, George	85TAS	703	$ .08	$ .35	Briggs, Dan	82TTR	11	$ .02	$ .10
Brett, George	86T	300	$ .10	$ .50	Briggs, Johnny	59T	177	$ .50	$1.95
Brett, George	86TAS	714	$ .03	$ .25	Briggs, Johnny	60T	376	$ .50	$1.95
Brett, George	87T	400	$ .25	$ .85	Briggs, Johnny	64T	482	$ .40	$1.25
Brett, George	88T	700	$ .01	$ .25	Briggs, Johnny	65T	163	$ .25	$ .65
Brett, George	88TBB	157	$ .05	$ .25	Briggs, Johnny	66T	359	$ .25	$ .85
Brett, George	89T	200	$ .01	$ .15	Briggs, Johnny	67T	268	$ .25	$ .65
Brett, George	89TBB	46	$ .01	$ .25	Briggs, Johnny	68T	284	$ .25	$ .65
Brett, George	90T	60	$ .01	$ .15	Briggs, Johnny	69T	73	$ .25	$ .65
Brett, Ken	69T	476	$ .25	$ .65	Briggs, Johnny	70T	564	$ .25	$ .85
Brett, Ken	71T	89	$ .10	$ .35	Briggs, Johnny	71T	297	$ .10	$ .35
Brett, Ken	72T	517	$ .10	$ .35	Briggs, Johnny	72T	197	$ .10	$ .35
Brett, Ken	73T	444	$ .10	$ .35	Briggs, Johnny	73T	71	$ .06	$ .25
Brett, Ken	74T	237	$ .06	$ .25	Briggs, Johnny	74T	218	$ .06	$ .25
Brett, Ken	75T	250	$ .06	$ .25	Briggs, Johnny	75T	123	$ .06	$ .25
Brett, Ken	76T	401	$ .05	$ .20	Briggs, Johnny	76T	373	$ .05	$ .20
Brett, Ken	76TTR	401	$ .05	$ .20	Bright, Harry	59T	523	$2.00	$7.00
Brett, Ken	77T	157	$ .05	$ .15	Bright, Harry	60T	277	$ .35	$1.10
Brett, Ken	77T	631	$ .50	$2.00	Bright, Harry	61T	447	$ .50	$2.00
Brett, Ken	78T	682	$ .02	$ .10	Bright, Harry	62T	551	$3.75	$11.00
Brett, Ken	79T	557	$ .02	$ .10	Bright, Harry	63T	304	$ .35	$1.20
Brett, Ken	80T	521	$ .01	$ .07	Bright, Harry	64T	259	$ .25	$ .85
Brett, Ken	81T	47	$ .01	$ .07					

GEORGE BRETT
3rd BASE
George Brett
ROYALS

Player	Year	No.	VG	EX/MT	Player	Year	No.	VG	EX/MT
Bright, Harry	65T	584	$1.50	$3.75	Brock, Lou	63T	472	$35.00	$100.00
Briles, Nelson	65T	431	$ .35	$1.10	Brock, Lou	64T	29	$7.50	$25.00
Briles, Nelson	66T	243	$ .25	$ .85	Brock, Lou	65T	540	$10.00	$35.00
Briles, Nelson	67T	404	$ .25	$ .85	Brock, Lou	66T	125	$2.85	$9.00
Briles, Nelson	68T	540	$ .30	$1.00	Brock, Lou	67T	63	$1.35	$4.00
Briles, Nelson	69T	60	$ .25	$ .65	Brock, Lou	67T	285	$3.00	$9.00
Briles, Nelson	70T	435	$ .10	$ .35	Brock, Lou	68T	520	$2.85	$9.00
Briles, Nelson	71T	257	$ .10	$ .35	Brock, Lou	68TAS	372	$1.25	$3.00
Briles, Nelson	72T	605	$ .25	$ .85	Brock, Lou	69T	85	$3.00	$9.00
Briles, Nelson	73T	303	$ .06	$ .25	Brock, Lou	69TAS	428	$1.35	$4.00
Briles, Nelson	74T	123	$ .06	$ .25	Brock, Lou	70T	330	$2.00	$8.00
Briles, Nelson	74TTR	123	$ .06	$ .25	Brock, Lou	71T	625	$4.50	$12.00
Briles, Nelson	75T	495	$ .06	$ .25	Brock, Lou	72T	200	$1.35	$4.00
Briles, Nelson	76T	569	$ .05	$ .20	Brock, Lou	73T	64	$ .35	$1.10
Briles, Nelson	77T	174	$ .05	$ .15	Brock, Lou	73T	320	$1.25	$4.50
Briles, Nelson	78T	717	$ .02	$ .10	Brock, Lou	74T	60	$1.25	$4.50
Briles, Nelson	79T	262	$ .02	$ .10	Brock, Lou	74T	204	$ .30	$1.00
Briley, Greg	89T	781	$ .01	$ .50	Brock, Lou	75T	309	$ .30	$1.00
Briley, Greg	89TBB	247	$ .01	$ .20	Brock, Lou	75T	540	$ .75	$3.00
Briley, Greg	90T	288	$ .01	$ .20	Brock, Lou	75THL	2	$ .50	$2.00
Brinkman, Charlie "Chuck"	71T	13	$ .10	$ .35	Brock, Lou	76T	10	$ .50	$3.00
Brinkman, Chuck	72T	786	$ .70	$2.10	Brock, Lou	76T	197	$ .15	$ .50
Brinkman, Chuck	73T	404	$ .06	$ .25	Brock, Lou	77T	355	$ .75	$2.00
Brinkman, Chuck	74T	641	$ .06	$ .25	Brock, Lou	78T	170	$ .85	$3.25
Brinkman, Ed	63T	479	$2.50	$6.50	Brock, Lou	78TRB	1	$1.00	$4.00
Brinkman, Ed	64T	46	$ .25	$ .85	Brock, Lou	79T	665	$ .35	$1.25
Brinkman, Ed	65T	417	$ .30	$1.00	Brock, Lou	79TRH	415	$ .15	$ .50
Brinkman, Ed	66T	251	$ .25	$ .85	Brock, Lou	80THL	1	$ .35	$1.25
Brinkman, Ed	67T	311	$ .25	$ .65	Brock, Lou	89TTB	662	$ .01	$ .04
Brinkman, Ed	68T	49	$ .25	$ .65	Brodowski, Dick	52T	404	$39.00	$135.00
Brinkman, Ed	69T	153	$ .25	$ .65	Brodowski, Dick	53T	69	$3.75	$13.00
Brinkman, Ed	70T	711	$ .50	$2.00	Brodowski, Dick	54T	221	$2.10	$7.50
Brinkman, Ed	71T	389	$ .10	$ .35	Brodowski, Dick	55T	171	$4.25	$13.00
Brinkman, Ed	72T	535	$ .25	$ .85	Brodowski, Dick	56T	157	$1.25	$4.50
Brinkman, Ed	73T	5	$ .06	$ .25	Brodowski, Dick	59T	371	$ .50	$1.95
Brinkman, Ed	74T	138	$ .06	$ .25	Broglio, Ernie	59T	296	$ .50	$1.95
Brinkman, Ed	75T	439	$ .06	$ .25	Broglio, Ernie	60T	16	$ .35	$1.10
Brissie, Lou	51Tbb	31	$5.50	$17.00	Broglio, Ernie	61T	45	$ .60	$2.75
Brissie, Lou	52T	270	$11.50	$38.00	Broglio, Ernie	61T	47	$ .60	$1.75
Bristol, Dave	67T	21	$ .25	$ .65	Broglio, Ernie	61T	49	$ .50	$1.50
Bristol, Dave	68T	148	$ .25	$ .65	Broglio, Ernie	61T	420	$ .35	$1.00
Bristol, Dave	69T	234	$ .25	$ .85	Broglio, Ernie	61T	451	$1.25	$3.50
Bristol, Dave	70T	556	$ .30	$1.00	Broglio, Ernie	62T	507	$ .50	$1.75
Bristol, Dave	71T	637	$ .30	$1.00	Broglio, Ernie	63T	313	$ .24	$ .60
Bristol, Dave	72T	602	$ .25	$ .85	Broglio, Ernie	64T	59	$ .25	$ .85
Bristol, Dave	73T	377	$ .10	$ .35	Broglio, Ernie	65T	565	$ .80	$2.00
Bristol, Dave	74T	531	$ .25	$ .85	Broglio, Ernie	66T	423	$ .15	$ .35
Britton, Jim	64T	94	$ .25	$ .85	Brohamer, Jack	73T	181	$ .06	$ .25
Britton, Jim	68T	76	$ .25	$ .65	Brohamer, Jack	75T	552	$ .05	$ .15
Britton, Jim	69T	154	$ .25	$ .65	Brohamer, Jack	76T	618	$ .05	$ .20
Britton, Jim	70T	646	$ .50	$2.00	Brohamer, Jack	77T	293	$ .05	$ .15
Britton, Jim	71T	699	$ .70	$2.10	Brohamer, Jack	78T	416	$ .02	$ .10
Britton, Jimmy	72T	351	$ .10	$ .35	Brohamer, Jack	79T	63	$ .02	$ .10
Brizzolara, Tony	80T	156	$ .01	$ .07	Brohamer, Jack	80T	349	$ .01	$ .07
Brklyn-Boston, 26 Inning Tie	61T	403	$ .60	$1.75	Brohamer, Jack	81T	462	$ .01	$ .07
Broberg, Pete	72T	64	$ .10	$ .35	Brookens, Tom	80T	416	$ .01	$ .07
Broberg, Pete	73T	162	$ .06	$ .25	Brookens, Tom	81T	251	$ .01	$ .07
Broberg, Pete	74T	425	$ .06	$ .25	Brookens, Tom	82T	753	$ .01	$ .06
Broberg, Pete	75T	542	$ .06	$ .25	Brookens, Tom	83T	119	$ .01	$ .06
Broberg, Pete	76T	39	$ .05	$ .20	Brookens, Tom	84T	14	$ .01	$ .05
Broberg. Pete	77T	409	$ .05	$ .15	Brookens, Tom	85T	512	$ .01	$ .04
Broberg, Pete	78T	722	$ .02	$ .10	Brookens, Tom	86T	643	$ .01	$ .03
Broberg, Pete	79T	578	$ .02	$ .10	Brookens, Tom	87T	713	$ .01	$ .03
Brock, Greg	83TTR	14	$ .25	$ .65	Brookens, Tom	88T	474	$ .01	$ .03
Brock, Greg	84T	555	$ .01	$ .05	Brookens, Tom	89T	342	$ .01	$ .04
Brock, Greg	85T	753	$ .01	$ .04	Brooks, Bobby	70T	381	$ .10	$ .35
Brock, Greg	86T	368	$ .01	$ .03	Brooks, Bobby	71T	633	$ .30	$1.00
Brock, Greg	87T	26	$ .01	$ .03	Brooks, Hubie	81T	259	$ .50	$1.50
Brock, Greg	87TTR	9	$ .01	$ .10	Brooks, Hubie	81TTR	742	$ .20	$1.00
Brock, Greg	88T	212	$ .01	$ .03	Brooks, Hubie	82T	246	$ .05	$ .25
Brock, Greg	88TBB	217	$ .01	$ .05	Brooks, Hubie	82T	494	$ .01	$ .06
Brock, Greg	89T	517	$ .01	$ .04	Brooks, Hubie	83T	134	$ .01	$ .06
Brock, Greg	89TBB	100	$ .01	$ .05	Brooks, Hubie	84T	368	$ .01	$ .05
Brock, Greg	90T	139	$ .01	$ .03	Brooks, Hubie	85T	222	$ .01	$ .04
Brock, Lou	62T	387	$27.50	$87.50	Brooks, Hubie	85TTR	9	$ .02	$ .10

TOPPS

Player	Year	No.	VG	EX/MT	Player	Year	No.	VG	EX/MT
Brooks, Hubie	86T	555	$ .01	$ .03	Brown, Jackie	75T	316	$ .06	$ .25
Brooks, Hubie	87T	650	$ .01	$ .10	Brown, Jackie	76T	301	$ .05	$ .20
Brooks, Hubie	88T	50	$ .01	$ .03	Brown, Jackie	77T	147	$ .05	$ .15
Brooks, Hubie	88TBB	81	$ .01	$ .05	Brown, Jackie	78T	699	$ .02	$ .10
Brooks, Hubie	89T	485	$ .01	$ .04	Brown, Kevin	89TTR	15	$ .01	$ .15
Brooks, Hubie	89TBB	301	$ .01	$ .05	Brown, Kevin	90T	136	$ .01	$ .10
Brooks, Hubie	90T	745	$ .01	$ .03	Brown, Larry	64T	301	$ .25	$ .85
Brosnan, Jim	57T	155	$ .95	$3.50	Brown, Larry	65T	468	$ .50	$2.00
Brosnan, Jim	58T	342	$ .65	$2.00	Brown, Larry	66T	16	$ .25	$ .85
Brosnan, Jim	59T	194	$ .60	$1.75	Brown, Larry	67T	145	$ .25	$ .65
Brosnan, Jim	60T	449	$ .60	$1.75	Brown, Larry	68T	197	$ .25	$ .65
Brosnan, Jim	61T	513	$ .50	$1.95	Brown, Larry	69T	503	$ .25	$ .65
Brosnan, Jim	62T	2	$ .50	$1.95	Brown, Larry	70T	391	$ .10	$ .35
Brosnan, Jim	63T	116	$ .25	$ .85	Brown, Larry	71T	539	$ .30	$1.00
Brouhard, Mark	82T	517	$ .01	$ .06	Brown, Larry	72T	279	$ .10	$ .35
Brouhard, Mark	83T	167	$ .01	$ .06	Brown, Mark	86T	451	$ .01	$ .03
Brouhard, Mark	84T	528	$ .01	$ .05	Brown, Mike	83TTR	15	$ .02	$ .10
Brouhard, Mark	85T	653	$ .01	$ .04	Brown, Mike	84T	472	$ .01	$ .05
Brouhard, Mark	86T	473	$ .01	$ .03	Brown, Mike	84T	643	$ .01	$ .05
Brower, Bob	87TTR	10	$ .01	$ .10	Brown, Mike	85T	258	$ .01	$ .04
Brower, Bob	88T	252	$ .01	$ .03	Brown, Mike	86T	114	$ .01	$ .03
Brower, Bob	89T	754	$ .01	$ .04	Brown, Mike	87T	271	$ .01	$ .03
Brown, Bobby	80T	670	$ .01	$ .07	Brown, Mike	87T	341	$ .01	$ .03
Brown, Bobby	81T	418	$ .01	$ .07	Brown, Ollie	66T	524	$4.00	$10.00
Brown, Bobby	82T	791	$ .01	$ .06	Brown, Ollie	67T	83	$ .25	$ .65
Brown, Bobby	82TTR	12	$ .02	$ .10	Brown, Ollie	68T	223	$ .25	$ .65
Brown, Bobby	83T	287	$ .01	$ .06	Brown, Ollie	69T	149	$ .25	$ .65
Brown, Bobby	84T	261	$ .01	$ .05	Brown, Ollie	70T	130	$ .10	$ .35
Brown, Bobby	85T	583	$ .01	$ .04	Brown, Ollie	71T	505	$ .10	$ .35
Brown, Bobby	86T	182	$ .01	$ .03	Brown, Ollie	72T	551	$ .25	$ .85
Brown, Chris	85TTR	10	$ .15	$ .50	Brown, Ollie	72TIA	552	$ .25	$ .85
Brown, Chris	86T	383	$ .05	$ .40	Brown, Ollie	73T	526	$ .10	$ .35
Brown, Chris	87T	180	$ .06	$ .25	Brown, Ollie	74T	625	$ .06	$ .25
Brown, Chris	88T	568	$ .01	$ .03	Brown, Ollie	75T	596	$ .06	$ .25
Brown, Chris	88TBB	130	$ .01	$ .05	Brown, Ollie	76T	223	$ .05	$ .20
Brown, Chris	89T	481	$ .01	$ .04	Brown, Ollie	77T	84	$ .05	$ .15
Brown, Darrell	84T	193	$ .01	$ .05	Brown, Oscar	71T	52	$ .10	$ .35
Brown, Darrell	85T	767	$ .01	$ .04	Brown, Oscar	72T	516	$ .10	$ .35
Brown, Dick	58T	456	$ .50	$1.95	Brown, Oscar	73T	312	$ .06	$ .25
Brown, Dick	59T	61	$1.00	$3.75	Brown, Paul	62T	181	$ .35	$1.10
Brown, Dick	60T	256	$ .35	$1.10	Brown, Paul	63T	478	$2.50	$6.50
Brown, Dick	61T	192	$ .30	$1.00	Brown, Paul	64T	319	$ .25	$ .85
Brown, Dick	62T	438	$ .70	$2.10	Brown, Scott	82T	351	$ .01	$ .06
Brown, Dick	63T	112	$ .25	$ .85	Brown, Tom	64T	311	$ .25	$ .85
Brown, Gates	64T	471	$ .40	$1.25	Brown, Tommy	52T	281	$14.00	$45.00
Brown, Gates	65T	19	$ .25	$ .65	Brown, Winston	61T	391	$ .50	$2.00
Brown, Gates	66T	362	$ .25	$ .85	Browne, Byron	66T	139	$ .25	$ .85
Brown, Gates	67T	134	$ .25	$ .65	Browne, Byron	67T	439	$ .25	$ .85
Brown, Gates	68T	583	$ .30	$1.00	Browne, Byron	68T	296	$ .25	$ .65
Brown, Gates	69T	256	$ .25	$ .85	Browne, Byron	70T	388	$ .10	$ .35
Brown, Gates	70T	98	$ .10	$ .35	Browne, Byron	71T	659	$ .70	$2.10
Brown, Gates	71T	503	$ .10	$ .35	Browne, Jerry	87TTR	11	$ .05	$ .20
Brown, Gates	72T	187	$ .10	$ .35	Browne, Jerry	88T	139	$ .01	$ .03
Brown, Gates	73T	508	$ .06	$ .25	Browne, Jerry	88TBB	163	$ .01	$ .05
Brown, Gates	74T	389	$ .06	$ .25	Browne, Jerry	89T	532	$ .01	$ .04
Brown, Gates	75T	371	$ .06	$ .25	Browne, Jerry	89TBB	236	$ .01	$ .10
Brown, Hal	53T	184	$3.75	$13.00	Browne, Jerry	89TTR	16	$ .01	$ .05
Brown, Hal	54T	172	$2.10	$7.50	Browne, Jerry	90T	442	$ .01	$ .03
Brown, Hal	55T	148	$1.35	$5.00	Browning, Brian	83T	442	$ .01	$ .06
Brown, Hal	57T	194	$ .95	$3.50	Browning, Tom	85TTR	11	$ .35	$1.10
Brown, Hal	58T	381	$ .50	$2.00	Browning, Tom	86T	652	$ .15	$ .50
Brown, Hal	59T	487	$ .50	$1.95	Browning, Tom	87T	65	$ .01	$ .25
Brown, Hal	60T	89	$ .35	$1.10	Browning, Tom	88T	577	$ .05	$ .10
Brown, Hal	61T	46	$ .50	$2.00	Browning, Tom	88TBB	96	$ .01	$ .10
Brown, Hal	61T	218	$ .30	$1.00	Browning, Tom	89T	234	$ .01	$ .10
Brown, Hal	62T	488	$ .70	$2.10	Browning, Tom	89TBB	14	$ .01	$ .10
Brown, Hal	63T	289	$ .50	$2.00	Browning, Tom	90T	418	$ .01	$ .10
Brown, Hal	64T	56	$ .25	$ .85	Brubaker, Bruce	65T	493	$ .50	$2.00
Brown, Ike	70T	152	$ .10	$ .35	Brubaker, Bruce	67T	276	$ .25	$ .65
Brown, Ike	71T	669	$ .70	$2.10	Bruce, Bob	60T	118	$ .35	$1.10
Brown, Ike	72T	284	$ .10	$ .35	Bruce, Bob	61T	83	$ .30	$1.00
Brown, Ike	73T	633	$ .35	$1.10	Bruce, Bob	62T	419	$ .70	$2.10
Brown, Ike	74T	409	$ .06	$ .25	Bruce, Bob	63T	24	$ .25	$ .85
Brown, Jackie	71T	591	$ .30	$1.00	Bruce, Bob	64T	282	$ .25	$ .85
Brown, Jackie	74T	89	$ .06	$ .25	Bruce, Bob	65T	240	$ .30	$1.00

Player	Year	No.	VG	EX/MT
Bruce, Bob	66T	64	$ .25	$ .85
Bruce, Bob	67T	417	$ .25	$ .85
Bruhert, Mike	79T	172	$ .02	$ .10
Brumley, Mike	64T	167	$4.00	$20.00
Brumley, Mike	65T	523	$1.50	$3.75
Brumley, Mike	66T	29	$ .25	$ .85
Brumley, Mike	89TBB	324	$ .01	$ .05
Brumley, Mike	90T	471	$ .01	$ .03
Brummer, Glenn	82T	561	$ .01	$ .06
Brummer, Glenn	83T	311	$ .01	$ .06
Brummer, Glenn	84T	152	$ .01	$ .05
Brummer, Glenn	86T	616	$ .01	$ .03
Brunansky, Tom	82T	653	$ .95	$3.50
Brunansky, Tom	82TTR	13	$ .50	$2.00
Brunansky, Tom	83T	232	$ .06	$ .30
Brunansky, Tom	84T	447	$ .10	$ .50
Brunansky, Tom	85T	122	$ .01	$ .04
Brunansky, Tom	86T	565	$ .02	$ .20

Player	Year	No.	VG	EX/MT
Brunansky, Tom	87T	776	$ .01	$ .10
Brunansky, Tom	88T	375	$ .01	$ .10
Brunansky, Tom	88TBB	211	$ .01	$ .05
Brunansky, Tom	88TTR	20	$ .01	$ .05
Brunansky, Tom	89T	60	$ .01	$ .04
Brunansky, Tom	89TBB	54	$ .01	$ .05
Brunansky, Tom	90T	409	$ .01	$ .03
Brunet, George	58T	139	$ .50	$2.00
Brunet, George	63T	538	$1.50	$3.75
Brunet, George	64T	322	$ .25	$ .85
Brunet, George	65T	242	$ .30	$1.00
Brunet, George	66T	393	$ .25	$ .85
Brunet, George	67T	122	$ .25	$ .65
Brunet, George	68T	347	$ .25	$ .65
Brunet, George	69T	645	$ .25	$ .85
Brunet, George	70T	328	$ .10	$ .35
Brunet, George	71T	73	$ .10	$ .35
Bruno, Tom	79T	724	$ .25	$ .65
Brusstar, Warren	78T	297	$ .02	$ .10
Brusstar, Warren	79T	653	$ .02	$ .10
Brusstar, Warren	80T	52	$ .01	$ .07
Brusstar, Warren	81T	426	$ .01	$ .07
Brusstar, Warren	82T	647	$ .01	$ .06
Brusstar, Warren	84T	304	$ .01	$ .05
Brusstar, Warren	85T	189	$ .01	$ .04

Player	Year	No.	VG	EX/MT
Brusstar, Warren	86T	564	$ .01	$ .03
Bruton, Bill	53T	214	$3.75	$13.00
Bruton, Bill	54T	109	$2.00	$7.00
Bruton, Bill	56T	185	$2.50	$8.00
Bruton, Bill	57T	48	$ .95	$3.50
Bruton, Bill	58T	355	$ .50	$2.00
Bruton, Bill	59T	165	$ .50	$1.95
Bruton, Bill	60T	37	$ .35	$1.10
Bruton, Bill	61T	251	$ .30	$1.00
Bruton, Bill	62T	335	$ .35	$1.10
Bruton, Bill	63T	437	$ .35	$1.20
Bruton, Bill	64T	98	$ .25	$ .85
Bryan, Bill	63T	236	$ .25	$ .85
Bryan, Bill	65T	51	$ .25	$ .65
Bryan, Bill	66T	332	$ .25	$ .85
Bryan, Bill	67T	601	$5.00	$15.00
Bryan, Bill	68T	498	$ .30	$1.00
Bryant, Clay	74T	521	$ .06	$ .25
Bryant, Derek	80T	671	$ .01	$ .07
Bryant, Don	69T	499	$ .25	$ .65
Bryant, Don	70T	473	$ .10	$ .35
Bryant, Don	74T	403	$ .06	$ .25
Bryant, Ralph	87TTR	12	$ .01	$ .07
Bryant, Ron	70T	433	$ .10	$ .35
Bryant, Ron	71T	621	$ .30	$1.00
Bryant, Ron	72T	185	$ .10	$ .35
Bryant, Ron	72TIA	186	$ .10	$ .35
Bryant, Ron	73T	298	$ .06	$ .25
Bryant, Ron	74T	104	$ .06	$ .25
Bryant, Ron	74T	205	$ .06	$ .25
Bryant, Ron	75T	265	$ .06	$ .25
Bryden, T.R.	87T	387	$ .01	$ .03
Brye, Steve	71T	391	$ .10	$ .35
Brye, Steve	72T	28	$ .10	$ .35
Brye, Steve	73T	353	$ .06	$ .25
Brye, Steve	74T	232	$ .06	$ .25
Brye, Steve	75T	151	$ .06	$ .25
Brye, Steve	76T	519	$ .05	$ .20
Brye, Steve	77T	424	$ .05	$ .15
Brye, Steve	78T	673	$ .02	$ .10
Brye, Steve	79T	28	$ .02	$ .10
Buchek, Jerry	62T	439	$ .70	$2.10
Buchek, Jerry	64T	314	$ .25	$ .85
Buchek, Jerry	65T	397	$ .30	$1.00
Buchek, Jerry	66T	454	$ .70	$2.10
Buchek, Jerry	67T	574	$6.00	$20.00
Buchek, Jerry	68T	277	$ .25	$ .65
Buchia, Johnny	52T	19	$14.00	$45.00
Buckner, Bill	70T	286	$1.35	$4.00
Buckner, Bill	71T	529	$ .70	$2.00
Buckner, Bill	72T	114	$ .30	$1.00
Buckner, Bill	73T	368	$ .30	$1.00
Buckner, Bill	74T	505	$ .25	$ .85
Buckner, Bill	75T	244	$ .25	$ .85
Buckner, Bill	76T	253	$ .10	$ .35
Buckner, Bill	77T	27	$ .06	$ .25
Buckner, Bill	78T	473	$ .05	$ .20
Buckner, Bill	79T	346	$ .05	$ .20
Buckner, Bill	80T	135	$ .03	$ .15
Buckner, Bill	81T	1	$ .15	$ .60
Buckner, Bill	81T	625	$ .03	$ .15
Buckner, Bill	82T	456	$ .01	$ .06
Buckner, Bill	82T	760	$ .02	$ .10
Buckner, Bill	83T	250	$ .01	$ .10
Buckner, Bill	84T	545	$ .02	$ .10
Buckner, Bill	84TTR	17	$ .05	$ .20
Buckner, Bill	85T	65	$ .01	$ .04
Buckner, Bill	86T	443	$ .01	$ .03
Buckner, Bill	87T	764	$ .01	$ .03
Buckner, Bill	88T	147	$ .01	$ .03
Budaska, Mark	82T	531	$ .01	$ .06
Buddin, Don	58T	297	$ .50	$2.00
Buddin, Don	59T	32	$1.00	$3.75
Buddin, Don	60T	520	$2.00	$7.00
Buddin, Don	61T	99	$ .30	$1.00

TOPPS

Player	Year	No.	VG	EX/MT	Player	Year	No.	VG	EX/MT
Buddin, Don	62T	332	$ .35	$1.10	Bunning, Jim	62T	460	$1.50	$4.50
Buechele, Steve	86T	397	$ .01	$ .03	Bunning, Jim	63T	8	$ .35	$1.10
Buechele, Steve	87T	176	$ .01	$ .03	Bunning, Jim	63T	10	$ .35	$1.10
Buechele, Steve	88T	537	$ .01	$ .03	Bunning, Jim	63T	218	$ .35	$1.10
Buechele, Steve	88TBB	104	$ .01	$ .05	Bunning, Jim	63T	365	$2.00	$6.00
Buechele, Steve	89T	732	$ .01	$ .04	Bunning, Jim	64T	6	$ .35	$1.10
Buechele, Steve	89TBB	156	$ .01	$ .05	Bunning, Jim	64T	265	$1.35	$4.00
Buechele, Steve	90T	279	$ .01	$ .03	Bunning, Jim	65T	20	$1.35	$4.00
Buford, Don	65T	81	$ .25	$ .65	Bunning, Jim	66T	435	$ .95	$2.75
Buford, Don	66T	465	$ .70	$2.10	Bunning, Jim	67T	238	$1.50	$3.75
Buford, Don	67T	143	$ .25	$ .65	Bunning, Jim	67T	560	$11.50	$45.00
Buford, Don	67T	232	$ .25	$ .65	Bunning, Jim	68T	7	$ .50	$1.95
Buford, Don	68T	194	$ .25	$ .65	Bunning, Jim	68T	9	$ .50	$1.95
Buford, Don	69T	478	$ .25	$ .65	Bunning, Jim	68T	11	$ .50	$1.95
Buford, Don	70T	428	$ .10	$ .35	Bunning, Jim	68T	215	$1.35	$4.00
Buford, Don	71T	29	$ .10	$ .35	Bunning, Jim	69T	175	$ .70	$2.00
Buford, Don	72T	370	$ .10	$ .35	Bunning, Jim	70T	403	$1.25	$4.50
Buford, Don	73T	183	$ .06	$ .25	Bunning, Jim	71T	574	$1.35	$4.00
Buhl, Bob	54T	210	$1.75	$7.00	Burbach, Bill	69T	658	$ .25	$ .85
Buhl, Bob	56T	244	$2.50	$8.00	Burbach, Bill	70T	167	$ .10	$ .35
Buhl, Bob	57T	127	$ .95	$3.50	Burbach, Bill	71T	683	$ .70	$2.10
Buhl, Bob	58T	176	$ .50	$2.00	Burbrink, Nelson	56T	27	$1.25	$4.50
Buhl, Bob	59T	347	$ .50	$1.95	Burchart, Larry	69T	597	$10.00	$40.00
Buhl, Bob	60T	230	.$1.25	$3.50	Burchart, Larry	70T	412	$ .10	$ .35
Buhl, Bob	60T	374	$ .50	$1.95	Burda, Bob	69T	392	$ .25	$ .65
Buhl, Bob	61T	145	$ .30	$1.00	Burda, Bob	70T	357	$ .10	$ .35
Buhl, Bob	62T	458	$ .70	$2.00	Burda, Bob	71T	541	$ .30	$1.00
Buhl, Bob	63T	175	$ .25	$ .85	Burda, Bob	72T	734	$ .70	$2.10
Buhl, Bob	64T	96	$ .25	$ .85	Burdette, Fred	64T	408	$ .40	$1.25
Buhl, Bob	65T	264	$ .30	$1.00	Burdette, Lew	56T	219	$2.50	$10.00
Buhl, Bob	66T	185	$ .25	$ .85	Burdette, Lew	57T	208	$2.10	$7.50
Buhl, Bob	67T	68	$ .25	$ .65	Burdette, Lou	58T	10	$ .80	$2.75
Buhner, Jay	88TTR	21	$ .01	$ .25	Burdette, Lou	58T	289	$ .75	$2.50
Buhner, Jay	89T	223	$ .01	$ .15	Burdette, Lou	59T	440	$1.35	$4.00
Buhner, Jay	89TBB	20	$ .01	$ .05	Burdette, Lou	60T	70	$ .70	$2.00
Buhner, Jay	90T	554	$ .01	$ .03	Burdette, Lou	60T	230	$1.25	$3.50
Buice, DeWayne	87TTR	13	$ .01	$ .07	Burdette, Lou	61T	47	$ .60	$1.75
Buice, DeWayne	88T	649	$ .01	$ .03	Burdette, Lou	61T	320	$1.00	$3.75
Buice, DeWayne	89T	147	$ .01	$ .04	Burdette, Lou	62T	380	$ .70	$2.00
Bulling, Terry	78T	432	$ .02	$ .10	Burdette, Lou	63T	429	$ .60	$1.75
Bulling, Terry	82T	98	$ .01	$ .06	Burdette, Lou	64T	523	$1.25	$3.50
Bulling, Terry	83T	519	$ .01	$ .06	Burdette, Lou	65T	64	$ .35	$1.10
Bumbry, Alonza "Al"	73T	614	$10.00	$40.00	Burdette, Lou	66T	299	$ .35	$1.10
Bumbry, Al	74T	137	$ .06	$ .25	Burdette, Lou	67T	265	$ .35	$1.10
Bumbry, Al	75T	358	$ .06	$ .25	Burdette, Lew "Lou"	73T	237	$ .30	$1.00
Bumbry, Al	76T	307	$ .05	$ .20	Burford, Don	64T	368	$ .25	$ .85
Bumbry, Al	77T	626	$ .05	$ .15	Burgess, Smoky	52T	357	$50.00	$150.00
Bumbry, Al	78T	188	$ .02	$ .10	Burgess, Smoky	53T	10	$4.50	$15.00
Bumbry, Al	79T	517	$ .02	$ .10	Burgess, Smoky	56T	192	$2.50	$8.00
Bumbry, Al	80T	65	$ .01	$ .07	Burgess, Smoky	57T	228	$ .60	$2.50
Bumbry, Al	81T	425	$ .01	$ .07	Burgess, Smoky	58T	49	$1.50	$3.75
Bumbry, Al	82T	265	$ .01	$ .06	Burgess, Smoky	59T	432	$ .50	$1.95
Bumbry, Al	83T	655	$ .01	$ .06	Burgess, Smoky	60T	393	$ .30	$1.35
Bumbry, Al	84T	319	$ .01	$ .05	Burgess, Smoky	61T	461	$ .60	$1.75
Bumbry, Al	85T	726	$ .01	$ .04	Burgess, Smoky	62T	389	$ .60	$1.75
Bumbry, Al	85TTR	12	$ .02	$ .10	Burgess, Smoky	63T	18	$2.35	$10.00
Bumbry, Al	86T	583	$ .01	$ .03	Burgess, Smoky	63T	425	$ .35	$1.10
Bunker, Wally	64T	201	$ .25	$ .85	Burgess, Smoky	64T	37	$ .25	$ .85
Bunker, Wally	65T	9	$ .30	$1.00	Burgess, Smoky	65T	198	$ .15	$ .50
Bunker, Wally	65T	290	$ .30	$1.00	Burgess, Smoky	66T	354	$ .15	$ .50
Bunker, Wally	66T	499	$ .70	$2.10	Burgess, Smoky	67T	506	$ .50	$2.00
Bunker, Wally	67T	585	$1.35	$4.00	Burgmeier, Tom	69T	558	$ .25	$ .85
Bunker, Wally	68T	489	$ .30	$1.00	Burgmeier, Tom	70T	108	$ .10	$ .35
Bunker, Wally	69T	137	$ .25	$ .65	Burgmeier, Tom	71T	431	$ .10	$ .35
Bunker, Wally	70T	266	$ .10	$ .35	Burgmeier, Tom	72T	246	$ .10	$ .35
Bunker, Wally	71T	528	$ .30	$1.00	Burgmeier, Tom	73T	306	$ .06	$ .25
Bunning, Jim	57T	338	$25.00	$90.00	Burgmeier, Tom	75T	478	$ .06	$ .25
Bunning, Jim	58T	115	$2.50	$8.50	Burgmeier, Tom	76T	87	$ .05	$ .20
Bunning, Jim	59T	149	$3.00	$9.00	Burgmeier, Tom	77T	398	$ .05	$ .15
Bunning, Jim	60T	502	$2.00	$8.00	Burgmeier, Tom	78T	678	$ .02	$ .10
Bunning, Jim	61T	46	$ .50	$2.00	Burgmeier, Tom	79T	524	$ .02	$ .10
Bunning, Jim	61T	50	$ .50	$3.00	Burgmeier, Tom	80T	128	$ .01	$ .07
Bunning, Jim	61T	490	$2.00	$6.00	Burgmeier, Tom	81T	320	$ .01	$ .07
Bunning, Jim	62T	57	$ .50	$1.95	Burgmeier, Tom	82T	455	$ .01	$ .06
Bunning, Jim	62T	59	$ .50	$1.95	Burgmeier, Tom	83T	213	$ .01	$ .06

Player	Year	No.	VG	EX/MT
Burgmeier, Tom	83TTR	16	$ .02	$ .10
Burgmeier, Tom	84T	33	$ .01	$ .05
Burk, Mack	57T	91	$ .95	$3.50
Burk, Mack	58T	278	$ .50	$2.00
Burke, Glenn	78T	562	$ .02	$ .10
Burke, Glenn	79T	163	$ .02	$ .10
Burke, Leo	63T	249	$ .25	$ .85
Burke, Leo	64T	557	$1.50	$3.75
Burke, Leo	65T	202	$ .30	$1.00
Burke, Steve	78T	709	$ .02	$ .10
Burke, Tim	86T	258	$ .01	$ .10
Burke, Tim	87T	624	$ .01	$ .03
Burke, Tim	88T	529	$ .01	$ .03
Burke, Tim	89T	48	$ .01	$ .04
Burke, Tim	90T	195	$ .01	$ .03
Burks, Ellis	87TTR	14	$ .25	$2.00
Burks, Ellis	88T	269	$ .25	$1.50
Burks, Ellis	88TBB	80	$ .10	$ .50
Burks, Ellis	89T	785	$ .05	$ .40
Burks, Ellis	89TBB	259	$ .01	$ .25
Burks, Ellis	90T	155	$ .01	$ .15
Burleson, Rick	75T	302	$ .06	$ .25
Burleson, Rick	76T	29	$ .05	$ .20
Burleson, Rick	77T	585	$ .05	$ .15
Burleson, Rick	78T	245	$ .02	$ .10
Burleson, Rick	79T	125	$ .02	$ .10
Burleson, Rick	80T	645	$ .01	$ .07
Burleson, Rick	81T	455	$ .01	$ .07
Burleson, Rick	81TTR	743	$ .02	$ .10
Burleson, Rick	82T	55	$ .01	$ .06
Burleson, Rick	83T	315	$ .01	$ .06
Burleson, Rick	84T	735	$ .01	$ .05
Burleson, Rick	86TTR	16	$ .02	$ .10
Burleson, Rick	87T	579	$ .01	$ .03
Burnette, Wally	57T	13	$ .95	$3.50
Burnette, Wally	58T	69	$1.00	$3.75
Burns, Britt	81T	412	$ .01	$ .07
Burns, Britt	82T	44	$ .01	$ .06
Burns, Britt	83T	541	$ .01	$ .06
Burns, Britt	84T	125	$ .01	$ .05

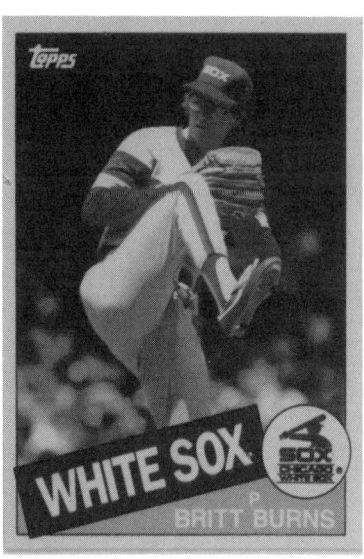

Player	Year	No.	VG	EX/MT
Burns, Britt	85T	338	$ .01	$ .04
Burns, Britt	86T	679	$ .01	$ .03
Burns, Todd	89T	174	$ .01	$ .25

Player	Year	No.	VG	EX/MT
Burns, Todd	89TBB	10	$ .01	$ .05
Burns, Todd	90T	369	$ .01	$ .03
Burnside, Pete	58T	211	$ .50	$2.00
Burnside, Pete	59T	354	$ .50	$1.95
Burnside, Pete	60T	261	$ .35	$1.10
Burnside, Pete	61T	507	$ .50	$2.00
Burnside, Pete	62T	207	$ .35	$1.10
Burnside, Pete	63T	19	$ .25	$ .85
Burright, Larry	62T	348	$ .35	$1.10
Burright, Larry	63T	174	$ .25	$ .85
Burris, Ray	74T	161	$ .06	$ .25
Burris, Ray	75T	566	$ .05	$ .15
Burris, Ray	76T	51	$ .05	$ .20
Burris, Ray	77T	190	$ .05	$ .15
Burris, Ray	78T	371	$ .02	$ .10
Burris, Ray	79T	98	$ .02	$ .10
Burris, Ray	80T	364	$ .01	$ .07
Burris, Ray	81T	654	$ .01	$ .07
Burris, Ray	81TTR	744	$ .02	$ .10
Burris, Ray	82T	227	$ .01	$ .06
Burris, Ray	83T	474	$ .01	$ .06
Burris, Ray	84T	552	$ .01	$ .05
Burris, Ray	84TTR	18	$ .02	$ .10
Burris, Ray	85T	758	$ .01	$ .04
Burris, Ray	85TTR	13	$ .02	$ .10
Burris, Ray	86T	106	$ .01	$ .03
Burroughs, Jeff	72T	191	$ .15	$ .50
Burroughs, Jeff	73T	489	$ .25	$ .65
Burroughs, Jeff	74T	223	$ .06	$ .25
Burroughs, Jeff	75T	212	$ .25	$ .85
Burroughs, Jeff	75T	308	$ .30	$1.00
Burroughs, Jeff	75T	470	$ .06	$ .25
Burroughs, Jeff	76T	360	$ .05	$ .20
Burroughs, Jeff	77T	55	$ .05	$ .15
Burroughs, Jeff	78T	130	$ .02	$ .10
Burroughs, Jeff	79T	245	$ .02	$ .10
Burroughs, Jeff	80T	545	$ .01	$ .07
Burroughs, Jeff	81T	20	$ .01	$ .07
Burroughs, Jeff	81TTR	745	$ .02	$ .10
Burroughs, Jeff	82T	440	$ .01	$ .06
Burroughs, Jeff	82TTR	14	$ .02	$ .10
Burroughs, Jeff	83T	648	$ .01	$ .06
Burroughs, Jeff	84T	354	$ .01	$ .05
Burroughs, Jeff	85T	91	$ .01	$ .04
Burroughs, Jeff	85T	272	$ .01	$ .04
Burroughs, Jeff	85TTR	14	$ .02	$ .10
Burroughs, Jeff	86T	168	$ .01	$ .03
Burton, Ellis	59T	231	$ .50	$1.95
Burton, Ellis	60T	446	$ .60	$1.75
Burton, Ellis	63T	262	$ .25	$ .85
Burton, Ellic	64T	269	$ .25	$ .85
Burton, Jim	76T	471	$ .05	$ .20
Burwell, Bill	60T	467	$ .95	$3.50
Busby, Jim	52T	309	$11.50	$38.00
Busby, Jim	56T	330	$1.80	$6.00
Busby, Jim	57T	309	$3.50	$13.00
Busby, Jim	58T	28	$1.00	$3.75
Busby, Jim	59T	185	$ .50	$1.95
Busby, Jim	60T	232	$ .35	$1.10
Busby, Jim	73T	237	$ .30	$1.00
Busby, Jim	74T	634	$ .30	$1.00
Busby, Steve	73T	608	$ .35	$1.10
Busby, Steve	74T	365	$ .06	$ .25
Busby, Steve	75T	120	$ .10	$ .35
Busby, Steve	75THL	7	$ .25	$ .85
Busby, Steve	76T	260	$ .05	$ .20
Busby, Steve	78T	336	$ .02	$ .10
Busby, Steve	80T	474	$ .01	$ .07
Buschhorn, Don	65T	577	$1.50	$3.75
Bush, Randy	83TTR	17	$ .02	$ .10
Bush, Randy	84T	429	$ .01	$ .05
Bush, Randy	85T	692	$ .01	$ .04
Bush, Randy	86T	214	$ .01	$ .03
Bush, Randy	87T	364	$ .01	$ .03
Bush, Randy	88T	73	$ .01	$ .03

Player	Year	No.	VG	EX/MT	Player	Year	No.	VG	EX/MT
Bush, Randy	89T	577	$ .01	$ .04	Cabell, Enos	76T	404	$ .05	$ .20
Bush, Randy	89TBB	282	$ .01	$ .05	Cabell, Enos	77T	567	$ .05	$ .15
Bush, Randy	90T	747	$ .01	$ .03	Cabell, Enos	78T	132	$ .02	$ .10
Buskey, Tom	75T	403	$ .06	$ .25	Cabell, Enos	79T	515	$ .02	$ .10
Buskey, Tom	76T	178	$ .05	$ .20	Cabell, Enos	80T	385	$ .01	$ .07
Buskey, Tom	77T	236	$ .05	$ .15	Cabell, Enos	81T	45	$ .01	$ .07
Buskey, Tom	80T	506	$ .01	$ .07	Cabell, Enos	81TTR	746	$ .02	$ .10
Busse, Ray	72T	101	$ .35	$1.25	Cabell, Enos	82T	627	$ .01	$ .06
Busse, Ray	73T	607	$ .35	$1.10	Cabell, Enos	82TTR	15	$ .02	$ .10
Butcher, John	81T	41	$ .01	$ .07	Cabell, Enos	83T	225	$ .01	$ .06
Butcher, John	82T	418	$ .03	$ .15	Cabell, Enos	84T	482	$ .01	$ .05
Butcher, John	83T	534	$ .01	$ .06	Cabell, Enos	84TTR	21	$ .02	$ .10
Butcher, John	84T	299	$ .30	$1.50	Cabell, Enos	85T	786	$ .01	$ .04
Butcher, John	84TTR	19	$ .02	$ .10	Cabell, Enos	86T	197	$ .01	$ .03
Butcher, John	85T	741	$ .01	$ .04	Cabell, Enos	87T	509	$ .01	$ .03
Butcher, John	86T	638	$ .01	$ .03	Cabrera, Francisco	89TMLD	20	$ .01	$ .25
Butcher, John	87T	107	$ .01	$ .03	Cabrera, Francisco	90T	254	$ .01	$ .15
Butera, Sal	81T	243	$ .01	$ .07	Cadaret, Greg	88T	328	$ .01	$ .10
Butera, Sal	82T	676	$ .01	$ .06	Cadaret, Greg	89T	552	$ .01	$ .10
Butera, Sal	83T	67	$ .01	$ .06	Cadaret, Greg	90T	659	$ .01	$ .03
Butera, Sal	86T	407	$ .01	$ .03	Caffie, Joe	58T	182	$ .50	$2.00
Butera, Sal	87T	358	$ .01	$ .03	Caffrey, Bob	85T	394	$ .01	$ .04
Butera, Sal	88T	772	$ .01	$ .03	Cage, Wayne	78T	706	$ .02	$ .10
Butler, Bill	69T	619	$ .25	$ .85	Cage, Wayne	79T	150	$ .02	$ .10
Butler, Bill	70T	377	$ .10	$ .35	Cage, Wayne	80T	208	$ .01	$ .07
Butler, Bill	71T	681	$ .70	$2.10	Cain, Bob	52T	349	$39.00	$135.00
Butler, Bill	75T	549	$ .06	$ .25	Cain, Bob	53T	266	$11.00	$37.50
Butler, Bill	76T	619	$ .05	$ .20	Cain, Bob	54T	61	$4.75	$14.00
Butler, Brett	82T	502	$ .50	$2.00	Cain, Les	69T	324	$ .25	$ .85
Butler, Brett	83T	364	$ .01	$ .06	Cain, Les	71T	101	$ .10	$ .35
Butler, Brett	84T	77	$ .01	$ .05	Cain, Les	72T	783	$ .70	$2.10
Butler, Brett	84TTR	20	$ .02	$ .10					
Butler, Brett	85T	637	$ .01	$ .04					
Butler, Brett	86T	149	$ .01	$ .03					
Butler, Brett	87T	723	$ .01	$ .03					
Butler, Brett	88T	479	$ .01	$ .03					
Butler, Brett	88TBB	166	$ .01	$ .05					
Butler, Brett	88TTR	22	$ .01	$ .05					
Butler, Brett	89T	241	$ .01	$ .04					
Butler, Brett	89TBB	62	$ .01	$ .05					
Butler, Brett	90T	571	$ .01	$ .03					
Butler, Cecil	62T	239	$ .35	$1.10					
Butler, Cecil	63T	201	$ .25	$ .85					
Butters, Tom	63T	299	$ .35	$1.20					
Butters, Tom	64T	74	$ .25	$ .85					
Butters, Tom	65T	246	$ .30	$1.00					
Buzhardt, John	59T	118	$ .30	$1.95					
Buzhardt, John	60T	549	$2.00	$7.00					
Buzhardt, John	61T	3	$ .30	$1.00					
Buzhardt, John	62T	555	$3.75	$11.00					
Buzhardt, John	63T	35	$ .25	$ .85					
Buzhardt, John	64T	323	$ .25	$ .85					
Buzhardt, John	65T	458	$ .50	$2.00					
Buzhardt, John	66T	245	$ .25	$ .85					
Buzhardt, John	67T	178	$ .25	$ .65					
Buzhardt, John	68T	403	$ .25	$ .65					
Byerly, Bud	52T	161	$6.00	$19.00					
Byerly, Bud	58T	72	$1.00	$3.75					
Byerly, Bud	60T	371	$ .50	$1.95					
Byrd, Harry	53T	131	$3.75	$13.00					
Byrd, Harry	58T	154	$ .50	$2.00					
Byrd, Jeff	78T	667	$ .02	$ .10					
Byrne, Tommy	51Tbb	35	$5.50	$17.00					
Byrne, Tommy	52T	241	$6.00	$19.00	Calderon, Ivan	86T	382	$ .03	$ .40
Byrne, Tommy	53T	123	$3.75	$13.00	Calderon, Ivan	87TTR	15	$ .05	$ .20
Byrne, Tommy	56T	215	$2.50	$8.00	Calderon, Ivan	88T	184	$ .01	$ .10
Byrne, Tommy	57T	108	$ .60	$2.50	Calderon, Ivan	88TBB	63	$ .01	$ .05
Bystrom, Marty	81T	526	$ .01	$ .07	Calderon, Ivan	89T	656	$ .01	$ .04
Bystrom, Marty	82T	416	$ .01	$ .06	Calderon, Ivan	89TBB	289	$ .01	$ .05
Bystrom, Marty	83T	199	$ .01	$ .06	Calderon, Ivan	90T	569	$ .01	$ .03
Bystrom, Marty	84T	511	$ .01	$ .05	Calderone, Sam	53T	260	$11.00	$37.50
Bystrom, Marty	85T	284	$ .01	$ .04	Calderone, Sammy	54T	68	$4.75	$14.00
Bystrom, Marty	86T	723	$ .01	$ .03	Caldwell, Mike	73T	182	$ .25	$ .65
Cabell, Enos	73T	605	$ .50	$2.00	Caldwell, Mike	74T	344	$ .06	$ .25
Cabell, Enos	75T	247	$ .06	$ .25	Caldwell, Mike	75T	347	$ .06	$ .25

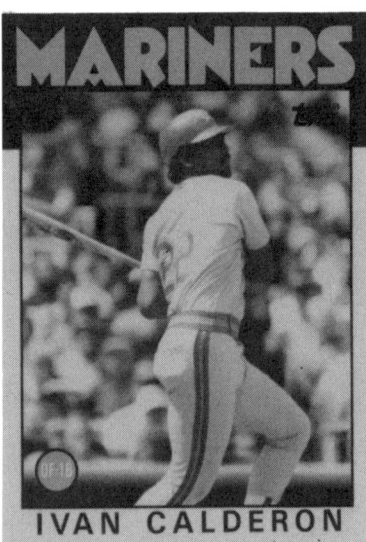

IVAN CALDERON

Player	Year	No.	VG	EX/MT	Player	Year	No.	VG	EX/MT
Caldwell, Mike	76T	157	$ .05	$ .20	Campaneris, Bert	69T	495	$ .25	$ .85
Caldwell, Mike	77T	452	$ .05	$ .15	Campaneris, Bert	69T	556	$ .30	$1.00
Caldwell, Mike	78T	212	$ .02	$ .10	Campaneris, Bert	69TAS	423	$ .25	$ .65
Caldwell, Mike	79T	651	$ .02	$ .10	Campaneris, Bert	70T	205	$ .25	$ .85
Caldwell, Mike	80T	515	$ .01	$ .07	Campaneris, Bert	71T	440	$ .25	$ .85
Caldwell, Mike	81T	85	$ .01	$ .07	Campaneris, Bert	72T	75	$ .25	$ .65
Caldwell, Mike	82T	378	$ .01	$ .06	Campaneris, Bert	73T	64	$ .35	$1.10
Caldwell, Mike	83T	142	$ .01	$ .06	Campaneris, Bert	73T	295	$ .25	$ .85
Caldwell, Mike	84T	605	$ .01	$ .05	Campaneris, Bert	74T	155	$ .25	$ .85
Caldwell, Mike	85T	419	$ .01	$ .04	Campaneris, Bert	74TAS	335	$ .10	$ .35
Calhoun, Jeff	86T	534	$ .01	$ .03	Campaneris, Bert	75T	170	$ .10	$ .35
Calhoun, Jeff	87T	282	$ .01	$ .03	Campaneris, Bert	76T	580	$ .06	$ .25
Calhoun, Jeff	87TTR	16	$ .01	$ .07	Campaneris, Bert	77T	373	$ .05	$ .15
Calhoun, Jeff	88T	38	$ .01	$ .03	Campaneris, Bert	78T	260	$ .05	$ .20
Callison, John	59T	119	$1.35	$4.00	Campaneris, Bert	79T	620	$ .05	$ .20
Callison, Johnny	60T	17	$ .35	$1.10	Campaneris, Bert	80T	505	$ .01	$ .07
Callison, Johnny	61T	468	$ .50	$2.00	Campaneris, Bert	81T	410	$ .02	$ .10
Callison, Johnny	62T	17	$ .50	$1.95	Campaneris, Bert	82T	772	$ .02	$ .10
Callison, Johnny	63T	434	$ .35	$1.10	Campaneris, Bert	83TTR	18	$ .05	$ .20
Callison, Johnny	64T	135	$ .25	$ .85	Campaneris, Bert	84T	139	$ .01	$ .05
Callison, Johnny	65T	4	$1.50	$3.75	Campaneris, Bert	84T	711	$ .04	$ .20
Callison, Johnny	65T	310	$ .35	$1.10	Campaneris, Bert	84T	714	$ .01	$ .05
Callison, Johnny	66T	52	$ .30	$1.00	Campanis, Jim	67T	12	$ .25	$ .65
Callison, Johnny	66T	230	$ .30	$1.00	Campanis, Jim	68T	281	$ .25	$ .65
Callison, Johnny	67T	85	$ .15	$ .50	Campanis, Jim	69T	396	$ .25	$ .65
Callison, Johnny	67T	309	$ .60	$1.20	Campanis, Jim	70T	671	$ .50	$2.00
Callison, Johnny	68T	415	$ .35	$1.10	Campanis, Jim	74T	513	$ .06	$ .25
Callison, Johnny	69T	133	$ .15	$ .50	Campanis, Jim	88TTR	23	$ .01	$ .35
Callison, Johnny	70T	375	$ .08	$ .30	Campbell, Bill	74T	26	$ .06	$ .25
Callison, Johnny	71T	12	$ .10	$ .35	Campbell, Bill	75T	226	$ .06	$ .25
Callison, Johnny	72T	364	$ .10	$ .35	Campbell, Bill	76T	288	$ .05	$ .20
Callison, Johnny	73T	535	$ .35	$1.10	Campbell, Bill	77T	8	$ .05	$ .15
Calmus, Dick	64T	231	$ .25	$ .85	Campbell, Bill	77T	166	$ .05	$ .15
Calmus, Dick	68T	427	$ .25	$ .65	Campbell, Bill	78T	208	$ .05	$ .20
Camacho, Ernie	81T	96	$ .01	$ .07	Campbell, Bill	78T	545	$ .02	$ .10
Camacho, Ernie	85T	739	$ .01	$ .04	Campbell, Bill	79T	375	$ .02	$ .10
Camacho, Ernie	86T	509	$ .01	$ .03	Campbell, Bill	80T	15	$ .01	$ .07
Camacho, Ernie	87T	353	$ .01	$ .03	Campbell, Bill	81T	396	$ .01	$ .07
Cambria, Fred	71T	27	$ .10	$ .35	Campbell, Bill	82T	619	$ .01	$ .06
Cambria, Fred	72T	392	$ .15	$ .50	Campbell, Bill	82TTR	16	$ .02	$ .10
Camilli, Doug	62T	594	$35.00	$125.00	Campbell, Bill	83T	436	$ .01	$ .06
Camilli, Doug	63T	196	$ .25	$ .85	Campbell, Bill	84T	787	$ .01	$ .05
Camilli, Doug	64T	249	$ .25	$ .85	Campbell, Bill	84TTR	22	$ .02	$ .10
Camilli, Doug	65T	77	$ .25	$ .65	Campbell, Bill	85T	209	$ .01	$ .04
Camilli, Doug	66T	593	$4.50	$15.00	Campbell, Bill	85TTR	15	$ .02	$ .10
Camilli, Doug	67T	551	$1.35	$4.00	Campbell, Bill	86T	112	$ .01	$ .03
Camilli, Doug	73T	131	$ .10	$ .35	Campbell, Bill	86TTR	17	$ .02	$ .10
Camilli, Lou	71T	612	$ .30	$1.00	Campbell, Bill	87T	674	$ .01	$ .03
Caminiti, Ken	88T	64	$ .01	$ .30	Campbell, Dave	69T	324	$ .25	$ .85
Caminiti, Ken	89T	369	$ .01	$ .04	Campbell, Dave	70T	639	$ .50	$2.00
Caminiti, Ken	89IBB	210	$ .01	$ .05	Campbell, Dave	71T	46	$1.35	$4.00
Caminiti, Ken	90T	531	$ .01	$ .03	Campbell, Dave	72T	384	$ .10	$ .35
Camp, Rick	77T	475	$ .05	$ .15	Campbell, Dave	73T	488	$ .06	$ .25
Camp, Rick	78T	349	$ .02	$ .10	Campbell, Dave	74T	556	$ .06	$ .25
Camp, Rick	79T	105	$ .02	$ .10	Campbell, Dave	78T	402	$ .02	$ .10
Camp, Rick	81T	87	$ .01	$ .07	Campbell, Dave	79T	9	$ .02	$ .10
Camp, Rick	82T	637	$ .01	$ .06	Campbell, Jim	63T	373	$ .35	$1.20
Camp, Rick	83T	207	$ .01	$ .06	Campbell, Jim	64T	303	$ .25	$ .85
Camp, Rick	84T	597	$ .01	$ .05	Campbell, Mike	88T	246	$ .01	$ .25
Camp, Rick	85T	491	$ .01	$ .04	Campbell, Mike	89T	143	$ .01	$ .04
Camp, Rick	86T	319	$ .01	$ .03	Campbell, Ron	67T	497	$ .50	$2.00
Campanella, Roy	52T	314	$500.00	$1500.00	Camper, Cardell	78T	711	$ .02	$ .10
Campanella, Roy	53T	27	$47.50	$165.00	Campisi, Sal	70T	716	$ .50	$2.00
Campanella, Roy	56T	101	$40.00	$145.00	Campisi, Sal	71T	568	$ .30	$1.00
Campanella, Roy	57T	210	$35.00	$100.00	Campos, Frank	52T	307	$11.50	$38.00
Campanella, Roy	57T	400	$40.00	$150.00	Campos, Frank	53T	51	$3.75	$13.00
Campanella, Roy	59T	550	$30.00	$110.00	Campusano, Sil	88TTR	24	$ .01	$ .15
Campanella, Roy	61TMVP	480	$7.50	$25.00	Campusano, Sil	89T	191	$ .01	$ .15
Campanella, Roy	75T	189	$ .50	$2.00	Canale, George	89TMLD	21	$ .01	$ .35
Campanella, Roy	75T	191	$ .35	$1.10	Canale, George	90T	344	$ .01	$ .25
Campanella, Roy	75T	193	$ .50	$2.00	Candaele, Casey	87TTR	17	$ .01	$ .07
Campaneris, Bert	65T	266	$1.00	$3.50	Candaele, Casey	88T	431	$ .01	$ .03
Campaneris, Bert	66T	175	$ .30	$1.00	Candelaria, John	76T	317	$ .50	$2.00
Campaneris, Bert	67T	515	$1.00	$3.75	Candelaria, John	77T	510	$ .15	$ .50
Campaneris, Bert	68T	109	$ .25	$ .85	Candelaria, John	78T	190	$ .05	$ .20

Player	Year	No.	VG	EX/MT	Player	Year	No.	VG	EX/MT
Candelaria, John	78T	207	$ .02	$ .10	Canseco, Jose	88TBB	13	$ .25	$1.50
					Canseco, Jose	89T	500	$ .10	$ .60
					Canseco, Jose	89TAS	401	$ .25	$ .65
					Canseco, Jose	89TBB	190	$ .01	$ .75
					Canseco, Jose	90T	250	$ .01	$ .50
					Capel, Mike	89T	767	$ .01	$ .15
					Capilla, Doug	78T	477	$ .02	$ .10
					Capilla, Doug	80T	628	$ .01	$ .07
					Capilla, Doug	81T	136	$ .01	$ .07
					Capilla, Doug	82T	537	$ .01	$ .06
					Cappuzzello, George	82T	137	$ .01	$ .06
					Cappuzzello, George	83T	422	$ .01	$ .06
					Capra, Buzz	72T	141	$ .10	$ .35
					Capra, Buzz	75T	105	$ .06	$ .25
					Capra, Buzz	75T	311	$ .25	$ .85
					Capra, Buzz	76T	153	$ .05	$ .20
					Capra, Buzz	77T	432	$ .05	$ .15
					Capra, Buzz	78T	578	$ .02	$ .10
					Carbo, Bernie	70T	36	$ .25	$ .85
					Carbo, Bernie	71T	478	$ .10	$ .35
					Carbo, Bernie	72T	463	$ .10	$ .35
					Carbo, Bernie	73T	171	$ .06	$ .25
					Carbo, Bernie	74T	621	$ .06	$ .25
					Carbo, Bernie	75T	379	$ .06	$ .25
					Carbo, Bernie	76T	278	$ .05	$ .20
					Carbo, Bernie	77T	159	$ .05	$ .15
					Carbo, Bernie	78T	524	$ .02	$ .10
					Carbo, Bernie	79T	38	$ .02	$ .10
					Carbo, Bernie	80T	266	$ .01	$ .07
					Cardenal, Jose	65T	374	$ .30	$1.00
					Cardenal, Jose	66T	505	$ .70	$2.10
					Cardenal, Jose	67T	193	$ .25	$ .65
					Cardenal, Jose	68T	102	$ .25	$ .65
Candelaria, John	79T	70	$ .03	$ .15	Cardenal, Jose	69T	325	$ .25	$ .85
Candelaria, John	80T	635	$ .02	$ .10	Cardenal, Jose	70T	675	$ .50	$2.00
Candelaria, John	81T	265	$ .02	$ .10	Cardenal, Jose	71T	435	$ .10	$ .35
Candelaria, John	82T	425	$ .03	$ .15	Cardenal, Jose	72T	12	$ .10	$ .35
Candelaria, John	83T	291	$ .01	$ .06	Cardenal, Jose	72TTR	757	$1.00	$3.75
Candelaria, John	83T	755	$ .01	$ .06	Cardenal, Jose	73T	393	$ .06	$ .25
Candelaria, John	84T	330	$ .02	$ .10	Cardenal, Jose	74T	185	$ .06	$ .25
Candelaria, John	85T	50	$ .01	$ .04	Cardenal, Jose	75T	15	$ .06	$ .25
Candelaria, John	86T	140	$ .01	$ .03	Cardenal, Jose	76T	430	$ .05	$ .20
Candelaria, John	87T	630	$ .01	$ .03	Cardenal, Jose	77T	610	$ .05	$ .15
Candelaria, John	88T	546	$ .01	$ .03	Cardenal, Jose	78T	210	$ .02	$ .10
Candelaria, John	88TTR	25	$ .01	$ .05	Cardenal, Jose	79T	317	$ .02	$ .10
Candelaria, John	89T	285	$ .01	$ .04	Cardenal, Jose	80T	512	$ .01	$ .07
Candelaria, John	90T	485	$ .01	$ .03	Cardenal, Jose	81T	473	$ .01	$ .07
Candiotti, Tom	84T	262	$ .01	$ .05	Cardenas, Chico	60T	119	$ .50	$2.00
Candiotti, Tom	86TTR	18	$ .02	$ .10	Cardenas, Chico	61T	244	$ .30	$1.00
Candiotti, Tom	87T	463	$ .01	$ .03	Cardenas, Chico	62T	381	$ .70	$2.10
Candiotti, Tom	88T	123	$ .01	$ .03	Cardenas, Chico	63T	203	$ .25	$ .85
Candiotti, Tom	88TBB	93	$ .01	$ .05	Cardenas, Chico	64T	72	$ .25	$ .85
Candiotti, Tom	89T	599	$ .01	$ .04	Cardenas, Chico	65T	437	$ .30	$1.00
Candiotti, Tom	89TBB	267	$ .01	$ .05	Cardenas, Chico	66T	370	$ .25	$ .85
Candiotti, Tom	90T	743	$ .01	$ .03	Cardenas, Chico	67T	325	$ .25	$ .65
Cangelosi, John	86TTR	19	$ .05	$ .20	Cardenas, Chico	68T	23	$ .25	$ .65
Cangelosi, John	87T	201	$ .06	$ .25	Cardenas, Chico	68T	480	$7.50	$22.50
Cangelosi, John	87TTR	18	$ .01	$ .07	Cardenas, Chico "Leo"	69T	265	$ .25	$ .85
Cangelosi, John	88T	506	$ .01	$ .03	Cardenas, Leo	70T	245	$ .10	$ .35
Cangelosi, John	89T	592	$ .01	$ .04	Cardenas, Leo	71T	405	$ .10	$ .35
Cangelosi, John	90T	29	$ .01	$ .03	Cardenas, Leo	72T	561	$ .25	$ .85
Cannizzaro, Chris	61T	118	$ .30	$1.00	Cardenas, Leo	72TIA	562	$ .25	$ .85
Cannizzaro, Chris	62T	26	$ .35	$1.10	Cardenas, Leo	73T	522	$ .06	$ .25
Cannizzaro, Chris	65T	61	$ .25	$ .65	Cardenas, Leo	75T	518	$ .06	$ .25
Cannizzaro, Chris	66T	497	$ .70	$2.10	Cardenas, Leo	76T	587	$ .05	$ .20
Cannizzaro, Chris	69T	131	$ .25	$ .65	Cardinal, Randy	63T	562	$3.00	$10.00
Cannizzaro, Chris	70T	329	$ .10	$ .35	Cardinals, Team	56T	134	$4.00	$12.00
Cannizzaro, Chris	71T	426	$ .10	$ .35	Cardinals, Team	57T	243	$2.00	$7.50
Cannizzaro, Chris	72T	759	$ .70	$2.10	Cardinals, Team	58T	216	$1.75	$6.50
Cannizzaro, Chris	75T	355	$ .06	$ .25	Cardinals, Team	59T	223	$1.75	$6.50
Cannon, Joe	80T	221	$ .01	$ .07	Cardinals, Team	60T	242	$1.75	$6.00
Cano, Jose	89TMLD	22	$ .01	$ .15	Cardinals, Team	61T	347	$ .60	$1.75
Canseco, Jose	86TTR	20	$2.50	$12.50	Cardinals, Team	62T	61	$ .60	$1.75
Canseco, Jose	87T	620	$1.25	$4.00	Cardinals, Team	63T	524	$2.50	$8.00
Canseco, Jose	88T	370	$ .10	$1.50	Cardinals, Team	64T	87	$1.35	$4.00

JOHN CANDELARIA P
PIRATES

Player	Year	No.	VG	EX/MT
Cardinals, Team	65T	57	$ .60	$1.75
Cardinals, Team	66T	379	$ .65	$1.75
Cardinals, Team	67T	173	$1.35	$4.00
Cardinals, Team	68T	497	$ .20	$2.50
Cardinals, Team	70T	549	$ .60	$1.75
Cardinals, Team	71T	308	$ .40	$1.25
Cardinals, Team	72T	688	$1.00	$3.75
Cardinals, Team	73T	219	$ .30	$1.00
Cardinals, Team	74T	36	$ .15	$ .50
Cardinals, Team Checklist	75T	246	$ .15	$ .50
Cardinals, Team Checklist	76T	581	$ .30	$1.00
Cardinals, Team Checklist	77T	183	$ .15	$ .50
Cardinals, Team Checklist	78T	479	$ .05	$ .25
Cardinals, Team Checklist	79T	192	$ .05	$ .25
Cardinals, Team Checklist	80T	244	$ .05	$ .25
Cardinals, Team Checklist	81T	684	$ .02	$ .20
Cardinals, Team Leaders	86T	66	$ .01	$ .03
Cardinals, Team Leaders	87T	181	$ .01	$ .03
Cardinals, Team Leaders	88T	351	$ .01	$ .03
Cardinals, Team Leaders	89T	261	$ .01	$ .04
Cardwell, Don	57T	374	$1.00	$3.75
Cardwell, Don	58T	372	$ .50	$2.00
Cardwell, Don	59T	314	$ .50	$1.95
Cardwell, Don	60T	384	$ .50	$1.95
Cardwell, Don	61T	393	$ .60	$1.75
Cardwell, Don	61T	564	$6.00	$18.00
Cardwell, Don	62T	495	$ .70	$2.10
Cardwell, Don	63T	575	$1.50	$3.75
Cardwell, Don	64T	417	$ .40	$1.25
Cardwell, Don	65T	502	$ .50	$2.00
Cardwell, Don	66T	235	$ .25	$ .85
Cardwell, Don	67T	555	$1.35	$4.00
Cardwell, Don	68T	437	$1.10	$ .30
Cardwell, Don	69T	193	$ .25	$ .65
Cardwell, Don	70T	83	$ .10	$ .35
Carew, Rod	67T	569	$85.00	$310.00
Carew, Rod	68T	80	$25.00	$100.00
Carew, Rod	68TAS	363	$2.00	$7.00
Carew, Rod	69T	510	$9.50	$37.50
Carew, Rod	69TAS	419	$1.25	$3.75
Carew, Rod	70T	62	$ .50	$2.00
Carew, Rod	70T	290	$7.50	$22.50
Carew, Rod	70TAS	453	$1.25	$3.50
Carew, Rod	71T	210	$4.00	$16.00
Carew, Rod	72T	695	$20.00	$65.00
Carew, Rod	72TIA	696	$9.00	$25.00
Carew, Rod	73T	61	$ .50	$2.00
Carew, Rod	73T	330	$2.50	$8.50
Carew, Rod	74T	50	$1.65	$5.00
Carew, Rod	74T	201	$1.25	$4.50
Carew, Rod	74TAS	333	$ .50	$2.00
Carew, Rod	75T	306	$ .30	$1.00
Carew, Rod	75T	600	$1.50	$4.50
Carew, Rod	76T	192	$ .50	$1.50
Carew, Rod	76T	400	$1.25	$3.75
Carew, Rod	77T	120	$1.25	$3.50
Carew, Rod	78T	201	$ .15	$ .60
Carew, Rod	78T	580	$ .75	$3.00
Carew, Rod	79T	1	$ .75	$2.25
Carew, Rod	79T	300	$ .60	$2.50
Carew, Rod	80T	700	$ .35	$1.25
Carew, Rod	81T	100	$ .35	$1.10
Carew, Rod	82T	276	$ .03	$ .15
Carew, Rod	82T	500	$ .15	$ .75
Carew, Rod	82TAS	547	$ .05	$ .25
Carew, Rod	82TIA	501	$ .07	$ .35
Carew, Rod	83T	200	$ .10	$ .50
Carew, Rod	83T	201	$ .05	$ .20
Carew, Rod	83T	651	$ .01	$ .06
Carew, Rod	83TAS	386	$ .05	$ .25
Carew, Rod	84T	276	$ .01	$ .05
Carew, Rod	84T	600	$ .12	$ .50
Carew, Rod	84T	710	$ .04	$ .20
Carew, Rod	84T	711	$ .04	$ .20
Carew, Rod	85T	300	$ .01	$ .30
Carew, Rod	86T	400	$ .03	$ .25
Carey, Andy	53T	188	$2.25	$8.00
Carey, Andy	54T	105	$3.50	$13.00
Carey, Andy	55T	20	$2.10	$7.50
Carey, Andy	56T	12	$1.25	$4.50
Carey, Andy	57T	290	$3.50	$13.00
Carey, Andy	58T	333	$ .50	$2.00
Carey, Andy	59T	45	$1.00	$3.75
Carey, Andy	60T	196	$ .35	$1.10
Carey, Andy	61T	518	$ .50	$2.00
Carey, Andy	62T	418	$ .70	$2.10
Carlos, Cisco	68T	287	$ .25	$ .65
Carlos, Cisco	69T	54	$ .25	$ .65
Carlos, Cisco	70T	487	$ .10	$ .35
Carlton, Steve	65T	477	$60.00	$250.00
Carlton, Steve	67T	146	$30.00	$95.00
Carlton, Steve	68T	408	$22.50	$65.00
Carlton, Steve	69T	255	$12.50	$45.00
Carlton, Steve	70T	67	$1.35	$4.75
Carlton, Steve	70T	220	$4.00	$16.00
Carlton, Steve	71T	55	$3.50	$12.50
Carlton, Steve	72T	93	$ .50	$2.00
Carlton, Steve	72T	420	$4.50	$18.00
Carlton, Steve	72TTR	751	$11.50	$38.00
Carlton, Steve	73T	65	$ .35	$1.10
Carlton, Steve	73T	66	$ .35	$1.10
Carlton, Steve	73T	67	$ .85	$3.50
Carlton, Steve	73T	300	$2.25	$8.50
Carlton, Steve	74T	95	$2.00	$7.00
Carlton, Steve	75T	185	$1.50	$5.50
Carlton, Steve	75T	312	$ .50	$2.50
Carlton, Steve	76T	355	$1.35	$4.00
Carlton, Steve	77T	110	$1.25	$4.50
Carlton, Steve	78T	205	$ .25	$ .65
Carlton, Steve	78T	540	$1.00	$3.75
Carlton, Steve	79T	25	$ .75	$2.25
Carlton, Steve	80T	210	$ .50	$2.00
Carlton, Steve	81T	5	$ .04	$ .20
Carlton, Steve	81T	6	$ .02	$ .10
Carlton, Steve	81T	630	$ .35	$1.25
Carlton, Steve	81TRB	202	$ .25	$ .65
Carlton, Steve	82T	480	$ .15	$ .75
Carlton, Steve	82T	636	$ .25	$ .65
Carlton, Steve	82THL	1	$ .25	$ .65
Carlton, Steve	82TIA	481	$ .07	$ .35
Carlton, Steve	83T	70	$ .15	$ .75
Carlton, Steve	83T	71	$ .05	$ .25
Carlton, Steve	83T	229	$ .01	$ .10
Carlton, Steve	83T	705	$ .01	$ .10
Carlton, Steve	83T	706	$ .01	$ .10
Carlton, Steve	83TAS	406	$ .05	$ .25
Carlton, Steve	84T	1	$ .25	$ .65
Carlton, Steve	84T	4	$ .05	$ .25
Carlton, Steve	84T	136	$ .02	$ .10
Carlton, Steve	84T	706	$ .05	$ .25
Carlton, Steve	84T	707	$ .05	$ .25
Carlton, Steve	84T	708	$ .04	$ .20
Carlton, Steve	84T	780	$ .10	$ .50
Carlton, Steve	84TAS	395	$ .05	$ .25
Carlton, Steve	85T	360	$ .07	$ .35
Carlton, Steve	86T	120	$ .03	$ .25
Carlton, Steve	87T	718	$ .10	$ .35
Carlton, Steve	87TTR	19	$ .05	$ .25
Carman, Don	85TTR	16	$ .05	$ .25
Carman, Don	86T	532	$ .01	$ .10
Carman, Don	87T	355	$ .01	$ .03
Carman, Don	88T	415	$ .01	$ .03
Carman, Don	89T	154	$ .01	$ .04
Carman, Don	90T	731	$ .01	$ .03
Carmel, Duke	60T	120	$ .35	$1.10
Carmel, Duke	63T	544	$8.50	$25.00
Carmel, Duke	64T	44	$ .25	$ .85
Carmel, Duke	65T	261	$ .30	$1.00
Carpenter, Cris	89T	282	$ .01	$ .20
Carpenter, Cris	89TBB	307	$ .01	$ .05

TOPPS

Player	Year	No.	VG	EX/MT	Player	Year	No.	VG	EX/MT
Carpenter, Cris	90T	443	$ .01	$ .03	Carter, Joe	86T	377	$ .05	$ .30
Carpin, Frank	66T	71	$ .25	$ .85	Carter, Joe	87T	220	$ .06	$ .25
Carrasquel, Chico	51Tbb	26	$5.50	$17.00	Carter, Joe	88T	75	$ .01	$ .10
Carrasquel, Chico	52T	251	$11.50	$38.00	Carter, Joe	88TBB	71	$ .01	$ .15
Carrasquel, Chico	56T	230	$2.50	$8.00	Carter, Joe	89T	420	$ .01	$ .10
Carrasquel, Chico	57T	67	$ .95	$3.50	Carter, Joe	89TBB	155	$ .01	$ .10
Carrasquel, Chico	58T	55	$1.00	$3.75	Carter, Joe	90T	580	$ .01	$ .10
Carrasquel, Chico	59T	264	$ .50	$1.95	Carter, Steve	89TMLD	23	$ .01	$ .10
Carreon, Camilo	60T	121	$ .35	$1.10	Carter, Steve	90T	482	$ .01	$ .10
Carreon, Camilo	61T	509	$ .50	$2.00	Carty, Rico	64T	476	$2.00	$10.00
Carreon, Camilo	62T	178	$ .35	$1.10	Carty, Rico	65T	2	$1.35	$4.00
Carreon, Camilo	63T	308	$ .35	$1.20	Carty, Rico	65T	305	$ .35	$1.10
Carreon, Camilo	64T	421	$ .40	$1.25	Carty, Rico	66T	153	$ .35	$1.10
Carreon, Camilo	65T	578	$1.50	$3.75	Carty, Rico	67T	35	$ .25	$ .65
Carreon, Camilo	66T	513	$ .70	$2.10	Carty, Rico	67T	240	$ .35	$1.10
Carreon, Mark	90T	434	$ .01	$ .03	Carty, Rico	68T	455	$ .15	$ .50
Carrithers, Don	72T	76	$ .10	$ .35	Carty, Rico	69T	590	$ .20	$ .50
Carrithers, Don	73T	651	$ .35	$1.10	Carty, Rico	70T	145	$ .25	$ .85
Carrithers, Don	74T	361	$ .06	$ .25	Carty, Rico	71T	62	$ .15	$ .50
Carrithers, Don	75T	438	$ .06	$ .25	Carty, Rico	71T	270	$ .15	$ .50
Carrithers, Don	76T	312	$ .05	$ .20	Carty, Rico	72T	740	$1.00	$3.75
Carrithers, Don	77T	579	$ .05	$ .15	Carty, Rico	73T	435	$ .25	$ .65
Carrithers, Don	78T	113	$ .02	$ .10	Carty, Rico	75T	655	$ .10	$ .35
Carroll, Clay	65T	461	$7.50	$32.50	Carty, Rico	76T	156	$ .06	$ .25
Carroll, Clay	66T	307	$ .25	$ .85	Carty, Rico	77T	465	$ .05	$ .15
Carroll, Clay	67T	219	$ .25	$ .65	Carty, Rico	78T	305	$ .02	$ .10
Carroll, Clay	68T	412	$ .25	$ .65	Carty, Rico	79T	565	$ .05	$ .20
Carroll, Clay	69T	26	$ .25	$ .65	Carty, Rico	80T	46	$ .02	$ .10
Carroll, Clay	70T	133	$ .10	$ .35	Cary, Chuck	87T	171	$ .01	$ .03
Carroll, Clay	71T	394	$ .10	$ .35	Cary, Chuck	89TTR	17	$ .01	$ .10
Carroll, Clay	72T	311	$ .10	$ .35	Cary, Chuck	90T	691	$ .01	$ .03
Carroll, Clay	72TIA	312	$ .10	$ .35	Casagrande, Tom	55T	167	$4.25	$13.00
Carroll, Clay	73T	68	$ .25	$ .65	Casale, Jerry	59T	456	$ .50	$1.95
Carroll, Clay	73T	195	$ .06	$ .25	Casale, Jerry	60T	38	$ .35	$1.10
Carroll, Clay	74T	111	$ .06	$ .25	Casale, Jerry	61T	195	$ .30	$1.00
Carroll, Clay	75T	345	$ .06	$ .25	Casanova, Paul	67T	115	$ .25	$ .65
Carroll, Clay	76T	211	$ .05	$ .20	Casanova, Paul	68T	560	$ .30	$1.00
Carroll, Clay	76TTR	211	$ .05	$ .20	Casanova, Paul	69T	486	$ .25	$ .65
Carroll, Clay	77T	497	$ .05	$ .15	Casanova, Paul	70T	84	$ .10	$ .35
Carroll, Clay	78T	615	$ .02	$ .10	Casanova, Paul	71T	139	$ .10	$ .35
Carroll, Tom	55T	158	$3.50	$10.00	Casanova, Paul	72T	591	$ .25	$ .85
Carroll, Tom	56T	139	$1.25	$3.50	Casanova, Paul	73T	452	$ .06	$ .25
Carroll, Tom	57T	164	$ .95	$3.50	Casanova, Paul	74T	272	$ .06	$ .25
Carroll, Tom	59T	513	$2.00	$7.00	Casanova, Paul	75T	633	$ .06	$ .25
Carroll, Tom	75T	507	$ .06	$ .25	Cash, Dave	70T	141	$ .25	$ .85
Carroll, Tom	76T	561	$ .05	$ .20	Cash, Dave	71T	582	$ .30	$1.00
Carter, Dick	60T	466	$ .95	$3.50	Cash, Dave	72T	125	$ .10	$ .35
Carter, Gary	75T	620	$12.00	$35.00	Cash, Dave	73T	397	$ .06	$ .25
Carter, Gary	76T	441	$4.00	$12.00	Cash, Dave	74T	198	$ .06	$ .25
Carter, Gary	77T	295	$2.25	$6.50	Cash, Dave	75T	22	$ .06	$ .25
Carter, Gary	78T	120	$ .80	$2.75	Cash, Dave	76T	295	$ .05	$ .20
Carter, Gary	79T	520	$ .95	$3.50	Cash, Dave	77T	649	$ .05	$ .15
Carter, Gary	80T	70	$ .40	$1.75	Cash, Dave	78T	495	$ .02	$ .10
Carter, Gary	81T	660	$ .35	$1.10	Cash, Dave	79T	395	$ .02	$ .10
Carter, Gary	82T	730	$ .15	$ .75	Cash, Dave	80T	14	$ .01	$ .07
Carter, Gary	82TAS	344	$ .05	$ .25	Cash, Dave	81T	707	$ .01	$ .07
Carter, Gary	83T	370	$ .10	$ .50	Cash, Norm	59T	509	$6.00	$18.00
Carter, Gary	83TAS	404	$ .05	$ .25	Cash, Norm	60T	488	$1.00	$4.00
Carter, Gary	84T	450	$ .10	$ .50	Cash, Norm	61T	95	$1.00	$2.75
Carter, Gary	84TAS	393	$ .05	$ .25	Cash, Norm	62T	51	$ .50	$1.95
Carter, Gary	85T	230	$ .05	$ .25	Cash, Norm	62T	250	$ .60	$1.75
Carter, Gary	85TAS	719	$ .01	$ .04	Cash, Norm	62TAS	466	$1.00	$3.75
Carter, Gary	85TTR	17	$ .15	$ .60	Cash, Norm	63T	4	$ .50	$2.00
Carter, Gary	86T	170	$ .03	$ .25	Cash, Norm	63T	445	$ .50	$1.95
Carter, Gary	86TAS	708	$ .02	$ .15	Cash, Norm	64T	331	$15.00	$45.00
Carter, Gary	87T	20	$ .10	$ .35	Cash, Norm	64T	425	$ .50	$2.00
Carter, Gary	87TAS	602	$ .01	$ .10	Cash, Norm	65T	153	$ .15	$ .50
Carter, Gary	88T	530	$ .01	$ .25	Cash, Norm	66T	218	$ .50	$2.00
Carter, Gary	88TBB	37	$ .01	$ .05	Cash, Norm	66T	315	$ .35	$1.10
Carter, Gary	89T	680	$ .01	$ .04	Cash, Norm	67T	216	$1.35	$4.00
Carter, Gary	89TAS	393	$ .01	$ .04	Cash, Norm	67T	540	$7.00	$22.50
Carter, Gary	89TBB	325	$ .01	$ .05	Cash, Norm	68T	256	$ .35	$1.10
Carter, Gary	89TRB	3	$ .01	$ .04	Cash, Norm	69T	80	$ .25	$ .65
Carter, Gary	90T	790	$ .01	$ .10	Cash, Norm	70T	611	$ .30	$1.00
Carter, Joe	85T	694	$ .60	$2.75	Cash, Norm	71T	599	$ .50	$2.00

Player	Year	No.	VG	EX/MT
Cash, Norm	72T	90	$ .50	$2.00
Cash, Norm	72T	150	$ .25	$ .85
Cash, Norm	73T	485	$ .15	$ .50
Cash, Norm	74T	367	$ .25	$ .85
Cash, Ron	74T	600	$1.00	$4.00
Castiglione. Pete	52T	260	$11.50	$38.00
Castillo, "Carmen", Carmelo	89TBB	91	$ .01	$ .05
Castillo, "Carmen", Carmelo	89TTR	18	$ .01	$ .05
Castillo, Bobby	79T	641	$ .02	$ .10
Castillo, Bobby	81T	146	$ .01	$ .07
Castillo, Bobby	82T	48	$ .01	$ .06
Castillo, Bobby	82TTR	17	$ .02	$ .10
Castillo, Bobby	83T	327	$ .01	$ .06
Castillo, Bobby	83T	771	$ .01	$ .06
Castillo, Bobby	84T	491	$ .01	$ .05
Castillo, Bobby	85T	588	$ .01	$ .04
Castillo, Bobby	85TTR	18	$ .02	$ .10
Castillo, Bobby	86T	252	$ .01	$ .03
Castillo, Carmelo	90T	427	$ .01	$ .03
Castillo, Carmen	85T	184	$ .01	$ .04
Castillo, Carmen	86TTR	21	$ .02	$ .10
Castillo, Carmen	87T	513	$ .01	$ .03
Castillo, Carmen	88T	341	$ .01	$ .03
Castillo, Carmen	89T	637	$ .01	$ .04
Castillo, Juan	87TTR	20	$ .01	$ .07
Castillo, Juan	88T	362	$ .01	$ .03
Castillo, Juan	88TBB	117	$ .01	$ .05
Castillo, Juan	89T	538	$ .01	$ .04
Castillo, Juan	89TBB	9	$ .01	$ .05
Castillo, Manny	81T	66	$ .01	$ .07
Castillo, Manny	83T	258	$ .01	$ .06
Castillo, Manny	84T	562	$ .01	$ .05
Castillo, Marty	82T	261	$ .01	$ .06
Castillo, Marty	84T	303	$ .01	$ .05
Castillo, Marty	85T	461	$ .01	$ .04
Castillo, Marty	86T	788	$ .01	$ .03
Castillo, Tony	90T	620	$ .01	$ .10
Castino, John	80T	137	$ .03	$ .15
Castino, John	81T	304	$ .01	$ .07
Castino, John	82T	396	$ .01	$ .06
Castino, John	82T	644	$ .01	$ .06
Castino, John	83T	93	$ .01	$ .06

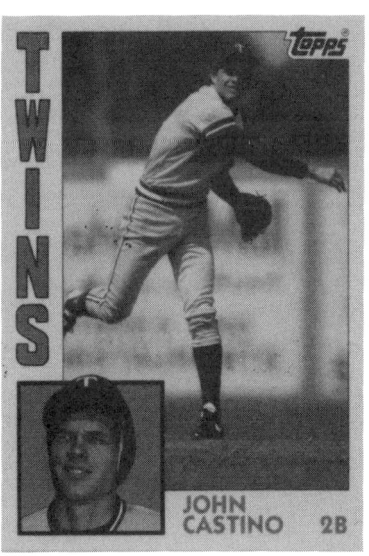

Player	Year	No.	VG	EX/MT
Castino, John	84T	237	$ .01	$ .05

Player	Year	No.	VG	EX/MT
Castino, John	85T	452	$ .01	$ .04
Castleman, Foster	56T	271	$1.80	$6.00
Castleman, Foster	57T	237	$ .95	$3.50
Castleman, Foster	58T	416	$ .50	$2.00
Castro, Bill	76T	293	$ .05	$ .20
Castro, Bill	77T	528	$ .05	$ .15
Castro, Bill	78T	448	$ .02	$ .10
Castro, Bill	79T	133	$ .02	$ .10
Castro, Bill	80T	303	$ .01	$ .07
Castro, Bill	81T	271	$ .01	$ .07
Cater, Danny	64T	482	$ .40	$1.25
Cater, Danny	65T	253	$ .35	$1.10
Cater, Danny	66T	398	$ .25	$ .85
Cater, Danny	67T	157	$ .25	$ .65
Cater, Danny	68T	535	$ .30	$1.00
Cater, Danny	69T	1	$1.75	$6.00
Cater, Danny	69T	44	$ .25	$ .65
Cater, Danny	69T	556	$ .30	$1.00
Cater, Danny	70T	437	$ .25	$ .85
Cater, Danny	71T	358	$ .10	$ .35
Cater, Danny	72T	676	$ .70	$2.10
Cater, Danny	73T	317	$ .06	$ .25
Cater, Danny	74T	543	$ .06	$ .25
Cater, Danny	75T	645	$ .06	$ .25
Cato, Keefe	85T	367	$ .01	$ .04
Caudill, Bill	80T	103	$ .03	$ .15
Caudill, Bill	81T	574	$ .01	$ .07
Caudill, Bill	82T	303	$ .01	$ .06
Caudill, Bill	82TTR	18	$ .02	$ .10
Caudill, Bill	83T	78	$ .01	$ .06
Caudill, Bill	84T	769	$ .01	$ .05
Caudill, Bill	84TTR	23	$ .02	$ .10
Caudill, Bill	85T	685	$ .01	$ .04
Caudill, Bill	85TTR	19	$ .02	$ .10
Caudill, Bill	86T	435	$ .01	$ .03
Caudill, Bill	87T	733	$ .01	$ .03
Causey, Wayne	62T	496	$ .70	$2.10
Causey, Wayne	63T	539	$1.50	$3.75
Causey, Wayne	64T	75	$ .25	$ .85
Causey, Wayne	65T	425	$ .30	$1.00
Causey, Wayne	66T	366	$ .25	$ .85
Causey, Wayne	67T	286	$ .25	$ .65
Causey, Wayne	68T	522	$ .30	$1.00
Causey, Wayne	69T	33	$ .25	$ .65
Cavarretta, Phil	52T	295	$15.00	$45.00
Cavarretta, Phil	54T	55	$3.75	$15.00
Ceccarelli, Art	58T	191	$ .50	$2.00
Ceccarelli, Art	59T	226	$ .50	$1.95
Ceccarelli, Art	60T	156	$ .35	$1.10
Cecena, Jose	88TTR	26	$ .01	$ .10
Cecena, Jose	89T	683	$ .01	$ .10
Cedeno, Cesar	71T	237	$ .25	$1.00
Cedeno, Cesar	72T	65	$ .25	$ .85
Cedeno, Cesar	73T	290	$ .06	$ .25
Cedeno, Cesar	74T	200	$ .25	$ .65
Cedeno, Cesar	74TAS	337	$ .06	$ .25
Cedeno, Cesar	75T	590	$ .10	$ .35
Cedeno, Cesar	76T	460	$ .06	$ .25
Cedeno, Cesar	77T	90	$ .05	$ .15
Cedeno, Cesar	78T	650	$ .02	$ .10
Cedeno, Cesar	79T	570	$ .05	$ .20
Cedeno, Cesar	80T	370	$ .01	$ .07
Cedeno, Cesar	81T	190	$ .01	$ .06
Cedeno, Cesar	82T	640	$ .01	$ .06
Cedeno, Cesar	82TTR	19	$ .02	$ .10
Cedeno, Cesar	83T	351	$ .01	$ .06
Cedeno, Cesar	83T	475	$ .01	$ .06
Cedeno, Cesar	84T	705	$ .02	$ .10
Cedeno, Cesar	84T	725	$ .01	$ .05
Cedeno, Cesar	85T	54	$ .01	$ .04
Cedeno, Cesar	86T	224	$ .01	$ .03
Cepeda, Orlando	58T	343	$13.00	$40.00
Cepeda, Orlando	59T	390	$3.00	$9.00
Cepeda, Orlando	59TAS	553	$2.75	$8.00
Cepeda, Orlando	60T	450	$2.50	$8.00

TOPPS

Player	Year	No.	VG	EX/MT	Player	Year	No.	VG	EX/MT
Cepeda, Orlando	61T	435	$1.35	$4.00	Chacon, Elio	60T	543	$2.00	$7.00
Cepeda, Orlando	62T	40	$1.25	$3.50	Chacon, Elio	62T	256	$ .35	$1.10
Cepeda, Orlando	62T	54	$ .50	$1.95	Chakales, Bob	52T	120	$6.00	$19.00
Cepeda, Orlando	62T	401	$6.00	$18.00	Chakales, Bob	57T	261	$ .95	$3.50
Cepeda, Orlando	62TAS	390	$ .70	$2.00	Chalk, Dave	74T	597	$ .15	$ .50
Cepeda, Orlando	63T	3	$2.35	$9.00	Chalk, Dave	75T	64	$ .06	$ .25
Cepeda, Orlando	63T	520	$3.50	$10.00	Chalk, Dave	76T	52	$ .05	$ .20
Cepeda, Orlando	64T	9	$2.50	$7.50	Chalk, Dave	77T	315	$ .05	$ .15
Cepeda, Orlando	64T	306	$6.50	$20.00	Chalk, Dave	78T	178	$ .02	$ .10
Cepeda, Orlando	64T	390	$1.15	$3.25	Chalk, Dave	79T	682	$ .02	$ .10
Cepeda, Orlando	65T	4	$1.50	$3.75	Chalk, Dave	80T	261	$ .01	$ .07
Cepeda, Orlando	65T	360	$1.35	$4.00	Chalk, Dave	82T	462	$ .01	$ .06
Cepeda, Orlando	66T	132	$1.25	$4.50	Chamberlain, Craig	80T	417	$ .01	$ .07
Cepeda, Orlando	67T	20	$1.35	$4.00	Chamberlain, Craig	81T	274	$ .01	$ .07
Cepeda, Orlando	68T	3	$1.35	$4.00	Chambers, Al	85T	277	$ .01	$ .04
Cepeda, Orlando	68T	200	$ .90	$2.75	Chambers, Cliff	51Trb	25	$1.35	$4.00
Cepeda, Orlando	68TAS	362	$ .70	$2.00	Chambers, Cliff	52T	68	$14.00	$45.00
Cepeda, Orlando	69T	385	$ .95	$3.50	Chambliss, Chris	72T	142	$ .40	$1.75
Cepeda, Orlando	70T	555	$ .95	$2.75	Chambliss, Chris	73T	11	$ .15	$ .50
Cepeda, Orlando	71T	605	$1.50	$3.75	Chambliss, Chris	74T	384	$ .25	$ .85
Cepeda, Orlando	72T	195	$ .60	$1.75	Chambliss, Chris	75T	585	$ .10	$ .35
Cepeda, Orlando	73T	545	$ .70	$2.00	Chambliss, Chris	76T	65	$ .06	$ .25
Cepeda, Orlando	74T	83	$ .35	$1.10	Chambliss, Chris	77T	220	$ .05	$ .15
Cepeda, Orlando	75T	205	$ .35	$1.10	Chambliss, Chris	78T	485	$ .05	$ .20
Cerone, Rick	77T	476	$20.00	$60.00	Chambliss, Chris	79T	335	$ .05	$ .20
Cerone, Rick	78T	469	$ .02	$ .10	Chambliss, Chris	80T	625	$ .01	$ .07
Cerone, Rick	79T	152	$ .02	$ .10	Chambliss, Chris	81T	155	$ .01	$ .07
Cerone, Rick	80T	591	$ .01	$ .07	Chambliss, Chris	82T	320	$ .01	$ .06
Cerone, Rick	81T	335	$ .01	$ .07	Chambliss, Chris	82TIA	321	$ .01	$ .06
Cerone, Rick	82T	45	$ .01	$ .06	Chambliss, Chris	83T	792	$ .01	$ .06
Cerone, Rick	83T	254	$ .01	$ .06	Chambliss, Chris	84T	50	$ .01	$ .05
Cerone, Rick	84T	617	$ .01	$ .05	Chambliss, Chris	85T	518	$ .01	$ .04
Cerone, Rick	85T	429	$ .01	$ .04	Chambliss, Chris	86T	293	$ .01	$ .03
Cerone, Rick	85TTR	20	$ .02	$ .10	Chambliss, Chris	87T	777	$ .01	$ .03
Cerone, Rick	86T	747	$ .01	$ .03	Champion, Billy	70T	149	$ .15	$ .20
Cerone, Rick	86TTR	22	$ .02	$ .10	Champion, Billy	71T	323	$ .10	$ .35
Cerone, Rick	87T	129	$ .01	$ .03	Champion, Billy	72T	599	$ .25	$ .85
Cerone, Rick	87TTR	21	$ .01	$ .07	Champion, Billy	73T	74	$ .06	$ .25
Cerone, Rick	88T	561	$ .01	$ .10	Champion, Billy	74T	391	$ .06	$ .25
Cerone, Rick	88TTR	27	$ .01	$ .05	Champion, Billy	75T	256	$ .06	$ .25
Cerone, Rick	89T	96	$ .01	$ .04	Champion, Billy	76T	501	$ .05	$ .20
Cerone, Rick	89TBB	119	$ .01	$ .05	Champion, Mike	77T	494	$ .12	$ .40
Cerone, Rick	90T	303	$ .01	$ .03	Champion, Mike	78T	683	$ .02	$ .10
Cerutti, John	86TTR	23	$ .05	$ .25	Championship, A.L.	75T	459	$ .25	$ .85
Cerutti, John	87T	557	$ .01	$ .10	Championship, A.L.	77T	276	$ .15	$ .50
Cerutti, John	88T	191	$ .01	$ .03	Championship, A.L.	78T	411	$ .15	$ .50
Cerutti, John	89T	347	$ .01	$ .04	Championship, A.L.	81T	401	$ .05	$ .25
Cerutti, John	90T	211	$ .01	$ .03	Championship, N.L.	75T	460	$ .25	$ .85
Cerv, Bob	53T	210	$2.25	$8.00	Championship, N.L.	77T	277	$ .15	$ .50
Cerv, Bob	56T	288	$1.80	$6.00	Championship, N.L.	78T	412	$ .08	$ .30
Cerv, Bob	57T	269	$3.50	$13.00	Championship, N.L.	81T	402	$ .03	$ .15
Cerv, Bob	58T	329	$ .50	$2.00	Chance, Bob	64T	146	$20.00	$60.00
Cerv, Bob	59T	100	$1.00	$3.75	Chance, Bob	65T	224	$ .30	$1.00
Cerv, Bob	60T	415	$ .50	$1.95	Chance, Bob	66T	564	$4.50	$15.00
Cerv, Bob	61T	563	$6.00	$18.00	Chance, Bob	67T	349	$ .25	$ .65
Cerv, Bob	62T	169	$ .50	$2.00	Chance, Bob	69T	523	$ .25	$ .85
Cey, Ron	72T	761	$4.00	$12.00	Chance, Dean	62T	194	$ .50	$ .50
Cey, Ron	73T	615	$120.00	$365.00	Chance, Dean	63T	6	$ .35	$1.10
Cey, Ron	74T	315	$ .12	$ .40	Chance, Dean	63T	355	$ .35	$1.10
Cey, Ron	75T	390	$ .25	$ .65	Chance, Dean	64T	32	$ .50	$2.00
Cey, Ron	76T	370	$ .10	$ .35	Chance, Dean	65T	7	$ .30	$1.00
Cey, Ron	77T	50	$ .06	$ .25	Chance, Dean	65T	9	$ .30	$1.00
Cey, Ron	78T	630	$ .02	$ .10	Chance, Dean	65T	11	$ .35	$1.10
Cey, Ron	79T	190	$ .02	$ .10	Chance, Dean	65T	140	$ .25	$ .65
Cey, Ron	80T	510	$ .01	$ .07	Chance, Dean	66T	340	$ .25	$ .85
Cey, Ron	81T	260	$ .03	$ .15	Chance, Dean	67T	380	$ .25	$ .85
Cey, Ron	82T	410	$ .01	$ .06	Chance, Dean	68T	10	$ .35	$1.10
Cey, Ron	82TIA	411	$ .01	$ .06	Chance, Dean	68T	12	$ .35	$1.10
Cey, Ron	83T	15	$ .01	$ .06	Chance, Dean	68T	255	$ .25	$ .65
Cey, Ron	83TTR	19	$ .02	$ .10	Chance, Dean	69T	620	$ .25	$ .85
Cey, Ron	84T	357	$ .01	$ .05	Chance, Dean	70T	625	$ .25	$ .85
Cey, Ron	85T	768	$ .01	$ .04	Chance, Dean	71T	36	$ .10	$ .35
Cey, Ron	86T	669	$ .01	$ .03	Chaney, Darrel	69T	624	$ .25	$ .85
Cey, Ron	87T	767	$ .01	$ .03	Chaney, Darrel	70T	3	$ .10	$ .35
Cey, Ron	87TTR	22	$ .01	$ .07	Chaney, Darrel	71T	632	$ .30	$1.00

Player	Year	No.	VG	EX/MT	Player	Year	No.	VG	EX/MT
Chaney, Darrel	72T	136	$ .10	$ .35	Checklist, Cards (1-88)	62T	22	$1.25	$3.50
Chaney, Darrel	73T	507	$ .06	$ .25	Checklist, Cards (1-88)	63T	79	$ .60	$1.75
Chaney, Darrel	74T	559	$ .06	$ .25	Checklist, Cards (1-88)	64T	76	$ .60	$1.75
Chaney, Darrel	75T	581	$ .06	$ .25	Checklist, Cards (1-88)	65T	79	$ .60	$1.75
Chaney, Darrel	76T	259	$ .05	$ .20	Checklist, Cards (1-88)	66T	34	$ .60	$1.75
Chaney, Darrel	76TTR	259	$ .05	$ .20	Checklist, Cards (1-88)	88TBB	28	$ .01	$ .05
Chaney, Darrel	77T	384	$ .05	$ .15	Checklist, Cards (110-196)	67T	103	$1.35	$4.00
Chaney, Darrel	78T	443	$ .02	$ .10	Checklist, Cards (110-196)	68T	107	$ .70	$2.00
Chaney, Darrel	79T	184	$ .02	$ .10	Checklist, Cards (110-218)	69T	107	$ .70	$2.00
Chapman, Ben	52T	391	$50.00	$150.00	Checklist, Cards (122-242)	78T	184	$ .25	$ .85
Chapman, Kelvin	85T	751	$ .01	$ .04	Checklist, Cards (122-242)	79T	241	$ .05	$ .25
Chapman, Kelvin	86T	492	$ .01	$ .03	Checklist, Cards (122-242)	80T	241	$ .05	$ .25
Chapman, Sam	51Tbb	52	$4.00	$18.00	Checklist, Cards (122-242)	81T	241	$ .01	$ .07
Chappas, Harry	80T	347	$ .01	$ .07	Checklist, Cards (122-263)	71T	123	$ .60	$1.75
Charboneau, Joe	81T	13	$ .02	$ .10	Checklist, Cards (133 -264)	88T	253	$ .01	$ .03
Charboneau, Joe	82T	630	$ .01	$ .06	Checklist, Cards (133 263)	72T	103	$ .50	$1.95
Charles, Ed	62T	595	$6.00	$18.00	Checklist, Cards (133-263)	70T	128	$ .08	$1.25
Charles, Ed	63T	67	$ .25	$ .85	Checklist, Cards (133-264)	73T	264	$ .50	$1.95
Charles, Ed	64T	475	$ .40	$1.25	Checklist, Cards (133-264)	74T	263	$ .35	$1.10
Charles, Ed	65T	35	$ .25	$ .65	Checklist, Cards (133-264)	75T	257	$ .50	$2.00
Charles, Ed	66T	422	$ .25	$ .85	Checklist, Cards (133-264)	76T	262	$ .35	$1.10
Charles, Ed	67T	182	$ .25	$ .65	Checklist, Cards (133-264)	77T	208	$ .35	$1.10
Charles, Ed	68T	563	$ .30	$1.00	Checklist, Cards (133-264)	82T	226	$ .01	$ .06
Charles, Ed	69T	245	$ .25	$ .85	Checklist, Cards (133-264)	83T	249	$ .01	$ .06
Charley (Charlie)	67T	329	$ .25	$ .65	Checklist, Cards (133-264)	84T	233	$ .01	$ .05
Charlton, Norm	89T	737	$ .01	$ .15	Checklist, Cards (133-264)	84T	379	$ .01	$ .05
Charlton, Norm	90T	289	$ .01	$ .10	Checklist, Cards (133-264)	85T	261	$ .01	$ .04
Charton, Pete	64T	459	$ .40	$1.25	Checklist, Cards (133-264)	86T	263	$ .01	$ .03
Charton, Pete	66T	329	$ .25	$ .85	Checklist, Cards (133-264)	87T	264	$ .01	$ .03
Chavarria, Ossie	67T	344	$ .25	$ .65	Checklist, Cards (133-264)	89T	258	$ .01	$ .04
Checklist '89, Cards(4/3-7/17)	89TMLD	151	$ .01	$ .05	Checklist, Cards (177-242)	59T	172	$1.35	$4.00
Checklist '89, Cards(7/24-9/23)	89TMLD	152	$ .01	$ .05	Checklist, Cards (177-264)	58T	158	$1.25	$3.50
Checklist TR, Cards (1T-132T)	82TTR	132	$ .15	$ .50	Checklist, Cards (177-264)	58T	216	$1.25	$3.50
Checklist TR, Cards (1T-132T)	83TTR	132	$ .25	$ .65	Checklist, Cards (177-264)	58T	246	$6.00	$18.00
Checklist TR, Cards (1T-132T)	84TTR	132	$ .08	$ .30	Checklist, Cards (177-264)	59T	248	$2.50	$7.50
Checklist TR, Cards (1T-132T)	85TTR	132	$ .05	$ .20	Checklist, Cards (177-264)	60T	151	$1.50	$4.50
Checklist TR, Cards (1T-132T)	86TTR	132	$ .02	$ .25	Checklist, Cards (177-264)	60T	164	$2.50	$8.00
Checklist TR, Cards (1T-132T)	87TTR	132	$ .05	$ .20	Checklist, Cards (177-264)	60T	208	$1.50	$6.00
Checklist TR, Cards (1T-132T)	88TTR	132	$ .01	$ .05	Checklist, Cards (177-264)	61T	189	$1.80	$6.00
Checklist TR, Cards (727-858)	81TTR	858	$ .15	$ .50	Checklist, Cards (177-264)	62T	192	$1.35	$4.00
Checklist, 1 of 6	90T	128	$ .01	$ .03	Checklist, Cards (177-264)	63T	191	$ .60	$1.75
Checklist, 2 of 6	90T	262	$ .01	$ .03	Checklist, Cards (177-264)	64T	188	$ .25	$ .85
Checklist, 3 of 6	90T	376	$ .01	$ .03					
Checklist, 4 of 6	90T	526	$ .01	$ .03					
Checklist, 5 of 6	90T	646	$ .01	$ .03					
Checklist, 6 of 6	90T	783	$ .01	$ .03					
Checklist, Cards (1-109)	67T	62	$ .70	$2.00					
Checklist, Cards (1-109)	68T	67	$ .70	$2.00					
Checklist, Cards (1-109)	69T	57	$ .70	$2.00					
Checklist, Cards (1-121)	78T	74	$ .15	$ .50					
Checklist Cards (1-121)	70T	121	$ .05	$ .20					
Checklist, Cards (1-121)	80T	121	$ .05	$ .25					
Checklist, Cards (1-121)	81T	31	$ .01	$ .07					
Checklist, Cards (1-132)	70T	9	$ .50	$1.95					
Checklist, Cards (1-132)	71T	54	$ .60	$1.75					
Checklist, Cards (1-132)	72T	4	$ .50	$1.95					
Checklist, Cards (1-132)	73T	54	$ .50	$1.95					
Checklist, Cards (1-132)	74T	126	$ .35	$1.10					
Checklist, Cards (1-132)	75T	126	$ .50	$2.00					
Checklist, Cards (1-132)	76T	119	$ .35	$1.10					
Checklist, Cards (1-132)	77T	32	$ .35	$1.10					
Checklist, Cards (1-132)	82T	129	$ .01	$ .06					
Checklist, Cards (1-132)	83T	129	$ .01	$ .06					
Checklist, Cards (1-132)	84T	114	$ .01	$ .05					
Checklist, Cards (1-132)	85T	121	$ .01	$ .04					
Checklist, Cards (1-132)	86T	131	$ .01	$ .03					
Checklist, Cards (1-132)	87T	128	$ .01	$ .03					
Checklist, Cards (1-132)	88T	121	$ .01	$ .03					
Checklist, Cards (1-132)	89T	118	$ .01	$ .04					
Checklist, Cards (1-88)	58T	71	$5.00	$20.00					
Checklist, Cards (1-88)	59T	8	$2.00	$6.00					
Checklist, Cards (1-88)	59T	48	$1.50	$4.50					
Checklist, Cards (1-88)	60T	18	$3.00	$9.00					
Checklist, Cards (1-88)	60T	43	$1.25	$3.50					
Checklist, Cards (1-88)	61T	17	$1.35	$4.00	Checklist, Cards (177-264)	65T	189	$ .60	$1.75

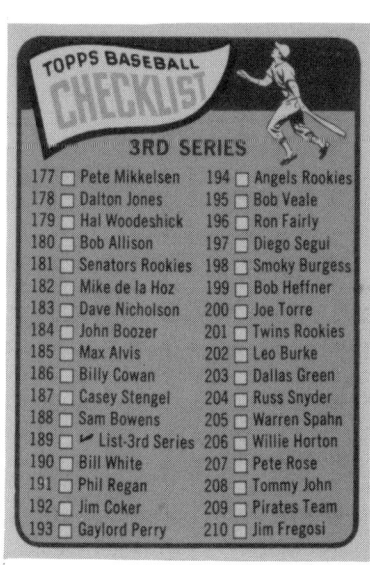

TOPPS

Player	Year	No.	VG	EX/MT	Player	Year	No.	VG	EX/MT
Checklist. Cards (177-264)	66T	183	$1.25	$4.50	Checklist. Cards (430-495)	59T	457	$4.00	$12.00
Checklist. Cards (177-264)	88TBB	216	$ .01	$ .05	Checklist. Cards (430-495)	60T	413	$1.35	$4.00
Checklist. Cards (197-283)	67T	191	$ .75	$2.50	Checklist. Cards (430-495)	60T	484	$4.00	$12.00
Checklist. Cards (197-283)	68T	192	$ .70	$2.00	Checklist. Cards (430-506)	61T	437	$1.50	$4.50
Checklist. Cards (219-327)	69T	214	$ .60	$1.75	Checklist. Cards (430-506)	62T	441	$2.00	$6.00
Checklist. Cards (243-363)	78T	289	$ .10	$ .45	Checklist. Cards (430-506)	63T	431	$1.35	$4.00
Checklist. Cards (243-363)	79T	353	$ .08	$ .30	Checklist. Cards (430-506)	64T	438	$1.35	$4.00
Checklist. Cards (243-363)	80T	348	$ .05	$ .25	Checklist. Cards (430-506)	65T	443	$ .60	$1.75
Checklist. Cards (243-363)	81T	338	$ .01	$ .07	Checklist. Cards (430-506)	66T	444	$1.35	$4.00
Checklist. Cards (264-372)	70T	244	$ .50	$1.95	Checklist. Cards (458-533)	67T	454	$2.00	$7.00
Checklist. Cards (264-393)	71T	206	$ .08	$1.50	Checklist. Cards (458-533)	68T	454	$1.35	$4.00
Checklist. Cards (264-394)	72T	251	$ .50	$1.95	Checklist. Cards (460-546)	70T	432	$ .50	$1.95
Checklist. Cards (265 352)	61T	273	$ .30	$1.00	Checklist. Cards (485-605)	78T	535	$ .15	$ .50
Checklist. Cards (265-332)	60T	332	$3.50	$10.00	Checklist. Cards (485-605)	79T	602	$ .08	$ .30
Checklist. Cards (265-352)	58T	327	$1.25	$3.50	Checklist. Cards (485-605)	80T	533	$ .05	$ .25
Checklist. Cards (265-352)	58T	341	$1.25	$3.50	Checklist. Cards (485-605)	81T	562	$ .01	$ .07
Checklist. Cards (265-352)	59T	223	$1.50	$4.50	Checklist. Cards (496-572)	59T	476	$1.50	$4.50
Checklist. Cards (265-352)	59T	304	$1.50	$4.50	Checklist. Cards (496-572)	59T	510	$10.50	$42.50
Checklist. Cards (265-352)	60T	242	$1.75	$6.00	Checklist. Cards (496-572)	59T	528	$4.25	$13.00
Checklist. Cards (265-352)	62T	277	$1.35	$4.00	Checklist. Cards (496-572)	60T	494	$2.25	$6.50
Checklist. Cards (265-352)	63T	274	$ .60	$1.75	Checklist. Cards (496-572)	60T	513	$5.00	$16.00
Checklist. Cards (265-352)	64T	274	$ .70	$2.00	Checklist. Cards (496-572)	60T	537	$6.00	$18.00
Checklist. Cards (265-352)	65T	273	$ .60	$1.75	Checklist. Cards (507-576)	63T	509	$2.70	$8.00
Checklist. Cards (265-352)	66T	279	$ .85	$2.75	Checklist. Cards (507-587)	61T	516	$3.00	$9.00
Checklist. Cards (265-362)	58T	256	$1.25	$3.50	Checklist. Cards (507-587)	64T	517	$2.00	$6.00
Checklist. Cards (265-396)	73T	338	$ .50	$1.95	Checklist. Cards (507-598)	62T	516	$3.00	$9.00
Checklist. Cards (265-396)	74T	273	$ .35	$1.10	Checklist. Cards (507-598)	65T	508	$1.80	$5.00
Checklist. Cards (265-396)	75T	386	$ .50	$2.00	Checklist. Cards (507-598)	66T	517	$2.25	$6.50
Checklist. Cards (265-396)	76T	392	$ .35	$1.10	Checklist. Cards (513-588)	69T	504	$1.35	$4.00
Checklist. Cards (265-396)	77T	356	$ .35	$1.10	Checklist. Cards (524-643)	71T	499	$ .60	$1.75
Checklist. Cards (265-396)	82T	394	$ .01	$ .06	Checklist. Cards (526-656)	72T	478	$ .50	$1.95
Checklist. Cards (265-396)	83T	349	$ .01	$ .06	Checklist. Cards (529-660)	73T	588	$2.75	$8.00
Checklist. Cards (265-396)	85T	377	$ .01	$ .04	Checklist. Cards (529-660)	74T	637	$ .35	$1.10
Checklist. Cards (265-396)	86T	394	$ .01	$ .03	Checklist. Cards (529-660)	75T	646	$ .50	$2.00
Checklist. Cards (265-396)	87T	392	$ .01	$ .03	Checklist. Cards (529-660)	76T	643	$ .35	$1.10
Checklist. Cards (265-396)	88T	373	$ .01	$ .03	Checklist. Cards (529-660)	77T	562	$ .35	$1.10
Checklist. Cards (265-396)	89T	378	$ .01	$ .04	Checklist. Cards (529-660)	82T	634	$ .01	$ .06
Checklist. Cards (284-370)	67T	278	$ .70	$2.00	Checklist. Cards (529-660)	83T	642	$ .01	$ .06
Checklist. Cards (284-370)	68T	278	$1.35	$4.00	Checklist. Cards (529-660)	84T	646	$ .01	$ .05
Checklist. Cards (328-425)	69T	314	$ .25	$ .85	Checklist. Cards (529-660)	85T	659	$ .01	$ .04
Checklist. Cards (353-429)	59T	329	$1.50	$4.50	Checklist. Cards (529-660)	86T	659	$ .01	$ .03
Checklist. Cards (353-429)	59T	419	$2.50	$9.50	Checklist. Cards (529-660)	87T	654	$ .01	$ .03
Checklist. Cards (353-429)	60T	302	$1.35	$4.00	Checklist. Cards (529-660)	88T	646	$ .01	$ .03
Checklist. Cards (353-429)	60T	381	$1.35	$4.00	Checklist. Cards (529-660)	89T	619	$ .01	$ .04
Checklist. Cards (353-429)	61T	361	$2.00	$6.00	Checklist. Cards (534 -598)	68T	518	$ .50	$2.50
Checklist. Cards (353-429)	62T	367	$1.35	$4.00	Checklist. Cards (534-609)	67T	531	$1.40	$4.00
Checklist. Cards (353-429)	63T	362	$ .70	$2.00	Checklist. Cards (547 -633)	70T	542	$ .70	$2.00
Checklist. Cards (353-429)	64T	362	$1.00	$3.75	Checklist. Cards (589-664)	69T	582	$ .95	$3.50
Checklist. Cards (353-429)	65T	361	$1.00	$3.75	Checklist. Cards (606-726)	78T	652	$ .25	$ .85
Checklist. Cards (353-429)	66T	363	$1.25	$4.50	Checklist. Cards (606-726)	79T	669	$ .08	$ .30
Checklist. Cards (353-440)	58T	312	$2.50	$7.50	Checklist. Cards (606-726)	80T	646	$ .05	$ .25
Checklist. Cards (364-484)	78T	435	$ .25	$ .85	Checklist. Cards (606-726)	81T	638	$ .01	$ .07
Checklist. Cards (364-484)	79T	483	$ .05	$ .25	Checklist. Cards (634-720)	70T	588	$ .75	$ .25
Checklist. Cards (364-484)	80T	484	$ .05	$ .25	Checklist. Cards (644-752)	71T	619	$1.35	$4.00
Checklist. Cards (364-484)	81T	446	$ .01	$ .07	Checklist. Cards (657-787)	72T	604	$1.35	$4.00
Checklist. Cards (371-457)	67T	361	$1.50	$3.75	Checklist. Cards (661-792)	82T	789	$ .01	$ .06
Checklist. Cards (371-457)	68T	356	$ .70	$2.00	Checklist. Cards (661-792)	83T	769	$ .01	$ .06
Checklist. Cards (373-459)	70T	343	$ .60	$1.75	Checklist. Cards (661-792)	84T	781	$ .01	$ .05
Checklist. Cards (394-523)	71T	369	$ .60	$1.75	Checklist. Cards (661-792)	85T	784	$ .01	$ .04
Checklist. Cards (395-525)	72T	378	$ .50	$1.95	Checklist. Cards (661-792)	86T	791	$ .01	$ .03
Checklist. Cards (397-528)	73T	453	$ .50	$1.95	Checklist. Cards (661-792)	87T	792	$ .01	$ .10
Checklist. Cards (397-528)	74T	414	$ .35	$1.10	Checklist. Cards (661-792)	88T	776	$ .01	$ .03
Checklist. Cards (397-528)	75T	517	$ .50	$2.00	Checklist. Cards (661-792)	89T	782	$ .01	$ .04
Checklist. Cards (397-528)	76T	526	$ .35	$1.10	Checklist. Cards (89-176)	58T	134	$3.00	$7.50
Checklist. Cards (397-528)	77T	451	$ .35	$1.10	Checklist. Cards (89-176)	58T	174	$1.25	$3.50
Checklist. Cards (397-528)	82T	491	$ .01	$ .06	Checklist. Cards (89-176)	59T	69	$2.75	$9.50
Checklist. Cards (397-528)	83T	526	$ .01	$ .06	Checklist. Cards (89-176)	59T	94	$3.00	$11.00
Checklist. Cards (397-528)	84T	527	$ .01	$ .05	Checklist. Cards (89-176)	59T	111	$2.55	$8.50
Checklist. Cards (397-528)	85T	527	$ .01	$ .04	Checklist. Cards (89-176)	60T	72	$2.50	$8.00
Checklist. Cards (397-528)	86T	527	$ .01	$ .03	Checklist. Cards (89-176)	60T	174	$1.35	$4.00
Checklist. Cards (397-528)	87T	522	$ .01	$ .03	Checklist. Cards (89-176)	61T	98	$1.80	$6.00
Checklist. Cards (397-528)	88T	528	$ .01	$ .03	Checklist. Cards (89-176)	62T	98	$1.35	$4.00
Checklist. Cards (397-528)	89T	524	$ .01	$ .04	Checklist. Cards (89-176)	63T	102	$1.50	$3.75
Checklist. Cards (426-512)	69T	412	$2.50	$8.00	Checklist. Cards (89-176)	64T	102	$ .60	$1.75
Checklist. Cards (430-495)	59T	397	$1.50	$4.50	Checklist. Cards (89-176)	65T	104	$1.75	$5.00

Player	Year	No.	VG	EX/MT
Checklist. Cards (89-176)	66T	101	$ .95	$2.75
Checklist. Cards (89-176)	88TBB	126	$ .01	$ .05
Checklist. Cards Traded	74TTR	0	$ .35	$1.10
Checklist. Cards Traded	76TTR	0	$ .15	$ .60
Checklist. Cards(1-110)	89TBB	59	$ .01	$ .05
Checklist. Cards(111-220)	89TBB	176	$ .01	$ .05
Checklist. Cards(1T-132T)	89TTR	132	$ .01	$ .05
Checklist. Cards(221-330))	89TBB	327	$ .01	$ .05
Checklist. Coins (1-161)	71T	161	$ .70	$2.00
Cheney. Tom	57T	359	$1.00	$3.75
Cheney. Tom	61T	494	$ .50	$2.00
Chesbro. Jack	61T	407	$ .50	$2.00
Chesbro. Jack	79TRH	416	$ .05	$ .20

FLOYD CHIFFER
PITCHER
PADRES

Player	Year	No.	VG	EX/MT
Chiffer. Floyd	83T	298	$ .01	$ .06
Childress. Rocky	88T	643	$ .01	$ .03
Chiles. Rich	72T	56	$ .10	$ .35
Chiles. Rich	73T	617	$ .35	$1.10
Chiles. Rich	78T	193	$ .02	$ .10
Chiles. Rich	79T	498	$ .02	$ .10
Chipman. Bob	52T	388	$39.00	$135.00
Chiti. Harry	56T	179	$1.25	$4.50
Chiti. Harry	58T	119	$ .50	$2.00
Chiti. Harry	59T	79	$1.00	$3.75
Chiti. Harry	60T	339	$ .50	$1.95
Chiti. Harry	61T	269	$ .30	$1.00
Chiti. Harry	62T	253	$ .35	$1.10
Chittum. Nelson	60T	296	$ .50	$1.95
Chlupsa. Bob	71T	594	$ .75	$2.00
Chris. Mike	80T	666	$ .01	$ .07
Chrisley. Neil	57T	320	$3.50	$13.00
Chrisley. Neil	58T	303	$ .50	$2.00
Chrisley. Neil	59T	189	$ .50	$1.95
Chrisley. Neil	60T	273	$ .35	$1.10
Chrisley. Neil	62T	308	$ .35	$1.10
Christensen. John	86T	287	$ .01	$ .03
Christensen. John	87TTR	23	$ .01	$ .07
Christensen. John	88T	413	$ .01	$ .03
Christensen. Larry	74T	587	$ .06	$ .25
Christensen. Larry	75T	551	$ .06	$ .25
Christensen. Larry	76T	634	$ .05	$ .20
Christensen. Larry	77T	59	$ .05	$ .15
Christensen. Larry	78T	247	$ .02	$ .10
Christensen. Larry	79T	493	$ .02	$ .10

Player	Year	No.	VG	EX/MT
Christenson, Larry	80T	161	$ .01	$ .07
Christenson, Larry	81T	346	$ .01	$ .07
Christenson, Larry	82T	544	$ .01	$ .06
Christenson, Larry	83T	668	$ .01	$ .06
Christenson, Larry	84T	252	$ .01	$ .05
Christian, Bob	69T	173	$ .25	$ .65
Christian, Bob	70T	51	$ .10	$ .35
Christiansen, Clay	85T	211	$ .01	$ .04
Christopher, Joe	61T	82	$ .30	$1.00
Christopher, Joe	63T	217	$ .25	$ .85
Christopher, Joe	64T	546	$1.50	$3.75
Christopher, Joe	65T	495	$ .50	$2.00
Christopher, Joe	66T	343	$ .25	$ .85
Church, Bubba	52T	323	$39.00	$135.00
Church, Bubba	53T	47	$3.75	$13.00
Ciardi, Mark	88T	417	$ .01	$ .03
Cias, Darryl	84T	159	$ .01	$ .05
Cicotte, Al	57T	398	$1.00	$3.75
Cicotte, Al	58T	382	$ .50	$2.00
Cicotte, Al	59T	57	$1.00	$3.75
Cicotte, Al	60T	473	$ .60	$1.75
Cicotte, Al	61T	241	$ .30	$1.00
Cicotte, Al	62T	126	$ .35	$1.10
Cimino, Pete	66T	563	$4.50	$15.00
Cimino, Pete	67T	34	$ .25	$ .65
Cimino, Pete	68T	143	$ .25	$ .65
Cimoli, Gino	57T	319	$3.50	$13.00
Cimoli, Gino	58T	286	$ .50	$2.00
Cimoli, Gino	59T	418	$ .50	$1.95
Cimoli, Gino	60T	58	$ .35	$1.10
Cimoli, Gino	61T	165	$ .30	$1.00
Cimoli, Gino	62T	402	$ .70	$2.10
Cimoli, Gino	63T	321	$ .35	$1.20
Cimoli, Gino	64T	26	$ .25	$ .85
Cimoli, Gino	65T	569	$1.50	$3.75
Cipriani, Frank	62T	333	$ .35	$1.10
Cisco. Galen	62T	301	$ .35	$1.10
Cisco. Galen	63T	93	$ .25	$ .85
Cisco. Galen	64T	202	$ .25	$ .85
Cisco. Galen	65T	364	$ .30	$1.00
Cisco. Galen	67T	596	$1.35	$4.00
Cisco. Galen	69T	211	$ .25	$ .65
Cisco. Galen	73T	593	$ .50	$2.00
Cisco. Galen	74T	166	$ .06	$ .25
Clancy, Jim	78T	496	$ .05	$ .20
Clancy, Jim	79T	131	$ .02	$ .10
Clancy, Jim	80T	249	$ .01	$ .07
Clancy, Jim	81T	19	$ .01	$ .07
Clancy, Jim	82T	665	$ .01	$ .06
Clancy, Jim	83T	345	$ .01	$ .06
Clancy, Jim	84T	575	$ .01	$ .05
Clancy, Jim	85T	746	$ .01	$ .04
Clancy, Jim	86T	412	$ .01	$ .03
Clancy, Jim	87T	122	$ .01	$ .03
Clancy, Jim	88T	54	$ .01	$ .03
Clancy, Jim	88TBB	258	$ .01	$ .05
Clancy, Jim	89T	219	$ .01	$ .04
Clancy, Jim	89TTR	19	$ .01	$ .05
Clancy, Jim	90T	648	$ .01	$ .03
Clark, Al	52T	278	$10 .00	$30.00
Clark, Bob	80T	663	$ .05	$ .20
Clark, Bob	81T	288	$ .01	$ .07
Clark, Bob	82T	74	$ .01	$ .06
Clark, Bob	83T	184	$ .01	$ .06
Clark, Bob	84T	626	$ .01	$ .05
Clark, Bob	84TTR	24	$ .02	$ .10
Clark, Bob	85T	553	$ .01	$ .04
Clark, Bob	86T	452	$ .01	$ .03
Clark, Bryan	82T	632	$ .01	$ .06
Clark, Bryan	83T	789	$ .01	$ .06
Clark, Bryan	84T	22	$ .01	$ .05
Clark, Bryan	84TTR	25	$ .02	$ .10
Clark, Bryan	85T	489	$ .01	$ .04
Clark, Bryan	85TTR	21	$ .02	$ .10
Clark, Dave	88T	49	$ .01	$ .10

TOPPS

Player	Year	No.	VG	EX/MT	Player	Year	No.	VG	EX/MT
Clark. Dave	89T	574	$ .01	$ .04	Clemens. Roger	87T	340	$ .50	$1.95
Clark. Dave	90T	339	$ .01	$ .03	Clemens. Roger	87TAS	614	$ .10	$ .35
Clark. Jack	77T	488	$5.00	$20.00	Clemens. Roger	87TRB	1	$ .25	$ .65
Clark. Jack	78T	384	$1.00	$3.00	Clemens. Roger	88T	70	$ .05	$ .50
Clark. Jack	79T	512	$ .60	$1.75	Clemens. Roger	88TAS	394	$ .01	$ .20
Clark. Jack	80T	167	$ .60	$1.75	Clemens. Roger	88TBB	118	$ .05	$ .35
Clark. Jack	81T	30	$ .10	$ .50	Clemens. Roger	89T	450	$ .05	$ .25
Clark. Jack	82T	460	$ .10	$ .50	Clemens. Roger	89TAS	405	$ .01	$ .15
Clark. Jack	83T	210	$ .05	$ .25	Clemens. Roger	89TBB	42	$ .01	$ .25
Clark. Jack	84T	690	$ .05	$ .25	Clemens. Roger	90T	245	$ .01	$ .15
Clark. Jack	85TTR	22	$ .25	$ .85	Clemente. Roberto	55T	164	$250.00	$900.00
Clark. Jack	86T	350	$ .02	$ .15	Clemente. Roberto	56T	33	$70.00	$250.00
Clark. Jack	87T	520	$ .06	$ .25	Clemente. Bob	57T	76	$50.00	$160.00
Clark. Jack	88T	100	$ .01	$ .10	Clemente. Bob	58T	52	$27.50	$110.00
Clark. Jack	88TAS	397	$ .01	$ .03	Clemente. Bob	59T	478	$24.00	$82.50
Clark. Jack	88TBB	262	$ .01	$ .05	Clemente. Roberto	59T	543	$11.50	$45.00
Clark. Jack	88TTR	28	$ .01	$ .10	Clemente. Bob	60T	326	$25.00	$85.00
Clark. Jack	89T	410	$ .01	$ .10	Clemente. Bob	61T	41	$1.50	$5.00
Clark. Jack	89TBB	240	$ .01	$ .10	Clemente. Bob	61T	388	$22.50	$77.50
Clark. Jack	89TTR	20	$ .01	$ .10	Clemente. Bob	62T	10	$18.00	$55.00
Clark. Jack	90T	90	$ .01	$ .10	Clemente. Bob	62T	52	$ .60	$1.75
Clark. Joe	85T	740	$ .01	$ .04	Clemente. Bob	63T	18	$2.35	$10.00
Clark. Mike	53T	193	$3.75	$13.00	Clemente. Bob	63T	540	$35.00	$140.00
Clark. Phil	58T	423	$ .50	$2.00	Clemente. Bob	64T	7	$1.70	$5.00
Clark. Phil	59T	454	$ .50	$1.95	Clemente. Bob	64T	440	$17.50	$67.50
Clark. Rickey	70T	586	$ .25	$ .85	Clemente. Bob	65T	2	$1.35	$4.00
Clark. Rickey	71T	697	$ .70	$2.10	Clemente. Bob	65T	160	$19.50	$65.00
Clark. Rickey	72T	462	$ .10	$ .35	Clemente. Bob	66T	215	$2.75	$9.50
Clark. Rickey	73T	636	$ .35	$1.10	Clemente. Bob	66T	300	$17.50	$68.00
Clark. Ron	67T	137	$ .25	$ .65	Clemente. Bob	67T	242	$1.50	$3.75
Clark. Ron	68T	589	$ .30	$1.00	Clemente. Bob	67T	400	$12.00	$50.00
Clark. Ron	69T	561	$ .25	$ .85	Clemente. Bob	68T	1	$2.50	$12.50
Clark. Ron	70T	531	$ .10	$ .35	Clemente. Bob	68T	3	$1.35	$4.00
Clark. Terry	89T	129	$ .01	$ .04	Clemente. Bob	68T	150	$9.00	$42.50
Clark. Will	86TTR	24	$3.00	$12.00	Clemente. Bob	68T	480	$7.50	$22.50
Clark. Will	87T	420	$1.25	$5.00	Clemente. Bob	68TAS	374	$3.00	$9.00
Clark. Will	88T	350	$ .10	$2.00	Clemente. Bob	69T	50	$10.00	$35.00
Clark. Will	88TBB	9	$ .25	$1.50	Clemente. Bob "Roberto"	70T	61	$1.50	$4.75
Clark. Will	89T	660	$ .05	$ .50	Clemente. Roberto	70T	350	$9.00	$30.00
Clark. Will	89TBB	146	$ .01	$ .75	Clemente. Roberto	71T	630	$9.00	$30.00
Clark. Will	90T	100	$ .01	$ .50	Clemente. Roberto	72T	309	$5.00	$20.00
Clark. Will	90TAS	397	$ .01	$ .25	Clemente. Roberto	72TIA	310	$2.00	$9.00
Clarke. Horace	66T	547	$10.00	$35.00	Clemente. Roberto	73T	50	$4.75	$18.50
Clarke. Horace	67T	169	$ .25	$ .65	Clemente. Roberto	75T	204	$ .50	$2.00
Clarke. Horace	68T	263	$ .25	$ .65	Clemente. Roberto	87TTB	313	$ .06	$ .25
Clarke. Horace	69T	87	$ .25	$ .65	Clements. Pat	85TTR	23	$ .02	$ .10
Clarke. Horace	70T	623	$ .25	$ .85	Clements. Pat	86T	754	$ .01	$ .03
Clarke. Horace	71T	715	$ .70	$2.10	Clements. Pat	87T	16	$ .01	$ .03
Clarke. Horace	72T	387	$ .10	$ .35	Clements. Pat	88T	484	$ .01	$ .03
Clarke. Horace	73T	198	$ .06	$ .25	Clements. Pat	89T	159	$ .01	$ .04
Clarke. Horace	74T	529	$ .06	$ .25	Clements. Pat	90T	548	$ .01	$ .03
Clarke. Stan	88T	556	$ .01	$ .03	Clemons. Lance	72T	372	$ .10	$ .35
Clary. Ellis	60T	470	$ .95	$3.50	Clendenon. Donn	62T	86	$ .50	$2.00
Clary. Marty	90T	304	$ .01	$ .03	Clendenon. Donn	63T	477	$2.50	$6.50
Clay. Ken	78T	89	$ .02	$ .10	Clendenon. Donn	64T	163	$ .25	$ .85
Clay. Ken	79T	434	$ .02	$ .10	Clendenon. Donn	65T	325	$ .30	$1.00
Clay. Ken	80T	159	$ .01	$ .07	Clendenon. Donn	66T	375	$ .25	$ .85
Clay. Ken	81T	305	$ .01	$ .07	Clendenon. Donn	67T	266	$ .25	$ .65
Clay. Ken	81TTR	747	$ .02	$ .10	Clendenon. Donn	67T	535	$1.50	$4.00
Clay. Ken	82T	649	$ .01	$ .06	Clendenon. Donn	68T	344	$ .25	$ .65
Clear. Mark	80T	638	$ .03	$ .15	Clendenon. Donn	69T	208	$ .15	$ .15
Clear. Mark	81T	12	$ .01	$ .07	Clendenon. Donn	70T	280	$ .10	$ .35
Clear. Mark	81TTR	748	$ .02	$ .10	Clendenon. Donn	71T	115	$ .10	$ .35
Clear. Mark	82T	421	$ .01	$ .06	Clendenon. Donn	72T	671	$ .60	$1.75
Clear. Mark	83T	162	$ .01	$ .06	Cleveland. Reggie	70T	716	$ .50	$2.00
Clear. Mark	84T	577	$ .01	$ .05	Cleveland. Reggie	71T	216	$ .10	$ .35
Clear. Mark	85T	207	$ .01	$ .04	Cleveland. Reggie	72T	375	$ .10	$ .35
Clear. Mark	86T	349	$ .01	$ .03	Cleveland. Reggie	73T	104	$ .06	$ .25
Clear. Mark	86TTR	25	$ .02	$ .10	Cleveland. Reggie	74T	175	$ .06	$ .25
Clear. Mark	87T	640	$ .01	$ .03	Cleveland. Reggie	74TTR	175	$ .06	$ .25
Clear. Mark	88T	742	$ .01	$ .03	Cleveland. Reggie	75T	32	$ .06	$ .25
Clear. Mark	89T	63	$ .01	$ .04	Cleveland. Reggie	76T	419	$ .05	$ .20
Clemens. Doug	67T	489	$ .50	$2.00	Cleveland. Reggie	77T	613	$ .05	$ .15
Clemens. Roger	85T	181	$2.50	$10.00	Cleveland. Reggie	78T	105	$ .02	$ .10
Clemens. Roger	86T	661	$1.00	$3.00	Cleveland. Reggie	79T	209	$ .02	$ .10

Player	Year	No.	VG	EX/MT
Cleveland, Reggie	80T	394	$ .01	$ .07
Cleveland, Reggie	81T	576	$ .01	$ .07
Cleveland, Reggie	82T	737	$ .01	$ .06
Clevenger, Tex	58T	31	$1.00	$3.75
Clevenger, Tex	59T	298	$ .50	$1.95
Clevenger, Tex	60T	392	$ .50	$1.95
Clevenger, Tex	61T	291	$ .30	$1.00
Clevenger, Tex	63T	457	$2.50	$6.50
Cliburn, Stewart	89T	649	$ .01	$ .04
Cliburn, Stu	86T	179	$ .01	$ .03
Cline, Ty	61T	421	$ .50	$2.00
Cline, Ty	62T	362	$ .35	$1.10
Cline, Ty	63T	414	$ .35	$1.20
Cline, Ty	64T	171	$ .25	$ .85

OUTFIELD
TY CLINE

Player	Year	No.	VG	EX/MT
Cline, Ty	65T	63	$ .25	$ .65
Cline, Ty	66T	306	$ .25	$ .85
Cline, Ty	67T	591	$1.35	$4.00
Cline, Ty	68T	469	$ .30	$1.00
Cline, Ty	69T	442	$ .25	$ .65
Cline, Ty	70T	164	$ .10	$ .35
Cline, Ty	71T	319	$ .10	$ .35
Clines, Gene	71T	27	$ .10	$ .35
Clines, Gene	72T	152	$ .10	$ .35
Clines, Gene	73T	333	$ .06	$ .25
Clines, Gene	74T	172	$ .06	$ .25
Clines, Gene	75T	575	$ .06	$ .25
Clines, Gene	76T	417	$ .05	$ .20
Clines, Gene	77T	237	$ .05	$ .15
Clines, Gene	78T	639	$ .02	$ .10
Clines, Gene	79T	171	$ .02	$ .10
Clinton, Lou	60T	533	$2.00	$7.00
Clinton, Lou	62T	457	$ .70	$2.10
Clinton, Lou	63T	96	$ .25	$ .85
Clinton, Lou	64T	526	$1.50	$3.75
Clinton, Lou	64T	527	$1.50	$3.75
Clinton, Lou	65T	229	$ .30	$1.00
Clinton, Lou	67T	426	$ .25	$ .85
Cloninger, Tony	62T	63	$ .50	$1.95
Cloninger, Tony	63T	367	$ .35	$1.10
Cloninger, Tony	64T	575	$1.50	$3.75
Cloninger, Tony	65T	520	$ .50	$2.00
Cloninger, Tony	66T	10	$ .25	$ .85
Cloninger, Tony	66T	223	$ .65	$1.75

Player	Year	No.	VG	EX/MT
Cloninger, Tony	67T	396	$ .35	$1.10
Cloninger, Tony	67T	490	$ .50	$2.00
Cloninger, Tony	68T	93	$ .25	$ .65
Cloninger, Tony	69T	492	$ .25	$ .65
Cloninger, Tony	70T	705	$ .50	$2.00
Cloninger, Tony	71T	218	$ .10	$ .35
Cloninger, Tony	72T	779	$ .70	$2.10
Closter, Alan	66T	549	$4.50	$15.00
Closter, Alan	69T	114	$ .25	$ .65
Closter, Alan	72T	124	$ .10	$ .35
Closter, Alan	73T	634	$ .35	$1.10
Clutterbuck, Bryan	87T	562	$ .01	$ .03
Clutterbuck, Bryan	89TTR	21	$ .01	$ .05
Clutterbuck, Bryan	90T	264	$ .01	$ .03
Clyde, David	74T	133	$ .06	$ .25
Clyde, David	75T	12	$ .06	$ .25
Clyde, David	79T	399	$ .02	$ .10
Clyde, David	80T	697	$ .01	$ .07
Coan, Gil	52T	291	$14.00	$45.00
Coan, Gil	53T	133	$3.75	$13.00
Coates, Jim	59T	525	$3.00	$9.00
Coates, Jim	60T	51	$ .35	$1.10
Coates, Jim	61T	531	$6.00	$18.00
Coates, Jim	62T	553	$3.00	$9.50
Coates, Jim	63T	237	$ .25	$ .85
Coates, Jim	67T	401	$ .25	$ .85
Cobb, Ty	73TATL	471	$ .70	$3.00
Cobb, Ty	73TATL	475	$ .60	$3.00
Cobb, Ty	76TAS	346	$ .70	$3.00
Cobb, Ty	79TRH	411	$ .15	$ .50
Cobb, Ty	79TRH	414	$ .15	$ .50
Cocanower, Jaime	84TTR	26	$ .02	$ .10
Cocanower, Jaime	85T	576	$ .01	$ .04
Cocanower, Jaime	86T	277	$ .01	$ .03
Cocanower, Jamie	87T	423	$ .01	$ .03
Cochrane, Dave	90T	491	$ .01	$ .10
Cochrane, Mickey	76TAS	348	$ .30	$1.00
Codiroli, Chris	83TTR	20	$ .02	$ .10
Codiroli, Chris	84T	61	$ .01	$ .05
Codiroli, Chris	85T	552	$ .01	$ .04
Codiroli, Chris	86T	433	$ .01	$ .03
Codiroli, Chris	87T	217	$ .01	$ .03
Coffman, Kevin	88TTR	29	$ .01	$ .05
Coffman, Kevin	89T	488	$ .01	$ .04
Coggins, Frank	68T	96	$ .25	$ .65
Coggins, Rich	73T	611	$ .35	$1.10
Coggins, Rich	74T	353	$ .06	$ .25
Coggins, Rich	75T	167	$ .06	$ .25
Coggins, Rich	76T	572	$ .05	$ .20
Cohen, Andy	60T	466	$ .95	$3.50
Coker, Jim	60T	438	$ .50	$1.95
Coker, Jim	61T	144	$ .30	$1.00
Coker, Jim	63T	456	$2.50	$6.50
Coker, Jim	64T	211	$ .25	$ .85
Coker, Jim	65T	192	$ .25	$ .65
Coker, Jim	66T	292	$ .25	$ .85
Coker, Jimmie	67T	158	$ .25	$ .65
Colavito, Rocco (Rocky)	57T	212	$12.00	$45.00
Colavito, Rocky	58T	368	$3.00	$10.00
Colavito, Rocky	59T	166	$ .60	$1.75
Colavito, Rocky	59T	420	$1.00	$3.00
Colavito, Rocky	59T	462	$1.50	$3.75
Colavito, Rocky	60T	260	$ .50	$2.00
Colavito, Rocky	60T	400	$ .60	$1.75
Colavito, Rocky	61T	44	$4.00	$16.00
Colavito, Rocky	61T	330	$ .95	$3.50
Colavito, Rocky	62T	20	$ .60	$1.75
Colavito, Rocky	62T	314	$1.25	$4.50
Colavito, Rocky	62TAS	472	$ .70	$2.00
Colavito, Rocky	63T	4	$ .50	$2.00
Colavito, Rocky	63T	240	$ .60	$1.75
Colavito, Rocky	64T	320	$ .60	$1.75
Colavito, Rocky	65T	380	$ .60	$1.75
Colavito, Rocky	66T	150	$ .50	$2.00
Colavito, Rocky	66T	220	$ .50	$2.00

Player	Year	No.	VG	EX/MT	Player	Year	No.	VG	EX/MT
Colavito, Rocky	67T	109	$ .15	$ .50	Coleman, Vince	86TRB	201	$ .03	$ .25
Colavito, Rocky	67T	580	$20.00	$75.00	Coleman, Vince	87T	590	$ .10	$ .35
Colavito, Rocky	68T	99	$ .50	$1.95	Coleman, Vince	88T	260	$ .01	$ .10
Colavito, Rocky	73T	449	$ .25	$ .65	Coleman, Vince	88TBB	5	$ .01	$ .10
Colbern, Mike	79T	704	$ .02	$ .10	Coleman, Vince	88TRB	1	$ .01	$ .10
Colbern, Mike	80T	664	$ .01	$ .07	Coleman, Vince	89T	90	$ .01	$ .10
Colbern, Mike	81T	522	$ .01	$ .07	Coleman, Vince	89TBB	124	$ .01	$ .10
Colbert, Nate	66T	596	$4.50	$15.00	Coleman, Vince	90T	660	$ .01	$ .10
Colbert, Nate	69T	408	$ .25	$ .65	Coleman, Vince	90TRB	6	$ .01	$ .10
Colbert, Nate	70T	11	$ .10	$ .35	Coles, Chuck	59T	120	$ .50	$1.95
Colbert, Nate	71T	235	$ .10	$ .35	Coles, Darnell	85T	108	$ .01	$ .04
Colbert, Nate	72T	571	$ .25	$ .85	Coles, Darnell	86T	337	$ .01	$ .03
Colbert, Nate	72TIA	572	$ .25	$ .85	Coles, Darnell	86TTR	26	$ .02	$ .10
Colbert, Nate	73T	340	$ .06	$ .25	Coles, Darnell	87	411	$ .01	$ .03
Colbert, Nate	74T	125	$ .06	$ .25	Coles, Darnell	88T	46	$ .01	$ .03
Colbert, Nate	75T	599	$ .06	$ .25	Coles, Darnell	88TBB	255	$ .01	$ .05
Colbert, Nate	76T	495	$ .05	$ .20	Coles, Darnell	89T	738	$ .01	$ .04
Colbert, Nate	77TB	433	$ .05	$ .15	Coles, Darnell	89TBB	133	$ .01	$ .05
Colbert, Vince	71T	231	$ .10	$ .35	Coles, Darnell	90T	232	$ .01	$ .03
Colbert, Vince	72T	84	$ .10	$ .35	Collins, Dave	76T	363	$ .25	$ .65
Colborn, Jim	71T	38	$ .10	$ .35	Collins, Dave	77T	431	$ .05	$ .15
Colborn, Jim	72T	386	$ .10	$ .35	Collins, Dave	78T	254	$ .02	$ .10
Colborn, Jim	73T	408	$ .06	$ .25	Collins, Dave	79T	622	$ .02	$ .10
Colborn, Jim	74T	75	$ .06	$ .25	Collins, Dave	80T	73	$ .01	$ .07
Colborn, Jim	75T	305	$ .06	$ .25	Collins, Dave	81T	175	$ .01	$ .07
Colborn, Jim	76T	521	$ .05	$ .20	Collins, Dave	82T	595	$ .01	$ .06
Colborn, Jim	77T	331	$ .05	$ .15	Collins, Dave	82TTR	20	$ .02	$ .10
Colborn, Jim	78T	129	$ .02	$ .10	Collins, Dave	83T	359	$ .01	$ .06
Colborn, Jim	79T	276	$ .02	$ .10	Collins, Dave	83TTR	21	$ .02	$ .10
Cole, Dick	54T	84	$2.10	$7.50	Collins, Dave	84T	733	$ .01	$ .05
Cole, Dick	57T	234	$ .95	$3.50	Collins, Dave	85T	463	$ .01	$ .04
Coleman, Claren. ChooChoo	61T	502	$ .50	$2.00	Collins, Dave	85TTR	25	$ .02	$ .10
Coleman, Choo Choo	63T	27	$ .25	$ .85	Collins, Dave	86T	271	$ .01	$ .03
Coleman, Choo Choo	64T	251	$ .25	$ .85	Collins, Dave	86TTR	27	$ .02	$ .10
Coleman, Choo Choo	66T	561	$10.00	$27.00	Collins, Dave	87T	148	$ .01	$ .03
Coleman, Gerry	51Trb	18	$1.35	$4.00	Collins, Joe	52T	202	$7.00	$20.00
Coleman, Gordy	60T	257	$ .35	$1.10	Collins, Joe	53T	9	$6.00	$18.00
Coleman, Gordy	61T	194	$ .30	$1.00	Collins, Joe	54T	83	$4.75	$14.00
Coleman, Gordy	62T	508	$ .70	$2.10	Collins, Joe	55T	63	$2.10	$7.50
Coleman, Gordy	63T	90	$ .25	$ .85	Collins, Joe	56T	21	$1.25	$4.50
Coleman, Gordy	64T	577	$1.50	$3.75	Collins, Joe	57T	295	$3.50	$13.00
Coleman, Gordy	65T	289	$ .30	$1.00	Collins, Kevin	65T	581	$20.00	$75.00
Coleman, Gordy	66T	494	$ .70	$2.10	Collins, Kevin	69T	127	$ .25	$ .65
Coleman, Gordy	67T	61	$ .25	$ .65	Collins, Kevin	70T	707	$ .50	$2.00
Coleman, Jerry	52T	237	$6.00	$8.00	Collins, Kevin	71T	553	$ .30	$1.00
Coleman, Jerry	56T	316	$3.00	$9.00	Collum, Jackie	57T	268	$3.50	$13.00
Coleman, Jerry	57T	192	$1.35	$5.00	Colpaert, Dick	73T	608	$ .35	$1.10
Coleman, Joe	53T	279	$11.00	$37.50	Colson, Loyd	71T	111	$ .10	$ .35
Coleman, Joe	54T	156	$2.10	$7.50	Colt .45's, Houston	63T	312	$3.00	$10.00
Coleman, Joe	55T	162	$4.25	$13.00	Colton, Larry	68T	348	$ .25	$ .65
Coleman, Joe	66T	333	$ .25	$ .85	Colton, Larry	69T	454	$ .25	$ .65
Coleman, Joe	67T	167	$ .25	$ .65	Coluccio, Bob	74T	124	$ .06	$ .25
Coleman, Joe	68T	573	$ .30	$1.00	Coluccio, Bob	75T	456	$ .06	$ .25
Coleman, Joe	69T	246	$ .25	$ .85	Coluccio, Bob	76T	333	$ .05	$ .20
Coleman, Joe	70T	127	$ .10	$ .35	Combe, Geoff	81T	606	$ .01	$ .07
Coleman, Joe	71T	403	$ .10	$ .35	Combe, Geoff	82T	351	$ .01	$ .06
Coleman, Joe	72T	96	$ .40	$1.50	Combs, Earle	54T	183	$4.00	$12.00
Coleman, Joe	72T	640	$ .25	$ .85	Combs, Merrill	52T	18	$14.00	$45.00
Coleman, Joe	73T	120	$ .06	$ .25	Combs, Pat	88TTR	30	$ .10	$1.50
Coleman, Joe	74T	240	$ .06	$ .25	Combs, Pat	89TBB	227	$ .01	$ .50
Coleman, Joe	75T	42	$ .06	$ .25	Combs, Pat	89TMLD	24	$ .01	$ .35
Coleman, Joe	76T	68	$ .06	$ .25	Combs, Pat	90T	384	$ .01	$ .35
Coleman, Joe	76T	456	$ .05	$ .20	Comer, Steve	79T	463	$ .02	$ .10
Coleman, Joe	77T	219	$ .05	$ .15	Comer, Steve	80T	144	$ .01	$ .07
Coleman, Joe	78T	554	$ .02	$ .10	Comer, Steve	81T	592	$ .01	$ .07
Coleman, Joe	79T	329	$ .02	$ .10	Comer, Steve	82T	16	$ .01	$ .06
Coleman, Joe	80T	542	$ .01	$ .07	Comer, Steve	83T	353	$ .01	$ .06
Coleman, Jr., Joe	76T	68	$ .06	$ .25	Comer, Steve	85T	788	$ .01	$ .04
Coleman, Paul	90T	654	$ .01	$ .35	Comer, Wayne	69T	346	$ .25	$ .65
Coleman, Ray	52T	211	$6.00	$19.00	Comer, Wayne	70T	323	$ .10	$ .35
Coleman, Rip	57T	354	$1.00	$3.75	Compton, Mike	71T	77	$ .10	$ .35
Coleman, Rip	59T	51	$1.00	$3.75	Comstock, Keith	88T	778	$ .01	$ .15
Coleman, Rip	60T	179	$ .35	$1.10	Concepcion, Dave	71T	14	$1.50	$5.00
Coleman, Vince	85TTR	24	$1.00	$4.00	Concepcion, Dave	72T	267	$ .20	$1.00
Coleman, Vince	86T	370	$ .25	$1.75	Concepcion, Dave	73T	554	$ .50	$2.25

Player	Year	No.	VG	EX/MT	Player	Year	No.	VG	EX/MT
Concepcion, Dave	74T	435	$ .30	$1.00	Cook, Cliff	61T	399	$ .50	$2.00
Concepcion, Dave	75T	17	$ .25	$ .85	Cook, Cliff	62T	41	$ .35	$1.10
Concepcion, Dave	76T	48	$ .08	$ .30	Cook, Cliff	63T	566	$1.50	$3.75
Concepcion, Dave	77T	560	$ .25	$ .65	Cook, Dennis	90T	633	$ .01	$ .20
Concepcion, Dave	78T	180	$ .06	$ .30	Cook, Glen	86T	502	$ .01	$ .03
Concepcion, Dave	79T	450	$ .05	$ .25	Cook, Ron	71T	583	$ .30	$1.00
Concepcion, Dave	80T	220	$ .05	$ .20	Cook, Ron	72T	339	$ .10	$ .35
Concepcion, Dave	81T	375	$ .05	$ .20	Coolbaugh, Scott	89TMLD	25	$ .01	$ .35
Concepcion, Dave	82T	660	$ .05	$ .20	Coombs, Dan	65T	553	$1.50	$3.75
Concepcion, Dave	82TAS	340	$ .03	$ .15	Coombs, Dan	66T	414	$ .25	$ .85
Concepcion, Dave	82TIA	661	$ .02	$ .10	Coombs, Dan	67T	464	$ .50	$2.00
Concepcion, Dave	83T	720	$ .01	$ .06	Coombs, Dan	68T	547	$ .30	$1.00
Concepcion, Dave	83TAS	400	$ .01	$ .10	Coombs, Dan	69T	389	$ .25	$ .65
Concepcion, Dave	84T	55	$ .01	$ .05	Coombs, Danny	71T	126	$ .10	$ .35
Concepcion, Dave	85T	515	$ .01	$ .04	Cooney, Johnny	60T	458	$ .95	$3.50
Concepcion, Dave	86T	195	$ .01	$ .03	Cooper, Cecil	72T	79	$15.00	$55.00
Concepcion, Dave	87T	731	$ .01	$ .10	Cooper, Cecil	74T	523	$ .50	$2.00
Concepcion, Dave	88T	422	$ .01	$ .10	Cooper, Cecil	75T	489	$ .30	$1.00
Concepcion, Dave	88TBB	144	$ .01	$ .05	Cooper, Cecil	76T	78	$ .25	$1.00
Concepcion, Onix	83T	52	$ .01	$ .06	Cooper, Cecil	77T	235	$ .25	$ .85
Concepcion, Onix	84T	247	$ .01	$ .05	Cooper, Cecil	78T	154	$ .08	$ .35
Concepcion, Onix	85T	697	$ .01	$ .04	Cooper, Cecil	79T	325	$ .25	$ .65
Concepcion, Onix	86T	596	$ .01	$ .03	Cooper, Cecil	80T	95	$ .05	$ .25
Cone, Dave	87TTR	24	$ .25	$1.50	Cooper, Cecil	81T	3	$ .05	$ .25
Cone, Dave	88T	181	$ .05	$ .75					
Cone, Dave	89T	710	$ .05	$ .25					
Cone, David	90T	30	$ .01	$ .10					
Conigliaro, Bill	69T	628	$ .25	$ .85					
Conigliaro, Billy	70T	317	$ .25	$ .85					
Conigliaro, Billy	71T	114	$ .10	$ .35					
Conigliaro, Billy	72T	481	$ .10	$ .35					
Conigliaro, Billy	74T	545	$ .06	$ .25					
Conigliaro, Tony	64T	287	$4.00	$14.00					
Conigliaro, Tony	65T	55	$ .60	$1.75					
Conigliaro, Tony	66T	218	$ .50	$2.00					
Conigliaro, Tony	66T	380	$ .50	$1.95					
Conigliaro, Tony	67T	280	$ .35	$1.10					
Conigliaro, Tony	68T	140	$ .50	$2.00					
Conigliaro, Tony	69T	330	$ .35	$1.10					
Conigliaro, Tony	70T	340	$ .15	$ .50					
Conigliaro, Tony	71T	63	$ .15	$ .50					
Conigliaro, Tony	71T	105	$ .30	$1.00					
Conley, Bob	59T	121	$ .50	$1.95					
Conley, Gene	53T	215	$2.25	$8.00					
Conley, Gene	54T	59	$3.25	$13.50					
Conley, Gene	55T	81	$2.00	$7.00					
Conley, Gene	56T	17	$1.25	$4.50					
Conley, Gene	57T	28	$1.35	$5.00					
Conley, Gene	58T	431	$ .65	$2.00					
Conley, Gene	59T	492	$ .50	$1.95					
Conley, Gene	60T	293	$ .50	$1.95					
Conley, Gene	61T	193	$ .30	$1.00					
Conley, Gene	62T	187	$ .35	$1.10					
Conley, Gene	63T	216	$ .25	$ .85					
Conley, Gene	64T	571	$1.35	$4.00					
Connelly, Bill	53T	126	$3.75	$13.00					
Connolly, Ed	65T	543	$1.50	$3.75	Cooper, Cecil	81T	555	$ .03	$ .15
Connors, Bill	67T	272	$ .25	$ .65	Cooper, Cecil	82T	675	$ .05	$ .25
Conroy, Tim	84T	156	$ .01	$ .10	Cooper, Cecil	82T	703	$ .03	$ .15
Conroy, Tim	84T	189	$ .01	$ .05	Cooper, Cecil	83T	190	$ .03	$ .15
Conroy, Tim	85T	503	$ .01	$ .04	Cooper, Cecil	84T	133	$ .06	$ .30
Conroy, Tim	86TTR	28	$ .02	$ .10	Cooper, Cecil	84T	420	$ .03	$ .15
Conroy, Tim	87T	338	$ .01	$ .03	Cooper, Cecil	84T	710	$ .04	$ .20
Conroy, Tim	88T	658	$ .01	$ .03	Cooper, Cecil	85T	290	$ .01	$ .10
Consolo, Bill	54T	195	$2.10	$7.50	Cooper, Cecil	86T	385	$ .02	$ .20
Consolo, Bill	55T	207	$4.25	$13.00	Cooper, Cecil	87T	10	$ .01	$ .10
Consolo, Billy	57T	399	$1.00	$3.75	Cooper, Cecil	88T	769	$ .01	$ .03
Consolo, Billy	58T	148	$ .50	$2.00	Cooper, Don	82T	409	$ .01	$ .06
Consolo, Billy	59T	112	$ .50	$1.95	Cooper, Walker	52T	294	$14.00	$45.00
Consolo, Billy	60T	508	$2.00	$7.00	Cooper, Walker	56T	273	$1.80	$6.00
Consolo, Billy	61T	504	$ .50	$2.00	Cooper, Walker	57T	380	$1.00	$3.75
Constable, Jimmy	59T	451	$ .50	$1.95	Cooper, Walker	60T	462	$ .95	$3.50
Constable, Jim	63T	411	$ .35	$1.20	Cora, Joey	88T	91	$ .01	$ .10
Consuegra, Sandy	56T	265	$1.80	$6.00	Corbett, Doug	81T	162	$ .01	$ .07
Coogan, Dale	52T	87	$6.00	$19.00	Corbett, Doug	82T	560	$ .01	$ .06

CECIL COOPER

Player	Year	No.	VG	EX/MT
Corbett, Doug	82TTR	21	$ .02	$ .10
Corbett, Doug	83T	27	$ .01	$ .06
Corbett, Doug	85T	682	$ .01	$ .04
Corbett, Doug	86T	234	$ .01	$ .03
Corbett, Doug	87T	359	$ .01	$ .03
Corbett, Sherman	89T	99	$ .01	$ .04
Corbin, Ray	72T	66	$ .10	$ .35
Corbin, Ray	73T	411	$ .06	$ .25
Corbin, Ray	74T	296	$ .06	$ .25
Corbin, Ray	75T	78	$ .06	$ .25
Corbin, Ray	76T	474	$ .05	$ .20
Corcoran, Tim	78T	515	$ .02	$ .10
Corcoran, Tim	79T	272	$ .02	$ .10
Corcoran, Tim	81T	448	$ .01	$ .07
Corcoran, Tim	85T	302	$ .01	$ .04
Corcoran, Tim	86T	664	$ .01	$ .03
Corey, Mark	79T	701	$ .02	$ .10
Corey, Mark	80T	661	$ .01	$ .07
Corey, Mark	81T	399	$ .35	$1.10
Corkins, Mike	70T	573	$ .25	$ .85

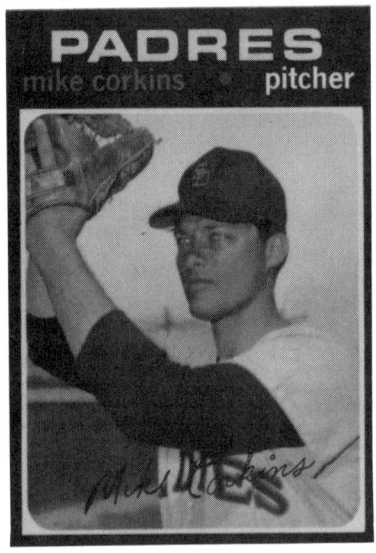

Player	Year	No.	VG	EX/MT
Corkins, Mike	71T	179	$ .10	$ .35
Corkins, Mike	72T	608	$ .25	$ .85
Corkins, Mike	73T	461	$ .06	$ .25
Corkins, Mike	74T	546	$ .06	$ .25
Cornell, Jeff	85T	514	$ .01	$ .04
Corrales, Pat	65T	107	$ .50	$2.00
Corrales, Pat	66T	137	$ .25	$ .85
Corrales, Pat	67T	78	$ .25	$ .65
Corrales, Pat	69T	382	$ .25	$ .65
Corrales, Pat	70T	507	$ .25	$ .85
Corrales, Pat	71T	293	$ .10	$ .35
Corrales, Pat	72T	705	$ .80	$2.25
Corrales, Pat	72TIA	706	$ .70	$2.10
Corrales, Pat	73T	542	$ .30	$1.00
Corrales, Pat	74T	498	$ .10	$ .35
Corrales, Pat	83T	637	$ .01	$ .06
Corrales, Pat	84T	141	$ .01	$ .05
Corrales, Pat	85T	119	$ .01	$ .04
Corrales, Pat	86T	699	$ .01	$ .03
Corrales, Pat	87T	268	$ .01	$ .03
Correa, Ed	87T	334	$ .01	$ .10
Correa, Ed	88T	227	$ .01	$ .03
Correll, Vic	75T	177	$ .06	$ .25

Player	Year	No.	VG	EX/MT
Correll, Vic	76T	608	$ .05	$ .20
Correll, Vic	77T	364	$ .05	$ .15
Correll, Vic	78T	527	$ .02	$ .10
Correll, Vic	79T	281	$ .02	$ .10
Correll, Vic	80T	419	$ .01	$ .07
Correll, Vic	81T	628	$ .01	$ .07
Corsi, Jim	89T	292	$ .01	$ .04
Corsi, Jim	90T	623	$ .01	$ .03
Cosgrove, Mike	75T	96	$ .06	$ .25
Cosgrove, Mike	76T	122	$ .05	$ .20
Cosgrove, Mike	77T	589	$ .05	$ .15
Cosman, Jim	67T	384	$ .25	$ .85
Cosman, Jim	70T	429	$ .10	$ .35
Costello, John	89T	184	$ .01	$ .10
Costello, John	90T	36	$ .01	$ .03
Cotes, Eugenio	79T	723	$ .05	$ .20
Cottier, Chuck	60T	417	$ .50	$1.95
Cottier, Chuck	61T	13	$ .30	$1.00
Cottier, Chuck	62T	27	$ .35	$1.10
Cottier, Chuck	63T	219	$ .25	$ .85
Cottier, Chuck	64T	397	$ .40	$1.25
Cottier, Chuck	69T	252	$ .25	$ .85
Cottier, Chuck	85T	656	$ .01	$ .04
Cottier, Chuck	86T	141	$ .01	$ .03
Cotto, Henry	85T	267	$ .01	$ .04
Cotto, Henry	87T	174	$ .01	$ .03
Cotto, Henry	88T	766	$ .01	$ .03
Cotto, Henry	88TBB	125	$ .01	$ .05
Cotto, Henry	88TTR	31	$ .01	$ .05
Cotto, Henry	89T	468	$ .01	$ .04
Cotto, Henry	89TBB	160	$ .01	$ .05
Cotto, Henry	90T	31	$ .01	$ .03
Coughtry, Marlan	62T	595	$6.00	$18.00
Courtney, Clint	53T	127	$3.75	$13.00
Courtney, Clint	56T	159	$1.25	$4.50
Courtney, Clint	57T	51	$ .95	$3.50
Courtney, Clint	58T	92	$1.00	$3.75
Courtney, Clint	59T	483	$ .50	$1.95
Courtney, Clint	60T	344	$ .50	$1.95
Courtney, Clint	61T	342	$ .30	$1.00
Covington, Wes	57T	283	$3.50	$13.00
Covington, Wes	58T	140	$ .65	$2.00
Covington, Wes	59T	290	$ .50	$1.95
Covington, Wes	59TAS	565	$2.00	$7.00
Covington, Wes	60T	158	$ .35	$1.10
Covington, Wes	61T	296	$ .30	$1.00
Covington, Wes	62T	157	$ .35	$1.10
Covington, Wes	63T	529	$1.50	$3.75
Covington, Wes	64T	208	$ .25	$ .85
Covington, Wes	65T	583	$1.50	$3.75
Covington, Wes	66T	52	$ .30	$1.00
Covington, Wes	66T	484	$ .50	$ .25
Cowan, Billy	64T	192	$ .25	$ .85
Cowan, Billy	65T	186	$ .25	$ .65
Cowan, Billy	69T	643	$ .25	$ .85
Cowan, Billy	71T	614	$ .30	$1.00
Cowan, Billy	72T	19	$ .10	$ .35
Cowens, Al	75T	437	$ .06	$ .25
Cowens, Al	76T	648	$ .05	$ .20
Cowens, Al	77T	262	$ .05	$ .15
Cowens, Al	78T	46	$ .02	$ .10
Cowens, Al	79T	490	$ .02	$ .10
Cowens, Al	80T	330	$ .01	$ .07
Cowens, Al	81T	123	$ .01	$ .07
Cowens, Al	82T	575	$ .01	$ .06
Cowens, Al	82TTR	22	$ .02	$ .10
Cowens, Al	83T	763	$ .01	$ .06
Cowens, Al	84T	622	$ .01	$ .05
Cowens, Al	85T	224	$ .01	$ .04
Cowens, Al	86T	92	$ .01	$ .03
Cowley, Joe	83T	288	$ .01	$ .06
Cowley, Joe	85T	769	$ .01	$ .04
Cowley, Joe	86T	427	$ .01	$ .03
Cowley, Joe	86TTR	29	$ .02	$ .10
Cowley, Joe	87T	27	$ .01	$ .03

Player	Year	No.	VG	EX/MT	Player	Year	No.	VG	EX/MT
Cox, Billy	51Tbb	48	$5.00	$20.00	Crandall, Del	62T	443	$ .70	$2.00
Cox, Billy	52T	232	$7.50	$22.00	Crandall, Del	63T	460	$ .60	$5.00
Cox, Bobby	69T	237	$ .15	$ .50	Crandall, Del	64T	169	$ .35	$1.10
Cox, Bobby	78T	93	$ .02	$ .10	Crandall, Del	65T	68	$ .25	$ .65
Cox, Bobby	83T	606	$ .01	$ .06	Crandall, Del	66T	339	$ .25	$ .85
Cox, Bobby	84T	202	$ .01	$ .05	Crandall, Del	73T	646	$ .50	$2.00
Cox, Bobby	85T	411	$ .01	$ .04	Crandall, Del	74T	99	$ .06	$ .25
Cox, Bobby	86T	471	$ .01	$ .03	Crandall, Del	84T	721	$ .01	$ .05
Cox, Casey	66T	549	$4.50	$15.00	Crawford, Jim	74T	279	$ .06	$ .25
Cox, Casey	67T	414	$ .25	$ .85	Crawford, Jim	76T	428	$ .05	$ .20
Cox, Casey	68T	66	$ .25	$ .65	Crawford, Jim	76TTR	428	$ .05	$ .20
Cox, Casey	69T	383	$ .25	$ .65	Crawford, Jim	77T	69	$ .05	$ .15
Cox, Casey	70T	281	$ .10	$ .35	Crawford, Steve	82T	157	$ .01	$ .06
Cox, Casey	71T	82	$ .10	$ .35	Crawford, Steve	83T	419	$ .01	$ .06
Cox, Casey	72T	231	$ .10	$ .35	Crawford, Steve	85T	661	$ .01	$ .04
Cox, Casey	73T	419	$ .06	$ .25	Crawford, Steve	86T	91	$ .01	$ .03
Cox, Danny	85T	499	$ .05	$ .25	Crawford, Steve	87T	589	$ .01	$ .03
Cox, Danny	86T	294	$ .01	$ .03	Crawford, Steve	88T	299	$ .01	$ .03
Cox, Danny	87T	621	$ .01	$ .03	Crawford, Willie	65T	453	$ .50	$2.00
Cox, Danny	88T	59	$ .01	$ .03	Crawford, Willie	68T	417	$ .25	$ .65
Cox, Danny	88TBB	111	$ .01	$ .05	Crawford, Willie	69T	327	$ .25	$ .85
Cox, Danny	89T	562	$ .01	$ .04	Crawford, Willie	70T	34	$ .10	$ .35
Cox, Danny	90T	184	$ .01	$ .03	Crawford, Willie	71T	519	$ .10	$ .35
Cox, Jeff	81T	133	$ .01	$ .07	Crawford, Willie	72T	669	$ .60	$1.75
Cox, Jim	74T	600	$1.00	$4.00	Crawford, Willie	73T	639	$ .35	$1.10
Cox, Larry	77T	379	$ .05	$ .15	Crawford, Willie	74T	480	$ .06	$ .25
Cox, Larry	78T	541	$ .02	$ .10	Crawford, Willie	75T	186	$ .06	$ .25
Cox, Larry	79T	489	$ .02	$ .10	Crawford, Willie	76T	76	$ .05	$ .20
Cox, Larry	80T	116	$ .01	$ .07	Crawford, Willie	77T	642	$ .05	$ .15
Cox, Larry	81T	249	$ .01	$ .07	Crawford, Willie	78T	507	$ .02	$ .10
Cox, Larry	81TTR	749	$ .02	$ .10	Crews, Tim	88T	57	$ .01	$ .25
Cox, Ted	78T	706	$ .02	$ .10	Crews, Tim	89T	22	$ .01	$ .04
Cox, Ted	79T	79	$ .02	$ .10	Crews, Tim	90T	551	$ .01	$ .03
Cox, Ted	80T	252	$ .01	$ .07	Crider, Jerry	69T	491	$ .25	$ .65
Cox, Terry	71T	559	$ .30	$1.00	Crider, Jerry	71T	113	$ .10	$ .35
Craddock, Walt	59T	281	$ .50	$1.95	Crim, Chuck	87TTR	25	$ .01	$ .07
Craft, Harry	62T	12	$ .35	$1.10	Crim, Chuck	88T	286	$ .01	$ .03
Craft, Harry	63T	491	$2.50	$6.50	Crim, Chuck	89T	466	$ .01	$ .04
Craft, Harry	64T	298	$ .25	$ .85	Crim, Chuck	90T	768	$ .01	$ .03
Craig, Pete	65T	466	$ .50	$2.00	Crimian, Jack	56T	319	$1.80	$6.00
Craig, Pete	66T	11	$ .25	$ .85	Crimian, Jack	57T	297	$3.50	$13.00
Craig, Pete	67T	459	$1.50	$5.50	Cromartie, Warren	78T	468	$ .02	$ .10
Craig, Rodney	80T	672	$ .01	$ .07	Cromartie, Warren	79T	76	$ .02	$ .10
Craig, Roger	56T	63	$5.00	$20.00	Cromartie, Warren	80T	180	$ .01	$ .07
Craig, Roger	57T	173	$3.00	$10.00	Cromartie, Warren	81T	345	$ .01	$ .07
Craig, Roger	58T	194	$ .65	$2.00	Cromartie, Warren	82T	526	$ .01	$ .06
Craig, Roger	60T	62	$ .50	$2.00	Cromartie, Warren	82T	695	$ .01	$ .06
Craig, Roger	61T	543	$10.00	$30.00	Cromartie, Warren	83T	495	$ .01	$ .06
Craig, Roger	62T	183	$ .50	$1.95	Cromartie, Warren	84T	287	$ .01	$ .05
Craig, Roger	63T	197	$ .50	$2.00	Crone, Ray	54T	206	$2.10	$7.50
Craig, Roger	64T	295	$ .35	$1.10	Crone, Ray	55T	149	$1.35	$5.00
Craig, Roger	65T	411	$ .50	$2.00	Crone, Ray	56T	76	$1.25	$4.50
Craig, Roger	66T	543	$10.00	$25.00	Crone, Ray	57T	68	$ .95	$3.50
Craig, Roger	74T	31	$ .06	$ .25	Crone, Ray	58T	272	$ .50	$2.00
Craig, Roger	81T	282	$ .01	$ .07	Crosby, Ed	71T	672	$ .70	$2.10
Craig, Roger	86T	111	$ .01	$ .03	Crosby, Ed	73T	599	$ .35	$1.10
Craig, Roger	87T	193	$ .01	$ .03	Crosby, Ed	76T	457	$ .05	$ .20
Craig, Roger	88T	654	$ .01	$ .03	Crosby, Ken	76T	593	$ .10	$ .35
Craig, Roger	89T	744	$ .01	$ .04	Crosetti, Frank	52T	384	$80.00	$235.00
Craig, Roger	90T	351	$ .01	$ .03	Crosetti, Frank	60T	465	$2.50	$9.00
Cram, Jerry	71T	247	$ .15	$ .50	Crowe, George	52T	360	$39.00	$135.00
Crandall, Del	52T	162	$6.00	$18.00	Crowe, George	53T	3	$4.50	$15.00
Crandall, Del	53T	197	$2.25	$8.00	Crowe, George	56T	254	$2.50	$8.00
Crandall, Del	54T	12	$3.50	$13.00	Crowe, George	57T	73	$ .95	$3.50
Crandall, Del	56T	175	$1.25	$3.50	Crowe, George	58T	12	$1.00	$3.75
Crandall, Del	57T	133	$1.35	$5.00	Crowe, George	59T	337	$ .50	$1.95
Crandall, Del	58T	351	$7.00	$20.00	Crowe, George	60T	419	$ .50	$1.95
Crandall, Del	58T	390	$ .65	$2.00	Crowe, George	61T	52	$ .30	$1.00
Crandall, Del	59T	425	$ .60	$1.75	Crowley, Terry	70T	121	$ .10	$ .35
Crandall, Del	59TAS	567	$2.00	$7.00	Crowley, Terry	71T	453	$ .10	$ .35
Crandall, Del	60T	170	$ .60	$1.75	Crowley, Terry	72T	628	$ .25	$ .85
Crandall, Del	60TAS	568	$2.00	$7.00	Crowley, Terry	73T	302	$ .06	$ .25
Crandall, Del	61T	390	$ .60	$1.75	Crowley, Terry	74T	648	$ .06	$ .25
Crandall, Del	61TAS	583	$6.00	$18.00	Crowley, Terry	74TTR	648	$ .06	$ .25
Crandall, Del	62T	351	$ .60	$1.75	Crowley, Terry	75T	447	$ .06	$ .25

Player	Year	No.	VG	EX/MT
Crowley, Terry	76T	491	$ .05	$ .20
Crowley, Terry	79T	91	$ .02	$ .10
Crowley, Terry	80T	188	$ .01	$ .07
Crowley, Terry	81T	543	$ .01	$ .07
Crowley, Terry	82T	232	$ .01	$ .06
Crowley, Terry	83T	372	$ .01	$ .06
Crowley, Terry	83TTR	22	$ .02	$ .10
Crowley, Terry	84T	732	$ .01	$ .05
Cruz, Hector	76T	598	$ .05	$ .20
Cruz, Hector	77T	624	$ .05	$ .15
Cruz, Hector	78T	257	$ .02	$ .10
Cruz, Hector	79T	436	$ .02	$ .10
Cruz, Hector	80T	516	$ .01	$ .07
Cruz, Hector	81T	52	$ .01	$ .07
Cruz, Hector	81TTR	750	$ .02	$ .10
Cruz, Hector	82T	663	$ .01	$ .06
Cruz, Henry	76T	590	$ .15	$ .50
Cruz, Henry	78T	316	$ .02	$ .10
Cruz, Jose	72T	107	$ .50	$2.00
Cruz, Jose	73T	292	$ .15	$ .50
Cruz, Jose	74T	464	$ .15	$ .50
Cruz, Jose	75T	514	$ .25	$ .65
Cruz, Jose	76T	321	$ .10	$ .35
Cruz, Jose	77T	42	$ .05	$ .15
Cruz, Jose	78T	625	$ .02	$ .10
Cruz, Jose	79T	289	$ .02	$ .10
Cruz, Jose	80T	722	$ .01	$ .07
Cruz, Jose	81T	105	$ .01	$ .07
Cruz, Jose	82T	325	$ .01	$ .06
Cruz, Jose	83T	585	$ .01	$ .06
Cruz, Jose	84T	66	$ .01	$ .05
Cruz, Jose	84T	422	$ .01	$ .05
Cruz, Jose	85T	95	$ .01	$ .04
Cruz, Jose	86T	640	$ .01	$ .03
Cruz, Jose	87T	670	$ .01	$ .03
Cruz, Jose	88T	278	$ .01	$ .03
Cruz, Julio	78T	687	$ .02	$ .10
Cruz, Julio	79T	583	$ .02	$ .10
Cruz, Julio	80T	32	$ .01	$ .07
Cruz, Julio	81T	397	$ .01	$ .07
Cruz, Julio	82T	130	$ .01	$ .06
Cruz, Julio	83T	414	$ .01	$ .06
Cruz, Julio	83TTR	23	$ .02	$ .10
Cruz, Julio	84T	257	$ .01	$ .05
Cruz, Julio	85T	749	$ .01	$ .04
Cruz, Julio	86T	14	$ .01	$ .03
Cruz, Julio	87T	790	$ .01	$ .03
Cruz, Todd	80T	492	$ .01	$ .07
Cruz, Todd	81T	571	$ .01	$ .07
Cruz, Todd	83T	132	$ .01	$ .06
Cruz, Todd	84T	773	$ .01	$ .05
Cruz, Todd	85T	366	$ .01	$ .04
Cruz, Victor	79T	714	$ .02	$ .10
Cruz, Victor	80T	99	$ .01	$ .07
Cruz, Victor	81T	252	$ .01	$ .07
Cruz, Victor	81TTR	751	$ .02	$ .10
Cruz, Victor	82T	263	$ .01	$ .06
Cubbage, Mike	75T	617	$ .35	$1.10
Cubbage, Mike	76T	615	$ .05	$ .20
Cubbage, Mike	77T	149	$ .05	$ .15
Cubbage, Mike	78T	219	$ .02	$ .10
Cubbage, Mike	79T	362	$ .02	$ .10
Cubbage, Mike	80T	503	$ .01	$ .07
Cubbage, Mike	81T	657	$ .01	$ .07
Cubbage, Mike	81TTR	752	$ .02	$ .10
Cubbage, Mike	82T	43	$ .01	$ .06
Cubs, Team	56T	11	$3.25	$9.50
Cubs, Team	57T	183	$2.10	$7.50
Cubs, Team	58T	327	$1.75	$6.50
Cubs, Team	59T	304	$2.25	$9.50
Cubs, Team	60T	513	$5.00	$16.00
Cubs, Team	61T	122	$ .90	$3.50
Cubs, Team	62T	552	$3.50	$15.00
Cubs, Team	63T	222	$1.00	$3.75
Cubs, Team	64T	237	$1.00	$3.75

Player	Year	No.	VG	EX/MT
Cubs, Team	65T	91	$ .60	$1.75
Cubs, Team	66T	204	$ .65	$1.75
Cubs, Team	67T	354	$ .60	$1.75
Cubs, Team	70T	593	$ .50	$1.95
Cubs, Team	71T	502	$ .35	$1.10
Cubs, Team	72T	192	$ .15	$ .50
Cubs, Team	73T	464	$ .15	$ .50
Cubs, Team	74T	211	$ .15	$ .50
Cubs, Team Checklist	75T	638	$ .15	$ .50
Cubs, Team Checklist	76T	277	$ .30	$1.00
Cubs, Team Checklist	77T	518	$ .15	$ .50
Cubs, Team Checklist	78T	302	$ .05	$ .25
Cubs, Team Checklist	79T	551	$ .05	$ .25
Cubs, Team Checklist	80T	381	$ .05	$ .25
Cubs, Team Checklist	81T	676	$ .02	$ .20
Cubs, Team Leaders	86T	636	$ .01	$ .03
Cubs, Team Leaders	87T	581	$ .01	$ .03
Cubs, Team Leaders	88T	171	$ .01	$ .03
Cubs, Team Leaders	89T	549	$ .01	$ .04
Cuccinello, Tony	60T	458	$ .95	$3.50
Cueller, Bobby	80T	665	$ .01	$ .07
Cueller (Cuellar), Mike	59T	518	$7.50	$22.50
Cuellar, Mike	60T	398	$ .45	$1.35
Cuellar, Mike	65T	337	$ .35	$1.10
Cuellar, Mike	66T	566	$3.00	$9.50

Player	Year	No.	VG	EX/MT
Cuellar, Mike	67T	97	$ .30	$1.00
Cuellar, Mike	67T	234	$1.50	$3.75
Cuellar, Mike	68T	274	$ .25	$ .65
Cuellar, Mike	69T	453	$ .35	$1.10
Cuellar, Mike	69T	532	$ .20	$ .50
Cuellar, Mike	70T	68	$ .50	$2.00
Cuellar, Mike	70T	70	$ .50	$2.00
Cuellar, Mike	70T	590	$ .25	$ .60
Cuellar, Mike	71T	69	$ .15	$ .50
Cuellar, Mike	71T	170	$ .15	$ .50
Cuellar, Mike	72T	70	$ .25	$ .65
Cuellar, Mike	73T	470	$ .10	$ .35
Cuellar, Mike	74T	560	$ .25	$ .65
Cuellar (Cueller), Mike	75T	410	$ .05	$ .25
Cuellar, Mike	76T	285	$ .10	$ .35
Cuellar, Mike	77T	162	$ .05	$ .15
Cullen, Jack	63T	54	$1.25	$4.50
Cullen, Jack	66T	31	$ .25	$ .85

Player	Year	No.	VG	EX/MT	Player	Year	No.	VG	EX/MT
Cullen, Tim	67T	167	$ .25	$ .65	Dailey, Bill	63T	391	$ .35	$1.20
Cullen, Tim	68T	209	$ .25	$ .65	Dailey, Bill	64T	156	$ .25	$ .85
Cullen, Tim	69T	586	$ .25	$ .85	Dal Canton, Bruce	69T	468	$ .25	$ .65
Cullen, Tim	70T	49	$ .10	$ .35	Dal Canton, Bruce	70T	52	$ .10	$ .35
Cullen, Tim	71T	566	$ .30	$1.00	Dal Canton, Bruce	71T	168	$ .10	$ .35
Cullen, Tim	72T	461	$ .10	$ .35	Dal Canton, Bruce	72T	717	$ .70	$2.10
Culp, Ray	63T	29	$ .35	$1.10	Dal Canton, Bruce	73T	487	$ .06	$ .25
Culp, Ray	64T	412	$ .40	$1.25	Dal Canton, Bruce	74T	308	$ .06	$ .25
Culp, Ray	65T	505	$ .50	$2.00	Dal Canton, Bruce	75T	472	$ .06	$ .25
Culp, Ray	66T	4	$ .25	$ .85	Dal Canton, Bruce	76T	486	$ .05	$ .20
Culp, Ray	67T	168	$ .25	$ .65	Dal Canton, Bruce	77T	114	$ .05	$ .15
Culp, Ray	68T	272	$ .25	$ .65	Dalena, Pete	89TMLD	27	$ .01	$ .15
Culp, Ray	69T	391	$ .25	$ .65	Daley, Bud	58T	222	$ .50	$2.00
Culp, Ray	70T	144	$ .10	$ .35	Daley, Bud	59T	263	$ .50	$1.95
Culp, Ray	71T	660	$ .70	$2.10	Daley, Bud	60T	8	$ .35	$1.10
Culp, Ray	72T	2	$ .10	$ .35	Daley, Bud	61T	48	$ .50	$2.00
Culver, George	65T	166	$ .50	$1.95	Daley, Bud	61T	422	$ .50	$2.00
Culver, George	67T	499	$ .50	$2.00	Daley, Bud	62T	376	$ .70	$2.10
Culver, George	68T	319	$ .25	$ .65	Daley, Bud	63T	38	$ .25	$ .85
Culver, George	69T	635	$ .25	$ .85	Daley, Bud	64T	164	$ .25	$ .85
Culver, George	70T	92	$ .10	$ .35	Daley, Bud	65T	262	$ .30	$1.00
Culver, George	71T	291	$ .10	$ .35	Daley, Pete	55T	206	$4.25	$13.00
Culver, George	72T	732	$ .70	$2.10	Daley, Pete	57T	388	$1.00	$3.75
Culver, George	73T	242	$ .06	$ .25	Daley, Pete	58T	73	$1.00	$3.75
Culver, George	74T	632	$ .06	$ .25	Daley, Pete	59T	276	$ .50	$1.95
Cumberland, John	69T	114	$ .25	$ .65	Daley, Pete	60T	108	$ .35	$1.10
Cumberland, John	71T	108	$ .10	$ .35	Daley, Pete	61T	158	$ .30	$1.00
Cumberland, John	72T	403	$ .10	$ .35	Dalkowski, Steve	63T	496	$2.50	$6.50
Cummings, Steve	89TMLD	26	$ .01	$ .15	Dalrymple, Clay	60T	523	$2.00	$7.00
Cummings, Steve	90T	374	$ .01	$ .10	Dalrymple, Clay	61T	299	$ .30	$1.00
Cunningham, Earl	90T	134	$ .01	$ .35	Dalrymple, Clay	62T	434	$ .70	$2.10
Cunningham, Joe	55T	37	$2.10	$7.50	Dalrymple, Clay	63T	192	$ .25	$ .85
Cunningham, Joe	57T	304	$3.50	$13.00	Dalrymple, Clay	64T	191	$ .25	$ .85
Cunningham, Joe	58T	168	$ .65	$2.00	Dalrymple, Clay	65T	372	$ .30	$1.00
Cunningham, Joe	59T	285	$ .60	$1.75	Dalrymple, Clay	66T	202	$ .25	$ .85
Cunningham, Joe	60T	40	$ .50	$2.00	Dalrymple, Clay	67T	53	$ .25	$ .65
Cunningham, Joe	60TAS	562	$2.00	$7.00	Dalrymple, Clay	68T	567	$ .30	$1.00
Cunningham, Joe	61T	520	$ .60	$1.75	Dalrymple, Clay	69T	151	$ .70	$2.00
Cunningham, Joe	62T	195	$ .50	$2.00	Dalrymple, Clay	71T	617	$ .30	$1.00
Cunningham, Joe	63T	100	$ .30	$1.00	Dalrymple, Clayton	70T	319	$ .10	$ .35
Cunningham, Joe	64T	340	$ .25	$ .85	Daniels, Bennie	58T	392	$ .50	$2.00
Cunningham, Joe	65T	496	$ .50	$2.00	Daniels, Bennie	59T	122	$ .50	$1.95
Cunningham, Joe	66T	531	$3.00	$8.50	Daniels, Bennie	60T	91	$ .35	$1.10
Curry, Steve	89T	471	$ .01	$ .04	Daniels, Bennie	61T	368	$ .30	$1.00
Curry, Tony	60T	541	$2.00	$7.00	Daniels, Bennie	62T	378	$ .70	$2.10
Curry, Tony	61T	262	$ .30	$1.00	Daniels, Bennie	63T	497	$2.50	$6.50
Curtis, Jack	61T	533	$6.00	$18.00	Daniels, Bennie	64T	587	$2.00	$8.00
Curtis, Jack	62T	372	$ .70	$2.10	Daniels, Bennie	65T	129	$ .25	$ .65
Curtis, John	72T	724	$1.00	$3.75	Daniels, Kal	87T	466	$ .25	$1.00
Curtis, John	73T	143	$ .06	$ .25	Daniels, Kal	88T	622	$ .01	$ .15
Curtis, John	74T	070	$ .06	$ .25	Daniels, Kal	88TBB	48	$ .01	$ .10
Curtis, John	74TTR	373	$ .06	$ .25	Daniels, Kal	89T	45	$ .01	$ .05
Curtis, John	75T	381	$ .06	$ .25	Daniels, Kal	89TBB	323	$ .01	$ .05
Curtis, John	76T	239	$ .05	$ .20	Daniels, Kal	90T	585	$ .01	$ .03
Curtis, John	77T	324	$ .05	$ .15	Darcy, Pat	75T	615	$ .25	$ .85
Curtis, John	78T	486	$ .02	$ .10	Darcy, Pat	76T	538	$ .05	$ .20
Curtis, John	79T	649	$ .02	$ .10	Dark, Al	52T	351	$60.00	$175.00
Curtis, John	80T	12	$ .01	$ .07	Dark, Al	53T	109	$3.50	$12.00
Curtis, John	81T	531	$ .01	$ .07	Dark, Al	56T	148	$1.50	$4.50
Curtis, John	82T	219	$ .01	$ .06	Dark, Al	57T	98	$1.35	$5.00
Curtis, John	83T	777	$ .01	$ .06	Dark, Al	58T	125	$ .65	$2.00
Curtis, John	84T	158	$ .01	$ .05	Dark, Al	59T	502	$ .60	$1.75
D'Acquisto, John	74T	608	$ .06	$ .25	Dark, Al	60T	472	$1.00	$3.75
D'Acquisto, John	75T	372	$ .06	$ .25	Dark, Al	61T	220	$ .30	$1.00
D'Acquisto, John	76T	628	$ .05	$ .20	Dark, Al	62T	322	$ .50	$2.00
D'Acquisto, John	77T	19	$ .05	$ .15	Dark, Al	63T	258	$ .30	$1.00
D'Acquisto, John	79T	506	$ .02	$ .10	Dark, Al	64T	529	$1.50	$3.75
D'Acquisto, John	80T	339	$ .01	$ .07	Dark, Al	66T	433	$ .35	$1.10
D'Acquisto, John	81T	427	$ .01	$ .07	Dark, Al	67T	389	$ .25	$ .85
D'Acquisto, John	82T	58	$ .01	$ .06	Dark, Al	69T	91	$ .25	$ .85
Daboll, Dennis	65T	561	$2.00	$7.00	Dark, Al	68T	237	$ .25	$ .85
Dade, Paul	78T	662	$ .02	$ .10	Dark, Alvin	70T	524	$ .15	$ .50
Dade, Paul	79T	13	$ .02	$ .10	Dark, Alvin	71T	397	$ .10	$ .35
Dade, Paul	80T	254	$ .01	$ .07	Dark, Alvin	78T	467	$ .02	$ .10
Dade, Paul	81T	496	$ .01	$ .07	Darling, Ron	84TTR	27	$1.25	$5.00

TOPPS

Player	Year	No.	VG	EX/MT	Player	Year	No.	VG	EX/MT
Darling, Ron	85T	415	$ .35	$1.10	Davenport, Jim	68T	525	$ .30	$1.00
Darling, Ron	86T	225	$ .01	$ .10	Davenport, Jim	69T	102	$ .25	$ .65
Darling, Ron	87T	75	$ .06	$ .25	Davenport, Jim	70T	378	$ .10	$ .35
Darling, Ron	88T	685	$ .01	$ .10	Davenport, Jim	85TTR	27	$ .02	$ .10
Darling, Ron	88TBB	85	$ .01	$ .10	David, Andre	85T	43	$ .01	$ .04
Darling, Ron	89T	105	$ .01	$ .10	Davidson, Bobby	89TMLD	29	$ .01	$ .15
Darling, Ron	89TBB	166	$ .01	$ .05	Davidson, Mark	88T	19	$ .01	$ .03
Darling, Ron	90T	330	$ .01	$ .05	Davidson, Mark	89T	451	$ .01	$ .04
Darwin, Bobby	69T	641	$ .25	$ .85	Davidson, Mark	89TBB	320	$ .01	$ .05
Darwin, Bobby	73T	228	$ .06	$ .25	Davidson, Mark	90T	267	$ .01	$ .03
Darwin, Bobby	74T	527	$ .06	$ .25	Davidson, Ted	65T	243	$ .60	$1.75
Darwin, Bobby	75T	346	$ .06	$ .25	Davidson, Ted	66T	89	$ .25	$ .85
Darwin, Bobby	76T	63	$ .05	$ .20	Davidson, Ted	67T	519	$ .50	$2.00
Darwin, Bobby	77T	617	$ .05	$ .15	Davidson, Ted	68T	48	$ .25	$ .65
Darwin, Danny	79T	713	$ .05	$ .20	Davie, Jerry	59T	256	$ .50	$1.95
Darwin, Danny	80T	498	$ .01	$ .07	Davie, Jerry	60T	301	$ .50	$1.95
Darwin, Danny	81T	22	$ .01	$ .07	Davis, Alvin	84TTR	28	$1.00	$4.00
Darwin, Danny	82T	298	$ .01	$ .06	Davis, Alvin	85T	145	$ .50	$1.75
Darwin, Danny	83T	609	$ .01	$ .06	Davis, Alvin	86T	440	$ .02	$ .30
Darwin, Danny	84T	377	$ .01	$ .05	Davis, Alvin	87T	235	$ .01	$ .15
Darwin, Danny	85T	227	$ .01	$ .04	Davis, Alvin	88T	785	$ .01	$ .10
Darwin, Danny	85TTR	26	$ .02	$ .10	Davis, Alvin	88TBB	64	$ .01	$ .05
Darwin, Danny	86T	519	$ .01	$ .03					
Darwin, Danny	87T	157	$ .01	$ .03					
Darwin, Danny	88T	461	$ .01	$ .03					
Darwin, Danny	89T	719	$ .01	$ .04					
Darwin, Danny	90T	64	$ .01	$ .03					
Dascenzo, Doug	89T	149	$ .01	$ .15					
Dascenzo, Doug	90T	762	$ .01	$ .03					
Datz, Jeff	89TMLD	28	$ .01	$ .15					
Dauer, Rich	77T	477	$ .05	$ .15					
Dauer, Rich	78T	237	$ .02	$ .10					
Dauer, Rich	79T	666	$ .02	$ .10					
Dauer, Rich	80T	102	$ .01	$ .07					
Dauer, Rich	81T	314	$ .01	$ .07					
Dauer, Rich	82T	8	$ .01	$ .06					
Dauer, Rich	83T	579	$ .01	$ .06					
Dauer, Rich	84T	723	$ .01	$ .05					
Dauer, Rich	85T	494	$ .01	$ .04					
Dauer, Rich	86T	251	$ .01	$ .03					
Daugherty, Jack	90T	52	$ .01	$ .03					
Daulton, Darren	86T	264	$ .01	$ .03					
Daulton, Darren	87T	636	$ .01	$ .03					
Daulton, Darren	88T	468	$ .01	$ .03					
Daulton, Darren	89T	187	$ .01	$ .04					
Daulton, Darren	90T	542	$ .01	$ .03					
Davalillo, Vic	63T	324	$ .35	$1.20					
Davalillo, Vic	64T	435	$ .40	$1.25					
Davalillo, Vic	65T	128	$ .25	$ .65					
Davalillo, Vic	66T	216	$ .75	$2.75					
Davalillo, Vic	66T	325	$ .25	$ .85					
Davalillo, Vic	67T	69	$ .25	$ .65					
Davalillo, Vic	68T	397	$ .25	$ .65					
Davalillo, Vic	69T	275	$ .25	$ .85					
Davalillo, Vic	70T	256	$ .10	$ .35	Davis, Alvin	89T	687	$ .01	$ .04
Davalillo, Vic	71T	4	$ .10	$ .35	Davis, Alvin	89TBB	218	$ .01	$ .05
Davalillo, Vic	72T	785	$ .70	$2.10	Davis, Alvin	90T	373	$ .01	$ .03
Davalillo, Vic	73T	163	$ .06	$ .25	Davis, Bill	65T	546	$1.50	$3.75
Davalillo, Vic	74T	444	$ .06	$ .25	Davis, Bill	66T	44	$ .25	$ .85
Davalillo, Vic	78T	539	$ .02	$ .10	Davis, Bill	67T	253	$ .25	$ .65
Davalillo, Vic	79T	228	$ .02	$ .10	Davis, Bill	68T	432	$ .25	$ .65
DaVanon, Jerry	69T	637	$ .25	$ .85	Davis, Bill	69T	304	$ .25	$ .85
DaVanon, Jerry	71T	32	$ .10	$ .35	Davis, Bob	61T	246	$ .30	$1.00
DaVanon, Jerry	76T	551	$ .05	$ .20	Davis, Bob	76T	472	$ .05	$ .20
DaVanon, Jerry	77T	283	$ .05	$ .15	Davis, Bob	77T	78	$ .05	$ .15
Davenport, Jim	58T	413	$ .50	$2.00	Davis, Bob	78T	713	$ .02	$ .10
Davenport, Jim	59T	198	$ .50	$1.95	Davis, Bob	80T	351	$ .01	$ .07
Davenport, Jim	60T	154	$ .35	$1.10	Davis, Bob	81T	221	$ .01	$ .07
Davenport, Jim	61T	55	$ .30	$1.00	Davis, Brock	63T	553	$60.00	$175.00
Davenport, Jim	62T	9	$ .35	$1.10	Davis, Brock	71T	576	$ .30	$1.00
Davenport, Jim	63T	388	$ .35	$1.20	Davis, Brock	72T	161	$ .10	$ .35
Davenport, Jim	64T	82	$ .25	$ .85	Davis, Brock	73T	366	$ .06	$ .25
Davenport, Jim	65T	213	$ .30	$1.00	Davis, Butch	85T	49	$ .01	$ .04
Davenport, Jim	66T	176	$ .25	$ .85	Davis, Chili	82T	171	$ .50	$1.50
Davenport, Jim	67T	441	$ .25	$ .85	Davis, Chili	82TTR	23	$ .25	$ .65

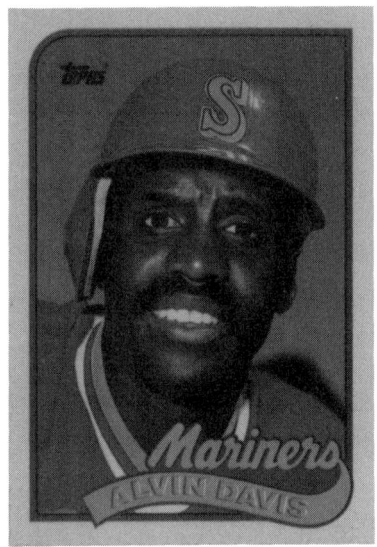

Player	Year	No.	VG	EX/MT	Player	Year	No.	VG	EX/MT
Davis, Chili	83T	115	$ .01	$ .06	Davis, Mike	89T	277	$ .01	$ .04
Davis, Chili	84T	494	$ .01	$ .05	Davis, Mike	89TBB	225	$ .01	$ .05
Davis, Chili	85T	245	$ .01	$ .04	Davis, Mike	90T	697	$ .01	$ .03
Davis, Chili	87T	672	$ .01	$ .03	Davis, Ron	67T	298	$ .25	$ .65
Davis, Chili	88T	15	$ .01	$ .03	Davis, Ron	68T	21	$ .25	$ .65
Davis, Chili	88TBB	235	$ .01	$ .05	Davis, Ron	69T	553	$ .25	$ .85
Davis, Chili	88TTR	32	$ .01	$ .05	Davis, Ron	80T	179	$ .05	$ .20
Davis, Chili	89T	525	$ .01	$ .04	Davis, Ron	81T	16	$ .01	$ .07
Davis, Chili	89TBB	294	$ .01	$ .05	Davis, Ron	82T	635	$ .01	$ .06
Davis, Chili	90T	765	$ .01	$ .03	Davis, Ron	82THL	2	$ .01	$ .06
Davis, Dick	79T	474	$ .02	$ .10	Davis, Ron	82TTR	25	$ .02	$ .10
Davis, Dick	80T	553	$ .01	$ .07	Davis, Ron	83T	380	$ .01	$ .06
Davis, Dick	81T	183	$ .01	$ .07	Davis, Ron	84T	519	$ .01	$ .05
Davis, Dick	81TTR	753	$ .02	$ .10	Davis, Ron	85T	430	$ .01	$ .04
Davis, Dick	82T	352	$ .01	$ .06	Davis, Ron	86T	265	$ .01	$ .03
Davis, Dick	82TTR	24	$ .02	$ .10	Davis, Ron	87T	383	$ .01	$ .03
Davis, Dick	83T	667	$ .01	$ .06	Davis, Steve	90T	428	$ .01	$ .03
Davis, Eric	85T	627	$4.00	$15.00	Davis, Storm	83T	268	$ .05	$ .50
Davis, Eric	86T	28	$ .50	$2.50	Davis, Storm	84T	140	$ .01	$ .10
Davis, Eric	87T	412	$ .35	$1.10	Davis, Storm	85T	599	$ .01	$ .04
Davis, Eric	88T	150	$ .15	$ .75	Davis, Storm	86T	469	$ .01	$ .03
Davis, Eric	88TBB	20	$ .25	$ .65	Davis, Storm	87T	349	$ .01	$ .03
Davis, Eric	89T	330	$ .05	$ .25	Davis, Storm	87TTR	26	$ .01	$ .07
Davis, Eric	89TBB	273	$ .01	$ .35	Davis, Storm	88T	248	$ .01	$ .03
Davis, Eric	90T	260	$ .01	$ .25	Davis, Storm	89T	701	$ .01	$ .04
Davis, Eric	90TAS	402	$ .01	$ .10	Davis, Storm	89TBB	121	$ .01	$ .05
Davis, Glenn	86T	389	$ .95	$2.75	Davis, Storm	90T	606	$ .01	$ .05
Davis, Glenn	87T	560	$ .10	$ .35	Davis, Tommy	60T	509	$4.25	$22.50
Davis, Glenn	88T	430	$ .01	$ .10	Davis, Tommy	61T	168	$ .60	$1.75
Davis, Glenn	88TBB	192	$ .01	$ .15	Davis, Tommy	62T	358	$ .50	$1.95
Davis, Glenn	89T	765	$ .01	$ .04	Davis, Tommy	63T	1	$4.35	$22.00
Davis, Glenn	89TBB	89	$ .01	$ .10	Davis, Tommy	63T	310	$ .50	$2.00
Davis, Glenn	90T	50	$ .01	$ .10	Davis, Tommy	64T	7	$1.70	$2.00
Davis, Jacke	62T	521	$ .70	$2.10	Davis, Tommy	64T	180	$ .35	$1.10
Davis, Jacke	63T	117	$ .25	$ .85	Davis, Tommy	65T	370	$ .50	$1.95
Davis, Jerry	85TTR	28	$ .02	$ .10	Davis, Tommy	66T	75	$ .30	$1.00
Davis, Jerry	86T	323	$ .01	$ .03	Davis, Tommy	67T	370	$ .30	$1.00
Davis, Jim	55T	68	$1.35	$5.00	Davis, Tommy	68T	265	$ .35	$1.10
Davis, Jim	56T	102	$1.25	$4.50	Davis, Tommy	69T	135	$ .15	$ .75
Davis, Jim	57T	273	$3.50	$13.00	Davis, Tommy	70T	559	$ .50	$2.00
Davis, Jody	82T	508	$ .25	$ .65	Davis, Tommy	71T	151	$ .25	$ .85
Davis, Jody	83T	542	$ .01	$ .06	Davis, Tommy	72T	41	$ .10	$ .35
Davis, Jody	84T	73	$ .01	$ .05	Davis, Tommy	72TIA	42	$ .10	$ .35
Davis, Jody	85T	384	$ .01	$ .04	Davis, Tommy	74T	396	$ .25	$ .85
Davis, Jody	86T	767	$ .01	$ .03	Davis, Tommy	75T	564	$ .10	$ .35
Davis, Jody	87T	270	$ .01	$ .03	Davis, Tommy	76T	149	$ .06	$ .25
Davis, Jody	88T	615	$ .01	$ .03	Davis, Tommy	77T	362	$ .05	$ .15
Davis, Jody	89T	115	$ .01	$ .04	Davis, Willie	61T	506	$1.35	$4.00
Davis, Jody	89TBB	3	$ .01	$ .05	Davis, Willie	62T	108	$ .50	$1.95
Davis, Jody	89TTR	22	$ .01	$ .05	Davis, Willie	63T	229	$ .35	$1.10
Davis, Jody	90T	453	$ .01	$ .03	Davis, Willie	64T	68	$ .35	$1.10
Davis, Joel	86TTR	30	$ .02	$ .10	Davis, Willie	65T	435	$ .35	$1.10
Davis, Joel	87T	299	$ .01	$ .03	Davis, Willie	66T	535	$4.00	$11.50
Davis, Joel	88T	511	$ .01	$ .03	Davis, Willie	67T	160	$ .30	$1.00
Davis, John	88T	672	$ .01	$ .20	Davis, Willie	68T	208	$ .25	$ .85
Davis, John	89T	162	$ .01	$ .04	Davis, Willie	69T	65	$ .15	$ .50
Davis, Mark	82T	231	$ .50	$1.50	Davis, Willie	70T	390	$ .10	$ .50
Davis, Mark	84T	343	$ .01	$ .05	Davis, Willie	71T	585	$ .30	$1.00
Davis, Mark	85T	541	$ .01	$ .04	Davis, Willie	72T	390	$ .25	$ .65
Davis, Mark	86T	138	$ .01	$ .03	Davis, Willie	73T	35	$ .25	$ .65
Davis, Mark	87T	21	$ .01	$ .03	Davis, Willie	74T	165	$ .10	$ .35
Davis, Mark	88T	482	$ .01	$ .03	Davis, Willie	74TTR	165	$ .10	$ .35
Davis, Mark	89T	59	$ .01	$ .04	Davis, Willie	75T	10	$ .06	$ .25
Davis, Mark	90T	205	$ .01	$ .03	Davis, Willie	76T	265	$ .06	$ .25
Davis, Mark	90TAS	407	$ .01	$ .03	Davis, Willie	77T	603	$ .05	$ .15
Davis, Mike	81T	364	$ .05	$ .20	Davison, Mike	71T	276	$1.75	$5.00
Davis, Mike	82T	671	$ .01	$ .06	Dawley, Bill	84T	248	$ .01	$ .05
Davis, Mike	83TTR	24	$ .02	$ .10	Dawley, Bill	85T	634	$ .01	$ .04
Davis, Mike	84T	558	$ .01	$ .05	Dawley, Bill	86T	376	$ .01	$ .03
Davis, Mike	85T	778	$ .01	$ .04	Dawley, Bill	87T	54	$ .01	$ .03
Davis, Mike	86T	165	$ .01	$ .03	Dawley, Bill	88T	509	$ .01	$ .03
Davis, Mike	87T	83	$ .01	$ .03	Dawson, Andre	77T	473	$9.00	$35.00
Davis, Mike	88T	448	$ .01	$ .03	Dawson, Andre	78T	72	$2.10	$7.50
Davis, Mike	88TBB	154	$ .01	$ .05	Dawson, Andre	79T	348	$1.00	$4.00
Davis, Mike	88TTR	33	$ .01	$ .05	Dawson, Andre	80T	235	$ .50	$2.50

Player	Year	No.	VG	EX/MT	Player	Year	No.	VG	EX/MT
Dawson, Andre	81T	125	$ .15	$ .90	De la Hoz, Mike	66T	346	$ .25	$ .85
Dawson, Andre	82T	540	$ .10	$ .65	De Los Santos, Luis	90T	452	$ .01	$ .10
Dawson, Andre	82TAS	341	$ .01	$ .15	De Maestri, Joe	52T	286	$14.00	$45.00
Dawson, Andre	83T	680	$ .10	$ .45	De Maestri, Joe	56T	161	$1.25	$4.50
Dawson, Andre	83TAS	402	$ .03	$ .15	De Maestri, Joe	57T	44	$ .95	$3.50
Dawson, Andre	84T	200	$ .10	$ .50	De Maestri, Joe	58T	62	$1.00	$3.75
Dawson, Andre	84TAS	392	$ .03	$ .15	De Maestri, Joe	59T	64	$1.00	$3.75
Dawson, Andre	85T	420	$ .05	$ .25	De Maestri, Joe	60T	358	$ .50	$1.95
Dawson, Andre	86T	760	$ .02	$ .20	De Maestri, Joe	61T	116	$ .30	$1.00
Dawson, Andre	87T	345	$ .10	$ .35	Deal, Cot	54T	192	$2.10	$7.50
Dawson, Andre	87TTR	27	$ .08	$ .30	Deal, Cot	60T	459	$ .95	$3.50
Dawson, Andre	88T	500	$ .01	$ .20	Dean, Tommy	69T	641	$ .25	$ .85
Dawson, Andre	88TAS	401	$ .01	$ .10	Dean, Tommy	70T	234	$ .10	$ .35
Dawson, Andre	88TBB	153	$ .01	$ .15	Dean, Tommy	71T	364	$ .10	$ .35
Dawson, Andre	89T	10	$ .01	$ .10	DeBusschere, Dave	63T	54	$1.25	$4.50
					DeBusschere, Dave	64T	247	$ .90	$3.75
					DeBusschere, Dave	65T	297	$ .75	$3.00
					DeCinces, Doug	75T	617	$ .35	$1.10
					DeCinces, Doug	76T	438	$ .25	$ .65
					DeCinces, Doug	77T	216	$ .05	$ .15
					DeCinces, Doug	78T	9	$ .02	$ .10
					DeCinces, Doug	79T	421	$ .05	$ .20
					DeCinces, Doug	80T	615	$ .01	$ .07
					DeCinces, Doug	81T	188	$ .01	$ .07
					DeCinces, Doug	82T	564	$ .01	$ .06
					DeCinces, Doug	82TTR	26	$ .02	$ .10
					DeCinces, Doug	83T	341	$ .01	$ .06
					DeCinces, Doug	84T	790	$ .01	$ .05
					DeCinces, Doug	85T	111	$ .01	$ .04
					DeCinces, Doug	86T	257	$ .01	$ .03
					DeCinces, Doug	87T	22	$ .01	$ .03
					DeCinces, Doug	88T	446	$ .01	$ .03
					Decker, Joe	71T	98	$ .10	$ .35
					Decker, Joe	72T	612	$ .25	$ .85
					Decker, Joe	73T	311	$ .06	$ .25
					Decker, Joe	74T	469	$ .06	$ .25
					Decker, Joe	75T	102	$ .06	$ .25
					Decker, Joe	76T	636	$ .05	$ .20
					Dedeaux, Rod	85T	389	$ .01	$ .04
					Dedmon, Jeff	84TTR	30	$ .02	$ .10
					Dedmon, Jeff	85T	602	$ .01	$ .04
					Dedmon, Jeff	86T	129	$ .01	$ .03
					Dedmon, Jeff	87T	373	$ .01	$ .03
					Dedmon, Jeff	88T	469	$ .01	$ .03
					Deer, Rob	86T	249	$ .04	$ .40
					Deer, Rob	86TTR	31	$ .05	$ .25
					Deer, Rob	87T	547	$ .06	$ .25
Dawson, Andre	89TAS	391	$ .01	$ .10	Deer, Rob	88T	33	$ .01	$ .10
Dawson, Andre	89TBB	120	$ .01	$ .15	Deer, Rob	88TBB	151	$ .01	$ .05
Dawson, Andre	89TRB	4	$ .01	$ .04	Deer, Rob	89T	364	$ .01	$ .04
Dawson, Andre	90T	140	$ .01	$ .15	Deer, Rob	89TBB	78	$ .01	$ .05
Day, Boots	70T	654	$ .70	$2.00	Deer, Rob	90T	615	$ .01	$ .03
Day, Boots	71T	42	$ .10	$ .35	Dees, Charlie	64T	159	$ .25	$ .85
Day, Boots	72T	254	$ .10	$ .35	DeFilippis, Art	76T	595	$ .05	$ .20
Day, Boots	73T	307	$ .06	$ .25	DeFreites, Art	80T	677	$ .01	$ .07
Day, Boots	74T	589	$ .06	$ .25	DeJesus, Ivan	78T	152	$ .02	$ .10
Dayett, Brian	85T	534	$ .01	$ .04	DeJesus, Ivan	79T	398	$ .02	$ .10
Dayett, Brian	85TTR	29	$ .02	$ .10	DeJesus, Ivan	80T	691	$ .01	$ .07
Dayett, Brian	86T	284	$ .01	$ .03	DeJesus, Ivan	81T	54	$ .01	$ .07
Dayett, Brian	87T	369	$ .01	$ .03	DeJesus, Ivan	82T	484	$ .03	$ .15
Dayett, Brian	88T	136	$ .01	$ .03	DeJesus, Ivan	82TTR	27	$ .02	$ .10
Dayley, Ken	83T	314	$ .01	$ .06	DeJesus, Ivan	83T	587	$ .01	$ .06
Dayley, Ken	84T	104	$ .01	$ .05	DeJesus, Ivan	84T	279	$ .01	$ .05
Dayley, Ken	84TTR	29	$ .02	$ .10	DeJesus, Ivan	85T	791	$ .01	$ .04
Dayley, Ken	86T	607	$ .01	$ .03	DeJesus, Ivan	85TTR	30	$ .02	$ .10
Dayley, Ken	87T	59	$ .01	$ .03	DeJesus, Ivan	86T	178	$ .01	$ .03
Dayley, Ken	88T	234	$ .01	$ .03	DeJesus, Jose	90T	596	$ .01	$ .03
Dayley, Ken	89T	409	$ .01	$ .04	Del Greco, Bob	52T	353	$39.00	$135.00
Dayley, Ken	90T	561	$ .01	$ .03	Del Greco, Bob	53T	48	$3.75	$13.00
De La Hoz, Mike	65T	182	$ .25	$ .65	Del Greco, Bob	57T	94	$ .95	$3.50
De La Hoz, Mike	67T	372	$ .25	$ .85	Del Greco, Bobby	60T	486	$ .60	$1.75
De la Hoz, Mike	61T	191	$ .30	$1.00	Del Greco, Bobby	61T	154	$ .30	$1.00
De la Hoz, Mike	62T	123	$ .35	$1.10	Del Greco, Bobby	62T	548	$3.75	$11.00
De la Hoz, Mike	63T	561	$1.50	$3.75	Del Greco, Bob	63T	282	$ .25	$ .85
De la Hoz, Mike	64T	216	$ .25	$ .85	DeLeon, Jose	84T	581	$ .02	$ .10

ANDRE DAWSON

Player	Year	No.	VG	EX/MT	Player	Year	No.	VG	EX/MT
DeLeon, Jose	85T	385	$ .01	$ .04	Denny, John	77T	7	$ .05	$ .15
DeLeon, Jose	86T	75	$ .01	$ .03	Denny, John	77T	541	$ .05	$ .15
DeLeon, Jose	87T	421	$ .01	$ .03	Denny, John	78T	609	$ .02	$ .10
DeLeon, Jose	88T	634	$ .01	$ .03	Denny, John	79T	59	$ .02	$ .10
DeLeon, Jose	88TBB	194	$ .01	$ .05	Denny, John	80T	464	$ .01	$ .07
DeLeon, Jose	88TTR	34	$ .01	$ .05	Denny, John	81T	122	$ .01	$ .07
DeLeon, Jose	89T	107	$ .01	$ .04	Denny, John	82T	773	$ .01	$ .06
DeLeon, Jose	90T	257	$ .01	$ .03	Denny, John	83T	211	$ .05	$ .25
DeLeon, Luis	82T	561	$ .01	$ .06	Denny, John	84T	17	$ .01	$ .05
DeLeon, Luis	83T	323	$ .01	$ .06	Denny, John	84T	135	$ .01	$ .05
DeLeon, Luis	84T	38	$ .01	$ .05	Denny, John	84T	637	$ .01	$ .05
DeLeon, Luis	85T	689	$ .01	$ .04	Denny, John	85T	325	$ .01	$ .04
DeLeon, Luis	86T	286	$ .01	$ .03	Denny, John	86T	556	$ .01	$ .03
Delock, Ike	52T	329	$39.00	$135.00	Denny, John	86TTR	32	$ .02	$ .10
Delock, Ike	56T	284	$1.80	$6.00	Denny, John	87T	644	$ .01	$ .03
Delock, Ike	57T	63	$ .95	$3.50	Denson, Drew	89TMLD	30	$ .01	$ .15
Delock, Ike	58T	328	$ .45	$1.50	Dent, Bucky	74T	582	$ .06	$ .25
Delock, Ike	59T	437	$ .50	$1.95	Dent, Bucky	75T	299	$ .25	$ .65
Delock, Ike	60T	336	$ .50	$1.95	Dent, Bucky	76T	154	$ .06	$ .25
Delock, Ike	61T	268	$ .30	$1.00	Dent, Bucky	77T	29	$ .05	$ .15
Delock, Ike	62T	201	$ .35	$1.10	Dent, Bucky	78T	335	$ .05	$ .20
Delock, Ike	63T	136	$ .25	$ .85	Dent, Bucky	79T	485	$ .05	$ .20
Delsing, Jim	52T	271	$11.50	$38.00	Dent, Bucky	80T	60	$ .01	$ .07
Delsing, Jim	53T	239	$11.00	$37.50	Dent, Bucky	81T	650	$ .01	$ .07
Delsing, Jim	54T	111	$2.10	$7.50	Dent, Bucky	82T	240	$ .01	$ .06
Delsing, Jim	55T	192	$4.25	$13.00	Dent, Bucky	82TAS	550	$ .01	$ .06
Delsing, Jim	56T	338	$1.80	$6.00	Dent, Bucky	82TIA	241	$ .01	$ .06
Delsing, Jim	59T	386	$ .50	$1.95					
DeMars, Billy	73T	486	$ .25	$ .85					
DeMars, Billy	74T	119	$ .06	$ .25					
DeMerit, John	61T	501	$ .50	$2.00					
DeMerit, John	62T	4	$ .35	$1.10					
Demery, Larry	75T	433	$ .06	$ .25					
Demery, Larry	76T	563	$ .05	$ .20					
Demery, Larry	77T	607	$ .05	$ .15					
Demery, Larry	78T	138	$ .02	$ .10					
Demeter, Don	58T	244	$ .45	$1.50					
Demeter, Don	59T	324	$ .60	$1.75					
Demeter, Don	60T	234	$ .35	$1.10					
Demeter, Don	61T	23	$ .30	$1.00					
Demeter, Don	62T	146	$ .35	$1.10					
Demeter, Don	63T	268	$ .25	$ .85					
Demeter, Don	64T	58	$ .25	$ .85					
Demeter, Don	65T	429	$ .30	$1.00					
Demeter, Don	66T	98	$ .25	$ .85					
Demeter, Don	67T	572	$2.50	$8.00					
DeMola, Don	75T	391	$ .06	$ .25					
DeMola, Don	76T	571	$ .05	$ .20					
Dempsey, Con	52T	44	$14.00	$45.00					
Dempsey, Pat	81T	96	$ .01	$ .07					
Dempsey, Rick	72T	778	$ .60	$1.75					
Dempsey, Rick	74T	569	$ .06	$ .25					
Dempsey, Rick	75T	451	$ .10	$ .35					
Dempsey, Rick	76T	272	$ .04	$ .15					
Dempsey, Rick	77T	189	$ .05	$ .15					
Dempsey, Rick	78T	367	$ .02	$ .10					
Dempsey, Rick	79T	593	$ .02	$ .10					
Dempsey, Rick	80T	91	$ .01	$ .07					
Dempsey, Rick	81T	615	$ .01	$ .07					
Dempsey, Rick	82T	489	$ .01	$ .06	Dent, Bucky	83T	565	$ .01	$ .06
Dempsey, Rick	83T	138	$ .02	$ .10	Dent, Bucky	84T	331	$ .01	$ .05
Dempsey, Rick	84T	272	$ .05	$ .20	Dent, Bucky	90T	519	$ .01	$ .03
Dempsey, Rick	85T	521	$ .01	$ .04	Dente, Sam	52T	304	$11.50	$38.00
Dempsey, Rick	86T	358	$ .01	$ .03	Dernier, Bob	82T	231	$ .50	$1.50
Dempsey, Rick	87T	28	$ .01	$ .03	Dernier, Bob	82TTR	28	$ .02	$ .10
Dempsey, Rick	87TTR	28	$ .01	$ .07	Dernier, Bob	83T	43	$ .01	$ .06
Dempsey, Rick	89T	606	$ .01	$ .04	Dernier, Bob	84T	358	$ .01	$ .05
Dempsey, Rick	89TBB	108	$ .01	$ .05	Dernier, Bob	84TTR	31	$ .02	$ .10
Dempsey, Rick	90T	736	$ .01	$ .03	Dernier, Bob	85T	589	$ .01	$ .04
Denehy, Bill	67T	581	$275.00	$825.00	Dernier, Bob	86T	188	$ .01	$ .03
Denehy, Bill	68T	526	$ .30	$1.00	Dernier, Bob	87T	715	$ .01	$ .03
Dennis, Don	66T	142	$ .25	$ .85	Dernier, Bob	88T	642	$ .01	$ .03
Dennis, Don	67T	259	$ .25	$ .65	Dernier, Bob	89T	418	$ .01	$ .04
Denny, John	75T	621	$ .15	$ .50	Dernier, Bob	89TBB	265	$ .01	$ .05
Denny, John	76T	339	$ .05	$ .20	Dernier, Bob	90T	204	$ .01	$ .03

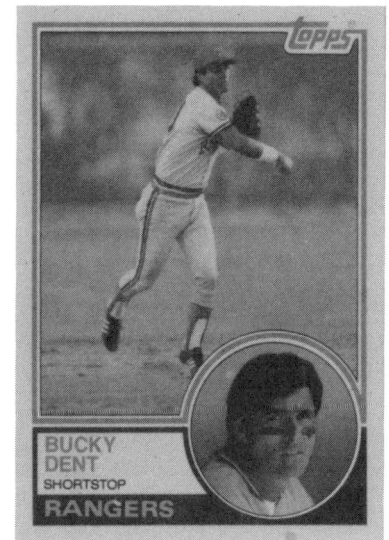

BUCKY DENT
SHORTSTOP
RANGERS

Player	Year	No.	VG	EX/MT	Player	Year	No.	VG	EX/MT
Derrington, Jim	58T	129	$ .50	$2.00	Dierker, Larry	76T	75	$ .05	$ .20
DeSa, Joe	86T	313	$ .01	$ .03	Dierker, Larry	77T	350	$ .05	$ .15
Deshaies, Jim	87T	167	$ .10	$ .35	Dierker, Larry	78T	195	$ .02	$ .10
Deshaies, Jim	87TRB	2	$ .01	$ .03	Dietz, Dick	67T	341	$ .25	$ .65
Deshaies, Jim	88T	24	$ .01	$ .10	Dietz, Dick	68T	104	$ .25	$ .65
Deshaies, Jim	89T	341	$ .01	$ .04	Dietz, Dick	69T	293	$ .25	$ .85
Deshaies, Jim	89TBB	29	$ .01	$ .05	Dietz, Dick	70T	135	$ .10	$ .35
Deshaies, Jim	90T	225	$ .01	$ .03	Dietz, Dick	71T	545	$ .30	$1.00
DeShields, Delino	90T	224	$ .01	$ .75	Dietz, Dick	72T	295	$ .10	$ .35
Destrade, Orestes	89T	27	$ .01	$ .15	Dietz, Dick	72TIA	296	$ .10	$ .35
Dettore, Tom	75T	469	$ .06	$ .25	Dietz, Dick	73T	442	$ .06	$ .25
Dettore, Tom	76T	126	$ .05	$ .20	DiLauro, Jack	70T	382	$ .10	$ .35
Devereaux, Mike	89TTR	23	$ .01	$ .10	DiLauro, Jack	71T	677	$ .70	$2.10
Devereaux, Mike	90T	127	$ .01	$ .03	Dillard, Don	59T	123	$ .50	$1.95
Devine, Adrian	74T	614	$ .06	$ .25	Dillard, Don	60T	122	$ .35	$1.10
Devine, Adrian	77T	339	$ .05	$ .15	Dillard, Don	61T	172	$ .30	$1.00
Devine, Adrian	78T	92	$ .02	$ .10	Dillard, Don	63T	298	$ .35	$1.20
Devine, Adrian	79T	257	$ .02	$ .10	Dillard, Steve	77T	142	$ .05	$ .15
Devine, Adrian	80T	528	$ .01	$ .07	Dillard, Steve	78T	597	$ .02	$ .10
Devine, Adrian	81T	464	$ .01	$ .07	Dillard, Steve	79T	217	$ .02	$ .10
Diaz, Bo	78T	708	$7.00	$25.00	Dillard, Steve	80T	452	$ .01	$ .07
Diaz, Bo	79T	61	$ .02	$ .10	Dillard, Steve	81T	78	$ .01	$ .07
Diaz, Bo	80T	483	$ .01	$ .07	Dillard, Steve	82T	324	$ .01	$ .06
Diaz, Bo	81T	362	$ .03	$ .15	Dillman, Bill	67T	558	$6.00	$20.00
Diaz, Bo	82T	258	$ .02	$ .10	Dillman, Bill	68T	466	$ .30	$1.00
Diaz, Bo	82TTR	29	$ .02	$ .10	Dillman, Bill	69T	141	$ .25	$ .65
Diaz, Bo	83T	175	$ .01	$ .06	Dillman, Bill	70T	386	$ .10	$ .35
Diaz, Bo	83T	229	$ .01	$ .06	Dillon, Steve	64T	556	$1.50	$3.75
Diaz, Bo	84T	535	$ .01	$ .05	Dilone, Miguel	78T	705	$ .02	$ .10
Diaz, Bo	85T	737	$ .01	$ .04	Dilone, Miguel	79T	487	$ .02	$ .10
Diaz, Bo	86T	639	$ .01	$ .03	Dilone, Miguel	80T	541	$ .01	$ .07
Diaz, Bo	87T	41	$ .01	$ .03	Dilone, Miguel	81T	141	$ .01	$ .07
Diaz, Bo	88T	265	$ .01	$ .03	Dilone, Miguel	82T	77	$ .01	$ .06
Diaz, Bo	89T	422	$ .01	$ .04	Dilone, Miguel	83T	303	$ .01	$ .06
Diaz, Carlos	84T	524	$ .01	$ .05	Dilone, Miguel	85T	178	$ .01	$ .04
Diaz, Carlos	84TTR	32	$ .02	$ .10	DiMaggio, Dom	51Trb	20	$3.50	$13.50
Diaz, Carlos	85T	159	$ .01	$ .04	DiMaggio, Dom	52T	22	$25.00	$75.00
Diaz, Carlos	86T	343	$ .01	$ .03	DiMaggio, Dom	53T	149	$4.00	$13.00
Diaz, Mario	89T	309	$ .01	$ .10	Diorio, Ron	74T	599	$ .15	$ .50
Diaz, Mario	90T	781	$ .01	$ .03	DiPino, Frank	82T	333	$ .01	$ .06
Diaz, Mike	87T	469	$ .01	$ .10	DiPino, Frank	83TTR	25	$ .02	$ .10
Diaz, Mike	88T	567	$ .01	$ .03	DiPino, Frank	84T	172	$ .01	$ .05
Diaz, Mike	89T	142	$ .01	$ .04	DiPino, Frank	85T	532	$ .01	$ .04
Dibble, Rob	89T	264	$ .01	$ .50	DiPino, Frank	86T	26	$ .01	$ .03
Dibble, Rob	90T	46	$ .01	$ .25	DiPino, Frank	87T	662	$ .01	$ .03
Dickey, Bill	52T	400	$160.00	$ 500.00	DiPino, Frank	88T	211	$ .01	$ .03
Dickey, Bill	60T	465	$2.50	$9.00	DiPino, Frank	89T	439	$ .01	$ .04
Dickson, Jim	64T	524	$1.50	$3.75	DiPino, Frank	89TTR	24	$ .01	$ .05
Dickson, Jim	65T	286	$ .30	$1.00	DiPino, Frank	90T	788	$ .01	$ .03
Dickson, Jim	66T	201	$ .25	$ .85	DiSarcina, Gary	89TMLD	31	$ .01	$ .05
Dickson, Murry	51Tbb	16	$5.50	$17.00	Distaso, Alec	69T	602	$ .25	$ .85
Dickson, Murry	52T	266	$11.50	$38.00	Distefano, Benny	85T	162	$ .01	$ .04
Dickson, Murry	56T	211	$2.50	$8.00	Distefano, Benny	87T	651	$ .01	$ .03
Dickson, Murry	57T	71	$ .95	$3.50	Distefano, Benny	89TTR	25	$ .01	$ .05
Dickson, Murry	58T	349	$ .50	$2.00	Ditmar, Art	56T	258	$2.50	$8.00
Dickson, Murry	59T	23	$ .95	$3.50	Ditmar, Art	57T	132	$ .95	$3.50
Didier, Bob	69T	611	$ .25	$ .85	Ditmar, Art	58T	354	$ .50	$2.00
Didier, Bob	70T	232	$ .10	$ .35	Ditmar, Art	59T	374	$ .60	$1.75
Didier, Bob	71T	432	$ .10	$ .35	Ditmar, Art	60T	430	$ .50	$1.95
Didier, Bob	73T	574	$ .35	$1.10	Ditmar, Art	61T	46	$ .50	$2.00
Didier, Bob	74T	482	$ .06	$ .25	Ditmar, Art	61T	48	$ .50	$2.00
Diering, Chuck	52T	265	$11.50	$38.00	Ditmar, Art	61T	510	$ .60	$1.75
Diering, Chuck	55T	105	$1.35	$5.00	Ditmar, Art	62T	246	$ .35	$1.10
Diering, Chuck	56T	19	$1.25	$4.50	Dittmer, Jack	53T	212	$3.75	$13.00
Dierker, Larry	65T	409	$ .30	$1.00	Dittmer, Jack	54T	53	$4.75	$14.00
Dierker, Larry	66T	228	$ .25	$ .85	Dittmer, Jack	57T	282	$3.50	$13.00
Dierker, Larry	67T	498	$ .50	$2.00	Dixon, Ken	85TTR	31	$ .02	$ .10
Dierker, Larry	68T	565	$ .30	$1.00	Dixon, Ken	86T	198	$ .01	$ .03
Dierker, Larry	69T	411	$ .25	$ .65	Dixon, Ken	87T	528	$ .01	$ .03
Dierker, Larry	70T	15	$ .10	$ .35	Dixon, Ken	88T	676	$ .01	$ .03
Dierker, Larry	71T	540	$ .30	$1.00	Dixon, Tom	79T	361	$ .02	$ .10
Dierker, Larry	72T	155	$ .10	$ .35	Dixon, Tom	80T	513	$ .01	$ .07
Dierker, Larry	73T	375	$ .06	$ .25	Dobbek, Dan	59T	124	$ .50	$1.95
Dierker, Larry	74T	660	$ .35	$1.10	Dobbek, Dan	60T	123	$ .35	$1.10
Dierker, Larry	75T	49	$ .06	$ .25	Dobbek, Dan	61T	108	$ .30	$1.00

Player	Year	No.	VG	EX/MT	Player	Year	No.	VG	EX/MT
Dobbek, Dan	62T	267	$ .35	$1.10	Donovan, Dick	57T	181	$ .95	$3.50
Dobson, Chuck	66T	588	$4.50	$15.00	Donovan, Dick	58T	290	$ .50	$2.00
Dobson, Chuck	67T	438	$ .25	$ .85	Donovan, Dick	59T	5	$1.00	$3.75
Dobson, Chuck	68T	62	$ .25	$ .65	Donovan, Dick	60T	199	$ .35	$1.10
Dobson, Chuck	69T	397	$ .25	$ .65	Donovan, Dick	61T	414	$ .50	$2.00
Dobson, Chuck	70T	331	$ .10	$ .35	Donovan, Dick	62T	15	$ .35	$1.10
Dobson, Chuck	71T	238	$ .10	$ .35	Donovan, Dick	62T	55	$ .50	$2.00
Dobson, Chuck	72T	523	$ .10	$ .35	Donovan, Dick	63T	8	$ .35	$1.10
Dobson, Chuck	75T	635	$ .06	$ .25	Donovan, Dick	63T	370	$ .35	$1.20
Dobson, Joe	52T	254	$11.50	$38.00	Dopson, John	89T	251	$ .01	$ .15
Dobson, Joe	53T	5	$3.75	$13.00	Dopson, John	89TTR	26	$ .01	$ .15
Dobson, Pat	67T	526	$ .50	$2.00	Dopson, John	90T	733	$ .01	$ .03
Dobson, Pat	68T	22	$ .25	$ .65	Doran, Bill	83TTR	26	$ .25	$1.25
Dobson, Pat	69T	231	$ .25	$ .85					
Dobson, Pat	70T	421	$ .10	$ .35					
Dobson, Pat	71T	547	$ .30	$1.00					
Dobson, Pat	72T	140	$ .10	$ .35					
Dobson, Pat	73T	34	$ .06	$ .25					
Dobson, Pat	74T	463	$ .06	$ .25					
Dobson, Pat	75T	44	$ .06	$ .25					
Dobson, Pat	76T	296	$ .05	$ .20					
Dobson, Pat	76TTR	296	$ .05	$ .20					
Dobson, Pat	77T	618	$ .05	$ .15					
Dobson, Pat	78T	575	$ .02	$ .10					
Doby, Larry	52T	243	$10.00	$30.00					
Doby, Larry	54T	70	$10.00	$35.00					
Doby, Larry	56T	250	$3.35	$10.00					
Doby, Larry	57T	85	$2.10	$7.50					
Doby, Larry	58T	424	$ .95	$3.00					
Doby, Larry	59T	166	$ .60	$1.75					
Doby, Larry	59T	455	$1.35	$4.00					
Doby, Larry	73T	377	$ .10	$ .35					
Doby, Larry	74T	531	$ .25	$ .85					
Dodgers, Team	56T	166	$50.00	$147.50					
Dodgers, Team	57T	324	$25.00	$100.00					
Dodgers, Team	58T	71	$5.00	$20.00					
Dodgers, Team	59T	457	$8.00	$20.00					
Dodgers, Team	60T	18	$3.00	$9.00					
Dodgers, Team	61T	86	$1.00	$3.00					
Dodgers, Team	62T	43	$1.25	$3.50					
Dodgers, Team	63T	337	$2.00	$7.00					
Dodgers, Team	64T	531	$2.00	$7.00					
Dodgers, Team	65T	126	$2.50	$8.00					
Dodgers, Team	66T	238	$ .95	$3.50					
Dodgers, Team	67T	503	$1.50	$3.50	Doran, Bill	84T	198	$ .25	$1.00
Dodgers, Team	68T	168	$ .70	$2.00	Doran, Bill	85T	684	$ .01	$ .04
Dodgers, Team	70T	411	$ .50	$2.00	Doran, Bill	86T	57	$ .01	$ .10
Dodgers, Team	71T	402	$ .35	$1.10	Doran, Bill	87T	472	$ .01	$ .03
Dodgers, Team	72T	522	$ .30	$1.00	Doran, Bill	88T	745	$ .01	$ .10
Dodgers, Team	73T	91	$ .30	$1.00	Doran, Bill	88TBB	51	$ .01	$ .05
Dodgers, Team	74T	643	$ .30	$1.00	Doran, Bill	89T	226	$ .01	$ .04
Dodgers, Team Checklist	75T	361	$ .35	$1.10	Doran, Bill	89TBB	168	$ .01	$ .05
Dodgers, Team Checklist	76T	46	$ .20	$ .75	Doran, Bill	90T	368	$ .01	$ .03
Dodgers, Team Checklist	77T	504	$ .35	$1.10	Dorish, Harry	52T	303	$11.50	$38.00
Dodgers, Team Checklist	78T	259	$ .25	$ .65	Dorish, Harry	53T	145	$3.75	$13.00
Dodgers, Team Checklist	79T	526	$ .08	$ .30	Dorish, Harry	54T	110	$2.10	$7.50
Dodgers, Team Checklist	80T	302	$ .08	$ .30	Dorish, Harry	56T	167	$1.25	$4.50
Dodgers, Team Checklist	81T	679	$ .02	$ .30	Dorsey, Jim	81T	214	$ .01	$ .07
Dodgers, Team Leaders	86T	696	$ .01	$ .03	Dotson, Rich	81T	138	$ .05	$ .25
Dodgers, Team Leaders	87T	431	$ .01	$ .03	Dotson, Rich	82T	461	$ .01	$ .06
Dodgers, Team Leaders	88T	489	$ .01	$ .03	Dotson, Richard	83T	46	$ .01	$ .06
Dodgers, Team Leaders	89T	669	$ .01	$ .04	Dotson, Richard	84T	216	$ .01	$ .05
Dodson, Pat	87T	449	$ .01	$ .03	Dotson, Richard	84T	759	$ .01	$ .05
Doerr, Bobby	51Tbb	37	$10.00	$42.50	Dotson, Richard	85T	364	$ .01	$ .04
Doherty, John	75T	524	$ .06	$ .25	Dotson, Richard	86T	612	$ .01	$ .03
Donaldson, John	68T	244	$ .25	$ .65	Dotson, Richard	87T	720	$ .01	$ .03
Donaldson, John	69T	217	$ .25	$ .65	Dotson, Richard	88T	209	$ .01	$ .03
Donaldson, John	70T	418	$ .10	$ .35	Dotson, Richard	88TTR	35	$ .01	$ .05
Donohue, Jim	60T	124	$ .35	$1.10	Dotson, Richard	89T	511	$ .01	$ .04
Donohue, Jim	61T	151	$ .30	$1.00	Dotson, Richard	90T	169	$ .01	$ .03
Donohue, Jim	62T	498	$ .70	$2.10	Dotter, Gary	65T	421	$ .30	$1.00
Donohue, Tom	80T	454	$ .01	$ .07	Dotterer, Dutch	58T	396	$ .50	$2.00
Donohue, Tom	81T	621	$ .01	$ .07	Dotterer, Dutch	59T	288	$ .50	$1.95
Donovan, Dick	55T	146	$1.35	$5.00	Dotterer, Dutch	60T	21	$ .35	$1.10
Donovan, Dick	56T	18	$1.25	$4.50					

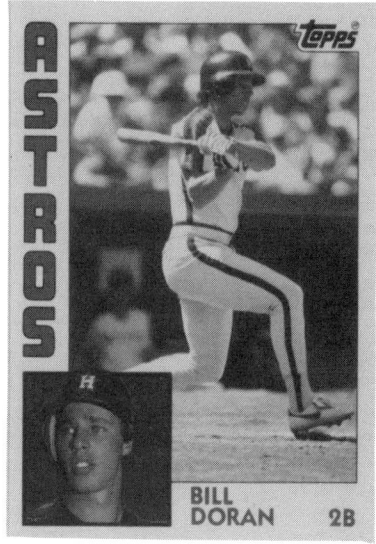

BILL DORAN 2B

Player	Year	No.	VG	EX/MT	Player	Year	No.	VG	EX/MT
Dotterer, Dutch	61T	332	$ .30	$1.00	Drabowsky, Moe	67T	125	$ .25	$ .65
Douglas, Whammy	58T	306	$ .50	$2.00	Drabowsky, Moe	68T	242	$ .25	$ .65
Douglas, Whammy	59T	431	$ .50	$1.95	Drabowsky, Moe	69T	508	$ .25	$ .65
Dowling, Dave	65T	116	$ .35	$1.10	Drabowsky, Moe	70T	653	$ .50	$2.00
Dowling, Dave	66T	482	$ .70	$2.10	Drabowsky, Moe	71T	685	$ .70	$2.10
Dowling, Dave	67T	272	$ .25	$ .65	Drabowsky, Moe	72T	627	$ .25	$ .85
Downing, Al	62T	219	$ .90	$2.75	Drago, Dick	69T	662	$ .25	$ .85
Downing, Al	64T	86	$ .35	$1.10	Drago, Dick	70T	37	$ .10	$ .35
Downing, Al	64T	219	$ .50	$2.00	Drago, Dick	71T	752	$1.80	$6.00
Downing, Al	65T	11	$ .35	$1.10	Drago, Dick	72T	205	$ .10	$ .35
Downing, Al	65T	598	$2.50	$9.00	Drago, Dick	73T	392	$ .06	$ .25
Downing, Al	66T	384	$ .35	$1.10	Drago, Dick	74T	113	$ .06	$ .25
Downing, Al	67T	308	$ .25	$ .65	Drago, Dick	75T	333	$ .06	$ .25
Downing, Al	68T	105	$ .25	$ .85	Drago, Dick	76T	142	$ .05	$ .20
Downing, Al	69T	292	$ .25	$ .85	Drago, Dick	77T	426	$ .05	$ .15
Downing, Al	70T	584	$ .25	$ .85	Drago, Dick	78T	567	$ .02	$ .10
Downing, Al	71T	182	$ .10	$ .35	Drago, Dick	79T	12	$ .02	$ .10
Downing, Al	72T	93	$ .50	$2.00	Drago, Dick	80T	271	$ .01	$ .07
Downing, Al	72T	460	$ .10	$ .35	Drago, Dick	81T	647	$ .01	$ .07
Downing, Al	73T	324	$ .06	$ .25	Drago, Dick	81TTR	755	$ .02	$ .10
Downing, Al	74T	620	$ .06	$ .25	Drago, Dick	82T	742	$ .01	$ .06
Downing, Al	75T	498	$ .06	$ .25	Drake, Sammy	62T	162	$ .35	$1.10
Downing, Al	76T	605	$ .05	$ .20	Drake, Solly	57T	159	$ .95	$3.50
Downing, Brian	74T	601	$ .35	$1.10	Drake, Solly	59T	406	$ .50	$1.95
Downing, Brian	75T	422	$ .06	$ .25	Dravecky, Dave	83T	384	$ .25	$1.25
Downing, Brian	76T	23	$ .05	$ .20	Dravecky, Dave	84T	290	$ .01	$ .15
Downing, Brian	77T	344	$ .05	$ .15	Dravecky, Dave	84T	366	$ .01	$ .05
Downing, Brian	78T	519	$ .02	$ .10	Dravecky, Dave	85T	530	$ .01	$ .04
Downing, Brian	79T	71	$ .02	$ .10	Dravecky, Dave	86T	735	$ .01	$ .03
Downing, Brian	80T	602	$ .01	$ .07	Dravecky, Dave	87T	470	$ .01	$ .03
Downing, Brian	81T	263	$ .01	$ .07	Dravecky, Dave	88T	68	$ .01	$ .03
Downing, Brian	82T	158	$ .01	$ .06	Dravecky, Dave	89T	601	$ .01	$ .04
Downing, Brian	84T	574	$ .01	$ .05	Dravecky, Dave	90T	124	$ .01	$ .03
Downing, Brian	85T	374	$ .01	$ .04	Dressen, Chuck	52T	377	$60.00	$175.00
Downing, Brian	86T	772	$ .01	$ .03	Dressen, Chuck	53T	50	$3.50	$13.00
Downing, Brian	87T	782	$ .01	$ .03	Dressen, Chuck	60T	213	$ .35	$1.10
Downing, Brian	88T	331	$ .01	$ .03	Dressen, Chuck	61T	137	$ .30	$1.00
Downing, Brian	88TBB	78	$ .01	$ .05	Dressen, Chuck	64T	443	$ .50	$2.00
Downing, Brian	89T	17	$ .01	$ .04	Dressen, Chuck	65T	538	$1.50	$3.75
Downing, Brian	90T	635	$ .01	$ .03	Dressen, Chuck	66T	187	$ .15	$ .50
Downs, Kelly	87T	438	$ .01	$ .03	Dressler, Rob	76T	599	$4.00	$12.00
Downs, Kelly	88T	629	$ .01	$ .03	Dressler, Rob	77T	11	$ .05	$ .15
Downs, Kelly	89T	361	$ .01	$ .04	Dressler, Rob	80T	366	$ .01	$ .07
Downs, Kelly	89TBB	112	$ .01	$ .05	Dressler, Rob	81T	508	$ .01	$ .07
Downs, Kelly	90T	17	$ .01	$ .03	Drews, Karl	52T	352	$39.00	$135.00
Doyle, Brian	79T	710	$ .05	$ .20	Drews, Karl	53T	59	$3.75	$13.00
Doyle, Brian	80T	582	$ .01	$ .07	Driessen, Dan	74T	341	$ .25	$ .85
Doyle, Brian	81T	159	$ .01	$ .07	Driessen, Dan	75T	133	$ .06	$ .25
Doyle, Brian	81TTR	754	$ .02	$ .10	Driessen, Dan	76T	514	$ .10	$ .35
Doyle, Dennis	70T	539	$1.35	$4.00	Driessen, Dan	77T	23	$ .05	$ .15
Doyle, Denny	71T	352	$ .10	$ .35	Driessen, Dan	78T	246	$ .05	$ .20
Doyle, Denny	72T	768	$ .70	$2.10	Driessen, Dan	79T	475	$ .02	$ .10
Doyle, Denny	73T	424	$ .06	$ .25	Driessen, Dan	80T	325	$ .01	$ .07
Doyle, Denny	74T	552	$ .06	$ .25	Driessen, Dan	81T	655	$ .01	$ .07
Doyle, Denny	75T	187	$ .06	$ .25	Driessen, Dan	82T	785	$ .01	$ .06
Doyle, Denny	76T	381	$ .05	$ .20	Driessen, Dan	83T	165	$ .01	$ .06
Doyle, Denny	77T	336	$ .05	$ .15	Driessen, Dan	84T	585	$ .01	$ .05
Doyle, Denny	78T	642	$ .02	$ .10	Driessen, Dan	85T	285	$ .01	$ .04
Doyle, Paul	70T	277	$ .10	$ .35	Driessen, Dan	86T	65	$ .01	$ .03
Doyle, Paul	72T	629	$ .25	$ .85	Driscoll, Jim	71T	317	$ .10	$ .35
Drabek, Doug	87T	283	$ .01	$ .10	Dropo, Walt	52T	235	$6.00	$18.00
Drabek, Doug	87TTR	29	$ .01	$ .07	Dropo, Walt	53T	121	$3.75	$13.00
Drabek, Doug	88T	591	$ .01	$ .03	Dropo, Walt	54T	18	$2.10	$7.50
Drabek, Doug	88TBB	124	$ .01	$ .05	Dropo, Walt	56T	238	$2.50	$8.00
Drabek, Doug	89T	478	$ .01	$ .04	Dropo, Walt	57T	257	$ .95	$3.50
Drabek, Doug	90T	197	$ .01	$ .03	Dropo, Walt	58T	338	$ .55	$1.75
Drabowsky, Moe	57T	84	$ .95	$3.50	Dropo, Walt	59T	158	$ .50	$1.95
Drabowsky, Moe (Mike)	58T	135	$ .50	$2.00	Dropo, Walt	60T	79	$ .35	$1.10
Drabowsky, Moe	59T	407	$ .50	$1.95	Dropo, Walt	61T	489	$ .50	$2.00
Drabowsky, Moe	60T	349	$ .50	$1.95	Drott, Dick	58T	80	$1.00	$3.75
Drabowsky, Moe	61T	364	$ .30	$1.00	Drott, Dick	59T	15	$1.00	$3.75
Drabowsky, Moe	62T	331	$ .35	$1.10	Drott, Dick	60T	27	$ .35	$1.10
Drabowsky, Moe	64T	42	$ .25	$ .85	Drott, Dick	61T	231	$ .30	$1.00
Drabowsky, Moe	65T	439	$ .30	$1.00	Drummond, Tim	90T	713	$ .01	$ .10
Drabowsky, Moe	66T	291	$ .25	$ .85	Drumright, Keith	82T	673	$ .01	$ .06

Player	Year	No.	VG	EX/MT	Player	Year	No.	VG	EX/MT
Drysdale, Don	57T	18	$67.50	$175.00	Duffy, Frank	74T	81	$ .06	$ .25
Drysdale, Don	58T	25	$13.00	$40.00	Duffy, Frank	75T	448	$ .06	$ .25
Drysdale, Don	59T	262	$3.00	$12.00	Duffy, Frank	76T	232	$ .05	$ .20
Drysdale, Don	59T	387	$12.50	$42.50	Duffy, Frank	77T	542	$ .05	$ .15
Drysdale, Don	60T	475	$7.00	$28.00	Duffy, Frank	78T	511	$ .02	$ .10
Drysdale, Don	60TAS	570	$10.00	$40.00	Duffy, Frank	79T	106	$ .02	$ .10
Drysdale, Don	61T	45	$ .60	$2.75	Dukes, Jan	70T	154	$ .10	$ .35
Drysdale, Don	61T	49	$ .60	$1.75	Dukes, Tom	68T	128	$ .25	$ .65
Drysdale, Don	61T	260	$6.00	$18.00	Dukes, Tom	69T	223	$ .25	$ .85
Drysdale, Don	62T	60	$ .65	$1.75	Dukes, Tom	71T	106	$ .10	$ .35
Drysdale, Don	62T	340	$9.00	$27.50	Duliba, Bob	60T	401	$ .50	$1.95
Drysdale, Don	62TAS	398	$3.00	$10.00	Duliba, Bob	62T	149	$ .35	$1.10
Drysdale, Don	63T	5	$ .60	$1.75	Duliba, Bob	63T	97	$ .25	$ .85
Drysdale, Don	63T	7	$ .35	$1.10	Duliba, Bob	64T	441	$ .40	$1.25
Drysdale, Don	63T	9	$ .60	$1.75	Duliba, Bob	66T	53	$ .25	$ .85
Drysdale, Don	63T	360	$4.50	$16.00	Duliba, Bob	67T	599	$1.35	$4.00
Drysdale, Don	63T	412	$10.00	$40.00	Dunbar, Tommy	85T	102	$ .01	$ .04
Drysdale, Don	64T	5	$1.75	$5.00	Dunbar, Tommy	86T	559	$ .01	$ .03
Drysdale, Don	64T	120	$4.00	$14.00	Duncan, Dave	64T	528	$1.50	$3.75
Drysdale, Don	65T	8	$1.50	$3.75	Duncan, Dave	68T	261	$ .25	$ .65
Drysdale, Don	65T	12	$1.50	$3.75	Duncan, Dave	69T	68	$ .25	$ .65
					Duncan, Dave	70T	678	$ .50	$2.00
					Duncan, Dave	71T	178	$ .10	$ .35
					Duncan, Dave	72T	17	$ .10	$ .35
					Duncan, Dave	73T	337	$ .06	$ .25
					Duncan, Dave	74T	284	$ .06	$ .25
					Duncan, Dave	75T	238	$ .06	$ .25
					Duncan, Dave	76T	49	$ .05	$ .20
					Duncan, Dave	77T	338	$ .05	$ .15
					Duncan, Mariano	85TTR	32	$ .05	$ .25
					Duncan, Mariano	86T	602	$ .01	$ .03
					Duncan, Mariano	87T	199	$ .01	$ .03
					Duncan, Mariano	88T	481	$ .01	$ .03
					Duncan, Mariano	90T	234	$ .01	$ .03
					Duncan, Taylor	79T	658	$ .02	$ .10
					Dunegan, Jim	71T	121	$ .10	$ .35
					Dunlop, Harry	73T	593	$ .50	$2.00
					Dunlop, Harry	74T	166	$ .06	$ .25
					Dunne, Mike	85T	395	$ .15	$ .50
					Dunne, Mike	87TTR	30	$ .05	$ .20
					Dunne, Mike	88T	619	$ .01	$ .15
					Dunne, Mike	88TBB	236	$ .01	$ .05
					Dunne, Mike	89T	165	$ .01	$ .04
					Dunne, Mike	90T	522	$ .01	$ .03
					Dunning, Steve	71T	294	$ .10	$ .35
					Dunning, Steve	72T	658	$ .70	$2.10
					Dunning, Steve	73T	53	$ .06	$ .25
					Dunning, Steve	78T	647	$ .02	$ .10
					Dunston, Shawon	85T	280	$ .15	$1.50
					Dunston, Shawon	86T	72	$ .01	$ .15
					Dunston, Shawon	87T	346	$ .01	$ .10
					Dunston, Shawon	88T	695	$ .01	$ .03
					Dunston, Shawon	88TBB	225	$ .01	$ .05
					Dunston, Shawon	89T	140	$ .01	$ .04
					Dunston, Shawon	89TBB	233	$ .01	$ .10
					Dunston, Shawon	90T	415	$ .01	$ .10
					Dupree, Mike	77T	491	$ .25	$1.00
					Duren, Ryne	58T	296	$1.35	$4.00
Drysdale, Don	65T	260	$3.75	$11.50	Duren, Ryne	59T	485	$ .70	$2.00
Drysdale, Don	66T	223	$ .65	$1.75	Duren, Ryne	60T	204	$ .60	$1.75
Drysdale, Don	66T	430	$2.25	$6.50	Duren, Ryne	61T	356	$ .30	$1.00
Drysdale, Don	67T	55	$3.00	$11.00	Duren, Ryne	62T	388	$1.00	$3.75
Drysdale, Don	68T	145	$3.00	$9.00	Duren, Ryne	63T	17	$ .25	$ .85
Drysdale, Don	69T	400	$2.00	$6.00	Duren, Ryne	64T	173	$ .30	$1.00
Dubiel, Walt	52T	164	$6.00	$19.00	Duren, Ryne	65T	339	$ .30	$1.00
DuBois, Brian	89TMLD	32	$ .01	$ .15	Durham, Don	73T	548	$ .35	$1.10
DuBois, Brian	90T	413	$ .01	$ .10	Durham, Joe	58T	96	$1.00	$3.75
Ducey, Rob	88T	438	$ .01	$ .20	Durham, Leon	81T	321	$ .35	$1.10
Ducey, Rob	89T	203	$ .01	$ .10	Durham, Leon	81TTR	756	$ .15	$ .50
Ducey, Rob	89TBB	280	$ .01	$ .05	Durham, Leon	82T	607	$ .03	$ .15
Ducey, Rob	90T	619	$ .01	$ .03	Durham, Leon	83T	51	$ .01	$ .06
Dues, Hal	79T	699	$ .02	$ .10	Durham, Leon	83T	125	$ .01	$ .06
Dues, Hal	81T	71	$ .01	$ .07	Durham, Leon	84T	565	$ .01	$ .05
Duffalo, Jim	62T	578	$3.75	$11.00	Durham, Leon	85T	330	$ .01	$ .04
Duffalo, Jim	63T	567	$1.50	$3.75	Durham, Leon	86T	460	$ .01	$ .10
Duffalo, Jim	64T	573	$1.50	$3.75					
Duffalo, Jim	65T	159	$ .25	$ .65					
Duffy, Frank	71T	164	$ .25	$ .85					
Duffy, Frank	72T	607	$ .25	$ .85					
Duffy, Frank	73T	376	$ .06	$ .25					

DON DRYSDALE
DODGERS
PITCHER

TOPPS

Player	Year	No.	VG	EX/MT	Player	Year	No.	VG	EX/MT
Durham, Leon	87T	290	$ .01	$ .03	Dyer, Duffy	77T	318	$ .05	$ .15
Durham, Leon	88T	65	$ .01	$ .03	Dyer, Duffy	78T	637	$ .02	$ .10
Durham, Leon	88TBB	42	$ .01	$ .05	Dyer, Duffy	79T	286	$ .02	$ .10
Durocher, Leo	52T	315	$80.00	$225.00	Dyer, Duffy	80T	446	$ .01	$ .07
Durocher, Leo	67T	481	$1.50	$3.75	Dyer, Duffy	81T	196	$ .01	$ .07
Durocher, Leo	68T	321	$ .50	$2.00	Dyer, Mike	89TMLD	33	$ .01	$ .15
Durocher, Leo	69T	147	$ .35	$1.10	Dyer, Mike	90T	576	$ .01	$ .10
Durocher, Leo	70T	291	$ .35	$1.10	Dykes, Jimmie	60T	214	$ .35	$1.10
Durocher, Leo	71T	609	$ .60	$1.75	Dykes, Jimmie	61T	222	$ .30	$1.00
Durocher, Leo	72T	576	$ .50	$2.00	Dykstra, Len	86T	53	$ .15	$2.00
Durocher, Leo	73T	624	$ .55	$1.75	Dykstra, Len	87T	295	$ .05	$ .50
Dusak, Erv	52T	183	$6.00	$19.00	Dykstra, Len	88T	655	$ .01	$ .25
Dustal, Bob	63T	299	$ .35	$1.20	Dykstra, Len	88TBB	203	$ .01	$ .10
Dwyer, Jim	75T	429	$ .06	$ .25	Dykstra, Len	89T	435	$ .01	$ .10
Dwyer, Jim	76T	94	$ .05	$ .20	Dykstra, Len	89TBB	41	$ .01	$ .10
Dwyer, Jim	78T	644	$ .02	$ .10	Dykstra, Len	89TTR	27	$ .01	$ .10
Dwyer, Jim	79T	236	$ .02	$ .10	Dykstra, Len	90T	515	$ .01	$ .10
Dwyer, Jim	80T	576	$ .01	$ .07	Earley, Arnold	67T	388	$ .25	$ .85
Dwyer, Jim	81T	184	$ .01	$ .07	Easler, Mike	78T	710	$ .15	$ .50
Dwyer, Jim	81TTR	757	$ .02	$ .10	Easler, Mike	80T	194	$ .03	$ .15
Dwyer, Jim	82T	359	$ .01	$ .06	Easler, Mike	81T	92	$ .01	$ .07
Dwyer, Jim	83T	718	$ .01	$ .06	Easler, Mike	82T	235	$ .01	$ .06
Dwyer, Jim	84T	473	$ .01	$ .05	Easler, Mike	83T	385	$ .01	$ .06
Dwyer, Jim	85T	56	$ .01	$ .04	Easler, Mike	84T	589	$ .01	$ .05
Dwyer, Jim	86T	653	$ .01	$ .03	Easler, Mike	84TTR	33	$ .02	$ .10
Dwyer, Jim	87T	246	$ .01	$ .03	Easler, Mike	85T	686	$ .01	$ .04
Dwyer, Jim	88T	521	$ .01	$ .03	Easler, Mike	86T	477	$ .01	$ .03
Dybzinski, Jerry	81T	198	$ .01	$ .07	Easler, Mike	86TTR	33	$ .02	$ .10
Dybzinski, Jerry	82T	512	$ .01	$ .06	Easler, Mike	87T	135	$ .01	$ .03
Dybzinski, Jerry	83T	289	$ .01	$ .06	Easler, Mike	88T	741	$ .01	$ .03
Dybzinski, Jerry	83TTR	27	$ .02	$ .10	Easter, Luke	51Trb	26	$1.35	$4.00
Dybzinski, Jerry	84T	619	$ .01	$ .05	Easter, Luke	52T	24	$15.00	$50.00
Dybzinski, Jerry	85T	52	$ .01	$ .04	Easter, Luke	53T	2	$4.50	$15.00
Dyck, Jim	53T	177	$3.75	$13.00	Easter, Luke	54T	23	$2.50	$9.00
Dyck, Jim	56T	303	$1.80	$6.00	Easterly, Jamie	75T	618	$ .60	$1.75
Dyer, Duffy	69T	624	$ .25	$ .85	Easterly, Jamie	76T	511	$ .05	$ .20
Dyer, Duffy	70T	692	$ .50	$2.00	Easterly, Jamie	78T	264	$ .02	$ .10
Dyer, Duffy	71T	136	$ .10	$ .35	Easterly, Jamie	79T	684	$ .02	$ .10
					Easterly, Jamie	82T	122	$ .01	$ .06
					Easterly, Jamie	83T	528	$ .01	$ .06
					Easterly, Jamie	83TTR	28	$ .02	$ .10
					Easterly, Jamie	84T	367	$ .01	$ .05
					Easterly, Jamie	85T	764	$ .01	$ .04
					Easterly, Jamie	86T	31	$ .01	$ .03
					Eastwick, Rawly	75T	621	$ .15	$ .50
					Eastwick, Rawly	76T	469	$ .05	$ .20
					Eastwick, Rawly	77T	8	$ .05	$ .15
					Eastwick, Rawly	77T	45	$ .05	$ .15
					Eastwick, Rawly	78T	405	$ .02	$ .10
					Eastwick, Rawly	79T	271	$ .02	$ .10
					Eastwick, Rawly	80T	692	$ .01	$ .07
					Eastwick, Rawly	82T	117	$ .01	$ .06
					Eckersley, Dennis	76T	98	$1.50	$6.00
					Eckersley, Dennis	76T	202	$ .35	$1.10
					Eckersley, Dennis	77T	525	$ .40	$1.50
					Eckersley, Dennis	78T	122	$ .35	$1.25
					Eckersley, Dennis	79T	40	$ .02	$ .20
					Eckersley, Dennis	80T	320	$ .01	$ .10
					Eckersley, Dennis	81T	620	$ .01	$ .10
					Eckersley, Dennis	82T	490	$ .01	$ .06
					Eckersley, Dennis	83T	270	$ .01	$ .06
					Eckersley, Dennis	84T	745	$ .01	$ .05
					Eckersley, Dennis	84TTR	34	$ .02	$ .10
					Eckersley, Dennis	85T	163	$ .01	$ .04
					Eckersley, Dennis	86T	538	$ .01	$ .03
					Eckersley, Dennis	87T	459	$ .01	$ .03
					Eckersley, Dennis	87TTR	31	$ .01	$ .07
					Eckersley, Dennis	88T	72	$ .01	$ .03
					Eckersley, Dennis	89T	370	$ .01	$ .04
					Eckersley, Dennis	90T	670	$ .01	$ .03
					Eddy, Don	72T	413	$ .10	$ .35
					Edge, Bruce	80T	674	$ .01	$ .07
					Edler, Dave	82T	711	$ .25	$1.00
					Edler, Dave	83T	622	$ .01	$ .06
					Edmondson, Paul	70T	414	$ .10	$ .35

DUFFY DYER

Player	Year	No.	VG	EX/MT
Dyer, Duffy	72T	127	$ .10	$ .35
Dyer, Duffy	73T	493	$ .06	$ .25
Dyer, Duffy	74T	536	$ .06	$ .25
Dyer, Duffy	75T	538	$ .06	$ .25
Dyer, Duffy	76T	88	$ .05	$ .20

Player	Year	No.	VG	EX/MT	Player	Year	No.	VG	EX/MT
Edwards, Bruce	51Tbb	42	$5.50	$17.00	Elliot, Larry	63T	407	$ .35	$1.20
Edwards, Bruce	52T	224	$6.00	$19.00	Elliot, Larry	64T	536	$1.50	$3.75
Edwards, Dave	80T	657	$ .01	$ .07	Elliot, Larry	67T	23	$ .25	$ .65
Edwards, Dave	81T	386	$ .01	$ .07	Elliott, Bob	51Tbb	32	$4.00	$18.00
Edwards, Dave	81TTR	758	$ .02	$ .10	Elliott, Bob	52T	14	$14.00	$45.00
Edwards, Dave	82T	151	$ .01	$ .06	Elliott, Bob	60T	215	$ .35	$1.10
Edwards, Dave	83T	94	$ .01	$ .06	Elliott, Harry	55T	137	$1.35	$5.00
Edwards, Doc	62T	594	$35.00	$125.00	Elliott, Randy	78T	719	$ .02	$ .10
Edwards, Doc	63T	296	$ .35	$1.20	Ellis, Dock	69T	286	$ .25	$ .85
Edwards, Doc	64T	174	$ .25	$ .85	Ellis, Dock	70T	551	$ .25	$ .85
Edwards, Doc	65T	239	$ .30	$1.00	Ellis, Dock	71T	2	$ .25	$ .85
Edwards, Doc	88T	374	$ .01	$ .03	Ellis, Dock	72T	179	$ .10	$ .35
Edwards, Doc	89T	534	$ .01	$ .04	Ellis, Dock	72TIA	180	$ .10	$ .35
Edwards, Hank	52T	176	$6.00	$19.00	Ellis, Dock	73T	575	$ .35	$1.10
Edwards, Hank	53T	90	$3.75	$13.00	Ellis, Dock	74T	145	$ .06	$ .25
Edwards, John	62T	302	$ .35	$1.10	Ellis, Dock	75T	385	$ .06	$ .25
Edwards, Johnny	63T	178	$ .25	$ .85	Ellis, Dock	76T	528	$ .05	$ .20
Edwards, Johnny	64T	507	$ .40	$1.25	Ellis, Dock	76TTR	528	$ .05	$ .20
Edwards, Johnny	65T	418	$ .30	$1.00	Ellis, Dock	77T	71	$ .05	$ .15
Edwards, Johnny	66T	507	$ .70	$2.10	Ellis, Dock	78T	209	$ .02	$ .10
Edwards, Johnny	67T	202	$ .25	$ .65	Ellis, Dock	79T	691	$ .02	$ .10
Edwards, John	68T	558	$ .30	$1.00	Ellis, Dock	80T	117	$ .01	$ .07
Edwards, Johnny	69T	186	$ .25	$ .65	Ellis, John	70T	516	$ .10	$ .35
Edwards, Johnny	70T	339	$ .10	$ .35	Ellis, John	71T	263	$ .10	$ .35
Edwards, Johnny	71T	44	$ .10	$ .35	Ellis, John	72T	47	$ .10	$ .35
Edwards, Johnny	72T	416	$ .10	$ .35	Ellis, John	72TIA	48	$ .10	$ .35
Edwards, Johnny	73T	519	$ .06	$ .25	Ellis, John	73T	656	$ .35	$1.10
Edwards, Johnny	74T	635	$ .06	$ .25	Ellis, John	74T	128	$ .06	$ .25
Edwards, Marshall	82T	333	$ .01	$ .06	Ellis, John	75T	605	$ .06	$ .25
Edwards, Marshall	83T	582	$ .01	$ .06	Ellis, John	76T	383	$ .05	$ .20
Edwards, Marshall	84T	167	$ .01	$ .05	Ellis, John	76TTR	383	$ .05	$ .20
Edwards, Mike	79T	613	$ .02	$ .10	Ellis, John	77T	36	$ .05	$ .15
Edwards, Mike	79TRB	201	$ .02	$ .10	Ellis, John	78T	438	$ .02	$ .10
Edwards, Mike	80T	301	$ .01	$ .07	Ellis, John	79T	539	$ .02	$ .10
Edwards, Wayne	89TMLD	34	$ .01	$ .15	Ellis, John	80T	283	$ .01	$ .07
Egan, Dick	63T	169	$6.00	$18.00	Ellis, John	81T	339	$ .01	$ .07
Egan, Dick	64T	572	$1.50	$3.75	Ellis, John	82T	177	$ .01	$ .06
Egan, Dick	66T	536	$4.50	$15.00	Ellis, Sam	66T	250	$ .25	$ .85
Egan, Dick	67T	539	$1.35	$4.00	Ellis, Sammy	63T	29	$ .35	$1.10
Egan, Tom	65T	486	$ .50	$2.00	Ellis, Sammy	64T	33	$ .25	$ .85
Egan, Tom	66T	263	$ .25	$ .85	Ellis, Sammy	65T	507	$ .50	$2.00
Egan, Tom	67T	147	$ .25	$ .65	Ellis, Sammy	67T	176	$ .25	$ .65
Egan, Tom	69T	407	$ .25	$ .65	Ellis, Sammy	68T	453	$ .25	$ .65
Egan, Tom	70T	4	$ .10	$ .35	Ellis, Sammy	69T	32	$ .25	$ .65
Egan, Tom	71T	537	$ .30	$1.00	Ellsworth, Dick	60T	125	$ .50	$2.00
Egan, Tom	72T	207	$ .10	$ .35	Ellsworth, Dick	61T	427	$ .50	$2.00
Egan, Tom	73T	648	$ .35	$1.10	Ellsworth, Dick	62T	264	$ .35	$1.10
Egan, Tom	75T	88	$ .06	$ .25	Ellsworth, Dick	63T	399	$ .35	$1.20
Eichelberger, Juan	81T	478	$ .01	$ .07	Ellsworth, Dick	64T	1	$3.00	$12.00
Eichelberger, Juan	82T	366	$ .01	$ .06	Ellsworth, Dick	64T	220	$ .25	$ .85
Eichelberger, Juan	82T	614	$ .01	$ .06	Ellsworth, Dick	65T	165	$ .25	$ .65
Eichelberger, Juan	83T	168	$ .01	$ .06	Ellsworth, Dick	66T	447	$ .70	$2.10
Eichelberger, Juan	83TTR	29	$ .02	$ .10	Ellsworth, Dick	67T	359	$ .25	$ .65
Eichelberger, Juan	84T	226	$ .01	$ .05	Ellsworth, Dick	68T	406	$ .25	$ .65
Eichhorn, Mark	86TTR	34	$ .01	$ .15	Ellsworth, Dick	69T	605	$ .25	$ .85
Eichhorn, Mark	87T	371	$ .01	$ .10	Ellsworth, Dick	70T	59	$ .10	$ .35
Eichhorn, Mark	88T	749	$ .01	$ .10	Ellsworth, Dick	71T	309	$ .10	$ .35
Eichhorn, Mark	88TBB	208	$ .01	$ .05	Ellsworth, Steve	89T	299	$ .01	$ .04
Eichhorn, Mark	89T	274	$ .01	$ .04	Elster, Kevin	88T	8	$ .01	$ .30
Eichhorn, Mark	89TBB	188	$ .01	$ .05	Elster, Kevin	89T	356	$ .01	$ .04
Eichhorn, Mark	90T	513	$ .01	$ .03	Elster, Kevin	89TBB	16	$ .01	$ .05
Eiland, Dave	89T		$ .01	$ .03	Elster, Kevin	90T	734	$ .01	$ .03
Eilers, Dave	66T	534	$4.50	$15.00	Elston, Don	57T	376	$1.00	$3.75
Eisenreich, Jim	83T	197	$ .25	$1.00	Elston, Don	58T	363	$ .50	$2.00
Eisenreich, Jim	88T	348	$ .01	$ .03	Elston, Don	59T	520	$2.00	$7.00
Eisenreich, Jim	89TTR	28	$ .01	$ .05	Elston, Don	60T	233	$ .35	$1.10
Eisenreich, Jim	90T	246	$ .01	$ .03	Elston, Don	61T	169	$ .30	$1.00
Elia, Lee	66T	529	$4.50	$15.00	Elston, Don	62T	446	$ .70	$2.10
Elia, Lee	67T	406	$ .25	$ .85	Elston, Don	63T	515	$1.50	$3.75
Elia, Lee	68T	561	$ .30	$1.00	Elston, Don	64T	111	$ .25	$ .85
Elia, Lee	69T	312	$ .25	$ .85	Elston, Don	65T	436	$ .30	$1.00
Elia, Lee	83T	456	$ .01	$ .06	Engle, Dave	81T	328	$ .01	$ .07
Elia, Lee	87TTR	32	$ .01	$ .07	Engle, Dave	82T	738	$ .01	$ .06
Elia, Lee	88T	254	$ .01	$ .03	Engle, Dave	83T	294	$ .01	$ .06
Ellingsen, Bruce	75T	288	$ .06	$ .25	Engle, Dave	84T	463	$ .01	$ .05

TOPPS

Player	Year	No.	VG	EX/MT	Player	Year	No.	VG	EX/MT
Engle, Dave	85T	667	$ .01	$ .04	Essian, Jim	82T	269	$ .01	$ .06
Engle, Dave	86T	43	$ .01	$ .03	Essian, Jim	82TTR	31	$ .02	$ .10
Engle, Dave	88T	196	$ .01	$ .03	Essian, Jim	83T	646	$ .01	$ .06
Ennis, Del	51Tbb	4	$4.50	$20.00	Essian, Jim	83TTR	30	$ .02	$ .10
Ennis, Del	52T	223	$6.00	$18.00	Essian, Jim	84T	737	$ .01	$ .05
Ennis, Del	56T	220	$3.00	$9.00	Essian, Jim	84TTR	35	$ .02	$ .10
Ennis, Del	57T	260	$ .60	$2.50	Essian, Jim	85T	472	$ .01	$ .04
Ennis, Del	58T	60	$ .70	$2.25	Estelle, Dick	65T	282	$ .30	$1.00
Ennis, Del	59T	255	$ .50	$1.95	Estelle, Dick	66T	373	$ .25	$ .85
Eppard, Jim	89T	42	$ .01	$ .10	Estrada, Chuck	60T	126	$ .35	$1.10
Epstein, Mike	67T	204	$ .25	$ .65	Estrada, Chuck	61T	48	$ .50	$2.00
Epstein, Mike	68T	358	$ .25	$ .65	Estrada, Chuck	61T	395	$ .50	$2.00
Epstein, Mike	69T	461	$ .25	$ .65	Estrada, Chuck	62T	560	$3.75	$11.00
Epstein, Mike	69T	539	$1.25	$4.50	Estrada, Chuck	63T	465	$2.50	$6.50
Epstein, Mike	70T	235	$ .10	$ .35	Estrada, Chuck	64T	263	$ .25	$ .85
Epstein, Mike	71T	655	$ .70	$2.10	Estrada, Chuck	65T	378	$ .30	$1.00
Epstein, Mike	72T	715	$ .70	$2.10	Estrada, Chuck	67T	537	$1.35	$4.00
Epstein, Mike	73T	38	$ .06	$ .25	Estrada, Chuck	73T	549	$ .30	$1.00
Epstein, Mike	74T	650	$ .06	$ .25	Etchebarren, Andy	66T	27	$ .25	$ .85
Erautt, Ed	52T	171	$6.00	$19.00	Etchebarren, Andy	67T	457	$ .25	$ .85
Erautt, Ed	53T	226	$11.00	$37.50	Etchebarren, Andy	68T	204	$ .25	$ .65
Erickson, Roger	79T	81	$ .02	$ .10	Etchebarren, Andy	69T	634	$ .25	$ .85
Erickson, Roger	80T	256	$ .01	$ .07	Etchebarren, Andy	70T	213	$ .10	$ .35
Erickson, Roger	81T	434	$ .01	$ .07	Etchebarren, Andy	71T	501	$ .10	$ .35
Erickson, Roger	82T	153	$ .01	$ .06	Etchebarren, Andy	72T	26	$ .10	$ .35
Erickson, Roger	82TTR	30	$ .02	$ .10	Etchebarren, Andy	73T	618	$ .35	$1.10
Erickson, Roger	83T	539	$ .01	$ .06	Etchebarren, Andy	74T	488	$ .06	$ .25
Ermer, Cal	68T	206	$ .25	$ .65	Etchebarren, Andy	75T	583	$ .06	$ .25
Erskine, Carl	52T	250	$18.00	$70.00	Etchebarren, Andy	76T	129	$ .05	$ .20
Erskine, Carl	56T	233	$6.00	$20.00	Etchebarren, Andy	77T	454	$ .05	$ .15
Erskine, Carl	57T	252	$2.10	$7.50	Etchebarren, Andy	78T	313	$ .02	$ .10
Erskine, Carl	58T	258	$1.35	$4.00	Etheridge, Bobby	68T	126	$ .25	$ .65
Erskine, Carl	59T	217	$1.35	$4.00	Etheridge, Bobby	69T	604	$ .25	$ .85
Esasky, Nick	84T	192	$ .50	$2.00	Etheridge, Bobby	70T	107	$ .10	$ .35
Esasky, Nick	85T	779	$ .01	$ .25	Eufemia, Frank	86T	236	$ .01	$ .05
Esasky, Nick	86T	677	$ .01	$ .10	Evans, Al	52T	152	$6.00	$19.00
Esasky, Nick	87T	13	$ .01	$ .05	Evans, Barry	81T	72	$ .01	$ .07
Esasky, Nick	88T	364	$ .01	$ .03	Evans, Barry	82T	541	$ .01	$ .06
Esasky, Nick	88TBB	167	$ .01	$ .05	Evans, Darrell	70T	621	$5.00	$14.00
Esasky, Nick	89T	554	$ .01	$ .04	Evans, Darrell	72T	171	$ .50	$2.00
Esasky, Nick	89TBB	316	$ .01	$ .10	Evans, Darrell	72TIA	172	$ .15	$ .50
Esasky, Nick	89TTR	29	$ .01	$ .25	Evans, Darrell	73T	374	$ .25	$ .85
Esasky, Nick	90T	206	$ .01	$ .10	Evans, Darrell	74T	140	$ .25	$ .85
Espino, Juan	87T	239	$ .01	$ .03	Evans, Darrell	75T	475	$ .25	$ .85
Espinosa, Nino	77T	376	$ .05	$ .15	Evans, Darrell	76T	81	$ .25	$ .65
Espinosa, Nino	78T	197	$ .02	$ .10	Evans, Darrell	77T	571	$ .25	$ .65
Espinosa, Nino	79T	566	$ .02	$ .10	Evans, Darrell	78T	215	$ .05	$ .20
Espinosa, Nino	80T	447	$ .01	$ .07	Evans, Darrell	79T	410	$ .05	$ .20
Espinosa, Nino	81T	405	$ .01	$ .07	Evans, Darrell	80T	145	$ .03	$ .15
Espinoza, Alvaro	87T	529	$ .01	$ .03	Evans, Darrell	81T	648	$ .01	$ .07
Espinoza, Alvaro	89TTR	30	$ .01	$ .25	Evans, Darrell	82T	17	$ .03	$ .15
Espinoza, Alvaro	90T	791	$ .01	$ .10	Evans, Darrell	83T	448	$ .01	$ .06
Esposito, Sam	57T	301	$3.50	$13.00	Evans, Darrell	84T	325	$ .01	$ .05
Esposito, Sam	58T	425	$ .50	$2.00	Evans, Darrell	84TTR	36	$ .02	$ .10
Esposito, Sam	59T	438	$ .50	$1.95	Evans, Darrell	85T	792	$ .01	$ .04
Esposito, Sammy	60T	31	$ .35	$1.10	Evans, Darrell	86T	515	$ .01	$ .03
Esposito, Sammy	61T	323	$ .30	$1.00	Evans, Darrell	87T	265	$ .01	$ .10
Esposito, Sammy	62T	586	$3.75	$11.00	Evans, Darrell	88T	630	$ .01	$ .03
Esposito, Sammy	63T	181	$ .25	$ .85	Evans, Darrell	88TBB	82	$ .01	$ .05
Espy, Cecil	88TTR	36	$ .01	$ .15	Evans, Darrell	89TTR	31	$ .01	$ .10
Espy, Cecil	89T	221	$ .01	$ .10	Evans, Darrell	90T	55	$ .01	$ .10
Espy, Cecil	89TBB	36	$ .01	$ .05	Evans, Dwight	73T	614	$10.00	$40.00
Espy, Cecil	90T	496	$ .01	$ .03	Evans, Dwight	74T	351	$1.25	$7.50
Essegian, Chuck	58T	460	$ .50	$1.95	Evans, Dwight	75T	255	$1.50	$5.00
Essegian, Chuck	59T	278	$ .50	$1.95	Evans, Dwight	76T	575	$ .65	$2.50
Essegian, Chuck	60T	166	$ .35	$1.10	Evans, Dwight	77T	25	$ .35	$1.50
Essegian, Chuck	61T	384	$ .50	$2.00	Evans, Dwight	78T	695	$ .35	$1.00
Essegian, Chuck	62T	379	$ .70	$2.10	Evans, Dwight	79T	155	$ .20	$ .85
Essegian, Chuck	63T	103	$ .25	$ .85	Evans, Dwight	80T	405	$ .15	$ .75
Essian, Jim	77T	529	$ .05	$ .15	Evans, Dwight	81T	275	$ .05	$ .20
Essian, Jim	78T	98	$ .02	$ .10	Evans, Dwight	82T	162	$ .05	$ .25
Essian, Jim	79T	458	$ .02	$ .10	Evans, Dwight	82T	355	$ .05	$ .20
Essian, Jim	80T	341	$ .01	$ .07	Evans, Dwight	83T	135	$ .03	$ .15
Essian, Jim	81T	178	$ .01	$ .07	Evans, Dwight	84T	720	$ .03	$ .15
Essian, Jim	81TTR	759	$ .02	$ .10	Evans, Dwight	85T	580	$ .01	$ .10

Player	Year	No.	VG	EX/MT
Evans, Dwight	86T	60	$ .01	$ .10
Evans, Dwight	87T	645	$ .01	$ .10
Evans, Dwight	87TRB	3	$ .01	$ .03
Evans, Dwight	88T	470	$ .01	$ .10
Evans, Dwight	88TBB	6	$ .01	$ .10
Evans, Dwight	89T	205	$ .01	$ .04
Evans, Dwight	89TBB	193	$ .01	$ .10
Evans, Dwight	90T	375	$ .01	$ .03
Evers, Hoot	52T	222	$6.00	$19.00
Ewing, Sam	78T	344	$ .02	$ .10
Ewing, Sam	79T	521	$ .02	$ .10
Expos, Team	70T	509	$ .35	$1.10
Expos, Team	71T	674	$1.00	$3.00
Expos, Team	72T	582	$ .65	$2.00
Expos, Team	73T	576	$ .60	$1.75
Expos, Team	74T	508	$ .20	$ .75
Expos, Team Checklist	75T	101	$ .25	$ .85
Expos, Team Checklist	76T	216	$ .15	$ .50
Expos, Team Checklist	77T	647	$ .15	$ .50
Expos, Team Checklist	78T	244	$ .02	$ .10
Expos, Team Checklist	79T	606	$ .05	$ .25
Expos, Team Checklist	80T	479	$ .05	$ .25
Expos, Team Checklist	81T	680	$ .02	$ .20
Expos, Team Leaders	86T	576	$ .01	$ .03
Expos, Team Leaders	87T	381	$ .01	$ .03
Expos, Team Leaders	88T	111	$ .01	$ .03
Expos, Team Leaders	89T	81	$ .01	$ .04
Face, Roy	53T	246	$15.00	$50.00
Face, Roy	54T	87	$2.00	$7.00
Face, Roy	56T	13	$1.25	$3.50
Face, Roy	57T	166	$ .60	$2.50
Face, Roy	58T	74	$ .70	$2.25
Face, Roy	59T	339	$ .50	$1.95
Face, Roy	59T	428	$ .50	$1.95
Face, Roy	60T	20	$ .50	$2.00
Face, Roy	60T	115	$1.30	$5.00
Face, Roy	61T	250	$ .50	$2.00
Face, Roy	61T	370	$ .50	$2.00
Face, Roy	62T	210	$ .50	$2.00
Face, Roy	62T	423	$1.35	$4.00
Face, Roy	63T	409	$ .50	$2.00
Face, Roy	64T	539	$1.35	$4.00
Face, Roy	65T	347	$ .35	$1.10
Face, Roy	66T	461	$ .60	$1.75
Face, Roy	67T	49	$ .25	$ .85
Face, Roy	68T	198	$ .25	$ .85
Face, Roy	69T	207	$ .25	$ .85
Faedo, Lenny	82T	766	$1.50	$4.50
Faedo, Lenny	83T	671	$ .01	$ .06
Faedo, Lenny	84T	84	$ .01	$ .05
Fahey, Bill	72T	334	$ .10	$ .05
Fahey, Bill	73T	186	$ .06	$ .25
Fahey, Bill	74T	558	$ .06	$ .25
Fahey, Bill	75T	644	$ .06	$ .25
Fahey, Bill	76T	436	$ .05	$ .20
Fahey, Bill	77T	511	$ .05	$ .15
Fahey, Bill	78T	388	$ .02	$ .10
Fahey, Bill	80T	44	$ .01	$ .07
Fahey, Bill	81T	653	$ .01	$ .07
Fahey, Bill	81TTR	760	$ .02	$ .10
Fahey, Bill	82T	286	$ .01	$ .06
Fahey, Bill	83T	196	$ .01	$ .06
Fain, Ferris	51Trb	3	$1.35	$4.00
Fain, Ferris	52T	21	$14.00	$45.00
Fain, Ferris	53T	24	$3.75	$13.00
Fain, Ferris	54T	27	$2.00	$7.00
Fain, Ferris	55T	11	$2.10	$7.50
Fairey, Jim	68T	228	$ .25	$ .85
Fairey, Jim	69T	117	$ .25	$ .65
Fairey, Jim	71T	474	$ .10	$ .35
Fairey, Jim	72T	653	$ .25	$ .85
Fairey, Jim	73T	429	$ .06	$ .25
Fairly, Ron	59T	125	$1.35	$4.00
Fairly, Ron	60T	321	$ .50	$1.95
Fairly, Ron	61T	492	$ .50	$2.00

Player	Year	No.	VG	EX/MT
Fairly, Ron	62T	375	$ .70	$2.10
Fairly, Ron	63T	105	$ .25	$ .85
Fairly, Ron	64T	490	$ .40	$1.25

Player	Year	No.	VG	EX/MT
Fairly, Ron	65T	196	$ .25	$ .65
Fairly, Ron	66T	330	$ .25	$ .85
Fairly, Ron	67T	94	$ .25	$ .65
Fairly, Ron	68T	510	$ .30	$1.00
Fairly, Ron	69T	122	$ .25	$ .85
Fairly, Ron	70T	690	$ .50	$2.00
Fairly, Ron	71T	315	$ .10	$ .35
Fairly, Ron	72T	405	$ .25	$ .65
Fairly, Ron	73T	125	$ .10	$ .35
Fairly, Ron	74T	146	$ .06	$ .25
Fairly, Ron	75T	270	$ .06	$ .25
Fairly, Ron	76T	375	$ .05	$ .20
Fairly, Ron	77T	127	$ .05	$ .15
Fairly, Ron	78T	85	$ .02	$ .10
Fairly, Ron	79T	580	$ .02	$ .10
Falcone, Pete	76T	524	$ .05	$ .20
Falcone, Pete	76TTR	524	$ .05	$ .20
Falcone, Pete	77T	205	$ .05	$ .15
Falcone, Pete	78T	669	$ .02	$ .10
Falcone, Pete	79T	87	$ .02	$ .10
Falcone, Pete	80T	401	$ .01	$ .07
Falcone, Pete	81T	117	$ .01	$ .07
Falcone, Pete	82T	326	$ .01	$ .06
Falcone, Pete	83T	764	$ .01	$ .06
Falcone, Pete	83TTR	31	$ .02	$ .10
Falcone, Pete	84T	521	$ .01	$ .05
Falcone, Pete	85T	618	$ .01	$ .04
Fannin, Cliff	51Tbb	36	$5.50	$17.00
Fannin, Cliff	52T	285	$14.00	$45.00
Fannin, Cliff	53T	203	$3.75	$13.00
Fanning, Jim	85T	759	$ .01	$ .04
Fanok, Harry	63T	54	$1.25	$4.50
Fanok, Harry	64T	262	$ .35	$1.10
Fanzone, Carmen	73T	139	$ .06	$ .25
Fanzone, Carmen	74T	484	$ .06	$ .25
Fanzone, Carmen	75T	363	$ .06	$ .25
Fariss, Monty	89T	177	$ .10	$ .40
Farley, Bob	62T	426	$ .70	$2.10
Farmer, Billy	70T	444	$ .10	$ .35
Farmer, Ed	72T	116	$ .10	$ .35

TOPPS

Player	Year	No.	VG	EX/MT	Player	Year	No.	VG	EX/MT
Farmer, Ed	73T	272	$ .06	$ .25	Fernandez, Chico	63T	278	$ .25	$ .85
Farmer, Ed	74T	506	$ .06	$ .25	Fernandez, Frank	66T	584	$4.50	$15.00
Farmer, Ed	80T	702	$ .01	$ .07	Fernandez, Frank	68T	214	$ .35	$1.10
Farmer, Ed	81T	36	$ .01	$ .07	Fernandez, Frank	69T	557	$ .25	$ .85
Farmer, Ed	82T	328	$ .01	$ .06	Fernandez, Frank	70T	82	$ .10	$ .35
Farmer, Ed	82TTR	32	$ .02	$ .10	Fernandez, Frank	71T	468	$ .10	$ .35
Farmer, Ed	83T	459	$ .01	$ .06	Fernandez, Sid	85T	649	$ .15	$ .75
Farr, Steve	85T	664	$ .01	$ .04	Fernandez, Sid	86T	104	$ .01	$ .20
Farr, Steve	86TTR	35	$ .02	$ .10	Fernandez, Sid	87T	570	$ .03	$ .15
Farr, Steve	87T	473	$ .01	$ .03	Fernandez, Sid	88T	30	$ .01	$ .10
Farr, Steve	88T	222	$ .01	$ .03	Fernandez, Sid	89T	790	$ .01	$ .10
Farr, Steve	89T	507	$ .01	$ .04	Fernandez, Sid	89TBB	276	$ .01	$ .05
Farr, Steve	90T	149	$ .01	$ .03	Fernandez, Sid	90T	480	$ .01	$ .03
Farrell, Dick	58T	76	$1.00	$3.75	Fernandez, Tony	85T	48	$ .25	$1.25
Farrell, Dick	59T	175	$ .50	$1.95	Fernandez, Tony	86T	241	$ .01	$ .10
Farrell, Dick	60T	103	$ .35	$1.10	Fernandez, Tony	87T	485	$ .01	$ .03
Farrell, Dick	61T	522	$ .50	$2.00	Fernandez, Tony	88T	290	$ .01	$ .10
Farrell, Dick	62T	304	$ .35	$1.10	Fernandez, Tony	88TBB	187	$ .01	$ .05
Farrell, Dick	63T	9	$ .60	$1.75	Fernandez, Tony	89T	170	$ .01	$ .10
Farrell, Dick	63T	277	$ .25	$ .85	Fernandez, Tony	89TBB	157	$ .01	$ .10
Farrell, Dick	64T	560	$1.50	$3.75	Fernandez, Tony	90T	685	$ .01	$ .10
Farrell, Dick	69T	531	$ .25	$ .85	Ferrara, Al	64T	337	$ .25	$ .85
Farrell, John	88T	533	$ .01	$ .25	Ferrara, Al	65T	331	$ .30	$1.00
Farrell, John	88TBB	213	$ .01	$ .20	Ferrara, Al	66T	487	$ .70	$2.10
Farrell, John	89T	227	$ .01	$ .20	Ferrara, Al	67T	557	$1.35	$4.00
Farrell, John	89TBB	135	$ .01	$ .10	Ferrara, Al	68T	34	$ .25	$ .65
Farrell, John	90T	32	$ .01	$ .10	Ferrara, Al	69T	452	$ .25	$ .65
Farrell, Turk	65T	80	$ .25	$ .65	Ferrara, Al	70T	345	$ .10	$ .35
Farrell, Turk	66T	377	$ .25	$ .85	Ferrara, Al	71T	214	$ .10	$ .35
Farrell, Turk	67T	190	$ .25	$ .65	Ferrarese, Don	55T	185	$4.25	$13.00
Farrell, Turk	68T	217	$ .25	$ .65	Ferrarese, Don	56T	266	$1.80	$6.00
Fast, Darcy	72T	457	$ .10	$ .35	Ferrarese, Don	57T	146	$ .95	$3.50
Faul, Bill	63T	558	$1.50	$3.75	Ferrarese, Don	58T	469	$ .50	$1.95
Faul, Bill	64T	236	$ .25	$ .85	Ferrarese, Don	59T	247	$ .50	$1.95
Faul, Bill	66T	322	$ .25	$ .85	Ferrarese, Don	60T	477	$ .60	$1.75
Felder, Mike	87T	352	$ .01	$ .03	Ferrarese, Don	61T	558	$6.00	$18.00
Felder, Mike	88T	718	$ .01	$ .03	Ferrarese, Don	62T	547	$3.75	$11.00
Felder, Mike	89T	263	$ .01	$ .04	Ferraro, Mike	68T	539	$ .30	$1.00
Felder, Mike	90T	159	$ .01	$ .03	Ferraro, Mike	69T	83	$ .25	$ .65
Felix, Junior	89TMLD	35	$ .01	$ .35	Ferraro, Mike	72T	613	$ .25	$ .85
Felix, Junior	89TTR	32	$ .01	$ .75	Ferraro, Mike	83TTR	32	$ .02	$ .10
Felix, Junior	90T	347	$ .01	$ .35	Ferrer, Sergio	79T	397	$ .02	$ .10
Feller, Bob	51Trb	22	$7.00	$22.00	Ferrer, Sergio	80T	619	$ .01	$ .07
Feller, Bob	52T	88	$35.00	$115.00	Ferrick, Tom	60T	461	$1.25	$4.50
Feller, Bob	53T	54	$27.50	$85.00	Fetters, Mike	89TMLD	36	$ .01	$ .35
Feller, Bob	56T	200	$20.00	$60.00	Fetters, Mike	90T	14	$ .01	$ .10
Felske, John	73T	332	$ .06	$ .25	Fidrych, Mark	77T	7	$ .05	$ .15
Felske, John	85TTR	33	$ .02	$ .10	Fidrych, Mark	77T	265	$ .25	$ .85
Felske, John	86T	621	$ .01	$ .03	Fidrych, Mark	78T	45	$ .05	$ .20
Felske, John	87T	443	$ .01	$ .03	Fidrych, Mark	79T	625	$ .05	$ .20
Felton, Terry	83T	181	$ .01	$ .06	Fidrych, Mark	80T	445	$ .01	$ .07
Fenwick, Bob	72T	679	$ .60	$1.75	Fidrych, Mark	81T	150	$ .01	$ .07
Fenwick, Bob	73T	567	$ .35	$1.10	Fielder, Cecil	86T	386	$ .50	$6.00
Ferguson, Joe	72T	616	$ .25	$ .85	Fielder, Cecil	87T	178	$ .15	$1.00
Ferguson, Joe	73T	621	$ .50	$2.00	Fielder, Cecil	88T	618	$ .10	$ .50
Ferguson, Joe	74T	86	$ .06	$ .25	Fielder, Cecil	89T	541	$ .01	$ .25
Ferguson, Joe	75T	115	$ .06	$ .25	Fields, Bruce	89T	556	$ .01	$ .04
Ferguson, Joe	76T	329	$ .05	$ .20	Fiesella, Dan	68T	191	$ .25	$ .65
Ferguson, Joe	77T	573	$ .05	$ .15	Fife, Dan	74T	421	$ .06	$ .25
Ferguson, Joe	78T	226	$ .02	$ .10	Figueroa, Ed	75T	476	$ .06	$ .25
Ferguson, Joe	79T	671	$ .02	$ .10	Figueroa, Ed	76T	27	$ .05	$ .20
Ferguson, Joe	80T	51	$ .01	$ .07	Figueroa, Ed	76TTR	27	$ .05	$ .20
Ferguson, Joe	81T	711	$ .01	$ .07	Figueroa, Ed	77T	195	$ .05	$ .15
Ferguson, Joe	82T	514	$ .01	$ .06	Figueroa, Ed	78T	365	$ .02	$ .10
Ferguson, Joe	83T	416	$ .01	$ .06	Figueroa, Ed	79T	35	$ .02	$ .10
Fermin, Felix	88T	547	$ .01	$ .03	Figueroa, Ed	80T	555	$ .01	$ .07
Fermin, Felix	89T	303	$ .01	$ .04	Figueroa, Ed	81T	245	$ .01	$ .07
Fermin, Felix	89TTR	33	$ .01	$ .05	Figueroa, Jesus	81T	533	$ .01	$ .07
Fermin, Felix	90T	722	$ .01	$ .03	Filer, Tom	83T	508	$ .01	$ .06
Fernandez, Chico	57T	305	$3.50	$13.00	Filer, Tom	86T	312	$ .01	$ .03
Fernandez, Chico	58T	348	$ .50	$2.00	Filer, Tom	88TTR	37	$ .01	$ .05
Fernandez, Chico	59T	452	$ .50	$1.95	Filer, Tom	89T	419	$ .01	$ .05
Fernandez, Chico	60T	314	$ .50	$1.95	Filson, Pete	84T	568	$ .01	$ .05
Fernandez, Chico	61T	112	$ .30	$1.00	Filson, Pete	85T	97	$ .01	$ .04
Fernandez, Chico	62T	173	$ .35	$1.10	Filson, Pete	86T	122	$ .01	$ .03

Player	Year	No.	VG	EX/MT
Fimple, Jack	84T	263	$ .01	$ .05
Finch, Joel	79T	702	$ .02	$ .10
Finch, Joel	80T	662	$ .01	$ .07
Fingers, Rollie	69T	597	$10.00	$40.00
Fingers, Rollie	70T	502	$ .90	$2.75
Fingers, Rollie	71T	384	$ .95	$3.50
Fingers, Rollie	72T	241	$ .70	$2.00
Fingers, Rollie	73T	84	$ .50	$2.00
Fingers, Rollie	74T	212	$ .50	$2.00
Fingers, Rollie	75T	21	$ .35	$1.10
Fingers, Rollie	76T	405	$ .35	$1.10
Fingers, Rollie	77T	523	$ .35	$1.10
Fingers, Rollie	78T	140	$ .08	$ .35
Fingers, Rollie	78T	208	$ .05	$ .20
Fingers, Rollie	79T	8	$ .05	$ .25
Fingers, Rollie	79T	390	$ .08	$ .35
Fingers, Rollie	80T	651	$ .05	$ .25
Fingers, Rollie	81T	8	$ .01	$ .07
Fingers, Rollie	81T	229	$ .10	$ .50
Fingers, Rollie	81TTR	761	$ .15	$ .50
Fingers, Rollie	82T	168	$ .03	$ .15
Fingers, Rollie	82T	585	$ .05	$ .25
Fingers, Rollie	82TIA	586	$ .01	$ .06
Fingers, Rollie	83T	35	$ .03	$ .15
Fingers, Rollie	83T	36	$ .01	$ .06
Fingers, Rollie	84T	495	$ .02	$ .10
Fingers, Rollie	84T	717	$ .01	$ .05
Fingers, Rollie	84T	718	$ .01	$ .05
Fingers, Rollie	85T	750	$ .01	$ .10
Fingers, Rollie	86T	185	$ .02	$ .15
Finigan, Jim	55T	14	$1.35	$5.00
Finigan, Jim	56T	22	$1.25	$4.50
Finigan, Jim	57T	248	$ .95	$3.50
Finigan, Jim	58T	136	$ .50	$2.00
Finigan, Jim	59T	47	$1.00	$3.75
Finley, Chuck	87T	446	$ .01	$ .03

Player	Year	No.	VG	EX/MT
Finley, Chuck	88T	99	$ .01	$ .03
Finley, Chuck	88TBB	254	$ .01	$ .05
Finley, Chuck	89T	708	$ .01	$ .04
Finley, Chuck	89TBB	76	$ .01	$ .05
Finley, Chuck	90T	147	$ .01	$ .10
Finley, Steve	89TMLD	37	$ .01	$ .35
Finley, Steve	90T	349	$ .01	$ .15

Player	Year	No.	VG	EX/MT
Fiore, Mike	69T	376	$ .25	$ .65
Fiore, Mike	70T	709	$ .50	$2.00
Fiore, Mike	71T	287	$ .10	$ .35
Fiore, Mike	72T	199	$ .10	$ .35
Fiore, Mike	88TTR	38	$ .01	$ .25
Fiore, Mike	89TBB	8	$ .01	$ .10
Fireovid, Steve	87T	357	$ .01	$ .03
Fischer, Bill	58T	56	$1.00	$3.75
Fischer, Bill	59T	230	$ .50	$1.95
Fischer, Bill	60T	76	$ .35	$1.10
Fischer, Bill	61T	553	$6.00	$18.00
Fischer, Bill	63T	301	$ .35	$1.20
Fischer, Bill	64T	409	$ .40	$1.25
Fischer, Hank	63T	554	$1.50	$3.75
Fischer, Hank	64T	218	$ .25	$ .85
Fischer, Hank	65T	585	$1.50	$3.75
Fischer, Hank	66T	381	$ .25	$ .85
Fischer, Hank	67T	342	$ .25	$ .65
Fischlin, Mike	79T	718	$ .02	$ .10
Fischlin, Mike	83T	182	$ .01	$ .06
Fischlin, Mike	84T	689	$ .01	$ .05
Fischlin, Mike	85T	41	$ .01	$ .04
Fischlin, Mike	86T	283	$ .01	$ .03
Fischlin, Mike	87T	434	$ .01	$ .03
Fisella, Danny	72TIA	294	$ .10	$ .35
Fisher, Brian	86T	584	$ .01	$ .10
Fisher, Brian	87T	316	$ .01	$ .03
Fisher, Brian	87TTR	33	$ .01	$ .07
Fisher, Brian	88T	193	$ .01	$ .03
Fisher, Brian	88TBB	159	$ .01	$ .05
Fisher, Brian	89T	423	$ .01	$ .04
Fisher, Brian	90T	666	$ .01	$ .03
Fisher, Eddie	60T	23	$ .35	$1.10
Fisher, Eddie	61T	366	$ .30	$1.00
Fisher, Eddie	63T	6	$ .35	$1.10
Fisher, Eddie	63T	223	$ .25	$ .85
Fisher, Eddie	64T	66	$ .25	$ .85
Fisher, Eddie	65T	328	$ .30	$1.00
Fisher, Eddie	66T	85	$ .25	$ .85
Fisher, Eddie	66T	222	$ .50	$2.00
Fisher, Eddie	67T	434	$ .25	$ .85
Fisher, Eddie	68T	418	$ .25	$ .65
Fisher, Eddie	69T	315	$ .25	$ .85
Fisher, Eddie	70T	156	$ .10	$ .35
Fisher, Eddie	71T	631	$ .30	$1.00
Fisher, Eddie	72T	689	$ .70	$2.10
Fisher, Eddie	73T	439	$ .06	$ .25
Fisher, Fritz	64T	312	$ .25	$ .85
Fisher, Fritz	66T	209	$ .30	$1.00
Fisher, Jack	60T	46	$ .35	$1.10
Fisher, Jack	60T	399	$ .60	$1.75
Fisher, Jack	61T	463	$ .60	$1.75
Fisher, Jack	62T	203	$ .35	$1.10
Fisher, Jack	63T	474	$2.50	$6.50
Fisher, Jack	64T	422	$ .40	$1.25
Fisher, Jack	65T	93	$ .25	$ .65
Fisher, Jack	66T	316	$ .25	$ .85
Fisher, Jack	67T	533	$ .50	$2.00
Fisher, Jack	68T	444	$ .25	$ .65
Fisher, Jack	69T	318	$ .25	$ .85
Fisher, Jack	70T	684	$ .50	$2.00
Fisk, Carlton	72T	79	$15.00	$55.00
Fisk, Carlton	73T	193	$4.00	$15.00
Fisk, Carlton	74T	105	$1.25	$5.00
Fisk, Carlton	74TAS	331	$1.50	$5.00
Fisk, Carlton	75T	80	$ .50	$2.00
Fisk, Carlton	76T	365	$ .75	$3.00
Fisk, Carlton	77T	640	$ .50	$2.00
Fisk, Carlton	78T	270	$ .30	$1.00
Fisk, Carlton	79T	680	$ .30	$1.00
Fisk, Carlton	80T	40	$ .25	$1.00
Fisk, Carlton	81T	480	$ .02	$ .25
Fisk, Carlton	81TTR	762	$ .35	$1.50
Fisk, Carlton	82T	110	$ .05	$ .25
Fisk, Carlton	82TAS	554	$ .02	$ .10

TOPPS

Player	Year	No.	VG	EX/MT	Player	Year	No.	VG	EX/MT
Fisk, Carlton	82TIA	111	$ .02	$ .10	Fletcher, Scott	87T	462	$ .01	$ .03
Fisk, Carlton	83T	20	$ .05	$ .20	Fletcher, Scott	88T	345	$ .01	$ .03
Fisk, Carlton	83TAS	393	$ .01	$ .06	Fletcher, Scott	88TBB	19	$ .01	$ .05
Fisk, Carlton	84T	216	$ .01	$ .05	Fletcher, Scott	89T	295	$ .01	$ .04
Fisk, Carlton	84T	560	$ .02	$ .10	Fletcher, Scott	89TBB	205	$ .01	$ .05
Fisk, Carlton	85T	770	$ .01	$ .10	Fletcher, Scott	90T	565	$ .01	$ .03
Fisk, Carlton	85TRB	1	$ .01	$ .10	Flinn, John	79T	701	$ .02	$ .10
Fisk, Carlton	86T	290	$ .01	$ .10	Flinn, John	81T	659	$ .01	$ .07
Fisk, Carlton	86TAS	719	$ .01	$ .03	Floethe, Chris	72T	268	$ .10	$ .35
Fisk, Carlton	87T	756	$ .01	$ .10	Flood, Curt	58T	464	$3.00	$10.00
Fisk, Carlton	88T	385	$ .01	$ .10	Flood, Curt	59T	353	$ .50	$1.95
Fisk, Carlton	88TBB	197	$ .01	$ .10	Flood, Curt	60T	275	$ .70	$2.00
Fisk, Carlton	89T	695	$ .01	$ .04	Flood, Curt	61T	438	$ .60	$1.75
Fisk, Carlton	89TBB	24	$ .01	$ .20	Flood, Curt	62T	590	$5.00	$16.00
Fisk, Carlton	90T	420	$ .01	$ .03	Flood, Curt	63T	505	$3.00	$9.00
Fisk, Carlton	90TAS	392	$ .01	$ .03	Flood, Curt	64T	103	$ .25	$ .85
Fitzgerald, Ed	52T	236	$6.00	$19.00	Flood, Curt	65T	415	$ .35	$1.10
Fitzgerald, Ed	56T	198	$2.50	$8.00	Flood, Curt	66T	60	$ .30	$1.00
Fitzgerald, Ed	57T	367	$1.00	$3.75	Flood, Curt	67T	63	$1.35	$4.00
Fitzgerald, Ed	58T	236	$ .50	$2.00	Flood, Curt	67T	245	$ .15	$ .50
Fitzgerald, Ed	59T	33	$1.00	$3.75	Flood, Curt	68T	180	$ .35	$1.10
Fitzgerald, Ed	60T	423	$ .50	$1.95	Flood, Curt	69T	540	$ .25	$ .85
Fitzgerald, Mike	84TTR	37	$ .02	$ .10	Flood, Curt	69TAS	426	$ .25	$ .65
Fitzgerald, Mike	85T	104	$ .01	$ .04	Flood, Curt	70T	360	$ .35	$1.10
Fitzgerald, Mike	85TTR	34	$ .02	$ .10	Flood, Curt	71T	535	$ .30	$1.00
Fitzgerald, Mike	86T	503	$ .01	$ .03	Flores, Gil	78T	268	$ .02	$ .10
Fitzgerald, Mike	87T	212	$ .01	$ .03	Flores, Gil	80T	478	$ .01	$ .07
Fitzgerald, Mike	88T	674	$ .01	$ .03	Floyd, Bob	69T	597	$10.00	$40.00
Fitzgerald, Mike	89T	23	$ .01	$ .04	Floyd, Bobby	70T	101	$ .10	$ .35
Fitzgerald, Mike	90T	484	$ .01	$ .03	Floyd, Bobby	71T	646	$ .70	$2.10
Fitzmorris, Al	70T	241	$ .10	$ .35	Floyd, Bobby	72T	273	$ .10	$ .35
Fitzmorris, Al	71T	564	$ .30	$1.00	Floyd, Bobby	74T	41	$ .06	$ .25
Fitzmorris, Al	72T	349	$ .10	$ .35	Flynn, Doug	76T	518	$ .06	$ .25
Fitzmorris, Al	73T	643	$ .35	$1.10	Flynn, Doug	77T	186	$ .05	$ .15
Fitzmorris, Al	74T	191	$ .06	$ .25	Flynn, Doug	78T	453	$ .02	$ .10
Fitzmorris, Al	75T	24	$ .06	$ .25	Flynn, Doug	79T	229	$ .02	$ .10
Fitzmorris, Al	76T	144	$ .05	$ .20	Flynn, Doug	80T	58	$ .01	$ .07
Fitzmorris, Al	77T	449	$ .05	$ .15	Flynn, Doug	81T	634	$ .01	$ .07
Fitzmorris, Al	78T	227	$ .02	$ .10	Flynn, Doug	82T	302	$ .01	$ .06
Fitzmorris, Al	79T	638	$ .02	$ .10	Flynn, Doug	82TTR	33	$ .02	$ .10
Fitzpatrick, John	54T	213	$2.10	$7.50	Flynn, Doug	83T	169	$ .01	$ .06
Fitzsimmons, Fred	60T	462	$ .95	$3.50	Flynn, Doug	84T	749	$ .01	$ .05
Flanagan, Mike	77T	106	$ .10	$ .35	Flynn, Doug	85T	554	$ .01	$ .04
Flanagan, Mike	76T	589	$ .35	$1.10	Flynn, Doug	86T	436	$ .01	$ .03
Flanagan, Mike	78T	341	$ .02	$ .10	Fodge, Gene	58T	449	$ .50	$1.95
Flanagan, Mike	79T	160	$ .08	$ .30	Foiles, Henry "Hank"	53T	252	$11.00	$37.50
Flanagan, Mike	80T	205	$ .05	$ .20	Foiles, Hank	57T	104	$ .95	$3.50
Flanagan, Mike	80T	640	$ .01	$ .07	Foiles, Hank	58T	4	$1.00	$3.75
Flanagan, Mike	81T	10	$ .01	$ .07	Foiles, Hank	59T	294	$ .50	$1.95
Flanagan, Mike	82T	520	$ .01	$ .06	Foiles, Hank	60T	77	$ .35	$1.10
Flanagan, Mike	83T	445	$ .01	$ .06	Foiles, Hank	61T	277	$ .30	$1.00
Flanagan, Mike	84T	295	$ .01	$ .05	Foiles, Hank	62T	112	$ .35	$1.10
Flanagan, Mike	85T	780	$ .01	$ .04	Foiles, Hank	63T	326	$ .35	$1.20
Flanagan, Mike	86T	365	$ .01	$ .03	Foiles, Hank	64T	554	$1.50	$3.75
Flanagan, Mike	87T	748	$ .01	$ .03	Foley, Marvis	81T	646	$ .01	$ .07
Flanagan, Mike	88T	623	$ .01	$ .03	Foley, Marvis	83T	409	$ .01	$ .06
Flanagan, Mike	89T	139	$ .01	$ .04	Foley, Marvis	85T	621	$ .01	$ .04
Flanagan, Mike	89TBB	243	$ .01	$ .05	Foley, Tom	84T	632	$ .01	$ .05
Flanagan, Mike	90T	78	$ .01	$ .03	Foley, Tom	85T	107	$ .01	$ .04
Flannery, Tim	80T	685	$ .01	$ .07	Foley, Tom	86T	466	$ .01	$ .03
Flannery, Tim	81T	579	$ .01	$ .07	Foley, Tom	87T	78	$ .01	$ .03
Flannery, Tim	82T	249	$ .01	$ .06	Foley, Tom	88T	251	$ .01	$ .03
Flannery, Tim	83T	38	$ .01	$ .06	Foley, Tom	89T	529	$ .01	$ .04
Flannery, Tim	84T	674	$ .01	$ .05	Foley, Tom	89TBB	261	$ .01	$ .05
Flannery, Tim	85T	182	$ .01	$ .04	Foley, Tom	90T	341	$ .01	$ .03
Flannery, Tim	86T	413	$ .01	$ .03	Foli, Tim	71T	83	$ .10	$ .35
Flannery, Tim	87T	763	$ .01	$ .03	Foli, Tim	72T	707	$ .70	$2.10
Flannery, Tim	88T	513	$ .01	$ .03	Foli, Tim	72TIA	708	$ .70	$2.10
Flannery, Tim	89T	379	$ .01	$ .04	Foli, Tim	73T	19	$ .06	$ .25
Flannery, Tim	89TBB	174	$ .01	$ .05	Foli, Tim	74T	217	$ .06	$ .25
Fletcher, Darrin	89TMLD	38	$ .01	$ .15	Foli, Tim	75T	149	$ .06	$ .25
Fletcher, Scott	84T	364	$ .01	$ .05	Foli, Tim	76T	397	$ .05	$ .20
Fletcher, Scott	85T	78	$ .01	$ .04	Foli, Tim	77T	76	$ .05	$ .15
Fletcher, Scott	86T	187	$ .01	$ .03	Foli, Tim	78T	167	$ .02	$ .10
Fletcher, Scott	86TTR	36	$ .02	$ .10	Foli, Tim	79T	403	$ .02	$ .10

Player	Year	No.	VG	EX/MT
Foli, Tim	80T	246	$ .01	$ .07
Foli, Tim	81T	501	$ .01	$ .07
Foli, Tim	82T	618	$ .01	$ .06
Foli, Tim	82TTR	34	$ .02	$ .10
Foli, Tim	83T	738	$ .01	$ .06
Foli, Tim	84T	342	$ .01	$ .05
Foli, Tim	84TTR	38	$ .02	$ .10
Foli, Tim	85T	271	$ .01	$ .04
Foli, Tim	85T	456	$ .01	$ .04
Folkers, Rich	71T	648	$1.00	$4.00
Folkers, Rich	73T	649	$ .35	$1.10
Folkers, Rich	74T	417	$ .06	$ .25
Folkers, Rich	75T	98	$ .06	$ .25
Folkers, Rich	76T	611	$ .05	$ .20
Folkers, Rich	77T	372	$ .05	$ .15
Fondy, Dee	52T	359	$39.00	$135.00
Fondy, Dee	56T	112	$1.25	$4.50
Fondy, Dee	57T	42	$ .95	$3.50
Fondy, Dee	58T	157	$ .50	$2.00
Fontenot, Ray	84T	19	$ .01	$ .05
Fontenot, Ray	85T	507	$ .01	$ .04
Fontenot, Ray	85TTR	35	$ .02	$ .10
Fontenot, Ray	86T	308	$ .01	$ .03
Fontenot, Ray	87T	124	$ .01	$ .03
Foor, Jim	72T	257	$ .10	$ .35
Foote, Barry	74T	603	$ .06	$ .25
Foote, Barry	75T	229	$ .06	$ .25
Foote, Barry	76T	42	$ .05	$ .20
Foote, Barry	77T	612	$ .05	$ .15
Foote, Barry	78T	513	$ .02	$ .10
Foote, Barry	79T	161	$ .02	$ .10
Foote, Barry	80T	398	$ .01	$ .07
Foote, Barry	81T	492	$ .01	$ .07
Foote, Barry	81TTR	763	$ .02	$ .10
Foote, Barry	82T	706	$ .01	$ .06
Foote, Barry	83T	697	$ .01	$ .06
Ford, Curt	87T	399	$ .01	$ .03
Ford, Curt	88T	612	$ .01	$ .03
Ford, Curt	89T	132	$ .01	$ .04
Ford, Curt	90T	39	$ .01	$ .03
Ford, Dan	76T	313	$ .05	$ .20
Ford, Dan	77T	555	$ .05	$ .15
Ford, Dan	78T	275	$ .02	$ .10
Ford, Dan	79T	385	$ .02	$ .10
Ford, Dan	80T	20	$ .01	$ .07
Ford, Dan	81T	422	$ .01	$ .07
Ford, Dan	82T	134	$ .01	$ .06
Ford, Dan	82TTR	35	$ .02	$ .10
Ford, Dan	83T	683	$ .01	$ .06
Ford, Dan	84T	530	$ .01	$ .05
Ford, Dan	85T	252	$ .01	$ .04
Ford, Dan	86T	753	$ .01	$ .03
Ford, Dave	80T	661	$ .01	$ .07
Ford, Dave	81T	706	$ .01	$ .07
Ford, Dave	82T	174	$ .01	$ .06
Ford, Ted	71T	612	$ .30	$1.00
Ford, Ted	72T	24	$ .10	$ .35
Ford, Ted	73T	299	$ .06	$ .25
Ford, Ted	74T	617	$ .06	$ .25
Ford, Whitey	53T	207	$45.00	$135.00
Ford, Whitey	54T	37	$30.00	$100.00
Ford, Whitey	56T	240	$35.00	$110.00
Ford, Whitey	57T	25	$30.00	$87.50
Ford, Whitey	58T	320	$20.00	$60.00
Ford, Whitey	59T	430	$14.00	$42.50
Ford, Whitey	60T	35	$10.00	$40.00
Ford, Whitey	61T	160	$6.00	$25.00
Ford, Whitey	61TAS	586	$22.00	$82.50
Ford, Whitey	62T	57	$ .50	$1.95
Ford, Whitey	62T	59	$ .50	$1.95
Ford, Whitey	62T	310	$7.00	$25.00
Ford, Whitey	62T	315	$1.50	$6.50
Ford, Whitey	62TAS	475	$4.00	$13.00
Ford, Whitey	63T	6	$ .35	$1.10
Ford, Whitey	63T	446	$10.00	$40.00

Player	Year	No.	VG	EX/MT
Ford, Whitey	64T	4	$1.50	$6.00
Ford, Whitey	64T	380	$6.00	$24.00
Ford, Whitey	65T	330	$10.00	$30.00

Player	Year	No.	VG	EX/MT
Ford, Whitey	66T	160	$6.25	$25.00
Ford, Whitey	67T	5	$5.50	$17.50
Fornieles, Mike	54T	154	$2.10	$7.50
Fornieles, Mike	57T	116	$ .95	$3.50
Fornieles, Mike	58T	361	$ .50	$2.00
Fornieles, Mike	59T	473	$ .50	$1.95
Fornieles, Mike	60T	54	$ .35	$1.10
Fornieles, Mike	61T	113	$ .30	$1.00
Fornieles, Mike	62T	512	$ .70	$2.10
Fornieles, Mike	63T	28	$ .25	$ .85
Forsch, Bob	75T	51	$ .12	$ .40
Forsch, Bob	76T	426	$ .05	$ .20
Forsch, Bob	77T	381	$ .05	$ .15
Forsch, Bob	77T	632	$ .05	$ .15
Forsch, Bob	70T	58	$ .02	$ .10
Forsch, Bob	79T	230	$ .02	$ .10
Forsch, Bob	80T	535	$ .01	$ .07
Forsch, Bob	81T	140	$ .01	$ .07
Forsch, Bob	82T	186	$ .05	$ .25
Forsch, Bob	82T	775	$ .01	$ .06
Forsch, Bob	83T	415	$ .01	$ .06
Forsch, Bob	84T	5	$ .02	$ .10
Forsch, Bob	84T	75	$ .01	$ .05
Forsch, Bob	85T	631	$ .01	$ .04
Forsch, Bob	86T	322	$ .01	$ .03
Forsch, Bob	87T	257	$ .01	$ .03
Forsch, Bob	88T	586	$ .01	$ .03
Forsch, Bob	89T	163	$ .01	$ .04
Forsch, Ken	71T	102	$ .10	$ .35
Forsch, Ken	72T	394	$ .10	$ .35
Forsch, Ken	73T	589	$ .35	$1.10
Forsch, Ken	74T	91	$ .06	$ .25
Forsch, Ken	75T	357	$ .06	$ .25
Forsch, Ken	76T	357	$ .05	$ .20
Forsch, Ken	77T	21	$ .05	$ .15
Forsch, Ken	77T	632	$ .05	$ .15
Forsch, Ken	78T	181	$ .02	$ .10
Forsch, Ken	79T	534	$ .02	$ .10
Forsch, Ken	80T	642	$ .01	$ .07
Forsch, Ken	81T	269	$ .01	$ .07

Player	Year	No.	VG	EX/MT	Player	Year	No.	VG	EX/MT
Forsch, Ken	81TTR	764	$ .02	$ .10	Foster, Leo	77T	458	$ .05	$ .15
Forsch, Ken	82T	276	$ .03	$ .15	Foster, Leo	78T	229	$ .02	$ .10
Forsch, Ken	82T	385	$ .01	$ .06	Foster, Roy	71T	107	$ .10	$ .35
Forsch, Ken	83T	625	$ .01	$ .06	Foster, Roy	72T	329	$ .10	$ .35
Forsch, Ken	84T	765	$ .01	$ .05	Foucault, Steve	74T	294	$ .06	$ .25
Forsch, Ken	85T	442	$ .01	$ .04	Foucault, Steve	75T	283	$ .06	$ .25
Forster, Terry	72T	539	$ .50	$2.00	Foucault, Steve	76T	303	$ .05	$ .20
Forster, Terry	73T	129	$ .10	$ .35	Foucault, Steve	77T	459	$ .05	$ .15
Forster, Terry	74T	310	$ .06	$ .25	Foucault, Steve	78T	68	$ .02	$ .10
Forster, Terry	75T	137	$ .06	$ .25	Fowler, Art	55T	3	$1.35	$5.00
Forster, Terry	75T	313	$ .25	$ .85	Fowler, Art	56T	47	$1.25	$4.50
Forster, Terry	76T	437	$ .05	$ .20	Fowler, Art	57T	233	$ .95	$3.50
Forster, Terry	77T	271	$ .05	$ .15	Fowler, Art	59T	508	$2.00	$7.00
Forster, Terry	78T	347	$ .02	$ .10	Fowler, Art	62T	128	$ .35	$1.10
Forster, Terry	79T	23	$ .02	$ .10	Fowler, Art	63T	454	$2.50	$6.50
Forster, Terry	80T	605	$ .01	$ .07	Fowler, Art	64T	349	$ .25	$ .85
Forster, Terry	81T	104	$ .01	$ .07	Fowler, Art	73T	323	$ .30	$1.00
Forster, Terry	82T	444	$ .01	$ .06	Fowler, Art	74T	379	$ .15	$ .50
Forster, Terry	83T	583	$ .01	$ .06	Fowler, Dick	52T	210	$6.00	$19.00
Forster, Terry	83TTR	33	$ .02	$ .10	Fowlkes, Alan	83T	543	$ .01	$ .06
Forster, Terry	84T	791	$ .01	$ .05	Fox, Charlie	71T	517	$ .10	$ .35
Forster, Terry	85T	248	$ .01	$ .04	Fox, Charlie	72T	129	$ .10	$ .35
Forster, Terry	86T	363	$ .01	$ .03	Fox, Charlie	73T	252	$ .25	$ .65
Forster, Terry	86TTR	37	$ .02	$ .10	Fox, Charlie	74T	78	$ .06	$ .25
Forster, Terry	87T	652	$ .01	$ .03	Fox, Howie	52T	209	$6.00	$19.00
Fosnow, Jerry	65T	529	$1.50	$3.75	Fox, Howie	53T	22	$3.75	$13.00
Fossas, Tony	90T	34	$ .01	$ .03	Fox, Howie	54T	246	$2.10	$7.50
Fosse, Ray	69T	244	$ .25	$ .85	Fox, Nellie	56T	118	$3.00	$12.00
Fosse, Ray	70T	184	$ .10	$ .35	Fox, Nellie	57T	38	$2.50	$9.50
Fosse, Ray	71T	125	$ .10	$ .35	Fox, Nellie	58T	400	$2.00	$6.00
Fosse, Ray	72T	470	$ .10	$ .35	Fox, Nellie	58TAS	479	$1.35	$4.00
Fosse, Ray	73T	226	$ .06	$ .25	Fox, Nellie	59T	30	$4.00	$16.00
Fosse, Ray	74T	420	$ .06	$ .25	Fox, Nellie	59T	408	$ .60	$1.80
Fosse, Ray	75T	486	$ .06	$ .25	Fox, Nellie	59TAS	556	$2.50	$7.50
Fosse, Ray	76T	554	$ .05	$ .20	Fox, Nellie	60T	100	$1.35	$4.00
Fosse, Ray	76TTR	554	$ .05	$ .20	Fox, Nellie	60T	429	$ .60	$1.75
Fosse, Ray	77T	267	$ .05	$ .15	Fox, Nellie	60TAS	555	$3.00	$9.00
Fosse, Ray	78T	415	$ .02	$ .10	Fox, Nellie	61T	30	$1.35	$4.00
Fosse, Ray	79T	51	$ .02	$ .10	Fox, Nellie	61TAS	570	$7.50	$22.50
Fosse, Ray	80T	327	$ .01	$ .07	Fox, Nellie	61TMVP	477	$ .75	$2.00
Foster, Alan	69T	266	$ .25	$ .85	Fox, Nellie	62T	73	$1.35	$4.00
Foster, Alan	70T	369	$ .10	$ .35	Fox, Nellie	63T	525	$2.50	$7.00
Foster, Alan	71T	207	$ .10	$ .35	Fox, Nellie	64T	81	$1.75	$7.00
Foster, Alan	72T	521	$ .10	$ .35	Fox, Nellie	64T	205	$ .70	$2.00
Foster, Alan	73T	543	$ .15	$ .75	Fox, Nellie	65T	485	$1.35	$4.00
Foster, Alan	74T	442	$ .06	$ .25	Fox, Nellie	75T	197	$ .30	$1.00
Foster, Alan	75T	296	$ .06	$ .25	Fox, Terry	61T	459	$ .50	$2.00
Foster, Alan	76T	266	$ .05	$ .20	Fox, Terry	62T	196	$ .35	$1.10
Foster, Alan	77T	108	$ .05	$ .15	Fox, Terry	63T	44	$ .25	$ .85
Foster, George	71T	276	$1.75	$5.00	Fox, Terry	64T	387	$ .40	$1.25
Foster, George	72T	256	$ .50	$1.50	Fox, Terry	65T	576	$1.50	$3.75
Foster, George	73T	399	$ .50	$1.50	Fox, Terry	66T	472	$ .70	$2.10
Foster, George	74T	646	$ .40	$1.25	Fox, Terry	67T	181	$ .25	$ .65
Foster, George	75T	87	$ .40	$1.25	Foy, Joe	66T	456	$ .70	$2.10
Foster, George	76T	179	$ .25	$1.00	Foy, Joe	67T	331	$ .25	$ .65
Foster, George	77T	3	$ .30	$1.00	Foy, Joe	68T	387	$ .25	$ .65
Foster, George	77T	347	$ .30	$1.00	Foy, Joe	69T	93	$ .25	$ .65
Foster, George	78T	202	$ .05	$ .20	Foy, Joe	70T	138	$ .10	$ .35
Foster, George	78T	203	$ .05	$ .20	Foy, Joe	71T	706	$ .70	$2.10
Foster, George	78T	500	$ .25	$ .65	Foytack, Paul	57T	77	$ .95	$3.50
Foster, George	79T	2	$ .25	$ .65	Foytack, Paul	58T	282	$ .50	$2.00
Foster, George	79T	3	$ .25	$ .65	Foytack, Paul	59T	233	$ .50	$1.95
Foster, George	79T	600	$ .10	$ .35	Foytack, Paul	60T	364	$ .50	$1.95
Foster, George	80T	400	$ .05	$ .25	Foytack, Paul	61T	171	$ .30	$1.00
Foster, George	81T	200	$ .05	$ .20	Foytack, Paul	62T	349	$ .35	$1.10
Foster, George	82T	700	$ .05	$ .25	Foytack, Paul	63T	327	$ .35	$1.20
Foster, George	82TAS	342	$ .10	$ .50	Foytack, Paul	64T	149	$ .25	$ .85
Foster, George	82TIA	701	$ .02	$ .15	Frailing, Ken	74T	605	$ .30	$1.50
Foster, George	82TTR	36	$ .05	$ .25	Frailing, Ken	75T	436	$ .06	$ .25
Foster, George	83T	80	$ .01	$ .06	Francis, Earl	61T	54	$ .30	$1.00
Foster, George	84T	350	$ .01	$ .05	Francis, Earl	62T	252	$ .35	$1.10
Foster, George	85T	170	$ .01	$ .04	Francis, Earl	63T	303	$ .35	$1.20
Foster, George	86T	680	$ .01	$ .03	Francis, Earl	64T	117	$ .25	$ .85
Foster, Leo	74T	607	$ .06	$ .25	Franco, John	85T	417	$ .35	$1.10
Foster, Leo	75T	418	$ .06	$ .25	Franco, John	86T	54	$ .05	$ .25

Player	Year	No.	VG	EX/MT
Franco, John	87T	305	$ .01	$ .10
Franco, John	88T	730	$ .01	$ .10
Franco, John	88TBB	232	$ .01	$ .10
Franco, John	89T	290	$ .01	$ .10
Franco, John	90T	120	$ .01	$ .10
Franco, Julio	83TTR	34	$ .90	$3.25
Franco, Julio	84T	48	$ .50	$1.50
Franco, Julio	85T	237	$ .10	$ .50
Franco, Julio	86T	391	$ .01	$ .20
Franco, Julio	87T	160	$ .01	$ .15
Franco, Julio	88T	683	$ .01	$ .10
Franco, Julio	88TBB	135	$ .01	$ .10
Franco, Julio	89T	55	$ .01	$ .10
Franco, Julio	89TAS	398	$ .01	$ .04
Franco, Julio	89TBB	288	$ .01	$ .10
Franco, Julio	89TTR	34	$ .01	$ .10
Franco, Julio	90T	550	$ .01	$ .03
Franco, Julio	90TAS	386	$ .01	$ .03
Francona, Terry	82T	118	$ .03	$ .15
Francona, Terry	83T	267	$ .01	$ .06
Francona, Terry	84T	496	$ .01	$ .05
Francona, Terry	85T	134	$ .01	$ .10
Francona, Terry	85T	578	$ .01	$ .04
Francona, Terry	86T	374	$ .01	$ .03
Francona, Terry	86TTR	38	$ .02	$ .10
Francona, Terry	87T	785	$ .01	$ .03
Francona, Terry	87TTR	34	$ .01	$ .07
Francona, Terry	88T	686	$ .01	$ .03
Francona, Terry	89T	31	$ .01	$ .04
Francona, Terry	89TTR	35	$ .01	$ .05
Francona, Terry	90T	214	$ .01	$ .03
Francona, Tito	57T	184	$ .95	$3.50
Francona, Tito	58T	316	$ .50	$2.00
Francona, Tito	59T	268	$ .50	$1.95
Francona, Tito	60T	30	$ .35	$1.10
Francona, Tito	60T	260	$ .50	$2.00
Francona, Tito	61T	503	$ .50	$2.00
Francona, Tito	62T	97	$ .35	$1.10
Francona, Tito	63T	248	$ .25	$ .85
Francona, Tito	63T	392	$ .24	$1.25
Francona, Tito	64T	583	$1.35	$4.00
Francona, Tito	65T	256	$ .30	$1.00
Francona, Tito	66T	163	$ .25	$ .85
Francona, Tito	67T	443	$ .25	$ .85
Francona, Tito	68T	527	$ .30	$1.00
Francona, Tito	69T	398	$ .25	$ .65
Francona, Tito	70T	663	$ .50	$2.00
Francona, Tito	85T	134	$ .01	$ .10
Franks, Herman	52T	385	$50.00	$150.00
Franks, Herman	65T	32	$ .25	$ .65
Franks, Herman	66T	537	$4.50	$15.00
Franks, Herman	67T	116	$ .25	$ .65
Franks, Herman	68T	267	$ .25	$ .65
Franks, Herman	78T	234	$ .02	$ .10
Fraser, Willie	87TTR	35	$ .05	$ .20
Fraser, Willie	88T	363	$ .01	$ .03
Fraser, Willie	88TBB	183	$ .01	$ .05
Fraser, Willie	89T	679	$ .01	$ .04
Fraser, Willie	89TBB	272	$ .01	$ .05
Fraser, Willie	90T	477	$ .01	$ .03
Frazier, George	79T	724	$ .25	$ .65
Frazier, George	80T	684	$ .08	$ .40
Frazier, George	82T	349	$ .01	$ .06
Frazier, George	83T	123	$ .01	$ .06
Frazier, George	84T	539	$ .01	$ .05
Frazier, George	84TTR	39	$ .02	$ .10
Frazier, George	85T	19	$ .01	$ .04
Frazier, George	86T	431	$ .01	$ .03
Frazier, George	87T	207	$ .01	$ .03
Frazier, George	88T	709	$ .01	$ .03
Frazier, Joe	55T	89	$1.35	$5.00
Frazier, Joe	56T	141	$1.25	$4.50
Freed, Roger	70T	477	$ .10	$ .35
Freed, Roger	71T	362	$ .10	$ .35
Freed, Roger	72T	69	$ .10	$ .35

ROGER FREED

Player	Year	No.	VG	EX/MT
Freed, Roger	78T	504	$ .02	$ .10
Freed, Roger	79T	111	$ .02	$ .10
Freed, Roger	80T	418	$ .01	$ .07
Freehan, Bill	63T	466	$6.00	$18.00
Freehan, Bill	64T	407	$ .40	$2.25
Freehan, Bill	65T	390	$ .35	$1.10
Freehan, Bill	66T	145	$ .25	$ .85
Freehan, Bill	67T	48	$ .25	$ .65
Freehan, Bill	68T	470	$ .30	$1.00
Freehan, Bill	68TAS	375	$ .25	$ .65
Freehan, Bill	69T	390	$ .25	$ .65
Freehan, Bill	69TAS	431	$ .25	$ .65
Freehan, Bill	70T	335	$ .10	$ .35
Freehan, Bill	70TAS	465	$ .10	$ .35
Freehan, Bill	71T	575	$ .35	$1.10
Freehan, Bill	72T	120	$ .25	$ .65
Freehan, Bill	73T	460	$ .25	$ .65
Freehan, Bill	74T	162	$ .25	$ 85
Freehan, Bill	75T	397	$ .25	$ .65
Freehan, Bill	76T	540	$ .05	$ .20
Freehan, Bill	77T	22	$ .05	$ .15
Freeman, Bud	58T	27	$1.00	$3.75
Freeman, Hershell	56T	242	$2.50	$8.00
Freeman, Hershell "Bud"	57T	32	$ .95	$3.50
Freeman, Jimmy	73T	610	$ .35	$1.10
Freeman, LaVel	89TMLD	39	$ .01	$ .15
Freeman, Mark	59T	532	$2.00	$7.00
Freeman, Marvin	89T	634	$ .01	$ .04
Freeman, Marvin	90T	103	$ .01	$ .03
Freese, Gene	55T	205	$4.25	$13.00
Freese, Gene	56T	46	$1.25	$4.50
Freese, Gene	58T	293	$ .50	$2.00
Freese, Gene	59T	472	$ .50	$1.95
Freese, Gene	60T	435	$ .50	$1.95
Freese, Gene	61T	175	$ .30	$1.00
Freese, Gene	62T	205	$ .35	$1.10
Freese, Gene	63T	133	$ .25	$ .85
Freese, Gene	64T	266	$ .25	$ .85
Freese, Gene	65T	492	$ .50	$2.00
Freese, Gene	66T	319	$ .25	$ .85
Fregosi, Jim	62T	209	$1.25	$3.50
Fregosi, Jim	63T	167	$ .35	$1.10
Fregosi, Jim	64T	97	$ .12	$ .75

TOPPS

Player	Year	No.	VG	EX/MT	Player	Year	No.	VG	EX/MT
Fregosi, Jim	65T	210	$ .35	$1.10	Frisella, Danny	74T	71	$ .06	$ .25
Fregosi, Jim	66T	5	$ .25	$ .85	Frisella, Danny	75T	343	$ .06	$ .25
Fregosi, Jim	67T	385	$ .35	$1.10	Frisella, Danny	76T	32	$ .05	$ .20
Fregosi, Jim	68T	170	$ .25	$ .85	Frisella, Danny	77T	278	$ .05	$ .15
Fregosi, Jim	68TAS	367	$ .25	$ .65	Frobel, Doug	84T	264	$ .01	$ .05
Fregosi, Jim	69T	365	$ .15	$ .50	Frobel, Doug	85T	587	$ .01	$ .04
Fregosi, Jim	70T	570	$ .35	$1.10	Frohwirth, Todd	88T	378	$ .01	$ .10
Fregosi, Jim	71T	360	$ .15	$ .50	Frohwirth, Todd	89T	542	$ .01	$ .04
Fregosi, Jim	72T	115	$ .25	$ .65	Frohwirth, Todd	90T	69	$ .01	$ .03
Fregosi, Jim	72T	346	$ .10	$ .35	Frost, Dave	79T	703	$ .02	$ .10
Fregosi, Jim	72TTR	755	$1.50	$3.75	Frost, Dave	80T	423	$ .01	$ .07
Fregosi, Jim	73T	525	$ .25	$ .85	Frost, Dave	81T	286	$ .01	$ .07
Fregosi, Jim	74T	196	$ .06	$ .25	Frost, Dave	82T	24	$ .01	$ .06
Fregosi, Jim	75T	339	$ .25	$ .65	Frost, Dave	82TTR	37	$ .02	$ .10
Fregosi, Jim	76T	635	$ .06	$ .25	Frost, Dave	83T	656	$ .01	$ .06
Fregosi, Jim	78T	323	$ .02	$ .10	Fry, Jerry	79T	720	$ .05	$ .20
Fregosi, Jim	86TTR	39	$ .02	$ .10	Fryman, Woodie	70T	677	$1.50	$3.75
Fregosi, Jim	87T	318	$ .01	$ .03	Fryman, Woodie	71T	414	$ .10	$ .35
Fregosi, Jim	88T	714	$ .01	$ .03	Fryman, Woodie	72T	357	$ .10	$ .35
Fregosi, Jim	89T	414	$ .01	$ .04	Fryman, Woodie	73T	146	$ .06	$ .25
Freisleben, Dave	74T	599	$ .15	$ .50	Fryman, Woodie	74T	555	$ .06	$ .25
Freisleben, Dave	75T	37	$ .06	$ .25	Fryman, Woodie	75T	166	$ .06	$ .25
Freisleben, Dave	76T	217	$ .05	$ .20	Fryman, Woodie	76T	467	$ .05	$ .20
Freisleben, Dave	77T	407	$ .05	$ .15	Fryman, Woodie	77T	28	$ .05	$ .15
Freisleben, Dave	78T	594	$ .02	$ .10	Fryman, Woodie	78T	585	$ .02	$ .10
Freisleben, Dave	79T	168	$ .02	$ .10	Fryman, Woodie	79T	269	$ .02	$ .10
Freisleben, Dave	80T	382	$ .01	$ .07	Fryman, Woodie	80T	607	$ .01	$ .07
French, Jim	66T	333	$ .25	$ .85	Fryman, Woodie	81T	394	$ .01	$ .07
French, Jim	69T	199	$ .25	$ .65	Fryman, Woodie	82T	788	$ .01	$ .06
French, Jim	70T	617	$ .25	$ .85	Fryman, Woodie	83T	137	$ .01	$ .06
French, Jim	71T	399	$ .10	$ .35	Fryman, Woody	66T	498	$ .65	$1.75
Frey, Jim	73T	136	$ .15	$ .50	Fryman, Woody	67T	221	$ .25	$ .65
Frey, Jim	74T	306	$ .15	$ .50	Fryman, Woody	68T	112	$ .25	$ .65
Frey, Jim	84T	51	$ .01	$ .05	Fryman, Woody "Woodie"	69T	51	$ .25	$ .65
Frey, Jim	85T	241	$ .01	$ .04	Fuentes, Miguel	70T	88	$ .10	$ .35
Frey, Jim	86T	231	$ .01	$ .03	Fuentes, Tito	66T	511	$ .70	$2.10
Frey, Steve	89TMLD	40	$ .01	$ .15	Fuentes, Tito	67T	177	$ .25	$ .65
Frey, Steve	90T	91	$ .01	$ .10	Fuentes, Tito	70T	42	$ .10	$ .35
Frias, Pepe	73T	607	$ .35	$1.10	Fuentes, Tito	71T	378	$ .10	$ .35
Frias, Pepe	74T	468	$ .06	$ .25	Fuentes, Tito	72T	427	$ .10	$ .35
Frias, Pepe	75T	496	$ .06	$ .25	Fuentes, Tito	72TIA	428	$ .10	$ .35
Frias, Pepe	76T	544	$ .05	$ .20	Fuentes, Tito	73T	236	$ .06	$ .25
Frias, Pepe	77T	199	$ .05	$ .15	Fuentes, Tito	74T	305	$ .06	$ .25
Frias, Pepe	78T	654	$ .02	$ .10	Fuentes, Tito	75T	425	$ .06	$ .25
Frias, Pepe	79T	294	$ .02	$ .10	Fuentes, Tito	76T	8	$ .05	$ .20
Frias, Pepe	80T	87	$ .01	$ .07	Fuentes, Tito	77T	63	$ .05	$ .15
Fricano, Marion	53T	199	$3.75	$13.00	Fuentes, Tito	78T	385	$ .02	$ .10
Fricano, Marion	54T	124	$2.10	$7.50	Fulgham, John	80T	152	$ .01	$ .07
Frick, Ford	59T	1	$17.50	$77.50	Fulgham, John	81T	523	$ .01	$ .07
Fridley, Jim	52T	399	$39.00	$135.00	Fuller, Jim	74T	606	$ .06	$ .25
Fridley, Jim	53T	187	$3.75	$13.00	Fuller, Jim	75T	594	$ .06	$ .25
Friend, Bob	52T	233	$6.00	$18.00	Fuller, Vern	68T	71	$ .25	$ .65
Friend, Bob	56T	221	$2.50	$8.00	Fuller, Vern	69T	291	$ .25	$ .85
Friend, Bob	57T	150	$ .60	$2.50	Fuller, Vern	70T	558	$ .25	$ .85
Friend, Bob	58T	315	$ .65	$2.00	Funk, Frank	61T	362	$ .30	$1.00
Friend, Bob	58T	334	$ .45	$1.50	Funk, Frank	62T	587	$3.75	$11.00
Friend, Bob	58TAS	492	$ .70	$2.25	Funk, Frank	63T	476	$2.50	$6.50
Friend, Bob	59T	428	$ .50	$1.95	Funk, Frank	64T	289	$ .25	$ .85
Friend, Bob	59T	460	$ .60	$1.75	Furillo, Carl	56T	190	$5.00	$18.00
Friend, Bob	59TAS	569	$3.00	$9.00	Furillo, Carl	57T	45	$2.10	$7.50
Friend, Bob	60T	437	$ .60	$1.75	Furillo, Carl	57T	400	$40.00	$150.00
Friend, Bob	61T	45	$ .60	$2.75	Furillo, Carl	58T	417	$ .95	$3.00
Friend, Bob	61T	270	$ .30	$1.00	Furillo, Carl	59T	206	$1.35	$4.00
Friend, Bob	61TAS	585	$6.00	$18.00	Furillo, Carl	60T	408	$1.35	$4.00
Friend, Bob	62T	520	$ .70	$2.10	Fusselman, Les	52T	378	$39.00	$135.00
Friend, Bob	63T	450	$2.50	$6.50	Fusselman, Les	53T	218	$3.75	$13.00
Friend, Bob	64T	1	$3.00	$12.00	Gabrielson, Len	63T	253	$ .25	$ .85
Friend, Bob	64T	20	$ .35	$1.10	Gabrielson, Len	64T	198	$ .25	$ .85
Friend, Bob	65T	392	$ .35	$1.10	Gabrielson, Len	65T	14	$ .25	$ .65
Friend, Bob	66T	519	$1.35	$4.00	Gabrielson, Len	66T	395	$ .25	$ .85
Friend, Owen	52T	160	$6.00	$19.00	Gabrielson, Len	67T	469	$ .50	$2.00
Frisella, Dan	69T	343	$ .25	$ .65	Gabrielson, Len	68T	357	$ .25	$ .65
Frisella, Dan	71T	104	$ .10	$ .35	Gabrielson, Len	69T	615	$ .25	$ .85
Frisella, Danny	72T	293	$ .10	$ .35	Gabrielson, Len	70T	204	$ .10	$ .35
Frisella, Danny	73T	432	$ .06	$ .25	Gaetti, Gary	83T	431	$1.50	$4.50

Player	Year	No.	VG	EX/MT	Player	Year	No.	VG	EX/MT
Gaetti, Gary	84T	157	$ .25	$1.00	Galarraga, Andres	89TBB	173	$ .01	$ .10
Gaetti, Gary	85T	304	$ .05	$ .25	Galarraga, Andres	90T	720	$ .01	$ .10
Gaetti, Gary	86T	97	$ .01	$ .15	Galasso, Bob	80T	711	$ .01	$ .07
Gaetti, Gary	87T	710	$ .01	$ .10	Galasso, Bob	82T	598	$ .01	$ .06
Gaetti, Gary	88T	578	$ .01	$ .10	Gale, Rich	79T	298	$ .02	$ .10
Gaetti, Gary	88TBB	127	$ .01	$ .15	Gale, Rich	80T	433	$ .01	$ .07
Gaetti, Gary	89T	220	$ .01	$ .10	Gale, Rich	81T	544	$ .01	$ .07
Gaetti, Gary	89TBB	264	$ .01	$ .10	Gale, Rich	82T	67	$ .01	$ .06
Gaetti, Gary	90T	630	$ .01	$ .03	Gale, Rich	82TTR	38	$ .02	$ .10
Gaff, Brent	85T	546	$ .01	$ .04	Gale, Rich	83T	719	$ .01	$ .06
Gaff, Brent	86T	18	$ .01	$ .03	Gale, Rich	83TTR	35	$ .25	$1.25
Gagliano, Phil	64T	568	$1.50	$3.75	Gale, Rich	84T	142	$ .01	$ .05
Gagliano, Phil	65T	503	$ .50	$2.00	Gale, Rich	84TTR	40	$ .02	$ .10
Gagliano, Phil	66T	418	$ .25	$ .85	Gale, Rich	85T	606	$ .01	$ .04
Gagliano, Phil	67T	304	$ .25	$ .65	Gallagher, Alan	71T	224	$ .10	$ .35
Gagliano, Phil	68T	479	$ .30	$1.00	Gallagher, Alan	72T	693	$ .70	$2.10
Gagliano, Phil	69T	609	$ .25	$ .85	Gallagher, Alan	72TIA	694	$ .70	$2.10
Gagliano, Phil	70T	143	$ .10	$ .35	Gallagher, Bob	74T	21	$ .06	$ .25
Gagliano, Phil	71T	302	$ .10	$ .35	Gallagher, Bob	75T	406	$ .06	$ .25
Gagliano, Phil	72T	472	$ .05	$ .25	Gallagher, Dave	89T	156	$ .01	$ .15
Gagliano, Phil	73T	69	$ .06	$ .25	Gallagher, Dave	89TBB	310	$ .01	$ .05
					Gallagher, Dave	90T	612	$ .01	$ .03
					Gallego, Mike	86T	304	$ .01	$ .03
					Gallego, Mike	88T	702	$ .01	$ .03
					Gallego, Mike	88TBB	103	$ .01	$ .05
					Gallego, Mike	89T	102	$ .01	$ .04
					Gallego, Mike	90T	293	$ .01	$ .03
					Gamble, John	74T	597	$ .15	$ .50
					Gamble, Oscar	70T	654	$ .70	$2.00
					Gamble, Oscar	71T	23	$ .10	$ .35
					Gamble, Oscar	72T	423	$ .05	$ .25
					Gamble, Oscar	73T	372	$ .06	$ .25
					Gamble, Oscar	74T	152	$ .06	$ .25
					Gamble, Oscar	75T	213	$ .06	$ .25
					Gamble, Oscar	76T	74	$ .05	$ .20
					Gamble, Oscar	76TTR	74	$ .05	$ .20
					Gamble, Oscar	77T	505	$ .03	$ .12
					Gamble, Oscar	78T	390	$ .02	$ .10
					Gamble, Oscar	79T	263	$ .02	$ .10
					Gamble, Oscar	80T	698	$ .01	$ .07
					Gamble, Oscar	81T	139	$ .01	$ .07
					Gamble, Oscar	82T	472	$ .01	$ .06
					Gamble, Oscar	83T	19	$ .01	$ .06
					Gamble, Oscar	84T	512	$ .01	$ .05
					Gamble, Oscar	85T	724	$ .01	$ .04
					Gamble, Oscar	85TTR	37	$ .02	$ .10
					Gant, Ron	88TBB	249	$ .01	$ .20
					Gant, Ron	88TTR	39	$ .01	$ .30
					Gant, Ron	89T	296	$ .01	$ .15
					Gant, Ron	89TBB	43	$ .01	$ .05
					Gant, Ron	90T	567	$ .01	$ .03
					Gantner, Jim	77T	494	$ .12	$ .40
					Gantner, Jim	79T	154	$ .02	$ .10
Gagliano, Phil	74T	622	$ .06	$ .25	Gantner, Jim	80T	374	$ .01	$ .07
Gagliano, Ralph	65T	501	$ .50	$2.00	Gantner, Jim	81T	482	$ .01	$ .07
Gagne, Greg	85TTR	36	$ .05	$ .25	Gantner, Jim	82T	613	$ .01	$ .06
Gagne, Greg	86T	162	$ .01	$ .03	Gantner, Jim	83T	88	$ .01	$ .06
Gagne, Greg	87T	558	$ .01	$ .03	Gantner, Jim	84T	298	$ .01	$ .05
Gagne, Greg	88T	343	$ .01	$ .03	Gantner, Jim	85T	781	$ .01	$ .04
Gagne, Greg	88TBB	58	$ .01	$ .05	Gantner, Jim	86T	582	$ .01	$ .03
Gagne, Greg	89T	19	$ .01	$ .04	Gantner, Jim	87T	108	$ .01	$ .03
Gagne, Greg	89TBB	186	$ .01	$ .05	Gantner, Jim	88T	337	$ .01	$ .03
Gagne, Greg	90T	448	$ .01	$ .03	Gantner, Jim	89T	671	$ .01	$ .04
Gaines, Joe	62T	414	$ .70	$2.10	Gantner, Jim	89TBB	184	$ .01	$ .05
Gaines, Joe	63T	319	$ .35	$1.20	Gantner, Jim	90T	417	$ .01	$ .03
Gaines, Joe	64T	364	$ .25	$ .85	Garagiola, Joe	52T	227	$17.50	$50.00
Gaines, Joe	65T	594	$1.50	$3.75	Garber, Gene	74T	431	$ .25	$ .85
Gaines, Joe	66T	122	$ .25	$ .85	Garber, Gene	75T	444	$ .06	$ .25
Galan, Augie	54T	233	$1.25	$6.00	Garber, Gene	76T	14	$ .05	$ .20
Galarraga, Andres	86TTR	40	$ .25	$1.75	Garber, Gene	77T	289	$ .03	$ .12
Galarraga, Andres	87T	272	$ .50	$2.00	Garber, Gene	78T	177	$ .02	$ .10
Galarraga, Andres	88T	25	$ .01	$ .40	Garber, Gene	79T	629	$ .02	$ .10
Galarraga, Andres	88TBB	55	$ .01	$ .15	Garber, Gene	80T	504	$ .01	$ .07
Galarraga, Andres	89T	590	$ .01	$ .10	Garber, Gene	81T	307	$ .01	$ .07
Galarraga, Andres	89TAS	386	$ .01	$ .04	Garber, Gene	82T	32	$ .01	$ .06

INFIELD

PHIL
GAGLIANO

REDS

Player	Year	No.	VG	EX/MT	Player	Year	No.	VG	EX/MT
Garber, Gene	83T	255	$ .01	$ .06	Garcia, Mike	58T	196	$ .45	$1.50
Garber, Gene	83T	256	$ .01	$ .06	Garcia, Mike	59T	516	$3.00	$9.00
Garber, Gene	84T	466	$ .01	$ .05	Garcia, Mike	60T	532	$3.75	13.00
Garber, Gene	84T	709	$ .01	$ .05	Garcia, Pedro	73T	609	$ .95	$3.50
Garber, Gene	85T	129	$ .01	$ .04	Garcia, Pedro	74T	142	$ .06	$ .25
Garber, Gene	86T	776	$ .01	$ .03	Garcia, Pedro	75T	147	$ .06	$ .25
Garber, Gene	87T	351	$ .01	$ .03	Garcia, Pedro	76T	187	$ .05	$ .20
Garber, Gene	88T	597	$ .01	$ .03	Garcia, Pedro	77T	453	$ .03	$ .12
Garbey, Barbaro	84TTR	41	$ .02	$ .10	Garcia, Ralph	73T	602	$ .35	$1.10
Garbey, Barbaro	85T	243	$ .01	$ .04	Gardenhire, Ron	82T	623	$ .20	$ .80
Garbey, Barbaro	86T	609	$ .01	$ .03	Gardenhire, Ron	82TTR	39	$ .02	$ .10
Garcia, Damaso	81T	488	$ .05	$ .25	Gardenhire, Ron	83T	469	$ .01	$ .06
Garcia, Damaso	82T	596	$ .01	$ .06	Gardenhire, Ron	85T	144	$ .01	$ .04
Garcia, Damaso	83T	202	$ .01	$ .06	Gardenhire, Ron	86T	274	$ .01	$ .03
Garcia, Damaso	83T	222	$ .01	$ .06	Gardner, Billy	55T	27	$1.35	$5.00
Garcia, Damaso	84T	124	$ .01	$ .05	Gardner, Billy	57T	17	$ .95	$3.50
Garcia, Damaso	85T	645	$ .01	$ .04	Gardner, Billy	58T	105	$1.00	$3.75
Garcia, Damaso	85TAS	702	$ .01	$ .04	Gardner, Billy	59T	89	$1.00	$3.75
Garcia, Damaso	86T	45	$ .01	$ .03	Gardner, Billy	60T	106	$ .35	$1.10
Garcia, Damaso	86TAS	713	$ .01	$ .03	Gardner, Billy	61T	123	$ .30	$1.00
Garcia, Damaso	87T	395	$ .01	$ .03	Gardner, Billy	62T	163	$ .50	$2.00
Garcia, Damaso	88T	241	$ .01	$ .03	Gardner, Billy	62T	338	$ .60	$1.75
Garcia, Damaso	89TBB	275	$ .01	$ .05	Gardner, Billy	63T	408	$ .35	$1.20
Garcia, Damaso	90T	432	$ .01	$ .03	Gardner, Billy	83T	11	$ .01	$ .06
Garcia, Dave	73T	12	$ .25	$ .65	Gardner, Billy	84T	771	$ .01	$ .05
Garcia, Dave	78T	656	$ .02	$ .10	Gardner, Billy	85T	213	$ .01	$ .04
Garcia, Dave	83T	546	$ .01	$ .06	Gardner, Billy	87TTR	36	$ .01	$ .07
Garcia, Kiko	77T	474	$ .05	$ .15	Gardner, Mark	89TMLD	41	$ .01	$ .05
Garcia, Kiko	78T	287	$ .02	$ .10	Gardner, Mark	90T	284	$ .01	$ .10
Garcia, Kiko	79T	543	$ .02	$ .10	Gardner, Rob	66T	534	$4.50	$15.00
Garcia, Kiko	80T	37	$ .01	$ .07	Gardner, Rob	67T	217	$ .25	$ .65
Garcia, Kiko	81T	688	$ .01	$ .07	Gardner, Rob	68T	219	$ .25	$ .65
Garcia, Kiko	81TTR	765	$ .02	$ .10	Gardner, Rob	71T	734	$ .70	$2.10
Garcia, Kiko	82T	377	$ .01	$ .06	Gardner, Rob	72T	22	$ .05	$ .25
Garcia, Kiko	83T	198	$ .01	$ .06	Gardner, Rob	73T	222	$ .06	$ .25
Garcia, Kiko	83TTR	36	$ .02	$ .10	Gardner, Wes	88T	189	$ .01	$ .03
Garcia, Kiko	84T	458	$ .01	$ .05	Gardner, Wes	89T	526	$ .01	$ .04
Garcia, Kiko	85T	763	$ .01	$ .04	Gardner, Wes	90T	38	$ .01	$ .03
Garcia, Mike	51Trb	40	$1.25	$3.50	Garibaldi, Bob	70T	681	$ .50	$2.00
					Garibaldi, Bob	71T	701	$ .70	$2.10
					Garland, Wayne	74T	596	$ .06	$ .25
					Garland, Wayne	76T	414	$ .05	$ .20
					Garland, Wayne	77T	33	$ .03	$ .12
					Garland, Wayne	78T	174	$ .02	$ .10
					Garland, Wayne	79T	636	$ .02	$ .10
					Garland, Wayne	80T	361	$ .01	$ .07
					Garland, Wayne	81T	511	$ .01	$ .07
					Garland, Wayne	82T	446	$ .01	$ .06
					Garman, Mike	71T	512	$ .10	$ .35
					Garman, Mike	72T	79	$15.00	$55.00
					Garman, Mike	73T	616	$ .35	$1.10
					Garman, Mike	75T	584	$ .06	$ .25
					Garman, Mike	76T	34	$ .05	$ .20
					Garman, Mike	77T	302	$ .03	$ .12
					Garman, Mike	78T	417	$ .02	$ .10
					Garman, Mike	79T	181	$ .02	$ .10
					Garner, Phil	75T	623	$6.00	$18.00
					Garner, Phil	76T	57	$ .05	$ .20
					Garner, Phil	77T	261	$ .03	$ .12
					Garner, Phil	78T	53	$ .02	$ .10
					Garner, Phil	79T	383	$ .02	$ .10
					Garner, Phil	80T	118	$ .01	$ .07
					Garner, Phil	81T	573	$ .01	$ .07
					Garner, Phil	82T	683	$ .01	$ .06
					Garner, Phil	83T	478	$ .01	$ .06
					Garner, Phil	84T	752	$ .01	$ .05
					Garner, Phil	85T	206	$ .01	$ .04
					Garner, Phil	86T	83	$ .01	$ .03
					Garner, Phil	87T	304	$ .01	$ .03
					Garner, Phil	88T	174	$ .01	$ .03
					Garr, Ralph	70T	172	$ .10	$ .35
Garcia, Mike	52T	272	$14.00	$40.00	Garr, Ralph	71T	494	$ .10	$ .35
Garcia, Mike	53T	75	$4.50	$15.00	Garr, Ralph	72T	85	$ .30	$1.00
Garcia, Mike	56T	210	$2.50	$8.00	Garr, Ralph	72T	260	$ .07	$ .25
Garcia, Mike	57T	300	$3.50	$13.00	Garr, Ralph	73T	15	$ .10	$ .35

MIKE GARCIA

Player	Year	No.	VG	EX/MT	Player	Year	No.	VG	EX/MT
Garr, Ralph	74T	570	$ .06	$ .25	Gaspar, Rod	71T	383	$ .10	$ .35
Garr, Ralph	75T	306	$ .30	$1.00	Gaston, Cito	89TTR	36	$ .01	$ .05
Garr, Ralph	75T	550	$ .06	$ .25	Gaston, Cito	90T	201	$ .01	$ .03
Garr, Ralph	76T	410	$ .05	$ .20	Gaston, Clarence	69T	304	$ .25	$ .85
Garr, Ralph	76TTR	410	$ .05	$ .20	Gaston, Clarence	70T	604	$ .25	$ .85
Garr, Ralph	77T	133	$ .03	$ .12	Gaston, Clarence	71T	25	$ .10	$ .35
Garr, Ralph	78T	628	$ .02	$ .10	Gaston, Clarence	72T	431	$ .05	$ .25
Garr, Ralph	79T	309	$ .02	$ .10	Gaston, Clarence	72TIA	432	$ .05	$ .25
Garr, Ralph	80T	272	$ .01	$ .07	Gaston, Clarence	73T	159	$ .06	$ .25
Garrelts, Scott	85TTR	38	$ .05	$ .20	Gaston, Clarence	74T	364	$ .06	$ .25
Garrelts, Scott	86T	395	$ .01	$ .03	Gaston, Clarence	75T	427	$ .06	$ .25
Garrelts, Scott	87T	475	$ .01	$ .03	Gaston, Clarence	76T	558	$ .05	$ .20
Garrelts, Scott	88T	97	$ .01	$ .03	Gaston, Clarence	77T	192	$ .03	$ .12
Garrelts, Scott	88TBB	240	$ .01	$ .05	Gaston, Clarence	78T	716	$ .02	$ .10
Garrelts, Scott	89T	703	$ .01	$ .04	Gaston, Clarence	79T	208	$ .02	$ .10
Garrelts, Scott	90T	602	$ .01	$ .03	Gates, Mike	83T	657	$ .01	$ .06
Garrett, Adrian	71T	576	$ .30	$1.00	Gatewood, Aubrey	64T	127	$ .25	$ .85
Garrett, Adrian	74T	656	$ .06	$ .25	Gatewood, Aubrey	65T	422	$ .30	$1.00
Garrett, Adrian	76T	562	$ .05	$ .20	Gatewood, Aubrey	66T	42	$ .25	$ .85
Garrett, Greg	70T	642	$ .50	$2.00	Gaudet, Jim	79T	707	$ .02	$ .10
Garrett, Greg	71T	377	$ .10	$ .35	Gebhard, Bob	72T	28	$ .10	$ .35
Garrett, Pat	66T	553	$4.50	$15.00	Geddes, Jim	73T	561	$ .35	$1.10
Garrett, Wayne	70T	628	$ .25	$ .85	Gedman, Rich	82T	59	$ .25	$ .65
Garrett, Wayne	71T	228	$ .10	$ .35	Gedman, Rich	83T	602	$ .01	$ .10
Garrett, Wayne	72T	518	$ .05	$ .25	Gedman, Rich	84T	498	$ .02	$ .10
Garrett, Wayne	73T	562	$ .35	$1.10	Gedman, Rich	85T	529	$ .01	$ .10
Garrett, Wayne	74T	510	$ .06	$ .25	Gedman, Rich	86T	375	$ .01	$ .10
Garrett, Wayne	75T	111	$ .06	$ .25	Gedman, Rich	87T	740	$ .01	$ .03
Garrett, Wayne	76T	222	$ .05	$ .20	Gedman, Rich	88T	245	$ .01	$ .03
Garrett, Wayne	77T	417	$ .03	$ .12	Gedman, Rich	88TBB	152	$ .01	$ .05
Garrett, Wayne	78T	679	$ .02	$ .10	Gedman, Rich	89T	652	$ .01	$ .04
Garrett, Wayne	79T	319	$ .02	$ .10	Gedman, Rich	89TBB	72	$ .01	$ .05
Garrido, Gil	64T	452	$ .50	$1.95	Gedman, Rich	90T	123	$ .01	$ .03
Garrido, Gil	69T	331	$ .25	$ .65	Gehrig, Lou	61T	405	$3.25	$12.50
Garrido, Gil	70T	48	$ .10	$ .35	Gehrig, Lou	73TATL	472	$ .60	$2.75
Garrido, Gil	71T	173	$ .10	$ .35	Gehrig, Lou	76TAS	341	$ .70	$2.00
Garrido, Gil	72T	758	$ .70	$2.10	Geiger, Gary	58T	462	$1.25	$3.50
Garver, Ned	51Tbb	18	$5.50	$17.00	Geiger, Gary	59T	521	$2.00	$7.00
Garver, Ned	52T	212	$6.00	$19.00	Geiger, Gary	60T	184	$ .35	$1.10
Garver, Ned	53T	112	$3.75	$13.00	Geiger, Gary	61T	33	$ .30	$1.00
Garver, Ned	54T	44	$2.10	$7.50	Geiger, Gary	62T	117	$ .35	$1.10
Garver, Ned	56T	189	$3.75	$13.00	Geiger, Gary	63T	513	$1.50	$3.75
Garver, Ned	57T	285	$3.50	$13.00	Geiger, Gary	64T	93	$ .25	$ .85
Garver, Ned	58T	292	$ .50	$2.00	Geiger, Gary	65T	452	$ .50	$2.00
Garver, Ned	59T	245	$ .50	$1.95	Geiger, Gary	66T	286	$ .25	$ .85
Garver, Ned	60T	471	$ .60	$1.75	Geiger, Gary	67T	566	$1.25	$3.50
Garver, Ned	61T	331	$ .30	$1.00	Geiger, Gary	69T	278	$ .25	$ .85
Garvey, Steve	71T	341	$22.50	$70.00	Geisel, Dave	79T	716	$ .02	$ .10
Garvey, Steve	72T	686	$25.00	$70.00	Geisel, Dave	80T	676	$ .01	$ .07
Garvey, Steve	73T	213	$3.00	$1200	Geisel, Dave	84T	256	$ .01	$ .05
Garvey, Steve	74T	575	$0.50	$12.50	Geishert, Vern	70T	683	$1.00	$3.50
Garvey, Steve	75T	140	$1.50	$4.50	Gelnar, John	65T	143	$ .25	$ .65
Garvey, Steve	75T	212	$ .25	$ .85	Gelnar, John	67T	472	$ .50	$2.00
Garvey, Steve	76T	150	$1.00	$4.00	Gelnar, John	70T	393	$ .10	$ .35
Garvey, Steve	77T	400	$1.00	$4.00	Gelnar, John	71T	604	$ .30	$1.00
Garvey, Steve	78T	350	$ .95	$3.50	Gentile, Jim	60T	448	$1.00	$4.25
Garvey, Steve	79T	50	$ .35	$1.10	Gentile, Jim	61T	559	$6.00	$15.00
Garvey, Steve	80T	290	$ .50	$2.00	Gentile, Jim	62T	53	$3.00	$12.50
Garvey, Steve	81T	530	$ .35	$1.10	Gentile, Jim	62T	290	$ .35	$1.10
Garvey, Steve	82T	179	$ .15	$ .75	Gentile, Jim	63T	4	$ .50	$2.00
Garvey, Steve	82TIA	180	$ .08	$ .35	Gentile, Jim	63T	260	$ .25	$ .85
Garvey, Steve	83T	610	$ .01	$ .06	Gentile, Jim	64T	196	$ .25	$ .85
Garvey, Steve	83TTR	37	$ .35	$1.10	Gentile, Jim	65T	365	$ .30	$1.00
Garvey, Steve	84T	380	$ .10	$ .50	Gentile, Jim	66T	45	$ .25	$ .85
Garvey, Steve	85T	450	$ .10	$ .35	Gentry, Gary	69T	31	$ .25	$ .85
Garvey, Steve	85TRB	2	$ .04	$ .20	Gentry, Gary	70T	153	$ .10	$ .35
Garvey, Steve	86T	660	$ .03	$ .25	Gentry, Gary	71T	725	$ .70	$2.10
Garvey, Steve	87T	150	$ .10	$ .35	Gentry, Gary	72T	105	$ .05	$ .25
Garvin, Jerry	78T	419	$ .02	$ .10	Gentry, Gary	73T	288	$ .06	$ .25
Garvin, Jerry	79T	293	$ .02	$ .10	Gentry, Gary	74T	415	$ .06	$ .25
Garvin, Jerry	80T	611	$ .01	$ .07	Gentry, Gary	75T	393	$ .06	$ .25
Garvin, Jerry	81T	124	$ .01	$ .07	Gerber, Craig	86T	222	$ .01	$ .03
Garvin, Jerry	82T	768	$ .01	$ .06	Geren, Bob	89TTR	37	$ .01	$ .50
Garvin, Jerry	83T	358	$ .01	$ .06	Geren, Bob	90T	536	$ .01	$ .10
Gaspar, Rod	70T	371	$ .10	$ .35	Gerhart, Ken	87TTR	37	$ .05	$ .25

TOPPS

Player	Year	No.	VG	EX/MT
Gerhart, Ken	88T	271	$ .01	$ .03
Gerhart, Ken	89T	598	$ .01	$ .04
Gernert, Dick	52T	343	$39.00	$135.00
Gernert, Dick	57T	202	$ .95	$3.50
Gernert, Dick	58T	38	$1.00	$3.75
Gernert, Dick	59T	13	$1.00	$3.75
Gernert, Dick	59T	519	$3.00	$9.00
Gernert, Dick	60T	86	$ .35	$1.10
Gernert, Dick	61T	284	$ .30	$1.00
Gernert, Dick	62T	536	$3.75	$11.00
Geronimo, Cesar	71T	447	$ .15	$ .50
Geronimo, Cesar	72T	719	$ .60	$1.75
Geronimo, Cesar	73T	156	$ .06	$ .25
Geronimo, Cesar	74T	181	$ .06	$ .25
Geronimo, Cesar	75T	41	$ .06	$ .25
Geronimo, Cesar	76T	24	$ .05	$ .20
Geronimo, Cesar	77T	535	$ .03	$ .12

CESAR GERONIMO

Player	Year	No.	VG	EX/MT
Geronimo, Cesar	78T	354	$ .02	$ .10
Geronimo, Cesar	79T	220	$ .02	$ .10
Geronimo, Cesar	80T	475	$ .01	$ .07
Geronimo, Cesar	81T	390	$ .01	$ .07
Geronimo, Cesar	81TTR	766	$ .02	$ .10
Geronimo, Cesar	82T	693	$ .01	$ .06
Geronimo, Cesar	83T	194	$ .01	$ .06
Geronimo, Cesar	84T	544	$ .01	$ .05
Giallombardo, Bob	59T	321	$ .50	$1.95
Giamatti, A. Bartlett	90T	396	$ .01	$ .50
Giants, Team	56T	226	$17.50	$65.00
Giants, Team	57T	317	$15.00	$50.00
Giants, Team	58T	19	$3.00	$10.00
Giants, Team	59T	69	$2.75	$9.50
Giants, Team	60T	151	$2.50	$7.50
Giants, Team	61T	167	$ .95	$3.50
Giants, Team	62T	226	$1.25	$3.50
Giants, Team	63T	417	$1.25	$3.50
Giants, Team	64T	257	$1.00	$3.75
Giants, Team	65T	379	$ .60	$1.75
Giants, Team	66T	19	$ .60	$1.75
Giants, Team	67T	516	$1.25	$3.50
Giants, Team	70T	696	$1.25	$3.50
Giants, Team	71T	563	$ .60	$1.75
Giants, Team	72T	771	$1.50	$3.75
Giants, Team	73T	434	$ .30	$1.00

Player	Year	No.	VG	EX/MT
Giants, Team	74T	281	$ .15	$ .50
Giants, Team Checklist	75T	216	$ .30	$1.00
Giants, Team Checklist	76T	443	$ .30	$1.00
Giants, Team Checklist	77T	211	$ .15	$ .50
Giants, Team Checklist	78T	82	$ .06	$ .30
Giants, Team Checklist	79T	356	$ .05	$ .25
Giants, Team Checklist	80T	499	$ .05	$ .25
Giants, Team Checklist	81T	686	$ .02	$ .20
Giants, Team Leaders	86T	516	$ .01	$ .03
Giants, Team Leaders	87T	231	$ .01	$ .03
Giants, Team Leaders	88T	261	$ .01	$ .03
Giants, Team Leaders	89T	351	$ .01	$ .04
Gibbon, Joe	60T	512	$2.00	$7.00
Gibbon, Joe	61T	523	$5.00	$20.00
Gibbon, Joe	62T	448	$ .70	$2.10
Gibbon, Joe	63T	101	$ .25	$ .85
Gibbon, Joe	64T	307	$ .25	$ .85
Gibbon, Joe	65T	54	$ .25	$ .65
Gibbon, Joe	66T	457	$ .70	$2.10
Gibbon, Joe	67T	541	$1.25	$3.50
Gibbon, Joe	68T	32	$ .25	$ .65
Gibbon, Joe	69T	158	$ .25	$ .65
Gibbon, Joe	70T	517	$ .10	$ .35
Gibbon, Joe	72T	382	$ .05	$ .25
Gibbs, Jake	62T	281	$ .50	$2.00
Gibbs, Jake	64T	281	$ .25	$ .85
Gibbs, Jake	65T	226	$ .35	$1.10
Gibbs, Jake	66T	117	$ .15	$ .50
Gibbs, Jake	67T	375	$ .25	$ .85
Gibbs, Jake	68T	89	$ .25	$ .65
Gibbs, Jake	69T	401	$ .25	$ .65
Gibbs, Jake	70T	594	$ .25	$ .85
Gibbs, Jake	71T	382	$ .10	$ .35
Gibson, Bob	59T	514	$75.00	$325.00
Gibson, Bob	60T	73	$10.00	$40.00
Gibson, Bob	61T	211	$5.00	$15.00
Gibson, Bob	62T	530	$20.00	$ 77.50
Gibson, Bob	63T	5	$ .60	$1.75
Gibson, Bob	63T	9	$ .60	$1.75
Gibson, Bob	63T	415	$7.00	$21.00
Gibson, Bob	64T	460	$6.50	$20.00
Gibson, Bob	65T	12	$1.50	$3.75
Gibson, Bob	65T	320	$6.00	$17.50
Gibson, Bob	66T	225	$1.00	$4.00
Gibson, Bob	66T	320	$4.50	$15.00
Gibson, Bob	67T	210	$4.00	$12.50
Gibson, Bob	67T	236	$2.50	$8.00
Gibson, Bob	68T	100	$4.00	$12.00
Gibson, Bob	68TAS	378	$1.25	$3.50
Gibson, Bob	69T	8	$ .50	$2.00
Gibson, Bob	69T	10	$1.50	$3.75
Gibson, Bob	69T	12	$1.00	$2.75
Gibson, Bob	69T	200	$2.00	$8.00
Gibson, Bob	69TAS	432	$1.25	$3.50
Gibson, Bob	70T	67	$1.35	$4.75
Gibson, Bob	70T	71	$ .50	$2.00
Gibson, Bob	70T	530	$2.00	$8.00
Gibson, Bob	71T	70	$ .50	$2.00
Gibson, Bob	71T	72	$ .50	$2.00
Gibson, Bob	71T	450	$2.50	$7.50
Gibson, Bob	72T	130	$1.75	$6.50
Gibson, Bob	73T	190	$1.00	$4.00
Gibson, Bob	74T	350	$1.00	$4.00
Gibson, Bob	75T	150	$1.00	$4.00
Gibson, Bob	75T	206	$ .35	$1.10
Gibson, Bob	75THL	3	$ .50	$2.00
Gibson, Bob	84T	349	$ .01	$ .05
Gibson, Bob	85TTR	39	$ .02	$ .10
Gibson, Bob	86T	499	$ .01	$ .03
Gibson, Bob	88TTB	664	$ .01	$ .10
Gibson, Joel	65T	368	$ .30	$1.00
Gibson, Kirk	81T	315	$1.25	$5.50
Gibson, Kirk	82T	105	$ .25	$ .90
Gibson, Kirk	83T	430	$ .10	$ .50
Gibson, Kirk	84T	65	$ .05	$ .35

Player	Year	No.	VG	EX/MT	Player	Year	No.	VG	EX/MT
Gibson, Kirk	85T	565	$ .05	$ .25	Giusti, Dave	68T	182	$ .25	$ .65
Gibson, Kirk	86T	295	$ .01	$ .25	Giusti, Dave	69T	98	$ .25	$ .65
Gibson, Kirk	87T	765	$ .03	$ .15	Giusti, Dave	70T	372	$ .10	$ .35
Gibson, Kirk	88T	605	$ .01	$ .10	Giusti, Dave	71T	562	$ .30	$1.00
Gibson, Kirk	88TBB	191	$ .01	$ .15	Giusti, Dave	72T	190	$ .05	$ .25
Gibson, Kirk	88TTR	40	$ .01	$ .15	Giusti, Dave	73T	465	$ .06	$ .25
Gibson, Kirk	89T	340	$ .01	$ .10	Giusti, Dave	74T	82	$ .06	$ .25
Gibson, Kirk	89TAS	396	$ .01	$ .04	Giusti, Dave	75T	53	$ .06	$ .25
Gibson, Kirk	89TBB	299	$ .01	$ .10	Giusti, Dave	76T	352	$ .05	$ .20
Gibson, Kirk	90T	150	$ .01	$ .03	Giusti, Dave	77T	154	$ .03	$ .12
Gibson, Paul	89T	583	$ .01	$ .04	Gladden, Dan	85T	386	$ .01	$ .10
Gibson, Paul	89TBB	230	$ .01	$ .05	Gladden, Dan	86T	678	$ .01	$ .03
Gibson, Paul	90T	11	$ .01	$ .03	Gladden, Danny	87T	46	$ .01	$ .03
Gibson, Russ	67T	547	$1.35	$4.00	Gladden, Danny	87TTR	38	$ .01	$ .07
Gibson, Russ	68T	297	$ .25	$ .65	Gladden, Danny	88T	502	$ .01	$ .03
Gibson, Russ	69T	89	$ .25	$ .65	Gladden, Danny	89T	426	$ .01	$ .04
Gibson, Russ	70T	237	$ .10	$ .35	Gladden, Danny	90T	298	$ .01	$ .03
Gibson, Russ	71T	738	$ .70	$2.10	Gladding, Fred	64T	312	$ .25	$ .85
Gibson, Russ	72T	643	$ .25	$ .85	Gladding, Fred	65T	37	$ .25	$ .65
Gideon, Jim	77T	478	$ .03	$ .12	Gladding, Fred	66T	337	$ .25	$ .85
Giel, Paul	58T	308	$ .50	$2.00	Gladding, Fred	67T	192	$ .25	$ .65
Giel, Paul	59T	9	$1.00	$3.75	Gladding, Fred	68T	423	$ .25	$ .65
Giel, Paul	60T	526	$2.00	$7.00	Gladding, Fred	69T	58	$ .25	$ .65
Giel, Paul	61T	374	$ .50	$2.00	Gladding, Fred	70T	208	$ .10	$ .35
Gigon, Norm	67T	576	$6.00	$20.00	Gladding, Fred	71T	381	$ .10	$ .35
Gil, Gus	67T	253	$ .25	$ .65	Gladding, Fred	72T	507	$ .05	$ .25
Gil, Gus	69T	651	$ .25	$ .85	Gladding, Fred	73T	17	$ .06	$ .25
Gilbert, Andy	73T	252	$ .25	$ .65	Glaviano, Tommy	51Trb	47	$1.25	$3.50
Gilbert, Andy	74T	78	$ .06	$ .25	Glaviano, Tommy	52T	56	$14.00	$45.00
Gilbert, Buddy	60T	359	$ .50	$1.95	Glaviano, Tommy	53T	140	$3.75	$13.00
Gilbert, Tookie	52T	61	$14.00	$45.00	Glavine, Tom	88T	779	$ .01	$ .25
Gilbreath, Rod	74T	93	$ .06	$ .25	Glavine, Tom	89T	157	$ .01	$ .04
Gilbreath, Rod	75T	431	$ .06	$ .25	Glavine, Tom	90T	506	$ .01	$ .03
Gilbreath, Rod	76T	306	$ .05	$ .20	Gleaton, Jerry Don	80T	673	$ .01	$ .07
Gilbreath, Rod	77T	126	$ .03	$ .12	Gleaton, Jerry Don	81T	41	$ .01	$ .07
Gilbreath, Rod	78T	217	$ .02	$ .10	Gleaton, Jerry Don	82T	371	$ .01	$ .06
Gilbreath, Rod	79T	572	$ .02	$ .10	Gleaton, Jerry Don	85T	216	$ .01	$ .04
Gile, Don	61T	236	$ .30	$1.00	Gleaton, Jerry Don	86T	447	$ .01	$ .03
Gile, Don	62T	244	$ .35	$1.10	Gleaton, Jerry Don	88T	116	$ .01	$ .03
Giles, Brian	83T	548	$ .01	$ .06	Gleaton, Jerry Don	89T	724	$ .01	$ .04
Giles, Brian	84T	676	$ .01	$ .05	Glynn, Bill	53T	171	$3.75	$13.00
Giles, Warren	56T	2	$2.75	$8.00	Glynn, Bill (Gylnn)	54T	178	$2.10	$7.50
Giles, Warren	57T	100	$2.10	$7.50	Glynn, Bill	55T	39	$1.35	$5.00
Giles, Warren	58T	300	$1.25	$3.50	Glynn, Ed	77T	487	$ .03	$ .12
Giles, Warren	59T	200	$ .70	$2.00	Glynn, Ed	79T	343	$ .02	$ .10
Gilliam, Jim	53T	258	$70.00	$200.00	Glynn, Ed	80T	509	$ .01	$ .07
Gilliam, Junior	54T	35	$7.00	$20.00	Glynn, Ed	81T	93	$ .01	$ .07
Gilliam, Jim	55T	5	$3.00	$11.00	Glynn, Ed	83T	614	$ .01	$ .06
Gilliam, Jim	56T	280	$3.00	$12.00	Goggin, Chuck	74T	457	$ .06	$ .25
Gilliam, Jim	57T	115	$2.50	$8.50	Gogolewski, Bill	71T	559	$ .30	$1.00
Gilliam, Jim	58T	215	$ .95	$3.00	Gogolewski, Bill	72T	424	$ .05	$ .25
Gilliam, Jim	59T	306	$1.25	$3.50	Gogolewski, Bill	73T	27	$ .06	$ .25
Gilliam, Jim	60T	255	$1.25	$3.50	Gogolewski, Bill	74T	242	$ .06	$ .25
Gilliam, Jim	61T	238	$ .70	$2.00	Golden, Jim	61T	298	$ .30	$1.00
Gilliam, Jim	62T	486	$1.25	$3.50	Golden, Jim	62T	568	$3.75	$11.00
Gilliam, Jim	63T	80	$1.00	$3.75	Golden, Jim	63T	297	$ .35	$1.20
Gilliam, Jim	64T	310	$ .70	$2.00	Goldsberry, Gordon	52T	46	$14.00	$45.00
Gilliam, Jim	73T	569	$1.00	$3.75	Goldsberry, Gordon	53T	200	$3.75	$13.00
Gilliam, Jim	74T	144	$ .50	$2.00	Goldy, Purnal	63T	516	$1.50	$3.75
Gilson, Hal	68T	162	$ .25	$ .65	Goltz, Dave	73T	148	$ .06	$ .25
Gilson, Hal	69T	156	$ .25	$ .65	Goltz, Dave	74T	636	$ .06	$ .25
Ginsberg, Joe	57T	236	$ .95	$3.50	Goltz, Dave	75T	419	$ .06	$ .25
Ginsberg, Joe	58T	67	$1.00	$3.75	Goltz, Dave	76T	136	$ .05	$ .20
Ginsberg, Joe	59T	66	$1.00	$3.75	Goltz, Dave	77T	321	$ .03	$ .12
Ginsberg, Joe	60T	304	$ .50	$1.95	Goltz, Dave	78T	205	$ .25	$ .65
Ginsberg, Joe	61T	79	$ .30	$1.00	Goltz, Dave	78T	249	$ .02	$ .10
Ginsberg, Myron	52T	192	$6.00	$19.00	Goltz, Dave	79T	27	$ .02	$ .10
Girardi, Joe	89TMLD	42	$ .01	$ .05	Goltz, Dave	80T	193	$ .01	$ .07
Girardi, Joe	90T	12	$ .01	$ .10	Goltz, Dave	81T	548	$ .01	$ .07
Giusti, Dave	62T	509	$ .70	$2.10	Goltz, Dave	82T	674	$ .01	$ .06
Giusti, Dave	63T	189	$ .25	$ .85	Goltz, Dave	83T	468	$ .01	$ .06
Giusti, Dave	64T	354	$ .25	$ .85	Gomez, Luis	77T	13	$ .03	$ .12
Giusti, Dave	65T	524	$1.50	$3.75	Gomez, Luis	78T	573	$ .02	$ .10
Giusti, Dave	66T	258	$ .25	$ .85	Gomez, Luis	79T	254	$ .02	$ .10
Giusti, Dave	67T	318	$ .25	$ .65	Gomez, Luis	80T	169	$ .01	$ .07

TOPPS

Player	Year	No.	VG	EX/MT	Player	Year	No.	VG	EX/MT
Gomez, Luis	81T	477	$ .01	$ .07	Gooden, Dwight "Doc"	89T	30	$ .01	$ .25
Gomez, Luis	82T	372	$ .01	$ .06	Gooden, Doc	89TBB	304	$ .01	$ .25
Gomez, Preston	69T	74	$ .25	$ .65	Gooden, Doc	90T	510	$ .01	$ .10
Gomez, Preston	70T	513	$ .10	$ .35	Goodman, Billy	51Trb	46	$1.25	$3.50
Gomez, Preston	71T	737	$ .70	$2.10	Goodman, Billy	52T	23	$12.50	$45.00
Gomez, Preston	72T	637	$ .25	$ .85	Goodman, Billy	56T	245	$3.00	$9.00
Gomez, Preston	73T	624	$ .55	$1.75	Goodman, Billy	57T	303	$3.50	$13.00
Gomez, Preston	74T	31	$ .06	$ .25	Goodman, Billy	58T	225	$ .50	$2.00
Gomez, Ruben	54T	220	$2.10	$7.50	Goodman, Billy	59T	103	$ .70	$2.00
Gomez, Ruben	55T	71	$1.35	$5.00	Goodman, Billy	60T	69	$ .50	$2.00
Gomez, Ruben	56T	9	$1.25	$4.50	Goodman, Billy	61T	247	$ .50	$2.00
Gomez, Ruben	57T	58	$ .95	$3.50	Goodson, Ed	73T	197	$ .06	$ .25
Gomez, Ruben	58T	335	$ .50	$2.00	Goodson, Ed	74T	494	$ .06	$ .25
Gomez, Ruben	59T	535	$2.00	$7.00	Goodson, Ed	75T	322	$ .06	$ .25
Gomez, Ruben	60T	82	$ .35	$1.10	Goodson, Ed	76T	386	$ .05	$ .20
Gomez, Ruben	61T	377	$ .50	$2.00	Goodson, Ed	77T	584	$ .03	$ .12
Gomez, Ruben	67T	427	$ .25	$ .85	Goodson, Ed	78T	586	$ .02	$ .10
Gonder, Jesse	63T	29	$ .35	$1.10	Goodwin, Danny	79T	322	$ .02	$ .10
Gonder, Jesse	64T	457	$ .40	$1.25	Goodwin, Danny	80T	362	$ .01	$ .07
Gonder, Jesse	65T	423	$ .30	$1.00	Goodwin, Danny	81T	527	$ .01	$ .07
Gonder, Jesse	66T	528	$4.00	$10.00	Goodwin, Danny	82T	123	$ .01	$ .06
Gonder, Jesse	67T	301	$ .25	$ .65	Goossen, Greg	67T	287	$ .25	$ .65
Gonder, Jesse	69T	617	$ .25	$ .85	Goossen, Greg	68T	386	$ .25	$ .65
Gonzales, Rene	88T	98	$ .01	$ .10	Goossen, Greg	70T	271	$ .10	$ .35
Gonzales, Rene	88TBB	209	$ .01	$ .05	Gorbous, Glen	56T	174	$1.25	$4.50
Gonzales, Rene	89T	213	$ .01	$ .04	Gordon, Don	88T	144	$ .01	$ .03
Gonzales, Rene	89TBB	87	$ .01	$ .05	Gordon, Joe	60T	216	$ .35	$1.10
Gonzales, Rene	90T	787	$ .01	$ .03	Gordon, Joe	61T	224	$ .30	$1.00
Gonzalez, Denny	86T	746	$ .01	$ .03	Gordon, Joe	69T	484	$ .25	$ .65
Gonzalez, Fernando	74T	649	$ .06	$ .25	Gordon, Sid	51Trb	2	$1.25	$3.50
Gonzalez, Fernando	74TTR	649	$ .06	$ .25	Gordon, Sid	52T	267	$11.50	$38.00
Gonzalez, Fernando	78T	433	$ .02	$ .10	Gordon, Sid	53T	117	$3.75	$13.00
Gonzalez, Fernando	79T	531	$ .02	$ .10	Gordon, Tom	89TTR	38	$ .01	$1.00
Gonzalez, Fernando	80T	171	$ .01	$ .07	Gordon, Tom	90T	752	$ .01	$ .50
Gonzalez, German	89T	746	$ .01	$ .04	Gorinski, Bob	78T	386	$ .02	$ .10
Gonzalez, German	90T	266	$ .01	$ .03	Gorman, Tom	56T	246	$2.50	$8.00
Gonzalez, Jose	90T	98	$ .01	$ .03	Gorman, Tom	57T	87	$ .95	$3.50
Gonzalez, Juan	89TMLD	43	$ .01	$ .50	Gorman, Tom	58T	235	$ .50	$2.00
Gonzalez, Juan	90T	331	$ .01	$ .40	Gorman, Tom	59T	449	$ .50	$1.95
Gonzalez, Julio	78T	389	$ .02	$ .10	Gorman, Tom	84T	774	$ .01	$ .05
Gonzalez, Julio	79T	268	$ .02	$ .10	Gorman, Tom	85T	53	$ .01	$ .04
Gonzalez, Julio	80T	696	$ .01	$ .07					
Gonzalez, Julio	82T	503	$ .01	$ .06					
Gonzalez, Julio	83T	74	$ .01	$ .06					
Gonzalez, Orlando	77T	477	$ .05	$ .15					
Gonzalez, Pedro	63T	537	$150.00	$450.00					
Gonzalez, Pedro	64T	581	$1.50	$3.75					
Gonzalez, Pedro	65T	97	$ .25	$ .65					
Gonzalez, Pedro	66T	266	$ .25	$ .85					
Gonzalez, Pedro	67T	424	$ .25	$ .85					
Gonzalez, Tony	60T	518	$2.00	$7.00					
Gonzalez, Tony	61T	93	$ .30	$1.00					
Gonzalez, Tony	62T	534	$3.75	$11.00					
Gonzalez, Tony	63T	32	$ .25	$ .85					
Gonzalez, Tony	64T	379	$ .40	$1.25					
Gonzalez, Tony	65T	72	$ .25	$ .65					
Gonzalez, Tony	66T	478	$ .70	$2.10					
Gonzalez, Tony	67T	548	$1.25	$3.50					
Gonzalez, Tony	68T	1	$2.50	$12.50					
Gonzalez, Tony	68T	245	$ .25	$ .65					
Gonzalez, Tony	69T	501	$ .25	$ .65					
Gonzalez, Tony	70T	105	$ .10	$ .35					
Gonzalez, Tony	71T	256	$ .10	$ .35					
Gooden, Dwight	84TTR	42	$12.50	$40.00					
Gooden, Dwight	85T	620	$3.00	$9.00					
Gooden, Dwight	85TRB	3	$ .20	$1.00					
Gooden, Dwight	86T	250	$ .50	$2.00					
Gooden, Dwight	86TAS	709	$ .03	$ .25					
Gooden, Dwight	86TRB	202	$ .03	$ .30					
Gooden, Dwight	87T	130	$ .25	$ .75					
Gooden, Dwight	87TAS	603	$ .25	$ .65					
Gooden, Dwight	88T	480	$ .10	$ .40					
Gooden, Dwight	88TAS	405	$ .01	$ .25					
Gooden, Dwight	88TBB	11	$ .05	$ .35	Gorman, Tom	86T	414	$ .01	$ .03
Gooden, Dwight	89TTB	661	$ .01	$ .10	Goryl, John	58T	384	$ .50	$2.00

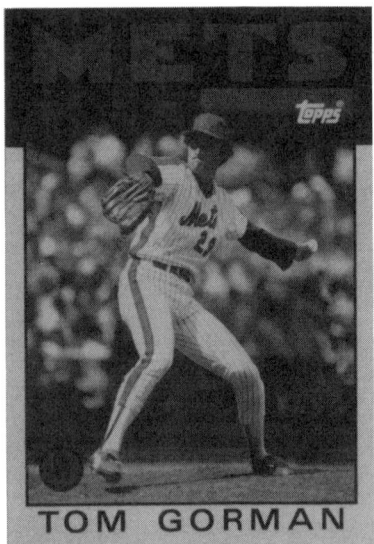

TOM GORMAN

Player	Year	No.	VG	EX/MT	Player	Year	No.	VG	EX/MT
Goryl, John	59T	77	$1.00	$3.75	Grammas, Alex	60T	168	$ .35	$1.10
Goryl, John	62T	558	$3.75	$11.00	Grammas, Alex	61T	64	$ .30	$1.00
Goryl, John	63T	314	$ .35	$1.20	Grammas, Alex	62T	223	$ .35	$1.10
Goryl, John	64T	194	$ .25	$ .85	Grammas, Alex	63T	416	$ .35	$1.20
Gosger, Jim	63T	553	$60.00	$175.00	Grammas, Alex	73T	296	$ .15	$ .50
Gosger, Jim	66T	114	$ .25	$ .85	Grammas, Alex	74T	326	$ .15	$ .50
Gosger, Jim	67T	17	$ .25	$ .65	Granger, Wayne	69T	551	$ .25	$ .85
Gosger, Jim	68T	343	$ .25	$ .65	Granger, Wayne	70T	73	$ .10	$ .35
Gosger, Jim	69T	482	$ .25	$ .65	Granger, Wayne	71T	379	$ .10	$ .35
Gosger, Jim	70T	651	$ .50	$2.00	Granger, Wayne	72T	545	$ .25	$ .85
Gosger, Jim	71T	284	$ .10	$ .35	Granger, Wayne	73T	523	$ .06	$ .25
Goss, Howie	62T	598	$12.00	$50.00	Granger, Wayne	74T	644	$ .06	$ .25
Goss, Howie	63T	364	$ .35	$1.20	Granger, Wayne	76T	516	$ .05	$ .20
Gossage, Rich	73T	174	$1.75	$5.00	Grant, Jim	58T	394	$ .65	$2.00
Gossage, Rich	74T	542	$ .60	$1.75	Grant, Jim "Mudcat"	59T	186	$ .50	$1.95
Gossage, Rich	75T	554	$ .35	$1.10	Grant, Jim	60T	14	$ .35	$1.10
Gossage, Rich	76T	180	$ .35	$1.10	Grant, Jim	61T	18	$ .30	$1.00
Gossage, Rich	76T	205	$ .10	$ .35	Grant, Jim	62T	307	$ .35	$1.10
Gossage, Rich	77T	319	$ .35	$1.10	Grant, Jim	63T	227	$ .25	$ .85
Gossage, Rich	78T	70	$ .15	$ .50	Grant, Jim	64T	133	$ .25	$ .85
Gossage, Rich	79T	8	$ .05	$ .25	Grant, Jim	65T	432	$ .30	$1.00
Gossage, Rich	79T	225	$ .25	$ .65	Grant, Jim	66T	40	$ .25	$ .85
Gossage, Rich	80T	140	$ .25	$ .65	Grant, Jim	66T	224	$ .60	$1.75
Gossage, Rich	81T	460	$ .05	$ .25	Grant, Jim	67T	545	$1.25	$3.50
Gossage, Rich	82T	770	$ .05	$ .25	Grant, Jim	68T	398	$ .25	$ .65
Gossage, Rich	82TAS	557	$ .01	$ .10	Grant, Jim	69T	306	$ .25	$ .85
Gossage, Rich	82TIA	771	$ .02	$ .10	Grant, Jim	71T	509	$ .10	$ .35
Gossage, Rich	83T	240	$ .05	$ .20	Grant, Jim	72T	111	$ .05	$ .25
Gossage, Rich	83T	241	$ .01	$ .06	Grant, Mark	88T	752	$ .01	$ .03
Gossage, Rich	84T	670	$ .03	$ .15	Grant, Mark	89T	178	$ .01	$ .04
Gossage, Rich	84T	718	$ .01	$ .05	Grant, Mark	89TBB	154	$ .01	$ .05
Gossage, Rich	84TTR	43	$ .10	$ .35	Grant, Mark	90T	537	$ .01	$ .03
Gossage, Rich	85T	90	$ .03	$ .15	Grasso, Mickey	52T	90	$6.00	$19.00
Gossage, Rich	86T	530	$ .01	$ .10	Grasso, Mickey	53T	148	$3.75	$13.00
Gossage, Rich	87T	380	$ .01	$ .10	Gray, Dave	64T	572	$1.50	$3.75
Gossage, Rich	88T	170	$ .01	$ .10	Gray, Dick	58T	146	$ .50	$2.00
Gossage, Rich	88TTR	41	$ .01	$ .05	Gray, Dick	59T	244	$ .50	$1.95
Gossage, Rich	89T	415	$ .01	$ .04	Gray, Dick	60T	24	$ .35	$1.10
Gotay, Julio	62T	489	$ .70	$2.10	Gray, Gary	81TTR	767	$ .02	$ .10
Gotay, Julio	63T	122	$ .25	$ .85	Gray, Gary	82T	523	$ .01	$ .06
Gotay, Julio	65T	552	$1.50	$3.75	Gray, Gary	83T	313	$ .01	$ .06
Gotay, Julio	68T	41	$ .25	$ .65	Gray, Johnny	55T	101	$1.35	$5.00
Gott, Jim	83T	506	$ .01	$ .06	Gray, Lorenzo	84T	163	$ .01	$ .05
Gott, Jim	84T	9	$ .01	$ .05	Gray, Ted	52T	86	$6.00	$19.00
Gott, Jim	85T	311	$ .01	$ .04	Gray, Ted	53T	52	$3.75	$13.00
Gott, Jim	85TTR	40	$ .02	$ .10	Grba, Eli	60T	183	$ .35	$1.10
Gott, Jim	86T	463	$ .01	$ .03	Grba, Eli	61T	121	$ .30	$1.00
Gott, Jim	87TTR	39	$ .01	$ .07	Grba, Eli	62T	96	$ .35	$1.10
Gott, Jim	88T	127	$ .01	$ .03	Grba, Eli	63T	231	$ .25	$ .85
Gott, Jim	89T	752	$ .01	$ .04	Green, Dallas	60T	366	$1.00	$4.00
Gott, Jim	90T	292	$ .01	$ .03	Green, Dallas	61T	359	$ .30	$1.00
Gozzo, Goose	89TMLD	44	$ .01	$ .05	Green, Dallas	62T	111	$ .35	$1.10
Gozzo, Goose	90T	274	$ .01	$ .10	Green, Dallas	63T	91	$ .25	$ .85
Grabarkewitz, Billy	70T	446	$ .10	$ .35	Green, Dallas	64T	464	$ .40	$1.25
Grabarkewitz, Billy	71T	85	$ .10	$ .35	Green, Dallas	65T	203	$ .30	$1.00
Grabarkewitz, Billy	72T	578	$ .25	$ .85	Green, Dallas	89T	104	$ .01	$ .04
Grabarkewitz, Billy	73T	301	$ .06	$ .25	Green, David	83T	578	$ .01	$ .06
Grabarkewitz, Billy	74T	214	$ .06	$ .25	Green, David	84T	362	$ .01	$ .05
Grabarkewitz, Billy	75T	233	$ .06	$ .25	Green, David	85T	87	$ .01	$ .04
Grace, Mark	88TTR	42	$1.25	$5.75	Green, David	85TTR	41	$ .02	$ .10
Grace, Mark	89T	465	$ .75	$2.25	Green, David	86T	727	$ .01	$ .03
Grace, Mark	89TBB	189	$ .01	$ .50	Green, Dick	64T	466	$ .40	$1.25
Grace, Mark	90T	240	$ .01	$ .35	Green, Dick	65T	168	$ .25	$ .65
Graff, Milt	57T	369	$1.00	$3.75	Green, Dick	66T	545	$4.50	$15.00
Graff, Milt	58T	192	$ .50	$2.00	Green, Dick	67T	54	$ .25	$ .65
Graff, Milt	59T	182	$ .50	$1.95	Green, Dick	68T	303	$ .25	$ .65
Graham, Dan	80T	669	$ .06	$ .30	Green, Dick	69T	515	$ .25	$ .85
Graham, Dan	81T	161	$ .01	$ .07	Green, Dick	70T	311	$ .10	$ .35
Graham, Dan	82T	37	$ .01	$ .06	Green, Dick	71T	258	$ .10	$ .35
Grammas, Alex	54T	151	$2.10	$7.50	Green, Dick	72T	780	$ .70	$2.10
Grammas, Alex	55T	21	$1.35	$5.00	Green, Dick	73T	456	$ .06	$ .25
Grammas, Alex	56T	37	$1.25	$4.50	Green, Dick	74T	392	$ .06	$ .25
Grammas, Alex	57T	222	$ .95	$3.50	Green, Dick	75T	91	$ .06	$ .25
Grammas, Alex	58T	254	$ .50	$2.00	Green, Fred	60T	272	$ .35	$1.10
Grammas, Alex	59T	6	$1.00	$3.75	Green, Fred	61T	181	$ .30	$1.00

Player	Year	No.	VG	EX/MT	Player	Year	No.	VG	EX/MT
Green, Gary	85T	396	$ .01	$ .04	Grich, Bob	71T	193	$ .50	$1.95
Green, Gene	58T	366	$ .50	$2.00	Grich, Bob	72T	338	$ .05	$ .25
Green, Gene	59T	37	$1.00	$3.75	Grich, Bob	73T	418	$ .25	$ .65
Green, Gene	60T	269	$ .35	$1.10	Grich, Bob	74T	109	$ .06	$ .25
Green, Gene	61T	206	$ .30	$1.00	Grich, Bob	75T	225	$ .10	$ .35
Green, Gene	62T	78	$ .35	$1.10	Grich, Bob	76T	335	$ .05	$ .20
Green, Gene	63T	506	$2.50	$6.50	Grich, Bob	77T	521	$ .03	$ .12
Green, Lenny	58T	471	$ .50	$1.95	Grich, Bob	78T	18	$ .02	$ .10
Green, Lenny	59T	209	$ .50	$1.95	Grich, Bob	79T	477	$ .02	$ .10
Green, Lenny	60T	99	$ .35	$1.10	Grich, Bob	80T	621	$ .01	$ .07
Green, Lenny	61T	4	$ .30	$1.00	Grich, Bob	81T	182	$ .01	$ .07
Green, Lenny	62T	84	$ .35	$1.10	Grich, Bob	82T	162	$ .05	$ .25
Green, Lenny	63T	198	$ .25	$ .85	Grich, Bob	82T	284	$ .01	$ .06
Green, Lenny	64T	386	$ .40	$1.25	Grich, Bob	83T	790	$ .01	$ .06
Green, Lenny	65T	588	$1.50	$3.75	Grich, Bob	83TAS	387	$ .01	$ .06
Green, Lenny	66T	502	$ .70	$2.10	Grich, Bob	84T	315	$ .01	$ .05
Green, Pumpsie	60T	317	$ .50	$1.95	Grich, Bob	85T	465	$ .01	$ .04
Green, Pumpsie	61T	454	$ .50	$2.00	Grich, Bob	86T	155	$ .01	$ .03
Green, Pumpsie	62T	153	$ .35	$1.10	Grich, Bob	87T	677	$ .01	$ .03
Green, Pumpsie	63T	292	$ .35	$1.20	Grieve, Tom	71T	167	$ .10	$ .35
Green, Pumpsie	64T	442	$ .40	$1.25	Grieve, Tom	72T	609	$ .25	$ .85
Greene, Al	80T	666	$ .01	$ .07	Grieve, Tom	73T	579	$ .35	$1.10
Greene, Tommy	89TMLD	45	$ .01	$ .05	Grieve, Tom	74T	268	$ .06	$ .25
Greengrass, Jim	53T	209	$3.75	$13.00	Grieve, Tom	75T	234	$ .06	$ .25
Greengrass, Jim	54T	22	$2.10	$7.50	Grieve, Tom	76T	106	$ .05	$ .20
Greengrass, Jim	56T	275	$1.80	$6.00	Grieve, Tom	77T	403	$ .03	$ .12
Greenwell, Mike	87T	259	$1.50	$4.50	Grieve, Tom	78T	337	$ .02	$ .10
Greenwell, Mike	88T	493	$ .30	$1.25	Grieve, Tom	79T	277	$ .02	$ .10
Greenwell, Mike	88TBB	233	$ .15	$1.00	Griffey, Jr., Ken	89TMLD	46	$ .01	$1.25
Greenwell, Mike	89T	630	$ .10	$ .50	Griffey, Jr., Ken	89TTR	41	$ .01	$4.50
Greenwell, Mike	89TAS	402	$ .05	$ .25	Griffey, Jr., Ken	90T	336	$ .01	$1.50
Greenwell, Mike	89TBB	211	$ .01	$ .40	Griffey, Ken	74T	598	$1.00	$4.00
Greenwell, Mike	90T	70	$ .01	$ .25	Griffey, Ken	75T	284	$ .25	$ .85
Greer, Brian	80T	685	$ .01	$ .07	Griffey, Ken	76T	128	$ .06	$ .25
Gregg, Hal	52T	318	$39.00	$135.00	Griffey, Ken	77T	320	$ .10	$ .35
Gregg, Tommy	89TTR	39	$ .01	$ .15	Griffey, Ken	78T	80	$ .05	$ .25
Gregg, Tommy	90T	223	$ .01	$ .03	Griffey, Ken	79T	420	$ .05	$ .20
Greif, Bill	72T	101	$ .35	$1.25	Griffey, Ken	80T	550	$ .06	$ .25
Greif, Bill	73T	583	$ .35	$1.10	Griffey, Ken	81T	280	$ .03	$ .15
Greif, Bill	74T	102	$ .06	$ .25	Griffey, Ken	82T	620	$ .03	$ .15
Greif, Bill	75T	168	$ .06	$ .25	Griffey, Ken	82T	756	$ .05	$ .20
					Griffey, Ken	82TIA	621	$ .01	$ .06
					Griffey, Ken	82TTR	40	$ .10	$ .35
					Griffey, Ken	83T	110	$ .01	$ .10
					Griffey, Ken	84T	770	$ .02	$ .10
					Griffey, Ken	85T	380	$ .01	$ .04
					Griffey, Ken	86T	40	$ .01	$ .03
					Griffey, Ken	86TTR	41	$ .02	$ .10
					Griffey, Ken	87T	711	$ .01	$ .03
					Griffey, Ken	88T	443	$ .01	$ .03
					Griffey, Ken	88TBB	110	$ .01	$ .10
					Griffey, Ken	89TTR	40	$ .01	$ .10
					Griffey, Ken	90T	581	$ .01	$ .03
					Griffin, Alfredo	79T	705	$ .35	$1.20
					Griffin, Alfredo	80T	558	$ .01	$ .07
					Griffin, Alfredo	81T	277	$ .01	$ .07
					Griffin, Alfredo	82T	677	$ .01	$ .06
					Griffin, Alfredo	83T	488	$ .01	$ .06
					Griffin, Alfredo	84T	76	$ .01	$ .05
					Griffin, Alfredo	85T	361	$ .01	$ .04
					Griffin, Alfredo	85TTR	42	$ .02	$ .10
					Griffin, Alfredo	86T	566	$ .01	$ .03
					Griffin, Alfredo	87T	111	$ .01	$ .03
					Griffin, Alfredo	88T	726	$ .01	$ .03
					Griffin, Alfredo	88TBB	247	$ .01	$ .05
					Griffin, Alfredo	88TTR	43	$ .01	$ .05
					Griffin, Alfredo	89T	62	$ .01	$ .04
					Griffin, Alfredo	90T	643	$ .01	$ .03
					Griffin, Doug	71T	176	$ .10	$ .35
					Griffin, Doug	72T	703	$ .70	$2.10
					Griffin, Doug	72TIA	704	$ .70	$2.10
					Griffin, Doug	73T	96	$ .06	$ .25
					Griffin, Doug	74T	219	$ .06	$ .25
Greif, Bill	76T	184	$ .05	$ .20	Griffin, Doug	75T	454	$ .06	$ .25
Greif, Bill	77T	112	$ .03	$ .12	Griffin, Doug	76T	654	$ .05	$ .20

BILL GREIF
PITCHER PADRES

Player	Year	No.	VG	EX/MT	Player	Year	No.	VG	EX/MT
Griffin, Doug	77T	191	$ .03	$ .12	Gromek, Steve	52T	258	$11.50	$38.00
Griffin, Mike	81T	483	$ .01	$ .07	Gromek, Steve	56T	310	$1.80	$6.00
Griffin, Mike	82T	146	$ .01	$ .06	Gromek, Steve	57T	258	$ .95	$3.50
Griffin, Tom	69T	614	$ .25	$ .85	Gross, Don	57T	341	$3.50	$13.00
Griffin, Tom	70T	578	$ .25	$ .85	Gross, Don	58T	172	$ .50	$2.00
Griffin, Tom	71T	471	$ .10	$ .35	Gross, Don	59T	228	$ .50	$1.95
Griffin, Tom	73T	468	$ .06	$ .25	Gross, Don	60T	284	$ .35	$1.10
Griffin, Tom	74T	256	$ .06	$ .25	Gross, Greg	75T	334	$ .06	$ .25
Griffin, Tom	75T	188	$ .06	$ .25	Gross, Greg	76T	171	$ .05	$ .20
Griffin, Tom	76T	454	$ .05	$ .20	Gross, Greg	77T	614	$ .03	$ .12
Griffin, Tom	77T	39	$ .03	$ .12	Gross, Greg	78T	397	$ .02	$ .10
Griffin, Tom	78T	318	$ .02	$ .10	Gross, Greg	79T	579	$ .02	$ .10
Griffin, Tom	79T	291	$ .02	$ .10	Gross, Greg	80T	718	$ .01	$ .07
Griffin, Tom	80T	649	$ .01	$ .07	Gross, Greg	81T	459	$ .01	$ .07
Griffin, Tom	81T	538	$ .01	$ .07	Gross, Greg	82T	53	$ .01	$ .06
Griffin, Tom	82T	777	$ .01	$ .06	Gross, Greg	83T	279	$ .01	$ .06
Griffin, Ty	88TTR	44	$ .30	$1.25	Gross, Greg	84T	613	$ .01	$ .05
Griffin, Ty	89T	713	$ .15	$ .75	Gross, Greg	85T	117	$ .01	$ .04
Griffin, Ty	89TBB	170	$ .01	$ .40	Gross, Greg	86T	302	$ .01	$ .03
Griffith, Derrell	65T	112	$ .25	$ .65	Gross, Greg	87T	702	$ .01	$ .03
Griffith, Derrell	66T	573	$4.50	$15.00	Gross, Greg	88T	518	$ .01	$ .03
Griffith, Derrell	67T	502	$ .50	$2.00	Gross, Greg	89T	438	$ .01	$ .04
Griggs, Hal	58T	455	$ .50	$1.95	Gross, Kevin	84T	332	$ .05	$ .25
Griggs, Hal	59T	434	$ .50	$1.95	Gross, Kevin	85T	584	$ .01	$ .04
Griggs, Hal	60T	244	$ .35	$1.10	Gross, Kevin	86T	764	$ .01	$ .03
Grilli, Guido	66T	558	$5.50	$17.50	Gross, Kevin	87T	163	$ .01	$ .03
Grilli, Steve	76T	591	$ .05	$ .20	Gross, Kevin	88T	20	$ .01	$ .03
Grilli, Steve	77T	506	$ .03	$ .12	Gross, Kevin	89T	215	$ .01	$ .04
Grim, Bob	55T	80	$2.10	$7.50	Gross, Kevin	89TTR	42	$ .01	$ .05
Grim, Bob	56T	52	$1.25	$4.50	Gross, Kevin	90T	465	$ .01	$ .03
Grim, Bob	57T	36	$ .95	$3.50	Gross, Wayne	77T	479	$ .03	$ .12
Grim, Bob	58T	224	$ .45	$1.50	Gross, Wayne	78T	139	$ .02	$ .10
Grim, Bob	59T	423	$ .50	$1.95	Gross, Wayne	79T	528	$ .02	$ .10
Grim, Bob	60T	78	$ .35	$1.10	Gross, Wayne	80T	363	$ .01	$ .07
Grim, Bob	62T	564	$3.75	$11.00	Gross, Wayne	81T	86	$ .01	$ .07
Grimm, Charley	60T	217	$ .35	$1.10	Gross, Wayne	82T	692	$ .01	$ .06
Grimsley, Jason	89TMLD	47	$ .01	$ .10	Gross, Wayne	83T	233	$ .01	$ .06
Grimsley, Jason	90T	493	$ .01	$ .10	Gross, Wayne	84T	741	$ .01	$ .05
Grimsley, Ross	72T	99	$ .25	$ .65	Gross, Wayne	84TTR	44	$ .02	$ .10
Grimsley, Ross	73T	357	$ .06	$ .25	Gross, Wayne	85T	416	$ .01	$ .04
Grimsley, Ross	74T	59	$ .06	$ .25	Gross, Wayne	86T	173	$ .01	$ .03
Grimsley, Ross	74TTR	59	$ .06	$ .25	Grote, Gerald "Jerry"	64T	226	$ .25	$ .85
Grimsley, Ross	75T	458	$ .06	$ .25	Grote, Jerry	65T	504	$ .50	$2.00
Grimsley, Ross	76T	257	$ .05	$ .20	Grote, Jerry	66T	328	$ .25	$ .85
Grimsley, Ross	77T	572	$ .03	$ .12	Grote, Jerry	67T	413	$ .25	$ .85
Grimsley, Ross	78T	691	$ .02	$ .10	Grote, Jerry	68T	582	$ .30	$1.00
Grimsley, Ross	79T	15	$ .02	$ .10	Grote, Jerry	69T	55	$ .25	$ .65
Grimsley, Ross	80T	375	$ .01	$ .07	Grote, Jerry	70T	183	$ .10	$ .35
Grimsley, Ross	81T	170	$ .01	$ .07	Grote, Jerry	71T	278	$ .10	$ .35
Grissom, Marquis	89TMLD	48	$ .01	$ .50	Grote, Jerry	72T	655	$ .25	$ .85
Grissom, Marquis	90T	714	¢ .01	$ .40	Grote, Jerry	73T	113	$ .06	$ .25
Grissom, Marv	56T	301	$1.80	$6.00	Grote, Jerry	74T	311	$ .06	$ .25
Grissom, Marv	57T	216	$ .95	$3.50	Grote, Jerry	75T	158	$ .06	$ .25
Grissom, Marv	58T	399	$ .50	$2.00	Grote, Jerry	76T	143	$ .05	$ .20
Grissom, Marv	59T	243	$ .50	$1.95	Grote, Jerry	78T	464	$ .02	$ .10
Groat, Dick	52T	369	$70.00	$210.00	Grote, Jerry	79T	279	$ .02	$ .10
Groat, Dick	53T	154	$6.00	$17.50	Groth, Johnny	51Tbb	11	$5.50	$17.00
Groat, Dick	54T	43	$2.00	$7.00	Groth, Johnny	52T	25	$14.00	$45.00
Groat, Dick	55T	26	$2.10	$7.50	Groth, Johnny	53T	36	$3.75	$13.00
Groat, Dick	56T	24	$1.25	$3.50	Groth, Johnny	56T	279	$1.80	$6.00
Groat, Dick	57T	12	$1.35	$5.00	Groth, Johnny	57T	360	$1.00	$3.75
Groat, Dick	58T	45	$ .70	$2.25	Groth, Johnny	58T	262	$ .50	$2.00
Groat, Dick	59T	160	$ .60	$1.75	Groth, Johnny	59T	164	$ .50	$1.95
Groat, Dick	60T	258	$ .25	$2.50	Groth, Johnny	60T	171	$ .35	$1.10
Groat, Dick	61T	1	$3.00	$18.00	Grove, Lefty	76TAS	350	$ .35	$1.10
Groat, Dick	61T	41	$1.50	$5.00	Grubb, John	74T	32	$ .06	$ .25
Groat, Dick	61TMVP	486	$ .60	$1.75	Grubb, Johnny	75T	298	$ .06	$ .25
Groat, Dick	62T	270	$ .50	$2.00	Grubb, Johnny	76T	422	$ .05	$ .20
Groat, Dick	63T	130	$ .30	$1.00	Grubb, Johnny	77T	286	$ .03	$ .12
Groat, Dick	64T	7	$1.70	$5.00	Grubb, Johnny	78T	608	$ .02	$ .10
Groat, Dick	64T	40	$ .15	$ .50	Grubb, Johnny	79T	198	$ .02	$ .10
Groat, Dick	65T	275	$ .50	$2.00	Grubb, Johnny	80T	313	$ .01	$ .07
Groat, Dick	66T	103	$ .35	$1.10	Grubb, Johnny	81T	545	$ .01	$ .07
Groat, Dick	67T	205	$ .35	$1.10	Grubb, Johnny	82T	496	$ .01	$ .06
Groat, Dick	75T	198	$ .50	$1.95	Grubb, Johnny	83T	724	$ .01	$ .06

TOPPS

Player	Year	No.	VG	EX/MT	Player	Year	No.	VG	EX/MT
Grubb, Johnny	83TTR	38	$ .02	$ .10	Guidry, Ron	83T	440	$ .05	$ .20
Grubb, Johnny	84T	42	$ .01	$ .05	Guidry, Ron	84T	110	$ .05	$ .25
Grubb, Johnny	85T	643	$ .01	$ .04	Guidry, Ron	84T	486	$ .01	$ .05
Grubb, Johnny	86T	243	$ .01	$ .03	Guidry, Ron	84T	717	$ .01	$ .05
Grubb, Johnny	87T	384	$ .01	$ .03	Guidry, Ron	84TAS	406	$ .01	$ .05
Grubb, Johnny	88T	128	$ .01	$ .03	Guidry, Ron	85T	790	$ .05	$ .20
Gruber, Kelly	87T	458	$ .01	$ .03	Guidry, Ron	86T	610	$ .01	$ .10
Gruber, Kelly	88T	113	$ .01	$ .03	Guidry, Ron	86TAS	721	$ .01	$ .03
Gruber, Kelly	88TBB	134	$ .01	$ .05	Guidry, Ron	87T	375	$ .01	$ .10
Gruber, Kelly	89T	29	$ .01	$ .04	Guidry, Ron	88T	535	$ .01	$ .10
Gruber, Kelly	89TBB	95	$ .01	$ .05	Guidry, Ron	88TBB	50	$ .01	$ .05
Gruber, Kelly	90T	505	$ .01	$ .03	Guidry, Ron	89T	255	$ .01	$ .04
Grunwald, Al	60T	427	$ .50	$1.95	Guillen, Ozzie	85TTR	43	$ .25	$ .85
Grzenda, Joe	69T	121	$ .25	$ .65	Guillen, Ozzie	86T	254	$ .02	$ .20
Grzenda, Joe	70T	691	$ .50	$2.00	Guillen, Ozzie	87T	89	$ .01	$ .10
Grzenda, Joe	71T	518	$ .10	$ .35	Guillen, Ozzie	88T	585	$ .01	$ .03
Grzenda, Joe	72T	13	$ .05	$ .25	Guillen, Ozzie	88TBB	27	$ .01	$ .05
Guante, Cecilio	84T	122	$ .01	$ .05	Guillen, Ozzie	89T	195	$ .01	$ .04
Guante, Cecilio	85T	457	$ .01	$ .04	Guillen, Ozzie	89TBB	148	$ .01	$ .05
Guante, Cecilio	86T	668	$ .01	$ .03	Guillen, Ozzie	90T	365	$ .01	$ .03
Guante, Cecilio	87T	219	$ .01	$ .03	Guindon, Bob	65T	509	$ .50	$2.00
Guante, Cecilio	87TTR	40	$ .01	$ .07	Guinn, Skip	69T	614	$ .25	$ .85
Guante, Cecilio	88T	84	$ .01	$ .03	Guinn, Skip	70T	316	$ .10	$ .35
Guante, Cecilio	89T	766	$ .01	$ .04	Guinn, Skip	71T	741	$ .70	$2.10
Guante, Cecilio	90T	532	$ .01	$ .03	Gulden, Brad	80T	670	$ .01	$ .07
Gubicza, Mark	84TTR	45	$1.00	$4.00					
Gubicza, Mark	85T	127	$ .50	$1.50					
Gubicza, Mark	86T	644	$ .01	$ .25					
Gubicza, Mark	87T	326	$ .01	$ .10					
Gubicza, Mark	88T	507	$ .01	$ .10					
Gubicza, Mark	88TBB	199	$ .01	$ .10					
Gubicza, Mark	89T	430	$ .01	$ .10					
Gubicza, Mark	89TBB	26	$ .01	$ .10					
Gubicza, Mark	90T	20	$ .01	$ .10					
Guerrero, Mario	73T	607	$ .35	$1.10					
Guerrero, Mario	74T	192	$ .06	$ .25					
Guerrero, Mario	75T	152	$ .06	$ .25					
Guerrero, Mario	76T	499	$ .05	$ .20					
Guerrero, Mario	77T	628	$ .03	$ .12					
Guerrero, Mario	78T	339	$ .02	$ .10					
Guerrero, Mario	79T	261	$ .02	$ .10					
Guerrero, Mario	80T	49	$ .01	$ .07					
Guerrero, Mario	81T	547	$ .01	$ .07					
Guerrero, Pedro	79T	719	$2.25	$9.00					
Guerrero, Pedro	81T	651	$ .30	$1.25					
Guerrero, Pedro	82T	247	$ .15	$ .60					
Guerrero, Pedro	83T	425	$ .06	$ .30					
Guerrero, Pedro	83T	681	$ .01	$ .06					
Guerrero, Pedro	84T	90	$ .08	$ .35					
Guerrero, Pedro	84T	306	$ .01	$ .05					
Guerrero, Pedro	85T	575	$ .05	$ .25					
Guerrero, Pedro	86T	145	$ .02	$ .20					
Guerrero, Pedro	86TAS	706	$ .01	$ .03	Gulden, Brad	85T	251	$ .01	$ .04
Guerrero, Pedro	87T	360	$ .06	$ .25	Gullett, Don	71T	124	$ .50	$2.00
Guerrero, Pedro	88T	550	$ .01	$ .10	Gullett, Don	72T	157	$ .25	$ .85
Guerrero, Pedro	88TBB	171	$ .01	$ .10	Gullett, Don	73T	595	$ .50	$1.95
Guerrero, Pedro	89T	780	$ .01	$ .10	Gullett, Don	74T	385	$ .06	$ .25
Guerrero, Pedro	89TBB	285	$ .01	$ .15	Gullett, Don	75T	65	$ .06	$ .25
Guerrero, Pedro	90T	610	$ .01	$ .10	Gullett, Don	76T	390	$ .06	$ .25
Guetterman, Lee	87T	307	$ .01	$ .10	Gullett, Don	77T	15	$ .03	$ .12
Guetterman, Lee	88T	656	$ .01	$ .03	Gullett, Don	78T	225	$ .02	$ .10
Guetterman, Lee	89TTR	43	$ .01	$ .05	Gullett, Don	79T	140	$ .02	$ .10
Guetterman, Lee	90T	286	$ .01	$ .03	Gullett, Don	80T	435	$ .01	$ .07
Guidry, Ron	76T	599	$4.00	$12.00	Gullickson, Bill	81T	578	$ .05	$ .25
Guidry, Ron	77T	656	$1.50	$3.75	Gullickson, Bill	81TRB	203	$ .01	$ .07
Guidry, Ron	78T	135	$ .20	$ .75	Gullickson, Bill	82T	172	$ .01	$ .06
Guidry, Ron	79T	5	$ .06	$ .30	Gullickson, Bill	82T	526	$ .01	$ .06
Guidry, Ron	79T	7	$ .03	$ .15	Gullickson, Bill	83T	31	$ .01	$ .06
Guidry, Ron	79T	500	$ .20	$ .75	Gullickson, Bill	84T	318	$ .01	$ .05
Guidry, Ron	79TRB	202	$ .05	$ .20	Gullickson, Bill	85T	687	$ .01	$ .04
Guidry, Ron	80T	207	$ .02	$ .10					
Guidry, Ron	80T	300	$ .01	$ .07					
Guidry, Ron	81T	250	$ .08	$ .35					
Guidry, Ron	82T	9	$ .05	$ .25					
Guidry, Ron	82TIA	10	$ .01	$ .06					

Player	Year	No.	VG	EX/MT
Gullickson, Bill	86T	229	$ .01	$ .03
Gullickson, Bill	86TTR	42	$ .02	$ .10
Gullickson, Bill	87T	489	$ .01	$ .03
Gullickson, Bill	88T	711	$ .01	$ .03
Gulliver, Glenn	83T	293	$ .01	$ .06
Gumpert, Dave	84T	371	$ .01	$ .05
Gumpert, Dave	87T	487	$ .01	$ .03
Gumpert, Randy	52T	247	$6.00	$19.00
Gura, Larry	71T	203	$ .15	$ .50
Gura, Larry	73T	501	$ .25	$ .85
Gura, Larry	74T	616	$ .06	$ .25
Gura, Larry	74TTR	616	$ .10	$ .35
Gura, Larry	75T	557	$ .06	$ .25
Gura, Larry	76T	319	$ .05	$ .20
Gura, Larry	77T	193	$ .03	$ .12
Gura, Larry	78T	441	$ .02	$ .10
Gura, Larry	79T	19	$ .02	$ .10
Gura, Larry	80T	295	$ .01	$ .07
Gura, Larry	81T	130	$ .01	$ .07
Gura, Larry	82T	96	$ .05	$ .25

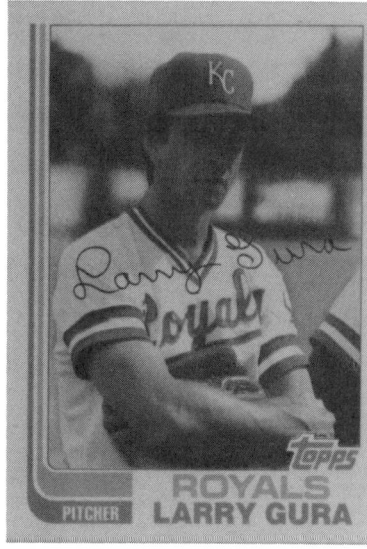

Player	Year	No.	VG	EX/MT
Gura, Larry	82T	790	$ .01	$ .06
Gura, Larry	83T	340	$ .01	$ .06
Gura, Larry	83TAS	395	$ .01	$ .06
Gura, Larry	84T	96	$ .01	$ .05
Gura, Larry	84T	625	$ .01	$ .05
Gura, Larry	85T	595	$ .01	$ .04
Guthrie, Mark	89TMLD	49	$ .01	$ .15
Guthrie, Mark	90T	317	$ .01	$ .10
Gutierrez, Cesar	69T	16	$ .25	$ .65
Gutierrez, Cesar	70T	269	$ .10	$ .35
Gutierrez, Cesar	71T	154	$ .10	$ .35
Gutierrez, Cesar	72T	743	$ .70	$2.10
Gutierrez, Jackie	84TTR	46	$ .02	$ .10
Gutierrez, Jackie	85T	89	$ .01	$ .04
Gutierrez, Jackie	86T	633	$ .01	$ .03
Gutierrez, Jackie	87T	276	$ .01	$ .03
Gutteridge, Don	60T	458	$ .95	$3.50
Gutteridge, Don	70T	123	$ .10	$ .35
Guzman, Jose	86TTR	43	$ .05	$ .25
Guzman, Jose	87T	363	$ .01	$ .03
Guzman, Jose	88T	563	$ .01	$ .03
Guzman, Jose	89T	462	$ .01	$ .04
Guzman, Jose	90T	308	$ .01	$ .03

Player	Year	No.	VG	EX/MT
Guzman, Santiago	70T	716	$ .50	$2.00
Guzman, Santiago	72T	316	$ .10	$ .35
Gwosdz, Doug	82T	731	$ .01	$ .06
Gwosdz, Doug	84T	753	$ .01	$ .05
Gwynn, Chris	90T	456	$ .01	$ .10
Gwynn, Tony	83T	482	$5.00	$18.00
Gwynn, Tony	84T	251	$ .60	$3.00
Gwynn, Tony	85T	660	$ .35	$1.25
Gwynn, Tony	85TAS	717	$ .05	$ .25
Gwynn, Tony	86T	10	$ .15	$ .50
Gwynn, Tony	87T	530	$ .25	$ .85
Gwynn, Tony	87TAS	599	$ .01	$ .10
Gwynn, Tony	88T	360	$ .01	$ .25
Gwynn, Tony	88TAS	402	$ .01	$ .10
Gwynn, Tony	88TBB	161	$ .05	$ .25
Gwynn, Tony	89T	570	$ .01	$ .10
Gwynn, Tony	89TBB	58	$ .01	$ .20
Gwynn, Tony	90T	730	$ .01	$ .10
Gwynn, Tony	90TAS	403	$ .01	$ .10
Haas, Bill	63T	544	$8.50	$25.00
Haas, Bill	64T	398	$ .40	$1.25
Haas, Eddie	59T	126	$ .50	$1.95
Haas, Eddie	85TTR	44	$ .02	$ .10
Haas, Moose	78T	649	$ .02	$ .10
Haas, Moose	79T	448	$ .02	$ .10
Haas, Moose	80T	181	$ .01	$ .07
Haas, Moose	81T	327	$ .01	$ .07
Haas, Moose	82T	12	$ .01	$ .06
Haas, Moose	83T	503	$ .01	$ .06
Haas, Moose	84T	271	$ .01	$ .05
Haas, Moose	84T	726	$ .01	$ .05
Haas, Moose	85T	151	$ .01	$ .04
Haas, Moose	86T	759	$ .01	$ .03
Haas, Moose	86TTR	44	$ .02	$ .10
Haas, Moose	87T	413	$ .01	$ .03
Haas, Moose	88T	606	$ .01	$ .03
Habyan, John	88T	153	$ .01	$ .03
Hack, Stan	55T	6	$2.10	$7.50
Hacker, Warren	52T	324	$39.00	$135.00
Hacker, Warren	56T	282	$1.80	$6.00
Hacker, Warren	57T	370	$1.00	$3.75
Hacker, Warren	58T	251	$ .50	$2.00
Haddix, Harvey	53T	273	$30.00	$100.00
Haddix, Harvey	54T	9	$2.50	$9.00
Haddix, Harvey	55T	43	$2.10	$7.50
Haddix, Harvey	56T	77	$1.25	$4.50
Haddix, Harvey	57T	265	$5.00	$20.00
Haddix, Harvey	58T	118	$ .50	$2.00
Haddix, Harvey	59T	184	$ .50	$1.95
Haddix, Harvey	60T	340	$ .60	$1.75
Haddix, Harvey	61T	100	$ .30	$1.00
Haddix, Harvey	61T	410	$ .70	$2.00
Haddix, Harvey	62T	67	$ .35	$1.10
Haddix, Harvey	63T	239	$ .25	$ .85
Haddix, Harvey	64T	439	$ .50	$1.95
Haddix, Harvey	65T	67	$ .25	$ .65
Hadley, Kent	59T	127	$ .50	$1.95
Hadley, Kent	60T	102	$ .35	$1.10
Hagen, Kevin	84T	337	$ .01	$ .05
Hagen, Mike	71T	415	$ .10	$ .35
Hague, Joe	69T	559	$ .25	$ .85
Hague, Joe	70T	362	$ .10	$ .35
Hague, Joe	71T	96	$ .10	$ .35
Hague, Joe	72T	546	$ .25	$ .85
Hague, Joe	73T	447	$ .06	$ .25
Hahn, Don	71T	94	$ .10	$ .35
Hahn, Don	72T	269	$ .05	$ .25
Hahn, Don	74T	291	$ .06	$ .25
Hahn, Don	75T	182	$ .06	$ .25
Hairston, Jerry	74T	96	$ .10	$ .35
Hairston, Jerry	75T	327	$ .06	$ .25
Hairston, Jerry	76T	391	$ .05	$ .20
Hairston, Jerry	83T	487	$ .01	$ .06
Hairston, Jerry	84T	177	$ .01	$ .05
Hairston, Jerry	85T	596	$ .01	$ .04

TOPPS

Player	Year	No.	VG	EX/MT	Player	Year	No.	VG	EX/MT
Hairston, Jerry	86T	778	$ .01	$ .03	Haller, Tom	69T	310	$ .25	$ .85
Hairston, Jerry	87T	685	$ .01	$ .03	Haller, Tom	70T	685	$ .50	$2.00
Hairston, Jerry	88T	281	$ .01	$ .03	Haller, Tom	71T	639	$ .30	$1.00
Hale, Bob	56T	231	$2.50	$8.00	Haller, Tom	72T	175	$ .05	$ .25
Hale, Bob	57T	406	$1.00	$3.75	Haller, Tom	72TIA	176	$ .05	$ .25
Hale, Bob	59T	507	$2.00	$7.00	Haller, Tom	73T	454	$ .06	$ .25
Hale, Bob	60T	309	$ .50	$1.95	Hambright, Roger	72T	124	$ .05	$ .25
Hale, Bob	61T	532	$6.00	$18.00	Hamilton, Darryl	89T	88	$ .01	$ .10
Hale, Chip	89TMLD	50	$ .01	$ .10	Hamilton, Dave	73T	214	$ .06	$ .25
Hale, Chip	90T	704	$ .01	$ .10	Hamilton, Dave	74T	633	$ .06	$ .25
Hale, John	76T	228	$ .05	$ .20	Hamilton, Dave	75T	428	$ .06	$ .25
Hale, John	77T	253	$ .03	$ .12	Hamilton, Dave	76T	237	$ .05	$ .20
Hale, John	78T	584	$ .02	$ .10	Hamilton, Dave	77T	367	$ .03	$ .12
Hale, John	79T	56	$ .02	$ .10	Hamilton, Dave	78T	288	$ .02	$ .10
Halicki, Ed	75T	467	$ .06	$ .25	Hamilton, Dave	79T	147	$ .02	$ .10
Halicki, Ed	76T	423	$ .05	$ .20	Hamilton, Dave	80T	86	$ .01	$ .07
Halicki, Ed	77T	343	$ .03	$ .12	Hamilton, Jack	62T	593	$6.00	$18.00
Halicki, Ed	78T	107	$ .02	$ .10	Hamilton, Jack	63T	132	$ .20	$ .75
Halicki, Ed	79T	672	$ .02	$ .10	Hamilton, Jack	65T	288	$ .30	$1.00
Halicki, Ed	80T	217	$ .01	$ .07	Hamilton, Jack	66T	262	$ .25	$ .85
Halicki, Ed	81T	69	$ .01	$ .07	Hamilton, Jack	67T	2	$ .25	$ .65
Hall, Albert	85T	676	$ .01	$ .04	Hamilton, Jack	68T	193	$ .25	$ .65
Hall, Albert	87TTR	41	$ .01	$ .07	Hamilton, Jack	69T	629	$ .25	$ .85
Hall, Albert	88T	213	$ .01	$ .03	Hamilton, Jeff	87T	266	$ .01	$ .10
Hall, Albert	89T	433	$ .01	$ .04	Hamilton, Jeff	88T	62	$ .01	$ .03
Hall, Albert	89TBB	104	$ .01	$ .05	Hamilton, Jeff	89T	736	$ .01	$ .04
Hall, Bill	59T	49	$1.00	$3.75	Hamilton, Jeff	90T	426	$ .01	$ .03
Hall, Dick	55T	126	$1.35	$5.00	Hamilton, Steve	63T	171	$ .25	$ .85
Hall, Dick	56T	331	$1.80	$6.00	Hamilton, Steve	64T	206	$ .35	$1.10
Hall, Dick	57T	308	$3.50	$13.00	Hamilton, Steve	65T	309	$ .35	$1.10
Hall, Dick	60T	308	$ .50	$1.95	Hamilton, Steve	66T	503	$1.00	$3.75
Hall, Dick	61T	197	$ .30	$1.00	Hamilton, Steve	67T	567	$5.00	$15.00
Hall, Dick	62T	189	$ .35	$1.10	Hamilton, Steve	68T	496	$ .30	$1.00
Hall, Dick	63T	526	$1.50	$3.75	Hamilton, Steve	69T	69	$ .15	$ .50
Hall, Dick	67T	508	$ .50	$2.00	Hamilton, Steve	70T	349	$ .25	$ .65
Hall, Dick	68T	17	$ .25	$ .65	Hamilton, Steve	71T	627	$ .30	$1.00
Hall, Dick	70T	182	$ .10	$ .35	Hamilton, Steve	72T	766	$ .70	$2.10
Hall, Dick	71T	417	$ .10	$ .35	Hamlin, Ken	60T	542	$2.00	$7.00
Hall, Drew	88T	262	$ .01	$ .03	Hamlin, Ken	61T	263	$ .30	$1.00
Hall, Drew	89T	593	$ .01	$ .04	Hamlin, Ken	62T	296	$ .35	$1.10
Hall, Drew	90T	463	$ .01	$ .03	Hamlin, Ken	66T	69	$ .25	$ .85
Hall, Jimmie	64T	73	$ .25	$ .85	Hamm, Pete	71T	74	$ .10	$ .35
Hall, Jimmie	65T	580	$1.50	$3.75	Hamm, Pete	72T	501	$ .05	$ .25
Hall, Jimmie	66T	190	$ .25	$ .85	Hammaker, Atlee	82T	471	$ .05	$ .20
Hall, Jimmie	67T	432	$ .25	$ .85	Hammaker, Atlee	83T	342	$ .01	$ .06
Hall, Jimmie	68T	121	$ .25	$ .65	Hammaker, Atlee	84T	85	$ .01	$ .05
Hall, Jimmie	69T	61	$ .25	$ .65	Hammaker, Atlee	84T	137	$ .01	$ .05
Hall, Jimmie	70T	649	$ .50	$2.00	Hammaker, Atlee	84T	576	$ .01	$ .05
Hall, Mel	83TTR	39	$ .15	$ .75	Hammaker, Atlee	85T	674	$ .01	$ .04
Hall, Mel	84T	508	$ .01	$ .35	Hammaker, Atlee	86T	223	$ .01	$ .03
Hall, Mel	84TTR	47	$ .02	$ .10	Hammaker, Atlee	87T	781	$ .01	$ .03
Hall, Mel	85T	263	$ .01	$ .04	Hammaker, Atlee	88T	157	$ .01	$ .03
Hall, Mel	86T	647	$ .01	$ .03	Hammaker, Atlee	88TBB	259	$ .01	$ .05
Hall, Mel	87T	51	$ .01	$ .03	Hammaker, Atlee	89T	572	$ .01	$ .04
Hall, Mel	88T	318	$ .01	$ .03	Hammaker, Atlee	89TBB	21	$ .01	$ .05
Hall, Mel	88TBB	114	$ .01	$ .05	Hammaker, Atlee	90T	447	$ .01	$ .03
Hall, Mel	89T	173	$ .01	$ .04	Hamner, Granny	52T	221	$6.00	$19.00
Hall, Mel	89TBB	13	$ .01	$ .05	Hamner, Granny	53T	146	$3.75	$13.00
Hall, Mel	89TTR	44	$ .01	$ .05	Hamner, Granny	54T	24	$2.10	$7.50
Hall, Mel	90T	436	$ .01	$ .03	Hamner, Granny	56T	197	$2.50	$8.00
Hall, Tom	69T	658	$ .25	$ .85	Hamner, Granny	57T	335	$3.50	$13.00
Hall, Tom	70T	169	$ .10	$ .35	Hamner, Granny	58T	268	$ .50	$2.00
Hall, Tom	71T	313	$ .10	$ .35	Hamner, Granny	59T	436	$ .50	$1.95
Hall, Tom	72T	417	$ .05	$ .25	Hamner, Granville " Granny"51Tbb		29	$5.50	$17.00
Hall, Tom	73T	8	$ .06	$ .25	Hampton, Ike	78T	503	$ .02	$ .10
Hall, Tom	74T	248	$ .06	$ .25	Hamric, Bert	55T	199	$4.25	$13.00
Hall, Tom	75T	108	$ .06	$ .25	Hamric, Bert	58T	336	$ .50	$2.00
Hall, Tom	76T	621	$ .05	$ .20	Hancock, Garry	79T	702	$ .02	$ .10
Haller, Tom	62T	356	$ .35	$1.10	Hancock, Garry	82T	322	$ .01	$ .06
Haller, Tom	63T	85	$ .25	$ .85	Hancock, Garry	84T	197	$ .01	$ .05
Haller, Tom	64T	485	$ .40	$1.25	Hand, Rich	71T	24	$ .10	$ .35
Haller, Tom	65T	465	$ .50	$2.00	Hand, Rich	72T	317	$ .05	$ .25
Haller, Tom	66T	308	$ .25	$ .85	Hand, Rich	73T	398	$ .06	$ .25
Haller, Tom	67T	65	$ .25	$ .65	Hand, Rich	74T	571	$ .06	$ .25
Haller, Tom	68T	185	$ .25	$ .65	Hands, Bill	66T	392	$ .25	$ .85

Player	Year	No.	VG	EX/MT
Hands, Bill	67T	16	$ .25	$ .65
Hands, Bill	68T	279	$ .25	$ .65
Hands, Bill	69T	115	$ .25	$ .65
Hands, Bill	70T	405	$ .10	$ .35
Hands, Bill	71T	670	$ .70	$2.10
Hands, Bill	72T	335	$ .05	$ .25
Hands, Bill	73T	555	$ .35	$1.10
Hands, Bill	74T	271	$ .06	$ .25
Hands, Bill	75T	412	$ .06	$ .25
Hands, Bill	76T	509	$ .05	$ .20
Hanebrink, Harry	58T	454	$ .50	$1.95
Hanebrink, Harry	59T	322	$ .50	$1.95
Haney, Fred	54T	75	$4.00	$14.00
Haney, Fred	58T	475	$5.00	$15.00
Haney, Fred	59TAS	551	$3.00	$9.00
Haney, Larry	67T	507	$ .50	$2.00
Haney, Larry	68T	42	$ .25	$ .65
Haney, Larry	69T	209	$ .25	$ .65
Haney, Larry	70T	648	$ .50	$2.00
Haney, Larry	73T	563	$ .35	$1.10
Haney, Larry	75T	626	$ .06	$ .25
Haney, Larry	76T	446	$ .05	$ .20
Haney, Larry	77T	12	$ .03	$ .12
Haney, Larry	78T	391	$ .02	$ .10
Hanna, Preston	79T	296	$ .02	$ .10
Hanna, Preston	80T	489	$ .01	$ .07
Hanna, Preston	81T	594	$ .01	$ .07
Hanna, Preston	83T	127	$ .01	$ .06
Hannan, Jim	63T	121	$ .25	$ .85
Hannan, Jim	64T	261	$ .25	$ .85
Hannan, Jim	65T	394	$ .30	$1.00
Hannan, Jim	66T	479	$ .70	$2.10
Hannan, Jim	67T	291	$ .25	$ .65
Hannan, Jim	69T	106	$ .25	$ .65
Hannan, Jim	70T	697	$ .50	$2.00
Hannan, Jim	71T	229	$ .10	$ .35
Hansen, Andy	52T	74	$14.00	$45.00
Hansen, Bob	75T	508	$ .06	$ .25
Hansen, Ronnie	59T	444	$ .50	$1.95
Hansen, Ron	60T	127	$ .35	$1.10
Hansen, Ron	61T	240	$ .30	$1.00
Hansen, Ron	62T	245	$ .35	$1.10
Hansen, Ron	63T	88	$ .25	$ .85
Hansen, Ron	64T	384	$ .40	$1.25
Hansen, Ron	65T	146	$ .25	$ .65
Hansen, Ron	66T	261	$ .25	$ .85
Hansen, Ron	67T	9	$ .25	$ .65
Hansen, Ron	68T	411	$ .25	$ .65
Hansen, Ron	69T	566	$ .25	$ .85
Hansen, Ron	70T	217	$ .10	$ .35
Hansen, Ron	71T	410	$ .10	$ .35
Hansen, Ron	72T	763	$ .70	$2.10
Hanson, Erik	89TTR	45	$ .01	$ .15
Hanson, Erik	90T	118	$ .01	$ .10
Harder, Mel	60T	460	$1.25	$4.50
Hardin, Jim	68T	222	$ .25	$ .65
Hardin, Jim	69T	532	$ .20	$ .50
Hardin, Jim	69T	610	$ .25	$ .85
Hardin, Jim	70T	656	$ .50	$2.00
Hardin, Jim	71T	491	$ .10	$ .35
Hardin, Jim	72T	287	$ .05	$ .25
Hardin, Jim	73T	124	$ .06	$ .25
Hardy, Carroll	58T	446	$1.25	$3.50
Hardy, Carroll	59T	168	$ .50	$1.95
Hardy, Carroll	60T	341	$ .50	$1.95
Hardy, Carroll	61T	257	$ .30	$1.00
Hardy, Carroll	62T	101	$ .35	$1.10
Hardy, Carroll	63T	468	$2.50	$6.50
Hardy, Jack	89TMLD	51	$ .01	$ .05
Hardy, Larry	75T	112	$ .06	$ .25
Hargan, Steve	66T	508	$ .70	$2.10
Hargan, Steve	67T	233	$ .35	$1.10
Hargan, Steve	67T	440	$ .25	$ .85
Hargan, Steve	68T	35	$ .25	$ .65
Hargan, Steve	69T	348	$ .25	$ .65

Player	Year	No.	VG	EX/MT
Hargan, Steve	70T	136	$ .10	$ .35
Hargan, Steve	71T	375	$ .10	$ .35
Hargan, Steve	72T	615	$ .25	$ .85
Hargan, Steve	75T	362	$ .06	$ .25
Hargan, Steve	76T	463	$ .05	$ .20
Hargan, Steve	77T	37	$ .03	$ .12
Hargesheimer, Al	81T	502	$ .01	$ .07
Hargrove, Mike	75T	106	$ .10	$ .35
Hargrove, Mike	76T	485	$ .05	$ .20
Hargrove, Mike	77T	275	$ .03	$ .12
Hargrove, Mike	78T	172	$ .02	$ .10
Hargrove, Mike	79T	591	$ .02	$ .10
Hargrove, Mike	80T	308	$ .01	$ .07
Hargrove, Mike	81T	74	$ .01	$ .07
Hargrove, Mike	82T	310	$ .01	$ .06
Hargrove, Mike	82T	559	$ .01	$ .06
Hargrove, Mike	83T	660	$ .01	$ .06
Hargrove, Mike	84T	546	$ .01	$ .05
Hargrove, Mike	84T	764	$ .01	$ .05
Hargrove, Mike	85T	425	$ .01	$ .04
Hargrove, Mike	86T	136	$ .01	$ .03
Harkey, Mike	89T	742	$ .05	$ .25
Harkness, Tim	62T	404	$ .70	$2.10
Harkness, Tim	63T	436	$ .35	$1.20
Harkness, Tim	64T	57	$ .25	$ .85
Harlow, Larry	78T	543	$ .02	$ .10
Harlow, Larry	79T	314	$ .02	$ .10
Harlow, Larry	80T	68	$ .01	$ .07
Harlow, Larry	81T	121	$ .01	$ .07
Harlow, Larry	82T	257	$ .01	$ .06
Harmon, Chuck	54T	182	$2.10	$7.50
Harmon, Chuck	55T	82	$1.35	$5.00
Harmon, Chuck	56T	308	$1.80	$6.00
Harmon, Chuck	57T	299	$3.50	$13.00
Harmon, Chuck	58T	48	$ .70	$2.25
Harmon, Terry	69T	624	$ .25	$ .85
Harmon, Terry	70T	486	$ .10	$ .35

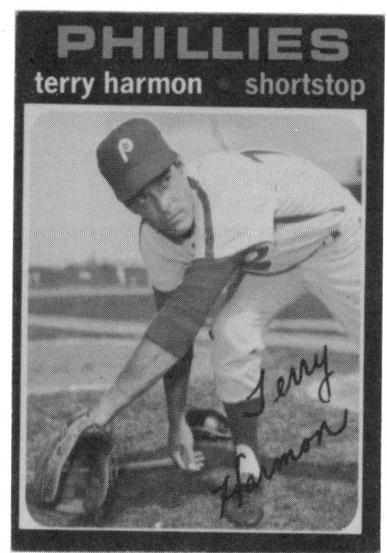

Player	Year	No.	VG	EX/MT
Harmon, Terry	71T	682	$ .70	$2.10
Harmon, Terry	72T	377	$ .05	$ .25
Harmon, Terry	73T	166	$ .05	$ .25
Harmon, Terry	74T	642	$ .06	$ .25
Harmon, Terry	75T	399	$ .06	$ .25
Harmon, Terry	76T	247	$ .05	$ .20

TOPPS

Player	Year	No.	VG	EX/MT	Player	Year	No.	VG	EX/MT
Harmon, Terry	77T	388	$ .03	$ .12	Harrelson, Ken	66T	55	$ .35	$1.10
Harmon, Terry	78T	118	$ .02	$ .10	Harrelson, Ken	67T	188	$ .30	$1.00
Harnisch, Pete	90T	324	$ .01	$ .03	Harrelson, Ken	68T	566	$ .35	$1.10
Harper, Brian	84T	144	$ .01	$ .05	Harrelson, Ken	69T	3	$ .30	$1.00
Harper, Brian	85T	332	$ .01	$ .04	Harrelson, Ken	69T	5	$ .30	$1.00
Harper, Brian	86T	656	$ .01	$ .03	Harrelson, Ken	69T	240	$ .35	$1.10
Harper, Brian	89T	472	$ .01	$ .04	Harrelson, Ken	69TAS	417	$ .25	$ .65
Harper, Brian	90T	47	$ .01	$ .03	Harrelson, Ken	70T	545	$ .35	$1.10
Harper, Terry	81T	192	$ .05	$ .20	Harrelson, Ken	71T	510	$ .30	$1.00
Harper, Terry	82T	507	$ .01	$ .06	Harridge, William	56T	1	$20.00	$80.00
Harper, Terry	83T	339	$ .01	$ .06	Harridge, William	57T	100	$2.10	$7.50
Harper, Terry	84T	624	$ .01	$ .05	Harridge, William	58T	300	$1.25	$3.50
Harper, Terry	85TTR	45	$ .02	$ .10	Harris, Alonzo	67T	564	$1.35	$4.00
Harper, Terry	86T	247	$ .01	$ .03	Harris, Alonzo	68T	128	$ .25	$ .65
Harper, Terry	87T	49	$ .01	$ .03	Harris, Bill	60T	128	$ .35	$1.10
Harper, Terry	87TTR	42	$ .01	$ .07	Harris, Billy	69T	569	$ .25	$ .85
Harper, Tommy	63T	158	$ .25	$ .85	Harris, Billy	70T	512	$ .10	$ .35
Harper, Tommy	64T	330	$ .25	$ .85	Harris, Buddy	71T	404	$ .10	$ .35
Harper, Tommy	65T	47	$ .25	$ .65	Harris, Donald	90T	314	$ .01	$ .15
Harper, Tommy	66T	214	$ .25	$ .85	Harris, Gail	56T	91	$1.25	$4.50
Harper, Tommy	67T	392	$ .25	$ .85	Harris, Gail	57T	281	$3.50	$13.00
Harper, Tommy	68T	590	$ .30	$1.00	Harris, Gail	58T	309	$ .50	$2.00
Harper, Tommy	69T	42	$ .15	$ .50	Harris, Gail	59T	378	$ .50	$1.95
Harper, Tommy	70T	370	$ .25	$ .65	Harris, Gail	60T	152	$ .35	$1.10
Harper, Tommy	71T	260	$ .10	$ .35	Harris, Gene	89TMLD	52	$ .01	$ .15
Harper, Tommy	72T	455	$ .05	$ .25	Harris, Gene	89TTR	46	$ .01	$ .15
Harper, Tommy	73T	620	$ .50	$2.00	Harris, Gene	90T	738	$ .01	$ .10
Harper, Tommy	74T	204	$ .30	$1.00	Harris, Greg	82T	783	$ .01	$ .06
Harper, Tommy	74T	325	$ .06	$ .25	Harris, Greg	82TTR	41	$ .02	$ .10
Harper, Tommy	75T	537	$ .06	$ .25	Harris, Greg	83T	296	$ .01	$ .06
Harper, Tommy	76T	274	$ .05	$ .20	Harris, Greg	85T	242	$ .01	$ .04
Harper, Tommy	77T	414	$ .03	$ .12	Harris, Greg	85TTR	47	$ .02	$ .10
Harrah, Toby	72T	104	$ .25	$ .65	Harris, Greg	86T	586	$ .01	$ .03
Harrah, Toby	73T	216	$ .25	$ .65	Harris, Greg	87T	44	$ .01	$ .03
Harrah, Toby	74T	511	$ .06	$ .25	Harris, Greg	88T	369	$ .01	$ .03
Harrah, Toby	75T	131	$ .06	$ .25	Harris, Greg	89T	194	$ .01	$ .04
Harrah, Toby	76T	412	$ .05	$ .20	Harris, Greg	89T	627	$ .01	$ .04
Harrah, Toby	77T	301	$ .03	$ .12	Harris, Greg	90T	529	$ .01	$ .03
Harrah, Toby	78T	44	$ .02	$ .10	Harris, Greg	90T	572	$ .01	$ .03
Harrah, Toby	79T	234	$ .02	$ .10	Harris, John	81T	214	$ .01	$ .07
Harrah, Toby	80T	636	$ .01	$ .07	Harris, John	82T	313	$ .01	$ .06
Harrah, Toby	81T	721	$ .01	$ .07	Harris, Lenny	90T	277	$ .01	$ .03
Harrah, Toby	82T	532	$ .01	$ .06	Harris, Lum	60T	455	$ .95	$3.50
Harrah, Toby	83T	141	$ .01	$ .06	Harris, Lum	65T	274	$ .30	$1.00
Harrah, Toby	83T	480	$ .01	$ .06	Harris, Lum	66T	147	$ .25	$ .85
Harrah, Toby	84T	348	$ .01	$ .05	Harris, Lum	68T	439	$ .25	$ .65
Harrah, Toby	84TTR	48	$ .02	$ .10	Harris, Lum	69T	196	$ .25	$ .65
Harrah, Toby	85T	94	$ .01	$ .04	Harris, Lum	70T	86	$ .10	$ .35
Harrah, Toby	85TTR	46	$ .02	$ .10	Harris, Lum	71T	346	$ .10	$ .35
Harrah, Toby	86T	535	$ .01	$ .03	Harris, Lum	72T	484	$ .05	$ .25
Harrah, Toby	87T	152	$ .01	$ .03	Harris, Mickey	52T	207	$6.00	$19.00
Harrell, Billy	58T	443	$1.25	$3.50	Harris, Vic	73T	594	$ .35	$1.10
Harrell, Billy	59T	433	$ .50	$1.95	Harris, Vic	74T	157	$ .06	$ .25
Harrell, Billy	61T	354	$ .30	$1.00	Harris, Vic	75T	658	$ .06	$ .25
Harrell, John	70T	401	$ .10	$ .35	Harris, Vic	78T	436	$ .02	$ .10
Harrelson, Bill	69T	224	$ .25	$ .85	Harris, Vic	79T	338	$ .02	$ .10
Harrelson, Bud	67T	306	$ .35	$1.10	Harrison, Chuck	66T	244	$ .25	$ .85
Harrelson, Bud	68T	132	$ .25	$ .85	Harrison, Chuck	67T	8	$ .25	$ .65
Harrelson, Bud	69T	456	$ .25	$ .65	Harrison, Chuck	69T	116	$ .25	$ .65
Harrelson, Bud	70T	634	$ .50	$2.00	Harrison, Roric	72T	474	$ .50	$2.35
Harrelson, Bud	71T	355	$ .10	$ .35	Harrison, Roric	73T	229	$ .06	$ .25
Harrelson, Bud	72T	53	$ .25	$ .65	Harrison, Roric	74T	298	$ .06	$ .25
Harrelson, Bud	72T	496	$ .05	$ .25	Harrison, Roric	75T	287	$ .06	$ .25
Harrelson, Bud	72TIA	54	$ .05	$ .25	Harrison, Roric	76T	547	$ .05	$ .20
Harrelson, Bud	73T	223	$ .06	$ .25	Harrison, Roric	78T	536	$ .02	$ .10
Harrelson, Bud	74T	380	$ .06	$ .25	Harrist, Earl	52T	402	$39.00	$135.00
Harrelson, Bud	75T	395	$ .06	$ .25	Harrist, Earl	53T	65	$3.75	$13.00
Harrelson, Bud	76T	337	$ .05	$ .20	Harshman, Jack	54T	173	$2.10	$7.50
Harrelson, Bud	77T	44	$ .03	$ .12	Harshman, Jack	55T	104	$1.35	$5.00
Harrelson, Bud	78T	403	$ .02	$ .10	Harshman, Jack	56T	29	$1.25	$4.50
Harrelson, Bud	79T	118	$ .02	$ .10	Harshman, Jack	57T	152	$ .95	$3.50
Harrelson, Bud	80T	566	$ .01	$ .07	Harshman, Jack	58T	217	$ .50	$2.00
Harrelson, Bud	81T	694	$ .01	$ .07	Harshman, Jack	59T	475	$ .50	$1.95
Harrelson, Ken	64T	419	$1.00	$4.00	Harshman, Jack	60T	112	$ .35	$1.10
Harrelson, Ken	65T	479	$ .50	$1.95	Hart, Jim	64T	452	$ .50	$1.95

Player	Year	No.	VG	EX/MT
Hart, Jim	65T	4	$1.50	$3.75
Hart, Jim	65T	395	$ .30	$1.00
Hart, Jim	66T	295	$ .25	$ .85
Hart, Jim	67T	220	$ .25	$ .65
Hart, Jim	68T	73	$ .25	$ .65
Hart, Jim	69T	555	$ .25	$ .85
Hart, Jim	70T	176	$ .35	$1.10
Hart, Jim	71T	461	$ .10	$ .35
Hart, Jim	72T	733	$ .70	$2.10
Hart, Jim	73T	538	$ .35	$1.10
Hart, Jim	74T	159	$ .06	$ .25
Hart, John	90T	141	$ .01	$ .03
Hart, Mike	88T	69	$ .01	$ .10
Hartenstein, Chuck	68T	13	$ .25	$ .65
Hartenstein, Chuck	69T	596	$ .25	$ .85
Hartenstein, Chuck	70T	216	$ .10	$ .35
Hartenstein, Chuck	77T	416	$ .03	$ .12
Hartley, Mike	89TMLD	53	$ .01	$ .05
Hartman, Bob	59T	128	$ .50	$1.95
Hartman, Bob	60T	129	$ .35	$1.10
Hartman, J. C.	63T	442	$ .35	$1.20
Hartsfield, Roy	52T	264	$11.50	$38.00
Hartsfield, Roy	73T	237	$ .30	$1.00
Hartsfield, Roy	78T	444	$ .02	$ .10
Hartung, Clint	52T	141	$6.00	$19.00
Hartzell, Paul	77T	179	$ .03	$ .12
Hartzell, Paul	78T	529	$ .02	$ .10
Hartzell, Paul	79T	402	$ .02	$ .10
Hartzell, Paul	80T	721	$ .01	$ .07
Harvey, Bryan	88TTR	45	$ .01	$ .25
Harvey, Bryan	89T	632	$ .01	$ .15
Harvey, Bryan	90T	272	$ .01	$ .03
Hassey, Ron	80T	222	$ .01	$ .07
Hassey, Ron	81T	564	$ .01	$ .07
Hassey, Ron	82T	54	$ .01	$ .06
Hassey, Ron	83T	689	$ .01	$ .06
Hassey, Ron	84T	308	$ .01	$ .05
Hassey, Ron	84TTR	49	$ .02	$ .10
Hassey, Ron	85T	742	$ .01	$ .04
Hassey, Ron	85TTR	48	$ .02	$ .10
Hassey, Ron	86T	157	$ .01	$ .03
Hassey, Ron	87T	667	$ .01	$ .03
Hassey, Ron	88T	458	$ .01	$ .03
Hassey, Ron	88TTR	46	$ .01	$ .05
Hassey, Ron	89T	272	$ .01	$ .04
Hassey, Ron	89TBB	171	$ .01	$ .05
Hassey, Ron	90T	527	$ .01	$ .03
Hassler, Andy	75T	261	$ .06	$ .25
Hassler, Andy	76T	207	$ .05	$ .20
Hassler, Andy	77T	602	$ .03	$ .12
Hassler, Andy	78T	73	$ .02	$ .10
Hassler, Andy	79T	696	$ .02	$ .10
Hassler, Andy	80T	353	$ .01	$ .07
Hassler, Andy	81T	454	$ .01	$ .07
Hassler, Andy	82T	94	$ .01	$ .06
Hassler, Andy	83T	573	$ .01	$ .06
Hassler, Andy	84T	719	$ .01	$ .05
Hatcher, Billy	86T	46	$ .01	$ .03
Hatcher, Billy	86TTR	45	$ .02	$ .10
Hatcher, Billy	87T	578	$ .01	$ .03
Hatcher, Billy	88T	306	$ .01	$ .03
Hatcher, Billy	88TBB	3	$ .01	$ .05
Hatcher, Billy	89T	252	$ .01	$ .04
Hatcher, Billy	89TBB	118	$ .01	$ .10
Hatcher, Billy	90T	119	$ .01	$ .10
Hatcher, Mickey	80T	679	$ .01	$ .07
Hatcher, Mickey	81T	289	$ .01	$ .07
Hatcher, Mickey	81TTR	768	$ .02	$ .10
Hatcher, Mickey	82T	467	$ .01	$ .06
Hatcher, Mickey	83T	121	$ .01	$ .06
Hatcher, Mickey	84T	746	$ .01	$ .05
Hatcher, Mickey	85T	18	$ .01	$ .04
Hatcher, Mickey	86T	356	$ .01	$ .03
Hatcher, Mickey	87T	504	$ .01	$ .03
Hatcher, Mickey	87TTR	43	$ .01	$ .07

Player	Year	No.	VG	EX/MT
Hatcher, Mickey	88T	607	$ .01	$ .03
Hatcher, Mickey	89T	483	$ .01	$ .04
Hatcher, Mickey	89TBB	63	$ .01	$ .05
Hatcher, Mickey	90T	226	$ .01	$ .03
Hatfield, Fred	52T	354	$39.00	$135.00
Hatfield, Fred	53T	163	$3.75	$13.00
Hatfield, Fred	56T	318	$1.80	$6.00
Hatfield, Fred	57T	278	$3.50	$13.00
Hatfield, Fred	58T	339	$ .50	$2.00
Hatten, Joe	52T	194	$6.00	$19.00
Hatton, Grady	51Trb	34	$1.25	$3.50
Hatton, Grady	52T	6	$14.00	$45.00
Hatton, Grady	53T	45	$4.50	$15.00
Hatton, Grady	54T	208	$2.10	$7.50
Hatton, Grady	55T	131	$1.35	$5.00
Hatton, Grady	56T	26	$1.25	$4.50
Hatton, Grady	66T	504	$ .70	$2.10
Hatton, Grady	67T	347	$ .25	$ .65
Hatton, Grady	68T	392	$ .25	$ .65
Hatton, Grady	73T	624	$ .55	$1.75
Hatton, Grady	74T	31	$ .06	$ .25
Haugstad, Phil	52T	198	$6.00	$18.00
Hausman, Tom	76T	452	$ .05	$ .20
Hausman, Tom	77T	99	$ .03	$ .12

Player	Year	No.	VG	EX/MT
Hausman, Tom	79T	643	$ .02	$ .10
Hausman, Tom	80T	151	$ .01	$ .07
Hausman, Tom	81T	359	$ .01	$ .07
Hausman, Tom	82T	524	$ .01	$ .06
Hausman, Tom	83T	417	$ .01	$ .06
Havens, Brad	82T	92	$ .01	$ .06
Havens, Brad	83T	751	$ .01	$ .06
Havens, Brad	84T	509	$ .01	$ .05
Havens, Brad	87T	398	$ .01	$ .03
Havens, Brad	87TTR	44	$ .01	$ .07
Havens, Brad	88T	698	$ .01	$ .03
Havens, Brad	89T	204	$ .01	$ .04
Hawkins, Andy	84T	778	$ .05	$ .35
Hawkins, Andy	85T	299	$ .01	$ .10
Hawkins, Andy	86T	478	$ .01	$ .03
Hawkins, Andy	87T	183	$ .01	$ .03
Hawkins, Andy	88T	9	$ .01	$ .03
Hawkins, Andy	88TBB	257	$ .01	$ .05
Hawkins, Andy	89T	533	$ .01	$ .04

Player	Year	No.	VG	EX/MT
Hawkins, Andy	89TTR	47	$ .01	$ .05
Hawkins, Andy	90T	335	$ .01	$ .03
Hawkins, Wynn	60T	536	$2.00	$7.00
Hawkins, Wynn	61T	34	$ .30	$1.00
Hawkins, Wynn	63T	334	$ .35	$1.20
Haydel, Hal	71T	692	$ .70	$2.10
Haydel, Hal	72T	28	$ .10	$ .35
Hayes, Ben	84T	448	$ .01	$ .05
Hayes, Charlie	90T	577	$ .01	$ .15
Hayes, Von	82T	141	$ .50	$1.95
Hayes, Von	82TTR	42	$ .35	$1.10
Hayes, Von	83T	325	$ .25	$ .65
Hayes, Von	83TTR	40	$ .25	$ .65
Hayes, Von	84T	587	$ .01	$ .10
Hayes, Von	85T	68	$ .01	$ .10
Hayes, Von	86T	420	$ .01	$ .03
Hayes, Von	87T	666	$ .01	$ .03
Hayes, Von	88T	215	$ .01	$ .03
Hayes, Von	88TBB	139	$ .01	$ .10
Hayes, Von	89T	385	$ .01	$ .04
Hayes, Von	89TBB	302	$ .01	$ .10
Hayes, Von	90T	710	$ .01	$ .03
Haynes, Joe	52T	145	$7.00	$20.00
Haynes, Joe	54T	223	$2.10	$7.50
Hayward, Ray	88TTR	47	$ .01	$ .05
Hazle, Bob	58T	83	$1.00	$3.75
Healy, Fran	72T	663	$ .70	$2.10
Healy, Fran	73T	361	$ .06	$ .25
Healy, Fran	74T	238	$ .06	$ .25
Healy, Fran	75T	251	$ .06	$ .25
Healy, Fran	76T	394	$ .05	$ .20
Healy, Fran	77T	148	$ .03	$ .12
Healy, Fran	78T	582	$ .02	$ .10
Heard, Jehosie	54T	226	$2.10	$7.50
Hearn, Ed	87T	433	$ .01	$ .10
Hearn, Ed	88T	56	$ .01	$ .03
Hearn, Ed	89T	348	$ .01	$ .04
Hearn, Jim	52T	337	$39.00	$135.00
Hearn, Jim	53T	38	$3.75	$13.00
Hearn, Jim	56T	202	$2.50	$8.00
Hearn, Jim	57T	348	$3.50	$13.00
Hearn, Jim	58T	298	$ .50	$2.00
Hearn, Jim	59T	63	$1.00	$3.75
Hearron, Jeff	87T	274	$ .01	$ .03
Heath, Bill	66T	539	$4.50	$15.00
Heath, Bill	67T	172	$ .25	$ .65
Heath, Bill	70T	541	$ .10	$ .35
Heath, Mike	79T	710	$ .05	$ .20
Heath, Mike	80T	687	$ .01	$ .07
Heath, Mike	81T	437	$ .01	$ .07
Heath, Mike	82T	318	$ .01	$ .06
Heath, Mike	83T	23	$ .01	$ .06
Heath, Mike	84T	567	$ .01	$ .05
Heath, Mike	85T	662	$ .01	$ .04
Heath, Mike	86T	148	$ .01	$ .03
Heath, Mike	86TTR	46	$ .02	$ .10
Heath, Mike	87T	492	$ .01	$ .03
Heath, Mike	88T	237	$ .01	$ .03
Heath, Mike	89T	743	$ .01	$ .04
Heath, Mike	90T	366	$ .01	$ .03
Heaton, Neal	87TTR	45	$ .01	$ .07
Heaton, Neal	88T	765	$ .01	$ .03
Heaton, Neal	88TBB	33	$ .01	$ .05
Heaton, Neal	89T	197	$ .01	$ .04
Heaton, Neal	90T	539	$ .01	$ .03
Heaverlo, Dave	76T	213	$ .05	$ .20
Heaverlo, Dave	77T	97	$ .03	$ .12
Heaverlo, Dave	78T	338	$ .02	$ .10
Heaverlo, Dave	79T	432	$ .02	$ .10
Heaverlo, Dave	80T	177	$ .01	$ .07
Hebert, Ray	54T	190	$2.10	$7.50
Hebner, Rich	69T	82	$2.50	$7.00
Hebner, Rich	70T	264	$ .10	$ .35
Hebner, Rich	71T	212	$ .10	$ .35
Hebner, Rich	72T	630	$ .25	$ .85
Hebner, Rich	73T	2	$ .06	$ .25
Hebner, Rich	74T	450	$ .06	$ .25
Hebner, Rich	75T	492	$ .06	$ .25
Hebner, Rich	76T	376	$ .05	$ .20
Hebner, Rich	77T	167	$ .03	$ .12
Hebner, Rich	78T	26	$ .02	$ .10
Hebner, Rich	79T	567	$ .02	$ .10
Hebner, Rich	80T	331	$ .01	$ .07
Hebner, Rich	81T	217	$ .01	$ .07
Hebner, Rich	82T	603	$ .01	$ .06
Hebner, Rich	83T	778	$ .01	$ .06
Hebner, Rich	84T	433	$ .01	$ .05
Hebner, Rich	84TTR	50	$ .02	$ .10
Hebner, Rich	85T	124	$ .01	$ .04
Hebner, Rich	86T	19	$ .02	$ .20
Hedlund, Mike	65T	546	$1.50	$3.75
Hedlund, Mike	69T	591	$ .25	$ .85
Hedlund, Mike	70T	187	$ .10	$ .35
Hedlund, Mike	71T	662	$ .70	$2.10
Hedlund, Mike	72T	81	$ .05	$ .25
Hedlund, Mike	73T	591	$ .35	$1.10
Heep, Danny	81T	82	$ .01	$ .07
Heep, Danny	82T	441	$ .01	$ .06
Heep, Danny	83T	538	$ .01	$ .06
Heep, Danny	83TTR	41	$ .02	$ .10
Heep, Danny	84T	29	$ .01	$ .05
Heep, Danny	85T	339	$ .01	$ .04
Heep, Danny	86T	619	$ .01	$ .03
Heep, Danny	87T	241	$ .01	$ .03
Heep, Danny	88T	753	$ .01	$ .03
Heep, Danny	89T	198	$ .01	$ .04
Heep, Danny	90T	573	$ .01	$ .03
Heffner, Bob	64T	79	$ .25	$ .85
Heffner, Bob	65T	199	$ .30	$1.00
Heffner, Bob	66T	432	$ .25	$ .85
Heffner, Don	60T	462	$ .95	$3.50
Heffner, Don	66T	269	$ .25	$ .85
Hegan, Jim	51Trb	12	$1.25	$3.50
Hegan, Jim	52T	17	$14.00	$45.00
Hegan, Jim	53T	80	$3.75	$13.00
Hegan, Jim	54T	29	$2.10	$7.50
Hegan, Jim	55T	7	$1.35	$5.00
Hegan, Jim	56T	48	$1.25	$4.50
Hegan, Jim	57T	136	$ .95	$3.50
Hegan, Jim	58T	345	$ .50	$2.00
Hegan, Jim	59T	372	$ .50	$1.95
Hegan, Jim	73T	116	$ .15	$ .50
Hegan, Jim	76T	69	$ .06	$ .25
Hegan, Mike	67T	553	$5.00	$20.00
Hegan, Mike	68T	402	$ .25	$ .65
Hegan, Mike	69T	577	$ .25	$ .85
Hegan, Mike	70T	111	$ .10	$ .35
Hegan, Mike	72T	632	$ .25	$ .85
Hegan, Mike	73T	382	$ .06	$ .25
Hegan, Mike	74T	517	$ .06	$ .25
Hegan, Mike	75T	99	$ .06	$ .25
Hegan, Mike	76T	69	$ .06	$ .25
Hegan, Mike	76T	377	$ .05	$ .20
Hegan, Mike	77T	507	$ .03	$ .12
Heidemann, Jack	71T	87	$ .10	$ .35
Heidemann, Jack	72T	374	$ .05	$ .25
Heidemann, Jack	73T	644	$ .35	$1.10
Heidemann, Jack	75T	649	$ .06	$ .25
Heidemann, Jack	77T	553	$ .03	$ .12
Heinkel, Don	89T	499	$ .01	$ .10
Heintzelman, Ken	52T	362	$39.00	$135.00
Heintzelman, Ken	53T	136	$3.75	$13.00
Heintzelman, Tom	74T	607	$ .06	$ .25
Heise, Bob	70T	478	$ .10	$ .35
Heise, Bob	71T	691	$ .70	$2.10
Heise, Bobby	72T	402	$ .05	$ .25
Heise, Bobby	73T	547	$ .35	$1.10
Heise, Bobby	74T	51	$ .06	$ .25
Heise, Bobby	74TTR	51	$ .06	$ .25
Heise, Bobby	75T	441	$ .06	$ .25

Player	Year	No.	VG	EX/MT
Heist, Al	61T	302	$ .30	$1.00
Heist, Al	62T	373	$ .70	$2.10
Held, Woody	58T	202	$ .50	$2.00
Held, Woody	59T	266	$ .50	$1.95
Held, Woody	60T	178	$ .35	$1.10
Held, Woodie (y)	61T	60	$ .30	$1.00
Held, Woody	62T	215	$ .35	$1.10
Held, Woody	63T	435	$ .35	$1.20
Held, Woody	64T	105	$ .25	$ .85

Player	Year	No.	VG	EX/MT
Held, Woody	65T	336	$ .30	$1.00
Held, Woody	66T	136	$ .25	$ .85
Held, Woody	67T	251	$10.00	$40.00
Held, Woody	68T	289	$ .25	$ .65
Held, Woody	69T	636	$ .25	$ .85
Helms, Tommy	65T	243	$ .60	$1.75
Helms, Tommy	66T	311	$ .35	$1.10
Helms, Tommy	67T	505	$ .50	$2.00
Helms, Tommy	68T	405	$ .25	$ .65
Helms, Tommy	69T	70	$ .25	$ .85
Helms, Tommy	69TAS	418	$ .15	$ .50
Helms, Tommy	70T	159	$ .10	$ .35
Helms, Tommy	71T	272	$ .10	$ .35
Helms, Tommy	72T	204	$ .05	$ .25
Helms, Tommy	73T	495	$ .06	$ .25
Helms, Tommy	74T	67	$ .06	$ .25
Helms, Tommy	75T	119	$ .06	$ .25
Helms, Tommy	76T	583	$ .05	$ .20
Helms, Tommy	76TTR	583	$ .05	$ .20
Helms, Tommy	77T	402	$ .03	$ .12
Helms, Tommy	78T	618	$ .02	$ .10
Helms, Tommy	90T	110	$ .01	$ .03
Heman, Russ	59T	283	$ .50	$1.95
Hemond, Scott	89TMLD	54	$ .01	$ .05
Hemsley, Rollie	54T	143	$2.10	$7.50
Hemus, Solly	52T	196	$6.00	$19.00
Hemus, Solly	53T	231	$11.00	$37.50
Hemus, Solly	54T	117	$2.10	$7.50
Hemus, Solly	57T	231	$ .95	$3.50
Hemus, Solly	58T	207	$ .50	$2.00
Hemus, Solly	59T	527	$2.00	$7.00
Hemus, Solly	60T	218	$ .35	$1.10
Hemus, Solly	61T	139	$ .30	$1.00
Henderson, Dave	82T	711	$ .25	$1.00

Player	Year	No.	VG	EX/MT
Henderson, Dave	83T	732	$ .01	$ .20
Henderson, Dave	84T	154	$ .01	$ .15
Henderson, Dave	85T	344	$ .01	$ .10
Henderson, Dave	86T	221	$ .01	$ .03
Henderson, Dave	87T	452	$ .01	$ .03
Henderson, Dave	88T	628	$ .01	$ .03
Henderson, Dave	88TBB	131	$ .01	$ .05
Henderson, Dave	88TTR	48	$ .01	$ .05
Henderson, Dave	89T	527	$ .01	$ .04
Henderson, Dave	89TBB	326	$ .01	$ .05
Henderson, Dave	90T	68	$ .01	$ .03
Henderson, Joe	77T	487	$ .03	$ .12
Henderson, Ken	65T	497	$ .50	$2.00
Henderson, Ken	66T	39	$ .25	$ .85
Henderson, Ken	67T	383	$ .25	$ .85
Henderson, Ken	68T	309	$ .25	$ .65
Henderson, Ken	70T	298	$ .10	$ .35
Henderson, Ken	71T	155	$ .10	$ .35
Henderson, Ken	72T	443	$ .05	$ .25
Henderson, Ken	72TIA	444	$ .05	$ .25
Henderson, Ken	73T	101	$ .06	$ .25
Henderson, Ken	74T	394	$ .06	$ .25
Henderson, Ken	75T	59	$ .06	$ .25
Henderson, Ken	76T	464	$ .05	$ .20
Henderson, Ken	76TTR	464	$ .05	$ .20
Henderson, Ken	77T	242	$ .03	$ .12
Henderson, Ken	78T	612	$ .02	$ .10
Henderson, Ken	79T	73	$ .02	$ .10
Henderson, Ken	80T	523	$ .01	$ .07
Henderson, Rickey	80T	482	$15.00	$75.00
Henderson, Rickey	81T	4	$ .04	$ .20
Henderson, Rickey	81T	261	$3.00	$9.00
Henderson, Rickey	82T	156	$ .05	$ .20
Henderson, Rickey	82T	164	$ .05	$ .25
Henderson, Rickey	82T	610	$1.00	$3.00
Henderson, Rickey	83T	180	$ .75	$2.00
Henderson, Rickey	83T	531	$ .01	$ .06
Henderson, Rickey	83T	704	$ .15	$ .75
Henderson, Rickey	83TAS	391	$ .06	$ .30
Henderson, Rickey	83TRB	2	$ .05	$ .25
Henderson, Rickey	84T	2	$ .05	$ .25
Henderson, Rickey	84T	134	$ .02	$ .10
Henderson, Rickey	84T	156	$ .01	$ .10
Henderson, Rickey	84T	230	$ .35	$1.25
Henderson, Rickey	85T	115	$ .05	$ .50
Henderson, Rickey	85TAS	706	$ .05	$ .25
Henderson, Rickey	85TTR	49	$ .50	$2.00
Henderson, Rickey	86T	500	$ .03	$ .30
Henderson, Rickey	86TAS	716	$ .02	$ .15
Henderson, Rickey	87T	735	$ .10	$ .35
Henderson, Rickey	87TTB	311	$ .01	$ .10
Henderson, Rickey	88T	60	$ .01	$ .20
Henderson, Rickey	88TBB	165	$ .05	$ .25
Henderson, Rickey	89T	380	$ .01	$ .15
Henderson, Rickey	89TBB	271	$ .01	$ .35
Henderson, Rickey	89TTR	48	$ .01	$ .15
Henderson, Rickey	90T	450	$ .01	$ .15
Henderson, Rickey	90TRB	7	$ .01	$ .15
Henderson, Steve	78T	134	$ .02	$ .10
Henderson, Steve	79T	445	$ .02	$ .10
Henderson, Steve	80T	299	$ .30	$1.00
Henderson, Steve	81T	619	$ .01	$ .07
Henderson, Steve	81TTR	769	$ .02	$ .10
Henderson, Steve	82T	89	$ .01	$ .06
Henderson, Steve	83T	335	$ .01	$ .06
Henderson, Steve	83TTR	42	$ .02	$ .10
Henderson, Steve	84T	501	$ .01	$ .05
Henderson, Steve	85T	640	$ .01	$ .04
Henderson, Steve	85TTR	50	$ .02	$ .10
Henderson, Steve	86T	748	$ .01	$ .03
Henderson, Steve	88T	527	$ .01	$ .03
Hendley, Bob	61T	372	$ .50	$2.00
Hendley, Bob	62T	361	$ .35	$1.10
Hendley, Bob	63T	62	$ .25	$ .85
Hendley, Bob	64T	189	$ .25	$ .85

Player	Year	No.	VG	EX/MT	Player	Year	No.	VG	EX/MT
Hendley, Bob	65T	444	$ .30	$1.00	Henneman, Mike	90T	177	$ .01	$ .03
Hendley, Bob	66T	82	$ .25	$ .85	Hennigan, Phil	71T	211	$ .10	$ .35
Hendley, Bob	67T	256	$ .25	$ .65	Hennigan, Phil	72T	748	$ .70	$2.10
Hendley, Bob	68T	345	$ .25	$ .65	Hennigan, Phil	73T	107	$ .06	$ .25
Hendley, Bob	69T	144	$ .25	$ .65	Henninger, Rick	74T	602	$ .06	$ .25
Hendrick, George	72T	406	$ .35	$1.20	Henrich, Bob	58T	131	$ .50	$2.00
Hendrick, George	73T	13	$ .15	$ .50	Henry, Bill	59T	46	$1.00	$3.75
Hendrick, George	74T	303	$ .06	$ .25	Henry, Bill	60T	524	$2.00	$7.00
Hendrick, George	75T	109	$ .06	$ .25	Henry, Bill	61T	66	$ .30	$1.00
Hendrick, George	76T	570	$ .05	$ .20	Henry, Bill	62T	562	$3.75	$11.00
Hendrick, George	77T	330	$ .03	$ .12	Henry, Bill	63T	378	$ .35	$1.20
Hendrick, George	78T	30	$ .02	$ .10	Henry, Bill	64T	49	$ .25	$ .85
Hendrick, George	79T	175	$ .02	$ .10	Henry, Bill	65T	456	$ .50	$2.00
Hendrick, George	80T	350	$ .05	$ .25	Henry, Bill	66T	115	$ .25	$ .85
Hendrick, George	81T	230	$ .01	$ .07	Henry, Bill	67T	579	$1.25	$3.50
Hendrick, George	82T	420	$ .01	$ .06	Henry, Bill	68T	239	$ .25	$ .65
Hendrick, George	83T	650	$ .01	$ .06	Henry, Bill	68T	384	$1.00	$4.00
Hendrick, George	84T	540	$ .01	$ .05	Henry, Dwayne	88T	178	$ .01	$ .03
Hendrick, George	84TAS	386	$ .01	$ .05	Henry, Dwayne	89T	496	$ .01	$ .04
					Hepler, Bill	66T	574	$4.50	$15.00
					Hepler, Bill	67T	144	$ .25	$ .65
					Herbel, Ron	63T	208	$ .25	$ .85
					Herbel, Ron	64T	47	$ .30	$1.00
					Herbel, Ron	65T	84	$ .25	$ .65
					Herbel, Ron	66T	331	$ .25	$ .85
					Herbel, Ron	67T	156	$ .25	$ .65
					Herbel, Ron	68T	333	$ .25	$ .65
					Herbel, Ron	69T	251	$ .25	$ .85
					Herbel, Ron	70T	526	$ .10	$ .35
					Herbel, Ron	71T	387	$ .10	$ .35
					Herbel, Ron	72T	469	$ .05	$ .25
					Herbert, Ray	55T	138	$1.35	$5.00
					Herbert, Ray	58T	379	$ .50	$2.00
					Herbert, Ray	59T	154	$ .50	$1.95
					Herbert, Ray	60T	252	$ .35	$1.10
					Herbert, Ray	61T	498	$ .50	$2.00
					Herbert, Ray	62T	8	$ .35	$1.10
					Herbert, Ray	63T	8	$ .35	$1.10
					Herbert, Ray	63T	560	$1.50	$3.75
					Herbert, Ray	64T	215	$ .25	$ .85
					Herbert, Ray	65T	399	$ .30	$1.00
					Herbert, Ray	66T	121	$ .25	$ .85
					Herman, Billy	52T	394	$60.00	$225.00
					Herman, Billy	54T	86	$5.00	$20.00
					Herman, Billy	55T	19	$2.50	$12.50
					Herman, Billy	60T	456	$1.25	$4.50
					Herman, Billy	65T	251	$ .50	$2.00
					Herman, Billy	66T	37	$ .35	$1.10
					Hermann, Ed	73T	73	$ .06	$ .25
					Hermann, Ed	75T	219	$ .06	$ .25
					Hermann, Ed	78T	677	$ .02	$ .10
Hendrick, George	85T	60	$ .01	$ .04	Hermann, Ed	79T	374	$ .02	$ .10
Hendrick, George	85TTR	51	$ .02	$ .10	Hermanski, Gene	51Trb	11	$1.25	$3.50
Hendrick, George	86T	190	$ .01	$ .03	Hermanski, Gene	52T	16	$14.00	$45.00
Hendrick, George	87T	725	$ .01	$ .03	Hermanski, Gene	53T	179	$3.75	$13.00
Hendrick, George	88T	304	$ .01	$ .03	Hermanski, Gene	54T	228	$2.10	$7.50
Hendricks, Rod	69T	277	$ .25	$ .85	Hermoso, Angel	70T	147	$ .10	$ .35
Hendricks, Elrod	70T	528	$ .10	$ .35	Hernandez, Enzo	71T	529	$ .70	$2.00
Hendricks, Elrod "Ellie"	71T	219	$ .10	$ .35	Hernandez, Enzo	72T	7	$ .05	$ .25
Hendricks, Ellie	72T	508	$ .05	$ .25	Hernandez, Enzo	73T	438	$ .06	$ .25
Hendricks, Ellie	75T	609	$ .06	$ .25	Hernandez, Enzo	74T	572	$ .06	$ .25
Hendricks, Ellie	76T	371	$ .05	$ .20	Hernandez, Enzo	75T	84	$ .06	$ .25
Hengel, Dave	89T	531	$ .01	$ .10	Hernandez, Enzo	76T	289	$ .05	$ .20
Henke, Tom	86T	333	$ .01	$ .03	Hernandez, Enzo	77T	522	$ .03	$ .12
Henke, Tom	87T	510	$ .01	$ .03	Hernandez, Guillermo	88TBB	206	$ .01	$ .05
Henke, Tom	88T	220	$ .01	$ .10	Hernandez, Guillermo	89T	43	$ .01	$ .04
Henke, Tom	88TAS	396	$ .01	$ .03	Hernandez, Jackie	68T	352	$ .25	$ .65
Henke, Tom	88TBB	41	$ .01	$ .05	Hernandez, Jackie	69T	258	$ .25	$ .85
Henke, Tom	89T	75	$ .01	$ .04	Hernandez, Jackie	70T	686	$ .50	$2.00
Henke, Tom	90T	695	$ .01	$ .03	Hernandez, Jackie	71T	144	$ .10	$ .35
Henneman, Mike	87TTR	46	$ .05	$ .25	Hernandez, Jackie	72T	502	$ .05	$ .25
Henneman, Mike	88T	582	$ .01	$ .15	Hernandez, Jackie	73T	363	$ .06	$ .25
Henneman, Mike	88TBB	256	$ .01	$ .05	Hernandez, Jackie	74T	566	$ .06	$ .25
Henneman, Mike	89T	365	$ .01	$ .04	Hernandez, Keith	75T	623	$6.00	$18.00
Henneman, Mike	89TBB	252	$ .01	$ .05	Hernandez, Keith	76T	542	$2.50	$6.50

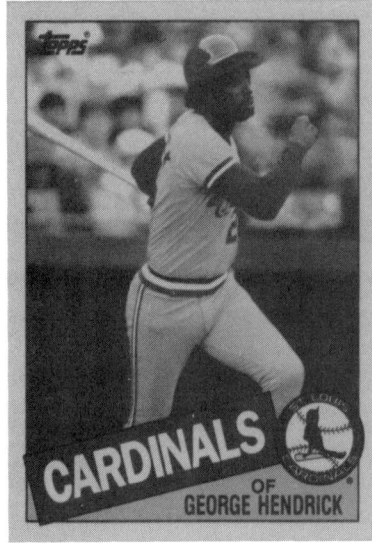

CARDINALS OF GEORGE HENDRICK

Player	Year	No.	VG	EX/MT	Player	Year	No.	VG	EX/MT
Hernandez, Keith	77T	95	$1.25	$4.50	Herr, Tom	89TBB	283	$ .01	$ .05
Hernandez, Keith	78T	143	$ .40	$1.75	Herr, Tom	89TTR	49	$ .01	$ .05
Hernandez, Keith	79T	695	$ .50	$2.00	Herr, Tom	90T	297	$ .01	$ .03
Hernandez, Keith	80T	201	$ .08	$ .30	Herrera, Frank "Pancho"	58T	433	$ .50	$2.00
Hernandez, Keith	80T	321	$ .30	$1.00	Herrera, Frank	59T	129	$ .50	$1.95
Hernandez, Keith	81T	420	$ .15	$ .75	Herrera, Frank	60T	130	$ .35	$1.10
Hernandez, Keith	82T	186	$ .05	$ .25	Herrera, Frank	61TAS	569	$6.00	$18.00
Hernandez, Keith	82T	210	$ .15	$ .60	Herrera, Jose	69T	378	$ .25	$ .65
Hernandez, Keith	83T	700	$ .01	$ .06	Herrmann, Ed	69T	439	$ .25	$ .65
Hernandez, Keith	83TTR	43	$ .35	$1.10	Herrmann, Ed	70T	368	$ .10	$ .35
Hernandez, Keith	84T	120	$ .07	$ .30	Herrmann, Ed	71T	169	$ .10	$ .35
Hernandez, Keith	85T	80	$ .05	$ .25	Herrmann, Ed	72T	452	$ .05	$ .25
Hernandez, Keith	85TAS	712	$ .01	$ .10	Herrmann, Ed	74T	438	$ .06	$ .25
Hernandez, Keith	86T	520	$ .03	$ .25	Herrmann, Ed	76T	406	$ .05	$ .20
Hernandez, Keith	86TAS	701	$ .01	$ .10	Herrmann, Ed	77T	143	$ .03	$ .12
Hernandez, Keith	86TRB	203	$ .01	$ .10	Herrnstein, John	63T	553	$60.00	$175.00
Hernandez, Keith	87T	350	$ .10	$ .35	Herrnstein, John	64T	243	$3.00	$10.00
Hernandez, Keith	87TAS	595	$ .01	$ .10	Herrnstein, John	65T	534	$1.50	$3.75
Hernandez, Keith	88T	610	$ .01	$ .10	Herrnstein, John	66T	304	$ .25	$ .85
Hernandez, Keith	88TBB	59	$ .01	$ .15	Hershberger, Mike	62T	341	$ .35	$1.10
Hernandez, Keith	89T	480	$ .01	$ .04	Hershberger, Mike	63T	254	$ .25	$ .85
Hernandez, Keith	89TBB	185	$ .01	$ .10	Hershberger, Mike	64T	465	$ .40	$1.25
Hernandez, Keith	90T	230	$ .01	$ .10	Hershberger, Mike	65T	89	$ .25	$ .65
Hernandez, Leo	83TTR	44	$ .02	$ .10	Hershberger, Mike	66T	236	$ .25	$ .85
Hernandez, Leo	84T	71	$ .01	$ .05	Hershberger, Mike	67T	323	$ .25	$ .65
Hernandez, Ramon	67T	576	$6.00	$20.00	Hershberger, Mike	68T	18	$ .25	$ .65
Hernandez, Ramon	68T	382	$ .25	$ .65	Hershberger, Mike	69T	655	$ .25	$ .85
Hernandez, Ramon	73T	117	$ .06	$ .25	Hershberger, Mike	70T	596	$ .25	$ .85
Hernandez, Ramon	74T	222	$ .06	$ .25	Hershberger, Mike	71T	149	$ .10	$ .35
Hernandez, Ramon	75T	224	$ .06	$ .25	Hershiser, Orel	85T	493	$2.00	$7.00
Hernandez, Ramon	76T	647	$ .05	$ .20	Hershiser, Orel	86T	159	$ .35	$1.10
Hernandez, Ramon	77T	468	$ .03	$ .12	Hershiser, Orel	87T	385	$ .05	$ .30
Hernandez, Rudy	61T	229	$ .30	$1.00	Hershiser, Orel	88T	40	$ .05	$ .25
Hernandez, Willie	78T	99	$ .20	$ .75	Hershiser, Orel	88TBB	91	$ .05	$ .35
Hernandez, Willie	79T	614	$ .02	$ .10	Hershiser, Orel	89T	550	$ .01	$ .15
Hernandez, Willie	80T	472	$ .05	$ .25	Hershiser, Orel	89TAS	394	$ .01	$ .10
Hernandez, Willie	81T	238	$ .01	$ .07	Hershiser, Orel	89TBB	1	$ .01	$ .25
Hernandez, Willie	82T	23	$ .01	$ .06	Hershiser, Orel	89TRB	5	$ .01	$ .10
Hernandez, Willie	83T	568	$ .01	$ .06	Hershiser, Orel	90T	780	$ .01	$ .10
Hernandez, Willie	83TTR	45	$ .02	$ .10	Hertz, Steve	64T	544	$1.50	$3.75
Hernandez, Willie	84T	199	$ .15	$ .60	Herzog, Whitey	57T	29	$5.00	$17.50
Hernandez, Willie	84TTR	51	$ .05	$ .25	Herzog, Whitey	58T	438	$ .45	$1.50
Hernandez, Willie	85T	333	$ .01	$ .04	Herzog, Whitey	59T	392	$ .50	$1.95
Hernandez, Willie	86T	670	$ .01	$ .03	Herzog, Whitey	60T	92	$ .65	$1.75
Hernandez, Willie	87T	515	$ .01	$ .03	Herzog, Whitey	61T	106	$ .50	$1.95
Hernandez, Willie	88T	713	$ .01	$ .03	Herzog, Whitey	62T	513	$ .70	$2.00
Hernandez, Xavier	89TMLD	55	$ .01	$ .05	Herzog, Whitey	63T	302	$ .50	$1.95
Herndon, Larry	77T	397	$ .03	$ .12	Herzog, Whitey	73T	549	$ .30	$1.00
Herndon, Larry	78T	512	$ .02	$ .10	Herzog, Whitey	78T	299	$ .05	$ .20
Herndon, Larry	79T	624	$ .02	$ .10	Herzog, Whitey	83T	186	$ .01	$ .06
Herndon, Larry	80T	257	$ .01	$ .07	Herzog, Whitey	84T	561	$ .01	$ .05
Herndon, Larry	81T	409	$ .01	$ .07	Herzog, Whitey	85T	683	$ .01	$ .04
Herndon, Larry	82T	182	$ .01	$ .06	Herzog, Whitey	86T	441	$ .01	$ .03
Herndon, Larry	82TTR	43	$ .02	$ .10	Herzog, Whitey	87T	243	$ .01	$ .03
Herndon, Larry	83T	13	$ .01	$ .06	Herzog, Whitey	88T	744	$ .01	$ .03
Herndon, Larry	83T	261	$ .01	$ .06	Herzog, Whitey	89T	654	$ .01	$ .04
Herndon, Larry	84T	333	$ .01	$ .05	Herzog, Whitey	90T	261	$ .01	$ .03
Herndon, Larry	85T	591	$ .01	$ .04	Hesketh, Joe	85TTR	52	$ .05	$ .20
Herndon, Larry	86T	688	$ .01	$ .03	Hesketh, Joe	86T	472	$ .01	$ .03
Herndon, Larry	87T	298	$ .01	$ .03	Hesketh, Joe	87T	189	$ .01	$ .03
Herndon, Larry	88T	743	$ .01	$ .03	Hesketh, Joe	88T	371	$ .01	$ .03
Herndon, Larry	88TBB	56	$ .01	$ .05	Hesketh, Joe	89T	614	$ .01	$ .04
Herr, Tom	80T	684	$ .08	$ .40	Hesketh, Joe	90T	24	$ .01	$ .03
Herr, Tom	81T	266	$ .01	$ .07	Hetki, John	53T	235	$11.00	$37.50
Herr, Tom	82T	27	$ .01	$ .06	Hetki, John	54T	161	$2.10	$7.50
Herr, Tom	83T	489	$ .01	$ .06	Hetzel, Eric	89TMLD	56	$ .01	$ .05
Herr, Tom	84T	649	$ .01	$ .05	Hetzel, Eric	90T	629	$ .01	$ .03
Herr, Tom	85T	113	$ .01	$ .04	Hiatt, Jack	65T	497	$ .50	$2.00
Herr, Tom	86T	550	$ .01	$ .03	Hiatt, Jack	66T	373	$ .25	$ .85
Herr, Tom	86TAS	702	$ .01	$ .03	Hiatt, Jack	67T	368	$ .25	$ .65
Herr, Tom	87T	721	$ .01	$ .03	Hiatt, Jack	68T	419	$ .25	$ .65
Herr, Tom	88T	310	$ .01	$ .03	Hiatt, Jack	69T	204	$ .25	$ .65
Herr, Tom	88TBB	31	$ .01	$ .05	Hiatt, Jack	70T	13	$ .10	$ .35
Herr, Tom	88TTR	49	$ .01	$ .05	Hiatt, Jack	71T	371	$ .10	$ .35
Herr, Tom	89T	709	$ .01	$ .04	Hiatt, Jack	72T	633	$ .25	$ .85

TOPPS

JACK HIATT
CALIFORNIA ANGELS   CATCHER

Player	Year	No.	VG	EX/MT
Hiatt, Jack	73T	402	$ .06	$ .25
Hibbard, Greg	89TMLD	57	$ .01	$ .10
Hibbard, Greg	90T	769	$ .01	$ .10
Hickey, Kevin	82T	778	$ .01	$ .06
Hickey, Kevin	83T	278	$ .01	$ .06
Hickey, Kevin	84T	459	$ .01	$ .05
Hickey, Kevin	90T	546	$ .01	$ .03
Hickman, Jim	62T	598	$12.00	$50.00
Hickman, Jim	63T	107	$ .25	$ .85
Hickman, Jim	64T	514	$ .40	$1.25
Hickman, Jim	65T	114	$ .25	$ .65
Hickman, Jim	66T	402	$ .25	$ .85
Hickman, Jim	67T	346	$ .25	$ .65
Hickman, Jim	69T	63	$ .25	$ .65
Hickman, Jim	70T	612	$ .25	$ .85
Hickman, Jim	71T	175	$ .10	$ .35
Hickman, Jim	72T	534	$ .25	$ .85
Hickman, Jim	73T	565	$ .35	$1.10
Hicks, Jim	67T	532	$ .50	$2.00
Hicks, Jim	69T	559	$ .25	$ .85
Hicks, Jim	70T	173	$ .10	$ .35
Hicks, Joe	61T	386	$ .50	$2.00
Hicks, Joe	62T	428	$ .70	$2.10
Higgins, Dennis	66T	529	$4.50	$15.00
Higgins, Dennis	67T	52	$ .25	$ .65
Higgins, Dennis	68T	509	$ .30	$1.00
Higgins, Dennis	69T	441	$ .25	$ .65
Higgins, Dennis	70T	257	$ .10	$ .35
Higgins, Dennis	71T	479	$ .10	$ .35
Higgins, Dennis	72T	278	$ .05	$ .25
Higgins, Mark	89TMLD	58	$ .01	$ .15
Higgins, Mike	55T	150	$1.35	$5.00
Higgins, Mike	61T	221	$ .30	$1.00
Higgins, Mike	62T	559	$3.75	$11.00
Higuera, Teddy	85TTR	53	$ .75	$2.50
Higuera, Teddy	86T	347	$ .35	$1.10
Higuera, Teddy	87T	250	$ .06	$ .25
Higuera, Teddy	87TAS	615	$ .01	$ .10
Higuera, Teddy	88T	110	$ .01	$ .10
Higuera, Teddy	88TBB	87	$ .01	$ .05
Higuera, Teddy	89T	595	$ .01	$ .04
Higuera, Teddy	90T	15	$ .01	$ .03
Hilgendorf, Tom	70T	482	$ .10	$ .35

Player	Year	No.	VG	EX/MT
Hilgendorf, Tom	74T	13	$ .06	$ .25
Hilgendorf, Tom	75T	377	$ .06	$ .25
Hilgendorf, Tom	76T	168	$ .05	$ .20
Hill, Donnie	84T	265	$ .01	$ .05
Hill, Donnie	85TTR	54	$ .02	$ .10
Hill, Donnie	86T	484	$ .01	$ .03
Hill, Donnie	87T	339	$ .01	$ .03
Hill, Donnie	87TTR	47	$ .01	$ .07
Hill, Donnie	88T	132	$ .01	$ .03
Hill, Donnie	88TBB	137	$ .01	$ .05
Hill, Donnie	89T	512	$ .01	$ .04
Hill, Garry	70T	172	$ .10	$ .35
Hill, Glenallen	89TMLD	59	$ .01	$ .15
Hill, Glenallen	90T	194	$ .01	$ .15
Hill, Herman	70T	267	$ .10	$ .35
Hill, Ken	89TTR	50	$ .01	$ .10
Hill, Ken	90T	233	$ .01	$ .03
Hill, Marc	75T	620	$12.00	$35.00
Hill, Marc	76T	577	$ .05	$ .20
Hill, Marc	77T	57	$ .03	$ .12
Hill, Marc	78T	359	$ .02	$ .10
Hill, Marc	79T	11	$ .02	$ .10
Hill, Marc	80T	236	$ .01	$ .07
Hill, Marc	81T	486	$ .01	$ .07
Hill, Marc	81TTR	770	$ .02	$ .10
Hill, Marc	82T	748	$ .01	$ .06
Hill, Marc	83T	124	$ .01	$ .06
Hill, Marc	84T	698	$ .01	$ .05
Hill, Marc	85T	312	$ .01	$ .04
Hill, Marc	86T	552	$ .01	$ .03
Hillegas, Shawn	88T	455	$ .01	$ .20
Hillegas, Shawn	89T	247	$ .01	$ .04
Hillegas, Shawn	90T	93	$ .01	$ .03
Hiller, Chuck	61T	538	$6.00	$18.00
Hiller, Chuck	62T	188	$ .35	$1.10
Hiller, Chuck	63T	185	$ .25	$ .85
Hiller, Chuck	64T	313	$ .25	$ .85
Hiller, Chuck	65T	531	$1.50	$3.75
Hiller, Chuck	66T	154	$ .25	$ .85
Hiller, Chuck	67T	198	$ .25	$ .65
Hiller, Chuck	68T	461	$ .30	$1.00
Hiller, Chuck	73T	549	$ .30	$1.00
Hiller, Frank	52T	156	$6.00	$19.00
Hiller, John	66T	209	$ .30	$1.00
Hiller, John	68T	307	$ .25	$ .65
Hiller, John	69T	642	$ .25	$ .85
Hiller, John	70T	12	$ .10	$ .35
Hiller, John	71T	629	$ .30	$1.00
Hiller, John	73T	448	$ .06	$ .25
Hiller, John	74T	24	$ .06	$ .25
Hiller, John	74T	208	$ .06	$ .25
Hiller, John	75T	415	$ .06	$ .25
Hiller, John	76T	37	$ .05	$ .20
Hiller, John	77T	595	$ .03	$ .12
Hiller, John	78T	258	$ .02	$ .10
Hiller, John	79T	151	$ .02	$ .10
Hiller, John	80T	614	$ .01	$ .07
Hillman, Dave	57T	351	$3.50	$13.00
Hillman, Dave	58T	41	$1.00	$3.75
Hillman, Dave	59T	319	$ .50	$1.95
Hillman, Dave	60T	68	$ .35	$1.10
Hillman, Dave	61T	326	$ .30	$1.00
Hillman, Dave	62T	282	$ .35	$1.10
Hilton, Dave	73T	615	$120.00	$365.00
Hilton, Dave	74T	148	$ .06	$ .25
Hilton, Dave	75T	509	$ .06	$ .25
Hilton, Dave	77T	163	$ .03	$ .12
Hinds, Sam	78T	303	$ .02	$ .10
Hinsley, Jerry	64T	576	$1.50	$3.75
Hinsley, Jerry	65T	449	$ .50	$2.00
Hinton, Chuck	62T	347	$ .35	$1.10
Hinton, Chuck	63T	2	$3.00	$12.00
Hinton, Chuck	63T	330	$ .35	$1.20
Hinton, Chuck	64T	52	$ .25	$ .85
Hinton, Chuck	65T	235	$ .30	$1.00

Player	Year	No.	VG	EX/MT	Player	Year	No.	VG	EX/MT
Hinton, Chuck	66T	391	$ .25	$ .85	Hodges, Gil	57T	400	$40.00	$150.00
Hinton, Chuck	67T	189	$ .25	$ .65	Hodges, Gil	58T	162	$8.50	$32.50
Hinton, Chuck	68T	531	$ .30	$1.00	Hodges, Gil	59T	270	$5.00	$20.00
Hinton, Chuck	69T	644	$ .25	$ .85	Hodges, Gil	60T	295	$5.00	$16.00
Hinton, Chuck	70T	27	$ .10	$ .35	Hodges, Gil	61T	460	$4.50	$14.00
Hinton, Chuck	71T	429	$ .10	$ .35	Hodges, Gil	62T	85	$4.50	$14.00
Hinton, Rich	72T	724	$1.00	$3.75	Hodges, Gil	63T	68	$2.50	$10.00
Hinton, Rich	73T	321	$ .06	$ .25	Hodges, Gil	63T	245	$4.50	$15.00
Hinton, Rich	76T	607	$ .05	$ .20	Hodges, Gil	64T	547	$5.00	$17.50
Hinzo, Tommy	88T	576	$ .01	$ .03	Hodges, Gil	65T	99	$2.50	$7.50
Hippauf, Herb	66T	518	$ .70	$2.10	Hodges, Gil	66T	386	$1.50	$4.50
Hiser, Gene	72T	61	$ .15	$ .60	Hodges, Gil	67T	228	$1.25	$3.50
Hiser, Gene	74T	452	$ .06	$ .25	Hodges, Gil	68T	27	$3.00	$10.00
Hisle, Larry	68T	579	$ .35	$1.10	Hodges, Gil	69T	564	$1.35	$4.00
Hisle, Larry	69T	206	$ .25	$ .65	Hodges, Gil	70T	394	$1.50	$6.00
Hisle, Larry	70T	288	$ .10	$ .35	Hodges, Gil	71T	183	$1.25	$3.50
Hisle, Larry	71T	616	$ .30	$1.00	Hodges, Gil	72T	465	$1.00	$4.00
Hisle, Larry	72T	398	$ .05	$ .25	Hodges, Gil	89TTB	664	$ .01	$ .04
Hisle, Larry	73T	622	$ .35	$1.10	Hodges, Ron	74T	448	$ .06	$ .25
Hisle, Larry	74T	366	$ .06	$ .25	Hodges, Ron	75T	134	$ .06	$ .25
Hisle, Larry	75T	526	$ .06	$ .25	Hodges, Ron	77T	329	$ .03	$ .12
Hisle, Larry	76T	59	$ .05	$ .20	Hodges, Ron	78T	653	$ .02	$ .10
Hisle, Larry	77T	375	$ .03	$ .12	Hodges, Ron	79T	46	$ .02	$ .10
Hisle, Larry	78T	203	$ .05	$ .20	Hodges, Ron	80T	172	$ .01	$ .07
Hisle, Larry	78T	520	$ .02	$ .10	Hodges, Ron	81T	537	$ .01	$ .07
Hisle, Larry	79T	180	$ .02	$ .10	Hodges, Ron	82T	234	$ .01	$ .06
Hisle, Larry	80T	430	$ .01	$ .07	Hodges, Ron	83T	713	$ .01	$ .06
Hisle, Larry	81T	215	$ .01	$ .07	Hodges, Ron	84T	418	$ .01	$ .05
Hisle, Larry	82T	93	$ .01	$ .06	Hodges, Ron	85T	363	$ .01	$ .04
Hisle, Larry	83T	773	$ .01	$ .06	Hoeft, Billy	52T	370	$39.00	$135.00
Hitchcock, Billy	52T	182	$6.00	$19.00	Hoeft, Billy	53T	165	$3.75	$13.00
Hitchcock, Billy	53T	17	$3.75	$13.00	Hoeft, Billy	56T	152	$1.25	$4.50
Hitchcock, Billy	60T	461	$1.25	$4.50	Hoeft, Billy	57T	60	$ .95	$3.50
Hitchcock, Billy	62T	121	$ .35	$1.10	Hoeft, Billy	58T	13	$1.00	$3.75
Hitchcock, Billy	63T	213	$ .25	$ .85	Hoeft, Billy	59T	343	$ .50	$1.95
Hitchcock, Billy	67T	199	$ .25	$ .65	Hoeft, Billy	60T	369	$ .50	$1.95
Hoak, Don	53T	176	$2.25	$8.00	Hoeft, Billy	61T	256	$ .30	$1.00
Hoak, Don	54T	211	$1.75	$7.00	Hoeft, Billy	62T	134	$ .50	$1.95
Hoak, Don	55T	40	$2.10	$7.50	Hoeft, Billy	63T	346	$ .35	$1.20
Hoak, Don	56T	335	$1.80	$6.00	Hoeft, Billy	64T	551	$1.50	$3.75
Hoak, Don	57T	274	$3.50	$13.00	Hoeft, Billy	65T	471	$ .50	$2.00
Hoak, Don	58T	160	$ .65	$2.00	Hoeft, Billy	66T	409	$ .25	$ .85
Hoak, Don	59T	25	$1.50	$3.75	Hoerner, Joe	64T	544	$1.50	$3.75
Hoak, Don	60T	373	$ .45	$1.35	Hoerner, Joe	66T	544	$4.00	$11.50
Hoak, Don	61T	230	$ .30	$1.00	Hoerner, Joe	67T	41	$ .25	$ .65
Hoak, Don	62T	95	$ .35	$1.10	Hoerner, Joe	68T	227	$ .25	$ .65
Hoak, Don	63T	305	$ .35	$1.20	Hoerner, Joe	69T	522	$ .25	$ .85
Hoak, Don	64T	254	$ .25	$ .85	Hoerner, Joe	70T	511	$ .10	$ .35
Hobaugh, Ed	60T	131	$ .35	$1.10	Hoerner, Joe	71T	166	$ .10	$ .35
Hobaugh, Ed	61T	129	$ .30	$1.00	Hoerner, Joe	72T	482	$ .05	$ .25
Hobaugh, Ed	62T	70	$ .05	$1.10	Hoerner, Joe	73T	653	$ .35	$1.10
Hobaugh, Ed	63T	423	$ .35	$1.20	Hoerner, Joe	74T	493	$ .06	$ .25
Hobbie, Glen	58T	467	$ .50	$1.95	Hoerner, Joe	75T	629	$ .06	$ .25
Hobbie, Glen	59T	334	$ .50	$1.95	Hoerner, Joe	77T	256	$ .03	$ .12
Hobbie, Glen	60T	182	$ .35	$1.10	Hoffman, Glenn	81T	349	$ .01	$ .07
Hobbie, Glen	61T	264	$ .30	$1.00	Hoffman, Glenn	82T	189	$ .01	$ .06
Hobbie, Glen	61T	393	$ .60	$1.75	Hoffman, Glenn	83T	108	$ .01	$ .06
Hobbie, Glen	62T	585	$3.75	$11.00	Hoffman, Glenn	84T	523	$ .01	$ .05
Hobbie, Glen	63T	212	$ .25	$ .85	Hoffman, Glenn	85T	633	$ .01	$ .04
Hobbie, Glen	64T	578	$1.50	$3.75	Hoffman, Glenn	86T	38	$ .01	$ .03
Hobson, Butch	77T	89	$ .03	$ .12	Hoffman, Glenn	87T	374	$ .01	$ .03
Hobson, Butch	78T	155	$ .02	$ .10	Hoffman, Glenn	88T	202	$ .01	$ .03
Hobson, Butch	79T	270	$ .02	$ .10	Hoffman, Guy	80T	664	$ .01	$ .07
Hobson, Butch	80T	420	$ .01	$ .07	Hoffman, Guy	87TTR	48	$ .01	$ .07
Hobson, Butch	81T	595	$ .01	$ .07	Hoffman, Guy	88T	496	$ .01	$ .03
Hobson, Butch	81TTR	771	$ .02	$ .10	Hofman, Bob	52T	371	$75.00	$225.00
Hobson, Butch	82T	357	$ .01	$ .06	Hofman, Bob	53T	182	$3.75	13.00
Hobson, Butch	83T	652	$ .01	$ .06	Hofman, Bob	54T	99	$2.10	$7.50
Hodge, Ed	85T	639	$ .01	$ .04	Hofman, Bobby	55T	17	$1.35	$5.00
Hodges, Gil	51Trb	31	$8.00	$30.00	Hofman, Bobby	56T	28	$1.25	$4.50
Hodges, Gil	52T	36	$65.00	$200.00	Hogue, Bobby	52T	9	$14.00	$45.00
Hodges, Gil	54T	102	$20.00	$80.00	Hogue, Cal	53T	238	$11.00	$37.50
Hodges, Gil	55T	187	$45.00	$175.00	Hogue, Cal	54T	134	$2.10	$7.50
Hodges, Gil	56T	145	$10.00	$42.50	Hoiles, Chris	89TMLD	60	$ .01	$ .05
Hodges, Gil	57T	80	$10.00	$40.00	Holcombe, Ken	52T	95	$6.00	$19.00

Player	Year	No.	VG	EX/MT
Holdsworth, Fred	74T	596	$ .06	$ .25
Holdsworth, Fred	75T	323	$ .06	$ .25
Holdsworth, Fred	77T	466	$ .03	$ .12
Holland, Al	81T	213	$ .01	$ .07
Holland, Al	82T	406	$ .01	$ .06
Holland, Al	83T	58	$ .01	$ .06
Holland, Al	83TTR	46	$ .02	$ .10
Holland, Al	84T	138	$ .02	$ .10
Holland, Al	84T	564	$ .01	$ .05
Holland, Al	85T	185	$ .01	$ .04
Holland, Al	85TTR	55	$ .02	$ .10
Holland, Al	86T	369	$ .01	$ .03
Holly, Jeff	79T	371	$ .02	$ .10
Holman, Brian	89TTR	51	$ .01	$ .15
Holman, Brian	90T	616	$ .01	$ .10
Holman, Gary	69T	361	$ .25	$ .65
Holman, Scott	84T	13	$ .01	$ .05
Holman, Shawn	89TMLD	61	$ .01	$ .25
Holmes, Tommy	51Trb	52	$3.25	$10.00
Holmes, Tommy	52T	289	$18.50	$55.00
Holt, Jim	71T	7	$ .10	$ .35
Holt, Jim	72T	588	$ .25	$ .85
Holt, Jim	73T	259	$ .06	$ .25
Holt, Jim	74T	122	$ .06	$ .25
Holt, Jim	75T	607	$ .06	$ .25
Holt, Jim	76T	603	$ .05	$ .20
Holt, Jim	77T	349	$ .03	$ .12
Holton, Brian	87TTR	49	$ .01	$ .07
Holton, Brian	88T	338	$ .01	$ .03
Holton, Brian	89T	368	$ .01	$ .04
Holton, Brian	89TTR	52	$ .01	$ .05
Holton, Brian	90T	179	$ .01	$ .03
Holtzman, Ken	67T	185	$ .30	$1.00
Holtzman, Ken	68T	60	$ .25	$ .65
Holtzman, Ken	68TAS	380	$ .25	$ .65
Holtzman, Ken	69T	288	$ .25	$ .85
Holtzman, Ken	70T	505	$ .10	$ .35
Holtzman, Ken	71T	410	$ .10	$ .35
Holtzman, Ken	72T	670	$ .60	$1.75
Holtzman, Ken	73T	60	$ .10	$ .35
Holtzman, Ken	74T	180	$ .06	$ .25
Holtzman, Ken	75T	145	$ .06	$ .25
Holtzman, Ken	76T	115	$ .05	$ .20
Holtzman, Ken	77T	625	$ .03	$ .12
Holtzman, Ken	78T	387	$ .02	$ .10
Holtzman, Ken	79T	522	$ .02	$ .10
Holtzman, Ken	80T	298	$ .01	$ .07
Honeycutt, Rick	79T	612	$ .05	$ .25
Honeycutt, Rick	80T	307	$ .01	$ .07
Honeycutt, Rick	81T	33	$ .01	$ .07
Honeycutt, Rick	81TTR	772	$ .02	$ .10
Honeycutt, Rick	82T	751	$ .01	$ .06
Honeycutt, Rick	83T	557	$ .01	$ .06
Honeycutt, Rick	84T	37	$ .01	$ .05
Honeycutt, Rick	84T	137	$ .01	$ .05
Honeycutt, Rick	84T	222	$ .01	$ .05
Honeycutt, Rick	85T	174	$ .01	$ .04
Honeycutt, Rick	86T	439	$ .01	$ .03
Honeycutt, Rick	87T	753	$ .01	$ .03
Honeycutt, Rick	88T	641	$ .01	$ .03
Honeycutt, Rick	89T	328	$ .01	$ .04
Honeycutt, Rick	90T	582	$ .01	$ .03
Hood, Don	74T	436	$ .06	$ .25
Hood, Don	75T	516	$ .06	$ .25
Hood, Don	76T	132	$ .05	$ .20
Hood, Don	77T	296	$ .03	$ .12
Hood, Don	78T	398	$ .02	$ .10
Hood, Don	79T	667	$ .02	$ .10
Hood, Don	80T	89	$ .01	$ .07
Hood, Don	83T	443	$ .01	$ .06
Hood, Don	84T	743	$ .01	$ .05
Hook, Jay	60T	187	$ .35	$1.10
Hook, Jay	61T	162	$ .30	$1.00
Hook, Jay	62T	94	$ .35	$1.10
Hook, Jay	63T	469	$2.50	$6.50

Player	Year	No.	VG	EX/MT
Hook, Jay	64T	361	$ .25	$ .85
Hooper, Bob	52T	340	$39.00	$135.00
Hooper, Bob	53T	84	$3.75	$13.00
Hooten, Leon	77T	478	$ .03	$ .12
Hooton, Burt	72T	61	$ .15	$ .60
Hooton, Burt	73T	367	$ .06	$ .25
Hooton, Burt	74T	378	$ .06	$ .25
Hooton, Burt	75T	176	$ .06	$ .25
Hooton, Burt	76T	280	$ .05	$ .20
Hooton, Burt	77T	484	$ .03	$ .12
Hooton, Burt	78T	41	$ .02	$ .10
Hooton, Burt	79T	694	$ .02	$ .10
Hooton, Burt	80T	170	$ .01	$ .07
Hooton, Burt	81T	565	$ .01	$ .07
Hooton, Burt	82T	311	$ .01	$ .06
Hooton, Burt	82T	315	$ .01	$ .06
Hooton, Burt	83T	775	$ .01	$ .06
Hooton, Burt	84T	15	$ .01	$ .05
Hooton, Burt	85T	201	$ .01	$ .04
Hooton, Burt	85TTR	56	$ .02	$ .10
Hooton, Burt	86T	454	$ .01	$ .03
Hoover, John	85T	397	$ .01	$ .04
Hopkins, Gail	70T	483	$ .10	$ .35
Hopkins, Gail	71T	269	$ .10	$ .35
Hopkins, Gail	72T	728	$ .70	$2.10
Hopkins, Gail	73T	441	$ .06	$ .25
Hopkins, Gail	74T	652	$ .06	$ .25

JOHNNY HOPP

Player	Year	No.	VG	EX/MT
Hopp, Johnny	52T	214	$7.00	$20.00
Hopp, Johnny	54T	193	$2.10	$7.50
Horlen, Joe	68T	8	$ .35	$1.10
Horlen, Joe	68TAS	377	$ .25	$ .65
Horlen, Joe	69T	328	$ .25	$ .65
Horlen, Joe	70T	35	$ .10	$ .35
Horlen, Joe	71T	345	$ .10	$ .35
Horlen, Joe	72T	685	$ .70	$2.10
Horlen, Joel	62T	479	$ .70	$2.10
Horlen, Joel	63T	332	$ .35	$1.20
Horlen, Joel	64T	584	$1.50	$3.75
Horlen, Joel	65T	7	$ .30	$1.00
Horlen, Joel	65T	480	$ .50	$2.00
Horlen, Joel	66T	560	$4.50	$15.00
Horlen, Joel	67T	107	$ .25	$ .65
Horlen, Joel	67T	233	$ .35	$1.10

Player	Year	No.	VG	EX/MT	Player	Year	No.	VG	EX/MT
Horlen, Joe "Joel"	68T	125	$ .25	$ .65	Hough, Charlie	88TBB	47	$ .01	$ .05
Horn, Sam	88T	377	$ .01	$ .10	Hough, Charlie	89T	345	$ .01	$ .04
Horn, Sam	88TBB	252	$ .01	$ .05	Hough, Charlie	90T	735	$ .01	$ .03
Horner, Bob	79T	586	$1.35	$5.00	Houk, Ralph	52T	200	$20.00	$60.00
Horner, Bob	80T	108	$ .15	$ .75	Houk, Ralph	60T	465	$2.50	$9.00
Horner, Bob	81T	355	$ .08	$ .35	Houk, Ralph	61T	133	$1.00	$3.00
Horner, Bob	82T	145	$ .05	$ .25	Houk, Ralph	62T	88	$ .60	$1.75
Horner, Bob	83T	50	$ .05	$ .20	Houk, Ralph	63T	382	$ .50	$2.00
Horner, Bob	84T	760	$ .04	$ .20	Houk, Ralph	67T	468	$ .70	$2.00
Horner, Bob	85T	276	$ .05	$ .20	Houk, Ralph	68T	47	$ .15	$ .50
Horner, Bob	85T	410	$ .05	$ .25	Houk, Ralph	69T	447	$ .25	$ .85
Horner, Bob	86T	220	$ .02	$ .15	Houk, Ralph	70T	273	$ .15	$ .50
Horner, Bob	87T	660	$ .01	$ .10	Houk, Ralph	71T	146	$ .15	$ .50
Horner, Bob	88TBB	245	$ .01	$ .10	Houk, Ralph	72T	533	$ .30	$1.00
Horner, Bob	88TTR	50	$ .01	$ .05	Houk, Ralph	73T	116	$ .15	$ .50
Horner, Bob	89T	510	$ .01	$ .04	Houk, Ralph	74T	578	$ .06	$ .25
Hornsby, Rogers	61T	404	$ .70	$2.00	Houk, Ralph	78T	684	$ .02	$ .10
Hornsby, Rogers	76TAS	342	$ .50	$2.00	Houk, Ralph	83T	786	$ .01	$ .06
Hornsby, Rogers	79TRH	414	$ .15	$ .50	Houk, Ralph	84T	381	$ .01	$ .05
Horton, Ricky	84TTR	52	$ .08	$ .30	Houk, Ralph	85T	11	$ .01	$ .04
Horton, Ricky	85T	321	$ .01	$ .10	House, Frank	52T	146	$6.00	$19.00
Horton, Ricky	86T	783	$ .01	$ .03	House, Frank	54T	163	$1.25	$5.00
Horton, Ricky	87T	542	$ .01	$ .03	House, Frank	55T	87	$1.35	$5.00
Horton, Ricky	88T	34	$ .01	$ .03	House, Frank	56T	32	$1.25	$4.50
Horton, Ricky	88TTR	51	$ .01	$ .05	House, Frank	57T	223	$ .95	$3.50
Horton, Ricky	89T	232	$ .01	$ .04	House, Frank	58T	318	$ .50	$2.00
Horton, Ricky	90T	133	$ .01	$ .03	House, Frank	59T	313	$ .50	$1.95
Horton, Willie	64T	512	$2.00	$8.00	House, Frank	60T	372	$ .50	$1.95
Horton, Willie	65T	206	$ .35	$1.10	House, Tom	69T	331	$ .25	$ .65
Horton, Willie	66T	20	$ .25	$ .85	House, Tom	72T	351	$ .10	$ .35
Horton, Willie	66T	218	$ .50	$2.00	House, Tom	74T	164	$ .06	$ .25
Horton, Willie	66T	220	$ .50	$2.00	House, Tom	75T	525	$ .06	$ .25
Horton, Willie	67T	465	$ .50	$2.00	House, Tom	76T	231	$ .05	$ .20
Horton, Willie	68T	360	$ .15	$ .50	House, Tom	76TTR	231	$ .05	$ .20
Horton, Willie	69T	5	$ .30	$1.00	House, Tom	77T	358	$ .03	$ .12
Horton, Willie	69T	180	$ .25	$ .65	House, Tom	78T	643	$ .02	$ .10
Horton, Willie	69TAS	429	$ .25	$ .65	House, Tom	79T	31	$ .02	$ .10
Horton, Willie	70T	520	$ .15	$ .50	Householder, Paul	81T	606	$ .01	$ .07
Horton, Willie	71T	120	$ .10	$ .35	Householder, Paul	82T	351	$ .01	$ .06
Horton, Willie	72T	494	$ .05	$ .25	Householder, Paul	83T	34	$ .01	$ .06
Horton, Willie	72T	750	$ .60	$1.75	Householder, Paul	84T	214	$ .01	$ .05
Horton, Willie	73T	433	$ .25	$ .65	Householder, Paul	86T	554	$ .01	$ .03
Horton, Willie	74T	115	$ .06	$ .25	Houston, Tyler	90T	564	$ .01	$ .35
Horton, Willie	75T	66	$ .06	$ .25	Houtteman, Art	52T	238	$6.00	$19.00
Horton, Willie	76T	320	$ .05	$ .20	Houtteman, Art	56T	281	$1.80	$6.00
Horton, Willie	77T	660	$ .15	$ .50	Houtteman, Art	57T	385	$1.00	$3.75
Horton, Willie	78T	290	$ .02	$ .10	Hovley, Steve	70T	514	$ .10	$ .35
Horton, Willie	79T	239	$ .02	$ .10	Hovley, Steve	71T	109	$ .10	$ .35
Horton, Willie	80T	532	$ .01	$ .07	Hovley, Steve	72T	683	$ .70	$2.10
Hoscheit, Vern	73T	179	$ .25	$ .85	Hovley, Steve	73T	282	$ .06	$ .25
Hoskins, Dave	54T	81	$2.10	$7.50	Howard, Bruce	64T	107	$ .25	$ .85
Hoskins, Dave	55T	133	$1.35	$5.00	Howard, Bruce	65T	41	$ .25	$ .65
Hosley, Tim	72T	257	$ .05	$ .25	Howard, Bruce	66T	281	$ .25	$ .85
Hosley, Tim	76T	482	$ .05	$ .20	Howard, Bruce	67T	159	$ .25	$ .65
Hosley, Tim	78T	261	$ .02	$ .10	Howard, Bruce	68T	293	$ .25	$ .65
Hostetler, Dave	83T	584	$ .01	$ .06	Howard, Bruce	69T	226	$ .25	$ .85
Hostetler, Dave	84T	62	$ .01	$ .05	Howard, Elston	56T	208	$10.00	$30.00
Hough, Charlie	72T	198	$ .60	$1.50	Howard, Elston	57T	82	$6.00	$18.00
Hough, Charlie	73T	610	$ .35	$1.10	Howard, Elston	58T	275	$2.50	$9.00
Hough, Charlie	74T	408	$ .06	$ .25	Howard, Elston	59T	395	$1.75	$7.00
Hough, Charlie	75T	71	$ .06	$ .25	Howard, Elston	60T	65	$1.50	$4.50
Hough, Charlie	76T	174	$ .05	$ .20	Howard, Elston	61T	495	$1.50	$4.50
Hough, Charlie	77T	298	$ .03	$ .12	Howard, Elston	62T	51	$ .50	$1.95
Hough, Charlie	78T	22	$ .02	$ .10	Howard, Elston	62T	400	$1.50	$4.50
Hough, Charlie	79T	508	$ .02	$ .10	Howard, Elston	62TAS	473	$1.00	$3.00
Hough, Charlie	80T	644	$ .01	$ .07	Howard, Elston	63T	60	$2.25	$6.50
Hough, Charlie	81T	371	$ .01	$ .07	Howard, Elston	63T	306	$1.00	$4.00
Hough, Charlie	82T	718	$ .01	$ .06	Howard, Elston	64T	100	$ .70	$2.00
Hough, Charlie	83T	412	$ .01	$ .06	Howard, Elston	65T	1	$2.50	$8.00
Hough, Charlie	83T	479	$ .01	$ .06	Howard, Elston	65T	3	$5.00	$15.00
Hough, Charlie	84T	118	$ .01	$ .05	Howard, Elston	65T	450	$1.50	$3.75
Hough, Charlie	85T	571	$ .01	$ .04	Howard, Elston	66T	405	$1.00	$3.00
Hough, Charlie	86T	275	$ .01	$ .03	Howard, Elston	67T	25	$1.00	$3.00
Hough, Charlie	87T	70	$ .01	$ .03	Howard, Elston	68T	167	$ .60	$1.75
Hough, Charlie	88T	680	$ .01	$ .03	Howard, Elston	73T	116	$ .15	$ .50

Player	Year	No.	VG	EX/MT
Howard, Elston	75T	201	$ .50	$2.00
Howard, Frank	60T	132	$3.00	$10.00
Howard, Frank	61T	280	$ .95	$3.50
Howard, Frank	62T	175	$ .75	$2.00
Howard, Frank	63T	123	$ .75	$2.00
Howard, Frank	64T	371	$ .60	$1.75
Howard, Frank	65T	40	$ .75	$2.00
Howard, Frank	66T	515	$2.00	$6.00
Howard, Frank	67T	255	$ .40	$1.50
Howard, Frank	68T	6	$2.00	$5.00
Howard, Frank	68T	320	$ .35	$1.10
Howard, Frank	69T	3	$ .30	$1.00
Howard, Frank	69T	5	$ .30	$1.00
Howard, Frank	69T	170	$ .35	$1.10
Howard, Frank	70T	66	$1.00	$4.00
Howard, Frank	70T	550	$ .35	$1.10
Howard, Frank	71T	63	$ .15	$ .50
Howard, Frank	71T	65	$ .60	$1.75
Howard, Frank	71T	620	$ .75	$2.00

FRANK HOWARD

Player	Year	No.	VG	EX/MT
Howard, Frank	72T	350	$ .25	$ .85
Howard, Frank	73T	560	$ .75	$2.00
Howard, Frank	83TTR	47	$ .02	$ .10
Howard, Frank	84T	621	$ .01	$ .05
Howard, Fred	80T	72	$ .01	$ .07
Howard, Larry	71T	102	$ .10	$ .35
Howard, Wilbur	74T	606	$ .06	$ .25
Howard, Wilbur	75T	563	$ .06	$ .25
Howard, Wilbur	76T	97	$ .05	$ .20
Howard, Wilbur	77T	248	$ .03	$ .12
Howard, Wilbur	78T	534	$ .02	$ .10
Howard, Wilbur	79T	642	$ .02	$ .10
Howarth, Jimmy	73T	459	$ .06	$ .25
Howarth, Jimmy	74T	404	$ .06	$ .25
Howe, Art	78T	13	$ .02	$ .10
Howe, Art	79T	327	$ .02	$ .10
Howe, Art	80T	554	$ .01	$ .07
Howe, Art	81T	129	$ .01	$ .07
Howe, Art	82T	66	$ .03	$ .15
Howe, Art	82T	453	$ .01	$ .06
Howe, Art	83T	639	$ .01	$ .06
Howe, Art	84T	679	$ .01	$ .05
Howe, Art	84TTR	53	$ .02	$ .10
Howe, Art	85T	204	$ .01	$ .04

Player	Year	No.	VG	EX/MT
Howe, Art	89TTR	53	$ .01	$ .05
Howe, Art	90T	579	$ .01	$ .03
Howe, Steve	81T	693	$ .04	$ .20
Howe, Steve	82T	14	$ .01	$ .06
Howe, Steve	83T	170	$ .01	$ .06
Howe, Steve	84T	425	$ .01	$ .05
Howell, Dixie	52T	135	$6.00	$19.00
Howell, Dixie	53T	255	$11.00	$37.50
Howell, Dixie	56T	149	$1.25	$4.50
Howell, Dixie	57T	221	$ .95	$3.50
Howell, Dixie	58T	421	$ .50	$2.00
Howell, Jack	86T	127	$ .01	$ .03
Howell, Jack	87T	422	$ .01	$ .03
Howell, Jack	88T	631	$ .01	$ .03
Howell, Jack	88TBB	121	$ .01	$ .05
Howell, Jack	89T	216	$ .01	$ .04
Howell, Jack	89TBB	228	$ .01	$ .05
Howell, Jack	90T	547	$ .01	$ .03
Howell, Jay	82T	51	$ .03	$ .15
Howell, Jay	84T	239	$ .01	$ .05
Howell, Jay	85T	559	$ .01	$ .04
Howell, Jay	85TTR	57	$ .02	$ .10
Howell, Jay	86T	115	$ .01	$ .03
Howell, Jay	87T	391	$ .01	$ .03
Howell, Jay	88T	690	$ .01	$ .03
Howell, Jay	88TTR	52	$ .01	$ .05
Howell, Jay	89T	425	$ .01	$ .04
Howell, Jay	89TBB	79	$ .01	$ .05
Howell, Jay	90T	40	$ .01	$ .03
Howell, Ken	85TTR	58	$ .02	$ .10
Howell, Ken	86T	654	$ .01	$ .03
Howell, Ken	87T	477	$ .01	$ .03
Howell, Ken	88T	149	$ .01	$ .03
Howell, Ken	89T	93	$ .01	$ .04
Howell, Ken	89TTR	54	$ .01	$ .05
Howell, Ken	90T	756	$ .01	$ .03
Howell, Roy	76T	279	$ .05	$ .20
Howell, Roy	77T	608	$ .03	$ .12
Howell, Roy	78T	394	$ .02	$ .10
Howell, Roy	79T	101	$ .02	$ .10
Howell, Roy	80T	488	$ .01	$ .07
Howell, Roy	81T	581	$ .01	$ .07
Howell, Roy	81TTR	773	$ .02	$ .10
Howell, Roy	82T	68	$ .01	$ .06
Howell, Roy	83T	218	$ .01	$ .06
Howell, Roy	84T	687	$ .01	$ .05
Howell, Roy	85T	372	$ .01	$ .04
Howerton, Bill	52T	167	$6.00	$19.00
Howitt, Dann	89TMLD	62	$ .01	$ .50
Howser, Dick	61T	416	$1.25	$4.00
Howser, Dick	62T	13	$ .50	$1.95
Howser, Dick	63T	124	$ .50	$2.00
Howser, Dick	64T	478	$ .60	$1.75
Howser, Dick	65T	92	$ .50	$2.00
Howser, Dick	66T	567	$3.00	$9.50
Howser, Dick	67T	411	$ .50	$2.00
Howser, Dick	68T	467	$ .50	$2.00
Howser, Dick	73T	116	$ .15	$ .50
Howser, Dick	83T	96	$ .01	$ .06
Howser, Dick	84T	471	$ .01	$ .05
Howser, Dick	85T	334	$ .01	$ .04
Howser, Dick	86T	199	$ .01	$ .03
Howser, Dick	87T	18	$ .01	$ .03
Howser, Dick	90TTB	661	$ .01	$ .03
Hoyt, LaMarr	81T	164	$ .05	$ .20
Hoyt, LaMarr	82T	428	$ .01	$ .06
Hoyt, LaMarr	83T	591	$ .01	$ .06
Hoyt, LaMarr	83T	618	$ .01	$ .06
Hoyt, LaMarr	83T	705	$ .01	$ .10
Hoyt, LaMarr	84T	97	$ .01	$ .05
Hoyt, LaMarr	84T	135	$ .01	$ .05
Hoyt, LaMarr	84TAS	405	$ .01	$ .05
Hoyt, LaMarr	85T	520	$ .01	$ .04
Hoyt, LaMarr	85TTR	59	$ .02	$ .10
Hoyt, LaMarr	86T	380	$ .01	$ .03

Player	Year	No.	VG	EX/MT	Player	Year	No.	VG	EX/MT
Hoyt, LaMarr	87T	275	$ .01	$ .03	Hughes, Terry	73T	603	$ .35	$1.10
Hrabosky, Al	71T	594	$ .75	$2.00	Hughes, Terry	74T	604	$1.00	$3.00
Hrabosky, Al	73T	153	$ .25	$ .65	Hughes, Terry	75T	612	$ .06	$ .25
Hrabosky, Al	74T	108	$ .06	$ .25	Huismann, Mark	85T	644	$ .01	$ .04
Hrabosky, Al	75T	122	$ .06	$ .25	Huismann, Mark	87T	187	$ .01	$ .03
Hrabosky, Al	76T	205	$ .10	$ .35	Hulett, Tim	85TTR	60	$ .02	$ .10
Hrabosky, Al	76T	315	$ .05	$ .20	Hulett, Tim	86T	724	$ .01	$ .03
Hrabosky, Al	77T	495	$ .03	$ .12	Hulett, Tim	87T	566	$ .01	$ .03
Hrabosky, Al	78T	230	$ .02	$ .10	Hulett, Tim	88T	158	$ .01	$ .03
Hrabosky, Al	79T	45	$ .02	$ .10	Hume, Tom	78T	701	$ .02	$ .10
Hrabosky, Al	80T	585	$ .01	$ .07	Hume, Tom	79T	301	$ .02	$ .10
Hrabosky, Al	81T	636	$ .01	$ .07	Hume, Tom	80T	149	$ .01	$ .07
Hrabosky, Al	82T	393	$ .01	$ .06	Hume, Tom	81T	8	$ .01	$ .07
Hrbek, Kent	82T	766	$1.50	$4.50	Hume, Tom	81T	419	$ .01	$ .07
Hrbek, Kent	82TTR	44	$1.35	$5.00	Hume, Tom	82T	763	$ .01	$ .06
Hrbek, Kent	83T	690	$ .10	$ .50	Hume, Tom	83T	86	$ .01	$ .06
Hrbek, Kent	83T	771	$ .10	$ .40	Hume, Tom	84T	607	$ .01	$ .05
Hrbek, Kent	84T	11	$ .01	$ .10	Hume, Tom	85T	223	$ .01	$ .04
Hrbek, Kent	84T	345	$ .01	$ .40	Hume, Tom	86T	573	$ .01	$ .03
Hrbek, Kent	85T	510	$ .05	$ .25	Hume, Tom	86TTR	47	$ .02	$ .10
Hrbek, Kent	86T	430	$ .02	$ .20	Hume, Tom	87T	719	$ .01	$ .03
Hrbek, Kent	87T	679	$ .01	$ .10	Humphrey, Terry	72T	489	$ .05	$ .25
Hrbek, Kent	88T	45	$ .01	$ .15	Humphrey, Terry	73T	106	$ .06	$ .25
Hrbek, Kent	88TBB	84	$ .01	$ .10	Humphrey, Terry	76T	552	$ .05	$ .20
Hrbek, Kent	89T	265	$ .01	$ .10	Humphrey, Terry	77T	369	$ .03	$ .12
Hrbek, Kent	89TBB	209	$ .01	$ .10	Humphrey, Terry	78T	71	$ .02	$ .10
Hrbek, Kent	90T	125	$ .01	$ .10	Humphrey, Terry	79T	503	$ .02	$ .10
Hriniak, Walt	69T	611	$ .25	$ .85	Humphreys, Bob	65T	154	$ .25	$ .65
Hriniak, Walt	70T	392	$ .10	$ .35	Humphreys, Bob	66T	342	$ .25	$ .85
Hubbard, Glenn	79T	715	$ .05	$ .20	Humphreys, Bob	67T	478	$ .50	$2.00
Hubbard, Glenn	81T	247	$ .01	$ .07	Humphreys, Bob	68T	268	$ .25	$ .65
Hubbard, Glenn	82T	482	$ .01	$ .06	Humphreys, Bob	69T	84	$ .25	$ .65
Hubbard, Glenn	83T	624	$ .01	$ .06	Humphreys, Bob	70T	538	$ .10	$ .35
Hubbard, Glenn	84T	25	$ .01	$ .05	Humphreys, Bob	71T	236	$ .10	$ .35
Hubbard, Glenn	85T	195	$ .01	$ .04	Hundley, Randy	66T	392	$ .25	$ .85
Hubbard, Glenn	86T	539	$ .01	$ .03	Hundley, Randy	67T	106	$ .25	$ .65
Hubbard, Glenn	87T	745	$ .01	$ .03	Hundley, Randy	68T	136	$ .25	$ .65
Hubbard, Glenn	88T	325	$ .01	$ .03	Hundley, Randy	69T	347	$ .25	$ .65
Hubbard, Glenn	88TBB	200	$ .01	$ .05	Hundley, Randy	70T	265	$ .10	$ .35
Hubbard, Glenn	88TTR	53	$ .01	$ .05	Hundley, Randy	71T	592	$ .30	$1.00
Hubbard, Glenn	89T	237	$ .01	$ .04	Hundley, Randy	72T	258	$ .05	$ .25
Hubbard, Glenn	89TBB	232	$ .01	$ .05	Hundley, Randy	73T	21	$ .06	$ .25
Hubbs, Ken	62T	461	$2.50	$7.50	Hundley, Randy	74T	319	$ .06	$ .25
Hubbs, Ken	63T	15	$ .45	$1.80	Hundley, Randy	74TTR	319	$ .06	$ .25
Hubbs, Ken	64T	550	$2.00	$8.00	Hundley, Randy	76T	351	$ .05	$ .20
Hudler, Rex	89T	346	$ .01	$ .04	Hundley, Randy	77T	502	$ .03	$ .12
Hudler, Rex	89TBB	248	$ .01	$ .05	Hunt, Ken	60T	522	$2.00	$7.00
Hudler, Rex	90T	647	$ .01	$ .03	Hunt, Ken	61T	156	$ .30	$1.00
Hudson, Charlie	84T	432	$ .02	$ .10	Hunt, Ken	61T	556	$6.00	$18.00
Hudson, Charles	85T	379	$ .01	$ .04	Hunt, Ken	62T	68	$ .35	$1.10
Hudson, Charles	0CT	792	$ .01	$ .03	Hunt, Ken	62T	364	$ .35	$1.10
Hudson, Charles	87T	191	$ .01	$ .03	Hunt, Ken	63T	207	$ .25	$ .85
Hudson, Charles	87TTR	50	$ .01	$ .07	Hunt, Ken	64T	294	$ .25	$ .85
Hudson, Charles	88T	636	$ .01	$ .03	Hunt, Randy	86T	218	$ .01	$ .03
Hudson, Charles	88TBB	212	$ .01	$ .05	Hunt, Ron	63T	558	$1.50	$3.75
Hudson, Charles	89T	236	$ .01	$ .04	Hunt, Ron	64T	235	$ .25	$ .85
Hudson, Charles	89TBB	88	$ .01	$ .05	Hunt, Ron	65T	285	$ .30	$1.00
Hudson, Jesse	70T	348	$ .10	$ .35	Hunt, Ron	66T	360	$ .25	$ .85
Hudson, Sid	51Trb	44	$1.25	$3.50	Hunt, Ron	67T	525	$ .50	$2.00
Hudson, Sid	52T	60	$14.00	$45.00	Hunt, Ron	68T	15	$ .25	$ .65
Hudson, Sid	53T	251	$11.00	$37.50	Hunt, Ron	69T	664	$1.25	$4.50
Hudson, Sid	54T	93	$2.10	$7.50	Hunt, Ron	70T	276	$ .10	$ .35
Huff, Mike	89TMLD	63	$ .01	$ .05	Hunt, Ron	71T	578	$ .30	$1.00
Huffman, Phil	80T	142	$ .01	$ .07	Hunt, Ron	72T	110	$ .05	$ .25
Huffman, Phil	81T	506	$ .01	$ .07	Hunt, Ron	73T	149	$ .06	$ .25
Hughes, Dick	67T	384	$ .25	$ .85	Hunt, Ron	74T	275	$ .06	$ .25
Hughes, Dick	68T	253	$ .25	$ .65	Hunt, Ron	75T	610	$ .06	$ .25
Hughes, Dick	69T	39	$ .25	$ .65	Hunter, Billy	53T	166	$3.75	$13.00
Hughes, Jim	53T	216	$3.75	$13.00	Hunter, Billy	54T	48	$2.10	$7.50
Hughes, Jim	54T	169	$2.00	$7.00	Hunter, Gordon (Billy)	57T	207	$ .95	$3.50
Hughes, Jim	55T	51	$1.35	$5.00	Hunter, Billy	58T	98	$1.00	$3.75
Hughes, Jim	76T	11	$ .05	$ .20	Hunter, Billy	59T	11	$1.00	$3.75
Hughes, Jim	77T	304	$ .03	$ .12	Hunter, Billy	73T	136	$ .15	$ .50
Hughes, Jim	78T	395	$ .02	$ .10	Hunter, Billy	74T	306	$ .15	$ .50
Hughes, Keith	88T	781	$ .01	$ .03	Hunter, Billy	78T	548	$ .02	$ .10

Player	Year	No.	VG	EX/MT
Hunter, Jim	65T	526	$40.00	$105.00
Hunter, Jim	66T	36	$8.00	$20.00
Hunter, Jim	67T	369	$3.00	$10.00
Hunter, Jim	68T	385	$1.50	$6.50
Hunter, Jim	69T	235	$1.75	$7.00
Hunter, Jim	70T	565	$3.00	$9.00
Hunter, Jim	71T	45	$2.50	$9.00
Hunter, Jim	72T	330	$1.65	$5.00
Hunter, Jim	73T	235	$1.50	$6.00
Hunter, Jim	73T	344	$ .30	$1.00
Hunter, Jim	74T	7	$2.00	$6.00
Hunter, Jim	74TAS	339	$ .25	$ .85
Hunter, Jim	75T	230	$1.25	$4.00
Hunter, Jim	75T	310	$ .30	$1.00
Hunter, Jim	75T	311	$ .25	$ .85
Hunter, Jim	76T	100	$1.00	$4.00
Hunter, Jim	76T	200	$ .35	$1.10
Hunter, Jim	76T	202	$ .35	$1.10
Hunter, Jim	77T	280	$1.00	$3.50
Hunter, Jim	78T	460	$ .75	$2.75
Hunter, Jim	79T	670	$ .65	$1.50
Huntz, Steve	69T	136	$ .25	$ .65
Huntz, Steve	70T	282	$ .10	$ .35
Huntz, Steve	71T	486	$ .10	$ .35
Huntz, Steve	72T	73	$ .05	$ .25
Hurd, Tom	55T	116	$1.35	$5.00
Hurd, Tom	56T	256	$2.50	$8.00
Hurdle, Clint	78T	705	$ .02	$ .10
Hurdle, Clint	79T	547	$ .02	$ .10
Hurdle, Clint	80T	525	$ .01	$ .07
Hurdle, Clint	81T	98	$ .01	$ .07
Hurdle, Clint	82T	297	$ .01	$ .06

CLINT HURDLE

Player	Year	No.	VG	EX/MT
Hurdle, Clint	86T	438	$ .01	$ .03
Hurdle, Clint	87T	317	$ .01	$ .03
Hurst, Bruce	81T	689	$ .75	$2.25
Hurst, Bruce	82T	381	$ .25	$ .85
Hurst, Bruce	83T	82	$ .01	$ .06
Hurst, Bruce	84T	213	$ .01	$ .05
Hurst, Bruce	85T	451	$ .01	$ .04
Hurst, Bruce	86T	581	$ .01	$ .03
Hurst, Bruce	87T	705	$ .01	$ .03
Hurst, Bruce	88T	125	$ .01	$ .03
Hurst, Bruce	89T	675	$ .01	$ .04

Player	Year	No.	VG	EX/MT
Hurst, Bruce	89TTR	55	$ .01	$ .05
Hurst, Bruce	90T	315	$ .01	$ .03
Huson, Jeff	90T	72	$ .01	$ .10
Hutchinson, Fred	52T	126	$6.00	$18.00
Hutchinson, Fred	53T	72	$4.50	$15.00
Hutchinson, Fred	60T	219	$ .35	$1.10
Hutchinson, Fred	61T	135	$ .30	$1.00
Hutchinson, Fred	62T	172	$ .50	$2.00
Hutchinson, Fred	63T	422	$ .35	$1.10
Hutchinson, Fred	64T	207	$ .25	$ .85
Hutton, Tom	67T	428	$ .25	$ .85
Hutton, Tom	69T	266	$ .25	$ .85
Hutton, Tom	72T	741	$1.00	$3.75
Hutton, Tom	73T	271	$ .06	$ .25
Hutton, Tom	74T	443	$ .06	$ .25
Hutton, Tom	75T	477	$ .06	$ .25
Hutton, Tom	76T	91	$ .05	$ .20
Hutton, Tom	77T	264	$ .03	$ .12
Hutton, Tom	78T	568	$ .02	$ .10
Hutton, Tom	79T	673	$ .02	$ .10
Hutton, Tom	80T	427	$ .01	$ .07
Hutton, Tom	81T	374	$ .01	$ .07
Hyde, Dick	57T	403	$1.00	$3.75
Hyde, Dick	58T	156	$ .50	$2.00
Hyde, Dick	59T	498	$ .50	$1.95
Hyde, Dick	60T	193	$ .35	$1.10
Incaviglia, Pete	86TTR	48	$ .35	$1.10
Incaviglia, Pete	87T	550	$ .15	$ .75
Incaviglia, Pete	88T	280	$ .01	$ .20
Incaviglia, Pete	88TBB	73	$ .01	$ .05
Incaviglia, Pete	89T	706	$ .01	$ .04
Incaviglia, Pete	89TBB	127	$ .01	$ .10
Incaviglia, Pete	90T	430	$ .01	$ .03
Indians, Team	56T	85	$3.25	$9.50
Indians, Team	57T	275	$7.50	$22.50
Indians, Team	58T	158	$2.00	$7.50
Indians, Team	59T	476	$2.00	$7.50
Indians, Team	60T	174	$1.75	$5.50
Indians, Team	61T	467	$1.25	$4.50
Indians, Team	62T	537	$5.00	$25.00
Indians, Team	63T	451	$2.50	$8.50
Indians, Team	64T	172	$1.00	$3.75
Indians, Team	65T	481	$1.50	$3.75
Indians, Team	66T	303	$ .75	$2.00
Indians, Team	67T	544	$4.00	$13.00
Indians, Team	70T	637	$1.00	$3.00
Indians, Team	71T	584	$ .60	$1.75
Indians, Team	72T	547	$ .50	$2.00
Indians, Team	73T	629	$ .60	$1.75
Indians, Team	74T	541	$ .15	$ .50
Indians, Team Checklist	75T	331	$ .30	$1.00
Indians, Team Checklist	76T	477	$ .30	$1.00
Indians, Team Checklist	77T	18	$ .03	$ .60
Indians, Team Checklist	78T	689	$ .05	$ .25
Indians, Team Checklist	79T	96	$ .05	$ .25
Indians, Team Checklist	80T	451	$ .05	$ .25
Indians, Team Checklist	81T	665	$ .02	$ .20
Indians, Team Leaders	86T	336	$ .01	$ .03
Indians, Team Leaders	87T	11	$ .01	$ .03
Indians, Team Leaders	88T	789	$ .01	$ .03
Indians, Team Leaders	89T	141	$ .01	$ .04
Innis, Jeff	88TTR	54	$ .01	$ .15
Innis, Jeff	90T	557	$ .01	$ .03
Iorg, Dane	80T	139	$ .01	$ .07
Iorg, Dane	81T	334	$ .01	$ .07
Iorg, Dane	82T	86	$ .01	$ .06
Iorg, Dane	83T	788	$ .01	$ .06
Iorg, Dane	84T	416	$ .01	$ .05
Iorg, Dane	84TTR	54	$ .02	$ .10
Iorg, Dane	85T	671	$ .01	$ .04
Iorg, Dane	86T	269	$ .01	$ .03
Iorg, Dane	86TTR	49	$ .02	$ .10
Iorg, Dane	87T	690	$ .01	$ .03
Iorg, Garth	78T	704	$3.00	$10.00
Iorg, Garth	81T	444	$ .01	$ .07

Player	Year	No.	VG	EX/MT
Iorg, Garth	82T	518	$ .01	$ .06
Iorg, Garth	83T	326	$ .01	$ .06
Iorg, Garth	84T	39	$ .01	$ .05
Iorg, Garth	85T	168	$ .01	$ .04
Iorg, Garth	86T	694	$ .01	$ .03
Iorg, Garth	87T	751	$ .01	$ .03
Iorg, Garth	88T	273	$ .01	$ .03
Ireland, Tim	81T	66	$ .01	$ .07
Irvin, Monte	51Trb	50	$3.25	$12.50
Irvin, Monte(y)	52T	26	$27.50	$77.50
Irvin, Monte	53T	62	$7.50	$27.50
Irvin, Monte	54T	3	$5.00	$20.00
Irvin, Monte	55T	100	$3.00	$12.00
Irvin, Monte	56T	194	$6.00	$18.00
Ivie, Mike	72T	457	$ .05	$ .25
Ivie, Mike	73T	613	$9.00	$35.00
Ivie, Mike	76T	134	$ .05	$ .20
Ivie, Mike	77T	325	$ .03	$ .12
Ivie, Mike	78T	445	$ .02	$ .10
Ivie, Mike	79T	538	$ .02	$ .10
Ivie, Mike	80T	62	$ .01	$ .07
Ivie, Mike	81T	236	$ .01	$ .07
Ivie, Mike	81TTR	774	$ .02	$ .10
Ivie, Mike	82T	734	$ .01	$ .06
Ivie, Mike	82TTR	45	$ .02	$ .10
Ivie, Mike	83T	613	$ .01	$ .06
Jablonski, Ray	53T	189	$3.75	$13.00
Jablonski, Ray	54T	26	$2.10	$7.50
Jablonski, Ray	55T	56	$1.35	$5.00
Jablonski, Ray	56T	86	$1.25	$4.50
Jablonski, Ray	57T	218	$ .95	$3.50
Jablonski, Ray	58T	362	$ .50	$2.00
Jablonski, Ray	59T	342	$ .50	$1.95
Jackson, Al	62T	464	$1.00	$3.75
Jackson, Al	63T	111	$ .25	$ .85
Jackson, Al	64T	494	$ .40	$1.25
Jackson, Al	65T	381	$ .30	$1.00
Jackson, Al	66T	206	$ .25	$ .85
Jackson, Al	67T	195	$ .25	$ .65
Jackson, Al	68T	503	$ .30	$1.00
Jackson, Al	69T	649	$ .25	$ .85
Jackson, Al	70T	443	$ .10	$ .35
Jackson, Bo	86TTR	50	$3.00	$12.00
Jackson, Bo	87T	170	$ .75	$4.50
Jackson, Bo	88T	750	$ .15	$1.00
Jackson, Bo	88TBB	49	$ .25	$1.25
Jackson, Bo	89T	540	$ .05	$ .50
Jackson, Bo	89TBB	238	$ .01	$ .75
Jackson, Bo	90T	300	$ .01	$ .75
Jackson, Chuck	88T	94	$ .01	$ .15
Jackson, Danny	87TTR	51	¢ .15	¢ .50
Jackson, Danny	88T	324	$ .01	$ .10
Jackson, Danny	88TTR	55	$ .01	$ .15
Jackson, Danny	89T	730	$ .01	$ .10
Jackson, Danny	89TAS	395	$ .01	$ .04
Jackson, Danny	90T	445	$ .01	$ .03
Jackson, Darrell	79T	246	$ .02	$ .10
Jackson, Darrell	80T	386	$ .01	$ .07
Jackson, Darrell	81T	89	$ .01	$ .07
Jackson, Darrell	82T	193	$ .01	$ .06
Jackson, Darrin	88TTR	56	$ .05	$ .25
Jackson, Darrin	89T	286	$ .01	$ .15
Jackson, Darrin	90T	624	$ .01	$ .03
Jackson, Grant	66T	591	$4.50	$15.00
Jackson, Grant	67T	402	$ .25	$ .85
Jackson, Grant	68T	512	$ .30	$1.00
Jackson, Grant	69T	174	$ .25	$ .65
Jackson, Grant	70T	6	$ .10	$ .35
Jackson, Grant	71T	392	$ .10	$ .35
Jackson, Grant	72T	212	$ .05	$ .25
Jackson, Grant	73T	396	$ .06	$ .25
Jackson, Grant	74T	68	$ .06	$ .25
Jackson, Grant	75T	303	$ .06	$ .25
Jackson, Grant	76T	233	$ .05	$ .20
Jackson, Grant	77T	49	$ .03	$ .12
Jackson, Grant	78T	661	$ .02	$ .10
Jackson, Grant	79T	117	$ .02	$ .10
Jackson, Grant	80T	426	$ .01	$ .07
Jackson, Grant	81T	518	$ .01	$ .07
Jackson, Grant	82T	779	$ .01	$ .06
Jackson, Grant	82TTR	46	$ .02	$ .10
Jackson, Jeff	90T	74	$ .01	$ .25
Jackson, Larry	56T	119	$1.50	$4.50
Jackson, Larry	57T	196	$ .95	$3.50
Jackson, Larry	58T	97	$1.00	$3.75
Jackson, Larry	59T	399	$ .50	$1.95
Jackson, Larry	60T	492	$ .60	$1.75
Jackson, Larry	61T	75	$ .50	$2.00
Jackson, Larry	61T	535	$6.00	$18.00
Jackson, Larry	62T	83	$ .35	$1.10
Jackson, Larry	62T	306	$ .50	$2.00
Jackson, Larry	63T	95	$ .25	$ .85
Jackson, Larry	64T	444	$ .40	$1.25
Jackson, Larry	65T	10	$ .35	$1.10
Jackson, Larry	65T	420	$ .30	$1.00
Jackson, Larry	66T	595	$4.50	$15.00
Jackson, Larry	67T	229	$ .25	$ .65
Jackson, Larry	68T	81	$ .25	$ .65
Jackson, Lou	59T	130	$ .50	$1.95
Jackson, Lou	64T	511	$ .40	$1.25
Jackson, Mike	88T	651	$ .01	$ .03
Jackson, Mike	89T	169	$ .01	$ .04
Jackson, Mike	90T	761	$ .01	$ .03
Jackson, Randy	52T	322	$39.00	$135.00
Jackson, Randy	56T	223	$2.50	$8.00
Jackson, Randy	57T	190	$ .95	$3.50
Jackson, Randy	58T	301	$ .50	$2.00
Jackson, Randy	59T	394	$ .50	$1.95
Jackson, Reggie	69T	260	$125.00	$475.00
Jackson, Reggie	70T	64	$1.00	$3.50
Jackson, Reggie	70T	66	$1.00	$4.00
Jackson, Reggie	70T	140	$25.00	$65.00
Jackson, Reggie	70TAS	459	$3.25	$12.50
Jackson, Reggie	71T	20	$8.50	$32.50
Jackson, Reggie	72T	90	$ .50	$2.00
Jackson, Reggie	72T	435	$6.00	$25.00
Jackson, Reggie	72TIA	436	$3.00	$9.00
Jackson, Reggie	73T	255	$4.00	$17.50
Jackson, Reggie	74T	130	$3.00	$12.00
Jackson, Reggie	74T	202	$ .60	$2.00
Jackson, Reggie	74T	203	$ .60	$2.00
Jackson, Reggie	74TAS	338	$ .35	$1.10
Jackson, Reggie	75T	211	$ .75	$3.00
Jackson, Reggie	75T	300	$3.00	$12.00
Jackson, Reggie	76T	194	$ .50	$1.95
Jackson, Reggie	76T	500	$3.00	$8.00
Jackson, Reggie	77T	10	$2.00	$7.00
Jackson, Reggie	78T	200	$ .75	$2.50
Jackson, Reggie	78T	413	$ .50	$2.00
Jackson, Reggie	78TRB	7	$ .50	$2.00
Jackson, Reggie	79T	700	$ .50	$1.75
Jackson, Reggie	80T	600	$ .70	$2.25
Jackson, Reggie	81T	2	$ .06	$ .30
Jackson, Reggie	81T	400	$ .45	$1.75
Jackson, Reggie	82T	300	$ .35	$1.20
Jackson, Reggie	82TAS	551	$ .25	$ .65
Jackson, Reggie	82TIA	301	$ .15	$ .50
Jackson, Reggie	82TTR	47	$ .95	$3.50
Jackson, Reggie	83T	500	$ .15	$ .75
Jackson, Reggie	83T	501	$ .06	$ .30
Jackson, Reggie	83T	702	$ .01	$ .06
Jackson, Reggie	83TAS	390	$ .06	$ .30
Jackson, Reggie	84T	100	$ .15	$ .60
Jackson, Reggie	84T	711	$ .04	$ .20
Jackson, Reggie	84T	712	$ .03	$ .15
Jackson, Reggie	84T	713	$ .03	$ .15
Jackson, Reggie	85T	200	$ .09	$ .45
Jackson, Reggie	86T	700	$ .04	$ .35
Jackson, Reggie	87T	300	$ .10	$ .35
Jackson, Reggie	87TTB	312	$ .03	$ .15

TOPPS

Player	Year	No.	VG	EX/MT	Player	Year	No.	VG	EX/MT
Jackson, Reggie	87TTR	52	$ .15	$ .50	Jacoby, Brook	89T	739	$ .01	$ .04
Jackson, Ron	55T	66	$1.35	$5.00	Jacoby, Brook	89TBB	195	$ .01	$ .05
Jackson, Ron	56T	186	$2.50	$8.00	Jacoby, Brook	90T	208	$ .01	$ .03
Jackson, Ron	58T	26	$1.00	$3.75	Jaeckel, Paul	65T	386	$ .30	$1.00
Jackson, Ron	59T	73	$1.00	$3.75	James, Bob	84T	579	$ .02	$ .10
Jackson, Ron	60T	426	$ .50	$1.95	James, Bob	85T	114	$ .01	$ .04
Jackson, Ron	77T	153	$ .03	$ .12	James, Bob	85TTR	61	$ .02	$ .10
Jackson, Ron	78T	718	$ .02	$ .10	James, Bob	86T	467	$ .01	$ .03
Jackson, Ron	79T	339	$ .02	$ .10	James, Bob	87T	342	$ .01	$ .03
Jackson, Ron	80T	18	$ .01	$ .07	James, Bob	88T	232	$ .01	$ .03
Jackson, Ron	81T	631	$ .01	$ .07	James, Charley	60T	517	$2.00	$7.00
Jackson, Ron	82T	488	$ .01	$ .06	James, Charley	61T	561	$6.00	$18.00
Jackson, Ron	82TTR	48	$ .02	$ .10	James, Charlie	62T	412	$ .70	$2.10
Jackson, Ron	83T	262	$ .01	$ .06	James, Charley	63T	83	$ .25	$ .85
Jackson, Ron	84T	548	$ .01	$ .05	James, Charley	64T	357	$ .25	$ .85
					James, Charlie	65T	141	$ .25	$ .65
					James, Chris	87TTR	53	$ .03	$ .15
					James, Chris	88T	572	$ .01	$ .10
					James, Chris	89T	298	$ .01	$ .04
					James, Chris	89TTR	56	$ .01	$ .05
					James, Chris	90T	178	$ .01	$ .03
					James, Cleo	72T	117	$ .05	$ .25
					James, Dion	85T	228	$ .01	$ .04
					James, Dion	86T	76	$ .01	$ .03
					James, Dion	87TTR	54	$ .03	$ .15
					James, Dion	88T	408	$ .01	$ .03
					James, Dion	88TBB	220	$ .01	$ .05
					James, Dion	89T	678	$ .01	$ .04
					James, Dion	89TBB	223	$ .01	$ .05
					James, Dion	90T	319	$ .01	$ .03
					James, Jeff	69T	477	$ .25	$ .65
					James, Jeff	70T	302	$ .10	$ .35
					James, Johnny	60T	499	$ .60	$1.75
					James, Johnny	61T	457	$ .50	$2.00
					Janeski, Gerry	71T	673	$ .70	$2.10
					Janowicz, Vic	53T	222	$14.00	$45.00
					Janowicz, Vic	54T	16	$2.00	$7.00
					Jansen, Larry	51Trb	21	$1.25	$3.50
					Jansen, Larry	52T	5	$14.00	$45.00
					Jansen, Larry	54T	200	$2.10	$7.50
					Jansen, Larry	73T	81	$ .25	$ .85
					Jarvis, Pat	67T	57	$ .25	$ .65
					Jarvis, Pat	68T	134	$ .25	$ .65
					Jarvis, Pat	69T	282	$ .25	$ .85
					Jarvis, Pat	70T	438	$ .10	$ .35
					Jarvis, Pat	71T	623	$ .30	$1.00
					Jarvis, Pat	72T	675	$ .70	$2.10
					Jarvis, Pat	73T	192	$ .06	$ .25
					Jarvis, Ray	70T	361	$ .10	$ .35
					Jarvis, Ray	71T	526	$ .30	$1.00
					Jaster, Larry	67T	356	$ .25	$ .65
					Jaster, Larry	68T	117	$ .25	$ .65
					Jaster, Larry	69T	496	$ .25	$ .65
					Jaster, Larry	70T	124	$ .10	$ .35
					Jata, Paul	72T	257	$ .10	$ .35
					Javier, Manuel "Julian"	60T	133	$ .50	$2.00
Jackson, Roy Lee	81T	223	$ .01	$ .07	Javier, Julian	61T	148	$ .30	$1.00
Jackson, Roy Lee	81TTR	775	$ .02	$ .10	Javier, Julian	62T	118	$ .35	$1.10
Jackson, Roy Lee	82T	71	$ .01	$ .06	Javier, Julian	63T	226	$ .25	$ .85
Jackson, Roy Lee	83T	427	$ .01	$ .06	Javier, Julian	64T	446	$ .40	$1.25
Jackson, Roy Lee	84T	339	$ .01	$ .05	Javier, Julian	65T	447	$ .50	$2.00
Jackson, Roy Lee	85T	516	$ .01	$ .04	Javier, Julian	66T	436	$ .25	$ .85
Jackson, Roy Lee	86T	634	$ .01	$ .03	Javier, Julian	67T	226	$ .25	$ .65
Jackson, Roy Lee	87T	138	$ .01	$ .03	Javier, Julian	68T	25	$ .25	$ .65
Jackson, Sonny	65T	16	$35.00	$125.00	Javier, Julian	69T	497	$ .25	$ .65
Jackson, Sonny	66T	244	$ .25	$ .85	Javier, Julian	70T	415	$ .10	$ .35
Jackson, Sonny	67T	415	$ .25	$ .85	Javier, Julian	71T	185	$ .10	$ .35
Jackson, Sonny	68T	187	$ .25	$ .65	Javier, Julian	72T	745	$ .70	$2.10
Jackson, Sonny	69T	53	$ .25	$ .65	Javier, Stan	87T	263	$ .01	$ .03
Jackson, Sonny	70T	413	$ .10	$ .35	Javier, Stan	89T	622	$ .01	$ .04
Jackson, Sonny	71T	587	$ .30	$1.00	Javier, Stan	89TBB	277	$ .01	$ .05
Jackson, Sonny	72T	318	$ .05	$ .25	Javier, Stan	90T	102	$ .01	$ .03
Jackson, Sonny	73T	403	$ .06	$ .25	Jay, Joe	54T	141	$2.00	$7.00
Jackson, Sonny	74T	591	$ .06	$ .25	Jay, Joe	55T	134	$1.35	$5.00
Jacobs, Forrest "Spook"	54T	129	$2.10	$7.50	Jay, Joe	58T	472	$ .50	$1.95
Jacobs, Spook	55T	61	$1.35	$5.00					
Jacobs, Spook	56T	151	$1.25	$4.50					
Jacobs, Tony	55T	183	$4.25	$13.00					
Jacoby, Brook	84TTR	55	$ .20	$1.00					
Jacoby, Brook	85T	327	$ .01	$ .10					
Jacoby, Brook	86T	116	$ .01	$ .03					
Jacoby, Brook	87T	405	$ .01	$ .10					
Jacoby, Brook	88T	555	$ .01	$ .03					
Jacoby, Brook	88TBB	17	$ .01	$ .05					

TOPPS

Player	Year	No.	VG	EX/MT	Player	Year	No.	VG	EX/MT
Jay, Joe	59T	273	$ .50	$1.95	Jenkins, Fergie	84T	706	$ .05	$ .25
Jay, Joe	60T	266	$ .35	$1.10	Jenkins, Ferguson	66T	254	$10.00	$40.00
Jay, Joe	61T	233	$ .30	$1.00	Jenkins, Ferguson	67T	333	$2.00	$7.00
Jay, Joe	62T	58	$ .50	$1.95	Jenkins, Ferguson	68T	9	$ .50	$1.95
Jay, Joe	62T	263	$ .50	$2.00	Jenkins, Ferguson	68T	11	$ .50	$1.95
Jay, Joe	62T	440	$ .70	$2.10	Jenkins, Ferguson "Fergie"	68T	410	$1.25	$3.50
Jay, Joe	63T	7	$ .35	$1.10	Jenkins, Jack	70T	286	$1.35	$4.00
Jay, Joe	63T	225	$ .25	$ .85	Jennings, Doug	89T	166	$ .01	$ .15
Jay, Joe	64T	346	$ .25	$ .85	Jensen, Jack	52T	122	$17.50	$60.00
Jay, Joe	65T	174	$ .25	$ .65	Jensen, Jackie	53T	265	$30.00	$125.00
Jay, Joe	66T	406	$ .25	$ .85	Jensen, Jackie	54T	80	$3.50	$13.00
Jeffcoat, Hal	52T	341	$39.00	$135.00	Jensen, Jackie	55T	200	$10.00	$42.50
Jeffcoat, Hal	53T	29	$3.75	$13.00	Jensen, Jackie	56T	115	$1.50	$6.00
Jeffcoat, Hal	56T	289	$1.80	$6.00	Jensen, Jackie	57T	220	$ .60	$2.50
Jeffcoat, Hal	57T	93	$ .95	$3.50	Jensen, Jackie	58T	130	$ .95	$3.00
Jeffcoat, Hal	58T	294	$ .50	$2.00	Jensen, Jackie	58TAS	489	$ .70	$2.25
Jeffcoat, Hal	59T	81	$1.00	$3.75	Jensen, Jackie	59T	400	$ .60	$1.75
Jeffcoat, Mike	84TTR	56	$ .02	$ .10	Jensen, Jackie	61T	173	$ .50	$2.00
Jeffcoat, Mike	85T	303	$ .01	$ .04	Jensen, Jackie	61T	540	$7.00	$20.00
Jeffcoat, Mike	86T	571	$ .01	$ .03	Jensen, Jackie	61TMVP	476	$ .75	$2.00
Jeffcoat, Mike	90T	778	$ .01	$ .03	Jensen, Jackie	75T	196	$ .30	$1.00
Jefferies, Gregg	89T	233	$ .25	$2.00	Jernigan, Pete	63T	253	$ .25	$ .85
Jefferies, Gregg	89TBB	253	$ .01	$ .50	Jestadt, Garry	70T	109	$ .10	$ .35
Jefferies, Gregg	90T	457	$ .01	$ .35	Jestadt, Garry	71T	576	$ .30	$1.00
Jefferson, Jesse	73T	604	$ .35	$1.10	Jestadt, Garry	72T	143	$ .05	$ .25
Jefferson, Jesse	74T	509	$ .06	$ .25	Jeter, Johnny	70T	141	$ .25	$ .85
Jefferson, Jesse	75T	539	$ .06	$ .25	Jeter, Johnny	71T	47	$ .10	$ .35
Jefferson, Jesse	76T	47	$ .05	$ .20	Jeter, Johnny	72T	288	$ .05	$ .25
Jefferson, Jesse	77T	326	$ .03	$ .12	Jeter, Johnny	73T	423	$ .06	$ .25
Jefferson, Jesse	78T	144	$ .02	$ .10	Jeter, Johnny	74T	615	$ .06	$ .25
Jefferson, Jesse	79T	221	$ .02	$ .10	Jethroe, Sam	51Tbb	12	$5.50	$17.00
Jefferson, Jesse	80T	467	$ .01	$ .07	Jethroe, Sam	52T	27	$14.00	$45.00
Jefferson, Jesse	82T	682	$ .01	$ .06	Jimenez, E. Manny	62T	598	$12.00	$50.00
Jefferson, Stan	87TTR	55	$ .05	$ .20	Jimenez, E. Manny	63T	195	$ .25	$ .85
Jefferson, Stan	88T	223	$ .01	$ .03	Jimenez, E. Manny	64T	574	$1.50	$3.75
Jefferson, Stan	88TBB	86	$ .01	$ .05	Jimenez, Elvio "Manny"	65T	226	$ .35	$1.10
Jefferson, Stan	89T	689	$ .01	$ .04	Jimenez, E. Manny	66T	458	$ .70	$2.10
Jefferson, Stan	89TBB	165	$ .01	$ .05	Jimenez, E. Manny	67T	586	$3.00	$9.00
Jeltz, Steve	85TTR	62	$ .02	$ .10	Jimenez, E. Manny	68T	538	$ .30	$1.00
Jeltz, Steve	86T	453	$ .01	$ .03	Jimenez, Elvio	69T	567	$ .25	$ .85
Jeltz, Steve	87T	294	$ .01	$ .03	Jimenez, German	89T	569	$ .01	$ .10
Jeltz, Steve	88T	126	$ .01	$ .03	Jimenez, Houston	84T	411	$ .01	$ .05
Jeltz, Steve	89T	707	$ .01	$ .04	Jimenez, Houston	85T	562	$ .01	$ .04
Jeltz, Steve	89TBB	52	$ .01	$ .05	John, Tommy	64T	146	$20.00	$60.00
Jeltz, Steve	90T	607	$ .01	$ .03	John, Tommy	65T	208	$3.00	$9.00
Jenkins, Fergie	69T	10	$1.50	$3.75	John, Tommy	66T	486	$3.50	$12.50
Jenkins, Fergie	69T	12	$1.00	$2.75	John, Tommy	67T	609	$22.50	$90.00
Jenkins, Fergie	69T	640	$ .65	$1.75	John, Tommy	68T	72	$1.50	$3.75
Jenkins, Fergie	70T	69	$ .50	$1.95	John, Tommy	69T	465	$ .95	$3.50
Jenkins, Fergie	70T	71	$ .50	$1.95	John, Tommy	70T	180	$ .70	$2.00
Jenkins, Fergie	70T	240	$1.00	$4.00	John, Tommy	71T	520	$ .70	$2.00
Jenkins, Fergie	71T	70	$ .50	$2.00	John, Tommy	72T	264	$ .35	$1.50
Jenkins, Fergie	71T	72	$ .50	$2.00	John, Tommy	73T	258	$ .50	$2.00
Jenkins, Fergie	71T	280	$1.50	$6.00	John, Tommy	74T	451	$ .35	$1.10
Jenkins, Fergie	72T	93	$ .50	$2.00	John, Tommy	75T	47	$ .35	$1.10
Jenkins, Fergie	72T	95	$ .35	$1.10	John, Tommy	76T	416	$ .35	$1.10
Jenkins, Fergie	72T	410	$1.00	$4.00	John, Tommy	77T	128	$ .30	$1.00
Jenkins, Fergie	73T	180	$1.75	$5.00	John, Tommy	78T	375	$ .15	$ .75
Jenkins, Fergie	74T	87	$1.00	$4.00	John, Tommy	79T	255	$ .25	$1.00
Jenkins, Fergie	75T	60	$ .60	$2.50	John, Tommy	80T	690	$ .10	$ .50
Jenkins, Fergie	75T	310	$ .30	$1.00	John, Tommy	81T	550	$ .05	$ .25
Jenkins, Fergie	76T	250	$ .50	$2.00	John, Tommy	82T	75	$ .05	$ .25
Jenkins, Fergie	76TTR	250	$ .15	$ .50	John, Tommy	82T	486	$ .03	$ .15
Jenkins, Fergie	77T	430	$ .15	$ .50	John, Tommy	83T	735	$ .01	$ .06
Jenkins, Fergie	78T	720	$ .25	$ .85	John, Tommy	83T	736	$ .01	$ .06
Jenkins, Fergie	79T	544	$ .05	$ .25	John, Tommy	84T	415	$ .05	$ .20
Jenkins, Fergie	80T	390	$ .25	$ .85	John, Tommy	84T	715	$ .04	$ .20
Jenkins, Fergie	81T	158	$ .05	$ .20	John, Tommy	85T	179	$ .04	$ .20
Jenkins, Fergie	82T	624	$ .05	$ .20	John, Tommy	86T	240	$ .01	$ .10
Jenkins, Fergie	82TTR	49	$ .25	$ .65	John, Tommy	87T	236	$ .01	$ .10
Jenkins, Fergie	83T	51	$ .01	$ .06	John, Tommy	88T	611	$ .01	$ .10
Jenkins, Fergie	83T	230	$ .01	$ .20	John, Tommy	89T	359	$ .01	$ .04
Jenkins, Fergie	83T	231	$ .01	$ .06	Johnson, Alex	65T	352	$ .30	$1.00
Jenkins, Fergie	84T	456	$ .01	$ .05	Johnson, Alex	66T	104	$ .15	$ .50
Jenkins, Fergie	84T	483	$ .05	$ .20	Johnson, Alex	67T	108	$ .25	$ .65

TOPPS

Player	Year	No.	VG	EX/MT
Johnson, Alex	68T	441	$ .25	$ .65
Johnson, Alex	69T	280	$ .25	$ .85
Johnson, Alex	70T	115	$ .10	$ .35
Johnson, Alex	71T	61	$ .50	$1.95
Johnson, Alex	71T	590	$ .30	$1.00
Johnson, Alex	72T	215	$ .05	$ .25
Johnson, Alex	73T	425	$ .06	$ .25
Johnson, Alex	74T	107	$ .06	$ .25
Johnson, Alex	75T	534	$ .06	$ .25
Johnson, Alex	77T	637	$ .03	$ .12
Johnson, Bart	70T	669	$ .50	$2.00
Johnson, Bart	71T	156	$ .10	$ .35
Johnson, Bart	72T	126	$ .05	$ .25
Johnson, Bart	73T	506	$ .06	$ .25
Johnson, Bart	74T	147	$ .06	$ .25
Johnson, Bart	75T	446	$ .06	$ .25
Johnson, Bart	76T	513	$ .05	$ .20
Johnson, Bart	77T	177	$ .03	$ .12
Johnson, Ben	60T	528	$2.00	$7.00
Johnson, Billy	51Tbb	21	$5.50	$17.00
Johnson, Billy	52T	83	$6.00	$19.00
Johnson, Billy	53T	21	$3.75	$13.00
Johnson, Bob D.	71T	71	$ .15	$ .50
Johnson, Bob D.	71T	365	$ .10	$ .35
Johnson, Bob D.	72T	27	$ .05	$ .25
Johnson, Bob D.	73T	657	$ .35	$1.10
Johnson, Bob D.	74T	269	$ .06	$ .25
Johnson, Bob D.	74TTR	269	$ .06	$ .25
Johnson, Bob W.	62T	519	$ .70	$2.10
Johnson, Bob W.	63T	504	$2.50	$6.50
Johnson, Bob W.	64T	304	$ .25	$ .85
Johnson, Bob W.	65T	363	$ .30	$1.00
Johnson, Bob W.	66T	148	$ .25	$ .85
Johnson, Bob W.	67T	38	$ .25	$ .65
Johnson, Bob W.	68T	338	$ .25	$ .65
Johnson, Bob W.	69T	261	$ .25	$ .85
Johnson, Bob W.	70T	693	$ .50	$2.00
Johnson, Bob W.	70T	702	$ .50	$2.00
Johnson, Bobby	82T	418	$ .03	$ .15
Johnson, Bobby	83TTR	48	$ .02	$ .10
Johnson, Bobby	84T	608	$ .01	$ .05
Johnson, Cliff	75T	143	$ .06	$ .25
Johnson, Cliff	76T	249	$ .05	$ .20
Johnson, Cliff	77T	514	$ .03	$ .12
Johnson, Cliff	78T	309	$ .02	$ .10
Johnson, Cliff	79T	114	$ .02	$ .10
Johnson, Cliff	80T	612	$ .01	$ .07
Johnson, Cliff	81T	17	$ .01	$ .07
Johnson, Cliff	81TTR	776	$ .02	$ .10
Johnson, Cliff	82T	422	$ .01	$ .06
Johnson, Cliff	83T	762	$ .01	$ .06
Johnson, Cliff	83TTR	49	$ .02	$ .10
Johnson, Cliff	84T	221	$ .01	$ .05
Johnson, Cliff	85T	568	$ .01	$ .04
Johnson, Cliff	85TRB	4	$ .01	$ .04
Johnson, Cliff	85TTR	63	$ .02	$ .10
Johnson, Cliff	86T	348	$ .01	$ .03
Johnson, Cliff	87T	663	$ .01	$ .03
Johnson, Connie	56T	326	$1.80	$6.00
Johnson, Connie	57T	43	$ .95	$3.50
Johnson, Connie	58T	266	$ .50	$2.00
Johnson, Connie	59T	21	$1.00	$3.75
Johnson, Darrell	57T	306	$3.50	$13.00
Johnson, Darrell	58T	61	$1.00	$3.75
Johnson, Darrell	59T	533	$3.00	$9.00
Johnson, Darrell	60T	263	$ .35	$1.10
Johnson, Darrell	62T	16	$ .35	$1.10
Johnson, Darrell	74T	403	$ .06	$ .25
Johnson, Darrell	78T	79	$ .02	$ .10
Johnson, Darrell	83T	37	$ .01	$ .06
Johnson, Dave	65T	473	$2.25	$9.00
Johnson, Dave	66T	579	$4.50	$15.00
Johnson, Dave	67T	363	$ .30	$1.00
Johnson, Dave	68T	273	$ .35	$1.10
Johnson, Dave	69T	203	$ .50	$2.00

Player	Year	No.	VG	EX/MT
Johnson, Dave	70T	45	$ .35	$1.10
Johnson, Dave	71T	595	$ .30	$1.00

DAVE JOHNSON

Player	Year	No.	VG	EX/MT
Johnson, Dave	72T	680	$1.50	$3.75
Johnson, Dave	73T	550	$ .60	$1.75
Johnson, Dave	74T	45	$ .25	$ .85
Johnson, Dave	75T	57	$ .25	$ .85
Johnson, Dave	77T	478	$ .03	$ .12
Johnson, Dave	78T	317	$ .05	$ .20
Johnson, Dave	78T	627	$ .02	$ .10
Johnson, Dave	79T	513	$ .05	$ .20
Johnson, Dave	84TTR	57	$ .02	$ .10
Johnson, Dave	85T	492	$ .01	$ .04
Johnson, Dave	86T	501	$ .01	$ .03
Johnson, Dave	87T	543	$ .01	$ .03
Johnson, Dave	88T	164	$ .01	$ .03
Johnson, Dave	89T	684	$ .01	$ .04
Johnson, Dave	90T	291	$ .01	$ .03
Johnson, Dave	90T	416	$ .01	$ .03
Johnson, Deron	59T	131	$ .90	$2.75
Johnson, Deron	60T	134	$ .60	$1.75
Johnson, Deron	61T	68	$ .30	$1.00
Johnson, Deron	62T	82	$ .35	$1.10
Johnson, Deron	64T	449	$ .40	$1.25
Johnson, Deron	65T	75	$ .25	$ .65
Johnson, Deron	66T	219	$ .65	$1.75
Johnson, Deron	66T	440	$ .25	$ .85
Johnson, Deron	67T	135	$ .25	$ .65
Johnson, Deron	68T	323	$ .25	$ .65
Johnson, Deron	69T	297	$ .25	$ .85
Johnson, Deron	70T	125	$ .10	$ .35
Johnson, Deron	71T	490	$ .10	$ .35
Johnson, Deron	72T	167	$ .05	$ .25
Johnson, Deron	72TIA	168	$ .05	$ .25
Johnson, Deron	73T	590	$ .35	$1.10
Johnson, Deron	74T	312	$ .06	$ .25
Johnson, Deron	76T	529	$ .05	$ .20
Johnson, Don	52T	190	$6.00	$19.00
Johnson, Don	54T	146	$2.10	$7.50
Johnson, Don	55T	165	$4.25	$13.00
Johnson, Ernie	56T	294	$1.80	$6.00
Johnson, Ernie	57T	333	$3.50	$13.00
Johnson, Ernie	58T	78	$1.00	$3.75
Johnson, Ernie	59T	279	$ .50	$1.95

Player	Year	No.	VG	EX/MT	Player	Year	No.	VG	EX/MT
Johnson, Ernie	60T	228	$ .35	$1.10	Johnson, Tim	80T	297	$ .01	$ .07
Johnson, Frank	69T	227	$ .25	$ .85	Johnson, Tom	75T	618	$ .60	$1.75
Johnson, Frank	71T	128	$ .10	$ .35	Johnson, Tom	76T	448	$ .05	$ .20
Johnson, Howard	85T	192	$1.00	$4.00	Johnson, Tom	77T	202	$ .03	$ .12
Johnson, Howard	85TTR	64	$ .50	$2.50	Johnson, Tom	78T	54	$ .02	$ .10
Johnson, Howard	86T	751	$ .10	$ .45	Johnson, Tom	79T	162	$ .02	$ .10
Johnson, Howard	87T	267	$ .05	$ .25	Johnson, Wallace	87T	588	$ .01	$ .03
Johnson, Howard	88T	85	$ .01	$ .10	Johnson, Wallace	88T	228	$ .01	$ .03
Johnson, Howard	88TBB	129	$ .05	$ .25	Johnson, Wallace	89T	138	$ .01	$ .04
Johnson, Howard	89T	383	$ .01	$ .20	Johnson, Wallace	90T	318	$ .01	$ .03
Johnson, Howard	89TBB	208	$ .01	$ .15	Johnson, Walter	61T	409	$ .70	$2.00
Johnson, Howard	90T	680	$ .01	$ .10	Johnson, Walter	73TATL	476	$ .50	$2.00
Johnson, Howard	90TAS	399	$ .01	$ .10	Johnson, Walter	73TATL	478	$ .50	$2.00
Johnson, Jerry	69T	253	$ .25	$ .85	Johnson, Walter	76TAS	349	$ .50	$2.00
Johnson, Jerry	70T	162	$ .10	$ .35	Johnson, Walter	79TRH	417	$ .05	$ .20
Johnson, Jerry	71T	412	$ .10	$ .35	Johnson, Walter	79TRH	418	$ .02	$ .10
Johnson, Jerry	72T	35	$ .05	$ .25	Johnston, Greg	79T	726	$ .05	$ .20
Johnson, Jerry	72TIA	36	$ .05	$ .25	Johnston, Greg	80T	686	$ .01	$ .07
Johnson, Jerry	73T	248	$ .06	$ .25	Johnston, Greg	81T	328	$ .01	$ .07
Johnson, Jerry	75T	218	$ .06	$ .25	Johnstone, Jay	67T	213	$ .30	$1.00
Johnson, Jerry	76T	658	$ .05	$ .20	Johnstone, Jay	68T	389	$ .25	$ .65
Johnson, Jerry	78T	169	$ .02	$ .10	Johnstone, Jay	69T	59	$ .25	$ .65
Johnson, Joe	87TTR	56	$ .01	$ .07	Johnstone, Jay	70T	485	$ .10	$ .35
Johnson, Joe	88T	347	$ .01	$ .03	Johnstone, Jay	71T	292	$ .10	$ .35
Johnson, John Henry	79T	681	$ .02	$ .10	Johnstone, Jay	72T	233	$ .07	$ .30
Johnson, John Henry	80T	173	$ .01	$ .07	Johnstone, Jay	75T	242	$ .06	$ .25
Johnson, John Henry	81T	216	$ .01	$ .07	Johnstone, Jay	76T	114	$ .05	$ .20
Johnson, John Henry	82T	527	$ .01	$ .06	Johnstone, Jay	77T	415	$ .03	$ .12
Johnson, John Henry	84T	419	$ .01	$ .05	Johnstone, Jay	78T	675	$ .02	$ .10
Johnson, John Henry	85T	734	$ .01	$ .04	Johnstone, Jay	79T	558	$ .02	$ .10
Johnson, John Henry	87T	377	$ .01	$ .03	Johnstone, Jay	80T	31	$ .01	$ .07
Johnson, Ken	60T	135	$ .35	$1.10	Johnstone, Jay	81T	372	$ .01	$ .07
Johnson, Ken	61T	24	$ .30	$1.00	Johnstone, Jay	82T	774	$ .01	$ .06
Johnson, Ken	62T	278	$ .35	$1.10	Johnstone, Jay	82TTR	52	$ .02	$ .10
Johnson, Ken	63T	352	$ .35	$1.20	Johnstone, Jay	83T	152	$ .01	$ .06
Johnson, Ken	64T	158	$ .25	$ .85	Johnstone, Jay	84T	249	$ .01	$ .05
Johnson, Ken	65T	359	$ .30	$1.00	Johnstone, Jay	86T	496	$ .01	$ .03
Johnson, Ken	66T	466	$ .70	$2.10	Jok, Stan	54T	196	$2.10	$7.50
Johnson, Ken	67T	101	$ .25	$ .65	Jolly, Dave	54T	188	$2.10	$7.50
Johnson, Ken	68T	342	$ .25	$ .65	Jolly, Dave	55T	35	$1.35	$5.00
Johnson, Ken	69T	238	$ .25	$ .85	Jolly, Dave	57T	389	$1.00	$3.75
Johnson, Lamar	76T	596	$ .10	$ .35	Jolly, Dave	58T	183	$ .50	$2.00
Johnson, Lamar	77T	443	$ .03	$ .12	Jones, Al	85T	437	$ .01	$ .04
Johnson, Lamar	78T	693	$ .02	$ .10	Jones, Al	86T	227	$ .01	$ .03
Johnson, Lamar	79T	372	$ .02	$ .10	Jones, Barry	87T	494	$ .10	$ .35
Johnson, Lamar	80T	242	$ .01	$ .07	Jones, Barry	88T	168	$ .01	$ .03
Johnson, Lamar	81T	589	$ .01	$ .07	Jones, Barry	89T	539	$ .01	$ .04
Johnson, Lamar	82T	13	$ .01	$ .06	Jones, Barry	90T	243	$ .01	$ .03
Johnson, Lamar	82TTR	50	$ .02	$ .10	Jones, Bob	77T	16	$ .03	$ .12
Johnson, Lamar	83T	453	$ .01	$ .06	Jones, Bob	84T	451	$ .01	$ .05
Johnson, Lance	88TBB	251	$ .01	$ .05	Jones, Bob	85T	648	$ .01	$ .04
Johnson, Lance	89T	122	$ .01	$ .04	Jones, Bob	86T	142	$ .01	$ .03
Johnson, Lance	90T	587	$ .01	$ .03	Jones, Clarence	68T	506	$ .30	$1.00
Johnson, Lou	60T	476	$ .60	$1.75	Jones, Cleon	65T	308	$ .35	$1.10
Johnson, Lou	63T	238	$ .25	$ .85	Jones, Cleon	66T	67	$ .25	$ .85
Johnson, Lou	66T	13	$ .25	$ .85	Jones, Cleon	67T	165	$ .25	$ .65
Johnson, Lou	67T	410	$ .25	$ .85	Jones, Cleon	68T	254	$ .25	$ .85
Johnson, Lou	68T	184	$ .25	$ .65	Jones, Cleon	69T	512	$ .25	$ .65
Johnson, Lou	69T	367	$ .25	$ .65	Jones, Cleon	70T	61	$1.50	$4.75
Johnson, Owen	66T	356	$ .25	$ .85	Jones, Cleon	70T	575	$ .25	$ .85
Johnson, Randy	89T	647	$ .01	$ .15	Jones, Cleon	71T	527	$ .30	$1.00
Johnson, Randy	89TBB	287	$ .01	$ .05	Jones, Cleon	72T	31	$ .05	$ .25
Johnson, Randy	89TTR	57	$ .01	$ .05	Jones, Cleon	72TIA	32	$ .05	$ .25
Johnson, Randy	90T	431	$ .01	$ .03	Jones, Cleon	73T	540	$ .35	$1.10
Johnson, Randy G.	83T	596	$ .01	$ .06	Jones, Cleon	74T	245	$ .06	$ .25
Johnson, Randy S.	82TTR	51	$ .02	$ .10	Jones, Cleon	75T	43	$ .06	$ .25
Johnson, Randy S.	83T	354	$ .01	$ .06	Jones, Dalton	64T	459	$ .40	$1.25
Johnson, Randy S.	84T	289	$ .01	$ .05	Jones, Dalton	65T	178	$ .25	$ .65
Johnson, Randy S.	85T	458	$ .01	$ .04	Jones, Dalton	66T	317	$ .25	$ .85
Johnson, Tim	74T	554	$ .06	$ .25	Jones, Dalton	67T	139	$ .25	$ .65
Johnson, Tim	75T	556	$ .06	$ .25	Jones, Dalton	68T	106	$ .25	$ .65
Johnson, Tim	76T	613	$ .05	$ .20	Jones, Dalton	69T	457	$ .25	$ .65
Johnson, Tim	77T	406	$ .03	$ .12	Jones, Dalton	70T	682	$ .50	$2.00
Johnson, Tim	78T	542	$ .02	$ .10	Jones, Dalton	71T	367	$ .10	$ .35
Johnson, Tim	79T	182	$ .02	$ .10	Jones, Dalton	72T	83	$ .05	$ .25

DALTON **JONES**
TEXAS RANGERS   2nd BASE

Player	Year	No.	VG	EX/MT
Jones, Dalton	73T	512	$ .06	$ .25
Jones, Darryl	80T	670	$ .01	$ .07
Jones, Deacon	63T	253	$ .25	$ .85
Jones, Doug	88T	293	$ .01	$ .25
Jones, Doug	89T	690	$ .01	$ .05
Jones, Doug	89TRB	6	$ .01	$ .04
Jones, Doug	90T	75	$ .01	$ .03
Jones, Gary	71T	559	$ .30	$1.00
Jones, Gordon	55T	78	$1.35	$5.00
Jones, Gordon	59T	458	$ .50	$1.95
Jones, Gordon	60T	98	$ .35	$1.10
Jones, Gordon	61T	442	$ .50	$2.00
Jones, Hal	62T	49	$ .35	$1.10
Jones, Jeff	81T	687	$ .01	$ .07
Jones, Jeff	82T	139	$ .01	$ .06
Jones, Jeff	83T	259	$ .01	$ .06
Jones, Jeff	84T	464	$ .01	$ .05
Jones, Jeff	85T	319	$ .01	$ .04
Jones, Jimmy	88T	63	$ .01	$ .03
Jones, Jimmy	89T	748	$ .01	$ .04
Jones, Jimmy	89TTR	58	$ .01	$ .05
Jones, Jimmy	90T	359	$ .01	$ .03
Jones, Lynn	80T	123	$ .01	$ .07
Jones, Lynn	81T	337	$ .01	$ .07
Jones, Lynn	82T	64	$ .01	$ .06
Jones, Lynn	83T	483	$ .01	$ .06
Jones, Lynn	84T	731	$ .01	$ .05
Jones, Lynn	84TTR	58	$ .02	$ .10
Jones, Lynn	85T	513	$ .01	$ .04
Jones, Lynn	86T	671	$ .01	$ .03
Jones, Mack	62T	186	$ .35	$1.10
Jones, Mack	63T	137	$ .25	$ .85
Jones, Mack	65T	241	$ .30	$1.00
Jones, Mack	66T	446	$ .25	$ .85
Jones, Mack	67T	435	$ .25	$ .85
Jones, Mack	68T	353	$ .25	$ .65
Jones, Mack	69T	625	$ .25	$ .85
Jones, Mack	70T	38	$ .10	$ .35
Jones, Mack	71T	142	$ .10	$ .35
Jones, Mike	81T	66	$ .01	$ .07
Jones, Mike	82T	471	$ .05	$ .20
Jones, Mike	85T	244	$ .01	$ .04
Jones, Mike	86T	514	$ .01	$ .03
Jones, Nippy	52T	213	$6.00	$19.00

Player	Year	No.	VG	EX/MT
Jones, Odell	78T	407	$ .02	$ .10
Jones, Odell	80T	342	$ .01	$ .07
Jones, Odell	83TTR	50	$ .02	$ .10
Jones, Odell	84T	734	$ .01	$ .05
Jones, Odell	85T	29	$ .01	$ .04
Jones, Randy	74T	173	$ .06	$ .25
Jones, Randy	75T	248	$ .06	$ .25
Jones, Randy	76T	199	$ .15	$ .50
Jones, Randy	76T	201	$ .30	$1.00
Jones, Randy	76T	310	$ .05	$ .20
Jones, Randy	77T	5	$ .15	$ .50
Jones, Randy	77T	550	$ .03	$ .12
Jones, Randy	78T	56	$ .02	$ .10
Jones, Randy	79T	194	$ .02	$ .10
Jones, Randy	80T	305	$ .01	$ .07
Jones, Randy	81T	458	$ .01	$ .07
Jones, Randy	81TTR	777	$ .02	$ .10
Jones, Randy	82T	626	$ .01	$ .06
Jones, Randy	83T	29	$ .01	$ .06
Jones, Rick	77T	118	$ .03	$ .12
Jones, Ron	89T	349	$ .05	$ .25
Jones, Ron	90T	129	$ .01	$ .10
Jones, Ross	88T	169	$ .01	$ .03
Jones, Ruppert	77T	488	$5.00	$20.00
Jones, Ruppert	78T	141	$ .02	$ .10
Jones, Ruppert	79T	422	$ .02	$ .10
Jones, Ruppert	80T	78	$ .01	$ .07
Jones, Ruppert	81T	225	$ .01	$ .07
Jones, Ruppert	81TTR	778	$ .02	$ .10
Jones, Ruppert	82T	511	$ .01	$ .06
Jones, Ruppert	83T	695	$ .01	$ .05
Jones, Ruppert	84T	327	$ .01	$ .05
Jones, Ruppert	84TTR	59	$ .02	$ .10
Jones, Ruppert	85T	126	$ .01	$ .04
Jones, Ruppert	85TTR	65	$ .02	$ .10
Jones, Ruppert	86T	464	$ .01	$ .03
Jones, Ruppert	87T	53	$ .01	$ .03
Jones, Sam	52T	382	$39.00	$135.00
Jones, Sam	53T	6	$3.75	$13.00
Jones, Sam	56T	259	$2.50	$8.00
Jones, Sam	57T	287	$3.50	$13.00
Jones, Sam	58T	287	$ .50	$2.00
Jones, Sam	59T	75	$1.00	$3.75
Jones, Sam	60T	410	$ .50	$1.95
Jones, Sam	61T	49	$ .60	$1.75
Jones, Sam	61T	555	$6.00	$18.00
Jones, Sam	62T	92	$ .35	$1.10
Jones, Sheldon	52T	130	$6.00	$19.00
Jones, Sherman	61T	161	$ .30	$1.00
Jones, Steve	69T	49	$ .35	$1.10
Jones, Tim	78T	703	$2.00	$7.00
Jones, Tim	90T	533	$ .01	$ .03
Jones, Tracy	87T	146	$ .15	$ .50
Jones, Tracy	88T	553	$ .01	$ .15
Jones, Tracy	89T	373	$ .01	$ .04
Jones, Tracy	90T	767	$ .01	$ .03
Jones, Willie	51Tbb	43	$5.50	$17.00
Jones, Willie	52T	47	$14.00	$45.00
Jones, Willie	53T	88	$3.75	$13.00
Jones, Willie	54T	41	$2.10	$7.50
Jones, Willie	56T	127	$1.25	$4.50
Jones, Willie	57T	174	$ .95	$3.50
Jones, Willie	58T	181	$ .50	$2.00
Jones, Willie	59T	208	$ .50	$1.95
Jones, Willie	60T	289	$ .50	$1.95
Jones, Willie	61T	497	$ .50	$2.00
Joost, Eddie	51Tbb	15	$5.50	$17.00
Joost, Eddie	52T	45	$14.00	$45.00
Jordan, Ricky	89T	358	$ .15	$1.25
Jordan, Ricky	89TBB	246	$ .01	$ .35
Jordan, Ricky	90T	216	$ .01	$ .25
Jorgensen, Mike	70T	348	$ .10	$ .35
Jorgensen, Mike	71T	596	$ .30	$1.00
Jorgensen, Mike	72T	16	$ .05	$ .25
Jorgensen, Mike	73T	281	$ .06	$ .25

Player	Year	No.	VG	EX/MT	Player	Year	No.	VG	EX/MT
Jorgensen, Mike	74T	549	$ .06	$ .25	Kaat, Jim	75T	243	$ .50	$2.00
Jorgensen, Mike	75T	286	$ .06	$ .25	Kaat, Jim	76T	80	$ .35	$1.10
Jorgensen, Mike	76T	117	$ .05	$ .20	Kaat, Jim	76TTR	80	$ .30	$1.00
Jorgensen, Mike	77T	368	$ .03	$ .12	Kaat, Jim	77T	638	$ .15	$ .50
Jorgensen, Mike	78T	406	$ .02	$ .10	Kaat, Jim	78T	715	$ .30	$1.00
Jorgensen, Mike	79T	22	$ .02	$ .10	Kaat, Jim	79T	136	$ .10	$ .45
Jorgensen, Mike	80T	213	$ .01	$ .07	Kaat, Jim	80T	250	$ .25	$ .65
Jorgensen, Mike	81T	698	$ .01	$ .07	Kaat, Jim	81T	563	$ .05	$ .25
Jorgensen, Mike	82T	566	$ .01	$ .06	Kaat, Jim	82T	367	$ .05	$ .25
Jorgensen, Mike	83T	107	$ .01	$ .06	Kaat, Jim	83T	672	$ .01	$ .06
Jorgensen, Mike	83TTR	51	$ .02	$ .10	Kaat, Jim	83T	673	$ .01	$ .06
Jorgensen, Mike	84T	313	$ .01	$ .05	Kaiser, Don	56T	124	$1.25	$4.50
Jorgensen, Mike	84TTR	60	$ .02	$ .10	Kaiser, Don	57T	134	$ .95	$3.50
Jorgensen, Mike	85T	783	$ .01	$ .04	Kaline, Al	54T	201	$150.00	$600.00
Jorgensen, Mike	86T	422	$ .01	$ .03	Kaline, Al	55T	4	$25.00	$85.00
Jorgensen, Terry	89TMLD	64	$ .01	$ .35	Kaline, Al	56T	20	$17.50	$52.50
Jose, Felix	90T	238	$ .01	$ .10	Kaline, Al	57T	125	$15.00	$50.00
Joseph, Ricardo	68T	434	$ .25	$ .65	Kaline, Al	58T	70	$7.50	$30.00
Joseph, Rick	69T	329	$ .25	$ .65	Kaline, Al	58T	304	$2.50	$10.00
Joseph, Rick	70T	186	$ .10	$ .35	Kaline, Al	59T	34	$2.00	$8.00
Josephson, Duane	67T	373	$ .25	$ .85	Kaline, Al	59T	360	$10.00	$42.50
Josephson, Duane	68T	329	$ .25	$ .65	Kaline, Al	59T	463	$1.50	$6.00
Josephson, Duane	69T	222	$ .25	$ .85	Kaline, Al	59TAS	562	$9.00	$35.00
Josephson, Duane	70T	263	$ .10	$ .35	Kaline, Al	60T	50	$5.00	$20.00
Josephson, Duane	71T	56	$ .10	$ .35	Kaline, Al	60TAS	561	$6.00	$18.00
Josephson, Duane	72T	543	$ .25	$ .85	Kaline, Al	61T	429	$6.00	$24.00
Joshua, Von	71T	57	$ .10	$ .35	Kaline, Al	61TAS	580	$20.00	$65.00
Joshua, Von	73T	544	$ .15	$ .75	Kaline, Al	62T	51	$ .50	$1.95
Joshua, Von	74T	551	$ .06	$ .25	Kaline, Al	62T	150	$4.00	$16.00
Joshua, Von	75T	547	$ .06	$ .25	Kaline, Al	62TAS	470	$3.00	$10.00
Joshua, Von	76T	82	$ .05	$ .20	Kaline, Al	63T	25	$5.00	$20.00
Joshua, Von	77T	651	$ .03	$ .12	Kaline, Al	64T	8	$1.35	$4.00
Joshua, Von	78T	108	$ .02	$ .10	Kaline, Al	64T	12	$ .50	$2.00
Joshua, Von	80T	209	$ .01	$ .07	Kaline, Al	64T	250	$4.00	$12.00
Joyce, Mike	63T	66	$ .25	$ .85	Kaline, Al	64T	331	$15.00	$45.00
Joyce, Mike	64T	477	$ .40	$1.25	Kaline, Al	65T	130	$4.00	$12.00
Joyner, Wally	86TTR	51	$ .75	$2.00	Kaline, Al	66T	410	$5.00	$15.00
Joyner, Wally	87T	80	$ .50	$1.95	Kaline, Al	67T	30	$3.00	$9.00
Joyner, Wally	88T	420	$ .25	$ .65	Kaline, Al	67T	216	$1.25	$4.00
Joyner, Wally	88TBB	52	$ .05	$ .25	Kaline, Al	67T	239	$1.50	$3.75
Joyner, Wally	89T	270	$ .01	$ .10	Kaline, Al	68T	2	$1.35	$4.00
Joyner, Wally	89TBB	201	$ .01	$ .10	Kaline, Al	68T	240	$3.00	$9.00
Joyner, Wally	90T	525	$ .01	$ .10	Kaline, Al	69T	410	$2.50	$8.00
Juden, Jeff	90T	164	$ .01	$ .15	Kaline, Al	70T	640	$7.50	$30.00
Judson, Howie	52T	169	$6.00	$19.00	Kaline, Al	71T	180	$2.50	$8.00
Judson, Howie	53T	12	$3.75	$13.00	Kaline, Al	72T	600	$4.00	$12.00
Jurak, Ed	84T	628	$ .01	$ .05	Kaline, Al	73T	280	$1.50	$4.50
Jurak, Ed	85T	233	$ .01	$ .04	Kaline, Al	74T	215	$1.50	$4.50
Jurak, Ed	86T	749	$ .01	$ .03	Kaline, Al	75THL	4	$ .50	$2.00
Jurges, Billy	60T	220	$ .35	$1.10	Kanehl, Rod	62T	597	$6.00	$18.00
Justice, Dave	89TMLD	65	$ .01	$ .05	Kanehl, Rod	63T	371	$ .35	$1.20
Jutze, Skip	73T	613	$9.00	$35.00	Kanehl, Rod	64T	582	$1.50	$3.75
Jutze, Skip	74T	328	$ .06	$ .25	Karkovice, Ron	87T	491	$ .01	$ .03
Jutze, Skip	76T	489	$ .05	$ .20	Karkovice, Ron	88T	86	$ .01	$ .03
Jutze, Skip	78T	532	$ .02	$ .10	Karkovice, Ron	89T	308	$ .01	$ .04
Kaat, Jim	60T	136	$7.00	$21.00	Karkovice, Ron	90T	717	$ .01	$ .03
Kaat, Jim	61T	63	$3.00	$9.00	Kasko, Eddie	57T	363	$1.00	$3.75
Kaat, Jim	62T	21	$1.25	$3.50	Kasko, Eddie	58T	8	$ .70	$2.25
Kaat, Jim	63T	10	$ .35	$1.10	Kasko, Eddie	59T	232	$ .50	$1.95
Kaat, Jim	63T	165	$ .80	$2.50	Kasko, Eddie	60T	61	$ .35	$1.10
Kaat, Jim	64T	567	$2.50	$8.50	Kasko, Eddie	61T	534	$6.00	$18.00
Kaat (Katt), Jim	65T	62	$ .75	$2.50	Kasko, Eddie	62T	193	$ .35	$1.10
Kaat, Jim	66T	224	$ .60	$1.75	Kasko, Eddie	63T	498	$2.50	$6.50
Kaat, Jim	66T	445	$1.25	$3.50	Kasko, Eddie	70T	489	$ .10	$ .35
Kaat, Jim	67T	235	$ .35	$1.10	Kasko, Eddie	71T	31	$ .10	$ .35
Kaat, Jim	67T	237	$ .35	$1.10	Kasko, Eddie	72T	218	$ .05	$ .25
Kaat, Jim	67T	300	$ .75	$2.50	Kasko, Eddie	73T	131	$ .10	$ .35
Kaat, Jim	68T	450	$1.25	$3.50	Katt, Ray	57T	331	$3.50	$13.00
Kaat, Jim	69T	290	$ .75	$3.00	Katt, Ray	58T	284	$ .50	$2.00
Kaat, Jim	70T	75	$1.00	$3.75	Katt, Ray	60T	468	$ .95	$3.50
Kaat, Jim	71T	245	$ .70	$2.00	Kaufman, Curt	85T	61	$ .01	$ .04
Kaat, Jim	72T	709	$2.00	$7.00	Kazak, Eddie	52T	165	$6.00	$19.00
Kaat, Jim	72TIA	710	$1.50	$3.75	Kazak, Eddie	53T	194	$3.75	13.00
Kaat, Jim	73T	530	$1.25	$4.50	Kazanski, Ted	54T	78	$2.10	$7.50
Kaat, Jim	74T	440	$ .50	$2.00	Kazanski, Ted	55T	46	$1.35	$5.00

299

TOPPS

Player	Year	No.	VG	EX/MT	Player	Year	No.	VG	EX/MT
Kazanski, Ted	57T	27	$ .95	$3.50	Kell, George	56T	195	$6.00	$18.00
Kazanski, Ted	58T	36	$1.00	$3.75	Kell, George	57T	230	$3.50	$13.00
Kazanski, Ted	59T	99	$1.00	$3.75	Kell, George	58T	40	$3.00	$9.00
Kealey, Steve	69T	224	$ .25	$ .85	Kelleher, Mick	77T	657	$ .03	$ .12
Kealey, Steve	71T	43	$ .10	$ .35	Kelleher, Mick	78T	564	$ .02	$ .10
Kealey, Steve	72T	146	$ .05	$ .25	Kelleher, Mick	79T	53	$ .02	$ .10
Kealey, Steve	73T	581	$ .35	$1.10	Kelleher, Mick	80T	323	$ .01	$ .07
Keane, Johnny	60T	468	$ .95	$3.50	Kelleher, Mick	81T	429	$ .01	$ .07
Keane, Johnny	62T	198	$ .35	$1.10	Kelleher, Mick	81TTR	779	$ .02	$ .10
Keane, Johnny	63T	166	$ .25	$ .85	Kelleher, Mick	82T	184	$ .01	$ .06
Keane, Johnny	64T	413	$ .40	$1.25	Kelleher, Mick	82TTR	53	$ .02	$ .10
Keane, Johnny	65T	131	$ .25	$ .65	Kelleher, Mick	83T	79	$ .01	$ .06
Keane, Johnny	66T	296	$ .25	$ .85	Kellert, Frank	56T	291	$1.80	$6.00
Kearney, Bob	83TTR	52	$ .02	$ .10	Kelley, Dick	64T	476	$1.50	$3.75
Kearney, Bob	84T	326	$ .01	$ .05	Kelley, Dick	66T	84	$ .25	$ .85
Kearney, Bob	84TTR	61	$ .02	$ .10	Kelley, Dick	67T	138	$ .25	$ .65
Kearney, Bob	85T	679	$ .01	$ .04	Kelley, Dick	68T	203	$ .25	$ .65
Kearney, Bob	86T	13	$ .01	$ .03	Kelley, Dick	69T	359	$ .25	$ .65
Kearney, Bob	87T	498	$ .01	$ .03	Kelley, Dick	70T	474	$ .10	$ .35
Keedy, Pat	88T	486	$ .01	$ .03	Kelley, Dick	72T	412	$ .05	$ .25
Keegan, Bob	53T	196	$3.75	$13.00	Kelley, Tom	64T	552	$1.50	$3.75
Keegan, Bob	54T	100	$2.10	$7.50	Kelley, Tom	66T	44	$ .25	$ .85
Keegan, Bob	55T	10	$1.35	$5.00	Kelley, Tom	67T	214	$ .25	$ .65
Keegan, Bob	56T	54	$1.25	$4.50	Kelley, Tom	71T	463	$ .10	$ .35
Keegan, Bob	57T	99	$ .95	$3.50	Kelley, Tom	72T	97	$ .05	$ .25
Keegan, Bob	58T	200	$ .50	$2.00	Kellner, Alex	52T	201	$6.00	$19.00
Keegan, Bob	59T	86	$1.00	$3.75	Kellner, Alex	56T	176	$1.25	$4.50
Keegan, Bob	60T	291	$ .50	$1.95	Kellner, Alex	57T	280	$3.50	$13.00
Keegan, Bob	77TB	436	$ .03	$ .12	Kellner, Alex	58T	3	$1.00	$3.75
Keegan, Ed	61T	248	$ .30	$1.00	Kellner, Alex	59T	101	$1.00	$3.75
Keegan, Ed	62T	249	$ .35	$1.10	Kelly, Bob	52T	348	$39.00	$135.00
Keely, Bob	54T	176	$2.10	$7.50	Kelly, Pat	69T	619	$ .25	$ .85
Keeton, Rickey	82T	268	$ .01	$ .06	Kelly, Pat	70T	57	$ .10	$ .35
Kekich, Mike	65T	561	$2.00	$7.00	Kelly, Pat	71T	413	$ .10	$ .35
Kekich, Mike	69T	262	$ .25	$ .85	Kelly, Pat	72T	326	$ .05	$ .25
					Kelly, Pat	73T	261	$ .06	$ .25
					Kelly, Pat	74T	46	$ .06	$ .25
					Kelly, Pat	75T	82	$ .06	$ .25
					Kelly, Pat	76T	212	$ .05	$ .20
					Kelly, Pat	77T	469	$ .03	$ .12
					Kelly, Pat	78T	616	$ .02	$ .10
					Kelly, Pat	79T	188	$ .02	$ .10
					Kelly, Pat	79T	714	$ .02	$ .10
					Kelly, Pat	80T	543	$ .01	$ .07
					Kelly, Pat	80T	674	$ .01	$ .07
					Kelly, Pat	82T	417	$ .01	$ .06
					Kelly, Roberto	88TTR	57	$ .01	$ .50
					Kelly, Roberto	89T	691	$ .01	$ .20
					Kelly, Roberto	89TBB	152	$ .01	$ .10
					Kelly, Roberto	90T	109	$ .01	$ .10
					Kelly, Tom	87T	618	$ .01	$ .03
					Kelly, Tom	88T	194	$ .01	$ .03
					Kelly, Tom	89T	14	$ .01	$ .04
					Kelly, Tom	90T	429	$ .01	$ .03
					Kelso, Bill	65T	194	$ .25	$ .65
					Kelso, Bill	67T	367	$ .25	$ .65
					Kelso, Bill	68T	511	$ .30	$1.00
					Kemmerer, Russ	55T	18	$1.35	$5.00
					Kemmerer, Russ	58T	137	$ .50	$2.00
					Kemmerer, Russ	59T	191	$ .50	$1.95
					Kemmerer, Russ	60T	362	$ .50	$1.95
					Kemmerer, Russ	61T	56	$ .30	$1.00
					Kemmerer, Russ	62T	576	$3.75	$11.00
					Kemmerer, Russ	63T	338	$ .35	$1.20
					Kemp, Steve	77T	492	$ .25	$ .80
					Kemp, Steve	78T	21	$ .02	$ .10
					Kemp, Steve	79T	196	$ .02	$ .10

Mike Kekich   PITCHER

Player	Year	No.	VG	EX/MT	Player	Year	No.	VG	EX/MT
Kekich, Mike	70T	536	$ .10	$ .35	Kemp, Steve	80T	315	$ .01	$ .07
Kekich, Mike	71T	703	$ .70	$2.10	Kemp, Steve	81T	593	$ .01	$ .07
Kekich, Mike	72T	138	$ .05	$ .25	Kemp, Steve	82T	666	$ .01	$ .06
Kekich, Mike	73T	371	$ .06	$ .25	Kemp, Steve	82T	670	$ .01	$ .06
Kekich, Mike	74T	199	$ .06	$ .25	Kemp, Steve	82TTR	54	$ .02	$ .10
Kekich, Mike	76T	582	$ .05	$ .20	Kemp, Steve	83T	260	$ .01	$ .06
Kell, George	52T	246	$16.00	$50.00	Kemp, Steve	83TTR	53	$ .02	$ .10
Kell, George	53T	138	$8.50	$35.00	Kemp, Steve	84T	440	$ .01	$ .05

Player	Year	No.	VG	EX/MT	Player	Year	No.	VG	EX/MT
Kemp, Steve	85T	120	$ .01	$ .04	Keough, Marty	63T	21	$ .25	$ .85
Kemp, Steve	85TTR	66	$ .02	$ .10	Keough, Marty	64T	166	$ .25	$ .85
Kemp, Steve	86T	387	$ .01	$ .03	Keough, Marty	65T	263	$ .30	$1.00
Kendall, Fred	72T	532	$ .25	$ .85	Keough, Marty	66T	334	$ .25	$ .85
Kendall, Fred	73T	221	$ .06	$ .25	Keough, Matt	78T	709	$ .02	$ .10
Kendall, Fred	74T	53	$ .06	$ .25	Keough, Matt	79T	554	$ .02	$ .10
Kendall, Fred	75T	332	$ .06	$ .25	Keough, Matt	80T	134	$ .01	$ .07
Kendall, Fred	76T	639	$ .05	$ .20	Keough, Matt	81T	301	$ .01	$ .07
Kendall, Fred	77T	576	$ .03	$ .12	Keough, Matt	82T	87	$ .01	$ .06
Kendall, Fred	78T	426	$ .02	$ .10	Keough, Matt	83T	413	$ .01	$ .06
Kendall, Fred	79T	83	$ .02	$ .10	Keough, Matt	83TTR	54	$ .02	$ .10
Kendall, Fred	80T	598	$ .01	$ .07	Keough, Matt	84T	203	$ .01	$ .05
Kennedy, Bill	52T	102	$6.00	$19.00	Kepshire, Kurt	85T	474	$ .01	$ .04
Kennedy, Bill	53T	94	$3.75	$13.00	Kepshire, Kurt	86T	256	$ .01	$ .03
Kennedy, Bob	51Trb	29	$1.25	$3.50	Kerfeld, Charlie	86TTR	52	$ .02	$ .10
Kennedy, Bob	52T	77	$14.00	$45.00	Kerfeld, Charlie	87T	145	$ .01	$ .03
Kennedy, Bob	53T	33	$3.75	$13.00	Kerfeld, Charlie	88T	608	$ .01	$ .03
Kennedy, Bob	54T	155	$2.10	$7.50	Kern, Jim	75T	621	$ .15	$ .50
Kennedy, Bob	55T	48	$1.35	$5.00	Kern, Jim	77T	41	$ .03	$ .12
Kennedy, Bob	56T	38	$1.25	$4.50	Kern, Jim	78T	253	$ .02	$ .10
Kennedy, Bob	57T	149	$ .95	$3.50	Kern, Jim	79T	573	$ .02	$ .10
Kennedy, Bob	64T	486	$ .40	$1.25	Kern, Jim	80T	369	$ .01	$ .07
Kennedy, Bob	65T	457	$ .50	$2.00	Kern, Jim	81T	197	$ .01	$ .07
Kennedy, Bob	68T	183	$ .25	$ .65	Kern, Jim	82T	463	$ .01	$ .06
Kennedy, Bob	85T	135	$ .01	$ .10	Kern, Jim	82TTR	56	$ .02	$ .10
Kennedy, John	64T	203	$ .25	$ .85	Kern, Jim	83T	772	$ .01	$ .06
Kennedy, John	65T	119	$ .25	$ .65	Kernek, George	66T	544	$4.00	$11.50
Kennedy, John	66T	407	$ .25	$ .85	Kerrigan, Joe	77T	341	$ .03	$ .12
Kennedy, John	67T	111	$ .25	$ .65	Kerrigan, Joe	78T	549	$ .02	$ .10
Kennedy, John	69T	631	$ .25	$ .85	Kerrigan, Joe	79T	37	$ .02	$ .10
Kennedy, John	70T	53	$ .10	$ .35	Kessinger, Don	66T	24	$2.50	$5.00
Kennedy, John	71T	498	$ .10	$ .35	Kessinger, Don	67T	419	$ .25	$ .85
Kennedy, John	72T	674	$ .70	$2.10	Kessinger, Don	68T	159	$ .25	$ .65
Kennedy, John	73T	437	$ .06	$ .25	Kessinger, Don	69T	225	$ .25	$ .85
Kennedy, Junior	79T	501	$ .02	$ .10	Kessinger, Don	69TAS	422	$ .25	$ .65
Kennedy, Junior	80T	377	$ .01	$ .07	Kessinger, Don	70T	80	$ .10	$ .35
Kennedy, Junior	81T	447	$ .01	$ .07	Kessinger, Don	70TAS	456	$ .10	$ .35
Kennedy, Junior	82T	723	$ .01	$ .06	Kessinger, Don	71T	455	$ .10	$ .35
Kennedy, Junior	82TTR	55	$ .02	$ .10	Kessinger, Don	72T	145	$ .05	$ .25
Kennedy, Junior	83T	204	$ .01	$ .06	Kessinger, Don	73T	285	$ .06	$ .25
Kennedy, Monte	52T	124	$6.00	$19.00	Kessinger, Don	74T	38	$ .06	$ .25
Kennedy, Terry	79T	724	$ .09	$ .35	Kessinger, Don	75T	315	$ .06	$ .25
Kennedy, Terry	80T	569	$ .03	$ .15	Kessinger, Don	76T	574	$ .05	$ .20
Kennedy, Terry	81T	353	$ .01	$ .07	Kessinger, Don	77T	229	$ .03	$ .12
Kennedy, Terry	81TTR	780	$ .02	$ .10	Kessinger, Don	78T	672	$ .02	$ .10
Kennedy, Terry	82T	65	$ .01	$ .06	Kessinger, Don	79T	467	$ .02	$ .10
Kennedy, Terry	83T	274	$ .01	$ .06	Kester, Rick	70T	621	$5.00	$14.00
Kennedy, Terry	83T	742	$ .01	$ .06	Kester, Rick	71T	494	$ .10	$ .35
Kennedy, Terry	84T	366	$ .01	$ .05	Kester, Rick	72T	351	$ .10	$ .35
Kennedy, Terry	84T	455	$ .01	$ .05	Key, Jimmy	84TTR	62	$ .75	$3.00
Kennedy, Terry	85T	135	$ .01	$ .10	Key, Jimmy	85T	193	$ .20	$1.00
Kennedy, Terry	85T	635	$ .01	$ .04	Key, Jimmy	86T	545	$ .01	$ .15
Kennedy, Terry	86T	540	$ .01	$ .03	Key, Jimmy	87T	29	$ .01	$ .10
Kennedy, Terry	87T	540	$ .01	$ .03	Key, Jimmy	88T	682	$ .01	$ .10
Kennedy, Terry	87TTR	57	$ .01	$ .07	Key, Jimmy	88TAS	395	$ .01	$ .03
Kennedy, Terry	88T	180	$ .01	$ .03	Key, Jimmy	89T	229	$ .01	$ .04
Kennedy, Terry	89T	705	$ .01	$ .04	Key, Jimmy	90T	371	$ .01	$ .03
Kennedy, Terry	89TBB	180	$ .01	$ .05	Khalifa, Sammy	86T	316	$ .01	$ .03
Kennedy, Terry	89TTR	59	$ .01	$ .05	Khalifa, Sammy	87T	164	$ .01	$ .03
Kennedy, Terry	90T	372	$ .01	$ .03	Kiefer, Steve	88T	187	$ .01	$ .03
Kenney, Gerry (Jerry)	69T	519	$ .25	$ .85	Kiely, Leo	52T	54	$14.00	$45.00
Kenney, Jerry	70T	219	$ .10	$ .35	Kiely, Leo	54T	171	$2.10	$7.50
Kenney, Jerry	71T	572	$ .30	$1.00	Kiely, Leo	55T	36	$1.35	$5.00
Kenney, Jerry	72T	158	$ .05	$ .25	Kiely, Leo	58T	204	$ .50	$2.00
Kenney, Jerry	73T	514	$ .06	$ .25	Kiely, Leo	59T	199	$ .50	$1.95
Kenworthy, Dick	68T	63	$ .25	$ .65	Kiely, Leo	60T	94	$ .35	$1.10
Keough, Joe	69T	603	$ .25	$ .85	Kilgus, Paul	88T	427	$ .01	$ .03
Keough, Joe	70T	589	$ .25	$ .85	Kilgus, Paul	89T	276	$ .01	$ .04
Keough, Joe	71T	451	$ .10	$ .35	Kilgus, Paul	89TTR	60	$ .01	$ .05
Keough, Joe	72T	133	$ .05	$ .25	Kilgus, Paul	90T	86	$ .01	$ .03
Keough, Marty	58T	371	$ .50	$2.00	Kilkenny, Mike	69T	544	$ .25	$ .85
Keough, Marty	59T	303	$ .50	$1.95	Kilkenny, Mike	70T	424	$ .10	$ .35
Keough, Marty	60T	71	$ .35	$1.10	Kilkenny, Mike	71T	86	$ .10	$ .35
Keough, Marty	61T	146	$ .30	$1.00	Kilkenny, Mike	72T	337	$ .05	$ .25
Keough, Marty	62T	258	$ .35	$1.10	Kilkenny, Mike	73T	551	$ .35	$1.10

Player	Year	No.	VG	EX/MT	Player	Year	No.	VG	EX/MT
Killebrew, Harmon	55T	124	$75.00	$225.00	Kindall, Jerry	58T	221	$ .50	$2.00
Killebrew, Harmon	56T	164	$20.00	$60.00	Kindall, Jerry	59T	274	$ .50	$1.95
					Kindall, Jerry	60T	444	$ .60	$1.75
					Kindall, Jerry	61T	27	$ .30	$1.00
					Kindall, Jerry	62T	292	$ .35	$1.10
					Kindall, Jerry	63T	36	$ .25	$ .85
					Kinder, Ellis	52T	78	$14.00	$45.00
					Kinder, Ellis	53T	44	$2.50	$8.00
					Kinder, Ellis	54T	47	$1.25	$5.00
					Kinder, Ellis	55T	115	$1.35	$5.00
					Kinder, Ellis	56T	336	$1.80	$6.00
					Kinder, Ellis	57T	352	$3.50	$13.00
					Kiner, Ralph	51Trb	15	$5.00	$20.00
					Kiner, Ralph	53T	191	$20.00	$60.00
					Kiner, Ralph	77TB	437	$ .30	$1.00
					King, Chick	59T	538	$2.00	$7.00
					King, Clyde	52T	205	$6.00	$18.00
					King, Clyde	69T	274	$ .25	$ .85
					King, Clyde	70T	624	$ .25	$ .85
					King, Clyde	83T	486	$ .01	$ .06
					King, Eric	86TTR	53	$ .03	$ .15
					King, Eric	87T	36	$ .01	$ .10
					King, Eric	88T	499	$ .01	$ .03
					King, Eric	89T	238	$ .01	$ .04
					King, Eric	89TTR	61	$ .01	$ .05
					King, Eric	90T	786	$ .01	$ .03
					King, Hal	70T	327	$ .10	$ .35
					King, Hal	71T	88	$ .10	$ .35
					King, Hal	72T	598	$ .25	$ .85
					King, Hal	74T	362	$ .06	$ .25
					King, Jeff	89TMLD	66	$ .01	$ .05
					King, Jeff	90T	454	$ .01	$ .03
					King, Jim	56T	74	$1.25	$4.50
					King, Jim	57T	186	$ .95	$3.50
Killebrew, Harmon	58T	288	$9.50	$37.50	King, Jim	58T	332	$ .50	$2.00
Killebrew, Harmon	59T	515	$25.00	$90.00	King, Jim	61T	351	$ .30	$1.00
Killebrew, Harmon	60T	210	$5.00	$15.00	King, Jim	62T	42	$ .35	$1.10
Killebrew, Harmon	61T	80	$5.00	$15.00	King, Jim	63T	176	$ .25	$ .85
Killebrew, Harmon	62T	53	$3.00	$12.50	King, Jim	64T	217	$ .25	$ .85
Killebrew, Harmon	62T	70	$3.50	$11.00	King, Jim	65T	38	$ .25	$ .65
Killebrew, Harmon	62T	316	$1.25	$3.50	King, Jim	66T	369	$ .25	$ .85
Killebrew, Harmon	63T	4	$ .50	$2.00	King, Jim	67T	509	$ .50	$2.00
Killebrew, Harmon	63T	500	$17.50	$50.00	King, Nelson	55T	112	$1.35	$5.00
Killebrew, Harmon	64T	10	$ .50	$2.00	King, Nelson	57T	349	$3.50	$13.00
Killebrew, Harmon	64T	12	$ .50	$2.00	Kingery, Mike	87T	203	$ .03	$ .15
Killebrew, Harmon	64T	81	$1.75	$7.00	Kingery, Mike	87TTR	58	$ .01	$ .07
Killebrew, Harmon	64T	177	$4.00	$12.00	Kingery, Mike	88T	532	$ .01	$ .03
Killebrew, Harmon	65T	3	$5.00	$15.00	Kingery, Mike	88TBB	160	$ .01	$ .05
Killebrew, Harmon	65T	5	$3.00	$12.00	Kingery, Mike	89T	413	$ .01	$ .04
Killebrew, Harmon	65T	400	$4.50	$12.50	Kingman, Brian	80T	671	$ .01	$ .07
Killebrew, Harmon	66T	120	$3.00	$9.00	Kingman, Brian	81T	284	$ .01	$ .07
Killebrew, Harmon	67T	241	$1.50	$3.75	Kingman, Brian	82T	476	$ .01	$ .06
Killebrew, Harmon	67T	243	$1.50	$3.75	Kingman, Brian	83T	312	$ .01	$ .06
Killebrew, Harmon	67T	334	$1.50	$3.75	Kingman, Dave	72T	147	$1.00	$3.00
Killebrew, Harmon	67T	460	$10.00	$38.00	Kingman, Dave	73T	23	$ .35	$1.00
Killebrew, Harmon	68T	4	$1.35	$4.00	Kingman, Dave	74T	610	$ .35	$1.00
Killebrew, Harmon	68T	6	$2.00	$5.00	Kingman, Dave	75T	156	$ .35	$1.20
Killebrew, Harmon	68T	220	$3.00	$9.00	Kingman, Dave	76T	40	$ .08	$ .30
Killebrew, Harmon	68T	490	$17.50	$60.00	Kingman, Dave	76T	193	$ .50	$1.95
Killebrew, Harmon	68TAS	361	$1.25	$3.50	Kingman, Dave	77T	500	$ .15	$ .50
Killebrew, Harmon	69T	375	$3.50	$9.50	Kingman, Dave	78T	570	$ .05	$ .25
Killebrew, Harmon	70T	64	$ .50	$1.95	Kingman, Dave	79T	370	$ .05	$ .20
Killebrew, Harmon	70T	66	$1.00	$4.00	Kingman, Dave	80T	202	$ .05	$ .20
Killebrew, Harmon	70T	150	$2.50	$7.50	Kingman, Dave	80T	240	$ .02	$ .20
Killebrew, Harmon	71T	65	$ .60	$1.75	Kingman, Dave	81T	450	$ .03	$ .15
Killebrew, Harmon	71T	550	$3.50	$10.00	Kingman, Dave	81TTR	781	$ .05	$ .25
Killebrew, Harmon	72T	51	$1.50	$6.00	Kingman, Dave	82T	690	$ .05	$ .20
Killebrew, Harmon	72T	88	$ .60	$2.00	Kingman, Dave	83T	160	$ .01	$ .10
Killebrew, Harmon	72TIA	52	$ .60	$1.75	Kingman, Dave	83T	161	$ .01	$ .06
Killebrew, Harmon	73T	170	$1.50	$6.00	Kingman, Dave	83T	702	$ .01	$ .06
Killebrew, Harmon	74T	400	$ .95	$3.50	Kingman, Dave	84T	573	$ .02	$ .10
Killebrew, Harmon	75T	207	$ .50	$2.00	Kingman, Dave	84T	703	$ .02	$ .10
Killebrew, Harmon	75T	640	$ .55	$1.75	Kingman, Dave	84TTR	63	$ .05	$ .20
Kimm, Bruce	77T	554	$ .03	$ .12	Kingman, Dave	85T	730	$ .01	$ .04
Kimm, Bruce	81T	272	$ .01	$ .07	Kingman, Dave	86T	410	$ .01	$ .03

Player	Year	No.	VG	EX/MT
Kingman, Dave	87T	709	$ .01	$ .03
Kinney, Dennis	81T	599	$ .01	$ .07
Kinzer, Matt	89TMLD	67	$ .01	$ .05
Kipp, Fred	59T	258	$ .50	$1.95
Kipp, Fred	60T	202	$ .35	$1.10
Kipper, Bob	86TTR	54	$ .02	$ .10
Kipper, Bob	87T	289	$ .01	$ .03
Kipper, Bob	88T	723	$ .01	$ .03
Kipper, Bob	88TBB	141	$ .01	$ .05
Kipper, Bob	89T	114	$ .01	$ .04
Kipper, Bob	90T	441	$ .01	$ .03
Kipper, Thornton	54T	108	$2.10	$7.50
Kipper, Thornton	55T	62	$1.35	$5.00
Kirby, Clay	69T	637	$ .25	$ .85
Kirby, Clay	70T	79	$ .10	$ .35
Kirby, Clay	71T	333	$ .10	$ .35
Kirby, Clay	72T	173	$ .05	$ .25
Kirby, Clay	72TIA	174	$ .05	$ .25
Kirby, Clay	73T	655	$ .35	$1.10
Kirby, Clay	74T	287	$ .06	$ .25
Kirby, Clay	75T	423	$ .06	$ .25
Kirby, Clay	76T	579	$ .05	$ .20
Kirby, Clay	76TTR	579	$ .05	$ .20
Kirkland, Willie	58T	128	$ .45	$1.50
Kirkland, Willie	59T	484	$ .50	$1.95
Kirkland, Willie	60T	172	$ .35	$1.10
Kirkland, Willie	61T	15	$ .30	$1.00
Kirkland, Willie	62T	447	$ .70	$2.10
Kirkland, Willie	63T	187	$ .25	$ .85
Kirkland, Willie	64T	17	$ .25	$ .85
Kirkland, Willie	65T	148	$ .25	$ .65
Kirkland, Willie	66T	434	$ .25	$ .85
Kirkpatrick, Ed	63T	386	$ .50	$1.95
Kirkpatrick, Ed	64T	296	$ .25	$ .85
Kirkpatrick, Ed	65T	393	$ .30	$1.00
Kirkpatrick, Ed	66T	102	$ .25	$ .85
Kirkpatrick, Ed	67T	293	$ .25	$ .65
Kirkpatrick, Ed	68T	552	$ .30	$1.00
Kirkpatrick, Ed	69T	529	$ .25	$ .85
Kirkpatrick, Ed	70T	165	$ .10	$ .35
Kirkpatrick, Ed	71T	299	$ .10	$ .35
Kirkpatrick, Ed	72T	569	$ .25	$ .85
Kirkpatrick, Ed	72TIA	570	$ .25	$ .85
Kirkpatrick, Ed	73T	233	$ .06	$ .25
Kirkpatrick, Ed	74T	262	$ .06	$ .25
Kirkpatrick, Ed	74TTR	262	$ .06	$ .25
Kirkpatrick, Ed	75T	171	$ .06	$ .25
Kirkpatrick, Ed	76T	294	$ .05	$ .20
Kirkpatrick, Ed	77T	582	$ .03	$ .12
Kirkpatrick, Ed	78T	77	$ .02	$ .10
Kirkwood, Don	76T	108	$ .05	$ .20
Kirkwood, Don	77T	519	$ .03	$ .12
Kirkwood, Don	78T	251	$ .02	$ .10
Kirkwood, Don	79T	632	$ .02	$ .10
Kison, Bruce	72T	72	$ .25	$ .65
Kison, Bruce	73T	141	$ .06	$ .25
Kison, Bruce	75T	598	$ .06	$ .25
Kison, Bruce	76T	161	$ .05	$ .20
Kison, Bruce	77T	563	$ .03	$ .12
Kison, Bruce	78T	223	$ .02	$ .10
Kison, Bruce	79T	661	$ .02	$ .10
Kison, Bruce	80T	28	$ .01	$ .07
Kison, Bruce	81T	340	$ .01	$ .07
Kison, Bruce	82T	442	$ .01	$ .06
Kison, Bruce	83T	712	$ .01	$ .06
Kison, Bruce	84T	201	$ .01	$ .05
Kison, Bruce	85T	544	$ .01	$ .04
Kison, Bruce	85TTR	67	$ .02	$ .10
Kison, Bruce	86T	117	$ .01	$ .03
Kissell, George	73T	497	$ .25	$ .65
Kissell, George	74T	236	$ .06	$ .25
Kittle, Hub	73T	624	$ .55	$1.75
Kittle, Hub	74T	31	$ .06	$ .25
Kittle, Ron	83TTR	55	$ .15	$ .50
Kittle, Ron	84T	480	$ .02	$ .10
Kittle, Ron	85T	105	$ .01	$ .04
Kittle, Ron	86T	574	$ .01	$ .03
Kittle, Ron	87T	584	$ .01	$ .03
Kittle, Ron	88T	259	$ .01	$ .03
Kittle, Ron	88TTR	58	$ .01	$ .05
Kittle, Ron	89T	771	$ .01	$ .04
Kittle, Ron	89TTR	62	$ .01	$ .05
Kittle, Ron	90T	79	$ .01	$ .03
Klages, Fred	67T	373	$ .25	$ .85
Klages, Fred	68T	229	$ .25	$ .65
Klaus, Billy	56T	217	$2.50	$8.00
Klaus, Billy	57T	292	$3.50	$13.00
Klaus, Billy	58T	89	$1.00	$3.75
Klaus, Billy	59T	299	$ .50	$1.95
Klaus, Billy	60T	406	$ .50	$1.95
Klaus, Billy	61T	187	$ .30	$1.00
Klaus, Billy	62T	571	$3.75	$11.00
Klaus, Billy	63T	551	$1.50	$3.75
Klaus, Bobby	64T	524	$1.50	$3.75
Klaus, Bobby	65T	227	$ .30	$1.00
Klaus, Bobby	66T	108	$ .25	$ .85
Klaus, Bobby	69T	387	$ .25	$ .65
Klein, Lou	60T	457	$ .95	$3.50
Klimchock, Lou	60T	137	$ .35	$1.10
Klimchock, Lou	61T	462	$ .50	$2.00
Klimchock, Lou	62T	259	$ .35	$1.10
Klimchock, Lou	63T	542	$1.50	$3.75
Klimchock, Lou	65T	542	$1.50	$3.75
Klimchock, Lou	66T	589	$4.50	$15.00
Klimchock, Lou	70T	247	$ .10	$ .35
Klimkowski, Ron	70T	702	$ .50	$2.00
Klimkowski, Ron	71T	28	$ .10	$ .35
Klimkowski, Ron	72T	363	$ .05	$ .25
Kline, Johnny	55T	173	$4.25	$13.00
Kline, Ron	53T	175	$3.75	$13.00
Kline, Ronnie	56T	94	$1.25	$4.50
Kline, Ronnie	57T	256	$ .95	$3.50
Kline, Ronnie	58T	82	$1.00	$3.75
Kline, Ron	59T	265	$ .50	$1.95
Kline, Ron	59T	428	$ .50	$1.95
Kline, Ron	60T	197	$ .35	$1.10
Kline, Ron	61T	127	$ .30	$1.00
Kline, Ron	62T	216	$ .35	$1.10
Kline, Ron	63T	84	$ .25	$ .85
Kline, Ron	64T	358	$ .25	$ .85
Kline, Ron	65T	56	$ .25	$ .65
Kline, Ron	66T	453	$ .70	$2.10
Kline, Ron	67T	133	$ .25	$ .65
Kline, Ron	68T	446	$ .25	$ .65
Kline, Ron "Ronnie"	69T	243	$ .25	$ .85
Kline, Steve	71T	51	$ .10	$ .35
Kline, Steve	72T	467	$ .05	$ .25
Kline, Steve	73T	172	$ .06	$ .25
Kline, Steve	74T	324	$ .06	$ .25
Kline, Steve	75T	639	$ .06	$ .25
Klippstein, Johnny	52T	148	$6.00	$19.00
Klippstein, Johnny	53T	46	$3.75	$13.00
Klippstein, Johnny	54T	31	$2.10	$7.50
Klippstein, Johnny	56T	249	$2.50	$8.00
Klippstein, Johnny	57T	296	$3.50	$13.00
Klippstein, Johnny	58T	242	$ .50	$2.00
Klippstein, Johnny	59T	152	$ .50	$1.95
Klippstein, Johnny	60T	191	$ .35	$1.10
Klippstein, Johnny	61T	539	$6.00	$18.00
Klippstein, Johnny	62T	151	$ .35	$1.10
Klippstein, Johnny	63T	571	$1.50	$3.75
Klippstein, Johnny	64T	533	$1.50	$3.75
Klippstein, Johnny	65T	384	$ .30	$1.00
Klippstein, Johnny	66T	493	$ .70	$2.10
Klippstein, Johnny	67T	588	$1.25	$3.50
Kluszewski, Ted	51Trb	39	$2.25	$6.75
Kluszewski, Ted	52T	29	$25.00	$75.00
Kluszewski, Ted	53T	162	$8.00	$30.00
Kluszewski, Ted	54T	7	$5.00	$15.00
Kluszewski, Ted	55T	120	$4.00	$12.50

TOPPS

Player	Year	No.	VG	EX/MT	Player	Year	No.	VG	EX/MT
Kluszewski, Ted	56T	25	$3.00	$9.00	Knowles, Darold	71T	261	$ .10	$ .35
Kluszewski, Ted	57T	165	$3.00	$9.00	Knowles, Darold	72T	583	$ .25	$ .85
Kluszewski, Ted	58T	178	$1.35	$4.00	Knowles, Darold	73T	274	$ .06	$ .25
Kluszewski, Ted	58T	321	$7.00	$30.00	Knowles, Darold	74T	57	$ .06	$ .25
Kluszewski, Ted	59T	17	$1.50	$3.75	Knowles, Darold	75T	352	$ .06	$ .25
Kluszewski, Ted	59T	35	$1.80	$6.00	Knowles, Darold	76T	617	$ .05	$ .20
Kluszewski, Ted	60T	505	$1.25	$4.50	Knowles, Darold	77T	169	$ .03	$ .12
Kluszewski, Ted	61T	65	$1.00	$3.00	Knowles, Darold	78T	414	$ .02	$ .10
Kluszewski, Ted	73T	296	$ .15	$ .50	Knowles, Darold	79T	581	$ .02	$ .10
Kluszewski, Ted	74T	326	$ .15	$ .50	Knowles, Darold	80T	286	$ .01	$ .07
Klutts, Mickey	77T	490	$ .03	$ .12	Knox, John	74T	604	$1.00	$3.00
Klutts, Mickey	78T	707	$10.00	$40.00	Knox, John	75T	546	$ .06	$ .25
Klutts, Mickey	80T	717	$ .01	$ .07	Knox, John	76T	218	$ .05	$ .20
Klutts, Mickey	81T	232	$ .01	$ .07	Knudson, Mark	88T	61	$ .01	$ .10
Klutts, Mickey	82T	148	$ .01	$ .06	Knudson, Mark	90T	566	$ .01	$ .03
Klutts, Mickey	83T	571	$ .01	$ .06	Kobel, Kevin	74T	605	$ .30	$1.50
Klutts, Mickey	83TTR	56	$ .02	$ .10	Kobel, Kevin	75T	337	$ .06	$ .25
Kluttz, Clyde	52T	132	$6.00	$19.00	Kobel, Kevin	76T	588	$ .05	$ .20
Knapp, Chris	77T	247	$ .03	$ .12	Kobel, Kevin	79T	21	$ .02	$ .10
Knapp, Chris	78T	361	$ .02	$ .10	Kobel, Kevin	80T	189	$ .01	$ .07
Knapp, Chris	79T	453	$ .02	$ .10	Koegel, Pete	71T	633	$ .30	$1.00
Knapp, Chris	80T	658	$ .01	$ .07	Koegel, Pete	72T	14	$ .10	$ .35
Knapp, Chris	81T	557	$ .01	$ .07	Kokos, Dick	51Trb	19	$1.25	$3.50
Knepper, Bob	78T	589	$ .05	$ .25	Kokos, Dick	53T	232	$11.00	$37.50
Knepper, Bob	79T	486	$ .02	$ .10	Kokos, Dick	54T	106	$2.10	$7.50
Knepper, Bob	80T	111	$ .01	$ .07	Kolb, Gary	64T	119	$ .25	$ .85
Knepper, Bob	81T	279	$ .01	$ .07	Kolb, Gary	65T	287	$ .30	$1.00
Knepper, Bob	81TTR	782	$ .02	$ .10	Kolb, Gary	68T	407	$ .25	$ .65
Knepper, Bob	82T	672	$ .01	$ .06	Kolb, Gary	69T	307	$ .25	$ .85
Knepper, Bob	83T	382	$ .01	$ .06	Kolloway, Don	52T	104	$6.00	$19.00
Knepper, Bob	84T	93	$ .01	$ .05	Kolloway, Don	53T	97	$3.75	$13.00
Knepper, Bob	85T	455	$ .01	$ .04	Kolstad, Hal	62T	276	$ .35	$1.10
Knepper, Bob	85TAS	721	$ .01	$ .04	Kolstad, Hal	63T	574	$1.50	$3.75
Knepper, Bob	86T	590	$ .01	$ .03	Komminsk, Brad	85T	292	$ .01	$ .04
Knepper, Bob	87T	722	$ .01	$ .03	Komminsk, Brad	86T	698	$ .01	$ .03
Knepper, Bob	88T	151	$ .01	$ .03	Komminsk, Brad	90T	476	$ .01	$ .03
Knepper, Bob	89T	280	$ .01	$ .04	Konieczny, Doug	75T	624	$ .06	$ .25
Knepper, Bob	90T	104	$ .01	$ .03	Konieczny, Doug	76T	602	$ .05	$ .20
Knicely, Alan	80T	678	$ .01	$ .07	Konstanty, Jim	52T	108	$6.00	$17.50
Knicely, Alan	81T	82	$ .01	$ .07	Konstanty, Jim	56T	321	$1.50	$4.50
Knicely, Alan	83T	117	$ .01	$ .06	Konstanty, Jim	61TMVP	479	$ .60	$1.75
Knicely, Alan	83TTR	57	$ .02	$ .10	Koonce, Cal	63T	31	$ .25	$ .85
Knicely, Alan	84T	323	$ .01	$ .05	Koonce, Cal	65T	34	$ .25	$ .65
Knicely, Alan	85TTR	68	$ .02	$ .10	Koonce, Cal	66T	278	$ .25	$ .85
Knicely, Alan	86T	418	$ .01	$ .03	Koonce, Cal	67T	171	$ .25	$ .65
Knight, Ray	78T	674	$ .30	$ .90	Koonce, Cal	68T	486	$ .30	$1.00
Knight, Ray	79T	401	$ .05	$ .20	Koonce, Cal	69T	303	$ .25	$ .85
Knight, Ray	80T	174	$ .01	$ .07	Koonce, Cal	70T	521	$ .10	$ .35
Knight, Ray	81T	325	$ .01	$ .07	Koonce, Cal "Calvin"	71T	254	$ .10	$ .35
Knight, Ray	82T	525	$ .01	$ .06	Koosman, Jerry	68T	177	$200.00	$700.00
Knight, Ray	82TTR	57	$ .05	$ .20	Koosman, Jerry	69T	90	$ .85	$2.25
Knight, Ray	83T	275	$ .01	$ .06	Koosman, Jerry	69TAS	434	$ .25	$ .65
Knight, Ray	83T	441	$ .01	$ .06	Koosman, Jerry	70T	610	$ .35	$1.10
Knight, Ray	84T	660	$ .01	$ .05	Koosman, Jerry	70TAS	468	$ .25	$ .85
Knight, Ray	85T	590	$ .01	$ .04	Koosman, Jerry	71T	335	$ .35	$1.10
Knight, Ray	86T	27	$ .01	$ .10	Koosman, Jerry	72T	697	$1.50	$5.00
Knight, Ray	87T	488	$ .01	$ .03	Koosman, Jerry	72TIA	698	$ .70	$2.75
Knight, Ray	87TTR	59	$ .01	$ .07	Koosman, Jerry	73T	184	$ .25	$ .65
Knight, Ray	88T	124	$ .01	$ .03	Koosman, Jerry	74T	356	$ .10	$ .35
Knight, Ray	88TTR	59	$ .01	$ .05	Koosman, Jerry	75T	19	$ .10	$ .35
Knoop, Bobby	64T	502	$ .40	$1.25	Koosman, Jerry	76T	64	$ .06	$ .25
Knoop, Bobby	65T	26	$ .25	$ .65	Koosman, Jerry	77T	300	$ .03	$ .12
Knoop, Bobby	66T	280	$ .25	$ .85	Koosman, Jerry	78T	565	$ .02	$ .10
Knoop, Bobby	67T	175	$ .25	$ .65	Koosman, Jerry	79T	655	$ .05	$ .20
Knoop, Bobby	68T	271	$ .25	$ .65	Koosman, Jerry	80T	275	$ .01	$ .07
Knoop, Bobby	69T	445	$ .25	$ .65	Koosman, Jerry	81T	476	$ .01	$ .07
Knoop, Bobby	70T	695	$ .50	$2.00	Koosman, Jerry	82T	714	$ .01	$ .06
Knoop, Bobby	71T	506	$ .10	$ .35	Koosman, Jerry	83T	153	$ .01	$ .06
Knoop, Bobby	72T	664	$ .70	$2.10	Koosman, Jerry	84T	311	$ .01	$ .05
Knowles, Darold	64T	418	$ .40	$1.25	Koosman, Jerry	84T	716	$ .01	$ .05
Knowles, Darold	65T	577	$1.50	$3.75	Koosman, Jerry	84TTR	64	$ .05	$ .20
Knowles, Darold	66T	27	$ .25	$ .85	Koosman, Jerry	85T	15	$ .01	$ .04
Knowles, Darold	67T	362	$ .25	$ .65	Koosman, Jerry	86T	505	$ .01	$ .03
Knowles, Darold	68T	483	$ .30	$1.00	Kopacz, George	71T	204	$ .10	$ .35
Knowles, Darold	70T	106	$ .10	$ .35	Koplitz, Howie	62T	114	$ .35	$1.10

Player	Year	No.	VG	EX/MT	Player	Year	No.	VG	EX/MT
Koplitz, Howie	63T	406	$ .35	$1.20	Kranepool, Ed	66T	212	$ .15	$ .50
Koplitz, Howie	64T	372	$ .40	$1.25	Kranepool, Ed	67T	186	$ .25	$ .65
Koplitz, Howie	66T	46	$ .25	$ .85	Kranepool, Ed	67T	452	$ .25	$ .85
Koppe, Joe	59T	517	$2.00	$7.00	Kranepool, Ed	68T	92	$ .25	$ .65
Koppe, Joe	60T	319	$ .50	$1.95	Kranepool, Ed	69T	381	$ .25	$ .85
Koppe, Joe	61T	179	$ .30	$1.00	Kranepool, Ed	70T	557	$ .25	$ .85
Koppe, Joe	62T	39	$ .35	$1.10	Kranepool, Ed	71T	573	$ .35	$1.10
Koppe, Joe	63T	396	$ .35	$1.20	Kranepool, Ed	72T	181	$ .05	$ .25
Koppe, Joe	64T	279	$ .25	$ .85	Kranepool, Ed	72TIA	182	$ .05	$ .25
Korcheck, Steve	58T	403	$ .50	$2.00	Kranepool, Ed	73T	329	$ .06	$ .25
Korcheck, Steve	59T	284	$ .50	$1.95	Kranepool, Ed	74T	561	$ .06	$ .25
Korcheck, Steve	60T	56	$ .35	$1.10	Kranepool, Ed	75T	324	$ .06	$ .25
Korince, George	67T	72	$ .25	$ .65	Kranepool, Ed	76T	314	$ .05	$ .20
Korince, George	67T	526	$ .50	$2.00	Kranepool, Ed	77T	201	$ .03	$ .12
Korince, George	68T	447	$ .25	$ .65	Kranepool, Ed	78T	49	$ .02	$ .10
Kosco, Andy	66T	264	$ .25	$ .85	Kranepool, Ed	79T	505	$ .02	$ .10
Kosco, Andy	67T	366	$ .25	$ .65	Kranepool, Ed	80T	641	$ .01	$ .07
Kosco, Andy	68T	524	$ .30	$1.00	Krausse, Lew	63T	104	$ .25	$ .85
Kosco, Andy	69T	139	$ .25	$ .65	Krausse, Lew	64T	334	$ .25	$ .85
Kosco, Andy	70T	535	$ .10	$ .35					
Kosco, Andy	71T	746	$ .70	$2.10					
Kosco, Andy	72T	376	$ .05	$ .25					
Kosco, Andy	74T	34	$ .06	$ .25					
Koshorek, Clem	52T	380	$39.00	$135.00					
Koshorek, Clem	53T	8	$3.75	$13.00					
Koslo, Dave	52T	336	$39.00	$135.00					
Kostro, Frank	63T	407	$ .35	$1.20					
Kostro, Frank	65T	459	$ .50	$2.00					
Kostro, Frank	68T	44	$ .25	$ .65					
Kostro, Frank	69T	242	$ .25	$ .85					
Koufax, Sandy	55T	123	$200.00	$800.00					
Koufax, Sandy	56T	79	$75.00	$225.00					
Koufax, Sandy	57T	302	$110.00	$350.00					
Koufax, Sandy	58T	187	$40.00	$120.00					
Koufax, Sandy	59T	163	$40.00	$120.00					
Koufax, Sandy	60T	343	$25.00	$75.00					
Koufax, Sandy	61T	49	$ .60	$1.75					
Koufax, Sandy	61T	207	$4.50	$14.00					
Koufax, Sandy	61T	344	$35.00	$110.00					
Koufax, Sandy	62T	5	$30.00	$100.00					
Koufax, Sandy	62T	60	$ .65	$1.75					
Koufax, Sandy	63T	5	$ .60	$1.75					
Koufax, Sandy	63T	9	$ .60	$1.75					
Koufax, Sandy	63T	210	$45.00	$135.00					
Koufax, Sandy	63T	412	$10.00	$40.00					
Koufax, Sandy	64T	1	$3.00	$12.00					
Koufax, Sandy	64T	3	$1.25	$3.50					
Koufax, Sandy	64T	5	$1.75	$5.00					
Koufax, Sandy	64T	200	$25.00	$77.50					
Koufax, Sandy	65T	8	$1.50	$3.75					
Koufax, Sandy	65T	300	$50.00	$150.00					
Koufax, Sandy	66T	100	$17.00	$57.50	Krausse, Lew	65T	462	$ .50	$2.00
Koufax, Sandy	66T	221	$ .65	$1.75	Krausse, Lew	66T	256	$ .25	$ .85
Koufax, Sandy	66T	223	$ .65	$1.75	Krausse, Lew	67T	565	$1.25	$3.50
Koufax, Sandy	66T	225	$1.00	$4.00	Krausse, Lew	68T	458	$ .30	$1.00
Koufax, Sandy	67T	234	$1.50	$3.75	Krausse, Lew	69T	23	$ .25	$ .65
Koufax, Sandy	67T	236	$2.50	$8.00	Krausse, Lew	70T	233	$ .10	$ .35
Koufax, Sandy	67T	238	$1.50	$3.75	Krausse, Lew	71T	372	$ .10	$ .35
Koufax, Sandy	75T	201	$ .50	$2.00	Krausse, Lew	72T	592	$ .25	$ .85
Koufax, Sandy	90TTB	665	$ .01	$ .05	Krausse, Lew	73T	566	$ .35	$1.10
Kraemer, Joe	89TMLD	68	$ .01	$ .05	Krausse, Lew	75T	603	$ .06	$ .25
Kralick, Jack	61T	36	$ .30	$1.00	Kravec, Ken	77T	389	$ .03	$ .12
Kralick, Jack	62T	346	$ .35	$1.10	Kravec, Ken	78T	439	$ .02	$ .10
Kralick, Jack	63T	448	$2.50	$6.50	Kravec, Ken	79T	283	$ .02	$ .10
Kralick, Jack	64T	338	$ .25	$ .85	Kravec, Ken	80T	575	$ .01	$ .07
Kralick, Jack	65T	535	$1.50	$3.75	Kravec, Ken	81T	67	$ .01	$ .07
Kralick, Jack	66T	129	$ .25	$ .85	Kravec, Ken	81TTR	783	$ .02	$ .10
Kralick, Jack	67T	316	$ .25	$ .65	Kravec, Ken	82T	639	$ .01	$ .06
Kraly, Steve	55T	139	$1.35	$5.00	Kravitz, Danny	57T	267	$3.50	$13.00
Kramer, Randy	89T	522	$ .01	$ .15	Kravitz, Danny	58T	444	$ .50	$1.95
Kramer, Randy	90T	126	$ .01	$ .03	Kravitz, Danny	59T	536	$2.00	$7.00
Kranepool, Ed	63T	228	$9.00	$35.00	Kravitz, Danny	60T	238	$ .35	$1.10
Kranepool, Ed	64T	393	$1.25	$3.50	Kravitz, Danny	61T	166	$ .30	$1.00
Kranepool, Ed	64T	566	$1.25	$3.50	Krenchicki, Wayne	80T	661	$ .01	$ .07
Kranepool, Ed	65T	144	$ .25	$ .65	Krenchicki, Wayne	82T	107	$ .01	$ .06

PITCHER
LEW KRAUSSE

TOPPS

Player	Year	No.	VG	EX/MT	Player	Year	No.	VG	EX/MT
Krenchicki, Wayne	82TTR	58	$ .02	$ .10	Kucab, John	52T	358	$39.00	$135.00
Krenchicki, Wayne	83T	374	$ .01	$ .06	Kucek, John "Jack"	75T	614	$ .06	$ .25
Krenchicki, Wayne	84T	223	$ .01	$ .05	Kucek, Jack	76T	597	$ .25	$ .65
Krenchicki, Wayne	84TTR	65	$ .02	$ .10	Kucek, Jack	77T	623	$ .03	$ .12
Krenchicki, Wayne	85T	468	$ .01	$ .04	Kucks, Johnny	56T	88	$1.25	$4.50
Krenchicki, Wayne	86T	777	$ .01	$ .03	Kucks, Johnny	57T	185	$ .60	$2.50
Krenchicki, Wayne	86TTR	55	$ .02	$ .10	Kucks, Johnny	58T	87	$1.00	$3.75
Krenchicki, Wayne	87T	774	$ .01	$ .03	Kucks, Johnny	59T	289	$ .50	$1.95
Kress, Chuck	54T	219	$2.10	$7.50	Kucks, Johnny	60T	177	$ .35	$1.10
Kress, Red	54T	160	$2.10	$7.50	Kucks, Johnny	61T	94	$ .30	$1.00
Kress, Red	55T	151	$2.00	$7.00	Kucks, Johnny	62T	241	$ .35	$1.10
Kress, Red	60T	460	$1.25	$4.50	Kuenn, Harvey	54T	25	$6.00	$20.00
Kretlow, Lou	52T	42	$14.00	$45.00	Kuenn, Harvey	56T	155	$1.75	$5.00
Kretlow, Lou	57T	139	$ .95	$3.50	Kuenn, Harvey	57T	88	$1.00	$4.00
Kreuter, Chad	89T	432	$ .01	$ .15	Kuenn, Harvey	58T	304	$3.25	$9.50
Kreuter, Chad	90T	562	$ .01	$ .03	Kuenn, Harvey	58T	434	$1.00	$3.00
Kreutzer, Frank	64T	107	$ .25	$ .85	Kuenn, Harvey	59T	70	$1.00	$3.00
Kreutzer, Frank	65T	371	$ .30	$1.00	Kuenn, Harvey	60T	330	$ .60	$1.75
Kreutzer, Frank	66T	211	$ .25	$ .85	Kuenn, Harvey	60T	429	$ .60	$1.75
Kroll, Gary	65T	449	$ .50	$2.00	Kuenn, Harvey	61T	500	$ .75	$2.00
Kroll, Gary	66T	548	$4.50	$15.00	Kuenn, Harvey	62T	480	$1.00	$3.75
Krsnich, Mike	62T	289	$ .35	$1.10	Kuenn, Harvey	63T	30	$ .35	$1.10
Krsnich, Rocky	53T	229	$11.00	$37.50	Kuenn, Harvey	64T	242	$ .25	$ .80
Krueger, Bill	84T	178	$ .01	$ .05	Kuenn, Harvey	65T	103	$ .15	$ .50
Krueger, Bill	85T	528	$ .01	$ .04	Kuenn, Harvey	66T	372	$ .30	$1.00
Krueger, Bill	86T	58	$ .01	$ .03	Kuenn, Harvey	73T	646	$ .50	$2.00
Krueger, Bill	87T	238	$ .01	$ .03	Kuenn, Harvey	74T	99	$ .06	$ .25
Krueger, Bill	90T	518	$ .01	$ .03	Kuenn, Harvey	83T	726	$ .01	$ .06
Krug, Chris	66T	166	$ .25	$ .85	Kuenn, Harvey	84T	321	$ .01	$ .05
Kruk, John	86TTR	56	$ .30	$1.50	Kuhaulua, Fred	82T	731	$ .01	$ .06
Kruk, John	87T	123	$ .30	$1.00	Kuhn, Ken	57T	266	$3.50	$13.00
Kruk, John	88T	596	$ .01	$ .25	Kuiper, Duane	76T	508	$ .05	$ .20
Kruk, John	88TBB	60	$ .01	$ .05	Kuiper, Duane	77T	85	$ .03	$ .12
Kruk, John	89T	235	$ .01	$ .04	Kuiper, Duane	78T	332	$ .02	$ .10
Kruk, John	89TBB	216	$ .01	$ .05	Kuiper, Duane	79T	146	$ .02	$ .10
Kruk, John	89TBV	63	$ .01	$ .05	Kuiper, Duane	80T	429	$ .01	$ .07
Kruk, John	90T	469	$ .01	$ .03	Kuiper, Duane	81T	612	$ .01	$ .07
Krukow, Mike	77T	493	$ .25	$ .80	Kuiper, Duane	82T	233	$ .01	$ .06
Krukow, Mike	78T	17	$ .02	$ .10	Kuiper, Duane	82TTR	60	$ .02	$ .10
Krukow, Mike	79T	592	$ .02	$ .10	Kuiper, Duane	83T	767	$ .01	$ .06
Krukow, Mike	80T	431	$ .01	$ .07	Kuiper, Duane	84T	542	$ .01	$ .05
Krukow, Mike	81T	176	$ .01	$ .07	Kuiper, Duane	85T	22	$ .01	$ .04
Krukow, Mike	82T	215	$ .01	$ .06	Kunkel, Bill	61T	322	$ .30	$1.00
Krukow, Mike	82TTR	59	$ .02	$ .10	Kunkel, Bill	62T	147	$ .60	$1.75
Krukow, Mike	83T	331	$ .01	$ .06	Kunkel, Bill	63T	523	$1.50	$3.75
Krukow, Mike	83TTR	58	$ .02	$ .10	Kunkel, Bill	85T	136	$ .01	$ .10
Krukow, Mike	84T	633	$ .01	$ .05	Kunkel, Jeff	85T	136	$ .01	$ .10
Krukow, Mike	85T	74	$ .01	$ .04	Kunkel, Jeff	85T	288	$ .01	$ .04
Krukow, Mike	86T	752	$ .01	$ .03	Kunkel, Jeff	89T	92	$ .01	$ .04
Krukow, Mike	87T	580	$ .01	$ .03	Kunkel, Jeff	90T	174	$ .01	$ .03
Krukow, Mike	88T	445	$ .01	$ .03	Kuntz, Rusty	81T	112	$ .01	$ .07
Krukow, Mike	89T	125	$ .01	$ .04	Kuntz, Rusty	82T	237	$ .01	$ .06
Krukow, Mike	90T	241	$ .01	$ .03	Kuntz, Rusty	84T	598	$ .01	$ .05
Kryhoski, Dick	52T	149	$4.50	$3.00	Kuntz, Rusty	84TTR	66	$ .02	$ .10
Kryhoski, Dick	54T	150	$2.10	$7.50	Kuntz, Rusty	85T	73	$ .01	$ .04
Kubek, Tony	57T	312	$35.00	$100.00	Kusick, Craig	75T	297	$ .06	$ .25
Kubek, Tony	58T	393	$3.00	$9.00	Kusick, Craig	77T	38	$ .03	$ .12
Kubek, Tony	59T	505	$3.00	$9.00	Kusick, Craig	78T	137	$ .02	$ .10
Kubek, Tony	60T	83	$1.25	$3.50	Kusick, Craig	79T	472	$ .02	$ .10
Kubek, Tony	61T	265	$1.35	$4.00	Kusick, Craig	80T	693	$ .01	$ .07
Kubek, Tony	62T	311	$1.25	$4.50	Kusnyer, Art	72T	213	$ .10	$ .35
Kubek, Tony	62T	430	$1.50	$4.00	Kutcher, Randy	89TTR	64	$ .01	$ .05
Kubek, Tony	63T	20	$ .70	$2.00	Kutcher, Randy	90T	676	$ .01	$ .03
Kubek, Tony	64T	415	$ .30	$2.50	Kutyna, Marty	60T	516	$2.00	$7.00
Kubek, Tony	65T	65	$1.50	$3.75	Kutyna, Marty	61T	546	$6.00	$18.00
Kubiak, Ted	68T	79	$ .25	$ .65	Kutyna, Marty	62T	566	$3.75	$11.00
Kubiak, Ted	69T	281	$ .25	$ .85	Kuzava, Bob	51Tbb	22	$5.50	$17.00
Kubiak, Ted	70T	688	$ .50	$2.00	Kuzava, Bob	52T	85	$7.00	$20.00
Kubiak, Ted	71T	516	$ .10	$ .35	Kuzava, Bob	54T	230	$4.75	$14.00
Kubiak, Ted	72T	23	$ .05	$ .25	Labine, Clem	52T	342	$70.00	$210.00
Kubiak, Ted	73T	652	$ .35	$1.10	Labine, Clem	53T	14	$4.50	$15.00
Kubiak, Ted	74T	228	$ .06	$ .25	Labine, Clem	54T	121	$1.75	$7.00
Kubiak, Ted	75T	329	$ .06	$ .25	Labine, Clem	55T	180	$1.25	$10.00
Kubiak, Ted	76T	578	$ .05	$ .20	Labine, Clem	56T	295	$2.00	$6.00
Kubiak, Ted	77T	158	$ .03	$ .12	Labine, Clem	57T	53	$ .95	$3.50

Player	Year	No.	VG	EX/MT
Labine, Clem	58T	305	$ .45	$1.50
Labine, Clem	59T	262	$3.00	$12.00
Labine, Clem	59T	403	$ .50	$1.95
Labine, Clem	60T	29	$ .35	$1.10
Labine, Clem	61T	22	$ .30	$1.00
Laboy, Jose	69T	524	$ .25	$ .85
Laboy, Jose	70T	238	$ .10	$ .35
Laboy, Jose	71T	132	$ .10	$ .35
Laboy, Jose	72T	727	$ .70	$2.10
Laboy, Jose	73T	642	$ .35	$1.10
Lacey, Bob	78T	29	$ .02	$ .10
Lacey, Bob	79T	647	$ .02	$ .10
Lacey, Bob	80T	316	$ .01	$ .07
Lacey, Bob	81T	481	$ .01	$ .07
Lacey, Bob	81TTR	784	$ .02	$ .10
Lacey, Bob	82T	103	$ .01	$ .06
Lachemann, Marcel	71T	84	$ .10	$ .35
Lachemann, Rene	65T	526	$40.00	$105.00
Lachemann, Rene	66T	157	$ .25	$ .85

RENE LACHEMANN • C

ATHLETICS

Player	Year	No.	VG	EX/MT
Lachemann, Rene	67T	471	$ .50	$2.00
Lachemann, Rene	68T	422	$ .25	$ .65
Lachemann, Rene	83T	336	$ .01	$ .06
Lachemann, Rene	84TTR	67	$ .02	$ .10
Lachemann, Rene	85T	628	$ .01	$ .04
LaCock, Pete	75T	494	$ .06	$ .25
LaCock, Pete	76T	101	$ .05	$ .20
LaCock, Pete	77T	561	$ .03	$ .12
LaCock, Pete	78T	157	$ .02	$ .10
LaCock, Pete	79T	248	$ .02	$ .10
LaCock, Pete	80T	389	$ .01	$ .07
LaCock, Pete	81T	9	$ .01	$ .07
LaCorte, Frank	76T	597	$ .25	$ .65
LaCorte, Frank	80T	411	$ .01	$ .07
LaCorte, Frank	81T	513	$ .01	$ .07
LaCorte, Frank	82T	248	$ .01	$ .06
LaCorte, Frank	83T	14	$ .01	$ .06
LaCorte, Frank	84T	301	$ .01	$ .05
LaCorte, Frank	84TTR	68	$ .02	$ .10
LaCorte, Frank	85T	153	$ .01	$ .04
LaCoss, Mike	79T	717	$ .05	$ .20
LaCoss, Mike	80T	199	$ .01	$ .07
LaCoss, Mike	81T	474	$ .01	$ .07
LaCoss, Mike	82T	294	$ .01	$ .06

Player	Year	No.	VG	EX/MT
LaCoss, Mike	82TTR	61	$ .02	$ .10
LaCoss, Mike	83T	92	$ .01	$ .06
LaCoss, Mike	84T	507	$ .01	$ .05
LaCoss, Mike	85T	666	$ .01	$ .04
LaCoss, Mike	85TTR	69	$ .02	$ .10
LaCoss, Mike	86T	359	$ .01	$ .03
LaCoss, Mike	86TTR	57	$ .02	$ .10
LaCoss, Mike	87T	151	$ .01	$ .03
LaCoss, Mike	88T	754	$ .01	$ .03
LaCoss, Mike	89T	417	$ .01	$ .04
LaCoss, Mike	90T	53	$ .01	$ .03
Lacy, Lee	73T	391	$ .06	$ .25
Lacy, Lee	74T	658	$ .06	$ .25
Lacy, Lee	75T	631	$ .06	$ .25
Lacy, Lee	76T	99	$ .05	$ .20
Lacy, Lee	76TTR	99	$ .05	$ .20
Lacy, Lee	77T	272	$ .03	$ .12
Lacy, Lee	78T	104	$ .02	$ .10
Lacy, Lee	79T	441	$ .02	$ .10
Lacy, Lee	80T	536	$ .01	$ .07
Lacy, Lee	81T	332	$ .01	$ .07
Lacy, Lee	82T	752	$ .01	$ .06
Lacy, Lee	83T	69	$ .01	$ .06
Lacy, Lee	84T	462	$ .01	$ .05
Lacy, Lee	85T	669	$ .01	$ .04
Lacy, Lee	85TTR	70	$ .02	$ .10
Lacy, Lee	86T	226	$ .01	$ .03
Lacy, Lee	87T	182	$ .01	$ .03
Lacy, Lee	88T	598	$ .01	$ .03
Ladd, Pete	80T	678	$ .01	$ .07
Ladd, Pete	84T	243	$ .01	$ .05
Ladd, Pete	85T	471	$ .01	$ .04
Ladd, Pete	86T	163	$ .01	$ .03
Ladd, Pete	86TTR	58	$ .02	$ .10
Ladd, Pete	87T	572	$ .01	$ .03
LaFrancois, Roger	83T	344	$ .01	$ .06
Laga, Mike	86TTR	59	$ .02	$ .10
Laga, Mike	87T	321	$ .01	$ .03
LaGrow, Lerrin	71T	39	$ .10	$ .35
LaGrow, Lerrin	73T	369	$ .06	$ .25
LaGrow, Lerrin	74T	433	$ .06	$ .25
LaGrow, Lerrin	75T	116	$ .06	$ .25
LaGrow, Lerrin	76T	138	$ .05	$ .20
LaGrow, Lerrin	78T	14	$ .02	$ .10
LaGrow, Lerrin	79T	527	$ .02	$ .10
LaGrow, Lerrin	80T	624	$ .01	$ .07
Lahoud, Joe	69T	189	$ .25	$ .65
Lahoud, Joe	70T	78	$ .10	$ .35
Lahoud, Joe	71T	622	$ .30	$1.00
Lahoud, Joe	72T	321	$ .05	$ .25
Lahoud, Joe	73T	212	$ .06	$ .25
Lahoud, Joe	74T	512	$ .06	$ .25
Lahoud, Joe	75T	317	$ .06	$ .25
Lahoud, Joe	76T	612	$ .05	$ .20
Lahoud, Joe	78T	382	$ .02	$ .10
Lahti, Jeff	83T	284	$ .01	$ .06
Lahti, Jeff	84T	593	$ .01	$ .05
Lahti, Jeff	85T	447	$ .01	$ .04
Lahti, Jeff	86T	33	$ .01	$ .03
Lahti, Jeff	87T	367	$ .01	$ .03
Lake, Steve	84T	691	$ .01	$ .05
Lake, Steve	85T	98	$ .01	$ .04
Lake, Steve	86T	588	$ .01	$ .03
Lake, Steve	87T	84	$ .01	$ .03
Lake, Steve	88T	208	$ .01	$ .03
Lake, Steve	89T	463	$ .01	$ .04
Lake, Steve	89TTR	65	$ .01	$ .05
Lake, Steve	90T	183	$ .01	$ .03
Lamabe, Jack	62T	593	$6.00	$18.00
Lamabe, Jack	63T	251	$ .25	$ .85
Lamabe, Jack	64T	305	$ .25	$ .85
Lamabe, Jack	65T	88	$ .25	$ .65
Lamabe, Jack	66T	577	$4.50	$15.00
Lamabe, Jack	67T	208	$ .25	$ .65
Lamabe, Jack	68T	311	$ .25	$ .65

Player	Year	No.	VG	EX/MT	Player	Year	No.	VG	EX/MT
Lamanczyk, Dave	81T	391	$ .01	$ .07	Landrum, Don	61T	338	$ .30	$1.00
LaMay, Dick	62T	71	$ .35	$1.10	Landrum, Don	62T	323	$ .35	$1.10
Lamb, Ray	70T	131	$ .10	$ .35	Landrum, Don	63T	113	$ .30	$1.00
Lamb, Ray	71T	727	$ .70	$2.10	Landrum, Don	64T	286	$ .25	$ .85
Lamb, Ray	72T	422	$ .05	$ .25	Landrum, Don	65T	596	$1.50	$3.75
Lamb, Ray	73T	496	$ .06	$ .25	Landrum, Don	66T	43	$ .25	$ .85
Lamont, Gene	71T	39	$ .10	$ .35	Landrum, Tito	81T	244	$ .01	$ .07
Lamont, Gene	75T	593	$ .06	$ .25	Landrum, Tito	82T	658	$ .01	$ .06
Lamp, Dennis	78T	711	$ .02	$ .10	Landrum, Tito	83T	337	$ .01	$ .06
Lamp, Dennis	79T	153	$ .02	$ .10	Landrum, Tito	85T	33	$ .01	$ .04
Lamp, Dennis	80T	54	$ .01	$ .07	Landrum, Tito	86T	498	$ .01	$ .03
Lamp, Dennis	81T	331	$ .01	$ .07	Landrum, Tito	87T	288	$ .01	$ .03
Lamp, Dennis	81TTR	785	$ .02	$ .10	Landrum, Tito	88T	581	$ .01	$ .03
Lamp, Dennis	82T	216	$ .01	$ .06	Lane, Jerry	54T	97	$2.10	$7.50
Lamp, Dennis	82T	622	$ .01	$ .06	Lang, Chip	77T	132	$ .03	$ .12
Lamp, Dennis	83T	434	$ .01	$ .06	Lange, Dick	74T	429	$ .06	$ .25
Lamp, Dennis	84T	541	$ .01	$ .05	Lange, Dick	75T	114	$ .06	$ .25
Lamp, Dennis	84TTR	69	$ .02	$ .10	Lange, Dick	76T	176	$ .05	$ .20
Lamp, Dennis	85T	774	$ .01	$ .04	Langford, Rick	78T	327	$ .02	$ .10
Lamp, Dennis	86T	219	$ .01	$ .03	Langford, Rick	79T	29	$ .02	$ .10
Lamp, Dennis	87T	768	$ .01	$ .03	Langford, Rick	80T	546	$ .01	$ .07
Lamp, Dennis	89T	188	$ .01	$ .04	Langford, Rick	81T	154	$ .01	$ .07
Lamp, Dennis	89TBB	169	$ .01	$ .05	Langford, Rick	82T	454	$ .01	$ .06
Lamp, Dennis	90T	338	$ .01	$ .03	Langford, Rick	83T	286	$ .01	$ .06
Lampard, Keith	70T	492	$ .10	$ .35	Langford, Rick	83T	531	$ .01	$ .06
Lampard, Keith	71T	728	$ .70	$2.10	Langford, Rick	84T	629	$ .01	$ .05
Lampard, Keith	72T	489	$ .05	$ .25	Langford, Rick	85T	347	$ .01	$ .04
Lampkin, Tom	90T	172	$ .01	$ .03	Langford, Rick	86T	766	$ .01	$ .03
Lancaster, Les	88T	112	$ .01	$ .15	Langston, Mark	84TTR	70	$5.50	$17.50
Lancaster, Les	89T	694	$ .01	$ .04	Langston, Mark	85T	625	$ .75	$3.00
Lancaster, Les	90T	437	$ .01	$ .03	Langston, Mark	86T	495	$ .01	$ .40
Landestoy, Rafael	79T	14	$ .02	$ .10	Langston, Mark	87T	215	$ .01	$ .20
Landestoy, Rafael	80T	268	$ .01	$ .07	Langston, Mark	88T	80	$ .01	$ .10
Landestoy, Rafael	81T	597	$ .01	$ .07	Langston, Mark	88TBB	176	$ .01	$ .15
Landestoy, Rafael	81TTR	786	$ .02	$ .10	Langston, Mark	89T	355	$ .01	$ .10
Landestoy, Rafael	82T	361	$ .01	$ .06	Langston, Mark	89TTR	66	$ .01	$ .10
Landestoy, Rafael	83T	684	$ .01	$ .06	Langston, Mark	90T	530	$ .01	$ .10
Landestoy, Rafael	83TTR	59	$ .02	$ .10	Lanier, Hal	65T	118	$ .35	$1.10
Landestoy, Rafael	84T	477	$ .01	$ .05	Lanier, Hal	66T	156	$ .15	$ .50
Landis, Bill	68T	189	$ .25	$ .65	Lanier, Hal	66T	271	$ .25	$ .85
Landis, Bill	69T	264	$ .25	$ .85	Lanier, Hal	67T	4	$ .25	$ .65
Landis, Jim	57T	375	$1.00	$3.75	Lanier, Hal	68T	436	$ .25	$ .85
Landis, Jim	58T	108	$1.00	$3.75	Lanier, Hal	69T	316	$ .30	$1.00
Landis, Jim	59T	493	$ .50	$1.95	Lanier, Hal	70T	583	$ .25	$ .85
Landis, Jim	60T	550	$2.00	$7.00	Lanier, Hal	71T	181	$ .10	$ .35
Landis, Jim	61T	271	$ .30	$1.00	Lanier, Hal	72T	589	$ .35	$1.10
Landis, Jim	62T	540	$3.75	$11.00	Lanier, Hal	73T	479	$ .25	$ .65
Landis, Jim	63T	485	$2.50	$6.50	Lanier, Hal	74T	588	$ .06	$ .25
Landis, Jim	64T	264	$ .25	$ .85	Lanier, Hal	86TTR	60	$ .02	$ .10
Landis, Jim	65T	376	$ .30	$1.00	Lanier, Hal	87T	343	$ .01	$ .03
Landis, Jim	66T	128	$ .25	$ .85	Lanier, Hal	88T	684	$ .01	$ .03
Landis, Jim	67T	483	$ .50	$2.00	Lanier, Hal	89T	164	$ .01	$ .04
Landreaux, Ken	79T	619	$ .05	$ .20	Lanier, Max	52T	101	$6.00	$19.00
Landreaux, Ken	80T	88	$ .01	$ .07	Lansford, Carney	79T	212	$1.50	$4.50
Landreaux, Ken	81T	219	$ .01	$ .07	Lansford, Carney	80T	337	$ .25	$1.25
Landreaux, Ken	81TTR	787	$ .02	$ .10	Lansford, Carney	81T	639	$ .15	$ .75
Landreaux, Ken	82T	114	$ .01	$ .06	Lansford, Carney	81TTR	788	$ .02	$ .20
Landreaux, Ken	83T	376	$ .01	$ .06	Lansford, Carney	82T	91	$ .01	$ .06
Landreaux, Ken	84T	533	$ .01	$ .05	Lansford, Carney	82T	161	$ .03	$ .15
Landreaux, Ken	85T	418	$ .01	$ .04	Lansford, Carney	82T	786	$ .01	$ .06
Landreaux, Ken	86T	782	$ .01	$ .03	Lansford, Carney	83T	523	$ .01	$ .06
Landreaux, Ken	87T	699	$ .01	$ .03	Lansford, Carney	83TTR	60	$ .02	$ .10
Landreaux, Ken	88T	23	$ .01	$ .03	Lansford, Carney	84T	767	$ .01	$ .05
Landreth, Larry	78T	701	$ .02	$ .10	Lansford, Carney	85T	422	$ .01	$ .04
Landrith, Hobie	56T	314	$1.80	$6.00	Lansford, Carney	86T	134	$ .01	$ .03
Landrith, Hobie	57T	182	$ .95	$3.50	Lansford, Carney	87T	678	$ .01	$ .03
Landrith, Hobie	58T	24	$1.00	$3.75	Lansford, Carney	88T	292	$ .01	$ .03
Landrith, Hobie	59T	422	$ .50	$1.95	Lansford, Carney	88TBB	221	$ .01	$ .05
Landrith, Hobie	60T	42	$ .35	$1.10	Lansford, Carney	89T	47	$ .01	$ .04
Landrith, Hobie	61T	114	$ .30	$1.00	Lansford, Carney	89TBB	57	$ .01	$ .05
Landrith, Hobie	62T	279	$ .35	$1.10	Lansford, Carney	90T	316	$ .01	$ .03
Landrith, Hobie	63T	209	$ .25	$ .85	LaPalme, Paul	52T	166	$6.00	$19.00
Landrum, Bill	88T	42	$ .01	$ .03	LaPalme, Paul	53T	201	$3.75	$13.00
Landrum, Bill	90T	425	$ .01	$ .03	LaPalme, Paul	57T	344	$3.50	$13.00
Landrum, Don	58T	291	$ .50	$2.00	LaPoint, Dave	83T	438	$ .05	$ .25

Player	Year	No.	VG	EX/MT
LaPoint, Dave	84T	627	$ .01	$ .05
LaPoint, Dave	85T	229	$ .01	$ .04
LaPoint, Dave	85TTR	71	$ .02	$ .10
LaPoint, Dave	86T	551	$ .01	$ .03
LaPoint, Dave	86TTR	61	$ .02	$ .10
LaPoint, Dave	87T	754	$ .01	$ .03
LaPoint, Dave	88T	334	$ .01	$ .03
LaPoint, Dave	89T	89	$ .01	$ .04
LaPoint, Dave	89TTR	67	$ .01	$ .05
LaPoint, Dave	90T	186	$ .01	$ .03
Larker, Norm	59T	107	$1.00	$3.75
Larker, Norm	60T	394	$ .50	$1.95
Larker, Norm	61T	41	$1.50	$5.00
Larker, Norm	61T	130	$ .30	$1.00
Larker, Norm	62T	23	$ .35	$1.10
Larker, Norm	63T	536	$1.50	$3.75
Larkin, Barry	87T	648	$ .50	$2.00
Larkin, Barry	88T	102	$ .01	$ .35
Larkin, Barry	88TBB	74	$ .01	$ .15
Larkin, Barry	89T	515	$ .01	$ .15
Larkin, Barry	89TBB	199	$ .01	$ .15
Larkin, Barry	90T	10	$ .01	$ .15
Larkin, Gene	87TTR	60	$ .05	$ .30
Larkin, Gene	88T	746	$ .01	$ .25
Larkin, Gene	88TBB	264	$ .01	$ .05
Larkin, Gene	89T	318	$ .01	$ .04
Larkin, Gene	89TBB	226	$ .01	$ .05
Larkin, Gene	90T	556	$ .01	$ .03
LaRoche, Dave	71T	174	$ .10	$ .35
LaRoche, Dave	72T	352	$ .05	$ .25
LaRoche, Dave	73T	426	$ .06	$ .25
LaRoche, Dave	74T	502	$ .06	$ .25
LaRoche, Dave	75T	258	$ .06	$ .25
LaRoche, Dave	76T	21	$ .05	$ .20
LaRoche, Dave	77T	385	$ .03	$ .12
LaRoche, Dave	78T	454	$ .02	$ .10
LaRoche, Dave	79T	601	$ .02	$ .10
LaRoche, Dave	80T	263	$ .01	$ .07
LaRoche, Dave	81T	529	$ .01	$ .07
LaRoche, Dave	81TTR	789	$ .02	$ .10
LaRoche, Dave	82T	142	$ .01	$ .06
LaRoche, Dave	83T	333	$ .01	$ .06
LaRoche, Dave	83T	334	$ .01	$ .06
LaRose, Vic	69T	404	$ .25	$ .65
Larsen, Don	56T	332	$7.00	$28.00
Larsen, Don	57T	175	$2.50	$10.00
Larsen, Don	58T	161	$4.00	$12.50
Larsen, Don	59T	205	$3.00	$9.00
Larsen, Don	59T	383	$1.35	$4.00
Larsen, Don	60T	353	$ .45	$1.35
Larsen, Don	61T	177	$ .50	$2.00
Larsen, Don	61T	402	$1.35	$4.00
Larsen, Don	62T	33	$ .50	$2.00
Larsen, Don	63T	163	$ .35	$1.10
Larsen, Don	64T	513	$ .50	$1.95
Larsen, Don	65T	389	$ .35	$1.10
Larson, Dan	77T	641	$ .03	$ .12
LaRussa, Tony	64T	244	$1.25	$5.50
LaRussa, Tony	68T	571	$ .50	$2.00
LaRussa, Tony	72T	451	$ .05	$ .25
LaRussa, Tony	83T	216	$ .01	$ .06
LaRussa, Tony	84T	591	$ .01	$ .05
LaRussa, Tony	85T	466	$ .01	$ .04
LaRussa, Tony	86T	531	$ .01	$ .03
LaRussa, Tony	87T	68	$ .01	$ .03
LaRussa, Tony	88T	344	$ .01	$ .03
LaRussa, Tony	89T	224	$ .01	$ .04
LaRussa, Tony	90T	639	$ .01	$ .03
Lary, Frank	56T	191	$2.50	$8.00
Lary, Frank	57T	168	$ .95	$3.50
Lary, Frank	58T	245	$ .50	$2.00
Lary, Frank	59T	393	$ .50	$1.95
Lary, Frank	60T	85	$ .35	$1.10
Lary, Frank	61T	48	$ .50	$2.00
Lary, Frank	61T	50	$ .50	$1.95

Player	Year	No.	VG	EX/MT
Lary, Frank	61T	243	$ .30	$1.00
Lary, Frank	62T	57	$ .50	$1.95
Lary, Frank	62TAS	474	$ .70	$2.10
Lary, Frank	63T	140	$ .25	$ .85
Lary, Frank	63T	218	$ .35	$1.10
Lary, Frank	64T	197	$ .25	$ .85
Lary, Frank	65T	127	$ .25	$ .65
Lasher, Fred	68T	447	$ .25	$ .65
Lasher, Fred	69T	373	$ .25	$ .65
Lasher, Fred	70T	356	$ .10	$ .35
Lasher, Fred	71T	707	$ .70	$2.10
Laskey, Bill	83T	171	$ .01	$ .06
Laskey, Bill	83T	518	$ .01	$ .06
Laskey, Bill	84T	129	$ .01	$ .05
Laskey, Bill	85T	331	$ .01	$ .04
Laskey, Bill	86T	603	$ .01	$ .03
Lasorda, Tom	54T	132	$40.00	$125.00
Lasorda, Tom	73T	569	$1.00	$3.75
Lasorda, Tom	74T	144	$ .06	$ .25
Lasorda, Tom	78T	189	$ .05	$ .25

TOM LASORDA
MANAGER
LOS ANGELES DODGERS

Player	Year	No.	VG	EX/MT
Lasorda, Tom	83T	306	$ .01	$ .15
Lasorda, Tom	84T	681	$ .02	$ .10
Lasorda, Tom	85T	601	$ .01	$ .04
Lasorda, Tom	86T	291	$ .01	$ .03
Lasorda, Tom	87T	493	$ .01	$ .03
Lasorda, Tom	88T	74	$ .01	$ .03
Lasorda, Tom	89T	254	$ .01	$ .04
Lasorda, Tom	90T	669	$ .01	$ .03
Latman, Barry	59T	477	$ .50	$1.95
Latman, Barry	60T	41	$ .35	$1.10
Latman, Barry	61T	560	$6.00	$18.00
Latman, Barry	62T	37	$ .50	$2.00
Latman, Barry	62T	145	$ .35	$1.10
Latman, Barry	63T	426	$ .35	$1.20
Latman, Barry	64T	227	$ .25	$ .85
Latman, Barry	65T	307	$ .30	$1.00
Latman, Barry	66T	451	$ .70	$2.10
Latman, Barry	67T	28	$ .25	$ .65
Lau, Charley	64T	229	$ .25	$ .85
Lau, Charlie	58T	448	$ .65	$2.00
Lau, Charlie	60T	312	$ .50	$1.95
Lau, Charlie	61T	261	$ .30	$1.00
Lau, Charlie	62T	533	$3.75	$11.00

Player	Year	No.	VG	EX/MT	Player	Year	No.	VG	EX/MT
Lau, Charlie	63T	41	$ .25	$ .85	Law, Vern	63T	184	$ .30	$1.00
Lau, Charlie	65T	94	$ .25	$ .65	Law, Vern	64T	472	$ .50	$1.95
Lau, Charlie	66T	368	$ .25	$ .85	Law, Vern	65T	515	$ .60	$1.75
Lau, Charlie	73T	593	$ .50	$2.00	Law, Vern	66T	15	$ .35	$1.10
Lau, Charlie	74T	166	$ .06	$ .25	Law, Vern	66T	221	$ .65	$1.75
Laudner, Tim	82T	766	$1.50	$4.50	Law, Vern	67T	351	$ .25	$ .65
Laudner, Tim	83T	529	$ .01	$ .06	Law, Vern	85T	137	$ .01	$ .10
Laudner, Tim	84T	363	$ .01	$ .05	Lawless, Tom	83T	423	$ .01	$ .06
Laudner, Tim	85T	71	$ .01	$ .04	Lawless, Tom	86T	228	$ .01	$ .03
Laudner, Tim	86T	184	$ .01	$ .03	Lawless, Tom	87T	647	$ .01	$ .03
Laudner, Tim	87T	478	$ .01	$ .03	Lawless, Tom	88T	183	$ .01	$ .03
Laudner, Tim	88T	671	$ .01	$ .03	Lawless, Tom	89T	312	$ .01	$ .04
Laudner, Tim	88TBB	243	$ .01	$ .05	Lawless, Tom	90T	49	$ .01	$ .03
Laudner, Tim	89T	239	$ .01	$ .04	Lawrence, Brooks	56T	305	$1.80	$6.00
Laudner, Tim	90T	777	$ .01	$ .03	Lawrence, Brooks	57T	66	$ .95	$3.50
Lauzerique, George	69T	358	$ .25	$ .65	Lawrence, Brooks	58T	374	$ .50	$2.00
Lauzerique, George	70T	41	$ .10	$ .35	Lawrence, Brooks	59T	67	$1.00	$3.75
Lavagetto, Cookie	52T	365	$50.00	$155.00	Lawrence, Brooks	60T	434	$ .50	$1.95
Lavagetto, Cookie	59T	74	$ .95	$3.50	Lawson, Steve	73T	612	$ .35	$1.10
Lavagetto, Cookie	60T	221	$ .35	$1.10	Lawton, Marcus	89TMLD	69	$ .01	$ .25
Lavagetto, Harry "Cookie"	61T	226	$ .30	$1.00	Lawton, Marcus	90T	302	$ .01	$ .10
LaValliere, Mike	87T	·162	$ .03	$ .15	Laxton, Bill	77T	394	$ .03	$ .12
LaValliere, Mike	87TTR	61	$ .01	$ .07	Lazar, Dan	69T	439	$ .25	$ .65
LaValliere, Mike	88T	539	$ .01	$ .03	Lazar, Dan	70T	669	$ .50	$2.00
LaValliere, Mike	88TBB	61	$ .01	$ .05	Lazorko, Jack	85T	317	$ .01	$ .04
LaValliere, Mike	89T	218	$ .01	$ .04	Lazorko, Jack	87TTR	62	$ .01	$ .07
LaValliere, Mike	89TBB	306	$ .01	$ .05	Lazorko, Jack	88T	601	$ .01	$ .03
LaValliere, Mike	90T	478	$ .01	$ .03	Lazorko, Jack	89T	362	$ .01	$ .04
Lavelle, Gary	75T	624	$ .06	$ .25	Lea, Charlie	81T	293	$ .01	$ .07
Lavelle, Gary	76T	105	$ .05	$ .20	Lea, Charlie	82T	38	$ .01	$ .06
Lavelle, Gary	77T	423	$ .03	$ .12	Lea, Charlie	83T	629	$ .01	$ .06
Lavelle, Gary	78T	671	$ .02	$ .10	Lea, Charlie	84T	421	$ .01	$ .05
Lavelle, Gary	79T	311	$ .02	$ .10	Lea, Charlie	84T	516	$ .01	$ .05
Lavelle, Gary	80T	84	$ .01	$ .07	Lea, Charlie	85T	345	$ .01	$ .04
Lavelle, Gary	81T	588	$ .01	$ .07	Lea, Charlie	86T	526	$ .01	$ .03
Lavelle, Gary	82T	209	$ .01	$ .06	Leach, Rick	82T	266	$ .01	$ .06
Lavelle, Gary	83T	791	$ .01	$ .06	Leach, Rick	83T	147	$ .01	$ .06
Lavelle, Gary	84T	145	$ .01	$ .05	Leach, Rick	84T	427	$ .01	$ .05
Lavelle, Gary	85T	462	$ .01	$ .04	Leach, Rick	84TTR	71	$ .02	$ .10
Lavelle, Gary	85TTR	72	$ .02	$ .10	Leach, Rick	85T	593	$ .01	$ .04
Lavelle, Gary	86T	622	$ .01	$ .03	Leach, Rick	86TTR	63	$ .02	$ .10
Law, Rudy	79T	719	$2.25	$9.00	Leach, Rick	87T	716	$ .01	$ .03
Law, Rudy	81T	127	$ .01	$ .07	Leach, Rick	88T	323	$ .01	$ .03
Law, Rudy	83T	514	$ .01	$ .06	Leach, Rick	89T	682	$ .01	$ .04
Law, Rudy	84T	47	$ .01	$ .05	Leach, Rick	89TTR	68	$ .01	$ .05
Law, Rudy	85T	286	$ .01	$ .04	Leach, Rick	90T	27	$ .01	$ .03
Law, Rudy	86T	637	$ .01	$ .03	Leach, Terry	82T	623	$ .20	$ .80
Law, Rudy	86TTR	62	$ .02	$ .10	Leach, Terry	83T	187	$ .01	$ .06
Law, Rudy	87T	382	$ .01	$ .03	Leach, Terry	86T	774	$ .01	$ .03
Law, Vance	81T	551	$ .50	$2.00	Leach, Terry	87TTR	63	$ .01	$ .07
Law, Vance	82T	291	$ .25	$1.00	Leach, Terry	88T	457	$ .01	$ .04
Law, Vance	83T	98	$ .01	$ .06	Leach, Terry	89T	207	$ .01	$ .04
Law, Vance	84T	667	$ .01	$ .05	Leach, Terry	89TBB	96	$ .01	$ .05
Law, Vance	85T	137	$ .01	$ .10	Leach, Terry	89TTR	69	$ .01	$ .05
Law, Vance	85T	413	$ .01	$ .04	Leach, Terry	90T	508	$ .01	$ .03
Law, Vance	85TTR	73	$ .02	$ .10	Leal, Luis	81T	577	$ .01	$ .07
Law, Vance	86T	787	$ .01	$ .03	Leal, Luis	82T	412	$ .01	$ .06
Law, Vance	87T	127	$ .01	$ .03	Leal, Luis	83T	109	$ .01	$ .06
Law, Vance	88T	346	$ .01	$ .03	Leal, Luis	84T	783	$ .01	$ .05
Law, Vance	88TTR	60	$ .01	$ .05	Leal, Luis	85T	622	$ .01	$ .04
Law, Vance	89T	501	$ .01	$ .04	Leal, Luis	86T	459	$ .01	$ .03
Law, Vance	89TBB	143	$ .01	$ .05	Leary, Tim	82T	623	$ .20	$ .80
Law, Vance	90T	287	$ .01	$ .03	Leary, Tim	86TTR	64	$ .02	$ .10
Law, Vern	52T	81	$7.00	$20.00	Leary, Tim	87T	32	$ .01	$ .03
Law, Vern	54T	235	$1.75	$7.00	Leary, Tim	87TTR	64	$ .01	$ .07
Law, Vernon	56T	252	$2.50	$7.00	Leary, Tim	88T	367	$ .01	$ .03
Law, Vernon	57T	199	$ .60	$2.50	Leary, Tim	89T	249	$ .01	$ .04
Law, Vernon "Vern"	58T	132	$ .75	$2.50	Leary, Tim	89TBB	17	$ .01	$ .05
Law, Vern	59T	12	$ .95	$3.50	Leary, Tim	90T	516	$ .01	$ .03
Law, Vern	59T	428	$ .50	$1.95	Lee, Bill	70T	279	$ .10	$ .35
Law, Vern	60T	453	$1.00	$4.00	Lee, Bill	71T	58	$ .10	$ .35
Law, Vern	61T	47	$ .60	$1.75	Lee, Bill	72T	636	$ .25	$ .85
Law, Vern	61T	250	$ .50	$2.00	Lee, Bill	73T	224	$ .06	$ .25
Law, Vern	61T	400	$ .60	$1.75	Lee, Bill	74T	118	$ .06	$ .25
Law, Vern	62T	295	$ .50	$2.00	Lee, Bill	75T	128	$ .06	$ .25

Player	Year	No.	VG	EX/MT
Lee, Bill	76T	396	$ .05	$ .20
Lee, Bill	77T	503	$ .03	$ .12
Lee, Bill	78T	295	$ .02	$ .10
Lee, Bill	79T	455	$ .02	$ .10
Lee, Bill	80T	97	$ .01	$ .07
Lee, Bill	81T	633	$ .01	$ .07
Lee, Bill	82T	323	$ .01	$ .06
Lee, Bob	64T	502	$ .40	$1.25

PITCHER
BOB LEE

Player	Year	No.	VG	EX/MT
Lee, Bob	65T	46	$ .25	$ .65
Lee, Bob	66T	481	$ .70	$2.10
Lee, Bob	67T	313	$ .25	$ .65
Lee, Bob	68T	543	$ .30	$1.00
Lee, Don	57T	379	$1.00	$3.75
Lee, Don	59T	132	$ .50	$1.95
Lee, Don	60T	503	$ .60	$1.75
Lee, Don	61T	153	$ .30	$1.00
Lee, Don	62T	166	$ .35	$1.10
Lee, Don	63T	372	$ .35	$1.20
Lee, Don	64T	493	$ .40	$1.25
Lee, Don	65T	595	$1.50	$3.75
Lee, Leron	70T	96	$ .50	$2.00
Lee, Leron	71T	521	$ .10	$ .35
Lee, Leron	72T	238	$ .05	$ .25
Lee, Leron	73T	83	$ .06	$ .25
Lee, Leron	74T	651	$ .06	$ .25
Lee, Leron	75T	506	$ .06	$ .25
Lee, Leron	76T	487	$ .05	$ .20
Lee, Manny	86T	23	$ .01	$ .03
Lee, Manny	87T	574	$ .01	$ .03
Lee, Manny	88T	722	$ .01	$ .03
Lee, Manny	89T	371	$ .01	$ .04
Lee, Manny	89TBB	70	$ .01	$ .05
Lee, Manny	90T	113	$ .01	$ .03
Lee, Mark	79T	138	$ .02	$ .10
Lee, Mark	80T	557	$ .01	$ .07
Lee, Mike	60T	521	$2.00	$7.00
Leek, Gene	61T	527	$6.00	$18.00
Lefebvre, Jim	65T	561	$2.00	$7.00
Lefebvre, Jim	66T	57	$ .25	$ .85
Lefebvre, Jim	67T	260	$ .25	$ .65
Lefebvre, Jim	68T	457	$ .25	$ .65
Lefebvre, Jim	69T	140	$ .25	$ .65
Lefebvre, Jim	70T	553	$ .25	$ .85

Player	Year	No.	VG	EX/MT
Lefebvre, Jim	71T	459	$ .10	$ .35
Lefebvre, Jim	72T	369	$ .05	$ .25
Lefebvre, Jim	89TTR	70	$ .01	$ .05
Lefebvre, Jim	90T	459	$ .01	$ .03
Lefebvre, Joe	81T	88	$ .01	$ .07
Lefebvre, Joe	81TTR	790	$ .02	$ .10
Lefebvre, Joe	82T	434	$ .01	$ .06
Lefebvre, Joe	83T	644	$ .01	$ .06
Lefebvre, Joe	83TTR	61	$ .02	$ .10
Lefebvre, Joe	84T	148	$ .01	$ .05
Lefebvre, Joe	85T	531	$ .01	$ .04
Lefferts, Craig	84T	99	$ .01	$ .05
Lefferts, Craig	84TTR	72	$ .02	$ .10
Lefferts, Craig	85T	608	$ .01	$ .04
Lefferts, Craig	86T	244	$ .01	$ .03
Lefferts, Craig	87T	501	$ .01	$ .03
Lefferts, Craig	88T	734	$ .01	$ .03
Lefferts, Craig	89T	372	$ .01	$ .04
Lefferts, Craig	90T	158	$ .01	$ .03
LeFlore, Ron	75T	628	$ .35	$1.10
LeFlore, Ron	76T	61	$ .06	$ .25
LeFlore, Ron	77T	240	$ .03	$ .12
LeFlore, Ron	78T	480	$ .02	$ .10
LeFlore, Ron	79T	4	$ .03	$ .15
LeFlore, Ron	79T	660	$ .02	$ .10
LeFlore, Ron	80T	80	$ .01	$ .07
LeFlore, Ron	81T	4	$ .04	$ .20
LeFlore, Ron	81T	710	$ .01	$ .07
LeFlore, Ron	81TRB	204	$ .01	$ .07
LeFlore, Ron	81TTR	791	$ .02	$ .10
LeFlore, Ron	82T	140	$ .01	$ .06
LeFlore, Ron	83T	560	$ .01	$ .06
Lehman, Ken	57T	366	$1.00	$3.75
Lehman, Ken	58T	141	$ .50	$2.00
Lehman, Ken	59T	31	$1.00	$3.75
Leibrandt, Charlie	81T	126	$ .25	$ .65
Leibrandt, Charlie	82T	169	$ .01	$ .06
Leibrandt, Charlie	83T	607	$ .01	$ .06
Leibrandt, Charlie	85T	459	$ .01	$ .04
Leibrandt, Charlie	86T	77	$ .01	$ .03
Leibrandt, Charlie	87T	223	$ .01	$ .03
Leibrandt, Charlie	88T	569	$ .01	$ .03
Leibrandt, Charlie	89T	301	$ .01	$ .04
Leibrandt, Charlie	90T	776	$ .01	$ .03
Leiper, Dave	87T	441	$ .01	$ .10
Leiper, Dave	89T	82	$ .01	$ .04
Leiper, Dave	90T	773	$ .01	$ .03
Leiter, Al	88T	18	$ .10	$ .75
Leiter, Al	89T	659	$ .01	$ .15
Leiter, Al	89TBB	125	$ .01	$ .10
Leiter, Al	89TTR	71	$ .01	$ .10
Leiter, Al	90T	138	$ .01	$ .03
Leja, Frank	54T	175	$1.75	$7.00
Leja, Frank	55T	99	$1.35	$5.00
LeJohn, Don	66T	41	$ .25	$ .85
Lemanczyk, Dave	75T	571	$ .06	$ .25
Lemanczyk, Dave	76T	409	$ .05	$ .20
Lemanczyk, Dave	77T	611	$ .03	$ .12
Lemanczyk, Dave	78T	33	$ .02	$ .10
Lemanczyk, Dave	79T	207	$ .02	$ .10
Lemanczyk, Dave	80T	124	$ .01	$ .07
Lemaster, Denver	63T	74	$ .25	$ .85
Lemaster, Denver	64T	152	$ .25	$ .85
Lemaster, Denver	65T	441	$ .30	$1.00
Lemaster, Denver	66T	252	$ .25	$ .85
Lemaster, Denver	67T	288	$ .25	$ .65
Lemaster, Denny	68T	491	$ .30	$1.00
Lemaster, Denny	69T	96	$ .25	$ .65
Lemaster, Denny	70T	178	$ .10	$ .35
Lemaster, Denny "Denver"	71T	636	$ .30	$1.00
Lemaster, Denny	72T	371	$ .05	$ .25
LeMaster, Johnnie	76T	596	$ .10	$ .35
LeMaster, Johnnie	77T	151	$ .03	$ .12
LeMaster, Johnnie	78T	538	$ .02	$ .10
LeMaster, Johnnie	79T	284	$ .02	$ .10

TOPPS

Player	Year	No.	VG	EX/MT
LeMaster, Johnnie	80T	434	$ .01	$ .07
LeMaster, Johnnie	81T	84	$ .01	$ .07
LeMaster, Johnnie	82T	304	$ .01	$ .06
LeMaster, Johnnie	83T	154	$ .01	$ .06
LeMaster, Johnnie	84T	663	$ .01	$ .05
LeMaster, Johnnie	85T	772	$ .01	$ .04
LeMaster, Johnnie	85TTR	74	$ .02	$ .10
LeMaster, Johnnie	86T	289	$ .01	$ .03
LeMay, Dick	63T	459	$2.50	$6.50
Lemke, Mark	89T	327	$ .01	$ .15
Lemke, Mark	90T	451	$ .01	$ .03
Lemon, Bob	52T	268	$35.00	$110.00
Lemon, Bob	56T	255	$7.00	$20.00
Lemon, Bob	57T	120	$3.50	$13.00
Lemon, Bob	58T	2	$3.50	$13.00
Lemon, Bob	60T	460	$1.25	$4.50
Lemon, Bob	61T	44	$4.00	$16.00
Lemon, Bob	71T	91	$ .35	$1.10
Lemon, Bob	72T	449	$ .30	$1.00
Lemon, Bob	78T	574	$ .05	$ .20
Lemon, Chet	76T	590	$ .15	$ .50
Lemon, Chet	77T	58	$ .03	$ .12
Lemon, Chet	78T	127	$ .02	$ .10
Lemon, Chet	79T	333	$ .02	$ .10
Lemon, Chet	80T	589	$ .01	$ .07
Lemon, Chet	81T	242	$ .01	$ .07
Lemon, Chet	82T	216	$ .01	$ .06
Lemon, Chet	82T	493	$ .01	$ .06
Lemon, Chet	82TTR	62	$ .02	$ .10
Lemon, Chet	83T	727	$ .01	$ .06
Lemon, Chet	84T	611	$ .01	$ .05
Lemon, Chet	85T	20	$ .01	$ .04
Lemon, Chet	86T	160	$ .01	$ .03
Lemon, Chet	87T	739	$ .01	$ .03
Lemon, Chet	88T	366	$ .01	$ .03
Lemon, Chet	88TBB	147	$ .01	$ .05
Lemon, Chet	89T	514	$ .01	$ .04
Lemon, Chet	89TBB	202	$ .01	$ .05
Lemon, Chet	90T	271	$ .01	$ .03
Lemon, Jim	54T	103	$1.75	$7.00
Lemon, Jim	57T	57	$ .95	$3.50
Lemon, Jim	58T	15	$1.00	$3.75
Lemon, Jim	59T	74	$ .95	$3.50
Lemon, Jim	59T	215	$ .50	$1.95
Lemon, Jim	60T	440	$ .50	$1.95
Lemon, Jim	61T	44	$4.00	$16.00
Lemon, Jim	61T	450	$ .50	$2.00
Lemon, Jim	62T	510	$ .70	$2.10
Lemon, Jim	63T	369	$ .35	$1.20
Lemon, Jim	68T	341	$ .25	$ .65
Lemon, Jim	69T	294	$ .25	$ .85
Lemonds, Dave	71T	458	$ .10	$ .35
Lemonds, Dave	72T	413	$ .05	$ .25
Lemonds, Dave	73T	534	$ .35	$1.10
Lemongello, Mark	77T	478	$ .03	$ .12
Lemongello, Mark	78T	358	$ .02	$ .10
Lemongello, Mark	79T	187	$ .02	$ .10
Lenhardt, Don	51Tbb	33	$5.50	$17.00
Lenhardt, Don	52T	4	$14.00	$45.00
Lenhardt, Don	54T	157	$2.10	$7.50
Lenhardt, Don	73T	131	$ .10	$ .35
Lennon, Bob	55T	119	$1.35	$5.00
Lennon, Bob	56T	104	$1.25	$4.50
Lennon, Bob	57T	371	$1.00	$3.75
Leon, Eddie	70T	292	$ .10	$ .35
Leon, Eddie	71T	252	$ .10	$ .35
Leon, Eddie	72T	721	$ .70	$2.10
Leon, Eddie	73T	287	$ .06	$ .25
Leon, Eddie	74T	501	$ .06	$ .25
Leon, Eddie	75T	528	$ .06	$ .25
Leon, Maximino	75T	442	$ .06	$ .25
Leon, Maximino	76T	576	$ .05	$ .20
Leon, Maximino	77T	213	$ .03	$ .12
Leonard, Dave	72T	527	$ .25	$ .85
Leonard, Dennis	75T	615	$ .25	$ .85
Leonard, Dennis	76T	334	$ .05	$ .20
Leonard, Dennis	77T	75	$ .03	$ .12
Leonard, Dennis	78T	205	$ .25	$ .65
Leonard, Dennis	78T	665	$ .02	$ .10
Leonard, Dennis	79T	218	$ .02	$ .10
Leonard, Dennis	80T	565	$ .01	$ .07
Leonard, Dennis	81T	185	$ .01	$ .07
Leonard, Dennis	82T	495	$ .01	$ .06
Leonard, Dennis	83T	785	$ .01	$ .06
Leonard, Dennis	84T	375	$ .01	$ .05
Leonard, Dennis	86TTR	65	$ .02	$ .10
Leonard, Dennis	87T	38	$ .01	$ .03
Leonard, Dutch	52T	110	$6.00	$19.00
Leonard, Dutch	53T	155	$3.75	$13.00
Leonard, Dutch	79TRH	418	$ .02	$ .10
Leonard, Jeff	80T	106	$ .60	$1.75
Leonard, Jeff	81T	469	$ .05	$ .20
Leonard, Jeff	82T	47	$ .01	$ .06
Leonard, Jeff	83T	309	$ .01	$ .06
Leonard, Jeff	84T	576	$ .01	$ .05
Leonard, Jeff	84T	748	$ .01	$ .05
Leonard, Jeff	85T	619	$ .01	$ .04
Leonard, Jeff	85TAS	718	$ .01	$ .04
Leonard, Jeff	86T	490	$ .01	$ .03
Leonard, Jeffrey	87T	280	$ .01	$ .03
Leonard, Jeffrey	88T	570	$ .01	$ .03
Leonard, Jeffrey	89T	160	$ .01	$ .04
Leonard, Jeffrey	89TTR	72	$ .01	$ .05
Leonard, Jeffrey	90T	455	$ .01	$ .03
Leonhard, Dave	68T	56	$ .25	$ .65
Leonhard, Dave	69T	228	$ .25	$ .85
Leonhard, Dave	70T	674	$ .50	$2.00
Leonhard, Dave	71T	716	$ .50	$1.25
Lepcio, Ted	52T	335	$39.00	$135.00
Lepcio, Ted	53T	18	$3.75	$13.00
Lepcio, Ted	54T	66	$4.75	$14.00
Lepcio, Ted	55T	128	$1.35	$5.00
Lepcio, Ted	57T	288	$3.50	$13.00
Lepcio, Ted	58T	29	$1.00	$3.75
Lepcio, Ted	59T	348	$ .50	$1.95
Lepcio, Ted	60T	97	$ .35	$1.10
Lepcio, Ted	61T	234	$ .30	$1.00
Leppert, Don	62T	36	$ .35	$1.10
Leppert, Don	63T	243	$ .25	$ .85
Leppert, Don	64T	463	$ .40	$1.25
Leppert, Don	73T	517	$ .25	$ .85
Leppert, Don	74T	489	$ .06	$ .25
Lerch, Randy	76T	595	$ .05	$ .20
Lerch, Randy	77T	489	$ .25	$ .65
Lerch, Randy	78T	271	$ .02	$ .10
Lerch, Randy	79T	52	$ .02	$ .10
Lerch, Randy	80T	344	$ .01	$ .07
Lerch, Randy	81T	584	$ .01	$ .07
Lerch, Randy	81TTR	792	$ .02	$ .10
Lerch, Randy	82T	466	$ .01	$ .06
Lerch, Randy	83T	686	$ .01	$ .06
Lerch, Randy	85T	103	$ .01	$ .04
Lersch, Barry	69T	206	$ .25	$ .65
Lersch, Barry	71T	739	$ .70	$2.10
Lersch, Barry	72T	453	$ .05	$ .25
Lersch, Barry	73T	559	$ .35	$1.10
Lersch, Barry	74T	313	$ .06	$ .25
Lersch, Barry	74TTR	313	$ .06	$ .25
Lesley, Brad	85T	597	$ .01	$ .04
Lewallyn, Denny	82T	356	$ .01	$ .06
Lewis, Johnny	64T	479	$ .40	$1.25
Lewis, Johnny	65T	277	$ .30	$1.00
Lewis, Johnny	66T	282	$ .25	$ .85
Lewis, Johnny	67T	91	$ .25	$ .65
Lewis, Johnny	74T	236	$ .06	$ .25
Lewis, Mark	89T	222	$ .01	$ .40
Ley, Terry	72T	506	$ .25	$ .65
Leyland, Jim	86TTR	66	$ .02	$ .10
Leyland, Jim	87T	93	$ .01	$ .03
Leyland, Jim	88T	624	$ .01	$ .03

Player	Year	No.	VG	EX/MT	Player	Year	No.	VG	EX/MT
Leyland, Jim	89T	284	$ .01	$ .04	Linz, Phil	66T	522	$ .70	$2.10
Leyland, Jim	90T	699	$ .01	$ .03	Linz, Phil	67T	14	$ .25	$ .65
Leyva, Nick	89T	74	$ .01	$ .04	Linz, Phil	68T	594	$ .30	$1.00
Leyva, Nick	90T	489	$ .01	$ .03	Linzy, Frank	65T	589	$1.50	$3.75
Lezcano, Carlos	81T	381	$ .01	$ .07	Linzy, Frank	66T	78	$ .25	$ .85
Lezcano, Carlos	82T	51	$ .03	$ .15	Linzy, Frank	67T	279	$ .25	$ .65
Lezcano, Sixto	76T	353	$ .06	$ .25	Linzy, Frank	68T	147	$ .25	$ .65
Lezcano, Sixto	77T	185	$ .03	$ .12	Linzy, Frank	69T	345	$ .25	$ .65
Lezcano, Sixto	78T	595	$ .02	$ .10	Linzy, Frank	70T	77	$ .10	$ .35
Lezcano, Sixto	79T	685	$ .02	$ .10	Linzy, Frank	71T	551	$ .30	$1.00
Lezcano, Sixto	80T	215	$ .01	$ .07	Linzy, Frank	72T	243	$ .05	$ .25
Lezcano, Sixto	81T	25	$ .01	$ .07	Linzy, Frank	73T	286	$ .06	$ .25
Lezcano, Sixto	81TTR	793	$ .02	$ .10	Lipon, John	53T	40	$3.75	$13.00
Lezcano, Sixto	82T	727	$ .01	$ .06	Lipon, Johnny	52T	89	$6.00	$19.00
Lezcano, Sixto	82TTR	63	$ .02	$ .10	Lipon, Johnny	54T	19	$2.10	$7.50
Lezcano, Sixto	83T	455	$ .01	$ .06	Lipski, Bob	63T	558	$1.50	$3.75
Lezcano, Sixto	84T	185	$ .01	$ .05	Liriano, Nelson	88T	205	$ .01	$ .10
Lezcano, Sixto	85T	556	$ .01	$ .04	Liriano, Nelson	88TBB	155	$ .01	$ .05
Lezcano, Sixto	85TTR	75	$ .02	$ .10	Liriano, Nelson	89T	776	$ .01	$ .04
Lezcano, Sixto	86T	278	$ .01	$ .03	Liriano, Nelson	89TBB	207	$ .01	$ .05
Liddle, Don	54T	225	$2.10	$7.50	Liriano, Nelson	90T	543	$ .01	$ .03
Liddle, Don	56T	325	$1.80	$6.00	Lis, Joe	70T	56	$ .10	$ .35
Lilliquist, Derek	89TMLD	70	$ .01	$ .10	Lis, Joe	71T	138	$ .10	$ .35
Lilliquist, Derek	89TTR	73	$ .01	$ .15	Lis, Joe	74T	659	$ .06	$ .25
Lilliquist, Derek	90T	282	$ .01	$ .10	Lis, Joe	75T	86	$ .06	$ .25
Lillis, Bob	59T	133	$ .50	$1.95	Lis, Joe	77T	269	$ .03	$ .12
Lillis, Bob	60T	354	$ .50	$1.95	Littell, Mark	74T	596	$ .06	$ .25
Lillis, Bob	61T	38	$ .30	$1.00	Littell, Mark	76T	593	$ .10	$ .35
Lillis, Bob	62T	74	$ .35	$1.10	Littell, Mark	77T	141	$ .03	$ .12
Lillis, Bob	63T	119	$ .25	$ .85	Littell, Mark	78T	331	$ .02	$ .10
Lillis, Bob	64T	321	$ .25	$ .85	Littell, Mark	79T	466	$ .02	$ .10
Lillis, Bob	74T	31	$ .06	$ .25	Littell, Mark	80T	631	$ .01	$ .07
Lillis, Bob	83T	66	$ .01	$ .06					
Lillis, Bob	84T	441	$ .01	$ .05					
Lillis, Bob	85T	186	$ .01	$ .04					
Lillis, Bob	86T	561	$ .01	$ .03					
Limmer, Lou	54T	232	$2.10	$7.50					
Limmer, Lou	55T	54	$1.35	$5.00					
Linares, Rufino	82T	244	$ .01	$ .06					
Linares, Rufino	83T	467	$ .01	$ .06					
Linares, Rufino	85T	167	$ .01	$ .04					
Lind, Jose	88T	767	$ .01	$ .10					
Lind, Jose	88TBB	107	$ .01	$ .05					
Lind, Jose	89T	273	$ .01	$ .04					
Lind, Jose	89TBB	25	$ .01	$ .05					
Lind, Jose	90T	168	$ .01	$ .03					
Lindblad, Paul	66T	568	$4.50	$15.00					
Lindblad, Paul	67T	227	$ .25	$ .65					
Lindblad, Paul	68T	127	$ .25	$ .65					
Lindblad, Paul	69T	449	$ .25	$ .65					
Lindblad, Paul	70T	408	$ .10	$ .35					
Lindblad, Paul	71T	658	$ .70	$2.10					
Lindblad, Paul	72T	396	$ .05	$ .25					
Lindblad, Paul	73T	406	$ .06	$ .25					
Lindblad, Paul	74T	369	$ .06	$ .25					
Lindblad, Paul	75T	278	$ .06	$ .25					
Lindblad, Paul	76T	9	$ .05	$ .20					
Lindblad, Paul	77T	583	$ .03	$ .12					
Lindblad, Paul	78T	314	$ .02	$ .10					
Lindblad, Paul	79T	634	$ .02	$ .10					
Lindell, Johnny	53T	230	$11.00	$37.50					
Lindell, Johnny	54T	51	$4.75	$14.00					
Lindeman, Jim	87TTR	65	$ .05	$ .20					
Lindeman, Jim	88T	562	$ .01	$ .03					
Lindeman, Jim	89T	791	$ .01	$ .04	Littell, Mark	81T	255	$ .01	$ .07
Lines, Dick	67T	273	$ .25	$ .65	Littell, Mark	82T	56	$ .01	$ .06
Lines, Dick	68T	291	$ 25	$ .65	Little, Bryan	83TTR	62	$ .02	$ .10
Lintz, Larry	74T	121	$ .06	$ .25	Little, Bryan	84T	188	$ .01	$ .05
Lintz, Larry	75T	416	$ .06	$ .25	Little, Bryan	85T	257	$ .01	$ .04
Lintz, Larry	76T	109	$ .05	$ .20	Little, Bryan	86T	346	$ .01	$ .03
Lintz, Larry	77T	323	$ .03	$ .12	Little, Jeff	83T	499	$ .01	$ .06
Linz, Phil	62T	596	$10.00	$30.00	Little, Scott	89TMLD	71	$ .01	$ .25
Linz, Phil	63T	264	$ .25	$ .85	Littlefield, Dick	57T	346	$3.50	$13.00
Linz, Phil	64T	344	$ .25	$ .85	Littlefield, Dick	58T	241	$ .50	$2.00
Linz, Phil	65T	369	$ .35	$1.10	Littlefield, John	81T	489	$ .01	$ .07

MARK LITTELL — CARDINALS

TOPPS

Player	Year	No.	VG	EX/MT	Player	Year	No.	VG	EX/MT
Littlefield, John	81TTR	794	$ .02	$ .10	Logan, Johnny	63T	259	$ .25	$ .85
Littlefield, John	82T	278	$ .01	$ .06	Lois, Alberto	80T	683	$ .01	$ .07
Littlejohn, Dennis	80T	686	$ .01	$ .07	Lolich, Mickey	64T	128	$2.50	$7.50
Littlejohn, Dennis	81T	561	$ .01	$ .07	Lolich, Mickey	65T	335	$ .50	$1.95
Litton, Greg	89TMLD	72	$ .01	$ .05	Lolich, Mickey	66T	226	$ .50	$2.00
Litton, Greg	90T	66	$ .01	$ .03	Lolich, Mickey	66T	455	$ .60	$1.75
Llenas, Winston	71T	152	$ .10	$ .35	Lolich, Mickey	67T	88	$ .35	$1.10
Llenas, Winston	74T	467	$ .06	$ .25	Lolich, Mickey	68T	414	$ .60	$1.75
Llenas, Winston	75T	597	$ .06	$ .25	Lolich, Mickey	69T	270	$ .60	$1.75
Lock, Don	63T	47	$ .25	$ .85	Lolich, Mickey	70T	72	$ .50	$2.00
Lock, Don	64T	114	$ .25	$ .85	Lolich, Mickey	70T	715	$ .90	$2.75
Lock, Don	65T	445	$ .30	$1.00	Lolich, Mickey	71T	71	$ .15	$ .50
Lock, Don	66T	165	$ .25	$ .85	Lolich, Mickey	71T	133	$ .15	$ .50
Lock, Don	67T	376	$ .25	$ .85	Lolich, Mickey	72T	94	$ .40	$1.50
Lock, Don	68T	59	$ .25	$ .65	Lolich, Mickey	72T	96	$ .40	$1.50
Lock, Don	69T	229	$ .25	$ .85	Lolich, Mickey	72T	450	$ .25	$ .85
Locke, Bobby	60T	44	$ .35	$1.10	Lolich, Mickey	73T	390	$ .25	$ .85
Locke, Bobby	61T	537	$6.00	$18.00	Lolich, Mickey	74T	9	$ .25	$ .85
Locke, Bobby	62T	359	$ .35	$1.10	Lolich, Mickey	75T	245	$ .25	$ .85
Locke, Bobby	65T	324	$ .30	$1.00	Lolich, Mickey	76T	385	$ .25	$ .85
Locke, Bobby	68T	24	$ .25	$ .65	Lolich, Mickey	76TRB	3	$ .05	$ .20
Locke, Ron	64T	556	$1.50	$3.75	Lolich, Mickey	76TTR	385	$ .25	$ .85
Locke, Ron	65T	511	$ .50	$2.00	Lolich, Mickey	77T	565	$ .25	$ .65
Locker, Bob	65T	541	$1.50	$3.75	Lolich, Mickey	79T	164	$ .05	$ .20
Locker, Bob	66T	374	$ .25	$ .85	Lolich, Mickey	80T	459	$ .01	$ .07
Locker, Bob	67T	338	$ .25	$ .65	Lolich, Ron	71T	458	$ .10	$ .35
Locker, Bob	68T	51	$ .25	$ .65	Lollar, Sherman	51Tbb	24	$4.00	$18.00
Locker, Bob	69T	548	$ .25	$ .85	Lollar, Sherman	52T	117	$6.00	$18.00
Locker, Bob	70T	249	$ .10	$ .35	Lollar, Sherman	53T	53	$3.75	$13.00
Locker, Bob	71T	356	$ .10	$ .35	Lollar, Sherm	54T	39	$2.00	$7.00
Locker, Bob	72T	537	$ .25	$ .85	Lollar, Sherm	55T	201	$2.85	$9.50
Locker, Bob	73T	645	$ .35	$1.10	Lollar, Sherm	56T	243	$2.50	$8.00
Locker, Bob	74T	62	$ .06	$ .25	Lollar, Sherm	57T	23	$ .95	$3.50
Locker, Bob	74TTR	62	$ .06	$ .25	Lollar, Sherm	58T	267	$ .50	$2.00
Locker, Bob	75T	434	$ .06	$ .25	Lollar, Sherm	58TAS	491	$ .40	$1.10
Locklear, Gene	75T	13	$ .06	$ .25	Lollar, Sherm	59T	385	$ .50	$1.95
Locklear, Gene	76T	447	$ .05	$ .20	Lollar, Sherm	60T	495	$ .60	$1.75
Lockman, Whitey	51Trb	41	$1.25	$3.50	Lollar, Sherm	60TAS	567	$2.00	$7.00
Lockman, Whitey	56T	205	$2.50	$8.00	Lollar, Sherm	61T	285	$ .30	$1.00
Lockman, Whitey	57T	232	$ .95	$3.50	Lollar, Sherm	62T	514	$ .70	$2.10
Lockman, Whitey	58T	195	$ .45	$1.50	Lollar, Sherm "Sherman"	63T	118	$ .25	$ .85
Lockman, Whitey	59T	411	$ .50	$1.95	Lollar, Tim	81T	424	$ .01	$ .07
Lockman, Whitey	60T	535	$2.00	$7.00	Lollar, Tim	82T	587	$ .01	$ .06
Lockman, Whitey	73T	81	$ .25	$ .85	Lollar, Tim	83T	185	$ .01	$ .06
Lockman, Whitey	74T	354	$ .06	$ .25	Lollar, Tim	83T	742	$ .01	$ .06
Lockwood, Skip	65T	526	$40.00	$105.00	Lollar, Tim	84T	644	$ .01	$ .05
Lockwood, Skip	70T	499	$ .10	$ .35	Lollar, Tim	85T	13	$ .01	$ .04
Lockwood, Skip	71T	433	$ .10	$ .35	Lollar, Tim	85TTR	76	$ .02	$ .10
Lockwood, Skip	72T	118	$ .05	$ .25	Lollar, Tim	86T	297	$ .01	$ .03
Lockwood, Skip	73T	308	$ .06	$ .25	Lollar, Tim	87T	396	$ .01	$ .03
Lockwood, Skip	74T	532	$ .06	$ .25	Lombardi, Phil	88T	283	$ .01	$ .03
Lockwood, Skip	75T	417	$ .06	$ .25	Lombardozzi, Steve	87TTR	66	$ .01	$ .07
Lockwood, Skip	76T	166	$ .05	$ .20	Lombardozzi, Steve	88T	697	$ .01	$ .03
Lockwood, Skip	77T	65	$ .03	$ .12	Lombardozzi, Steve	89T	376	$ .01	$ .04
Lockwood, Skip	78T	379	$ .02	$ .10	Lonborg, Jim	65T	573	$1.75	$8.50
Lockwood, Skip	79T	481	$ .02	$ .10	Lonborg, Jim	66T	93	$ .15	$ .50
Lockwood, Skip	80T	567	$ .01	$ .07	Lonborg, Jim	67T	371	$ .30	$1.00
Lockwood, Skip	81T	233	$ .01	$ .07	Lonborg, Jim	68T	10	$ .35	$1.10
Loes, Billy	52T	20	$22.50	$85.00	Lonborg, Jim	68T	12	$ .35	$1.10
Loes, Billy	53T	174	$2.25	$8.00	Lonborg, Jim	68T	460	$ .30	$1.00
Loes, Billy	56T	270	$3.00	$9.00	Lonborg, Jim	69T	109	$ .15	$ .50
Loes, Billy	57T	244	$ .95	$3.50	Lonborg, Jim	70T	665	$1.00	$3.75
Loes, Billy	58T	359	$ .50	$2.00	Lonborg, Jim	71T	577	$ .35	$1.10
Loes, Billy	59T	336	$ .50	$1.95	Lonborg, Jim	72T	255	$ .05	$ .25
Loes, Billy	60T	181	$ .35	$1.10	Lonborg, Jim	73T	3	$ .25	$ .65
Loes, Billy	61T	237	$ .30	$1.00	Lonborg, Jim	74T	342	$ .06	$ .25
Logan, Johnny	53T	158	$3.75	$13.00	Lonborg, Jim	75T	94	$ .06	$ .25
Logan, Johnny	54T	122	$2.00	$7.00	Lonborg, Jim	76T	271	$ .05	$ .20
Logan, Johnny	56T	136	$1.25	$3.50	Lonborg, Jim	77T	569	$ .03	$ .12
Logan, Johnny	57T	4	$ .95	$3.50	Lonborg, Jim	78T	52	$ .02	$ .10
Logan, Johnny	58T	110	$1.00	$3.75	Lonborg, Jim	79T	446	$ .02	$ .10
Logan, Johnny	59T	225	$ .50	$1.95	Long, Bill	87TTR	67	$ .01	$ .07
Logan, Johnny	60T	205	$ .35	$1.10	Long, Bill	88T	309	$ .01	$ .03
Logan, Johnny	61T	524	$6.00	$18.00	Long, Bill	89T	133	$ .01	$ .04
Logan, Johnny	62T	573	$2.50	$7.50	Long, Bill	90T	499	$ .01	$ .03

Player	Year	No.	VG	EX/MT	Player	Year	No.	VG	EX/MT
Long, Bob	82T	291	$ .25	$1.00	Lopez, Hector	56T	16	$1.25	$4.50
Long, Dale	55T	127	$1.35	$5.00	Lopez, Hector	57T	6	$ .95	$3.50
Long, Dale	56T	56	$1.25	$4.50	Lopez, Hector	58T	155	$ .50	$2.00
Long, Dale	57T	3	$ .95	$3.50	Lopez, Hector	59T	402	$ .50	$1.95
Long, Dale	58T	7	$1.50	$3.75	Lopez, Hector	60T	163	$ .35	$1.10
Long, Dale	59T	147	$3.50	$10.00	Lopez, Hector	61T	28	$ .30	$1.00
Long, Dale	59T	414	$ .50	$1.95	Lopez, Hector	62T	502	$ .60	$1.75
Long, Dale	60T	375	$ .50	$1.95	Lopez, Hector	63T	92	$ .25	$ .85
Long, Dale	61T	117	$ .30	$1.00	Lopez, Hector	64T	325	$ .25	$ .85
Long, Dale	62T	228	$ .35	$1.10	Lopez, Hector	65T	532	$1.50	$3.75
Long, Dale	63T	484	$2.50	$6.50	Lopez, Hector	66T	177	$ .25	$ .85
Long, Jeoff	64T	497	$ .40	$1.25	Lopez, Marcelino	63T	549	$1.50	$3.75
Lonnett, Joe	57T	241	$ .95	$3.50	Lopez, Marcelino	65T	537	$1.35	$4.00
Lonnett, Joe	58T	64	$1.00	$3.75	Lopez, Marcelino	66T	155	$ .25	$ .85
Lonnett, Joe	73T	356	$ .10	$ .35	Lopez, Marcelino	67T	513	$ .50	$2.00
Lonnett, Joe	74T	221	$ .06	$ .25	Lopez, Marcelino	70T	344	$ .10	$ .35
Look, Bruce	69T	317	$ .25	$ .85	Lopez, Marcelino	71T	137	$ .10	$ .35
Lopat, Ed	51Tbb	39	$7.50	$28.00	Lopez, Marcelino	72T	652	$ .25	$ .85
Lopat, Ed	52T	57	$25.00	$75.00	Loun, Don	65T	181	$ .25	$ .65
Lopat, Ed	53T	87	$9.00	$35.00	Loviglio, Jay	81T	526	$ .01	$ .07
Lopat, Ed	54T	5	$5.50	$18.00	Loviglio, Jay	82T	599	$ .01	$ .06
Lopat, Ed	55T	109	$3.00	$12.00	Lovitto, Joe	73T	276	$ .06	$ .25
Lopat, Ed	60T	465	$2.50	$9.00	Lovitto, Joe	74T	639	$ .06	$ .25
Lopat, Ed	63T	23	$ .30	$1.00	Lovitto, Joe	75T	36	$ .06	$ .25
Lopat, Ed	64T	348	$ .35	$1.10	Lovitto, Joe	76T	604	$ .05	$ .20
Lopata, Stan	56T	183	$2.50	$8.00	Lovrich, Pete	63T	549	$1.50	$3.75
Lopata, Stan	57T	119	$ .95	$3.50	Lovrich, Pete	64T	212	$ .25	$ .85
Lopata, Stan	58T	353	$ .50	$2.00	Lowenstein, John	71T	231	$ .10	$ .35
Lopata, Stan	59T	412	$ .50	$1.95	Lowenstein, John	72T	486	$ .05	$ .25
Lopata, Stan	60T	515	$2.00	$7.00	Lowenstein, John	73T	327	$ .06	$ .25
Lopes, Dave	73T	609	$ .95	$3.50	Lowenstein, John	74T	176	$ .06	$ .25
Lopes, Dave	74T	112	$ .25	$ .85	Lowenstein, John	75T	424	$ .06	$ .25
Lopes, Dave	75T	93	$ .10	$ .35	Lowenstein, John	76T	646	$ .05	$ .20
Lopes, Dave	76T	197	$ .15	$ .50	Lowenstein, John	77T	393	$ .03	$ .12
Lopes, Dave	76T	660	$ .35	$1.10	Lowenstein, John	78T	87	$ .02	$ .10
Lopes, Dave	76TRB	4	$ .05	$ .20	Lowenstein, John	79T	173	$ .02	$ .10
Lopes, Dave	77T	4	$ .03	$ .12	Lowenstein, John	80T	287	$ .01	$ .07
Lopes, Dave	77T	180	$ .03	$ .12					
Lopes, Dave	78T	440	$ .05	$ .20					
Lopes, Dave	79T	290	$ .02	$ .10					
Lopes, Dave	80T	560	$ .03	$ .15					
Lopes, Dave	81T	50	$ .02	$ .10					
Lopes, Dave	82T	740	$ .01	$ .06					
Lopes, Dave	82TAS	338	$ .01	$ .06					
Lopes, Dave	82TIA	741	$ .01	$ .06					
Lopes, Dave	82TTR	64	$ .05	$ .25					
Lopes, Dave	83T	365	$ .01	$ .06					
Lopes, Dave	84T	669	$ .02	$ .10					
Lopes, Dave	84T	714	$ .01	$ .05					
Lopes, Dave	85T	12	$ .01	$ .04					
Lopes, Dave	86T	125	$ .05	$ .60					
Lopes, Dave	87T	445	$ .01	$ .03					
Lopes, Dave	87TRB	4	$ .01	$ .03					
Lopes, Dave	88T	226	$ .01	$ .10					
Lopez, Al	60T	222	$ .90	$3.00					
Lopez, Al	61T	132	$ .60	$1.75					
Lopez, Al	61T	337	$ .70	$2.00					
Lopez, Al	62T	286	$ .75	$2.00					
Lopez, Al	63T	458	$3.00	$9.00					
Lopez, Al	64T	232	$ .60	$1.75					
Lopez, Al	65T	414	$ .60	$1.75					
Lopez, Al	69T	527	$ .75	$2.50					
Lopez, Art	65T	566	$1.75	$5.75					
Lopez, Aurelio	79T	444	$ .05	$ .20					
Lopez, Aurelio	80T	101	$ .01	$ .07	Lowenstein, John	81T	591	$ .01	$ .07
Lopez, Aurelio	81T	291	$ .01	$ .07	Lowenstein, John	82T	747	$ .01	$ .06
Lopez, Aurelio	82T	728	$ .01	$ .06	Lowenstein, John	83T	473	$ .01	$ .06
Lopez, Aurelio	83TTR	63	$ .02	$ .10	Lowenstein, John	84T	604	$ .01	$ .05
Lopez, Aurelio	84T	95	$ .01	$ .05	Lowenstein, John	85T	316	$ .01	$ .04
Lopez, Aurelio	85T	539	$ .01	$ .04	Lown, Turk	52T	330	$39.00	$135.00
Lopez, Aurelio	86T	367	$ .01	$ .03					
Lopez, Aurelio	87T	659	$ .01	$ .03					
Lopez, Carlos	77T	492	$ .25	$ .80					
Lopez, Carlos	78T	166	$ .02	$ .10					
Lopez, Carlos	79T	568	$ .02	$ .10					

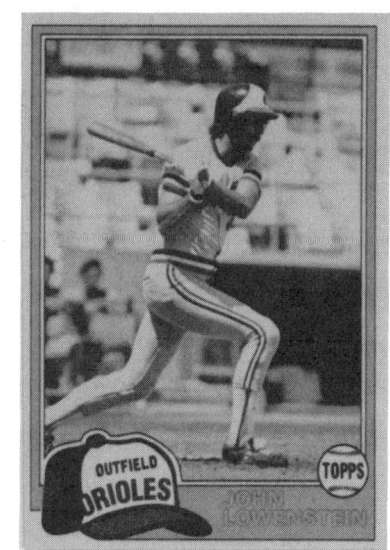

TOPPS

Player	Year	No.	VG	EX/MT	Player	Year	No.	VG	EX/MT
Lown, Turk	53T	130	$3.75	$13.00	Lum, Mike	76T	208	$ .05	$ .20
Lown, Turk	57T	247	$ .95	$3.50	Lum, Mike	76TTR	208	$ .05	$ .20
Lown, Turk	58T	261	$ .50	$2.00	Lum, Mike	77T	601	$ .03	$ .12
Lown, Turk	59T	277	$ .50	$1.95	Lum, Mike	78T	326	$ .02	$ .10
Lown, Turk	60T	57	$ .50	$2.00	Lum, Mike	79T	556	$ .02	$ .10
Lown, Turk	60T	313	$ .50	$1.95	Lum, Mike	80T	7	$ .01	$ .07
Lown, Turk	61T	424	$ .50	$2.00	Lum, Mike	81T	457	$ .01	$ .07
Lown, Turk	62T	528	$3.75	$11.00	Lum, Mike	81TTR	795	$ .02	$ .10
Lowrey, Harry	52T	111	$6.00	$19.00	Lum, Mike	82T	732	$ .01	$ .06
Lowrey, Harry "Peanuts"	53T	16	$3.75	$13.00	Lumenti, Ralph	58T	369	$ .50	$2.00
Lowrey, Peanuts	54T	158	$2.10	$7.50	Lumenti, Ralph	59T	316	$ .50	$1.95
Lowry, Dwight	87T	483	$ .01	$ .03	Lumenti, Ralph	61T	469	$ .50	$2.00
Loynd, Mike	87T	126	$ .06	$ .25	Lumpe, Jerry	58T	193	$ .50	$2.00
Loynd, Mike	88T	319	$ .01	$ .03	Lumpe, Jerry	59T	272	$ .50	$1.95
Lubratich, Steve	84T	266	$ .01	$ .05	Lumpe, Jerry	60T	290	$ .50	$1.95
Lucas, Gary	81T	436	$ .01	$ .07	Lumpe, Jerry	61T	119	$ .35	$1.10
Lucas, Gary	82T	120	$ .01	$ .06	Lumpe, Jerry	61T	365	$ .30	$1.00
					Lumpe, Jerry	62T	127	$ .50	$2.00
					Lumpe, Jerry	62T	305	$ .35	$1.10
					Lumpe, Jerry	63T	256	$ .25	$ .85
					Lumpe, Jerry	64T	165	$ .25	$ .85
					Lumpe, Jerry	65T	353	$ .30	$1.00
					Lumpe, Jerry	66T	161	$ .25	$ .85
					Lumpe, Jerry	67T	247	$ .25	$ .65
					Lund, Don	53T	277	$11.00	$37.50
					Lund, Don	54T	167	$2.10	$7.50
					Lund, Gordon	70T	642	$ .50	$2.00
					Lundstedt, Tom	74T	603	$ .06	$ .25
					Luplow, Al	62T	598	$12.00	$50.00
					Luplow, Al	63T	351	$ .35	$1.20
					Luplow, Al	64T	184	$ .25	$ .85
					Luplow, Al	66T	188	$ .25	$ .85
					Luplow, Al	67T	433	$ .25	$ .85
					Lusader, Scott	89T	487	$ .01	$ .10
					Lusader, Scott	90T	632	$ .01	$ .03
					Luttrell, Lyle	57T	386	$1.00	$3.75
					Lutz, Joe	73T	449	$ .25	$ .65
					Luzinski, Greg	71T	439	$ .60	$2.00
					Luzinski, Greg	72T	112	$ .25	$ .85
					Luzinski, Greg	73T	189	$ .25	$ .85
					Luzinski, Greg	74T	360	$ .15	$ .50

Player	Year	No.	VG	EX/MT	Player	Year	No.	VG	EX/MT
Lucas, Gary	83T	761	$ .01	$ .06	Luzinski, Greg	75T	630	$ .25	$ .85
Lucas, Gary	84T	7	$ .01	$ .05	Luzinski, Greg	76T	193	$ .50	$1.95
Lucas, Gary	84TTR	73	$ .02	$ .10	Luzinski, Greg	76T	195	$ .30	$1.00
Lucas, Gary	85T	297	$ .01	$ .04	Luzinski, Greg	76T	610	$ .10	$ .35
Lucas, Gary	86T	601	$ .01	$ .03	Luzinski, Greg	77T	30	$ .25	$ .65
Lucas, Gary	87T	696	$ .01	$ .03	Luzinski, Greg	78T	420	$ .05	$ .20
Lucas, Gary	88T	524	$ .01	$ .03	Luzinski, Greg	79T	540	$ .05	$ .20
Lucchesi, Frank	70T	662	$ .50	$2.00	Luzinski, Greg	80T	120	$ .01	$ .07
Lucchesi, Frank	71T	119	$ .10	$ .35	Luzinski, Greg	81T	270	$ .03	$ .15
Lucchesi, Frank	72T	188	$ .05	$ .25	Luzinski, Greg	81TTR	796	$ .02	$ .10
Lucchesi, Frank	74T	379	$ .15	$ .50	Luzinski, Greg	82T	720	$ .03	$ .15
Lucchesi, Frank	88T	564	$ .01	$ .03	Luzinski, Greg	82TIA	721	$ .01	$ .06
Luebber, Steve	72T	678	$ .70	$2.10	Luzinski, Greg	83T	310	$ .01	$ .06
Luebber, Steve	77T	457	$ .03	$ .12	Luzinski, Greg	83T	591	$ .01	$ .06
Luecken, Rick	89TMLD	73	$ .01	$ .05	Luzinski, Greg	84T	20	$ .01	$ .05
Luecken, Rick	90T	87	$ .01	$ .10	Luzinski, Greg	84T	712	$ .03	$ .15
Lugo, Urbano	86T	373	$ .01	$ .03	Luzinski, Greg	85T	650	$ .01	$ .04
Lugo, Urbano	87T	92	$ .01	$ .03	Lyle, Sparky	69T	311	$1.00	$4.00
Lum, Mike	68T	579	$ .35	$1.10	Lyle, Sparky	70T	116	$ .25	$1.00
Lum, Mike	69T	514	$ .25	$ .85	Lyle, Sparky	71T	649	$1.50	$3.75
Lum, Mike	70T	367	$ .10	$ .35	Lyle, Sparky	72T	259	$ .25	$1.00
Lum, Mike	71T	194	$ .10	$ .35	Lyle, Sparky	73T	68	$ .25	$ .65
Lum, Mike	72T	641	$ .25	$ .85	Lyle, Sparky	73T	394	$ .25	$ .65
Lum, Mike	73T	266	$ .06	$ .25	Lyle, Sparky	74T	66	$ .25	$ .85
Lum, Mike	74T	227	$ .06	$ .25	Lyle, Sparky	75T	485	$ .10	$ .35
Lum, Mike	75T	154	$ .06	$ .25	Lyle, Sparky	76T	545	$ .10	$ .35
					Lyle, Sparky	77T	598	$ .25	$ .65
					Lyle, Sparky	78T	35	$ .02	$ .10
					Lyle, Sparky	78TRB	2	$ .02	$ .10
					Lyle, Sparky	79T	365	$ .05	$ .20
					Lyle, Sparky	80T	115	$ .03	$ .15
					Lyle, Sparky	81T	719	$ .01	$ .07
					Lyle, Sparky	82T	285	$ .01	$ .06
					Lyle, Sparky	83T	693	$ .01	$ .06

Player	Year	No.	VG	EX/MT	Player	Year	No.	VG	EX/MT
Lyle, Sparky	83T	694	$ .01	$ .06	Macfarlane, Mike	89TBB	86	$ .01	$ .05
Lynch, Ed	82T	121	$ .01	$ .06	Macfarlane, Mike	90T	202	$ .01	$ .03
Lynch, Ed	83T	601	$ .01	$ .06	Macha, Ken	78T	483	$ .02	$ .10
Lynch, Ed	84T	293	$ .01	$ .05	Macha, Ken	82T	282	$ .01	$ .06
Lynch, Ed	85T	467	$ .01	$ .04	Machado, Julio	89TMLD	74	$ .01	$ .15
Lynch, Ed	86T	68	$ .01	$ .03	Machado, Julio	90T	684	$ .01	$ .10
Lynch, Ed	87T	697	$ .01	$ .03	Mack, Shane	85T	398	$ .10	$ .40
Lynch, Ed	88T	336	$ .01	$ .03	Mack, Shane	87TTR	69	$ .05	$ .25
Lynch, Jerry	54T	234	$1.75	$7.00	Mack, Shane	88T	548	$ .01	$ .03
Lynch, Jerry	55T	142	$1.35	$5.00	Mackanin, Pete	74T	597	$ .15	$ .50
Lynch, Jerry	56T	97	$1.25	$4.50	Mackanin, Pete	76T	287	$ .05	$ .20
Lynch, Jerry	57T	358	$1.00	$3.75	Mackanin, Pete	77T	156	$ .03	$ .12
Lynch, Jerry	58T	103	$1.00	$3.75	Mackanin, Pete	78T	399	$ .02	$ .10
Lynch, Jerry	59T	97	$1.00	$3.75	Mackanin, Pete	81T	509	$ .01	$ .07
Lynch, Jerry	60T	198	$ .35	$1.10	Mackanin, Pete	82T	438	$ .01	$ .06
Lynch, Jerry	60T	352	$ .90	$3.50	MacKenzie, Ken	60T	534	$2.00	$7.00
Lynch, Jerry	61T	97	$ .30	$1.00	MacKenzie, Ken	61T	496	$ .50	$2.00
Lynch, Jerry	62T	487	$ .70	$2.10	MacKenzie, Ken	62T	421	$ .70	$2.10
Lynch, Jerry	63T	37	$ .25	$ .85	MacKenzie, Ken	63T	393	$ .35	$1.20
Lynch, Jerry	64T	193	$ .25	$ .85	MacKenzie, Ken	64T	297	$ .25	$ .85
Lynch, Jerry	65T	291	$ .30	$1.00	Macko, Steve	80T	676	$ .01	$ .07
Lynch, Jerry	66T	182	$ .25	$ .85	Macko, Steve	81T	381	$ .01	$ .07
Lynn, Fred	75T	622	$2.25	$11.00	MacWhorter, Keith	81T	689	$ .75	$2.25
Lynn, Fred	76T	50	$ .50	$2.00	Madden, Mike	83TTR	64	$ .02	$ .10
Lynn, Fred	76T	192	$ .50	$1.50	Madden, Mike	84T	127	$ .01	$ .05
Lynn, Fred	76T	196	$ .25	$ .85	Madden, Mike	85T	479	$ .01	$ .04
Lynn, Fred	77T	210	$ .50	$1.50	Madden, Mike	86T	691	$ .01	$ .03
Lynn, Fred	78T	320	$ .30	$ .90	Maddox, Elliott	71T	11	$ .10	$ .35
Lynn, Fred	79T	480	$ .30	$1.00	Maddox, Elliott	72T	277	$ .05	$ .25
Lynn, Fred	80T	110	$ .05	$ .25	Maddox, Elliott	73T	658	$ .35	$1.10
Lynn, Fred	80T	201	$ .08	$ .30	Maddox, Elliott	74T	401	$ .06	$ .25
Lynn, Fred	81T	720	$ .05	$ .20	Maddox, Elliott	75T	113	$ .06	$ .25
Lynn, Fred	81TTR	797	$ .25	$ .65	Maddox, Elliott	76T	503	$ .05	$ .20
Lynn, Fred	82T	251	$ .05	$ .20	Maddox, Elliott	77T	332	$ .03	$ .12
Lynn, Fred	82TIA	252	$ .02	$ .10	Maddox, Elliott	78T	442	$ .02	$ .10
Lynn, Fred	83T	520	$ .03	$ .15	Maddox, Elliott	79T	69	$ .02	$ .10
Lynn, Fred	83TAS	392	$ .01	$ .10	Maddox, Elliott	80T	707	$ .01	$ .07
Lynn, Fred	84T	680	$ .05	$ .20	Maddox, Elliott	81T	299	$ .01	$ .07
Lynn, Fred	85T	220	$ .03	$ .15	Maddox, Garry	73T	322	$ .25	$ .85
Lynn, Fred	85TTR	77	$ .05	$ .25	Maddox, Garry	74T	178	$ .06	$ .25
Lynn, Fred	86T	55	$ .02	$ .20	Maddox, Garry	75T	240	$ .06	$ .25
Lynn, Fred	87T	370	$ .01	$ .10	Maddox, Garry	76T	38	$ .05	$ .20
Lynn, Fred	88T	707	$ .01	$ .10	Maddox, Garry	77T	520	$ .03	$ .12
Lynn, Fred	88TBB	169	$ .01	$ .10	Maddox, Garry	78T	610	$ .02	$ .10
Lynn, Fred	89T	416	$ .01	$ .04	Maddox, Garry	79T	470	$ .02	$ .10
Lynn, Fred	90T	107	$ .01	$ .03	Maddox, Garry	80T	380	$ .01	$ .07
Lynn, Fred	90TTB	663	$ .01	$ .03	Maddox, Garry	81T	160	$ .01	$ .07
Lyons, Barry	87TTR	68	$ .01	$ .07	Maddox, Garry	82T	20	$ .01	$ .06
Lyons, Barry	88T	633	$ .01	$ .03	Maddox, Garry	83T	615	$ .01	$ .06
Lyons, Barry	89T	412	$ .01	$ .04	Maddox, Garry	84T	755	$ .01	$ .05
Lyons, Barry	90T	258	$ .01	$ .03	Maddox, Garry	85T	235	$ .01	$ .04
Lyons, Steve	86T	233	$ .01	$ .03	Maddox, Garry	86T	585	$ .01	$ .03
Lyons, Steve	86TTR	67	$ .02	$ .10	Maddux, Greg	87TTR	70	$ .15	$1.00
Lyons, Steve	88T	108	$ .01	$ .03	Maddux, Greg	88T	361	$ .01	$ .50
Lyons, Steve	89T	334	$ .01	$ .04	Maddux, Greg	89T	240	$ .01	$ .04
Lyons, Steve	89TBB	105	$ .01	$ .05	Maddux, Greg	90T	715	$ .01	$ .10
Lyons, Steve	90T	751	$ .01	$ .03	Maddux, Mike	87T	553	$ .01	$ .10
Lysander, Rick	84T	639	$ .01	$ .05	Maddux, Mike	88T	756	$ .01	$ .03
Lysander, Rick	85T	383	$ .01	$ .04	Maddux, Mike	89T	39	$ .01	$ .04
Lysander, Rick	86T	482	$ .01	$ .03	Maddux, Mike	89TBB	74	$ .01	$ .05
Lyttle, Jim	70T	516	$ .10	$ .35	Maddux, Mike	90T	154	$ .01	$ .05
Lyttle, Jim	71T	234	$ .10	$ .35	Madison, Dave	52T	366	$39.00	$135.00
Lyttle, Jim	72T	648	$ .25	$ .85	Madison, Dave	53T	99	$2.50	$8.00
Lyttle, Jim	74T	437	$ .06	$ .25	Madison, Scotti	88TTR	63	$ .01	$ .05
Maas, Duke	56T	57	$1.25	$4.50	Madlock, Bill	74T	600	$1.00	$4.00
Maas, Duke	57T	405	$1.00	$3.75	Madlock, Bill	75T	104	$ .50	$2.00
Maas, Duke	58T	228	$ .50	$2.00	Madlock, Bill	76T	191	$ .25	$ .85
Maas, Duke	59T	167	$ .50	$1.95	Madlock, Bill	76T	640	$ .50	$2.00
Maas, Duke	60T	421	$ .50	$1.95	Madlock, Bill	77T	1	$1.00	$4.00
Maas, Duke	61T	387	$ .50	$2.00	Madlock, Bill	77T	250	$ .25	$ .85
Mabe, Bob	59T	356	$ .50	$1.95	Madlock, Bill	78T	410	$ .07	$ .30
Mabe, Bob	60T	288	$ .50	$1.95	Madlock, Bill	79T	195	$ .05	$ .20
MacDonald, Bill	52T	138	$6.00	$19.00	Madlock, Bill	80T	55	$ .05	$ .25
Macfarlane, Mike	88TTR	62	$ .01	$ .15	Madlock, Bill	81T	715	$ .05	$ .20
Macfarlane, Mike	89T	479	$ .01	$ .15	Madlock, Bill	82T	161	$ .03	$ .15

TOPPS

Player	Year	No.	VG	EX/MT
Madlock, Bill	82T	365	$ .03	$ .15
Madlock, Bill	82T	696	$ .01	$ .06
Madlock, Bill	83T	291	$ .01	$ .06
Madlock, Bill	83T	645	$ .01	$ .06
Madlock, Bill	84T	131	$ .08	$ .35
Madlock, Bill	84T	250	$ .02	$ .10
Madlock, Bill	84T	696	$ .01	$ .05
Madlock, Bill	84T	701	$ .06	$ .30
Madlock, Bill	85T	560	$ .01	$ .10
Madlock, Bill	86T	470	$ .01	$ .03
Madlock, Bill	87T	734	$ .01	$ .03
Madlock, Bill	87TTR	71	$ .03	$ .15
Madlock, Bill	88T	145	$ .01	$ .10
Magadan, Dave	87T	512	$ .25	$ .85
Magadan, Dave	88T	58	$ .01	$ .10
Magadan, Dave	89T	655	$ .01	$ .04
Magadan, Dave	89TBB	71	$ .01	$ .05
Magadan, Dave	90T	135	$ .01	$ .03
Maglie, Sal	57T	5	$3.00	$9.50
Maglie, Sal	58T	43	$2.10	$7.50
Maglie, Sal	59T	309	$1.25	$3.50
Maglie, Sal	60T	456	$1.25	$4.50
Magnuson, Jim	72T	597	$ .25	$ .85
Magrane, Joe	87TTR	72	$ .25	$1.25
Magrane, Joe	88T	380	$ .01	$ .50
Magrane, Joe	89T	657	$ .01	$ .15
Magrane, Joe	89TBB	203	$ .01	$ .05
Magrane, Joe	90T	578	$ .01	$ .03
Magrane, Joe	90TAS	406	$ .01	$ .03
Magrann, Tom	89TMLD	75	$ .01	$ .05
Magrini, Pete	66T	558	$5.50	$17.50
Mahaffey, Art	60T	138	$ .35	$1.10
Mahaffey, Art	61T	433	$ .50	$2.00
Mahaffey, Art	62T	550	$3.75	$11.00
Mahaffey, Art	63T	7	$ .35	$1.10
Mahaffey, Art	63T	385	$ .35	$1.20
Mahaffey, Art	64T	104	$ .25	$ .85
Mahaffey, Art	65T	446	$ .30	$1.00
Mahaffey, Art	66T	570	$3.50	$10.00
Mahlberg, Greg	80T	673	$ .01	$ .07
Mahler, Mickey	78T	703	$2.00	$7.00
Mahler, Mickey	79T	331	$ .02	$ .10
Mahler, Mickey	86TTR	68	$ .02	$ .10
Mahler, Rick	82T	126	$ .01	$ .06
Mahler, Rick	82T	579	$ .05	$ .20
Mahler, Rick	83T	76	$ .01	$ .06
Mahler, Rick	85T	79	$ .01	$ .04
Mahler, Rick	86T	437	$ .01	$ .03
Mahler, Rick	87T	242	$ .01	$ .03
Mahler, Rick	88T	706	$ .01	$ .03
Mahler, Rick	89T	621	$ .01	$ .04
Mahler, Rick	89TTR	74	$ .01	$ .05
Mahler, Rick	90T	151	$ .01	$ .03
Mahoney, Bob	52T	58	$14.00	$45.00
Mahoney, Jim	73T	356	$ .10	$ .35
Mahoney, Jim	74T	221	$ .06	$ .25
Main, Forrest	52T	397	$39.00	$135.00
Main, Forrest	53T	198	$3.75	$13.00
Majeski, Hank	51Tbb	2	$5.50	$17.00
Majeski, Henry	52T	112	$6.00	$19.00
Maldonado, Candy	84T	244	$ .05	$ .20
Maldonado, Candy	85T	523	$ .01	$ .04
Maldonado, Candy	86T	87	$ .01	$ .03
Maldonado, Candy	86TTR	69	$ .02	$ .10
Maldonado, Candy	87T	335	$ .01	$ .03
Maldonado, Candy	88T	190	$ .01	$ .03
Maldonado, Candy	88TBB	35	$ .01	$ .05
Maldonado, Candy	89T	495	$ .01	$ .04
Maldonado, Candy	89TBB	197	$ .01	$ .05
Maldonado, Candy	90T	628	$ .01	$ .03
Maler, Jim	83T	54	$ .01	$ .06
Maler, Jim	84T	461	$ .01	$ .05
Malkmus, Bob	58T	356	$ .50	$2.00
Malkmus, Bob	59T	151	$ .50	$1.95
Malkmus, Bobby	60T	251	$ .35	$1.10

Player	Year	No.	VG	EX/MT
Malkmus, Bobby	61T	530	$6.00	$18.00
Maloney, Jim	61T	436	$ .70	$2.00
Maloney, Jim	63T	444	$ .50	$2.00
Maloney, Jim	64T	3	$1.25	$3.50
Maloney, Jim	64T	5	$1.75	$5.00
Maloney, Jim	64T	420	$ .50	$2.00
Maloney, Jim	65T	530	$1.50	$3.75
Maloney, Jim	66T	140	$ .25	$ .85
Maloney, Jim	67T	80	$ .25	$ .65

JIM MALONEY
PITCHER REDS

Player	Year	No.	VG	EX/MT
Maloney, Jim	68T	425	$ .25	$ .85
Maloney, Jim	69T	362	$ .25	$ .65
Maloney, Jim	70T	320	$ .25	$ .65
Maloney, Jim	71T	645	$ .60	$1.75
Maloney, Jim	72T	645	$ .25	$ .85
Malzone, Frank	56T	304	$1.80	$6.00
Malzone, Frank	57T	355	$1.00	$3.75
Malzone, Frank	58T	260	$ .50	$2.00
Malzone, Frank	58TAS	481	$ .40	$1.10
Malzone, Frank	59T	220	$ .50	$1.95
Malzone, Frank	59T	519	$3.00	$9.00
Malzone, Frank	59TAS	558	$2.00	$7.00
Malzone, Frank	60T	310	$ .50	$1.95
Malzone, Frank	60TAS	557	$2.00	$7.00
Malzone, Frank	61T	173	$ .50	$2.00
Malzone, Frank	61T	445	$ .50	$2.00
Malzone, Frank	62T	225	$ .35	$1.10
Malzone, Frank	63T	232	$ .25	$ .85
Malzone, Frank	64T	60	$ .15	$ .50
Malzone, Frank	65T	315	$ .30	$1.00
Malzone, Frank	66T	152	$ .25	$ .85
Mangual, Angel	70T	654	$ .70	$2.00
Mangual, Angel	71T	317	$ .10	$ .35
Mangual, Angel	72T	6	$ .10	$ .35
Mangual, Angel	72T	62	$ .05	$ .25
Mangual, Angel	73T	625	$ .35	$1.10
Mangual, Angel	75T	452	$ .06	$ .25
Mangual, Pepe	75T	616	$8.50	$27.50
Mangual, Pepe	76T	164	$ .05	$ .20
Mangual, Pepe	77T	552	$ .03	$ .12
Mankowski, Phil	77T	477	$ .05	$ .15
Mankowski, Phil	78T	559	$ .02	$ .10
Mankowski, Phil	79T	93	$ .02	$ .10
Mankowski, Phil	80T	216	$ .01	$ .07

Player	Year	No.	VG	EX/MT	Player	Year	No.	VG	EX/MT
Mann, Kelly	89TMLD	76	$ .01	$ .15	Manwaring, Kirt	88TTR	64	$ .01	$ .10
Mann, Kelly	90T	744	$ .01	$ .10	Manwaring, Kirt	89T	506	$ .01	$ .10
Manning, Rick	76T	275	$ .05	$ .20	Manwaring, Kirt	90T	678	$ .01	$ .03
Manning, Rick	77T	115	$ .03	$ .12	Mapes, Cliff	52T	103	$6.00	$19.00
Manning, Rick	78T	11	$ .02	$ .10	Maranda, Georges	60T	479	$ .60	$1.75
Manning, Rick	79T	425	$ .02	$ .10	Margoneri, Joe	57T	191	$ .95	$3.50
Manning, Rick	80T	564	$ .01	$ .07	Marichal, Juan	C1T	417	$22.50	$70.00
Manning, Rick	81T	308	$ .01	$ .07	Marichal, Juan	62T	505	$7.50	$22.50
Manning, Rick	82T	202	$ .01	$ .06	Marichal, Juan	63T	440	$4.50	$18.00
Manning, Rick	83T	757	$ .01	$ .06	Marichal, Juan	64T	3	$1.25	$3.50
Manning, Rick	83TTR	65	$ .02	$ .10	Marichal, Juan	64T	280	$3.00	$9.00
Manning, Rick	84T	128	$ .01	$ .05	Marichal, Juan	65T	10	$ .35	$1.10
Manning, Rick	85T	603	$ .01	$ .04	Marichal, Juan	65T	50	$3.00	$9.00
Manning, Rick	86T	49	$ .01	$ .03	Marichal, Juan	66T	221	$ .65	$1.75
Manning, Rick	87T	706	$ .01	$ .03	Marichal, Juan	66T	420	$3.00	$9.00
Manning, Rick	88T	441	$ .01	$ .03	Marichal, Juan	67T	234	$1.50	$3.75
Manrique, Fred	88T	437	$ .01	$ .03	Marichal, Juan	67T	236	$2.50	$8.00
Manrique, Fred	89T	108	$ .01	$ .04	Marichal, Juan	67T	500	$3.75	$13.00
Manrique, Fred	89TBB	84	$ .01	$ .05	Marichal, Juan	68T	205	$2.00	$6.00
Manrique, Fred	90T	242	$ .01	$ .03	Marichal, Juan	69T	10	$1.50	$3.75
Mantilla, Felix	57T	188	$ .95	$3.50	Marichal, Juan	69T	370	$1.35	$4.00
Mantilla, Felix	58T	17	$1.00	$3.75	Marichal, Juan	69T	572	$2.50	$7.50
Mantilla, Felix	59T	157	$ .50	$1.95	Marichal, Juan	70T	67	$1.35	$4.75
Mantilla, Felix	60T	19	$ .35	$1.10	Marichal, Juan	70T	69	$ .50	$1.95
Mantilla, Felix	61T	164	$ .30	$1.00	Marichal, Juan	70T	210	$2.00	$8.00
Mantilla, Felix	62T	436	$1.00	$3.75	Marichal, Juan	70TAS	466	$ .95	$3.50
Mantilla, Felix	63T	447	$2.50	$6.50	Marichal, Juan	71T	325	$2.00	$7.50
Mantilla, Felix	64T	228	$ .25	$ .85	Marichal, Juan	72T	567	$1.35	$4.00
Mantilla, Felix	65T	29	$ .25	$ .65	Marichal, Juan	72TIA	568	$ .70	$2.00
Mantilla, Felix	66T	557	$4.50	$15.00	Marichal, Juan	73T	480	$1.25	$4.50
Mantilla, Felix	67T	524	$ .50	$2.00	Marichal, Juan	74T	330	$ .95	$3.50
Mantle, Mickey	52T	311	$1850.00	$7250.00	Marichal, Juan	74TTR	330	$ .50	$1.95
Mantle, Mickey	53T	82	$550.00	$1650.00	Mariners, Team Checklist	77T	597	$ .03	$ .12
Mantle, Mickey	56T	135	$200.00	$595.00	Mariners, Team Checklist	78T	499	$ .05	$ .25
Mantle, Mickey	57T	95	$200.00	$575.00	Mariners, Team Checklist	79T	659	$ .05	$ .25
Mantle, Mickey	57T	407	$100.00	$350.00	Mariners, Team Checklist	80T	282	$ .06	$ .25
Mantle, Mickey	58T	150	$160.00	$475.00	Mariners, Team Checklist	81T	672	$ .02	$ .20
Mantle, Mickey	58T	418	$35.00	$130.00	Mariners, Team Leaders	86T	546	$ .01	$ .03
Mantle, Mickey	58TAS	487	$15.00	$55.00	Mariners, Team Leaders	87T	156	$ .01	$ .03
Mantle, Mickey	59T	10	$110.00	$325.00	Mariners, Team Leaders	88T	519	$ .01	$ .03
Mantle, Mickey	59T	461	$7.50	$22.50	Mariners, Team Leaders	89T	459	$ .01	$ .04
Mantle, Mickey	59TAS	564	$50.00	$200.00	Maris, Roger	58T	47	$85.00	$275.00
Mantle, Mickey	60T	160	$8.00	$35.00	Maris, Roger	59T	202	$30.00	$100.00
Mantle, Mickey	60T	350	$100.00	$300.00	Maris, Roger	60T	377	$19.50	$67.50
Mantle, Mickey	60TAS	563	$60.00	$175.00	Maris, Roger	60TAS	565	$17.50	$57.50
Mantle, Mickey	61T	44	$4.00	$16.00	Maris, Roger	61T	2	$35.00	$125.00
Mantle, Mickey	61T	300	$80.00	$250.00	Maris, Roger	61T	44	$4.00	$16.00
Mantle, Mickey	61T	406	$7.50	$22.50	Maris, Roger	61TAS	576	$25.00	$75.00
Mantle, Mickey	61TAS	578	$85.00	$275.00	Maris, Roger	61TMVP	478	$8.00	$25.00
Mantle, Mickey	61TMVP	475	$12.50	$50.00	Maris, Roger	62T	1	$40.00	$160.00
Mantle, Mickey	62T	18	$30.00	$95.00	Maris, Roger	62T	53	$3.00	$12.50
Mantle, Mickey	62T	53	$3.00	$12.50	Maris, Roger	62T	313	$3.00	$12.50
Mantle, Mickey	62T	200	$125.00	$325.00	Maris, Roger	62T	401	$6.00	$18.00
Mantle, Mickey	62T	318	$9.00	$27.50	Maris, Roger	63T	4	$ .50	$2.00
Mantle, Mickey	62TAS	471	$15.00	$50.00	Maris, Roger	63T	120	$10.00	$37.50
Mantle, Mickey	63T	2	$3.00	$12.00	Maris, Roger	64T	225	$10.00	$37.50
Mantle, Mickey	63T	173	$7.50	$30.00	Maris, Roger	64T	331	$15.00	$45.00
Mantle, Mickey	63T	200	$95.00	$275.00	Maris, Roger	65T	155	$15.00	$45.00
Mantle, Mickey	64T	50	$65.00	$195.00	Maris, Roger	66T	365	$10.00	$37.50
Mantle, Mickey	64T	331	$15.00	$45.00	Maris, Roger	67T	45	$7.50	$22.50
Mantle, Mickey	65T	3	$5.00	$15.00	Maris, Roger	68T	330	$15.00	$45.00
Mantle, Mickey	65T	5	$3.00	$12.00	Maris, Roger	75T	198	$ .50	$1.95
Mantle, Mickey	65T	350	$100.00	$300.00	Maris, Roger	75T	199	$ .50	$2.00
Mantle, Mickey	66T	50	$80.00	$235.00	Maris, Roger	79T	413	$ .20	$ .75
Mantle, Mickey	67T	150	$60.00	$175.00	Maris, Roger	86TB	405	$ .03	$ .15
Mantle, Mickey	68T	280	$50.00	$150.00	Marone, Lou	70T	703	$ .50	$2.00
Mantle, Mickey	68T	490	$17.50	$60.00	Marquess, Mark	88TTR	65	$ .01	$ .05
Mantle, Mickey	69T	500	$55.00	$160.00	Marquez, Gonzalo	73T	605	$ .50	$2.00
Mantle, Mickey	75T	194	$1.75	$5.00	Marquez, Gonzalo	74T	422	$ .06	$ .25
Mantle, Mickey	75T	195	$1.75	$5.00	Marrero, Connie	52T	317	$39.00	$135.00
Mantle, Mickey	75T	200	$1.25	$4.00	Marrero, Connie	53T	13	$3.75	$13.00
Manual, Jerry	76T	596	$ .10	$ .35	Marsh, Fred	52T	8	$14.00	$45.00
Manuel, Chuck	70T	194	$ .10	$ .35	Marsh, Fred	54T	218	$2.10	$7.50
Manuel, Chuck	71T	744	$ .70	$2.10	Marsh, Fred	55T	13	$1.35	$5.00
Manush, Heinie	54T	187	$3.75	$11.00	Marsh, Freddie	53T	240	$11.00	$37.50

Player	Year	No.	VG	EX/MT
Marsh, Freddie	56T	23	$1.25	$4.50
Marshall, Clarence	52T	174	$6.00	$19.00
Marshall, Dave	69T	464	$ .25	$ .65
Marshall, Dave	70T	58	$ .10	$ .35
Marshall, Dave	71T	259	$ .10	$ .35
Marshall, Dave	72T	673	$ .70	$2.10
Marshall, Dave	73T	513	$ .06	$ .25
Marshall, Jim	58T	441	$ .50	$1.95
Marshall, Jim	59T	153	$ .50	$1.95
Marshall, Jim	60T	267	$ .35	$1.10
Marshall, Jim	61T	188	$ .30	$1.00
Marshall, Jim	62T	337	$ .35	$1.10
Marshall, Jim	74T	354	$ .06	$ .25
Marshall, Mike	68T	201	$ .50	$2.00
Marshall, Mike	69T	17	$ .25	$ .65
Marshall, Mike	71T	713	$1.00	$3.75
Marshall, Mike	72T	505	$ .25	$ .65
Marshall, Mike	73T	355	$ .25	$ .65
Marshall, Mike	74T	73	$ .15	$ .50
Marshall, Mike	74T	208	$ .06	$ .25
Marshall, Mike	74TTR	73	$ .25	$ .85
Marshall, Mike	75T	313	$ .25	$ .85
Marshall, Mike	75T	330	$ .06	$ .25
Marshall, Mike	75THL	6	$ .10	$ .35
Marshall, Mike	76T	465	$ .06	$ .25
Marshall, Mike	77T	263	$ .03	$ .12
Marshall, Mike	82T	681	$ .75	$3.50
Marshall, Mike	83T	324	$ .03	$ .15
Marshall, Mike	84T	634	$ .02	$ .10
Marshall, Mike	85T	85	$ .01	$ .04
Marshall, Mike	86T	728	$ .01	$ .10
Marshall, Mike	87T	664	$ .01	$ .10
Marshall, Mike	88T	249	$ .01	$ .10
Marshall, Mike	88TBB	133	$ .01	$ .05
Marshall, Mike	89T	582	$ .01	$ .04
Marshall, Mike	89TBB	48	$ .01	$ .05
Marshall, Mike	90T	198	$ .01	$ .03
Marshall, Willard	52T	96	$6.00	$19.00
Marshall, Willard	53T	95	$3.75	$13.00
Martin, Billy	52T	175	$75.00	$250.00
Martin, Billy	53T	86	$25.00	$90.00
Martin, Billy	54T	13	$25.00	$75.00
Martin, Billy	56T	181	$15.00	$45.00
Martin, Billy	57T	62	$8.50	$32.50
Martin, Billy	58T	271	$2.75	$8.50
Martin, Billy	59T	295	$2.75	$8.50
Martin, Billy	60T	173	$2.00	$6.00
Martin, Billy	61T	89	$1.50	$4.50
Martin, Billy	62T	208	$1.50	$4.50
Martin, Billy	69T	547	$ .70	$2.00
Martin, Billy	71T	208	$ .50	$2.00
Martin, Billy	72T	33	$1.00	$4.00
Martin, Billy	72TIA	34	$ .15	$ .50
Martin, Billy	73T	323	$ .30	$1.00
Martin, Billy	74T	379	$ .15	$ .50
Martin, Billy	78T	721	$ .25	$ .85
Martin, Billy	83T	156	$ .01	$ .10
Martin, Billy	83TTR	66	$ .05	$ .25
Martin, Billy	84T	81	$ .03	$ .15
Martin, Billy	85TTR	78	$ .10	$ .35
Martin, Billy	86T	651	$ .01	$ .03
Martin, Gene	70T	599	$ .25	$ .85
Martin, J. C.	60T	346	$ .50	$1.95
Martin, J. C.	61T	124	$ .30	$1.00
Martin, J. C.	62T	91	$ .35	$1.10
Martin, J. C.	63T	499	$2.50	$6.50
Martin, J. C.	64T	148	$ .25	$ .85
Martin, J. C.	65T	382	$ .30	$1.00
Martin, J. C.	66T	47	$ .25	$ .85
Martin, J. C.	67T	538	$1.25	$3.50
Martin, J. C.	68T	211	$ .25	$ .65
Martin, J. C.	69T	112	$ .25	$ .65
Martin, J. C.	70T	488	$ .10	$ .35
Martin, J. C.	71T	704	$ .70	$2.10
Martin, J. C.	72T	639	$ .25	$ .85

Player	Year	No.	VG	EX/MT
Martin, J. C.	73T	552	$ .35	$1.10
Martin, J. C.	74T	354	$ .06	$ .25
Martin, Jake	56T	129	$1.25	$4.50
Martin, Jerry	77T	596	$ .03	$ .12
Martin, Jerry	78T	222	$ .02	$ .10
Martin, Jerry	79T	382	$ .02	$ .10

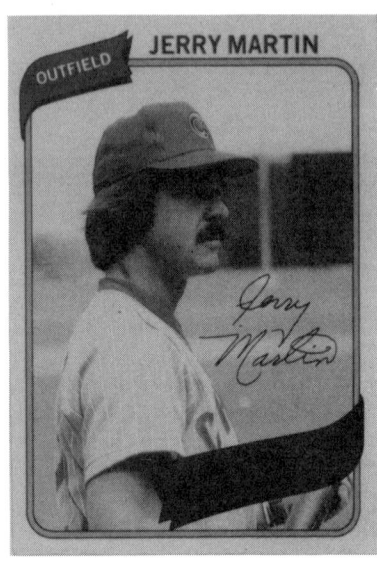

Player	Year	No.	VG	EX/MT
Martin, Jerry	80T	493	$ .01	$ .07
Martin, Jerry	81T	103	$ .01	$ .07
Martin, Jerry	81TTR	798	$ .02	$ .10
Martin, Jerry	82T	722	$ .01	$ .06
Martin, Jerry	82TTR	65	$ .02	$ .10
Martin, Jerry	83T	626	$ .01	$ .06
Martin, Jerry	84T	74	$ .01	$ .05
Martin, Jerry	84TTR	74	$ .02	$ .10
Martin, Jerry	85T	517	$ .01	$ .04
Martin, John	82T	236	$ .01	$ .06
Martin, John	83T	721	$ .01	$ .06
Martin, John	84T	24	$ .01	$ .05
Martin, Morrie	52T	131	$6.00	$19.00
Martin, Morrie	53T	227	$11.00	$37.50
Martin, Morrie	54T	168	$2.10	$7.50
Martin, Morrie	58T	53	$1.00	$3.75
Martin, Morrie	59T	38	$1.00	$3.75
Martin, Renie	80T	667	$ .30	$1.25
Martin, Renie	81T	452	$ .01	$ .07
Martin, Renie	82T	594	$ .01	$ .06
Martin, Renie	82TTR	66	$ .02	$ .10
Martin, Renie	83T	263	$ .01	$ .06
Martin, Renie	84T	603	$ .01	$ .05
Martinez, Buck	70T	609	$ .25	$ .85
Martinez, Buck	71T	163	$ .10	$ .35
Martinez, Buck	72T	332	$ .05	$ .25
Martinez, Buck	75T	314	$ .06	$ .25
Martinez, Buck	76T	616	$ .05	$ .20
Martinez, Buck	77T	46	$ .03	$ .12
Martinez, Buck	78T	571	$ .02	$ .10
Martinez, Buck	79T	243	$ .02	$ .10
Martinez, Buck	80T	477	$ .01	$ .07
Martinez, Buck	81T	56	$ .01	$ .07
Martinez, Buck	81TTR	799	$ .02	$ .10
Martinez, Buck	82T	314	$ .01	$ .06
Martinez, Buck	83T	733	$ .01	$ .06
Martinez, Buck	84T	179	$ .01	$ .05

Player	Year	No.	VG	EX/MT	Player	Year	No.	VG	EX/MT
Martinez, Buck	85T	673	$ .01	$ .04	Marting, Tim	71T	423	$ .10	$ .35
Martinez, Buck	86T	518	$ .01	$ .03	Martyn, Bob	58T	39	$ .65	$2.00
Martinez, Carlos	90T	461	$ .01	$ .10	Martyn, Bob	59T	41	$ .60	$1.80
Martinez, Carmelo	84T	267	$ .03	$ .25	Martz, Randy	81T	381	$ .01	$ .07
Martinez, Carmelo	84TTR	75	$ .02	$ .10	Martz, Randy	82T	188	$ .01	$ .06
Martinez, Carmelo	85T	558	$ .01	$ .04	Martz, Randy	82T	456	$ .01	$ .06
Martinez, Carmelo	86T	67	$ .01	$ .03	Martz, Randy	83T	22	$ .01	$ .06
Martinez, Carmelo	87T	348	$ .01	$ .03	Marzano, John	85T	399	$ .50	$2.00
Martinez, Carmelo	88T	148	$ .01	$ .03	Marzano, John	88T	757	$ .01	$ .25
Martinez, Carmelo	88TBB	238	$ .01	$ .05	Mashore, Clyde	71T	376	$ .10	$ .35
Martinez, Carmelo	89T	449	$ .01	$ .04	Mashore, Clyde	73T	401	$ .06	$ .25
Martinez, Carmelo	89TBB	11	$ .01	$ .05	Masi, Phil	51Tbb	19	$5.50	$17.00
Martinez, Carmelo	90T	686	$ .01	$ .03	Masi, Phil	52T	283	$14.00	$45.00
Martinez, Dave	87TTR	73	$ .15	$ .50	Mason, Don	66T	524	$4.00	$10.00
Martinez, Dave	88T	439	$ .01	$ .20	Mason, Don	69T	584	$ .25	$ .85
Martinez, Dave	89T	763	$ .01	$ .04	Mason, Don	71T	548	$ .30	$1.00
Martinez, Dave	90T	228	$ .01	$ .03	Mason, Don	72T	739	$ .70	$2.10
Martinez, Denny	77T	491	$ .25	$1.00	Mason, Henry	60T	331	$ .50	$1.95
Martinez, Denny	78T	119	$ .02	$ .10	Mason, Jim	72T	334	$ .10	$ .35
Martinez, Denny	79T	211	$ .02	$ .10	Mason, Jim	73T	458	$ .06	$ .25
Martinez, Denny	80T	10	$ .01	$ .07	Mason, Jim	74T	618	$ .06	$ .25
Martinez, Denny	81T	367	$ .01	$ .07	Mason, Jim	74TTR	618	$ .06	$ .25
Martinez, Denny	82T	165	$ .03	$ .15	Mason, Jim	75T	136	$ .06	$ .25
Martinez, Denny	82T	712	$ .01	$ .06	Mason, Jim	77T	212	$ .03	$ .12
Martinez, Denny	83T	553	$ .01	$ .06	Mason, Jim	78T	588	$ .02	$ .10
Martinez, Denny	84T	631	$ .01	$ .05	Mason, Jim	79T	67	$ .02	$ .10
Martinez, Denny	85T	199	$ .01	$ .04	Mason, Jim	80T	497	$ .01	$ .07
Martinez, Denny	86T	416	$ .01	$ .03	Mason, Mike	84TTR	76	$ .02	$ .10
Martinez, Denny	87T	252	$ .01	$ .03	Mason, Mike	85T	464	$ .01	$ .04
Martinez, Denny	88T	76	$ .01	$ .03	Mason, Mike	86T	189	$ .01	$ .03
Martinez, Denny	89T	313	$ .01	$ .04	Mason, Mike	87T	646	$ .01	$ .03
Martinez, Denny	90T	763	$ .01	$ .03	Mason, Mike	88T	87	$ .01	$ .03
Martinez, Edgar	90T	148	$ .01	$ .03	Mason, Roger	86TTR	70	$ .02	$ .10
Martinez, Fred	81T	227	$ .01	$ .07	Mason, Roger	87T	526	$ .01	$ .03
Martinez, Fred	82T	659	$ .01	$ .06	Masse, Billy	88TTR	67	$ .01	$ .20
Martinez, Jose	70T	8	$ .10	$ .35	Masse, Billy	89TBB	179	$ .01	$ .05
Martinez, Jose	71T	712	$ .70	$2.10	Masterson, Walt	52T	186	$6.00	$19.00
Martinez, Orlando "Marty"	67T	504	$ .50	$2.00	Matchick, John (Tom)	67T	72	$ .25	$ .65
Martinez, Orlando	68T	578	$ .30	$1.00	Matchick, Tom	68T	113	$ .25	$ .65
Martinez, Marty	69T	337	$ .25	$ .65	Matchick, Tom	69T	344	$ .25	$ .65
Martinez, Marty	70T	126	$ .10	$ .35	Matchick, Tom	70T	647	$ .50	$2.00
Martinez, Marty	71T	602	$ .30	$1.00	Matchick, Tom	71T	321	$ .10	$ .35
Martinez, Marty	72T	336	$ .05	$ .25	Matchick, Tom	73T	631	$ .35	$1.10
Martinez, Ramon	89T	225	$ .05	$ .25	Mathew, Nelson	63T	54	$1.25	$4.50
Martinez, Ramon	90T	62	$ .01	$ .25	Mathews, Ed	52T	407	$350.00	$1500.00
Martinez, Silvio	79T	609	$ .02	$ .10	Mathews, Ed	53T	37	$17.50	$55.00
Martinez, Silvio	80T	496	$ .01	$ .07	Mathews, Ed	54T	30	$13.50	$42.50
Martinez, Silvio	81T	586	$ .01	$ .07	Mathews, Ed	55T	155	$22.50	$67.50
Martinez, Silvio	82T	181	$ .01	$ .06	Mathews, Ed	56T	107	$10.00	$30.00
Martinez, Ted	71T	648	$ .50	$4.00	Mathews, Ed	57T	250	$5.50	$20.00
Martinez, Ted	72T	544	$ .25	$ .85	Mathews, Ed	58T	351	$7.00	$20.00
Martinez, Ted	73T	161	$ .06	$ .25	Mathews, Ed	58T	440	$6.00	$18.00
Martinez, Ted	74T	487	$ .06	$ .25	Mathews, Ed	58TAS	480	$3.50	$9.50
Martinez, Ted	75T	637	$ .06	$ .25	Mathews, Ed	59T	212	$7.00	$28.00
Martinez, Ted	76T	356	$ .05	$ .20	Mathews, Ed	59T	450	$6.50	$20.00
Martinez, Ted	78T	546	$ .02	$ .10	Mathews, Ed	60T	420	$6.00	$18.00
Martinez, Ted	79T	128	$ .02	$ .10	Mathews, Ed	60TAS	558	$4.50	$13.50
Martinez, Ted	80T	191	$ .01	$ .07	Mathews, Ed	61T	43	$1.50	$5.75
Martinez, Tino	88TTR	66	$ .20	$1.75	Mathews, Ed	61T	120	$3.50	$12.50
Martinez, Tino	89TBB	93	$ .01	$ .25	Mathews, Ed	62T	30	$2.75	$9.00
Martinez, Tippy	76T	41	$ .06	$ .25	Mathews, Ed	63T	275	$3.00	$9.00
Martinez, Tippy	77T	238	$ .03	$ .12	Mathews, Ed	64T	35	$3.00	$9.00
Martinez, Tippy	78T	393	$ .02	$ .10	Mathews, Ed	65T	500	$4.00	$15.00
Martinez, Tippy	79T	491	$ .02	$ .10	Mathews, Ed	66T	200	$2.50	$7.50
Martinez, Tippy	80T	706	$ .01	$ .07	Mathews, Ed	67T	166	$2.50	$8.00
Martinez, Tippy	81T	119	$ .01	$ .07	Mathews, Ed	68T	58	$2.50	$8.00
Martinez, Tippy	82T	583	$ .01	$ .06	Mathews, Eddie	73T	237	$ .30	$1.00
Martinez, Tippy	83T	631	$ .01	$ .06	Mathews, Eddie	74T	634	$ .30	$1.00
Martinez, Tippy	84T	215	$ .01	$ .05	Mathews, Greg	87T	567	$ .01	$ .10
Martinez, Tippy	85T	445	$ .01	$ .04	Mathews, Greg	88T	133	$ .01	$ .03
Martinez, Tippy	86T	82	$ .01	$ .03	Mathews, Greg	88TBB	177	$ .01	$ .05
Martinez, Tippy	87T	728	$ .01	$ .03	Mathews, Greg	89T	97	$ .01	$ .04
Martinez, Tony	63T	466	$6.00	$18.00	Mathews, Greg	90T	209	$ .01	$ .03
Martinez, Tony	64T	404	$ .40	$1.25	Mathews, Nelson	64T	366	$ .25	$ .85
Martinez, Tony	66T	581	$4.50	$15.00	Mathews, Nelson	65T	87	$ .25	$ .65

TOPPS

Player	Year	No.	VG	EX/MT
Mathewson, Christy	61T	408	$ .70	$2.00
Mathias, Carl	60T	139	$ .35	$1.10
Mathis, Ron	85TTR	79	$ .02	$ .10
Mathis, Ron	86T	476	$ .01	$ .03
Matias, John	70T	444	$ .10	$ .35
Matias, John	71T	546	$ .30	$1.00
Matlack, Jon	71T	648	$ .50	$4.00
Matlack, Jon	72T	141	$ .10	$ .35
Matlack, Jon	73T	55	$ .10	$ .35
Matlack, Jon	74T	153	$ .06	$ .25
Matlack, Jon	75T	290	$ .06	$ .25
Matlack, Jon	76T	190	$ .05	$ .20
Matlack, Jon	77T	440	$ .03	$ .12
Matlack, Jon	78T	25	$ .02	$ .10
Matlack, Jon	79T	315	$ .02	$ .10
Matlack, Jon	80T	592	$ .01	$ .07
Matlack, Jon	81T	656	$ .01	$ .07
Matlack, Jon	82T	239	$ .01	$ .06
Matlack, Jon	83T	749	$ .01	$ .06
Matlack, Jon	84T	149	$ .01	$ .05
Matthews, Gary	73T	606	$ .95	$3.50
Matthews, Gary	74T	386	$ .25	$ .85
Matthews, Gary	75T	79	$ .10	$ .35
Matthews, Gary	76T	133	$ .05	$ .20
Matthews, Gary	77T	194	$ .03	$ .12
Matthews, Gary	78T	475	$ .02	$ .10
Matthews, Gary	79T	85	$ .02	$ .10
Matthews, Gary	80T	355	$ .01	$ .07
Matthews, Gary	81T	528	$ .01	$ .07
Matthews, Gary	81TTR	800	$ .02	$ .10
Matthews, Gary	82T	680	$ .01	$ .06
Matthews, Gary	83T	780	$ .01	$ .06
Matthews, Gary	84T	70	$ .01	$ .05
Matthews, Gary	84T	637	$ .01	$ .05
Matthews, Gary	84TTR	77	$ .02	$ .10
Matthews, Gary	85T	210	$ .01	$ .04
Matthews, Gary	86T	485	$ .01	$ .03
Matthews, Gary	87T	390	$ .01	$ .03
Matthews, Gary	88T	156	$ .01	$ .03
Mattingly, Don	84T	8	$7.50	$30.00
Mattingly, Don	85T	665	$2.00	$9.00
Mattingly, Don	86T	180	$ .75	$3.00
Mattingly, Don	86TAS	712	$ .20	$1.00
Mattingly, Don	87T	500	$ .70	$2.10
Mattingly, Don	87TAS	606	$ .50	$1.95
Mattingly, Don	88T	300	$ .35	$1.10
Mattingly, Don	88TAS	386	$ .10	$ .50
Mattingly, Don	88TBB	229	$ .15	$1.00
Mattingly, Don	88TRB	2	$ .05	$ .60
Mattingly, Don	89T	700	$ .10	$ .50
Mattingly, Don	89TAS	397	$ .05	$ .25
Mattingly, Don	89TBB	50	$ .01	$ .75
Mattingly, Don	90T	200	$ .01	$ .50
Matula, Rick	80T	596	$ .01	$ .07
Matula, Rick	81T	611	$ .01	$ .07
Matuszek, Len	83T	357	$ .01	$ .06
Matuszek, Len	84T	275	$ .01	$ .05
Matuszek, Len	85T	688	$ .01	$ .04
Matuszek, Len	85TTR	80	$ .02	$ .10
Matuszek, Len	86T	109	$ .01	$ .03
Matuszek, Len	87T	457	$ .01	$ .03
Matuszek, Len	88T	92	$ .01	$ .03
Mauch, Gene	57T	342	$5.00	$15.00
Mauch, Gene	61T	219	$ .60	$1.75
Mauch, Gene	62T	374	$ .60	$1.75
Mauch, Gene	63T	318	$ .35	$1.10
Mauch, Gene	64T	157	$ .15	$ .50
Mauch, Gene	65T	489	$ .50	$1.95
Mauch, Gene	66T	411	$ .15	$ .50
Mauch, Gene	67T	248	$ .25	$ .65
Mauch, Gene	68T	122	$ .15	$ .50
Mauch, Gene	69T	606	$ .20	$ .50
Mauch, Gene	70T	442	$ .25	$ .85
Mauch, Gene	71T	59	$ .15	$ .50
Mauch, Gene	72T	276	$ .25	$ .65

Player	Year	No.	VG	EX/MT
Mauch, Gene	73T	377	$ .10	$ .35

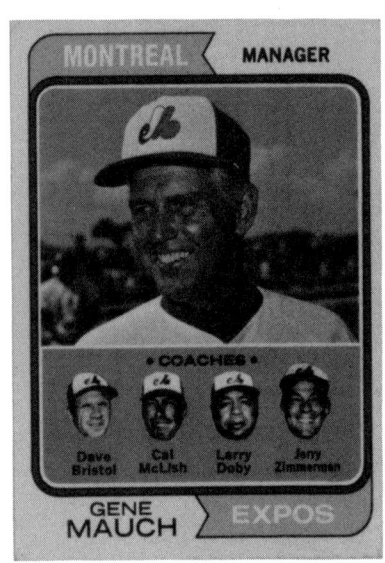

Player	Year	No.	VG	EX/MT
Mauch, Gene	74T	531	$ .25	$ .85
Mauch, Gene	78T	601	$ .02	$ .10
Mauch, Gene	83T	276	$ .01	$ .06
Mauch, Gene	85TTR	81	$ .02	$ .10
Mauch, Gene	86T	81	$ .01	$ .03
Mauch, Gene	87T	518	$ .01	$ .03
Mauch, Gene	88T	774	$ .01	$ .03
Maxie, Larry	64T	94	$ .25	$ .85
Maxvill, Dal	63T	49	$ .30	$1.00
Maxvill, Dal	64T	563	$1.50	$3.75
Maxvill, Dal	65T	78	$ .25	$ .65
Maxvill, Dal	66T	338	$ .15	$ .75
Maxvill, Dal	67T	421	$ .25	$ .85
Maxvill, Dal	68T	141	$ .25	$ .65
Maxvill, Dal	69T	320	$ .25	$ .85
Maxvill, Dal	70T	503	$ .10	$ .35
Maxvill, Dal	71T	476	$ .10	$ .35
Maxvill, Dal	72T	206	$ .05	$ .25
Maxvill, Dal	73T	483	$ .06	$ .25
Maxvill, Dal	74T	358	$ .06	$ .25
Maxwell, Charley	52T	180	$6.00	$18.00
Maxwell, Charley	57T	205	$ .95	$3.50
Maxwell, Charley	58T	380	$ .50	$2.00
Maxwell, Charlie	59T	34	$2.00	$8.00
Maxwell, Charlie	59T	481	$ .50	$1.95
Maxwell, Charlie	60T	443	$ .60	$1.75
Maxwell, Charlie	61T	37	$ .30	$1.00
Maxwell, Charley	62T	506	$ .70	$2.10
Maxwell, Charlie	63T	86	$ .25	$ .85
Maxwell, Charley	64T	401	$ .40	$1.25
May, Carlos	69T	654	$ .25	$ .85
May, Carlos	70T	18	$ .10	$ .35
May, Carlos	71T	243	$ .10	$ .35
May, Carlos	72T	525	$ .05	$ .25
May, Carlos	73T	105	$ .06	$ .25
May, Carlos	74T	195	$ .06	$ .25
May, Carlos	75T	480	$ .06	$ .25
May, Carlos	76T	110	$ .05	$ .20
May, Carlos	77T	568	$ .03	$ .12
May, Carlos	77T	633	$ .03	$ .12
May, Dave	68T	56	$ .25	$ .65
May, Dave	69T	113	$ .25	$ .65

Player	Year	No.	VG	EX/MT	Player	Year	No.	VG	EX/MT
May, Dave	70T	81	$ .10	$ .35	Mayberry, John	72T	373	$ .05	$ .25
May, Dave	71T	493	$ .10	$ .35	Mayberry, John	73T	118	$ .10	$ .35
May, Dave	72T	549	$ .25	$ .85	Mayberry, John	74T	150	$ .06	$ .25
May, Dave	73T	152	$ .06	$ .25	Mayberry, John	75T	95	$ .06	$ .25
May, Dave	74T	12	$ .06	$ .25	Mayberry, John	76T	194	$ .50	$1.95
May, Dave	75T	650	$ .06	$ .25	Mayberry, John	76T	196	$ .25	$ .85
May, Dave	76T	281	$ .05	$ .20	Mayberry, John	76T	440	$ .05	$ .20
May, Dave	78T	362	$ .02	$ .10	Mayberry, John	77T	244	$ .03	$ .12
May, Jerry	65T	143	$ .25	$ .65	Mayberry, John	78T	550	$ .02	$ .10
May, Jerry	66T	123	$ .25	$ .85	Mayberry, John	79T	380	$ .02	$ .10
May, Jerry	67T	379	$ .25	$ .85	Mayberry, John	80T	643	$ .01	$ .07
May, Jerry	68T	598	$1.25	$3.50	Mayberry, John	81T	169	$ .01	$ .07
May, Jerry	69T	263	$ .25	$ .85	Mayberry, John	82T	470	$ .01	$ .06
May, Jerry	70T	423	$ .10	$ .35	Mayberry, John	82T	606	$ .01	$ .06
May, Jerry	71T	719	$ .70	$2.10	Mayberry, John	82TTR	67	$ .02	$ .10
May, Jerry	72T	109	$ .05	$ .25	Mayberry, John	83T	45	$ .01	$ .06
May, Jerry	73T	558	$ .35	$1.10	Maye, Lee	60T	246	$ .35	$1.10
May, Lee	66T	424	$ .95	$3.50	Maye, Lee	61T	84	$ .30	$1.00
May, Lee	67T	222	$ .30	$1.00	Maye, Lee	62T	518	$ .70	$2.10
May, Lee	68T	487	$ .50	$2.00	Maye, Lee	63T	109	$ .25	$ .85
May, Lee	69T	405	$ .30	$1.00	Maye, Lee	64T	416	$ .40	$1.25
May, Lee	70T	65	$ .60	$1.75	Maye, Lee	65T	407	$ .30	$1.00
May, Lee	70T	225	$ .15	$ .50	Maye, Lee	66T	162	$ .25	$ .85
May, Lee	71T	40	$ .15	$ .50	Maye, Lee	67T	258	$ .25	$ .65
May, Lee	72T	89	$ .60	$2.00	Maye, Lee	68T	94	$ .25	$ .65
May, Lee	72T	480	$ .25	$ .85	Maye, Lee	69T	595	$ .25	$ .85
May, Lee	73T	135	$ .25	$ .65	Maye, Lee	70T	439	$ .10	$ .35
May, Lee	74T	500	$ .25	$ .85	Maye, Lee	71T	733	$ .70	$2.10
May, Lee	75T	25	$ .10	$ .35	Mayer, Ed	58T	461	$ .50	$1.95
May, Lee	76T	210	$ .05	$ .20	Mayo, Eddie	54T	247	$2.10	$7.50
May, Lee	77T	3	$ .30	$1.00	Mays, Willie	52T	261	$325.00	$900.00
May, Lee	77T	380	$ .03	$ .12	Mays, Willie	53T	244	$375.00	$1250.00
May, Lee	77T	633	$ .03	$ .12	Mays, Willie	54T	90	$95.00	$285.00
May, Lee	78T	640	$ .02	$ .10	Mays, Willie	55T	194	$100.00	$350.00
May, Lee	79T	10	$ .02	$ .10	Mays, Willie	56T	130	$70.00	$200.00
May, Lee	80T	490	$ .01	$ .07	Mays, Willie	57T	10	$87.50	$200.00
May, Lee	82T	132	$ .01	$ .06	Mays, Willie	58T	5	$40.00	$120.00
May, Lee	83T	377	$ .01	$ .06	Mays, Willie	58T	436	$11.50	$38.00
May, Lee	83T	378	$ .01	$ .06	Mays, Willie	58TAS	486	$9.50	$27.50
May, Milt	71T	343	$ .10	$ .35	Mays, Willie	59T	50	$35.00	$100.00
May, Milt	72T	247	$ .05	$ .25	Mays, Willie	59T	317	$4.00	$16.00
May, Milt	73T	529	$ .35	$1.10	Mays, Willie	59T	464	$4.00	$15.00
May, Milt	74T	293	$ .06	$ .25	Mays, Willie	59TAS	563	$30.00	$95.00
May, Milt	75T	279	$ .06	$ .25	Mays, Willie	60T	7	$3.00	$9.50
May, Milt	76T	532	$ .05	$ .20	Mays, Willie	60T	200	$32.50	$100.00
May, Milt	76TTR	532	$ .05	$ .20	Mays, Willie	60TAS	564	$20.00	$70.00
May, Milt	77T	98	$ .03	$ .12	Mays, Willie	61T	41	$1.50	$5.00
May, Milt	78T	176	$ .02	$ .10	Mays, Willie	61T	150	$22.50	$72.50
May, Milt	79T	316	$ .02	$ .10	Mays, Willie	61TAS	579	$40.00	$115.00
May, Milt	80T	647	$ .01	$ .07	Mays, Willie	61TMVP	402	$7.00	$25.00
May, Milt	81T	463	$ .01	$ .07	Mays, Willie	62T	18	$30.00	$95.00
May, Milt	82T	242	$ .01	$ .06	Mays, Willie	62T	54	$ .50	$1.95
May, Milt	82T	576	$ .01	$ .06	Mays, Willie	62T	300	$35.00	$100.00
May, Milt	83T	84	$ .01	$ .06	Mays, Willie	62TAS	395	$7.00	$25.00
May, Milt	84T	788	$ .01	$ .05	Mays, Willie	63T	3	$2.35	$9.00
May, Milt	85T	509	$ .01	$ .04	Mays, Willie	63T	138	$8.00	$25.00
May, Rudy	65T	537	$1.35	$4.00	Mays, Willie	63T	300	$32.50	$87.50
May, Rudy	70T	203	$ .10	$ .35	Mays, Willie	64T	9	$2.50	$7.50
May, Rudy	71T	318	$ .10	$ .35	Mays, Willie	64T	150	$17.50	$57.50
May, Rudy	72T	656	$ .25	$ .85	Mays, Willie	64T	306	$6.50	$20.00
May, Rudy	73T	102	$ .06	$ .25	Mays, Willie	64T	423	$15.00	$45.00
May, Rudy	74T	302	$ .06	$ .25	Mays, Willie	65T	4	$1.50	$3.75
May, Rudy	75T	321	$ .06	$ .25	Mays, Willie	65T	6	$ .95	$3.50
May, Rudy	76T	481	$ .05	$ .20	Mays, Willie	65T	250	$20.00	$65.00
May, Rudy	77T	56	$ .03	$ .12	Mays, Willie	66T	1	$35.00	$135.00
May, Rudy	78T	262	$ .02	$ .10	Mays, Willie	66T	215	$2.75	$9.50
May, Rudy	79T	603	$ .02	$ .10	Mays, Willie	66T	217	$1.25	$3.50
May, Rudy	80T	539	$ .01	$ .07	Mays, Willie	66T	219	$ .65	$1.75
May, Rudy	81T	7	$ .02	$ .10	Mays, Willie	67T	200	$22.00	$65.00
May, Rudy	81T	179	$ .01	$ .07	Mays, Willie	67T	244	$1.35	$4.00
May, Rudy	82T	735	$ .01	$ .06	Mays, Willie	67T	423	$7.50	$22.50
May, Rudy	83T	408	$ .01	$ .06	Mays, Willie	68T	50	$17.50	$57.50
May, Rudy	84T	652	$ .01	$ .05	Mays, Willie	68T	490	$17.50	$60.00
Mayberry, John	70T	227	$ .30	$1.00	Mays, Willie	69T	190	$8.50	$32.50
Mayberry, John	71T	148	$ .10	$ .35	Mays, Willie	70T	600	$11.25	$45.00

Player	Year	No.	VG	EX/MT
Mays, Willie	71T	600	$11.00	$42.50
Mays, Willie	72T	49	$4.00	$16.00
Mays, Willie	72TIA	50	$2.50	$8.00
Mays, Willie	73T	1	$3.50	$12.50

WILLIE MAYS
NEW YORK METS   **OUTFIELD**

Player	Year	No.	VG	EX/MT
Mays, Willie	73T	305	$7.50	$22.50
Mays, Willie	75T	192	$ .50	$2.00
Mays, Willie	75T	203	$ .35	$1.10
Mays, Willie	86TB	403	$ .03	$ .15
Mazeroski, Bill	57T	24	$7.50	$22.50
Mazeroski, Bill	58T	238	$1.75	$5.00
Mazeroski, Bill	59T	415	$1.25	$3.50
Mazeroski, Bill	59TAS	555	$3.00	$9.00
Mazeroski, Bill	60T	55	$ .75	$2.50
Mazeroski, Bill	61T	430	$ .75	$2.00
Mazeroski, Bill	61TAS	571	$6.00	$17.50
Mazeroski, Bill	62T	353	$1.00	$3.75
Mazeroski, Bill	62TAS	391	$ .70	$2.00
Mazeroski, Bill	63T	323	$1.00	$3.75
Mazeroski, Bill	64T	570	$2.00	$7.50
Mazeroski, Bill	65T	95	$ .50	$2.00
Mazeroski, Bill	66T	210	$1.00	$4.00
Mazeroski, Bill	67T	510	$1.25	$3.50
Mazeroski, Bill	68T	390	$ .50	$1.95
Mazeroski, Bill	69T	335	$ .50	$2.00
Mazeroski, Bill	70T	440	$ .35	$1.00
Mazeroski, Bill	71T	110	$ .30	$1.00
Mazeroski, Bill	72T	760	$ .90	$2.75
Mazeroski, Bill	73T	517	$ .25	$ .85
Mazeroski, Bill	74T	489	$ .06	$ .25
Mazilli, Lee	90T	721	$ .01	$ .03
Mazzilli, Lee	77T	488	$5.00	$20.00
Mazzilli, Lee	78T	147	$ .02	$ .10
Mazzilli, Lee	79T	355	$ .02	$ .10
Mazzilli, Lee	80T	25	$ .01	$ .07
Mazzilli, Lee	81T	510	$ .01	$ .07
Mazzilli, Lee	82T	465	$ .01	$ .06
Mazzilli, Lee	82TTR	68	$ .02	$ .10
Mazzilli, Lee	83T	685	$ .01	$ .06
Mazzilli, Lee	83TTR	67	$ .02	$ .10
Mazzilli, Lee	84T	225	$ .01	$ .05
Mazzilli, Lee	85T	748	$ .01	$ .04
Mazzilli, Lee	86T	578	$ .01	$ .03
Mazzilli, Lee	87T	198	$ .01	$ .03

Player	Year	No.	VG	EX/MT
Mazzilli, Lee	88T	308	$ .01	$ .03
Mazzilli, Lee	89T	58	$ .01	$ .04
McAnally, Ernie	71T	376	$ .10	$ .35
McAnally, Ernie	72T	58	$ .05	$ .25
McAnally, Ernie	73T	484	$ .06	$ .25
McAnally, Ernie	74T	322	$ .06	$ .25
McAnally, Ernie	75T	318	$ .06	$ .25
McAndrew, Jim	69T	321	$ .25	$ .85
McAndrew, Jim	70T	246	$ .10	$ .35
McAndrew, Jim	71T	428	$ .10	$ .35
McAndrew, Jim	72T	781	$ .70	$2.10
McAndrew, Jim	73T	436	$ .06	$ .25
McAuliffe, Dick	62T	527	$2.70	$7.00
McAuliffe, Dick	63T	64	$ .25	$ .85
McAuliffe, Dick	64T	363	$ .25	$ .65
McAuliffe, Dick	65T	53	$ .25	$ .65
McAuliffe, Dick	66T	495	$ .70	$2.10
McAuliffe, Dick	67T	170	$ .25	$ .65
McAuliffe, Dick	68T	285	$ .25	$ .65
McAuliffe, Dick	69T	305	$ .25	$ .85
McAuliffe, Dick	70T	475	$ .10	$ .35
McAuliffe, Dick	71T	3	$ .10	$ .35
McAuliffe, Dick	72T	725	$ .70	$2.10
McAuliffe, Dick	73T	349	$ .06	$ .25
McAuliffe, Dick	74T	495	$ .06	$ .25
McBean, Al	62T	424	$ .70	$2.10
McBean, Al	63T	387	$ .35	$1.20
McBean, Al	64T	525	$1.50	$3.75
McBean, Al	65T	25	$ .25	$ .65
McBean, Al	66T	353	$ .25	$ .85
McBean, Al	67T	203	$ .25	$ .65
McBean, Al	68T	514	$ .30	$1.00
McBean, Al	69T	14	$ .25	$ .65
McBean, Al	70T	641	$ .50	$2.00
McBride, Bake	74T	601	$ .35	$1.10
McBride, Bake	75T	174	$ .06	$ .25
McBride, Bake	76T	135	$ .05	$ .20
McBride, Bake	77T	516	$ .03	$ .12
McBride, Bake	78T	340	$ .02	$ .10
McBride, Bake	79T	630	$ .05	$ .20
McBride, Bake	80T	495	$ .01	$ .07
McBride, Bake	81T	90	$ .03	$ .15
McBride, Bake	82T	745	$ .01	$ .06
McBride, Bake	82TTR	69	$ .02	$ .10
McBride, Bake	83T	248	$ .01	$ .06
McBride, Bake	84T	569	$ .01	$ .05
McBride, Ken	60T	276	$ .35	$1.10
McBride, Ken	61T	209	$ .30	$1.00
McBride, Ken	62T	268	$ .35	$1.10
McBride, Ken	63T	510	$1.50	$3.75
McBride, Ken	64T	405	$ .40	$1.25
McBride, Ken	65T	268	$ .30	$1.00
McCabe, Joe	64T	564	$1.50	$3.75
McCabe, Joe	65T	181	$ .25	$ .65
McCall, Windy	55T	42	$1.35	$5.00
McCall, Windy	56T	44	$1.25	$4.50
McCall, Windy	57T	291	$3.50	$13.00
McCament, Randy	89TMLD	77	$ .01	$ .05
McCament, Randy	90T	361	$ .01	$ .10
McCarthy, Tom	89TTR	75	$ .01	$ .15
McCarthy, Tom	90T	326	$ .01	$ .03
McCarver, Tim	62T	167	$4.00	$12.00
McCarver, Tim	63T	394	$1.50	$5.00
McCarver, Tim	64T	429	$1.00	$4.00
McCarver, Tim	65T	294	$ .60	$1.75
McCarver, Tim	66T	275	$ .50	$1.95
McCarver, Tim	67T	485	$ .70	$2.00
McCarver, Tim	68T	275	$ .35	$1.10
McCarver, Tim	68TAS	376	$ .50	$2.00
McCarver, Tim	69T	475	$ .25	$ .65
McCarver, Tim	70T	90	$ .15	$ .50
McCarver, Tim	71T	465	$ .15	$ .50
McCarver, Tim	72T	139	$ .25	$ .85
McCarver, Tim	73T	269	$ .25	$ .85
McCarver, Tim	74T	520	$ .25	$ .65

Player	Year	No.	VG	EX/MT	Player	Year	No.	VG	EX/MT
McCarver, Tim	75T	586	$ .25	$ .85	McCosky, Barney	52T	300	$14.00	$45.00
McCarver, Tim	76T	502	$ .25	$ .65	McCovey, Willie	60T	316	$35.00	$115.00
McCarver, Tim	77T	357	$ .25	$ .65	McCovey, Willie	60TAS	554	$11.50	$38.00
McCarver, Tim	78T	235	$ .05	$ .20	McCovey, Willie	61T	517	$11.50	$38.00
McCarver, Tim	79T	675	$ .05	$ .20	McCovey, Willie	62T	544	$32.50	$97.50
McCarver, Tim	80T	178	$ .03	$ .15	McCovey, Willie	63T	490	$22.00	$65.00
McCaskill, Kirk	86T	628	$ .04	$ .35	McCovey, Willie	64T	9	$2.50	$7.50
McCaskill, Kirk	87T	194	$ .01	$ .03	McCovey, Willie	64T	41	$ .70	$2.00
McCaskill, Kirk	88T	16	$ .01	$ .03	McCovey, Willie	64T	350	$6.00	$17.50
McCaskill, Kirk	88TBB	168	$ .01	$ .05	McCovey, Willie	65T	176	$4.00	$12.00
McCaskill, Kirk	89T	421	$ .01	$ .04	McCovey, Willie	66T	217	$1.25	$3.50
McCaskill, Kirk	89TBB	149	$ .01	$ .05	McCovey, Willie	66T	550	$30.00	$87.50
McCaskill, Kirk	90T	215	$ .01	$ .03	McCovey, Willie	67T	423	$7.50	$22.50
McCatty, Steve	78T	701	$ .02	$ .10	McCovey, Willie	67T	480	$4.00	$12.00
McCatty, Steve	80T	231	$ .01	$ .07	McCovey, Willie	68T	5	$1.35	$5.00
McCatty, Steve	81T	503	$ .01	$ .07	McCovey, Willie	68T	290	$3.00	$8.00
McCatty, Steve	82T	113	$ .01	$ .06	McCovey, Willie	69T	4	$ .70	$2.00
McCatty, Steve	82T	156	$ .05	$ .20	McCovey, Willie	69T	6	$ .80	$2.50
McCatty, Steve	82T	165	$ .03	$ .15	McCovey, Willie	69T	440	$3.00	$12.00
McCatty, Steve	82T	167	$ .03	$ .15	McCovey, Willie	69T	572	$2.50	$7.50
McCatty, Steve	83T	493	$ .01	$ .06	McCovey, Willie	69TAS	416	$1.25	$3.50
McCatty, Steve	84T	369	$ .01	$ .05	McCovey, Willie	70T	63	$ .50	$1.95
McCatty, Steve	85T	63	$ .01	$ .04	McCovey, Willie	70T	65	$ .60	$1.75
McCatty, Steve	86T	624	$ .01	$ .03	McCovey, Willie	70T	250	$1.75	$5.25
McClain, Joe	61T	488	$ .50	$2.00	McCovey, Willie	70TAS	450	$1.25	$3.50
McClain, Joe	62T	324	$ .35	$1.10	McCovey, Willie	71T	50	$1.50	$5.00
McClain, Joe	63T	311	$ .35	$1.20	McCovey, Willie	72T	280	$1.25	$3.50
McClendon, Lloyd	88T	172	$ .01	$ .10	McCovey, Willie	73T	410	$1.50	$4.75
McClendon, Lloyd	89T	644	$ .01	$ .04	McCovey, Willie	74T	250	$1.35	$4.00
McClendon, Lloyd	89TTR	76	$ .01	$ .05	McCovey, Willie	75T	207	$ .50	$2.00
McClendon, Lloyd	90T	337	$ .01	$ .03	McCovey, Willie	75T	450	$ .95	$3.50
McClure, Bob	76T	599	$4.00	$12.00	McCovey, Willie	76T	520	$1.00	$3.75
McClure, Bob	77T	472	$ .03	$ .12	McCovey, Willie	77T	547	$1.00	$3.75
McClure, Bob	78T	243	$ .02	$ .10	McCovey, Willie	78T	34	$ .45	$1.50
McClure, Bob	79T	623	$ .02	$ .10	McCovey, Willie	78TRB	3	$ .35	$1.00
McClure, Bob	80T	357	$ .01	$ .07	McCovey, Willie	79T	215	$ .75	$3.00
McClure, Bob	81T	156	$ .01	$ .07					
McClure, Bob	82T	487	$ .01	$ .06					
McClure, Bob	83T	62	$ .01	$ .06					
McClure, Bob	84T	582	$ .01	$ .05					
McClure, Bob	85T	203	$ .01	$ .04					
McClure, Bob	86T	684	$ .01	$ .03					
McClure, Bob	86TTR	71	$ .02	$ .10					
McClure, Bob	87T	707	$ .01	$ .03					
McClure, Bob	88T	313	$ .01	$ .03					
McClure, Bob	89T	182	$ .01	$ .04					
McClure, Bob	90T	458	$ .01	$ .03					
McClure, Jack	65T	553	$1.50	$3.75					
McCool, Bill	64T	356	$ .25	$ .85					
McCool, Bill	65T	18	$ .25	$ .65					
McCool, Bill	66T	459	$ .70	$2.10					
McCool, Bill	67T	353	$ .25	$ .65					
McCool, Bill	68T	597	$ .30	$1.00					
McCool, Bill	69T	129	$ .25	$ .65					
McCool, Bill	70T	314	$ .10	$ .35					
McCormick, Mike	58T	37	$ .70	$2.25					
McCormick, Mike	59T	148	$ .50	$1.95					
McCormick, Mike	60T	530	$2.00	$7.00					
McCormick, Mike	61T	45	$ .60	$2.75					
McCormick, Mike	61T	305	$ .30	$1.00					
McCormick, Mike	61T	383	$ .50	$2.00					
McCormick, Mike	62T	56	$ .50	$2.00					
McCormick, Mike	62T	107	$ .35	$1.10					
McCormick, Mike	62T	319	$ .50	$2.00					
McCormick, Mike	63T	563	$1.50	$3.75					
McCormick, Mike	64T	487	$ .40	$1.25					
McCormick, Mike	65T	343	$ .30	$1.00					
McCormick, Mike	66T	118	$ .25	$ .85	McCovey, Willie	80T	335	$ .35	$1.25
McCormick, Mike	67T	86	$ .30	$1.00	McCovey, Willie	80THL	2	$ .15	$ .50
McCormick, Mike	68T	9	$ .50	$1.95	McCraw, Tommy	64T	283	$ .25	$ .85
McCormick, Mike	68T	400	$ .25	$ .65	McCraw, Tommy	65T	586	$1.50	$3.75
McCormick, Mike	69T	521	$ .25	$ .85	McCraw, Tom	66T	141	$ .25	$ .85
McCormick, Mike	70T	337	$ .10	$ .35	McCraw, Tommy	67T	29	$ .25	$ .65
McCormick, Mike	71T	438	$ .10	$ .35	McCraw, Tommy	68T	413	$ .25	$ .65
McCormick, Mike	72T	682	$ .70	$2.10					

Player	Year	No.	VG	EX/MT	Player	Year	No.	VG	EX/MT
McCraw, Tom	69T	388	$ .25	$ .65	McDowell, Roger	88T	355	$ .01	$ .03
McCraw, Tom	70T	561	$ .25	$ .85	McDowell, Roger	88TBB	101	$ .01	$ .05
McCraw, Tom	71T	373	$ .10	$ .35	McDowell, Roger	89T	735	$ .01	$ .04
McCraw, Tom	72T	767	$ .70	$2.10	McDowell, Roger	89TTR	79	$ .01	$ .05
McCraw, Tom	73T	86	$ .06	$ .25	McDowell, Roger	90T	625	$ .01	$ .03
McCraw, Tom	74T	449	$ .06	$ .25	McDowell, Sam	62T	591	$8.00	$22.50
McCraw, Tom	75T	482	$ .06	$ .25	McDowell, Sam	63T	317	$ .35	$1.10
McCullers, Lance	86T	44	$ .02	$ .20	McDowell, Sam	64T	391	$ .50	$2.00
McCullers, Lance	87T	559	$ .01	$ .10	McDowell, Sam	65T	76	$ .15	$ .50
McCullers, Lance	88T	197	$ .01	$ .03	McDowell, Sam	66T	222	$ .50	$2.00
McCullers, Lance	88TBB	38	$ .01	$ .05	McDowell, Sam	66T	226	$ .50	$2.00
McCullers, Lance	89T	307	$ .01	$ .04	McDowell, Sam	66T	470	$ .65	$1.75
McCullers, Lance	89TTR	77	$ .01	$ .05	McDowell, Sam	67T	237	$ .35	$1.10
McCullers, Lance	90T	259	$ .01	$ .03	McDowell, Sam	67T	295	$ .25	$ .65
McCullough, Clyde	52T	218	$6.00	$19.00	McDowell, Sam	67T	463	$ .50	$2.00
McDaniel, Jim	59T	134	$ .50	$1.95	McDowell, Sam	68T	12	$ .35	$1.10
McDaniel, Lindy	57T	79	$ .60	$2.50	McDowell, Sam	68T	115	$ .25	$ .85
McDaniel, Lindy	58T	180	$ .50	$2.00	McDowell, Sam	69T	7	$ .30	$1.00
McDaniel, Lindy	59T	479	$ .50	$1.95	McDowell, Sam	69T	11	$ .50	$2.00
McDaniel, Lindy	60T	195	$ .35	$1.10	McDowell, Sam	69T	220	$ .30	$1.00
McDaniel, Lindy	61T	75	$ .30	$1.00	McDowell, Sam	69TAS	435	$ .25	$ .65
McDaniel, Lindy	61T	266	$ .30	$1.00	McDowell, Sam	70T	72	$ .50	$2.00
McDaniel, Lindy	62T	306	$ .50	$2.00	McDowell, Sam	70T	650	$ .50	$2.00
McDaniel, Lindy	62T	522	$ .70	$2.10	McDowell, Sam	70TAS	469	$ .25	$ .85
McDaniel, Lindy	63T	329	$ .35	$1.20	McDowell, Sam	71T	71	$ .15	$ .50
McDaniel, Lindy	64T	510	$ .40	$1.25	McDowell, Sam	71T	150	$ .25	$ .85
McDaniel, Lindy	65T	244	$ .30	$1.00	McDowell, Sam	72T	720	$1.00	$3.75
McDaniel, Lindy	66T	496	$ .70	$2.10	McDowell, Sam	73T	342	$ .06	$ .25
McDaniel, Lindy	67T	46	$ .25	$ .65	McDowell, Sam	73T	511	$ .10	$ .35
McDaniel, Lindy	68T	545	$ .30	$1.00	McDowell, Sam	74T	550	$ .25	$ .65
McDaniel, Lindy	69T	191	$ .25	$ .65	McElroy, Chuck	89TMLD	79	$ .01	$ .15
McDaniel, Lindy	70T	493	$ .10	$ .35	McEnaney, Will	75T	481	$ .06	$ .25
McDaniel, Lindy	71T	303	$ .10	$ .35	McEnaney, Will	76T	362	$ .05	$ .20
McDaniel, Lindy	72T	513	$ .05	$ .25	McEnaney, Will	77T	160	$ .03	$ .12
McDaniel, Lindy	73T	46	$ .06	$ .25	McEnaney, Will	78T	603	$ .02	$ .10
McDaniel, Lindy	74T	182	$ .06	$ .25	McEnaney, Will	80T	563	$ .01	$ .07
McDaniel, Lindy	74TTR	182	$ .06	$ .25	McFadden, Leon	69T	156	$ .25	$ .65
McDaniel, Lindy	75T	652	$ .06	$ .25	McFadden, Leon	70T	672	$ .50	$2.00
McDaniel, Von	58T	65	$1.00	$3.75	McFarlane, Jesus "Orlando"	62T	229	$ .35	$1.10
McDermott, Maurice	51Trb	43	$1.25	$3.50	McFarlane, Orlando	64T	509	$ .40	$1.25
McDermott, Maurice	52T	119	$6.00	$19.00	McFarlane, Orlando	66T	569	$4.50	$15.00
McDermott, Maurice	53T	55	$3.75	$13.00	McFarlane, Orlando	67T	496	$ .50	$2.00
McDermott, Mickey	56T	340	$6.00	$27.50	McGaffigan, Andy	82T	83	$ .10	$ .50
McDermott, Mickey	57T	318	$3.50	$13.00	McGaffigan, Andy	83TTR	68	$ .02	$ .10
McDevitt, Danny	58T	357	$ .50	$2.00	McGaffigan, Andy	84T	31	$ .01	$ .05
McDevitt, Danny	59T	364	$ .50	$1.95	McGaffigan, Andy	84TTR	78	$ .02	$ .10
McDevitt, Danny	60T	333	$ .50	$1.95	McGaffigan, Andy	85T	323	$ .01	$ .04
McDevitt, Danny	61T	349	$ .30	$1.00	McGaffigan, Andy	86T	133	$ .01	$ .03
McDevitt, Danny	62T	493	$ .70	$2.10	McGaffigan, Andy	86TTR	72	$ .02	$ .10
McDonald, Ben	89TMLD	78	$ .01	$1.25	McGaffigan, Andy	87T	742	$ .01	$ .03
McDonald, Ben	90T	774	$ .01	$2.00	McGaffigan, Andy	88T	488	$ .01	$ .03
McDonald, Dave	70T	189	$20.00	$67.50	McGaffigan, Andy	89T	278	$ .01	$ .04
McDougald, Gil	52T	372	$75.00	$225.00	McGaffigan, Andy	89TBB	315	$ .01	$ .05
McDougald, Gil	53T	43	$10.00	$40.00	McGaffigan, Andy	90T	559	$ .01	$ .03
McDougald, Gil	56T	225	$6.00	$18.00	McGaha, Mel	62T	242	$ .35	$1.10
McDougald, Gil	57T	200	$3.00	$10.00	McGaha, Mel	65T	391	$ .30	$1.00
McDougald, Gil	58T	20	$3.00	$9.00	McGee, Willie	83T	49	$ .40	$1.75
McDougald, Gil	59T	237	$ .60	$1.75	McGee, Willie	84T	310	$ .05	$ .25
McDougald, Gil	59T	345	$2.00	$7.00	McGee, Willie	85T	757	$ .05	$ .25
McDougald, Gil	60T	247	$1.75	$6.50	McGee, Willie	86T	580	$ .01	$ .10
McDowell, Jack	88TTR	68	$ .01	$ .15	McGee, Willie	86TAS	707	$ .01	$ .03
McDowell, Jack	89T	486	$ .01	$ .10	McGee, Willie	87T	440	$ .03	$ .15
McDowell, Oddibe	85T	400	$ .35	$1.00	McGee, Willie	88T	160	$ .01	$ .10
McDowell, Oddibe	85TTR	82	$ .20	$ .50	McGee, Willie	88TBB	79	$ .01	$ .05
McDowell, Oddibe	86T	480	$ .03	$ .25	McGee, Willie	89T	640	$ .01	$ .04
McDowell, Oddibe	87T	95	$ .01	$ .10	McGee, Willie	89TBB	183	$ .01	$ .10
McDowell, Oddibe	88T	617	$ .01	$ .03	McGee, Willie	90T	285	$ .01	$ .03
McDowell, Oddibe	88TBB	198	$ .01	$ .10	McGhee, Ed	53T	195	$3.75	$13.00
McDowell, Oddibe	89T	183	$ .01	$ .04	McGhee, Ed	54T	215	$2.10	$7.50
McDowell, Oddibe	89TBB	245	$ .01	$ .05	McGhee, Ed	55T	32	$1.35	$5.00
McDowell, Oddibe	89TTR	78	$ .01	$ .05	McGilberry, Randy	79T	707	$ .02	$ .10
McDowell, Oddibe	90T	329	$ .01	$ .03	McGinn, Dan	69T	646	$ .25	$ .85
McDowell, Roger	85TTR	83	$ .15	$ .60	McGinn, Dan	70T	364	$ .10	$ .35
McDowell, Roger	86T	547	$ .03	$ .35	McGinn, Dan	71T	21	$ .10	$ .35
McDowell, Roger	87T	185	$ .01	$ .10	McGinn, Dan	72T	473	$ .05	$ .25

Player	Year	No.	VG	EX/MT
McGinn, Dan	73T	527	$ .06	$ .25
McGlothen, Lynn	73T	114	$ .06	$ .25
McGlothen, Lynn	75T	272	$ .06	$ .25
McGlothen, Lynn	76T	478	$ .05	$ .20
McGlothen, Lynn	77T	47	$ .03	$ .12
McGlothen, Lynn	78T	581	$ .02	$ .10
McGlothen, Lynn	79T	323	$ .02	$ .10
McGlothen, Lynn	80T	716	$ .01	$ .07
McGlothen, Lynn	81T	609	$ .01	$ .07
McGlothen, Lynn	82T	85	$ .01	$ .06
McGlothin, Jim	74T	557	$ .06	$ .25
McGlothlin, Jim	66T	417	$ .25	$ .85
McGlothlin, Jim	67T	19	$ .25	$ .65
McGlothlin, Jim	68T	493	$ .30	$1.00
McGlothlin, Jim	69T	386	$ .25	$ .65
McGlothlin, Jim	70T	132	$ .10	$ .35
McGlothlin, Jim	71T	556	$ .30	$1.00
McGlothlin, Jim	72T	236	$ .05	$ .25
McGlothlin, Jim	73T	318	$ .06	$ .25
McGraw, Tug	65T	533	$3.00	$12.00
McGraw, Tug	66T	124	$ .60	$1.75
McGraw, Tug	67T	348	$1.00	$3.00
McGraw, Tug	68T	236	$ .75	$3.00
McGraw, Tug	69T	601	$ .50	$2.00
McGraw, Tug	70T	26	$ .35	$1.10
McGraw, Tug	71T	618	$ .50	$2.00
McGraw, Tug	72T	163	$ .20	$ .70
McGraw, Tug	72TIA	164	$ .25	$ .85
McGraw, Tug	73T	30	$ .25	$ .85
McGraw, Tug	74T	265	$ .06	$ .25
McGraw, Tug	75T	67	$ .25	$ .85
McGraw, Tug	76T	565	$ .10	$ .35
McGraw, Tug	77T	164	$ .10	$ .35
McGraw, Tug	78T	446	$ .05	$ .25
McGraw, Tug	79T	345	$ .05	$ .20
McGraw, Tug	80T	655	$ .01	$ .07
McGraw, Tug	81T	40	$ .03	$ .15
McGraw, Tug	82T	250	$ .01	$ .06
McGraw, Tug	83T	510	$ .01	$ .06
McGraw, Tug	83T	511	$ .01	$ .06
McGraw, Tug	84T	709	$ .01	$ .05
McGraw, Tug	84T	728	$ .01	$ .05
McGraw, Tug	85T	157	$ .01	$ .04
McGregor, Scott	75T	618	$ .60	$1.75
McGregor, Scott	77T	475	$ .05	$ .15
McGregor, Scott	78T	491	$ .02	$ .10
McGregor, Scott	79T	393	$ .02	$ .10
McGregor, Scott	80T	237	$ .02	$ .10
McGregor, Scott	81T	65	$ .01	$ .07
McGregor, Scott	82T	617	$ .01	$ .06
McGregor, Scott	82TAS	555	$ .01	$ .06
McGregor, Scott	83T	745	$ .01	$ .06
McGregor, Scott	84T	260	$ .01	$ .05
McGregor, Scott	85T	550	$ .01	$ .04
McGregor, Scott	86T	110	$ .01	$ .03
McGregor, Scott	87T	708	$ .01	$ .03
McGregor, Scott	88T	419	$ .01	$ .03
McGriff, Fred	87TTR	74	$ .35	$2.00
McGriff, Fred	88T	463	$ .15	$1.00
McGriff, Fred	89T	745	$ .01	$ .15
McGriff, Fred	89BB	15	$ .01	$ .10
McGriff, Fred	90T	295	$ .01	$ .15
McGriff, Fred	90TAS	385	$ .01	$ .10
McGriff, Terry	88T	644	$ .01	$ .10
McGriff, Terry	89T	151	$ .01	$ .04
McGwire, Mark	85T	401	$5.50	$16.50
McGwire, Mark	87T	366	$1.25	$3.50
McGwire, Mark	88T	580	$ .01	$1.00
McGwire, Mark	88TBB	179	$ .10	$ .50
McGwire, Mark	88TRB	3	$ .05	$ .35
McGwire, Mark	89T	70	$ .05	$ .25
McGwire, Mark	89BB	34	$ .01	$ .50
McGwire, Mark	90T	690	$ .01	$ .25
McIntosh, Joe	76T	497	$ .05	$ .20
McIntosh, Joe	76TTR	497	$ .05	$ .20

Player	Year	No.	VG	EX/MT
McKay, Dave	76T	592	$1.25	$3.75
McKay, Dave	77T	377	$ .03	$ .12
McKay, Dave	79T	608	$ .02	$ .10
McKay, Dave	81T	461	$ .01	$ .07

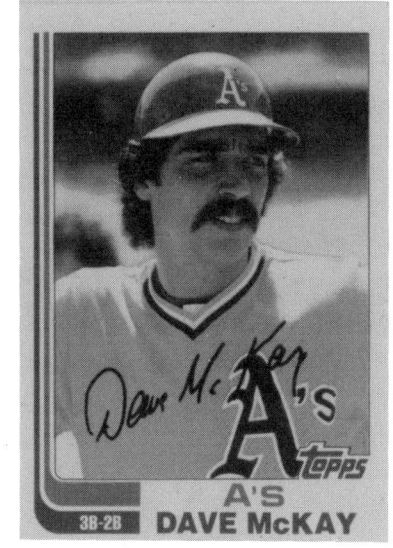

3B-2B **DAVE McKAY**

Player	Year	No.	VG	EX/MT
McKay, Dave	82T	534	$ .01	$ .06
McKay, Dave	83T	47	$ .01	$ .06
McKeon, Jack	73T	593	$ .50	$2.00
McKeon, Jack	74T	166	$ .06	$ .25
McKeon, Jack	88TTR	69	$ .01	$ .05
McKeon, Jack	89T	624	$ .01	$ .04
McKeon, Jack	90T	231	$ .01	$ .03
McKeon, Joel	88T	409	$ .01	$ .03
McKinney, Rich	71T	37	$ .10	$ .35
McKinney, Rich	72T	619	$ .25	$ .85
McKinney, Rich	73T	587	$ .35	$1.10
McKnight, Jeff	89TMLD	80	$ .01	$ .05
McKnight, Jim	62T	597	$6.00	$18.00
McLain, Dennis	65T	236	$3.00	$12.00
McLain, Dennis	66T	226	$ .50	$2.00
McLain, Denny	66T	540	$15.00	$50.00
McLain, Denny	67T	235	$ .35	$1.10
McLain, Dennis	67T	420	$ .50	$2.50
McLain, Denny	68T	40	$1.00	$4.00
McLain, Denny	69T	9	$ .30	$1.00
McLain, Denny	69T	11	$ .50	$2.00
McLain, Denny	69T	150	$1.00	$3.00
McLain, Denny	69TAS	433	$ .50	$2.00
McLain, Denny	70T	70	$ .50	$2.00
McLain, Denny	70T	400	$ .50	$2.00
McLain, Denny	70TAS	467	$ .30	$1.00
McLain, Denny	71T	750	$1.25	$3.50
McLain, Denny	72T	210	$ .15	$ .50
McLain, Denny	72TTR	753	$1.25	$3.50
McLain, Denny	73T	630	$ .75	$1.50
McLain, Denny	75T	206	$ .35	$1.10
McLaughlin, Bo	77T	184	$ .03	$ .12
McLaughlin, Bo	78T	437	$ .02	$ .10
McLaughlin, Bo	80T	326	$ .01	$ .07
McLaughlin, Bo	82T	217	$ .01	$ .06
McLaughlin, Byron	79T	712	$ .02	$ .10
McLaughlin, Byron	80T	197	$ .01	$ .07
McLaughlin, Byron	81T	344	$ .01	$ .07
McLaughlin, Byron	84T	442	$ .01	$ .05

Player	Year	No.	VG	EX/MT	Player	Year	No.	VG	EX/MT
McLaughlin, Joey	80T	384	$ .01	$ .07	McMillan, Roy	58T	360	$ .50	$2.00
McLaughlin, Joey	81T	248	$ .01	$ .07	McMillan, Roy	59T	405	$ .50	$1.95
McLaughlin, Joey	82T	739	$ .01	$ .06	McMillan, Roy	60T	45	$ .35	$1.10
McLaughlin, Joey	83T	9	$ .01	$ .06	McMillan, Roy	61T	465	$ .50	$2.00
McLaughlin, Joey	84T	556	$ .01	$ .05	McMillan, Roy	62T	211	$ .50	$2.00
McLaughlin, Joey	85T	678	$ .01	$ .04	McMillan, Roy	62TAS	393	$ .60	$1.75
McLemore, Mark	87TTR	75	$ .01	$ .07	McMillan, Roy	63T	156	$ .25	$ .85
McLemore, Mark	88T	162	$ .01	$ .03	McMillan, Roy	64T	238	$ .25	$ .85
McLemore, Mark	89T	547	$ .01	$ .04	McMillan, Roy	65T	45	$ .25	$ .65
McLemore, Mark	89TBB	30	$ .01	$ .05	McMillan, Roy	66T	421	$ .25	$ .85
McLish, Cal	57T	364	$1.00	$3.75	McMillan, Roy	73T	257	$ .50	$2.00
McLish, Cal	58T	208	$ .50	$2.00	McMillan, Roy	74T	179	$ .50	$2.00
McLish, Cal	59T	445	$ .50	$1.95	McMillan, Tommy	77T	490	$ .03	$ .12
McLish, Cal	60T	110	$ .35	$1.10	McMullen, Ken	63T	537	$150.00	$450.00
McLish, Cal	61T	157	$ .30	$1.00	McMullen, Ken	64T	214	$ .25	$ .85
McLish, Cal	62T	453	$ .70	$2.10	McMullen, Ken	65T	319	$ .30	$1.00
McLish, Cal	63T	512	$1.50	$3.75	McMullen, Ken	66T	401	$ .25	$ .85
McLish, Cal	64T	365	$ .25	$ .85	McMullen, Ken	67T	47	$ .25	$ .65
McLish, Cal	73T	377	$ .10	$ .35	McMullen, Ken	68T	116	$ .25	$ .65
McLish, Cal	74T	531	$ .25	$ .85	McMullen, Ken	69T	319	$ .25	$ .85
McMahon, Don	58T	147	$ .50	$2.00	McMullen, Ken	70T	420	$ .10	$ .35
McMahon, Don	59T	3	$1.00	$3.75	McMullen, Ken	71T	485	$ .10	$ .35
McMahon, Don	60T	189	$ .35	$1.10	McMullen, Ken	72T	765	$ .70	$2.10
McMahon, Don	61T	278	$ .30	$1.00	McMullen, Ken	73T	196	$ .06	$ .25
McMahon, Don	62T	483	$ .70	$2.10	McMullen, Ken	74T	434	$ .06	$ .25
McMahon, Don	63T	395	$ .35	$1.20	McMullen, Ken	75T	473	$ .06	$ .25
McMahon, Don	64T	122	$ .25	$ .85	McMullen, Ken	76T	566	$ .05	$ .20
McMahon, Don	65T	317	$ .30	$1.00	McMullen, Ken	77T	181	$ .03	$ .12
					McMurtry, Craig	83TTR	69	$ .02	$ .10
					McMurtry, Craig	84T	126	$ .01	$ .05
					McMurtry, Craig	84T	543	$ .01	$ .05
					McMurtry, Craig	85T	362	$ .01	$ .04
					McMurtry, Craig	86T	194	$ .01	$ .03
					McMurtry, Craig	87T	461	$ .01	$ .03
					McMurtry, Craig	89T	779	$ .01	$ .04
					McMurtry, Craig	90T	294	$ .01	$ .03
					McNally, Dave	63T	562	$3.00	$10.00
					McNally, Dave	64T	161	$ .15	$ .50
					McNally, Dave	65T	249	$ .35	$1.10
					McNally, Dave	66T	193	$ .30	$1.00
					McNally, Dave	67T	382	$ .25	$ .85
					McNally, Dave	68T	478	$ .35	$1.10
					McNally, Dave	69T	7	$ .30	$1.00
					McNally, Dave	69T	9	$ .30	$1.00
					McNally, Dave	69T	340	$ .25	$ .85
					McNally, Dave	69T	532	$ .20	$ .50
					McNally, Dave	70T	20	$ .25	$ .65
					McNally, Dave	70T	70	$ .50	$2.00
					McNally, Dave	71T	69	$ .15	$ .50
					McNally, Dave	71T	320	$ .25	$ .85
					McNally, Dave	72T	344	$ .05	$ .25
					McNally, Dave	72T	490	$ .25	$ .65
					McNally, Dave	73T	600	$ .50	$1.95
					McNally, Dave	74T	235	$ .06	$ .25
					McNally, Dave	75T	26	$ .06	$ .25
					McNamara, John	70T	706	$ .70	$2.00
					McNamara, John	73T	252	$ .25	$ .65
					McNamara, John	74T	78	$ .06	$ .25
					McNamara, John	83TTR	70	$ .02	$ .10
					McNamara, John	84T	651	$ .01	$ .05

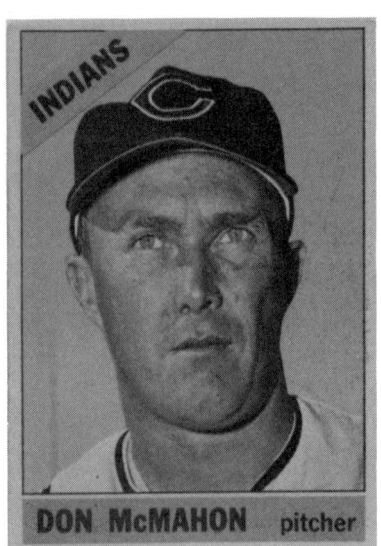

DON McMAHON pitcher

Player	Year	No.	VG	EX/MT	Player	Year	No.	VG	EX/MT
McMahon, Don	66T	133	$ .25	$ .85	McNamara, John	85T	732	$ .01	$ .04
McMahon, Don	67T	7	$ .25	$ .65	McNamara, John	85TTR	84	$ .02	$ .10
McMahon, Don	68T	464	$ .30	$1.00	McNamara, John	86T	771	$ .01	$ .03
McMahon, Don	69T	616	$ .25	$ .85	McNamara, John	87T	368	$ .01	$ .03
McMahon, Don	70T	519	$ .10	$ .35	McNamara, John	88T	414	$ .01	$ .03
McMahon, Don	71T	354	$ .10	$ .35	McNertney, Jerry	64T	564	$1.50	$3.75
McMahon, Don	72T	509	$ .05	$ .25	McNertney, Jerry	68T	14	$ .25	$ .65
McMahon, Don	73T	252	$ .25	$ .65	McNertney, Jerry	69T	534	$ .25	$ .85
McMahon, Don	74T	78	$ .06	$ .25	McNertney, Jerry	70T	158	$ .10	$ .35
McMillan, Roy	52T	137	$7.00	$20.00	McNertney, Jerry	71T	286	$ .10	$ .35
McMillan, Roy	53T	259	$11.00	$37.50	McNertney, Jerry	72T	584	$ .25	$ .85
McMillan, Roy	54T	120	$2.10	$7.50	McNulty, Bill	73T	603	$ .35	$1.10
McMillan, Roy	55T	181	$4.25	$13.00	McQueen, Mike	70T	621	$5.00	$14.00
McMillan, Roy	56T	123	$1.25	$4.50	McQueen, Mike	71T	8	$ .10	$ .35
McMillan, Roy	57T	69	$ .95	$3.50	McQueen, Mike	72T	214	$ .05	$ .25

Player	Year	No.	VG	EX/MT	Player	Year	No.	VG	EX/MT
McRae, Hal	68T	384	$1.00	$4.00	Mejias, Roman	63T	432	$ .35	$1.20
McRae, Hal	70T	683	$1.00	$3.50	Mejias, Roman	64T	186	$ .25	$ .85
McRae, Hal	71T	177	$ .15	$ .50	Mejias, Sam	77T	479	$ .03	$ .12
McRae, Hal	72T	291	$ .25	$ .85	Mejias, Sam	78T	576	$ .02	$ .10
McRae, Hal	72TIA	292	$ .05	$ .25	Mejias, Sam	79T	97	$ .02	$ .10
McRae, Hal	73T	28	$ .25	$ .65	Mejias, Sam	81T	521	$ .01	$ .07
McRae, Hal	74T	563	$ .25	$ .65	Mejias, Sam	82T	228	$ .01	$ .06
McRae, Hal	75T	268	$ .10	$ .35	Mele, Sam	51Tbb	25	$5.50	$17.00
McRae, Hal	76T	72	$ .04	$ .20	Mele, Sam	52T	94	$6.00	$19.00
McRae, Hal	77T	340	$ .03	$ .12	Mele, Sam	54T	240	$2.10	$7.50
McRae, Hal	78T	465	$ .05	$ .20	Mele, Sam	60T	470	$ .95	$3.50
McRae, Hal	79T	585	$ .02	$ .10	Mele, Sam	62T	482	$ .70	$2.10
McRae, Hal	80T	185	$ .01	$ .07	Mele, Sam	63T	531	$1.50	$3.75
McRae, Hal	81T	295	$ .01	$ .07	Mele, Sam	64T	54	$ .25	$ .85
McRae, Hal	82T	625	$ .01	$ .06	Mele, Sam	65T	506	$ .50	$2.00
McRae, Hal	83T	25	$ .01	$ .06	Mele, Sam	66T	3	$ .25	$ .85
McRae, Hal	83T	703	$ .01	$ .06	Mele, Sam	67T	418	$ .25	$ .85
McRae, Hal	84T	96	$ .01	$ .05	Melendez, Luis	71T	216	$ .10	$ .35
McRae, Hal	84T	340	$ .01	$ .05	Melendez, Luis	72T	606	$ .25	$ .85
McRae, Hal	85T	773	$ .01	$ .04	Melendez, Luis	73T	47	$ .06	$ .25
McRae, Hal	86T	415	$ .01	$ .03	Melendez, Luis	74T	307	$ .06	$ .25
McRae, Hal	87T	573	$ .01	$ .03	Melendez, Luis	75T	353	$ .06	$ .25
McRae, Norman	70T	207	$ .10	$ .35	Melendez, Luis	76T	399	$ .05	$ .20
McRae, Norman	71T	93	$ .10	$ .35	Melton, Bill	69T	481	$ .25	$ .65
McReynolds, Kevin	87TTR	76	$ .15	$ .50	Melton, Bill	70T	518	$ .10	$ .35
McReynolds, Kevin	88T	735	$ .01	$ .15	Melton, Bill	71T	80	$ .10	$ .35
McReynolds, Kevin	88TBB	158	$ .01	$ .15	Melton, Bill	72T	90	$ .50	$2.00
McReynolds, Kevin	89T	85	$ .01	$ .10	Melton, Bill	72T	183	$ .05	$ .25
McReynolds, Kevin	89TBB	116	$ .01	$ .10	Melton, Bill	72T	495	$ .05	$ .25
McReynolds, Kevin	89TRB	7	$ .01	$ .04	Melton, Bill	72TIA	184	$ .05	$ .25
McReynolds, Kevin	90T	545	$ .01	$ .03	Melton, Bill	73T	455	$ .06	$ .25
McWilliams, Larry	79T	504	$ .02	$ .10	Melton, Bill	74T	170	$ .06	$ .25
McWilliams, Larry	80T	309	$ .01	$ .07	Melton, Bill	75T	11	$ .06	$ .25
McWilliams, Larry	81T	44	$ .01	$ .07	Melton, Bill	76T	309	$ .05	$ .20
McWilliams, Larry	82T	733	$ .01	$ .06	Melton, Bill	76TTR	309	$ .05	$ .20
McWilliams, Larry	83T	253	$ .01	$ .06	Melton, Bill	77T	107	$ .03	$ .12
McWilliams, Larry	84T	668	$ .01	$ .05	Melton, Dave	58T	391	$ .50	$2.00
McWilliams, Larry	85T	183	$ .01	$ .04	Melvin, Bob	86T	479	$ .01	$ .03
McWilliams, Larry	86T	425	$ .01	$ .03	Melvin, Bob	87T	549	$ .01	$ .03
McWilliams, Larry	87T	564	$ .01	$ .03	Melvin, Bob	88T	41	$ .01	$ .03
McWilliams, Larry	88TBB	261	$ .01	$ .05	Melvin, Bob	89T	329	$ .01	$ .04
McWilliams, Larry	88TTR	70	$ .01	$ .05	Melvin, Bob	90T	626	$ .01	$ .03
McWilliams, Larry	89T	259	$ .01	$ .04	Mendoza, Mario	75T	457	$ .06	$ .25
McWilliams, Larry	89TTR	80	$ .01	$ .05	Mendoza, Mario	78T	383	$ .02	$ .10
Meacham, Bobby	84T	204	$ .01	$ .05	Mendoza, Mario	79T	509	$ .02	$ .10
Meacham, Bobby	85T	16	$ .01	$ .04	Mendoza, Mario	80T	652	$ .01	$ .07
Meacham, Bobby	86T	379	$ .01	$ .03	Mendoza, Mario	81T	76	$ .01	$ .07
Meacham, Bobby	87T	62	$ .01	$ .03	Mendoza, Mario	81TTR	801	$ .02	$ .10
Meacham, Bobby	88T	659	$ .01	$ .03	Mendoza, Mario	82T	212	$ .01	$ .06
Meacham, Bobby	89T	436	$ .01	$ .04	Menke, Denis	62T	597	$6.00	$18.00
Meadows, Louie	89T	643	$ .01	$ .15	Menke, Denis	63T	433	$ .35	$1.10
Meadows, Louie	90T	534	$ .01	$ .03	Menke, Denis	64T	53	$ .25	$ .85
Meads, Dave	87TTR	77	$ .01	$ .07	Menke, Denis	65T	327	$ .30	$1.00
Meads, Dave	88T	199	$ .01	$ .03	Menke, Denis	66T	184	$ .25	$ .85
Meads, Dave	89T	589	$ .01	$ .04	Menke, Denis	67T	396	$ .35	$1.10
Medich, George	73T	608	$ .35	$1.10	Menke, Denis	67T	518	$ .50	$2.00
Medich, George	74T	445	$ .06	$ .25	Menke, Denis	68T	232	$ .25	$ .65
Medich, George	75T	426	$ .06	$ .25	Menke, Denis	69T	487	$ .25	$ .65
Medich, George	76T	146	$ .05	$ .20	Menke, Denis	70T	155	$ .10	$ .35
Medich, George	76TTR	146	$ .05	$ .20	Menke, Denis	71T	130	$ .10	$ .35
Medich, George	77T	294	$ .03	$ .12	Menke, Denis	72T	586	$ .25	$ .85
Medich, George	78T	583	$ .02	$ .10	Menke, Denis	73T	52	$ .06	$ .25
Medich, George	79T	657	$ .02	$ .10	Menke, Denis	74T	134	$ .06	$ .25
Medich, George	80T	336	$ .01	$ .07	Meoli, Rudy	75T	533	$ .06	$ .25
Medich, George	81T	702	$ .01	$ .07	Meoli, Rudy	76T	254	$ .05	$ .20
Medich, George	82T	36	$ .01	$ .06	Meoli, Rudy	78T	489	$ .02	$ .10
Medich, George	82T	78	$ .01	$ .06	Mercado, Orlando	83TTR	71	$ .02	$ .10
Medina, Luis	89T	528	$ .05	$ .35	Mercado, Orlando	84T	314	$ .01	$ .05
Medvin, Scott	89T	756	$ .01	$ .04	Mercado, Orlando	85T	58	$ .01	$ .04
Meier, Dave	85T	356	$ .01	$ .04	Mercado, Orlando	87T	514	$ .01	$ .03
Mejias, Roman	57T	362	$1.00	$3.75	Merchant, Andy	76T	594	$ .05	$ .20
Mejias, Roman	58T	452	$ .50	$1.95	Mercker, Kent	89TMLD	81	$ .01	$ .25
Mejias, Roman	59T	218	$ .50	$1.95	Merritt, Jim	66T	97	$ .25	$ .85
Mejias, Roman	60T	2	$ .35	$1.10	Merritt, Jim	67T	523	$ .50	$2.00
Mejias, Roman	62T	354	$ .35	$1.10	Merritt, Jim	68T	64	$ .25	$ .65

TOPPS

Player	Year	No.	VG	EX/MT	Player	Year	No.	VG	EX/MT
Merritt, Jim	69T	661	$ .25	$ .85	Meyer, Dan	78T	57	$ .02	$ .10
Merritt, Jim	70T	616	$ .25	$ .85	Meyer, Dan	79T	683	$ .02	$ .10
Merritt, Jim	71T	420	$ .10	$ .35	Meyer, Dan	80T	396	$ .01	$ .07
Merritt, Jim	72T	738	$ .70	$2.10	Meyer, Dan	81T	143	$ .01	$ .07
Merritt, Jim	74T	318	$ .06	$ .25	Meyer, Dan	82T	413	$ .01	$ .06
Merritt, Jim	75T	83	$ .06	$ .25	Meyer, Dan	82TTR	70	$ .02	$ .10
Merritt, Lloyd	58T	231	$ .50	$2.00	Meyer, Dan	83T	208	$ .01	$ .06
Merson, Jack	52T	375	$39.00	$135.00	Meyer, Dan	84T	609	$ .01	$ .05
Merullo, Matt	89TMLD	82	$ .01	$ .05	Meyer, Jack	56T	269	$1.80	$6.00
Messersmith, Andy	69T	296	$ .35	$1.10	Meyer, Jack	57T	162	$ .95	$3.50
Messersmith, Andy	70T	72	$ .50	$2.00	Meyer, Jack	58T	186	$ .50	$2.00
Messersmith, Andy	70T	430	$ .10	$ .35	Meyer, Jack	59T	269	$ .50	$1.95
Messersmith, Andy	71T	15	$ .10	$ .35	Meyer, Jack	60T	64	$ .35	$1.10
Messersmith, Andy	72T	160	$ .25	$ .65	Meyer, Jack	61T	111	$ .30	$1.00
Messersmith, Andy	73T	515	$ .10	$ .35	Meyer, Joey	88T	312	$ .01	$ .15
Messersmith, Andy	74T	267	$ .06	$ .25	Meyer, Joey	89T	136	$ .01	$ .04
Messersmith, Andy	75T	310	$ .30	$1.00	Meyer, Joey	89TBB	153	$ .01	$ .05
Messersmith, Andy	75T	440	$ .06	$ .25	Meyer, Joey	90T	673	$ .01	$ .03
Messersmith, Andy	76T	199	$ .15	$ .50	Meyer, Russ	52T	339	$39.00	$135.00
Messersmith, Andy	76T	201	$ .30	$1.00	Meyer, Russ	56T	227	$2.50	$8.00
Messersmith, Andy	76T	203	$ .30	$1.00	Meyer, Russ	59T	482	$ .50	$1.95
Messersmith, Andy	76T	305	$ .05	$ .20	Micelotta, Bob	54T	212	$2.10	$7.50
Messersmith, Andy	77T	80	$ .03	$ .12	Michael, Gene	67T	428	$ .25	$ .85
Messersmith, Andy	78T	156	$ .02	$ .10	Michael, Gene	68T	299	$ .15	$ .50
Messersmith, Andy	79T	278	$ .02	$ .10	Michael, Gene	69T	626	$ .20	$ .50
Metcalf, Tom	64T	281	$ .25	$ .85	Michael, Gene	70T	114	$ .25	$ .65
Metkovich, George	52T	310	$11.50	$38.00	Michael, Gene	71T	483	$ .10	$ .35
Metkovich, George	53T	58	$3.75	$13.00	Michael, Gene	72T	713	$1.00	$3.75
Metro, Charlie	70T	16	$ .10	$ .35	Michael, Gene	72T	714	$ .70	$2.10
Mets, Team	63T	473	$20.00	$55.00	Michael, Gene	73T	265	$ .25	$ .65
Mets, Team	64T	27	$1.75	$6.00	Michael, Gene	74T	299	$ .06	$ .25
Mets, Team	65T	551	$5.00	$20.00	Michael, Gene	75T	608	$ .06	$ .25
Mets, Team	66T	172	$ .85	$1.75	Michael, Gene	86TTR	73	$ .02	$ .10
Mets, Team	67T	42	$1.25	$3.50	Michael, Gene	87T	43	$ .01	$ .03
Mets, Team	68T	401	$1.50	$3.75	Michaels, Cass	52T	178	$6.00	$19.00
Mets, Team	70T	1	$3.00	$10.00	Mielke, Gary	90T	221	$ .01	$ .10
Mets, Team	71T	641	$1.50	$4.50	Mikkelsen, Pete	64T	488	$ .40	$1.25
Mets, Team	72T	362	$ .35	$1.10	Mikkelsen, Pete	65T	177	$ .25	$ .65
Mets, Team	73T	389	$ .50	$2.00	Mikkelsen, Pete	66T	248	$ .25	$ .85
Mets, Team	74T	56	$ .35	$1.10	Mikkelsen, Pete	67T	425	$ .25	$ .85
Mets, Team Checklist	75T	421	$ .35	$1.10	Mikkelsen, Pete	68T	516	$ .30	$1.00
Mets, Team Checklist	76T	531	$ .30	$1.00	Miksis, Eddie	52T	172	$6.00	$19.00
Mets, Team Checklist	77T	259	$ .30	$1.00	Miksis, Eddie	53T	39	$3.75	$13.00
Mets, Team Checklist	78T	356	$ .02	$ .10	Miksis, Eddie	56T	285	$1.80	$6.00
Mets, Team Checklist	79T	82	$ .08	$ .30	Miksis, Eddie	57T	350	$3.50	$13.00
Mets, Team Checklist	80T	259	$ .10	$ .35	Miksis, Eddie	58T	121	$ .50	$2.00
Mets, Team Checklist	81T	681	$ .02	$ .20	Miksis, Eddie	59T	58	$1.00	$3.75
Mets, Team Leaders	86T	126	$ .01	$ .03	Milacki, Bob	89T	324	$ .01	$ .25
Mets, Team Leaders	87T	331	$ .01	$ .03	Milacki, Bob	90T	73	$ .01	$ .10
Mets, Team Leaders	88T	579	$ .01	$ .03	Milbourne, Larry	75T	512	$ .06	$ .25
Mets, Team Leaders	89T	291	$ .01	$ .10	Milbourne, Larry	78T	366	$ .02	$ .10
Metzger, Butch	76T	593	$ .10	$ .35	Milbourne, Larry	79T	199	$ .02	$ .10
Metzger, Butch	77T	215	$ .03	$ .12	Milbourne, Larry	80T	422	$ .01	$ .07
Metzger, Butch	78T	431	$ .02	$ .10	Milbourne, Larry	81T	583	$ .01	$ .07
Metzger, Roger	71T	404	$ .10	$ .35	Milbourne, Larry	81TTR	802	$ .02	$ .10
Metzger, Roger	72T	217	$ .05	$ .25	Milbourne, Larry	82T	669	$ .01	$ .06
Metzger, Roger	73T	395	$ .06	$ .25	Milbourne, Larry	82TTR	71	$ .02	$ .10
Metzger, Roger	74T	224	$ .06	$ .25	Milbourne, Larry	83T	91	$ .01	$ .06
Metzger, Roger	75T	541	$ .06	$ .25	Milbourne, Larry	83TTR	72	$ .02	$ .10
Metzger, Roger	76T	297	$ .05	$ .20	Milbourne, Larry	84T	281	$ .01	$ .05
Metzger, Roger	77T	481	$ .03	$ .12	Milbourne, Larry	84TTR	79	$ .02	$ .10
Metzger, Roger	78T	697	$ .02	$ .10	Milbourne, Larry	85T	754	$ .01	$ .04
Metzger, Roger	79T	167	$ .02	$ .10	Miles, Jim	69T	658	$ .25	$ .85
Metzger, Roger	80T	311	$ .01	$ .07	Miles, Jim	70T	154	$ .10	$ .35
Meulens, Hensley	89TMLD	83	$ .01	$ .10	Miley, Mike	76T	387	$ .05	$ .20
Meulens, Hensley	90T	83	$ .01	$ .10	Miley, Mike	77T	257	$ .03	$ .12
Meyer, Billy	52T	387	$39.00	$135.00	Millan, Felix	67T	89	$ .25	$ .65
Meyer, Bob	64T	488	$ .40	$1.25	Millan, Felix	68T	241	$ .25	$ .65
Meyer, Bob	65T	219	$ .30	$1.00	Millan, Felix	69T	210	$ .25	$ .65
Meyer, Bob	70T	667	$ .50	$2.00	Millan, Felix	70T	710	$ .50	$2.00
Meyer, Bob	71T	456	$ .10	$ .35	Millan, Felix	70TAS	452	$ .10	$ .35
Meyer, Brian	90T	766	$ .01	$ .03	Millan, Felix	71T	81	$ .10	$ .35
Meyer, Danny	75T	620	$12.00	$35.00	Millan, Felix	72T	540	$ .25	$ .85
Meyer, Dan	76T	242	$ .05	$ .20	Millan, Felix	73T	407	$ .06	$ .25
Meyer, Dan	77T	527	$ .03	$ .12	Millan, Felix	74T	132	$ .06	$ .25

Player	Year	No.	VG	EX/MT
Millan, Felix	75T	445	$ .06	$ .25
Millan, Felix	76T	245	$ .05	$ .20
Millan, Felix	77T	605	$ .03	$ .12
Millan, Felix	78T	505	$ .02	$ .10
Miller, Bill	52T	403	$45.00	$140.00
Miller, Bill	53T	100	$3.75	$13.00
Miller, Bob	52T	187	$6.00	$19.00
Miller, Bob	54T	241	$2.10	$7.50
Miller, Bob	55T	9	$1.35	$5.00
Miller, Bob	55T	157	$2.00	$7.00
Miller, Bob	56T	263	$1.80	$6.00
Miller, Bob	56T	334	$1.80	$6.00
Miller, Bob	57T	46	$ .95	$3.50
Miller, Bob	58T	326	$ .50	$2.00
Miller, Bob	59T	379	$ .50	$1.95
Miller, Bob	60T	101	$ .35	$1.10
Miller, Bob	61T	314	$ .30	$1.00
Miller, Bob	62T	293	$ .35	$1.10
Miller, Bob	62T	572	$3.75	$11.00
Miller, Bob	63T	261	$ .25	$ .85
Miller, Bob	64T	394	$ .40	$1.25
Miller, Bob	65T	98	$ .25	$ .65
Miller, Bob	66T	208	$ .25	$ .85

Player	Year	No.	VG	EX/MT
Miller, Bob	67T	461	$ .50	$2.00
Miller, Bob	68T	534	$ .30	$1.00
Miller, Bob	69T	403	$ .25	$ .65
Miller, Bob	70T	47	$ .10	$ .35
Miller, Bob	71T	542	$ .30	$1.00
Miller, Bob	72T	414	$ .05	$ .25
Miller, Bob	73T	277	$ .06	$ .25
Miller, Bob	74T	624	$ .06	$ .25
Miller, Bruce	75T	606	$ .06	$ .25
Miller, Bruce	76T	367	$ .05	$ .20
Miller, Darrell	86T	524	$ .01	$ .03
Miller, Darrell	87T	337	$ .01	$ .03
Miller, Darrell	88T	679	$ .01	$ .03
Miller, Darrell	89T	68	$ .01	$ .04
Miller, Dyar	75T	614	$ .06	$ .25
Miller, Dyar	76T	555	$ .05	$ .20
Miller, Dyar	77T	77	$ .03	$ .12
Miller, Dyar	78T	239	$ .02	$ .10
Miller, Dyar	79T	313	$ .02	$ .10
Miller, Dyar	81T	472	$ .01	$ .07

Player	Year	No.	VG	EX/MT
Miller, Dyar	82T	178	$ .01	$ .07
Miller, Eddie	80T	675	$ .01	$ .06
Miller, Ed	81T	192	$ .05	$ .20
Miller, Ed	82T	451	$ .01	$ .06
Miller, John	63T	208	$ .25	$ .85
Miller, John	65T	49	$ .50	$2.00
Miller, John	66T	427	$ .25	$ .85
Miller, John	67T	141	$ .25	$ .65
Miller, John	69T	641	$ .25	$ .85
Miller, Keith	88T	382	$ .01	$ .20
Miller, Keith	89T	268	$ .01	$ .15
Miller, Keith	89T	557	$ .01	$ .10
Miller, Keith	90T	58	$ .01	$ .03
Miller, Larry	65T	349	$ .30	$1.00
Miller, Larry	69T	323	$ .25	$ .85
Miller, Norm	67T	412	$ .25	$ .85
Miller, Norm	68T	161	$ .25	$ .65
Miller, Norm	69T	76	$ .25	$ .65
Miller, Norm	70T	619	$ .25	$ .85
Miller, Norm	71T	18	$ .10	$ .35
Miller, Norm	72T	466	$ .05	$ .25
Miller, Norm	73T	637	$ .35	$1.10
Miller, Norm	74T	439	$ .06	$ .25
Miller, Randy	80T	680	$ .05	$ .20
Miller, Ray	86T	381	$ .01	$ .03
Miller, Rick	72T	741	$1.00	$3.75
Miller, Rick	74T	247	$ .06	$ .25
Miller, Rick	75T	103	$ .06	$ .25
Miller, Rick	76T	302	$ .05	$ .20
Miller, Rick	77T	566	$ .03	$ .12
Miller, Rick	78T	482	$ .02	$ .10
Miller, Rick	79T	654	$ .02	$ .10
Miller, Rick	80T	48	$ .01	$ .07
Miller, Rick	81T	239	$ .01	$ .07
Miller, Rick	81TTR	803	$ .02	$ .10
Miller, Rick	82T	717	$ .01	$ .06
Miller, Rick	83T	188	$ .01	$ .06
Miller, Rick	84T	344	$ .01	$ .05
Miller, Rick	85T	502	$ .01	$ .04
Miller, Rick	86T	424	$ .01	$ .03
Miller, Stu	53T	183	$3.75	$13.00
Miller, Stu	54T	164	$2.10	$7.50
Miller, Stu	56T	293	$1.80	$6.00
Miller, Stu	58T	111	$ .50	$2.00
Miller, Stu	59T	183	$ .50	$1.95
Miller, Stu	60T	378	$ .50	$1.95
Miller, Stu	61T	72	$ .30	$1.00
Miller, Stu	62T	155	$ .35	$1.10
Miller, Stu	63T	286	$ .35	$1.20
Miller, Stu	64T	565	$1.50	$3.75
Miller, Stu	65T	499	$ .50	$2.00
Miller, Stu	66T	265	$ .25	$ .85
Miller, Stu	67T	345	$ .25	$ .65
Milligan, Randy	89TTR	81	$ .01	$ .10
Milligan, Randy	90T	153	$ .01	$ .03
Milliken, Bob	53T	221	$11.00	$37.50
Milliken, Bob	54T	177	$2.10	$7.50
Milliken, Bob	55T	111	$1.35	$5.00
Mills, Brad	82T	118	$ .03	$ .15
Mills, Brad	83T	744	$ .01	$ .06
Mills, Buster	54T	227	$2.10	$7.50
Mills, Dick	71T	512	$ .10	$ .35
Milner, Brian	81T	577	$ .01	$ .07
Milner, Brian	82T	203	$ .70	$3.50
Milner, Eddie	82TTR	72	$ .05	$ .20
Milner, Eddie	83T	449	$ .01	$ .06
Milner, Eddie	84T	34	$ .01	$ .05
Milner, Eddie	85T	198	$ .01	$ .04
Milner, Eddie	86T	544	$ .01	$ .03
Milner, Eddie	87T	253	$ .01	$ .03
Milner, Eddie	87TTR	78	$ .01	$ .07
Milner, Eddie	88T	677	$ .01	$ .03
Milner, John	72T	741	$1.00	$3.75
Milner, John	73T	4	$ .06	$ .25
Milner, John	74T	234	$ .06	$ .25

Player	Year	No.	VG	EX/MT
Milner, John	75T	264	$ .06	$ .25
Milner, John	76T	517	$ .05	$ .20
Milner, John	77T	172	$ .03	$ .12
Milner, John	78T	304	$ .02	$ .10
Milner, John	79T	523	$ .02	$ .10
Milner, John	80T	71	$ .01	$ .07
Milner, John	81T	618	$ .01	$ .07
Milner, John	82T	638	$ .01	$ .06
Minarcin, Rudy	55T	174	$4.25	$13.00
Minarcin, Rudy	56T	36	$1.25	$4.50
Mincher, Don	60T	548	$2.00	$7.00
Mincher, Don	61T	336	$ .30	$1.00
Mincher, Don	62T	386	$ .70	$2.10
Mincher, Don	63T	269	$ .25	$ .85
Mincher, Don	64T	542	$1.50	$3.75
Mincher, Don	65T	108	$ .25	$ .65
Mincher, Don	66T	388	$ .25	$ .85

Player	Year	No.	VG	EX/MT
Mincher, Don	67T	312	$ .25	$ .65
Mincher, Don	68T	75	$ .25	$ .65
Mincher, Don	69T	285	$ .25	$ .85
Mincher, Don	70T	185	$ .10	$ .35
Mincher, Don	71T	680	$ .70	$2.10
Mincher, Don	72T	242	$ .05	$ .25
Minetto, Craig	80T	494	$ .01	$ .07
Minetto, Craig	81T	316	$ .01	$ .07
Mingori, Steve	69T	339	$ .25	$ .65
Mingori, Steve	71T	612	$ .30	$1.00
Mingori, Steve	72T	261	$ .05	$ .25
Mingori, Steve	73T	532	$ .35	$1.10
Mingori, Steve	74T	537	$ .06	$ .25
Mingori, Steve	75T	544	$ .06	$ .25
Mingori, Steve	76T	541	$ .05	$ .20
Mingori, Steve	77T	314	$ .03	$ .12
Mingori, Steve	78T	696	$ .02	$ .10
Mingori, Steve	79T	72	$ .02	$ .10
Mingori, Steve	80T	219	$ .01	$ .07
Minner, Paul	52T	127	$6.00	$19.00
Minner, Paul	53T	92	$3.75	$13.00
Minner, Paul	54T	28	$2.10	$7.50
Minner, Paul	56T	182	$2.50	$8.00
Minoso, Orestes	52T	195	$15.00	$50.00
Minoso, Orestes	53T	66	$7.50	$22.50
Minoso, Minnie	56T	125	$3.00	$9.00

Player	Year	No.	VG	EX/MT
Minoso, Minnie	57T	138	$2.10	$7.50
Minoso, Minnie	58T	295	$1.00	$3.00
Minoso, Minnie	59T	80	$1.25	$3.50
Minoso, Minnie	59T	166	$ .60	$1.75
Minoso, Minnie	60T	365	$1.00	$3.75
Minoso, Minnie	61T	42	$ .50	$2.00
Minoso, Minnie	61T	380	$ .60	$1.75
Minoso, Minnie	62T	28	$ .60	$1.75
Minoso, Minnie	63T	190	$ .50	$1.95
Minoso, Minnie	64T	538	$1.75	$5.00
Minoso, Minnie "Orestes"	77TRB	232	$ .10	$ .35
Minton, Greg	77T	489	$ .25	$ .65
Minton, Greg	78T	312	$ .02	$ .10
Minton, Greg	79T	84	$ .02	$ .10
Minton, Greg	80T	588	$ .01	$ .07
Minton, Greg	81T	111	$ .01	$ .07
Minton, Greg	82T	687	$ .01	$ .06
Minton, Greg	83T	470	$ .01	$ .06
Minton, Greg	83TRB	3	$ .01	$ .06
Minton, Greg	84T	205	$ .01	$ .05
Minton, Greg	85T	45	$ .01	$ .04
Minton, Greg	86T	310	$ .01	$ .03
Minton, Greg	87T	724	$ .01	$ .03
Minton, Greg	87TTR	79	$ .01	$ .07
Minton, Greg	88T	129	$ .01	$ .03
Minton, Greg	89T	576	$ .01	$ .04
Minton, Greg	90T	421	$ .01	$ .03
Mirabella, Paul	81T	382	$ .01	$ .07
Mirabella, Paul	82T	499	$ .01	$ .06
Mirabella, Paul	83T	12	$ .01	$ .06
Mirabella, Paul	85T	766	$ .01	$ .04
Mirabella, Paul	89T	192	$ .01	$ .04
Miranda, Willie	53T	278	$11.00	$37.50
Miranda, Willie	54T	56	$3.00	$12.50
Miranda, Willie	55T	154	$2.00	$7.00
Miranda, Willie	56T	103	$1.25	$4.50
Miranda, Willie (Willy)	57T	151	$ .95	$3.50
Miranda, Willy	58T	179	$ .50	$2.00
Miranda, Willy	59T	540	$2.00	$7.00
Mitchell, Bobby	71T	111	$ .10	$ .35
Mitchell, Bobby	74T	497	$ .06	$ .25
Mitchell, Bobby	75T	468	$ .06	$ .25
Mitchell, Bobby	76T	479	$ .05	$ .20
Mitchell, Bobby	83T	647	$ .01	$ .06
Mitchell, Bobby	84T	307	$ .01	$ .05
Mitchell, Craig	76T	591	$ .05	$ .20
Mitchell, Craig	77T	491	$ .25	$1.00
Mitchell, Craig	78T	711	$ .02	$ .10
Mitchell, Dale	51Trb	13	$1.25	$3.50
Mitchell, Dale	52T	92	$6.00	$18.00
Mitchell, Dale	53T	26	$3.75	$13.00
Mitchell, Dale	56T	268	$1.50	$4.50
Mitchell, John	87TTR	80	$ .01	$ .07
Mitchell, John	88T	207	$ .01	$ .10
Mitchell, Kevin	86TTR	74	$1.00	$5.50
Mitchell, Kevin	87T	653	$ .50	$4.00
Mitchell, Kevin	87TTR	81	$ .25	$1.50
Mitchell, Kevin	88T	497	$ .10	$ .50
Mitchell, Kevin	88TBB	57	$ .15	$1.00
Mitchell, Kevin	89T	189	$ .10	$ .35
Mitchell, Kevin	89TBB	129	$ .01	$ .35
Mitchell, Kevin	90T	500	$ .01	$ .25
Mitchell, Kevin	90TAS	401	$ .01	$ .15
Mitchell, Paul	76T	393	$ .05	$ .20
Mitchell, Paul	77T	53	$ .03	$ .12
Mitchell, Paul	78T	558	$ .02	$ .10
Mitchell, Paul	79T	233	$ .02	$ .10
Mitchell, Paul	80T	131	$ .01	$ .07
Mitchell, Paul	81T	449	$ .01	$ .07
Mitterwald, George	68T	301	$ .25	$ .65
Mitterwald, George	69T	491	$ .25	$ .65
Mitterwald, George	70T	118	$ .10	$ .35
Mitterwald, George	71T	189	$ .10	$ .35
Mitterwald, George	72T	301	$ .05	$ .25
Mitterwald, George	72TIA	302	$ .05	$ .25

Player	Year	No.	VG	EX/MT	Player	Year	No.	VG	EX/MT
Mitterwald, George	74T	249	$ .06	$ .25	Monbouquette, Bill	68T	234	$ .25	$ .65
Mitterwald, George	74TTR	249	$ .06	$ .25	Monbouquette, Bill	69T	64	$ .25	$ .65
Mitterwald, George	75T	411	$ .06	$ .25	Monchak, Al	73T	356	$ .10	$ .35
Mitterwald, George	76T	506	$ .05	$ .20	Monchak, Alex	74T	221	$ .06	$ .25
Mitterwald, George	77T	124	$ .03	$ .12	Monday, Rick	67T	542	$3.00	$10.00
Mitterwald, George	78T	688	$ .02	$ .10	Monday, Rick	68T	282	$ .15	$ .50
Mize, Johnny	51Tbb	50	$20.00	$65.00	Monday, Rick	69T	105	$ .25	$ .65
Mize, Johnny	52T	129	$22.50	$70.00	Monday, Rick	70T	547	$ .15	$ .50
Mize, John	53T	77	$22.50	$67.50	Monday, Rick	71T	135	$ .10	$ .35
Mizell, Wilmer	52T	334	$39.00	$135.00	Monday, Rick	72T	730	$1.00	$3.75
Mizell, Wilmer	53T	128	$3.75	$13.00	Monday, Rick	73T	44	$ .10	$ .35
Mizell, Wilmer	54T	249	$2.10	$7.50	Monday, Rick	74T	295	$ .06	$ .25
Mizell, Wilmer	56T	193	$2.50	$8.00	Monday, Rick	75T	129	$ .06	$ .25
Mizell, Wilmer	57T	113	$ .95	$3.50	Monday, Rick	76T	251	$ .05	$ .20
Mizell, Wilmer	58T	385	$ .50	$2.00	Monday, Rick	77T	360	$ .03	$ .12
Mizerock, John	87T	408	$ .01	$ .03	Monday, Rick	78T	145	$ .02	$ .10
Mmahat, Kevin	89TMLD	84	$ .01	$ .25	Monday, Rick	79T	605	$ .02	$ .10
Moates, Dave	76T	327	$ .05	$ .20	Monday, Rick	80T	465	$ .01	$ .07
Moates, Dave	77T	588	$ .03	$ .12	Monday, Rick	81T	726	$ .05	$ .20
Moeller, Joe	63T	53	$ .25	$ .85	Monday, Rick	82T	577	$ .01	$ .06
Moeller, Joe	64T	549	$1.50	$3.75	Monday, Rick	83T	63	$ .01	$ .06
Moeller, Joe	65T	238	$ .30	$1.00	Monday, Rick	84T	274	$ .01	$ .05
Moeller, Joe	66T	449	$ .70	$2.10	Money, Don	69T	454	$ .25	$ .65
Moeller, Joe	67T	149	$ .25	$ .65	Money, Don	70T	645	$ .50	$2.00
Moeller, Joe	68T	359	$ .25	$ .65	Money, Don	71T	49	$ .10	$ .35
Moeller, Joe	69T	444	$ .25	$ .65	Money, Don	72T	635	$ .25	$ .85
Moeller, Joe	70T	97	$ .10	$ .35	Money, Don	73T	386	$ .06	$ .25
Moeller, Joe	71T	288	$ .10	$ .35	Money, Don	74T	413	$ .06	$ .25
Moeller, Ron	61T	466	$ .50	$2.00	Money, Don	75T	175	$ .06	$ .25
Moeller, Ron	63T	541	$1.50	$3.75	Money, Don	76T	402	$ .05	$ .20
Moffitt, Randy	73T	43	$ .06	$ .25	Money, Don	77T	79	$ .03	$ .12
Moffitt, Randy	74T	156	$ .06	$ .25	Money, Don	78T	24	$ .02	$ .10
Moffitt, Randy	75T	132	$ .06	$ .25	Money, Don	79T	265	$ .02	$ .10
Moffitt, Randy	76T	553	$ .05	$ .20	Money, Don	80T	595	$ .01	$ .07
Moffitt, Randy	77T	464	$ .03	$ .12	Money, Don	81T	106	$ .01	$ .07
Moffitt, Randy	78T	284	$ .02	$ .10	Money, Don	82T	709	$ .01	$ .06
Moffitt, Randy	79T	62	$ .02	$ .10	Money, Don	83T	608	$ .01	$ .06
Moffitt, Randy	80T	359	$ .01	$ .07	Money, Don	84T	374	$ .01	$ .05
Moffitt, Randy	81T	622	$ .01	$ .07	Moneyham, Bill	87T	548	$ .01	$ .03
Moffitt, Randy	83T	723	$ .01	$ .06	Monge, Sid	76T	595	$ .05	$ .20
Moffitt, Randy	83TTR	73	$ .02	$ .10	Monge, Sid	77T	282	$ .03	$ .12
Moffitt, Randy	84T	108	$ .01	$ .05	Monge, Sid	78T	101	$ .02	$ .10
Moford, Herb	59T	91	$1.00	$3.75	Monge, Sid	79T	459	$ .02	$ .10
Mohorcic, Dale	87T	497	$ .01	$ .10	Monge, Sid	80T	74	$ .01	$ .07
Mohorcic, Dale	88T	163	$ .01	$ .03	Monge, Sid	81T	333	$ .01	$ .07
Mohorcic, Dale	89T	26	$ .01	$ .04	Monge, Sid	82T	601	$ .01	$ .06
Molinaro, Bob	79T	88	$ .02	$ .10	Monge, Sid	82TTR	73	$ .02	$ .10
Molinaro, Bob	81T	466	$ .01	$ .07	Monge, Sid	83T	564	$ .01	$ .06
Molinaro, Bob	82T	363	$ .01	$ .06	Monge, Sid	83TTR	74	$ .02	$ .10
Molinaro, Bob	83T	664	$ .01	$ .06	Monge, Sid	84T	224	$ .01	$ .05
Molitor, Paul	70T	707	$10.00	$40.00	Monge, Sid	84TTH	80	$ .02	$ .10
Molitor, Paul	79T	24	$1.00	$4.00	Monge, Sid	85T	408	$ .01	$ .04
Molitor, Paul	80T	406	$ .35	$1.25	Monroe, Zack	59T	108	$1.00	$3.75
Molitor, Paul	81T	300	$ .05	$ .25	Monroe, Zack	60T	329	$ .50	$1.95
Molitor, Paul	82T	195	$ .05	$ .25	Montague, John	75T	405	$ .06	$ .25
Molitor, Paul	83T	630	$ .01	$ .06	Montague, John	78T	117	$ .02	$ .10
Molitor, Paul	84T	60	$ .03	$ .15	Montague, John	79T	337	$ .02	$ .10
Molitor, Paul	85T	522	$ .01	$ .10	Montague, John	80T	253	$ .01	$ .07
Molitor, Paul	86T	267	$ .01	$ .03	Montague, John	81T	652	$ .01	$ .07
Molitor, Paul	87T	741	$ .01	$ .10	Montanez, Willie	71T	138	$ .10	$ .35
Molitor, Paul	88T	465	$ .01	$ .10	Montanez, Willie	72T	690	$ .70	$2.10
Molitor, Paul	88TBB	1	$ .01	$ .10	Montanez, Willie	73T	97	$ .06	$ .25
Molitor, Paul	89T	110	$ .01	$ .04	Montanez, Willie	74T	515	$ .06	$ .25
Molitor, Paul	89TBB	330	$ .01	$ .10	Montanez, Willie	75T	162	$ .06	$ .25
Molitor, Paul	90T	360	$ .01	$ .03	Montanez, Willie	76T	181	$ .05	$ .20
Moloney, Dick	71T	13	$ .10	$ .35	Montanez, Willie	77T	410	$ .03	$ .12
Monbouquette, Bill	59T	173	$ .50	$1.95	Montanez, Willie	78T	38	$ .02	$ .10
Monbouquette, Bill	60T	544	$2.00	$7.00	Montanez, Willie	79T	305	$ .02	$ .10
Monbouquette, Bill	61T	562	$6.00	$18.00	Montanez, Willie	80T	224	$ .01	$ .07
Monbouquette, Bill	62T	580	$3.75	$11.00	Montanez, Willie	81T	559	$ .01	$ .07
Monbouquette, Bill	63T	480	$2.50	$6.50	Montanez, Willie	82T	458	$ .01	$ .06
Monbouquette, Bill	64T	25	$ .25	$ .85	Monteagudo, Aurelio	64T	466	$ .40	$1.25
Monbouquette, Bill	65T	142	$ .25	$ .65	Monteagudo, Aurelio	65T	286	$ .30	$1.00
Monbouquette, Bill	66T	429	$ .25	$ .85	Monteagudo, Aurelio	66T	532	$4.50	$15.00
Monbouquette, Bill	67T	482	$ .50	$2.00	Monteagudo, Aurelio	67T	453	$ .25	$ .85

Player	Year	No.	VG	EX/MT
Monteagudo, Aurelio	71T	129	$ .10	$ .35
Monteagudo, Aurelio	72T	458	$ .05	$ .25
Monteagudo, Aurelio	74T	139	$ .06	$ .25
Monteagudo, Aurelio	74TTR	139	$ .06	$ .25
Montefusco, John	76T	30	$ .10	$ .35
Montefusco, John	76T	203	$ .30	$1.00
Montefusco, John	77T	370	$ .03	$ .12
Montefusco, John	78T	142	$ .02	$ .10
Montefusco, John	79T	560	$ .02	$ .10
Montefusco, John	80T	195	$ .01	$ .07
Montefusco, John	81T	438	$ .01	$ .07
Montefusco, John	81TTR	804	$ .02	$ .10
Montefusco, John	82T	697	$ .01	$ .06
Montefusco, John	82TTR	74	$ .02	$ .10
Montefusco, John	83T	223	$ .01	$ .06
Montefusco, John	84T	761	$ .01	$ .05
Montefusco, John	85T	301	$ .01	$ .04
Monteleone, Rich	90T	99	$ .01	$ .03
Montgomery, Bob	71T	176	$ .10	$ .35
Montgomery, Bob	72T	411	$ .05	$ .25
Montgomery, Bob	73T	491	$ .06	$ .25
Montgomery, Bob	74T	301	$ .06	$ .25
Montgomery, Bob	75T	559	$ .06	$ .25
Montgomery, Bob	76T	523	$ .05	$ .20
Montgomery, Bob	77T	288	$ .03	$ .12
Montgomery, Bob	78T	83	$ .02	$ .10
Montgomery, Bob	79T	423	$ .02	$ .10
Montgomery, Bob	80T	618	$ .01	$ .07
Montgomery, Jeff	88T	447	$ .01	$ .30
Montgomery, Jeff	89T	116	$ .01	$ .10
Montgomery, Jeff	90T	638	$ .01	$ .10
Montgomery, Monty	72T	372	$ .10	$ .35
Montgomery, Monty	73T	164	$ .06	$ .25
Monzant, Ray	56T	264	$1.80	$6.00
Monzant, Ray	58T	447	$ .50	$1.95
Monzant, Ray	59T	332	$ .50	$1.95
Monzant, Ray	60T	338	$ .50	$1.95
Monzon, Dan	73T	469	$ .06	$ .25
Monzon, Dan	74T	613	$ .06	$ .25
Moon, Wally	54T	137	$5.00	$15.00
Moon, Wally	55T	67	$1.00	$4.00
Moon, Wally	56T	55	$1.25	$3.50
Moon, Wally	57T	65	$ .50	$2.00
Moon, Wally	58T	210	$ .45	$1.50
Moon, Wally	59T	530	$3.00	$9.00
Moon, Wally	60T	5	$ .35	$1.00
Moon, Wally	61T	325	$ .30	$1.00
Moon, Wally	62T	52	$ .60	$1.75
Moon, Wally	62T	190	$ .60	$1.75
Moon, Wally	63T	279	$ .30	$1.00
Moon, Wally	64T	353	$ .25	$ .85
Moon, Wally	65T	247	$ .30	$1.00
Moore, Archie	64T	581	$1.50	$3.75
Moore, Balor	71T	747	$ .70	$2.10
Moore, Balor	73T	211	$ .06	$ .25
Moore, Balor	74T	453	$ .06	$ .25
Moore, Balor	75T	592	$ .06	$ .25
Moore, Balor	78T	368	$ .02	$ .10
Moore, Balor	79T	238	$ .02	$ .10
Moore, Balor	80T	19	$ .01	$ .07
Moore, Barry	67T	11	$ .25	$ .65
Moore, Barry	68T	462	$ .30	$1.00
Moore, Barry	69T	639	$ .25	$ .85
Moore, Barry	70T	366	$ .10	$ .35
Moore, Brad	89T	202	$ .01	$ .04
Moore, Charlie	74T	379	$ .15	$ .50
Moore, Charlie	74T	603	$ .06	$ .25
Moore, Charlie	75T	636	$ .06	$ .25
Moore, Charlie	76T	116	$ .05	$ .20
Moore, Charlie	77T	382	$ .03	$ .12
Moore, Charlie	78T	51	$ .02	$ .10
Moore, Charlie	79T	408	$ .02	$ .10
Moore, Charlie	80T	579	$ .01	$ .07
Moore, Charlie	81T	237	$ .01	$ .07
Moore, Charlie	82T	308	$ .01	$ .06

Player	Year	No.	VG	EX/MT
Moore, Charlie	83T	659	$ .01	$ .06
Moore, Charlie	84T	751	$ .01	$ .05
Moore, Charlie	85T	83	$ .01	$ .04
Moore, Charlie	86T	137	$ .01	$ .03
Moore, Charlie	87T	676	$ .01	$ .03
Moore, Charlie	87TTR	82	$ .01	$ .07
Moore, Donnie	78T	523	$ .05	$ .20
Moore, Donnie	79T	17	$ .02	$ .10

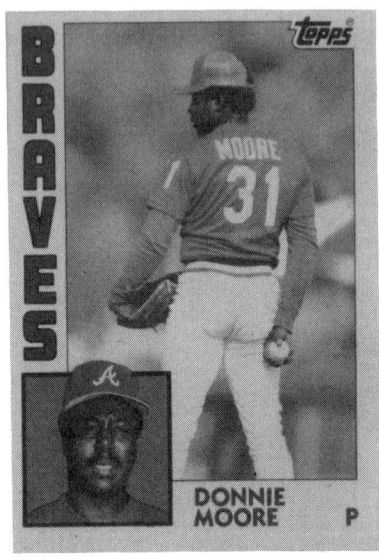

DONNIE MOORE P

Player	Year	No.	VG	EX/MT
Moore, Donnie	84T	207	$ .01	$ .05
Moore, Donnie	85T	699	$ .01	$ .04
Moore, Donnie	85TTR	85	$ .02	$ .10
Moore, Donnie	86T	345	$ .01	$ .03
Moore, Donnie	87T	115	$ .01	$ .03
Moore, Donnie	88T	471	$ .01	$ .03
Moore, Jackie	65T	593	$1.50	$3.75
Moore, Jackie	73T	549	$ .30	$1.00
Moore, Jackie	84TTR	81	$ .02	$ .10
Moore, Jackie	85T	38	$ .01	$ .04
Moore, Jackie	86T	591	$ .01	$ .03
Moore, Junior	78T	421	$ .02	$ .10
Moore, Junior	79T	275	$ .02	$ .10
Moore, Junior	80T	186	$ .01	$ .07
Moore, Junior	82T	531	$ .01	$ .06
Moore, Kelvin	83T	209	$ .50	$2.00
Moore, Mike	84T	547	$ .01	$ .25
Moore, Mike	85T	279	$ .01	$ .10
Moore, Mike	85T	373	$ .01	$ .04
Moore, Mike	86T	646	$ .01	$ .03
Moore, Mike	87T	727	$ .01	$ .03
Moore, Mike	88T	432	$ .01	$ .03
Moore, Mike	88TBB	241	$ .01	$ .05
Moore, Mike	89T	28	$ .01	$ .04
Moore, Mike	89TTR	82	$ .01	$ .10
Moore, Mike	90T	175	$ .01	$ .03
Moore, Ray	55T	208	$4.25	$13.00
Moore, Ray	56T	43	$1.25	$4.50
Moore, Ray	57T	106	$ .95	$3.50
Moore, Ray	58T	249	$ .50	$2.00
Moore, Ray	59T	293	$ .50	$1.95
Moore, Ray	60T	447	$ .60	$1.75
Moore, Ray	61T	289	$ .30	$1.00
Moore, Ray	62T	437	$ .70	$2.10
Moore, Ray	63T	26	$ .25	$ .85

Player	Year	No.	VG	EX/MT
Moorhead, Bob	62T	593	$6.00	$18.00
Moose, Bob	68T	36	$ .15	$ .50
Moose, Bob	69T	409	$ .25	$ .65
Moose, Bob	70T	110	$ .10	$ .35
Moose, Bob	71T	690	$ .70	$2.10
Moose, Bob	72T	647	$ .25	$ .85
Moose, Bob	73T	499	$ .06	$ .25
Moose, Bob	74T	382	$ .06	$ .25
Moose, Bob	75T	536	$ .06	$ .25
Moose, Bob	76T	476	$ .05	$ .20
Mora, Andres	77T	646	$ .03	$ .12
Mora, Andres	78T	517	$ .02	$ .10
Mora, Andres	79T	287	$ .02	$ .10
Morales, Jerry	70T	262	$ .10	$ .35
Morales, Jerry	71T	696	$ .70	$2.10
Morales, Jerry	73T	268	$ .06	$ .25
Morales, Jerry	74T	258	$ .06	$ .25
Morales, Jerry	75T	282	$ .06	$ .25
Morales, Jerry	76T	79	$ .05	$ .20
Morales, Jerry	77T	639	$ .03	$ .12
Morales, Jerry	78T	175	$ .02	$ .10
Morales, Jerry	79T	452	$ .02	$ .10
Morales, Jerry	80T	572	$ .01	$ .07
Morales, Jerry	81T	377	$ .01	$ .07
Morales, Jerry	81TTR	805	$ .02	$ .10
Morales, Jerry	82T	33	$ .01	$ .06
Morales, Jerry	83T	729	$ .01	$ .06
Morales, Jose	76T	418	$ .05	$ .20
Morales, Jose	77T	102	$ .03	$ .12
Morales, Jose	77TRB	233	$ .03	$ .12
Morales, Jose	78T	374	$ .02	$ .10
Morales, Jose	79T	552	$ .02	$ .10
Morales, Jose	80T	218	$ .01	$ .07
Morales, Jose	81T	43	$ .01	$ .07
Morales, Jose	81TTR	806	$ .02	$ .10
Morales, Jose	82T	648	$ .01	$ .06
Morales, Jose	82TTR	75	$ .02	$ .10
Morales, Jose	83TTR	75	$ .02	$ .10
Morales, Jose	84T	143	$ .01	$ .05
Morales, Rich	69T	654	$ .25	$ .85
Morales, Rich	70T	91	$ .10	$ .35
Morales, Rich	71T	267	$ .10	$ .35
Morales, Rich	72T	593	$ .25	$ .85
Morales, Rich	73T	494	$ .06	$ .25
Morales, Rich	74T	387	$ .06	$ .25
Moran, Al	63T	558	$1.50	$3.75
Moran, Al	64T	288	$ .25	$ .85
Moran, Billy	58T	388	$ .50	$2.00
Moran, Billy	59T	196	$ .50	$1.95
Moran, Billy	62T	539	$3.75	$11.00
Moran, Billy	63T	57	$ .25	$ .85
Moran, Billy	64T	333	$ .25	$ .85
Moran, Billy	65T	562	$1.50	$3.75
Morandini, Mickey	88TTR	71	$ .05	$ .50
Morandini, Mickey	89TBB	162	$ .01	$ .10
Morehead, Dave	63T	299	$ .35	$1.20
Morehead, Dave	64T	376	$ .40	$1.25
Morehead, Dave	65T	434	$ .30	$1.00
Morehead, Dave	66T	135	$ .25	$ .85
Morehead, Dave	67T	297	$ .25	$ .65
Morehead, Dave	68T	212	$ .25	$ .65
Morehead, Dave	69T	29	$ .25	$ .65
Morehead, Dave	70T	495	$ .10	$ .35
Morehead, Dave	71T	221	$ .10	$ .35
Morehead, Seth	59T	253	$ .50	$1.95
Morehead, Seth	60T	504	$ .60	$1.75
Morehead, Seth	61T	107	$ .30	$1.00
Moreland, Keith	81T	131	$ .05	$ .25
Moreland, Keith	82T	384	$ .01	$ .15
Moreland, Keith	82TTR	76	$ .02	$ .10
Moreland, Keith	83T	619	$ .01	$ .06
Moreland, Keith	84T	23	$ .01	$ .05
Moreland, Keith	84T	456	$ .01	$ .05
Moreland, Keith	85T	538	$ .01	$ .04
Moreland, Keith	86T	266	$ .01	$ .03
Moreland, Keith	87T	177	$ .01	$ .03
Moreland, Keith	88T	416	$ .01	$ .03
Moreland, Keith	88TBB	207	$ .01	$ .05
Moreland, Keith	88TTR	72	$ .01	$ .05
Moreland, Keith	89T	773	$ .01	$ .04
Moreland, Keith	89TTR	83	$ .01	$ .05
Moreno, Omar	77T	104	$ .03	$ .12
Moreno, Omar	78T	283	$ .02	$ .10
Moreno, Omar	79T	4	$ .03	$ .15
Moreno, Omar	79T	607	$ .02	$ .10
Moreno, Omar	80T	165	$ .01	$ .07
Moreno, Omar	80T	204	$ .02	$ .10
Moreno, Omar	81T	535	$ .01	$ .07
Moreno, Omar	82T	395	$ .01	$ .06
Moreno, Omar	83T	485	$ .01	$ .06
Moreno, Omar	83TTR	76	$ .02	$ .10
Moreno, Omar	84T	16	$ .01	$ .05
Moreno, Omar	84T	714	$ .01	$ .05
Moreno, Omar	85T	738	$ .01	$ .04
Moreno, Omar	86TTR	75	$ .02	$ .10
Moreno, Omar	87T	214	$ .01	$ .03
Moret, Rogelio	71T	692	$ .70	$2.10
Moret, Rogelio	72T	113	$ .05	$ .25
Moret, Rogelio	73T	291	$ .06	$ .25
Moret, Rogelio	74T	590	$ .06	$ .25
Moret, Rogelio	75T	8	$ .06	$ .25
Moret, Rogelio	76T	632	$ .05	$ .20
Moret, Rogelio	76TTR	632	$ .05	$ .20
Moret, Rogelio	77T	292	$ .03	$ .12
Moret, Rogelio	78T	462	$ .02	$ .10
Morgan, Bobby	52T	355	$39.00	$135.00
Morgan, Bobby	53T	85	$3.75	$13.00
Morgan, Bobby	56T	337	$1.80	$6.00
Morgan, Bobby	58T	144	$ .50	$2.00
Morgan, Joe	60T	229	$ .35	$1.10
Morgan, Joe	61T	511	$ .50	$2.00
Morgan, Joe	89T	714	$ .01	$ .04
Morgan, Joe	90T	321	$ .01	$ .03
Morgan, Joe L.	65T	16	$35.00	$125.00
Morgan, Joe L.	66T	195	$7.00	$35.00
Morgan, Joe L.	67T	337	$4.00	$15.00
Morgan, Joe L.	68T	144	$3.00	$9.00
Morgan, Joe L.	68TAS	364	$ .75	$3.00
Morgan, Joe L.	69T	35	$2.50	$7.50
Morgan, Joe L.	70T	537	$2.50	$7.50
Morgan, Joe L.	71T	264	$2.50	$7.50
Morgan, Joe L.	72T	132	$1.75	$5.00
Morgan, Joe L.	72TTR	752	$11.50	$38.00
Morgan, Joe L.	73T	230	$2.00	$6.00
Morgan, Joe L.	74T	85	$1.00	$4.00
Morgan, Joe L.	74TAS	333	$ .50	$2.00
Morgan, Joe L.	75T	180	$ .95	$3.50
Morgan, Joe L.	76T	197	$ .15	$ .50
Morgan, Joe L.	76T	420	$ .95	$3.50
Morgan, Joe L.	77T	100	$1.00	$4.00
Morgan, Joe L.	78T	300	$ .50	$2.00
Morgan, Joe L.	79T	20	$ .10	$ .50
Morgan, Joe L.	80T	650	$ .20	$1.00
Morgan, Joe L.	81T	560	$ .15	$ .60
Morgan, Joe L.	81TTR	807	$ .35	$1.25
Morgan, Joe L.	82T	754	$ .25	$ .65
Morgan, Joe L.	82TIA	755	$ .05	$ .20
Morgan, Joe L.	83T	171	$ .01	$ .06
Morgan, Joe L.	83T	603	$ .07	$ .35
Morgan, Joe L.	83T	604	$ .01	$ .15
Morgan, Joe L.	83TTR	77	$ .35	$1.50
Morgan, Joe L.	84T	210	$ .05	$ .25
Morgan, Joe L.	84T	705	$ .02	$ .10
Morgan, Joe L.	84TTR	82	$ .15	$ .60
Morgan, Joe L.	85T	352	$ .05	$ .25
Morgan, Joe L.	85TRB	5	$ .01	$ .10
Morgan, Mike	80T	671	$ .01	$ .07
Morgan, Mike	83T	203	$ .01	$ .06
Morgan, Mike	83TTR	78	$ .02	$ .10
Morgan, Mike	84T	423	$ .01	$ .05

TOPPS

Player	Year	No.	VG	EX/MT	Player	Year	No.	VG	EX/MT
Morgan, Mike	86T	152	$ .01	$ .03	Morton, Carl	74T	244	$ .06	$ .25
Morgan, Mike	87T	546	$ .01	$ .03	Morton, Carl	75T	237	$ .06	$ .25
Morgan, Mike	88T	32	$ .01	$ .03	Morton, Carl	76T	328	$ .05	$ .20
Morgan, Mike	88TBB	98	$ .01	$ .05	Morton, Craig	77T	24	$ .03	$ .12
Morgan, Mike	88TTR	73	$ .01	$ .05	Moryn, Milt	59T	147	$3.50	$10.00
Morgan, Mike	89T	788	$ .01	$ .04	Moryn, Walt	57T	16	$ .95	$3.50
Morgan, Mike	89TTR	84	$ .01	$ .05	Moryn, Walt	58T	122	$ .50	$2.00
Morgan, Mike	90T	367	$ .01	$ .03	Moryn, Walt	59T	488	$ .50	$1.95
Morgan, Tom	52T	331	$50.00	$145.00	Moryn, Walt	60T	74	$ .35	$1.10
Morgan, Tom	53T	132	$3.75	$13.00	Moryn, Walt	61T	91	$ .30	$1.00
Morgan, Tom	57T	239	$ .95	$3.50	Moschitto, Ross	65T	566	$2.00	$6.00
Morgan, Tom	58T	365	$ .50	$2.00	Moseby, LLoyd	87T	210	$ .01	$ .03
Morgan, Tom	59T	545	$2.00	$7.00	Moseby, Lloyd	81T	643	$ .35	$1.10
Morgan, Tom	60T	33	$ .35	$1.10	Moseby, Lloyd	82T	223	$ .01	$ .20
Morgan, Tom	61T	272	$ .30	$1.00	Moseby, Lloyd	83T	452	$ .03	$ .15
Morgan, Tom	62T	11	$ .35	$1.10	Moseby, Lloyd	84T	92	$ .02	$ .10
Morgan, Tom	63T	421	$ .35	$1.20	Moseby, Lloyd	84T	606	$ .01	$ .05
Morgan, Tom	73T	421	$ .06	$ .25	Moseby, Lloyd	84TAS	403	$ .01	$ .05
Morgan, Tom	74T	276	$ .06	$ .25	Moseby, Lloyd	85T	545	$ .01	$ .10
Morgan, Vern	73T	49	$ .25	$ .65	Moseby, Lloyd	86T	360	$ .01	$ .03
Morgan, Vern	74T	447	$ .06	$ .25	Moseby, Lloyd	88T	565	$ .01	$ .03
Morhardt, Moe	62T	309	$ .35	$1.10	Moseby, Lloyd	88TBB	113	$ .01	$ .05
Morlan, John	75T	651	$ .06	$ .25	Moseby, Lloyd	89T	113	$ .01	$ .04
Morman, Russ	87T	233	$ .01	$ .10	Moseby, Lloyd	89TBB	262	$ .01	$ .05
Morogiello, Dan	84T	682	$ .01	$ .05	Moseby, Lloyd	90T	779	$ .01	$ .03
Morris, Danny	69T	99	$3.75	$11.50	Moses, Gerry	65T	573	$2.50	$9.00
Morris, Hal	90T	236	$ .10	$ .10	Moses, Gerry	69T	476	$ .25	$ .65
Morris, Jack	78T	703	$2.00	$7.00	Moses, Gerry	70T	104	$ .10	$ .35
Morris, Jack	79T	251	$ .50	$1.50	Moses, Gerry	71T	205	$ .10	$ .35
Morris, Jack	80T	371	$ .35	$1.10	Moses, Gerry	72T	356	$ .05	$ .25
Morris, Jack	81T	572	$ .10	$ .50	Moses, Gerry	73T	431	$ .06	$ .25
Morris, Jack	82T	165	$ .03	$ .15	Moses, Gerry	74T	19	$ .06	$ .25
Morris, Jack	82T	450	$ .15	$ .50	Moses, Jerry	75T	271	$ .06	$ .25
Morris, Jack	82TAS	556	$ .02	$ .10	Moses, John	84T	517	$ .01	$ .05
Morris, Jack	83T	65	$ .06	$ .30	Moses, John	87T	284	$ .01	$ .03
Morris, Jack	84T	136	$ .02	$ .10	Moses, John	88T	712	$ .01	$ .03
Morris, Jack	84T	195	$ .05	$ .20	Moses, John	89T	72	$ .01	$ .04
Morris, Jack	84T	666	$ .01	$ .05	Moses, John	90T	653	$ .01	$ .03
Morris, Jack	85T	610	$ .05	$ .20	Moses, Wally	60T	459	$ .95	$3.50
Morris, Jack	86T	270	$ .02	$ .15	Moskau, Paul	78T	126	$ .02	$ .10
Morris, Jack	87T	778	$ .01	$ .10	Moskau, Paul	79T	377	$ .02	$ .10
Morris, Jack	88T	340	$ .01	$ .10	Moskau, Paul	80T	258	$ .01	$ .07
Morris, Jack	88TBB	170	$ .01	$ .05	Moskau, Paul	81T	546	$ .01	$ .07
Morris, Jack	89T	645	$ .01	$ .04	Moskau, Paul	82T	97	$ .01	$ .06
Morris, Jack	89TBB	61	$ .01	$ .10	Moss, Les	52T	143	$6.00	$19.00
Morris, Jack	90T	555	$ .01	$ .03	Moss, Les	57T	213	$ .95	$3.50
Morris, Johnny	69T	111	$ .25	$ .65	Moss, Les	58T	153	$ .50	$2.00
Morris, John	71T	721	$ .70	$2.10	Moss, Les	59T	453	$ .50	$1.95
Morris, John	75T	577	$ .06	$ .25	Mossi, Don	55T	85	$2.10	$7.50
Morris, John	87T	211	$ .01	$ .10	Mossi, Don	56T	39	$1.25	$4.50
Morris, John	88T	536	$ .01	$ .03	Mossi, Don	57T	8	$ .95	$3.50
Morris, John	89T	578	$ .01	$ .04	Mossi, Don	58T	35	$1.00	$3.75
Morris, John	90T	383	$ .01	$ .03	Mossi, Don	59T	302	$ .50	$1.95
Morrison, Jim	79T	722	$ .50	$1.50	Mossi, Don	60T	418	$ .50	$1.95
Morrison, Jim	80T	522	$ .01	$ .07	Mossi, Don	61T	14	$ .30	$1.00
Morrison, Jim	81T	323	$ .01	$ .07	Mossi, Don	62T	55	$ .50	$2.00
Morrison, Jim	82T	654	$ .01	$ .06	Mossi, Don	62T	105	$ .35	$1.10
Morrison, Jim	82TTR	77	$ .02	$ .10	Mossi, Don	63T	218	$ .35	$1.10
Morrison, Jim	83T	173	$ .01	$ .06	Mossi, Don	63T	530	$1.50	$3.75
Morrison, Jim	84T	44	$ .01	$ .05	Mossi, Don	64T	335	$ .25	$ .85
Morrison, Jim	85T	433	$ .01	$ .04	Mossi, Don	66T	74	$ .25	$ .85
Morrison, Jim	86T	553	$ .01	$ .03	Mota, Manny	63T	141	$1.00	$4.00
Morrison, Jim	87T	237	$ .01	$ .03	Mota, Manny	64T	246	$ .15	$ .50
Morrison, Jim	88T	751	$ .01	$ .03	Mota, Manny	65T	463	$ .50	$2.00
Morrison, Jim	88TBB	237	$ .01	$ .05	Mota, Manny	66T	112	$ .30	$1.00
Morton, Bubba	62T	554	$3.75	$11.00	Mota, Manny	67T	66	$ .25	$ .65
Morton, Bubba	63T	164	$ .25	$ .85	Mota, Manny	68T	325	$ .15	$ .50
Morton, Bubba	67T	79	$ .25	$ .65	Mota, Manny	69T	236	$ .35	$1.10
Morton, Bubba	68T	216	$ .25	$ .65	Mota, Manny	70T	157	$ .25	$ .85
Morton, Bubba	69T	342	$ .25	$ .65	Mota, Manny	71T	112	$ .30	$1.00
Morton, Carl	69T	646	$ .25	$ .85	Mota, Manny	72T	596	$ .35	$1.10
Morton, Carl	70T	109	$ .10	$ .35	Mota, Manny	73T	412	$ .25	$ .65
Morton, Carl	71T	515	$ .10	$ .35	Mota, Manny	74T	368	$ .10	$ .35
Morton, Carl	72T	134	$ .05	$ .25	Mota, Manny	75T	414	$ .06	$ .25
Morton, Carl	73T	331	$ .06	$ .25	Mota, Manny	76T	548	$ .05	$ .20

Player	Year	No.	VG	EX/MT	Player	Year	No.	VG	EX/MT
Mota, Manny	77T	386	$ .03	$ .12	Munson, Thurman	73T	142	$2.00	$6.00
Mota, Manny	78T	228	$ .02	$ .10	Munson, Thurman	74T	340	$1.75	$5.00
Mota, Manny	79T	644	$ .05	$ .20	Munson, Thurman	75T	20	$1.75	$5.00
Mota, Manny	80T	104	$ .03	$ .15	Munson, Thurman	76T	192	$ .50	$1.50
Mota, Manny	80THL	3	$ .01	$ .07	Munson, Thurman	76T	650	$1.75	$5.00
Motley, Darryl	82T	471	$ .05	$ .20	Munson, Thurman	77T	170	$1.00	$4.00
Motley, Darryl	85T	561	$ .01	$ .04	Munson, Thurman	78T	60	$ .65	$2.25
Motley, Darryl	86T	332	$ .01	$ .03	Munson, Thurman	79T	310	$ .45	$1.75
Motley, Darryl	87T	99	$ .01	$ .03	Mura, Steve	79T	725	$ .02	$ .10
Motton, Curt	68T	549	$ .30	$1.00	Mura, Steve	80T	491	$ .01	$ .07
Motton, Curt	69T	37	$ .25	$ .65	Mura, Steve	81T	134	$ .01	$ .07
Motton, Curt	70T	261	$ .10	$ .35	Mura, Steve	82T	641	$ .01	$ .06
Motton, Curt	71T	684	$ .70	$2.10	Mura, Steve	82TTR	79	$ .02	$ .10
Motton, Curt	72T	393	$ .05	$ .25	Mura, Steve	83T	24	$ .01	$ .06
Moyer, Jamie	87T	227	$ .06	$ .25	Mura, Steve	86T	281	$ .01	$ .03
Moyer, Jamie	88T	36	$ .01	$ .03	Murakami, Masanori	65T	282	$ .30	$1.00
Moyer, Jamie	89T	717	$ .01	$ .04	Murcer, Bobby	66T	469	$3.00	$12.00
Moyer, Jamie	89TTR	85	$ .01	$ .05	Murcer, Bobby	67T	93	$ .75	$2.25
Moyer, Jamie	90T	412	$ .01	$ .03	Murcer, Bobby	69T	657	$ .50	$1.50
Moyer, Jim	72T	506	$ .25	$ .65	Murcer, Bobby	70T	333	$ .25	$ .75
Mueller, Don	52T	52	$12.50	$45.00	Murcer, Bobby	71T	635	$ .50	$1.50
Mueller, Don	54T	42	$2.00	$7.00	Murcer, Bobby	72T	86	$ .30	$1.00
Mueller, Don	56T	241	$3.00	$9.00	Murcer, Bobby	72T	699	$ .75	$2.50
Mueller, Don	57T	148	$ .95	$3.50	Murcer, Bobby	72TIA	700	$ .80	$2.25
Mueller, Don	58T	253	$ .50	$2.00	Murcer, Bobby	73T	240	$ .25	$ .85
Mueller, Don	59T	368	$ .50	$1.95	Murcer, Bobby	73T	343	$ .06	$ .25
Mueller, Willie	80T	668	$ .01	$ .07	Murcer, Bobby	74T	90	$ .10	$ .35
Muffett, Billy	58T	143	$ .50	$2.00	Murcer, Bobby	74TAS	336	$ .75	$2.50
Muffett, Billy	59T	241	$ .50	$1.95	Murcer, Bobby	75T	350	$ .25	$ .65
Muffett, Billy	61T	16	$ .30	$1.00	Murcer, Bobby	76T	470	$ .10	$ .35
Muffett, Billy	62T	336	$ .35	$1.10	Murcer, Bobby	77T	40	$ .03	$ .12
Muir, Joe	52T	154	$6.00	$19.00	Murcer, Bobby	78T	590	$ .05	$ .20
Mulholland, Terry	87T	536	$ .01	$ .03	Murcer, Bobby	79T	135	$ .05	$ .20
Mulholland, Terry	89T	41	$ .01	$ .04	Murcer, Bobby	80T	365	$ .01	$ .07
Mulholland, Terry	90T	657	$ .01	$ .03	Murcer, Bobby	81T	602	$ .01	$ .07
Mulleavy, Greg	60T	463	$ .85	$2.25	Murcer, Bobby	82T	208	$ .01	$ .06
Mullin, Pat	52T	275	$11.50	$38.00					
Mulliniks, Rance	78T	579	$ .05	$ .20					
Mulliniks, Rance	81T	433	$ .01	$ .07					
Mulliniks, Rance	82T	104	$ .01	$ .06					
Mulliniks, Rance	82TTR	78	$ .02	$ .10					
Mulliniks, Rance	83T	277	$ .01	$ .06					
Mulliniks, Rance	84T	762	$ .01	$ .05					
Mulliniks, Rance	85T	336	$ .01	$ .04					
Mulliniks, Rance	86T	74	$ .01	$ .03					
Mulliniks, Rance	87T	537	$ .01	$ .03					
Mulliniks, Rance	88T	167	$ .01	$ .03					
Mulliniks, Rance	89T	618	$ .01	$ .04					
Mulliniks, Rance	90T	466	$ .01	$ .03					
Mullins, Fran	81T	112	$ .01	$ .07					
Mullins, Fran	85T	283	$ .01	$ .04					
Mumphrey, Jerry	77T	136	$ .25	$ .65					
Mumphrey, Jerry	78T	452	$ .02	$ .10					
Mumphrey, Jerry	79T	32	$ .02	$ .10					
Mumphrey, Jerry	80T	378	$ .01	$ .07					
Mumphrey, Jerry	81T	556	$ .01	$ .07					
Mumphrey, Jerry	81TTR	808	$ .02	$ .10					
Mumphrey, Jerry	82T	175	$ .01	$ .06					
Mumphrey, Jerry	82T	486	$ .03	$ .15					
Mumphrey, Jerry	83T	81	$ .01	$ .06					
Mumphrey, Jerry	83T	670	$ .01	$ .06					
Mumphrey, Jerry	84T	45	$ .01	$ .05					
Mumphrey, Jerry	85T	736	$ .01	$ .04					
Mumphrey, Jerry	86T	282	$ .01	$ .03					
Mumphrey, Jerry	86TTR	76	$ .02	$ .10					
Mumphrey, Jerry	87T	372	$ .01	$ .03					
Mumphrey, Jerry	88T	466	$ .01	$ .03					
Mumphrey, Jerry	88TBB	70	$ .01	$ .05					
Munger, Red	51Tbb	14	$5.50	$17.00	Murcer, Bobby	83T	782	$ .01	$ .06
Munger, George "Red"	52T	115	$6.00	$19.00	Murcer, Bobby	83T	783	$ .01	$ .06
Munoz, Mike	89TMLD	85	$ .01	$ .05	Murff, Red	57T	321	$3.50	$13.00
Munson, Thurman	70T	189	$20.00	$67.50	Murphy, Bill	66T	574	$4.50	$15.00
Munson, Thurman	71T	5	$6.00	$18.00	Murphy, Dale	77T	476	$20.00	$60.00
Munson, Thurman	72T	441	$4.00	$15.00	Murphy, Dale	78T	708	$7.00	$25.00
Munson, Thurman	72TIA	442	$2.00	$7.50	Murphy, Dale	79T	39	$2.00	$7.50

BOBBY MURCER
DESIGNATED HITTER
YANKEES

TOPPS

Player	Year	No.	VG	EX/MT	Player	Year	No.	VG	EX/MT
Murphy, Dale	80T	274	$2.00	$7.00	Murphy, Tom	69T	474	$ .25	$ .65
Murphy, Dale	81T	504	$ .60	$2.50	Murphy, Tom	70T	351	$ .10	$ .35
Murphy, Dale	82T	668	$ .95	$3.50	Murphy, Tom	71T	401	$ .10	$ .35
Murphy, Dale	83T	502	$ .01	$ .06	Murphy, Tom	72T	354	$ .05	$ .25
Murphy, Dale	83T	703	$ .01	$ .06	Murphy, Tom	73T	539	$ .35	$1.10
Murphy, Dale	83T	760	$ .25	$1.00	Murphy, Tom	74T	496	$ .06	$ .25
Murphy, Dale	83TAS	401	$ .15	$ .60	Murphy, Tom	74TTR	496	$ .06	$ .25
Murphy, Dale	84T	126	$ .01	$ .05	Murphy, Tom	75T	28	$ .06	$ .25
Murphy, Dale	84T	133	$ .06	$ .30	Murphy, Tom	76T	219	$ .05	$ .20
Murphy, Dale	84T	150	$ .20	$ .75	Murphy, Tom	77T	396	$ .03	$ .12
Murphy, Dale	84TAS	391	$ .06	$ .30	Murphy, Tom	78T	103	$ .02	$ .10
Murphy, Dale	85T	320	$ .10	$ .50	Murphy, Tom	79T	588	$ .02	$ .10
Murphy, Dale	85TAS	716	$ .05	$ .25	Murray, Dale	75T	568	$ .06	$ .25
Murphy, Dale	86T	600	$ .04	$ .35	Murray, Dale	76T	18	$ .05	$ .20
Murphy, Dale	86TAS	705	$ .02	$ .20	Murray, Dale	77T	252	$ .03	$ .12
Murphy, Dale	87T	490	$ .25	$ .85	Murray, Dale	78T	149	$ .02	$ .10
Murphy, Dale	88T	90	$ .01	$ .30	Murray, Dale	79T	379	$ .02	$ .10
Murphy, Dale	88TBB	14	$ .01	$ .15	Murray, Dale	80T	559	$ .01	$ .07
Murphy, Dale	89T	210	$ .01	$ .10	Murray, Dale	83T	42	$ .01	$ .06
Murphy, Dale	89TBB	172	$ .01	$ .20	Murray, Dale	83TTR	79	$ .02	$ .10
Murphy, Dale	90T	750	$ .01	$ .10	Murray, Dale	84T	697	$ .01	$ .05
					Murray, Dale	85T	481	$ .01	$ .04
					Murray, Eddie	78T	36	$10.00	$33.00
					Murray, Eddie	79T	640	$2.10	$7.50
					Murray, Eddie	80T	160	$ .50	$2.25
					Murray, Eddie	81T	490	$ .25	$1.25
					Murray, Eddie	82T	162	$ .05	$ .25
					Murray, Eddie	82T	163	$ .05	$ .25
					Murray, Eddie	82T	390	$ .35	$1.10
					Murray, Eddie	82T	426	$ .05	$ .25
					Murray, Eddie	83T	21	$ .05	$ .25
					Murray, Eddie	83T	530	$ .15	$ .75
					Murray, Eddie	84T	240	$ .25	$ .65
					Murray, Eddie	84TAS	397	$ .05	$ .25
					Murray, Eddie	85T	700	$ .25	$ .65
					Murray, Eddie	85TAS	701	$ .06	$ .30
					Murray, Eddie	86T	30	$ .03	$ .25
					Murray, Eddie	87T	120	$ .06	$ .25
					Murray, Eddie	88T	495	$ .01	$ .20
					Murray, Eddie	88TBB	215	$ .01	$ .20
					Murray, Eddie	88TRB	4	$ .01	$ .30
					Murray, Eddie	89T	625	$ .01	$ .15
					Murray, Eddie	89TBB	319	$ .01	$ .15
					Murray, Eddie	89TTR	87	$ .01	$ .10
					Murray, Eddie	90T	305	$ .01	$ .10
					Murray, Larry	80T	284	$ .01	$ .07
					Murray, Ray	52T	299	$14.00	$45.00
					Murray, Ray	53T	234	$11.00	$37.50
					Murray, Ray	54T	49	$2.10	$7.50
					Murray, Rich	81T	195	$ .01	$ .07
					Murrell, Ivan	68T	569	$ .30	$1.00
					Murrell, Ivan	69T	333	$ .25	$ .65
					Murrell, Ivan	70T	179	$ .10	$ .35
Murphy, Dan	89TMLD	86	$ .01	$ .05	Murrell, Ivan	71T	569	$ .30	$1.00
Murphy, Dan	90T	649	$ .01	$ .10	Murrell, Ivan	72T	677	$ .70	$2.10
Murphy, Danny	61T	214	$ .30	$1.00	Murrell, Ivan	73T	409	$ .06	$ .25
Murphy, Danny	62T	119	$ .35	$1.10	Murrell, Ivan	74T	628	$ .06	$ .25
Murphy, Danny	63T	272	$ .25	$ .85	Murtaugh, Danny	59T	17	$1.50	$3.75
Murphy, Danny	70T	146	$ .10	$ .35	Murtaugh, Danny	60T	223	$ .60	$1.75
Murphy, Dwayne	79T	711	$ .08	$ .30	Murtaugh, Danny	61T	138	$ .30	$1.00
Murphy, Dwayne	80T	461	$ .01	$ .07	Murtaugh, Danny	61TAS	567	$5.50	$16.50
Murphy, Dwayne	81T	341	$ .01	$ .07	Murtaugh, Danny	62T	503	$ .70	$2.10
Murphy, Dwayne	82T	29	$ .01	$ .06	Murtaugh, Danny	63T	559	$1.50	$3.75
Murphy, Dwayne	83T	598	$ .01	$ .06	Murtaugh, Danny	64T	141	$ .25	$ .85
Murphy, Dwayne	84T	103	$ .01	$ .05	Murtaugh, Danny	64T	268	$ .25	$ .85
Murphy, Dwayne	85T	231	$ .01	$ .04	Murtaugh, Danny	70T	532	$ .10	$ .35
Murphy, Dwayne	86T	8	$ .01	$ .03	Murtaugh, Danny	71T	437	$ .10	$ .35
Murphy, Dwayne	87T	743	$ .01	$ .03	Murtaugh, Danny	74T	489	$ .06	$ .25
Murphy, Dwayne	88T	424	$ .01	$ .03	Muser, Tony	73T	238	$ .06	$ .25
Murphy, Dwayne	89T	667	$ .01	$ .04	Muser, Tony	74T	286	$ .06	$ .25
Murphy, Rob	87T	82	$ .03	$ .15	Muser, Tony	75T	348	$ .06	$ .25
Murphy, Rob	88T	603	$ .01	$ .03	Muser, Tony	76T	537	$ .05	$ .20
Murphy, Rob	89T	446	$ .01	$ .04	Muser, Tony	77T	251	$ .03	$ .12
Murphy, Rob	89TTR	86	$ .01	$ .05	Muser, Tony	78T	418	$ .05	$ .20
Murphy, Rob	90T	268	$ .01	$ .03	Musial, Stan	58TAS	476	$7.50	$22.50

AUGUST 10, 1989
MAJOR LEAGUE DEBUT

DAN MURPHY

Player	Year	No.	VG	EX/MT	Player	Year	No.	VG	EX/MT
Musial, Stan	59T	150	$45.00	$150.00	Neal, Charley	56T	299	$3.00	$9.00
Musial, Stan	59T	470	$3.00	$10.00	Neal, Charley	57T	242	$ .60	$2.50
Musial, Stan	60T	250	$25.00	$90.00	Neal, Charley	58T	16	$1.00	$3.75
Musial, Stan	61T	290	$20.00	$60.00	Neal, Charlie	59T	427	$ .50	$1.95
Musial, Stan	62T	50	$20.00	$60.00	Neal, Charlie	60T	155	$ .35	$1.10
Musial, Stan	62T	317	$3.00	$12.00	Neal, Charlie	60TAS	556	$2.00	$7.00
Musial, Stan	63T	1	$4.35	$22.00	Neal, Charlie	61T	423	$ .50	$2.00
Musial, Stan	63T	138	$8.00	$25.00	Neal, Charley	62T	365	$ .50	$2.00
Musial, Stan	63T	250	$24.00	$90.00	Neal, Charlie	63T	511	$1.50	$3.75
Musial, Stan	88TTB	665	$ .01	$ .20	Neal, Charlie	64T	436	$ .40	$1.25
Musselman, Jeff	87TTR	83	$ .10	$ .35	Neeman, Cal	57T	353	$1.00	$3.75
Musselman, Jeff	88T	229	$ .01	$ .10	Neeman, Cal	58T	33	$1.00	$3.75
Musselman, Jeff	88TBB	69	$ .01	$ .05	Neeman, Cal	59T	367	$ .50	$1.95
Musselman, Jeff	89T	591	$ .01	$ .04	Neeman, Cal	60T	337	$ .50	$1.95
Musselman, Jeff	90T	382	$ .01	$ .03	Negray, Ron	56T	7	$1.25	$4.50
Myatt, George	60T	464	$ .95	$3.50	Negray, Ron	57T	254	$ .95	$3.50
Myers, Greg	90T	438	$ .01	$ .03	Neibauer, Gary	69T	611	$ .25	$ .85
Myers, Randy	87T	213	$ .06	$ .25	Neibauer, Gary	70T	384	$ .10	$ .35
Myers, Randy	88T	412	$ .01	$ .03	Neibauer, Gary	71T	668	$ .70	$2.10
Myers, Randy	89T	610	$ .01	$ .04	Neibauer, Gary	72T	149	$ .05	$ .25
Myers, Randy	90T	105	$ .01	$ .03	Neiger, Al	61T	202	$ .30	$1.00
Myrick, Bob	77T	627	$ .03	$ .12	Nelson, "Rocky" Glenn	52T	390	$39.00	$135.00
Myrick, Bob	78T	676	$ .02	$ .10	Nelson, Bob	56T	169	$1.25	$4.50
Nagelson, Russ	70T	7	$ .10	$ .35	Nelson, Dave	69T	579	$ .25	$ .85
Nagelson, Russ	71T	708	$ .70	$2.10	Nelson, Dave	70T	112	$ .10	$ .35
Nagy, Charles	88TTR	74	$ .10	$ .50	Nelson, Dave	71T	241	$ .10	$ .35
Nagy, Charles	89TBB	217	$ .10	$ .50	Nelson, Dave	72T	529	$ .25	$ .85
Nagy, Mike	70T	39	$ .10	$ .35	Nelson, Dave	73T	111	$ .06	$ .25
Nagy, Mike	71T	363	$ .10	$ .35	Nelson, Dave	74T	355	$ .06	$ .25
Nagy, Mike	72T	488	$ .05	$ .25	Nelson, Dave	75T	435	$ .06	$ .25
Nahorodny, Bill	78T	702	$ .02	$ .10	Nelson, Dave	76T	535	$ .05	$ .20
Nahorodny, Bill	79T	169	$ .02	$ .10	Nelson, Gene	81TTR	809	$ .02	$ .10
Nahorodny, Bill	80T	552	$ .01	$ .07	Nelson, Gene	82T	373	$ .01	$ .06
Nahorodny, Bill	81T	296	$ .01	$ .07	Nelson, Gene	82TTR	80	$ .02	$ .10
Nahorodny, Bill	83T	616	$ .01	$ .06	Nelson, Gene	83T	106	$ .01	$ .06
Napoleon, Dan	65T	533	$3.00	$12.00	Nelson, Gene	85TTR	86	$ .02	$ .10
Napoleon, Dan	66T	87	$ .25	$ .85	Nelson, Gene	86T	493	$ .01	$ .03
Naragon, Hal	56T	311	$1.80	$6.00	Nelson, Gene	87T	273	$ .01	$ .03
Naragon, Hal	57T	347	$3.50	$13.00	Nelson, Gene	87TTR	84	$ .01	$ .07
Naragon, Hal	58T	22	$1.00	$3.75	Nelson, Gene	88T	621	$ .01	$ .03
Naragon, Hal	59T	376	$ .50	$1.95	Nelson, Gene	89T	581	$ .01	$ .04
Naragon, Hal	60T	231	$ .35	$1.10	Nelson, Gene	90T	726	$ .01	$ .03
Naragon, Hal	61T	92	$ .30	$1.00	Nelson, Jamie	84T	166	$ .01	$ .05
Naragon, Hal	62T	164	$ .35	$1.10	Nelson, Jim	71T	298	$ .10	$ .35
Narleski, Ray	55T	160	$2.00	$7.00	Nelson, Mel	63T	522	$1.35	$4.00
Narleski, Ray	56T	133	$1.25	$4.50	Nelson, Mel	64T	273	$ .25	$ .85
Narleski, Ray	57T	144	$ .95	$3.50	Nelson, Mel	65T	564	$1.50	$3.75
Narleski, Ray	58T	439	$ .50	$2.00	Nelson, Mel	66T	367	$ .25	$ .85
Narleski, Ray	59T	442	$ .50	$1.95	Nelson, Mel	69T	181	$ .25	$ .65
Narleski, Ray	60T	161	$ .35	$1.10	Nelson, Ricky	84T	672	$ .01	$ .05
Narron, Jerry	80T	16	$ .01	$ .07	Nelson, Ricky	85T	296	$ .01	$ .04
Narron, Jerry	81T	637	$ .01	$ .07	Nelson, Rocky	54T	199	$2.10	$7.50
Narron, Jerry	82T	719	$ .01	$ .06	Nelson, Rocky	59T	446	$ .50	$1.95
Narron, Jerry	85T	234	$ .01	$ .04	Nelson, Rocky	60T	157	$ .35	$1.10
Narron, Jerry	86T	543	$ .01	$ .03	Nelson, Rocky	61T	304	$ .30	$1.00
Narron, Jerry	87T	474	$ .01	$ .03	Nelson, Roger	68T	549	$ .30	$1.00
Narron, Sam	60T	467	$ .95	$3.50	Nelson, Roger	69T	279	$ .25	$ .85
Narum, Les	64T	418	$ .40	$1.25	Nelson, Roger	70T	633	$ .25	$ .85
Narum, Les	65T	86	$ .25	$ .65	Nelson, Roger	71T	581	$ .30	$1.00
Narum, Les "Buster"	66T	274	$ .25	$ .85	Nelson, Roger	73T	251	$ .06	$ .25
Nash, Cotton	71T	391	$ .10	$ .35	Nelson, Roger	74T	491	$ .06	$ .25
Nash, Jim	67T	90	$ .25	$ .65	Nelson, Roger	75T	572	$ .06	$ .25
Nash, Jim	68T	324	$ .25	$ .65	Nen, Dick	64T	14	$ .25	$ .85
Nash, Jim	69T	546	$ .25	$ .85	Nen, Dick	65T	466	$ .50	$2.00
Nash, Jim	70T	171	$ .10	$ .35	Nen, Dick	66T	149	$ .25	$ .85
Nash, Jim	71T	306	$ .10	$ .35	Nen, Dick	67T	403	$ .25	$ .85
Nash, Jim	72T	401	$ .05	$ .25	Nen, Dick	68T	591	$ .30	$1.00
Nash, Jim	73T	509	$ .06	$ .25	Nettles, Graig	69T	99	$3.75	$11.50
Nastu, Phil	80T	686	$ .01	$ .07	Nettles, Graig	70T	491	$1.25	$3.50
Navarro, Jaime	89TMLD	87	$ .01	$ .25	Nettles, Graig	71T	324	$ .95	$3.50
Navarro, Julio	60T	140	$ .35	$1.10	Nettles, Graig	72T	590	$ .60	$1.75
Navarro, Julio	63T	169	$6.00	$18.00	Nettles, Graig	73T	498	$ .60	$1.75
Navarro, Julio	64T	489	$ .40	$1.25	Nettles, Graig	74T	251	$ .50	$2.00
Navarro, Julio	65T	563	$1.50	$3.75	Nettles, Graig	75T	160	$ .50	$2.00
Navarro, Julio	66T	527	$4.50	$15.00	Nettles, Graig	76T	169	$ .35	$1.10

TOPPS

Player	Year	No.	VG	EX/MT	Player	Year	No.	VG	EX/MT
Nettles, Graig	77T	2	$ .50	$2.00	Nichols, Reid	87TTR	87	$ .01	$ .07
Nettles, Graig	77T	20	$ .15	$ .50	Nichols, Reid	88T	748	$ .01	$ .03
Nettles, Graig	78T	250	$ .02	$ .20	Nichols, Rod	89T	443	$ .01	$ .04
Nettles, Graig	79T	460	$ .25	$ .65	Nichols, Rod	90T	108	$ .01	$ .03
Nettles, Graig	80T	710	$ .05	$ .20	Nicholson, Bill	52T	185	$6.00	$19.00
Nettles, Graig	81T	365	$ .03	$ .15	Nicholson, Dave	61T	182	$ .30	$1.00
Nettles, Graig	82T	505	$ .05	$ .20	Nicholson, Dave	62T	577	$3.75	$11.00
Nettles, Graig	82TIA	506	$ .02	$ .10	Nicholson, Dave	63T	234	$ .25	$ .85
Nettles, Graig	83T	635	$ .01	$ .06	Nicholson, Dave	64T	31	$ .25	$ .85
Nettles, Graig	83T	636	$ .01	$ .06	Nicholson, Dave	65T	183	$ .25	$ .65
Nettles, Graig	84T	175	$ .03	$ .15	Nicholson, Dave	66T	576	$4.50	$15.00
Nettles, Graig	84T	712	$ .03	$ .15	Nicholson, Dave	67T	113	$ .25	$ .65
Nettles, Graig	84T	713	$ .03	$ .15	Nicholson, Dave	69T	298	$ .25	$ .85
Nettles, Graig	84TTR	83	$ .25	$ .65	Nicosia, Steve	80T	519	$ .01	$ .07
Nettles, Graig	85T	35	$ .01	$ .10	Nicosia, Steve	81T	212	$ .01	$ .07
Nettles, Graig	86T	450	$ .01	$ .03	Nicosia, Steve	82T	652	$ .01	$ .06
Nettles, Graig	87T	205	$ .01	$ .03	Nicosia, Steve	83T	462	$ .01	$ .06
Nettles, Graig	87TTR	85	$ .05	$ .20	Nicosia, Steve	84T	98	$ .01	$ .05
Nettles, Graig	88T	574	$ .01	$ .03	Nicosia, Steve	85T	191	$ .01	$ .04
Nettles, Jim	71T	74	$ .10	$ .35	Nicosia, Steve	85TTR	87	$ .02	$ .10
Nettles, Jim	72T	131	$ .05	$ .25	Niedenfuer, Tom	83T	477	$ .01	$ .06
Nettles, Jim	73T	358	$ .06	$ .25	Niedenfuer, Tom	84T	112	$ .01	$ .05
Nettles, Jim	75T	497	$ .06	$ .25	Niedenfuer, Tom	85T	782	$ .01	$ .04
Nettles, Morris	75T	632	$ .06	$ .25	Niedenfuer, Tom	86T	56	$ .01	$ .03
Nettles, Morris	76T	434	$ .05	$ .20	Niedenfuer, Tom	87T	538	$ .01	$ .03
Neville, Dan	65T	398	$ .35	$1.10	Niedenfuer, Tom	87TTR	88	$ .01	$ .07
Newcombe, Don	56T	235	$8.50	$35.00	Niedenfuer, Tom	88T	242	$ .01	$ .03
Newcombe, Don	57T	130	$3.00	$9.00	Niedenfuer, Tom	89T	651	$ .01	$ .04
Newcombe, Don	58T	340	$ .75	$2.50	Niedenfuer, Tom	90T	306	$ .01	$ .03
Newcombe, Don	59T	312	$ .70	$2.00	Niekro, Joe	67T	536	$8.25	$28.00
Newcombe, Don	60T	345	$ .70	$2.00	Niekro, Joe	68T	475	$ .70	$2.00
Newcombe, Don	61TMVP	483	$1.25	$3.50	Niekro, Joe	69T	43	$ .35	$1.10
Newcombe, Don	75T	194	$1.75	$5.00	Niekro, Joe	70T	508	$ .15	$ .50
Newhauser, Don	74T	33	$ .06	$ .25	Niekro, Joe	71T	695	$1.50	$3.75
Newhouser, Hal	53T	228	$22.00	$85.00	Niekro, Joe	72T	216	$ .25	$ .65
Newhouser, Hal	55T	24	$2.10	$7.50	Niekro, Joe	73T	585	$ .60	$2.25
Newman, Al	87T	323	$ .01	$ .03					
Newman, Al	87TTR	86	$ .01	$ .07					
Newman, Al	88T	648	$ .01	$ .03					
Newman, Al	89T	503	$ .01	$ .04					
Newman, Al	90T	19	$ .01	$ .03					
Newman, Fred	63T	496	$2.50	$6.50					
Newman, Fred	64T	569	$1.50	$3.75					
Newman, Fred	65T	101	$ .25	$ .65					
Newman, Fred	66T	213	$ .25	$ .85					
Newman, Fred	67T	451	$ .25	$ .85					
Newman, Fred	69T	543	$ .25	$ .85					
Newman, Jeff	77T	204	$ .03	$ .12					
Newman, Jeff	78T	458	$ .02	$ .10					
Newman, Jeff	79T	604	$ .02	$ .10					
Newman, Jeff	80T	34	$ .01	$ .07					
Newman, Jeff	81T	587	$ .01	$ .07					
Newman, Jeff	82T	187	$ .01	$ .06					
Newman, Jeff	83T	784	$ .01	$ .06					
Newman, Jeff	83TTR	80	$ .02	$ .10					
Newman, Jeff	84T	296	$ .01	$ .05					
Newman, Jeff	85T	376	$ .01	$ .04					
Newman, Ray	72T	667	$ .70	$2.10					
Newman, Ray	73T	568	$ .35	$1.10					
Newsom, Bobo	53T	15	$3.75	$13.00					
Niarhos, Gus	52T	121	$6.00	$19.00					
Niarhos, Gus	53T	63	$3.75	$13.00					
Nichols, Chet	52T	288	$14.00	$45.00					
Nichols, Chet	56T	278	$1.80	$6.00					
Nichols, Chet	61T	301	$ .30	$1.00					
Nichols, Chet	62T	403	$ .70	$2.10					
Nichols, Chet	63T	307	$ .35	$1.20					
Nichols, Dolan	59T	362	$ .50	$1.95					
Nichols, Reid	81T	689	$ .75	$2.25	Niekro, Joe	74T	504	$ .25	$ .85
Nichols, Reid	82T	124	$ .01	$ .06	Niekro, Joe	75T	595	$ .10	$ .35
Nichols, Reid	83T	446	$ .01	$ .06	Niekro, Joe	76T	273	$ .06	$ .25
Nichols, Reid	84T	238	$ .01	$ .05	Niekro, Joe	77T	116	$ .03	$ .12
Nichols, Reid	85T	37	$ .01	$ .04	Niekro, Joe	78T	306	$ .02	$ .10
Nichols, Reid	86T	364	$ .01	$ .03	Niekro, Joe	79T	68	$ .02	$ .10
Nichols, Reid	87T	539	$ .01	$ .03	Niekro, Joe	80T	205	$ .05	$ .20

ATLANTA — PITCHER

JOE NIEKRO — BRAVES

340

Player	Year	No.	VG	EX/MT	Player	Year	No.	VG	EX/MT
Niekro, Joe	80T	437	$ .01	$ .07	Nipper, Al	88TTR	75	$ .01	$ .05
Niekro, Joe	81T	722	$ .01	$ .07	Nipper, Al	89T	86	$ .01	$ .04
Niekro, Joe	82T	611	$ .03	$ .15	Nischwitz, Ron	62T	591	$8.00	$22.50
Niekro, Joe	83T	221	$ .01	$ .06	Nischwitz, Ron	63T	152	$ .25	$ .85
Niekro, Joe	83T	441	$ .01	$ .06	Nischwitz, Ron	66T	38	$ .25	$ .85
Niekro, Joe	84T	586	$ .01	$ .05	Nixon, Donell	88T	146	$ .01	$ .03
Niekro, Joe	85T	295	$ .01	$ .04	Nixon, Donell	89T	447	$ .01	$ .04
Niekro, Joe	86T	135	$ .01	$ .03	Nixon, Donell	89TBB	214	$ .01	$ .05
Niekro, Joe	87T	344	$ .01	$ .03	Nixon, Donell	90T	658	$ .01	$ .03
Niekro, Joe	87TTR	89	$ .01	$ .07	Nixon, Otis	86TTR	80	$ .02	$ .10
Niekro, Joe	88T	473	$ .01	$ .03	Nixon, Otis	87T	486	$ .01	$ .03
Niekro, Joe	88TRB	5	$ .01	$ .10	Nixon, Otis	89T	674	$ .01	$ .04
Niekro, Phil	64T	541	$40.00	$125.00	Nixon, Otis	89TBB	234	$ .01	$ .05
Niekro, Phil	65T	461	$7.50	$32.50	Nixon, Otis	90T	252	$ .01	$ .03
Niekro, Phil	66T	28	$3.00	$8.50	Nixon, Russ	58T	133	$ .50	$2.00
Niekro, Phil	67T	456	$2.00	$7.00	Nixon, Russ	59T	344	$ .50	$1.95
Niekro, Phil	68T	7	$ .50	$1.95	Nixon, Russ	60T	36	$ .35	$1.10
Niekro, Phil	68T	257	$1.25	$3.50	Nixon, Russ	61T	53	$ .30	$1.00
Niekro, Phil	69T	355	$2.00	$7.50	Nixon, Russ	62T	523	$3.75	$11.00
Niekro, Phil	70T	69	$ .50	$1.95	Nixon, Russ	63T	168	$ .25	$ .85
Niekro, Phil	70T	160	$1.25	$3.50	Nixon, Russ	64T	329	$ .25	$ .85
Niekro, Phil	71T	30	$1.25	$3.50	Nixon, Russ	65T	162	$ .25	$ .65
Niekro, Phil	72T	620	$1.50	$4.50	Nixon, Russ	66T	227	$ .25	$ .85
Niekro, Phil	73T	503	$ .95	$3.50	Nixon, Russ	67T	446	$ .25	$ .85
Niekro, Phil	74T	29	$ .60	$1.75	Nixon, Russ	68T	515	$ .30	$1.00
Niekro, Phil	75T	130	$ .60	$1.75	Nixon, Russ	69T	363	$ .25	$ .65
Niekro, Phil	75T	310	$ .30	$1.00	Nixon, Russ	83T	756	$ .01	$ .06
Niekro, Phil	76T	435	$ .50	$1.95	Nixon, Russ	84T	351	$ .01	$ .05
Niekro, Phil	77T	615	$ .50	$1.95	Nixon, Russ	88TTR	76	$ .01	$ .05
Niekro, Phil	78T	10	$ .35	$1.10	Nixon, Russ	89T	564	$ .01	$ .04
Niekro, Phil	78T	206	$ .05	$ .20	Nixon, Russ	90T	171	$ .01	$ .03
Niekro, Phil	79T	595	$ .35	$1.10	Nixon, Willard	52T	269	$11.50	$38.00
Niekro, Phil	80T	205	$ .05	$ .20	Nixon, Willard	53T	30	$3.75	$13.00
Niekro, Phil	80T	245	$ .15	$ .60	Nixon, Willard	56T	122	$1.25	$4.50
Niekro, Phil	81T	387	$ .15	$ .60	Nixon, Willard	57T	189	$ .95	$3.50
Niekro, Phil	82T	185	$ .10	$ .50	Nixon, Willard	58T	395	$ .50	$2.00
Niekro, Phil	83T	410	$ .08	$ .40	Nixon, Willard	59T	361	$ .50	$1.95
Niekro, Phil	83T	411	$ .03	$ .15	Noboa, Junior	88T	503	$ .01	$ .10
Niekro, Phil	83T	502	$ .01	$ .06	Noce, Paul	88T	542	$ .01	$ .03
Niekro, Phil	84T	650	$ .06	$ .30	Nokes, Matt	87TTR	91	$ .20	$ .75
Niekro, Phil	84TTR	84	$ .15	$ .60	Nokes, Matt	88T	645	$ .10	$ .50
Niekro, Phil	85T	40	$ .05	$ .25	Nokes, Matt	88TAS	393	$ .01	$ .20
Niekro, Phil	86T	790	$ .03	$ .25	Nokes, Matt	88TBB	185	$ .01	$ .05
Niekro, Phil	86TRB	204	$ .01	$ .10	Nokes, Matt	89T	445	$ .01	$ .04
Niekro, Phil	86TTR	77	$ .10	$ .35	Nokes, Matt	89TBB	303	$ .01	$ .05
Niekro, Phil	87T	694	$ .06	$ .25	Nokes, Matt	90T	131	$ .01	$ .05
Niekro, Phil	88TRB	5	$ .01	$ .10	Nolan, Gary	68T	196	$ .25	$ .65
Nielsen, Scott	87T	57	$ .01	$ .03	Nolan, Gary	69T	581	$ .25	$ .85
Nieman, Bob	56T	267	$1.80	$6.00	Nolan, Gary	70T	484	$ .10	$ .35
Nieman, Bob	57T	14	$ .95	$3.50	Nolan, Gary	71T	75	$ .10	$ .35
Nieman, Bob	58T	165	$ .50	$2.00	Nolan, Gary	72T	475	$ .05	$ .25
Nieman, Bob	59T	375	$ .50	$1.95	Nolan, Gary	73T	260	$ .06	$ .25
Nieman, Bob	60T	149	$ .35	$1.10	Nolan, Gary	74T	277	$ .06	$ .25
Nieman, Bob	61T	178	$ .30	$1.00	Nolan, Gary	75T	562	$ .06	$ .25
Nieman, Bob	62T	182	$ .35	$1.10	Nolan, Gary	76T	444	$ .05	$ .20
Niemann, Randy	80T	469	$ .01	$ .07	Nolan, Gary	77T	121	$ .03	$ .12
Niemann, Randy	81T	148	$ .01	$ .07	Nolan, Gary	78T	115	$ .02	$ .10
Niemann, Randy	83T	329	$ .01	$ .06	Nolan, Joe	78T	617	$ .02	$ .10
Niemann, Randy	86TTR	78	$ .02	$ .10	Nolan, Joe	79T	464	$ .02	$ .10
Niemann, Randy	87T	147	$ .01	$ .03	Nolan, Joe	80T	64	$ .01	$ .07
Nieto, Tom	85T	294	$ .01	$ .04	Nolan, Joe	81T	149	$ .01	$ .07
Nieto, Tom	86T	88	$ .01	$ .03	Nolan, Joe	82T	327	$ .01	$ .06
Nieto, Tom	87T	416	$ .01	$ .03	Nolan, Joe	82TTR	81	$ .02	$ .10
Nieto, Tom	87TTR	90	$ .01	$ .07	Nolan, Joe	83T	242	$ .01	$ .06
Nieto, Tom	88T	317	$ .01	$ .03	Nolan, Joe	84T	553	$ .01	$ .05
Nieves, Juan	86TTR	79	$ .10	$ .35	Nolan, Joe	85T	652	$ .01	$ .04
Nieves, Juan	87T	79	$ .06	$ .25	Nolan, Joe	86T	781	$ .01	$ .03
Nieves, Juan	88T	515	$ .01	$ .10	Nold, Dick	68T	96	$ .25	$ .65
Nieves, Juan	88TBB	190	$ .01	$ .05	Noles, Dickie	80T	682	$ .01	$ .07
Nieves, Juan	89T	287	$ .01	$ .04	Noles, Dickie	81T	406	$ .01	$ .07
Nieves, Juan	90T	467	$ .01	$ .03	Noles, Dickie	82T	530	$ .01	$ .06
Nipper, Al	85T	424	$ .01	$ .10	Noles, Dickie	82TTR	82	$ .02	$ .10
Nipper, Al	86T	181	$ .01	$ .03	Noles, Dickie	83T	99	$ .01	$ .06
Nipper, Al	87T	617	$ .01	$ .03	Noles, Dickie	84T	618	$ .01	$ .05
Nipper, Al	88T	326	$ .01	$ .03	Noles, Dickie	85T	149	$ .01	$ .04

Player	Year	No.	VG	EX/MT	Player	Year	No.	VG	EX/MT
Noles, Dickie	86T	388	$ .01	$ .03	Northrup, Jim	69T	3	$ .30	$1.00
Noles, Dickie	87T	244	$ .01	$ .03	Northrup, Jim	69T	580	$ .25	$ .85
Noles, Dickie	87TTR	92	$ .01	$ .07	Northrup, Jim	70T	177	$ .10	$ .35
Noles, Dickie	88T	768	$ .01	$ .03	Northrup, Jim	.71T	265	$ .10	$ .35
Nolte, Eric	88T	694	$ .01	$ .03	Northrup, Jim	72T	408	$ .05	$ .25
Nordbrook, Tim	76T	252	$ .05	$ .20	Northrup, Jim	73T	168	$ .06	$ .25
Nordbrook, Tim	78T	369	$ .02	$ .10	Northrup, Jim	74T	266	$ .06	$ .25
Nordhagen, Wayne	78T	231	$ .02	$ .10	Northrup, Jim	75T	641	$ .06	$ .25
Nordhagen, Wayne	79T	351	$ .02	$ .10	Norwood, Willie	78T	705	$ .02	$ .10
Nordhagen, Wayne	80T	487	$ .01	$ .07	Norwood, Willie	79T	274	$ .02	$ .10
Nordhagen, Wayne	81T	186	$ .01	$ .07	Norwood, Willie	80T	432	$ .01	$ .07
Nordhagen, Wayne	82T	597	$ .01	$ .06	Nosek, Randy	89TMLD	88	$ .01	$ .05
Nordhagen, Wayne	83T	714	$ .01	$ .06	Nossek, Joe	64T	532	$1.50	$3.75
Noren, Irv	51Tbb	38	$5.50	$17.00	Nossek, Joe	65T	597	$1.50	$3.75
Noren, Irv	52T	40	$14.00	$45.00	Nossek, Joe	66T	22	$ .25	$ .85
Noren, Irv	53T	35	$3.75	$13.00	Nossek, Joe	67T	209	$ .25	$ .65
Noren, Irv	56T	253	$2.55	$7.50	Nossek, Joe	69T	143	$ .25	$ .65
Noren, Irv	57T	298	$3.50	$13.00	Nossek, Joe	73T	646	$ .50	$2.00
Noren, Irv	58T	114	$2.35	$7.00	Nossek, Joe	74T	99	$ .06	$ .25
Noren, Irv	59T	59	$1.00	$3.75	Nottebart, Don	60T	351	$ .50	$1.95
Noren, Irv	60T	433	$ .50	$1.95	Nottebart, Don	61T	29	$ .30	$1.00
Noren, Irv	73T	179	$ .25	$ .85	Nottebart, Don	62T	541	$3.75	$11.00
Norman, Bill	53T	245	$11.00	$37.50	Nottebart, Don	63T	204	$ .25	$ .85
Norman, Dan	79T	721	$ .05	$ .20	Nottebart, Don	64T	434	$ .40	$1.25
Norman, Dan	80T	681	$3.00	$9.00	Nottebart, Don	65T	469	$ .50	$2.00
Norman, Dan	83T	237	$ .01	$ .06	Nottebart, Don	66T	21	$ .25	$ .85
Norman, Fred	64T	469	$ .40	$1.25	Nottebart, Don	67T	269	$ .25	$ .65
Norman, Fred	65T	386	$ .30	$1.00	Nottebart, Don	68T	171	$ .25	$ .65
Norman, Fred	70T	427	$ .10	$ .35	Nottebart, Don	69T	593	$ .25	$ .85
Norman, Fred	71T	348	$ .10	$ .35	Nunez, Ed	85T	34	$ .01	$ .04
Norman, Fred	72T	194	$ .05	$ .25	Nunez, Ed	86T	511	$ .01	$ .03
Norman, Fred	73T	32	$ .06	$ .25	Nunez, Ed	87T	427	$ .01	$ .03
Norman, Fred	74T	581	$ .06	$ .25	Nunez, Ed	88T	258	$ .01	$ .03
Norman, Fred	75T	396	$ .06	$ .25	Nunez, Ed	90T	586	$ .01	$ .03
Norman, Fred	76T	609	$ .05	$ .20	Nunez, Jose	88T	28	$ .01	$ .03
Norman, Fred	77T	139	$ .03	$ .12	Nunn, Howie	59T	549	$2.00	$7.00
Norman, Fred	78T	273	$ .02	$ .10	Nunn, Howie	61T	346	$ .30	$1.00
Norman, Fred	79T	47	$ .02	$ .10	Nunn, Howie	62T	524	$3.75	$11.00
Norman, Fred	80T	714	$ .01	$ .07	Nuxhall, Joe	52T	406	$60.00	$175.00
Norman, Fred	81T	497	$ .01	$ .07	Nuxhall, Joe	53T	105	$4.00	$12.50
Norman, Nelson	80T	518	$ .01	$ .07	Nuxhall, Joe	56T	218	$2.50	$8.00
Norrid, Tim	79T	705	$ .35	$1.20	Nuxhall, Joe	57T	103	$1.35	$5.00
Norris, Jim	78T	484	$ .02	$ .10	Nuxhall, Joe	58T	63	$1.25	$3.50
Norris, Jim	79T	611	$ .02	$ .10	Nuxhall, Joe	59T	389	$ .70	$2.00
Norris, Jim	80T	333	$ .01	$ .07	Nuxhall, Joe	60T	282	$1.00	$3.75
Norris, Jim	81T	264	$ .01	$ .07	Nuxhall, Joe	61T	444	$ .50	$2.00
Norris, Mike	76T	653	$ .06	$ .25	Nuxhall, Joe	63T	194	$ .50	$2.00
Norris, Mike	77T	284	$ .03	$ .12	Nuxhall, Joe	64T	106	$ .35	$1.10
Norris, Mike	78T	434	$ .02	$ .10	Nuxhall, Joe	65T	312	$ .35	$1.10
Norris, Mike	79T	191	$ .02	$ .10	Nuxhall, Joe	66T	483	$ .75	$2.00
Norris, Mike	80T	599	$ .01	$ .07	Nuxhall, Joe	67T	44	$ .25	$ .65
Norris, Mike	81T	55	$ .01	$ .07	Nye, Rich	67T	608	$2.00	$6.00
Norris, Mike	82T	370	$ .01	$ .06	Nye, Rich	68T	339	$ .25	$ .65
Norris, Mike	83T	620	$ .01	$ .06	Nye, Rich	69T	88	$ .25	$ .65
Norris, Mike	84T	493	$ .01	$ .05	Nye, Rich	70T	139	$ .10	$ .35
Norris, Mike	85T	246	$ .01	$ .04	Nyman, Chris	84T	382	$ .01	$ .05
North, Bill	73T	234	$ .06	$ .25	Nyman, Gerry	69T	173	$ .25	$ .65
North, Bill	74T	345	$ .06	$ .25	Nyman, Gerry	70T	644	$ .50	$2.00
North, Bill	75T	121	$ .06	$ .25	Nyman, Gerry	71T	656	$ .70	$2.10
North, Bill	75T	309	$ .30	$1.00	Nyman, Nyls	75T	619	$ .06	$ .25
North, Bill	76T	33	$ .05	$ .20	Nyman, Nyls	76T	258	$ .05	$ .20
North, Bill	77T	4	$ .03	$ .12	O'Berry, Mike	80T	662	$ .01	$ .07
North, Bill	77T	551	$ .03	$ .12	O'Berry, Mike	82T	562	$ .01	$ .06
North, Bill	78T	163	$ .02	$ .10	O'Berry, Mike	84T	184	$ .01	$ .05
North, Bill	79T	668	$ .02	$ .10	O'Berry, Mike	84TTR	86	$ .02	$ .10
North, Bill	80T	408	$ .01	$ .07	O'Brien, Bob	72T	198	$ .60	$1.50
North, Bill	81T	713	$ .01	$ .07	O'Brien, Charlie	90T	106	$ .01	$ .03
Northey, Ron	52T	204	$6.00	$19.00	O'Brien, Charlie	88T	566	$ .01	$ .03
Northey, Ron	57T	31	$ .95	$3.50	O'Brien, Charlie	89T	214	$ .01	$ .04
Northey, Scott	70T	241	$ .10	$ .35	O'Brien, Dan	80T	684	$ .08	$ .40
Northey, Scott	71T	633	$ .30	$1.00	O'Brien, Ed	53T	249	$11.00	$37.50
Northrup, Jim	65T	259	$ .35	$1.10	O'Brien, Eddie	54T	139	$3.75	$13.00
Northrup, Jim	66T	554	$4.50	$15.00	O'Brien, Eddie	56T	116	$1.25	$4.50
Northrup, Jim	67T	408	$ .25	$ .85	O'Brien, Eddie	57T	259	$ .95	$3.50
Northrup, Jim	68T	78	$ .25	$ .65	O'Brien, John	53T	223	$11.00	$37.50

Player	Year	No.	VG	EX/MT
O'Brien, Johnny	54T	139	$3.75	$13.00
O'Brien, Johnny	55T	135	$1.35	$5.00
O'Brien, Johnny	56T	65	$1.25	$4.50

Player	Year	No.	VG	EX/MT
O'Brien, Johnny	58T	426	$ .50	$2.00
O'Brien, Johnny	59T	499	$ .50	$1.95
O'Brien, Pete	83TTR	81	$ .05	$1.50
O'Brien, Pete	84T	534	$ .10	$1.00
O'Brien, Pete	85T	196	$ .01	$ .20
O'Brien, Pete	86T	328	$ .01	$ .15
O'Brien, Pete	87T	17	$ .01	$ .10
O'Brien, Pete	88T	721	$ .01	$ .05
O'Brien, Pete	88TBB	227	$ .01	$ .10
O'Brien, Pete	89T	629	$ .01	$ .04
O'Brien, Pete	89TBB	115	$ .01	$ .05
O'Brien, Pete	89TTR	88	$ .01	$ .05
O'Brien, Pete	90T	265	$ .01	$ .03
O'Brien, Syd	69T	628	$ .25	$ .85
O'Brien, Syd	70T	163	$ .10	$ .35
O'Brien, Syd	71T	561	$ .30	$1.00
O'Brien, Syd	72T	289	$ .05	$ .25
O'Connell, Danny	53T	107	$3.75	$13.00
O'Connell, Danny	56T	272	$1.80	$6.00
O'Connell, Danny	57T	271	$3.50	$13.00
O'Connell, Danny	58T	166	$ .50	$2.00
O'Connell, Danny	59T	87	$1.00	$3.75
O'Connell, Danny	60T	192	$ .35	$1.10
O'Connell, Danny	61T	318	$ .30	$1.00
O'Connell, Danny	62T	411	$ .70	$2.10
O'Connor, Jack	82T	353	$ .01	$ .06
O'Connor, Jack	83T	33	$ .01	$ .06
O'Connor, Jack	84T	268	$ .01	$ .05
O'Dell, Billy	55T	57	$2.10	$7.50
O'Dell, Billy	57T	316	$3.50	$13.00
O'Dell, Billy	58T	84	$1.00	$3.75
O'Dell, Billy	59T	250	$ .50	$1.95
O'Dell, Billy	60T	303	$ .50	$1.95
O'Dell, Billy	61T	96	$ .30	$1.00
O'Dell, Billy	61T	383	$ .50	$2.00
O'Dell, Billy	62T	429	$ .70	$2.10
O'Dell, Billy	63T	7	$ .35	$1.10
O'Dell, Billy	63T	9	$ .60	$1.75
O'Dell, Billy	63T	235	$ .25	$ .85
O'Dell, Billy	64T	18	$ .25	$ .85

Player	Year	No.	VG	EX/MT
O'Dell, Billy	65T	476	$ .50	$2.00
O'Dell, Billy	66T	237	$ .25	$ .85
O'Dell, Billy	67T	162	$ .25	$ .65
O'Donoghue, John	64T	388	$ .40	$1.25
O'Donoghue, John	65T	71	$ .25	$ .65
O'Donoghue, John	66T	501	$ .70	$2.10
O'Donoghue, John	67T	127	$ .25	$ .65
O'Donoghue, John	68T	456	$ .25	$ .65
O'Donoghue, John	70T	441	$ .10	$ .35
O'Donoghue, John	71T	743	$ .70	$2.10
O'Malley, Tom	90T	504	$ .01	$ .03
O'Malley, Tom	83T	663	$ .01	$ .06
O'Malley, Tom	84T	469	$ .01	$ .05
O'Malley, Tom	87T	154	$ .01	$ .03
O'Malley, Tom	88T	77	$ .01	$ .03
O'Neal, Randy	86T	73	$ .01	$ .03
O'Neal, Randy	87T	196	$ .01	$ .03
O'Neill, Paul	89TBB	39	$ .01	$ .10
O'Neill, Paul	90T	332	$ .01	$ .03
O'Neill, Paul	88T	204	$ .01	$ .25
O'Neill, Paul	89T	604	$ .01	$ .04
O'Neill, Steve	54T	127	$2.10	$7.50
O'Riley, Don	70T	552	$ .25	$ .85
O'Riley, Don	71T	679	$ .70	$2.10
O'Toole, Dennis	73T	604	$ .35	$1.10
O'Toole, Jim	59T	136	$ .70	$2.00
O'Toole, Jim	60T	32	$ .50	$1.95
O'Toole, Jim	60T	325	$ .45	$1.35
O'Toole, Jim	61T	328	$ .30	$1.00
O'Toole, Jim	62T	56	$ .50	$2.00
O'Toole, Jim	62T	58	$ .50	$1.95
O'Toole, Jim	62T	60	$ .65	$1.75
O'Toole, Jim	62T	450	$ .70	$2.10
O'Toole, Jim	63T	70	$ .25	$ .85
O'Toole, Jim	64T	185	$ .25	$ .85
O'Toole, Jim	65T	60	$ .25	$ .65
O'Toole, Jim	66T	389	$ .25	$ .85
O'Toole, Jim	67T	467	$ .50	$2.00
Oates, Johnny	72T	474	$ .50	$2.35
Oates, Johnny	73T	9	$ .06	$ .25
Oates, Johnny	74T	183	$ .06	$ .25
Oates, Johnny	75T	319	$ .06	$ .25
Oates, Johnny	76T	62	$ .05	$ .20
Oates, Johnny	77T	619	$ .05	$ .15
Oates, Johnny	78T	508	$ .02	$ .10
Oates, Johnny	79T	104	$ .02	$ .10
Oates, Johnny	80T	228	$ .01	$ .07
Oates, Johnny	81T	303	$ .01	$ .07
Oberkfell, Ken	80T	701	$ .05	$ .20
Oberkfell, Ken	81T	32	$ .01	$ .07
Oberkfell, Ken	82T	474	$ .01	$ .06
Oberkfell, Ken	83T	206	$ .01	$ .06
Oberkfell, Ken	84T	102	$ .01	$ .05
Oberkfell, Ken	84TTR	85	$ .02	$ .10
Oberkfell, Ken	85T	569	$ .01	$ .04
Oberkfell, Ken	86T	334	$ .01	$ .03
Oberkfell, Ken	87T	627	$ .01	$ .03
Oberkfell, Ken	88T	67	$ .01	$ .03
Oberkfell, Ken	89T	751	$ .01	$ .04
Oberkfell, Ken	90T	488	$ .01	$ .03
Oceak, Frank	60T	467	$ .95	$3.50
Odom, Johnny	65T	526	$40.00	$105.00
Odom, Johnny	67T	282	$ .25	$ .65
Odom, John	68T	501	$ .30	$1.00
Odom, John	69T	195	$ .25	$ .65
Odom, John	70T	55	$ .10	$ .35
Odom, John	71T	523	$ .10	$ .35
Odom, John	72T	557	$ .25	$ .85
Odom, John	72TIA	558	$ .25	$ .85
Odom, John	73T	315	$ .06	$ .25
Odom, John	74T	461	$ .06	$ .25
Odom, John	75T	69	$ .06	$ .25
Odom, John	76T	651	$ .05	$ .20
Oelkers, Bryan	87T	77	$ .01	$ .03
Oester, Ron	79T	717	$ .05	$ .20

TOPPS

Player	Year	No.	VG	EX/MT	Player	Year	No.	VG	EX/MT
Oester, Ron	81T	21	$ .01	$ .07	Oliva, Tony	70T	62	$ .50	$2.00
Oester, Ron	82T	427	$ .01	$ .06	Oliva, Tony	70T	510	$ .50	$1.95
Oester, Ron	83T	269	$ .01	$ .06	Oliva, Tony	71T	61	$ .50	$1.95
Oester, Ron	84T	526	$ .01	$ .05	Oliva, Tony	71T	290	$ .35	$1.10
Oester, Ron	84T	756	$ .01	$ .05	Oliva, Tony	72T	86	$ .30	$1.00
Oester, Ron	85T	314	$ .01	$ .04	Oliva, Tony	72T	400	$ .35	$1.10
Oester, Ron	86T	627	$ .01	$ .03	Oliva, Tony	73T	80	$ .30	$1.00
Oester, Ron	87T	172	$ .01	$ .03	Oliva, Tony	74T	190	$ .15	$ .50
Oester, Ron	88T	17	$ .01	$ .03	Oliva, Tony	75T	325	$ .25	$ .85
Oester, Ron	89T	772	$ .01	$ .04	Oliva, Tony	76T	35	$ .10	$ .35
Oester, Ron	89TBB	229	$ .01	$ .05	Oliva, Tony	89TTB	665	$ .01	$ .04
Oester, Ron	90T	492	$ .01	$ .03	Olivares, Ed	62T	598	$12.00	$50.00
Off, Ed	78T	28	$ .02	$ .10	Oliver, Al	69T	82	$2.50	$7.00
Office, Rowland	75T	262	$ .06	$ .25	Oliver, Al	70T	166	$ .50	$2.00
Office, Rowland	76T	256	$ .05	$ .20	Oliver, Al	71T	388	$ .60	$1.75
Office, Rowland	77T	524	$ .05	$ .15	Oliver, Al	72T	575	$ .60	$1.75
Office, Rowland	78T	632	$ .02	$ .10	Oliver, Al	73T	225	$ .30	$1.00
Office, Rowland	79T	132	$ .02	$ .10	Oliver, Al	74T	52	$ .50	$2.00
Office, Rowland	80T	39	$ .01	$ .07	Oliver, Al	75T	555	$ .15	$ .50
Office, Rowland	81T	319	$ .01	$ .07	Oliver, Al	76T	620	$ .25	$ .85
Office, Rowland	82T	479	$ .01	$ .06	Oliver, Al	77T	130	$ .15	$ .50
Ogier, Moe	68T	589	$ .30	$1.00	Oliver, Al	78T	430	$ .08	$ .30
Oglivie, Ben	72T	761	$4.00	$12.00	Oliver, Al	79T	391	$ .05	$ .20
Oglivie, Ben	73T	388	$ .25	$ .65	Oliver, Al	80T	260	$ .05	$ .20
Oglivie, Ben	75T	344	$ .06	$ .25	Oliver, Al	81T	70	$ .03	$ .15
Oglivie, Ben	76T	659	$ .06	$ .25	Oliver, Al	82T	36	$ .01	$ .06
Oglivie, Ben	77T	122	$ .05	$ .15	Oliver, Al	82T	590	$ .03	$ .15
Oglivie, Ben	78T	286	$ .02	$ .10	Oliver, Al	82TIA	591	$ .01	$ .06
Oglivie, Ben	79T	519	$ .02	$ .10	Oliver, Al	82TTR	83	$ .25	$ .65
Oglivie, Ben	80T	53	$ .01	$ .07	Oliver, Al	83T	111	$ .01	$ .06
Oglivie, Ben	81T	2	$ .06	$ .30	Oliver, Al	83T	420	$ .03	$ .15
Oglivie, Ben	81T	415	$ .01	$ .07	Oliver, Al	83T	421	$ .01	$ .06
Oglivie, Ben	82T	280	$ .01	$ .06	Oliver, Al	83T	701	$ .01	$ .06
Oglivie, Ben	83T	750	$ .01	$ .06	Oliver, Al	83T	703	$ .01	$ .06
Oglivie, Ben	84T	190	$ .01	$ .05	Oliver, Al	84T	516	$ .01	$ .05
Oglivie, Ben	85T	681	$ .01	$ .04	Oliver, Al	84T	620	$ .02	$ .10
Oglivie, Ben	86T	372	$ .01	$ .03	Oliver, Al	84T	704	$ .03	$ .15
Oglivie, Ben	87T	586	$ .01	$ .03	Oliver, Al	84TTR	87	$ .05	$ .20
Ojeda, Bob	82T	274	$ .10	$ .50	Oliver, Al	85T	130	$ .01	$ .10
Ojeda, Bob	83T	654	$ .01	$ .06	Oliver, Al	85TTR	88	$ .08	$ .30
Ojeda, Bob	84T	162	$ .01	$ .05	Oliver, Al	86T	775	$ .01	$ .03
Ojeda, Bob	84T	786	$ .06	$ .30	Oliver, Bob	69T	662	$ .25	$ .85
Ojeda, Bob	85T	477	$ .01	$ .04	Oliver, Bob	70T	567	$ .25	$ .85
Ojeda, Bob	86T	11	$ .01	$ .03	Oliver, Bob	71T	470	$ .10	$ .35
Ojeda, Bob	86TTR	81	$ .02	$ .10	Oliver, Bob	72T	57	$ .10	$ .35
Ojeda, Bob	87T	746	$ .01	$ .03	Oliver, Bob	73T	289	$ .06	$ .25
Ojeda, Bob	88T	558	$ .01	$ .03	Oliver, Bob	74T	243	$ .06	$ .25
Ojeda, Bob	88TBB	234	$ .01	$ .05	Oliver, Bob	75T	657	$ .06	$ .25
Ojeda, Bob	89T	333	$ .01	$ .04	Oliver, Dave	78T	704	$3.00	$10.00
Ojeda, Bob	90T	207	$ .01	$ .03	Oliver, Dave	79T	705	$ .35	$1.20
Oldis, Bob	53T	262	$11.00	$37.50	Oliver, Gene	59T	135	$ .50	$1.95
Oldis, Bob	54T	91	$2.10	$7.50	Oliver, Gene	60T	307	$ .50	$1.95
Oldis, Bob	55T	169	$4.25	$13.00	Oliver, Gene	61T	487	$ .50	$2.00
Oldis, Bob	60T	361	$ .50	$1.95	Oliver, Gene	62T	561	$3.75	$11.00
Oldis, Bob	61T	149	$ .30	$1.00	Oliver, Gene	63T	172	$ .25	$ .85
Oldis, Bob	62T	269	$ .35	$1.10	Oliver, Gene	64T	316	$ .25	$ .85
Oldis, Bob	63T	404	$ .35	$1.20	Oliver, Gene	65T	106	$ .25	$ .65
Olerud, John	89TMLD	89	$ .01	$1.50	Oliver, Gene	66T	541	$4.50	$15.00
Olin, Steve	89TMLD	90	$ .01	$ .15	Oliver, Gene	67T	18	$ .25	$ .65
Olin, Steve	90T	433	$ .01	$ .03	Oliver, Gene	68T	449	$ .25	$ .65
Oliva, Pedro "Tony"	63T	228	$9.00	$35.00	Oliver, Gene	69T	247	$ .25	$ .85
Oliva, Tony	64T	116	$3.00	$12.00	Oliver, Joe	89TMLD	91	$ .01	$ .35
Oliva, Tony	65T	1	$2.50	$8.00	Oliver, Joe	90T	668	$ .01	$ .25
Oliva, Tony	65T	340	$1.25	$5.00	Oliver, Nate	63T	466	$6.00	$18.00
Oliva, Tony	66T	216	$ .75	$2.75	Oliver, Nate	65T	59	$ .25	$ .65
Oliva, Tony	66T	220	$ .50	$2.00	Oliver, Nate	66T	364	$ .25	$ .85
Oliva, Tony	66T	450	$2.00	$6.00	Oliver, Nate	68T	124	$ .25	$ .65
Oliva, Tony	67T	50	$ .60	$1.75	Oliver, Nate	69T	354	$ .25	$ .65
Oliva, Tony	67T	239	$1.50	$3.75	Oliver, Nate	70T	223	$ .10	$ .35
Oliva, Tony	68T	165	$5.00	$15.00	Oliver, Tom	54T	207	$2.10	$7.50
Oliva, Tony	68T	480	$ .30	$1.00	Oliveras, Francisco	89TMLD	92	$ .01	$ .05
Oliva, Tony	68TAS	371	$ .50	$1.95	Olivo, Chi Chi	66T	578	$4.50	$15.00
Oliva, Tony	69T	1	$1.75	$6.00	Olivo, Mike	70T	381	$ .10	$ .35
Oliva, Tony	69T	600	$ .50	$2.00	Ollom, Jim	67T	137	$ .25	$ .65
Oliva, Tony	69TAS	427	$ .50	$2.00	Ollom, Jim	68T	91	$ .25	$ .65

Player	Year	No.	VG	EX/MT
Olmsted, Al	81T	244	$ .01	$ .07
Olson, Gregg	89T	161	$ .05	$1.00
Olson, Gregg	89TMLD	93	$ .01	$ .05
Olson, Gregg	89TTR	89	$ .01	$ .75
Olson, Gregg	90T	655	$ .01	$ .25
Olson, Karl	52T	72	$14.00	$45.00
Olson, Karl	54T	186	$2.10	$7.50
Olson, Karl	55T	72	$1.35	$5.00
Olson, Karl	56T	322	$1.80	$6.00
Olson, Karl	57T	153	$ .95	$3.50
Olwine, Ed	87T	159	$ .01	$ .03
Olwine, Ed	88T	353	$ .01	$ .03
Ontiveros, Steve	74T	598	$1.00	$4.00
Ontiveros, Steve	75T	483	$ .06	$ .25
Ontiveros, Steve	76T	284	$ .05	$ .20
Ontiveros, Steve	78T	76	$ .02	$ .10
Ontiveros, Steve	79T	299	$ .02	$ .10
Ontiveros, Steve	80T	514	$ .01	$ .07
Ontiveros, Steve	86T	507	$ .01	$ .10
Ontiveros, Steve	87T	161	$ .01	$ .03
Ontiveros, Steve	88T	272	$ .01	$ .03
Ontiveros, Steve	89T	692	$ .01	$ .04
Ontiveros, Steve	89TTR	90	$ .01	$ .05
Oquendo, Jose	84T	208	$ .10	$ .45
Oquendo, Jose	85T	598	$ .01	$ .10
Oquendo, Jose	86TTR	82	$ .02	$ .10
Oquendo, Jose	87T	133	$ .01	$ .03
Oquendo, Jose	88T	83	$ .01	$ .03
Oquendo, Jose	89T	442	$ .01	$ .04
Oquendo, Jose	89TBB	77	$ .01	$ .05
Oquendo, Jose	90T	645	$ .01	$ .03
Oravetz, Ernie	56T	51	$1.25	$4.50
Oravetz, Ernie	57T	179	$ .95	$3.50
Orioles, Team	56T	100	$3.00	$9.00
Orioles, Team	57T	251	$2.10	$7.50
Orioles, Team	58T	408	$3.00	$9.00
Orioles, Team	59T	48	$1.50	$4.50
Orioles, Team	60T	494	$2.25	$6.50
Orioles, Team	61T	159	$1.00	$3.00
Orioles, Team	62T	476	$1.25	$4.50
Orioles, Team	63T	377	$1.35	$4.00
Orioles, Team	64T	473	$1.50	$3.75
Orioles, Team	65T	572	$1.50	$4.50
Orioles, Team	66T	348	$1.25	$4.50
Orioles, Team	67T	302	$ .60	$1.75
Orioles, Team	68T	334	$ .50	$2.00
Orioles, Team	70T	387	$ .50	$1.95
Orioles, Team	71T	1	$2.00	$7.50
Orioles, Team	72T	731	$1.50	$3.75
Orioles, Team	73T	278	$ .30	$1.00
Orioles, Team	74T	16	$ .15	$ .50
Orioles, Team Checklist	75T	117	$ .35	$1.10
Orioles, Team Checklist	76T	73	$ .15	$ .60
Orioles, Team Checklist	77T	546	$ .15	$ .50
Orioles, Team Checklist	78T	96	$ .06	$ .30
Orioles, Team Checklist	79T	689	$ .10	$ .35
Orioles, Team Checklist	80T	404	$ .08	$ .30
Orioles, Team Checklist	81T	661	$ .02	$ .20
Orioles, Team Leaders	86T	726	$ .01	$ .03
Orioles, Team Leaders	87T	506	$ .01	$ .03
Orioles, Team Leaders	88T	51	$ .01	$ .03
Orioles, Team Leaders	89T	381	$ .01	$ .04
Oritz, Junior	87T	583	$ .01	$ .03
Orosco, Jesse	80T	681	$3.00	$9.50
Orosco, Jesse	83T	369	$ .01	$ .06
Orosco, Jesse	84T	54	$ .01	$ .05
Orosco, Jesse	84TAS	396	$ .01	$ .05
Orosco, Jesse	85T	250	$ .01	$ .04
Orosco, Jesse	86T	465	$ .01	$ .03
Orosco, Jesse	87T	704	$ .01	$ .03
Orosco, Jesse	88T	105	$ .01	$ .03
Orosco, Jesse	88TTR	77	$ .01	$ .05
Orosco, Jesse	89T	513	$ .01	$ .04
Orosco, Jesse	89TTR	91	$ .01	$ .05
Orosco, Jesse	90T	636	$ .01	$ .03

Player	Year	No.	VG	EX/MT
Orsino, Johnny	62T	377	$ .70	$2.10
Orsino, Johnny	63T	418	$ .35	$1.20
Orsino, Johnny	64T	63	$ .25	$ .85
Orsino, Johnny	65T	303	$ .30	$1.00
Orsino, Johnny	66T	77	$ .25	$ .85
Orsino, Johnny	67T	207	$ .25	$ .65
Orsulak, Joe	85TTR	89	$ .05	$ .20
Orsulak, Joe	86T	102	$ .01	$ .03
Orsulak, Joe	87	414	$ .01	$ .03

Player	Year	No.	VG	EX/MT
Orsulak, Joe	88TTR	78	$ .01	$ .05
Orsulak, Joe	89T	727	$ .01	$ .04
Orsulak, Joe	89TBB	181	$ .01	$ .05
Orsulak, Joe	90T	212	$ .01	$ .03
Orta, Jorge	73T	194	$ .25	$ .65
Orta, Jorge	74T	376	$ .06	$ .25
Orta, Jorge	75T	184	$ .06	$ .25
Orta, Jorge	76T	560	$ .05	$ .20
Orta, Jorge	77T	109	$ .05	$ .15
Orta, Jorge	78T	42	$ .02	$ .10
Orta, Jorge	79T	631	$ .02	$ .10
Orta, Jorge	80T	442	$ .01	$ .07
Orta, Jorge	81T	222	$ .01	$ .07
Orta, Jorge	82T	26	$ .01	$ .06
Orta, Jorge	82TTR	84	$ .02	$ .10
Orta, Jorge	83T	722	$ .01	$ .06
Orta, Jorge	83TTR	82	$ .02	$ .10
Orta, Jorge	84T	312	$ .01	$ .05
Orta, Jorge	84TTR	88	$ .02	$ .10
Orta, Jorge	85T	164	$ .01	$ .04
Orta, Jorge	86T	541	$ .01	$ .03
Orta, Jorge	87T	738	$ .01	$ .03
Ortega, Phil	62T	69	$ .35	$1.10
Ortega, Phil	63T	467	$2.50	$6.50
Ortega, Phil	64T	291	$ .25	$ .85
Ortega, Phil	65T	152	$ .25	$ .65
Ortega, Phil	66T	416	$ .25	$ .85
Ortega, Phil	67T	493	$ .50	$2.00
Ortega, Phil	68T	595	$ .30	$1.00
Ortega, Phil	69T	406	$ .25	$ .65
Ortiz, Junior	84T	161	$ .01	$ .05
Ortiz, Junior	85T	439	$ .01	$ .04
Ortiz, Junior	86T	682	$ .01	$ .03
Ortiz, Junior	88T	274	$ .01	$ .03

TOPPS

Player	Year	No.	VG	EX/MT	Player	Year	No.	VG	EX/MT
Ortiz, Junior	89T	769	$ .01	$ .04	Otto, Dave	89T	131	$ .01	$ .10
Ortiz, Junior	89TBB	66	$ .01	$ .05	Overmire, Frank	52T	155	$6.00	$19.00
Ortiz, Junior	90T	322	$ .01	$ .03	Overy, Mike	77T	489	$ .25	$ .65
Ortiz, Lou	55T	114	$1.35	$5.00	Owchinko, Bob	78T	164	$ .02	$ .10
Orton, John	89TMLD	94	$ .01	$ .05	Owchinko, Bob	79T	488	$ .02	$ .10
Osborn, Dan	76T	282	$ .05	$ .20	Owchinko, Bob	80T	79	$ .01	$ .07
Osborn, Don	74T	489	$ .06	$ .25	Owchinko, Bob	81T	536	$ .01	$ .07
Osborne, Larry	59T	524	$2.00	$7.00	Owchinko, Bob	81TTR	811	$ .02	$ .10
Osborne, Larry	60T	201	$ .35	$1.10	Owchinko, Bob	82T	243	$ .01	$ .06
Osborne, Larry	61T	208	$ .30	$1.00	Owchinko, Bob	83T	338	$ .01	$ .06
Osborne, Larry	62T	583	$3.75	$11.00	Owchinko, Bob	85T	752	$ .01	$ .04
Osborne, Larry	63T	514	$1.50	$3.75	Owen, Dave	85T	642	$ .01	$ .04
Osinski, Dan	63T	114	$ .25	$ .85	Owen, Larry	82T	502	$ .50	$2.00
Osinski, Dan	64T	537	$1.50	$3.75	Owen, Larry	89T	87	$ .01	$ .04
Osinski, Dan	65T	223	$ .30	$1.00	Owen, Spike	84T	413	$ .01	$ .05
Osinski, Dan	66T	168	$ .25	$ .85	Owen, Spike	85T	84	$ .01	$ .04
Osinski, Dan	67T	594	$1.35	$4.00	Owen, Spike	86T	248	$ .01	$ .03
Osinski, Dan	68T	331	$ .25	$ .65	Owen, Spike	87T	591	$ .01	$ .03
Osinski, Dan	69T	622	$ .25	$ .85	Owen, Spike	88T	733	$ .01	$ .03
Osteen, Claude	59T	224	$1.35	$4.00	Owen, Spike	89T	123	$ .01	$ .04
Osteen, Claude	60T	206	$ .60	$1.75	Owen, Spike	89TBB	221	$ .01	$ .05
Osteen, Claude	62T	501	$ .70	$2.00	Owen, Spike	89TTR	92	$ .01	$ .05
Osteen, Claude	63T	374	$ .35	$1.20	Owen, Spike	90T	674	$ .01	$ .03
Osteen, Claude	64T	28	$ .25	$ .85	Owens, Jim	55T	202	$4.25	$13.00
Osteen, Claude	65T	570	$1.35	$4.00	Owens, Jim	56T	114	$1.25	$4.50
Osteen, Claude	66T	270	$ .25	$ .85	Owens, Jim	59T	503	$ .50	$1.95
Osteen, Claude	67T	330	$ .25	$ .65	Owens, Jim	60T	185	$ .35	$1.10
Osteen, Claude	68T	440	$ .15	$ .50	Owens, Jim	61T	341	$ .30	$1.00
Osteen, Claude	68T	9	$ .50	$1.95	Owens, Jim	62T	212	$ .35	$1.10
Osteen, Claude	69T	528	$ .20	$ .50	Owens, Jim	63T	483	$2.50	$6.50
Osteen, Claude	70T	260	$ .25	$ .85	Owens, Jim	64T	241	$ .25	$ .85
Osteen, Claude	71T	10	$ .10	$ .35	Owens, Jim	65T	451	$ .50	$2.00
Osteen, Claude	72T	297	$ .10	$ .35	Owens, Jim	66T	297	$ .30	$1.00
Osteen, Claude	72TIA	298	$ .10	$ .35	Owens, Jim	67T	582	$1.35	$4.00
Osteen, Claude	73T	490	$ .25	$ .65	Owens, Jim	73T	624	$ .55	$1.75
Osteen, Claude	74T	42	$ .06	$ .25	Owens, Paul	84T	229	$ .01	$ .05
Osteen, Claude	74TTR	42	$ .06	$ .25	Owens, Paul	85T	92	$ .01	$ .04
Osteen, Claude	75T	453	$ .06	$ .25	Ownbey, Rick	83T	739	$ .01	$ .06
Osteen, Claude	76T	488	$ .05	$ .20	Oyler, Ray	65T	259	$ .35	$1.10
Osteen, Darrell	66T	424	$1.00	$2.75	Oyler, Ray	66T	81	$ .25	$ .85
Osteen, Darrell	67T	222	$ .30	$1.00	Oyler, Ray	67T	352	$ .25	$ .65
Osteen, Darrell	68T	199	$ .25	$ .65	Oyler, Ray	68T	399	$ .25	$ .65
Ostrowski, Joe	52T	206	$6.00	$18.00	Oyler, Ray	69T	178	$ .25	$ .65
Otero, Reggie	60T	459	$ .95	$3.50	Oyler, Ray	70T	603	$ .25	$ .85
Otis, Amos	69T	31	$ .25	$ .85	Oyler, Ray	73T	486	$ .25	$ .85
Otis, Amos	70T	354	$ .25	$ .65	Ozark, Danny	74T	119	$ .06	$ .25
Otis, Amos	71T	610	$ .35	$1.10	Ozark, Danny	78T	631	$ .02	$ .10
Otis, Amos	72T	10	$ .25	$ .65	Ozark, Danny	85T	365	$ .01	$ .04
Otis, Amos	73T	510	$ .10	$ .35	Pacella, John	81T	414	$ .01	$ .07
Otis, Amos	74T	65	$ .06	$ .25	Pacella, John	83T	166	$ .01	$ .06
Otis, Amos	74TAS	337	$ .06	$ .25	Pacheco, Tony	74T	521	$ .06	$ .25
Otis, Amos	75T	520	$ .06	$ .25	Pacillo, Pat	85T	402	$ .05	$ .25
Otis, Amos	76T	198	$ .10	$ .35	Pacillo, Pat	87TTR	93	$ .01	$ .07
Otis, Amos	76T	510	$ .06	$ .25	Pacillo, Pat	88T	288	$ .01	$ .03
Otis, Amos	77T	290	$ .05	$ .15	Paciorek, Tom	71T	709	$7.00	$22.50
Otis, Amos	78T	490	$ .02	$ .10	Paciorek, Tom	73T	606	$ .95	$3.50
Otis, Amos	79T	360	$ .02	$ .10	Paciorek, Tom	74T	127	$ .06	$ .25
Otis, Amos	80T	130	$ .01	$ .07	Paciorek, Tom	75T	523	$ .06	$ .25
Otis, Amos	81T	585	$ .01	$ .07	Paciorek, Tom	76T	641	$ .05	$ .20
Otis, Amos	82T	725	$ .01	$ .06	Paciorek, Tom	77T	48	$ .05	$ .15
Otis, Amos	82TIA	726	$ .01	$ .06	Paciorek, Tom	78T	322	$ .02	$ .10
Otis, Amos	83T	75	$ .01	$ .06	Paciorek, Tom	79T	141	$ .02	$ .10
Otis, Amos	84T	655	$ .01	$ .05	Paciorek, Tom	80T	481	$ .01	$ .07
Otis, Amos	84TTR	89	$ .02	$ .10	Paciorek, Tom	81T	228	$ .01	$ .07
Ott, Billy	65T	354	$ .30	$1.00	Paciorek, Tom	82T	336	$ .01	$ .06
Ott, Ed	76T	594	$ .05	$ .20	Paciorek, Tom	82T	678	$ .01	$ .06
Ott, Ed	77T	197	$ .05	$ .15	Paciorek, Tom	82TTR	85	$ .02	$ .10
Ott, Ed	79T	561	$ .02	$ .10	Paciorek, Tom	83T	72	$ .01	$ .06
Ott, Ed	80T	383	$ .01	$ .07	Paciorek, Tom	84T	777	$ .01	$ .05
Ott, Ed	81T	246	$ .01	$ .07	Paciorek, Tom	85T	572	$ .01	$ .04
Ott, Ed	81TTR	810	$ .02	$ .10	Paciorek, Tom	86T	362	$ .01	$ .03
Ott, Ed	82T	469	$ .01	$ .06	Paciorek, Tom	86TTR	83	$ .02	$ .10
Ott, Ed	83T	131	$ .01	$ .06	Paciorek, Tom	87T	729	$ .01	$ .03
Otten, Jim	75T	624	$ .06	$ .25	Pactwa, Joe	76T	589	$ .35	$1.10
Otten, Jim	77T	493	$ .25	$ .80	Padres, Team	70T	657	$ .70	$2.00

Player	Year	No.	VG	EX/MT
Padres, Team	71T	482	$ .35	$1.10
Padres, Team	72T	262	$ .15	$ .50
Padres, Team	73T	316	$ .30	$1.00
Padres, Team	74T	226	$ .30	$1.00
Padres, Team Checklist	75T	146	$ .15	$ .50
Padres, Team Checklist	76T	331	$ .30	$1.00
Padres, Team Checklist	77T	134	$ .15	$ .50
Padres, Team Checklist	78T	192	$ .05	$ .25
Padres, Team Checklist	79T	479	$ .05	$ .25
Padres, Team Checklist	80T	356	$ .05	$ .25
Padres, Team Checklist	81T	685	$ .02	$ .20
Padres, Team Leaders	86T	306	$ .01	$ .03
Padres, Team Leaders	87T	81	$ .01	$ .03
Padres, Team Leaders	88T	699	$ .01	$ .03
Padres, Team Leaders	89T	231	$ .01	$ .04
Paepke, Dennis	70T	552	$ .25	$ .85
Pafko, Andy	51Tbb	27	$5.50	$17.00
Pafko, Andy	52T	1	$100.00	$1000.00
Pafko, Andy	54T	79	$3.50	$13.00
Pafko, Andy	56T	312	$2.00	$6.00
Pafko, Andy	57T	143	$ .60	$2.50
Pafko, Andy	58T	223	$ .45	$1.50
Pafko, Andy	59T	27	$1.00	$3.75
Pafko, Andy	60T	464	$ .95	$3.50

DAVE PAGAN — Pitcher

Player	Year	No.	VG	EX/MT
Pagan, Dave	75T	648	$ .06	$ .25
Pagan, Dave	77T	508	$ .05	$ .15
Pagan, Jose	60T	67	$ .35	$1.10
Pagan, Jose	61T	279	$ .30	$1.00
Pagan, Jose	62T	565	$3.75	$11.00
Pagan, Jose	63T	545	$1.50	$3.75
Pagan, Jose	64T	123	$ .25	$ .85
Pagan, Jose	65T	575	$1.50	$3.75
Pagan, Jose	66T	54	$ .25	$ .85
Pagan, Jose	67T	322	$ .25	$ .65
Pagan, Jose	68T	482	$ .30	$1.00
Pagan, Jose	69T	192	$ .25	$ .65
Pagan, Jose	70T	643	$ .50	$2.00
Pagan, Jose	71T	282	$ .10	$ .35
Pagan, Jose	72T	701	$ .70	$2.10
Pagan, Jose	72TIA	702	$ .70	$2.10
Pagan, Jose	73T	659	$ .35	$1.10
Page, Joe	51Tbb	10	$4.00	$18.00
Page, Joe	52T	48	$25.00	$75.00

Player	Year	No.	VG	EX/MT
Page, Mitchell	78T	55	$ .02	$ .10
Page, Mitchell	79T	295	$ .02	$ .10
Page, Mitchell	80T	586	$ .01	$ .07
Page, Mitchell	81T	35	$ .01	$ .07
Page, Mitchell	82T	633	$ .01	$ .06
Page, Mitchell	83T	737	$ .01	$ .06
Page, Mitchell	84T	414	$ .01	$ .05
Pagel, Karl	79T	716	$ .02	$ .10
Pagel, Karl	80T	676	$ .01	$ .07
Pagliaroni, Jim	61T	519	$ .50	$2.00
Pagliaroni, Jim	62T	81	$ .35	$1.10
Pagliaroni, Jim	63T	159	$ .25	$ .85
Pagliaroni, Jim	64T	392	$ .40	$1.25
Pagliaroni, Jim	65T	265	$ .30	$1.00
Pagliaroni, Jim	66T	33	$ .25	$ .85
Pagliaroni, Jim	67T	183	$ .25	$ .65
Pagliaroni, Jim	68T	586	$ .30	$1.00
Pagliaroni, Jim	69T	302	$ .25	$ .85
Pagliarulo, Mike	85T	638	$ .15	$ .60
Pagliarulo, Mike	86T	327	$ .02	$ .20
Pagliarulo, Mike	87T	195	$ .01	$ .10
Pagliarulo, Mike	88T	435	$ .01	$ .10
Pagliarulo, Mike	88TBB	138	$ .01	$ .10
Pagliarulo, Mike	89T	211	$ .01	$ .04
Pagliarulo, Mike	89TBB	28	$ .01	$ .05
Pagliarulo, Mike	90T	63	$ .01	$ .03
Pagnozzi, Tom	88T	689	$ .01	$ .03
Pagnozzi, Tom	89T	208	$ .01	$ .04
Pagnozzi, Tom	90T	509	$ .01	$ .03
Paige, Satchell	53T	220	$80.00	$300.00
Paine, Phil	58T	442	$ .50	$1.95
Palacios, Vicente	88T	322	$ .01	$ .20
Palica, Erv	52T	273	$12.00	$35.00
Palica, Erv	56T	206	$2.50	$8.00
Pall, Donn	89T	458	$ .01	$ .04
Pall, Donn	90T	219	$ .01	$ .03
Palmeiro, Rafael	87T	634	$ .35	$1.25
Palmeiro, Rafael	88T	186	$ .05	$ .30
Palmeiro, Rafael	89T	310	$ .01	$ .10
Palmeiro, Rafael	89TBB	257	$ .01	$ .10
Palmeiro, Rafael	89TTR	93	$ .01	$ .10
Palmeiro, Rafael	90T	755	$ .01	$ .03
Palmer, Dave	80T	42	$ .05	$ .20
Palmer, Dave	81T	607	$ .01	$ .07
Palmer, Dave	82T	292	$ .01	$ .06
Palmer, Dave	83T	164	$ .01	$ .06
Palmer, Dave	84T	750	$ .25	$ .65
Palmer, Dave	85T	526	$ .01	$ .04
Palmer, Dave	86T	421	$ .01	$ .03
Palmer, Dave	86TTR	84	$ .02	$ .10
Palmer, Dave	87T	324	$ .01	$ .03
Palmer, Dave	88T	732	$ .01	$ .03
Palmer, Dave	88TTR	79	$ .01	$ .05
Palmer, Dave	89T	67	$ .01	$ .04
Palmer, Dean	89TMLD	95	$ .01	$ .25
Palmer, Jim	66T	126	$70.00	$200.00
Palmer, Jim	67T	475	$15.00	$60.00
Palmer, Jim	68T	575	$15.00	$55.00
Palmer, Jim	69T	573	$10.00	$35.00
Palmer, Jim	70T	68	$ .50	$2.00
Palmer, Jim	70T	449	$3.00	$13.00
Palmer, Jim	71T	67	$ .15	$ .50
Palmer, Jim	71T	570	$3.00	$10.00
Palmer, Jim	72T	92	$ .65	$2.20
Palmer, Jim	72T	270	$2.00	$8.00
Palmer, Jim	73T	160	$2.00	$7.50
Palmer, Jim	73T	341	$ .30	$1.00
Palmer, Jim	74T	40	$ .95	$2.75
Palmer, Jim	74T	206	$ .50	$2.00
Palmer, Jim	75T	335	$1.50	$5.00
Palmer, Jim	76T	200	$ .35	$1.10
Palmer, Jim	76T	202	$ .35	$1.10
Palmer, Jim	76T	450	$ .90	$2.75
Palmer, Jim	77T	5	$ .15	$ .50
Palmer, Jim	77T	600	$1.00	$3.75

TOPPS

Player	Year	No.	VG	EX/MT	Player	Year	No.	VG	EX/MT
Palmer, Jim	78T	160	$ .75	$3.00	Parker, Dave	88T	315	$ .01	$ .15
Palmer, Jim	78T	205	$ .25	$ .65	Parker, Dave	88TBB	242	$ .01	$ .10
Palmer, Jim	79T	340	$ .75	$3.00	Parker, Dave	88TTR	81	$ .01	$ .05
Palmer, Jim	80T	590	$ .50	$2.00	Parker, Dave	89T	475	$ .01	$ .04
Palmer, Jim	81T	210	$ .40	$1.50	Parker, Dave	89TBB	144	$ .01	$ .10
Palmer, Jim	82T	80	$ .10	$ .50	Parker, Dave	90T	45	$ .01	$ .10
Palmer, Jim	82TIA	81	$ .05	$ .25	Parker, Harry	74T	106	$ .06	$ .25
Palmer, Jim	83T	21	$ .05	$ .25	Parker, Harry	75T	214	$ .06	$ .25
Palmer, Jim	83T	490	$ .10	$ .50	Parker, Salty	60T	469	$ .95	$3.50
Palmer, Jim	83T	491	$ .03	$ .15	Parker, Salty	73T	421	$ .06	$ .25
Palmer, Jim	84T	715	$ .04	$ .20	Parker, Salty	74T	276	$ .06	$ .25
Palmer, Jim	84T	717	$ .01	$ .05	Parker, Wes	64T	456	$ .60	$1.75
Palmer, Lowell	70T	252	$ .10	$ .35	Parker, Wes	65T	344	$ .30	$1.00
Palmer, Lowell	71T	554	$ .30	$1.00	Parker, Wes	66T	134	$ .25	$ .85
Palmer, Lowell	72T	746	$ .50	$ .25	Parker, Wes	67T	218	$ .25	$ .65
Palys, Stan	58T	126	$ .50	$2.00	Parker, Wes	68T	533	$ .30	$1.00
Pankovits, Jim	86T	618	$ .01	$ .03	Parker, Wes	69T	493	$ .25	$ .85
Pankovits, Jim	87T	249	$ .01	$ .03	Parker, Wes	70T	5	$ .10	$ .35
Pankovits, Jim	88T	487	$ .01	$ .03	Parker, Wes	71T	430	$ .10	$ .35
Pankovits, Jim	88TBB	109	$ .01	$ .05	Parker, Wes	72T	265	$ .10	$ .35
Pankovits, Jim	89T	153	$ .01	$ .04	Parker, Wes	73T	151	$ .06	$ .25
Papi, Stan	79T	652	$ .02	$ .10	Parks, Jack	55T	23	$1.35	$5.00
Papi, Stan	81T	273	$ .01	$ .07	Parnell, Mel	51Trb	10	$1.35	$4.00
Papi, Stan	82T	423	$ .01	$ .06	Parnell, Mel	52T	30	$12.50	$45.00
Pappas, Milt	58T	457	$ .65	$2.00	Parnell, Mel	53T	19	$3.75	$13.00
Pappas, Milt	59T	391	$ .50	$1.95	Parnell, Mel	54T	40	$2.00	$7.00
Pappas, Milt	60T	12	$ .50	$2.00	Parnell, Mel	55T	140	$2.10	$7.50
Pappas, Milt	60T	399	$ .60	$1.75	Parnell, Mel	57T	313	$3.50	$13.00
Pappas, Milt	61T	48	$ .50	$2.00	Parrett, Jeff	88T	588	$ .01	$ .20
Pappas, Milt	61T	295	$ .50	$2.00	Parrett, Jeff	89T	176	$ .01	$ .04
Pappas, Milt	62T	55	$ .50	$2.00	Parrett, Jeff	89TTR	95	$ .01	$ .05
Pappas, Milt	62T	75	$ .50	$2.00	Parrett, Jeff	90T	439	$ .01	$ .03
Pappas, Milt	63T	358	$ .35	$1.20	Parrish, Lance	78T	708	$7.00	$25.00
Pappas, Milt	64T	45	$ .15	$ .50	Parrish, Lance	79T	469	$ .60	$3.00
Pappas, Milt	65T	270	$ .30	$1.00	Parrish, Lance	80T	196	$ .20	$ .75
Pappas, Milt	66T	105	$ .60	$1.75	Parrish, Lance	81T	392	$ .10	$ .50
Pappas, Milt	67T	254	$ .25	$ .65	Parrish, Lance	82T	535	$ .05	$ .25
Pappas, Milt	68T	74	$ .25	$ .65	Parrish, Lance	83T	285	$ .05	$ .20
Pappas, Milt	69T	79	$ .25	$ .65	Parrish, Lance	83TRB	4	$ .01	$ .06
Pappas, Milt	70T	576	$ .25	$ .85	Parrish, Lance	84T	640	$ .05	$ .20
Pappas, Milt	71T	441	$ .25	$ .65	Parrish, Lance	85T	160	$ .04	$ .20
Pappas, Milt	72T	208	$ .10	$ .35	Parrish, Lance	85TAS	708	$ .01	$ .04
Pappas, Milt	73T	70	$ .10	$ .35	Parrish, Lance	86T	740	$ .02	$ .15
Pappas, Milt	74T	640	$ .06	$ .25	Parrish, Lance	87T	791	$ .06	$ .25
Pardo, Al	86T	279	$ .01	$ .03	Parrish, Lance	87TAS	613	$ .01	$ .10
Paredes, Johnny	89T	367	$ .01	$ .10	Parrish, Lance	87TTR	94	$ .01	$ .10
Parent, Mark	88TTR	80	$ .01	$ .10	Parrish, Lance	88T	95	$ .01	$ .10
Parent, Mark	89T	617	$ .01	$ .10	Parrish, Lance	88TBB	45	$ .01	$ .05
Parent, Mark	90T	749	$ .01	$ .03	Parrish, Lance	89T	470	$ .01	$ .04
Paris, Kelly	84T	113	$ .01	$ .05	Parrish, Lance	89TBB	250	$ .01	$ .10
Parker, Billy	72T	213	$ .10	$ .35	Parrish, Lance	89TTR	96	$ .01	$ .10
Parker, Billy	73T	354	$ .06	$ .25	Parrish, Lance	90T	575	$ .01	$ .10
Parker, Clay	89TTR	94	$ .01	$ .15	Parrish, Larry	76T	141	$ .30	$1.25
Parker, Clay	90T	511	$ .01	$ .03	Parrish, Larry	77T	526	$ .25	$ .65
Parker, Dave	74T	252	$7.00	$22.50	Parrish, Larry	78T	294	$ .02	$ .10
Parker, Dave	75T	29	$ .75	$3.00	Parrish, Larry	79T	677	$ .05	$ .20
Parker, Dave	76T	185	$ .75	$3.00	Parrish, Larry	80T	345	$ .01	$ .07
Parker, Dave	77T	270	$ .75	$3.00	Parrish, Larry	81T	15	$ .01	$ .07
Parker, Dave	78T	201	$ .15	$ .60	Parrish, Larry	82T	445	$ .01	$ .06
Parker, Dave	78T	560	$1.00	$3.75	Parrish, Larry	82TTR	86	$ .02	$ .10
Parker, Dave	79T	1	$ .75	$2.25	Parrish, Larry	83T	776	$ .01	$ .06
Parker, Dave	79T	430	$ .35	$1.10	Parrish, Larry	84T	169	$ .01	$ .05
Parker, Dave	80T	310	$ .25	$1.00	Parrish, Larry	85T	548	$ .01	$ .04
Parker, Dave	81T	640	$ .15	$ .60	Parrish, Larry	86T	238	$ .01	$ .03
Parker, Dave	82T	40	$ .01	$ .06	Parrish, Larry	87T	629	$ .01	$ .03
Parker, Dave	82TAS	343	$ .05	$ .20	Parrish, Larry	88T	490	$ .01	$ .03
Parker, Dave	82TIA	41	$ .25	$ .65	Parrish, Larry	89T	354	$ .01	$ .04
Parker, Dave	83T	205	$ .05	$ .25	Parrott, Mike	79T	576	$ .02	$ .10
Parker, Dave	84T	701	$ .06	$ .30	Parrott, Mike	80T	443	$ .01	$ .07
Parker, Dave	84T	775	$ .05	$ .25	Parrott, Mike	81T	187	$ .01	$ .07
Parker, Dave	84TTR	90	$ .20	$ .90	Parrott, Mike	82T	358	$ .01	$ .06
Parker, Dave	85T	175	$ .05	$ .25	Parsons, Bill	72T	281	$ .10	$ .35
Parker, Dave	86T	595	$ .03	$ .25	Parsons, Bill	73T	231	$ .06	$ .25
Parker, Dave	87T	691	$ .03	$ .15	Parsons, Bill	74T	574	$ .06	$ .25
Parker, Dave	87TAS	600	$ .01	$ .10	Parsons, Bill	75T	613	$ .06	$ .25

Player	Year	No.	VG	EX/MT	Player	Year	No.	VG	EX/MT
Parsons, Tom	62T	326	$ .35	$1.10	Pastore, Frank	85T	727	$ .01	$ .04
Parsons, Tom	65T	308	$ .35	$1.10	Pastore, Frank	86T	314	$ .01	$ .03
Paschall, Bill	80T	667	$ .30	$1.25	Pastore, Frank	86TTR	85	$ .02	$ .10
Pascual, Camilo	55T	84	$2.10	$7.50	Pastore, Frank	87T	576	$ .01	$ .03
Pascual, Camilo	56T	98	$1.25	$4.50	Pate, Bobby	81T	479	$2.00	$8.00
Pascual, Camilo	57T	211	$ .95	$3.50	Patek, Freddie	69T	219	$ .15	$ .50
					Patek, Freddie	70T	94	$ .10	$ .35
					Patek, Freddie	71T	626	$ .30	$1.00
					Patek, Freddie	72T	531	$ .25	$ .85
					Patek, Freddie	73T	334	$ .06	$ .25
					Patek, Freddie	74T	88	$ .06	$ .25
					Patek, Freddie	75T	48	$ .06	$ .25
					Patek, Freddie	76T	167	$ .05	$ .20
					Patek, Freddie	77T	422	$ .05	$ .15
					Patek, Freddie	78T	204	$ .02	$ .10
					Patek, Freddie	78T	274	$ .02	$ .10
					Patek, Freddie	79T	525	$ .02	$ .10
					Patek, Freddie	80T	705	$ .01	$ .07
					Patek, Freddie	81T	311	$ .01	$ .07
					Patek, Freddie	82T	602	$ .01	$ .06
					Patterson, Bob	88T	522	$ .01	$ .10
					Patterson, Daryl	68T	113	$ .25	$ .65
					Patterson, Daryl	69T	101	$ .25	$ .65
					Patterson, Daryl	70T	592	$ .25	$ .85
					Patterson, Daryl	71T	481	$ .10	$ .35
					Patterson, Dave	80T	679	$ .01	$ .07
					Patterson, Gil	77T	472	$ .05	$ .15
					Patterson, Ken	89T	434	$ .01	$ .04
					Patterson, Ken	90T	156	$ .01	$ .03
					Patterson, Reggie	82T	599	$ .01	$ .06
					Pattin, Marty	69T	563	$ .25	$ .85
					Pattin, Marty	70T	31	$ .10	$ .35
					Pattin, Marty	71T	579	$ .30	$1.00
					Pattin, Marty	72T	144	$ .10	$ .35
					Pattin, Marty	73T	415	$ .06	$ .25
					Pattin, Marty	74T	583	$ .06	$ .25
					Pattin, Marty	75T	413	$ .06	$ .25
					Pattin, Marty	76T	492	$ .05	$ .20
Pascual, Camilo	58T	219	$ .50	$2.00	Pattin, Marty	77T	658	$ .05	$ .15
Pascual, Camilo	59T	291	$ .50	$1.95	Pattin, Marty	78T	218	$ .02	$ .10
Pascual, Camillo (Camilo)	59T	413	$ .50	$1.95	Pattin, Marty	79T	129	$ .02	$ .10
Pascual, Camilo	60T	483	$ .60	$1.75	Pattin, Marty	80T	26	$ .01	$ .07
Pascual, Camilo	60TAS	569	$2.00	$7.00	Pattin, Marty	81T	389	$ .01	$ .07
Pascual, Camilo	61T	235	$ .30	$1.00	Paul, Mike	69T	537	$ .25	$ .85
Pascual, Camilo	62T	59	$ .50	$1.95	Paul, Mike	70T	582	$ .25	$ .85
Pascual, Camilo	62T	230	$ .35	$1.10	Paul, Mike	71T	454	$ .10	$ .35
Pascual, Camilo	63T	8	$ .35	$1.10	Paul, Mike	72T	577	$ .25	$ .85
Pascual, Camilo	63T	10	$ .35	$1.10	Paul, Mike	73T	58	$ .06	$ .25
Pascual, Camilo	63T	220	$ .25	$ .85	Paul, Mike	74T	399	$ .06	$ .25
Pascual, Camilo	64T	2	$ .50	$2.00	Paula, Carlos	55T	97	$1.35	$5.00
Pascual, Camilo	64T	4	$1.50	$6.00	Paula, Carlos	56T	4	$1.25	$4.50
Pascual, Camilo	64T	6	$ .35	$1.10	Pavletich, Don	59T	494	$ .50	$1.95
Pascual, Camilo	64T	500	$ .40	$1.25	Pavletich, Don	62T	594	$35.00	$125.00
Pascual, Camilo	65T	11	$ .35	$1.10	Pavletich, Don	65T	472	$ .50	$2.00
Pascual, Camilo	65T	255	$ .30	$1.00	Pavletich, Don	66T	196	$ .25	$ .85
Pascual, Camilo	66T	305	$ .25	$ .85	Pavletich, Don	67T	292	$ .25	$ .65
Pascual, Camilo	67T	71	$ .25	$ .65	Pavletich, Don	68T	108	$ .25	$ .65
Pascual, Camilo	68T	395	$ .15	$ .50	Pavletich, Don	69T	179	$ .25	$ .65
Pascual, Camilo	69T	513	$ .25	$ .85	Pavletich, Don	70T	504	$ .10	$ .35
Pascual, Camilo	70T	254	$ .10	$ .35	Pavletich, Don	71T	409	$ .10	$ .35
Pasley, Kevin	77T	476	$20.00	$60.00	Pavletich, Don	72T	359	$ .10	$ .35
Pasley, Kevin	78T	702	$ .02	$ .10	Paxton, Mike	78T	216	$ .02	$ .10
Pasqua, Dan	86T	259	$ .03	$ .30	Paxton, Mike	79T	122	$ .02	$ .10
Pasqua, Dan	87T	74	$ .01	$ .10	Paxton, Mike	80T	388	$ .01	$ .07
Pasqua, Dan	88T	691	$ .01	$ .03	Pazik, Mike	76T	597	$ .25	$ .65
Pasqua, Dan	88TBB	164	$ .01	$ .05	Pazik, Mike	77T	643	$ .05	$ .15
Pasqua, Dan	88TTR	82	$ .01	$ .05	Pearce, Jim	55T	170	$3.25	$9.00
Pasqua, Dan	89T	558	$ .01	$ .04	Pearson, Albie	58T	317	$ .50	$2.00
Pasqua, Dan	89TBB	44	$ .01	$ .05	Pearson, Albie	59T	4	$1.00	$3.75
Pasqua, Dan	90T	446	$ .01	$ .03	Pearson, Albie	60T	241	$ .35	$1.10
Pastore, Frank	80T	677	$ .01	$ .07	Pearson, Albie	61T	288	$ .30	$1.00
Pastore, Frank	81T	499	$ .01	$ .07	Pearson, Albie	62T	343	$ .35	$1.10
Pastore, Frank	82T	128	$ .01	$ .06	Pearson, Albie	63T	182	$ .25	$ .85
Pastore, Frank	83T	658	$ .01	$ .06	Pearson, Albie	64T	110	$ .25	$ .85
Pastore, Frank	84T	87	$ .01	$ .05	Pearson, Albie	65T	358	$ .30	$1.00

Player	Year	No.	VG	EX/MT
Pearson, Albie	66T	83	$ .25	$ .85
Pecota, Bill	88T	433	$ .01	$ .03
Pecota, Bill	89T	148	$ .01	$ .04
Pecota, Bill	89TBB	292	$ .01	$ .05
Peden, Les	53T	256	$11.00	$37.50
Pedrique, Al	88T	294	$ .01	$ .03
Pedrique, Al	89T	566	$ .01	$ .04
Pellagrini, Eddie	52T	405	$39.00	$135.00
Pellagrini, Eddie	53T	28	$3.75	$13.00
Pena, Alejandro	83TTR	83	$ .05	$ .25
Pena, Alejandro	84T	324	$ .02	$ .10
Pena, Alejandro	85T	110	$ .01	$ .04
Pena, Alejandro	86T	665	$ .01	$ .03
Pena, Alejandro	87T	787	$ .01	$ .03
Pena, Alejandro	88T	277	$ .01	$ .03
Pena, Alejandro	89T	57	$ .01	$ .04
Pena, Alejandro	90T	483	$ .01	$ .03
Pena, George	73T	601	$ .35	$1.10
Pena, Hipolito	89T	109	$ .01	$ .04
Pena, Jose	69T	339	$ .25	$ .65
Pena, Jose	70T	523	$ .10	$ .35
Pena, Jose	71T	693	$ .70	$2.10
Pena, Jose	72T	322	$ .10	$ .35
Pena, Orlando	59T	271	$ .50	$1.95
Pena, Orlando	63T	214	$ .25	$ .85
Pena, Orlando	64T	124	$ .25	$ .85
Pena, Orlando	65T	311	$ .30	$1.00
Pena, Orlando	66T	239	$ .25	$ .85
Pena, Orlando	67T	449	$ .25	$ .85
Pena, Orlando	68T	471	$ .30	$1.00
Pena, Orlando	74T	393	$ .06	$ .25
Pena, Orlando	75T	573	$ .06	$ .25
Pena, Ramon	89TMLD	96	$ .01	$ .15
Pena, Roberto	66T	559	$2.00	$5.00
Pena, Roberto	69T	184	$ .25	$ .65
Pena, Roberto	70T	44	$ .10	$ .35
Pena, Roberto	71T	334	$ .10	$ .35
Pena, Tony	81T	551	$ .50	$2.00
Pena, Tony	82T	138	$ .05	$ .25
Pena, Tony	83T	590	$ .03	$ .15
Pena, Tony	84T	645	$ .05	$ .20
Pena, Tony	85T	358	$ .01	$ .10
Pena, Tony	86T	260	$ .01	$ .10
Pena, Tony	87T	60	$ .01	$ .10
Pena, Tony	87TTR	95	$ .01	$ .10
Pena, Tony	88T	410	$ .01	$ .10
Pena, Tony	89T	715	$ .01	$ .04
Pena, Tony	90T	115	$ .01	$ .03
Pendleton, Jim	53T	185	$3.75	$13.00
Pendleton, Jim	54T	165	$2.10	$7.50
Pendleton, Jim	55T	15	$1.35	$5.00
Pendleton, Jim	57T	327	$3.50	$13.00
Pendleton, Jim	58T	104	$1.00	$3.75
Pendleton, Jim	59T	174	$ .50	$1.95
Pendleton, Jim	62T	432	$ .70	$2.10
Pendleton, Terry	85T	346	$ .10	$ .50
Pendleton, Terry	86T	528	$ .01	$ .03
Pendleton, Terry	87T	8	$ .01	$ .03
Pendleton, Terry	88T	635	$ .01	$ .03
Pendleton, Terry	88TBB	53	$ .01	$ .05
Pendleton, Terry	89T	375	$ .01	$ .04
Pendleton, Terry	89TBB	151	$ .01	$ .05
Pendleton, Terry	90T	725	$ .01	$ .03
Penson, Paul	54T	236	$2.10	$7.50
Pentz, Gene	77T	308	$ .05	$ .15
Pentz, Gene	78T	64	$ .02	$ .10
Penz, Roberto	65T	549	$1.35	$4.00
Pepe, Dave	56T	154	$1.25	$4.50
Pepitone, Joe	62T	596	$10.00	$30.00
Pepitone, Joe	63T	183	$1.30	$3.00
Pepitone, Joe	64T	360	$ .50	$1.95
Pepitone, Joe	65T	245	$ .50	$2.00
Pepitone, Joe	66T	79	$ .35	$1.10
Pepitone, Joe	67T	340	$ .30	$1.00
Pepitone, Joe	68T	195	$ .15	$ .50

Player	Year	No.	VG	EX/MT
Pepitone, Joe	69T	589	$ .20	$ .50
Pepitone, Joe	70T	598	$ .35	$1.10

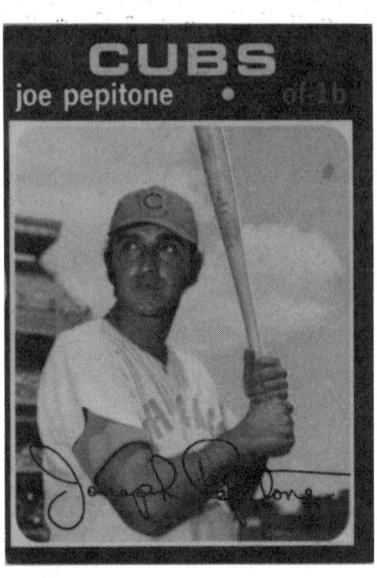

Player	Year	No.	VG	EX/MT
Pepitone, Joe	71T	90	$ .15	$ .50
Pepitone, Joe	72T	303	$ .10	$ .35
Pepitone, Joe	72TIA	304	$ .10	$ .35
Pepitone, Joe	73T	580	$ .35	$1.10
Pepper, Laurin	55T	147	$1.35	$5.00
Pepper, Laurin	56T	108	$1.25	$4.50
Peraza, Oswald	89T	297	$ .01	$ .10
Peraza, Oswald	89TBB	219	$ .01	$ .05
Perconte, Jack	81T	302	$ .90	$4.50
Perconte, Jack	82TTR	87	$ .02	$ .10
Perconte, Jack	83T	569	$ .01	$ .06
Perconte, Jack	85T	172	$ .01	$ .04
Perconte, Jack	86T	146	$ .01	$ .03
Perez, Marty	71T	529	$ .70	$2.00
Perez, Marty	72T	119	$ .10	$ .35
Perez, Marty	73T	144	$ .06	$ .25
Perez, Marty	74T	374	$ .06	$ .25
Perez, Marty	75T	499	$ .06	$ .25
Perez, Marty	76T	177	$ .05	$ .20
Perez, Marty	77T	438	$ .05	$ .15
Perez, Marty	78T	613	$ .02	$ .10
Perez, Melido	88TTR	83	$ .01	$ .25
Perez, Melido	89T	786	$ .01	$ .15
Perez, Melido	89TBB	235	$ .01	$ .05
Perez, Melido	90T	621	$ .01	$ .03
Perez, Pascual	81T	551	$ .50	$2.00
Perez, Pascual	82T	383	$ .01	$ .20
Perez, Pascual	83TTR	84	$ .02	$ .10
Perez, Pascual	84T	675	$ .01	$ .05
Perez, Pascual	85T	106	$ .01	$ .04
Perez, Pascual	86T	491	$ .01	$ .10
Perez, Pascual	88T	647	$ .01	$ .10
Perez, Pascual	88TBB	196	$ .01	$ .05
Perez, Pascual	90T	278	$ .01	$ .03
Perez, Pasqual	89T	73	$ .01	$ .04
Perez, Tony	65T	581	$20.00	$75.00
Perez, Tony	66T	72	$3.75	$13.00
Perez, Tony	67T	476	$12.50	$47.50
Perez, Tony	68T	130	$1.35	$4.00
Perez, Tony	69T	295	$1.25	$4.50
Perez, Tony	70T	380	$ .90	$2.75

Player	Year	No.	VG	EX/MT	Player	Year	No.	VG	EX/MT
Perez, Tony	70T	63	$ .50	$1.95	Perry, Gaylord	76T	55	$ .75	$3.00
Perez, Tony	71T	64	$ .60	$1.75	Perry, Gaylord	77T	152	$ .90	$3.50
Perez, Tony	71T	66	$ .60	$1.75	Perry, Gaylord	78T	686	$1.00	$4.00
Perez, Tony	71T	580	$1.25	$3.75	Perry, Gaylord	79T	5	$ .06	$ .30
Perez, Tony	72T	80	$ .65	$1.75	Perry, Gaylord	79T	321	$ .55	$2.25
Perez, Tony	73T	275	$ .50	$2.00	Perry, Gaylord	80T	280	$ .15	$ .50
Perez, Tony	74T	230	$ .50	$1.95	Perry, Gaylord	81T	582	$ .15	$ .60
Perez, Tony	75T	560	$ .50	$2.00	Perry, Gaylord	81TTR	812	$ .35	$1.25
Perez, Tony	76T	195	$ .30	$1.00	Perry, Gaylord	82T	115	$ .06	$ .30
Perez, Tony	76T	325	$ .35	$1.10	Perry, Gaylord	82TTR	88	$ .35	$1.10
Perez, Tony	77T	655	$ .35	$1.10	Perry, Gaylord	83T	463	$ .08	$ .40
Perez, Tony	78T	15	$ .05	$ .25	Perry, Gaylord	83T	464	$ .01	$ .06
Perez, Tony	79T	495	$ .15	$ .50	Perry, Gaylord	84T	4	$ .05	$ .25
Perez, Tony	80T	125	$ .25	$ .65	Perry, Gaylord	84T	6	$ .10	$ .50
Perez, Tony	81T	575	$ .07	$ .35	Perry, Gerald	84TTR	92	$ .05	$ .25
Perez, Tony	82T	255	$ .06	$ .30	Perry, Gerald	85T	219	$ .01	$ .04
Perez, Tony	82TIA	256	$ .03	$ .15	Perry, Gerald	86T	557	$ .01	$ .03
Perez, Tony	83T	715	$ .01	$ .06	Perry, Gerald	87T	639	$ .01	$ .03
Perez, Tony	83T	716	$ .01	$ .06	Perry, Gerald	88T	39	$ .01	$ .03
Perez, Tony	83TTR	85	$ .20	$ .70	Perry, Gerald	88TBB	40	$ .01	$ .05
Perez, Tony	84T	385	$ .05	$ .25	Perry, Gerald	89T	130	$ .01	$ .04
Perez, Tony	84T	702	$ .06	$ .30	Perry, Gerald	89TBB	279	$ .01	$ .05
Perez, Tony	84T	703	$ .02	$ .10	Perry, Gerald	90T	792	$ .01	$ .03
Perez, Tony	84T	704	$ .03	$ .15	Perry, Jim	59T	542	$11.50	$45.00
Perez, Tony	84TTR	91	$ .15	$ .60	Perry, Jim	60T	324	$ .45	$1.35
Perez, Tony	85T	675	$ .01	$ .04	Perry, Jim	61T	385	$ .60	$1.75
Perez, Tony	86T	85	$ .02	$ .20	Perry, Jim	61T	48	$ .50	$2.00
Perez, Tony	86TRB	205	$ .01	$ .10	Perry, Jim	61TAS	584	$6.00	$18.00
Perkins, Broderick	79T	725	$ .02	$ .10	Perry, Jim	62T	37	$ .50	$2.00
Perkins, Broderick	81T	393	$ .01	$ .07	Perry, Jim	62T	405	$1.00	$3.75
Perkins, Broderick	82T	192	$ .01	$ .06	Perry, Jim	63T	535	$1.35	$4.00
Perkins, Broderick	83T	593	$ .01	$ .06	Perry, Jim	64T	34	$ .15	$ .50
Perkins, Broderick	83TTR	86	$ .02	$ .10	Perry, Jim	65T	351	$ .35	$1.10
Perkins, Broderick	84T	212	$ .01	$ .05	Perry, Jim	66T	283	$ .30	$1.00
Perkins, Broderick	85T	609	$ .01	$ .04	Perry, Jim	67T	246	$ .15	$ .50
Perkowski, Harry	52T	142	$6.00	$19.00	Perry, Jim	68T	393	$ .15	$ .50
Perkowski, Harry	53T	236	$11.00	$37.50	Perry, Jim	69T	146	$ .15	$ .50
Perkowski, Harry	54T	125	$2.10	$7.50	Perry, Jim	70T	70	$ .50	$2.00
Perkowski, Harry	55T	184	$3.25	$9.00	Perry, Jim	70T	620	$ .50	$2.00
Perlman, Jon	89T	476	$ .01	$ .04	Perry, Jim	71T	69	$ .15	$ .50
Perlozzo, Sam	78T	704	$3.00	$10.00	Perry, Jim	71T	500	$ .10	$ .35
Perlozzo, Sam	79T	709	$ .02	$ .10	Perry, Jim	72T	220	$ .07	$ .25
Perranoski, Ron	61T	525	$6.00	$18.00	Perry, Jim	72T	497	$ .10	$ .35
Perranoski, Ron	62T	297	$ .35	$1.10	Perry, Jim	73T	385	$ .25	$ .65
Perranoski, Ron	63T	403	$ .35	$1.20	Perry, Jim	74T	316	$ .06	$ .25
Perranoski, Ron	64T	30	$ .25	$ .85	Perry, Jim	75T	263	$ .10	$ .35
Perranoski, Ron	65T	484	$ .50	$2.00	Perry, Pat	87T	417	$ .01	$ .10
Perranoski, Ron	66T	555	$4.50	$15.00	Perry, Pat	88T	282	$ .01	$ .03
Perranoski, Ron	67T	197	$ .25	$ .65	Perry, Pat	89T	186	$ .01	$ .04
Perranoski, Ron	68T	435	$ .25	$ .65	Perry, Pat	89TBB	329	$ .01	$ .05
Perranoski, Ron	69T	77	$ .25	$ .65	Perry, Pat	90T	541	$ .01	$ .03
Perranoski, Ron	70T	226	$ .10	$ .35	Perzanowski, Stan	76T	388	$ .05	$ .20
Perranoski, Ron	71T	475	$ .10	$ .35	Pesky, Johnny	51Tbb	5	$4.50	$18.00
Perranoski, Ron	72T	367	$ .10	$ .35	Pesky, Johnny	52T	15	$12.50	$45.00
Perry, Bob	64T	48	$ .25	$ .85	Pesky, Johnny	54T	63	$3.75	$15.00
Perry, Gaylord	62T	199	$37.50	$110.00	Pesky, Johnny	63T	343	$ .35	$1.20
Perry, Gaylord	63T	169	$6.00	$18.00	Pesky, Johnny	64T	248	$ .25	$ .85
Perry, Gaylord	64T	468	$7.50	$22.50	Peterek, Jeff	89TMLD	97	$ .01	$ .05
Perry, Gaylord	65T	193	$2.50	$10.00	Peters, Frank	68T	409	$ .25	$ .65
Perry, Gaylord	66T	598	$75.00	$250.00	Peters, Gary	60T	407	$ .50	$1.95
Perry, Gaylord	67T	236	$2.50	$8.00	Peters, Gary	61T	303	$ .30	$1.00
Perry, Gaylord	67T	320	$2.00	$7.00	Peters, Gary	63T	522	$1.35	$4.00
Perry, Gaylord	68T	11	$ .50	$1.95	Peters, Gary	64T	2	$ .50	$2.00
Perry, Gaylord	68T	85	$1.35	$4.00	Peters, Gary	64T	130	$ .25	$ .85
Perry, Gaylord	69T	485	$1.35	$4.00	Peters, Gary	65T	9	$ .30	$1.00
Perry, Gaylord	70T	560	$1.40	$4.00	Peters, Gary	65T	430	$ .30	$1.00
Perry, Gaylord	71T	70	$ .50	$2.00	Peters, Gary	66T	111	$ .25	$ .85
Perry, Gaylord	71T	140	$2.35	$7.00	Peters, Gary	67T	233	$ .35	$1.10
Perry, Gaylord	72T	285	$1.35	$4.00	Peters, Gary	67T	310	$ .25	$ .65
Perry, Gaylord	73T	66	$ .35	$1.10	Peters, Gary	68T	8	$ .35	$1.10
Perry, Gaylord	73T	346	$ .30	$1.00	Peters, Gary	68T	210	$ .25	$ .65
Perry, Gaylord	73T	400	$ .95	$3.50	Peters, Gary	68TAS	379	$ .25	$ .65
Perry, Gaylord	74T	35	$1.00	$3.75	Peters, Gary	69T	34	$ .25	$ .65
Perry, Gaylord	75T	530	$1.00	$4.00	Peters, Gary	70T	540	$ .10	$ .35
Perry, Gaylord	76T	204	$ .15	$ .50	Peters, Gary	71T	225	$ .10	$ .35

Player	Year	No.	VG	EX/MT
Peters, Gary	72T	503	$ .10	$ .35
Peters, Rick	81T	177	$ .01	$ .07
Peters, Rick	82T	504	$ .01	$ .06
Peters, Rick	84T	436	$ .01	$ .05
Peters, Steve	88TTR	84	$ .01	$ .05
Peters, Steve	89T	482	$ .01	$ .10
Peterson, Adam	90T	299	$ .01	$ .10
Peterson, Cap	64T	568	$1.50	$3.75
Peterson, Cap	65T	512	$ .50	$2.00
Peterson, Cap	66T	349	$ .25	$ .85
Peterson, Cap	67T	387	$ .25	$ .85
Peterson, Cap	68T	188	$ .25	$ .65
Peterson, Cap	69T	571	$ .25	$ .85
Peterson, Fritz	66T	584	$4.50	$15.00
Peterson, Fritz	67T	495	$ .50	$2.00
Peterson, Fritz	68T	246	$ .25	$ .65
Peterson, Fritz	69T	46	$ .25	$ .65
Peterson, Fritz	70T	142	$ .10	$ .35

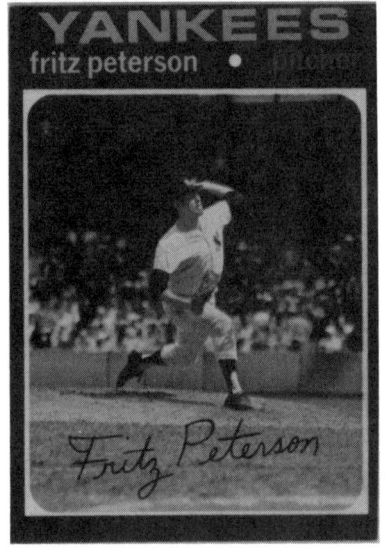

Player	Year	No.	VG	EX/MT
Peterson, Fritz	71T	460	$ .10	$ .35
Peterson, Fritz	72T	573	$ .25	$ .85
Peterson, Fritz	72TIA	574	$ .25	$ .85
Peterson, Fritz	73T	82	$ .06	$ .25
Peterson, Fritz	74T	229	$ .06	$ .25
Peterson, Fritz	75T	62	$ .06	$ .25
Peterson, Fritz	76T	255	$ .05	$ .20
Peterson, Harding	58T	322	$ .50	$2.00
Petralli, Geno	86T	296	$ .01	$ .03
Petralli, Geno	87T	388	$ .01	$ .03
Petralli, Geno	88T	589	$ .01	$ .03
Petralli, Geno	89T	137	$ .01	$ .04
Petralli, Geno	89TBB	12	$ .01	$ .05
Petralli, Geno	90T	706	$ .01	$ .03
Petrocelli, Rico	65T	74	$ .35	$1.10
Petrocelli, Rico	66T	298	$ .30	$1.00
Petrocelli, Rico	67T	528	$ .50	$2.00
Petrocelli, Rico	68T	430	$ .25	$ .85
Petrocelli, Rico	69T	215	$ .25	$ .85
Petrocelli, Rico	70T	680	$ .50	$2.00
Petrocelli, Rico	70TAS	457	$ .10	$ .35
Petrocelli, Rico	71T	340	$ .10	$ .35
Petrocelli, Rico	72T	30	$ .25	$ .65
Petrocelli, Rico	73T	365	$ .06	$ .25
Petrocelli, Rico	74T	609	$ .06	$ .25

Player	Year	No.	VG	EX/MT
Petrocelli, Rico	75T	356	$ .06	$ .25
Petrocelli, Rico	76T	445	$ .05	$ .20
Petrocelli, Rico	77T	111	$ .05	$ .15
Petry, Dan	80T	373	$ .15	$ .50
Petry, Dan	81T	59	$ .03	$ .15
Petry, Dan	82T	211	$ .01	$ .06
Petry, Dan	82T	666	$ .01	$ .06
Petry, Dan	83T	261	$ .01	$ .06
Petry, Dan	83T	638	$ .01	$ .06
Petry, Dan	84T	147	$ .01	$ .05
Petry, Dan	85T	435	$ .01	$ .04
Petry, Dan	86T	540	$ .01	$ .03
Petry, Dan	87T	752	$ .01	$ .03
Petry, Dan	88T	78	$ .01	$ .03
Petry, Dan	88TTR	85	$ .01	$ .05
Petry, Dan	89TBB	178	$ .01	$ .05
Petry, Dan	90T	363	$ .01	$ .03
Pettini, Joe	81T	62	$ .01	$ .07
Pettini, Joe	82T	568	$ .01	$ .06
Pettini, Joe	83T	143	$ .01	$ .06
Pettini, Joe	84T	449	$ .01	$ .05
Pettis, Gary	84TTR	93	$ .05	$ .25
Pettis, Gary	85T	497	$ .01	$ .04
Pettis, Gary	86T	604	$ .01	$ .03
Pettis, Gary	87T	278	$ .01	$ .03
Pettis, Gary	88T	71	$ .01	$ .03
Pettis, Gary	88TTR	86	$ .01	$ .05
Pettis, Gary	89T	146	$ .01	$ .04
Pettis, Gary	90T	512	$ .01	$ .03
Pevey, Marty	89TMLD	98	$ .01	$ .05
Pevey, Marty	90T	137	$ .01	$ .03
Pfeil, Bobby	70T	99	$ .10	$ .35
Pfeil, Bobby	72T	681	$ .70	$2.10
Pfister, Dan	62T	592	$13.00	$40.00
Pfister, Dan	63T	521	$1.00	$2.00
Pfister, Dan	64T	302	$ .25	$ .85
Phelps, Ken	85T	582	$ .01	$ .04
Phelps, Ken	86T	34	$ .01	$ .03
Phelps, Ken	87T	333	$ .01	$ .03
Phelps, Ken	88T	182	$ .01	$ .03
Phelps, Ken	88TBB	189	$ .01	$ .05
Phelps, Ken	89T	741	$ .01	$ .04
Phelps, Ken	89TBB	293	$ .01	$ .05
Phelps, Ken	90T	411	$ .01	$ .03
Philley, Dave	52T	226	$6.00	$18.00
Philley, Dave	53T	64	$3.75	$13.00
Philley, Dave	54T	159	$2.00	$7.00
Philley, Dave	56T	222	$2.50	$8.00
Philley, Dave	57T	124	$ .95	$3.50
Philley, Dave	58T	116	$ .50	$2.00
Philley, Dave	59T	92	$ .70	$2.00
Philley, Dave	60T	52	$ .35	$1.10
Philley, Dave	61T	369	$ .30	$1.00
Philley, Dave	62T	542	$3.75	$11.00
Phillies, Team	56T	72	$3.00	$9.00
Phillies, Team	57T	214	$2.00	$6.00
Phillies, Team	58T	134	$3.00	$9.00
Phillies, Team	59T	8	$2.00	$6.00
Phillies, Team	60T	302	$2.00	$6.00
Phillies, Team	61T	491	$1.25	$4.50
Phillies, Team	62T	294	$ .75	$2.00
Phillies, Team	63T	13	$ .50	$1.95
Phillies, Team	64T	293	$ .85	$3.50
Phillies, Team	65T	338	$ .75	$2.25
Phillies, Team	66T	463	$1.35	$4.00
Phillies, Team	67T	102	$ .25	$ .65
Phillies, Team	68T	477	$ .60	$1.75
Phillies, Team	70T	436	$ .35	$1.10
Phillies, Team	71T	268	$ .35	$1.10
Phillies, Team	72T	397	$ .15	$ .50
Phillies, Team	73T	536	$ .60	$1.75
Phillies, Team	74T	383	$ .15	$ .50
Phillies, Team Checklist	75T	46	$ .15	$ .50
Phillies, Team Checklist	76T	384	$ .30	$1.00
Phillies, Team Checklist	77T	467	$ .15	$ .50

Player	Year	No.	VG	EX/MT
Phillies, Team Checklist	78T	381	$ .10	$ .35
Phillies, Team Checklist	79T	112	$ .05	$ .25
Phillies, Team Checklist	80T	526	$ .25	$ .65
Phillies, Team Checklist	81T	682	$ .02	$ .20
Phillies, Team Leaders	86T	246	$ .01	$ .03
Phillies, Team Leaders	87T	481	$ .01	$ .03
Phillies, Team Leaders	88T	669	$ .01	$ .03
Phillies, Team Leaders	89T	489	$ .01	$ .04
Phillips, Adolfo	66T	32	$ .25	$ .85
Phillips, Adolfo	67T	148	$ .25	$ .65
Phillips, Adolfo	68T	202	$ .25	$ .65
Phillips, Adolfo	69T	372	$ .25	$ .65
Phillips, Adolfo	70T	666	$ .50	$2.00
Phillips, Adolfo	71T	418	$ .10	$ .35
Phillips, Bubba	57T	395	$ .85	$3.50
Phillips, Bubba	58T	212	$ .50	$2.00
Phillips, Bubba	59T	187	$ .50	$1.95
Phillips, Bubba	60T	243	$ .35	$1.10
Phillips, Bubba	61T	101	$ .30	$1.00
Phillips, Bubba	62T	511	$ .70	$2.10
Phillips, Bubba	63T	177	$ .25	$ .85
Phillips, Bubba	64T	143	$ .25	$ .85
Phillips, Bubba	65T	306	$ .30	$1.00
Phillips, Dick	63T	544	$8.50	$25.00
Phillips, Dick	64T	559	$1.50	$3.75
Phillips, Jack	52T	240	$6.00	$19.00
Phillips, Jack	57T	307	$3.50	$13.00
Phillips, Lefty	70T	376	$ .10	$ .35
Phillips, Lefty	71T	279	$ .10	$ .35
Phillips, Mike	74T	533	$ .06	$ .25
Phillips, Mike	75T	642	$ .06	$ .25
Phillips, Mike	76T	93	$ .05	$ .20
Phillips, Mike	77T	352	$ .05	$ .15
Phillips, Mike	78T	88	$ .02	$ .10
Phillips, Mike	79T	258	$ .02	$ .10
Phillips, Mike	80T	439	$ .01	$ .07
Phillips, Mike	81T	113	$ .01	$ .07
Phillips, Mike	81TTR	813	$ .02	$ .10
Phillips, Mike	82T	762	$ .01	$ .06
Phillips, Taylor	57T	343	$3.50	$13.00
Phillips, Taylor	58T	159	$ .50	$2.00
Phillips, Taylor	59T	113	$ .50	$1.95
Phillips, Taylor	60T	211	$ .35	$1.10
Phillips, Tony	83TTR	87	$ .02	$ .10
Phillips, Tony	84T	309	$ .01	$ .05
Phillips, Tony	85T	444	$ .01	$ .04
Phillips, Tony	86T	29	$ .01	$ .03
Phillips, Tony	87T	188	$ .01	$ .03
Phillips, Tony	88T	673	$ .01	$ .03
Phillips, Tony	89T	248	$ .01	$ .04
Phillips, Tony	90T	702	$ .01	$ .03
Phoebus, Tom	67T	204	$ .25	$ .65
Phoebus, Tom	68T	97	$ .25	$ .65
Phoebus, Tom	69T	185	$ .25	$ .65
Phoebus, Tom	69T	532	$ .20	$ .50
Phoebus, Tom	70T	717	$ .50	$2.00
Phoebus, Tom	71T	611	$ .30	$1.00
Phoebus, Tom	72T	477	$ .10	$ .35
Picciolo, Rob	78T	528	$ .02	$ .10
Picciolo, Rob	79T	378	$ .02	$ .10
Picciolo, Rob	80T	158	$ .01	$ .07
Picciolo, Rob	81T	604	$ .01	$ .07
Picciolo, Rob	82T	293	$ .01	$ .06
Picciolo, Rob	82TTR	89	$ .02	$ .10
Picciolo, Rob	83T	476	$ .01	$ .06
Picciolo, Rob	84T	88	$ .01	$ .05
Picciolo, Rob	84TTR	94	$ .02	$ .10
Picciolo, Rob	85T	756	$ .01	$ .04
Picciolo, Rob	85TTR	90	$ .02	$ .10
Picciolo, Rob	86T	672	$ .01	$ .03
Piche, Ron	61T	61	$ .30	$1.00
Piche, Ron	62T	582	$3.75	$11.00
Piche, Ron	63T	179	$ .25	$ .85
Piche, Ron	65T	464	$ .50	$2.00
Pico, Jeff	88TTR	87	$ .01	$ .15
Pico, Jeff	89T	262	$ .01	$ .10
Pico, Jeff	90T	613	$ .01	$ .03
Pierce, Billy	51Tbb	45	$7.50	$22.50
Pierce, Billy	52T	98	$6.00	$12.50
Pierce, Billy	53T	143	$3.75	$13.00
Pierce, Billy	56T	160	$1.50	$4.50
Pierce, Billy	57T	160	$ .60	$2.50
Pierce, Billy	58T	334	$ .45	$1.50
Pierce, Billy	58T	50	$ .90	$3.50
Pierce, Billy	59T	156	$1.30	$5.00
Pierce, Billy	59T	410	$ .50	$1.95
Pierce, Billy	59T	466	$ .60	$1.75
Pierce, Billy	59TAS	572	$6.00	$18.00
Pierce, Billy	60T	150	$ .50	$2.00
Pierce, Billy	60TAS	571	$2.50	$8.00
Pierce, Bill	61T	205	$ .50	$2.00
Pierce, Bill	62T	260	$ .50	$2.00
Pierce, Bill	63T	50	$ .30	$1.00
Pierce, Bill	63T	331	$ .50	$1.95
Pierce, Bill	64T	222	$ .15	$ .50
Pierce, Jack	76T	162	$ .05	$ .20
Pierce, Tony	67T	542	$3.00	$10.00
Pierce, Tony	68T	38	$ .25	$ .65
Piersall, Jim	56T	143	$1.75	$5.00
Piersall, Jim	57T	75	$1.00	$4.00
Piersall, Jim	58T	280	$1.00	$3.00
Piersall, Jim	59T	355	$ .60	$1.75
Piersall, Jim	60T	159	$ .60	$1.75
Piersall, Jim	61T	345	$ .60	$1.75
Piersall, Jim	62T	51	$ .50	$1.95
Piersall, Jim	62T	90	$ .50	$1.95
Piersall, Jim	63T	443	$ .50	$2.00
Piersall, Jim	64T	586	$1.35	$4.00
Piersall, Jim	65T	172	$ .50	$2.00
Piersall, Jim	66T	565	$8.00	$25.00
Piersall, Jim	67T	584	$5.00	$20.00
Pignatano, Joe	58T	373	$ .50	$2.00
Pignatano, Joe	59T	16	$ .85	$3.50
Pignatano, Joe	60T	292	$ .45	$1.35
Pignatano, Joe	60T	442	$ .60	$1.75
Pignatano, Joe	61T	74	$ .30	$1.00
Pignatano, Joe	62T	247	$ .35	$1.10
Pignatano, Joe	73T	257	$ .50	$2.00
Pignatano, Joe	74T	179	$ .50	$2.00
Pilarcik, Al	57T	311	$3.50	$13.00
Pilarcik, Al	58T	259	$ .50	$2.00
Pilarcik, Al	59T	7	$ .85	$3.50
Pilarcik, Al	60T	498	$ .60	$1.75
Pilarcik, Al	61T	62	$ .30	$1.00
Pillette, Duane	52T	82	$6.00	$19.00
Pillette, Duane	53T	269	$11.00	$37.50
Pillette, Duane	54T	107	$2.00	$7.00
Pillette, Duane	55T	168	$4.25	$13.00
Pilots, Team	70T	713	$3.00	$12.00
Pina, Horacio	71T	497	$ .10	$ .35
Pina, Horacio	72T	654	$ .25	$ .85
Pina, Horacio	73T	138	$ .06	$ .25
Pina, Horacio	74T	516	$ .06	$ .25
Pina, Horacio	74TTR	516	$ .06	$ .25
Pina, Horacio	75T	139	$ .06	$ .25
Piniella, Lou	64T	167	$4.00	$20.00
Piniella, Lou	68T	16	$ .75	$3.00
Piniella, Lou	69T	394	$ .75	$3.00
Piniella, Lou	70T	321	$ .50	$2.00
Piniella, Lou	71T	35	$ .15	$ .50
Piniella, Lou	72T	491	$ .15	$ .50
Piniella, Lou	72T	580	$ .35	$1.10
Piniella, Lou	73T	140	$ .15	$ .50
Piniella, Lou	74T	390	$ .25	$ .85
Piniella, Lou	74TTR	390	$ .25	$ .65
Piniella, Lou	75T	217	$ .15	$ .50
Piniella, Lou	76T	453	$ .25	$ .65
Piniella, Lou	77T	96	$ .25	$ .65
Piniella, Lou	78T	159	$ .05	$ .25
Piniella, Lou	79T	648	$ .05	$ .20

Player	Year	No.	VG	EX/MT
Piniella, Lou	80T	225	$ .02	$ .15
Piniella, Lou	81T	724	$ .05	$ .20
Piniella, Lou	82T	538	$ .03	$ .15
Piniella, Lou	83T	307	$ .01	$ .06
Piniella, Lou	84T	408	$ .01	$ .05
Piniella, Lou	86TTR	86	$ .02	$ .10
Piniella, Lou	87T	168	$ .01	$ .03
Piniella, Lou	88T	44	$ .01	$ .03
Pinson, Vada	58T	420	$5.00	$12.00
Pinson, Vada	59T	448	$ .30	$2.50
Pinson, Vada	60T	32	$1.15	$3.50
Pinson, Vada	60T	176	$ .95	$3.50
Pinson, Vada	61T	25	$1.35	$4.00
Pinson, Vada	61T	110	$ .95	$3.50
Pinson, Vada	62T	52	$ .60	$1.75
Pinson, Vada	62T	80	$ .75	$2.00
Pinson, Vada	63T	265	$ .60	$1.75
Pinson, Vada	64T	80	$ .50	$2.00
Pinson, Vada	64T	162	$ .15	$ .50
Pinson, Vada	65T	355	$ .60	$1.75
Pinson, Vada	66T	180	$ .50	$2.00
Pinson, Vada	67T	550	$3.00	$10.00
Pinson, Vada	68T	90	$ .60	$1.75
Pinson, Vada	69T	160	$ .10	$1.00
Pinson, Vada	70T	445	$ .50	$2.00
Pinson, Vada	71T	275	$ .35	$1.10
Pinson, Vada	72T	135	$ .15	$ .50
Pinson, Vada	73T	75	$ .15	$ .50
Pinson, Vada	74T	490	$ .15	$ .50
Pinson, Vada	75T	295	$ .25	$ .85
Pinson, Vada	76T	415	$ .10	$ .35
Pirates, Team	56T	121	$4.00	$12.00
Pirates, Team	57T	161	$1.25	$5.00
Pirates, Team	58T	341	$1.25	$5.00
Pirates, Team	59T	528	$7.50	$22.50
Pirates, Team	60T	484	$4.00	$12.00
Pirates, Team	61T	554	$9.00	$35.00
Pirates, Team	62T	409	$1.50	$3.75
Pirates, Team	63T	151	$ .50	$1.95
Pirates, Team	64T	373	$ .70	$2.00
Pirates, Team	65T	209	$ .60	$1.75
Pirates, Team	66T	404	$ .65	$1.75
Pirates, Team	67T	492	$1.35	$4.00
Pirates, Team	68T	308	$ .50	$2.00
Pirates, Team	70T	608	$ .60	$1.75
Pirates, Team	71T	603	$1.75	$6.00
Pirates, Team	72T	1	$1.10	$3.25
Pirates, Team	73T	26	$ .10	$ .50
Pirates, Team	74T	626	$ .15	$ .50
Pirates, Team Checklist	75T	304	$ .30	$1.00
Pirates, Team Checklist	76T	504	$ .30	$1.00
Pirates, Team Checklist	77T	354	$ .15	$ .50
Pirates, Team Checklist	78T	606	$ .05	$ .25
Pirates, Team Checklist	79T	244	$ .25	$ .65
Pirates, Team Checklist	80T	551	$ .05	$ .25
Pirates, Team Checklist	81T	683	$ .02	$ .20
Pirates, Team Leaders	86T	756	$ .01	$ .03
Pirates, Team Leaders	87T	131	$ .01	$ .03
Pirates, Team Leaders	88T	231	$ .01	$ .03
Pirates, Team Leaders	89T	699	$ .01	$ .04
Pirtle, Jerry	79T	720	$ .05	$ .20
Pisker, Don	79T	718	$ .02	$ .10
Pisoni, Jim	57T	402	$ .85	$3.50
Pisoni, Jim	59T	259	$ .50	$1.95
Pitler, Jake	52T	395	$39.00	$135.00
Pitlock, Skip	71T	19	$ .10	$ .35
Pitlock, Skip	75T	579	$ .06	$ .25
Pittaro, Chris	85TTR	91	$ .02	$ .10
Pittaro, Chris	86T	393	$ .01	$ .03
Pittman, Joe	82T	119	$ .01	$ .06
Pittman, Joe	82TTR	90	$ .02	$ .10
Pittman, Joe	83T	346	$ .01	$ .06
Pizarro, Juan	57T	383	$ .85	$3.50
Pizarro, Juan	59T	188	$ .50	$1.95
Pizarro, Juan	60T	59	$ .35	$1.10
Pizarro, Juan	61T	227	$ .30	$1.00
Pizarro, Juan	62T	255	$ .35	$1.10
Pizarro, Juan	63T	10	$ .35	$1.10
Pizarro, Juan	63T	160	$ .25	$ .85
Pizarro, Juan	64T	2	$ .50	$2.00
Pizarro, Juan	64T	430	$ .40	$1.25
Pizarro, Juan	65T	9	$ .30	$1.00
Pizarro, Juan	65T	125	$ .25	$ .65
Pizarro, Juan	66T	335	$ .25	$ .85
Pizarro, Juan	67T	602	$1.35	$4.00
Pizarro, Juan	68T	19	$ .25	$ .65
Pizarro, Juan	69T	498	$ .25	$ .65
Pizarro, Juan	71T	647	$ .70	$2.10
Pizarro, Juan	72T	18	$ .10	$ .35
Pizzaro, Juan	62T	59	$ .50	$1.95
Pladson, Gordy	81T	491	$ .01	$ .07
Plaskett, Elmo	63T	549	$1.50	$3.75
Playoff '69, A. L./Game 1	70T	199	$ .35	$1.00
Playoff '69, A. L./Game 2	70T	200	$ .35	$1.00
Playoff '69, A. L./Game 3	70T	201	$ .35	$1.00
Playoff '69, Mets	70T	198	$ .50	$2.00
Playoff '69, N.L./Game 1	70T	195	$ .60	$1.75
Playoff '69, N.L./Game 2	70T	196	$ .50	$2.00
Playoff '69, N.L./Game 3	70T	197	$ .60	$1.75
Playoff '69, Orioles	70T	202	$ .35	$1.10
Playoffs '70, A. L./Game 1	71T	195	$ .35	$1.10
Playoffs '70, A. L./Game 2	71T	196	$ .35	$1.10
Playoffs '70, A. L./Game 3	71T	197	$ .50	$1.95
Playoffs '70, A. L./Orioles	71T	198	$ .35	$1.10
Playoffs '70, N. L./Game 1	71T	199	$ .35	$1.10
Playoffs '70, N. L./Game 2	71T	200	$ .35	$1.10
Playoffs '70, N. L./Game 3	71T	201	$ .35	$1.10
Playoffs '70, N. L./Reds	71T	202	$ .50	$1.95
Playoffs '71, A. L.	72T	222	$ .50	$2.00
Playoffs '71, N. L.	72T	221	$ .35	$1.10
Playoffs '72, A. L.	73T	201	$ .15	$ .50
Playoffs '72, N. L.	73T	202	$ .15	$ .50
Playoffs '73, A.L.	74T	470	$ .60	$1.75
Playoffs '73, N.L.	74T	471	$ .15	$ .50
Playoffs '75, NL & AL	76T	461	$ .25	$ .85
Pleis, Bill	62T	124	$ .35	$1.10
Pleis, Bill	63T	293	$ .35	$1.20
Pleis, Bill	64T	484	$ .40	$1.25
Pleis, Bill	65T	122	$ .25	$ .65
Plesac, Dan	86TTR	87	$ .05	$ .25
Plesac, Dan	87T	279	$ .10	$ .50
Plesac, Dan	88T	670	$ .01	$ .03
Plesac, Dan	89T	740	$ .01	$ .04
Plesac, Dan	90T	490	$ .01	$ .03
Pless, Rance	56T	339	$1.30	$5.00
Plews, Herb	57T	169	$ .95	$3.50
Plews, Herb	58T	109	$ .85	$3.50
Plews, Herb	59T	373	$ .50	$1.95
Plummer, Bill	73T	177	$ .06	$ .25
Plummer, Bill	74T	524	$ .06	$ .25
Plummer, Bill	75T	656	$ .06	$ .25
Plummer, Bill	76T	627	$ .05	$ .20
Plummer, Bill	77T	239	$ .05	$ .15
Plummer, Bill	78T	106	$ .02	$ .10
Plummer, Bill	79T	396	$ .02	$ .10
Plunk, Eric	87T	587	$ .01	$ .03
Plunk, Eric	88T	173	$ .01	$ .03
Plunk, Eric	89T	448	$ .01	$ .04
Plunk, Eric	90T	9	$ .01	$ .03
Pocoroba, Biff	76T	103	$ .05	$ .20
Pocoroba, Biff	77T	594	$ .05	$ .15
Pocoroba, Biff	78T	296	$ .02	$ .10
Pocoroba, Biff	79T	555	$ .02	$ .10
Pocoroba, Biff	80T	132	$ .01	$ .07
Pocoroba, Biff	81T	326	$ .01	$ .07
Pocoroba, Biff	82T	88	$ .01	$ .06
Pocoroba, Biff	83T	676	$ .01	$ .06
Pocoroba, Biff	84T	438	$ .01	$ .05
Podbielan, Clarence "Bud"	52T	188	$6.00	$18.00
Podbielan, Bud	53T	237	$11.00	$37.50

Player	Year	No.	VG	EX/MT	Player	Year	No.	VG	EX/MT
Podbielan, Bud	54T	69	$4.75	$14.00	Porter, Darrell	75T	52	$ .06	$ .25
Podbielan, Bud	55T	153	$2.00	$7.00	Porter, Darrell	76T	645	$ .05	$ .20
Podbielan, Bud	56T	224	$2.50	$8.00	Porter, Darrell	77T	214	$ .05	$ .15
Podres, Johnny	53T	263	$70.00	$200.00	Porter, Darrell	78T	19	$ .02	$ .10
Podres, Johnny	54T	166	$6.00	$18.00	Porter, Darrell	79T	571	$ .02	$ .10
Podres, Johnny	55T	25	$5.50	$17.50	Porter, Darrell	80T	360	$ .01	$ .07
Podres, Johnny	56T	173	$4.50	12.50	Porter, Darrell	81T	610	$ .01	$ .07
Podres, Johnny	57T	277	$19.50	$57.50	Porter, Darrell	81TTR	814	$ .02	$ .10
Podres, Johnny	58T	120	$ 1.50	$4.50	Porter, Darrell	82T	447	$ .05	$ .20
Podres, Johnny	59T	262	$3.00	$12.00	Porter, Darrell	82TIA	448	$ .02	$ .10
Podres, Johnny	59T	495	$ .85	$3.50	Porter, Darrell	83T	103	$ .01	$ .06
Podres, Johnny	60T	425	$ .50	$1.95	Porter, Darrell	84T	285	$ .01	$ .05
Podres, Johnny	61T	109	$ .50	$1.95	Porter, Darrell	85T	525	$ .01	$ .04
Podres, Johnny	61T	207	$2.70	$8.00	Porter, Darrell	86T	757	$ .01	$ .03
Podres, Johnny	62T	280	$ .50	$1.95	Porter, Darrell	86TTR	88	$ .02	$ .10
Podres, Johnny	63T	150	$ .35	$1.10	Porter, Darrell	87T	689	$ .01	$ .03
Podres, Johnny	63T	412	$10.00	$40.00	Porter, J. W.	53T	211	$3.75	$13.00
Podres, Johnny	64T	580	$1.30	$5.00	Porter, J. W.	55T	49	$1.35	$5.00
Podres, Johnny	65T	387	$ .50	$2.00	Porter, J. W.	58T	32	$ .85	$3.50
Podres, Johnny	66T	468	$ .95	$3.50	Porter, J. W.	59T	246	$ .50	$1.95
Podres, Johnny	67T	284	$ .25	$ .65	Porterfield, Bob	52T	301	$11.50	$38.00
Podres, Johnny	69T	659	$ .30	$1.00	Porterfield, Bob	53T	108	$3.75	$13.00
Podres, Johnny	73T	12	$ .25	$ .65	Porterfield, Bob	56T	248	$2.50	$8.00
Poholsky, Tom	52T	242	$6.00	$19.00	Porterfield, Bob	57T	118	$ .95	$3.50
Poholsky, Tom	54T	142	$2.00	$7.00	Porterfield, Bob	58T	344	$ .50	$2.00
Poholsky, Tom	56T	196	$2.50	$8.00	Porterfield, Bob	59T	181	$ .50	$1.95
Poholsky, Tom	57T	235	$ .95	$3.50	Portocarrero, Arnold	54T	214	$2.00	$7.00
Pointer, Aaron	67T	564	$1.35	$4.00	Portocarrero, Arnold	55T	77	$1.35	$5.00
Pole, Dick	74T	596	$ .06	$ .25	Portocarrero, Arnold	56T	53	$1.25	$4.50
Pole, Dick	75T	513	$ .06	$ .25	Portocarrero, Arnie	58T	465	$ .50	$1.95
Pole, Dick	76T	326	$ .05	$ .20	Portocarrero, Arnie	59T	98	$ .85	$3.50
Pole, Dick	77T	187	$ .05	$ .15	Portocarrero, Arnie	60T	254	$ .35	$1.10
Pole, Dick	78T	233	$ .02	$ .10	Portugal, Mark	87T	419	$ .01	$ .10
Polidor, Gus	88T	708	$ .01	$ .03	Portugal, Mark	89T	46	$ .01	$ .04
Polidor, Gus	90T	313	$ .01	$ .03					
Pollet, Howie	51Trb	7	$1.00	$6.00					
Pollet, Howie	52T	63	$14.00	$45.00					
Pollet, Howie	53T	83	$3.75	$13.00					
Pollet, Howie	54T	89	$2.00	$7.00					
Pollet, Howie	55T	76	$1.35	$5.00					
Pollet, Howie	56T	262	$1.30	$5.00					
Pollet, Howie	60T	468	$ .95	$3.50					
Polonia, Luis	87TTR	96	$ .01	$ .30					
Polonia, Luis	88T	238	$ .01	$ .20					
Polonia, Luis	88TBB	65	$ .01	$ .05					
Polonia, Luis	89T	424	$ .01	$ .04					
Polonia, Luis	90T	634	$ .01	$ .03					
Poole, Jim	88TTR	88	$ .01	$ .25					
Poole, Jim	89TBB	263	$ .01	$ .05					
Pope, Dave	57T	249	$ .95	$3.50					
Popovich, Paul	67T	536	$8.25	$28.00					
Popovich, Paul	68T	266	$ .25	$ .65					
Popovich, Paul	69T	47	$ .15	$ .50					
Popovich, Paul	70T	258	$ .10	$ .35					
Popovich, Paul	71T	726	$ .70	$2.10					
Popovich, Paul	72T	512	$ .10	$ .35					
Popovich, Paul	73T	309	$ .06	$ .25					
Popovich, Paul	74T	14	$ .06	$ .25					
Popovich, Paul	75T	359	$ .06	$ .25					
Popowski, Eddie	73T	131	$ .10	$ .35					
Popowski, Eddie	74T	403	$ .06	$ .25					
Poquette, Tom	75T	622	$2.25	$11.00					
Poquette, Tom	77T	93	$ .05	$ .15					
Poquette, Tom	78T	357	$ .02	$ .10					
Poquette, Tom	79T	476	$ .02	$ .10					
Poquette, Tom	80T	597	$ .01	$ .07					
Poquette, Tom	81T	153	$ .01	$ .07	Portugal, Mark	90T	253	$ .01	$ .03
Poquette, Tom	82T	657	$ .01	$ .06	Posada, Leo	61T	39	$ .30	$1.00
Porter, Chuck	82T	333	$ .01	$ .06	Posada, Leo	62T	168	$ .35	$1.10
Porter, Chuck	84T	452	$ .01	$ .05	Posedel, Bill	52T	361	$39.00	$135.00
Porter, Chuck	85T	32	$ .01	$ .04	Posedel, Bill	60T	469	$ .95	$3.50
Porter, Chuck	86T	292	$ .01	$ .03	Post, Wally	52T	151	$6.00	$19.00
Porter, Darrell	72T	162	$ .25	$ .75	Post, Wally	56T	158	$1.25	$4.50
Porter, Darrell	73T	582	$ .35	$1.10	Post, Wally	57T	157	$ .95	$3.50
Porter, Darrell	74T	194	$ .06	$ .25	Post, Wally	58T	387	$ .50	$2.00

MARK PORTUGAL

TOPPS

Player	Year	No.	VG	EX/MT	Player	Year	No.	VG	EX/MT
Post, Wally	59T	398	$ .50	$1.95	Power, Ted	86T	108	$ .01	$ .03
Post, Wally	60T	13	$ .35	$1.10	Power, Ted	87T	437	$ .01	$ .03
Post, Wally	61T	378	$ .50	$2.00	Power, Ted	88T	236	$ .01	$ .03
Post, Wally	62T	148	$ .35	$1.10	Power, Ted	88TTR	89	$ .01	$ .05
Post, Wally	63T	462	$2.50	$6.50	Power, Ted	89T	777	$ .01	$ .04
Post, Wally	64T	253	$ .25	$ .85	Power, Ted	90T	59	$ .01	$ .03
Powell, "Boog" John	62T	99	$3.00	$11.00	Power, Vic	54T	52	$4.75	$14.00
Powell, Boog	63T	398	$1.75	$5.00	Power, Vic	55T	30	$1.35	$5.00
Powell, Boog	64T	89	$ .60	$1.75	Power, Vic	56T	67	$1.25	$4.50
Powell, Boog	65T	3	$5.00	$15.00	Power, Vic	57T	167	$ .95	$3.50
Powell, Boog	65T	560	$1.50	$6.00	Power, Vic	58T	406	$ .50	$2.00
Powell, Boog	66T	167	$ .50	$2.00	Power, Vic	59T	229	$ .50	$1.95
Powell, Boog	67T	230	$ .50	$1.95	Power, Vic	60T	75	$ .35	$1.10
Powell, Boog	67T	241	$1.50	$3.75	Power, Vic	61T	255	$ .30	$1.00
Powell, Boog	67T	243	$1.50	$3.75	Power, Vic	62T	445	$ .70	$2.10
Powell, Boog	67T	521	$ .60	$1.75	Power, Vic	63T	40	$ .25	$ .85
Powell, Boog	68T	381	$ .60	$1.75	Power, Vic	64T	355	$ .25	$ .85
Powell, Boog	69T	15	$ .15	$ .50	Power, Vic	65T	442	$ .30	$1.00
Powell, Boog	70T	64	$1.00	$3.50	Power, Vic	66T	192	$ .25	$ .85
Powell, Boog	70T	410	$ .60	$1.75	Powers, John	58T	432	$ .50	$2.00
Powell, Boog	70TAS	451	$ .35	$1.10	Powers, John	59T	489	$ .50	$1.95
Powell, Boog	71T	63	$ .15	$ .50	Powers, Johnny	60T	422	$ .50	$1.95
Powell, Boog	71T	700	$1.35	$4.00	Pramesa, John	52T	105	$6.00	$19.00
Powell, Boog	72T	250	$ .15	$ .50	Presko, Joe	52T	220	$6.00	$19.00
Powell, Boog	73T	325	$ .15	$ .50	Presko, Joe	54T	135	$2.00	$7.00
Powell, Boog	74T	460	$ .35	$1.10	Presley, Jim	85TTR	92	$ .35	$1.10
Powell, Boog	75T	208	$ .45	$1.75	Presley, Jim	86T	598	$ .04	$ .40
Powell, Boog	75T	625	$ .10	$ .35	Presley, Jim	87T	45	$ .01	$ .10
Powell, Boog	76T	45	$ .08	$ .30	Presley, Jim	88T	285	$ .01	$ .10
Powell, Boog	77T	206	$ .25	$ .85	Presley, Jim	88TBB	90	$ .01	$ .05
					Presley, Jim	89T	112	$ .01	$ .04
					Presley, Jim	89TBB	75	$ .01	$ .05
					Presley, Jim	90T	346	$ .01	$ .03
					Price, Jimmie	67T	123	$ .25	$ .65
					Price, Jimmie	68T	226	$ .25	$ .65
					Price, Jimmie	69T	472	$ .25	$ .65
					Price, Jimmie	70T	129	$ .10	$ .35
					Price, Jimmie	71T	444	$ .10	$ .35
					Price, Joe	81T	258	$ .01	$ .07
					Price, Joe	82T	492	$ .01	$ .06
					Price, Joe	83T	191	$ .01	$ .06
					Price, Joe	84T	686	$ .01	$ .05
					Price, Joe	85T	82	$ .01	$ .04
					Price, Joe	86T	523	$ .01	$ .03
					Price, Joe	87T	332	$ .01	$ .03
					Price, Joe	88T	786	$ .01	$ .03
					Price, Joe	89T	217	$ .01	$ .04
					Price, Joe	90T	473	$ .01	$ .03
					Priddy, Bob	64T	74	$ .25	$ .85
					Priddy, Bob	65T	482	$ .50	$2.00
					Priddy, Bob	66T	572	$4.50	$15.00
					Priddy, Bob	67T	26	$ .25	$ .65
					Priddy, Bob	68T	391	$ .25	$ .65
					Priddy, Bob	69T	248	$ .25	$ .85
					Priddy, Bob	70T	687	$ .50	$2.00
					Priddy, Bob	71T	147	$ .10	$ .35
					Priddy, Gerry (Jerry)	51Tbb	46	$5.50	$17.00
					Priddy, Jerry	52T	28	$14.00	$45.00
					Priddy, Jerry	53T	113	$3.75	$13.00
					Prince, Tom	89T	453	$ .01	$ .04
					Pritchard, Buddy	58T	151	$ .50	$2.00
					Proctor, Jim	60T	141	$ .35	$1.10
					Proly, Mike	79T	514	$ .02	$ .10
					Proly, Mike	80T	399	$ .01	$ .07
					Proly, Mike	81T	83	$ .01	$ .07
					Proly, Mike	81TTR	815	$ .02	$ .10
					Proly, Mike	82T	183	$ .01	$ .06
					Proly, Mike	82TTR	92	$ .02	$ .10
					Proly, Mike	83T	597	$ .01	$ .06
					Proly, Mike	84T	437	$ .01	$ .05
					Pruitt, Ron	77T	654	$ .05	$ .15
					Pruitt, Ron	78T	198	$ .02	$ .10
					Pruitt, Ron	79T	226	$ .02	$ .10
					Pruitt, Ron	80T	13	$ .01	$ .07
					Pruitt, Ron	81T	442	$ .01	$ .07

DENNIS POWELL

Player	Year	No.	VG	EX/MT
Powell, Dennis	87T	47	$ .01	$ .03
Powell, Dennis	88T	453	$ .01	$ .03
Powell, Dennis	89TTR	97	$ .01	$ .05
Powell, Grover	64T	113	$ .25	$ .85
Powell, Hosken	79T	656	$ .02	$ .10
Powell, Hosken	80T	471	$ .01	$ .07
Powell, Hosken	81T	137	$ .01	$ .07
Powell, Hosken	82T	584	$ .01	$ .06
Powell, Hosken	82TTR	91	$ .02	$ .10
Powell, Hosken	83T	77	$ .01	$ .06
Powell, Leroy	56T	144	$1.25	$4.50
Power, Ted	84T	554	$ .01	$ .05
Power, Ted	85T	342	$ .01	$ .04

Player	Year	No.	VG	EX/MT	Player	Year	No.	VG	EX/MT
Pryor, Greg	79T	559	$ .02	$ .10	Putnam, Pat	85T	535	$ .01	$ .04
Pryor, Greg	80T	164	$ .01	$ .07	Pyburn, Jim	57T	276	$3.50	$13.00
Pryor, Greg	81T	608	$ .01	$ .07	Pyznarski, Tim	87T	429	$ .01	$ .10
Pryor, Greg	82T	76	$ .01	$ .06	Qualls, Jim	69T	602	$ .25	$ .85
Pryor, Greg	82TTR	93	$ .02	$ .10	Qualls, Jim	70T	192	$ .10	$ .35
Pryor, Greg	83T	418	$ .01	$ .06	Qualls, Jim	71T	731	$ .70	$2.10
Pryor, Greg	84T	317	$ .01	$ .05	Qualters, Tom	54T	174	$2.00	$7.00
Pryor, Greg	85T	188	$ .01	$ .04	Qualters, Tom	55T	33	$1.35	$5.00
Pryor, Greg	86T	773	$ .01	$ .03	Qualters, Tom	58T	453	$ .50	$1.95
Pryor, Greg	87T	761	$ .01	$ .03	Qualters, Tom	59T	341	$ .50	$1.95
Puckett, Kirby	85T	536	$3.50	$14.00	Queen, Mel	64T	33	$ .25	$ .85
Puckett, Kirby	86T	329	$ .75	$3.00	Queen, Mel	66T	556	$3.50	$10.00
Puckett, Kirby	87T	450	$ .15	$ .75	Queen, Mel	67T	374	$ .25	$ .85
Puckett, Kirby	87TAS	611	$ .01	$ .10	Queen, Mel	68T	283	$ .25	$ .65
Puckett, Kirby	88T	120	$ .01	$ .20	Queen, Mel	69T	81	$ .25	$ .65
Puckett, Kirby	88TAS	391	$ .01	$ .10	Queen, Mel	71T	736	$ .70	$2.10
Puckett, Kirby	88TBB	36	$ .05	$ .30	Queen, Mel	72T	196	$ .10	$ .35
Puckett, Kirby	89T	650	$ .01	$ .15	Quilici, Frank	66T	207	$ .25	$ .85
Puckett, Kirby	89TAS	403	$ .01	$ .10	Quilici, Frank	68T	557	$ .30	$1.00
Puckett, Kirby	89TBB	167	$ .01	$ .25	Quilici, Frank	69T	356	$ .25	$ .65
Puckett, Kirby	90T	700	$ .01	$ .20	Quilici, Frank	70T	572	$ .25	$ .85
Puckett, Kirby	90TAS	391	$ .01	$ .10	Quilici, Frank	71T	141	$ .10	$ .35
Puhl, Terry	78T	553	$ .05	$ .20	Quilici, Frank	73T	49	$ .25	$ .65
Puhl, Terry	79T	617	$ .02	$ .10	Quilici, Frank	74T	447	$ .06	$ .25
Puhl, Terry	80T	147	$ .01	$ .07	Quinones, Luis	87T	362	$ .01	$ .10
Puhl, Terry	81T	411	$ .01	$ .07	Quinones, Luis	88T	667	$ .01	$ .03
Puhl, Terry	82T	277	$ .01	$ .06	Quinones, Luis	90T	176	$ .01	$ .03
Puhl, Terry	83T	39	$ .01	$ .06	Quinones, Rey	86TTR	89	$ .05	$ .20
Puhl, Terry	84T	383	$ .01	$ .05	Quinones (nez), Rey	87T	561	$ .01	$ .10
Puhl, Terry	85T	613	$ .01	$ .04	Quinones, Rey	88T	358	$ .01	$ .03
Puhl, Terry	86T	763	$ .01	$ .03	Quinones, Rey	89T	246	$ .01	$ .04
Puhl, Terry	87T	693	$ .01	$ .03	Quinones, Rey	89TTR	98	$ .01	$ .05
Puhl, Terry	88T	587	$ .01	$ .03	Quintana, Carlos	89T	704	$ .01	$ .30
Puhl, Terry	89T	119	$ .01	$ .04	Quintana, Carlos	89TBB	142	$ .01	$ .05
Puhl, Terry	90T	494	$ .01	$ .03	Quintana, Carlos	90T	18	$ .01	$ .10
Pujols, Luis	79T	139	$ .02	$ .10	Quirk, Art	62T	591	$8.00	$22.50
Pujols, Luis	81T	313	$ .01	$ .07	Quirk, Art	63T	522	$1.35	$4.00
Pujols, Luis	82T	582	$ .01	$ .06	Quirk, Jamie	76T	598	$ .05	$ .20
Pujols, Luis	83T	752	$ .01	$ .06	Quirk, Jamie	77T	463	$ .05	$ .15
Pujols, Luis	84T	446	$ .01	$ .05	Quirk, Jamie	78T	95	$ .02	$ .10
Puleo, Charlie	82TTR	94	$ .02	$ .10	Quirk, Jamie	79T	26	$ .02	$ .10
Puleo, Charlie	83T	549	$ .01	$ .06	Quirk, Jamie	80T	248	$ .01	$ .07
Puleo, Charlie	83TTR	88	$ .02	$ .10	Quirk, Jamie	81T	507	$ .01	$ .07
Puleo, Charlie	84T	273	$ .01	$ .05	Quirk, Jamie	82T	173	$ .01	$ .06
Puleo, Charlie	88T	179	$ .01	$ .03	Quirk, Jamie	83T	264	$ .01	$ .06
Puleo, Charlie	89T	728	$ .01	$ .04	Quirk, Jamie	83TTR	90	$ .02	$ .10
Pulido, Al	87T	642	$ .01	$ .03	Quirk, Jamie	84T	671	$ .01	$ .05
Purdin, John	65T	331	$ .30	$1.00	Quirk, Jamie	87T	354	$ .01	$ .03
Purdin, John	68T	336	$ .25	$ .65	Quirk, Jamie	88T	477	$ .01	$ .03
Purdin, John	69T	161	$ .25	$ .65	Quirk, Jamie	89T	702	$ .01	$ .04
Purdin, John	71T	748	$ .70	$2.10	Quisenberry, Dan	80T	667	$ .30	$1.25
Purkey, Bob	54T	202	$2.00	$7.00	Quisenberry, Dan	81T	8	$ .01	$ .07
Purkey, Bob	55T	118	$1.35	$5.00	Quisenberry, Dan	81T	493	$ .05	$ .25
Purkey, Bob	57T	368	$ .85	$3.50	Quisenberry, Dan	82T	264	$ .03	$ .15
Purkey, Bob	58T	311	$ .50	$2.00	Quisenberry, Dan	83T	155	$ .01	$ .10
Purkey, Bob	59T	506	$ .50	$1.95	Quisenberry, Dan	83T	708	$ .01	$ .06
Purkey, Bob	60T	4	$ .35	$1.10	Quisenberry, Dan	83TAS	396	$ .01	$ .06
Purkey, Bob	61T	9	$ .30	$1.00	Quisenberry, Dan	84T	3	$ .02	$ .10
Purkey, Bob	62T	120	$ .35	$1.10	Quisenberry, Dan	84T	138	$ .02	$ .10
Purkey, Bob	62T	263	$ .50	$2.00	Quisenberry, Dan	84T	570	$ .02	$ .10
Purkey, Bob	63T	5	$ .60	$1.75	Quisenberry, Dan	84T	718	$ .01	$ .05
Purkey, Bob	63T	7	$ .35	$1.10	Quisenberry, Dan	84TAS	407	$ .01	$ .05
Purkey, Bob	63T	350	$ .35	$1.20	Quisenberry, Dan	85T	270	$ .01	$ .04
Purkey, Bob	64T	480	$ .40	$1.25	Quisenberry, Dan	85TAS	711	$ .01	$ .04
Purkey, Bob	65T	214	$ .30	$1.00	Quisenberry, Dan	86T	50	$ .01	$ .03
Purkey, Bob	66T	551	$4.00	$11.50	Quisenberry, Dan	86TAS	722	$ .01	$ .03
Putnam, Eddy	80T	59	$ .01	$ .07	Quisenberry, Dan	87T	714	$ .01	$ .10
Putnam, Pat	78T	706	$ .02	$ .10	Quisenberry, Dan	88T	195	$ .01	$ .10
Putnam, Pat	79T	713	$ .05	$ .20	Quisenberry, Dan	89T	612	$ .01	$ .04
Putnam, Pat	80T	22	$ .01	$ .07	Quisenberry, Dan	90T	312	$ .01	$ .03
Putnam, Pat	81T	498	$ .01	$ .07	Rabb, John	84T	228	$ .01	$ .05
Putnam, Pat	82T	149	$ .01	$ .06	Rabb, John	85T	696	$ .01	$ .04
Putnam, Pat	83TTR	89	$ .02	$ .10	Rabe, Charley	58T	376	$ .50	$2.00
Putnam, Pat	84T	336	$ .01	$ .05	Radatz, Dick	62T	591	$8.00	$22.50
Putnam, Pat	84T	636	$ .01	$ .05	Radatz, Dick	63T	363	$ .35	$1.20

TOPPS

Player	Year	No.	VG	EX/MT	Player	Year	No.	VG	EX/MT
Radatz, Dick	64T	170	$ .25	$ .85	Rakow, Ed	65T	454	$ .50	$2.00
Radatz, Dick	65T	295	$ .30	$1.00	Ramazzotti, Bob	52T	184	$6.00	$19.00
Radatz, Dick	66T	475	$ .70	$2.10	Ramirez, Allan	84T	347	$ .01	$ .05
Radatz, Dick	67T	174	$ .25	$ .65	Ramirez, Mario	84T	94	$ .01	$ .05
Radatz, Dick	69T	663	$ .25	$ .85	Ramirez, Mario	85T	427	$ .01	$ .04
Rader, Dave	72T	232	$ .10	$ .35	Ramirez, Mario	86T	262	$ .01	$ .03
Rader, Dave	73T	121	$ .06	$ .25	Ramirez, Milt	71T	702	$ .70	$2.10
Rader, Dave	74T	213	$ .06	$ .25	Ramirez, Orlando	77T	131	$ .05	$ .15
Rader, Dave	75T	31	$ .06	$ .25	Ramirez, Rafael	81T	192	$ .05	$ .20
Rader, Dave	76T	54	$ .05	$ .20	Ramirez, Rafael	82T	536	$ .01	$ .06
Rader, Dave	77T	427	$ .05	$ .15	Ramirez, Rafael	83T	439	$ .01	$ .06
Rader, Dave	78T	563	$ .02	$ .10	Ramirez, Rafael	84T	234	$ .01	$ .05
Rader, Dave	79T	693	$ .02	$ .10	Ramirez, Rafael	85T	647	$ .01	$ .04
Rader, Dave	80T	296	$ .01	$ .07	Ramirez, Rafael	86T	107	$ .01	$ .03
Rader, Dave	81T	378	$ .01	$ .07	Ramirez, Rafael	87T	76	$ .01	$ .03
Rader, Doug	67T	412	$ .25	$ .85	Ramirez, Rafael	88T	379	$ .01	$ .03
Rader, Doug	68T	332	$ .25	$ .65	Ramirez, Rafael	88TTR	90	$ .01	$ .05
Rader, Doug	69T	119	$ .25	$ .65	Ramirez, Rafael	89T	749	$ .01	$ .04
Rader, Doug	70T	355	$ .10	$ .35	Ramirez, Rafael	89TBB	268	$ .01	$ .05
Rader, Doug	71T	425	$ .10	$ .35	Ramirez, Rafael	90T	558	$ .01	$ .03
Rader, Doug	72T	536	$ .25	$ .85	Ramos, Bobby	83TTR	93	$ .02	$ .10
Rader, Doug	73T	76	$ .06	$ .25	Ramos, Bobby	84T	32	$ .01	$ .05
Rader, Doug	74T	395	$ .06	$ .25	Ramos, Bobby	85T	407	$ .01	$ .04
Rader, Doug	75T	165	$ .06	$ .25	Ramos, Domingo	84T	194	$ .01	$ .05
Rader, Doug	76T	44	$ .05	$ .20	Ramos, Domingo	85T	349	$ .01	$ .04
Rader, Doug	76TTR	44	$ .05	$ .20	Ramos, Domingo	86T	462	$ .01	$ .03
Rader, Doug	77T	9	$ .05	$ .15	Ramos, Domingo	87T	641	$ .01	$ .03
Rader, Doug	78T	651	$ .02	$ .10	Ramos, Domingo	88T	206	$ .01	$ .03
Rader, Doug	83TTR	91	$ .02	$ .10	Ramos, Domingo	90T	37	$ .01	$ .03
Rader, Doug	84T	412	$ .01	$ .05	Ramos, Pedro	56T	49	$1.25	$4.50
Rader, Doug	85T	519	$ .01	$ .04	Ramos, Pedro	57T	326	$3.50	$13.00
Rader, Doug	89TTR	99	$ .01	$ .05	Ramos, Pedro	58T	331	$ .50	$2.00
Rader, Doug	90T	51	$ .01	$ .03	Ramos, Pedro	59T	78	$ .85	$3.50
Raffensberger, Ken	52T	118	$6.00	$19.00	Ramos, Pedro	59T	291	$ .50	$1.95
Raffensberger, Ken	53T	276	$11.00	$37.50	Ramos, Pedro	60T	175	$ .35	$1.10
Raffensberger, Ken	54T	46	$1.25	$5.00	Ramos, Pedro	61T	50	$ .50	$1.95
Ragland, Tom	72T	334	$ .10	$ .35	Ramos, Pedro	61T	528	$6.00	$18.00
Ragland, Tom	74T	441	$ .06	$ .25	Ramos, Pedro	62T	485	$ .70	$2.10
Raich, Eric	76T	484	$ .05	$ .20	Ramos, Pedro	63T	14	$ .25	$ .85
Raich, Eric	77T	62	$ .05	$ .15	Ramos, Pedro	64T	562	$1.50	$3.75
Raines, Larry	58T	243	$ .50	$2.00	Ramos, Pedro	65T	13	$ .25	$ .65
Raines, Tim	81T	479	$2.00	$8.00	Ramos, Pedro	66T	439	$ .25	$ .85
Raines, Tim	81TTR	816	$2.00	$7.00	Ramos, Pedro	67T	187	$ .25	$ .65
Raines, Tim	82T	70	$ .50	$2.00	Ramos, Roberto	81T	479	$2.00	$8.00
Raines, Tim	82T	164	$ .15	$ .25	Ramos, Roberto	82T	354	$ .01	$ .06
Raines, Tim	82THL	3	$ .05	$ .75	Ramsdell, Willard	52T	114	$6.00	$19.00
Raines, Tim	83T	595	$ .10	$ .75	Ramsey, Mike	81T	366	$ .01	$ .07
Raines, Tim	83T	704	$ .15	$ .75	Ramsey, Mike	82T	574	$ .01	$ .06
Raines, Tim	83TAS	403	$ .05	$ .25	Ramsey, Mike	83T	128	$ .01	$ .06
Raines, Tim	84T	134	$ .02	$ .10	Ramsey, Mike	84T	467	$ .01	$ .05
Raines, Tim	84T	370	$ .10	$ .50	Ramsey, Mike	85T	62	$ .01	$ .04
Raines, Tim	84TAS	390	$ .05	$ .25	Rand, Dick	58T	218	$ .50	$2.00
Raines, Tim	85T	630	$ .05	$ .25	Randall, Bob	77T	578	$ .05	$ .15
Raines, Tim	86T	280	$ .03	$ .25	Randall, Bob	78T	363	$ .02	$ .10
Raines, Tim	87T	30	$ .06	$ .25	Randall, Bob	79T	58	$ .02	$ .10
Raines, Tim	88T	720	$ .01	$ .15	Randall, Bob	80T	162	$ .01	$ .07
Raines, Tim	88TAS	403	$ .01	$ .10	Randle, Lenny	72T	737	$ .70	$2.10
Raines, Tim	88TBB	116	$ .01	$ .15	Randle, Lenny	73T	378	$ .06	$ .25
Raines, Tim "Rock"	89T	560	$ .01	$ .10	Randle, Len	74T	446	$ .06	$ .25
Raines, Rock	89TBB	73	$ .01	$ .15	Randle, Len	75T	259	$ .06	$ .25
Raines, Rock	90T	180	$ .01	$ .10	Randle, Len	76T	31	$ .05	$ .20
Rainey, Chuck	80T	662	$ .01	$ .07	Randle, Len	77T	196	$ .05	$ .15
Rainey, Chuck	81T	199	$ .01	$ .07	Randle, Len	78T	544	$ .02	$ .10
Rainey, Chuck	82T	522	$ .01	$ .06	Randle, Len	79T	454	$ .02	$ .10
Rainey, Chuck	83T	56	$ .01	$ .06	Randle, Lenny	81T	692	$ .01	$ .07
Rainey, Chuck	83TTR	92	$ .02	$ .10	Randle, Lenny	81TTR	817	$ .02	$ .10
Rainey, Chuck	84T	334	$ .01	$ .05	Randle, Lenny	82T	312	$ .01	$ .06
Rajsich, Dave	79T	710	$ .05	$ .20	Randolph, Willie	76T	592	$1.25	$3.75
Rajsich, Dave	80T	548	$ .01	$ .07	Randolph, Willie	76TTR	592	$ .30	$1.00
Rajsich, Gary	83T	317	$ .01	$ .06	Randolph, Willie	77T	359	$ .15	$ .50
Rakow, Ed	60T	551	$2.00	$7.00	Randolph, Willie	78T	620	$ .05	$ .20
Rakow, Ed	61T	147	$ .30	$1.00	Randolph, Willie	79T	250	$ .02	$ .10
Rakow, Ed	62T	342	$ .35	$1.10	Randolph, Willie	80T	460	$ .01	$ .07
Rakow, Ed	63T	82	$ .25	$ .85	Randolph, Willie	81T	60	$ .01	$ .07
Rakow, Ed	64T	491	$ .40	$1.25	Randolph, Willie	82T	569	$ .01	$ .06

Player	Year	No.	VG	EX/MT
Randolph, Willie	82TAS	548	$ .01	$ .06
Randolph, Willie	82TIA	570	$ .01	$ .06
Randolph, Willie	83T	140	$ .01	$ .06
Randolph, Willie	84T	360	$ .01	$ .05
Randolph, Willie	85T	765	$ .01	$ .04
Randolph, Willie	86T	455	$ .01	$ .03
Randolph, Willie	87T	701	$ .01	$ .03
Randolph, Willie	88T	210	$ .01	$ .03
Randolph, Willie	88TAS	387	$ .01	$ .03
Randolph, Willie	88TBB	76	$ .01	$ .05
Randolph, Willie	89T	635	$ .01	$ .04
Randolph, Willie	89TBB	244	$ .01	$ .05
Randolph, Willie	89TTR	100	$ .01	$ .05
Randolph, Willie	90T	25	$ .01	$ .03
Ranew, Merritt	62T	156	$ .35	$1.10
Ranew, Merritt	64T	78	$ .25	$ .85
Ranew, Merritt	66T	62	$ .30	$1.00
Rangers, Team	72T	668	$ .80	$2.50
Rangers, Team	73T	7	$ .30	$1.00
Rangers, Team	74T	184	$ .15	$ .50
Rangers, Team Checklist	75T	511	$ .15	$ .50
Rangers, Team Checklist	76T	172	$ .15	$ .50
Rangers, Team Checklist	77T	428	$ .15	$ .50
Rangers, Team Checklist	78T	659	$ .05	$ .25
Rangers, Team Checklist	79T	499	$ .05	$ .25
Rangers, Team Checklist	80T	41	$ .05	$ .25
Rangers, Team Checklist	81T	673	$ .02	$ .20
Rangers, Team Leaders	86T	666	$ .01	$ .03
Rangers, Team Leaders	87T	656	$ .01	$ .03
Rangers, Team Leaders	88T	201	$ .01	$ .03
Rangers, Team Leaders	89T	729	$ .01	$ .04
Rapp, Vern	78T	324	$ .02	$ .10
Rapp, Vern	84TTR	95	$ .02	$ .10
Rasmussen, Dennis	85T	691	$ .05	$ .25
Rasmussen, Dennis	86T	301	$ .01	$ .03
Rasmussen, Dennis	87T	555	$ .01	$ .03
Rasmussen, Dennis	88T	135	$ .01	$ .10
Rasmussen, Dennis	88TTR	91	$ .01	$ .05
Rasmussen, Dennis	89T	32	$ .01	$ .04
Rasmussen, Dennis	90T	449	$ .01	$ .03
Rasmussen, "Eric" Harry	76T	182	$ .05	$ .20
Rasmussen, Eric	77T	404	$ .05	$ .15
Rasmussen, Eric	78T	281	$ .02	$ .10
Rasmussen, Eric	79T	57	$ .02	$ .10
Rasmussen, Eric	80T	531	$ .01	$ .07
Rasmussen, Eric	81T	342	$ .01	$ .07
Rasmussen, Eric	83T	594	$ .01	$ .06
Rasmussen, Eric	84T	724	$ .01	$ .05
Ratliff, Gene	65T	553	$1.50	$3.75
Ratliff, Paul	63T	549	$1.50	$3.75
Ratliff, Paul	70T	267	$ .10	$ .35
Ratliff, Paul	71T	607	$ .30	$1.00
Rau, Doug	73T	602	$ .35	$1.10
Rau, Doug	74T	64	$ .06	$ .25
Rau, Doug	75T	269	$ .06	$ .25
Rau, Doug	76T	124	$ .05	$ .20
Rau, Doug	77T	421	$ .05	$ .15
Rau, Doug	78T	641	$ .02	$ .10
Rau, Doug	79T	347	$ .02	$ .10
Rau, Doug	80T	527	$ .01	$ .07
Rau, Doug	81T	174	$ .01	$ .07
Rau, Doug	81TTR	818	$ .02	$ .10
Rautzhan, Lance	78T	709	$ .02	$ .10
Rautzhan, Lance	79T	373	$ .02	$ .10
Rawley, Shane	79T	74	$ .20	$ .75
Rawley, Shane	80T	723	$ .01	$ .07
Rawley, Shane	81T	423	$ .01	$ .07
Rawley, Shane	82T	197	$ .01	$ .06
Rawley, Shane	82TTR	95	$ .02	$ .10
Rawley, Shane	83T	592	$ .01	$ .06
Rawley, Shane	84T	254	$ .01	$ .05
Rawley, Shane	85T	636	$ .01	$ .04
Rawley, Shane	86T	361	$ .01	$ .03
Rawley, Shane	87T	771	$ .01	$ .03
Rawley, Shane	88T	66	$ .01	$ .03

Player	Year	No.	VG	EX/MT
Rawley, Shane	88TAS	406	$ .01	$ .03

Player	Year	No.	VG	EX/MT
Rawley, Shane	89T	494	$ .01	$ .04
Rawley, Shane	89TTR	101	$ .01	$ .05
Rawley, Shane	90T	101	$ .01	$ .03
Ray, Jim	68T	539	$ .30	$1.00
Ray, Jim	69T	257	$ .25	$ .85
Ray, Jim	70T	113	$ .10	$ .35
Ray, Jim	71T	242	$ .10	$ .35
Ray, Jim	72T	603	$ .25	$ .85
Ray, Jim	73T	313	$ .06	$ .25
Ray, Jim	74T	458	$ .06	$ .25
Ray, Jim	74TTR	458	$ .06	$ .25
Ray, Jim	75T	89	$ .06	$ .25
Ray, Johnny	82T	291	$ .25	$1.00
Ray, Johnny	82TTR	96	$ .25	$1.00
Ray, Johnnie (y)	83T	149	$ .03	$ .15
Ray, Johnny	84T	537	$ .02	$ .10
Ray, Johnny	84TAS	387	$ .01	$ .05
Ray, Johnny	85T	96	$ .01	$ .10
Ray, Johnny	86T	615	$ .01	$ .10
Ray, Johnny	87T	747	$ .01	$ .03
Ray, Johnny	88T	115	$ .01	$ .03
Ray, Johnny	88TBB	97	$ .01	$ .05
Ray, Johnny	89T	455	$ .01	$ .04
Ray, Johnny	89TBB	7	$ .01	$ .05
Ray, Johnny	90T	334	$ .01	$ .03
Raydon, Curt	59T	305	$ .50	$1.95
Raydon, Curt	60T	49	$ .35	$1.10
Rayford, Floyd	81T	399	$ .35	$1.10
Rayford, Floyd	83T	192	$ .01	$ .06
Rayford, Floyd	84T	514	$ .01	$ .05
Rayford, Floyd	84TTR	96	$ .02	$ .10
Rayford, Floyd	85T	341	$ .01	$ .04
Rayford, Floyd	86T	623	$ .01	$ .03
Rayford, Floyd	87T	426	$ .01	$ .03
Rayford, Floyd	88T	296	$ .01	$ .03
Raymond, Claude	63T	519	$1.50	$3.75
Raymond, Claude	64T	504	$ .40	$1.25
Raymond, Claude	65T	48	$ .25	$ .65
Raymond, Claude	66T	586	$4.50	$15.00
Raymond, Claude	67T	364	$ .25	$ .65
Raymond, Claude	68T	166	$ .25	$ .65
Raymond, Claude	69T	446	$ .25	$ .65

TOPPS

Player	Year	No.	VG	EX/MT
Raymond, Claude	70T	268	$ .10	$ .35
Raymond, Claude	71T	536	$ .30	$1.00
Ready, Randy	84TTR	97	$ .02	$ .10
Ready, Randy	86T	209	$ .01	$ .03
Ready, Randy	87TTR	97	$ .01	$ .07
Ready, Randy	88T	426	$ .01	$ .03
Ready, Randy	88TBB	102	$ .01	$ .05
Ready, Randy	89T	551	$ .01	$ .04
Ready, Randy	89TTR	102	$ .01	$ .05
Ready, Randy	90T	356	$ .01	$ .03

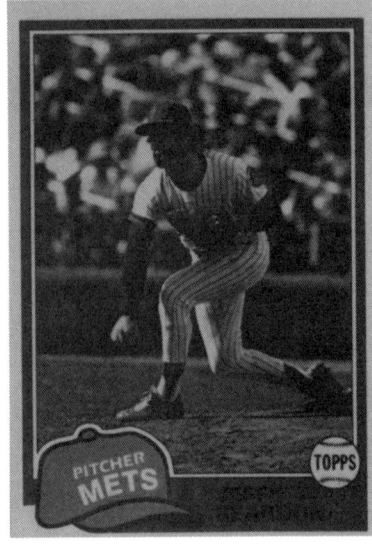

Player	Year	No.	VG	EX/MT
Reardon, Jeff	81T	456	$ .25	$1.25
Reardon, Jeff	81TTR	819	$ .15	$ .75
Reardon, Jeff	82T	667	$ .05	$ .35
Reardon, Jeff	83T	290	$ .01	$ .15
Reardon, Jeff	84T	595	$ .01	$ .10
Reardon, Jeff	85T	375	$ .01	$ .04
Reardon, Jeff	86T	35	$ .01	$ .03
Reardon, Jeff	86TAS	711	$ .01	$ .03
Reardon, Jeff	87T	165	$ .01	$ .03
Reardon, Jeff	87TTR	98	$ .01	$ .07
Reardon, Jeff	88T	425	$ .01	$ .03
Reardon, Jeff	88TBB	10	$ .01	$ .05
Reardon, Jeff	89T	775	$ .01	$ .04
Reardon, Jeff	90T	235	$ .01	$ .03
Reberger, Frank	69T	637	$ .25	$ .85
Reberger, Frank	70T	103	$ .10	$ .35
Reberger, Frank	71T	251	$ .10	$ .35
Reberger, Frank	72T	548	$ .25	$ .85
Red Sox, Team	56T	111	$3.50	$12.50
Red Sox, Team	57T	171	$1.50	$6.00
Red Sox, Team	58T	312	$2.50	$7.50
Red Sox, Team	59T	248	$2.50	$7.50
Red Sox, Team	60T	537	$6.00	$18.00
Red Sox, Team	61T	373	$1.35	$4.00
Red Sox, Team	62T	334	$1.25	$4.50
Red Sox, Team	63T	202	$ .50	$1.95
Red Sox, Team	64T	579	$3.50	$10.00
Red Sox, Team	65T	403	$ .60	$1.75
Red Sox, Team	66T	259	$ .65	$1.75
Red Sox, Team	67T	604	$15.00	$75.00
Red Sox, Team	70T	563	$ .60	$1.75
Red Sox, Team	71T	386	$ .35	$1.10
Red Sox, Team	72T	328	$ .30	$1.00

Player	Year	No.	VG	EX/MT
Red Sox, Team	73T	596	$ .60	$1.75
Red Sox, Team	74T	567	$ .30	$1.00
Red Sox, Team Checklist	75T	172	$ .35	$1.10
Red Sox, Team Checklist	76T	118	$ .15	$ .50
Red Sox, Team Checklist	77T	309	$ .30	$1.00
Red Sox, Team Checklist	78T	424	$ .10	$ .35
Red Sox, Team Checklist	79T	214	$ .08	$ .30
Red Sox, Team Checklist	80T	689	$ .06	$ .30
Red Sox, Team Checklist	81T	662	$ .02	$ .20
Red Sox, Team Leaders	86T	396	$ .01	$ .03
Red Sox, Team Leaders	87T	306	$ .01	$ .03
Red Sox, Team Leaders	88T	21	$ .01	$ .03
Red Sox, Team Leaders	89T	321	$ .01	$ .04
Redfern, Pete	77T	249	$ .05	$ .15
Redfern, Pete	78T	81	$ .02	$ .10
Redfern, Pete	79T	113	$ .02	$ .10
Redfern, Pete	80T	403	$ .01	$ .07
Redfern, Pete	81T	714	$ .01	$ .07
Redfern, Pete	82T	309	$ .01	$ .06
Redfern, Pete	83T	559	$ .01	$ .06
Redlegs, Team	56T	90	$4.50	$15.00
Redmond, Wayne	71T	728	$ .70	$2.10
Reds, Team	57T	322	$13.00	$40.00
Reds, Team	58T	428	$3.00	$9.00
Reds, Team	59T	111	$2.55	$8.50
Reds, Team	60T	164	$2.50	$8.00
Reds, Team	61T	249	$1.25	$4.50
Reds, Team	62T	465	$1.35	$4.00
Reds, Team	63T	63	$ .85	$3.50
Reds, Team	64T	403	$ .30	$2.50
Reds, Team	65T	316	$ .70	$2.00
Reds, Team	66T	59	$ .85	$3.50
Reds, Team	67T	407	$ .75	$2.00
Reds, Team	68T	574	$ .50	$2.50
Reds, Team	70T	544	$ .60	$1.75
Reds, Team	71T	357	$ .50	$2.00
Reds, Team	72T	651	$ .60	$1.75
Reds, Team	73T	641	$ .65	$2.00
Reds, Team	74T	459	$ .35	$1.10
Reds, Team Checklist	75T	531	$ .50	$2.00
Reds, Team Checklist	76T	104	$ .50	$1.95
Reds, Team Checklist	77T	287	$ .30	$1.00
Reds, Team Checklist	78T	526	$ .10	$ .35
Reds, Team Checklist	79T	259	$ .10	$ .35
Reds, Team Checklist	80T	606	$ .10	$ .35
Reds, Team Checklist	81T	677	$ .02	$ .20
Reds, Team Leaders	86T	366	$ .01	$ .03
Reds, Team Leaders	87T	281	$ .01	$ .03
Reds, Team Leaders	88T	81	$ .01	$ .03
Reds, Team Leaders	89T	111	$ .01	$ .04
Redus, Gary	83TTR	94	$ .02	$ .10
Redus, Gary	84T	475	$ .03	$ .15
Redus, Gary	85T	146	$ .01	$ .04
Redus, Gary	86T	342	$ .01	$ .03
Redus, Gary	86TTR	90	$ .02	$ .10
Redus, Gary	87T	42	$ .01	$ .03
Redus, Gary	87TTR	99	$ .01	$ .07
Redus, Gary	88T	657	$ .01	$ .03
Redus, Gary	89T	281	$ .01	$ .04
Redus, Gary	89TBB	131	$ .01	$ .05
Redus, Gary	90T	507	$ .01	$ .03
Reed, Bob	70T	207	$ .10	$ .35
Reed, Bob	71T	732	$ .70	$2.10
Reed, Howie	65T	544	$1.50	$3.75
Reed, Howie	66T	387	$ .25	$ .85
Reed, Howie	70T	548	$ .25	$ .85
Reed, Howie	71T	398	$ .10	$ .35
Reed, Jeff	87T	247	$ .01	$ .03
Reed, Jeff	87TTR	100	$ .01	$ .07
Reed, Jeff	88T	176	$ .01	$ .03
Reed, Jeff	89T	626	$ .01	$ .04
Reed, Jeff	89TBB	158	$ .01	$ .05
Reed, Jeff	90T	772	$ .01	$ .03
Reed, Jerry	86T	172	$ .01	$ .03
Reed, Jerry	87T	619	$ .01	$ .03

Player	Year	No.	VG	EX/MT	Player	Year	No.	VG	EX/MT
Reed, Jerry	88T	332	$ .01	$ .03	Reitz, Ken	81T	441	$ .01	$ .07
Reed, Jerry	89T	441	$ .01	$ .04	Reitz, Ken	81TTR	820	$ .02	$ .10
Reed, Jerry	90T	247	$ .01	$ .03	Reitz, Ken	82T	245	$ .01	$ .06
Reed, Jody	88T	152	$ .01	$ .35	Remmerswaal, Win	81T	38	$ .01	$ .07
Reed, Jody	88TBB	202	$ .01	$ .15	Remy, Jerry	76T	229	$ .05	$ .20
Reed, Jody	89T	734	$ .01	$ .15	Remy, Jerry	77T	342	$ .05	$ .15
Reed, Jody	89TBB	97	$ .01	$ .05	Remy, Jerry	78T	478	$ .02	$ .10
Reed, Jody	90T	96	$ .01	$ .03	Remy, Jerry	79T	618	$ .02	$ .10
Reed, Ron	68T	76	$ .25	$ .65	Remy, Jerry	80T	155	$ .01	$ .07
Reed, Ron	69T	177	$ .25	$ .65	Remy, Jerry	81T	549	$ .01	$ .07
Reed, Ron	70T	546	$ .10	$ .35	Remy, Jerry	82T	25	$ .01	$ .06
Reed, Ron	71T	359	$ .10	$ .35	Remy, Jerry	83T	295	$ .01	$ .06
Reed, Ron	72T	787	$1.35	$4.00	Remy, Jerry	84T	445	$ .01	$ .05
Reed, Ron	73T	72	$ .06	$ .25	Remy, Jerry	85T	761	$ .01	$ .04
Reed, Ron	74T	346	$ .06	$ .25	Renick, Rick	68T	301	$ .25	$ .65
Reed, Ron	75T	81	$ .06	$ .25	Renick, Rick	70T	93	$ .10	$ .35
Reed, Ron	76T	58	$ .05	$ .20	Renick, Rick	71T	694	$ .70	$2.10
Reed, Ron	76TTR	58	$ .05	$ .20	Renick, Rick	72T	459	$ .10	$ .35
Reed, Ron	77T	243	$ .05	$ .15	Reniff, Hal	62T	139	$3.00	$9.00
Reed, Ron	78T	472	$ .02	$ .10	Reniff, Hal	62T	159	$ .60	$1.75
Reed, Ron	79T	177	$ .02	$ .10	Reniff, Hal	63T	546	$1.50	$3.75
Reed, Ron	80T	609	$ .01	$ .07	Reniff, Hal	64T	36	$ .25	$ .85
Reed, Ron	81T	376	$ .01	$ .07	Reniff, Hal	65T	413	$ .30	$1.00
Reed, Ron	82T	581	$ .01	$ .06	Reniff, Hal	66T	68	$ .25	$ .85
Reed, Ron	83T	728	$ .01	$ .06	Reniff, Hal	67T	201	$ .25	$ .65
Reed, Ron	84T	43	$ .01	$ .05	Renko, Steve	70T	87	$ .10	$ .35
Reed, Ron	84TTR	98	$ .02	$ .10	Renko, Steve	71T	209	$ .10	$ .35
Reed, Ron	85T	221	$ .01	$ .04	Renko, Steve	72T	307	$ .10	$ .35
Reese, Dick	65T	597	$1.50	$3.75	Renko, Steve	72TIA	308	$ .10	$ .35
Reese, Jimmie	73T	421	$ .06	$ .25	Renko, Steve	73T	623	$ .55	$1.75
Reese, Jimmie	74T	276	$ .06	$ .25	Renko, Steve	74T	49	$ .06	$ .25
Reese, Pee Wee	52T	333	$250.00	$750.00	Renko, Steve	75T	34	$ .06	$ .25
Reese, Pee Wee	53T	76	$40.00	$160.00	Renko, Steve	76T	264	$ .05	$ .20
Reese, Pee Wee	56T	260	$30.00	$90.00	Renko, Steve	77T	586	$ .05	$ .15
Reese, Pee Wee	57T	30	$25.00	$70.00	Renko, Steve	78T	493	$ .02	$ .10
Reese, Pee Wee	58T	375	$10.00	$40.00	Renko, Steve	79T	352	$ .02	$ .10
Reese, Rich	67T	486	$ .50	$2.00	Renko, Steve	80T	184	$ .01	$ .07
Reese, Rich	68T	111	$ .25	$ .65	Renko, Steve	81T	63	$ .01	$ .07
Reese, Rich	69T	56	$ .25	$ .65	Renko, Steve	81TTR	821	$ .02	$ .10
Reese, Rich	70T	404	$ .10	$ .35	Renko, Steve	82T	702	$ .01	$ .06
Reese, Rich	71T	349	$ .10	$ .35	Renko, Steve	83T	236	$ .01	$ .06
Reese, Rich	72T	611	$ .25	$ .85	Renko, Steve	83TTR	95	$ .02	$ .10
Regan, Phil	61T	439	$ .50	$2.00	Renko, Steve	84T	444	$ .01	$ .05
Regan, Phil	62T	366	$ .35	$1.10	Renna, Bill	54T	112	$2.00	$7.00
Regan, Phil	63T	494	$2.50	$6.50	Renna, Bill	55T	121	$1.35	$5.00
Regan, Phil	64T	535	$1.50	$3.75	Renna, Bill	56T	82	$1.25	$4.50
Regan, Phil	65T	191	$ .25	$ .65	Renna, Bill	58T	473	$ .50	$1.95
Regan, Phil	66T	347	$ .25	$ .85	Renna, Bill	59T	72	$ .85	$3.50
Regan, Phil	67T	130	$ .25	$ .65	Renteria, Rich	89TBB	109	$ .01	$ .05
Regan, Phil	68T	88	$ .25	$ .65	Replogle, Andy	79T	427	$ .02	$ .10
Regan, Phil	69T	535	$ .25	$ .85	Repoz, Roger	66T	138	$ .25	$ .85
Regan, Phil	70T	334	$ .10	$ .35	Repoz, Roger	67T	416	$ .25	$ .85
Regan, Phil	71T	634	$ .30	$1.00	Repoz, Roger	68T	587	$ .30	$1.00
Regan, Phil	72T	485	$ .10	$ .35	Repoz, Roger	69T	103	$ .25	$ .65
Reichardt, Rick	65T	194	$ .25	$ .65	Repoz, Roger	70T	397	$ .10	$ .35
Reichardt, Rick	66T	321	$ .25	$ .85	Repoz, Roger	71T	508	$ .10	$ .35
Reichardt, Rick	67T	40	$ .25	$ .65	Repoz, Roger	72T	541	$ .25	$ .85
Reichardt, Rick	68T	570	$ .30	$1.00	Repulski, Rip	53T	172	$3.75	$13.00
Reichardt, Rick	69T	205	$ .25	$ .65	Repulski, Rip	54T	115	$2.00	$7.00
Reichardt, Rick	70T	720	$1.25	$3.75	Repulski, Rip	55T	55	$1.35	$5.00
Reichardt, Rick	71T	643	$ .30	$1.00	Repulski, Rip	56T	201	$2.50	$8.00
Reid, Scott	70T	56	$ .10	$ .35	Repulski, Rip	57T	245	$ .95	$3.50
Reid, Scott	71T	439	$ .60	$2.00	Repulski, Rip	58T	14	$ .85	$3.50
Reiser, Pete	52T	189	$10.00	$30.00	Repulski, Rip	59T	195	$ .50	$1.95
Reiser, Pete	60T	463	$ .85	$2.25	Repulski, Rip	60T	265	$ .35	$1.10
Reiser, Pete	73T	81	$ .25	$ .85	Repulski, Rip	61T	128	$ .30	$1.00
Reitz, Ken	73T	603	$ .35	$1.10	Rettenmund, Merv	69T	66	$ .25	$ .65
Reitz, Ken	74T	372	$ .06	$ .25	Rettenmund, Merv	70T	629	$ .25	$ .85
Reitz, Ken	75T	27	$ .06	$ .25	Rettenmund, Merv	71T	393	$ .10	$ .35
Reitz, Ken	76T	158	$ .05	$ .20	Rettenmund, Merv	72T	86	$ .30	$1.00
Reitz, Ken	76TTR	158	$ .05	$ .20	Rettenmund, Merv	72T	235	$ .10	$ .35
Reitz, Ken	77T	297	$ .05	$ .15	Rettenmund, Merv	73T	56	$ .06	$ .25
Reitz, Ken	78T	692	$ .02	$ .10	Rettenmund, Merv	74T	585	$ .06	$ .25
Reitz, Ken	79T	587	$ .02	$ .10	Rettenmund, Merv	74TTR	585	$ .06	$ .25
Reitz, Ken	80T	182	$ .01	$ .07	Rettenmund, Merv	75T	369	$ .06	$ .25

TOPPS

Player	Year	No.	VG	EX/MT	Player	Year	No.	VG	EX/MT
Rettenmund, Merv	76T	283	$ .05	$ .20	Reynolds, Craig	79T	482	$ .02	$ .10
Rettenmund, Merv	77T	659	$ .05	$ .15	Reynolds, Craig	80T	129	$ .01	$ .07
Rettenmund, Merv	78T	566	$ .02	$ .10	Reynolds, Craig	81T	617	$ .01	$ .07
Rettenmund, Merv	79T	48	$ .02	$ .10	Reynolds, Craig	82T	57	$ .01	$ .06
Rettenmund, Merv	80T	402	$ .01	$ .07	Reynolds, Craig	83T	328	$ .01	$ .06
Retzer, Ken	62T	594	$35.00	$125.00	Reynolds, Craig	84T	776	$ .01	$ .05
Retzer, Ken	63T	471	$2.50	$6.50	Reynolds, Craig	85T	156	$ .01	$ .04
Retzer, Ken	64T	277	$ .25	$ .85	Reynolds, Craig	86T	298	$ .01	$ .03
Retzer, Ken	65T	278	$ .30	$1.00	Reynolds, Craig	87T	779	$ .01	$ .03
Reuschel, Paul	77T	333	$ .05	$ .15	Reynolds, Craig	88T	557	$ .01	$ .03
Reuschel, Paul	77T	634	$ .05	$ .25	Reynolds, Craig	88TBB	219	$ .01	$ .05
Reuschel, Paul	78T	663	$ .02	$ .10	Reynolds, Craig	89T	428	$ .01	$ .04
Reuschel, Paul	79T	511	$ .02	$ .10	Reynolds, Craig	89TBB	312	$ .01	$ .05
Reuschel, Rick	73T	482	$1.25	$3.75	Reynolds, Craig	90T	637	$ .01	$ .03
Reuschel, Rick	74T	136	$ .35	$1.10	Reynolds, Don	79T	292	$ .02	$ .10
Reuschel, Rick	75T	153	$ .10	$ .35	Reynolds, Harold	86T	769	$ .01	$ .50
Reuschel, Rick	76T	359	$ .10	$ .35	Reynolds, Harold	87T	91	$ .01	$ .10
Reuschel, Rick	77T	530	$ .05	$ .25	Reynolds, Harold	88T	485	$ .01	$ .03
Reuschel, Rick	77T	634	$ .05	$ .25	Reynolds, Harold	88TBB	142	$ .01	$ .05
Reuschel, Rick	78T	50	$ .05	$ .25	Reynolds, Harold	89T	580	$ .01	$ .04
Reuschel, Rick	79T	240	$ .02	$ .10	Reynolds, Harold	89TBB	2	$ .01	$ .10
Reuschel, Rick	80T	175	$ .01	$ .07	Reynolds, Harold	90T	161	$ .01	$ .03
Reuschel, Rick	81T	645	$ .01	$ .07	Reynolds, Ken	71T	664	$ .70	$2.10
Reuschel, Rick	81TTR	822	$ .02	$ .10	Reynolds, Ken	72T	252	$ .10	$ .35
Reuschel, Rick	82T	405	$ .01	$ .06	Reynolds, Ken	73T	638	$ .35	$1.10
Reuschel, Rick	85T	306	$ .01	$ .04	Reynolds, R. J.	85T	369	$ .03	$ .15
Reuschel, Rick	85TTR	93	$ .02	$ .10	Reynolds, R. J.	86T	417	$ .01	$ .03
Reuschel, Rick	86T	779	$ .01	$ .03	Reynolds, R. J.	87T	109	$ .01	$ .03
Reuschel, Rick	87T	521	$ .01	$ .03	Reynolds, R. J.	88T	27	$ .01	$ .03
Reuschel, Rick	88T	660	$ .01	$ .03	Reynolds, R. J.	89T	658	$ .01	$ .04
Reuschel, Rick	88TBB	188	$ .01	$ .10	Reynolds, R. J.	90T	592	$ .01	$ .03
Reuschel, Rick	89T	65	$ .01	$ .04	Reynolds, Ronn	86T	649	$ .01	$ .03
Reuschel, Rick	90T	190	$ .01	$ .03	Reynolds, Ronn	87T	471	$ .01	$ .03
Reuss, Jerry	70T	96	$ .50	$2.00	Reynolds, Tom	64T	528	$1.50	$3.75
Reuss, Jerry	71T	158	$ .30	$1.00	Reynolds, Tom	65T	333	$ .30	$1.00
Reuss, Jerry	72T	775	$ .85	$3.50	Reynolds, Tom	67T	487	$ .50	$2.00
Reuss, Jerry	73T	446	$ .25	$ .65	Reynolds, Tom	69T	467	$ .25	$ .65
Reuss, Jerry	74T	116	$ .06	$ .25	Reynolds, Tommie	70T	259	$ .10	$ .35
Reuss, Jerry	75T	124	$ .10	$ .35	Reynolds, Tommie	71T	676	$ .70	$2.10
Reuss, Jerry	76T	60	$ .06	$ .25	Rhoden, Rick	75T	618	$ .60	$1.75
Reuss, Jerry	77T	645	$ .05	$ .15					
Reuss, Jerry	78T	255	$ .02	$ .10					
Reuss, Jerry	79T	536	$ .02	$ .10					
Reuss, Jerry	80T	318	$ .01	$ .07					
Reuss, Jerry	81T	440	$ .01	$ .07					
Reuss, Jerry	82T	710	$ .01	$ .06					
Reuss, Jerry	83T	90	$ .01	$ .06					
Reuss, Jerry	84T	170	$ .01	$ .05					
Reuss, Jerry	85T	680	$ .01	$ .04					
Reuss, Jerry	86T	577	$ .01	$ .03					
Reuss, Jerry	87T	682	$ .01	$ .03					
Reuss, Jerry	88T	216	$ .01	$ .03					
Reuss, Jerry	89T	357	$ .01	$ .04					
Reuss, Jerry	90T	424	$ .01	$ .03					
Revering, Dave	78T	706	$ .02	$ .10					
Revering, Dave	79T	224	$ .02	$ .10					
Revering, Dave	80T	438	$ .01	$ .07					
Revering, Dave	81T	568	$ .01	$ .07					
Revering, Dave	81TTR	823	$ .02	$ .10					
Revering, Dave	82T	109	$ .01	$ .06					
Revering, Dave	82TTR	97	$ .02	$ .10					
Revering, Dave	83T	677	$ .01	$ .06					
Reynolds, Allie	51Trb	6	$3.00	$12.00					
Reynolds, Allie	52T	67	$27.50	$77.50					
Reynolds, Allie	53T	141	$7.50	$22.50					
Reynolds, Archie	71T	664	$ .70	$2.10					
Reynolds, Archie	72T	672	$ .70	$2.10					
Reynolds, Bob	71T	664	$ .70	$2.10					
Reynolds, Bob	72T	162	$ .25	$ .75					
Reynolds, Bob	73T	612	$ .35	$1.10					
Reynolds, Bob	74T	259	$ .06	$ .25					
Reynolds, Bob	75T	142	$ .06	$ .25					
Reynolds, Craig	76T	596	$ .10	$ .35	Rhoden, Rick	76T	439	$ .25	$ .65
Reynolds, Craig	77T	474	$ .05	$ .15	Rhoden, Rick	77T	245	$ .05	$ .15
Reynolds, Craig	78T	199	$ .02	$ .10	Rhoden, Rick	78T	605	$ .02	$ .10

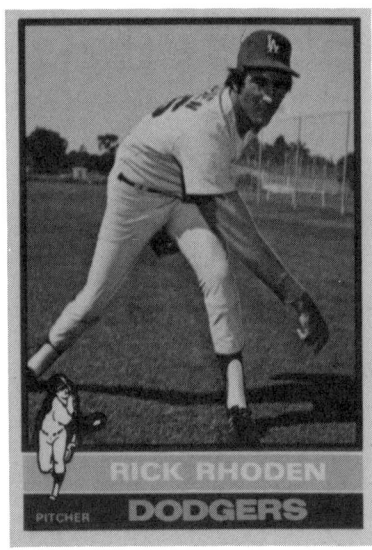

RICK RHODEN
PITCHER DODGERS

Player	Year	No.	VG	EX/MT	Player	Year	No.	VG	EX/MT
Rhoden, Rick	79T	145	$ .02	$ .10	Richard, J. R.	80T	207	$ .02	$ .10
Rhoden, Rick	80T	92	$ .01	$ .07	Richard, J. R.	80T	50	$ .01	$ .07
Rhoden, Rick	81T	312	$ .01	$ .07	Richard, J. R.	81T	350	$ .01	$ .07
Rhoden, Rick	82T	513	$ .01	$ .06	Richard, J. R.	82T	190	$ .01	$ .06
Rhoden, Rick	83T	781	$ .01	$ .06	Richard, Lee	72T	476	$ .10	$ .35
Rhoden, Rick	84T	485	$ .01	$ .05	Richard, Lee	75T	653	$ .06	$ .25
Rhoden, Rick	84T	696	$ .01	$ .05	Richard, Lee	76T	533	$ .05	$ .20
Rhoden, Rick	85T	695	$ .01	$ .04	Richards, Gene	77T	473	$9.00	$35.00
Rhoden, Rick	86T	232	$ .01	$ .03	Richards, Gene	78T	292	$ .02	$ .10
Rhoden, Rick	87T	365	$ .01	$ .03	Richards, Gene	79T	364	$ .02	$ .10
Rhoden, Rick	87TTR	101	$ .01	$ .07	Richards, Gene	80T	616	$ .01	$ .07
Rhoden, Rick	88T	185	$ .01	$ .03	Richards, Gene	81T	171	$ .01	$ .07
Rhoden, Rick	88TBB	108	$ .01	$ .05	Richards, Gene	82T	708	$ .01	$ .06
Rhoden, Rick	89T	18	$ .01	$ .04	Richards, Gene	83T	7	$ .01	$ .06
Rhoden, Rick	89TBB	237	$ .01	$ .05	Richards, Gene	84T	594	$ .01	$ .05
Rhoden, Rick	90T	588	$ .01	$ .03	Richards, Gene	84TTR	99	$ .02	$ .10
Rhodes, "Dusty" Jim	54T	170	$2.00	$7.00	Richards, Gene	85T	434	$ .01	$ .04
Rhodes, Dusty	55T	1	$5.00	$35.00	Richards, Paul	52T	305	$14.00	$40.00
Rhodes, Dusty	56T	50	$1.25	$3.50	Richards, Paul	60T	224	$ .35	$1.10
Rhodes, Dusty	57T	61	$ .95	$3.50	Richards, Paul	61T	131	$ .30	$1.00
Ribant, Dennis	65T	73	$ .25	$ .65	Richards, Paul	61TAS	566	$5.50	$16.50
Ribant, Dennis	66T	241	$ .25	$ .85	Richards, Rusty	89TMLD	99	$ .01	$ .05
Ribant, Dennis	67T	527	$ .50	$2.00	Richardson, Bobby	57T	286	$20.00	$80.00
Ribant, Dennis	69T	463	$ .25	$ .65	Richardson, Bobby	58T	101	$2.50	$10.00
Ribant, Denny	68T	326	$ .25	$ .65	Richardson, Bobby	59T	76	$3.00	$9.00
Riccelli, Frank	74T	599	$ .15	$ .50	Richardson, Bobby	59T	237	$ .60	$1.75
Riccelli, Frank	80T	247	$ .01	$ .07	Richardson, Bobby	60T	405	$1.50	$6.00
Rice, Del	52T	100	$6.00	$19.00	Richardson, Bobby	61T	180	$1.75	$5.00
Rice, Del	53T	68	$4.50	$15.00	Richardson, Bobby	62T	65	$1.35	$4.00
Rice, Del	57T	193	$ .95	$3.50	Richardson, Bobby	63T	173	$7.50	$30.00
Rice, Del	58T	51	$ .85	$3.50	Richardson, Bobby	63T	420	$1.50	$5.00
Rice, Del	59T	104	$ .85	$3.50	Richardson, Bobby	64T	190	$1.00	$4.00
Rice, Del	60T	248	$ .35	$1.10	Richardson, Bobby	65T	115	$1.00	$4.00
Rice, Del	61T	448	$ .50	$2.00	Richardson, Bobby	66T	490	$3.00	$12.00
Rice, Del	72T	718	$ .70	$2.10	Richardson, Gordon	66T	51	$ .25	$ .85
Rice, Hal	52T	398	$39.00	$135.00	Richardson, Jeff	89TMLD	100	$ .01	$ .25
Rice, Hal	53T	93	$3.75	$13.00	Richardt, Mike	83T	371	$ .01	$ .06
Rice, Hal	54T	95	$2.00	$7.00	Richardt, Mike	84T	641	$ .01	$ .05
Rice, Jim	75T	616	$8.50	$27.50	Richert, Pete	62T	131	$ .35	$1.10
Rice, Jim	76T	340	$2.75	$8.50	Richert, Pete	63T	383	$ .35	$1.20
Rice, Jim	77T	60	$1.75	$5.00	Richert, Pete	64T	51	$ .25	$ .85
Rice, Jim	78T	202	$ .05	$ .20	Richert, Pete	65T	252	$ .30	$1.00
Rice, Jim	78T	670	$1.00	$3.75	Richert, Pete	66T	95	$ .25	$ .85
Rice, Jim	79T	2	$ .25	$ .65	Richert, Pete	67T	590	$1.35	$4.00
Rice, Jim	79T	3	$ .25	$ .65	Richert, Pete	68T	354	$ .25	$ .65
Rice, Jim	79T	400	$ .75	$2.25	Richert, Pete	69T	86	$ .25	$ .65
Rice, Jim	80T	200	$ .50	$1.50	Richert, Pete	70T	601	$ .25	$ .85
Rice, Jim	81T	500	$ .15	$ .75	Richert, Pete	71T	273	$ .10	$ .35
Rice, Jim	82T	750	$ .10	$ .50	Richert, Pete	72T	649	$ .25	$ .85
Rice, Jim	83T	30	$ .25	$ .65	Richert, Pete	73T	239	$ .06	$ .25
Rice, Jim	83T	381	$ .01	$ .00	Richert, Pete	74T	348	$ .06	$ .25
Rice, Jim	84T	132	$ .08	$ .35	Richert, Pete	74TTR	348	$ .06	$ .25
Rice, Jim	84T	133	$ .06	$ .30	Richie, Rob	89TMLD	101	$ .01	$ .05
Rice, Jim	84T	550	$ .25	$ .65	Richie, Rob	90T	146	$ .01	$ .03
Rice, Jim	84TAS	401	$ .05	$ .20	Rickert, Marv	52T	50	$14.00	$45.00
Rice, Jim	85T	150	$ .05	$ .25	Ricketts, Dave	65T	581	$20.00	$75.00
Rice, Jim	86T	320	$ .01	$ .10	Ricketts, Dave	67T	589	$1.35	$4.00
Rice, Jim	87T	480	$ .10	$ .35	Ricketts, Dave	68T	46	$ .25	$ .65
Rice, Jim	87TAS610	610	$ .01	$ .10	Ricketts, Dave	69T	232	$ .25	$ .85
Rice, Jim	88T	675	$ .01	$ .15	Ricketts, Dave	70T	626	$ .25	$ .85
Rice, Jim	88TBB	181	$ .01	$ .10	Ricketts, Dave	73T	517	$ .25	$ .85
Rice, Jim	88TTB	662	$ .01	$ .03	Ricketts, Dick	59T	137	$ .50	$1.95
Rice, Jim	89T	245	$ .01	$ .04	Ricketts, Dick	60T	236	$ .35	$1.10
Rice, Jim	89TBB	18	$ .01	$ .05	Rico, Fred	70T	552	$ .25	$ .85
Rice, Jim	90T	785	$ .01	$ .10	Riddle, John	53T	274	$11.00	$37.50
Richard, J. R.	72T	101	$ .35	$1.25	Riddle, John	54T	147	$2.00	$7.00
Richard, J. R.	74T	522	$ .06	$ .25	Riddle, Johnny	55T	98	$1.35	$5.00
Richard, J. R.	75T	73	$ .06	$ .25	Riddleberger, Denny	71T	93	$ .10	$ .35
Richard, J. R.	76T	625	$ .06	$ .25	Riddleberger, Denny	72T	642	$ .25	$ .85
Richard, J. R.	77T	260	$ .05	$ .15	Riddleberger, Denny	73T	157	$ .06	$ .25
Richard, J. R.	78T	470	$ .05	$ .20	Ridzik, Steve	57T	123	$ .95	$3.50
Richard, J. R.	79T	590	$ .02	$ .10	Ridzik, Steve	60T	489	$ .60	$1.75
Richard, J. R.	79T	6	$ .06	$ .30	Ridzik, Steve	64T	92	$ .25	$ .85
Richard, J. R.	79TRB	203	$ .02	$ .10	Ridzik, Steve	65T	211	$ .30	$1.00
Richard, J. R.	80T	206	$ .05	$ .25	Ridzik, Steve	66T	294	$ .25	$ .85

Player	Year	No.	VG	EX/MT
Righetti, Dave	82T	439	$ .95	$3.50
Righetti, Dave	83T	81	$ .01	$ .06
Righetti, Dave	83T	176	$ .05	$ .25
Righetti, Dave	84T	5	$ .02	$ .10
Righetti, Dave	84T	635	$ .03	$ .15
Righetti, Dave	85T	260	$ .04	$ .20
Righetti, Dave	86T	560	$ .01	$ .10
Righetti, Dave	87T	40	$ .01	$ .10
Righetti, Dave	87TAS	616	$ .01	$ .10
Righetti, Dave	87TRB	5	$ .01	$ .03
Righetti, Dave	88T	790	$ .01	$ .10

Player	Year	No.	VG	EX/MT
Righetti, Dave	89T	335	$ .01	$ .04
Righetti, Dave	90T	160	$ .01	$ .03
Rigney, Bill	52T	125	$6.00	$18.00
Rigney, Bill	60T	7	$3.00	$9.50
Rigney, Bill	60T	225	$ .35	$1.10
Rigney, Bill	61T	225	$ .30	$1.00
Rigney, Bill	62T	549	$3.75	$11.00
Rigney, Bill	63T	294	$ .35	$1.20
Rigney, Bill	64T	383	$ .40	$1.25
Rigney, Bill	65T	66	$ .25	$ .65
Rigney, Bill	66T	249	$ .25	$ .85
Rigney, Bill	67T	494	$ .50	$2.00
Rigney, Bill	68T	416	$ .25	$ .65
Rigney, Bill	69T	182	$ .25	$ .65
Rigney, Bill	70T	426	$ .10	$ .35
Rigney, Bill	71T	532	$ .30	$1.00
Rigney, Bill	72T	389	$ .10	$ .35
Rijo, Jose	84TTR	100	$ .15	$1.25
Rijo, Jose	85T	238	$ .10	$ .45
Rijo, Jose	86T	536	$ .05	$ .25
Rijo, Jose	87T	34	$ .05	$ .20
Rijo, Jose	88T	316	$ .01	$ .10
Rijo, Jose	88TTR	92	$ .01	$ .15
Rijo, Jose	89T	135	$ .01	$ .10
Rijo, Jose	90T	627	$ .01	$ .03
Riles, Earnie	86T	398	$ .02	$ .20
Riles, Earnie	87T	523	$ .01	$ .03
Riles, Earnie	88T	88	$ .01	$ .03
Riles, Ernie (Earnie)	88TTR	93	$ .01	$ .05
Riles, Ernie	89T	676	$ .01	$ .04
Riles, Ernie	90T	732	$ .01	$ .03
Riley, George	81T	514	$ .01	$ .07

Player	Year	No.	VG	EX/MT
Rincon, Andy	81T	244	$ .01	$ .07
Rincon, Andy	82T	135	$ .01	$ .06
Rios, Juan	69T	619	$ .25	$ .85
Rios, Juan	70T	89	$ .10	$ .35
Ripken, Billy	88T	352	$ .05	$ .30
Ripken, Billy	89T	571	$ .01	$ .04
Ripken, Billy	89TBB	27	$ .01	$ .05
Ripken, Billy	90T	468	$ .01	$ .03
Ripken, Cal	82T	21	$3.25	$12.50
Ripken, Cal	82TTR	98	$3.00	$11.00
Ripken, Cal	83T	163	$1.00	$3.00
Ripken, Cal	84T	426	$ .01	$ .05
Ripken, Cal	84T	490	$ .10	$ .85
Ripken, Cal	84TAS	400	$ .06	$ .30
Ripken, Cal	85T	30	$ .07	$ .50
Ripken, Cal	85TAS	704	$ .05	$ .25
Ripken, Cal	86T	340	$ .03	$ .40
Ripken, Cal	86TAS	715	$ .03	$ .25
Ripken, Cal	87T	784	$ .10	$ .30
Ripken, Cal	87TAS	609	$ .01	$ .10
Ripken, Jr., Cal	88TBB	62	$ .01	$ .25
Ripken, Cal	88T	650	$ .01	$ .25
Ripken, Jr., Cal	89T	250	$ .01	$ .15
Ripken, Cal	89TBB	286	$ .01	$ .15
Ripken, Cal	90T	570	$ .01	$ .10
Ripken, Cal	90TAS	388	$ .01	$ .10
Ripken, Cal	90TRB	8	$ .01	$ .10
Ripken, Sr., Cal	87TTR	102	$ .01	$ .07
Ripken, Sr., Cal	88T	444	$ .01	$ .03
Ripley, Allen	79T	702	$ .02	$ .10
Ripley, Allen	80T	413	$ .01	$ .07
Ripley, Allen	81T	144	$ .01	$ .07
Ripley, Allen	82T	529	$ .01	$ .06
Ripley, Allen	82TTR	99	$ .02	$ .10
Ripley, Allen	83T	73	$ .01	$ .06
Rippelmeyer, Ray	61T	276	$ .30	$1.00
Rippelmeyer, Ray	62T	271	$ .35	$1.10
Rippelmeyer, Ray	73T	486	$ .25	$ .85
Rippelmeyer, Ray	74T	119	$ .06	$ .25
Ritchie, Jay	65T	494	$ .50	$2.00
Ritchie, Wally	87TTR	103	$ .05	$ .25
Ritchie, Wally	88T	494	$ .01	$ .03
Rittwage, Jim	65T	501	$ .50	$2.00
Ritz, Kevin	89TMLD	102	$ .01	$ .05
Ritz, Kevin	90T	237	$ .01	$ .10
Rivera, Bombo	77T	178	$ .05	$ .15
Rivera, Bombo	78T	657	$ .02	$ .10
Rivera, Bombo	79T	449	$ .02	$ .10
Rivera, Bombo	80T	43	$ .01	$ .07
Rivera, Bombo	81T	256	$ .01	$ .07
Rivera, German	85T	626	$ .01	$ .04
Rivera, Jim	53T	156	$3.75	$13.00
Rivera, Jim	54T	34	$1.25	$5.00
Rivera, Jim	55T	58	$1.35	$5.00
Rivera, Jim	56T	70	$1.25	$4.50
Rivera, Jim	57T	107	$ .95	$3.50
Rivera, Jim	58T	11	$ .85	$3.50
Rivera, Jim	59T	213	$ .50	$1.95
Rivera, Jim	60T	116	$ .35	$1.10
Rivera, Jim	61T	367	$ .30	$1.00
Rivera, Luis	88TBB	223	$ .01	$ .05
Rivera, Luis	88TTR	94	$ .01	$ .10
Rivera, Luis	89T	431	$ .01	$ .04
Rivera, Luis	90T	601	$ .01	$ .03
Rivers, Mickey	72T	272	$ .15	$ .50
Rivers, Mickey	73T	597	$ .50	$2.00
Rivers, Mickey	74T	76	$ .06	$ .25
Rivers, Mickey	75T	164	$ .06	$ .25
Rivers, Mickey	76T	85	$ .06	$ .25
Rivers, Mickey	76T	198	$ .10	$ .35
Rivers, Mickey	76TTR	85	$ .05	$ .20
Rivers, Mickey	77T	305	$ .05	$ .15
Rivers, Mickey	78T	690	$ .02	$ .10
Rivers, Mickey	79T	60	$ .02	$ .10
Rivers, Mickey	80T	485	$ .01	$ .07

Player	Year	No.	VG	EX/MT
Rivers, Mickey	81T	145	$ .02	$ .10
Rivers, Mickey	82T	704	$ .03	$ .15
Rivers, Mickey	82TIA	705	$ .01	$ .06
Rivers, Mickey	83T	224	$ .01	$ .06
Rivers, Mickey	84T	504	$ .01	$ .05
Rivers, Mickey	85T	371	$ .01	$ .04
Rizzuto, Phil	51Trb	5	$5.50	$20.00
Rizzuto, Phil	52T	11	$75.00	$225.00
Rizzuto, Phil	53T	114	$45.00	$135.00
Rizzuto, Phil	54T	17	$25.00	$75.00
Rizzuto, Phil	55T	189	$42.50	$125.00
Rizzuto, Phil	56T	113	$12.50	$37.50
Rizzuto, Phil	61TMVP	471	$3.00	$9.00
Roach, Mel	54T	181	$2.00	$7.00
Roach, Mel	55T	117	$1.35	$5.00
Roach, Mel	59T	54	$ .85	$3.50
Roach, Mel	60T	491	$ .60	$1.75
Roach, Mel	61T	217	$ .30	$1.00
Roach, Mel	62T	581	$3.75	$11.00
Roarke, Mike	61T	376	$ .50	$2.00
Roarke, Mike	62T	87	$ .35	$1.10
Roarke, Mike	63T	224	$ .25	$ .85
Roarke, Mike	64T	292	$ .25	$ .85
Robbins, Bruce	80T	666	$ .01	$ .07
Robbins, Bruce	81T	79	$ .01	$ .07
Robbins, Doug	88TTR	95	$ .01	$ .25
Robbins, Doug	89TBB	49	$ .01	$ .05
Roberge, Bert	80T	329	$ .01	$ .07
Roberge, Bert	83T	611	$ .01	$ .06
Roberge, Bert	85T	388	$ .01	$ .04
Roberge, Bert	85TTR	94	$ .02	$ .10
Roberge, Bert	86T	154	$ .01	$ .03
Roberts, Bip	86TTR	91	$ .02	$ .10
Roberts, Bip	87T	637	$ .01	$ .03
Roberts, Bip	89TTR	103	$ .01	$ .05
Roberts, Bip	90T	307	$ .01	$ .03
Roberts, Curt	54T	242	$2.00	$7.00
Roberts, Curt	55T	107	$1.35	$5.00
Roberts, Curt	56T	306	$1.30	$5.00
Roberts, Dave	63T	158	$ .25	$ .85
Roberts, Dave	66T	571	$4.50	$15.00
Roberts, Dave	69T	536	$ .25	$ .85

Player	Year	No.	VG	EX/MT
Roberts, Dave	71T	448	$ .10	$ .35
Roberts, Dave	72T	91	$ .35	$1.10
Roberts, Dave	72T	360	$ .10	$ .35
Roberts, Dave	73T	39	$ .06	$ .25
Roberts, Dave	73T	133	$ .06	$ .25
Roberts, Dave	74T	177	$ .06	$ .25
Roberts, Dave	74T	309	$ .06	$ .25
Roberts, Dave	75T	301	$ .06	$ .25
Roberts, Dave	75T	558	$ .06	$ .25
Roberts, Dave	76T	107	$ .05	$ .20
Roberts, Dave	76T	649	$ .05	$ .20
Roberts, Dave	76TTR	649	$ .05	$ .20
Roberts, Dave	77T	363	$ .05	$ .15
Roberts, Dave	77T	537	$ .05	$ .15
Roberts, Dave	78T	501	$ .02	$ .10
Roberts, Dave	79T	342	$ .02	$ .10
Roberts, Dave	79T	473	$ .02	$ .10
Roberts, Dave	80T	93	$ .01	$ .07
Roberts, Dave	80T	212	$ .01	$ .07
Roberts, Dave	81T	57	$ .01	$ .07
Roberts, Dave	81T	431	$ .01	$ .07
Roberts, Dave	81TTR	824	$ .02	$ .10
Roberts, Dave	82T	218	$ .01	$ .06
Roberts, Dave	83T	148	$ .01	$ .06
Roberts, Leon	75T	620	$12.00	$35.00
Roberts, Leon	76T	292	$ .05	$ .20
Roberts, Leon	76TTR	292	$ .05	$ .20
Roberts, Leon	77T	456	$ .05	$ .15
Roberts, Leon	79T	166	$ .02	$ .10
Roberts, Leon	80T	507	$ .01	$ .07
Roberts, Leon	81T	368	$ .01	$ .07
Roberts, Leon	81TTR	825	$ .02	$ .10
Roberts, Leon	82T	688	$ .01	$ .06
Roberts, Leon	83T	89	$ .01	$ .06
Roberts, Leon	83TTR	96	$ .02	$ .10
Roberts, Leon	84T	784	$ .01	$ .05
Roberts, Leon	85T	217	$ .01	$ .04
Roberts, Robin	52T	59	$40.00	$125.00
Roberts, Robin	56T	180	$7.00	$20.00
Roberts, Robin	57T	15	$5.00	$15.00
Roberts, Robin	58T	90	$2.50	$10.00
Roberts, Robin	59T	156	$1.30	$5.00
Roberts, Robin	59T	352	$3.50	$12.50
Roberts, Robin	60T	264	$3.50	$12.50
Roberts, Robin	61T	20	$3.00	$9.00
Roberts, Robin	62T	243	$2.35	$7.00
Roberts, Robin	63T	6	$ .35	$1.10
Roberts, Robin	63T	125	$2.50	$8.00
Roberts, Robin	64T	285	$2.50	$8.00
Roberts, Robin	65T	15	$1.50	$6.00
Roberts, Robin	66T	530	$10.00	$32.50
Robertson, Andre	82T	83	$ .10	$ .50
Robertson, Andre	83T	281	$ .01	$ .06
Robertson, Andre	84T	592	$ .01	$ .05
Robertson, Andre	85T	354	$ .01	$ .04
Robertson, Andre	86T	738	$ .01	$ .03
Robertson, Bob	68T	36	$ .15	$ .50
Robertson, Bob	69T	468	$ .25	$ .65
Robertson, Bob	70T	664	$ .50	$2.00
Robertson, Bob	71T	255	$ .10	$ .35
Robertson, Bob	72T	429	$ .10	$ .35
Robertson, Bob	72TIA	430	$ .10	$ .35
Robertson, Bob	73T	422	$ .06	$ .25
Robertson, Bob	74T	540	$ .06	$ .25
Robertson, Bob	75T	409	$ .06	$ .25
Robertson, Bob	76T	449	$ .05	$ .20
Robertson, Bob	77T	176	$ .05	$ .15
Robertson, Bob	79T	312	$ .02	$ .10
Robertson, Jerry	69T	284	$ .25	$ .85
Robertson, Jerry	70T	661	$ .50	$2.00
Robertson, Jerry	71T	651	$ .70	$2.10
Robertson, Jim	54T	149	$2.00	$7.00
Robertson, Jim	55T	177	$4.25	$13.00
Robertson, Rich	69T	16	$ .25	$ .65
Robertson, Rich	70T	229	$ .10	$ .35

Roberts, Dave   70T   151 $ .10 $ .35

TOPPS

Player	Year	No.	VG	EX/MT
Robertson, Rich	71T	443	$ .10	$ .35
Robertson, Rich	72T	618	$ .25	$ .85
Robertson, Sherry	52T	245	$6.00	$19.00
Robidoux, Billy Jo	86TTR	92	$ .05	$ .20
Robidoux, Billy Jo	87T	401	$ .01	$ .10
Robinson, Bill	67T	442	$ .25	$ .85
Robinson, Bill	68T	337	$ .25	$ .65
Robinson, Bill	69T	313	$ .25	$ .85
Robinson, Bill	70T	23	$ .10	$ .35
Robinson, Bill	73T	37	$ .06	$ .25
Robinson, Bill	74T	174	$ .06	$ .25
Robinson, Bill	75T	501	$ .06	$ .25

BILL ROBINSON
OUTFIELD PIRATES

Player	Year	No.	VG	EX/MT
Robinson, Bill	76T	137	$ .05	$ .20
Robinson, Bill	77T	335	$ .05	$ .15
Robinson, Bill	78T	455	$ .02	$ .10
Robinson, Bill	79T	637	$ .02	$ .10
Robinson, Bill	80T	264	$ .01	$ .07
Robinson, Bill	81T	51	$ .01	$ .07
Robinson, Bill	82T	543	$ .01	$ .06
Robinson, Bill	82TTR	100	$ .02	$ .10
Robinson, Bill	83T	754	$ .01	$ .06
Robinson, Brooks	57T	328	$100.00	$300.00
Robinson, Brooks	58T	307	$15.00	$45.00
Robinson, Brooks	59T	439	$8.50	$32.50
Robinson, Brooks	60T	28	$8.00	$25.00
Robinson, Brooks	61T	10	$8.00	$25.00
Robinson, Brooks	61TAS	572	$22.50	$67.50
Robinson, Brooks	62T	45	$6.00	$25.00
Robinson, Brooks	62TAS	468	$4.00	$12.00
Robinson, Brooks	63T	345	$9.00	$27.50
Robinson, Brooks	64T	230	$7.00	$20.00
Robinson, Brooks	65T	1	$2.50	$8.00
Robinson, Brooks	65T	5	$3.00	$12.00
Robinson, Brooks	65T	150	$5.00	$15.00
Robinson, Brooks	66T	390	$7.50	$25.00
Robinson, Brooks	67T	1	$5.00	$15.00
Robinson, Brooks	67T	600	$60.00	$180.00
Robinson, Brooks	68T	20	$4.00	$16.00
Robinson, Brooks	68T	530	$3.00	$10.00
Robinson, Brooks	68TAS	365	$1.40	$4.00
Robinson, Brooks	69T	550	$3.50	$12.50
Robinson, Brooks	69TAS	421	$1.35	$4.00
Robinson, Brooks	70T	230	$2.25	$8.50

Player	Year	No.	VG	EX/MT
Robinson, Brooks	70TAS	455	$1.35	$4.00
Robinson, Brooks	71T	300	$3.00	$10.00
Robinson, Brooks	72T	498	$ .50	$2.00
Robinson, Brooks	72T	550	$3.50	$10.50
Robinson, Brooks	73T	90	$1.35	$4.00
Robinson, Brooks	74T	160	$1.35	$4.00
Robinson, Brooks	74TAS	334	$ .35	$1.10
Robinson, Brooks	75T	50	$1.35	$4.00
Robinson, Brooks	75T	202	$ .35	$1.10
Robinson, Brooks	76T	95	$ .95	$3.50
Robinson, Brooks	77T	285	$1.00	$4.00
Robinson, Brooks	78TRB	4	$ .15	$ .50
Robinson, Bruce	79T	711	$ .08	$ .30
Robinson, Bruce	81T	424	$ .01	$ .07
Robinson, Craig	74T	23	$ .06	$ .25
Robinson, Craig	74TTR	23	$ .06	$ .25
Robinson, Craig	75T	367	$ .06	$ .25
Robinson, Dave	71T	262	$ .10	$ .35
Robinson, Dewey	80T	664	$ .01	$ .07
Robinson, Dewey	81T	487	$ .01	$ .07
Robinson, Dewey	82T	176	$ .01	$ .06
Robinson, Don	79T	264	$ .05	$ .20
Robinson, Don	80T	719	$ .01	$ .07
Robinson, Don	81T	168	$ .01	$ .07
Robinson, Don	82T	332	$ .01	$ .06
Robinson, Don	83T	44	$ .01	$ .06
Robinson, Don	84T	616	$ .01	$ .05
Robinson, Don	85T	537	$ .01	$ .04
Robinson, Don	86T	731	$ .01	$ .03
Robinson, Don	87T	712	$ .01	$ .03
Robinson, Don	88T	52	$ .01	$ .03
Robinson, Don	89T	473	$ .01	$ .04
Robinson, Don	90T	217	$ .01	$ .03
Robinson, Earl	61T	343	$ .30	$1.00
Robinson, Earl	62T	272	$ .35	$1.10
Robinson, Eddie	51Trb	51	$1.35	$4.00
Robinson, Eddie	52T	32	$14.00	$45.00
Robinson, Eddie	53T	73	$3.75	$13.00
Robinson, Eddie	54T	62	$3.00	$12.00
Robinson, Eddie	56T	302	$2.00	$6.00
Robinson, Eddie	57T	238	$ .95	$3.50
Robinson, Eddie	60T	455	$ .95	$3.50
Robinson, Floyd	62T	454	$ .70	$2.10
Robinson, Floyd	63T	2	$3.00	$12.00
Robinson, Floyd	63T	405	$ .35	$1.20
Robinson, Floyd	64T	195	$ .25	$ .85
Robinson, Floyd	65T	345	$ .30	$1.00
Robinson, Floyd	66T	8	$ .25	$ .85
Robinson, Floyd	66T	199	$ .30	$1.00
Robinson, Floyd	67T	120	$ .25	$ .65
RobInson, Floyd	68T	404	$ .25	$ .65
Robinson, Frank	57T	35	$75.00	$225.00
Robinson, Frank	58T	285	$17.50	$52.50
Robinson, Frank	58T	386	$2.00	$6.00
Robinson, Frank	58TAS	484	$3.00	$9.00
Robinson, Frank	59T	435	$10.00	$30.00
Robinson, Frank	60T	352	$ .90	$3.50
Robinson, Frank	60T	490	$7.00	$28.00
Robinson, Frank	61T	25	$1.35	$4.00
Robinson, Frank	61T	360	$7.00	$21.00
Robinson, Frank	61TAS	581	$19.50	$62.50
Robinson, Frank	62T	54	$ .50	$1.95
Robinson, Frank	62T	350	$7.50	$22.50
Robinson, Frank	62TAS	396	$4.00	$12.00
Robinson, Frank	63T	1	$4.35	$22.00
Robinson, Frank	63T	3	$2.35	$9.00
Robinson, Frank	63T	400	$9.00	$30.00
Robinson, Frank	64T	260	$3.00	$9.00
Robinson, Frank	65T	120	$2.75	$8.00
Robinson, Frank	66T	219	$ .65	$1.75
Robinson, Frank	66T	310	$5.00	$22.50
Robinson, Frank	67T	1	$5.00	$15.00
Robinson, Frank	67T	100	$4.00	$12.00
Robinson, Frank	67T	239	$1.50	$3.75
Robinson, Frank	67T	241	$1.50	$3.75

Player	Year	No.	VG	EX/MT
Robinson, Frank	67T	243	$1.50	$3.75
Robinson, Frank	68T	2	$1.35	$4.00
Robinson, Frank	68T	4	$1.35	$4.00
Robinson, Frank	68T	500	$2.50	$7.50
Robinson, Frank	68T	530	$3.00	$10.00
Robinson, Frank	68TAS	373	$1.35	$4.00
Robinson, Frank	69T	250	$2.75	$8.00
Robinson, Frank	70T	700	$6.00	$18.00
Robinson, Frank	70TAS	463	$1.35	$4.00
Robinson, Frank	71T	640	$4.00	$12.00
Robinson, Frank	72T	88	$ .60	$2.00
Robinson, Frank	72T	100	$1.50	$6.00
Robinson, Frank	72TTR	754	$5.00	$20.00
Robinson, Frank	73T	175	$1.50	$3.75
Robinson, Frank	74T	55	$1.25	$4.50
Robinson, Frank	75T	199	$ .50	$2.00
Robinson, Frank	75T	204	$ .50	$2.00
Robinson, Frank	75T	580	$ .95	$3.50
Robinson, Frank	83T	576	$ .05	$ .20
Robinson, Frank	84T	171	$ .05	$ .25
Robinson, Frank	86TB	404	$ .03	$ .15
Robinson, Frank	88TTR	96	$ .01	$ .10
Robinson, Frank	89T	774	$ .01	$ .10
Robinson, Frank	90T	381	$ .01	$ .10
Robinson, Humberto	55T	182	$4.25	$13.00
Robinson, Humberto	59T	366	$ .50	$1.95
Robinson, Humberto	60T	416	$ .50	$1.95
Robinson, Jackie	52T	312	$300.00	$900.00
Robinson, Jackie	53T	1	$100.00	$600.00
Robinson, Jackie	54T	10	$80.00	$250.00
Robinson, Jackie	55T	50	$75.00	$225.00
Robinson, Jackie	56T	30	$40.00	$125.00
Robinson, Jeff	84TTR	101	$ .02	$ .10
Robinson, Jeff	85T	592	$ .01	$ .04
Robinson, Jeff	86TTR	93	$ .02	$ .10
Robinson, Jeff	87T	390	$ .01	$ .03
Robinson, Jeff	87TTR	104	$ .05	$ .20
Robinson, Jeff	88T	449	$ .01	$ .30
Robinson, Jeff	89T	681	$ .01	$ .10
Robinson, Jeff	89TBB	45	$ .01	$ .05
Robinson, Jeff	90T	723	$ .01	$ .03
Robinson, Jeff M.	88T	244	$ .01	$ .03
Robinson, Jeff M.	88TBB	123	$ .01	$ .10
Robinson, Jeff M.	89T	267	$ .01	$ .10
Robinson, Jeff M.	89TBB	274	$ .01	$ .05
Robinson, Jeff M.	90T	42	$ .01	$ .03
Robinson, Jerry	63T	466	$6.00	$18.00
Robinson, Ron	86T	442	$ .01	$ .03
Robinson, Ron	87T	119	$ .01	$ .03
Robinson, Ron	88T	517	$ .01	$ .03
Robinson, Ron	89T	16	$ .01	$ .10
Robinson, Ron	89TBB	132	$ .01	$ .05
Robinson, Ron	90T	604	$ .01	$ .03
Robles, Rafael	69T	592	$ .25	$ .85
Robles, Rafael	70T	573	$ .25	$ .85
Robles, Rafael	71T	408	$ .10	$ .35
Robles, Sergio	73T	601	$ .35	$1.10
Robles, Sergio	74T	603	$ .06	$ .25
Rockett, Pat	78T	502	$ .02	$ .10
Rodgers, Andre	57T	377	$ .85	$3.50
Rodgers, Andre	59T	216	$ .50	$1.95
Rodgers, Andre	60T	431	$ .50	$1.95
Rodgers, Andre	61T	183	$ .30	$1.00
Rodgers, Andre	62T	477	$ .70	$2.10
Rodgers, Andre	63T	193	$ .25	$ .85
Rodgers, Andre	64T	336	$ .25	$ .85
Rodgers, Andre	65T	536	$1.50	$3.75
Rodgers, Andre	66T	592	$4.50	$15.00
Rodgers, Andre	67T	554	$1.35	$4.00
Rodgers, Bob	62T	431	$ .70	$2.00
Rodgers, Bob	63T	280	$ .30	$1.00
Rodgers, Bob	64T	426	$ .40	$1.25
Rodgers, Bob	64T	61	$ .25	$ .85
Rodgers, Bob	65T	342	$ .30	$1.00
Rodgers, Bob	66T	462	$ .70	$2.10
Rodgers, Bob	67T	281	$ .25	$ .65
Rodgers, Bob	68T	433	$ .25	$ .65
Rodgers, Bob	69T	157	$ .25	$ .65
Rodgers, Bob	73T	49	$ .25	$ .65
Rodgers, Bob	74T	447	$ .06	$ .25
Rodgers, Bob	85TTR	95	$ .02	$ .10
Rodgers, Bob	86T	171	$ .01	$ .03
Rodgers, Bob	87T	293	$ .01	$ .03
Rodgers, Bob	88T	504	$ .01	$ .03
Rodgers, Bob	89T	474	$ .01	$ .04
Rodgers, Bob	90T	81	$ .01	$ .03
Rodriguez, Aurelio	69T	653	$ .50	$1.50
Rodriguez, Aurelio	70T	228	$ .10	$ .35
Rodriguez, Aurelio	71T	464	$ .10	$ .35
Rodriguez, Aurelio	72T	319	$ .10	$ .35
Rodriguez, Aurelio	73T	218	$ .06	$ .25
Rodriguez, Aurelio	74T	72	$ .06	$ .25
Rodriguez, Aurelio	75T	221	$ .06	$ .25
Rodriguez, Aurelio	76T	267	$ .05	$ .20
Rodriguez, Aurelio	77T	574	$ .05	$ .15
Rodriguez, Aurelio	78T	342	$ .02	$ .10
Rodriguez, Aurelio	79T	176	$ .02	$ .10
Rodriguez, Aurelio	80T	468	$ .01	$ .07
Rodriguez, Aurelio	81T	34	$ .01	$ .07
Rodriguez, Aurelio	82T	334	$ .01	$ .06
Rodriguez, Aurelio	82TTR	101	$ .02	$ .10
Rodriguez, Aurelio	83T	758	$ .01	$ .06
Rodriguez, Aurelio	83TTR	97	$ .02	$ .10
Rodriguez, Aurelio	84T	269	$ .01	$ .05
Rodriguez, Eduardo	74T	171	$ .06	$ .25
Rodriguez, Eduardo	75T	582	$ .06	$ .25
Rodriguez, Eduardo	76T	92	$ .05	$ .20
Rodriguez, Eduardo	77T	361	$ .05	$ .15
Rodriguez, Eduardo	78T	623	$ .02	$ .10
Rodriguez, Eduardo	79T	108	$ .02	$ .10
Rodriguez, Eduardo	80T	273	$ .01	$ .07
Rodriguez, Eliseo "Ellie"	69T	49	$ .35	$1.10
Rodriguez, Ellie	70T	402	$ .10	$ .35
Rodriguez, Ellie	71T	344	$ .10	$ .35
Rodriguez, Ellie	72T	421	$ .10	$ .35
Rodriguez, Ellie	73T	45	$ .06	$ .25
Rodriguez, Ellie	74T	405	$ .06	$ .25
Rodriguez, Ellie	75T	285	$ .06	$ .25
Rodriguez, Ellie	76T	512	$ .05	$ .20
Rodriguez, Ellie	77T	448	$ .05	$ .15
Rodriguez, Rick	88T	166	$ .01	$ .10
Rodriguez, Roberto	68T	199	$ .25	$ .65
Rodriguez, Roberto	69T	358	$ .25	$ .65
Rodriguez, Roberto	71T	424	$ .10	$ .35
Rodriguez, Rosario	89TMLD	103	$ .01	$ .15
Roe, Preacher	51Trb	16	$2.50	$8.00
Roe, Preacher	52T	66	$32.50	$85.00
Roe, Preacher	53T	254	$20.00	$60.00
Roe, Preacher	54T	14	$6.00	$18.00
Roebuck, Ed	55T	195	$2.85	$9.50
Roebuck, Ed	56T	58	$1.25	$4.50
Roebuck, Ed	58T	435	$ .50	$2.00
Roebuck, Ed	60T	519	$2.00	$7.00
Roebuck, Ed	61T	6	$ .30	$1.00
Roebuck, Ed	62T	535	$2.50	$16.50
Roebuck, Ed	63T	295	$ .35	$1.20
Roebuck, Ed	64T	187	$ .25	$ .85
Roebuck, Ed	65T	52	$ .25	$ .65
Roenicke, Gary	80T	568	$ .01	$ .07
Roenicke, Gary	81T	37	$ .01	$ .07
Roenicke, Gary	82T	204	$ .01	$ .06
Roenicke, Gary	83T	605	$ .01	$ .06
Roenicke, Gary	84T	372	$ .01	$ .05
Roenicke, Gary	85T	109	$ .01	$ .04
Roenicke, Gary	86T	494	$ .01	$ .03
Roenicke, Gary	86TTR	94	$ .02	$ .10
Roenicke, Gary	87T	683	$ .01	$ .03
Roenicke, Gary	87TTR	105	$ .01	$ .07
Roenicke, Gary	88T	523	$ .01	$ .03
Roenicke, Ron	82T	681	$ .75	$3.50

Player	Year	No.	VG	EX/MT	Player	Year	No.	VG	EX/MT
Roenicke, Ron	83T	113	$ .01	$ .06	Rollins, Rich	68T	243	$ .25	$ .65
Roenicke, Ron	84T	647	$ .01	$ .05	Rollins, Rich	69T	451	$ .25	$ .65
Roenicke, Ron	86T	63	$ .01	$ .03	Rollins, Rich	70T	652	$ .50	$2.00
Roenicke, Ron	87T	329	$ .01	$ .03	Roman, Bill	65T	493	$ .50	$2.00
Roenicke, Ron	88T	783	$ .01	$ .03	Romanick, Ron	84TTR	102	$ .02	$ .10
Roesler, Mike	89TMLD	104	$ .01	$ .10	Romanick, Ron	85T	579	$ .01	$ .04
Roesler, Mike	90T	203	$ .01	$ .10	Romanick, Ron	86T	733	$ .01	$ .03
Rogan, Pat	65T	486	$ .50	$2.00	Romanick, Ron	87T	136	$ .01	$ .03
Rogers, Kenny	89TMLD	105	$ .01	$ .10	Romano, John	59T	138	$ .50	$1.95
Rogers, Kenny	89TTR	104	$ .01	$ .15	Romano, Johnny	60T	323	$ .50	$1.95
Rogers, Kenny	90T	683	$ .01	$ .15	Romano, Johnny	61T	5	$ .30	$1.00
Rogers, Steve	74T	169	$ .10	$ .35	Romano, Johnny	62T	330	$ .35	$1.10
Rogers, Steve	75T	173	$ .06	$ .25	Romano, Johnny	63T	72	$ .25	$ .85
Rogers, Steve	76T	71	$ .05	$ .20	Romano, Johnny	63T	392	$ .24	$1.25
Rogers, Steve	77T	316	$ .05	$ .15	Romano, Johnny	64T	515	$ .40	$1.25
Rogers, Steve	78T	425	$ .02	$ .10	Romano, Johnny	65T	17	$ .25	$ .65
Rogers, Steve	79T	235	$ .02	$ .10	Romano, Johnny	66T	199	$ .30	$1.00
Rogers, Steve	80T	520	$ .01	$ .07	Romano, Johnny	66T	413	$ .25	$ .85
Rogers, Steve	81T	725	$ .01	$ .07	Romano, Johnny	67T	196	$ .25	$ .65
Rogers, Steve	82T	605	$ .01	$ .06	Romero, "Eddie"	79T	708	$ .35	$1.10
Rogers, Steve	83T	111	$ .01	$ .06	Romero, Ed	81T	659	$ .01	$ .07
Rogers, Steve	83T	320	$ .01	$ .06	Romero, Ed	82T	408	$ .01	$ .06
Rogers, Steve	83T	707	$ .01	$ .06	Romero, Ed	83T	271	$ .01	$ .06
Rogers, Steve	83TAS	405	$ .01	$ .06	Romero, Ed	84T	146	$ .01	$ .05
Rogers, Steve	84T	80	$ .01	$ .05	Romero, Ed	85T	498	$ .01	$ .04
Rogers, Steve	84T	708	$ .04	$ .20	Romero, Ed	86T	317	$ .01	$ .03
Rogers, Steve	84TAS	394	$ .01	$ .05	Romero, Ed	86TTR	95	$ .02	$ .10
Rogers, Steve	85T	205	$ .01	$ .04	Romero, Ed	87T	675	$ .01	$ .03
Roggenburk, Garry	63T	386	$ .50	$1.95	Romero, Ed	88T	37	$ .01	$ .03
Roggenburk, Garry	64T	258	$ .25	$ .85	Romero, Ed	89TTR	105	$ .01	$ .05
Roggenburk, Garry	66T	582	$4.50	$15.00	Romero, Ramon	86T	208	$ .01	$ .03
Roggenburk, Garry	67T	429	$ .25	$ .85	Romine, Kevin	87T	121	$ .01	$ .03
Roggenburk, Garry	68T	581	$ .30	$1.00	Romo, Enrique	78T	278	$ .02	$ .10
Rogodzinski, Mike	74T	492	$ .06	$ .25	Romo, Enrique	79T	548	$ .02	$ .10
Rogovin, Saul	52T	159	$6.00	$19.00	Romo, Enrique	80T	332	$ .01	$ .07
Rogovin, Saul	57T	129	$ .95	$3.50	Romo, Enrique	81T	28	$ .01	$ .07
Rohr, Bill	67T	547	$1.35	$4.00	Romo, Enrique	82T	106	$ .01	$ .06
Rohr, Bill	68T	314	$ .25	$ .65	Romo, Enrique	83T	226	$ .01	$ .06
Rohr, Les	68T	569	$ .30	$1.00	Romo, Vicente	69T	267	$ .25	$ .85
Rojas, Cookie	63T	221	$ .25	$ .85	Romo, Vicente	70T	191	$ .10	$ .35
Rojas, Cookie	64T	448	$ .40	$1.25	Romo, Vicente	71T	723	$ .70	$2.10
Rojas, Cookie	65T	474	$ .50	$2.00	Romo, Vicente	72T	499	$ .10	$ .35
Rojas, Cookie	66T	170	$ .25	$ .85	Romo, Vicente	73T	381	$ .06	$ .25
Rojas, Cookie	67T	595	$1.35	$4.00	Romo, Vicente	74T	197	$ .06	$ .25
Rojas, Cookie	68T	39	$ .25	$ .65	Romo, Vicente	75T	274	$ .06	$ .25
Rojas, Cookie	69T	507	$ .25	$ .65	Romo, Vicente	83T	633	$ .01	$ .06
Rojas, Cookie	70T	569	$ .25	$ .85	Romonosky, John	59T	267	$ .50	$1.95
Rojas, Cookie	71T	118	$ .10	$ .35	Romonosky, John	60T	87	$ .35	$1.10
Rojas, Cookie	72T	415	$ .10	$ .35	Roof, Gene	82T	561	$ .01	$ .06
Rojas, Cookie	73T	188	$ .06	$ .25	Roof, Phil	63T	324	$ .35	$1.20
Rojas, Cookie	74T	278	$ .06	$ .25	Roof, Phil	64T	541	$40.00	$125.00
Rojas, Cookie	75T	169	$ .06	$ .25	Roof, Phil	65T	537	$1.35	$4.00
Rojas, Cookie	76T	311	$ .05	$ .20	Roof, Phil	66T	382	$ .25	$ .85
Rojas, Cookie	77T	509	$ .05	$ .15	Roof, Phil	67T	129	$ .25	$ .65
Rojas, Cookie	88TTR	97	$ .01	$ .05	Roof, Phil	68T	484	$ .30	$1.00
Rojas, Minnie	67T	104	$ .25	$ .65	Roof, Phil	69T	334	$ .25	$ .65
Rojas, Minnie	68T	305	$ .25	$ .65	Roof, Phil	70T	359	$ .10	$ .35
Rojas, Minnie	69T	502	$ .25	$ .65	Roof, Phil	71T	22	$ .10	$ .35
Rojek, Stan	52T	163	$6.00	$19.00	Roof, Phil	72T	201	$ .10	$ .35
Roland, Jim	63T	522	$1.35	$4.00	Roof, Phil	73T	598	$ .35	$1.10
Roland, Jim	64T	341	$ .25	$ .85	Roof, Phil	74T	388	$ .06	$ .25
Roland, Jim	65T	171	$ .25	$ .65	Roof, Phil	75T	576	$ .06	$ .25
Roland, Jim	68T	276	$ .25	$ .65	Roof, Phil	76T	424	$ .05	$ .20
Roland, Jim	69T	336	$ .25	$ .65	Roof, Phil	77T	392	$ .05	$ .15
Roland, Jim	70T	719	$ .60	$1.75	Rooker, Jim	69T	376	$ .25	$ .65
Roland, Jim	71T	642	$ .30	$1.00	Rooker, Jim	70T	222	$ .10	$ .35
Roland, Jim	72T	464	$ .10	$ .35	Rooker, Jim	71T	730	$ .70	$2.10
Rolfe, Red	52T	296	$15.00	$45.00	Rooker, Jim	72T	742	$ .70	$2.10
Rollins, Rich	62T	596	$10.00	$30.00	Rooker, Jim	74T	402	$ .06	$ .25
Rollins, Rich	63T	110	$ .25	$ .85	Rooker, Jim	75T	148	$ .06	$ .25
Rollins, Rich	64T	270	$ .25	$ .85	Rooker, Jim	77T	82	$ .05	$ .15
Rollins, Rich	64T	8	$1.35	$4.00	Rooker, Jim	78T	308	$ .02	$ .10
Rollins, Rich	65T	90	$ .25	$ .65	Rooker, Jim	79T	584	$ .02	$ .10
Rollins, Rich	66T	473	$ .70	$2.10	Rooker, Jim	80T	694	$ .01	$ .07
Rollins, Rich	67T	98	$ .25	$ .65	Roomes, Rolando	90T	364	$ .01	$ .10

Player	Year	No.	VG	EX/MT
Root, Charlie	60T	457	$ .95	$3.50
Roque, Jorge	72T	316	$ .10	$ .35
Roque, Jorge	73T	606	$ .95	$3.50
Rosario, Jimmy	72T	366	$ .10	$ .35
Rose, Bobby	89TMLD	106	$ .01	$ .25
Rose, Don	73T	178	$ .06	$ .25
Rose, Pete	63T	537	$150.00	$450.00
Rose, Pete	64T	125	$50.00	$140.00
Rose, Pete	65T	207	$50.00	$150.00
Rose, Pete	66T	30	$20.00	$60.00
Rose, Pete	67T	430	$12.00	$60.00
Rose, Pete	68T	230	$10.00	$45.00
Rose, Pete	69T	2	$1.35	$4.00
Rose, Pete	69T	120	$12.00	$35.00
Rose, Pete	69TAS	424	$3.00	$9.00
Rose, Pete	70T	61	$1.50	$4.75
Rose, Pete	70T	580	$24.00	$70.00
Rose, Pete	70TAS	458	$2.75	$8.00
Rose, Pete	71T	100	$15.00	$45.00
Rose, Pete	72T	559	$18.50	$55.00

Player	Year	No.	VG	EX/MT
Rose, Pete	72TIA	560	$9.25	$27.50
Rose, Pete	73T	130	$6.00	$17.50
Rose, Pete	74T	201	$1.25	$4.50
Rose, Pete	74T	300	$6.00	$18.00
Rose, Pete	74TAS	336	$ .75	$2.50
Rose, Pete	75T	211	$ .75	$3.00
Rose, Pete	75T	320	$6.00	$18.00
Rose, Pete	76T	240	$6.00	$18.00
Rose, Pete	77T	450	$3.00	$9.00
Rose, Pete	78T	20	$ .90	$3.50
Rose, Pete	78TRB	5	$ .95	$3.50
Rose, Pete	79T	650	$1.25	$4.25
Rose, Pete	79TRB	204	$ .50	$2.00
Rose, Pete	80T	540	$1.00	$4.00
Rose, Pete	80THL	4	$ .70	$2.10
Rose, Pete	81T	180	$ .75	$2.50
Rose, Pete	81TRR	205	$ .15	$ .75
Rose, Pete	82T	636	$ .25	$ .65
Rose, Pete	82T	780	$ .50	$2.50
Rose, Pete	82TAS	337	$ .15	$ .75
Rose, Pete	82THL	4	$ .15	$ .75
Rose, Pete	82TIA	781	$ .25	$1.25
Rose, Pete	83T	100	$ .50	$2.25

Player	Year	No.	VG	EX/MT
Rose, Pete	83T	101	$ .35	$1.10
Rose, Pete	83TAS	397	$ .20	$ .75
Rose, Pete	84T	300	$ .01	$ .05
Rose, Pete	84T	701	$ .06	$ .30
Rose, Pete	84T	702	$ .06	$ .30
Rose, Pete	84TTR	103	$2.00	$7.00
Rose, Pete	85T	547	$ .20	$ .75
Rose, Pete	85T	600	$ .25	$1.00
Rose, Pete	85TRB	6	$ .10	$ .50
Rose, Pete	86T	1	$ .10	$1.00
Rose, Pete (1963-1966)	86T	2	$ .03	$ .30
Rose, Pete (1967-1970)	86T	3	$ .03	$ .30
Rose, Pete (1971-1974)	86T	4	$ .03	$ .30
Rose, Pete (1975-1978)	86T	5	$ .03	$ .30
Rose, Pete (1979-1982)	86T	6	$ .03	$ .30
Rose, Pete (1983-1986)	86T	7	$ .03	$ .30
Rose, Pete	86T	741	$ .10	$ .50
Rose, Pete	86TRB	206	$ .01	$ .50
Rose, Pete	87T	200	$ .15	$ .50
Rose, Pete	87T	393	$ .15	$ .45
Rose, Pete	88T	475	$ .01	$ .25
Rose, Pete	89T	505	$ .01	$ .10
Roseboro, John	58T	42	$1.50	$3.75
Roseboro, John	59T	441	$ .50	$1.95
Roseboro, John	60T	88	$ .35	$1.10
Roseboro, John	60T	292	$ .45	$1.35
Roseboro, John	61T	363	$ .30	$1.00
Roseboro, John	62T	32	$ .50	$1.95
Roseboro, John	62TAS	397	$ .70	$2.10
Roseboro, John	63T	487	$2.50	$6.50
Roseboro, John	64T	88	$ .25	$ .85
Roseboro, John	65T	405	$ .30	$1.00
Roseboro, John	66T	189	$ .25	$ .85
Roseboro, John	67T	365	$ .25	$ .65
Roseboro, John	68T	65	$ .15	$ .50
Roseboro, John	69T	218	$ .25	$ .65
Roseboro, John	70T	655	$ .50	$2.00
Roseboro, John	73T	421	$ .06	$ .25
Roseboro, John	74T	276	$ .06	$ .25
Roselli, Bob	56T	131	$1.25	$4.50
Roselli, Bob	61T	529	$6.00	$18.00
Roselli, Bob	62T	363	$ .35	$1.10
Rosello, Dave	74T	607	$ .06	$ .25
Rosello, Dave	76T	546	$ .05	$ .20
Rosello, Dave	77T	92	$ .05	$ .15
Rosello, Dave	78T	423	$ .02	$ .10
Rosello, Dave	80T	122	$ .01	$ .07
Rosello, Dave	82T	724	$ .01	$ .06
Rosen, Al	51Trb	35	$1.75	$7.00
Rosen, Al	52T	10	$20.00	$70.00
Rosen, Al	53T	135	$7.50	$22.50
Rosen, Al	54T	15	$3.00	$9.00
Rosen, Al	55T	70	$3.00	$9.00
Rosen, Al	56T	35	$1.75	$5.00
Rosen, Al	61TMVP	474	$ .75	$2.00
Rosen, Al	75T	191	$ .35	$1.10
Rosenberg, Steve	89T	616	$ .01	$ .04
Rosenberg, Steve	90T	379	$ .01	$ .03
Ross, Bob	52T	298	$14.00	$45.00
Ross, Bob	54T	189	$2.00	$7.00
Ross, Gary	69T	404	$ .25	$ .65
Ross, Gary	70T	694	$ .50	$2.00
Ross, Gary	71T	153	$ .10	$ .35
Ross, Gary	73T	112	$ .06	$ .25
Ross, Gary	77T	544	$ .05	$ .15
Ross, Gary	78T	291	$ .02	$ .10
Rossi, Joe	52T	379	$39.00	$135.00
Rossi, Joe	53T	74	$3.75	$13.00
Rowdon, Wade	87T	569	$ .01	$ .03
Rowe, Don	63T	562	$3.00	$10.00
Rowe, Ken	63T	562	$3.00	$10.00
Rowe, Ken	65T	518	$ .50	$2.00
Rowe, Ralph	73T	49	$ .25	$ .65
Rowe, Ralph	74T	447	$ .06	$ .25
Rowe, Schoolboy	54T	197	$1.75	$7.00

Player	Year	No.	VG	EX/MT	Player	Year	No.	VG	EX/MT
Rowland, Mike	81T	502	$ .01	$ .07	Rudolph, Don	64T	427	$ .40	$1.25
Royals, Team	70T	422	$ .40	$1.75	Rudolph, Ken	70T	46	$ .10	$ .35
Royals, Team	71T	742	$1.35	$4.00	Rudolph, Ken	71T	472	$ .10	$ .35
Royals, Team	72T	617	$ .75	$2.25	Rudolph, Ken	72T	271	$ .10	$ .35
Royals, Team	73T	347	$ .30	$1.00	Rudolph, Ken	73T	414	$ .06	$ .25
Royals, Team	74T	343	$ .15	$ .50	Rudolph, Ken	74T	584	$ .06	$ .25
Royals, Team Checklist	75T	72	$ .15	$ .50	Rudolph, Ken	75T	289	$ .06	$ .25
Royals, Team Checklist	76T	236	$ .30	$1.00	Rudolph, Ken	76T	601	$ .05	$ .20
Royals, Team Checklist	77T	371	$ .15	$ .50	Ruffin, Bruce	87T	499	$ .10	$ .35
Royals, Team Checklist	78T	724	$ .25	$ .85	Ruffin, Bruce	88T	268	$ .01	$ .03
Royals, Team Checklist	79T	451	$ .05	$ .25	Ruffin, Bruce	89T	518	$ .01	$ .04
Royals, Team Checklist	80T	66	$ .06	$ .30	Ruffin, Bruce	90T	22	$ .01	$ .03
Royals, Team Checklist	81T	667	$ .02	$ .20	Ruhle, Vern	75T	614	$ .06	$ .25
Royals, Team Leaders	86T	606	$ .01	$ .03	Ruhle, Vern	76T	89	$ .05	$ .20
Royals, Team Leaders	87T	256	$ .01	$ .03	Ruhle, Vern	77T	311	$ .05	$ .15
Royals, Team Leaders	88T	141	$ .01	$ .03	Ruhle, Vern	78T	456	$ .02	$ .10
Royals, Team Leaders	89T	789	$ .01	$ .04	Ruhle, Vern	79T	49	$ .02	$ .10
Royster, Jerry	76T	592	$1.25	$3.75	Ruhle, Vern	80T	234	$ .01	$ .07
Royster, Jerry	77T	549	$ .05	$ .15	Ruhle, Vern	81T	642	$ .01	$ .07
Royster, Jerry	78T	187	$ .02	$ .10	Ruhle, Vern	82T	539	$ .01	$ .06
Royster, Jerry	79T	344	$ .02	$ .10	Ruhle, Vern	83T	172	$ .01	$ .06
Royster, Jerry	80T	463	$ .01	$ .07	Ruhle, Vern	84T	328	$ .01	$ .05
Royster, Jerry	81T	268	$ .01	$ .07	Ruhle, Vern	85T	426	$ .01	$ .04
Royster, Jerry	82T	608	$ .01	$ .06	Ruhle, Vern	85TTR	99	$ .02	$ .10
Royster, Jerry	83T	26	$ .01	$ .06	Ruhle, Vern	86T	768	$ .01	$ .03
Royster, Jerry	84T	572	$ .01	$ .05	Ruhle, Vern	87T	221	$ .01	$ .03
Royster, Jerry	85T	776	$ .01	$ .04	Ruiz, Chico	63T	407	$ .35	$1.20
Royster, Jerry	85TTR	96	$ .02	$ .10	Ruiz, Chico	64T	356	$ .25	$ .85
Royster, Jerry	86T	118	$ .01	$ .03	Ruiz, Chico	65T	554	$1.50	$3.75
Royster, Jerry	87T	403	$ .01	$ .03	Ruiz, Chico	66T	159	$ .25	$ .85
Royster, Jerry	87TTR	106	$ .01	$ .07	Ruiz, Chico	67T	339	$ .25	$ .65
Royster, Jerry	88T	257	$ .01	$ .03	Ruiz, Chico	68T	213	$ .25	$ .65
Rozek, Dick	52T	363	$39.00	$135.00	Ruiz, Chico	69T	469	$ .25	$ .65
Rozema, Dave	78T	124	$ .02	$ .10	Ruiz, Chico	70T	606	$ .25	$ .85
Rozema, Dave	79T	33	$ .02	$ .10	Ruiz, Chico	71T	686	$ .70	$2.10
Rozema, Dave	80T	288	$ .01	$ .07	Runge, Paul	85TTR	100	$ .02	$ .10
Rozema, Dave	81T	614	$ .01	$ .07	Runge, Paul	86T	409	$ .01	$ .03
Rozema, Dave	82T	319	$ .01	$ .06	Runge, Paul	89T	38	$ .01	$ .04
Rozema, Dave	83T	562	$ .01	$ .06	Runge, Paul	89TBB	23	$ .01	$ .05
Rozema, Dave	84T	457	$ .01	$ .05	Runnels, James "Pete"	52T	2	$20.00	$65.00
Rozema, Dave	85T	47	$ .01	$ .04	Runnels, Pete	53T	219	$3.75	$13.00
Rozema, Dave	85TTR	97	$ .02	$ .10	Runnels, Pete	54T	6	$2.00	$7.00
Rozema, Dave	86T	739	$ .01	$ .03	Runnels, Pete	56T	234	$2.50	$8.00
Roznovsky, Vic	65T	334	$ .30	$1.00	Runnels, Pete	57T	64	$ .95	$3.50
Roznovsky, Vic	66T	467	$ .70	$2.10	Runnels, Pete	58T	265	$ .50	$2.00
Roznovsky, Vic	67T	163	$ .25	$ .65	Runnels, Pete	59T	370	$ .50	$1.95
Roznovsky, Vic	68T	428	$ .25	$ .65	Runnels, Pete	59T	519	$3.00	$9.00
Roznovsky, Vic	69T	368	$ .25	$ .65	Runnels, Pete	60T	15	$ .35	$1.10
Rucker, Dave	82T	261	$ .01	$ .06	Runnels, Pete	61T	42	$ .50	$2.00
Rucker, Dave	83T	304	$ .01	$ .06	Runnels, Pete	61T	210	$ .30	$1.00
Rucker, Dave	84T	699	$ .01	$ .05	Runnels, Pete	62T	3	$ .35	$1.10
Rucker, Dave	85T	421	$ .01	$ .04	Runnels, Pete	63T	2	$3.00	$12.00
Rucker, Dave	85TTR	98	$ .02	$ .10	Runnels, Pete	63T	230	$ .25	$ .85
Rucker, Dave	86T	39	$ .01	$ .03	Runnels, Pete	64T	121	$ .25	$ .85
Rudi, Joe	69T	587	$ .60	$1.60	Rush, Bob	52T	153	$6.00	$19.00
Rudi, Joe	70T	102	$ .25	$ .65	Rush, Bob	56T	214	$2.50	$8.00
Rudi, Joe	71T	407	$ .10	$ .35	Rush, Bob	57T	137	$ .95	$3.50
Rudi, Joe	72T	209	$ .25	$ .85	Rush, Bob	58T	313	$ .50	$2.00
Rudi, Joe	73T	360	$ .10	$ .35	Rush, Bob	59T	396	$ .50	$1.95
Rudi, Joe	74T	264	$ .06	$ .25	Rush, Bob	60T	404	$ .50	$1.95
Rudi, Joe	75T	45	$ .06	$ .25	Russell, Bill	70T	304	$ .10	$ .35
Rudi, Joe	76T	475	$ .06	$ .25	Russell, Bill	71T	226	$ .10	$ .35
Rudi, Joe	77T	155	$ .05	$ .15	Russell, Bill	72T	736	$ .85	$3.50
Rudi, Joe	78T	635	$ .02	$ .10	Russell, Bill	73T	108	$ .10	$ .35
Rudi, Joe	79T	267	$ .02	$2.10	Russell, Bill	74T	239	$ .06	$ .25
Rudi, Joe	80T	556	$ .01	$ .07	Russell, Bill	75T	23	$ .06	$ .25
Rudi, Joe	81T	701	$ .01	$ .07	Russell, Bill	76T	22	$ .05	$ .20
Rudi, Joe	81TTR	826	$ .02	$ .10	Russell, Bill	77T	322	$ .05	$ .15
Rudi, Joe	82T	388	$ .01	$ .06	Russell, Bill	78T	128	$ .02	$ .10
Rudi, Joe	82TTR	102	$ .02	$ .10	Russell, Bill	79T	546	$ .02	$ .10
Rudi, Joe	83T	87	$ .01	$ .06	Russell, Bill	80T	75	$ .01	$ .07
Rudolph, Don	58T	347	$ .50	$2.00	Russell, Bill	81T	465	$ .01	$ .07
Rudolph, Don	59T	179	$ .50	$1.95	Russell, Bill	82T	279	$ .01	$ .06
Rudolph, Don	62T	224	$ .35	$1.10	Russell, Bill	83T	661	$ .01	$ .06
Rudolph, Don	63T	291	$ .35	$1.20	Russell, Bill	84T	792	$ .01	$ .05

Player	Year	No.	VG	EX/MT
Russell, Bill	85T	343	$ .01	$ .04
Russell, Bill	86T	506	$ .01	$ .03
Russell, Bill	87T	116	$ .01	$ .03
Russell, Jeff	84T	270	$ .01	$ .25
Russell, Jeff	85T	651	$ .01	$ .10
Russell, Jeff	87	444	$ .01	$ .03
Russell, Jeff	88T	114	$ .01	$ .03
Russell, Jeff	89T	565	$ .01	$ .04
Russell, Jeff	89TBB	309	$ .01	$ .05
Russell, Jeff	90T	80	$ .01	$ .03
Russell, Jeff	90TAS	395	$ .01	$ .03
Russell, Jim	52T	51	$14.00	$45.00
Russell, John	86T	392	$ .01	$ .03
Russell, John	87T	379	$ .01	$ .03
Russell, John	88T	188	$ .01	$ .03
Ruth, Babe	61T	401	$3.35	$10.00
Ruth, Babe, Special 1	62T	135	$5.00	$15.00
Ruth, Babe, Special 2	62T	136	$2.50	$8.00
Ruth, Babe, Special 3	62T	137	$2.50	$8.00
Ruth, Babe, Special 4	62T	138	$2.50	$8.00
Ruth, Babe, Special 5	62T	139	$3.00	$12.00
Ruth, Babe, Special 6	62T	140	$3.00	$10.00
Ruth, Babe, Special 7	62T	141	$2.50	$8.00
Ruth, Babe, Special 8	62T	142	$2.50	$8.00
Ruth, Babe, Special 9	62T	143	$2.50	$8.00
Ruth, Babe, Special 10	62T	144	$2.50	$8.00
Ruth, Babe	73T	1	$3.50	$12.50
Ruth, Babe	73TATL	474	$1.30	$5.00
Ruth, Babe	76TAS	345	$1.10	$3.25
Rutherford, John	52T	320	$39.00	$135.00
Rutherford, John	53T	137	$3.75	$13.00
Ruthven, Dick	74T	47	$ .06	$ .25
Ruthven, Dick	75T	267	$ .06	$ .25
Ruthven, Dick	76T	431	$ .05	$ .20
Ruthven, Dick	77T	575	$ .05	$ .15
Ruthven, Dick	78T	75	$ .02	$ .10
Ruthven, Dick	79T	419	$ .02	$ .10
Ruthven, Dick	80T	136	$ .01	$ .07
Ruthven, Dick	81T	691	$ .01	$ .07
Ruthven, Dick	82T	317	$ .01	$ .06
Ruthven, Dick	83T	484	$ .01	$ .06
Ruthven, Dick	83TTR	98	$ .02	$ .10
Ruthven, Dick	84T	736	$ .01	$ .05
Ruthven, Dick	85T	563	$ .01	$ .04
Ruthven, Dick	86T	98	$ .01	$ .03
Ryal, Mark	88T	243	$ .01	$ .03
Ryan, Connie	52T	107	$6.00	$19.00
Ryan, Connie	53T	102	$3.75	$13.00
Ryan, Connie	54T	136	$2.00	$7.00
Ryan, Connie	74T	634	$ .30	$1.00
Ryan, Mike	65T	573	$2.50	$9.00
Ryan, Mike	66T	419	$ .25	$ .85
Ryan, Mike	67T	223	$ .25	$ .65
Ryan, Mike	68T	306	$ .25	$ .65
Ryan, Mike	69T	28	$ .25	$ .65
Ryan, Mike	70T	591	$ .25	$ .85
Ryan, Mike	71T	533	$ .30	$1.00
Ryan, Mike	72T	324	$ .10	$ .35
Ryan, Mike	73T	467	$ .06	$ .25
Ryan, Mike	74T	564	$ .06	$ .25
Ryan, Nolan	68T	177	$200.00	$700.00
Ryan, Nolan	69T	533	$100.00	$250.00
Ryan, Nolan	70T	712	$100.00	$250.00
Ryan, Nolan	71T	513	$25.00	$90.00
Ryan, Nolan	72T	595	$20.00	$75.00
Ryan, Nolan	73T	220	$10.00	$35.00
Ryan, Nolan	73T	67	$ .85	$3.50
Ryan, Nolan	74T	20	$5.00	$17.50
Ryan, Nolan	74T	207	$ .50	$2.00
Ryan, Nolan	75T	312	$ .50	$2.50
Ryan, Nolan	75T	500	$5.00	$20.00
Ryan, Nolan	75THL	7	$ .25	$ .85
Ryan, Nolan	75THL	75	$1.50	$4.50
Ryan, Nolan	76T	330	$5.00	$15.00
Ryan, Nolan	77T	6	$ .50	$2.00

Player	Year	No.	VG	EX/MT
Ryan, Nolan	77T	650	$4.50	$14.00
Ryan, Nolan	77TRB	234	$ .50	$2.50
Ryan, Nolan	78T	206	$ .05	$ .20

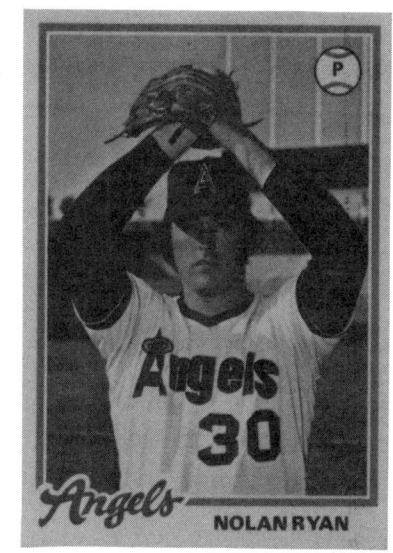

NOLAN RYAN

Player	Year	No.	VG	EX/MT
Ryan, Nolan	78T	400	$2.00	$8.00
Ryan, Nolan	78TRB	6	$ .75	$3.00
Ryan, Nolan	79T	6	$ .06	$ .30
Ryan, Nolan	79T	115	$2.00	$8.00
Ryan, Nolan	79TRH	417	$ .05	$ .20
Ryan, Nolan	80T	206	$ .05	$ .25
Ryan, Nolan	80T	580	$1.50	$6.00
Ryan, Nolan	81T	240	$ .95	$3.50
Ryan, Nolan	82T	66	$ .03	$ .15
Ryan, Nolan	82T	90	$ .50	$2.00
Ryan, Nolan	82T	167	$ .03	$ .15
Ryan, Nolan	82THL	5	$ .05	$ .25
Ryan, Nolan	83T	360	$ .50	$2.00
Ryan, Nolan	83T	361	$ .01	$ .06
Ryan, Nolan	84T	4	$ .05	$ .25
Ryan, Nolan	84T	66	$ .01	$ .05
Ryan, Nolan	84T	470	$ .40	$1.50
Ryan, Nolan	84T	707	$ .05	$ .25
Ryan, Nolan	85T	760	$ .15	$ .75
Ryan, Nolan	85TRB	7	$ .04	$ .20
Ryan, Nolan	86T	100	$ .15	$ .75
Ryan, Nolan	87T	757	$ .10	$ .65
Ryan, Nolan	88T	250	$ .01	$ .50
Ryan, Nolan	88TBB	29	$ .05	$ .25
Ryan, Nolan	88TRB	6	$ .01	$ .10
Ryan, Nolan	88TTB	661	$ .05	$ .35
Ryan, Nolan	89T	530	$ .05	$ .50
Ryan, Nolan	89TTR	106	$ .01	$1.00
Ryan, Nolan	90T	1	$ .01	$ .50
Ryan, Nolan (Angels)	90T	3	$ .01	$ .15
Ryan, Nolan (Astros)	90T	4	$ .01	$ .15
Ryan, Nolan (Mets)	90T	2	$ .01	$ .15
Ryan, Nolan (Rangers)	90T	5	$ .01	$ .15
Ryba, Mike	54T	237	$2.00	$7.00
Saberhagen, Bret	84TTR	104	$5.00	$20.00
Saberhagen, Bret	85T	23	$1.25	$5.00
Saberhagen, Bret	86T	487	$ .10	$ .50
Saberhagen, Bret	86TAS	720	$ .02	$ .15
Saberhagen, Bret	87T	140	$ .10	$ .35
Saberhagen, Bret	88T	540	$ .01	$ .20

TOPPS

Player	Year	No.	VG	EX/MT	Player	Year	No.	VG	EX/MT
Saberhagen, Bret	88TBB	94	$ .01	$ .10	Salazar, Luis	82T	366	$ .01	$ .06
Saberhagen, Bret	89T	750	$ .01	$ .10	Salazar, Luis	82T	662	$ .01	$ .06
Saberhagen, Bret	89TBB	6	$ .01	$ .20	Salazar, Luis	83T	533	$ .01	$ .06
Saberhagen, Bret	90T	350	$ .01	$ .10	Salazar, Luis	84T	68	$ .01	$ .05
Saberhagen, Bret	90TAS	393	$ .01	$ .10	Salazar, Luis	85T	789	$ .01	$ .04
Sabo, Chris	88TTR	98	$ .15	$1.50	Salazar, Luis	85TTR	102	$ .02	$ .10
Sabo, Chris	89T	490	$ .10	$1.00	Salazar, Luis	86T	103	$ .01	$ .03
Sabo, Chris	89TBB	251	$ .01	$ .25	Salazar, Luis	87T	454	$ .01	$ .03
Sabo, Chris	90T	737	$ .01	$ .20	Salazar, Luis	87TTR	108	$ .01	$ .07
Sadecki, Ray	60T	327	$ .50	$1.95	Salazar, Luis	88T	276	$ .01	$ .03
Sadecki, Ray	61T	32	$ .30	$1.00	Salazar, Luis	88TTR	100	$ .01	$ .05
Sadecki, Ray	62T	383	$ .70	$2.10	Salazar, Luis	89T	553	$ .01	$ .04
Sadecki, Ray	63T	486	$2.50	$6.50	Salazar, Luis	89TTR	107	$ .01	$ .05
Sadecki, Ray	64T	147	$ .25	$ .85	Salazar, Luis	90T	378	$ .01	$ .03
Sadecki, Ray	65T	10	$ .35	$1.10	Salkeld, Roger	90T	44	$ .01	$ .25
Sadecki, Ray	65T	230	$ .30	$1.00	Salmon, Chico	64T	499	$ .40	$1.25
Sadecki, Ray	66T	26	$ .25	$ .85	Salmon, Chico	65T	105	$ .25	$ .65
Sadecki, Ray	67T	409	$ .25	$ .85	Salmon, Chico	66T	594	$4.50	$15.00
Sadecki, Ray	68T	494	$ .30	$1.00	Salmon, Chico	67T	43	$ .25	$ .65
Sadecki, Ray	69T	125	$ .25	$ .65	Salmon, Chico	68T	318	$ .25	$ .65
Sadecki, Ray	70T	679	$ .50	$2.00	Salmon, Chico	69T	62	$ .25	$ .65
Sadecki, Ray	71T	406	$ .10	$ .35	Salmon, Chico	70T	301	$ .10	$ .35
Sadecki, Ray	72T	563	$ .25	$ .85	Salmon, Chico	71T	249	$ .10	$ .35
Sadecki, Ray	72TIA	564	$ .25	$ .85	Salmon, Chico	72T	646	$ .25	$ .85
Sadecki, Ray	73T	283	$ .06	$ .25	Sambito, Joe	77T	227	$ .05	$ .15
Sadecki, Ray	74T	216	$ .06	$ .25	Sambito, Joe	78T	498	$ .02	$ .10
Sadecki, Ray	75T	349	$ .06	$ .25	Sambito, Joe	79T	158	$ .02	$ .10
Sadecki, Ray	77T	26	$ .05	$ .15	Sambito, Joe	80T	571	$ .01	$ .07
Sadek, Mike	74T	577	$ .06	$ .25	Sambito, Joe	81T	385	$ .01	$ .07
Sadek, Mike	76T	234	$ .05	$ .20	Sambito, Joe	82T	34	$ .01	$ .06
Sadek, Mike	77T	129	$ .05	$ .15	Sambito, Joe	83T	662	$ .01	$ .06
Sadek, Mike	78T	8	$ .02	$ .10	Sambito, Joe	85T	264	$ .01	$ .04
Sadek, Mike	79T	256	$ .02	$ .10	Sambito, Joe	85TTR	103	$ .02	$ .10
Sadek, Mike	80T	462	$ .01	$ .07	Sambito, Joe	86TTR	97	$ .02	$ .10
Sadek, Mike	81T	384	$ .01	$ .07	Sambito, Joe	87T	451	$ .01	$ .03
Sadowski, Bob	62T	595	$6.00	$18.00	Sambito, Joe	88T	784	$ .01	$ .03
Sadowski, Bob	63T	568	$1.50	$3.75	Samford, Ron	59T	242	$ .50	$1.95
Sadowski, Bob	64T	271	$ .25	$ .85	Samford, Ron	60T	409	$ .50	$1.95
Sadowski, Bob	65T	156	$ .25	$ .65	Sample, Billy	79T	713	$ .05	$ .20
Sadowski, Bob	66T	523	$4.50	$15.00	Sample, Billy	80T	458	$ .01	$ .07
Sadowski, Ed	59T	139	$ .50	$1.95	Sample, Billy	81T	283	$ .01	$ .07
Sadowski, Ed	60T	403	$ .50	$1.95	Sample, Billy	82T	112	$ .01	$ .06
Sadowski, Ed	61T	163	$ .30	$1.00	Sample, Billy	83T	641	$ .01	$ .06
Sadowski, Ed	62T	569	$3.75	$11.00	Sample, Billy	84T	12	$ .01	$ .05
Sadowski, Ed	63T	527	$1.50	$3.75	Sample, Billy	85T	337	$ .01	$ .04
Sadowski, Ed	64T	61	$ .25	$ .85	Sample, Billy	86T	533	$ .01	$ .03
Sadowski, Ted	61T	254	$ .30	$1.00	Sample, Billy	86TTR	98	$ .02	$ .10
Saferight, Harry	80T	683	$ .01	$ .07	Sample, Billy	87T	104	$ .01	$ .03
Sain, Johnny	51Tbb	9	$6.50	$25.00	Samuel, Amado	62T	597	$6.00	$18.00
Sain, Johnny	52T	49	$25.00	$75.00	Samuel, Amado	64T	129	$ .25	$ .85
Sain, Johnny	53T	119	$8.00	$25.00	Samuel, Juan	84TTR	105	$ .95	$3.50
Sain, Johnny	54T	205	$8.00	$25.00	Samuel, Juan	85T	265	$ .25	$ .65
Sain, Johnny	55T	193	$7.50	$30.00	Samuel, Juan	85TRB	8	$ .01	$ .10
Sain, Johnny	73T	356	$ .10	$ .35	Samuel, Juan	86T	475	$ .01	$ .10
Sain, Johnny	74T	221	$ .06	$ .25	Samuel, Juan	87T	255	$ .01	$ .10
Sakata, Lenn	80T	668	$ .01	$ .07	Samuel, Juan	88T	705	$ .01	$ .10
Sakata, Lenn	81T	287	$ .01	$ .07	Samuel, Juan	88TAS	398	$ .01	$ .03
Sakata, Lenn	82T	136	$ .01	$ .06	Samuel, Juan	88TBB	67	$ .01	$ .10
Sakata, Lenn	83T	319	$ .01	$ .06	Samuel, Juan	89T	575	$ .01	$ .04
Sakata, Lenn	84T	578	$ .01	$ .05	Samuel, Juan	89TBB	321	$ .01	$ .05
Sakata, Lenn	85T	81	$ .01	$ .04	Samuel, Juan	89TTR	108	$ .01	$ .10
Sakata, Lenn	86T	446	$ .01	$ .03	Samuel, Juan	90T	85	$ .01	$ .03
Sakata, Lenn	88T	716	$ .01	$ .03	Sanchez, Alejandro	86T	563	$ .01	$ .03
Salas, Mark	85TTR	101	$ .02	$ .10	Sanchez, Alex	89TMLD	107	$ .01	$ .15
Salas, Mark	86T	537	$ .01	$ .03	Sanchez, Alex	89TTR	109	$ .01	$ .25
Salas, Mark	87T	87	$ .01	$ .03	Sanchez, Alex	90T	563	$ .01	$ .15
Salas, Mark	87TTR	107	$ .01	$ .07	Sanchez, Celerino	73T	103	$ .06	$ .25
Salas, Mark	88TTR	99	$ .01	$ .05	Sanchez, Celerino	74T	623	$ .06	$ .25
Salas, Mark	89T	384	$ .01	$ .04	Sanchez, Israel	89T	452	$ .01	$ .10
Salazar, Argenis	85T	154	$ .01	$ .04	Sanchez, Luis	82T	653	$ .95	$3.50
Salazar, Argenis	86TTR	96	$ .02	$ .10	Sanchez, Luis	83T	623	$ .01	$ .06
Salazar, Argenis	87T	533	$ .01	$ .03	Sanchez, Luis	84T	258	$ .01	$ .05
Salazar, Argenis	88T	29	$ .01	$ .03	Sanchez, Luis	85T	42	$ .01	$ .04
Salazar, Argenis	89T	642	$ .01	$ .04	Sanchez, Luis	86T	124	$ .01	$ .03
Salazar, Luis	81T	309	$ .01	$ .07	Sanchez, Orlando	82T	604	$ .01	$ .06

Player	Year	No.	VG	EX/MT
Sanchez, Raul	57T	393	$ .85	$3.50
Sanchez, Raul	60T	311	$ .50	$1.95
Sandberg, Ryne	83T	83	$3.50	$15.00
Sandberg, Ryne	84T	596	$ .65	$3.00
Sandberg, Ryne	85T	460	$ .05	$ .50
Sandberg, Ryne	85TAS	713	$ .01	$ .10
Sandberg, Ryne	86T	690	$ .03	$ .30
Sandberg, Ryne	87T	680	$ .10	$ .35
Sandberg, Ryne	88T	10	$ .01	$ .10
Sandberg, Ryne	88TBB	16	$ .01	$ .15
Sandberg, Ryne	89T	360	$ .01	$ .15
Sandberg, Ryne	89TAS	387	$ .01	$ .04
Sandberg, Ryne	89TBB	212	$ .01	$ .25
Sandberg, Ryne	90T	210	$ .01	$ .10
Sandberg, Ryne	90TAS	398	$ .01	$ .10
Sanders, Deion	89TMLD	108	$ .01	$ .50
Sanders, Deion	89TTR	110	$ .01	$1.00
Sanders, Deion	90T	61	$ .01	$ .50
Sanders, Ken	66T	356	$ .25	$ .85
Sanders, Ken	71T	116	$ .10	$ .35
Sanders, Ken	72T	391	$ .10	$ .35
Sanders, Ken	73T	246	$ .06	$ .25
Sanders, Ken	74T	638	$ .06	$ .25
Sanders, Ken	75T	366	$ .06	$ .25
Sanders, Ken	76T	291	$ .05	$ .20
Sanders, Ken	77T	171	$ .05	$ .15
Sanders, Reggie	74T	600	$1.00	$4.00
Sanders, Reggie	75T	617	$ .35	$1.10
Sanderson, Scott	79T	720	$ .05	$ .20
Sanderson, Scott	80T	578	$ .01	$ .07
Sanderson, Scott	81T	235	$ .01	$ .07
Sanderson, Scott	82T	7	$ .01	$ .06
Sanderson, Scott	83T	717	$ .01	$ .06
Sanderson, Scott	84T	164	$ .01	$ .05
Sanderson, Scott	84TTR	106	$ .02	$ .10
Sanderson, Scott	85T	616	$ .01	$ .04
Sanderson, Scott	86T	406	$ .01	$ .03
Sanderson, Scott	87T	534	$ .01	$ .03
Sanderson, Scott	88T	311	$ .01	$ .03
Sanderson, Scott	89T	212	$ .01	$ .04
Sanderson, Scott	90T	67	$ .01	$ .03
Sandlock, Mike	53T	247	$11.00	$37.50
Sandlock, Mike	54T	104	$2.00	$7.00
Sands, Charlie	72T	538	$ .25	$ .85
Sands, Charlie	74T	381	$ .06	$ .25
Sands, Charlie	75T	548	$ .06	$ .25
Sandt, Tommy	77T	616	$ .05	$ .15
Sanford, Jack	57T	387	$1.00	$4.25
Sanford, Jack	58T	264	$ .50	$2.00
Sanford, Jack	59T	275	$ .50	$1.95
Sanford, Jack	60T	165	$ .35	$1.10
Sanford, Jack	61T	258	$ .30	$1.00
Sanford, Jack	61T	383	$ .50	$2.00
Sanford, Jack	62T	538	$3.75	$11.00
Sanford, Jack	63T	7	$ .35	$1.10
Sanford, Jack	63T	325	$ .35	$1.20
Sanford, Jack	64T	414	$ .40	$1.25
Sanford, Jack	65T	228	$ .30	$1.00
Sanford, Jack	66T	23	$ .25	$ .85
Sanford, Jack	67T	549	$2.00	$6.00
Sanguillen, Manny	68T	251	$ .15	$ .50
Sanguillen, Manny	69T	509	$ .25	$ .85
Sanguillen, Manny	70T	188	$ .10	$ .35
Sanguillen, Manny	71T	62	$ .15	$ .50
Sanguillen, Manny	71T	480	$ .10	$ .35
Sanguillen, Manny	72T	60	$ .25	$ .65
Sanguillen, Manny	73T	250	$ .06	$ .25
Sanguillen, Manny	74T	28	$ .06	$ .25
Sanguillen, Manny	75T	515	$ .06	$ .25
Sanguillen, Manny	76T	191	$ .25	$ .85
Sanguillen, Manny	76T	220	$ .05	$ .20
Sanguillen, Manny	77T	61	$ .05	$ .15
Sanguillen, Manny	78T	658	$ .02	$ .10
Sanguillen, Manny	79T	447	$ .02	$ .10
Sanguillen, Manny	80T	148	$ .01	$ .07

Player	Year	No.	VG	EX/MT
Sanguillen, Manny	81T	226	$ .01	$ .07
Santana, Rafael	85T	67	$ .01	$ .04
Santana, Rafael	86T	587	$ .01	$ .03
Santana, Rafael	87T	378	$ .01	$ .03
Santana, Rafael	88T	233	$ .01	$ .03
Santana, Rafael	88TBB	246	$ .01	$ .05
Santana, Rafael	88TTR	101	$ .01	$ .05
Santana, Rafael	89T	792	$ .01	$ .04
Santana, Rafael	89TBB	192	$ .01	$ .05
Santana, Rafael	90T	651	$ .01	$ .03
Santiago, Benny	87TTR	109	$ .20	$1.00
Santiago, Benny	88T	693	$ .10	$ .50
Santiago, Benito "Benny"	88TRB	7	$ .01	$ .05
Santiago, Benny	88TAS	404	$ .01	$ .25
Santiago, Benny	88TBB	12	$ .01	$ .10
Santiago, Benny	89T	256	$ .01	$ .04
Santiago, Benny	89TBB	134	$ .01	$ .15
Santiago, Benny	90T	35	$ .01	$ .10
Santiago, Jose	56T	59	$1.25	$4.50
Santiago, Jose	65T	557	$1.50	$3.75
Santiago, Jose	66T	203	$ .25	$ .85
Santiago, Jose	67T	473	$ .50	$2.00

JOSE SANTIAGO — PITCHER RED SOX

Player	Year	No.	VG	EX/MT
Santiago, Jose	68T	123	$ .25	$ .65
Santiago, Jose	69T	21	$ .25	$ .65
Santiago, Jose	70T	708	$ .50	$2.00
Santo, Ron	61T	35	$2.50	$10.00
Santo, Ron	62T	170	$ .70	$2.00
Santo, Ron	63T	252	$ .85	$2.50
Santo, Ron	64T	375	$ .50	$2.00
Santo, Ron	65T	6	$ .95	$3.50
Santo, Ron	65T	110	$ .15	$ .50
Santo, Ron	66T	290	$ .35	$1.10
Santo, Ron	67T	70	$ .30	$1.00
Santo, Ron	68T	5	$1.35	$4.00
Santo, Ron	68T	235	$ .35	$1.10
Santo, Ron	68TAS	366	$ .35	$1.10
Santo, Ron	69T	4	$ .70	$2.00
Santo, Ron	69T	570	$ .20	$ .50
Santo, Ron	69TAS	420	$ .25	$ .65
Santo, Ron	70T	63	$ .50	$1.95
Santo, Ron	70T	670	$ .70	$2.00
Santo, Ron	70TAS	454	$ .10	$ .35
Santo, Ron	71T	220	$ .15	$ .50

TOPPS

Player	Year	No.	VG	EX/MT	Player	Year	No.	VG	EX/MT
Santo, Ron	72T	555	$ .25	$ .85	Sawatski, Carl	61T	198	$ .30	$1.00
Santo, Ron	72TIA	556	$ .25	$ .85	Sawatski, Carl	62T	106	$ .35	$1.10
Santo, Ron	73T	115	$ .06	$ .25	Sawatski, Carl	63T	267	$ .25	$ .85
Santo, Ron	74T	270	$ .25	$ .85	Sawatski, Carl	64T	24	$ .25	$ .85
Santo, Ron	74TAS	334	$ .35	$1.10	Sawyer, Eddie	60T	226	$ .35	$1.10
Santo, Ron	74TTR	270	$ .25	$ .65	Sawyer, Rick	77T	268	$ .05	$ .15
Santo, Ron	75T	35	$ .10	$ .35	Sax, Dave	86T	307	$ .01	$ .03
Santorini, Al	69T	592	$ .25	$ .85	Sax, Steve	82T	681	$ .75	$3.50
Santorini, Al	70T	212	$ .10	$ .35	Sax, Steve	82TTR	103	$1.00	$4.00
Santorini, Al	71T	467	$ .10	$ .35	Sax, Steve	83T	245	$ .05	$ .50
Santorini, Al	72T	723	$ .70	$2.10	Sax, Steve	84T	610	$ .04	$ .25
Santorini, Al	73T	24	$ .06	$ .25	Sax, Steve	85T	470	$ .01	$ .15
Santovenia, Nelson	88TTR	102	$ .01	$ .10	Sax, Steve	86T	175	$ .02	$ .15
Santovenia, Nelson	89T	228	$ .01	$ .10	Sax, Steve	87T	769	$ .01	$ .10
Santovenia, Nelson	89TBB	98	$ .01	$ .05	Sax, Steve	87TAS	596	$ .01	$ .03
Santovenia, Nelson	90T	614	$ .01	$ .03	Sax, Steve	88T	305	$ .01	$ .10
Sarmiento, Manny	77T	475	$ .05	$ .15	Sax, Steve	88TBB	46	$ .01	$ .15
Sarmiento, Manny	78T	377	$ .02	$ .10	Sax, Steve	89T	40	$ .01	$ .10
Sarmiento, Manny	79T	149	$ .02	$ .10	Sax, Steve	89TBB	111	$ .01	$ .05
Sarmiento, Manny	80T	21	$ .01	$ .07	Sax, Steve	89TTR	111	$ .01	$ .10
Sarmiento, Manny	81T	649	$ .01	$ .07	Sax, Steve	90T	560	$ .01	$ .03
Sarmiento, Manny	83T	566	$ .01	$ .06	Scanlon, Pat	78T	611	$ .02	$ .10
Sarmiento, Manny	84T	209	$ .01	$ .05	Scarbery, Randy	80T	291	$ .01	$ .07
Sarni, Bill	54T	194	$2.00	$7.00	Scarborough, Ray	51Trb	42	$1.35	$4.00
Sarni, Bill	56T	247	$2.50	$8.00	Scarborough, Ray	52T	43	$14.00	$45.00
Sarni, Bill	57T	86	$ .95	$3.50	Scarborough, Ray	53T	213	$3.75	$13.00
Sasser, Mackey	88TTR	103	$ .01	$ .05	Scarce, Mac	73T	6	$ .06	$ .25
Sasser, Mackey	89T	457	$ .01	$ .04	Scarce, Mac	74T	149	$ .06	$ .25
Sasser, Mackey	90T	656	$ .01	$ .03	Scarce, Mac	75T	527	$ .06	$ .25
Satriano, Tom	63T	548	$1.50	$3.75	Schaal, Paul	65T	517	$ .50	$2.00
Satriano, Tom	64T	521	$ .40	$1.25	Schaal, Paul	66T	376	$ .25	$ .85
Satriano, Tom	65T	124	$ .25	$ .65	Schaal, Paul	67T	58	$ .25	$ .65
Satriano, Tom	66T	361	$ .25	$ .85	Schaal, Paul	68T	474	$ .30	$1.00
Satriano, Tom	67T	343	$ .25	$ .65	Schaal, Paul	69T	352	$ .25	$ .65
Satriano, Tom	68T	238	$ .25	$ .65	Schaal, Paul	70T	338	$ .10	$ .35
Satriano, Tom	69T	78	$ .25	$ .65	Schaal, Paul	71T	487	$ .10	$ .35
Satriano, Tom	70T	581	$ .25	$ .85	Schaal, Paul	72T	177	$ .10	$ .35
Satriano, Tom	71T	557	$ .30	$1.00	Schaal, Paul	72TIA	178	$ .10	$ .35
Saucier, Kevin	80T	682	$ .01	$ .07	Schaal, Paul	73T	416	$ .06	$ .25
Saucier, Kevin	81T	53	$ .01	$ .07	Schaal, Paul	74T	514	$ .06	$ .25
Saucier, Kevin	81TTR	827	$ .02	$ .10	Schaefer, Jeff	89TMLD	109	$ .01	$ .05
Saucier, Kevin	82T	238	$ .01	$ .06	Schaffer, Jim	62T	579	$3.75	$11.00
Saucier, Kevin	83T	373	$ .01	$ .06	Schaffer, Jimmie	63T	81	$ .25	$ .85
Sauer, Henry "Hank"	51Tbb	49	$5.00	$20.00	Schaffer, Jim	64T	359	$ .25	$ .85
Sauer, Hank	52T	35	$15.00	$50.00	Schaffer, Jimmie	65T	313	$ .30	$1.00
Sauer, Hank	53T	111	$3.75	$13.00	Schaffer, Jimmie	68T	463	$ .30	$1.00
Sauer, Hank	54T	4	$2.00	$7.00	Schaffernoth, Joe	61T	58	$ .30	$1.00
Sauer, Hank	55T	45	$1.25	$5.00	Schaffernoth, Joe	63T	463	$2.50	$6.50
Sauer, Hank	56T	41	$1.25	$3.50	Schaive, John	61T	259	$ .30	$1.00
Sauer, Hank	57T	197	$ .60	$2.50	Schaive, John	62T	529	$3.75	$11.00
Sauer, Hank	58T	378	$ .55	$1.75	Schaive, John	63T	356	$ .35	$1.20
Sauer, Hank	59T	404	$ .50	$1.95	Schatzeder, Dan	78T	709	$ .02	$ .10
Sauer, Hank	61TMVP	481	$ .60	$1.75	Schatzeder, Dan	79T	124	$ .02	$ .10
Sauer, Hank	75T	190	$ .10	$ .35	Schatzeder, Dan	80T	267	$ .01	$ .07
Saunders, Dennis	71T	423	$ .10	$ .35	Schatzeder, Dan	81T	417	$ .01	$ .07
Savage, Ted	62T	104	$ .35	$1.10	Schatzeder, Dan	82T	691	$ .01	$ .06
Savage, Ted	63T	508	$1.50	$3.75	Schatzeder, Dan	82TTR	104	$ .02	$ .10
Savage, Ted	64T	62	$ .25	$ .85	Schatzeder, Dan	83T	189	$ .01	$ .06
Savage, Ted	67T	552	$1.35	$4.00	Schatzeder, Dan	84T	57	$ .01	$ .05
Savage, Ted	68T	119	$ .25	$ .65	Schatzeder, Dan	85T	501	$ .01	$ .04
Savage, Ted	69T	471	$ .25	$ .65	Schatzeder, Dan	86T	324	$ .01	$ .03
Savage, Ted	70T	602	$ .25	$ .85	Schatzeder, Dan	87T	789	$ .01	$ .03
Savage, Ted	71T	76	$ .10	$ .35	Schatzeder, Dan	88T	218	$ .01	$ .03
Saverine, Bob	63T	158	$ .25	$ .85	Scheffing, Bob	54T	76	$2.00	$7.00
Saverine, Bob	64T	221	$ .25	$ .85	Scheffing, Bob	60T	464	$ .95	$3.50
Saverine, Bob	65T	427	$ .30	$1.00	Scheffing, Bob	61T	223	$ .30	$1.00
Saverine, Bob	66T	312	$ .25	$ .85	Scheffing, Bob	62T	72	$ .35	$1.10
Saverine, Bob	67T	27	$ .25	$ .65	Scheffing, Bob	62T	416	$ .70	$2.10
Saverine, Bob	68T	149	$ .25	$ .65	Scheffing, Bob	63T	134	$ .25	$ .85
Sawatski, Carl	53T	202	$3.75	$13.00	Scheib, Carl	52T	116	$6.00	$19.00
Sawatski, Carl	54T	198	$2.00	$7.00	Scheib, Carl	53T	57	$3.75	$13.00
Sawatski, Carl	55T	122	$1.35	$5.00	Scheib, Carl	54T	118	$2.00	$7.00
Sawatski, Carl	58T	234	$ .50	$2.00	Scheinblum, Richie	65T	577	$1.50	$3.75
Sawatski, Carl	59T	56	$ .85	$3.50	Scheinblum, Richie	68T	16	$1.00	$3.50
Sawatski, Carl	60T	545	$2.00	$7.00	Scheinblum, Richie	69T	479	$ .25	$ .65

Player	Year	No.	VG	EX/MT
Scheinblum, Richie	70T	161	$ .10	$ .35
Scheinblum, Richie	71T	326	$ .10	$ .35
Scheinblum, Richie	72T	468	$ .10	$ .35
Scheinblum, Richie	73T	78	$ .06	$ .25
Scheinblum, Richie	74T	323	$ .06	$ .25
Schell, Danny	55T	79	$1.35	$5.00
Scherger, George	73T	296	$ .15	$ .50
Scherger, George	74T	326	$ .15	$ .50
Scherman, Fred	71T	316	$ .10	$ .35
Scherman, Fred	72T	6	$ .10	$ .35
Scherman, Fred	73T	660	$ .70	$2.10
Scherman, Fred	74T	186	$ .06	$ .25
Scherman, Fred	74TTR	186	$ .06	$ .25
Scherman, Fred	75T	252	$ .06	$ .25
Scherman, Fred	76T	188	$ .05	$ .20

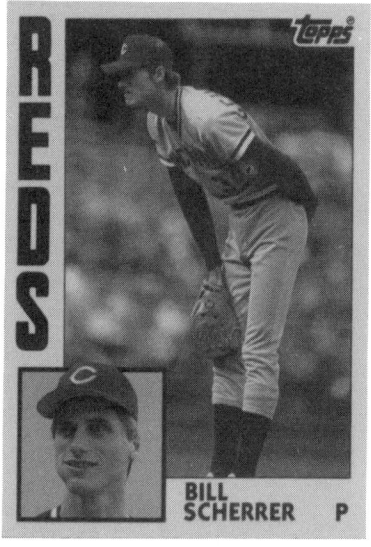

BILL SCHERRER P

Player	Year	No.	VG	EX/MT
Scherrer, Bill	84T	373	$ .01	$ .05
Scherrer, Bill	85T	586	$ .01	$ .04
Scherrer, Bill	86T	217	$ .01	$ .03
Scherrer, Bill	87T	98	$ .01	$ .03
Schilling, Chuck	61T	499	$ .50	$2.00
Schilling, Chuck	62T	345	$ .35	$1.10
Schilling, Chuck	62TAS	467	$ .70	$2.10
Schilling, Chuck	63T	52	$ .25	$ .85
Schilling, Chuck	64T	182	$2.00	$8.00
Schilling, Chuck	64T	481	$ .40	$1.25
Schilling, Chuck	65T	272	$ .30	$1.00
Schilling, Chuck	66T	6	$ .25	$ .85
Schilling, Curt	90T	97	$ .01	$ .10
Schiraldi, Calvin	86T	210	$ .01	$ .03
Schiraldi, Calvin	87T	94	$ .01	$ .03
Schiraldi, Calvin	88T	599	$ .01	$ .03
Schiraldi, Calvin	88TTR	104	$ .01	$ .05
Schiraldi, Calvin	89T	337	$ .01	$ .04
Schiraldi, Calvin	90T	693	$ .01	$ .03
Schlesinger, Bill	65T	573	$2.50	$9.00
Schlesinger, Bill	68T	258	$ .25	$ .65
Schmidt, Bob	58T	468	$ .50	$1.95
Schmidt, Bob	59T	109	$ .85	$3.50
Schmidt, Bob	60T	501	$ .60	$1.75
Schmidt, Bob	61T	31	$ .30	$1.00
Schmidt, Bob	62T	262	$ .35	$1.10
Schmidt, Bob	63T	94	$ .25	$ .85
Schmidt, Bob	65T	582	$1.50	$3.75

Player	Year	No.	VG	EX/MT
Schmidt, Dave	82T	381	$ .05	$ .20
Schmidt, Dave	82T	418	$ .03	$ .15
Schmidt, Dave	83T	116	$ .01	$ .06
Schmidt, Dave	84T	584	$ .01	$ .05
Schmidt, Dave	85T	313	$ .01	$ .04
Schmidt, Dave	86T	79	$ .01	$ .03
Schmidt, Dave	86TTR	99	$ .02	$ .10
Schmidt, Dave	87T	703	$ .01	$ .03
Schmidt, Dave	87TTR	110	$ .01	$ .07
Schmidt, Dave	88T	214	$ .01	$ .03
Schmidt, Dave	89T	677	$ .01	$ .04
Schmidt, Dave	89TBB	130	$ .01	$ .05
Schmidt, Dave	90T	497	$ .01	$ .03
Schmidt, Mike	73T	615	$120.00	$365.00
Schmidt, Mike	74T	283	$22.50	$67.50
Schmidt, Mike	75T	307	$ .30	$1.00
Schmidt, Mike	75T	70	$10.00	$37.50
Schmidt, Mike	76T	193	$ .50	$1.95
Schmidt, Mike	76T	480	$7.50	$22.50
Schmidt, Mike	77T	2	$ .50	$2.00
Schmidt, Mike	77T	140	$3.50	$12.50
Schmidt, Mike	78T	360	$2.00	$7.00
Schmidt, Mike	79T	610	$1.25	$5.00
Schmidt, Mike	80T	270	$ .50	$2.00
Schmidt, Mike	81T	2	$ .06	$ .30
Schmidt, Mike	81T	3	$ .05	$ .25
Schmidt, Mike	81T	540	$ .35	$1.10
Schmidt, Mike	81TRB	206	$ .10	$ .50
Schmidt, Mike	82T	100	$ .35	$1.10
Schmidt, Mike	82T	162	$ .05	$ .25
Schmidt, Mike	82T	163	$ .05	$ .25
Schmidt, Mike	82TAS	339	$ .25	$ .65
Schmidt, Mike	82TIA	101	$ .15	$ .50
Schmidt, Mike	83T	300	$ .50	$2.00
Schmidt, Mike	83T	301	$ .10	$ .50
Schmidt, Mike	83TAS	399	$ .08	$ .40
Schmidt, Mike	84T	132	$ .08	$ .35
Schmidt, Mike	84T	700	$ .25	$1.00
Schmidt, Mike	84T	703	$ .02	$ .10
Schmidt, Mike	84TAS	388	$ .07	$ .30
Schmidt, Mike	85T	500	$ .10	$ .50
Schmidt, Mike	85TAS	714	$ .05	$ .25
Schmidt, Mike	86T	200	$ .05	$ .45
Schmidt, Mike	87T	430	$ .25	$ .85
Schmidt, Mike	87TAS	597	$ .03	$ .15
Schmidt, Mike	88T	600	$ .01	$ .25
Schmidt, Mike	88TBB	88	$ .05	$ .30
Schmidt, Mike	89T	100	$ .01	$ .15
Schmidt, Mike	89TBB	220	$ .01	$ .60
Schmidt, Mike	90TTB	662	$ .01	$ .03
Schmidt, Willard	53T	168	$3.75	$13.00
Schmidt, Willard	56T	323	$1.30	$5.00
Schmidt, Willard	57T	206	$ .95	$3.50
Schmidt, Willard	58T	214	$ .50	$2.00
Schmidt, Willard	59T	171	$ .50	$1.95
Schmitz, Johnny	51Tbb	41	$5.50	$17.00
Schmitz, Johnny	52T	136	$6.00	$18.00
Schmitz, Johnny	54T	33	$1.25	$5.00
Schmitz, Johnny	55T	159	$2.00	$7.00
Schmitz, Johnny	56T	298	$1.30	$5.00
Schneider, Dan	63T	299	$ .35	$1.20
Schneider, Dan	64T	351	$ .25	$ .85
Schneider, Dan	65T	366	$ .30	$1.00
Schneider, Dan	67T	543	$1.35	$4.00
Schneider, Dan	68T	57	$ .25	$ .65
Schneider, Dan	69T	656	$ .25	$ .85
Schneider, Jeff	82T	21	$3.25	$12.50
Schoendienst, Al	51Tbb	6	$7.50	$30.00
Schoendienst, Al	52T	91	$19.50	$57.50
Schoendienst, Al	53T	78	$16.50	$50.00
Schoendienst, Al "Red"	56T	165	$6.00	$18.00
Schoendienst, Red	57T	154	$5.00	$15.00
Schoendienst, Red	58T	190	$2.50	$10.00
Schoendienst, Red	59T	480	$2.50	$10.00
Schoendienst, Red	60T	335	$2.00	$8.00

Player	Year	No.	VG	EX/MT
Schoendienst, Red	61T	505	$2.00	$8.00
Schoendienst, Red	62T	575	$8.00	$25.00
Schoendienst, Red	65T	556	$2.00	$7.00
Schoendienst, Red	66T	76	$1.00	$3.00
Schoendienst, Red	67T	512	$ .70	$2.00
Schoendienst, Red	68T	294	$ .35	$1.10
Schoendienst, Red	69T	462	$ .15	$ .50
Schoendienst, Red	70T	346	$ .75	$3.00
Schoendienst, Red	71T	239	$ .50	$2.00
Schoendienst, Red	72T	67	$ .25	$ .65
Schoendienst, Red	73T	497	$ .25	$ .65
Schoendienst, Red	74T	236	$ .06	$ .25
Schofield, Dick	54T	191	$1.75	$7.00
Schofield, Dick	55T	143	$1.35	$5.00
Schofield, Dick	58T	106	$ .85	$3.50
Schofield, Dick	59T	68	$ .85	$3.50
Schofield, Dick	60T	104	$ .35	$1.10
Schofield, Dick	61T	453	$ .50	$2.00
Schofield, Dick	62T	484	$ .70	$2.10
Schofield, Dick	63T	34	$ .25	$ .85
Schofield, Dick	64T	284	$ .25	$ .85
Schofield, Dick	65T	218	$ .30	$1.00
Schofield, Dick	66T	156	$ .15	$ .50
Schofield, Dick	66T	474	$ .70	$2.10
Schofield, Dick	67T	381	$ .25	$ .85
Schofield, Dick	68T	588	$ .30	$1.00
Schofield, Dick	69T	18	$ .25	$ .65
Schofield, Dick	70T	251	$ .10	$ .35
Schofield, Dick	71T	396	$ .10	$ .35
Schofield, Dick	84TTR	107	$ .08	$ .30
Schofield, Dick	85T	138	$ .01	$ .10
Schofield, Dick	89TBB	53	$ .01	$ .05
Schofield, Dick	90T	189	$ .01	$ .03
Schofield, Dick, Jr.	85T	138	$ .01	$ .10
Schofield, Dick, Jr.	85T	629	$ .01	$ .04
Schofield, Dick, Jr.	86T	311	$ .01	$ .03
Schofield, Dick, Jr.	87T	502	$ .01	$ .03
Schofield, Dick, Jr.	88T	43	$ .01	$ .03
Schofield, Dick, Jr.	88TBB	204	$ .01	$ .05
Schofield, Dick, Jr.	89T	477	$ .01	$ .04
Schooler, Mike	88TTR	105	$ .01	$ .30
Schooler, Mike	89T	199	$ .01	$ .30
Schooler, Mike	90T	681	$ .01	$ .03
Schoonmaker, Jerry	56T	216	$2.50	$8.00
Schoonmaker, Jerry	57T	334	$3.50	$13.00
Schreiber, Paul	54T	217	$2.00	$7.00
Schroder, Bob	65T	589	$1.50	$3.75
Schroeder, Bill	84T	738	$ .01	$ .05
Schroeder, Bill	85T	176	$ .01	$ .04
Schroeder, Bill	86T	662	$ .01	$ .03
Schroeder, Bill	87T	302	$ .01	$ .03
Schroeder, Bill	88T	12	$ .01	$ .03
Schroeder, Bill	89T	563	$ .01	$ .04
Schroeder, Bill	90T	244	$ .01	$ .03
Schroll, Al	59T	546	$2.00	$7.00
Schroll, Al	60T	357	$ .50	$1.95
Schroll, Al	62T	102	$ .35	$1.10
Schrom, Ken	81T	577	$ .01	$ .07
Schrom, Ken	84T	11	$ .01	$ .05
Schrom, Ken	84T	322	$ .01	$ .05
Schrom, Ken	85T	161	$ .01	$ .04
Schrom, Ken	86T	71	$ .01	$ .03
Schrom, Ken	86TTR	100	$ .02	$ .10
Schrom, Ken	87T	635	$ .01	$ .03
Schrom, Ken	88T	256	$ .01	$ .03
Schu, Rick	85TTR	104	$ .02	$ .10
Schu, Rick	86T	16	$ .01	$ .03
Schu, Rick	87T	209	$ .01	$ .03
Schu, Rick	88T	731	$ .01	$ .03
Schu, Rick	88TBB	122	$ .01	$ .05
Schu, Rick	89T	352	$ .01	$ .04
Schu, Rick	89TBB	164	$ .01	$ .05
Schu, Rick	89TTR	112	$ .01	$ .05
Schu, Rick	90T	498	$ .01	$ .03
Schueler, Ron	73T	169	$ .06	$ .25

Player	Year	No.	VG	EX/MT
Schueler, Ron	74T	544	$ .06	$ .25
Schueler, Ron	74TTR	544	$ .06	$ .25
Schueler, Ron	75T	292	$ .06	$ .25
Schueler, Ron	76T	586	$ .05	$ .20
Schueler, Ron	77T	337	$ .05	$ .15
Schueler, Ron	78T	409	$ .02	$ .10
Schueler, Ron	79T	686	$ .02	$ .10
Schult, Art	53T	167	$3.75	$13.00
Schult, Art	58T	58	$ .85	$3.50
Schult, Art	60T	93	$ .35	$1.10
Schultz, Barney	62T	89	$ .35	$1.10
Schultz, Barney	63T	452	$2.50	$6.50
Schultz, Barney	65T	28	$ .25	$ .65
Schultz, Barney	73T	497	$ .25	$ .65
Schultz, Barney	74T	236	$ .06	$ .25
Schultz, Bob	52T	401	$39.00	$135.00
Schultz, Bob	53T	144	$3.75	$13.00
Schultz, Buddy	78T	301	$ .02	$ .10
Schultz, Buddy	79T	532	$ .02	$ .10
Schultz, Buddy	80T	601	$ .01	$ .07
Schultz, Joe	69T	254	$ .25	$ .85
Schultz, Joseph	73T	323	$ .30	$1.00
Schulz, Jeff	89TMLD	110	$ .01	$ .15
Schulze, Don	85T	93	$ .01	$ .04
Schulze, Don	86T	542	$ .01	$ .03
Schulze, Don	87T	297	$ .01	$ .03
Schulze, Don	88T	131	$ .01	$ .03
Schurr, Wayne	64T	548	$1.50	$3.75

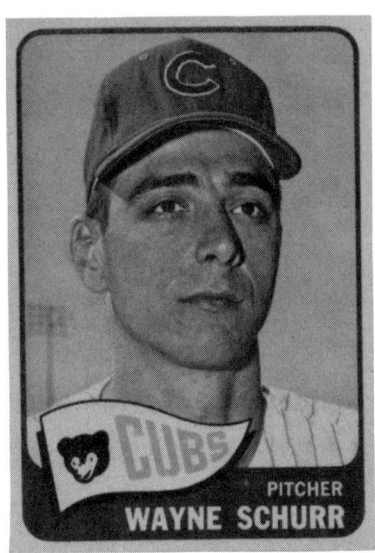

Player	Year	No.	VG	EX/MT
Schurr, Wayne	65T	149	$ .25	$ .65
Schwabe, Mike	89TMLD	111	$ .01	$ .05
Schwall, Don	62T	35	$ .35	$1.10
Schwall, Don	63T	344	$ .35	$1.20
Schwall, Don	64T	558	$1.50	$3.75
Schwall, Don	65T	362	$ .30	$1.00
Schwall, Don	66T	144	$ .25	$ .85
Schwall, Don	67T	267	$ .25	$ .65
Schwartz, Randy	67T	33	$ .50	$2.00
Scioscia, Mike	81T	302	$ .90	$4.50
Scioscia, Mike	82T	642	$ .01	$ .06
Scioscia, Mike	83T	352	$ .01	$ .06
Scioscia, Mike	84T	64	$ .01	$ .05
Scioscia, Mike	85T	549	$ .01	$ .04
Scioscia, Mike	86T	468	$ .01	$ .03

Player	Year	No.	VG	EX/MT	Player	Year	No.	VG	EX/MT
Scioscia, Mike	87T	144	$ .01	$ .03	Scott, Tony	81TTR	828	$ .02	$ .10
Scioscia, Mike	88T	225	$ .01	$ .03	Scott, Tony	82T	698	$ .01	$ .06
Scioscia, Mike	88TBB	72	$ .01	$ .05	Scott, Tony	83T	507	$ .01	$ .06
Scioscia, Mike	89T	755	$ .01	$ .04	Scott, Tony	84T	292	$ .01	$ .05
Scioscia, Mike	89TBB	281	$ .01	$ .05	Scott, Tony	85T	733	$ .01	$ .04
Scioscia, Mike	90T	605	$ .01	$ .03	Scrivener, Chuck	77T	173	$ .05	$ .15
Sconiers, Daryl	82T	653	$ .95	$3.50	Scrivener, Chuck	78T	94	$ .02	$ .10
Sconiers, Daryl	83TTR	99	$ .02	$ .10	Scudder, Scott	89TMLD	113	$ .01	$ .25
Sconiers, Daryl	84T	27	$ .01	$ .05	Scudder, Scott	90T	553	$ .01	$ .15
Sconiers, Daryl	85T	604	$ .01	$ .04	Scull, Angel	54T	204	$2.00	$7.00
Sconiers, Daryl	86T	193	$ .01	$ .03	Scurry, Rod	81T	194	$ .01	$ .07
Score, Herb	56T	140	$5.50	$17.50	Scurry, Rod	82T	207	$ .01	$ .06
Score, Herb	57T	50	$1.25	$3.75	Scurry, Rod	83T	537	$ .01	$ .06
Score, Herb	58T	352	$ .45	$1.50	Scurry, Rod	84T	69	$ .01	$ .05
Score, Herb	58TAS	495	$1.50	$6.00	Scurry, Rod	85T	641	$ .01	$ .04
Score, Herb	59T	88	$ .70	$2.00	Scurry, Rod	86T	449	$ .01	$ .03
Score, Herb	60T	360	$ .60	$1.75	Scurry, Rod	87T	665	$ .01	$ .03
Score, Herb	61T	185	$ .50	$2.00	Seanez, Rudy	89TMLD	114	$ .01	$ .05
Score, Herb	61T	337	$ .70	$2.00	Searage, Ray	82T	478	$ .01	$ .06
Score, Herb	62T	116	$ .50	$2.00	Searage, Ray	86T	642	$ .01	$ .03
Scott, Dick	89TMLD	112	$ .01	$ .05	Searage, Ray	87T	149	$ .01	$ .03
Scott, Donnie	85T	496	$ .01	$ .04	Searage, Ray	88T	788	$ .01	$ .03
Scott, Donnie	85TTR	105	$ .02	$ .10	Searage, Ray	90T	84	$ .01	$ .03
Scott, Donnie	86T	568	$ .01	$ .03	Searcy, Steve	89T	167	$ .05	$ .25
Scott, George	66T	558	$5.50	$17.50	Searcy, Steve	90T	487	$ .01	$ .03
Scott, George	67T	75	$ .15	$ .50	Seaver, Tom	67T	581	$275.00	$825.00
Scott, George	68T	233	$ .15	$ .50	Seaver, Tom	68T	45	$50.00	$150.00
Scott, George	69T	574	$ .25	$ .85	Seaver, Tom	69T	480	$27.50	$77.50
Scott, George	70T	385	$ .25	$ .65	Seaver, Tom	70T	69	$ .50	$1.95
Scott, George	71T	9	$ .10	$ .35	Seaver, Tom	70T	300	$14.00	$42.50
Scott, George	72T	585	$ .25	$ .85	Seaver, Tom	71T	68	$ .15	$ .50
Scott, George	73T	263	$ .06	$ .25	Seaver, Tom	71T	72	$ .50	$2.00
Scott, George	74T	27	$ .06	$ .25	Seaver, Tom	71T	160	$7.50	$30.00
Scott, George	75T	360	$ .06	$ .25	Seaver, Tom	72T	91	$ .35	$1.10
Scott, George	76T	15	$ .05	$ .20	Seaver, Tom	72T	93	$ .50	$2.00
Scott, George	76T	194	$ .50	$1.95	Seaver, Tom	72T	95	$ .35	$1.10
Scott, George	76T	196	$ .25	$ .85	Seaver, Tom	72T	347	$ .50	$2.00
Scott, George	77T	255	$ .05	$ .15	Seaver, Tom	72T	445	$6.00	$18.00
Scott, George	78T	125	$ .02	$ .10	Seaver, Tom	72TIA	446	$2.00	$5.50
Scott, George	79T	645	$ .02	$ .10	Seaver, Tom	73T	350	$4.50	$12.50
Scott, George	80T	414	$ .01	$ .07	Seaver, Tom	74T	80	$3.00	$9.00
Scott, John	75T	616	$8.50	$27.50	Seaver, Tom	74T	206	$ .50	$2.00
Scott, John	77T	473	$9.00	$35.00	Seaver, Tom	74T	207	$ .50	$2.00
Scott, John	78T	547	$ .02	$ .10	Seaver, Tom	75T	370	$2.50	$8.00
Scott, Mickey	70T	669	$ .50	$2.00	Seaver, Tom	76T	199	$ .15	$ .50
Scott, Mickey	72T	724	$1.00	$3.75	Seaver, Tom	76T	201	$ .30	$1.00
Scott, Mickey	73T	553	$ .35	$1.10	Seaver, Tom	76T	203	$ .30	$1.00
Scott, Mickey	76T	276	$ .05	$ .20	Seaver, Tom	76T	600	$2.00	$6.00
Scott, Mickey	77T	401	$ .05	$ .15	Seaver, Tom	76TRB	5	$ .35	$1.10
Scott, Mike	80T	681	$3.00	$9.50	Seaver, Tom	77T	6	$ .50	$2.00
Scott, Mike	81T	109	$ .35	$1.25	Seaver, Tom	77T	150	$1.35	$4.00
Scott, Mike	82T	246	$ .05	$ .25	Seaver, Tom	78T	450	$ .75	$3.00
Scott, Mike	82T	432	$ .05	$ .20	Seaver, Tom	79T	100	$ .60	$2.50
Scott, Mike	83T	679	$ .01	$ .15	Seaver, Tom	80T	500	$ .50	$2.00
Scott, Mike	83TTR	100	$ .50	$1.50	Seaver, Tom	81T	220	$ .30	$1.25
Scott, Mike	84T	559	$ .01	$ .15	Seaver, Tom	82T	30	$ .15	$ .60
Scott, Mike	85T	17	$ .01	$ .15	Seaver, Tom	82T	165	$ .03	$ .15
Scott, Mike	86T	268	$ .02	$ .15	Seaver, Tom	82T	756	$ .05	$ .20
Scott, Mike	87T	330	$ .03	$ .15	Seaver, Tom	82TAS	346	$ .05	$ .25
Scott, Mike	88T	760	$ .01	$ .10	Seaver, Tom	82TIA	31	$ .06	$ .30
Scott, Mike	88TBB	140	$ .01	$ .15	Seaver, Tom	83T	580	$ .15	$1.00
Scott, Mike	89T	180	$ .01	$ .10	Seaver, Tom	83T	581	$ .05	$ .25
Scott, Mike	89TBB	51	$ .01	$ .10	Seaver, Tom	83TTR	101	$ .35	$1.10
Scott, Mike	90T	460	$ .01	$ .03	Seaver, Tom	84T	246	$ .01	$ .05
Scott, Mike	90TAS	405	$ .01	$ .03	Seaver, Tom	84T	706	$ .05	$ .25
Scott, Rodney	78T	191	$ .02	$ .10	Seaver, Tom	84T	707	$ .05	$ .25
Scott, Rodney	79T	86	$ .02	$ .10	Seaver, Tom	84T	708	$ .04	$ .20
Scott, Rodney	80T	712	$ .01	$ .07	Seaver, Tom	84T	740	$ .25	$ .65
Scott, Rodney	81T	539	$ .01	$ .07	Seaver, Tom	84TTR	108	$ .75	$3.00
Scott, Rodney	81TRB	204	$ .01	$ .07	Seaver, Tom	85T	670	$ .05	$ .25
Scott, Rodney	82T	259	$ .01	$ .06	Seaver, Tom	86T	390	$ .03	$ .25
Scott, Tony	78T	352	$ .02	$ .10	Seaver, Tom	86TB	402	$ .02	$ .15
Scott, Tony	79T	143	$ .02	$ .10	Seaver, Tom	86TTR	101	$ .15	$ .50
Scott, Tony	80T	33	$ .01	$ .07	Seaver, Tom	87T	425	$ .10	$ .35
Scott, Tony	81T	165	$ .01	$ .07	Sebra, Bob	87T	479	$ .01	$ .03

Player	Year	No.	VG	EX/MT	Player	Year	No.	VG	EX/MT
Sebra, Bob	88T	93	$ .01	$ .03	Seyfried, Gordon	64T	499	$ .40	$1.25
Secrest, Charlie	59T	140	$ .50	$1.95	Shamsky, Art	65T	398	$ .35	$1.10
Secrist, Don	69T	654	$ .25	$ .85	Shamsky, Art	66T	119	$ .25	$ .85
Seelbach, Chuck	73T	51	$ .06	$ .25	Shamsky, Art	67T	96	$ .25	$ .65
Seelbach, Chuck	74T	292	$ .06	$ .25					
Segui, Diego	63T	157	$ .25	$ .85					
Segui, Diego	64T	508	$ .40	$1.25					
Segui, Diego	65T	197	$ .25	$ .65					
Segui, Diego	66T	309	$ .25	$ .85					
Segui, Diego	68T	517	$ .30	$1.00					
Segui, Diego	69T	511	$ .25	$ .65					
Segui, Diego	71T	67	$ .15	$ .50					
Segui, Diego	71T	215	$ .10	$ .35					
Segui, Diego	72T	735	$ .70	$2.10					
Segui, Diego	73T	383	$ .06	$ .25					
Segui, Diego	74T	151	$ .06	$ .25					
Segui, Diego	74TTR	151	$ .06	$ .25					
Segui, Diego	75T	232	$ .06	$ .25					
Segui, Diego	77T	653	$ .05	$ .15					
Seitzer, Kevin	87TTR	111	$ .30	$1.00					
Seitzer, Kevin	88T	275	$ .20	$ .75					
Seitzer, Kevin	88TBB	115	$ .01	$ .15					
Seitzer, Kevin	89T	670	$ .01	$ .15					
Seitzer, Kevin	89TBB	313	$ .01	$ .10					
Seitzer, Kevin	90T	435	$ .01	$ .03					
Sellers, Jeff	87T	12	$ .01	$ .10					
Sellers, Jeff	88T	653	$ .01	$ .03					
Sellers, Jeff	89T	544	$ .01	$ .04					
Sells, Dave	74T	37	$ .06	$ .25					
Selma, Dick	66T	67	$ .25	$ .85					
Selma, Dick	67T	386	$ .25	$ .85					
Selma, Dick	68T	556	$ .30	$1.00					
Selma, Dick	69T	197	$ .25	$ .65					
Selma, Dick	70T	24	$ .10	$ .35					
Selma, Dick	71T	705	$ .70	$2.10					
Selma, Dick	72T	726	$ .70	$2.10					
Selma, Dick	73T	632	$ .35	$1.10	Shamsky, Art	68T	292	$ .25	$ .85
Sembera, Carroll	66T	539	$4.50	$15.00	Shamsky, Art	69T	221	$ .25	$ .85
Sembera, Carroll	67T	136	$ .25	$ .65	Shamsky, Art	70T	137	$ .10	$ .35
Sembera, Carroll	68T	207	$ .25	$ .65	Shamsky, Art	71T	445	$ .10	$ .35
Sembera, Carroll	69T	351	$ .25	$ .65	Shamsky, Art	72T	353	$ .10	$ .35
Seminick, Andy	51Trb	45	$1.35	$4.00	Shanahan, Greg	74T	599	$ .15	$ .50
Seminick, Andy	52T	297	$14.00	$45.00	Shannon, Mike	64T	262	$ .35	$1.10
Seminick, Andy	53T	153	$3.75	$13.00	Shannon, Mike	65T	43	$ .25	$ .65
Seminick, Andy	56T	296	$1.30	$5.00	Shannon, Mike	66T	293	$ .25	$ .85
Semproch, "Ray" Roman	58T	474	$ .50	$1.95	Shannon, Mike	67T	605	$13.00	$40.00
Semproch, Ray	59T	197	$ .50	$1.95	Shannon, Mike	68T	445	$ .25	$ .65
Semproch, Ray	60T	286	$ .35	$1.10	Shannon, Mike	69T	110	$ .25	$ .65
Semproch, Ray	61T	174	$ .30	$1.00	Shannon, Mike	70T	614	$ .25	$ .85
Senators, Team	57T	270	$6.00	$18.00	Shannon, Mike	71T	735	$ .70	$2.10
Senators, Team	58T	44	$3.00	$9.00	Shantz, Bobby	52T	219	$7.50	$22.00
Senators, Team	60T	43	$2.50	$7.50	Shantz, Bobby	53T	225	$11.00	$35.00
Senators, Team	62T	206	$ .75	$2.00	Shantz, Bobby	54T	21	$2.50	$9.00
Senators, Team	63T	131	$ .75	$2.55	Shantz, Bobby	56T	261	$2.25	$6.50
Senators, Team	64T	343	$ .85	$3.50	Shantz, Bobby	57T	272	$7.50	$22.50
Senators, Team	65T	267	$ .60	$1.75	Shantz, Bobby	58T	289	$ .75	$2.50
Senators, Team	66T	194	$ .65	$1.75	Shantz, Bobby	58T	419	$ .75	$2.50
Senators, Team	67T	437	$ .70	$2.00	Shantz, Bobby	59T	222	$1.35	$4.00
Senators, Team	70T	676	$1.00	$4.00	Shantz, Bobby	60T	315	$ .70	$2.00
Senators, Team	71T	462	$ .35	$1.10	Shantz, Bobby	61T	379	$ .60	$1.75
Sequi, Diego	70T	2	$ .10	$ .35	Shantz, Bobby	61TMVP	473	$ .75	$2.00
Serena, Bill	52T	325	$39.00	$135.00	Shantz, Bobby	62T	177	$ .35	$1.10
Serna, Paul	83T	492	$ .01	$ .06	Shantz, Bobby	63T	533	$1.35	$4.00
Serum, Gary	79T	627	$ .02	$ .10	Shantz, Bobby	64T	278	$ .35	$1.10
Serum, Gary	80T	61	$ .01	$ .07	Shantz, Bobby	75T	190	$ .10	$ .35
Servais, Scott	88TTR	106	$ .01	$ .25	Sharon, Dick	74T	48	$ .06	$ .25
Servais, Scott	89TBB	291	$ .01	$ .10	Sharon, Dick	75T	293	$ .06	$ .25
Sevcik, John	65T	597	$1.50	$3.75	Sharp, Bill	74T	519	$ .06	$ .25
Severinsen, Al	70T	477	$ .10	$ .35	Sharp, Bill	75T	373	$ .06	$ .25
Severinsen, Al	71T	747	$ .70	$2.10	Sharp, Bill	76T	244	$ .05	$ .20
Severinsen, Al	72T	274	$ .10	$ .35	Sharperson, Mike	90T	117	$ .01	$ .03
Severson, Rich	71T	103	$ .10	$ .35	Shaw, Bob	58T	206	$ .35	$ .00
Sexton, Jimmy	79T	232	$ .02	$ .10	Shaw, Bob	59T	159	$ .50	$1.95
Sexton, Jimmy	80T	11	$ .01	$ .07	Shaw, Bob	60T	380	$ .50	$1.95
Sexton, Jimmy	83T	709	$ .01	$ .06	Shaw, Bob	61T	352	$ .30	$1.00

TOPPS

Player	Year	No.	VG	EX/MT
Shaw, Bob	62T	109	$ .35	$1.10
Shaw, Bob	63T	5	$ .60	$1.75
Shaw, Bob	63T	255	$ .25	$ .85
Shaw, Bob	64T	328	$ .25	$ .85
Shaw, Bob	65T	428	$ .30	$1.00
Shaw, Bob	66T	260	$ .25	$ .85
Shaw, Bob	67T	470	$ .50	$2.00
Shaw, Bob	73T	646	$ .50	$2.00
Shaw, Don	67T	587	$4.00	$12.00
Shaw, Don	68T	521	$ .30	$1.00
Shaw, Don	69T	183	$ .25	$ .65
Shaw, Don	70T	476	$ .10	$ .35
Shaw, Don	71T	654	$ .70	$2.10
Shaw, Don	72T	479	$ .10	$ .35
Shea, Frank	52T	248	$6.00	$19.00
Shea, Frank	53T	164	$3.75	$13.00
Shea, Steve	69T	499	$ .25	$ .65
Shearer, Ray	58T	283	$ .50	$2.00
Sheets, Larry	85TTR	106	$ .20	$ .75
Sheets, Larry	86T	147	$ .01	$ .03
Sheets, Larry	87T	552	$ .01	$ .03
Sheets, Larry	88T	327	$ .01	$ .10
Sheets, Larry	88TBB	26	$ .01	$ .05
Sheets, Larry	89T	98	$ .01	$ .04
Sheets, Larry	89TBB	113	$ .01	$ .05
Sheets, Larry	90T	708	$ .01	$ .03
Sheffield, Gary	89T	343	$ .25	$1.00
Sheffield, Gary	89TBB	55	$ .01	$ .25
Sheffield, Gary	90T	718	$ .01	$ .25
Shelby, John	83TTR	102	$ .02	$ .10
Shelby, John	84T	86	$ .01	$ .05
Shelby, John	85T	508	$ .01	$ .04
Shelby, John	86T	309	$ .01	$ .03
Shelby, John	87T	208	$ .01	$ .03
Shelby, John	87TTR	112	$ .01	$ .07
Shelby, John	88T	428	$ .01	$ .03
Shelby, John	88TBB	218	$ .01	$ .05
Shelby, John	89T	175	$ .01	$ .04
Sheldon, Bob	75T	623	$6.00	$18.00
Sheldon, Bob	76T	626	$ .05	$ .20
Sheldon, Roland	61T	541	$6.00	$18.00
Sheldon, Roland	62T	185	$ .35	$1.10
Sheldon, Roland	63T	507	$1.50	$3.75
Sheldon, Roland	65T	254	$ .30	$1.00
Sheldon, Roland	66T	18	$ .25	$ .85
Sheldon, Roland	69T	413	$ .25	$ .65
Shelenback, Jim	67T	592	$5.00	$15.00
Shellenback, Jim	69T	567	$ .25	$ .85
Shellenback, Jim	70T	389	$ .10	$ .35
Shellenback, Jim	71T	351	$ .10	$ .35
Shellenback, Jim	74T	657	$ .06	$ .25
Shepard, Jack	55T	73	$1.35	$5.00
Shepard, Larry	68T	584	$ .30	$1.00
Shepard, Larry	69T	384	$ .25	$ .65
Shepard, Larry	73T	296	$ .15	$ .50
Shepard, Larry	74T	326	$ .15	$ .50
Shepherd, Ron	87T	643	$ .01	$ .03
Sheridan, Pat	84T	121	$ .01	$ .05
Sheridan, Pat	85T	359	$ .01	$ .04
Sheridan, Pat	86T	743	$ .01	$ .03
Sheridan, Pat	87T	234	$ .01	$ .03
Sheridan, Pat	88T	514	$ .01	$ .03
Sheridan, Pat	89T	288	$ .01	$ .04
Sheridan, Pat	89TBB	150	$ .01	$ .05
Sheridan, Pat	90T	422	$ .01	$ .03
Sherry, Larry	60T	105	$ .65	$1.75
Sherry, Larry	61T	412	$ .50	$2.00
Sherry, Larry	61T	521	$ .60	$1.75
Sherry, Larry	62T	435	$ .70	$2.10
Sherry, Larry	63T	565	$1.50	$3.75
Sherry, Larry	64T	474	$ .40	$1.25
Sherry, Larry	65T	408	$ .30	$1.00
Sherry, Larry	66T	289	$ .25	$ .85
Sherry, Larry	67T	571	$2.50	$8.00
Sherry, Larry	68T	468	$ .30	$1.00

Player	Year	No.	VG	EX/MT
Sherry, Norm	60T	529	$2.00	$7.00
Sherry, Norm	61T	521	$ .60	$1.75
Sherry, Norm	62T	238	$ .35	$1.10
Sherry, Norm	63T	316	$ .35	$1.10
Shetrone, Barry	60T	348	$ .50	$1.95
Shetrone, Barry	63T	276	$ .25	$ .85
Shields, Steve	87TTR	113	$ .01	$ .07
Shields, Steve	88T	632	$ .01	$ .03
Shields, Steve	89T	484	$ .01	$ .04
Shines, Razor	86T	132	$ .01	$ .03
Shipley, Joe	59T	141	$ .50	$1.95
Shipley, Joe	60T	239	$ .35	$1.10
Shirley, Bart	66T	591	$4.50	$15.00
Shirley, Bart	67T	287	$ .25	$ .65
Shirley, Bart	69T	289	$ .25	$ .85
Shirley, Bob	78T	266	$ .02	$ .10
Shirley, Bob	79T	594	$ .02	$ .10
Shirley, Bob	80T	476	$ .01	$ .07
Shirley, Bob	81T	49	$ .01	$ .07
Shirley, Bob	81TTR	829	$ .02	$ .10
Shirley, Bob	82T	749	$ .01	$ .06
Shirley, Bob	82TTR	105	$ .02	$ .10
Shirley, Bob	83T	112	$ .01	$ .06
Shirley, Bob	83TTR	103	$ .02	$ .10
Shirley, Bob	84T	684	$ .01	$ .05
Shirley, Bob	85T	328	$ .01	$ .04
Shirley, Bob	86T	213	$ .01	$ .03
Shirley, Bob	87T	524	$ .01	$ .03
Shockley, Costen	65T	107	$ .50	$2.00
Shopay, Tom	70T	363	$ .10	$ .35
Shopay, Tom	72T	418	$ .10	$ .35
Short, Bill	60T	142	$ .50	$2.00
Short, Bill	61T	252	$ .30	$1.00
Short, Bill	62T	221	$ .35	$1.10
Short, Bill	67T	577	$1.35	$4.00
Short, Bill	68T	536	$ .30	$1.00
Short, Bill	69T	259	$ .25	$ .85
Short, Chris	67T	395	$ .25	$ .85
Short, Chris	68T	7	$ .50	$1.95
Short, Chris	68T	139	$ .25	$ .65
Short, Chris	69T	395	$ .25	$ .65
Short, Chris	70T	270	$ .10	$ .35
Short, Chris	71T	511	$ .10	$ .35
Short, Chris	72T	665	$ .70	$2.10
Show, Eric	82TTR	106	$ .02	$ .10
Show, Eric	83T	68	$ .01	$ .06
Show, Eric	84T	532	$ .01	$ .05
Show, Eric	85T	118	$ .01	$ .04
Show, Eric	86T	762	$ .01	$ .03
Show, Eric	87T	730	$ .01	$ .03
Show, Eric	88T	303	$ .01	$ .03
Show, Eric	89T	427	$ .01	$ .04
Show, Eric	89TBB	35	$ .01	$ .05
Show, Eric	90T	239	$ .01	$ .03
Shuba, George	52T	326	$39.00	$135.00
Shuba, George	53T	34	$3.75	$13.00
Siebern, Norm	58T	54	$1.50	$3.75
Siebern, Norm	59T	308	$ .70	$2.00
Siebern, Norm	60T	11	$ .35	$1.10
Siebern, Norm	61T	119	$ .35	$1.10
Siebern, Norm	61T	267	$ .30	$1.00
Siebern, Norm	62T	127	$ .50	$2.00
Siebern, Norm	62T	275	$ .35	$1.10
Siebern, Norm	63T	2	$3.00	$12.00
Siebern, Norm	63T	430	$ .35	$1.20
Siebern, Norm	64T	145	$ .25	$ .85
Siebern, Norm	65T	455	$ .50	$2.00
Siebern, Norm	66T	14	$ .25	$ .85
Siebern, Norm	67T	299	$ .25	$ .65
Siebern, Norm	68T	537	$ .30	$1.00
Siebert, Paul	75T	614	$ .06	$ .25
Siebert, Sonny	64T	552	$1.50	$3.75
Siebert, Sonny	65T	96	$ .25	$ .65
Siebert, Sonny	66T	197	$ .25	$ .85
Siebert, Sonny	66T	222	$ .50	$2.00

Player	Year	No.	VG	EX/MT	Player	Year	No.	VG	EX/MT
Siebert, Sonny	66T	226	$ .50	$2.00	Silvera, Charlie	52T	168	$6.00	$19.00
Siebert, Sonny	67T	95	$ .25	$ .65	Silvera, Charlie	53T	242	$11.00	$35.00
Siebert, Sonny	67T	463	$ .50	$2.00	Silvera, Charlie	54T	96	$1.75	$7.00
Siebert, Sonny	68T	8	$ .35	$1.10	Silvera, Charlie	55T	188	$2.85	$9.50
					Silvera, Charlie	57T	255	$ .95	$3.50
					Silvera, Charlie	73T	323	$ .30	$1.00
					Silvera, Charlie	74T	379	$ .15	$ .50
					Silverio, Tom	72T	213	$ .10	$ .35
					Silvestri, Dave	88TTR	107	$ .01	$ .25
					Silvestri, Dave	89TBB	141	$ .01	$ .05
					Silvestri, Ken	60T	466	$ .95	$3.50
					Silvestri, Ken	73T	237	$ .30	$1.00
					Silvestri, Ken	74T	634	$ .30	$1.00
					Sima, Al	52T	93	$6.00	$19.00
					Sima, Al	53T	241	$11.00	$37.50
					Sima, Al	54T	216	$2.00	$7.00
					Simmons, Curt	52T	203	$6.00	$18.00
					Simmons, Curt	56T	290	$1.30	$5.00
					Simmons, Curt	57T	158	$ .60	$2.50
					Simmons, Curt	58T	404	$ .45	$1.50
					Simmons, Curt	59T	382	$ .50	$1.95
					Simmons, Curt	60T	451	$ .95	$3.50
					Simmons, Curt	61T	11	$ .30	$1.00
					Simmons, Curt	62T	56	$ .50	$2.00
					Simmons, Curt	62T	285	$ .50	$2.00
					Simmons, Curt	63T	22	$ .25	$ .85
					Simmons, Curt	64T	385	$ .50	$1.95
					Simmons, Curt	65T	373	$ .30	$1.00
					Simmons, Curt	66T	489	$ .65	$1.75
					Simmons, Curt	67T	39	$ .25	$ .65
					Simmons, Nelson	86T	121	$ .01	$ .03
					Simmons, Ted	71T	117	$1.50	$6.00
					Simmons, Ted	72T	154	$ .50	$1.50
					Simmons, Ted	73T	85	$ .35	$1.10
					Simmons, Ted	74T	260	$ .15	$ .50
					Simmons, Ted	75T	75	$ .15	$ .50
Siebert, Sonny	68T	295	$ .25	$ .65	Simmons, Ted	76T	191	$ .25	$ .85
Siebert, Sonny	69T	455	$ .25	$ .65	Simmons, Ted	76T	290	$ .25	$ .65
Siebert, Sonny	70T	597	$ .25	$ .85	Simmons, Ted	77T	470	$ .15	$ .50
Siebert, Sonny	71T	710	$6.00	$18.00	Simmons, Ted	78T	380	$ .05	$ .25
Siebert, Sonny	72T	290	$ .10	$ .35	Simmons, Ted	79T	510	$ .05	$ .20
Siebert, Sonny	73T	14	$ .06	$ .25	Simmons, Ted	80T	85	$ .05	$ .20
Siebert, Sonny	74T	548	$ .06	$ .25	Simmons, Ted	81T	705	$ .03	$ .15
Siebert, Sonny	75T	328	$ .06	$ .25	Simmons, Ted	81TTR	830	$ .25	$ .65
Siebler, Dwight	64T	516	$ .40	$1.25	Simmons, Ted	82T	150	$ .03	$ .15
Siebler, Dwight	65T	326	$ .30	$1.00	Simmons, Ted	83T	450	$ .03	$ .15
Siebler, Dwight	66T	546	$4.50	$15.00	Simmons, Ted	83T	451	$ .01	$ .06
Siebler, Dwight	67T	164	$ .25	$ .65	Simmons, Ted	84T	630	$ .02	$ .10
Sierra, Candy	89T	711	$ .01	$ .04	Simmons, Ted	84T	713	$ .03	$ .15
Sierra, Ruben	87T	261	$ .40	$3.00	Simmons, Ted	84T	726	$ .01	$ .05
Sierra, Ruben	87TRB	6	$ .01	$ .25	Simmons, Ted	84TAS	404	$ .01	$ .05
Sierra, Ruben	88T	771	$ .10	$1.00	Simmons, Ted	85T	318	$ .01	$ .10
Sierra, Ruben	89T	53	$ .01	$ .40	Simmons, Ted	86T	237	$ .01	$ .10
Sierra, Ruben	89TBB	82	$ .01	$ .35	Simmons, Ted	86TTR	102	$ .02	$ .10
Sierra, Ruben	90T	185	$ .01	$ .15	Simmons, Ted	87T	516	$ .01	$ .03
Sierra, Ruben	90TAS	390	$ .01	$ .10	Simmons, Ted	88T	791	$ .01	$ .10
Sievers, Roy	51Trb	9	$1.35	$4.00	Simpson, Dick	63T	407	$ .35	$1.20
Sievers, Roy	52T	64	$12.50	$45.00	Simpson, Dick	64T	127	$ .25	$ .85
Sievers, Roy	53T	67	$3.75	$13.00	Simpson, Dick	65T	374	$ .30	$1.00
Sievers, Roy	54T	245	$3.50	$13.00	Simpson, Dick	66T	311	$ .35	$1.10
Sievers, Roy	55T	16	$1.25	$5.00	Simpson, Dick	67T	6	$ .25	$ .65
Sievers, Roy	56T	75	$1.25	$4.50	Simpson, Dick	68T	459	$ .30	$1.00
Sievers, Roy	57T	89	$ .60	$2.50	Simpson, Dick	69T	608	$ .25	$ .85
Sievers, Roy	58T	250	$ .65	$2.00	Simpson, Harry	52T	193	$6.00	$19.00
Sievers, Roy	59T	74	$ .95	$3.50	Simpson, Harry	53T	150	$3.75	$13.00
Sievers, Roy	59T	340	$ .50	$1.95	Simpson, Harry	56T	239	$2.50	$8.00
Sievers, Roy	59T	465	$ .60	$1.75	Simpson, Harry	57T	225	$ .95	$3.50
Sievers, Roy	59TAS	566	$2.00	$7.00	Simpson, Harry	58T	299	$ .50	$2.00
Sievers, Roy	60T	25	$ .35	$1.10	Simpson, Harry	59T	333	$ .50	$1.95
Sievers, Roy	61T	470	$ .50	$2.00	Simpson, Harry	60T	180	$ .35	$1.10
Sievers, Roy	62T	220	$ .35	$1.10	Simpson, Joe	79T	719	$2.25	$9.00
Sievers, Roy	63T	283	$ .30	$1.00	Simpson, Joe	80T	637	$ .01	$ .07
Sievers, Roy	64T	43	$ .15	$ .50	Simpson, Joe	81T	116	$ .01	$ .07
Sievers, Roy	65T	574	$1.50	$3.75	Simpson, Joe	82T	382	$ .01	$ .06
Silvera, Al	56T	137	$1.25	$4.50	Simpson, Joe	83T	567	$ .01	$ .06

SONNY SIEBERT

PITCHER INDIANS

Player	Year	No.	VG	EX/MT	Player	Year	No.	VG	EX/MT
Simpson, Joe	83TTR	104	$ .02	$ .10	Sisler, Dick	52T	113	$6.00	$19.00
Simpson, Joe	84T	219	$ .01	$ .05	Sisler, Dick	64T	162	$ .15	$ .50
Simpson, Wayne	70T	683	$1.00	$3.50	Sisler, Dick	65T	158	$ .25	$ .65
Simpson, Wayne	71T	68	$ .15	$ .50	Sisler, George	79TRH	411	$ .15	$ .50
Simpson, Wayne	71T	339	$ .10	$ .35	Sisti, Sibby	52T	293	$14.00	$45.00
Simpson, Wayne	72T	762	$ .70	$2.10	Sisti, Sibby	53T	124	$3.75	$13.00
Simpson, Wayne	73T	428	$ .06	$ .25	Sizemore, Ted	69T	552	$ .25	$ .85
Sims, Duke	66T	169	$ .25	$ .85	Sizemore, Ted	70T	174	$ .10	$ .35
Sims, Duke	67T	3	$ .25	$ .65	Sizemore, Ted	71T	571	$ .30	$1.00
Sims, Duke	68T	508	$ .30	$1.00	Sizemore, Ted	72T	514	$ .10	$ .35
Sims, Duke	69T	414	$ .25	$ .65	Sizemore, Ted	73T	128	$ .06	$ .25
Sims, Duke	70T	275	$ .10	$ .35	Sizemore, Ted	74T	209	$ .06	$ .25
Sims, Duke	71T	172	$ .10	$ .35	Sizemore, Ted	75T	404	$ .06	$ .25
Sims, Duke	72T	63	$ .10	$ .35	Sizemore, Ted	76T	522	$ .05	$ .20
Sims, Duke	73T	304	$ .06	$ .25	Sizemore, Ted	77T	366	$ .05	$ .15
Sims, Duke	74T	398	$ .06	$ .25	Sizemore, Ted	78T	136	$ .02	$ .10
Sims, Greg	66T	596	$4.50	$15.00	Sizemore, Ted	79T	297	$ .02	$ .10
Singer, Bill	66T	288	$27.50	$90.00	Sizemore, Ted	80T	81	$ .01	$ .07
Singer, Bill	67T	12	$ .25	$ .65	Skaggs, Dave	78T	593	$ .02	$ .10
Singer, Bill	68T	249	$ .25	$ .65	Skaggs, Dave	79T	367	$ .02	$ .10
Singer, Bill	69T	12	$1.00	$2.75	Skaggs, Dave	80T	211	$ .01	$ .07
Singer, Bill	69T	575	$ .25	$ .85	Skaggs, Dave	81T	48	$ .01	$ .07
Singer, Bill	70T	71	$ .50	$1.95	Skalski, Joe	89TMLD	115	$ .01	$ .05
Singer, Bill	70T	490	$ .10	$ .35	Skeen, Archie	64T	428	$ .40	$1.25
Singer, Bill	71T	145	$ .10	$ .35	Skidmore, Roe	71T	121	$ .10	$ .35
Singer, Bill	72T	25	$ .10	$ .35	Skinner, Bob	55T	88	$2.00	$7.00
Singer, Bill	73T	570	$ .35	$1.10	Skinner, Bob	56T	297	$1.30	$5.00
Singer, Bill	74T	210	$ .06	$ .25	Skinner, Bob	57T	209	$ .95	$3.50
Singer, Bill	75T	40	$ .06	$ .25	Skinner, Bob	58T	94	$ .70	$2.25
Singer, Bill	76T	411	$ .05	$ .20	Skinner, Bob	59T	320	$ .50	$1.95
Singer, Bill	76TTR	411	$ .05	$ .20	Skinner, Bob	59T	543	$11.50	$45.00
Singer, Bill	77T	346	$ .05	$ .15	Skinner, Bob	60T	113	$ .35	$1.10
Singleton, Elmer	57T	378	$ .85	$3.50	Skinner, Bob	61T	204	$ .30	$1.00
Singleton, Elmer	59T	548	$2.00	$7.00	Skinner, Bob	62T	115	$ .35	$1.10
Singleton, Ken	71T	16	$ .50	$2.00	Skinner, Bob	63T	18	$2.35	$10.00
Singleton, Ken	72T	425	$ .15	$ .50	Skinner, Bob	63T	215	$ .25	$ .85
Singleton, Ken	72TIA	426	$ .10	$ .35	Skinner, Bob	64T	377	$ .40	$1.25
Singleton, Ken	73T	232	$ .25	$ .65	Skinner, Bob	65T	591	$1.35	$4.00
Singleton, Ken	74T	25	$ .10	$ .35	Skinner, Bob	66T	471	$ .70	$2.10
Singleton, Ken	75T	125	$ .10	$ .35	Skinner, Bob	69T	369	$ .25	$ .65
Singleton, Ken	76T	175	$ .10	$ .35	Skinner, Bob	73T	12	$ .25	$ .65
Singleton, Ken	77T	445	$ .05	$ .15	Skinner, Bob	74T	188	$ .06	$ .25
Singleton, Ken	78T	65	$ .05	$ .20	Skinner, Bob	74T	489	$ .06	$ .25
Singleton, Ken	79T	615	$ .02	$ .10	Skinner, Bob	85T	139	$ .01	$ .10
Singleton, Ken	80T	340	$ .01	$ .07	Skinner, Joel	85T	139	$ .01	$ .10
Singleton, Ken	81T	570	$ .01	$ .07	Skinner, Joel	85T	488	$ .01	$ .04
Singleton, Ken	82T	290	$ .01	$ .06	Skinner, Joel	86T	239	$ .01	$ .03
Singleton, Ken	82TAS	552	$ .01	$ .06	Skinner, Joel	87T	626	$ .01	$ .03
Singleton, Ken	83T	85	$ .01	$ .06	Skinner, Joel	88T	109	$ .01	$ .03
Singleton, Ken	84T	165	$ .01	$ .05	Skinner, Joel	89T	536	$ .01	$ .04
Singleton, Ken	85T	755	$ .01	$ .04	Skinner, Joel	90T	54	$ .01	$ .03
Sisk, Doug	83TTR	105	$ .02	$ .10	Skizas, Lou	57T	83	$ .95	$3.50
Sisk, Doug	84T	599	$ .01	$ .05	Skizas, Lou	58T	319	$ .50	$2.00
Sisk, Doug	85T	315	$ .01	$ .04	Skizas, Lou	59T	328	$ .50	$1.95
Sisk, Doug	86T	144	$ .01	$ .03	Skok, Craig	79T	363	$ .02	$ .10
Sisk, Doug	87T	404	$ .01	$ .03	Skowron, Bill	54T	239	$20.00	$65.00
Sisk, Doug	88T	763	$ .01	$ .03	Skowron, Bill	55T	22	$5.00	$20.00
Sisk, Doug	89T	13	$ .01	$ .04	Skowron, Bill	56T	61	$2.50	$10.00
Sisk, Tommie	63T	169	$6.00	$18.00	Skowron, Bill	57T	135	$2.50	$10.00
Sisk, Tommie	64T	224	$ .25	$ .85	Skowron, "Moose" Bill	58T	240	$2.00	$7.00
Sisk, Tommie	65T	558	$1.50	$3.75	Skowron, Bill	58TAS	477	$ .70	$2.50
Sisk, Tommie	66T	441	$ .25	$ .85	Skowron, Bill	59T	90	$3.00	$9.00
Sisk, Tommie	67T	84	$ .25	$ .65	Skowron, Bill	59TAS	554	$3.00	$9.00
Sisk, Tommie	68T	429	$ .25	$ .65	Skowron, Bill	60T	370	$1.35	$4.00
Sisk, Tommie	69T	152	$ .25	$ .65	Skowron, Bill	60TAS	553	$1.85	$5.50
Sisk, Tommie	70T	374	$ .10	$ .35	Skowron, Bill	61T	42	$ .50	$2.00
Sisler, Dave	57T	56	$ .95	$3.50	Skowron, Bill	61T	371	$1.35	$4.00
Sisler, Dave	58T	59	$ .85	$3.50	Skowron, Bill	61TAS	568	$6.00	$17.50
Sisler, Dave	59T	346	$ .50	$1.95	Skowron, Bill	62T	110	$1.35	$4.00
Sisler, Dave	59T	384	$ .50	$1.95	Skowron, Bill	63T	180	$ .30	$1.00
Sisler, Dave	60T	186	$ .35	$1.10	Skowron, Bill	64T	445	$ .50	$2.00
Sisler, Dave	61T	239	$ .30	$1.00	Skowron, Bill	65T	70	$ .15	$ .50
Sisler, Dave	62T	171	$ .35	$1.10	Skowron, Bill	66T	199	$ .20	$ .35
Sisler, Dave	63T	284	$ .35	$1.20	Skowron, Bill	66T	590	$5.00	$14.50
Sisler, Dick	51Tbb	8	$5.50	$17.00	Skowron, Bill	67T	357	$ .30	$1.00

TOPPS

Player	Year	No.	VG	EX/MT	Player	Year	No.	VG	EX/MT
Slater, Bob	79T	703	$ .02	$ .10	Smith, Al	54T	248	$2.00	$7.00
Slaton, Jim	72T	744	$ .70	$2.10	Smith, Al	55T	197	$4.25	$13.00
Slaton, Jim	73T	628	$ .35	$1.10	Smith, Al	56T	105	$1.25	$4.50
Slaton, Jim	74T	371	$ .06	$ .25	Smith, Al	57T	145	$ .95	$3.50
Slaton, Jim	75T	281	$ .06	$ .25	Smith, Al	58T	177	$ .50	$2.00
Slaton, Jim	76T	163	$ .05	$ .20	Smith, Al	59T	22	$ .85	$3.50
Slaton, Jim	77T	604	$ .05	$ .15	Smith, Al	60T	428	$ .50	$1.95
Slaton, Jim	78T	474	$ .02	$ .10	Smith, Al	61T	42	$ .50	$2.00
Slaton, Jim	79T	541	$ .02	$ .10	Smith, Al	61T	170	$ .30	$1.00
Slaton, Jim	80T	24	$ .01	$ .07	Smith, Al	62T	410	$ .70	$2.10
Slaton, Jim	81T	357	$ .01	$ .07	Smith, Al	63T	16	$ .25	$ .85
Slaton, Jim	82T	221	$ .01	$ .06	Smith, Al	64T	317	$ .25	$ .85
Slaton, Jim	83T	114	$ .01	$ .06	Smith, Bernie	71T	204	$ .10	$ .35
Slaton, Jim	84TTR	109	$ .02	$ .10	Smith, Billy	63T	241	$ .25	$ .85
Slaton, Jim	85T	657	$ .01	$ .04	Smith, Billy	78T	666	$ .02	$ .10
Slaton, Jim	86T	579	$ .01	$ .03	Smith, Billy	79T	237	$ .02	$ .10
Slaught, Don	84T	196	$ .01	$ .05	Smith, Billy	80T	367	$ .01	$ .07
Slaught, Don	85T	542	$ .01	$ .04	Smith, Billy	82T	441	$ .01	$ .06
Slaught, Don	85TTR	107	$ .02	$ .10	Smith, Billy	82T	593	$ .01	$ .06
Slaught, Don	86T	761	$ .01	$ .03	Smith, Bob G.	58T	226	$ .50	$2.00
Slaught, Don	87T	308	$ .01	$ .03	Smith, Bob G.	59T	83	$ .85	$3.50
Slaught, Don	88T	462	$ .01	$ .03	Smith, Bob W.	58T	445	$ .50	$1.95
Slaught, Don	88TTR	108	$ .01	$ .05	Smith, Bobby Gene	57T	384	$ .85	$3.50
Slaught, Don	89T	611	$ .01	$ .04	Smith, Bobby Gene	58T	402	$ .50	$2.00
Slaught, Don	89TBB	138	$ .01	$ .05	Smith, Bobby Gene	59T	162	$ .50	$1.95
Slaught, Don	90T	26	$ .01	$ .03	Smith, Bobby Gene	60T	194	$ .35	$1.10
Slaughter, Enos	51Tbb	30	$10.00	$40.00	Smith, Bobby Gene	61T	316	$ .30	$1.00
Slaughter, Enos	52T	65	$35.00	$100.00	Smith, Bobby Gene	62T	531	$3.75	$11.00
Slaughter, Enos	53T	41	$20.00	$57.50	Smith, Bryn	82T	118	$ .03	$ .15
Slaughter, Enos	56T	109	$8.00	$25.00	Smith, Bryn	83T	447	$ .01	$ .06
Slaughter, Enos	57T	215	$7.00	$20.00	Smith, Bryn	84T	656	$ .01	$ .05
Slaughter, Enos	58T	142	$5.00	$15.00	Smith, Bryn	85T	88	$ .01	$ .04
Slaughter, Enos	59T	155	$5.50	$17.50	Smith, Bryn	86T	299	$ .01	$ .03
Slaughter, Sterling	64T	469	$ .40	$1.25	Smith, Bryn	87T	505	$ .01	$ .03
Slaughter, Sterling	65T	314	$ .30	$1.00	Smith, Bryn	88T	161	$ .01	$ .03
Slayback, Bill	73T	537	$ .35	$1.10	Smith, Bryn	88TBB	250	$ .01	$ .05
Slayton, Jim	84T	772	$ .01	$ .05	Smith, Bryn	89T	464	$ .01	$ .04
Slayton, Jim	87T	432	$ .01	$ .03	Smith, Bryn	89TBB	47	$ .01	$ .05
Sleater, Lou	52T	306	$11.50	$38.00	Smith, Bryn	90T	352	$ .01	$ .03
Sleater, Lou	53T	224	$11.00	$37.50	Smith, Charlie	62T	283	$ .35	$1.10
Sleater, Lou	58T	46	$ .85	$3.50	Smith, Charley (ie)	63T	424	$ .35	$1.20
Slocum, Ron	70T	573	$ .25	$ .85	Smith, Charlie	64T	519	$ .40	$1.25
Slocum, Ron	71T	274	$ .10	$ .35	Smith, Charlie	65T	22	$ .25	$ .65
Slusarski, Joe	88TTR	109	$ .01	$ .25	Smith, Charlie	66T	358	$ .25	$ .85
Slusarski, Joe	89TBB	213	$ .01	$ .05	Smith, Charlie	67T	257	$ .25	$ .65
Small, Jim	56T	207	$2.50	$8.00	Smith, Charlie	68T	596	$ .30	$1.00
Small, Jim	57T	33	$ .95	$3.50	Smith, Charlie	69T	538	$ .25	$ .85
Smalley, Jr., Roy	76T	70	$ .05	$ .25	Smith, Dave	81T	534	$ .05	$ .20
Smalley, Jr., Roy	76T	657	$ .25	$ .85	Smith, Dave	82T	761	$ .01	$ .06
Smalley, Jr., Roy	77T	66	$ .05	$ .15	Smith, Dave	83T	247	$ .01	$ .06
Smalley, Jr., Roy	78T	471	$ .02	$ .10	Smith, Dave	84T	361	$ .01	$ .05
Smalley, Jr., Roy	79T	219	$ .02	$ .10	Smith, Dave	85T	123	$ .01	$ .04
Smalley, Jr., Roy	80T	570	$ .01	$ .07	Smith, Dave	86T	408	$ .01	$ .03
Smalley, Jr., Roy	81T	115	$ .01	$ .07	Smith, Dave	87T	50	$ .01	$ .03
Smalley, Jr., Roy	82T	767	$ .01	$ .06	Smith, Dave	88T	520	$ .01	$ .03
Smalley, Jr., Roy	82TTR	107	$ .02	$ .10	Smith, Dave	89T	305	$ .01	$ .04
Smalley, Jr., Roy	83T	460	$ .01	$ .06	Smith, Dave	90T	746	$ .01	$ .03
Smalley, Jr., Roy	84T	305	$ .01	$ .05	Smith, Dick	64T	398	$ .40	$1.25
Smalley, Jr., Roy	85T	26	$ .01	$ .04	Smith, Dick	65T	579	$1.50	$3.75
Smalley, Jr., Roy	85T	140	$ .01	$ .10	Smith, Dwight	89TMLD	116	$ .01	$ .50
Smalley, Jr., Roy	85TTR	108	$ .02	$ .10	Smith, Dwight	89TTR	113	$ .01	$1.25
Smalley, Jr., Roy	86T	613	$ .01	$ .03	Smith, Dwight	90T	311	$ .01	$ .50
Smalley, Jr., Roy	87T	744	$ .01	$ .03	Smith, Frank	52T	179	$6.00	$19.00
Smalley, Jr., Roy	88T	239	$ .01	$ .03	Smith, Frank	53T	116	$3.75	$13.00
Smalley, Roy	51Tbb	17	$5.50	$17.00	Smith, Frank	54T	71	$4.75	$14.00
Smalley, Roy	52T	173	$6.00	$19.00	Smith, Frank	55T	204	$4.25	$13.00
Smalley, Roy	54T	231	$2.00	$7.00	Smith, George	65T	483	$ .50	$2.00
Smalley, Roy	57T	397	$ .85	$3.50	Smith, George	66T	542	$4.50	$15.00
Smalley, Roy	76T	70	$ .05	$ .25	Smith, George	67T	444	$ .25	$ .85
Smalley, Roy	85T	140	$ .01	$ .10	Smith, Greg	89TMLD	117	$ .01	$ .15
Smiley, John	87TTR	114	$ .05	$ .40	Smith, Hal	55T	8	$1.35	$5.00
Smiley, John	88T	423	$ .01	$ .30	Smith, Hal	56T	62	$1.25	$4.50
Smiley, John	89T	322	$ .01	$ .10	Smith, Hal	56T	283	$1.30	$5.00
Smiley, John	89TBB	85	$ .01	$ .10	Smith, Hal	57T	41	$ .95	$3.50
Smiley, John	90T	568	$ .01	$ .03	Smith, Hal	57T	111	$ .95	$3.50

Player	Year	No.	VG	EX/MT	Player	Year	No.	VG	EX/MT
Smith, Hal	58T	257	$ .50	$2.00	Smith, Mayo	67T	321	$ .25	$ .65
Smith, Hal	58T	273	$ .50	$2.00	Smith, Mayo	68T	544	$ .30	$1.00
Smith, Hal	59T	227	$ .50	$1.95	Smith, Mayo	69T	40	$ .25	$ .65
Smith, Hal	59T	497	$ .50	$1.95	Smith, Mayo	70T	313	$ .10	$ .35
Smith, Hal	60T	48	$ .35	$1.10	Smith, Mike	89TMLD	118	$ .01	$ .05
Smith, Hal	60T	84	$ .35	$1.10	Smith, Mike	90T	249	$ .01	$ .10
Smith, Hal	61T	242	$ .30	$1.00	Smith, Mike	90T	552	$ .01	$ .10
Smith, Hal	61T	549	$6.00	$18.00	Smith, Ozzie	79T	116	$10.00	$30.00
Smith, Hal	62T	492	$ .70	$2.10	Smith, Ozzie	80T	393	$1.50	$4.50
Smith, Hal	63T	153	$ .25	$ .85	Smith, Ozzie	81T	254	$ .50	$1.50
Smith, Hal	64T	233	$ .25	$ .85	Smith, Ozzie	81TRB	207	$ .03	$ .15
Smith, Jack	63T	496	$2.50	$6.50	Smith, Ozzie	82T	95	$ .40	$1.50
Smith, Jack	64T	378	$ .40	$1.25	Smith, Ozzie	82TTR	109	$1.00	$4.00
Smith, Jimmy	83T	122	$ .01	$ .06	Smith, Ozzie	83T	540	$ .05	$ .75
Smith, Keith	78T	710	$ .15	$ .50	Smith, Ozzie	84T	130	$ .01	$ .35
Smith, Lee	82T	452	$ .35	$1.10	Smith, Ozzie	84TAS	389	$ .01	$ .05
Smith, Lee	83T	699	$ .01	$ .06	Smith, Ozzie	85T	605	$ .01	$ .10
Smith, Lee	84T	176	$ .01	$ .05	Smith, Ozzie	85TAS	715	$ .01	$ .10
Smith, Lee	85T	511	$ .01	$ .04	Smith, Ozzie	86T	730	$ .02	$ .15
Smith, Lee	86T	355	$ .01	$ .03	Smith, Ozzie	86TAS	704	$ .01	$ .10
Smith, Lee	87T	23	$ .01	$ .03	Smith, Ozzie	87T	749	$ .01	$ .10
Smith, Lee	88T	240	$ .01	$ .10	Smith, Ozzie	87TAS	598	$ .01	$ .03
Smith, Lee	88TTR	110	$ .01	$ .05	Smith, Ozzie	88T	460	$ .01	$ .10
Smith, Lee	89T	760	$ .01	$ .04	Smith, Ozzie	88TAS	400	$ .01	$ .03
Smith, Lee	90T	495	$ .01	$ .03	Smith, Ozzie	88TBB	228	$ .01	$ .15
Smith, Lonnie	79T	722	$ .50	$1.50	Smith, Ozzie	89T	230	$ .01	$ .10
Smith, Lonnie	81T	317	$ .01	$ .07	Smith, Ozzie	89TAS	389	$ .01	$ .04
Smith, Lonnie	82T	127	$ .01	$ .06	Smith, Ozzie	89TBB	110	$ .01	$ .10
Smith, Lonnie	82TTR	108	$ .02	$ .10	Smith, Ozzie	90T	590	$ .01	$ .03
Smith, Lonnie	83T	465	$ .01	$ .06	Smith, Ozzie	90TAS	389	$ .01	$ .10
Smith, Lonnie	83T	561	$ .01	$ .06	Smith, Paul	54T	11	$1.25	$5.00
Smith, Lonnie	84T	186	$ .01	$ .05	Smith, Paul	57T	345	$3.50	$13.00
Smith, Lonnie	84T	580	$ .01	$ .05	Smith, Paul	58T	269	$ .50	$2.00
Smith, Lonnie	85T	255	$ .01	$ .04	Smith, Pete	64T	428	$ .40	$1.25
Smith, Lonnie	85TTR	109	$ .02	$ .10	Smith, Pete	88TTR	111	$ .01	$ .10
Smith, Lonnie	86T	617	$ .01	$ .03	Smith, Pete	89T	537	$ .01	$ .10
Smith, Lonnie	87T	69	$ .01	$ .03	Smith, Pete	90T	771	$ .01	$ .03
Smith, Lonnie	88T	777	$ .01	$ .03	Smith, Ray	84T	46	$ .01	$ .05
Smith, Lonnie	89TBB	242	$ .01	$ .05	Smith, Reggie	67T	314	$1.35	$4.00
Smith, Lonnie	89TTR	114	$ .01	$ .05	Smith, Reggie	68T	61	$ .15	$ .50
					Smith, Reggie	69T	660	$ .30	$1.00
					Smith, Reggie	70T	62	$ .50	$2.00
					Smith, Reggie	70T	215	$ .25	$ .65
					Smith, Reggie	71T	305	$ .35	$1.10
					Smith, Reggie	72T	88	$ .60	$2.00
					Smith, Reggie	72T	565	$ .30	$1.00
					Smith, Reggie	72TIA	566	$ .25	$ .85
					Smith, Reggie	73T	40	$ .25	$ .65
					Smith, Reggie	74T	285	$ .06	$ .25
					Smith, Reggie	75T	490	$ .06	$ .25
					Smith, Reggie	76T	215	$ .05	$ .20
					Smith, Reggie	77T	345	$ .05	$ .15
					Smith, Reggie	78T	168	$ .02	$ .10
					Smith, Reggie	79T	465	$ .05	$ .20
					Smith, Reggie	80T	695	$ .01	$ .07
					Smith, Reggie	81T	75	$ .01	$ .07
					Smith, Reggie	82T	545	$ .01	$ .06
					Smith, Reggie	82TIA	546	$ .01	$ .06
					Smith, Reggie	82TTR	110	$ .02	$ .10
					Smith, Reggie	83T	282	$ .01	$ .06
					Smith, Reggie	83T	283	$ .01	$ .06
					Smith, Roy	85T	381	$ .01	$ .04
					Smith, Roy	86T	9	$ .01	$ .03
					Smith, Roy	90T	672	$ .01	$ .03
					Smith, Tommy	74T	606	$ .06	$ .25
					Smith, Tommy	75T	619	$ .06	$ .25
					Smith, Tommy	77T	14	$ .05	$ .15
					Smith, Willie	65T	85	$ .25	$ .65
					Smith, Willie	66T	438	$ .25	$ .85
					Smith, Willie	67T	397	$ .25	$ .85
					Smith, Willie	68T	568	$ .30	$1.00
					Smith, Willie	69T	198	$ .25	$ .65
					Smith, Willie	70T	318	$ .10	$ .35
					Smith, Willie	71T	457	$ .10	$ .35

LONNIE SMITH

Player	Year	No.	VG	EX/MT
Smith, Lonnie	90T	152	$ .01	$ .03
Smith, Mayo	55T	130	$1.35	$5.00
Smith, Mayo	56T	60	$1.25	$4.50
Smith, Zane	86T	167	$ .02	$ .20

Player	Year	No.	VG	EX/MT
Smith, Zane	87T	544	$ .01	$ .03
Smith, Zane	88T	297	$ .01	$ .03
Smith, Zane	88TBB	193	$ .01	$ .05
Smith, Zane	89T	688	$ .01	$ .04
Smith, Zane	90T	48	$ .01	$ .03
Smithson, Mike	83TTR	106	$ .02	$ .10
Smithson, Mike	84T	89	$ .01	$ .05
Smithson, Mike	84TTR	110	$ .02	$ .10
Smithson, Mike	85T	483	$ .01	$ .04
Smithson, Mike	86T	695	$ .01	$ .03
Smithson, Mike	87T	225	$ .01	$ .03
Smithson, Mike	88T	554	$ .01	$ .03
Smithson, Mike	89T	377	$ .01	$ .04
Smithson, Mike	89TBB	222	$ .01	$ .05
Smithson, Mike	90T	188	$ .01	$ .03
Smoltz, John	89T	382	$ .05	$ .35
Smoltz, John	89TBB	260	$ .01	$ .25
Smoltz, John	90T	535	$ .01	$ .15
Snell, Nate	85TTR	110	$ .05	$ .25
Snell, Nate	86T	521	$ .01	$ .03
Snell, Nate	87T	86	$ .01	$ .03
Snider, Duke	51Trb	38	$15.00	$50.00
Snider, Duke	52T	37	$100.00	$300.00
Snider, Duke	54T	32	$50.00	$150.00
Snider, Duke	55T	210	$100.00	$400.00
Snider, Duke	56T	150	$32.50	$100.00
Snider, Duke	57T	170	$45.00	$125.00
Snider, Duke	57T	400	$40.00	$150.00
Snider, Duke	58T	88	12.00	$37.50
Snider, Duke	58T	314	$8.00	$35.00
Snider, Duke	58T	436	$11.50	$38.00
Snider, Duke	59T	20	$12.00	$45.00
Snider, Duke	59T	468	$3.00	$9.00
Snider, Duke	60T	493	$11.50	$37.50
Snider, Duke	61T	443	$9.00	$30.00
Snider, Duke	62T	500	$20.00	$60.00
Snider, Duke	63T	68	$2.50	$10.00
Snider, Duke	63T	550	$20.00	$62.50
Snider, Duke	64T	155	$4.00	$16.00
Snyder, Brian	86T	174	$ .01	$ .03
Snyder, Cory	85T	403	$1.00	$4.00
Snyder, Cory	87T	192	$ .25	$ .60
Snyder, Cory	88T	620	$ .01	$ .20
Snyder, Cory	88TBB	43	$ .01	$ .10
Snyder, Cory	89T	80	$ .01	$ .10
Snyder, Cory	89TBB	175	$ .01	$ .10
Snyder, Cory	90T	770	$ .01	$ .10
Snyder, Gene	59T	522	$2.00	$7.00
Snyder, Jerry	57T	22	$ .95	$3.50
Snyder, Jim	88TTR	112	$ .01	$ .05
Snyder, Jim	89T	44	$ .01	$ .04
Snyder, Russ	60T	81	$ .35	$1.10
Snyder, Russ	61T	143	$ .30	$1.00
Snyder, Russ	62T	64	$ .35	$1.10
Snyder, Russ	63T	543	$1.50	$3.75
Snyder, Russ	64T	126	$ .25	$ .85
Snyder, Russ	65T	204	$ .30	$1.00
Snyder, Russ	66T	562	$4.50	$15.00
Snyder, Russ	67T	405	$ .25	$ .85
Snyder, Russ	68T	504	$ .30	$1.00
Snyder, Russ	69T	201	$ .25	$ .65
Snyder, Russ	70T	347	$ .10	$ .35
Snyder, Russ	71T	653	$ .70	$2.10
Soderholm, Eric	73T	577	$ .35	$1.10
Soderholm, Eric	74T	503	$ .06	$ .25
Soderholm, Eric	75T	54	$ .06	$ .25
Soderholm, Eric	76T	214	$ .05	$ .20
Soderholm, Eric	77T	273	$ .05	$ .15
Soderholm, Eric	78T	602	$ .02	$ .10
Soderholm, Eric	79T	186	$ .02	$ .10
Soderholm, Eric	80T	441	$ .01	$ .07
Soderholm, Eric	81T	383	$ .01	$ .07
Soff, Ray	87T	671	$ .01	$ .03
Sofield, Rick	79T	709	$ .02	$ .10
Sofield, Rick	80T	669	$ .06	$ .30

Player	Year	No.	VG	EX/MT
Sofield, Rick	81T	278	$ .01	$ .07
Sofield, Rick	82T	42	$ .05	$ .20
Sojo, Luis	90T	594	$ .01	$ .10

Player	Year	No.	VG	EX/MT
Solaita, Tony	75T	389	$ .06	$ .25
Solaita, Tony	76T	121	$ .06	$ .25
Solaita, Tony	77T	482	$ .05	$ .15
Solaita, Tony	78T	557	$ .02	$ .10
Solaita, Tony	79T	18	$ .02	$ .10
Solaita, Tony	80T	407	$ .01	$ .07
Solano, Julio	85T	353	$ .01	$ .04
Solis, Marcelino	59T	214	$ .50	$1.95
Solomon, "Eddie"	75T	624	$ .06	$ .25
Solomon, "Eddie"(Buddy)	78T	598	$ .02	$ .10
Solomon, Buddy	79T	156	$ .02	$ .10
Solomon, Buddy	80T	346	$ .01	$ .07
Solomon, Buddy	81T	298	$ .01	$ .07
Solomon, Buddy	82T	73	$ .01	$ .06
Solomon, Buddy	82T	696	$ .01	$ .06
Sorensen, Lary	78T	569	$ .02	$ .10
Sorensen, Lary	79T	303	$ .02	$ .10
Sorensen, Lary	80T	154	$ .01	$ .07
Sorensen, Lary	81T	379	$ .01	$ .07
Sorensen, Lary	81TTR	831	$ .02	$ .10
Sorensen, Lary	82T	689	$ .01	$ .06
Sorensen, Lary	82TTR	111	$ .02	$ .10
Sorensen, Lary	83T	48	$ .01	$ .06
Sorensen, Lary	84T	286	$ .01	$ .05
Sorensen, Lary	84T	546	$ .01	$ .05
Sorensen, Lary	84TTR	111	$ .02	$ .10
Sorensen, Lary	86T	744	$ .01	$ .07
Sorrell, Bill	66T	254	$10.00	$40.00
Sorrell, Bill	67T	341	$ .25	$ .65
Sorrell, Billy	71T	17	$ .10	$ .35
Sorrento, Paul	89TMLD	119	$ .01	$ .15
Sosa, Elias	74T	54	$ .06	$ .25
Sosa, Elias	75T	398	$ .06	$ .25
Sosa, Elias	76T	364	$ .05	$ .20
Sosa, Elias	77T	558	$ .05	$ .15
Sosa, Elias	78T	694	$ .02	$ .10
Sosa, Elias	79T	78	$ .02	$ .10
Sosa, Elias	80T	293	$ .01	$ .07
Sosa, Elias	81T	181	$ .01	$ .07
Sosa, Elias	82T	414	$ .01	$ .06

Player	Year	No.	VG	EX/MT	Player	Year	No.	VG	EX/MT
Sosa, Elias	82TTR	112	$ .02	$ .10	Speier, Chris	72TIA	166	$ .10	$ .35
Sosa, Elias	83T	753	$ .01	$ .06	Speier, Chris	73T	273	$ .06	$ .25
Sosa, Elias	83TTR	107	$ .02	$ .10	Speier, Chris	73T	345	$ .06	$ .25
Sosa, Elias	84T	503	$ .01	$ .05	Speier, Chris	74T	129	$ .06	$ .25
Sosa, Jose	76T	591	$ .05	$ .20	Speier, Chris	74TAS	335	$ .10	$ .35
Sosa, Sammy	89TMLD	120	$ .01	$ .20	Speier, Chris	75T	505	$ .06	$ .25
Sosa, Sammy	90T	692	$ .01	$ .25	Speier, Chris	76T	630	$ .05	$ .20
Soto, Mario	78T	427	$ .35	$1.10	Speier, Chris	77T	515	$ .05	$ .15
Soto, Mario	80T	622	$ .05	$ .20	Speier, Chris	78T	221	$ .02	$ .10
Soto, Mario	81T	354	$ .01	$ .07	Speier, Chris	79T	426	$ .02	$ .10
Soto, Mario	82T	63	$ .01	$ .06	Speier, Chris	80T	319	$ .01	$ .07
Soto, Mario	83T	215	$ .01	$ .06	Speier, Chris	81T	97	$ .01	$ .07
Soto, Mario	83T	351	$ .01	$ .06	Speier, Chris	82T	198	$ .01	$ .06
Soto, Mario	84T	160	$ .01	$ .05	Speier, Chris	83T	768	$ .01	$ .06
Soto, Mario	84T	756	$ .01	$ .05	Speier, Chris	84T	678	$ .01	$ .05
Soto, Mario	85T	495	$ .01	$ .04	Speier, Chris	85T	577	$ .01	$ .04
Soto, Mario	86T	725	$ .01	$ .10	Speier, Chris	85TTR	111	$ .02	$ .10
Soto, Mario	87T	517	$ .01	$ .03	Speier, Chris	86T	212	$ .01	$ .03
Soto, Mario	88T	666	$ .01	$ .10	Speier, Chris	87T	424	$ .01	$ .03
Soto, Mario	88TBB	120	$ .01	$ .05	Speier, Chris	87TTR	115	$ .01	$ .07
Souchock, Steve	52T	234	$6.00	$19.00	Speier, Chris	88T	329	$ .01	$ .03
Spahn, Warren	51Trb	30	$9.50	$27.50	Speier, Chris	89T	94	$ .01	$ .04
Spahn, Warren	52T	33	$75.00	$225.00	Speier, Chris	90T	753	$ .01	$ .03
Spahn, Warren	53T	147	$35.00	$100.00	Spence, Bob	71T	186	$ .10	$ .35
Spahn, Warren	54T	20	$22.50	$87.50	Spencer, Daryl	56T	277	$1.30	$5.00
Spahn, Warren	55T	31	$22.50	$65.00	Spencer, Daryl	57T	49	$ .95	$3.50
Spahn, Warren	56T	10	$10.00	$40.00	Spencer, Daryl	58T	68	$ .85	$3.50
Spahn, Warren	57T	90	$13.00	$40.00	Spencer, Daryl	59T	443	$ .50	$1.95
Spahn, Warren	58T	270	$9.00	$28.00	Spencer, Daryl	60T	368	$ .50	$1.95
Spahn, Warren	58TAS	494	$3.00	$9.00	Spencer, Daryl	61T	357	$ .30	$1.00
Spahn, Warren	59T	40	$12.00	$35.00	Spencer, Daryl	61T	451	$1.25	$3.50
Spahn, Warren	59TAS	571	$11.00	$35.00	Spencer, Daryl	62T	197	$ .35	$1.10
Spahn, Warren	60T	230	$1.25	$3.50	Spencer, Daryl	63T	502	$2.50	$6.50
Spahn, Warren	60T	445	$9.00	$35.00	Spencer, George	52T	346	$39.00	$135.00
Spahn, Warren	61T	47	$ .60	$1.75	Spencer, George	53T	115	$3.75	$13.00
Spahn, Warren	61T	200	$7.00	$20.00	Spencer, Jim	70T	255	$ .10	$ .35
Spahn, Warren	61TAS	589	$30.00	$100.00	Spencer, Jim	71T	78	$ .10	$ .35
Spahn, Warren	62T	56	$ .50	$2.00	Spencer, Jim	72T	419	$ .10	$ .35
Spahn, Warren	62T	58	$ .50	$1.95	Spencer, Jim	73T	319	$ .06	$ .25
Spahn, Warren	62T	100	$7.50	$22.50	Spencer, Jim	74T	580	$ .06	$ .25
Spahn, Warren	62T	312	$1.25	$5.00	Spencer, Jim	75T	387	$ .06	$ .25
Spahn, Warren	62TAS	399	$3.00	$11.00	Spencer, Jim	76T	83	$ .05	$ .20
Spahn, Warren	63T	320	$8.00	$25.00	Spencer, Jim	76TTR	83	$ .05	$ .20
Spahn, Warren	64T	3	$1.25	$3.50	Spencer, Jim	77T	648	$ .05	$ .15
Spahn, Warren	64T	400	$10.00	$30.00	Spencer, Jim	78T	182	$ .02	$ .10
Spahn, Warren	65T	205	$9.50	$25.00	Spencer, Jim	79T	599	$ .02	$ .10
Spahn, Warren	73T	449	$ .25	$ .65	Spencer, Jim	80T	278	$ .01	$ .07
Spangler, Al	60T	143	$ .35	$1.10	Spencer, Jim	81T	435	$ .01	$ .07
Spangler, Al	61T	73	$ .30	$1.00	Spencer, Jim	81TTR	832	$ .02	$ .10
Spangler, Al	62T	556	$3.75	$11.00	Spencer, Jim	82T	729	$ .01	$ .06
Spangler, Al	63T	77	$ .25	$ .85	Sperring, Rob	76T	323	$ .05	$ .20
Spangler, Al	64T	406	$ .40	$1.25	Sperring, Rob	78T	514	$ .02	$ .10
Spangler, Al	65T	164	$ .25	$ .65	Spiers, Billy	89TMLD	121	$ .01	$ .10
Spangler, Al	66T	173	$ .25	$ .85	Spiers, Billy	89TTR	115	$ .01	$ .20
Spangler, Al	68T	451	$ .25	$ .65	Spiers, Billy	90T	538	$ .01	$ .10
Spangler, Al	69T	268	$ .25	$ .85	Spiezio, Ed	67T	128	$ .25	$ .65
Spangler, Al	70T	714	$ .50	$2.00	Spiezio, Ed	68T	349	$ .25	$ .65
Spangler, Al	74T	354	$ .06	$ .25	Spiezio, Ed	69T	249	$ .25	$ .85
Spanswick, Bill	64T	287	$4.00	$15.00	Spiezio, Ed	70T	718	$ .50	$2.00
Spanswick, Bill	65T	356	$ .30	$1.00	Spiezio, Ed	71T	6	$ .10	$ .35
Sparma, Joe	64T	512	$2.00	$8.00	Spiezio, Ed	72T	504	$ .10	$ .35
Sparma, Joe	65T	587	$1.50	$3.75	Spiezio, Wayne	65T	431	$ .35	$1.10
Sparma, Joe	66T	267	$ .25	$ .85	Spikes, Charlie	73T	614	$10.00	$40.00
Sparma, Joe	67T	13	$ .25	$ .65	Spikes, Charlie	74T	58	$ .06	$ .25
Sparma, Joe	68T	505	$ .30	$1.00	Spikes, Charlie	75T	135	$ .06	$ .25
Sparma, Joe	69T	488	$ .25	$ .65	Spikes, Charlie	76T	408	$ .05	$ .20
Sparma, Joe	70T	243	$ .10	$ .35	Spikes, Charlie	77T	168	$ .05	$ .15
Speake, Bob	56T	66	$1.25	$4.50	Spikes, Charlie	78T	459	$ .02	$ .10
Speake, Bob	57T	339	$3.50	$13.00	Spikes, Charlie	80T	294	$ .01	$ .07
Speake, Bob	58T	437	$ .50	$2.00	Spillner, Dan	75T	222	$ .06	$ .25
Speake, Bob	59T	526	$2.00	$7.00	Spillner, Dan	76T	557	$ .05	$ .20
Speck, Cliff	87T	269	$ .01	$ .03	Spillner, Dan	77T	182	$ .05	$ .15
Speckenbach, Paul	64T	548	$1.50	$3.75	Spillner, Dan	78T	488	$ .02	$ .10
Speed, Horace	79T	438	$ .02	$ .10	Spillner, Dan	79T	359	$ .02	$ .10
Speier, Chris	72T	165	$ .10	$ .35	Spillner, Dan	80T	38	$ .01	$ .07

TOPPS

Player	Year	No.	VG	EX/MT	Player	Year	No.	VG	EX/MT
Spillner, Dan	81T	276	$ .01	$ .07	Stafford, Bill	63T	331	$ .50	$1.95
Spillner, Dan	82T	664	$ .01	$ .06	Stafford, Bill	64T	299	$ .25	$ .85
Spillner, Dan	83T	725	$ .01	$ .06	Stafford, Bill	65T	281	$ .30	$1.00
Spillner, Dan	84T	91	$ .01	$ .05	Staggs, Steve	78T	521	$ .02	$ .10
Spillner, Dan	85T	169	$ .01	$ .04	Stahl, Larry	66T	107	$ .25	$ .85
Spillner, Dan	86T	423	$ .01	$ .03	Stahl, Larry	69T	271	$ .25	$ .85
Spilman, Harry	79T	717	$ .05	$ .20	Stahl, Larry	70T	494	$ .10	$ .35
Spilman, Harry	80T	677	$ .01	$ .07	Stahl, Larry	71T	711	$ .70	$2.10
Spilman, Harry	81T	94	$ .01	$ .07	Stahl, Larry	72T	782	$ .70	$2.10
Spilman, Harry	81TTR	833	$ .02	$ .10	Stahl, Larry	73T	533	$ .35	$1.10
Spilman, Harry	82T	509	$ .01	$ .06	Stahl, Larry	74T	507	$ .06	$ .25
Spilman, Harry	83T	193	$ .01	$ .06	Staiger, Roy	76T	592	$1.25	$3.75
Spilman, Harry	84T	612	$ .01	$ .05	Staiger, Roy	77T	281	$ .05	$ .15
Spilman, Harry	85T	482	$ .01	$ .04	Staley, Gerry	51Tbb	7	$5.50	$17.00
Spilman, Harry	86T	352	$ .01	$ .03	Staley, Gerald	52T	79	$14.00	$45.00
Spilman, Harry	87T	64	$ .01	$ .03	Staley, Gerald (Gerry)	53T	56	$3.75	$13.00
Spilman, Harry	88T	217	$ .01	$ .03	Staley, Jerry	57T	227	$ .95	$3.50
Spinks, Scipio	70T	492	$ .10	$ .35	Staley, Jerry	58T	412	$ .50	$2.00
Spinks, Scipio	71T	747	$ .70	$2.10	Staley, Jerry	59T	426	$ .50	$1.95
Spinks, Scipio	72T	202	$ .10	$ .35	Staley, Gerry (Jerry)	60T	57	$ .50	$2.00
Spinks, Scipio	73T	417	$ .06	$ .25	Staley, Jerry	60T	510	$2.00	$7.00
Spinks, Scipio	74T	576	$ .06	$ .25	Staley, Jerry	61T	90	$ .30	$1.00
Splittorff, Paul	71T	247	$ .15	$ .50	Staley, Jerry	61T	81	$ .30	$1.00
Splittorff, Paul	72T	315	$ .10	$ .35	Stallard, Tracy	62T	567	$3.75	$11.00
Splittorff, Paul	73T	48	$ .06	$ .25	Stallard, Tracy	63T	419	$ .35	$1.20
Splittorff, Paul	74T	225	$ .06	$ .25	Stallard, Tracy	64T	176	$ .25	$ .85
Splittorff, Paul	75T	340	$ .06	$ .25	Stallard, Tracy	65T	491	$ .50	$2.00
Splittorff, Paul	76T	43	$ .05	$ .20	Stallard, Tracy	66T	7	$ .25	$ .85
Splittorff, Paul	77T	534	$ .05	$ .15	Stallcup, Virgil	52T	69	$14.00	$45.00
Splittorff, Paul	78T	638	$ .02	$ .10	Stallcup, Virgil	53T	180	$3.75	$13.00
Splittorff, Paul	79T	183	$ .02	$ .10	Staller, George	73T	136	$ .15	$ .50
Splittorff, Paul	80T	409	$ .01	$ .07	Staller, George	74T	307	$ .06	$ .25
Splittorff, Paul	81T	218	$ .01	$ .07	Stanek, Al	64T	99	$ .25	$ .85
Splittorff, Paul	82T	759	$ .01	$ .06	Stanek, Al	65T	302	$ .30	$1.00
Splittorff, Paul	83T	316	$ .01	$ .06	Stanek, Al	66T	437	$ .25	$ .85
Splittorff, Paul	84T	52	$ .01	$ .05	Stanfield, Kevin	79T	709	$ .02	$ .10
Spooner, Karl	55T	90	$1.35	$5.00	Stange, Lee	62T	321	$ .35	$1.10
Spooner, Karl	56T	83	$1.25	$4.50	Stange, Lee	63T	246	$ .25	$ .85
Sprague, Ed	69T	638	$ .25	$ .85	Stange, Lee	64T	555	$1.50	$3.75
Sprague, Ed	72T	121	$ .10	$ .35	Stange, Lee	65T	448	$ .50	$2.00
Sprague, Ed	75T	76	$ .06	$ .25	Stange, Lee	66T	371	$ .25	$ .85
Sprague, Ed	88TTR	113	$ .01	$ .40	Stange, Lee	67T	99	$ .25	$ .65
Sprague, Ed	89TBB	40	$ .01	$ .05	Stange, Lee	68T	593	$ .30	$1.00
Spriggs, George	67T	472	$ .50	$2.00	Stange, Lee	69T	148	$ .25	$ .65
Spriggs, George	68T	314	$ .25	$ .65	Stange, Lee	70T	447	$ .10	$ .35
Spriggs, George	69T	662	$ .25	$ .85	Stange, Lee	71T	311	$ .10	$ .35
Spriggs, George	71T	411	$ .10	$ .35	Stange, Lee	73T	131	$ .10	$ .35
Spring, Jack	62T	257	$ .35	$1.10	Stange, Lee	74T	403	$ .06	$ .25
Spring, Jack	63T	572	$1.50	$3.75	Stanhouse, Don	73T	352	$ .06	$ .25
Spring, Jack	64T	71	$ .25	$ .85	Stanhouse, Don	75T	493	$ .06	$ .25
Sprowl, Bobby	81T	82	$ .01	$ .07	Stanhouse, Don	77T	274	$ .05	$ .15
Sprowl, Bobby	82T	441	$ .01	$ .06	Stanhouse, Don	78T	629	$ .02	$ .10
Squires, Mike	79T	704	$ .02	$ .10	Stanhouse, Don	79T	119	$ .02	$ .10
Squires, Mike	80T	466	$ .01	$ .07	Stanhouse, Don	80T	517	$ .01	$ .07
Squires, Mike	81T	292	$ .01	$ .07	Stanhouse, Don	81T	24	$ .01	$ .07
Squires, Mike	82T	398	$ .01	$ .06	Stanicek, Pete	88TTR	114	$ .01	$ .15
Squires, Mike	83T	669	$ .01	$ .06	Stanicek, Pete	89T	497	$ .01	$ .10
Squires, Mike	84T	72	$ .01	$ .05	Stanky, Eddie	51Trb	48	$1.35	$4.00
Squires, Mike	85T	543	$ .01	$ .04	Stanky, Eddie	52T	76	$20.00	$60.00
St. Claire, Ebba	52T	393	$39.00	$135.00	Stanky, Eddie	54T	38	$2.00	$7.00
St. Claire, Ebba	53T	91	$3.75	$13.00	Stanky, Ed (Eddie)	55T	191	$2.65	$8.50
St. Claire, Randy	86T	89	$ .01	$ .03	Stanky, Eddie	66T	448	$ .60	$1.75
St. Claire, Randy	87T	467	$ .01	$ .03	Stanky, Eddie	67T	81	$ .25	$ .65
St. Claire, Randy	88T	279	$ .01	$ .03	Stanky, Eddie	68T	564	$ .35	$1.10
St. Claire, Randy	89T	666	$ .01	$ .04	Stanley, Bob	78T	186	$ .05	$ .20
St. Claire, Randy	90T	503	$ .01	$ .03	Stanley, Bob	79T	597	$ .02	$ .10
Stablein, George	81T	356	$ .01	$ .07	Stanley, Bob	80T	63	$ .01	$ .07
Staehle, Marv	65T	41	$ .25	$ .65	Stanley, Bob	81T	421	$ .01	$ .07
Staehle, Marv	66T	164	$ .25	$ .85	Stanley, Bob	82T	289	$ .01	$ .06
Staehle, Marv	69T	394	$ .60	$1.75	Stanley, Bob	83T	381	$ .01	$ .06
Staehle, Marv	71T	663	$ .75	$2.25	Stanley, Bob	83T	682	$ .01	$ .06
Stafford, Bill	61T	213	$ .30	$1.00	Stanley, Bob	84T	320	$ .01	$ .05
Stafford, Bill	62T	55	$ .50	$2.00	Stanley, Bob	85T	555	$ .01	$ .04
Stafford, Bill	62T	570	$3.75	$11.00	Stanley, Bob	86T	785	$ .01	$ .03
Stafford, Bill	63T	155	$ .25	$ .85	Stanley, Bob	87T	175	$ .01	$ .03

Player	Year	No.	VG	EX/MT
Stanley, Bob	88T	573	$ .01	$ .03
Stanley, Bob	89T	37	$ .01	$ .04
Stanley, Fred	72T	59	$ .10	$ .35
Stanley, Fred	74T	423	$ .06	$ .25
Stanley, Fred	75T	503	$ .06	$ .25
Stanley, Fred	76T	429	$ .05	$ .20
Stanley, Fred	77T	123	$ .05	$ .15
Stanley, Fred	78T	664	$ .02	$ .10
Stanley, Fred	79T	16	$ .02	$ .10
Stanley, Fred	80T	387	$ .01	$ .07
Stanley, Fred	81T	281	$ .01	$ .07
Stanley, Fred	81TTR	834	$ .02	$ .10
Stanley, Fred	82T	787	$ .01	$ .06
Stanley, Fred	83T	513	$ .01	$ .06
Stanley, Mickey	66T	198	$ .30	$1.00
Stanley, Mickey	67T	607	$7.00	$21.00
Stanley, Mickey	68T	129	$ .25	$ .65
Stanley, Mickey	69T	13	$ .25	$ .65
Stanley, Mickey	70T	383	$ .10	$ .35
Stanley, Mickey	71T	524	$ .30	$1.00
Stanley, Mickey	72T	385	$ .10	$ .35
Stanley, Mickey	73T	88	$ .06	$ .25
Stanley, Mickey	74T	530	$ .06	$ .25
Stanley, Mickey	75T	141	$ .06	$ .25
Stanley, Mickey	76T	483	$ .05	$ .20
Stanley, Mickey	77T	533	$ .05	$ .15
Stanley, Mickey	78T	232	$ .02	$ .10
Stanley, Mickey	79T	692	$ .02	$ .10
Stanley, Mike	87TTR	116	$ .01	$ .07
Stanley, Mike	88T	219	$ .01	$ .03
Stanley, Mike	89T	587	$ .01	$ .04
Stanley, Mike	90T	92	$ .01	$ .03
Stanton, Leroy	72T	141	$ .10	$ .35
Stanton, Leroy	73T	18	$ .06	$ .25
Stanton, Leroy	74T	594	$ .06	$ .25
Stanton, Leroy	75T	342	$ .06	$ .25
Stanton, Leroy	76T	152	$ .05	$ .20
Stanton, Leroy	77T	226	$ .05	$ .15
Stanton, Leroy	78T	447	$ .02	$ .10
Stanton, Leroy	79T	533	$ .02	$ .10
Stanton, Mike	82T	473	$ .01	$ .06
Stanton, Mike	82TTR	113	$ .02	$ .10
Stanton, Mike	83T	159	$ .01	$ .06
Stanton, Mike	84T	694	$ .01	$ .05
Stanton, Mike	85T	256	$ .01	$ .04
Stanton, Mike	89TMLD	122	$ .01	$ .05
Stanton, Mike	90T	694	$ .01	$ .10
Stapleton, Dave	81T	81	$ .01	$ .07
Stapleton, Dave	82T	589	$ .01	$ .06
Stapleton, Dave	83T	239	$ .01	$ .06
Stapleton, Dave	84T	053	$ .01	$ .05
Stapleton, Dave	85T	322	$ .01	$ .04
Stapleton, Dave	86T	151	$ .01	$ .03
Stapleton, Dave	87T	507	$ .01	$ .03
Stargell, Willie	63T	553	$60.00	$175.00
Stargell, Willie	64T	342	$10.00	$30.00
Stargell, Willie	65T	377	$6.00	$18.00
Stargell, Willie	66T	99	$ .75	$2.00
Stargell, Willie	66T	255	$4.00	$14.00
Stargell, Willie	67T	140	$5.50	$17.50
Stargell, Willie	67T	266	$1.50	$3.75
Stargell, Willie	68T	86	$2.50	$8.00
Stargell, Willie	69T	545	$2.75	$8.50
Stargell, Willie	70T	470	$2.00	$7.00
Stargell, Willie	71T	230	$1.50	$6.00
Stargell, Willie	72T	87	$ .60	$2.00
Stargell, Willie	72T	89	$ .60	$2.00
Stargell, Willie	72T	343	$ .35	$1.10
Stargell, Willie	72T	447	$1.25	$3.50
Stargell, Willie	72TIA	448	$ .60	$1.75
Stargell, Willie	73T	370	$1.25	$4.50
Stargell, Willie	74T	100	$1.00	$4.00
Stargell, Willie	74T	202	$ .60	$2.00
Stargell, Willie	74T	203	$ .60	$2.00
Stargell, Willie	75T	100	$ .65	$2.00

Player	Year	No.	VG	EX/MT
Stargell, Willie	76T	270	$ .70	$2.00
Stargell, Willie	77T	460	$1.00	$4.00
Stargell, Willie	78T	510	$1.00	$4.00
Stargell, Willie	79T	55	$ .50	$2.00
Stargell, Willie	80T	610	$ .35	$1.10
Stargell, Willie	81T	380	$ .35	$1.10
Stargell, Willie	82T	715	$ .15	$ .60
Stargell, Willie	82TIA	716	$ .08	$ .30
Starrette, Herm	64T	239	$ .25	$ .85
Starrette, Herm	65T	539	$1.50	$3.75
Starrette, Herm	74T	634	$ .06	$ .25
Staub, Rusty	63T	544	$8.50	$25.00
Staub, Rusty	64T	109	$1.75	$6.50
Staub, Rusty	65T	321	$2.00	$6.00
Staub, Rusty	66T	106	$1.00	$4.00
Staub, Rusty	66T	273	$ .50	$2.00
Staub, Rusty	67T	73	$ .75	$3.00
Staub, Rusty	68T	300	$ .75	$3.00

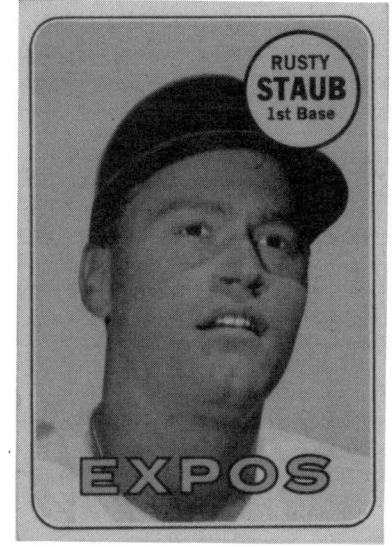

Player	Year	No.	VG	EX/MT
Staub, Rusty	69T	230	$ .50	$2.00
Staub, Rusty	70T	585	$ .60	$1.75
Staub, Rusty	71T	560	$ .70	$2.00
Staub, Rusty	74T	629	$ .25	$ .85
Staub, Rusty	75T	90	$ .10	$ .35
Staub, Rusty	76T	120	$ .05	$ .20
Staub, Rusty	76TTR	120	$ .06	$ .25
Staub, Rusty	77T	420	$ .10	$ .35
Staub, Rusty	78T	370	$ .05	$ .20
Staub, Rusty	79T	440	$ .05	$ .20
Staub, Rusty	80T	660	$ .02	$ .10
Staub, Rusty	81T	80	$ .02	$ .10
Staub, Rusty	81TTR	835	$ .08	$ .30
Staub, Rusty	82T	270	$ .02	$ .10
Staub, Rusty	83T	740	$ .01	$ .06
Staub, Rusty	83T	741	$ .01	$ .06
Staub, Rusty	84T	430	$ .02	$ .10
Staub, Rusty	84T	702	$ .06	$ .30
Staub, Rusty	84T	704	$ .03	$ .15
Staub, Rusty	85T	190	$ .01	$ .04
Staub, Rusty	86T	570	$ .01	$ .03
Stearns, John	76T	633	$ .10	$ .35
Stearns, John	77T	119	$ .05	$ .15
Stearns, John	78T	334	$ .02	$ .10
Stearns, John	79T	545	$ .02	$ .10

TOPPS

Player	Year	No.	VG	EX/MT	Player	Year	No.	VG	EX/MT
Stearns, John	79TRB	205	$ .02	$ .10	Stephens, Gene	64T	308	$ .25	$ .85
Stearns, John	80T	76	$ .01	$ .07	Stephens, Gene	65T	498	$ .50	$2.00
Stearns, John	81T	428	$ .01	$ .07	Stephens, Verne	51Trb	4	$1.35	$4.00
Stearns, John	82T	743	$ .01	$ .06					
Stearns, John	83T	212	$ .01	$ .06					
Steels, James	88T	117	$ .01	$ .10					
Stefero, John	87T	563	$ .01	$ .03					
Steffen, Dave	81T	626	$ .01	$ .07					
Stegman, Dave	79T	706	$ .02	$ .10					
Stegman, Dave	84T	664	$ .01	$ .05					
Stegman, Dave	85T	194	$ .01	$ .04					
Stein, Bill	76T	131	$ .05	$ .20					
Stein, Bill	77T	334	$ .05	$ .15					
Stein, Bill	78T	476	$ .02	$ .10					
Stein, Bill	79T	698	$ .02	$ .10					
Stein, Bill	80T	226	$ .01	$ .07					
Stein, Bill	81T	532	$ .01	$ .07					
Stein, Bill	81TTR	836	$ .02	$ .10					
Stein, Bill	82T	402	$ .01	$ .06					
Stein, Bill	83T	64	$ .01	$ .06					
Stein, Bill	84T	758	$ .01	$ .05					
Stein, Bill	85T	171	$ .01	$ .04					
Stein, Bill	86T	371	$ .01	$ .03					
Stein, Randy	79T	394	$ .02	$ .10					
Stein, Randy	80T	613	$ .01	$ .07					
Steinbach, Terry	87TTR	117	$ .10	$ .50					
Steinbach, Terry	88T	551	$ .01	$ .15					
Steinbach, Terry	88TBB	39	$ .01	$ .10					
Steinbach, Terry	89T	725	$ .01	$ .10					
Steinbach, Terry	89TBB	80	$ .01	$ .05					
Steinbach, Terry	90T	145	$ .01	$ .03					
Stelmaszek, Rick	70T	599	$ .25	$ .85					
Stelmaszek, Rick	73T	601	$ .35	$1.10					
Stelmaszek, Rick	74T	611	$ .06	$ .25					
Stelmaszek, Rick	75T	338	$ .06	$ .25					
Stengel, Casey	58T	475	$5.00	$15.00	Stephens, Vern(e)	52T	84	$6.00	$19.00
Stengel, Casey	59T	383	$1.35	$4.00	Stephens, Vern	53T	270	$11.00	$37.50
Stengel, Casey	59TAS	552	$7.50	$25.00	Stephens, Vern	54T	54	$4.75	$14.00
Stengel, Casey	60T	227	$5.50	$17.50	Stephenson, Earl	72T	61	$ .15	$ .60
Stengel, Casey	62T	29	$3.50	$12.50	Stephenson, Jerry	65T	74	$ .35	$1.10
Stengel, Casey	63T	43	$1.25	$4.50	Stephenson, Jerry	66T	396	$ .25	$ .85
Stengel, Casey	63T	233	$7.00	$20.00	Stephenson, Jerry	68T	519	$ .30	$1.00
Stengel, Casey	64T	324	$3.00	$10.00	Stephenson, Jerry	69T	172	$ .25	$ .65
Stengel, Casey	64T	393	$1.35	$4.00	Stephenson, Jerry	71T	488	$ .10	$ .35
Stengel, Casey	65T	187	$5.00	$15.00	Stephenson, John	64T	536	$1.50	$3.75
Stenhouse, Dave	62T	592	$13.00	$40.00	Stephenson, John	66T	17	$ .25	$ .85
Stenhouse, Dave	63T	263	$ .25	$ .85	Stephenson, John	67T	522	$ .50	$2.00
Stenhouse, Dave	64T	498	$ .40	$1.25	Stephenson, John	68T	83	$ .25	$ .65
Stenhouse, Dave	65T	304	$ .30	$1.00	Stephenson, John	71T	421	$ .10	$ .35
Stenhouse, Dave	85T	141	$ .01	$ .10	Stephenson, Phil	89TMLD	123	$ .01	$ '.15
Stenhouse, Mike	85T	141	$ .01	$ .10	Stephenson, Phil	90T	584	$ .01	$ .03
Stenhouse, Mike	85T	658	$ .01	$ .04	Steve, Lyons	87T	511	$ .01	$ .03
Stenhouse, Mike	85TTR	112	$ .02	$ .10	Stevens, Morrie	65T	521	$ .50	$2.00
Stenhouse, Mike	86T	17	$ .01	$ .03	Stevens, R. C.	58T	470	$ .50	$1.95
Stennett, Rennie	72T	219	$ .10	$ .35	Stevens, R. C.	59T	282	$ .50	$1.95
Stennett, Rennie	73T	348	$ .06	$ .25	Stevens, R. C.	61T	526	$6.00	$18.00
Stennett, Rennie	74T	426	$ .06	$ .25	Stewart, Bunky	55T	136	$1.35	$5.00
Stennett, Rennie	75T	336	$ .06	$ .25	Stewart, Dave	82T	213	$1.25	$4.50
Stennett, Rennie	76T	425	$ .05	$ .20	Stewart, Dave	83T	532	$ .01	$ .75
Stennett, Rennie	76TRB	6	$ .05	$ .20	Stewart, Dave	84T	352	$ .01	$ .50
Stennett, Rennie	77T	35	$ .05	$ .15	Stewart, Dave	85T	723	$ .01	$ .25
Stennett, Rennie	78T	165	$ .02	$ .10	Stewart, Dave	86T	689	$ .01	$ .15
Stennett, Rennie	79T	687	$ .02	$ .10	Stewart, Dave	87T	14	$ .01	$ .10
Stennett, Rennie	80T	501	$ .01	$ .07	Stewart, Dave	88T	476	$ .01	$ .03
Stennett, Rennie	81T	257	$ .01	$ .07	Stewart, Dave	89T	145	$ .01	$ .04
Stennett, Rennie	82T	84	$ .01	$ .06	Stewart, Dave	89TBB	101	$ .01	$ .10
Stephen, Buzz	70T	533	$ .10	$ .35	Stewart, Dave	90T	270	$ .01	$ .03
Stephens, Gene	53T	248	$11.00	$37.50	Stewart, Ed	52T	279	$11.50	$38.00
Stephens, Gene	56T	313	$1.30	$5.00	Stewart, Jim	64T	408	$ .40	$1.25
Stephens, Gene	57T	217	$ .95	$3.50	Stewart, Jim	65T	298	$ .30	$1.00
Stephens, Gene	58T	227	$ .50	$2.00	Stewart, Jim	66T	63	$ .25	$ .85
Stephens, Gene	59T	261	$ .50	$1.95	Stewart, Jim	67T	124	$ .25	$ .65
Stephens, Gene	60T	363	$ .50	$1.95	Stewart, Jim	70T	636	$ .50	$2.00
Stephens, Gene	61T	102	$ .30	$1.00	Stewart, Jim	71T	644	$ .70	$2.10
Stephens, Gene	62T	38	$ .35	$1.10	Stewart, Jim	72T	747	$ .70	$2.10

VERN STEPHENS
Vernon D. Stephens

Player	Year	No.	VG	EX/MT	Player	Year	No.	VG	EX/MT
Stewart, Jimmy	73T	351	$ .06	$ .25	Stock, Wes	61T	26	$ .30	$1.00
Stewart, Sammy	79T	701	$ .02	$ .10	Stock, Wes	62T	442	$ .70	$2.10
Stewart, Sammy	79TRB	206	$ .02	$ .10	Stock, Wes	63T	438	$ .35	$1.20
Stewart, Sammy	80T	119	$ .01	$ .07	Stock, Wes	64T	382	$ .40	$1.25
Stewart, Sammy	81T	262	$ .01	$ .07	Stock, Wes	65T	117	$ .25	$ .65
Stewart, Sammy	82T	426	$ .05	$ .25	Stock, Wes	67T	74	$ .25	$ .65
Stewart, Sammy	82T	679	$ .01	$ .06	Stock, Wes	73T	179	$ .25	$ .85
Stewart, Sammy	83T	347	$ .01	$ .06	Stoddard, Bob	83T	195	$ .01	$ .06
Stewart, Sammy	84T	59	$ .01	$ .05	Stoddard, Bob	84T	439	$ .01	$ .05
Stewart, Sammy	85T	469	$ .01	$ .04	Stoddard, Tim	80T	314	$ .01	$ .07
Stewart, Sammy	86T	597	$ .01	$ .03	Stoddard, Tim	81T	91	$ .01	$ .07
Stewart, Sammy	86TTR	103	$ .02	$ .10	Stoddard, Tim	82T	457	$ .01	$ .06
Stewart, Sammy	87T	204	$ .01	$ .03	Stoddard, Tim	83T	217	$ .01	$ .06
Stewart, Sammy	88T	701	$ .01	$ .03	Stoddard, Tim	84T	106	$ .01	$ .05
Stieb, Dave	80T	77	$ .90	$3.00	Stoddard, Tim	84TTR	112	$ .02	$ .10
Stieb, Dave	81T	467	$ .15	$ .75	Stoddard, Tim	85T	693	$ .01	$ .04
Stieb, Dave	82T	380	$ .05	$ .25	Stoddard, Tim	85TTR	113	$ .02	$ .10
Stieb, Dave	82T	606	$ .01	$ .06	Stoddard, Tim	86T	558	$ .01	$ .03
Stieb, Dave	83T	130	$ .03	$ .15	Stoddard, Tim	87T	788	$ .01	$ .03
Stieb, Dave	83T	202	$ .01	$ .06	Stoddard, Tim	88T	359	$ .01	$ .03
Stieb, Dave	84T	590	$ .05	$ .20	Stone, Dean	54T	114	$2.00	$7.00
Stieb, Dave	84T	606	$ .01	$ .05	Stone, Dean	55T	60	$1.35	$5.00
Stieb, Dave	85T	240	$ .01	$ .10	Stone, Dean	56T	87	$1.25	$4.50
Stieb, Dave	86T	650	$ .01	$ .10	Stone, Dean	57T	381	$ .85	$3.50
Stieb, Dave	87T	90	$ .01	$ .10	Stone, Dean	59T	286	$ .50	$1.95
Stieb, Dave	88T	775	$ .01	$ .03	Stone, Dean	62T	574	$3.75	$11.00
Stieb, Dave	88TBB	172	$ .01	$ .05	Stone, Dean	63T	271	$ .25	$ .85
Stieb, Dave	89T	460	$ .01	$ .04	Stone, George	69T	627	$ .25	$ .85
Stieb, Dave	89TBB	128	$ .01	$ .10	Stone, George	70T	122	$ .10	$ .35
Stieb, Dave	90T	320	$ .01	$ .10	Stone, George	71T	507	$ .10	$ .35
Stieglitz, Al	60T	144	$ .35	$1.10	Stone, George	72T	601	$ .25	$ .85
Stigman, Dick	59T	142	$ .50	$1.95	Stone, George	73T	647	$ .35	$1.10
Stigman, Dick	60T	507	$2.00	$7.00	Stone, George	74T	397	$ .06	$ .25
Stigman, Dick	61T	77	$ .30	$1.00	Stone, George	75T	239	$ .06	$ .25
Stigman, Dick	62T	37	$ .50	$2.00	Stone, George	76T	567	$ .05	$ .20
Stigman, Dick	62T	532	$3.75	$11.00	Stone, Jeff	85T	476	$ .01	$ .04
Stigman, Dick	63T	89	$ .25	$ .85	Stone, Jeff	86T	686	$ .01	$ .03
Stigman, Dick	64T	6	$ .35	$1.10	Stone, Jeff	87T	532	$ .01	$ .03
Stigman, Dick	64T	245	$ .25	$ .85	Stone, Jeff	88T	154	$ .01	$ .03
Stigman, Dick	65T	548	$1.50	$3.75	Stone, Jeff	88TBB	146	$ .01	$ .05
Stigman, Dick	66T	512	$ .70	$2.10	Stone, Ron	66T	568	$4.50	$15.00
Stillman, Royle	76T	594	$ .05	$ .20	Stone, Ron	68T	409	$ .25	$ .65
Stillman, Royle	78T	272	$ .02	$ .10	Stone, Ron	69T	576	$ .25	$ .85
Stillwell, Kurt	86TTR	104	$ .08	$ .30	Stone, Ron	70T	218	$ .10	$ .35
Stillwell, Kurt	87T	623	$ .25	$ .85	Stone, Ron	71T	366	$ .10	$ .35
Stillwell, Kurt	88T	339	$ .01	$ .10	Stone, Ron	72T	528	$ .25	$ .85
Stillwell, Kurt	88TBB	136	$ .01	$ .05	Stone, Steve	72T	327	$ .15	$ .50
Stillwell, Kurt	88TTR	115	$ .01	$ .05	Stone, Steve	73T	167	$ .25	$ .65
Stillwell, Kurt	89T	596	$ .01	$ .04	Stone, Steve	74T	486	$ .06	$ .25
Stillwell, Kurt	89TBB	161	$ .01	$ .05	Stone, Steve	74TTR	486	$ .06	$ .25
Stillwell, Kurt	90T	222	$ .01	$ .03	Stone, Steve	75T	388	$ .06	$ .25
Stimac, Craig	81T	356	$ .01	$ .07	Stone, Steve	76T	378	$ .05	$ .20
Stinson, Bob	70T	131	$ .75	$1.75	Stone, Steve	77T	17	$ .03	$ .12
Stinson, Bob	71T	594	$ .75	$2.00	Stone, Steve	78T	153	$ .05	$ .20
Stinson, Bob	72T	679	$ .60	$1.75	Stone, Steve	79T	227	$ .02	$ .10
Stinson, Bob	74T	653	$ .06	$ .25	Stone, Steve	80T	688	$ .05	$ .20
Stinson, Bob	75T	471	$ .06	$ .25	Stone, Steve	81T	5	$ .04	$ .20
Stinson, Bob	76T	466	$ .05	$ .20	Stone, Steve	81T	520	$ .01	$ .07
Stinson, Bob	77T	138	$ .03	$ .12	Stone, Steve	82T	419	$ .01	$ .06
Stinson, Bob	78T	396	$ .02	$ .10	Stoneman, Bill	68T	179	$ .25	$ .65
Stinson, Bob	79T	252	$ .02	$ .10	Stoneman, Bill	69T	67	$ .25	$ .65
Stinson, Bob	80T	583	$ .01	$ .07	Stoneman, Bill	70T	398	$ .10	$ .35
Stirnweiss, George	52T	217	$6.00	$19.00	Stoneman, Bill	71T	266	$ .10	$ .35
Stobbs, Chuck	52T	62	$14.00	$45.00	Stoneman, Bill	72T	95	$ .35	$1.10
Stobbs, Chuck	53T	89	$3.75	$13.00	Stoneman, Bill	72T	610	$ .25	$ .85
Stobbs, Chuck	54T	185	$2.00	$7.00	Stoneman, Bill	73T	254	$ .06	$ .25
Stobbs, Chuck	55T	41	$1.35	$5.00	Stoneman, Bill	74T	352	$ .06	$ .25
Stobbs, Chuck	56T	68	$1.25	$4.50	Stottlemyre, Jr., Mel	90T	263	$ .01	$ .10
Stobbs, Chuck	57T	101	$ .95	$3.50	Stottlemyre, Mel	65T	550	$5.00	$15.00
Stobbs, Chuck	58T	239	$ .50	$2.00	Stottlemyre, Mel	66T	224	$ .60	$1.75
Stobbs, Chuck	59T	26	$ .85	$3.50	Stottlemyre, Mel	66T	350	$ .50	$2.00
Stobbs, Chuck	60T	432	$ .50	$1.95	Stottlemyre, Mel	67T	225	$ .35	$1.10
Stobbs, Chuck	61T	431	$ .50	$2.00	Stottlemyre, Mel	68T	120	$ .25	$ .65
Stock, Milton	52T	381	$39.00	$135.00	Stottlemyre, Mel	69T	9	$ .30	$1.00
Stock, Wes	60T	481	$ .60	$1.75	Stottlemyre, Mel	69T	470	$ .15	$ .50

TOPPS

Player	Year	No.	VG	EX/MT
Stottlemyre, Mel	70T	70	$ .50	$2.00
Stottlemyre, Mel	70T	100	$ .25	$ .85
Stottlemyre, Mel	71T	615	$ .30	$1.00
Stottlemyre, Mel	72T	325	$ .25	$ .65
Stottlemyre, Mel	72T	492	$ .05	$ .25
Stottlemyre, Mel	73T	520	$ .10	$ .35
Stottlemyre, Mel	74T	44	$ .06	$ .25
Stottlemyre, Mel	75T	183	$ .10	$ .35
Stottlemyre, Todd	88TTR	116	$ .05	$ .25
Stottlemyre, Todd	89T	722	$ .01	$ .10
Stottlemyre, Todd	89TBB	298	$ .01	$ .05
Stottlemyre, Todd	90T	591	$ .01	$ .03
Stowe, Hal	62T	291	$ .35	$1.10
Strahler, Mike	71T	188	$ .60	$1.75
Strahler, Mike	72T	198	$ .60	$1.50
Strahler, Mike	73T	279	$ .06	$ .25
Strain, Joe	79T	726	$ .05	$ .20
Strain, Joe	80T	538	$ .01	$ .07
Strain, Joe	81T	361	$ .01	$ .07
Strain, Joe	81TTR	837	$ .02	$ .10
Strain, Joe	82T	436	$ .01	$ .06
Straker, Les	87TTR	118	$ .01	$ .07
Straker, Les	88T	264	$ .01	$ .03
Straker, Les	89T	101	$ .01	$ .04
Straker, Les	89TBB	90	$ .01	$ .05
Strampe, Bob	73T	604	$ .35	$1.10
Strange, Doug	89TMLD	124	$ .01	$ .05
Strange, Doug	90T	641	$ .01	$ .03
Strawberry, Darryl	83TTR	108	$15.00	$60.00
Strawberry, Darryl	84T	182	$5.00	$15.00
Strawberry, Darryl	85T	278	$ .55	$1.75
Strawberry, Darryl	85T	570	$ .75	$3.00
Strawberry, Darryl	86T	80	$ .15	$ .75
Strawberry, Darryl	87T	460	$ .15	$ .50
Strawberry, Darryl	87TAS	601	$ .06	$ .25
Strawberry, Darryl	88T	710	$ .01	$ .25
Strawberry, Darryl	88TBB	253	$ .10	$ .45
Strawberry, Darryl	89T	300	$ .05	$ .25
Strawberry, Darryl	89TAS	390	$ .01	$ .15
Strawberry, Darryl	89TBB	139	$ .01	$ .25
Strawberry, Darryl	90T	600	$ .01	$ .15
Strickland, George	52T	197	$6.00	$19.00
Strickland, George	57T	263	$ .95	$3.50
Strickland, George	58T	102	$ .85	$3.50
Strickland, George	59T	207	$ .50	$1.95
Strickland, George	60T	63	$ .35	$1.10
Strickland, Jim	72T	778	$ .60	$1.75
Strickland, Jim	73T	122	$ .06	$ .25
Striker, Jake	60T	169	$ .35	$1.10
Strohmayer, John	71T	232	$ .10	$ .35
Strohmayer, John	72T	631	$ .25	$ .85
Strohmayer, John	73T	457	$ .06	$ .25
Strom, Brent	73T	612	$ .35	$1.10
Strom, Brent	74T	359	$ .06	$ .25
Strom, Brent	75T	643	$ .06	$ .25
Strom, Brent	76T	84	$ .05	$ .20
Strom, Brent	77T	348	$ .03	$ .12
Strom, Brent	78T	509	$ .02	$ .10
Stroud, Ed	67T	598	$2.00	$6.00
Stroud, Ed	68T	31	$ .25	$ .65
Stroud, Ed	69T	272	$ .25	$ .85
Stroud, Ed	70T	506	$ .10	$ .35
Stroud, Ed	71T	217	$ .10	$ .35
Stroughter, Steve	82TTR	114	$ .02	$ .10
Stuart, Dick	59T	357	$ .60	$1.75
Stuart, Dick	60T	402	$ .50	$1.95
Stuart, Dick	61T	126	$ .30	$1.00
Stuart, Dick	62T	160	$ .35	$1.10
Stuart, Dick	63T	18	$2.35	$10.00
Stuart, Dick	63T	285	$ .35	$1.10
Stuart, Dick	64T	10	$ .50	$2.00
Stuart, Dick	64T	12	$ .50	$2.00
Stuart, Dick	64T	410	$ .40	$1.25
Stuart, Dick	65T	5	$3.00	$12.00
Stuart, Dick	65T	280	$ .30	$1.00

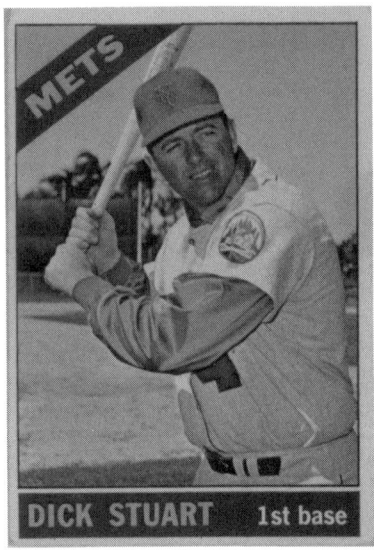

DICK STUART   1st base

Player	Year	No.	VG	EX/MT
Stuart, Dick	66T	480	$ .65	$1.75
Stuart, Marlin	52T	208	$6.00	$19.00
Stubbs, Franklin	85T	506	$ .05	$ .25
Stubbs, Franklin	86TTR	105	$ .02	$ .10
Stubbs, Franklin	87T	292	$ .01	$ .10
Stubbs, Franklin	88T	198	$ .01	$ .03
Stubbs, Franklin	88TBB	112	$ .01	$ .05
Stubbs, Franklin	89T	697	$ .01	$ .04
Stubbs, Franklin	89TBB	32	$ .01	$ .05
Stubbs, Franklin	90T	56	$ .01	$ .03
Stubing, Moose	89T	444	$ .01	$ .04
Stuper, John	83T	363	$ .01	$ .06
Stuper, John	84T	49	$ .01	$ .05
Stuper, John	84T	186	$ .01	$ .05
Stuper, John	86T	497	$ .01	$ .03
Sturdivant, Tom	57T	34	$ .95	$3.50
Sturdivant, Tom	58T	127	$ .50	$2.00
Sturdivant, Tom	59T	471	$ .50	$1.95
Sturdivant, Tom	60T	487	$ .60	$1.75
Sturdivant, Tom	61T	293	$ .30	$1.00
Sturdivant, Tom	62T	179	$ .35	$1.10
Sturdivant, Tom	63T	281	$ .25	$ .85
Sturdivant, Tom	64T	402	$ .40	$1.25
Suarez, Ken	66T	588	$4.50	$15.00
Suarez, Ken	68T	218	$ .25	$ .65
Suarez, Ken	69T	19	$ .25	$ .65
Suarez, Ken	70T	209	$ .10	$ .35
Suarez, Ken	71T	597	$ .30	$1.00
Suarez, Ken	72T	483	$ .05	$ .25
Suarez, Ken	74T	39	$ .06	$ .25
Such, Dick	70T	599	$ .25	$ .85
Such, Dick	71T	283	$ .10	$ .35
Sudakis, Bill	69T	552	$ .25	$ .85
Sudakis, Bill	70T	341	$ .10	$ .35
Sudakis, Bill	71T	253	$ .10	$ .35
Sudakis, Bill	72T	722	$ .70	$2.10
Sudakis, Bill	73T	586	$ .35	$1.10
Sudakis, Bill	74T	63	$ .06	$ .25
Sudakis, Bill	74TTR	63	$ .06	$ .25
Sudakis, Bill	75T	291	$ .06	$ .25
Suder, Pete	52T	256	$11.50	$38.00
Sukeforth, Clyde	52T	364	$39.00	$135.00
Sukla, Ed	66T	417	$ .25	$ .85

Player	Year	No.	VG	EX/MT	Player	Year	No.	VG	EX/MT
Sularz, Guy	83T	379	$ .01	$ .06	Sutcliffe, Rick	85T	72	$ .01	$ .04
Sullivan, Frank	55T	106	$1.35	$5.00	Sutcliffe, Rick	85TAS	720	$ .01	$ .10
Sullivan, Frank	56T	71	$1.25	$4.50	Sutcliffe, Rick	86T	330	$ .01	$ .03
Sullivan, Frank	57T	21	$ .95	$3.50	Sutcliffe, Rick	87T	142	$ .01	$ .10
Sullivan, Frank	58T	18	$ .85	$3.50	Sutcliffe, Rick	88T	740	$ .01	$ .10
Sullivan, Frank	59T	323	$ .50	$1.95	Sutcliffe, Rick	88TBB	128	$ .01	$ .10
Sullivan, Frank	60T	280	$ .35	$1.10	Sutcliffe, Rick	89T	520	$ .01	$ .04
Sullivan, Frank	61T	281	$ .30	$1.00	Sutcliffe, Rick	90T	640	$ .01	$ .03
Sullivan, Frank	62T	352	$ .35	$1.10	Sutherland, Darrell	66T	191	$ .25	$ .85
Sullivan, Frank	63T	389	$ .35	$1.20	Sutherland, Darrell	68T	551	$ .30	$1.00
Sullivan, Haywood	57T	336	$3.50	$13.00	Sutherland, Gary	67T	587	$4.00	$12.00
Sullivan, Haywood	58T	197	$ .50	$2.00	Sutherland, Gary	68T	98	$ .25	$ .65
Sullivan, Haywood	59T	416	$ .50	$1.95	Sutherland, Gary	69T	326	$ .25	$ .85
Sullivan, Haywood	60T	474	$ .60	$1.75	Sutherland, Gary	70T	632	$ .25	$ .85
Sullivan, Haywood	61T	212	$ .30	$1.00	Sutherland, Gary	71T	434	$ .10	$ .35
Sullivan, Haywood	62T	184	$ .35	$1.10	Sutherland, Gary	72T	211	$ .05	$ .25
Sullivan, Haywood	63T	359	$ .35	$1.20	Sutherland, Gary	73T	572	$ .35	$1.10
Sullivan, John	65T	593	$1.50	$3.75	Sutherland, Gary	74T	428	$ .06	$ .25
Sullivan, John	66T	597	$4.50	$15.00	Sutherland, Gary	74TTR	428	$ .06	$ .25
Sullivan, John	67T	568	$1.25	$3.50	Sutherland, Gary	75T	522	$ .06	$ .25
Sullivan, Marc	86T	529	$ .01	$ .03	Sutherland, Gary	76T	113	$ .05	$ .20
Sullivan, Marc	87T	66	$ .01	$ .03	Sutherland, Gary	77T	307	$ .03	$ .12
Sullivan, Marc	88T	354	$ .01	$ .03	Sutherland, Leo	81T	112	$ .01	$ .07
Summers, Champ	76T	299	$ .05	$ .20	Sutherland, Leo	82T	599	$ .01	$ .06
Summers, Champ	78T	622	$ .02	$ .10	Sutter, Bruce	77T	144	$ .60	$1.75
Summers, Champ	79T	516	$ .02	$ .10	Sutter, Bruce	78T	325	$ .25	$ .65
Summers, Champ	80T	176	$ .01	$ .07	Sutter, Bruce	79T	457	$ .15	$ .50
Summers, Champ	81T	27	$ .01	$ .07	Sutter, Bruce	80T	17	$ .08	$ .30
Summers, Champ	82T	369	$ .01	$ .06	Sutter, Bruce	81T	590	$ .05	$ .20
Summers, Champ	82TTR	115	$ .02	$ .10	Sutter, Bruce	81TTR	838	$ .02	$ .10
Summers, Champ	83T	428	$ .01	$ .06	Sutter, Bruce	82T	168	$ .03	$ .15
Summers, Champ	84T	768	$ .01	$ .05	Sutter, Bruce	82T	260	$ .02	$ .10
Summers, Champ	84TTR	113	$ .02	$ .10	Sutter, Bruce	82TAS	347	$ .02	$ .10
Summers, Champ	85T	208	$ .01	$ .04	Sutter, Bruce	83T	150	$ .01	$ .06
Sundberg, Jim	75T	567	$ .25	$ .85	Sutter, Bruce	83T	151	$ .01	$ .06
Sundberg, Jim	76T	226	$ .05	$ .20	Sutter, Bruce	83T	708	$ .01	$ .06
Sundberg, Jim	77T	351	$ .03	$ .12	Sutter, Bruce	83TAS	407	$ .01	$ .10
Sundberg, Jim	78T	492	$ .02	$ .10	Sutter, Bruce	84T	709	$ .01	$ .05
Sundberg, Jim	79T	120	$ .02	$ .10	Sutter, Bruce	84T	730	$ .03	$ .15
Sundberg, Jim	80T	530	$ .01	$ .07	Sutter, Bruce	85T	370	$ .01	$ .04
Sundberg, Jim	81T	95	$ .01	$ .07	Sutter, Bruce	85TAS	722	$ .01	$ .04
Sundberg, Jim	82T	335	$ .01	$ .06	Sutter, Bruce	85TRB	9	$ .01	$ .10
Sundberg, Jim	83T	665	$ .01	$ .06	Sutter, Bruce	85TTR	115	$ .05	$ .20
Sundberg, Jim	84T	779	$ .01	$ .05	Sutter, Bruce	86T	620	$ .01	$ .03
Sundberg, Jim	84TTR	114	$ .02	$ .10	Sutter, Bruce	87T	435	$ .01	$ .10
Sundberg, Jim	85T	446	$ .01	$ .04	Sutter, Bruce	88T	155	$ .01	$ .03
Sundberg, Jim	85TTR	114	$ .02	$ .10	Sutter, Bruce	89T	11	$ .01	$ .04
Sundberg, Jim	86T	245	$ .01	$ .03	Sutter, Bruce	89TBB	64	$ .01	$ .05
Sundberg, Jim	87T	190	$ .01	$ .03	Sutton, Don	66T	288	$27.50	$90.00
Sundberg, Jim	87TTR	119	$ .01	$ .07	Sutton, Don	67T	445	$5.00	$15.00
Sundberg, Jim	88T	516	$ .01	$ .03	Sutton, Don	68T	103	$1.25	$5.00
Sundberg, Jim	88TBB	100	$ .01	$ .05	Sutton, Don	69T	216	$1.25	$3.50
Sundberg, Jim	89T	78	$ .01	$ .04	Sutton, Don	70T	622	$1.50	$4.50
Sundberg, Jim	89TBB	103	$ .01	$ .05	Sutton, Don	71T	361	$1.25	$3.50
Surhoff, B. J.	90T	696	$ .01	$ .03	Sutton, Don	72T	530	$1.50	$3.75
Surhoff, B.J.	87T	216	$ .10	$ .50	Sutton, Don	73T	10	$ .85	$3.50
Surhoff, B.J.	88T	491	$ .01	$ .25	Sutton, Don	74T	220	$ .50	$2.50
Surhoff, B.J.	88TBB	22	$ .01	$ .05	Sutton, Don	75T	220	$ .60	$1.75
Surhoff, B.J.	89T	33	$ .01	$ .04	Sutton, Don	76T	530	$ .50	$2.00
Surkont, Max	52T	302	$11.50	$38.00	Sutton, Don	77T	620	$ .50	$1.95
Surkont, Max	56T	209	$2.50	$8.00	Sutton, Don	78T	310	$ .35	$1.10
Surkont, Max	57T	310	$3.50	$13.00	Sutton, Don	79T	170	$ .35	$1.10
Susce, George	56T	93	$1.25	$4.50	Sutton, Don	80T	440	$ .20	$ .75
Susce, George	57T	229	$ .95	$3.50	Sutton, Don	81T	605	$ .15	$ .75
Susce, George	58T	189	$ .50	$2.00	Sutton, Don	81T	7	$ .02	$ .10
Susce, George	59T	511	$2.00	$7.00	Sutton, Don	81TTR	839	$ .02	$ .10
Sutcliffe, Rick	80T	544	$1.00	$3.35	Sutton, Don	82T	305	$ .25	$ .65
Sutcliffe, Rick	81T	191	$ .25	$ .65	Sutton, Don	82TIA	306	$ .05	$ .20
Sutcliffe, Rick	82T	609	$ .05	$ .20	Sutton, Don	83T	145	$ .08	$ .35
Sutcliffe, Rick	82TTR	116	$ .15	$ .50	Sutton, Don	83T	146	$ .03	$ .15
Sutcliffe, Rick	83T	141	$ .01	$ .06	Sutton, Don	84T	35	$ .05	$ .25
Sutcliffe, Rick	83T	497	$ .01	$ .10	Sutton, Don	84T	715	$ .04	$ .20
Sutcliffe, Rick	83T	707	$ .01	$ .06	Sutton, Don	85T	729	$ .05	$ .25
Sutcliffe, Rick	84T	245	$ .07	$ .30	Sutton, Don	85TRB	10	$ .01	$ .04
Sutcliffe, Rick	84TTR	115	$ .08	$ .30	Sutton, Don	85TTR	116	$ .15	$ .60

TOPPS

Player	Year	No.	VG	EX/MT	Player	Year	No.	VG	EX/MT
Sutton, Don	86T	335	$ .02	$ .15	Tabler, Pat	85T	158	$ .01	$ .04
Sutton, Don	87T	673	$ .06	$ .25	Tabler, Pat	86T	674	$ .01	$ .03
Sutton, Don	88T	575	$ .01	$ .10	Tabler, Pat	87T	575	$ .01	$ .03
Sutton, Johnny	79T	676	$ .02	$ .10	Tabler, Pat	88T	230	$ .01	$ .03
Sveum, Dale	86TTR	106	$ .08	$ .30	Tabler, Pat	88TBB	173	$ .01	$ .05
Sveum, Dale	87T	327	$ .10	$ .35	Tabler, Pat	88TTR	118	$ .01	$ .05
Sveum, Dale	88T	592	$ .01	$ .03	Tabler, Pat	89T	56	$ .01	$ .04
Sveum, Dale	88TBB	44	$ .01	$ .05	Tabler, Pat	89TBB	67	$ .01	$ .05
Sveum, Dale	89T	12	$ .01	$ .04	Tabler, Pat	90T	727	$ .01	$ .03
Sveum, Dale	89TBB	126	$ .01	$ .05	Talbot, Bob	54T	229	$2.00	$7.00
Sveum, Dale	90T	739	$ .01	$ .03	Talbot, Fred	65T	58	$ .25	$ .65
Swaggerty, Bill	85T	147	$ .01	$ .04	Talbot, Fred	66T	403	$ .25	$ .85
Swan, Craig	74T	602	$ .06	$ .25	Talbot, Fred	67T	517	$ .50	$2.00
Swan, Craig	76T	494	$ .05	$ .20	Talbot, Fred	68T	577	$ .30	$1.00
Swan, Craig	77T	94	$ .03	$ .12	Talbot, Fred	69T	332	$ .25	$ .65
Swan, Craig	78T	621	$ .02	$ .10	Talbot, Fred	70T	287	$ .10	$ .35
Swan, Craig	79T	7	$ .03	$ .15	Talton, Tim	67T	603	$1.25	$3.50
Swan, Craig	79T	334	$ .02	$ .10	Tamargo, John	79T	726	$ .05	$ .20
Swan, Craig	80T	8	$ .01	$ .07	Tamargo, John	80T	680	$ .05	$ .20
Swan, Craig	81T	189	$ .01	$ .07	Tamargo, John	81T	519	$ .01	$ .07
Swan, Craig	82T	592	$ .01	$ .06	Tanana, Frank	74T	605	$ .30	$1.50
Swan, Craig	83T	292	$ .01	$ .06	Tanana, Frank	75T	16	$ .10	$ .35
Swan, Craig	83T	621	$ .01	$ .06	Tanana, Frank	76T	204	$ .15	$ .50
Swan, Craig	84T	763	$ .01	$ .05	Tanana, Frank	76T	490	$ .06	$ .25
Swan, Craig	84TTR	116	$ .02	$ .10	Tanana, Frank	77T	200	$ .03	$ .12
Swan, Russ	89TMLD	125	$ .01	$ .25	Tanana, Frank	78T	207	$ .02	$ .10
Swanson, Art	56T	204	$2.50	$8.00	Tanana, Frank	78T	600	$ .02	$ .10
Swanson, Stan	72T	331	$ .05	$ .25	Tanana, Frank	79T	530	$ .05	$ .20
Sweet, Rick	78T	702	$ .02	$ .10	Tanana, Frank	80T	105	$ .01	$ .07
Sweet, Rick	79T	646	$ .02	$ .10	Tanana, Frank	81T	369	$ .01	$ .07
Sweet, Rick	83T	437	$ .01	$ .06	Tanana, Frank	81TTR	841	$ .02	$ .10
Sweet, Rick	84T	211	$ .01	$ .05	Tanana, Frank	82T	792	$ .02	$ .10
Swift, Billy	85T	404	$ .01	$ .04	Tanana, Frank	82TTR	117	$ .02	$ .10
Swift, Bill	86T	399	$ .01	$ .03	Tanana, Frank	83T	272	$ .01	$ .06
Swift, Bill	87T	67	$ .01	$ .03	Tanana, Frank	84T	479	$ .01	$ .05
Swift, Bill	88TTR	117	$ .01	$ .05	Tanana, Frank	85T	55	$ .01	$ .04
Swift, Bill	89T	712	$ .01	$ .04	Tanana, Frank	86T	592	$ .01	$ .03
Swift, Bill	90T	574	$ .01	$ .03	Tanana, Frank	87T	726	$ .01	$ .03
Swift, Bob	52T	181	$6.00	$19.00	Tanana, Frank	88T	177	$ .01	$ .03
Swift, Bob	54T	65	$4.75	$14.00	Tanana, Frank	89T	603	$ .01	$ .04
Swift, Bob	60T	470	$ .95	$3.50	Tanana, Frank	90T	343	$ .01	$ .03
Swindell, Greg	87T	319	$ .25	$1.00	Tanner, Chuck	55T	161	$5.50	$17.50
Swindell, Greg	88T	22	$ .01	$ .10	Tanner, Chuck	56T	69	$1.50	$5.00
Swindell, Greg	88TBB	156	$ .01	$ .15	Tanner, Chuck	57T	392	$1.35	$5.00
Swindell, Greg	89T	315	$ .01	$ .15	Tanner, Chuck	58T	91	$ .70	$2.25
Swindell, Greg	89TBB	68	$ .01	$ .10	Tanner, Chuck	59T	234	$ .50	$1.95
Swindell, Greg	90T	595	$ .01	$ .10	Tanner, Chuck	60T	279	$ .50	$2.00
Swisher, Steve	75T	63	$ .06	$ .25	Tanner, Chuck	71T	661	$ .85	$3.50
Swisher, Steve	76T	173	$ .05	$ .20	Tanner, Chuck	72T	98	$ .25	$ .65
Swisher, Steve	77T	419	$ .03	$ .12	Tanner, Chuck	73T	356	$ .10	$ .35
Swisher, Steve	78T	252	$ .02	$ .10	Tanner, Chuck	74T	221	$ .06	$ .25
Swisher, Steve	79T	304	$ .02	$ .10	Tanner, Chuck	78T	494	$ .02	$ .10
Swisher, Steve	80T	163	$ .01	$ .07	Tanner, Chuck	83T	696	$ .01	$ .06
Swisher, Steve	81T	541	$ .01	$ .07	Tanner, Chuck	84T	291	$ .01	$ .05
Swisher, Steve	81TTR	840	$ .02	$ .10	Tanner, Chuck	85T	268	$ .01	$ .04
Swisher, Steve	82T	764	$ .01	$ .06	Tanner, Chuck	86T	351	$ .01	$ .03
Swisher, Steve	83T	612	$ .01	$ .06	Tanner, Chuck	86TTR	107	$ .02	$ .10
Swoboda, Ron	65T	533	$3.00	$12.00	Tanner, Chuck	87T	593	$ .01	$ .03
Swoboda, Ron	66T	35	$ .25	$ .85	Tanner, Chuck	88T	134	$ .01	$ .03
Swoboda, Ron	67T	186	$ .25	$ .65	Tapani, Kevin	89TMLD	126	$ .01	$ .25
Swoboda, Ron	67T	264	$ .25	$ .65	Tapani, Kevin	90T	227	$ .01	$ .25
Swoboda, Ron	68T	114	$ .25	$ .65	Tappe, Elvin	55T	129	$1.35	$5.00
Swoboda, Ron	69T	585	$ .25	$ .85	Tappe, Elvin	58T	184	$ .50	$2.00
Swoboda, Ron	70T	431	$ .10	$ .35	Tappe, Elvin	60T	457	$ .95	$3.50
Swoboda, Ron	71TTR	665	$ .70	$2.10	Tartabull, Danny	86TTR	108	$ .25	$1.00
Swoboda, Ron	72T	8	$ .05	$ .25	Tartabull, Danny	87T	476	$ .30	$ .75
Swoboda, Ron	73T	314	$ .06	$ .25	Tartabull, Danny	87TTR	120	$ .12	$ .40
Sykes, Bob	77T	491	$ .25	$1.00	Tartabull, Danny	88T	724	$ .01	$ .15
Sykes, Bob	79T	569	$ .02	$ .10	Tartabull, Danny	88TBB	230	$ .05	$ .25
Sykes, Bob	80T	223	$ .01	$ .07	Tartabull, Danny	89T	275	$ .01	$ .10
Sykes, Bob	81T	348	$ .01	$ .07	Tartabull, Danny	89TBB	107	$ .01	$ .10
Sykes, Bob	82T	108	$ .01	$ .06	Tartabull, Danny	90T	540	$ .01	$ .03
Szotkiewicz, Ken	71T	749	$ .70	$2.10	Tartabull, Jose	62T	451	$ .60	$1.75
Tabb, Jerry	78T	224	$ .02	$ .10	Tartabull, Jose	63T	449	$2.50	$6.50
Tabler, Pat	84T	329	$ .01	$ .05	Tartabull, Jose	64T	276	$ .25	$ .85

Player	Year	No.	VG	EX/MT	Player	Year	No.	VG	EX/MT
Tartabull, Jose	66T	143	$ .25	$ .85	Taylor, Carl	69T	357	$ .25	$ .65
Tartabull, Jose	67T	56	$ .25	$ .65	Taylor, Carl	70T	76	$ .10	$ .35
Tartabull, Jose	68T	555	$ .30	$1.00	Taylor, Carl	71T	353	$ .10	$ .35
Tartabull, Jose	69T	287	$ .25	$ .85	Taylor, Carl	73T	99	$ .06	$ .25
Tartabull, Jose	70T	481	$ .10	$ .35	Taylor, Carl	74T	627	$ .06	$ .25
Tasby, Willie	59T	143	$ .50	$1.95	Taylor, Chuck	70T	119	$ .10	$ .35
Tasby, Willie	60T	322	$ .50	$1.95	Taylor, Chuck	71T	606	$ .30	$1.00
Tasby, Willie	61T	458	$ .50	$2.00	Taylor, Chuck	72T	407	$ .05	$ .25
Tasby, Willie	62T	462	$ .70	$2.00	Taylor, Chuck	73T	176	$ .06	$ .25
Tate, Lee	59T	544	$2.00	$7.00	Taylor, Chuck	74T	412	$ .06	$ .25
Tate, Randy	76T	549	$ .05	$ .20	Taylor, Chuck	75T	58	$ .06	$ .25
Tate, Stu	89TMLD	127	$ .01	$ .05	Taylor, Joe	58T	451	$ .50	$1.95
Tatum, Jarvis	70T	642	$ .50	$2.00	Taylor, Rob	69T	239	$ .25	$ .85
Tatum, Jarvis	71T	159	$ .10	$ .35	Taylor, Ron	62T	591	$8.00	$22.50
Tatum, Ken	70T	658	$ .50	$2.00	Taylor, Ron	63T	208	$ .25	$ .85
Tatum, Ken	71T	601	$ .30	$1.00	Taylor, Ron	64T	183	$ .25	$ .85
Tatum, Ken	72T	772	$ .70	$2.10	Taylor, Ron	65T	568	$1.50	$3.75
Tatum, Ken	73T	463	$ .06	$ .25	Taylor, Ron	66T	174	$ .25	$ .85
Taussig, Don	62T	44	$ .35	$1.10	Taylor, Ron	67T	606	$4.00	$12.00
Taveras, Alex	77T	474	$ .05	$ .15	Taylor, Ron	68T	421	$ .25	$ .65
Taveras, Frank	74T	607	$ .06	$ .25	Taylor, Ron	69T	72	$ .25	$ .65
Taveras, Frank	75T	277	$ .06	$ .25	Taylor, Ron	70T	419	$ .10	$ .35
Taveras, Frank	76T	36	$ .05	$ .20	Taylor, Ron	71T	687	$ .70	$2.10
Taveras, Frank	77T	538	$ .03	$ .12	Taylor, Ron	72T	234	$ .05	$ .25
Taveras, Frank	78T	204	$ .02	$ .10	Taylor, Sam	58T	281	$ .50	$2.00
Taveras, Frank	78T	685	$ .02	$ .10	Taylor, Sammy	59T	193	$ .50	$1.95
Taveras, Frank	79T	165	$ .02	$ .10	Taylor, Sammy	60T	162	$ .35	$1.10
Taveras, Frank	80T	456	$ .01	$ .07	Taylor, Sammy	61T	253	$ .30	$1.00
Taveras, Frank	81T	343	$ .01	$ .07	Taylor, Sammy	62T	274	$ .35	$1.10
Taveras, Frank	82T	782	$ .01	$ .06	Taylor, Sammy	63T	273	$ .25	$ .85
Taveras, Frank	82TTR	118	$ .02	$ .10	Taylor, Terry	89T	597	$ .01	$ .04
Taylor, Bill	54T	74	$4.75	$14.00	Taylor, Tony	58T	411	$ .35	$2.00
Taylor, Bill	55T	53	$1.35	$5.00	Taylor, Tony	59T	62	$ .85	$3.50
Taylor, Bill	58T	389	$ .50	$2.00	Taylor, Tony	60T	294	$ .50	$1.95
Taylor, Bob	58T	164	$ .50	$2.00	Taylor, Tony	61T	411	$ .50	$2.00
Taylor, Bob "Hawk"	61T	446	$ .50	$2.00	Taylor, Tony	62T	77	$ .35	$1.10
Taylor, Bob	62T	406	$ .70	$2.10	Taylor, Tony	63T	366	$ .35	$1.20
Taylor, Bob	63T	481	$2.50	$6.50	Taylor, Tony	64T	585	$1.50	$3.75
Taylor, Bob	64T	381	$ .40	$1.25	Taylor, Tony	65T	296	$ .30	$1.00
					Taylor, Tony	66T	585	$4.50	$15.00
					Taylor, Tony	67T	126	$ .25	$ .65
					Taylor, Tony	68T	327	$ .25	$ .65
					Taylor, Tony	69T	108	$ .25	$ .65
					Taylor, Tony	70T	324	$ .10	$ .35
					Taylor, Tony	71T	246	$ .10	$ .35
					Taylor, Tony	72T	511	$ .05	$ .25
					Taylor, Tony	73T	29	$ .06	$ .25
					Taylor, Tony	75T	574	$ .06	$ .25
					Taylor, Tony	76T	624	$ .05	$ .20
					Tebbetts, Birdie	52T	282	$14.00	$45.00
					Tebbetts, Birdie	58T	386	$2.00	$6.00
					Tebbetts, Birdie	62T	588	$3.75	$11.00
					Tebbetts, Birdie	63T	48	$ .25	$ .85
					Tebbetts, Birdie	64T	462	$ .40	$1.25
					Tebbetts, Birdie	65T	301	$ .30	$1.00
					Tebbetts, Birdie	66T	552	$4.50	$15.00
					Tejada, Wil	89T	747	$ .01	$ .04
					Tekulve, Kent	76T	112	$ .35	$1.10
					Tekulve, Kent	77T	374	$ .05	$ .25
					Tekulve, Kent	78T	84	$ .02	$ .10
					Tekulve, Kent	79T	223	$ .02	$ .10
					Tekulve, Kent	80T	573	$ .01	$ .07
					Tekulve, Kent	81T	695	$ .01	$ .07
					Tekulve, Kent	82T	485	$ .01	$ .06
					Tekulve, Kent	83T	17	$ .01	$ .06
					Tekulve, Kent	83T	18	$ .01	$ .06
					Tekulve, Kent	84T	754	$ .01	$ .05
					Tekulve, Kent	85T	125	$ .01	$ .04
					Tekulve, Kent	85TTR	117	$ .02	$ .10
					Tekulve, Kent	86T	326	$ .01	$ .03
					Tekulve, Kent	87T	684	$ .01	$ .03
					Tekulve, Kent	88T	543	$ .01	$ .03
					Tekulve, Kent	89TTR	116	$ .01	$ .05
Taylor, Bob "Hawk"	65T	329	$ .30	$1.00	Tellmann, Tom	81T	356	$ .01	$ .07
Taylor, Bob "Hawk"	68T	52	$ .25	$ .65	Tellmann, Tom	83TTR	109	$ .02	$ .10
Taylor, Bruce	78T	701	$ .02	$ .10					
Taylor, Carl	68T	559	$ .30	$1.00					

Player	Year	No.	VG	EX/MT	Player	Year	No.	VG	EX/MT
Tellmann, Tom	84T	476	$ .01	$ .05	Terry, Ralph	63T	8	$ .35	$1.10
Tellmann, Tom	85T	112	$ .01	$ .04	Terry, Ralph	63T	10	$ .35	$1.10
Tellmann, Tom	85TTR	118	$ .02	$ .10	Terry, Ralph	63T	315	$ .50	$2.00
Tellmann, Tom	86T	693	$ .01	$ .03	Terry, Ralph	64T	458	$ .50	$2.00
Temple, Johnny	56T	212	$2.50	$8.00	Terry, Ralph	65T	406	$ .30	$1.00
Temple, Johnny	57T	9	$ .95	$3.50	Terry, Ralph	66T	109	$ .25	$ .85
Temple, Johnny	58T	205	$ .50	$2.00	Terry, Ralph	67T	59	$ .25	$ .65
Temple, Johnny	58TAS	478	$ .70	$2.25	Terry, Scott	87T	453	$ .01	$ .03
Temple, Johnny	59T	335	$ .50	$1.95	Terry, Scott	88TTR	119	$ .01	$ .05
Temple, Johnny	60T	500	$ .85	$3.50	Terry, Scott	89T	686	$ .01	$ .04
Temple, Johnny	61T	155	$ .30	$1.00	Terry, Scott	89TBB	31	$ .01	$ .05
Temple, Johnny	62T	34	$ .35	$1.10	Terry, Scott	90T	82	$ .01	$ .03
Temple, Johnny	63T	576	$3.00	$9.00	Terwilliger, Wayne	51Trb	14	$1.25	$3.50
Templeton, Garry	77T	161	$ .35	$1.10	Terwilliger, Wayne	52T	7	$15.00	$50.00
Templeton, Garry	78T	32	$ .07	$ .30	Terwilliger, Wayne	53T	159	$3.75	$13.00
Templeton, Garry	79T	350	$ .05	$ .20	Terwilliger, Wayne	54T	73	$4.75	$14.00
Templeton, Garry	80T	587	$ .01	$ .07	Terwilliger, Wayne	55T	34	$1.35	$5.00
Templeton, Garry	80THL	5	$ .05	$ .20	Terwilliger, Wayne	56T	73	$1.25	$4.50
Templeton, Garry	81T	485	$ .01	$ .07	Terwilliger, Wayne	59T	496	$ .50	$1.95
Templeton, Garry	82T	288	$ .01	$ .06	Terwilliger, Wayne	60T	26	$ .35	$1.10
Templeton, Garry	82TTR	119	$ .02	$ .10	Tettleton, Mickey	85TTR	120	$ .20	$1.00
Templeton, Garry	83T	505	$ .01	$ .06	Tettleton, Mickey	86T	457	$ .10	$ .50
Templeton, Garry	84T	615	$ .01	$ .05	Tettleton, Mickey	87T	649	$ .01	$ .03
Templeton, Garry	85T	735	$ .01	$ .04	Tettleton, Mickey	88T	143	$ .01	$ .03
Templeton, Garry	86T	90	$ .01	$ .03	Tettleton, Mickey	88TTR	120	$ .01	$ .05
Templeton, Garry	87T	325	$ .01	$ .03	Tettleton, Mickey	89T	521	$ .01	$ .04
Templeton, Garry	88T	640	$ .01	$ .03	Tettleton, Mickey	89TBB	198	$ .01	$ .05
Templeton, Garry	89T	121	$ .01	$ .04	Tettleton, Mickey	90T	275	$ .01	$ .03
Templeton, Garry	89TBB	328	$ .01	$ .05	Teufel, Tim	84TTR	117	$ .08	$ .30
Templeton, Garry	90T	481	$ .01	$ .03	Teufel, Tim	85T	239	$ .01	$ .04
Tenace, Gene	70T	21	$1.00	$3.00	Teufel, Tim	86T	667	$ .01	$ .03
Tenace, Gene	71T	338	$ .10	$ .35	Teufel, Tim	86TTR	109	$ .02	$ .10
Tenace, Gene	72T	189	$ .25	$ .85	Teufel, Tim	87T	158	$ .01	$ .03
Tenace, Gene	73T	524	$ .06	$ .25	Teufel, Tim	88T	508	$ .01	$ .03
Tenace, Gene	74T	79	$ .06	$ .25	Teufel, Tim	89T	9	$ .01	$ .04
Tenace, Gene	75T	535	$ .06	$ .25	Teufel, Tim	90T	764	$ .01	$ .03
Tenace, Gene	76T	165	$ .05	$ .20	Tewksbury, Bob	86TTR	110	$ .05	$ .20
Tenace, Gene	77T	303	$ .03	$ .12	Tewksbury, Bob	87T	254	$ .01	$ .10
Tenace, Gene	78T	240	$ .02	$ .10	Tewksbury, Bob	88T	593	$ .01	$ .03
Tenace, Gene	79T	435	$ .02	$ .10	Thacker, Moe	59T	474	$ .50	$1.95
Tenace, Gene	80T	704	$ .01	$ .07	Thacker, Moe	61T	12	$ .30	$1.00
Tenace, Gene	81T	29	$ .01	$ .07	Thacker, Moe	62T	546	$3.75	$11.00
Tenace, Gene	81TTR	842	$ .02	$ .10	Theobald, Ron	72T	77	$ .05	$ .25
Tenace, Gene	82T	631	$ .01	$ .06	Theodore, George	74T	8	$ .06	$ .25
Tenace, Gene	83T	515	$ .01	$ .06	Thibdeau, John	69T	189	$ .25	$ .65
Tenace, Gene	83TTR	110	$ .02	$ .10	Thies, Jake	55T	12	$1.35	$5.00
Tenace, Gene	84T	729	$ .01	$ .05	Thigpen, Bobby	87T	61	$ .01	$ .10
Tepedino, Frank	70T	689	$ .50	$2.00	Thigpen, Bobby	88T	613	$ .01	$ .03
Tepedino, Frank	71T	342	$ .10	$ .35	Thigpen, Bobby	89T	762	$ .01	$ .04
Tepedino, Frank	74T	526	$ .06	$ .25	Thigpen, Bobby	90T	255	$ .01	$ .03
Tepedino, Frank	75T	9	$ .06	$ .25	Thoenen, Dick	68T	348	$ .25	$ .65
Terlecky, Greg	77T	487	$ .03	$ .12	Thomas, Andres	86TTR	111	$ .05	$ .20
Terpko, Jeff	77T	137	$ .03	$ .12	Thomas, Andres	87T	296	$ .03	$ .15
Terrell, Jerry	74T	481	$ .06	$ .25	Thomas, Andres	88T	13	$ .01	$ .03
Terrell, Jerry	75T	654	$ .06	$ .25	Thomas, Andres	88TBB	68	$ .01	$ .05
Terrell, Jerry	76T	159	$ .05	$ .20	Thomas, Andres	89T	523	$ .01	$ .04
Terrell, Jerry	77T	513	$ .03	$ .12	Thomas, Andres	90T	358	$ .01	$ .03
Terrell, Jerry	78T	525	$ .02	$ .10	Thomas, Dan	77T	488	$5.00	$20.00
Terrell, Jerry	79T	273	$ .02	$ .10	Thomas, Derrel	72T	457	$ .05	$ .25
Terrell, Jerry	80T	98	$ .01	$ .07	Thomas, Derrel	73T	57	$ .06	$ .25
Terrell, Walt	84T	549	$ .15	$ .45	Thomas, Derrel	74T	518	$ .06	$ .25
Terrell, Walt	85T	287	$ .01	$ .10	Thomas, Derrel	75T	378	$ .06	$ .25
Terrell, Walt	85TTR	119	$ .02	$ .10	Thomas, Derrel	76T	493	$ .05	$ .20
Terrell, Walt	86T	461	$ .01	$ .03	Thomas, Derrel	77T	266	$ .03	$ .12
Terrell, Walt	87T	72	$ .01	$ .03	Thomas, Derrel	78T	194	$ .02	$ .10
Terrell, Walt	88T	668	$ .01	$ .03	Thomas, Derrel	79T	679	$ .02	$ .10
Terrell, Walt	89T	127	$ .01	$ .04	Thomas, Derrel	80T	23	$ .01	$ .07
Terrell, Walt	89TTR	117	$ .01	$ .05	Thomas, Derrel	81T	211	$ .01	$ .07
Terrell, Walt	90T	611	$ .01	$ .03	Thomas, Derrel	82T	348	$ .01	$ .06
Terry, Ralph	57T	391	$2.50	$7.50	Thomas, Derrel	83T	748	$ .01	$ .06
Terry, Ralph	58T	169	$ .65	$2.00	Thomas, Derrel	84T	583	$ .01	$ .05
Terry, Ralph	59T	358	$ .50	$1.95	Thomas, Derrel	84TTR	118	$ .02	$ .10
Terry, Ralph	60T	96	$ .60	$1.75	Thomas, Derrel	85T	448	$ .01	$ .04
Terry, Ralph	61T	389	$ .65	$1.75	Thomas, Derrel	85TTR	121	$ .02	$ .10
Terry, Ralph	62T	48	$ .50	$1.95	Thomas, Derrel	86T	158	$ .01	$ .03

Player	Year	No.	VG	EX/MT	Player	Year	No.	VG	EX/MT
Thomas, Frank	56T	153	$1.25	$4.50	Thomas, Lee	65T	111	$ .25	$ .65
Thomas, Frank	57T	140	$ .95	$3.50	Thomas, Lee	66T	408	$ .25	$ .85
Thomas, Frank	58T	409	$ .50	$2.00	Thomas, Lee	67T	458	$ .50	$2.00
Thomas, Frank	59T	17	$1.50	$3.75	Thomas, Lee	68T	438	$ .25	$ .65
Thomas, Frank	59T	490	$ .50	$1.95	Thomas, Roy	78T	711	$ .02	$ .10
Thomas, Frank	60T	95	$ .35	$1.10	Thomas, Roy	79T	563	$ .02	$ .10
Thomas, Frank	61T	382	$ .50	$2.00	Thomas, Roy	80T	397	$ .01	$ .07
Thomas, Frank	62T	7	$ .50	$1.95	Thomas, Roy	84T	181	$ .01	$ .05
Thomas, Frank	63T	495	$2.50	$6.50	Thomas, Roy	86T	626	$ .01	$ .03
Thomas, Frank	64T	345	$ .25	$ .85	Thomas, Stan	76T	148	$ .05	$ .20
Thomas, Frank	65T	123	$ .25	$ .65	Thomas, Stan	77T	353	$ .03	$ .12
Thomas, Frank	90T	414	$ .01	$ .30	Thomas, Valmy	58T	86	$ .85	$3.50
Thomas, George	61T	544	$6.00	$18.00	Thomas, Valmy	59T	235	$ .50	$1.95
Thomas, George	62T	525	$3.75	$11.00	Thomas, Valmy	60T	167	$ .35	$1.10
Thomas, George	63T	98	$ .25	$ .85	Thomas, Valmy	61T	319	$ .30	$1.00
Thomas, George	64T	461	$ .40	$1.25	Thomasson, Gary	74T	18	$ .06	$ .25
Thomas, George	65T	83	$ .25	$ .65	Thomasson, Gary	75T	529	$ .06	$ .25
Thomas, George	66T	277	$ .25	$ .85	Thomasson, Gary	76T	261	$ .05	$ .20
					Thomasson, Gary	77T	496	$ .03	$ .12
					Thomasson, Gary	78T	648	$ .02	$ .10
					Thomasson, Gary	79T	387	$ .02	$ .10
					Thomasson, Gary	80T	127	$ .01	$ .07
					Thomasson, Gary	81T	512	$ .01	$ .07
					Thompson, Bobby	79T	336	$ .02	$ .10
					Thompson, Charlie (y)	54T	209	$2.00	$7.00
					Thompson, Charley	57T	142	$ .95	$3.50
					Thompson, Danny	71T	127	$ .10	$ .35
					Thompson, Danny	72T	368	$ .05	$ .25
					Thompson, Danny	73T	443	$ .06	$ .25
					Thompson, Danny	74T	168	$ .06	$ .25
					Thompson, Danny	75T	249	$ .06	$ .25
					Thompson, Danny	76T	111	$ .05	$ .20
					Thompson, Hank	51Trb	32	$1.25	$3.50
					Thompson, Hank	52T	3	$14.00	$45.00
					Thompson, Hank	53T	20	$4.50	$15.00
					Thompson, Hank	54T	64	$4.75	$14.00
					Thompson, Hank	56T	199	$2.50	$8.00
					Thompson, Hank	57T	109	$ .95	$3.50
					Thompson, Jason	77T	291	$ .10	$ .35
					Thompson, Jason	78T	660	$ .02	$ .10
					Thompson, Jason	79T	80	$ .02	$ .10
					Thompson, Jason	80T	150	$ .01	$ .07
					Thompson, Jason	81T	505	$ .01	$ .07
					Thompson, Jason	81TTR	843	$ .02	$ .10
					Thompson, Jason	82T	295	$ .01	$ .06
					Thompson, Jason	83T	730	$ .01	$ .06
					Thompson, Jason	84T	355	$ .01	$ .05
					Thompson, Jason	85T	490	$ .01	$ .04
					Thompson, Jason	86T	635	$ .01	$ .03
					Thompson, Mike	73T	564	$ .35	$1.10
Thomas, George	67T	184	$ .25	$ .85	Thompson, Mike	76T	536	$ .05	$ .20
Thomas, George	69T	521	$ .25	$ .85	Thompson, Milt	86T	517	$ .02	$ .20
Thomas, George	71T	678	$ .70	$2.10	Thompson, Milt	86TTR	112	$ .02	$ .10
Thomas, Gorman	74T	288	$ .35	$1.10	Thompson, Milt	87T	409	$ .01	$ .03
Thomas, Gorman	75T	532	$ .06	$ .25	Thompson, Milt	88T	298	$ .01	$ .10
Thomas, Gorman	76T	139	$ .06	$ .25	Thompson, Milt	88TBB	2	$ .01	$ .05
Thomas, Gorman	77T	439	$ .03	$ .12	Thompson, Milt	89T	128	$ .01	$ .04
Thomas, Gorman	79T	376	$ .05	$ .20	Thompson, Milt	89TTR	118	$ .01	$ .05
Thomas, Gorman	80T	202	$ .05	$ .20	Thompson, Milt	90T	688	$ .01	$ .03
Thomas, Gorman	80T	623	$ .01	$ .07	Thompson, Rich	85TTR	122	$ .02	$ .10
Thomas, Gorman	81T	135	$ .01	$ .07	Thompson, Rich	86T	242	$ .01	$ .03
Thomas, Gorman	82T	765	$ .01	$ .06	Thompson, Rich	90T	474	$ .01	$ .03
Thomas, Gorman	83T	10	$ .01	$ .10	Thompson, Robby	86TTR	113	$ .15	$ .50
Thomas, Gorman	83T	702	$ .01	$ .06	Thompson, Robby	87T	658	$ .10	$ .35
Thomas, Gorman	83TTR	111	$ .02	$ .10	Thompson, Robby	88T	472	$ .01	$ .03
Thomas, Gorman	84T	515	$ .01	$ .05	Thompson, Robby	88TBB	83	$ .01	$ .05
Thomas, Gorman	84TTR	119	$ .02	$ .10	Thompson, Robby	89T	15	$ .01	$ .04
Thomas, Gorman	85T	202	$ .01	$ .04	Thompson, Robby	89TBB	163	$ .01	$ .05
Thomas, Gorman	86T	750	$ .01	$ .03	Thompson, Robby	90T	325	$ .01	$ .03
Thomas, Gorman	87T	495	$ .01	$ .03	Thompson, Scot	79T	716	$ .02	$ .10
Thomas, Keith	53T	129	$3.75	$13.00	Thompson, Scot	80T	574	$ .01	$ .07
Thomas, Leroy (Lee)	61T	464	$ .50	$2.00	Thompson, Scot	81T	395	$ .01	$ .07
Thomas, Lee	62T	154	$ .35	$1.10	Thompson, Scot	83T	481	$ .01	$ .06
Thomas, Lee	63T	441	$ .35	$1.20	Thompson, Scot	85T	646	$ .01	$ .04
Thomas, Lee	64T	255	$ .25	$ .85	Thompson, Scot	86T	93	$ .01	$ .03

Player	Year	No.	VG	EX/MT	Player	Year	No.	VG	EX/MT
Thompson, Tim	58T	57	$ .85	$3.50	Tiant, Luis	73T	270	$ .25	$ .85
Thomson, Bobby	52T	313	$55.00	$165.00	Tiant, Luis	74T	167	$ .25	$ .85
Thomson, Bobby	56T	257	$2.50	$8.00	Tiant, Luis	75T	430	$ .06	$ .25
Thomson, Bobby	57T	262	$1.35	$5.00	Tiant, Luis	76T	130	$ .10	$ .35
Thomson, Bobby	58T	430	$1.00	$3.50	Tiant, Luis	77T	258	$ .10	$ .35
Thomson, Bobby	59T	429	$ .50	$1.95	Tiant, Luis	78T	345	$ .05	$ .20
Thomson, Bobby	60T	153	$ .60	$1.75	Tiant, Luis	79T	575	$ .05	$ .20
Thon, Dickie	80T	663	$ .05	$ .20	Tiant, Luis	80T	35	$ .05	$ .20
Thon, Dickie	81T	209	$ .01	$ .07	Tiant, Luis	81T	627	$ .03	$ .15
Thon, Dickie	81TTR	844	$ .02	$ .10	Tiant, Luis	82T	160	$ .01	$ .06
Thon, Dickie	82T	404	$ .01	$ .06	Tiant, Luis	83T	178	$ .01	$ .06
Thon, Dickie	83T	558	$ .01	$ .06	Tiant, Luis	83T	179	$ .01	$ .06
Thon, Dickie	84T	692	$ .01	$ .05	Tibbs, Jay	85T	573	$ .01	$ .04
Thon, Dickie	85T	44	$ .01	$ .04	Tibbs, Jay	86T	176	$ .01	$ .03
Thon, Dickie	86T	166	$ .01	$ .03	Tibbs, Jay	86TTR	114	$ .02	$ .10
Thon, Dickie	87T	386	$ .01	$ .03	Tibbs, Jay	87T	9	$ .01	$ .03
Thon, Dickie	88TTR	121	$ .01	$ .05	Tibbs, Jay	88T	464	$ .01	$ .03
Thon, Dickie	89T	726	$ .01	$ .04	Tibbs, Jay	89T	271	$ .01	$ .04
Thon, Dickie	89TTR	119	$ .01	$ .05	Tibbs, Jay	90T	677	$ .01	$ .03
Thon, Dickie	90T	269	$ .01	$ .03	Tidrow, Dick	72T	506	$ .25	$ .65
Thormodsgard, Paul	78T	162	$ .02	$ .10					
Thormodsgard, Paul	79T	249	$ .02	$ .10					
Thornton, Andy	74T	604	$1.00	$3.00					
Thornton, Andy	75T	39	$ .06	$ .25					
Thornton, Andy	76T	26	$ .05	$ .20					
Thornton, Andre	78T	148	$ .02	$ .10					
Thornton, Andre	79T	280	$ .02	$ .10					
Thornton, Andre	80T	534	$ .01	$ .07					
Thornton, Andre	81T	388	$ .01	$ .07					
Thornton, Andre	82T	746	$ .01	$ .06					
Thornton, Andre	83T	640	$ .01	$ .06					
Thornton, Andre	84T	115	$ .01	$ .05					
Thornton, Andre	85T	475	$ .01	$ .04					
Thornton, Andre	86T	59	$ .01	$ .03					
Thornton, Andre	87T	780	$ .01	$ .03					
Thornton, Lou	86T	488	$ .01	$ .03					
Thorpe, Bob	52T	367	$39.00	$135.00					
Throedson, Rich	74T	77	$ .06	$ .25					
Throneberry, Faye	52T	376	$39.00	$135.00					
Throneberry, Faye	53T	49	$3.75	$13.00					
Throneberry, Faye	55T	163	$4.25	$13.00					
Throneberry, Faye	57T	356	$ .85	$3.50					
Throneberry, Faye	59T	534	$2.00	$7.00					
Throneberry, Faye	60T	9	$ .35	$1.10					
Throneberry, Faye	61T	282	$ .30	$1.00					
Throneberry, Marv	58T	175	$2.50	$8.00					
Throneberry, Marv	59T	326	$ .50	$1.95					
Throneberry, Marv	60T	436	$ .60	$1.75					
Throneberry, Marv	61T	57	$ .50	$2.00					
Throneberry, Marv	63T	78	$ .85	$3.50					
Throop, George	76T	591	$ .05	$ .20	Tidrow, Dick	73T	339	$ .06	$ .25
Thurman, Bob	57T	279	$3.50	$13.00	Tidrow, Dick	74T	231	$ .06	$ .25
Thurman, Bob	58T	34	$ .85	$3.50	Tidrow, Dick	75T	241	$ .06	$ .25
Thurman, Bob	59T	541	$2.00	$7.00	Tidrow, Dick	76T	248	$ .05	$ .20
Thurman, Gary	88T	89	$ .01	$ .50	Tidrow, Dick	77T	461	$ .03	$ .12
Thurman, Gary	89T	323	$ .01	$ .04	Tidrow, Dick	78T	179	$ .02	$ .10
Thurman, Gary	90T	276	$ .01	$ .03	Tidrow, Dick	79T	89	$ .02	$ .10
Thurmond, Mark	84T	481	$ .02	$ .10	Tidrow, Dick	80T	594	$ .01	$ .07
Thurmond, Mark	85T	236	$ .01	$ .04	Tidrow, Dick	81T	352	$ .01	$ .07
Thurmond, Mark	86T	37	$ .01	$ .03	Tidrow, Dick	82T	699	$ .01	$ .06
Thurmond, Mark	87T	361	$ .01	$ .03	Tidrow, Dick	83T	787	$ .01	$ .06
Thurmond, Mark	88T	552	$ .01	$ .03	Tidrow, Dick	83TTR	112	$ .02	$ .10
Thurmond, Mark	89T	152	$ .01	$ .04	Tidrow, Dick	84T	153	$ .01	$ .05
Thurmond, Mark	90T	758	$ .01	$ .03	Tiefenauer, Bobby	59T	501	$ .50	$1.95
Tiant, Luis	65T	145	$3.00	$9.00	Tiefenauer, Bobby	62T	227	$ .35	$1.10
Tiant, Luis	66T	285	$ .50	$2.00	Tiefenauer, Bobby	64T	522	$ .40	$1.25
Tiant, Luis	67T	377	$ .50	$2.00	Tiefenauer, Bob	65T	23	$ .25	$ .65
Tiant, Luis	68T	532	$ .20	$1.25	Tiefenauer, Bob	68T	269	$ .25	$ .65
Tiant, Luis	69T	7	$ .30	$1.00	Tigers, Team	56T	213	$4.00	$1500
Tiant, Luis	69T	9	$ .30	$1.00	Tigers, Team	57T	198	$1.50	$6.00
Tiant, Luis	69T	11	$ .50	$2.00	Tigers, Team	58T	397	$2.00	$8.00
Tiant, Luis	69T	560	$ .20	$ .50	Tigers, Team	59T	329	$2.50	$7.50
Tiant, Luis	70T	231	$ .30	$1.00	Tigers, Team	60T	72	$2.50	$8.00
Tiant, Luis	71T	95	$ .35	$1.10					
Tiant, Luis	73T	65	$ .35	$1.10					

DICK
TIDROW
CLEVELAND INDIANS · PITCHER

Player	Year	No.	VG	EX/MT	Player	Year	No.	VG	EX/MT
Tigers, Team	61T	51	$ .50	$2.00	Toliver, Fred	87T	63	$ .01	$ .03
Tigers, Team	62T	24	$ .70	$2.00	Toliver, Fred	88T	203	$ .01	$ .03
Tigers, Team	63T	552	$3.00	$8.00	Toliver, Fred	89T	623	$ .01	$ .04
Tigers, Team	64T	67	$ .50	$2.50	Toliver, Fred	90T	423	$ .01	$ .03
Tigers, Team	65T	173	$ .70	$2.00	Tolleson, Wayne	83TTR	114	$ .02	$ .10
Tigers, Team	66T	583	$25.00	$75.00	Tolleson, Wayne	84T	557	$ .01	$ .05
Tigers, Team	67T	378	$ .70	$2.00	Tolleson, Wayne	C5T	247	$ .01	$ .04
Tigers, Team	68T	528	$3.35	$10.00	Tolleson, Wayne	86T	641	$ .01	$ .03
Tigers, Team	70T	579	$ .60	$1.75	Tolleson, Wayne	86TTR	115	$ .02	$ .10
Tigers, Team	71T	336	$ .35	$1.10	Tolleson, Wayne	87T	224	$ .01	$ .03
Tigers, Team	72T	487	$ .35	$1.10	Tolleson, Wayne	88T	411	$ .01	$ .03
Tigers, Team	73T	191	$ .35	$1.10	Tolleson, Wayne	89T	716	$ .01	$ .04
Tigers, Team	74T	94	$ .35	$1.10	Tolman, Tim	86T	272	$ .01	$ .03
Tigers, Team Checklist	75T	18	$ .15	$ .50	Tomanek, Dick	58T	123	$ .50	$2.00
Tigers, Team Checklist	76T	361	$ .35	$1.10	Tomanek, Dick	59T	369	$ .50	$1.95
Tigers, Team Checklist	77T	621	$ .30	$1.00	Tomlin, Dave	75T	578	$ .06	$ .25
Tigers, Team Checklist	78T	404	$ .08	$ .30	Tomlin, Dave	76T	398	$ .05	$ .20
Tigers, Team Checklist	79T	66	$ .08	$ .30	Tomlin, Dave	77T	241	$ .03	$ .12
Tigers, Team Checklist	80T	626	$ .08	$ .30	Tomlin, Dave	78T	86	$ .02	$ .10
Tigers, Team Checklist	81T	666	$ .02	$ .20	Tomlin, Dave	79T	674	$ .02	$ .10
Tigers, Team Leaders	86T	36	$ .01	$ .10	Tomlin, Dave	80T	126	$ .01	$ .07
Tigers, Team Leaders	87T	631	$ .01	$ .03	Tompkins, Ron	66T	107	$ .25	$ .85
Tigers, Team Leaders	88T	429	$ .01	$ .03	Tompkins, Ron	68T	247	$90.00	$325.00
Tigers, Team Leaders	89T	609	$ .01	$ .04	Torborg, Jeff	64T	337	$ .25	$ .85
Tillman, Bob	62T	368	$ .35	$1.10	Torborg, Jeff	65T	527	$1.50	$3.75
Tillman, Bob	63T	384	$ .35	$1.20	Torborg, Jeff	66T	257	$ .25	$ .85
Tillman, Bob	64T	112	$ .25	$ .85	Torborg, Jeff	67T	398	$ .25	$ .85
Tillman, Bob	65T	222	$ .30	$1.00	Torborg, Jeff	68T	492	$ .30	$1.00
Tillman, Bob	66T	178	$ .25	$ .85	Torborg, Jeff	69T	353	$ .25	$ .65
Tillman, Bob	67T	36	$ .25	$ .65	Torborg, Jeff	70T	54	$ .10	$ .35
Tillman, Bob	68T	174	$ .25	$ .65	Torborg, Jeff	71T	314	$ .10	$ .35
Tillman, Bob	69T	374	$ .25	$ .65	Torborg, Jeff	72T	404	$ .05	$ .25
Tillman, Bob	70T	668	$ .50	$2.00	Torborg, Jeff	73T	154	$ .06	$ .25
Tillman, Bob	71T	244	$ .10	$ .35	Torborg, Jeff	78T	351	$ .02	$ .10
Tillotson, Thad	67T	553	$5.00	$20.00	Torborg, Jeff	89TTR	120	$ .01	$ .05
Timmermann, Tom	70T	554	$ .25	$ .85	Torborg, Jeff	90T	21	$ .01	$ .03
Timmermann, Tom	71T	296	$ .10	$ .35	Torgeson, Earl	51Tbb	34	$5.50	$17.00
Timmermann, Tom	72T	239	$ .05	$ .25	Torgeson, Earl	52T	97	$6.00	$19.00
Timmermann, Tom	73T	413	$ .06	$ .25	Torgeson, Earl	56T	147	$1.25	$4.50
Timmermann, Tom	74T	327	$ .06	$ .25	Torgeson, Earl	57T	357	$ .85	$3.50
Tingley, Ron	89T	721	$ .01	$ .04	Torgeson, Earl	58T	138	$ .50	$2.00
Tingley, Ron	89TBB	37	$ .01	$ .05	Torgeson, Earl	59T	351	$ .50	$1.95
Tipton, Joe	52T	134	$6.00	$19.00	Torgeson, Earl	60T	299	$ .50	$1.95
Tischinski, Tom	70T	379	$ .10	$ .35	Torgeson, Earl	61T	152	$ .30	$1.00
Tischinski, Tom	71T	724	$ .70	$2.10	Torre, Frank	56T	172	$1.35	$4.00
Tobik, Dave	79T	706	$ .02	$ .10	Torre, Frank	57T	37	$ .95	$3.50
Tobik, Dave	80T	269	$ .01	$ .07	Torre, Frank	58T	117	$ .50	$2.00
Tobik, Dave	81T	102	$ .01	$ .07	Torre, Frank	59T	65	$ .85	$3.50
Tobik, Dave	82T	391	$ .01	$ .06	Torre, Frank	60T	478	$ .60	$1.75
Tobik, Dave	83T	691	$ .01	$ .06	Torre, Frank	62T	303	$ .35	$1.10
Tobik, Dave	83IIH	113	$ .02	$ .10	Torre, Frank	63T	161	$ .25	$ .85
Tobik, Dave	84T	341	$ .01	$ .05	Torre, Joe	62T	218	$3.00	$12.00
Todd, Jackson	78T	481	$ .02	$ .10	Torre, Joe	62T	351	$ .60	$1.75
Todd, Jackson	81T	142	$ .01	$ .07	Torre, Joe	63T	347	$ .95	$3.50
Todd, Jackson	82T	565	$ .01	$ .06	Torre, Joe	64T	70	$ .60	$1.75
Todd, Jim	75T	519	$ .06	$ .25	Torre, Joe	65T	200	$ .50	$2.00
Todd, Jim	76T	221	$ .05	$ .20	Torre, Joe	66T	130	$ .50	$2.00
Todd, Jim	77T	31	$ .03	$ .12	Torre, Joe	67T	350	$ .35	$1.10
Todd, Jim	78T	333	$ .02	$ .10	Torre, Joe	68T	30	$ .15	$ .50
Todd, Jim	79T	103	$ .02	$ .10	Torre, Joe	69T	460	$ .15	$ .50
Todd, Jim	80T	629	$ .01	$ .07	Torre, Joe	70T	190	$ .35	$1.10
Tolan, Bob	65T	116	$ .35	$1.10	Torre, Joe	71T	62	$ .15	$ .50
Tolan, Bob	66T	179	$ .25	$ .85	Torre, Joe	71T	370	$ .60	$1.75
Tolan, Bob	67T	474	$ .50	$2.00	Torre, Joe	72T	85	$ .30	$1.00
Tolan, Bob	68T	84	$ .25	$ .65	Torre, Joe	72T	87	$ .60	$2.00
Tolan, Bob	69T	448	$ .25	$ .65	Torre, Joe	72T	341	$ .05	$ .25
Tolan, Bob	70T	409	$ .25	$ .65	Torre, Joe	72T	500	$ .15	$ .50
Tolan, Bob	71T	190	$ .10	$ .35	Torre, Joe	73T	450	$ .25	$ .85
Tolan, Bob	72T	3	$ .05	$ .25	Torre, Joe	74T	15	$ .25	$ .65
Tolan, Bob	73T	335	$ .06	$ .25	Torre, Joe	75T	209	$ .25	$ .65
Tolan, Bob	74T	535	$ .06	$ .25	Torre, Joe	75T	565	$ .25	$ .85
Tolan, Bob	75T	402	$ .06	$ .25	Torre, Joe	76T	585	$ .10	$ .35
Tolan, Bob	76T	56	$ .05	$ .20	Torre, Joe	77T	425	$ .25	$ .65
Tolan, Bob	77T	188	$ .03	$ .12	Torre, Joe	78T	109	$ .05	$ .20
Tolan, Bob	80T	708	$ .01	$ .07	Torre, Joe	83T	126	$ .01	$ .06

TOPPS

Player	Year	No.	VG	EX/MT	Player	Year	No.	VG	EX/MT
Torre, Joe	84T	502	$ .01	$ .05	Trammell, Alan	88TBB	8	$ .01	$ .15
Torre, Joe	85T	438	$ .01	$ .04	Trammell, Alan	89T	770	$ .01	$ .10
Torrealba, Pablo	76T	589	$ .35	$1.10	Trammell, Alan	89TAS	400	$ .01	$ .04
Torrealba, Pablo	77T	499	$ .03	$ .12	Trammell, Alan	89TBB	123	$ .01	$ .10
Torrealba, Pablo	78T	78	$ .02	$ .10	Trammell, Alan	90T	440	$ .01	$ .10
Torrealba, Pablo	79T	242	$ .02	$ .10	Travers, Bill	75T	488	$ .06	$ .25
Torres, Felix	62T	595	$6.00	$18.00	Travers, Bill	76T	573	$ .05	$ .20
Torres, Felix	63T	482	$2.50	$6.50	Travers, Bill	77T	125	$ .03	$ .12
Torres, Hector	69T	526	$ .25	$ .85	Travers, Bill	78T	355	$ .02	$ .10
Torres, Hector	70T	272	$ .10	$ .35	Travers, Bill	79T	213	$ .02	$ .10
Torres, Hector	71T	558	$ .30	$1.00	Travers, Bill	80T	109	$ .01	$ .07
Torres, Hector	72T	666	$ .70	$2.10	Travers, Bill	81T	704	$ .01	$ .07
Torres, Hector	76T	241	$ .05	$ .20	Travers, Bill	81TTR	845	$ .02	$ .10
Torres, Rusty	72T	124	$ .05	$ .25	Travers, Bill	82T	628	$ .01	$ .06
Torres, Rusty	73T	571	$ .35	$1.10	Traynor, Pie	76TAS	343	$ .30	$1.00
Torres, Rusty	74T	499	$ .06	$ .25	Treadway, Jeff	88TBB	214	$ .05	$ .25
Torres, Rusty	77T	224	$ .03	$ .12	Treadway, Jeff	88TTR	122	$ .05	$ .25
Torres, Rusty	80T	36	$ .01	$ .07	Treadway, Jeff	89T	685	$ .01	$ .15
Torrez, Mike	68T	162	$ .25	$ .65	Treadway, Jeff	89TTR	121	$ .01	$ .05
Torrez, Mike	69T	136	$ .25	$ .65	Treadway, Jeff	90T	486	$ .01	$ .03
Torrez, Mike	70T	312	$ .10	$ .35	Trebelhorn, Tom	87TTR	121	$ .05	$ .20
Torrez, Mike	71T	531	$ .30	$1.00	Trebelhorn, Tom	88T	224	$ .01	$ .03
Torrez, Mike	73T	77	$ .06	$ .25	Trebelhorn, Tom	89T	344	$ .01	$ .04
Torrez, Mike	74T	568	$ .06	$ .25	Trebelhorn, Tom	90T	759	$ .01	$ .03
Torrez, Mike	75T	254	$ .06	$ .25	Tremel, Bill	55T	52	$1.35	$5.00
Torrez, Mike	76T	25	$ .05	$ .20	Tremel, Bill	56T	96	$1.25	$4.50
Torrez, Mike	77T	365	$ .03	$ .12	Tresh, Tom	62T	31	$2.50	$7.50
Torrez, Mike	78T	645	$ .02	$ .10	Tresh, Tom	63T	173	$7.50	$30.00
Torrez, Mike	79T	185	$ .02	$ .10	Tresh, Tom	63T	470	$6.00	$20.00
Torrez, Mike	80T	455	$ .01	$ .07	Tresh, Tom	64T	395	$ .50	$1.95
Torrez, Mike	81T	525	$ .01	$ .07	Tresh, Tom	65T	440	$ .50	$2.00
Torrez, Mike	82T	225	$ .01	$ .06	Tresh, Tom	66T	205	$ .50	$2.00
Torrez, Mike	82T	786	$ .01	$ .06	Tresh, Tom	67T	289	$ .35	$1.10
Torrez, Mike	83T	743	$ .01	$ .06	Tresh, Tom	68T	69	$ .35	$1.10
Torrez, Mike	83TTR	115	$ .02	$ .10	Tresh, Tom	69T	212	$ .15	$ .50
Torrez, Mike	84T	78	$ .01	$ .05	Tresh, Tom	70T	698	$ .50	$2.00
Toth, Paul	63T	489	$2.50	$6.50	Trevino, Alex	80T	537	$ .01	$ .07
Toth, Paul	64T	309	$ .25	$ .85	Trevino, Alex	81T	23	$ .01	$ .07
Tovar, Cesar	65T	201	$ .30	$1.00	Trevino, Alex	82T	368	$ .01	$ .06
Tovar, Cesar	66T	563	$4.50	$15.00	Trevino, Alex	82TTR	120	$ .02	$ .10
Tovar, Cesar	67T	317	$ .25	$ .65	Trevino, Alex	83T	632	$ .01	$ .06
Tovar, Cesar	68T	420	$ .25	$ .65	Trevino, Alex	84T	242	$ .01	$ .05
Tovar, Cesar	69T	530	$ .25	$ .85	Trevino, Alex	84TTR	120	$ .02	$ .10
Tovar, Cesar	70T	25	$ .10	$ .35	Trevino, Alex	85T	747	$ .01	$ .04
Tovar, Cesar	71T	165	$ .10	$ .35	Trevino, Alex	85TTR	123	$ .02	$ .10
Tovar, Cesar	72T	275	$ .05	$ .25	Trevino, Alex	86T	444	$ .01	$ .03
Tovar, Cesar	73T	405	$ .06	$ .25	Trevino, Alex	86TTR	116	$ .02	$ .10
Tovar, Cesar	74T	538	$ .06	$ .25	Trevino, Alex	87T	173	$ .01	$ .03
Tovar, Cesar	74TTR	538	$ .06	$ .25	Trevino, Alex	88T	512	$ .01	$ .03
Tovar, Cesar	75T	178	$ .06	$ .25	Trevino, Alex	89T	64	$ .01	$ .04
Tovar, Cesar	76T	246	$ .05	$ .20	Trevino, Alex	90T	342	$ .01	$ .03
Tovar, Cesar	77T	408	$ .03	$ .12	Triandos, Gus	55T	64	$2.00	$7.00
Traber, Jim	87T	484	$ .01	$ .03	Triandos, Gus	56T	80	$1.25	$4.50
Traber, Jim	88T	544	$ .01	$ .03	Triandos, Gus	57T	156	$ .95	$3.50
Traber, Jim	89T	124	$ .01	$ .04	Triandos, Gus	58T	429	$ .50	$2.00
Tracewski, Dick	64T	154	$ .25	$ .85	Triandos, Gus	59T	330	$ .50	$1.95
Tracewski, Dick	65T	279	$ .30	$1.00	Triandos, Gus	59TAS	568	$2.00	$7.00
Tracewski, Dick	66T	378	$ .25	$ .85	Triandos, Gus	60T	60	$ .35	$1.10
Tracewski, Dick	67T	559	$1.25	$3.50	Triandos, Gus	61T	140	$ .30	$1.00
Tracewski, Dick	68T	488	$ .30	$1.00	Triandos, Gus	62T	420	$ .70	$2.10
Tracewski, Dick	69T	126	$ .25	$ .65	Triandos, Gus	63T	475	$2.50	$6.50
Tracewski, Dick	73T	323	$ .30	$1.00	Triandos, Gus	64T	83	$ .25	$ .85
Tracy, Jim	82T	403	$ .01	$ .06	Triandos, Gus	65T	248	$ .30	$1.00
Trammell, Alan	78T	707	$10.00	$40.00	Trice, Bob	54T	148	$2.00	$7.00
Trammell, Alan	79T	358	$1.50	$6.00	Trice, Bob	55T	132	$1.35	$5.00
Trammell, Alan	80T	232	$ .50	$2.00	Trillo, Manny	74T	597	$ .15	$ .50
Trammell, Alan	81T	709	$ .05	$ .30	Trillo, Manny	75T	617	$ .35	$1.10
Trammell, Alan	82T	475	$ .25	$ .65	Trillo, Manny	76T	206	$ .10	$ .35
Trammell, Alan	83T	95	$ .25	$ .65	Trillo, Manny	77T	395	$ .03	$ .12
Trammell, Alan	84T	510	$ .05	$ .25	Trillo, Manny	78T	123	$ .02	$ .10
Trammell, Alan	85T	690	$ .03	$ .15	Trillo, Manny	79T	639	$ .02	$ .10
Trammell, Alan	86T	130	$ .02	$ .20	Trillo, Manny	80T	90	$ .01	$ .07
Trammell, Alan	87T	687	$ .01	$ .10	Trillo, Manny	81T	470	$ .01	$ .07
Trammell, Alan	88T	320	$ .01	$ .10	Trillo, Manny	82T	220	$ .01	$ .06
Trammell, Alan	88TAS	389	$ .01	$ .03	Trillo, Manny	83T	535	$ .01	$ .06

Player	Year	No.	VG	EX/MT
Trillo, Manny	83TAS	398	$ .01	$ .06
Trillo, Manny	83TRB	5	$ .01	$ .06
Trillo, Manny	83TTR	116	$ .02	$ .10
Trillo, Manny	84T	180	$ .01	$ .05
Trillo, Manny	84TTR	121	$ .02	$ .10
Trillo, Manny	85T	310	$ .01	$ .04
Trillo, Manny	86T	655	$ .01	$ .03
Trillo, Manny	86TTR	117	$ .02	$ .10
Trillo, Manny	87T	732	$ .01	$ .03
Trillo, Manny	88T	287	$ .01	$ .03
Trillo, Manny	89T	66	$ .01	$ .04
Trillo, Manny	89TBB	295	$ .01	$ .05
Trout, Dizzy	51Tbb	23	$5.50	$17.00
Trout, Dizzy	52T	39	$14.00	$45.00
Trout, Dizzy	53T	169	$2.25	$8.00
Trout, Dizzy	85T	142	$ .01	$ .10
Trout, Steve	80T	83	$ .05	$ .20
Trout, Steve	81T	552	$ .01	$ .07
Trout, Steve	82T	299	$ .01	$ .06
Trout, Steve	83T	461	$ .01	$ .06
Trout, Steve	83TTR	117	$ .02	$ .10
Trout, Steve	84T	151	$ .01	$ .05
Trout, Steve	85T	142	$ .01	$ .10
Trout, Steve	85T	668	$ .01	$ .04
Trout, Steve	86T	384	$ .01	$ .03
Trout, Steve	87T	750	$ .01	$ .03
Trout, Steve	88T	584	$ .01	$ .03
Trout, Steve	88TBB	106	$ .01	$ .05
Trout, Steve	89T	54	$ .01	$ .04
Trowbridge, Bob	58T	252	$ .50	$2.00
Trowbridge, Bob	59T	239	$ .50	$1.95
Trowbridge, Bob	60T	66	$ .35	$1.10
Trucks, Virgil	52T	262	$14.00	$40.00
Trucks, Virgil	53T	96	$3.75	$13.00
Trucks, Virgil	56T	117	$1.25	$3.50
Trucks, Virgil	57T	187	$ .95	$3.50
Trucks, Virgil	58T	277	$ .50	$2.00
Trucks, Virgil	59T	417	$ .50	$1.95

MIKE TRUJILLO

Player	Year	No.	VG	EX/MT
Trujillo, Mike	86T	687	$ .01	$ .03
Trujillo, Mike	87T	402	$ .01	$ .03
Trujillo, Mike	88T	307	$ .01	$ .03
Tsitouris, John	60T	497	$ .60	$1.75
Tsitouris, John	63T	244	$ .25	$ .85

Player	Year	No.	VG	EX/MT
Tsitouris, John	64T	275	$ .25	$ .85
Tsitouris, John	65T	221	$ .30	$1.00
Tsitouris, John	66T	12	$ .25	$ .85
Tsitouris, John	68T	523	$ .30	$1.00
Tudor, John	81T	14	$ .35	$1.10
Tudor, John	82T	558	$ .05	$ .20
Tudor, John	83T	318	$ .01	$ .06
Tudor, John	84T	601	$ .01	$ .05
Tudor, John	84TTR	122	$ .02	$ .10
Tudor, John	85T	214	$ .01	$ .04
Tudor, John	85TTR	124	$ .02	$ .10
Tudor, John	86T	474	$ .01	$ .03
Tudor, John	86TAS	710	$ .01	$ .03
Tudor, John	87T	110	$ .01	$ .03
Tudor, John	88T	792	$ .01	$ .10
Tudor, John	89T	35	$ .01	$ .04
Tufts, Bob	82T	171	$ .50	$1.50
Tunnell, Lee	83TTR	118	$ .02	$ .10
Tunnell, Lee	84T	384	$ .01	$ .05
Tunnell, Lee	85T	21	$ .01	$ .04
Tunnell, Lee	86T	161	$ .01	$ .03
Turley, Bob	54T	85	$4.75	$14.00
Turley, Bob	55T	38	$3.75	$11.00
Turley, Bob	56T	40	$1.35	$4.00
Turley, Bob	57T	264	$2.00	$7.00
Turley, Bob	58T	255	$1.35	$4.00
Turley, Bob	58TAS	493	$ .70	$2.25
Turley, Bob	59T	60	$1.25	$3.50
Turley, Bob	59T	237	$ .60	$1.75
Turley, Bob	59TAS	570	$2.35	$7.00
Turley, Bob	60T	270	$ .60	$1.75
Turley, Bob	61T	40	$ .50	$1.95
Turley, Bob	62T	589	$6.00	$18.00
Turley, Bob	63T	322	$ .35	$1.10
Turner, Jerry	75T	619	$ .06	$ .25
Turner, Jerry	76T	598	$ .05	$ .20
Turner, Jerry	77T	447	$ .03	$ .12
Turner, Jerry	78T	364	$ .02	$ .10
Turner, Jerry	79T	564	$ .02	$ .10
Turner, Jerry	80T	133	$ .01	$ .07
Turner, Jerry	81T	285	$ .01	$ .07
Turner, Jerry	82T	736	$ .01	$ .06
Turner, Jerry	82TTR	121	$ .02	$ .10
Turner, Jerry	83T	41	$ .01	$ .06
Turner, Jim	52T	373	$50.00	$150.00
Turner, Jim	62T	263	$ .50	$2.00
Turner, Jim	73T	116	$ .15	$ .50
Tuttle, Bill	56T	203	$2.50	$8.00
Tuttle, Bill	57T	72	$ .95	$3.50
Tuttle, Bill	58T	23	$ .85	$3.50
Tuttle, Bill	59T	459	$ .50	$1.95
Tuttle, Bill	60T	367	$ .50	$1.95
Tuttle, Bill	61T	536	$6.00	$18.00
Tuttle, Bill	62T	298	$ .35	$1.10
Tuttle, Bill	63T	127	$ .25	$ .85
Twins, Team	61T	542	$8.50	$35.00
Twins, Team	62T	584	$5.00	$15.00
Twins, Team	63T	162	$ .50	$1.95
Twins, Team	64T	318	$ .85	$3.50
Twins, Team	65T	24	$ .70	$2.00
Twins, Team	66T	526	$15.00	$45.00
Twins, Team	67T	211	$ .60	$1.75
Twins, Team	68T	137	$ .50	$2.00
Twins, Team	70T	534	$ .50	$2.00
Twins, Team	71T	522	$ .35	$1.10
Twins, Team	72T	156	$ .15	$ .50
Twins, Team	73T	654	$ .60	$1.75
Twins, Team	74T	74	$ .15	$ .50
Twins, Team Checklist	75T	443	$ .15	$ .50
Twins, Team Checklist	76T	556	$ .30	$1.00
Twins, Team Checklist	77T	228	$ .15	$ .50
Twins, Team Checklist	78T	451	$ .05	$ .25
Twins, Team Checklist	79T	41	$ .05	$ .25
Twins, Team Checklist	80T	328	$ .05	$ .25
Twins, Team Checklist	81T	669	$ .02	$ .20

TOPPS

Player	Year	No.	VG	EX/MT	Player	Year	No.	VG	EX/MT
Twins, Team Leaders	86T	786	$ .01	$ .03	Unser, Del	80T	27	$ .01	$ .07
Twins, Team Leaders	87T	206	$ .01	$ .03	Unser, Del	80THL	6	$ .01	$ .07
Twins, Team Leaders	88T	609	$ .01	$ .03	Unser, Del	81T	566	$ .01	$ .07
Twins, Team Leaders	89T	429	$ .01	$ .04	Unser, Del	82T	713	$ .01	$ .06
Twitchell, Wayne	71T	692	$ .70	$2.10	Upham, John	67T	608	$2.00	$6.00
Twitchell, Wayne	72T	14	$ .10	$ .35	Upshaw, Cecil	67T	179	$ .25	$ .65
Twitchell, Wayne	73T	227	$ .06	$ .25	Upshaw, Cecil	68T	286	$ .25	$ .65
Twitchell, Wayne	74T	419	$ .06	$ .25	Upshaw, Cecil	69T	568	$ .25	$ .85
Twitchell, Wayne	75T	326	$ .06	$ .25	Upshaw, Cecil	70T	295	$ .10	$ .35
Twitchell, Wayne	76T	543	$ .05	$ .20	Upshaw, Cecil	71T	223	$ .10	$ .35
Twitchell, Wayne	77T	444	$ .03	$ .12	Upshaw, Cecil	72T	74	$ .05	$ .25
Twitchell, Wayne	78T	269	$ .02	$ .10	Upshaw, Cecil	73T	359	$ .06	$ .25
Twitchell, Wayne	79T	43	$ .02	$ .10	Upshaw, Cecil	74T	579	$ .06	$ .25
Tyrone, Jim	74T	598	$1.00	$4.00	Upshaw, Cecil	74TTR	579	$ .06	$ .25
Tyrone, Jim	78T	487	$ .02	$ .10	Upshaw, Cecil	75T	92	$ .06	$ .25
Tyson, Mike	74T	655	$ .06	$ .25	Upshaw, Willie	79T	341	$ .10	$ .35
Tyson, Mike	75T	231	$ .06	$ .25	Upshaw, Willie	82T	196	$ .01	$ .06
Tyson, Mike	76T	86	$ .05	$ .20	Upshaw, Willie	83T	556	$ .01	$ .06
Tyson, Mike	77T	599	$ .03	$ .12	Upshaw, Willie	84T	453	$ .01	$ .05
Tyson, Mike	78T	111	$ .02	$ .10	Upshaw, Willie	85T	75	$ .01	$ .04
Tyson, Mike	79T	324	$ .02	$ .10	Upshaw, Willie	86T	745	$ .01	$ .03
Tyson, Mike	80T	486	$ .01	$ .07	Upshaw, Willie	87T	245	$ .01	$ .03
Tyson, Mike	81T	294	$ .01	$ .07	Upshaw, Willie	88T	505	$ .01	$ .03
Tyson, Mike	82T	62	$ .01	$ .06	Upshaw, Willie	88TTR	123	$ .01	$ .05
Uecker, Bob	62T	594	$35.00	$125.00	Upshaw, Willie	89T	106	$ .01	$ .04
Uecker, Bob	63T	126	$11.50	$38.00	Upton, Tom	52T	71	$14.00	$45.00
Uecker, Bob	64T	543	$11.50	$38.00	Urban, Jack	58T	367	$ .50	$2.00
Uecker, Bob	65T	519	$10.00	$30.00	Urban, Jack	59T	18	$ .85	$3.50
Uecker, Bob	66T	91	$3.00	$15.00	Uribe, Jose	85TTR	125	$ .05	$ .20
Uecker, Bob	67T	326	$4.00	$12.00	Uribe, Jose	86T	12	$ .01	$ .10
Uhlaender, Ted	66T	264	$ .25	$ .85	Uribe, Jose	87T	633	$ .01	$ .03
Uhlaender, Ted	67T	431	$ .25	$ .85	Uribe, Jose	88T	302	$ .01	$ .03
Uhlaender, Ted	68T	28	$ .25	$ .65	Uribe, Jose	88TBB	95	$ .01	$ .05
Uhlaender, Ted	69T	194	$ .25	$ .65	Uribe, Jose	89T	753	$ .01	$ .04
Uhlaender, Ted	70T	673	$ .50	$2.00	Uribe, Jose	89TBB	258	$ .01	$ .05
Uhlaender, Ted	71T	347	$ .10	$ .35	Uribe, Jose	90T	472	$ .01	$ .03
Uhlaender, Ted	72T	614	$ .25	$ .85	Urrea, John	78T	587	$ .02	$ .10
Ujdur, Jerry	81T	626	$ .01	$ .07	Urrea, John	79T	429	$ .02	$ .10
Ujdur, Jerry	83T	174	$ .01	$ .06	Urrea, John	81T	152	$ .01	$ .07
Ullger, Scott	84T	551	$ .01	$ .05	Urrea, John	81TTR	847	$ .02	$ .10
Umbach, Arnie	66T	518	$ .70	$2.10	Urrea, John	82T	28	$ .01	$ .06
Umbarger, Jim	76T	7	$ .05	$ .20	Usher, Bob	52T	157	$6.00	$19.00
Umbarger, Jim	77T	378	$ .03	$ .12	Usher, Bobby	58T	124	$ .50	$2.00
Umbarger, Jim	79T	518	$ .02	$ .10	Vail, Mike	76T	655	$ .05	$ .20
Umbricht, Jim	60T	145	$ .35	$1.10	Vail, Mike	77T	246	$ .03	$ .12
Umbricht, Jim	63T	99	$ .25	$ .85	Vail, Mike	78T	69	$ .02	$ .10
Umbricht, Jim	64T	389	$ .40	$1.25	Vail, Mike	79T	663	$ .02	$ .10
Underwood, Pat	80T	709	$ .01	$ .07	Vail, Mike	80T	343	$ .01	$ .07
Underwood, Pat	81T	373	$ .01	$ .07	Vail, Mike	81T	471	$ .01	$ .07
Underwood, Pat	82T	133	$ .01	$ .06	Vail, Mike	81TTR	848	$ .02	$ .10
Underwood, Pat	83T	588	$ .01	$ .06	Vail, Mike	82T	194	$ .01	$ .06
Underwood, Tom	75T	615	$ .25	$ .85	Vail, Mike	83T	554	$ .01	$ .06
Underwood, Tom	76T	407	$ .05	$ .20	Vail, Mike	83TTR	119	$ .02	$ .10
Underwood, Tom	77T	217	$ .03	$ .12	Vail, Mike	84T	766	$ .01	$ .05
Underwood, Tom	78T	531	$ .02	$ .10	Vail, Mike	84TTR	124	$ .02	$ .10
Underwood, Tom	79T	64	$ .02	$ .10	Valdes, Rene	57T	337	$3.50	$13.00
Underwood, Tom	80T	324	$ .01	$ .07	Valdespino, Sandy	65T	201	$ .30	$1.00
Underwood, Tom	81T	114	$ .01	$ .07	Valdespino, Sandy	66T	56	$ .25	$ .85
Underwood, Tom	81TTR	846	$ .02	$ .10	Valdespino, Sandy	68T	304	$ .25	$ .65
Underwood, Tom	82T	757	$ .01	$ .06	Valdez, Julio	82T	381	$ .05	$ .20
Underwood, Tom	83T	466	$ .01	$ .06	Valdez, Julio	83T	628	$ .01	$ .06
Underwood, Tom	84T	642	$ .01	$ .05	Valdez, Sergio	90T	199	$ .01	$ .10
Underwood, Tom	84TTR	123	$ .02	$ .10	Valdivielso, Jose	56T	237	$2.50	$8.00
Underwood, Tom	85T	289	$ .01	$ .04	Valdivielso, Jose	57T	246	$ .95	$3.50
Unser, Del	69T	338	$ .25	$ .65	Valdivielso, Jose	60T	527	$2.00	$7.00
Unser, Del	70T	336	$ .10	$ .35	Valdivielso, Jose	61T	557	$6.00	$18.00
Unser, Del	71T	33	$ .10	$ .35	Valdivielso, Jose	62T	339	$ .35	$1.10
Unser, Del	72T	687	$ .70	$2.10	Valentine, Bob	71T	188	$ .60	$1.75
Unser, Del	73T	247	$ .06	$ .25	Valentine, Bobby	72T	11	$ .05	$ .25
Unser, Del	74T	69	$ .06	$ .25	Valentine, Bobby	73T	502	$ .06	$ .25
Unser, Del	75T	138	$ .06	$ .25	Valentine, Bobby	74T	101	$ .06	$ .25
Unser, Del	76T	268	$ .05	$ .20	Valentine, Bobby	75T	215	$ .06	$ .25
Unser, Del	77T	471	$ .03	$ .12	Valentine, Bobby	76T	366	$ .05	$ .20
Unser, Del	78T	348	$ .02	$ .10	Valentine, Bobby	77T	629	$ .03	$ .12
Unser, Del	79T	628	$ .02	$ .10	Valentine, Bobby	78T	712	$ .05	$ .20

Player	Year	No.	VG	EX/MT	Player	Year	No.	VG	EX/MT
Valentine, Bobby	79T	428	$ .02	$ .10	Van Slyke, Andy	89TAS	392	$ .01	$ .05
Valentine, Bobby	80T	56	$ .01	$ .07	Van Slyke, Andy	89TBB	255	$ .01	$ .10
Valentine, Bobby	85TTR	126	$ .02	$ .10	Van Slyke, Andy	90T	775	$ .01	$ .03
Valentine, Bobby	86T	261	$ .01	$ .03	Vance, Sandy	71T	34	$ .10	$ .35
Valentine, Bobby	87T	118	$ .01	$ .03	VandeBerg, Ed	82TTR	122	$ .02	$ .10
Valentine, Bobby	88T	594	$ .01	$ .03	VandeBerg, Ed	83T	183	$ .01	$ .06
Valentine, Bobby	89T	314	$ .01	$ .04	VandeBerg, Ed	84T	63	$ .01	$ .05
Valentine, Bobby	90T	729	$ .01	$ .03	VandeBerg, Ed	85T	566	$ .01	$ .04
Valentine, Corky	55T	44	$1.35	$5.00	VandeBerg, Ed	86T	357	$ .01	$ .03
Valentine, Ellis	76T	590	$ .15	$ .50	VandeBerg, Ed	86TTR	118	$ .02	$ .10
Valentine, Ellis	77T	52	$ .03	$ .12	VandeBerg, Ed	87T	717	$ .01	$ .03
Valentine, Ellis	78T	185	$ .02	$ .10	VandeBerg, Ed	87TTR	123	$ .01	$ .07
Valentine, Ellis	79T	535	$ .02	$ .10	VandeBerg, Ed	88T	421	$ .01	$ .03
Valentine, Ellis	80T	395	$ .01	$ .07	VandeBerg, Ed	89T	242	$ .01	$ .04
Valentine, Ellis	81T	445	$ .01	$ .07	Varney, Pete	76T	413	$ .05	$ .20
Valentine, Ellis	81TTR	849	$ .02	$ .10	Varsho, Gary	89T	613	$ .01	$ .10
Valentine, Ellis	82T	15	$ .01	$ .06	Vasquez, Rafael	80T	672	$ .01	$ .07
Valentine, Ellis	83T	653	$ .01	$ .06	Vaughn, Charley	67T	179	$ .25	$ .65
Valentine, Ellis	83TTR	120	$ .02	$ .10	Vaughn, Greg	89TMLD	128	$ .01	$1.00
Valentine, Ellis	84T	236	$ .01	$ .05	Vaughn, Greg	90T	57	$ .01	$1.00
Valentine, Fred	64T	483	$ .40	$1.25	Veal, Coot	59T	52	$ .85	$3.50
Valentine, Fred	66T	351	$ .25	$ .85	Veal, Coot	61T	432	$ .50	$2.00
Valentine, Fred	67T	64	$ .25	$ .65	Veal, Coot	63T	573	$1.50	$3.75
Valentine, Fred	68T	248	$ .25	$ .65	Veale, Bob	62T	593	$6.00	$18.00
Valentinetti, Vito	57T	74	$ .95	$3.50	Veale, Bob	63T	87	$ .25	$ .85
Valentinetti, Vito	58T	463	$ .50	$1.95	Veale, Bob	64T	501	$ .40	$1.25
Valentinetti, Vito	59T	44	$ .85	$3.50	Veale, Bob	65T	12	$1.50	$3.75
Valenzuela, Fernando	81T	302	$ .90	$4.50	Veale, Bob	65T	195	$ .25	$ .65
Valenzuela, Fernando	81TTR	850	$1.00	$4.50	Veale, Bob	66T	225	$1.00	$4.00
Valenzuela, Fernando	82T	166	$ .03	$ .15	Veale, Bob	66T	425	$ .25	$ .85
Valenzuela, Fernando	82T	510	$ .25	$ .50	Veale, Bob	67T	238	$1.50	$3.75
Valenzuela, Fernando	82TAS	345	$ .05	$ .25	Veale, Bob	67T	335	$ .25	$ .65
Valenzuela, Fernando	82THL	6	$ .05	$ .25	Veale, Bob	68T	70	$ .25	$ .65
Valenzuela, Fernando	83T	40	$ .10	$ .50	Veale, Bob	69T	8	$ .50	$2.00
Valenzuela, Fernando	83T	681	$ .01	$ .06	Veale, Bob	69T	520	$ .25	$ .85
Valenzuela, Fernando	84T	220	$ .25	$ .65	Veale, Bob	70T	236	$ .10	$ .35
Valenzuela, Fernando	85T	440	$ .05	$ .25					
Valenzuela, Fernando	86T	630	$ .03	$ .25					
Valenzuela, Fernando	86TB	401	$ .02	$ .15					
Valenzuela, Fernando	86TRB	207	$ .01	$ .10					
Valenzuela, Fernando	87T	410	$ .03	$ .15					
Valenzuela, Fernando	87TAS	604	$ .01	$ .10					
Valenzuela, Fernando	88T	780	$ .01	$ .10					
Valenzuela, Fernando	88TBB	18	$ .01	$ .10					
Valenzuela, Fernando	89T	150	$ .01	$ .10					
Valenzuela, Fernando	90T	340	$ .01	$ .03					
Valle, Dave	87TTR	122	$ .01	$ .07					
Valle, Dave	88T	583	$ .01	$ .03					
Valle, Dave	88TBB	210	$ .01	$ .05					
Valle, Dave	89T	498	$ .01	$ .04					
Valle, Dave	89TRR	56	$ .01	$ .05					
Valle, Dave	90T	76	$ .01	$ .03					
Valle, Hector	65T	561	$2.00	$7.00					
Valle, Hector	66T	314	$ .25	$ .85					
Valo, Elmer	51Trb	28	$1.25	$3.50					
Valo, Elmer	52T	34	$14.00	$45.00					
Valo, Elmer	53T	122	$3.75	$13.00					
Valo, Elmer	54T	145	$2.00	$7.00					
Valo, Elmer	55T	145	$1.35	$5.00					
Valo, Elmer	56T	3	$1.25	$4.50					
Valo, Elmer	57T	54	$ .95	$3.50					
Valo, Elmer	58T	323	$ .45	$1.50					
Valo, Elmer	60T	237	$ .50	$2.00					
Valo, Elmer	61T	186	$ .30	$1.00					
Van Cuyk, Chris	52T	53	$14.00	$45.00					
Van Gorder, Dave	83T	322	$ .01	$ .06					
Van Gorder, Dave	86T	143	$ .01	$ .03					
Van Slyke, Andy	84T	206	$ .50	$2.00					
Van Slyke, Andy	85T	551	$ .10	$ .40	Veale, Bob	71T	368	$ .10	$ .35
Van Slyke, Andy	86T	683	$ .01	$ .25	Veale, Bob	72T	729	$ .70	$2.10
Van Slyke, Andy	87T	33	$ .01	$ .10	Veale, Bob	73T	518	$ .10	$ .35
Van Slyke, Andy	87TTR	124	$ .01	$ .07	Vega, Jesus	83T	308	$ .01	$ .06
Van Slyke, Andy	88T	142	$ .01	$ .03	Veintidos, Juan	75T	621	$ .15	$ .50
Van Slyke, Andy	88TBB	184	$ .01	$ .10	Velarde, Randy	89T	584	$ .01	$ .04
Van Slyke, Andy	89T	350	$ .01	$ .10	Velarde, Randy	89TBB	239	$ .01	$ .05

Player	Year	No.	VG	EX/MT
Velarde, Randy	90T	23	$ .01	$ .03
Velez, Otto	74T	606	$ .06	$ .25
Velez, Otto	77T	299	$ .03	$ .12
Velez, Otto	78T	59	$ .02	$ .10
Velez, Otto	79T	462	$ .02	$ .10
Velez, Otto	80T	703	$ .01	$ .07
Velez, Otto	81T	351	$ .01	$ .07
Velez, Otto	82T	155	$ .01	$ .06
Venable, Max	81T	484	$ .01	$ .07
Venable, Max	83T	634	$ .01	$ .06
Venable, Max	84T	58	$ .01	$ .05
Venable, Max	86T	428	$ .01	$ .03
Venable, Max	87T	226	$ .01	$ .03
Ventura, Robin	88TTR	124	$ .50	$2.50
Ventura, Robin	89T	764	$ .15	$1.00
Ventura, Robin	89TBB	65	$ .01	$ .25
Ventura, Robin	89TMLD	129	$ .01	$ .35
Ventura, Robin	90T	121	$ .01	$ .35
Verbanic, Joe	67T	442	$ .25	$ .85
Verbanic, Joe	68T	29	$ .25	$ .65

Player	Year	No.	VG	EX/MT
Verbanic, Joe	69T	541	$ .25	$ .85
Verbanic, Joe	70T	416	$ .10	$ .35
Veres, Randy	89TMLD	130	$ .01	$ .05
Verhoeven, John	77T	91	$ .03	$ .12
Verhoeven, John	78T	329	$ .02	$ .10
Verhoeven, John	81T	603	$ .01	$ .07
Verhoeven, John	82T	281	$ .01	$ .06
Vernon, Mickey	51Tbb	13	$4.00	$18.00
Vernon, Mickey	52T	106	$6.00	$17.50
Vernon, Mickey	56T	228	$3.00	$9.00
Vernon, Mickey	57T	92	$ .95	$3.50
Vernon, Mickey	58T	233	$ .45	$1.50
Vernon, Mickey	59T	115	$ .60	$1.75
Vernon, Mickey	60T	467	$ .95	$3.50
Vernon, Mickey	61T	134	$ .30	$1.00
Vernon, Mickey	62T	152	$ .35	$1.10
Vernon, Mickey	63T	402	$ .30	$1.20
Versalles, Zorro "Zoilo"	61T	21	$ .30	$1.00
Versalles, Zoilo	62T	499	$ .70	$2.10
Versalles, Zoilo	63T	349	$ .35	$1.20
Versalles, Zoilo	64T	15	$ .25	$ .85
Versalles, Zoilo	65T	157	$ .35	$1.10
Versalles, Zoilo	66T	400	$ .25	$ .85

Player	Year	No.	VG	EX/MT
Versalles, Zoilo	67T	270	$ .25	$ .65
Versalles, Zoilo	68T	315	$ .25	$ .65
Versalles, Zoilo	69T	38	$ .25	$ .65
Versalles, Zoilo	70T	365	$ .10	$ .35
Versalles, Zoilo	75T	203	$ .35	$1.10
Veryzer, Tom	75T	623	$6.00	$18.00
Veryzer, Tom	76T	432	$ .05	$ .20
Veryzer, Tom	77T	145	$ .03	$ .12
Veryzer, Tom	78T	633	$ .02	$ .10
Veryzer, Tom	79T	537	$ .02	$ .10
Veryzer, Tom	80T	276	$ .01	$ .07
Veryzer, Tom	81T	39	$ .01	$ .07
Veryzer, Tom	82T	387	$ .01	$ .06
Veryzer, Tom	82TTR	123	$ .02	$ .10
Veryzer, Tom	83T	496	$ .01	$ .06
Veryzer, Tom	83TTR	121	$ .02	$ .10
Veryzer, Tom	84T	117	$ .01	$ .05
Veryzer, Tom	85T	405	$ .01	$ .04
Vezendy, Gerry	65T	509	$ .50	$2.00
Vidal, Jose	67T	499	$ .50	$2.00
Vidal, Jose	68T	432	$ .25	$ .65
Vidal, Jose	69T	322	$ .25	$ .85
Vineyard, Dave	65T	169	$ .25	$ .65
Vinson, Chuck	68T	328	$ .25	$ .65
Viola, Frank	83T	586	$2.00	$6.50
Viola, Frank	84T	28	$ .25	$1.00
Viola, Frank	85T	266	$ .10	$ .50
Viola, Frank	85TAS	710	$ .01	$ .10
Viola, Frank	86T	742	$ .01	$ .35
Viola, Frank	87T	310	$ .25	$ .65
Viola, Frank	88T	625	$ .01	$ .15
Viola, Frank	88TBB	201	$ .01	$ .15
Viola, Frank	89T	120	$ .01	$ .15
Viola, Frank	89TAS	406	$ .01	$ .10
Viola, Frank	89TBB	140	$ .01	$ .25
Viola, Frank	90T	470	$ .01	$ .10
Virdon, Bill	56T	170	$1.25	$3.50
Virdon, Bill	57T	110	$ .60	$2.50
Virdon, Bill	58T	198	$ .45	$1.50
Virdon, Bill	59T	190	$ .50	$1.95
Virdon, Bill	59T	543	$8.50	$25.00
Virdon, Bill	60T	496	$ .85	$3.50
Virdon, Bill	61T	70	$ .50	$2.00
Virdon, Bill	62T	415	$ .85	$3.50
Virdon, Bill	63T	55	$ .30	$1.00
Virdon, Bill	64T	495	$ .50	$1.95
Virdon, Bill	65T	69	$ .15	$ .50
Virdon, Bill	72T	661	$ .60	$1.75
Virdon, Bill	73T	517	$ .25	$ .85
Virdon, Bill	78T	279	$ .02	$ .10
Virdon, Bill	83T	516	$ .01	$ .06
Virdon, Bill	84T	111	$ .01	$ .05
Virgil, Jr., Ozzie	82T	231	$ .50	$1.50
Virgil, Jr., Ozzie	83T	383	$ .01	$ .06
Virgil, Jr., Ozzie	84T	484	$ .01	$ .05
Virgil, Jr., Ozzie	85T	143	$ .01	$ .10
Virgil, Jr., Ozzie	85T	611	$ .01	$ .04
Virgil, Jr., Ozzie	86T	95	$ .01	$ .03
Virgil, Jr., Ozzie	86TTR	119	$ .02	$ .10
Virgil, Jr., Ozzie	87T	571	$ .01	$ .03
Virgil, Jr., Ozzie	88T	755	$ .01	$ .03
Virgil, Ossie	57T	365	$ .85	$3.50
Virgil, Ossie	58T	107	$ .85	$3.50
Virgil, Ossie	59T	203	$ .50	$1.95
Virgil, Ossie	61T	67	$ .30	$1.00
Virgil, Ozzie (Ossie)	62T	327	$ .35	$1.10
Virgil, Ossie	65T	571	$1.50	$3.75
Virgil, Ozzie (Ossie)	67T	132	$ .25	$ .65
Virgil, Ossie	85T	143	$ .01	$ .10
Virgil, Ozzie	88TBB	148	$ .01	$ .05
Virgil, Ozzie	89T	179	$ .01	$ .05
Vizcaino, Jose	89TMLD	131	$ .01	$ .05
Vizquel, Omar	89TMLD	132	$ .01	$ .05
Vizquel, Omar	89TTR	122	$ .01	$ .25
Vizquel, Omar	90T	698	$ .01	$ .03

TOPPS

Player	Year	No.	VG	EX/MT	Player	Year	No.	VG	EX/MT
Vollmer, Clyde	52T	255	$11.50	$38.00	Wagner, Mark	83T	144	$ .01	$ .06
Vollmer, Clyde	53T	32	$3.75	$13.00	Wagner, Mark	85T	581	$ .01	$ .04
Von Hoff, Bruce	68T	529	$ .30	$1.00	Waitkus, Eddie	51Tbb	51	$5.50	$17.00
Von Ohlen, Dave	84T	489	$ .01	$ .05	Waitkus, Eddie	52T	158	$6.00	$19.00
Von Ohlen, Dave	85T	177	$ .01	$ .04	Waits, Rick	76T	433	$ .05	$ .20
Von Ohlen, Dave	85TTR	127	$ .02	$ .10	Waits, Rick	77T	306	$ .03	$ .12
Von Ohlen, Dave	86T	632	$ .01	$ .03	Waits, Rick	78T	37	$ .02	$ .10
Von Ohlen, Dave	87T	287	$ .01	$ .03	Waits, Rick	79T	484	$ .02	$ .10
Voss, Bill	66T	529	$4.50	$15.00	Waits, Rick	80T	168	$ .01	$ .07
Voss, Bill	68T	142	$ .25	$ .65	Waits, Rick	81T	697	$ .01	$ .07
Voss, Bill	69T	621	$ .25	$ .85	Waits, Rick	82T	573	$ .01	$ .06
Voss, Bill	70T	326	$ .10	$ .35	Waits, Rick	83T	779	$ .01	$ .06
Voss, Bill	71T	671	$ .70	$2.10	Waits, Rick	83TTR	123	$ .02	$ .10
Voss, Bill	72T	776	$ .70	$2.10	Waits, Rick	84T	218	$ .01	$ .05
Vossler, Dan	74T	602	$ .06	$ .25	Waits, Rick	85T	59	$ .01	$ .04
Vuckovich, Pete	77T	517	$ .12	$ .40	Waits, Rick	86T	614	$ .01	$ .03
Vuckovich, Pete	78T	241	$ .02	$ .10	Wakefield, Bill	64T	576	$1.50	$3.75
Vuckovich, Pete	79T	407	$ .02	$ .10	Wakefield, Bill	65T	167	$ .25	$ .65
Vuckovich, Pete	80T	57	$ .01	$ .07	Wakefield, Bill	66T	443	$ .25	$ .85
Vuckovich, Pete	81T	193	$ .01	$ .07	Walewander, Jim	88T	106	$ .01	$ .10
Vuckovich, Pete	81TTR	851	$ .02	$ .10	Walewander, Jim	89T	467	$ .01	$ .04
Vuckovich, Pete	82T	165	$ .03	$ .15	Walk, Bob	81T	494	$ .01	$ .07
Vuckovich, Pete	82T	643	$ .02	$ .10	Walk, Bob	81TTR	853	$ .02	$ .10
Vuckovich, Pete	82T	703	$ .03	$ .15	Walk, Bob	82T	296	$ .01	$ .06
Vuckovich, Pete	83T	321	$ .01	$ .10	Walk, Bob	83T	104	$ .01	$ .06
Vuckovich, Pete	83T	375	$ .01	$ .06	Walk, Bob	86TTR	120	$ .02	$ .10
Vuckovich, Pete	83TAS	394	$ .01	$ .06	Walk, Bob	87T	628	$ .01	$ .03
Vuckovich, Pete	84T	505	$ .01	$ .05	Walk, Bob	88T	349	$ .01	$ .03
Vuckovich, Pete	85T	254	$ .01	$ .04	Walk, Bob	89T	504	$ .01	$ .04
Vuckovich, Pete	86T	737	$ .01	$ .03	Walk, Bob	90T	754	$ .01	$ .03
Vukovich, George	81T	598	$ .01	$ .07	Walker, Al "Rube"	52T	319	$39.00	$135.00
Vukovich, George	82T	389	$ .01	$ .06	Walker, "Rube"	53T	134	$3.75	$13.00
Vukovich, George	83T	16	$ .01	$ .06	Walker, "Rube"	54T	153	$2.00	$7.00
Vukovich, George	83TTR	122	$ .02	$ .10	Walker, "Rube"	55T	108	$1.35	$5.00
Vukovich, George	84T	638	$ .01	$ .05	Walker, "Rube"	56T	333	$1.30	$5.00
Vukovich, George	85T	212	$ .01	$ .04	Walker, Al	57T	147	$ .95	$3.50
Vukovich, George	86T	483	$ .01	$ .03	Walker, Al	58T	203	$ .50	$2.00
Vukovich, John	73T	451	$ .06	$ .25	Walker, "Rube"	73T	257	$ .50	$2.00
Vukovich, John	74T	349	$ .06	$ .25	Walker, "Rube"	74T	179	$ .50	$2.00
Vukovich, John	75T	602	$ .06	$ .25	Walker, Chico	87T	695	$ .01	$ .03
Waddell, Tom	84TTR	125	$ .02	$ .10	Walker, Dixie	53T	190	$3.75	$13.00
Waddell, Tom	85T	453	$ .01	$ .04	Walker, Duane	83T	243	$ .01	$ .06
Waddell, Tom	86T	86	$ .01	$ .03	Walker, Duane	84T	659	$ .01	$ .05
Waddell, Tom	87T	657	$ .01	$ .03	Walker, Duane	85T	441	$ .01	$ .04
Wade, Ben	52T	389	$39.00	$135.00	Walker, Duane	86T	22	$ .01	$ .03
Wade, Ben	53T	4	$3.75	$13.00	Walker, Greg	83TTR	124	$ .35	$1.10
Wade, Ben	54T	126	$2.00	$7.00	Walker, Greg	84T	518	$ .07	$ .35
Wade, Gale	55T	196	$4.25	$13.00	Walker, Greg	85T	623	$ .01	$ .04
Wagner, Gary	66T	151	$ .25	$ .85	Walker, Greg	86T	123	$ .01	$ .03
Wagner, Gary	67T	529	$ .50	$2.00	Walker, Greg	87T	397	$ .01	$ .03
Wagner, Gary	08T	448	$ .25	$ .65	Walker, Greg	88T	764	$ .01	$ .03
Wagner, Gary	69T	276	$ .25	$ .85	Walker, Greg	88IBB	105	$ .01	$ .05
Wagner, Gary	70T	627	$ .25	$ .85	Walker, Greg	89T	408	$ .01	$ .04
Wagner, Gary	71T	473	$ .10	$ .35	Walker, Greg	89TBB	4	$ .01	$ .05
Wagner, Honus	76TAS	344	$ .50	$2.00	Walker, Greg	90T	33	$ .01	$ .03
Wagner, Leon	59T	257	$ .60	$1.75	Walker, Harry	60T	468	$ .95	$3.50
Wagner, Leon	60T	383	$ .50	$1.95	Walker, Harry	65T	438	$ .30	$1.00
Wagner, Leon	61T	547	$6.00	$17.00	Walker, Harry	66T	318	$ .15	$ .50
Wagner, Leon	62T	491	$ .70	$2.10	Walker, Harry	67T	448	$ .25	$ .85
Wagner, Leon	63T	4	$ .50	$2.00	Walker, Harry	69T	633	$ .25	$ .85
Wagner, Leon	63T	335	$ .35	$1.20	Walker, Harry	70T	32	$ .10	$ .35
Wagner, Leon	64T	41	$ .70	$2.00	Walker, Harry	71T	312	$ .10	$ .35
Wagner, Leon	64T	530	$1.50	$3.75	Walker, Harry	72T	249	$ .05	$ .25
Wagner, Leon	65T	367	$ .30	$1.00	Walker, Jerry	58T	113	$ .50	$2.00
Wagner, Leon	66T	65	$ .25	$ .85	Walker, Jerry	59T	144	$ .50	$1.95
Wagner, Leon	67T	109	$ .15	$ .50	Walker, Jerry	60T	399	$ .60	$1.75
Wagner, Leon	67T	360	$ .25	$ .65	Walker, Jerry	60T	540	$2.00	$7.00
Wagner, Leon	68T	495	$ .30	$1.00	Walker, Jerry	61T	85	$ .30	$1.00
Wagner, Leon	69T	187	$ .25	$ .65	Walker, Jerry	62T	357	$ .35	$1.10
Wagner, Mark	77T	490	$ .03	$ .12	Walker, Jerry	63T	413	$ .35	$1.20
Wagner, Mark	79T	598	$ .02	$ .10	Walker, Jerry	64T	77	$ .25	$ .85
Wagner, Mark	80T	29	$ .01	$ .07	Walker, Larry	89TMLD	133	$ .01	$ .15
Wagner, Mark	81T	358	$ .01	$ .07	Walker, Larry	90T	757	$ .01	$ .25
Wagner, Mark	81TTR	852	$ .02	$ .10	Walker, Luke	66T	498	$ .65	$1.75
Wagner, Mark	82T	443	$ .01	$ .06	Walker, Luke	67T	123	$ .25	$ .65

TOPPS

Player	Year	No.	VG	EX/MT	Player	Year	No.	VG	EX/MT
Walker, Luke	68T	559	$ .30	$1.00	Walton, Danny	71T	281	$ .10	$ .35
Walker, Luke	69T	36	$ .25	$ .65	Walton, Danny	73T	516	$ .06	$ .25
Walker, Luke	70T	322	$ .10	$ .35	Walton, Danny	78T	263	$ .02	$ .10
Walker, Luke	71T	68	$ .15	$ .50	Walton, Jerome	89TMLD	134	$ .01	$1.00
Walker, Luke	71T	534	$ .30	$1.00	Walton, Jerome	89TTR	123	$ .01	$3.00
Walker, Luke	72T	471	$ .05	$ .25	Walton, Jerome	90T	464	$ .01	$1.00
Walker, Luke	73T	187	$ .06	$ .25	Walton, Jim	73T	646	$ .50	$2.00
Walker, Luke	74T	612	$ .06	$ .25	Walton, Jim	74T	99	$ .06	$ .25
Walker, Luke	74TTR	612	$ .06	$ .25	Walton, Reggie	82T	711	$ .25	$1.00
Walker, Luke	75T	474	$ .06	$ .25	Ward, Chris	75T	587	$ .06	$ .25
Walker, Tom	73T	41	$ .06	$ .25	Ward, Duane	87T	153	$ .01	$ .03
Walker, Tom	74T	193	$ .06	$ .25	Ward, Duane	88T	696	$ .01	$ .03
Walker, Tom	75T	627	$ .06	$ .25	Ward, Duane	89T	502	$ .01	$ .04
Walker, Tom	76T	186	$ .05	$ .20	Ward, Duane	90T	28	$ .01	$ .03
Walker, Tom	77T	652	$ .03	$ .12	Ward, Gary	80T	669	$ .06	$ .30
Walker, Tony	87T	24	$ .01	$ .10	Ward, Gary	81T	328	$ .01	$ .07
Wall, Murray	53T	217	$3.75	$13.00	Ward, Gary	82T	612	$ .01	$ .06
Wall, Murray	58T	410	$ .50	$2.00	Ward, Gary	83T	517	$ .01	$ .06
Wall, Murray	59T	42	$ .85	$3.50	Ward, Gary	84T	67	$ .01	$ .05
Wall, Stan	76T	584	$ .05	$ .20	Ward, Gary	84TTR	126	$ .02	$ .10
Wall, Stan	77T	88	$ .03	$ .12	Ward, Gary	85T	414	$ .01	$ .04
Wallace, Don	67T	367	$ .25	$ .65	Ward, Gary	86T	105	$ .01	$ .03
Wallace, Mike	74T	608	$ .06	$ .25	Ward, Gary	87T	762	$ .01	$ .03
Wallace, Mike	75T	401	$ .06	$ .25	Ward, Gary	87TTR	125	$ .01	$ .07
Wallace, Mike	77T	539	$ .03	$ .12	Ward, Gary	88T	235	$ .01	$ .03
Wallach, Tim	82T	191	$ .50	$1.50	Ward, Gary	88TBB	195	$ .01	$ .05
Wallach, Tim	83T	552	$ .01	$ .06	Ward, Gary	89T	302	$ .01	$ .04
Wallach, Tim	84T	232	$ .01	$ .05	Ward, Gary	89TBB	206	$ .01	$ .05
Wallach, Tim	85T	473	$ .01	$ .04	Ward, Gary	89TTR	124	$ .01	$ .05
Wallach, Tim	86T	685	$ .01	$ .03	Ward, Gary	90T	679	$ .01	$ .03
Wallach, Tim	86TAS	703	$ .01	$ .03	Ward, Jay	64T	116	$3.00	$12.00
Wallach, Tim	87T	55	$ .01	$ .03	Ward, Jay	65T	421	$ .30	$1.00
Wallach, Tim	88T	560	$ .01	$ .10	Ward, Pete	63T	324	$ .35	$1.20
Wallach, Tim	88TAS	399	$ .01	$ .03	Ward, Pete	64T	85	$ .25	$ .85
Wallach, Tim	88TBB	7	$ .01	$ .05	Ward, Pete	65T	215	$ .30	$1.00
Wallach, Tim	89T	720	$ .01	$ .04	Ward, Pete	66T	25	$ .25	$ .85
Wallach, Tim	89TBB	215	$ .01	$ .05	Ward, Pete	67T	143	$ .25	$ .65
Wallach, Tim	90T	370	$ .01	$ .03					
Waller, Ty	82T	51	$ .03	$ .15					
Walling, Denny	77T	473	$9.00	$35.00					
Walling, Denny	79T	553	$ .02	$ .10					
Walling, Denny	80T	306	$ .01	$ .07					
Walling, Denny	81T	439	$ .01	$ .07					
Walling, Denny	82T	147	$ .01	$ .06					
Walling, Denny	83T	692	$ .01	$ .06					
Walling, Denny	84T	36	$ .01	$ .05					
Walling, Denny	85T	382	$ .01	$ .04					
Walling, Denny	86T	504	$ .01	$ .03					
Walling, Denny	87T	222	$ .01	$ .03					
Walling, Denny	88T	719	$ .01	$ .03					
Walling, Denny	89T	196	$ .01	$ .04					
Walling, Denny	90T	462	$ .01	$ .03					
Wallis, Joe	76T	598	$ .05	$ .20					
Wallis, Joe	77T	279	$ .03	$ .12					
Wallis, Joe	78T	614	$ .02	$ .10					
Wallis, Joe	79T	406	$ .02	$ .10					
Wallis, Joe	80T	562	$ .01	$ .07					
Walls, Lee	57T	52	$ .95	$3.50					
Walls, Lee	58T	66	$ .85	$3.50					
Walls, Lee	59T	105	$ .85	$3.50					
Walls, Lee	60T	506	$ .60	$1.75					
Walls, Lee	61T	78	$ .30	$1.00					
Walls, Lee	62T	129	$ .25	$1.25					
Walls, Lee	63T	11	$ .25	$ .85					
Walls, Lee	64T	411	$ .40	$1.25					
Walter, Gene	86TTR	121	$ .02	$ .10					
Walter, Gene	87T	248	$ .01	$ .03					
Walter, Gene	89T	758	$ .01	$ .04	Ward, Pete	67T	436	$ .25	$ .85
Walters, Ken	60T	511	$2.00	$7.00	Ward, Pete	68T	33	$ .25	$ .65
Walters, Ken	61T	394	$ .50	$2.00	Ward, Pete	69T	155	$ .25	$ .65
Walters, Ken	62T	328	$ .35	$1.10	Ward, Pete	70T	659	$ .50	$2.00
Walters, Ken	63T	534	$1.50	$3.75	Ward, Pete	71T	667	$ .70	$2.10
Walters, Mike	84T	673	$ .01	$ .05	Ward, Preston	53T	173	$3.75	$13.00
Walters, Mike	85T	187	$ .01	$ .04					
Walton, Danny	70T	134	$ .10	$ .35					

404

Player	Year	No.	VG	EX/MT	Player	Year	No.	VG	EX/MT
Ward, Preston	54T	72	$4.75	$14.00	Waslewski, Gary	69T	438	$ .25	$ .65
Ward, Preston	55T	95	$1.35	$5.00	Waslewski, Gary	70T	607	$ .25	$ .85
Ward, Preston	56T	328	$1.30	$5.00	Waslewski, Gary	71T	277	$ .10	$ .35
Ward, Preston	57T	226	$ .95	$3.50	Waslewski, Gary	72T	108	$ .05	$ .25
Ward, Preston	58T	450	$1.25	$3.50	Wathan, John	77T	218	$ .25	$ .65
Ward, Preston	59T	176	$ .50	$1.95	Wathan, John	78T	343	$ .02	$ .10
Warden, Jon	69T	632	$ .25	$ .85	Wathan, John	79T	99	$ .02	$ .10
Wardle, Curt	86T	303	$ .01	$ .03	Wathan, John	80T	547	$ .01	$ .07
Warner, Jack D.	65T	354	$ .30	$1.00	Wathan, John	81T	157	$ .01	$ .07
Warner, Jackie	65T	517	$ .50	$2.00	Wathan, John	82T	429	$ .01	$ .06
Warner, Jackie	66T	553	$4.50	$15.00	Wathan, John	83T	746	$ .01	$ .06
Warren, Mike	84T	5	$ .02	$ .10	Wathan, John	83TRB	6	$ .01	$ .06
Warren, Mike	84T	338	$ .01	$ .05	Wathan, John	84T	602	$ .01	$ .05
Warren, Mike	85T	197	$ .01	$ .04	Wathan, John	85T	308	$ .01	$ .04
Warthen, Dan	76T	374	$ .05	$ .20	Wathan, John	86T	128	$ .01	$ .03
Warthen, Dan	77T	391	$ .03	$ .12	Wathan, John	88T	534	$ .01	$ .03
Warwick, Carl	62T	202	$ .35	$1.10	Wathan, John	89T	374	$ .01	$ .04
Warwick, Carl	63T	333	$ .35	$1.20	Wathan, John	90T	789	$ .01	$ .03
Warwick, Carl	64T	179	$ .25	$ .85	Watkins, Bob	70T	227	$ .30	$1.00
Warwick, Carl	65T	357	$ .30	$1.00	Watkins, Dave	70T	168	$ .10	$ .35
Warwick, Carl	66T	247	$ .25	$ .85	Watson, Bob	69T	562	$ .35	$1.10
Washburn, Greg	70T	74	$ .10	$ .35	Watson, Bob	70T	407	$ .10	$ .35
Washburn, Ray	62T	19	$ .35	$1.10	Watson, Bob	71T	222	$ .10	$ .35
Washburn, Ray	63T	206	$ .25	$ .85	Watson, Bob	72T	355	$ .05	$ .25
Washburn, Ray	64T	332	$ .25	$ .85	Watson, Bob	73T	110	$ .06	$ .25
Washburn, Ray	65T	467	$ .50	$2.00	Watson, Bob	74T	370	$ .06	$ .25
Washburn, Ray	66T	399	$ .25	$ .85	Watson, Bob	75T	227	$ .06	$ .25
Washburn, Ray	67T	92	$ .25	$ .65	Watson, Bob	76T	20	$ .05	$ .20
Washburn, Ray	68T	388	$ .25	$ .65	Watson, Bob	77T	540	$ .03	$ .12
Washburn, Ray	69T	415	$ .25	$ .65	Watson, Bob	78T	330	$ .05	$ .20
Washburn, Ray	70T	22	$ .10	$ .35	Watson, Bob	79T	130	$ .02	$ .10
Washington Team, N.L.	74T	226	$1.50	$4.50	Watson, Bob	80T	480	$ .01	$ .07
Washington, Claudell	75T	647	$ .75	$2.00	Watson, Bob	81T	690	$ .02	$ .10
Washington, Claudell	76T	189	$ .06	$ .25	Watson, Bob	82T	275	$ .01	$ .06
Washington, Claudell	76T	198	$ .10	$ .35	Watson, Bob	82TTR	125	$ .05	$ .20
Washington, Claudell	77T	405	$ .03	$ .12	Watson, Bob	83T	572	$ .01	$ .06
Washington, Claudell	78T	67	$ .05	$ .20	Watson, Bob	84T	739	$ .01	$ .05
Washington, Claudell	79T	574	$ .05	$ .20	Watson, Bob	85T	51	$ .01	$ .04
Washington, Claudell	80T	322	$ .01	$ .07	Watt, Eddie	66T	442	$ .25	$ .85
Washington, Claudell	81T	151	$ .01	$ .07	Watt, Eddie	67T	271	$ .25	$ .65
Washington, Claudell	81TTR	854	$ .02	$ .10	Watt, Eddie	68T	186	$ .25	$ .65
Washington, Claudell	82T	126	$ .01	$ .06	Watt, Eddie	69T	652	$ .25	$ .85
Washington, Claudell	82T	758	$ .01	$ .06	Watt, Eddie	70T	497	$ .10	$ .35
Washington, Claudell	83T	235	$ .01	$ .06	Watt, Eddie	71T	122	$ .10	$ .35
Washington, Claudell	84T	410	$ .01	$ .05	Watt, Eddie	72T	128	$ .05	$ .25
Washington, Claudell	85T	540	$ .01	$ .04	Watt, Eddie	73T	362	$ .06	$ .25
Washington, Claudell	86T	675	$ .01	$ .03	Watt, Eddie	74T	534	$ .06	$ .25
Washington, Claudell	86TTR	122	$ .02	$ .10	Watt, Eddie	74TTR	534	$ .06	$ .25
Washington, Claudell	87T	15	$ .01	$ .03	Watt, Eddie	75T	374	$ .06	$ .25
Washington, Claudell	88T	335	$ .01	$ .03	Waugh, Jim	53T	178	$3.75	$13.00
Washington, Claudell	88TBB	1/8	$ .01	$ .06	Wayne, Gary	89TMLD	135	$ .01	$ .05
Washington, Claudell	89T	185	$ .01	$ .04	Wayne, Gary	90T	348	$ .01	$ .03
Washington, Claudell	89TTR	125	$ .01	$ .05	Weaver, Earl	69T	516	$1.25	$4.50
Washington, Claudell	90T	705	$ .01	$ .03	Weaver, Earl	70T	148	$ .15	$ .75
Washington, Herb	75T	407	$ .06	$ .25	Weaver, Earl	71T	477	$ .35	$1.10
Washington, LaRue	80T	233	$ .01	$ .07	Weaver, Earl	72T	323	$ .25	$ .65
Washington, Ron	82TTR	124	$ .02	$ .10	Weaver, Earl	73T	136	$ .15	$ .50
Washington, Ron	83T	458	$ .01	$ .06	Weaver, Earl	74T	306	$ .15	$ .50
Washington, Ron	84T	623	$ .01	$ .05	Weaver, Earl	78T	211	$ .02	$ .10
Washington, Ron	85T	329	$ .01	$ .04	Weaver, Earl	83T	426	$ .01	$ .10
Washington, Ron	86T	513	$ .01	$ .03	Weaver, Earl	85TTR	129	$ .05	$ .20
Washington, Ron	87T	169	$ .01	$ .03	Weaver, Earl	86T	321	$ .01	$ .03
Washington, Ron	88TTR	125	$ .01	$ .05	Weaver, Earl	87T	568	$ .01	$ .03
Washington, Team	56T	146	$3.00	$9.00	Weaver, Floyd	65T	546	$1.50	$3.75
Washington, Team	59T	397	$1.50	$4.50	Weaver, Floyd	66T	231	$ .25	$ .85
Washington, U. L.	78T	707	$10.00	$40.00	Weaver, Floyd	71T	227	$ .10	$ .35
Washington, U. L.	79T	157	$ .02	$ .10	Weaver, Jim	68T	328	$ .25	$ .65
Washington, U. L.	80T	508	$ .01	$ .07	Weaver, Jim	69T	134	$ .25	$ .65
Washington, U. L.	81T	26	$ .01	$ .07	Weaver, Roger	81T	626	$ .01	$ .07
Washington, U. L.	82T	329	$ .01	$ .06	Webb, Hank	73T	610	$ .35	$1.10
Washington, U. L.	83T	687	$ .01	$ .06	Webb, Hank	75T	615	$ .25	$ .85
Washington, U. L.	84T	294	$ .01	$ .05	Webb, Hank	76T	442	$ .05	$ .20
Washington, U. L.	85T	431	$ .01	$ .04	Webster, Lenny	89TMLD	136	$ .01	$ .15
Washington, U. L.	85TTR	128	$ .02	$ .10	Webster, Mitch	86T	629	$ .02	$ .15
Washington, U. L.	86T	113	$ .01	$ .03	Webster, Mitch	87T	442	$ .01	$ .03

Player	Year	No.	VG	EX/MT
Webster, Mitch	88T	138	$ .01	$ .03
Webster, Mitch	88TBB	150	$ .01	$ .05
Webster, Mitch	89T	36	$ .01	$ .04
Webster, Mitch	90T	502	$ .01	$ .03
Webster, Ramon	67T	603	$3.00	$12.00
Webster, Ramon	68T	164	$ .25	$ .65
Webster, Ramon	69T	618	$ .25	$ .85
Webster, Ray	59T	531	$2.00	$7.00
Webster, Ray	60T	452	$ .60	$1.75
Weekly, Johnny	62T	204	$ .35	$1.10
Weekly, Johnny	64T	256	$ .25	$ .85
Wegener, Mike	69T	284	$ .25	$ .85
Wegener, Mike	70T	193	$ .10	$ .35
Wegener, Mike	71T	608	$ .30	$1.00
Wegman, Bill	86TTR	123	$ .02	$ .10
Wegman, Bill	87T	179	$ .01	$ .03
Wegman, Bill	88T	538	$ .01	$ .03
Wegman, Bill	88TBB	244	$ .01	$ .05
Wegman, Bill	89T	768	$ .01	$ .04
Wegman, Bill	90T	333	$ .01	$ .03
Wehmeier, Herman	51Tbb	47	$5.50	$17.00
Wehmeier, Herman	52T	80	$14.00	$45.00
Wehmeier, Herman	53T	110	$3.75	$13.00
Wehmeier, Herman	54T	162	$2.00	$7.00
Wehmeier, Herman	55T	29	$1.35	$5.00
Wehmeier, Herman	56T	78	$1.25	$4.50
Wehmeier, Herm	57T	81	$ .95	$3.50
Wehmeier, Herm	58T	248	$ .50	$2.00
Wehmeier, Herm	59T	421	$ .50	$1.95
Wehrmeister, Dave	77T	472	$ .03	$ .12
Wehrmeister, Dave	82T	694	$ .01	$ .06
Weik, Dick	54T	224	$2.00	$7.00
Weis, Al	63T	537	$150.00	$450.00
Weis, Al	64T	168	$ .25	$ .85
Weis, Al	65T	516	$ .50	$2.00
Weis, Al	66T	66	$ .25	$ .85
Weis, Al	67T	556	$1.25	$3.50
Weis, Al	68T	313	$ .25	$ .65
Weis, Al	69T	269	$ .25	$ .85
Weis, Al	70T	498	$ .10	$ .35
Weis, Al	71T	751	$ .60	$1.75
Weiss, Walt	88TBB	263	$ .10	$ .45
Weiss, Walt	88TTR	126	$ .01	$ .40
Weiss, Walt	89T	316	$ .10	$ .25
Weiss, Walt	89TBB	305	$ .01	$ .15
Weiss, Walt	90T	165	$ .01	$ .10
Welch, Bob	79T	318	$ .35	$1.10
Welch, Bob	80T	146	$ .05	$ .25
Welch, Bob	81T	624	$ .03	$ .15
Welch, Bob	82T	82	$ .01	$ .06
Welch, Bob	83T	454	$ .01	$ .10
Welch, Bob	84T	306	$ .01	$ .05
Welch, Bob	84T	722	$ .02	$ .10
Welch, Bob	85T	291	$ .01	$ .04
Welch, Bob	86T	549	$ .01	$ .03
Welch, Bob	87T	328	$ .01	$ .03
Welch, Bob	88T	118	$ .01	$ .03
Welch, Bob	88TTR	127	$ .01	$ .05
Welch, Bob	89T	605	$ .01	$ .04
Welch, Bob	90T	475	$ .01	$ .03
Wellman, Bob	52T	41	$14.00	$45.00
Wellman, Brad	84T	109	$ .01	$ .05
Wellman, Brad	85T	409	$ .01	$ .04
Wellman, Brad	86T	41	$ .01	$ .03
Wells, Boomer	82T	203	$ .70	$3.50
Wells, David	88TTR	128	$ .01	$ .10
Wells, David	89T	567	$ .01	$ .10
Wells, David	90T	229	$ .01	$ .03
Welsh, Chris	82T	376	$ .01	$ .06
Welsh, Chris	83T	118	$ .01	$ .06
Welsh, Chris	83TTR	125	$ .02	$ .10
Welsh, Chris	86T	52	$ .01	$ .03
Welsh, Chris	87T	592	$ .01	$ .03
Wenz, Fred	69T	628	$ .25	$ .85
Wenz, Fred	71T	92	$ .10	$ .35

Player	Year	No.	VG	EX/MT
Werhas, John	64T	456	$ .40	$1.25
Werhas, John	65T	453	$ .50	$2.00
Werhas, John	67T	514	$ .50	$2.00
Werle, William	51Trb	33	$1.25	$3.50
Werle, William	52T	73	$14.00	$45.00
Werle, Bill	53T	170	$3.75	$13.00
Werle, Bill	54T	144	$2.00	$7.00
Werner, Don	78T	702	$ .02	$ .10
Werner, Don	83T	504	$ .01	$ .06
Wert, Don	62T	299	$ .35	$1.10
Wert, Don	64T	19	$ .25	$ .85
Wert, Don	65T	271	$ .30	$1.00
Wert, Don	66T	253	$ .25	$ .85
Wert, Don	67T	511	$ .50	$2.00
Wert, Don	68T	178	$ .25	$ .65
Wert, Don	69T	443	$ .25	$ .65
Wert, Don	70T	33	$ .10	$ .35
Wert, Don	71T	307	$ .10	$ .35
Werth, Dennis	81T	424	$ .01	$ .07
Werth, Dennis	82T	154	$ .01	$ .06
Werth, Dennis	82TTR	126	$ .02	$ .10
Wertz, Vic	51Tbb	40	$4.00	$18.00

Player	Year	No.	VG	EX/MT
Wertz, Vic	52T	244	$5.50	$17.50
Wertz, Vic	53T	142	$3.75	$13.00
Wertz, Vic	56T	300	$1.30	$5.00
Wertz, Vic	57T	78	$ .60	$2.50
Wertz, Vic	58T	170	$ .65	$2.00
Wertz, Vic	59T	500	$ .50	$1.95
Wertz, Vic	60T	111	$ .60	$1.75
Wertz, Vic	61T	173	$ .50	$2.00
Wertz, Vic	61T	340	$ .30	$1.00
Wertz, Vic	62T	481	$ .70	$2.10
Wertz, Vic	63T	348	$ .50	$2.00
West, Dave	89T	787	$ .10	$ .50
West, Dave	90T	357	$ .01	$ .10
Westlake, Wally	51Trb	27	$1.25	$3.50
Westlake, Wally	52T	38	$12.50	$45.00
Westlake, Wally	53T	192	$3.75	$13.00
Westlake, Wally	54T	92	$2.00	$7.00
Westlake, Wally	55T	102	$1.35	$5.00
Westlake, Wally	56T	81	$1.25	$4.50
Weston, Mickey	89TMLD	137	$ .01	$ .25
Weston, Mickey	90T	377	$ .01	$ .10

Player	Year	No.	VG	EX/MT
Westrum, Wes	51Trb	37	$1.25	$3.50
Westrum, Wes	52T	75	$14.00	$45.00
Westrum, Wes	54T	180	$2.00	$7.00
Westrum, Wes	56T	156	$1.50	$4.00
Westrum, Wes	57T	323	$3.50	$13.00
Westrum, Wes	60T	469	$ .95	$3.50
Westrum, Wes	66T	341	$ .25	$ .85
Westrum, Wes	67T	593	$5.00	$15.00
Wetherby, Jeff	89TMLD	138	$ .01	$ .05
Wetherby, Jeff	90T	142	$ .01	$ .10
Wetteland, John	89TMLD	139	$ .01	$ .25
Wetteland, John	90T	631	$ .01	$ .15
Wheat, Leroy	54T	244	$2.00	$7.00
Wheelock, Gary	77T	493	$ .25	$ .80
Wheelock, Gary	78T	596	$ .02	$ .10
Whisenant, Pete	57T	373	$ .85	$3.50
Whisenant, Pete	58T	466	$ .50	$1.95
Whisenant, Pete	59T	14	$ .85	$3.50
Whisenant, Pete	60T	424	$ .50	$1.95
Whisenant, Pete	61T	201	$ .30	$1.00
Whisenton, Larry	79T	715	$ .05	$ .20
Whisenton, Larry	83T	544	$ .01	$ .06
Whitaker, Lou	78T	704	$3.00	$10.00
Whitaker, Lou	79T	123	$ .85	$2.50
Whitaker, Lou	80T	358	$ .45	$1.25
Whitaker, Lou	81T	234	$ .10	$ .50
Whitaker, Lou	82T	39	$ .05	$ .25
Whitaker, Lou	83T	509	$ .01	$ .20
Whitaker, Lou	84T	666	$ .02	$ .10
Whitaker, Lou	84T	695	$ .05	$ .25
Whitaker, Lou	84TAS	398	$ .02	$ .10
Whitaker, Lou	85T	480	$ .03	$ .15
Whitaker, Lou	86T	20	$ .01	$ .03
Whitaker, Lou	87T	661	$ .01	$ .10
Whitaker, Lou	88T	770	$ .01	$ .10
Whitaker, Lou	88TBB	99	$ .01	$ .10
Whitaker, Lou	89T	320	$ .01	$ .04
Whitaker, Lou	89TBB	22	$ .01	$ .10
Whitaker, Lou	90T	280	$ .01	$ .10
Whitaker, Steve	67T	277	$ .25	$ .65
Whitaker, Steve	68T	383	$ .25	$ .65
Whitaker, Steve	69T	71	$ .25	$ .65
Whitaker, Steve	70T	496	$ .10	$ .35
Whitby, Bill	67T	486	$ .50	$2.00
White Sox, Team	56T	188	$3.75	$12.50
White Sox, Team	57T	329	$5.00	$20.00
White Sox, Team	58T	256	$1.25	$5.00
White Sox, Team	59T	94	$3.00	$11.00
White Sox, Team	60T	208	$1.50	$6.00
White Sox, Team	61T	7	$ .85	$3.50
White Sox, Team	62T	113	$ .65	$1.75
White Sox, Team	63T	288	$1.25	$3.50
White Sox, Team	64T	496	$ .95	$3.50
White Sox, Team	65T	234	$ .60	$1.75
White Sox, Team	66T	426	$ .65	$1.75
White Sox, Team	67T	573	$5.00	$15.00
White Sox, Team	68T	424	$ .50	$2.00
White Sox, Team	70T	501	$ .35	$1.10
White Sox, Team	71T	289	$ .35	$1.10
White Sox, Team	72T	381	$ .15	$ .50
White Sox, Team	73T	481	$ .15	$ .50
White Sox, Team	74T	416	$ .15	$ .50
White Sox, Team Checklist	75T	276	$ .15	$ .50
White Sox, Team Checklist	76T	656	$ .30	$1.00
White Sox, Team Checklist	77T	418	$ .15	$ .50
White Sox, Team Checklist	78T	66	$ .05	$ .25
White Sox, Team Checklist	79T	404	$ .05	$ .25
White Sox, Team Checklist	80T	112	$ .05	$ .25
White Sox, Team Checklist	81T	664	$ .02	$ .20
White Sox, Team Leaders	86T	156	$ .01	$ .03
White Sox, Team Leaders	87T	356	$ .01	$ .03
White Sox, Team Leaders	88T	321	$ .01	$ .03
White Sox, Team Leaders	89T	21	$ .01	$ .04
White, Bill	59T	359	$5.00	$15.00
White, Bill	60T	355	$1.00	$4.00
White, Bill	61T	232	$ .50	$2.00
White, Bill	61T	451	$1.25	$3.50
White, Bill	62T	14	$ .35	$1.10
White, Bill	63T	1	$4.35	$22.00
White, Bill	63T	290	$ .35	$1.10
White, Bill	64T	11	$1.00	$4.00
White, Bill	64T	240	$ .35	$1.10
White, Bill	65T	190	$ .15	$ .50
White, Bill	66T	397	$ .30	$1.00
White, Bill	67T	290	$ .35	$1.10
White, Bill	68T	190	$ .15	$ .50
White, Bill	69T	588	$ .20	$ .50
White, Charlie	55T	103	$1.35	$5.00
White, Devon	87T	139	$ .30	$1.00
White, Devon	88T	192	$ .01	$ .25
White, Devon	88TBB	145	$ .01	$ .15
White, Devon	89T	602	$ .01	$ .15
White, Devon	89TBB	122	$ .01	$ .10
White, Devon	90T	65	$ .01	$ .03
White, Frank	74T	604	$1.00	$3.00
White, Frank	75T	569	$ .10	$ .35
White, Frank	76T	369	$ .05	$ .20
White, Frank	77T	117	$ .03	$ .12
White, Frank	78T	248	$ .02	$ .10
White, Frank	79T	439	$ .02	$ .10
White, Frank	80T	45	$ .01	$ .07
White, Frank	81T	330	$ .01	$ .07
White, Frank	82T	645	$ .01	$ .06
White, Frank	82TIA	646	$ .01	$ .06
White, Frank	83T	525	$ .01	$ .06
White, Frank	84T	155	$ .01	$ .05
White, Frank	85T	743	$ .01	$ .04
White, Frank	86T	215	$ .01	$ .03
White, Frank	87T	692	$ .01	$ .03
White, Frank	88T	595	$ .01	$ .03
White, Frank	88TBB	75	$ .01	$ .05
White, Frank	89T	25	$ .01	$ .04
White, Frank	89BB	200	$ .01	$ .05
White, Frank	90T	479	$ .01	$ .03
White, Jerry	76T	594	$ .05	$ .20
White, Jerry	77T	557	$ .03	$ .12
White, Jerry	79T	494	$ .02	$ .10
White, Jerry	80T	724	$ .01	$ .07
White, Jerry	81T	42	$ .01	$ .07
White, Jerry	82T	386	$ .01	$ .06
White, Jerry	83T	214	$ .01	$ .06
White, Jo-Jo	60T	460	$1.25	$4.50
White, Mike	64T	492	$ .40	$1.25
White, Mike	65T	31	$ .25	$ .65
White, Roy	66T	234	$1.50	$5.00
White, Roy	68T	546	$ .50	$2.00
White, Roy	69T	25	$ .15	$ .50
White, Roy	70T	373	$ .15	$ .50
White, Roy	71T	395	$ .15	$ .50
White, Roy	72T	340	$ .25	$ .85
White, Roy	73T	25	$ .10	$ .35
White, Roy	74T	135	$ .06	$ .25
White, Roy	75T	375	$ .10	$ .35
White, Roy	76T	225	$ .05	$ .20
White, Roy	77T	485	$ .03	$ .12
White, Roy	78T	16	$ .02	$ .10
White, Roy	79T	159	$ .02	$ .10
White, Roy	80T	648	$ .01	$ .07
White, Sam	52T	345	$39.00	$135.00
White, Sam	53T	139	$2.50	$8.00
White, Sammy	56T	168	$1.25	$4.50
White, Sammy	57T	163	$ .95	$3.50
White, Sammy	58T	414	$ .50	$2.00
White, Sammy	59T	486	$ .50	$1.95
White, Sammy	60T	203	$ .35	$1.10
White, Sammy	62T	494	$ .70	$2.10
Whited, Ed	89TMLD	140	$ .01	$ .05
Whited, Ed	90T	111	$ .01	$ .03
Whitehouse, Len	83TTR	126	$ .02	$ .10
Whitehouse, Len	84T	648	$ .01	$ .05

TOPPS

Player	Year	No.	VG	EX/MT	Player	Year	No.	VG	EX/MT
Whitehouse, Len	85T	406	$ .01	$ .04	Wight, Bill	56T	286	$2.25	$6.50
Whitehurst, Wally	89TMLD	141	$ .01	$ .15	Wight, Bill	57T	340	$3.50	$13.00
Whitehurst, Wally	90T	719	$ .01	$ .10	Wight, Bill	58T	237	$ .50	$2.00
Whitfield, Fred	63T	211	$ .25	$ .85	Wihtol, Sandy	80T	665	$ .01	$ .07
Whitfield, Fred	64T	367	$ .25	$ .85	Wihtol, Sandy	81T	451	$ .01	$ .07
Whitfield, Fred	65T	283	$ .30	$1.00	Wilber, Del	52T	383	$39.00	$135.00
Whitfield, Fred	66T	88	$ .25	$ .85	Wilborn, Ted	80T	674	$ .01	$ .07
Whitfield, Fred	67T	275	$ .25	$ .65	Wilcox, Milt	71T	164	$ .25	$ .85
Whitfield, Fred	68T	133	$ .25	$ .65	Wilcox, Milt	72T	399	$ .05	$ .25
Whitfield, Fred	69T	518	$ .25	$ .85	Wilcox, Milt	73T	134	$ .06	$ .25
Whitfield, Terry	75T	622	$2.25	$11.00	Wilcox, Milt	74T	565	$ .06	$ .25
Whitfield, Terry	76T	590	$ .15	$ .50	Wilcox, Milt	75T	14	$ .06	$ .25
Whitfield, Terry	78T	236	$ .02	$ .10	Wilcox, Milt	78T	151	$ .02	$ .10
Whitfield, Terry	79T	589	$ .02	$ .10	Wilcox, Milt	79T	288	$ .02	$ .10
Whitfield, Terry	80T	713	$ .01	$ .07	Wilcox, Milt	80T	392	$ .01	$ .07
Whitfield, Terry	81T	167	$ .01	$ .07	Wilcox, Milt	81T	658	$ .01	$ .07
Whitfield, Terry	85T	31	$ .01	$ .04	Wilcox, Milt	82T	784	$ .01	$ .06
Whitfield, Terry	86T	318	$ .01	$ .03	Wilcox, Milt	83T	457	$ .01	$ .06
Whitson, Eddie	79T	189	$ .08	$ .30	Wilcox, Milt	84T	588	$ .01	$ .05
Whitson, Eddie	80T	561	$ .01	$ .07	Wilcox, Milt	85T	99	$ .01	$ .04
Whitson, Eddie	81T	336	$ .01	$ .07	Wilcox, Milt	86T	192	$ .01	$ .03
Whitson, Eddie	82T	656	$ .01	$ .06	Wilfong, Rob	79T	633	$ .02	$ .10
Whitson, Eddie	82TTR	127	$ .02	$ .10	Wilfong, Rob	80T	238	$ .01	$ .07
Whitson, Eddie	83T	429	$ .01	$ .06	Wilfong, Rob	81T	453	$ .01	$ .07
Whitson, Eddie	83TTR	127	$ .02	$ .10	Wilfong, Rob	82T	379	$ .01	$ .06
Whitson, Eddie	84T	277	$ .01	$ .05	Wilfong, Rob	82TTR	128	$ .02	$ .10
Whitson, Eddie	85T	762	$ .01	$ .04	Wilfong, Rob	83T	158	$ .01	$ .06
Whitson, Eddie	85TTR	130	$ .02	$ .10	Wilfong, Rob	84T	79	$ .01	$ .05
Whitson, Eddie	86T	15	$ .01	$ .03	Wilfong, Rob	85T	524	$ .01	$ .04
Whitson, Eddie	87T	155	$ .01	$ .03	Wilfong, Rob	86T	658	$ .01	$ .03
Whitson, Eddie	88T	330	$ .01	$ .03	Wilfong, Rob	87T	251	$ .01	$ .03
Whitson, Eddie	88TBB	186	$ .01	$ .05	Wilhelm, Hoyt	52T	392	$135.00	$400.00
Whitson, Eddie	89T	516	$ .01	$ .04	Wilhelm, Hoyt	53T	151	$15.00	$42.50
Whitson, Eddie	89TBB	81	$ .01	$ .05	Wilhelm, Hoyt	54T	36	$12.00	$35.00
Whitson, Eddie	90T	618	$ .01	$ .03	Wilhelm, Hoyt	56T	307	$7.50	$22.50
Whitt, Ernie	78T	708	$7.00	$25.00	Wilhelm, Hoyt	57T	203	$5.50	$17.50
Whitt, Ernie	79T	714	$ .02	$ .10	Wilhelm, Hoyt	58T	324	$3.00	$10.00
Whitt, Ernie	81T	407	$ .01	$ .07	Wilhelm, Hoyt	59T	349	$4.00	$12.50
Whitt, Ernie	82T	19	$ .01	$ .06	Wilhelm, Hoyt	60T	115	$ .70	$2.00
Whitt, Ernie	83T	302	$ .01	$ .06	Wilhelm, Hoyt	60T	395	$2.25	$6.50
Whitt, Ernie	84T	506	$ .01	$ .05	Wilhelm, Hoyt	61T	545	$14.00	$40.00
Whitt, Ernie	85T	128	$ .01	$ .04	Wilhelm, Hoyt	62T	423	$1.25	$3.50
Whitt, Ernie	86T	673	$ .01	$ .03	Wilhelm, Hoyt	62T	545	$15.00	$50.00
Whitt, Ernie	87T	698	$ .01	$ .03	Wilhelm, Hoyt	63T	108	$2.75	$8.50
Whitt, Ernie	88T	79	$ .01	$ .03	Wilhelm, Hoyt	64T	13	$2.00	$8.00
Whitt, Ernie	88TBB	239	$ .01	$ .05	Wilhelm, Hoyt	65T	276	$2.00	$6.00
Whitt, Ernie	89T	289	$ .01	$ .04	Wilhelm, Hoyt	66T	510	$5.00	$15.00
Whitt, Ernie	89TBB	224	$ .01	$ .05	Wilhelm, Hoyt	67T	422	$3.00	$9.00
Whitt, Ernie	90T	742	$ .01	$ .03	Wilhelm, Hoyt	68T	350	$1.35	$4.00
Wickander, Kevin	89TMLD	142	$ .01	$ .10	Wilhelm, Hoyt	69T	565	$1.50	$6.00
Wickander, Kevin	90T	528	$ .01	$ .10	Wilhelm, Hoyt	70T	17	$1.75	$7.00
Wicker, Floyd	69T	524	$ .25	$ .85	Wilhelm, Hoyt	71T	248	$1.25	$4.50
Wicker, Floyd	71T	97	$ .10	$ .35	Wilhelm, Hoyt	72T	777	$3.00	$9.00
Wickersham, Dave	61T	381	$ .50	$2.00	Wilhelm, Jim	80T	685	$ .01	$ .07
Wickersham, Dave	62T	517	$ .70	$2.10	Wilkerson, Curt	84TTR	127	$ .02	$ .10
Wickersham, Dave	63T	492	$2.50	$6.50	Wilkerson, Curt	85T	594	$ .01	$ .04
Wickersham, Dave	64T	181	$ .25	$ .85	Wilkerson, Curt	86T	434	$ .01	$ .03
Wickersham, Dave	65T	9	$ .30	$1.00	Wilkerson, Curt	87T	228	$ .01	$ .03
Wickersham, Dave	65T	375	$ .30	$1.00	Wilkerson, Curt	88T	53	$ .01	$ .03
Wickersham, Dave	66T	58	$ .25	$ .85	Wilkerson, Curt	88TBB	132	$ .01	$ .05
Wickersham, Dave	67T	112	$ .25	$ .65	Wilkerson, Curt	89T	331	$ .01	$ .04
Wickersham, Dave	68T	288	$ .25	$ .65	Wilkerson, Curt	89TTR	126	$ .01	$ .05
Wickersham, Dave	69T	647	$ .25	$ .85	Wilkerson, Curt	90T	667	$ .01	$ .03
Widmar, Al	52T	133	$6.00	$19.00	Wilkins, Dean	89TMLD	143	$ .01	$ .05
Widmar, Al	74T	99	$ .06	$ .25	Wilkins, Eric	80T	511	$ .01	$ .07
Wieand, Ted	60T	146	$ .35	$1.10	Wilkins, Eric	81T	99	$ .01	$ .07
Wiesler, Bob	56T	327	$1.30	$5.00	Wilkinson, Bill	87TTR	127	$ .01	$ .07
Wiesler, Bob	57T	126	$ .95	$3.50	Wilkinson, Bill	88T	376	$ .01	$ .03
Wietelmann, Whitey	73T	12	$ .25	$ .65	Wilkinson, Bill	89T	636	$ .01	$ .04
Wiggins, Alan	83T	251	$ .01	$ .06	Wilks, Ted	52T	109	$6.00	$19.00
Wiggins, Alan	84T	693	$ .01	$ .05	Wilks, Ted	53T	101	$3.75	$13.00
Wiggins, Alan	85T	378	$ .01	$ .04	Will, Bob	59T	388	$ .50	$1.95
Wiggins, Alan	86T	508	$ .01	$ .03	Will, Bob	60T	147	$ .35	$1.10
Wiggins, Alan	87TTR	126	$ .01	$ .07	Will, Bob	61T	512	$ .50	$2.00
Wight, Bill	52T	177	$6.00	$19.00	Will, Bob	62T	47	$ .35	$1.10

Player	Year	No.	VG	EX/MT
Will, Bob	63T	58	$ .25	$ .85
Willard, Jerry	85T	504	$ .01	$ .04
Willard, Jerry	86T	273	$ .01	$ .03
Willard, Jerry	87T	137	$ .01	$ .03
Willey, 'Carlton" (Carl)	58T	407	$ .50	$2.00
Willey, Carl	59T	95	$ .85	$3.50
Willey, Carl	60T	107	$ .35	$1.10
Willey, Carl	61T	105	$ .30	$1.00
Willey, Carl	62T	174	$ .60	$1.75
Willey, Carl	63T	528	$1.50	$3.75
Willey, Carl	64T	84	$ .25	$ .85
Willey, Carl	65T	401	$ .30	$1.00
Willhite, Nick	64T	14	$ .25	$ .85
Willhite, Nick	65T	284	$ .30	$1.00
Willhite, Nick	66T	171	$ .25	$ .85
Willhite, Nick	67T	249	$ .25	$ .65
Williams, Al	81T	569	$ .01	$ .07
Williams, Al	82T	69	$ .01	$ .06
Williams, Al	83T	731	$ .01	$ .06
Williams, Al	84T	183	$ .01	$ .05

Player	Year	No.	VG	EX/MT
Williams, Al	85T	614	$ .01	$ .04
Williams, Bernie	70T	401	$ .10	$ .35
Williams, Bernie	71T	728	$ .70	$2.10
Williams, Bernie	72T	761	$4.00	$12.00
Williams, Bernie	73T	557	$ .35	$1.10
Williams, Bernie	90T	701	$ .01	$ .25
Williams, Billy	61T	141	$17.50	$65.00
Williams, Billy	62T	288	$6.00	$18.00
Williams, Billy	63T	353	$6.00	$18.00
Williams, Billy	64T	175	$3.00	$9.00
Williams, Billy	65T	4	$1.50	$3.75
Williams, Billy	65T	220	$3.00	$9.00
Williams, Billy	66T	217	$1.25	$3.50
Williams, Billy	66T	580	$18.00	$55.00
Williams, Billy	67T	315	$2.00	$7.00
Williams, Billy	68T	37	$1.40	$4.00
Williams, Billy	69T	4	$ .70	$2.00
Williams, Billy	69T	450	$1.15	$3.25
Williams, Billy	70T	170	$1.25	$3.50
Williams, Billy	71T	64	$ .60	$1.75
Williams, Billy	71T	66	$ .60	$1.75
Williams, Billy	71T	350	$1.30	$5.00
Williams, Billy	72T	439	$ .95	$3.50

Player	Year	No.	VG	EX/MT
Williams, Billy	72TIA	440	$ .30	$1.00
Williams, Billy	73T	61	$ .50	$2.00
Williams, Billy	73T	200	$ .70	$2.00
Williams, Billy	74T	110	$ .95	$3.50
Williams, Billy	74TAS	338	$ .35	$1.10
Williams, Billy	75T	545	$1.00	$4.00
Williams, Billy	76T	525	$ .75	$3.00
Williams, Charlie	72T	388	$ .05	$ .25
Williams, Charlie	75T	449	$ .06	$ .25
Williams, Charlie	76T	332	$ .05	$ .20
Williams, Charlie	77T	73	$ .03	$ .12
Williams, Charlie	78T	561	$ .02	$ .10
Williams, Charlie	79T	142	$ .02	$ .10
Williams, Dana	89TMLD	144	$ .01	$ .05
Williams, Davey	52T	316	$39.00	$135.00
Williams, Davey	53T	120	$3.75	$13.00
Williams, Dick	52T	396	$70.00	$200.00
Williams, Dick	53T	125	$4.00	$13.00
Williams, Dick	57T	59	$ .60	$2.50
Williams, Dick	58T	79	$ .70	$2.25
Williams, Dick	59T	292	$ .50	$1.95
Williams, Dick	60T	188	$ .50	$2.00
Williams, Dick	61T	8	$ .50	$2.00
Williams, Dick	62T	382	$ .85	$3.50
Williams, Dick	63T	328	$ .35	$1.10
Williams, Dick	64T	153	$ .15	$ .50
Williams, Dick	67T	161	$ .30	$1.00
Williams, Dick	68T	87	$ .15	$ .50
Williams, Dick	69T	349	$ .25	$ .85
Williams, Dick	71T	714	$ .85	$3.50
Williams, Dick	72T	137	$ .25	$ .65
Williams, Dick	73T	179	$ .25	$ .85
Williams, Dick	78T	522	$ .02	$ .10
Williams, Dick	83T	366	$ .01	$ .06
Williams, Dick	84T	742	$ .01	$ .05
Williams, Dick	85T	66	$ .01	$ .04
Williams, Dick	86T	681	$ .01	$ .03
Williams, Dick	86TTR	124	$ .02	$ .10
Williams, Dick	87T	418	$ .01	$ .03
Williams, Dick	88T	104	$ .01	$ .03
Williams, Don	60T	414	$ .50	$1.95
Williams, Earl	71T	52	$ .10	$ .35
Williams, Earl	72T	380	$ .05	$ .25
Williams, Earl	73T	504	$ .06	$ .25
Williams, Earl	74T	375	$ .06	$ .25
Williams, Earl	75T	97	$ .06	$ .25
Williams, Earl	76T	458	$ .05	$ .20
Williams, Earl	77T	223	$ .03	$ .12
Williams, Earl	78T	604	$ .02	$ .10
Williams, Eddie	88T	758	$ .01	$ .25
Williams, Eddie	89TTR	127	$ .01	$ .05
Williams, Frank	84TTR	128	$ .05	$ .20
Williams, Frank	85T	487	$ .01	$ .04
Williams, Frank	86T	341	$ .01	$ .03
Williams, Frank	87T	96	$ .01	$ .03
Williams, Frank	87TTR	128	$ .01	$ .07
Williams, Frank	88T	773	$ .01	$ .03
Williams, Frank	89T	172	$ .01	$ .04
Williams, Frank	89TTR	128	$ .01	$ .05
Williams, Frank	90T	599	$ .01	$ .03
Williams, George	63T	324	$ .35	$1.20
Williams, George	64T	388	$ .40	$1.25
Williams, Jim A.	70T	262	$ .10	$ .35
Williams, Jim A.	71T	262	$ .10	$ .35
Williams, Jimmy F.	66T	544	$4.00	$11.50
Williams, Jimy	87T	786	$ .01	$ .03
Williams, Jimy	88T	314	$ .01	$ .03
Williams, Jimy	89T	594	$ .01	$ .04
Williams, Ken	88T	559	$ .01	$ .03
Williams, Ken	89T	34	$ .01	$ .04
Williams, Ken	89TTR	129	$ .01	$ .05
Williams, Ken	90T	327	$ .01	$ .03
Williams, Matt	87TTR	129	$ .12	$1.50
Williams, Matt	88T	372	$ .01	$ .75
Williams, Matt	89T	628	$ .01	$ .04

TOPPS

Player	Year	No.	VG	EX/MT
Williams, Matt	90T	41	$ .01	$ .10
Williams, Mitch	86TTR	125	$ .05	$ .50
Williams, Mitch	87T	291	$ .06	$ .35
Williams, Mitch	88T	26	$ .01	$ .10
Williams, Mitch	89T	411	$ .01	$ .10
Williams, Mitch	89TTR	130	$ .01	$ .15
Williams, Mitch	90T	520	$ .01	$ .03
Williams, Reggie	87T	232	$ .01	$ .03
Williams, Rick	79T	437	$ .02	$ .10
Williams, Rick	80T	69	$ .01	$ .07
Williams, Stan	59T	53	$ .85	$3.50
Williams, Stan	60T	278	$ .35	$1.10
Williams, Stan	61T	45	$ .60	$1.75
Williams, Stan	61T	190	$ .30	$1.00
Williams, Stan	62T	60	$ .65	$1.75
Williams, Stan	62T	515	$ .70	$2.10
Williams, Stan	63T	42	$ .30	$1.00
Williams, Stan	64T	505	$ .50	$1.95
Williams, Stan	65T	404	$ .30	$1.00
Williams, Stan	68T	54	$ .25	$ .65
Williams, Stan	69T	118	$ .25	$ .65
Williams, Stan	70T	353	$ .10	$ .35
Williams, Stan	71T	638	$ .30	$1.00
Williams, Stan	72T	9	$ .05	$ .25
Williams, Ted	54T	1	$125.00	$500.00
Williams, Ted	54T	250	$165.00	$550.00
Williams, Ted	55T	2	$100.00	$300.00
Williams, Ted	56T	5	$70.00	$200.00
Williams, Ted	57T	1	$90.00	$350.00
Williams, Ted	58T	1	$85.00	$325.00
Williams, Ted	58T	321	$7.00	$30.00
Williams, Ted	58TAS	485	$10.00	$40.00
Williams, Ted	69T	539	$1.25	$4.50
Williams, Ted	69T	650	$2.50	$8.00
Williams, Ted	70T	211	$1.50	$4.00
Williams, Ted	71T	380	$1.25	$3.50
Williams, Ted	72T	510	$1.25	$3.50
Williams, Ted	76TAS	347	$ .70	$2.00
Williams, Walt	67T	598	$2.00	$6.00
Williams, Walt	68T	172	$ .25	$ .65
Williams, Walt	69T	309	$ .25	$ .85
Williams, Walt	70T	395	$ .10	$ .35
Williams, Walt	71T	555	$ .30	$1.00
Williams, Walt	72T	15	$ .05	$ .25
Williams, Walt	73T	297	$ .06	$ .25
Williams, Walt	74T	418	$ .06	$ .25
Williams, Walt	76T	123	$ .05	$ .20
Williamson, Mark	88T	571	$ .01	$ .03
Williamson, Mark	89T	546	$ .01	$ .04
Williamson, Mark	89TBB	147	$ .01	$ .05
Williamson, Mark	90T	13	$ .01	$ .03
Willis, Carl	87T	101	$ .01	$ .03
Willis, Jim	54T	67	$4.75	$14.00
Willis, Mike	77T	493	$ .25	$ .80
Willis, Mike	78T	293	$ .02	$ .10
Willis, Mike	79T	688	$ .02	$ .10
Willis, Mike	81T	324	$ .01	$ .07
Willis, Ron	67T	592	$5.00	$15.00
Willis, Ron	68T	68	$ .25	$ .65
Willis, Ron	69T	273	$ .25	$ .85
Willoughby, Jim	73T	79	$ .06	$ .25
Willoughby, Jim	74T	553	$ .06	$ .25
Willoughby, Jim	76T	102	$ .05	$ .20
Willoughby, Jim	77T	532	$ .03	$ .12
Willoughby, Jim	78T	373	$ .02	$ .10
Willoughby, Jim	79T	266	$ .02	$ .10
Wills, Bump	77T	494	$ .12	$ .40
Wills, Bump	78T	23	$ .02	$ .10
Wills, Bump	79T	369	$ .75	$3.00
Wills, Bump	80T	473	$ .01	$ .07
Wills, Bump	81T	173	$ .01	$ .07
Wills, Bump	82T	272	$ .01	$ .06
Wills, Bump	82TTR	129	$ .02	$ .10
Wills, Bump	83T	643	$ .01	$ .06
Wills, Frank	86T	419	$ .01	$ .03
Wills, Frank	87T	551	$ .01	$ .03
Wills, Maury	67T	570	$30.00	$80.00
Wills, Maury	68T	175	$ .70	$2.00
Wills, Maury	69T	45	$ .60	$1.75
Wills, Maury	70T	595	$ .50	$2.00
Wills, Maury	71T	385	$ .50	$2.00
Wills, Maury	72T	437	$ .15	$ .50
Wills, Maury	72TIA	438	$ .07	$ .25
Wills, Maury	75T	200	$1.25	$4.00
Wills, Maury	77TB	435	$ .25	$ .65
Wills, Maury	87TTB	315	$ .01	$ .03
Wills, Ted	61T	548	$6.00	$18.00
Wills, Ted	62T	444	$ .70	$2.10
Wills, Ted	65T	488	$ .50	$2.00
Wilmet, Paul	89TMLD	145	$ .01	$ .05
Wilson, Archie	52T	327	$39.00	$135.00
Wilson, Bill D.	54T	222	$2.00	$7.00
Wilson, Bill D.	55T	86	$1.35	$5.00
Wilson, Billy H.	67T	402	$ .25	$ .85
Wilson, Billy H.	69T	576	$ .25	$ .85
Wilson, Billy H.	70T	28	$ .10	$ .35
Wilson, Billy H.	71T	192	$ .10	$ .35
Wilson, Billy H.	72T	587	$ .25	$ .85
Wilson, Billy H.	73T	619	$ .35	$1.10
Wilson, Bob	53T	250	$11.00	$37.50
Wilson, Bob	54T	58	$4.75	$14.00
Wilson, Bob "Red"	56T	92	$1.25	$4.50
Wilson, Bob	57T	19	$ .95	$3.50
Wilson, Bob "Red"	58T	213	$ .50	$2.00
Wilson, Bob "Red"	59T	24	$ .85	$3.50
Wilson, Bob "Red"	60T	379	$ .50	$1.95
Wilson, Craig	89TMLD	146	$ .01	$ .15
Wilson, Don	68T	77	$ .15	$ .50
Wilson, Don	69T	202	$ .25	$ .65
Wilson, Don	70T	515	$ .10	$ .35
Wilson, Don	71T	484	$ .10	$ .35
Wilson, Don	72T	20	$ .05	$ .25
Wilson, Don	72T	91	$ .35	$1.10
Wilson, Don	73T	217	$ .06	$ .25
Wilson, Don	74T	304	$ .06	$ .25
Wilson, Don	75T	455	$ .06	$ .25
Wilson, Earl	60T	249	$ .35	$1.10
Wilson, Earl	61T	69	$ .30	$1.00
Wilson, Earl	63T	76	$ .25	$ .85
Wilson, Earl	64T	503	$ .40	$1.25
Wilson, Earl	65T	42	$ .25	$ .65
Wilson, Earl	66T	575	$4.50	$15.00
Wilson, Earl	67T	235	$ .35	$1.10
Wilson, Earl	67T	237	$ .35	$1.10
Wilson, Earl	67T	305	$ .25	$ .65
Wilson, Earl	68T	10	$ .35	$1.10
Wilson, Earl	68T	160	$ .25	$ .65
Wilson, Earl	69T	525	$ .25	$ .85
Wilson, Earl	70T	95	$ .10	$ .35
Wilson, Earl	71T	301	$ .10	$ .35
Wilson, Glenn	83T	332	$ .10	$ .45
Wilson, Glenn	84T	563	$ .03	$ .15
Wilson, Glenn	84TTR	129	$ .05	$ .20
Wilson, Glenn	85T	454	$ .01	$ .04
Wilson, Glenn	86T	736	$ .01	$ .03
Wilson, Glenn	87T	97	$ .01	$ .03
Wilson, Glenn	88T	626	$ .01	$ .03
Wilson, Glenn	88TBB	260	$ .01	$ .05
Wilson, Glenn	88TTR	129	$ .01	$ .05
Wilson, Glenn	89T	293	$ .01	$ .04
Wilson, Glenn	89TBB	284	$ .01	$ .05
Wilson, Glenn	90T	112	$ .01	$ .03
Wilson, Hack	79TRH	412	$ .15	$ .50
Wilson, Jim	52T	276	$11.50	$38.00
Wilson, Jim	53T	208	$1.75	$6.00
Wilson, Jim	56T	171	$1.25	$4.50
Wilson, Jim	57T	330	$3.50	$13.00
Wilson, Jim	58T	163	$ .01	$2.00
Wilson, Mookie	81T	259	$ .50	$1.50
Wilson, Mookie	82T	143	$ .01	$ .06

MOOKIE WILSON
OUTFIELD
METS

Player	Year	No.	VG	EX/MT
Wilson, Mookie	83T	55	$ .01	$ .06
Wilson, Mookie	83T	621	$ .01	$ .06
Wilson, Mookie	84T	246	$ .01	$ .05
Wilson, Mookie	84T	465	$ .01	$ .05
Wilson, Mookie	85T	775	$ .01	$ .04
Wilson, Mookie	86T	315	$ .01	$ .03
Wilson, Mookie	87T	625	$ .01	$ .03
Wilson, Mookie	88T	255	$ .01	$ .03
Wilson, Mookie	88TBB	182	$ .01	$ .05
Wilson, Mookie	89T	545	$ .01	$ .04
Wilson, Mookie	89TBB	231	$ .01	$ .05
Wilson, Mookie	90T	182	$ .01	$ .03
Wilson, Steve	89TTR	131	$ .01	$ .15
Wilson, Steve	90T	741	$ .01	$ .03
Wilson, Trevor	89T	783	$ .01	$ .04
Wilson, Trevor	90T	408	$ .01	$ .03
Wilson, Willie	79T	409	$ .35	$1.10
Wilson, Willie	80T	157	$ .03	$ .15
Wilson, Willie	80T	204	$ .02	$ .10
Wilson, Willie	81T	360	$ .05	$ .25
Wilson, Willie	81TRB	208	$ .01	$ .07
Wilson, Willie	82T	230	$ .03	$ .15
Wilson, Willie	83T	471	$ .01	$ .06
Wilson, Willie	83T	701	$ .01	$ .06
Wilson, Willie	83T	710	$ .01	$ .06
Wilson, Willie	84T	525	$ .05	$ .10
Wilson, Willie	85T	617	$ .01	$ .04
Wilson, Willie	86T	25	$ .01	$ .03
Wilson, Willie	87T	783	$ .01	$ .10
Wilson, Willie	88T	452	$ .01	$ .03
Wilson, Willie	88TBB	21	$ .01	$ .05
Wilson, Willie	89T	168	$ .01	$ .04
Wilson, Willie	89TBB	136	$ .01	$ .05
Wilson, Willie	90T	323	$ .01	$ .03
Wiltbank, Ben	79T	723	$ .05	$ .20
Windhorn, Gordon	62T	254	$ .35	$1.10
Wine, Bobby	63T	71	$ .25	$ .85
Wine, Bobby	64T	347	$ .25	$ .85
Wine, Bobby	65T	36	$ .25	$ .65
Wine, Bobby	66T	284	$ .25	$ .85
Wine, Bobby	67T	466	$ .50	$2.00
Wine, Bobby	68T	396	$ .25	$ .65
Wine, Bobby	69T	648	$ .25	$ .85

Player	Year	No.	VG	EX/MT
Wine, Bobby	70T	332	$ .10	$ .35
Wine, Bobby	71T	171	$ .10	$ .35
Wine, Bobby	72T	657	$ .70	$2.10
Wine, Bobby	73T	486	$ .25	$ .85
Wine, Bobby	74T	119	$ .06	$ .25
Wine, Bobby	86T	51	$ .01	$ .03
Wine, Robbie	88T	119	$ .01	$ .10
Winfield, Dave	74T	456	$13.00	$40.00
Winfield, Dave	75T	61	$4.00	$12.00
Winfield, Dave	76T	160	$1.50	$5.00
Winfield, Dave	77T	390	$1.00	$4.00
Winfield, Dave	78T	530	$ .70	$2.00
Winfield, Dave	79T	30	$ .50	$2.00
Winfield, Dave	80T	203	$ .08	$ .30
Winfield, Dave	80T	230	$ .50	$2.00
Winfield, Dave	81T	370	$ .35	$1.10
Winfield, Dave	81TTR	855	$ .30	$1.25
Winfield, Dave	82T	600	$ .25	$ .65
Winfield, Dave	82TAS	553	$ .06	$ .30
Winfield, Dave	83T	770	$ .10	$ .40
Winfield, Dave	84T	460	$ .08	$ .35
Winfield, Dave	84TAS	402	$ .05	$ .25
Winfield, Dave	85T	180	$ .05	$ .25
Winfield, Dave	85TAS	705	$ .03	$ .15
Winfield, Dave	86T	70	$ .03	$ .25
Winfield, Dave	86TAS	717	$ .02	$ .15
Winfield, Dave	87T	770	$ .10	$ .35
Winfield, Dave	88T	510	$ .01	$ .20
Winfield, Dave	88TAS	392	$ .01	$ .10
Winfield, Dave	88TBB	24	$ .05	$ .25
Winfield, Dave	89T	260	$ .01	$ .10
Winfield, Dave	89TAS	407	$ .01	$ .04
Winfield, Dave	89TBB	314	$ .01	$ .15
Winfield, Dave	90T	380	$ .01	$ .10
Winkles, Bobby	73T	421	$ .06	$ .25
Winkles, Bobby	74T	276	$ .06	$ .25
Winkles, Bobby	78T	378	$ .02	$ .10
Winn, Jim	85T	69	$ .01	$ .04
Winn, Jim	86T	489	$ .01	$ .03
Winn, Jim	87T	262	$ .01	$ .03
Winn, Jim	87TTR	130	$ .01	$ .07
Winn, Jim	88T	688	$ .01	$ .03
Winningham, Herm	85TTR	131	$ .05	$ .20
Winningham, Herm	86T	448	$ .01	$ .03
Winningham, Herm	87T	141	$ .01	$ .03
Winningham, Herm	88T	614	$ .01	$ .03
Winningham, Herm	89T	366	$ .01	$ .04
Winningham, Herm	89TBB	94	$ .01	$ .05
Winningham, Herm	90T	94	$ .01	$ .03
Winters, Matt	89TMLD	147	$ .01	$ .05
Wirth, Alan	79T	711	₵ .08	$ .30
Wise, Casey	57T	396	$ .85	$3.50
Wise, Casey	58T	247	$ .50	$2.00
Wise, Casey	59T	204	$ .50	$1.95
Wise, Casey	60T	342	$ .50	$1.95
Wise, Rick	64T	561	$1.35	$4.00
Wise, Rick	65T	322	$ .30	$1.00
Wise, Rick	67T	37	$ .25	$ .65
Wise, Rick	68T	262	$ .25	$ .65
Wise, Rick	69T	188	$ .25	$ .65
Wise, Rick	70T	605	$ .25	$ .85
Wise, Rick	71T	598	$ .30	$1.00
Wise, Rick	72T	43	$ .05	$ .25
Wise, Rick	72T	345	$ .05	$ .25
Wise, Rick	72TIA	44	$ .05	$ .25
Wise, Rick	72TTR	756	$ .70	$2.00
Wise, Rick	73T	364	$ .06	$ .25
Wise, Rick	74T	84	$ .06	$ .25
Wise, Rick	74TAS	339	$ .25	$ .85
Wise, Rick	75T	56	$ .06	$ .25
Wise, Rick	76T	170	$ .05	$ .20
Wise, Rick	77T	455	$ .03	$ .12
Wise, Rick	78T	572	$ .02	$ .10
Wise, Rick	79T	253	$ .02	$ .10
Wise, Rick	80T	725	$ .01	$ .07

Player	Year	No.	VG	EX/MT	Player	Year	No.	VG	EX/MT
Wise, Rick	81T	616	$ .01	$ .07	Wood, Wilbur	70T	342	$ .10	$ .35
Wise, Rick	82T	330	$ .01	$ .06	Wood, Wilbur	71T	436	$ .10	$ .35
Witt, Bobby	86TTR	126	$ .08	$ .30	Wood, Wilbur	72T	92	$ .65	$2.25
Witt, Bobby	87T	415	$ .10	$ .35	Wood, Wilbur	72T	94	$ .40	$1.50
Witt, Bobby	88T	747	$ .01	$ .10	Wood, Wilbur	72T	342	$ .05	$ .25
Witt, Bobby	89T	548	$ .01	$ .04	Wood, Wilbur	72T	553	$ .35	$1.10
Witt, Bobby	89TBB	191	$ .01	$ .05	Wood, Wilbur	72TIA	554	$ .25	$ .85
Witt, Bobby	90T	166	$ .01	$ .03	Wood, Wilbur	73T	66	$ .35	$1.10
Witt, George	59T	110	$ .85	$3.50	Wood, Wilbur	73T	150	$ .10	$ .35
Witt, George	60T	298	$ .50	$1.95	Wood, Wilbur	74T	120	$ .06	$ .25
Witt, George	61T	286	$ .30	$1.00	Wood, Wilbur	74T	205	$ .06	$ .25
Witt, George	62T	287	$ .35	$1.10	Wood, Wilbur	75T	110	$ .06	$ .25
Witt, Mike	82T	744	$ .50	$2.00	Wood, Wilbur	76T	368	$ .05	$ .20
Witt, Mike	83T	53	$ .05	$ .20	Wood, Wilbur	77T	198	$ .03	$ .12
Witt, Mike	83T	651	$ .01	$ .06	Wood, Wilbur	78T	726	$ .05	$ .20
Witt, Mike	84T	499	$ .01	$ .05	Wood, Wilbur	79T	216	$ .02	$ .10
Witt, Mike	85T	309	$ .01	$ .04	Woodard, Mike	87T	286	$ .01	$ .03
Witt, Mike	87T	760	$ .03	$ .15	Woodeshick, Hal	59T	106	$ .85	$3.50
Witt, Mike	88T	270	$ .01	$ .10	Woodeshick, Hal	60T	454	$ .60	$1.75
Witt, Mike	88TBB	4	$ .01	$ .05	Woodeshick, Hal	61T	397	$ .50	$2.00
Witt, Mike	89T	190	$ .01	$ .04	Woodeshick, Hal	62T	526	$3.75	$11.00
Witt, Mike	90T	650	$ .01	$ .03	Woodeshick, Hal	63T	517	$1.50	$3.75
Wockenfuss, Johnny	76T	13	$ .05	$ .20	Woodeshick, Hal	64T	370	$ .25	$ .85
Wockenfuss, Johnny	78T	723	$ .02	$ .10	Woodeshick, Hal	65T	179	$ .25	$ .65
Wockenfuss, Johnny	79T	231	$ .02	$ .10	Woodeshick, Hal	66T	514	$ .70	$2.10
Wockenfuss, Johnny	80T	338	$ .01	$ .07	Woodeshick, Hal	67T	324	$ .25	$ .65
Wockenfuss, Johnny	81T	468	$ .01	$ .07	Woodling, Gene	52T	99	$10.00	$35.00
Wockenfuss, Johnny	82T	629	$ .01	$ .06	Woodling, Gene	53T	264	$18.00	$50.00
Wockenfuss, Johnny	83T	536	$ .01	$ .06	Woodling, Gene	54T	101	$5.00	$15.00
Wockenfuss, Johnny	84T	119	$ .01	$ .05	Woodling, Gene	55T	190	$2.85	$9.50
Wockenfuss, Johnny	84TTR	130	$ .02	$ .10	Woodling, Gene	56T	163	$1.25	$3.50
Wockenfuss, Johnny	85T	39	$ .01	$ .04	Woodling, Gene	57T	172	$ .60	$2.50
Wohlford, Jim	73T	611	$ .35	$1.10	Woodling, Gene	58T	398	$ .45	$1.50
Wohlford, Jim	74T	407	$ .06	$ .25	Woodling, Gene	59T	170	$ .50	$1.95
Wohlford, Jim	75T	144	$ .06	$ .25	Woodling, Gene	60T	190	$ .50	$2.00
Wohlford, Jim	76T	286	$ .05	$ .20	Woodling, Gene	61T	275	$ .30	$1.00
Wohlford, Jim	77T	622	$ .03	$ .12	Woodling, Gene	62T	125	$ .50	$2.00
Wohlford, Jim	78T	376	$ .02	$ .10	Woodling, Gene	63T	43	$1.25	$4.50
Wohlford, Jim	79T	596	$ .02	$ .10	Woodling, Gene	63T	342	$ .50	$2.00
Wohlford, Jim	80T	448	$ .01	$ .07	Woods, Alvis	77T	479	$ .03	$ .12
Wohlford, Jim	81T	11	$ .01	$ .07	Woods, Alvis	78T	121	$ .02	$ .10
Wohlford, Jim	82T	116	$ .01	$ .06	Woods, Alvis	79T	178	$ .02	$ .10
Wohlford, Jim	83T	688	$ .01	$ .06	Woods, Alvis	80T	444	$ .01	$ .07
Wohlford, Jim	83TTR	128	$ .02	$ .10	Woods, Alvis	81T	703	$ .01	$ .07
Wohlford, Jim	84T	253	$ .01	$ .05	Woods, Alvis	82T	49	$ .01	$ .06
Wohlford, Jim	85T	787	$ .01	$ .04	Woods, Alvis	83T	589	$ .01	$ .06
Wohlford, Jim	86T	344	$ .01	$ .03	Woods, Gary	77T	492	$ .25	$ .80
Wohlford, Jim	87T	527	$ .01	$ .03	Woods, Gary	78T	599	$ .02	$ .10
Wojcik, John	63T	253	$ .25	$ .85	Woods, Gary	81T	172	$ .01	$ .07
Wojna, Ed	86T	211	$ .01	$ .03	Woods, Gary	82T	483	$ .01	$ .06
Wojna, Ed	87T	88	$ .01	$ .03	Woods, Gary	82TTR	130	$ .02	$ .10
Wolf, Wally	63T	208	$ .25	$ .85	Woods, Gary	83T	356	$ .01	$ .06
Wolf, Wally	70T	74	$ .10	$ .35	Woods, Gary	84T	231	$ .01	$ .05
Wolfe, Larry	79T	137	$ .02	$ .10	Woods, Gary	85T	46	$ .01	$ .04
Wolfe, Larry	80T	549	$ .01	$ .07	Woods, Gary	86T	611	$ .01	$ .03
Womack, Dooley	66T	469	$3.00	$12.00	Woods, Jim	61T	59	$ .30	$1.00
Womack, Dooley	67T	77	$ .25	$ .65	Woods, Ron	69T	544	$ .25	$ .85
Womack, Dooley	68T	431	$ .25	$ .65	Woods, Ron	70T	253	$ .10	$ .35
Womack, Dooley	69T	594	$ .25	$ .85	Woods, Ron	71T	514	$ .10	$ .35
Wood, Jake	61T	514	$ .50	$2.00	Woods, Ron	72T	82	$ .05	$ .25
Wood, Jake	62T	72	$ .35	$1.10	Woods, Ron	73T	531	$ .35	$1.10
Wood, Jake	62T	427	$ .70	$2.10	Woods, Ron	74T	377	$ .06	$ .25
Wood, Jake	63T	453	$2.50	$6.50	Woodson, Dick	70T	479	$ .10	$ .35
Wood, Jake	64T	272	$ .25	$ .85	Woodson, Dick	71T	586	$ .30	$1.00
Wood, Jake	65T	547	$1.50	$3.75	Woodson, Dick	72T	634	$ .25	$ .85
Wood, Jake	66T	509	$ .70	$2.10	Woodson, Dick	73T	98	$ .06	$ .25
Wood, Jake	67T	394	$ .25	$ .85	Woodson, Dick	74T	143	$ .06	$ .25
Wood, Ken	52T	139	$6.00	$19.00	Woodson, George	69T	244	$ .25	$ .85
Wood, Ted	88TTR	130	$ .05	$ .40	Woodson, Tracy	89T	306	$ .01	$ .04
Wood, Ted	89TBB	308	$ .01	$ .05	Woodson, Tracy	89TBB	92	$ .01	$ .05
Wood, Wilbur	64T	267	$ .35	$1.10	Woodward, Rob	87T	632	$ .01	$ .03
Wood, Wilbur	65T	478	$ .50	$2.00	Woodward, Woody	64T	378	$ .40	$1.25
Wood, Wilbur	67T	391	$ .25	$ .85	Woodward, Woody	65T	487	$ .50	$2.00
Wood, Wilbur	68T	585	$ .35	$1.10	Woodward, Woody	66T	49	$ .25	$ .85
Wood, Wilbur	69T	123	$ .25	$ .85	Woodward, Woody	67T	546	$1.50	$4.00

Player	Year	No.	VG	EX/MT
Woodward, Woody	68T	476	$ .30	$1.00
Woodward, Woody	69T	142	$ .25	$ .65
Woodward, Woody	70T	296	$ .10	$ .35
Woodward, Woody	71T	496	$ .10	$ .35
World Series '59, Celebration	60T	391	$1.25	$4.50
World Series '59, Game 1	60T	385	$ .60	$1.75
World Series '59, Game 2	60T	386	$ .60	$1.75
World Series '59, Game 3	60T	387	$ .70	$2.00
World Series '59, Game 4	60T	388	$1.25	$4.50
World Series '59, Game 5	60T	389	$1.25	$4.50
World Series '59, Game 6	60T	390	$ .60	$1.75
World Series '60, Celebrate	61T	313	$ .95	$3.50
World Series '60, Game 1	61T	306	$ .95	$3.50
World Series '60, Game 2	61T	307	$6.50	$20.00
World Series '60, Game 3	61T	308	$ .95	$3.50
World Series '60, Game 4	61T	309	$ .60	$1.75
World Series '60, Game 5	61T	310	$ .60	$1.75
World Series '60, Game 6	61T	311	$1.50	$3.75
World Series '60, Game 7	61T	312	$ .95	$3.50
World Series '61, Celebrate	62T	237	$ .60	$1.75
World Series '61, Game 1	62T	232	$ .50	$2.00
World Series '61, Game 2	62T	233	$ .50	$2.00
World Series '61, Game 3	62T	234	$2.50	$7.50
World Series '61, Game 4	62T	235	$1.75	$6.00
World Series '61, Game 5	62T	236	$ .50	$2.00
World Series '62, Game 1	63T	142	$1.00	$3.00
World Series '62, Game 2	63T	143	$ .50	$2.00
World Series '62, Game 3	63T	144	$1.50	$4.50
World Series '62, Game 4	63T	145	$ .50	$2.00
World Series '62, Game 5	63T	146	$ .50	$2.00
World Series '62, Game 6	63T	147	$ .50	$2.00
World Series '62, Game 7	63T	148	$ .60	$1.75
World Series '63, Game 1	64T	136	$5.00	$15.00
World Series '63, Game 2	64T	137	$ .50	$2.00
World Series '63, Game 3	64T	138	$ .50	$2.00
World Series '63, Game 4	64T	139	$ .50	$2.00
World Series '63, Summary	64T	140	$ .70	$2.00
World Series '64, Cards Celeb.	65T	139	$ .85	$2.50
World Series '64, Game 1	65T	132	$ .75	$2.25
World Series '64, Game 2	65T	133	$ .75	$2.25
World Series '64, Game 3	65T	134	$9.00	$35.00
World Series '64, Game 4	65T	135	$ .75	$2.25
World Series '64, Game 5	65T	136	$ .75	$2.25
World Series '64, Game 6	65T	137	$1.00	$3.00
World Series '64, Game 7	65T	138	$1.00	$3.00
World Series '66, Celebrate	67T	155	$ .60	$1.75
World Series '66, Game 1	67T	151	$ .35	$1.10
World Series '66, Game 2	67T	152	$ .60	$1.75
World Series '66, Game 3	67T	153	$ .35	$1.10
World Series '66, Game 4	67T	154	$ .35	$1.10
World Series '67, Cards Celeb.	68T	158	$ .50	$2.00
World Series '67, Game 1	68T	151	$ .70	$2.00
World Series '67, Game 2	68T	152	$1.25	$3.50
World Series '67, Game 3	68T	153	$ .35	$1.10
World Series '67, Game 4	68T	154	$ .60	$1.75
World Series '67, Game 5	68T	155	$ .50	$2.00
World Series '67, Game 6	68T	156	$ .50	$2.00
World Series '67, Game 7	68T	157	$ .50	$1.95
World Series '68, Game 1	69T	162	$1.50	$3.75
World Series '68, Game 2	69T	163	$ .50	$2.00
World Series '68, Game 3	69T	164	$ .50	$2.00
World Series '68, Game 4	69T	165	$ .70	$2.00
World Series '68, Game 5	69T	166	$1.50	$3.75
World Series '68, Game 6	69T	167	$ .50	$2.00
World Series '68, Game 7	69T	168	$ .70	$2.00
World Series '68, Tigers Celeb.	69T	169	$ .50	$1.95
World Series '69, Celeb. Mets	70T	310	$ .50	$2.00
World Series '69, Game 1	70T	305	$ .35	$1.10
World Series '69, Game 2	70T	306	$ .35	$1.10
World Series '69, Game 3	70T	307	$ .35	$1.10
World Series '69, Game 4	70T	308	$ .35	$1.10
World Series '69, Game 5	70T	309	$ .35	$1.10
World Series '70, Game 1	71T	327	$ .35	$1.10
World Series '70, Game 2	71T	328	$ .35	$1.10
World Series '70, Game 3	71T	329	$ .60	$1.75

Player	Year	No.	VG	EX/MT
World Series '70, Game 4	71T	330	$ .35	$1.10
World Series '70, Game 5	71T	331	$ .60	$1.75
World Series '70, Summary	71T	332	$ .35	$1.10
World Series '71, Celebration	72T	230	$ .35	$1.10
World Series '71, Game 1	72T	223	$ .15	$ .50
World Series '71, Game 2	72T	224	$ .15	$ .50
World Series '71, Game 3	72T	225	$ .15	$ .50
World Series '71, Game 4	72T	226	$ .60	$1.75
World Series '71, Game 5	72T	227	$ .15	$ .50
World Series '71, Game 6	72T	228	$ .15	$ .50
World Series '71, Game 7	72T	229	$ .15	$ .50
World Series '72, Game 1	73T	203	$ .15	$ .50
World Series '72, Game 2	73T	204	$ .15	$ .50
World Series '72, Game 3	73T	205	$ .15	$ .50
World Series '72, Game 4	73T	206	$ .15	$ .50
World Series '72, Game 5	73T	207	$ .15	$ .50
World Series '72, Game 6	73T	208	$ .15	$ .50
World Series '72, Game 7	73T	209	$ .15	$ .50
World Series '72, Summary	73T	210	$ .15	$ .50
World Series '73, Game #1	74T	472	$ .35	$1.10
World Series '73, Game #2	74T	473	$ .65	$1.75
World Series '73, Game #3	74T	474	$ .35	$1.10
World Series '73, Game #4	74T	475	$ .35	$1.10
World Series '73, Game #5	74T	476	$ .35	$1.10
World Series '73, Game #6	74T	477	$ .65	$1.75
World Series '73, Game #7	74T	478	$ .35	$1.10
World Series '73, Summary	74T	479	$ .35	$1.10
World Series '74, Game 1	75T	461	$ .60	$1.75
World Series '74, Game 2	75T	462	$ .25	$ .85
World Series '74, Game 3	75T	463	$ .30	$1.00
World Series '74, Game 4	75T	464	$ .30	$1.00

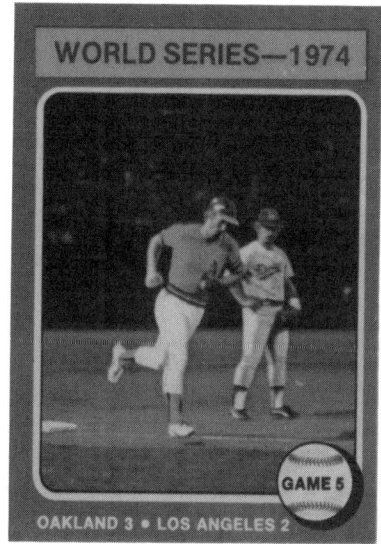

WORLD SERIES—1974

GAME 5

OAKLAND 3 • LOS ANGELES 2

Player	Year	No.	VG	EX/MT
World Series '74, Game 5	75T	465	$ .30	$1.00
World Series '74, Summary	75T	466	$ .30	$1.00
World Series '75, Reds	76T	462	$ .25	$ .85
World Series '76, Reds	77T	411	$ .15	$ .50
World Series '76, Summary	77T	413	$ .03	$ .60
World Series '76, Yankees	77T	412	$ .15	$ .50
World Series, Phillies	81T	403	$ .03	$ .15
World Series, Phillies	81T	404	$ .03	$ .15
Worrell, Todd	86TTR	127	$ .35	$1.10
Worrell, Todd	87T	465	$ .10	$ .35
Worrell, Todd	87TAS	605	$ .01	$ .10
Worrell, Todd	87TRB	7	$ .01	$ .03

Player	Year	No.	VG	EX/MT
Worrell, Todd	88T	715	$ .01	$ .10
Worrell, Todd	88TBB	149	$ .01	$ .05
Worrell, Todd	89T	535	$ .01	$ .04

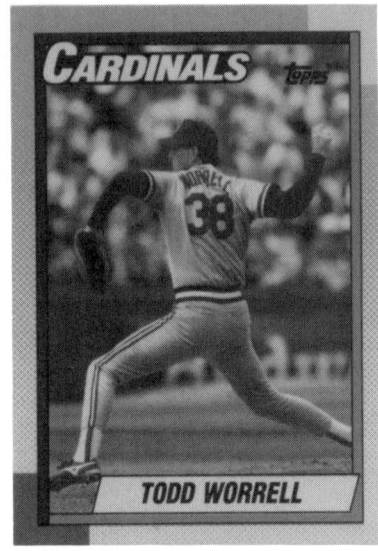

Player	Year	No.	VG	EX/MT
Worrell, Todd	90T	95	$ .01	$ .03
Wortham, Rich	80T	502	$ .01	$ .07
Wortham, Rich	81T	107	$ .01	$ .07
Worthington, Al	57T	39	$ .95	$3.50
Worthington, Al	58T	427	$ .50	$2.00
Worthington, "Red" Al	59T	28	$ .60	$ .75
Worthington, Al	60T	268	$ .35	$1.10
Worthington, Al	63T	556	$1.50	$3.75
Worthington, Al	64T	144	$ .25	$ .85
Worthington, Al	65T	216	$ .30	$1.00
Worthington, Al	66T	181	$ .25	$ .85
Worthington, Al	67T	399	$ .25	$ .85
Worthington, Al	68T	473	$ .30	$1.00
Worthington, Al	73T	49	$ .25	$ .65
Worthington, Craig	89T	181	$ .01	$ .35
Worthington, Craig	90T	521	$ .01	$ .10
Wright, Clyde	69T	583	$ .25	$ .85
Wright, Clyde	70T	543	$ .10	$ .35
Wright, Clyde	71T	67	$ .15	$ .50
Wright, Clyde	71T	240	$ .10	$ .35
Wright, Clyde	72T	55	$ .05	$ .25
Wright, Clyde	73T	373	$ .06	$ .25
Wright, Clyde	74T	525	$ .06	$ .25
Wright, Clyde	75T	408	$ .06	$ .25
Wright, Clyde	76T	559	$ .05	$ .20
Wright, Ed	52T	368	$39.00	$135.00
Wright, George	83T	299	$ .01	$ .06
Wright, George	84T	688	$ .01	$ .05
Wright, George	85T	443	$ .01	$ .04
Wright, George	86T	169	$ .01	$ .03
Wright, George	86TTR	128	$ .02	$ .10
Wright, Jim	79T	349	$ .02	$ .10
Wright, Jim	81T	526	$ .01	$ .07
Wright, Jim L.	79T	722	$ .50	$1.50
Wright, Jim L.	80T	524	$ .01	$ .07
Wright, Jim L.	82T	362	$ .01	$ .06
Wright, Ken	71T	504	$ .10	$ .35
Wright, Ken	72T	638	$ .25	$ .85
Wright, Ken	73T	578	$ .35	$1.10
Wright, Mel	73T	517	$ .25	$ .85

Player	Year	No.	VG	EX/MT
Wright, Ricky	86TTR	129	$ .02	$ .10
Wright, Ricky	87T	202	$ .01	$ .03
Wright, Tom	54T	140	$2.00	$7.00
Wright, Tom	55T	141	$1.35	$5.00
Wrona, Rick	90T	187	$ .01	$ .03
Wyatt, Johnnie	63T	376	$ .25	$ .50
Wyatt, John	64T	108	$ .25	$ .85
Wyatt, Johnnie	65T	590	$1.50	$3.75
Wyatt, John	66T	521	$ .70	$2.10
Wyatt, John	67T	261	$ .25	$ .65
Wyatt, John	68T	481	$ .30	$1.00
Wyatt, Whitlow	60T	464	$ .95	$3.50
Wynegar, Butch	77T	175	$ .25	$ .65
Wynegar, Butch	78T	555	$ .02	$ .10
Wynegar, Butch	79T	405	$ .02	$ .10
Wynegar, Butch	80T	304	$ .01	$ .07
Wynegar, Butch	81T	61	$ .01	$ .07
Wynegar, Butch	82T	222	$ .01	$ .06
Wynegar, Butch	82TTR	131	$ .02	$ .10
Wynegar, Butch	83T	617	$ .01	$ .06
Wynegar, Butch	84T	123	$ .01	$ .05
Wynegar, Butch	85T	585	$ .01	$ .04
Wynegar, Butch	86T	235	$ .01	$ .03
Wynegar, Butch	87T	464	$ .01	$ .03
Wynegar, Butch	88T	737	$ .01	$ .03
Wynn, Early	51Trb	8	$3.00	$9.00
Wynn, Early	52T	277	$35.00	$110.00
Wynn, Early	53T	61	$22.50	$67.50
Wynn, Early	56T	187	$6.00	$18.00
Wynn, Early	57T	40	$3.50	$11.00
Wynn, Early	58T	100	$3.25	$10.00
Wynn, Early	59T	260	$2.75	$10.50
Wynn, Early	60T	1	$5.00	$30.00
Wynn, Early	61T	50	$ .50	$1.95
Wynn, Early	61T	337	$ .70	$2.00
Wynn, Early	61T	455	$3.00	$9.00
Wynn, Early	62T	385	$3.00	$9.00
Wynn, Jim	64T	38	$ .35	$1.10
Wynn, Jim	65T	257	$ .35	$1.10
Wynn, Jim	66T	520	$ .95	$3.50
Wynn, Jim	67T	390	$ .35	$1.10
Wynn, Jim	68T	5	$1.35	$4.00
Wynn, Jim	68T	260	$ .15	$ .50
Wynn, Jim	69T	360	$ .25	$ .85
Wynn, Jim	70T	60	$ .25	$ .85
Wynn, Jim	71T	565	$ .30	$1.00
Wynn, Jim	72T	770	$ .85	$3.50
Wynn, Jim	73T	185	$ .25	$ .65
Wynn, Jim	74T	43	$ .06	$ .25
Wynn, Jim	74TTR	43	$ .10	$ .35
Wynn, Jim	75T	570	$ .06	$ .25
Wynn, Jim	76T	395	$ .10	$ .35
Wynn, Jim	77T	165	$ .03	$ .12
Wynne, Billy	70T	618	$ .25	$ .85
Wynne, Billy	71T	718	$ .70	$2.10
Wynne, Marvell	84T	173	$ .01	$ .05
Wynne, Marvell	85T	615	$ .01	$ .04
Wynne, Marvell	86T	525	$ .01	$ .03
Wynne, Marvell	87T	37	$ .01	$ .03
Wynne, Marvell	88T	454	$ .01	$ .03
Wynne, Marvell	89T	353	$ .01	$ .04
Wynne, Marvell	90T	256	$ .01	$ .03
Wyrostek, Johnny	51Tbb	44	$5.50	$17.00
Wyrostek, Johnny	52T	13	$14.00	$45.00
Wyrostek, Johnny	53T	79	$3.75	$13.00
Yankees, Team	56T	251	$55.00	$175.00
Yankees, Team	57T	97	$10.00	$30.00
Yankees, Team	58T	246	$8.00	$25.00
Yankees, Team	59T	510	$10.50	$42.50
Yankees, Team	60T	332	$6.00	$18.00
Yankees, Team	61T	228	$3.00	$10.00
Yankees, Team	62T	251	$3.00	$9.00
Yankees, Team	63T	247	$3.00	$9.00
Yankees, Team	64T	433	$2.50	$7.50
Yankees, Team	65T	513	$5.00	$15.00

Player	Year	No.	VG	EX/MT	Player	Year	No.	VG	EX/MT
Yankees, Team	66T	92	$1.25	$3.50	Yeager, Steve	86T	32	$ .01	$ .03
Yankees, Team	67TT	131	$1.25	$3.50	Yeager, Steve	86TTR	130	$ .02	$ .10
Yankees, Team	70T	399	$ .50	$1.95	Yeager, Steve	87T	258	$ .01	$ .03
Yankees, Team	71T	543	$1.50	$3.75	Yelding, Eric	89TMLD	148	$ .01	$ .10
Yankees, Team	72T	237	$ .35	$1.10	Yelding, Eric	90T	309	$ .01	$ .10
Yankees, Team	73T	556	$ .95	$3.50	Yellen, Larry	64T	226	$ .25	$ .85
Yankees, Team	74T	363	$ .50	$2.00	Yellen, Larry	65T	292	$ .30	$1.00
Yankees, Team Checklist	75T	611	$ .50	$1.95	Yett, Rich	87T	134	$ .01	$ .03
Yankees, Team Checklist	76T	17	$ .20	$ .75	Yett, Rich	88T	531	$ .01	$ .03
Yankees, Team Checklist	77T	387	$ .50	$2.00	Yett, Rich	89T	363	$ .01	$ .04
Yankees, Team Checklist	78T	282	$ .20	$ .75	Yett, Rich	89TBB	290	$ .01	$ .05
Yankees, Team Checklist	79T	626	$ .25	$ .65	Yett, Rich	90T	689	$ .01	$ .03
Yankees, Team Checklist	80T	424	$ .25	$ .85	York, Jim	72T	68	$ .05	$ .25
Yankees, Team Checklist	81T	670	$ .02	$ .30	York, Jim	73T	546	$ .35	$1.10
Yankees, Team Leaders	86T	276	$ .01	$ .03	York, Jim	75T	383	$ .06	$ .25
Yankees, Team Leaders	87T	406	$ .01	$ .03	York, Jim	76T	224	$ .05	$ .20
Yankees, Team Leaders	88T	459	$ .01	$ .03	York, Rudy	60T	456	$1.25	$4.50
Yankees, Team Leaders	89T	519	$ .01	$ .04	Yost, Eddie	51Tbb	1	$7.50	$30.00
Yastrzemski, Carl	60T	148	$75.00	$300.00	Yost, Eddie	52T	123	$6.00	$18.00
Yastrzemski, Carl	61T	287	$40.00	$125.00	Yost, Eddie	56T	128	$1.25	$4.50
Yastrzemski, Carl	62T	425	$60.00	$175.00	Yost, Eddie	57T	177	$ .95	$3.50
Yastrzemski, Carl	63T	115	$25.00	$75.00	Yost, Eddie	58T	173	$ .65	$2.00
Yastrzemski, Carl	64T	8	$1.35	$4.00	Yost, Eddie	59T	2	$ .95	$3.50
Yastrzemski, Carl	64T	182	$2.00	$8.00	Yost, Eddie	60T	245	$ .35	$1.10
Yastrzemski, Carl	64T	210	$20.00	$60.00	Yost, Eddie	61T	413	$ .50	$2.00
Yastrzemski, Carl	65T	385	$22.00	$75.00	Yost, Eddie	62T	176	$ .35	$1.10
Yastrzemski, Carl	66T	70	$22.50	$65.00	Yost, Eddie	73T	257	$ .50	$2.00
Yastrzemski, Carl	66T	216	$ .75	$2.75	Yost, Eddie	74T	179	$ .50	$2.00
Yastrzemski, Carl	67T	355	$27.50	$80.00	Yost, Ned	79T	708	$ .35	$1.10
Yastrzemski, Carl	68T	2	$1.35	$4.00	Yost, Ned	81T	659	$ .01	$ .07
Yastrzemski, Carl	68T	4	$1.35	$4.00	Yost, Ned	82T	542	$ .01	$ .06
Yastrzemski, Carl	68T	6	$2.00	$5.00	Yost, Ned	83T	297	$ .01	$ .06
Yastrzemski, Carl	68T	250	$10.00	$35.00	Yost, Ned	84T	107	$ .01	$ .05
Yastrzemski, Carl	68TAS	369	$3.00	$9.00	Yost, Ned	84TTR	131	$ .02	$ .10
Yastrzemski, Carl	69T	1	$1.75	$6.00	Yost, Ned	85T	777	$ .01	$ .04
Yastrzemski, Carl	69T	130	$8.00	$25.00	Youmans, Floyd	86T	732	$ .10	$ .50
Yastrzemski, Carl	69TAS	425	$2.00	$7.00	Youmans, Floyd	87T	105	$ .01	$ .10
Yastrzemski, Carl	70T	10	$7.50	$22.50	Youmans, Floyd	88T	365	$ .01	$ .10
Yastrzemski, Carl	70TAS	461	$1.50	$4.50	Youmans, Floyd	89T	91	$ .01	$ .04
Yastrzemski, Carl	71T	61	$ .50	$1.95	Young, Bob	52T	147	$4.50	$13.00
Yastrzemski, Carl	71T	65	$ .60	$1.75	Young, Bob	53T	160	$2.50	$8.00
Yastrzemski, Carl	71T	530	$10.00	$30.00	Young, Bobby	54T	8	$2.10	$7.50
Yastrzemski, Carl	72T	37	$4.00	$12.00	Young, Curt	85T	293	$ .06	$ .30
Yastrzemski, Carl	72TIA	38	$2.50	$8.00	Young, Curt	86T	84	$ .01	$ .03
Yastrzemski, Carl	73T	245	$3.50	$12.50	Young, Curt	87T	519	$ .01	$ .03
Yastrzemski, Carl	74T	280	$3.00	$9.00	Young, Curt	88T	103	$ .01	$ .03
Yastrzemski, Carl	75T	205	$ .35	$1.10	Young, Curt	89T	641	$ .01	$ .04
Yastrzemski, Carl	75T	280	$2.50	$10.00	Young, Curt	89TBB	254	$ .01	$ .05
Yastrzemski, Carl	76T	230	$2.50	$8.00	Young, Curt	90T	328	$ .01	$ .03
Yastrzomcki, Carl	77T	480	$1.30	$5.00	Young, Cy	73TATL	477	$ .50	$2.00
Yastrzemski, Carl	77TB	434	$ .85	$3.50	Young, Cy	70TRH	416	$ .05	$ .20
Yastrzemski, Carl	78T	40	$1.00	$4.00	Young, Don	66T	139	$ .25	$ .85
Yastrzemski, Carl	79T	320	$ .85	$3.50	Young, Don	69T	602	$ .25	$ .85
Yastrzemski, Carl	80T	720	$ .45	$1.75	Young, Don	70T	117	$ .10	$ .35
Yastrzemski, Carl	80THL	1	$ .35	$1.25	Young, Gerald	88T	368	$ .01	$ .25
Yastrzemski, Carl	81T	110	$ .35	$1.50	Young, Gerald	89T	95	$ .01	$ .04
Yastrzemski, Carl	82T	650	$ .30	$1.25	Young, Gerald	90T	196	$ .01	$ .03
Yastrzemski, Carl	82TIA	651	$ .15	$ .60	Young, Kip	79T	706	$ .02	$ .10
Yastrzemski, Carl	83T	550	$ .15	$ .75	Young, Kip	80T	251	$ .01	$ .07
Yastrzemski, Carl	83T	551	$ .01	$ .06	Young, Matt	83TTR	129	$ .02	$ .10
Yastrzemski, Carl	84T	6	$ .10	$ .50	Young, Matt	84T	235	$ .01	$ .05
Yastrzemski, Carl	87TTB	314	$ .06	$ .25	Young, Matt	84T	336	$ .01	$ .05
Yeager, Steve	73T	59	$ .12	$ .40	Young, Matt	85T	485	$ .01	$ .04
Yeager, Steve	74T	593	$ .06	$ .25	Young, Matt	86T	676	$ .01	$ .03
Yeager, Steve	75T	376	$ .06	$ .25	Young, Matt	87T	19	$ .01	$ .03
Yeager, Steve	76T	515	$ .05	$ .20	Young, Matt	87TTR	131	$ .01	$ .07
Yeager, Steve	77T	105	$ .03	$ .12	Young, Matt	88T	736	$ .01	$ .03
Yeager, Steve	78T	285	$ .02	$ .10	Young, Matt	90T	501	$ .01	$ .03
Yeager, Steve	79T	75	$ .02	$ .10	Young, Mike	85T	173	$ .01	$ .10
Yeager, Steve	80T	726	$ .05	$ .20	Young, Mike	86T	548	$ .01	$ .03
Yeager, Steve	81T	318	$ .01	$ .07	Young, Mike	87T	309	$ .01	$ .03
Yeager, Steve	82T	477	$ .01	$ .06	Young, Mike	88T	11	$ .01	$ .03
Yeager, Steve	83T	555	$ .01	$ .06	Young, Mike	89T	731	$ .01	$ .04
Yeager, Steve	84T	661	$ .01	$ .05	Youngblood, Joel	77T	548	$ .03	$ .12
Yeager, Steve	85T	148	$ .01	$ .04	Youngblood, Joel	78T	428	$ .02	$ .10

Player	Year	No.	VG	EX/MT	Player	Year	No.	VG	EX/MT
Youngblood, Joel	79T	109	$ .02	$ .10	Zauchin, Norm	55T	176	$4.25	$13.00
Youngblood, Joel	80T	372	$ .01	$ .07	Zauchin, Norm	56T	89	$1.25	$4.50
Youngblood, Joel	81T	58	$ .01	$ .07	Zauchin, Norm	57T	372	$ .85	$3.50
Youngblood, Joel	82T	655	$ .01	$ .06	Zauchin, Norm	58T	422	$ .50	$2.00
Youngblood, Joel	83T	265	$ .01	$ .06	Zauchin, Norm	59T	311	$ .50	$1.95
Youngblood, Joel	83TTR	130	$ .02	$ .10	Zavaras, Clint	89TMLD	149	$ .01	$ .10
Youngblood, Joel	84T	727	$ .01	$ .05	Zavaras, Clint	90T	89	$ .01	$ .10
Youngblood, Joel	85T	567	$ .01	$ .04	Zdeb, Joe	78T	408	$ .02	$ .10
Youngblood, Joel	86T	177	$ .01	$ .03	Zdeb, Joe	79T	389	$ .02	$ .10
Youngblood, Joel	87T	759	$ .01	$ .03	Zeber, George	78T	591	$ .02	$ .10
Youngblood, Joel	88T	418	$ .01	$ .03	Zeile, Todd	89TMLD	150	$ .01	$1.00
Youngblood, Joel	89T	304	$ .01	$ .04	Zeile, Todd	90T	162	$ .01	$1.50
Yount, Robin	75T	223	$25.00	$125.00	Zepp, Bill	70T	702	$ .50	$2.00
Yount, Robin	76T	316	$8.50	$32.50	Zepp, Bill	71T	271	$ .10	$ .35
Yount, Robin	77T	635	$5.00	$20.00	Zernial, Gus	51Trb	36	$2.50	$10.00
Yount, Robin	78T	173	$2.50	$7.50	Zernial, Gus	52T	31	$12.50	$45.00
Yount, Robin	79T	95	$1.50	$6.00	Zernial, Gus	53T	42	$2.50	$8.00
Yount, Robin	80T	265	$1.00	$4.00	Zernial, Gus	54T	2	$2.50	$9.00
Yount, Robin	81T	515	$ .75	$2.25	Zernial, Gus	55T	110	$1.25	$5.00
Yount, Robin	82T	435	$ .65	$1.75	Zernial, Gus	56T	45	$1.25	$4.50
Yount, Robin	83T	321	$ .01	$ .10	Zernial, Gus	57T	253	$ .95	$3.50
Yount, Robin	83T	350	$ .25	$1.00	Zernial, Gus	58T	112	$ .50	$2.00
Yount, Robin	83TAS	389	$ .03	$ .35	Zernial, Gus	59T	409	$ .50	$1.95
Yount, Robin	84T	10	$ .25	$1.00	Zimmer, Don	55T	92	$6.00	$25.00
Yount, Robin	85T	340	$ .10	$ .50	Zimmer, Don	56T	99	$3.00	$9.00
Yount, Robin	86T	780	$ .10	$ .50	Zimmer, Don	57T	284	$8.00	$25.00
Yount, Robin	87T	773	$ .06	$ .25	Zimmer, Don	58T	77	$ .90	$3.25
Yount, Robin	88T	165	$ .01	$ .20	Zimmer, Don	59T	287	$ .60	$1.75
Yount, Robin	88TBB	66	$ .01	$ .15	Zimmer, Don	60T	47	$ .50	$2.00
Yount, Robin	89T	615	$ .01	$ .10	Zimmer, Don	61T	493	$ .60	$1.75
Yount, Robin	89TBB	249	$ .01	$ .25	Zimmer, Don	62T	478	$ .85	$3.50
Yount, Robin	90T	290	$ .01	$ .20	Zimmer, Don	63T	439	$ .35	$1.10
Yount, Robin	90TAS	389	$ .01	$ .10	Zimmer, Don	64T	134	$ .15	$ .50
Yuhas, Eddie	52T	386	$39.00	$135.00	Zimmer, Don	65T	233	$ .35	$1.10
Yuhas, Ed	53T	70	$3.75	$13.00	Zimmer, Don	73T	12	$ .25	$ .65
Yvars, Sal	52T	338	$39.00	$135.00	Zimmer, Don	74T	403	$ .06	$ .25
Yvars, Sal	53T	11	$3.75	$13.00	Zimmer, Don	78T	63	$ .02	$ .10
Zachary, Chris	64T	23	$ .25	$ .85	Zimmer, Don	88TTR	131	$ .01	$ .05
Zachary, Chris	66T	313	$ .25	$ .85	Zimmer, Don	89T	134	$ .01	$ .04
Zachary, Chris	67T	212	$ .25	$ .65	Zimmer, Don	90T	549	$ .01	$ .03
Zachary, Chris	70T	471	$ .10	$ .35	Zimmerman, Jerry	59T	146	$ .50	$1.95
Zachary, Chris	73T	256	$ .06	$ .25	Zimmerman, Jerry	62T	222	$ .35	$1.10
Zachry, Pat	76T	599	$4.00	$12.00	Zimmerman, Jerry	63T	186	$ .25	$ .85
Zachry, Pat	77T	86	$ .03	$ .12	Zimmerman, Jerry	64T	369	$ .25	$ .85
Zachry, Pat	78T	171	$ .02	$ .10	Zimmerman, Jerry	66T	73	$ .25	$ .85
Zachry, Pat	79T	621	$ .02	$ .10	Zimmerman, Jerry	67T	501	$ .50	$2.00
Zachry, Pat	80T	428	$ .01	$ .07	Zimmerman, Jerry	68T	181	$ .25	$ .65
Zachry, Pat	81T	224	$ .01	$ .07	Zimmerman, Jerry	73T	377	$ .10	$ .35
Zachry, Pat	82T	399	$ .01	$ .06	Zimmerman, Jerry	74T	531	$ .25	$ .85
Zachry, Pat	83T	522	$ .01	$ .06	Zimmerman, Jerry	65T	299	$ .30	$1.00
Zachry, Pat	83TTR	131	$ .02	$ .10	Zipfel, Bud	63T	69	$ .25	$ .85
Zachry, Pat	84T	747	$ .01	$ .05	Zisk, Richie	72T	392	$ .15	$ .50
Zachry, Pat	85T	57	$ .01	$ .04	Zisk, Richie	73T	611	$ .35	$1.10
Zahn, Geoff	75T	294	$ .06	$ .25	Zisk, Richie	74T	317	$ .06	$ .25
Zahn, Geoff	76T	403	$ .05	$ .20	Zisk, Richie	75T	77	$ .06	$ .25
Zahn, Geoff	78T	27	$ .02	$ .10	Zisk, Richie	76T	12	$ .05	$ .20
Zahn, Geoff	79T	678	$ .02	$ .10	Zisk, Richie	77T	483	$ .03	$ .12
Zahn, Geoff	80T	113	$ .01	$ .07	Zisk, Richie	78T	110	$ .02	$ .10
Zahn, Geoff	81T	363	$ .01	$ .07	Zisk, Richie	79T	260	$ .02	$ .10
Zahn, Geoff	81TTR	856	$ .02	$ .10	Zisk, Richie	80T	620	$ .01	$ .07
Zahn, Geoff	82T	229	$ .01	$ .06	Zisk, Richie	81T	517	$ .01	$ .07
Zahn, Geoff	83T	547	$ .01	$ .06	Zisk, Richie	81TTR	857	$ .02	$13.00
Zahn, Geoff	84T	276	$ .01	$ .05	Zisk, Richie	82T	769	$ .01	$ .06
Zahn, Geoff	84T	468	$ .01	$ .05	Zisk, Richie	83T	368	$ .01	$ .06
Zahn, Geoff	85T	771	$ .01	$ .04	Zisk, Richie	84T	83	$ .01	$ .05
Zahn, Geoff	86T	42	$ .01	$ .03	Zoldak, Sam	52T	231	$6.00	$19.00
Zamora, Oscar	75T	604	$ .06	$ .25	Zupo, Frank	58T	229	$ .50	$2.00
Zamora, Oscar	76T	227	$ .05	$ .20	Zuvella, Paul	86T	572	$ .01	$ .03
Zamora, Oscar	78T	91	$ .02	$ .10	Zuvella, Paul	86TTR	131	$ .02	$ .10
Zanni, Dom	59T	145	$ .50	$1.95	Zuvella, Paul	87T	102	$ .01	$ .03
Zanni, Dom	62T	214	$ .35	$1.10	Zuverink, George	52T	199	$6.00	$19.00
Zanni, Dom	63T	354	$ .35	$1.20	Zuverink, George	56T	276	$1.30	$5.00
Zanni, Dom	66T	233	$ .25	$ .85	Zuverink, George	57T	11	$ .95	$3.50
Zarilla, Al	51Trb	49	$1.25	$3.50	Zuverink, George	58T	6	$ .85	$3.50
Zarilla, Al	52T	70	$14.00	$45.00	Zuverink, George	59T	219	$ .50	$1.95
Zarilla, Al	53T	181	$3.75	$13.00					

UPPER DECK COMPANY 1989

The Upper Deck Company began production of cards in 1989 joining all the other baseball card producers in searching for a share of the collector's market. Promising a better product than has ever been seen before, they actively sought dealer support. An unproven company in an already saturated market, caused many dealers to take a wait and see attitude. Many who hesitated in ordering wished that they had not done so when the product finally begin to arrive. After a slow beginning, the product found wide collector acceptance with the photo-like quality cards.

There are several good things that Upper Deck has done. Card dealers received the first shipments and candy wholesalers did not get to charge retail prices or allow someone to buy the total allotment for a change.

Distribution and cost (double the other card companies' prices) may be determining factors in the longevity of this product. Collectors will be the ultimate determining factor.

Looking back at 1989, Upper Deck shows that there is room for more cards in today's marketplace, but their saturation point is at hand. Today, early summer 1990, the new Upper Deck product is being offered at near cost and last year at this time dealers were paying full retail to obtain cards for resale. Supply has surpassed demand once again.

To answer all those readers who wrote to ask if I ever did receive the 1989 factory set promised from the company to use for my book - No!

As I go to press with an earlier deadline this year the extended set of Upper Deck cards (701-800) has not been released and so they are not included in my listing.

The listing for each card shown appears immediately following the photograph.

UPPER DECK

Player	Year	No.	VG	EX/MT	Player	Year	No.	VG	EX/MT
Aase, Don	89UD	450	$ .01	$ .07	Ashby, Alan	89UD	305	$ .01	$ .07
Aase, Don	90UD	131	$ .01	$ .07	Assenmacher, Paul	89UD	566	$ .01	$ .07
Abbott, Jim	89UD	755	$ .25	$5.00	Assenmacher, Paul	90UD	660	$ .01	$ .07
Abbott, Jim	90UD	645	$ .01	$1.50	Atherton, Keith	89UD	599	$ .01	$ .07
Abner, Shawn	90UD	301	$ .01	$ .07	August, Don	89UD	325	$ .01	$ .10
					August, Don	90UD	295	$ .01	$ .07
					Avery, Steve	90UD	65	$ .01	$1.00
					Backman, Wally	89UD	188	$ .01	$ .07
					Backman, Wally	89UD	732	$ .01	$ .10
					Backman, Wally	90UD	158	$ .01	$ .07
					Bailes, Scott	89UD	209	$ .01	$ .07
					Baines, Harold	89UD	211	$ .01	$ .10
					Baines, Harold	89UD	692	$ .01	$ .10
					Baines, Harold	90UD	353	$ .01	$ .07
					Balboni, Steve	89UD	111	$ .01	$ .07
					Balboni, Steve	90UD	497	$ .01	$ .07
					Ballard, Jeff	89UD	595	$ .01	$ .15
					Ballard, Jeff	90UD	259	$ .01	$ .07
					Bankhead, Scott	89UD	316	$ .01	$ .07
					Bankhead, Scott	90UD	561	$ .01	$ .07
					Bannister, Floyd	89UD	549	$ .01	$ .07
					Bannister, Floyd	90UD	695	$ .01	$ .07
					Barfield, Jesse	89UD	149	$ .01	$ .15
					Barfield, Jesse	89UD	702	$ .01	$ .15
					Barfield, Jesse	90UD	476	$ .01	$ .07
					Barrett, Marty	89UD	173	$ .01	$ .07
					Barrett, Marty	90UD	133	$ .01	$ .07
					Bass, Kevin	89UD	425	$ .01	$ .07
					Bass, Kevin	90UD	302	$ .01	$ .07
					Batiste, Kevin	90UD	115	$ .01	$ .15
					Bautista, Jose	89UD	574	$ .01	$ .10
					Baylor, Don	89UD	601	$ .01	$ .07
					Beatty, Blaine	90UD	23	$ .01	$ .15
					Bedrosian, Steve	89UD	511	$ .01	$ .07
					Bedrosian, Steve	90UD	618	$ .01	$ .07
					Belcher, Tim	89UD	648	$ .01	$ .15
					Bell, Buddy	89UD	112	$ .01	$ .07
Acker, Jim	89UD	52	$ .01	$ .07	Bell, George	89UD	255	$ .01	$ .07
Agosto, Juan	89UD	251	$ .01	$ .07	Bell, George	90UD	127	$ .01	$ .10
Agosto, Juan	90UD	450	$ .01	$ .07	Bell, George	90UD	95	$ .01	$ .07
Aguayo, Luis	89UD	156	$ .01	$ .07	Bell, Jay	89UD	489	$ .01	$ .07
Aguilera, Rick	89UD	563	$ .01	$ .07	Bell, Jay	90UD	517	$ .01	$ .07
Aguilera, Rick	90UD	11	$ .01	$ .07	Bell, Juan	89UD	20	$ .05	$ .40
Aldrete, Mike	89UD	239	$ .01	$ .07	Bell, Juan	89UD	747	$ .01	$ .25
Aldrete, Mike	89UD	738	$ .01	$ .10	Belle, Joey	90UD	446	$ .01	$ .90
Aldrete, Mike	90UD	415	$ .01	$ .07	Belliard, Rafael	89UD	90	$ .01	$ .07
Alexander, Doyle	89UD	298	$ .01	$ .07	Belliard, Rafael	90UD	208	$ .01	$ .07
Alexander, Doyle	90UD	330	$ .01	$ .07	Benedict, Bruce	89UD	121	$ .01	$ .07
Alicea, Luis	89UD	281	$ .01	$ .10	Benes, Andy	90UD	55	$ .01	$1.00
Allanson, Andy	89UD	217	$ .01	$ .07	Benzinger, Todd	89UD	184	$ .01	$ .07
Allanson, Andy	90UD	590	$ .01	$ .07	Benzinger, Todd	89UD	785	$ .01	$ .15
Allen, Neil	89UD	567	$ .01	$ .07	Benzinger, Todd	90UD	186	$ .01	$ .10
Alomar, Jr., Sandy	89UD	5	$ .10	$1.00	Berenguer, Juan	89UD	232	$ .01	$ .07
Alomar, Jr., Sandy	90UD	655	$ .01	$ .35	Berenguer, Juan	90UD	440	$ .01	$ .07
Alomar, Roberto	89UD	471	$ .01	$ .25	Bergman, Dave	89UD	266	$ .01	$ .07
Alomar, Roberto	90UD	346	$ .01	$ .15	Bergman, Dave	90UD	381	$ .01	$ .07
Alvarez, Jose	89UD	734	$ .01	$ .10	Berroa, Geronimo	90UD	531	$ .01	$ .10
Alvarez, Jose	90UD	634	$ .01	$ .07	Berryhill, Damon	89UD	455	$ .01	$ .15
Andersen, Larry	89UD	404	$ .01	$ .07	Berryhill, Damon	90UD	322	$ .01	$ .10
Andersen, Larry	90UD	407	$ .01	$ .07	Bichette, Dante	89UD	24	$ .01	$ .10
Anderson, Allan	89UD	85	$ .01	$ .15	Bichette, Dante	90UD	688	$ .01	$ .15
Anderson, Allan	90UD	219	$ .01	$ .07	Bielecki, Mike	90UD	359	$ .01	$ .07
Anderson, Brady	89UD	408	$ .01	$ .15	Biggio, Craig	89UD	273	$ .01	$ .75
Anderson, Brady	90UD	290	$ .01	$ .07	Biggio, Craig	90UD	104	$ .01	$ .25
Anderson, Dave	89UD	89	$ .01	$ .07	Birtsas, Tim	89UD	638	$ .01	$ .07
Anderson, Dave	90UD	510	$ .01	$ .07	Birtsas, Tim	90UD	137	$ .01	$ .07
Anderson, Kent	90UD	691	$ .01	$ .15	Bittiger, Jeff	89UD	509	$ .01	$ .07
Andujar, Joaquin	89UD	79	$ .01	$ .07	Black, Bud	89UD	466	$ .01	$ .07
Anthony, Eric	90UD	28	$ .01	$3.00	Black, Bud	90UD	498	$ .01	$ .07
Appier, Kevin	90UD	102	$ .01	$ .20	Blankenship, Kevin	89UD	762	$ .01	$ .10
Aquino, Luis	90UD	274	$ .01	$ .10	Blankenship, Kevin	90UD	47	$ .01	$ .15
Armas, Tony	89UD	212	$ .01	$ .07	Blankenship, Lance	89UD	15	$ .01	$ .10
Armas, Tony	90UD	58	$ .01	$ .07	Blankenship, Lance	90UD	687	$ .01	$ .07
Armstrong, Jack	89UD	257	$ .10	$ .75	Blauser, Jeff	89UD	132	$ .01	$ .15
Armstrong, Jack	90UD	684	$ .01	$ .35	Blauser, Jeff	90UD	406	$ .01	$ .07

Jim Acker

Player	Year	No.	VG	EX/MT
Blecher, Tim	90UD	547	$ .01	$ .25
Blocker, Terry	89UD	399	$ .01	$ .10
Blyleven, Bert	89UD	225	$ .01	$ .10
Blyleven, Bert	89UD	712	$ .01	$ .15
Blyleven, Bert	90UD	527	$ .01	$ .10
Boddicker, Mike	89UD	542	$ .01	$ .07
Boddicker, Mike	90UD	652	$ .01	$ .07
Boever, Joe	90UD	408	$ .01	$ .07
Boggs, Wade	89UD	389	$ .10	$ .50
Boggs, Wade	89UD	687	$ .01	$ .25
Boggs, Wade	90UD	555	$ .01	$1.00
Bolton, Tom	89UD	545	$ .01	$ .07
Bolton, Tom	90UD	351	$ .01	$ .07
Bonds, Barry	89UD	440	$ .01	$ .10
Bonds, Barry	90UD	227	$ .01	$ .15
Bonilla, Bobby	89UD	578	$ .01	$ .25
Bonilla, Bobby	90UD	16	$ .01	$ .07
Bonilla, Bobby	90UD	366	$ .01	$ .15
Booker, Greg	89UD	641	$ .01	$ .07
Booker, Rod	89UD	644	$ .01	$ .10
Boone, Bob	89UD	119	$ .01	$ .07
Boone, Bob	89UD	767	$ .01	$ .10
Boone, Bob	90UD	271	$ .01	$ .07
Borders, Pat	89UD	593	$ .01	$ .15
Borders, Pat	90UD	113	$ .01	$ .07
Bosio, Chris	89UD	292	$ .01	$ .07
Bosio, Chris	90UD	293	$ .01	$ .07
Bosley, Thad	89UD	591	$ .01	$ .07
Boston, Daryl	89UD	496	$ .01	$ .07
Boston, Daryl	90UD	529	$ .01	$ .07
Boyd, Oil Can	89UD	415	$ .01	$ .15
Boyd, Oil Can	90UD	484	$ .01	$ .07
Bradley, Phil	89UD	229	$ .01	$ .07
Bradley, Phil	89UD	749	$ .01	$ .10
Bradley, Phil	90UD	194	$ .01	$ .07
Bradley, Scott	89UD	226	$ .01	$ .07
Bradley, Scott	90UD	383	$ .01	$ .07

Glenn Braggs

Player	Year	No.	VG	EX/MT
Braggs, Glenn	89UD	504	$ .01	$ .07
Braggs, Glenn	90UD	456	$ .01	$ .07
Brantley, Jeff	90UD	358	$ .01	$ .10
Brantley, Mickey	89UD	550	$ .01	$ .07
Bream, Sid	89UD	556	$ .01	$ .07
Bream, Sid	90UD	250	$ .01	$ .07

Player	Year	No.	VG	EX/MT
Brenly, Bob	89UD	479	$ .01	$ .07
Brennan, William	89UD	16	$ .01	$ .10
Brett, George	89UD	215	$ .01	$ .25
Brett, George	89UD	689	$ .01	$ .25
Brett, George	90UD	124	$ .01	$ .15
Briley, Greg	89UD	770	$ .01	$ .25
Briley, Greg	90UD	455	$ .01	$ .25
Brock, Greg	89UD	543	$ .01	$ .07
Brock, Greg	90UD	514	$ .01	$ .07
Brookens, Tom	89UD	106	$ .01	$ .07
Brookens, Tom	90UD	138	$ .01	$ .07
Brooks, Hubie	89UD	122	$ .01	$ .07
Brooks, Hubie	90UD	197	$ .01	$ .07
Brower, Bob	89UD	439	$ .01	$ .07
Brown, Chris	89UD	193	$ .01	$ .07
Brown, Chris	89UD	784	$ .01	$ .10
Brown, Kevin	89UD	752	$ .01	$ .10
Brown, Kevin	90UD	123	$ .01	$ .15
Browne, Jerry	89UD	314	$ .01	$ .07
Browne, Jerry	90UD	426	$ .01	$ .07
Browning, Tom	89UD	617	$ .01	$ .10
Browning, Tom	90UD	189	$ .01	$ .07
Brumley, Mike	90UD	312	$ .01	$ .07
Brunansky, Tom	89UD	272	$ .01	$ .07
Brunansky, Tom	90UD	257	$ .01	$ .07
Buckner, Bill	89UD	639	$ .01	$ .07
Buckner, Bill	90UD	252	$ .01	$ .07
Buechele, Steve	89UD	418	$ .01	$ .07
Buechele, Steve	90UD	685	$ .01	$ .07
Buhner, Jay	89UD	220	$ .01	$ .10
Buhner, Jay	90UD	534	$ .01	$ .07
Buice, DeWayne	89UD	147	$ .01	$ .07
Burke, Tim	89UD	456	$ .01	$ .10
Burke, Tim	90UD	515	$ .01	$ .07
Burks, Ellis	89UD	434	$ .10	$ .55
Burks, Ellis	90UD	343	$ .01	$ .20
Burns, Todd	89UD	718	$ .01	$ .10
Burns, Todd	90UD	689	$ .01	$ .10
Bush, Randy	89UD	158	$ .01	$ .07
Bush, Randy	90UD	493	$ .01	$ .07
Butler, Brett	89UD	218	$ .01	$ .07
Butler, Brett	90UD	119	$ .01	$ .07
Cabrera, Francisco	90UD	64	$ .01	$ .20
Cadaret, Greg	90UD	549	$ .01	$ .07
Calderon, Ivan	89UD	650	$ .01	$ .07
Calderon, Ivan	90UD	503	$ .01	$ .07
Calhoun, Jeff	89UD	33	$ .01	$ .07
Caminiti, Ken	89UD	141	$ .01	$ .07
Caminiti, Ken	90UD	122	$ .01	$ .07
Campbell, Mike	89UD	337	$ .01	$ .07
Campusano, Sil	89UD	45	$ .01	$ .15
Canale, George	90UD	59	$ .01	$ .25
Candaele, Casey	89UD	58	$ .01	$ .07
Candelaria, John	89UD	248	$ .01	$ .07
Candiotti, Tom	89UD	470	$ .01	$ .07
Candiotti, Tom	90UD	388	$ .01	$ .07
Cangelosi, John	89UD	67	$ .01	$ .07
Cangelosi, John	90UD	370	$ .01	$ .07
Cano, Jose	90UD	43	$ .01	$ .25
Canseco, Jose	89UD	371	$ .15	$1.00
Canseco, Jose	89UD	659	$ .05	$ .35
Canseco, Jose	89UD	670	$ .01	$ .45
Canseco, Jose	90UD	66	$ .01	$ .75
Canseco, Ozzie	89UD	756	$ .10	$1.25
Carman, Don	89UD	409	$ .01	$ .07
Carman, Don	90UD	420	$ .01	$ .07
Carpenter, Cris	89UD	8	$ .01	$ .25
Carpenter, Cris	90UD	523	$ .01	$ .10
Carreon, Mark	90UD	135	$ .01	$ .15
Carter, Gary	89UD	390	$ .01	$ .10
Carter, Gary	90UD	168	$ .01	$ .07
Carter, Joe	89UD	190	$ .01	$ .15
Carter, Joe	90UD	375	$ .01	$ .07
Carter, Joe	90UD	53	$ .01	$ .07
Carter, Steve	90UD	368	$ .01	$ .15

Player	Year	No.	VG	EX/MT
Cary, Chuck	89UD	396	$ .01	$ .07
Cary, Chuck	90UD	528	$ .01	$ .07
Castillo, Carmen	89UD	487	$ .01	$ .07
Castillo, Carmen	90UD	281	$ .01	$ .07
Castillo, Juan	89UD	522	$ .01	$ .07
Castillo, Tony	90UD	551	$ .01	$ .07
Cecena, Jose	89UD	560	$ .01	$ .10
Cerone, Rick	89UD	152	$ .01	$ .07
Cerone, Rick	90UD	405	$ .01	$ .07
Cerutti, John	89UD	129	$ .01	$ .07
Cerutti, John	90UD	485	$ .01	$ .07
Chance, Tony	89UD	3	$ .01	$ .10
Charlton, Norm	89UD	783	$ .01	$ .25
Charlton, Norm	90UD	566	$ .01	$ .10
Checklist, Cards (1-100)	89UD	694	$ .01	$ .07
Checklist, Cards (1-100)	90UD	100	$ .01	$ .07
Checklist, Cards (101-200)	89UD	695	$ .01	$ .07
Checklist, Cards (101-200)	90UD	200	$ .01	$ .07
Checklist, Cards (201-300)	89UD	696	$ .01	$ .07
Checklist, Cards (201-300)	90UD	300	$ .01	$ .07
Checklist, Cards (301-400)	89UD	697	$ .01	$ .07
Checklist, Cards (301-400)	90UD	400	$ .01	$ .07
Checklist, Cards (401-500)	89UD	698	$ .01	$ .07
Checklist, Cards (401-500)	90UD	500	$ .01	$ .07
Checklist, Cards (501-600)	89UD	699	$ .01	$ .07
Checklist, Cards (501-600)	90UD	600	$ .01	$ .07
Checklist, Cards (601-700)	89UD	700	$ .01	$ .07
Checklist, Cards (601-700)	90UD	700	$ .01	$ .07
Checklist, Cards (701-800)	89UD	701	$ .01	$ .10
Checklist, Rookies (1-26)	89UD	27	$ .01	$ .07
Checklist, Rookies	90UD	1	$ .01	$ .07
Clancy, Jim	89UD	282	$ .01	$ .07
Clancy, Jim	90UD	203	$ .01	$ .07
Clark, Dave	89UD	517	$ .01	$ .07
Clark, Dave	90UD	449	$ .01	$ .07
Clark, Jack	89UD	346	$ .01	$ .10
Clark, Jack	89UD	773	$ .01	$ .15
Clark, Jack	90UD	342	$ .01	$ .07
Clark, Jerald	89UD	30	$ .01	$ .07
Clark, Jerald	90UD	624	$ .01	$ .07
Clark, Terry	89UD	234	$ .01	$ .10
Clark, Will	89UD	155	$ .15	$ .75
Clark, Will	89UD	678	$ .10	$ .75
Clark, Will	90UD	50	$ .01	$ .75
Clark, Will	90UD	556	$ .01	$ .75
Clemens, Roger	89UD	195	$ .05	$ .35
Clemens, Roger	90UD	323	$ .01	$ .25
Clemens, Roger	90UD	57	$ .01	$ .10
Cliburn, Stu	89UD	483	$ .01	$ .07
Clutterbuck, Bryan	90UD	239	$ .01	$ .07
Coleman, Vince	89UD	253	$ .01	$ .10
Coleman, Vince	90UD	223	$ .01	$ .07
Coleman, Vince	90UD	68	$ .01	$ .07
Coles, Darnell	89UD	339	$ .01	$ .07
Coles, Darnell	90UD	311	$ .01	$ .07
Collins, Dave	89UD	351	$ .01	$ .07
Concepcion, Dave	89UD	196	$ .01	$ .07
Cone, David	89UD	584	$ .01	$ .25
Cone, David	90UD	224	$ .01	$ .10
Cook, Dennis	89UD	779	$ .01	$1.00
Cook, Dennis	90UD	71	$ .01	$ .35
Coolbaugh, Scott	90UD	42	$ .01	$ .35
Cora, Joey	90UD	601	$ .01	$ .07
Corbett, Sherman	89UD	464	$ .01	$ .07
Correa, Edwin	89UD	598	$ .01	$ .07
Corsi, Jim	90UD	521	$ .01	$ .07
Costello, John	89UD	625	$ .01	$ .10
Costello, John	90UD	486	$ .01	$ .07
Cotto, Henry	89UD	134	$ .01	$ .07
Cotto, Henry	90UD	207	$ .01	$ .07
Cox, Danny	89UD	535	$ .01	$ .07
Crews, Jim	89UD	611	$ .01	$ .07
Crews, Tim	90UD	670	$ .01	$ .07
Crim, Chuck	89UD	501	$ .01	$ .07
Crim, Chuck	90UD	511	$ .01	$ .07

Player	Year	No.	VG	EX/MT
Daniels, Kal	89UD	160	$ .01	$ .10
Daniels, Kal	90UD	603	$ .01	$ .07
Darling, Ron	89UD	159	$ .01	$ .10
Darling, Ron	90UD	241	$ .01	$ .07

Danny Darwin

Player	Year	No.	VG	EX/MT
Darwin, Danny	89UD	97	$ .01	$ .07
Darwin, Danny	90UD	305	$ .01	$ .07
Dascenzo, Doug	89UD	10	$ .01	$ .10
Dascenzo, Doug	90UD	211	$ .01	$ .07
Daugherty, Jack	90UD	614	$ .01	$ .15
Daulton, Darren	89UD	448	$ .01	$ .07
Daulton, Darren	90UD	418	$ .01	$ .07
Davidson, Mark	89UD	577	$ .01	$ .07
Davis, Alvin	89UD	105	$ .01	$ .15
Davis, Alvin	89UD	680	$ .01	$ .10
Davis, Alvin	90UD	364	$ .01	$ .10
Davis, Chili	89UD	126	$ .01	$ .07
Davis, Chili	90UD	38	$ .01	$ .07
Davis, Eric	89UD	410	$ .01	$ .35
Davis, Eric	89UD	688	$ .01	$ .25
Davis, Eric	90UD	116	$ .01	$ .20
Davis, Glenn	89UD	443	$ .01	$ .10
Davis, Glenn	90UD	245	$ .01	$ .15
Davis, Jody	89UD	148	$ .01	$ .07
Davis, Jody	90UD	429	$ .01	$ .07
Davis, John	89UD	548	$ .01	$ .07
Davis, Mark	89UD	268	$ .01	$ .07
Davis, Mark	90UD	431	$ .01	$ .07
Davis, Mike	89UD	146	$ .01	$ .07
Davis, Mike	90UD	258	$ .01	$ .07
Davis, Storm	89UD	153	$ .01	$ .07
Davis, Storm	90UD	292	$ .01	$ .07
Dawson, Andre	89UD	205	$ .01	$ .10
Dawson, Andre	90UD	357	$ .01	$ .15
Dawson, Andre	90UD	73	$ .01	$ .15
Dayley, Ken	89UD	114	$ .01	$ .07
Dayley, Ken	90UD	280	$ .01	$ .07
De Los Santos, Luis	89UD	12	$ .01	$ .25
Deer, Rob	89UD	442	$ .01	$ .07
Deer, Rob	90UD	176	$ .01	$ .07
DeJesus, Ivan	89UD	355	$ .01	$ .07
DeJesus, Jose	89UD	769	$ .01	$ .10
DeJesus, Jose	90UD	255	$ .01	$ .07
DeLeon, Jose	89UD	293	$ .01	$ .07

Player	Year	No.	VG	EX/MT	Player	Year	No.	VG	EX/MT
DeLeon, Jose	90UD	697	$ .01	$ .07	Finley, Chuck	90UD	667	$ .01	$ .07
Dempsey, Rick	89UD	713	$ .01	$ .10	Finley, Steve	89UD	742	$ .01	$ .25
Dernier, Bob	89UD	340	$ .01	$ .07	Finley, Steve	90UD	602	$ .01	$ .15
Deshaies, Jim	89UD	76	$ .01	$ .07	Firova, Dan	89UD	32	$ .01	$ .07
Deshaies, Jim	90UD	221	$ .01	$ .07	Fisher, Brian	89UD	69	$ .01	$ .07
Devereaux, Mike	89UD	68	$ .01	$ .15	Fisher, Brian	90UD	97	$ .01	$ .07
Devereaux, Mike	90UD	681	$ .01	$ .07	Fisk, Carlton	89UD	609	$ .01	$ .07
Diaz, Bo	89UD	169	$ .01	$ .07	Fisk, Carlton	90UD	367	$ .01	$ .07
Diaz, Bo	90UD	664	$ .01	$ .07	Fitzgerald, Mike	89UD	133	$ .01	$ .07
Diaz, Mario	89UD	318	$ .01	$ .10	Fitzgerald, Mike	90UD	558	$ .01	$ .07
Diaz, Mike	89UD	606	$ .01	$ .07	Flanagan, Mike	89UD	385	$ .01	$ .07
Dibble, Rob	89UD	375	$ .01	$1.00	Flanagan, Mike	90UD	483	$ .01	$ .07
Dibble, Rob	90UD	586	$ .01	$ .50	Flannery, Tim	89UD	603	$ .01	$ .07
DiPino, Frank	89UD	61	$ .01	$ .07	Fletcher, Scott	89UD	420	$ .01	$ .07
DiPino, Frank	90UD	202	$ .01	$ .07	Fletcher, Scott	90UD	310	$ .01	$ .07
Dopson, John	89UD	57	$ .01	$ .15	Foley, Tom	89UD	441	$ .01	$ .07
Dopson, John	90UD	671	$ .01	$ .07	Foley, Tom	90UD	489	$ .01	$ .07
Doran, Bill	89UD	101	$ .01	$ .07	Ford, Curt	89UD	309	$ .01	$ .07
Doran, Bill	90UD	198	$ .01	$ .07	Ford, Curt	90UD	490	$ .01	$ .07
Dotson, Richard	89UD	80	$ .01	$ .07	Franco, John	89UD	407	$ .01	$ .15
Downing, Brian	89UD	485	$ .01	$ .07	Franco, John	90UD	139	$ .01	$ .07
Downing, Brian	90UD	146	$ .01	$ .07	Franco, Julio	89UD	186	$ .01	$ .10
Downs, Kelly	89UD	476	$ .01	$ .07	Franco, Julio	89UD	793	$ .01	$ .15
Downs, Kelly	90UD	699	$ .01	$ .07	Franco, Julio	90UD	103	$ .01	$ .07
Drabek, Doug	89UD	597	$ .01	$ .07	Franco, Julio	90UD	82	$ .01	$ .07
Drabek, Doug	90UD	422	$ .01	$ .07	Francona, Terry	89UD	536	$ .01	$ .07
Dravecky, Dave	89UD	39	$ .01	$ .07	Francona, Terry	90UD	180	$ .01	$ .07
Dravecky, Dave	90UD	679	$ .01	$ .07	Fraser, Willie	89UD	613	$ .01	$ .07
Drees, Tom	90UD	3	$ .01	$ .25	Fraser, Willie	90UD	85	$ .01	$ .07
DuBois, Brian	90UD	78	$ .01	$ .15	Freeman, LaVel	89UD	788	$ .05	$ .60
Ducey, Rob	89UD	721	$ .01	$ .15	Frohwirth, Todd	90UD	443	$ .01	$ .07
Ducey, Rob	90UD	464	$ .01	$ .07	Gaetti, Gary	89UD	203	$ .01	$ .15
Duncan, Mariano	90UD	430	$ .01	$ .07	Gaetti, Gary	90UD	454	$ .01	$ .15
Dunne, Mike	89UD	518	$ .01	$ .07	Gagne, Greg	89UD	166	$ .01	$ .07
Dunston, Shawon	89UD	107	$ .01	$ .10	Gagne, Greg	90UD	217	$ .01	$ .07
Dunston, Shawon	90UD	231	$ .01	$ .10	Galarraga, Andres	89UD	115	$ .01	$ .15
Durham, Leon	89UD	354	$ .01	$ .07	Galarraga, Andres	89UD	677	$ .01	$ .07
Dyer, Mike	90UD	374	$ .01	$ .15	Galarraga, Andres	90UD	356	$ .01	$ .07
Dykstra, Len	89UD	369	$ .01	$ .10	Gallagher, Dave	89UD	164	$ .01	$ .10
Dykstra, Len	90UD	472	$ .01	$ .10	Gallagher, Dave	90UD	328	$ .01	$ .07
Eckersley, Dennis	89UD	289	$ .01	$ .07					
Eckersley, Dennis	89UD	664	$ .01	$ .10					
Eckersley, Dennis	90UD	513	$ .01	$ .07					
Eisenreich, Jim	89UD	44	$ .01	$ .07					
Eisenreich, Jim	90UD	294	$ .01	$ .07					
Elster, Kevin	89UD	269	$ .01	$ .07					
Elster, Kevin	90UD	187	$ .01	$ .07					
Eppard, Jim	89UD	614	$ .01	$ .10					
Esasky, Nick	89UD	299	$ .01	$ .07					
Esasky, Nick	89UD	757	$ .01	$ .10					
Esasky, Nick	90UD	463	$ .01	$ .07					
Espinoza, Alvaro	90UD	163	$ .01	$ .15					
Espy, Cecil	89UD	92	$ .01	$ .15					
Espy, Cecil	90UD	371	$ .01	$ .07					
Evans, Darrell	89UD	394	$ .01	$ .07					
Evans, Darrell	90UD	143	$ .01	$ .07					
Evans, Dwight	89UD	366	$ .01	$ .07					
Evans, Dwight	90UD	112	$ .01	$ .07					
Farr, Steve	89UD	308	$ .01	$ .07					
Farr, Steve	90UD	680	$ .01	$ .07					
Farrell, John	89UD	468	$ .01	$ .10					
Farrell, John	90UD	570	$ .01	$ .07					
Felder, Mike	89UD	252	$ .01	$ .07					
Felder, Mike	90UD	178	$ .01	$ .07					
Felix, Junior	89UD	743	$ .01	$3.00					
Felix, Junior	90UD	106	$ .01	$1.00					
Fermin, Felix	89UD	88	$ .01	$ .07					
Fermin, Felix	90UD	409	$ .01	$ .07					
Fernandez, Sid	89UD	168	$ .01	$ .15					
Fernandez, Sid	90UD	261	$ .01	$ .07	Gallego, Mike	89UD	583	$ .01	$ .07
Fernandez, Tony	89UD	139	$ .01	$ .15	Gallego, Mike	90UD	230	$ .01	$ .07
Fernandez, Tony	90UD	130	$ .01	$ .10	Gant, Ron	89UD	378	$ .01	$ .15
Fielder, Cecil	89UD	364	$ .01	$ .35					
Fields, Bruce	89UD	238	$ .01	$ .07					
Finley, Chuck	89UD	632	$ .01	$ .07					

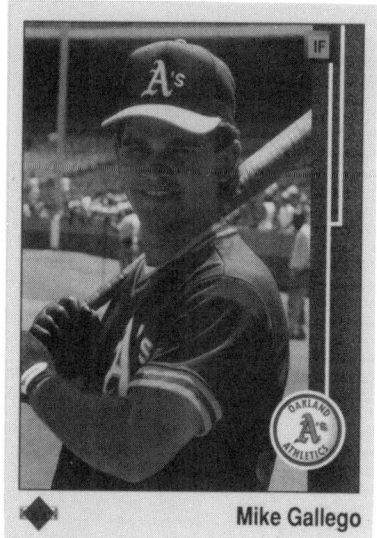

Mike Gallego

Player	Year	No.	VG	EX/MT	Player	Year	No.	VG	EX/MT
Gant, Ron	90UD	232	$ .01	$ .07	Gwynn, Chris	90UD	526	$ .01	$ .07
Gantner, Jim	89UD	274	$ .01	$ .07	Gwynn, Tony	89UD	384	$ .01	$ .25
Gantner, Jim	90UD	218	$ .01	$ .07	Gwynn, Tony	89UD	683	$ .01	$ .15
Garcia, Damaso	90UD	649	$ .01	$ .07	Gwynn, Tony	90UD	344	$ .01	$ .20
Garcia, Miguel	90UD	538	$ .01	$ .07	Hale, Chip	90UD	475	$ .01	$ .15
Garrelts, Scott	89UD	50	$ .01	$ .07	Hall, Albert	89UD	93	$ .01	$ .07
Garrelts, Scott	90UD	478	$ .01	$ .07	Hall, Drew	89UD	324	$ .01	$ .07
Gedman, Rich	89UD	368	$ .01	$ .07	Hall, Drew	90UD	631	$ .01	$ .07
Gedman, Rich	90UD	402	$ .01	$ .07	Hall, Mel	89UD	538	$ .01	$ .07
Geren, Bob	90UD	608	$ .01	$ .20	Hall, Mel	89UD	729	$ .01	$ .10
Gerhart, Ken	89UD	426	$ .01	$ .07	Hall, Mel	90UD	458	$ .01	$ .07
Gibson, Kirk	89UD	633	$ .01	$ .15	Hamelin, Bob	90UD	45	$ .01	$1.00
Gibson, Kirk	89UD	662	$ .01	$ .15	Hamilton, Darryl	89UD	301	$ .01	$ .10
Gibson, Kirk	89UD	666	$ .01	$ .15	Hamilton, Jeff	89UD	615	$ .01	$ .07
Gibson, Kirk	89UD	676	$ .01	$ .10	Hamilton, Jeff	90UD	296	$ .01	$ .07
Gibson, Kirk	90UD	264	$ .01	$ .07	Hammaker, Atlee	89UD	544	$ .01	$ .07
Gibson, Paul	89UD	47	$ .01	$ .07	Hammaker, Atlee	90UD	620	$ .01	$ .07
Gibson, Paul	90UD	496	$ .01	$ .07	Hammond, Chris	90UD	52	$ .01	$ .15
Girardi, Joe	89UD	776	$ .01	$ .10	Hanson, Erik	89UD	766	$ .01	$ .10
Girardi, Joe	90UD	304	$ .01	$ .10	Hanson, Erik	90UD	235	$ .01	$ .07
Gladden, Dan	89UD	400	$ .01	$ .07					
Gladden, Dan	90UD	238	$ .01	$ .07					
Glavine, Tom	89UD	360	$ .01	$ .07					
Glavine, Tom	90UD	571	$ .01	$ .07					
Gonzalez, German	90UD	352	$ .01	$ .10					
Gonzalez, Jose	89UD	626	$ .01	$ .07					
Gonzalez, Jose	90UD	666	$ .01	$ .10					
Gonzalez, Juan	90UD	72	$ .01	$1.00					
Gooden, Dwight	89UD	565	$ .01	$ .25					
Gooden, Dwight	90UD	114	$ .01	$ .20					
Gooden, Dwight	90UD	62	$ .01	$ .07					
Gordon, Tom	89UD	736	$ .01	$1.50					
Gordon, Tom	90UD	365	$ .01	$ .65					
Gossage, Goose	89UD	452	$ .01	$ .07					
Gott, Jim	89UD	539	$ .01	$ .07					
Gott, Jim	90UD	89	$ .01	$ .07					
Grace, Mark	89UD	140	$ .15	$1.25					
Grace, Mark	90UD	128	$ .01	$ .50					
Grant, Mark	89UD	622	$ .01	$ .07					
Grant, Mark	90UD	412	$ .01	$ .07					
Green, Gary	89UD	722	$ .01	$ .10					
Greene, Tommy	90UD	49	$ .01	$ .50					
Greenwell, Mike	89UD	432	$ .10	$1.00					
Greenwell, Mike	90UD	354	$ .01	$ .25					
Gregg, Tommy	89UD	751	$ .01	$ .10					
Gregg, Tommy	90UD	121	$ .01	$ .10					
Griffey, Jr., Ken	89UD	1	$1.00	$20.00					
Griffey, Jr., Ken	90UD	24	$ .01	$1.00					
Griffey, Jr., Ken	90UD	156	$ .01	$3.00					
Griffey, Sr., Ken	90UD	682	$ .01	$ .07					
Griffin, Alfredo	89UD	631	$ .01	$ .25					
Griffin, Alfredo	90UD	338	$ .01	$ .07	Harkey, Mike	89UD	14	$ .05	$ .40
Grimsley, Jaxon	90UD	27	$ .01	$ .20	Harkey, Mike	90UD	107	$ .01	$ .25
Grissom, Marquis	90UD	8	$ .01	$1.25	Harnisch, Pete	89UD	744	$ .01	$ .10
Gross, Greg	89UD	534	$ .01	$ .07	Harnisch, Pete	90UD	623	$ .01	$ .10
Gross, Kevin	89UD	31	$ .01	$ .07	Harper, Brian	89UD	379	$ .01	$ .07
Gross, Kevin	89UD	719	$ .01	$ .10	Harper, Brian	90UD	391	$ .01	$ .07
Gross, Kevin	90UD	468	$ .01	$ .07	Harris, Gene	90UD	565	$ .01	$ .10
Gruber, Kelly	89UD	575	$ .01	$ .07	Harris, Greg W.	89UD	724	$ .01	$ .10
Gruber, Kelly	90UD	111	$ .01	$ .15	Harris, Greg W.	90UD	622	$ .01	$ .10
Guante, Cecilio	89UD	576	$ .01	$ .07	Harris, Lenny	89UD	781	$ .01	$ .10
Gubicza, Mark	89UD	202	$ .01	$ .10	Harris, Lenny	90UD	423	$ .01	$ .10
Gubicza, Mark	90UD	676	$ .01	$ .07	Harvey, Bryan	89UD	594	$ .01	$ .15
Guerrero, Pedro	90UD	244	$ .01	$ .10	Harvey, Bryan	90UD	686	$ .01	$ .07
Guerrero, Pedro	89UD	306	$ .01	$ .07	Hassey, Ron	89UD	564	$ .01	$ .07
Guetterman, Lee	90UD	318	$ .01	$ .07	Hassey, Ron	90UD	195	$ .01	$ .07
Guidry, Ron	89UD	307	$ .01	$ .07	Hatcher, Billy	89UD	344	$ .01	$ .07
Guillen, Ozzie	89UD	175	$ .01	$ .10	Hatcher, Billy	90UD	598	$ .01	$ .07
Guillen, Ozzie	90UD	267	$ .01	$ .07	Hatcher, Mickey	89UD	709	$ .01	$ .10
Guillen, Ozzie	90UD	79	$ .01	$ .07	Hatcher, Mickey	90UD	283	$ .01	$ .07
Guthrie, Mark	90UD	436	$ .01	$ .15	Hawkins, Andy	89UD	495	$ .01	$ .07
Gutierrez, Jackie	89UD	430	$ .01	$ .07	Hawkins, Andy	89UD	708	$ .01	$ .10
Guzman, Jose	89UD	73	$ .01	$ .07	Hawkins, Andy	90UD	339	$ .01	$ .07
Guzman, Jose	90UD	617	$ .01	$ .07	Hayes, Charlie	89UD	707	$ .01	$ .75
Gwynn, Chris	89UD	607	$ .01	$ .07					

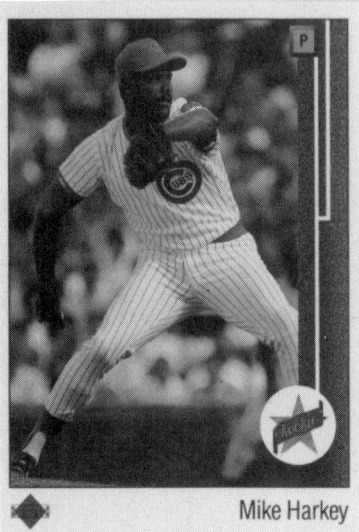

Mike Harkey

Player	Year	No.	VG	EX/MT
Hayes, Charlie	90UD	437	$ .01	$ .10
Hayes, Von	89UD	246	$ .01	$ .10
Hayes, Von	90UD	453	$ .01	$ .07
Hayes, Von	90UD	7	$ .01	$ .07
Hearn, Ed	89UD	42	$ .01	$ .07
Heath, Mike	89UD	654	$ .01	$ .07
Heath, Mike	90UD	306	$ .01	$ .07
Heaton, Neal	89UD	99	$ .01	$ .07
Heaton, Neal	90UD	86	$ .01	$ .07
Henderson, Dave	89UD	174	$ .01	$ .07
Henderson, Dave	90UD	206	$ .01	$ .10
Henderson, Rickey	89UD	210	$ .01	$ .25
Henderson, Rickey	90UD	334	$ .01	$ .25
Henke, Tom	89UD	264	$ .01	$ .07
Henke, Tom	90UD	282	$ .01	$ .07
Henneman, Mike	89UD	373	$ .01	$ .07
Henneman, Mike	90UD	537	$ .01	$ .07
Henry, Dwayne	89UD	51	$ .01	$ .07
Hernandez, Guillermo	89UD	279	$ .01	$ .07
Hernandez, Guillermo	90UD	518	$ .01	$ .07
Hernandez, Keith	89UD	612	$ .01	$ .10
Hernandez, Keith	90UD	222	$ .01	$ .07
Hernandez, Xavier	90UD	26	$ .01	$ .15
Herndon, Larry	89UD	49	$ .01	$ .07
Herr, Tommy	89UD	558	$ .01	$ .07
Herr, Tommy	89UD	720	$ .01	$ .10
Herr, Tommy	90UD	488	$ .01	$ .07
Hershiser, Orel	89UD	130	$ .01	$ .25
Hershiser, Orel	89UD	661	$ .01	$ .15
Hershiser, Orel	89UD	665	$ .01	$ .15
Hershiser, Orel	89UD	667	$ .01	$ .15
Hershiser, Orel	90UD	10	$ .01	$ .07
Hershiser, Orel	90UD	256	$ .01	$ .10
Hershiser, Orel	90UD	9	$ .01	$ .07
Hesketh, Joe	90UD	512	$ .01	$ .07
Hesketh, Jose	89UD	60	$ .01	$ .07
Hetzel, Eric	90UD	673	$ .01	$ .10
Hibbard, Greg	90UD	543	$ .01	$ .15
Hickey, Kevin	90UD	299	$ .01	$ .07
Higuera, Ted	89UD	424	$ .01	$ .07
Higuera, Ted	90UD	627	$ .01	$ .07
Hill, Donnie	89UD	527	$ .01	$ .07
Hill, Ken	90UD	336	$ .01	$ .07
Hillegas, Shawn	89UD	478	$ .01	$ .07
Hillegas, Shawn	90UD	541	$ .01	$ .07
Hinzo, Tommy	89UD	34	$ .01	$ .07
Holman, Brian	89UD	356	$ .01	$ .07
Holman, Brian	90UD	362	$ .01	$ .07
Holton, Brian	89UD	72	$ .01	$ .07
Holton, Brian	00UD	175	$ .01	$ .07
Honeycutt, Rick	89UD	278	$ .01	$ .07
Honeycutt, Rick	90UD	151	$ .01	$ .07
Horner, Bob	89UD	125	$ .01	$ .07
Horton, Ricky	89UD	629	$ .01	$ .07
Hough, Charlie	89UD	437	$ .01	$ .07
Hough, Charlie	90UD	314	$ .01	$ .07
Howard, Tom	89UD	726	$ .01	$ .50
Howell, Jack	89UD	138	$ .01	$ .07
Howell, Jack	90UD	19	$ .01	$ .07
Howell, Jay	89UD	610	$ .01	$ .07
Howell, Jay	90UD	508	$ .01	$ .07
Howell, Ken	90UD	559	$ .01	$ .07
Hrbek, Kent	89UD	213	$ .01	$ .10
Hrbek, Kent	90UD	452	$ .01	$ .07
Hubbard, Glenn	89UD	395	$ .01	$ .07
Hudler, Rex	89UD	405	$ .01	$ .07
Hudler, Rex	90UD	411	$ .01	$ .07
Hudson, Charles	89UD	586	$ .01	$ .07
Hudson, Charles	90UD	520	$ .01	$ .07
Hurst, Bruce	89UD	387	$ .01	$ .07
Hurst, Bruce	89UD	792	$ .01	$ .15
Hurst, Bruce	90UD	433	$ .01	$ .07
Huson, Jeff	90UD	434	$ .01	$ .15
Incaviglia, Pete	89UD	484	$ .01	$ .15
Incaviglia, Pete	90UD	333	$ .01	$ .07

Player	Year	No.	VG	EX/MT
Innis, Jeff	90UD	562	$ .01	$ .10
Jackson, Bo	89UD	221	$ .10	$1.00
Jackson, Bo	90UD	105	$ .01	$1.00
Jackson, Bo	90UD	32	$ .01	$ .45
Jackson, Bo	90UD	75	$ .01	$1.00
Jackson, Chuck	89UD	323	$ .01	$ .07
Jackson, Danny	89UD	640	$ .01	$ .10
Jackson, Danny	90UD	120	$ .01	$ .07
Jackson, Darrin	89UD	214	$ .01	$ .15
Jackson, Darrin	90UD	414	$ .01	$ .07
Jackson, Mike	89UD	142	$ .01	$ .07
Jackson, Mike	90UD	494	$ .01	$ .07
Jacoby, Brook	89UD	198	$ .01	$ .07
Jacoby, Brook	90UD	459	$ .01	$ .07
James, Chris	89UD	513	$ .01	$ .07
James, Chris	90UD	435	$ .01	$ .07
James, Dion	89UD	587	$ .01	$ .07
James, Dion	90UD	591	$ .01	$ .07
Javier, Stan	89UD	581	$ .01	$ .07
Javier, Stan	90UD	209	$ .01	$ .07
Jefferies, Gregg	89UD	9	$ .25	$3.00
Jefferies, Gregg	90UD	166	$ .01	$ .50
Jeltz, Steve	89UD	219	$ .01	$ .07
Jeltz, Steve	90UD	495	$ .01	$ .07
Jennings, Doug	89UD	585	$ .01	$ .15
Jimenez, German	89UD	113	$ .01	$ .10
Jody, Davis	89UD	795	$ .01	$ .10
John, Tommy	89UD	230	$ .01	$ .10
Johnson, Dave	90UD	425	$ .01	$ .25
Johnson, Howard	89UD	582	$ .01	$ .15
Johnson, Howard	90UD	263	$ .01	$ .15
Johnson, Lance	90UD	90	$ .01	$ .07
Johnson, Randy	89UD	25	$ .01	$ .10
Johnson, Randy	90UD	563	$ .01	$ .07
Johnson, Wallace	89UD	124	$ .01	$ .07
Jones, Barry	89UD	457	$ .01	$ .07
Jones, Doug	89UD	540	$ .01	$ .07
Jones, Doug	90UD	632	$ .01	$ .07
Jones, Jimmy	89UD	286	$ .01	$ .07
Jones, Odell	89UD	608	$ .01	$ .07

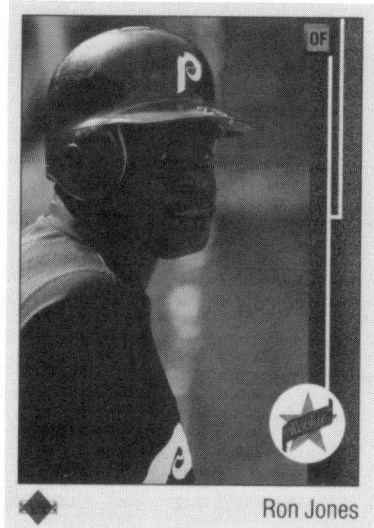

Ron Jones

Player	Year	No.	VG	EX/MT
Jones, Ron	89UD	11	$ .01	$ .35
Jones, Ron	90UD	94	$ .01	$ .07
Jones, Timmy	89UD	348	$ .01	$ .07

Player	Year	No.	VG	EX/MT
Jones, Timmy	90UD	501	$ .01	$ .07
Jones, Tracy	89UD	798	$ .01	$ .10
Jones, Tracy	89UD	96	$ .01	$ .07
Jones, Tracy	90UD	309	$ .01	$ .07
Jordan, Ricky	89UD	35	$ .01	$1.50
Jordan, Ricky	90UD	576	$ .01	$ .20
Jose, Felix	89UD	22	$ .05	$ .35
Jose, Felix	90UD	228	$ .01	$ .15
Joyner, Wally	89UD	573	$ .01	$ .15
Joyner, Wally	89UD	668	$ .01	$ .15
Joyner, Wally	90UD	693	$ .01	$ .15
Karkovice, Ron	89UD	183	$ .01	$ .07
Karkovice, Ron	90UD	69	$ .01	$ .07
Kelly, Roberto	89UD	590	$ .01	$ .25
Kelly, Roberto	90UD	193	$ .01	$ .15
Kennedy, Terry	89UD	469	$ .01	$ .07
Kennedy, Terry	90UD	397	$ .01	$ .07
Key, Jimmy	89UD	291	$ .01	$ .15
Key, Jimmy	90UD	462	$ .01	$ .07
Kilgus, Paul	89UD	335	$ .01	$ .07

Paul Kilgus

Player	Year	No.	VG	EX/MT
Kilgus, Paul	89UD	797	$ .01	$ .10
Kilgus, Paul	90UD	155	$ .01	$ .07
King, Eric	89UD	493	$ .01	$ .07
King, Eric	90UD	651	$ .01	$ .07
King, Jeff	90UD	557	$ .01	$ .10
Kipper, Bob	89UD	520	$ .01	$ .07
Kipper, Bob	90UD	560	$ .01	$ .07
Kittle, Ron	89UD	228	$ .01	$ .07
Kittle, Ron	89UD	711	$ .01	$ .10
Knepper, Bob	89UD	422	$ .01	$ .07
Knepper, Bob	90UD	599	$ .01	$ .07
Knight, Ray	89UD	259	$ .01	$ .07
Komminsk, Brad	90UD	428	$ .01	$ .07
Kramer, Randy	90UD	519	$ .01	$ .07
Kreuter, Chad	89UD	312	$ .01	$ .10
Kreuter, Chad	90UD	609	$ .01	$ .07
Kruk, John	89UD	280	$ .01	$ .07
Kruk, John	90UD	668	$ .01	$ .07
Krukow, Mike	89UD	46	$ .01	$ .07
Krukow, Mike	90UD	639	$ .01	$ .07
Kunkel, Jeff	89UD	463	$ .01	$ .07
Kunkel, Jeff	90UD	394	$ .01	$ .07
LaCoss, Mike	89UD	48	$ .01	$ .07

Player	Year	No.	VG	EX/MT
LaCoss, Mike	90UD	140	$ .01	$ .07
Lake, Steve	90UD	491	$ .01	$ .07
Lamp, Dennis	89UD	503	$ .01	$ .07
Lancaster, Les	89UD	84	$ .01	$ .07
Lancaster, Les	90UD	584	$ .01	$ .07
Landrum, Bill	90UD	442	$ .01	$ .07
Langston, Mark	89UD	526	$ .01	$ .20
Langston, Mark	90UD	647	$ .01	$ .10
Lansford, Carney	89UD	562	$ .01	$ .07
Lansford, Carney	90UD	253	$ .01	$ .07
LaPoint, Dave	89UD	600	$ .01	$ .07
LaPoint, Dave	89UD	706	$ .01	$ .10
LaPoint, Dave	90UD	507	$ .01	$ .07
Larkin, Barry	89UD	270	$ .01	$ .40
Larkin, Barry	90UD	167	$ .01	$ .15
Larkin, Barry	90UD	99	$ .01	$ .15
Larkin, Gene	89UD	580	$ .01	$ .10
Larkin, Gene	90UD	471	$ .01	$ .07
Laudner, Tim	89UD	62	$ .01	$ .07
Laudner, Tim	90UD	419	$ .01	$ .07
LaValliere, Mike	89UD	417	$ .01	$ .07
LaValliere, Mike	90UD	578	$ .01	$ .07
Law, Vance	89UD	473	$ .01	$ .07
Law, Vance	90UD	380	$ .01	$ .07
Lea, Charlie	89UD	81	$ .01	$ .07
Leach, Rick	89UD	554	$ .01	$ .07
Leach, Rick	90UD	640	$ .01	$ .07
Leach, Terry	89UD	288	$ .01	$ .07
Leach, Terry	90UD	642	$ .01	$ .07
Leary, Tim	89UD	94	$ .01	$ .07
Leary, Tim	90UD	662	$ .01	$ .07
Lee, Manny	89UD	271	$ .01	$ .07
Lee, Manny	90UD	285	$ .01	$ .07
Lefferts, Craig	89UD	541	$ .01	$ .07
Lefferts, Craig	90UD	399	$ .01	$ .07
Leibrandt, Charlie	89UD	637	$ .01	$ .07
Leibrandt, Charlie	90UD	658	$ .01	$ .07
Leiper, Dave	89UD	363	$ .01	$ .07
Leiter, Al	89UD	588	$ .01	$ .15
Leiter, Al	89UD	705	$ .01	$ .15
Lemke, Mark	89UD	19	$ .01	$ .10
Lemke, Mark	90UD	665	$ .01	$ .07
Lemon, Chet	89UD	128	$ .01	$ .07
Lemon, Chet	90UD	348	$ .01	$ .07
Leonard, Jeffrey	89UD	263	$ .01	$ .07
Leonard, Jeffrey	89UD	789	$ .01	$ .15
Leonard, Jeffrey	90UD	331	$ .01	$ .07
Lilliquist, Derek	89UD	753	$ .05	$ .75
Lilliquist, Derek	90UD	234	$ .01	$ .10
Lind, Jose	89UD	334	$ .01	$ .07
Lind, Jose	90UD	424	$ .01	$ .07
Liriano, Nelson	89UD	109	$ .01	$ .07
Liriano, Nelson	90UD	134	$ .01	$ .07
Litton, Greg	90UD	677	$ .01	$ .15
Lombardozzi, Steve	89UD	179	$ .01	$ .07
Long, Bill	89UD	499	$ .01	$ .07
Lovullo, Torey	89UD	782	$ .01	$ .10
Lovullo, Torey	90UD	332	$ .01	$ .10
Luecken, Rick	90UD	621	$ .01	$ .10
Lynn, Fred	89UD	761	$ .01	$ .15
Lynn, Fred	90UD	247	$ .01	$ .07
Lyons, Barry	89UD	176	$ .01	$ .07
Lyons, Barry	90UD	473	$ .01	$ .07
Lyons, Steve	89UD	224	$ .01	$ .07
Lyons, Steve	90UD	390	$ .01	$ .07
Maas, Kevin	90UD	70	$ .01	$ .35
MacFarlane (f), Mike	89UD	546	$ .01	$ .15
MacFarlane, Mike	90UD	307	$ .01	$ .07
Machado, Julio	90UD	93	$ .01	$ .20
Mack, Shane	89UD	182	$ .01	$ .15
Maddux, Greg	89UD	241	$ .01	$ .10
Maddux, Greg	90UD	213	$ .01	$ .07
Maddux, Mike	89UD	338	$ .01	$ .07
Magadan, Dave	89UD	388	$ .01	$ .07
Magadan, Dave	90UD	243	$ .01	$ .07

Player	Year	No.	VG	EX/MT	Player	Year	No.	VG	EX/MT
Magrane, Joe	89UD	103	$ .01	$ .15	McDowell, Jack	90UD	625	$ .01	$ .07
Magrane, Joe	90UD	242	$ .01	$ .07	McDowell, Oddibbe	90UD	145	$ .01	$ .07
Mahler, Rick	89UD	74	$ .01	$ .07	McDowell, Oddibbe	89UD	333	$ .01	$ .07
					McDowell, Oddibbe	89UD	796	$ .01	$ .15
					McDowell, Roger	89UD	296	$ .01	$ .07
					McDowell, Roger	90UD	416	$ .01	$ .07
					McGaffigan, Andy	89UD	359	$ .01	$ .07
					McGaffigan, Andy	90UD	597	$ .01	$ .07
					McGee, Willie	89UD	621	$ .01	$ .07
					McGee, Willie	90UD	505	$ .01	$ .07
					McGriff, Fred	89UD	572	$ .01	$ .25
					McGriff, Fred	89UD	671	$ .01	$ .15
					McGriff, Fred	90UD	108	$ .01	$ .20
					McGwire, Mark	89UD	300	$ .15	$ .75
					McGwire, Mark	90UD	171	$ .01	$ .35
					McGwire, Mark	90UD	36	$ .01	$ .10
					McKnight, Jeff	90UD	162	$ .01	$ .20
					McLemore, Mark	89UD	245	$ .01	$ .07
					McReynolds, Kevin	89UD	367	$ .01	$ .10
					McReynolds, Kevin	90UD	265	$ .01	$ .10
					McWilliams, Larry	89UD	143	$ .01	$ .07
					Meacham, Bobby	89UD	77	$ .01	$ .07
					Meadows, Louie	89UD	401	$ .01	$ .15
					Meadows, Louie	90UD	160	$ .01	$ .07
					Medina, Luis	89UD	2	$ .05	$ .40
					Melvin, Bob	89UD	227	$ .01	$ .07
					Melvin, Bob	90UD	644	$ .01	$ .07
					Mercado, Orlando	89UD	624	$ .01	$ .07
					Mercker, Kent	90UD	63	$ .01	$ .65
					Merullo, Matt	90UD	67	$ .01	$ .15
					Meulens, Hensley	89UD	746	$ .01	$ .25
					Meulens, Hensley	90UD	546	$ .01	$ .15
					Meyer, Brian	90UD	22	$ .01	$ .15
					Meyer, Joey	89UD	403	$ .01	$ .07
					Mielke, Gary	90UD	612	$ .01	$ .10

Rick Mahler

Player	Year	No.	VG	EX/MT	Player	Year	No.	VG	EX/MT
Mahler, Rick	89UD	760	$ .01	$ .10	Milacki, Bob	89UD	735	$ .01	$ .10
Mahler, Rick	90UD	220	$ .01	$ .07	Milacki, Bob	90UD	635	$ .01	$ .10
Maldonado, Candy	89UD	502	$ .01	$ .07	Miller, Darrell	89UD	462	$ .01	$ .07
Maldonado, Candy	90UD	136	$ .01	$ .07	Miller, Keith	89UD	739	$ .01	$ .15
Mann, Kelly	90UD	33	$ .01	$ .15	Miller, Keith	90UD	190	$ .01	$ .07
Manrique, Fred	89UD	628	$ .01	$ .07	Milligan, Randy	89UD	559	$ .01	$ .10
Manrique, Fred	90UD	392	$ .01	$ .07	Milligan, Randy	89UD	740	$ .01	$ .10
Manwaring, Kirt	89UD	500	$ .01	$ .10	Milligan, Randy	90UD	663	$ .01	$ .07
Manwaring, Kirt	90UD	457	$ .01	$ .07	Minton, Greg	89UD	635	$ .01	$ .07
Marshall, Mike	89UD	70	$ .01	$ .07	Minton, Greg	90UD	83	$ .01	$ .07
Marshall, Mike	90UD	262	$ .01	$ .07	Mirabella, Paul	89UD	322	$ .01	$ .07
Martinez, Carlos	90UD	347	$ .01	$ .15	Mitchell, Kevin	89UD	163	$ .15	$ .75
Martinez, Carmelo	89UD	365	$ .01	$ .07	Mitchell, Kevin	90UD	117	$ .01	$ .30
Martinez, Carmelo	90UD	592	$ .01	$ .07	Mitchell, Kevin	90UD	40	$ .01	$ .10
Martinez, Dave	89UD	444	$ .01	$ .07	Mohorcic, Dale	89UD	727	$ .01	$ .10
Martinez, Dave	90UD	470	$ .01	$ .07	Mohorcic, Dale	90UD	530	$ .01	$ .07
Martinez, Dennis	89UD	377	$ .01	$ .07	Molitor, Paul	89UD	525	$ .01	$ .10
Martinez, Dennis	90UD	413	$ .01	$ .07	Molitor, Paul	89UD	673	$ .01	$ .10
Martinez, Edgar	89UD	768	$ .01	$ .35	Molitor, Paul	90UD	254	$ .01	$ .07
Martinez, Edgar	90UD	532	$ .01	$ .15	Montgomery, Jeff	89UD	618	$ .01	$ .15
Martinez, Ramon	89UD	18	$ .05	$ .50	Montgomery, Jeff	90UD	698	$ .01	$ .07
Martinez, Ramon	90UD	675	$ .01	$ .10	Moore, Mike	89UD	123	$ .01	$ .07
Martinez, Tino	90UD	37	$ .01	$ .65	Moore, Mike	89UD	758	$ .01	$ .10
Mathews, Greg	89UD	531	$ .01	$ .07	Moore, Mike	90UD	275	$ .01	$ .07
Mathews, Greg	90UD	678	$ .01	$ .07	Moreland, Keith	89UD	361	$ .01	$ .07
Mattingly, Don	89UD	200	$ .15	$1.00	Moreland, Keith	90UD	401	$ .01	$ .07
Mattingly, Don	89UD	693	$ .01	$ .25	Morgan, Mike	89UD	653	$ .01	$ .07
Mattingly, Don	90UD	191	$ .01	$ .50	Morgan, Mike	90UD	317	$ .01	$ .07
Mazzilli, Lee	89UD	657	$ .01	$ .07	Morris, Hal	90UD	31	$ .01	$ .15
McCament, Randy	90UD	657	$ .01	$ .15	Morris, Jack	89UD	352	$ .01	$ .07
McCaskill, Kirk	89UD	223	$ .01	$ .07	Morris, Jack	90UD	573	$ .01	$ .07
McCaskill, Kirk	90UD	506	$ .01	$ .07	Morrison, Jim	89UD	568	$ .01	$ .07
McClendon, Lloyd	89UD	446	$ .01	$ .20	Moseby, Lloyd	89UD	381	$ .01	$ .07
McClendon, Lloyd	90UD	398	$ .01	$ .07	Moseby, Lloyd	90UD	421	$ .01	$ .07
McClure, Bob	90UD	81	$ .01	$ .07	Moses, John	89UD	242	$ .01	$ .07
McCullers, Lance	89UD	382	$ .01	$ .07	Moses, John	90UD	240	$ .01	$ .07
McCullers, Lance	89UD	710	$ .01	$ .10	Moyer, Jamie	89UD	63	$ .01	$ .07
McCullers, Lance	90UD	615	$ .01	$ .07	Moyer, Jamie	89UD	791	$ .01	$ .10
McDonald, Ben	90UD	54	$ .01	$3.00	Moyer, Jamie	90UD	619	$ .01	$ .07
McDowell, Jack	89UD	530	$ .01	$ .10	Mulholland, Terry	90UD	474	$ .01	$ .07

UPPER DECK

Player	Year	No.	VG	EX/MT	Player	Year	No.	VG	EX/MT
Mulliniks, Rance	89UD	43	$ .01	$ .07	Ojeda, Bob	90UD	204	$ .01	$ .07
Mulliniks, Rance	90UD	132	$ .01	$ .07	Olerud, John	90UD	56	$ .01	$4.25
Murphy, Dale	89UD	357	$ .05	$ .35	Olin, Steve	90UD	553	$ .01	$ .10
Murphy, Dale	89UD	672	$ .01	$ .15	Oliver, Joe	90UD	568	$ .01	$ .35
Murphy, Dale	90UD	533	$ .01	$ .10	Olson, Gregg	89UD	723	$ .01	$ .35
Murphy, Rob	89UD	372	$ .01	$ .07	Olson, Gregg	90UD	604	$ .01	$ .35
Murphy, Rob	89UD	759	$ .01	$ .10	Olwine, Ed	89UD	435	$ .01	$ .07
Murphy, Rob	90UD	461	$ .01	$ .07	Oquendo, Jose	89UD	514	$ .01	$ .07
Murray, Eddie	89UD	275	$ .01	$ .15	Oquendo, Jose	90UD	319	$ .01	$ .07
Murray, Eddie	89UD	763	$ .01	$ .15	Orosco, Jesse	89UD	87	$ .01	$ .07
Murray, Eddie	90UD	277	$ .01	$ .07	Orosco, Jesse	90UD	588	$ .01	$ .07
Musselman, Jeff	89UD	41	$ .01	$ .07	Orsulak, Joe	89UD	429	$ .01	$ .07
Musselman, Jeff	90UD	585	$ .01	$ .07	Orsulak, Joe	90UD	270	$ .01	$ .07
Myers, Randy	89UD	634	$ .01	$ .07	Ortiz, Junior	89UD	86	$ .01	$ .07
Myers, Randy	90UD	581	$ .01	$ .07	Ortiz, Junior	90UD	389	$ .01	$ .07
Navarro, Jaime	90UD	646	$ .01	$ .15	Orton, John	90UD	672	$ .01	$ .25
Nelson, Gene	89UD	643	$ .01	$ .07	Otto, David	89UD	4	$ .01	$ .10
Nelson, Gene	90UD	80	$ .01	$ .07	Owen, Larry	89UD	528	$ .01	$ .07
Nelson, Rob	90UD	51	$ .01	$ .07	Owen, Spike	89UD	161	$ .01	$ .07
Newman, Al	89UD	197	$ .01	$ .07	Owen, Spike	89UD	717	$ .01	$ .10
Newman, Al	90UD	199	$ .01	$ .07	Own, Spike	90UD	291	$ .01	$ .07
Nichols, Rod	90UD	572	$ .01	$ .07	Pagliarulo, Mike	89UD	569	$ .01	$ .07
Niedenfuer, Tom	89UD	488	$ .01	$ .07	Pagliarulo, Mike	90UD	329	$ .01	$ .07
Nieves, Juan	89UD	646	$ .01	$ .07	Pagnozzi, Tom	89UD	602	$ .01	$ .07
Nieves, Juan	90UD	648	$ .01	$ .07	Palacios, Ray	89UD	21	$ .01	$ .10
Nipper, Al	89UD	494	$ .01	$ .07	Pall, Donn	90UD	386	$ .01	$ .07
Nixon, Otis	89UD	480	$ .01	$ .07	Palmeiro, Rafael	89UD	235	$ .01	$ .25
Nixon, Otis	90UD	379	$ .01	$ .07	Palmeiro, Rafael	89UD	772	$ .01	$ .20
Nokes, Matt	89UD	150	$ .01	$ .07	Palmeiro, Rafael	90UD	335	$ .01	$ .07
Nokes, Matt	90UD	226	$ .01	$ .07	Palmer, David	89UD	515	$ .01	$ .07
Nosek, Randy	90UD	2	$ .01	$ .10	Palmer, Dean	90UD	74	$ .01	$ .35
O'Brien, Charlie	90UD	650	$ .01	$ .07	Pankovits, Jim	89UD	100	$ .01	$ .07
O'Brien, Pete	89UD	54	$ .01	$ .07	Paredes, Johnny	89UD	477	$ .01	$ .15
O'Brien, Pete	89UD	800	$ .01	$ .15	Parent, Mark	89UD	492	$ .01	$ .10
O'Brien, Pete	90UD	110	$ .01	$ .07	Parent, Mark	90UD	569	$ .01	$ .07
O'Neill, Paul	90UD	161	$ .01	$ .10	Paris, Kelly	89UD	192	$ .01	$ .07
O'Neill, Paul	89UD	428	$ .01	$ .07	Parker, Dave	89UD	605	$ .01	$ .07
Oberkfell, Ken	89UD	313	$ .01	$ .07	Parker, Dave	90UD	192	$ .01	$ .07
Oberkfell, Ken	90UD	360	$ .01	$ .07	Parrett, Jeff	89UD	398	$ .01	$ .15
					Parrett, Jeff	89UD	741	$ .01	$ .15
					Parrett, Jeff	90UD	92	$ .01	$ .07
					Parrish, Lance	89UD	240	$ .01	$ .07
					Parrish, Lance	89UD	775	$ .01	$ .10
					Parrish, Lance	90UD	674	$ .01	$ .07
					Parrish, Larry	89UD	36	$ .01	$ .07
					Pasqua, Dan	89UD	204	$ .01	$ .07
					Pasqua, Dan	90UD	286	$ .01	$ .07
					Pecota, Bill	89UD	507	$ .01	$ .07
					Pena, Alejandro	89UD	137	$ .01	$ .07
					Pena, Alejandro	90UD	279	$ .01	$ .07
					Pena, Tony	89UD	330	$ .01	$ .07
					Pena, Tony	90UD	276	$ .01	$ .07
					Pendleton, Terry	89UD	131	$ .01	$ .07
					Pendleton, Terry	90UD	469	$ .01	$ .07
					Peraza, Oswald	89UD	651	$ .01	$ .15
					Perez, Melido	89UD	243	$ .01	$ .10
					Perez, Melido	90UD	525	$ .01	$ .07
					Perez, Pascual	89UD	498	$ .01	$ .07
					Perez, Pascual	90UD	487	$ .01	$ .07
					Perry, Gerald	89UD	431	$ .01	$ .07
					Perry, Gerald	90UD	101	$ .01	$ .07
					Perry, Pat	89UD	345	$ .01	$ .07
					Peters, Steve	89UD	771	$ .01	$ .10
					Petralli, Geno	89UD	482	$ .01	$ .07
					Petralli, Geno	90UD	633	$ .01	$ .07
					Petry, Dan	89UD	552	$ .01	$ .07
					Petry, Dan	90UD	690	$ .01	$ .07
					Pettis, Gary	89UD	117	$ .01	$ .07
					Pettis, Gary	90UD	385	$ .01	$ .07
					Pevey, Marty	90UD	628	$ .01	$ .10
					Phelps, Ken	89UD	167	$ .01	$ .07
					Phillips, Tony	89UD	267	$ .01	$ .07
					Phillips, Tony	90UD	154	$ .01	$ .07
					Pico, Jeff	89UD	491	$ .01	$ .15
					Plesac, Dan	89UD	630	$ .01	$ .07

Ron Oester

Player	Year	No.	VG	EX/MT
Oester, Ron	89UD	287	$ .01	$ .07
Oester, Ron	90UD	118	$ .01	$ .07
Offerman, Jose	90UD	46	$ .01	$2.50
Ojeda, Bob	89UD	386	$ .01	$ .07

Player	Year	No.	VG	EX/MT	Player	Year	No.	VG	EX/MT
Plesac, Dan	90UD	477	$ .01	$ .07	Ripken, Billy	89UD	283	$ .01	$ .07
Plunk, Eric	89UD	353	$ .01	$ .07	Ripken, Billy	90UD	184	$ .01	$ .07
Plunk, Eric	90UD	630	$ .01	$ .07	Ripken, Jr., Cal	89UD	467	$ .01	$ .15
Polidor, Gus	90UD	480	$ .01	$ .07					
Polonia, Luis	89UD	162	$ .01	$ .10					
Polonia, Luis	90UD	316	$ .01	$ .07					
Portugal, Mark	89UD	358	$ .01	$ .07					
Portugal, Mark	90UD	502	$ .01	$ .07					
Powell, Dennis	90UD	229	$ .01	$ .07					
Power, Ted	90UD	340	$ .01	$ .07					
Presley, Jim	89UD	642	$ .01	$ .07					
Presley, Jim	90UD	315	$ .01	$ .07					
Price, Joe	89UD	505	$ .01	$ .07					
Prince, Tom	89UD	311	$ .01	$ .07					
Puckett, Kirby	89UD	376	$ .01	$ .35					
Puckett, Kirby	90UD	236	$ .01	$ .30					
Puckett, Kirby	90UD	48	$ .01	$ .07					
Puhl, Terry	90UD	201	$ .01	$ .07					
Puleo, Charlie	89UD	589	$ .01	$ .07					
Quinones, Luis	90UD	593	$ .01	$ .07					
Quinones, Rey	89UD	508	$ .01	$ .07					
Quinones, Rey	89UD	750	$ .01	$ .10					
Quintana, Carlos	89UD	26	$ .01	$ .25					
Quintana, Carlos	90UD	465	$ .01	$ .07					
Quirk, Jamie	89UD	620	$ .01	$ .07					
Quisenberry, Dan	89UD	533	$ .01	$ .07					
Quisenberry, Dan	90UD	659	$ .01	$ .07					
Raines, Tim	89UD	402	$ .01	$ .15					
Raines, Tim	90UD	177	$ .01	$ .10					
Raines, Tim	90UD	29	$ .01	$ .07					
Ramirez, Rafael	89UD	341	$ .01	$ .07					
Ramirez, Rafael	90UD	144	$ .01	$ .07					
Ramos, Domingo	90UD	150	$ .01	$ .07					
Randolph, Willie	89UD	237	$ .01	$ .07					
Randolph, Willie	89UD	777	$ .01	$ .10					
Randolph, Willie	90UD	183	$ .01	$ .07	Ripken, Jr., Cal	89UD	682	$ .01	$ .25
Rasmussen, Dennis	89UD	645	$ .01	$ .07	Ripken, Jr., Cal	90UD	266	$ .01	$ .10
Rasmussen, Dennis	90UD	594	$ .01	$ .07	Ritz, Kevin	90UD	98	$ .01	$ .20
Rawley, Shane	89UD	427	$ .01	$ .07	Rivera, Luis	89UD	423	$ .01	$ .10
Rawley, Shane	89UD	786	$ .01	$ .10	Rivera, Luis	90UD	482	$ .01	$ .07
Rawley, Shane	90UD	438	$ .01	$ .07	Roberts, Bip	90UD	303	$ .01	$ .07
Ray, Johnny	89UD	481	$ .01	$ .07	Robinson, Don	89UD	523	$ .01	$ .07
Ray, Johnny	90UD	509	$ .01	$ .07	Robinson, Don	90UD	616	$ .01	$ .07
Ready, Randy	89UD	474	$ .01	$ .07	Robinson, Jeff (Det.)	89UD	472	$ .01	$ .15
Ready, Randy	90UD	404	$ .01	$ .07	Robinson, Jeff	90UD	552	$ .01	$ .07
Reardon, Jeff	89UD	596	$ .01	$ .07	Robinson, Jeff (Pitts.)	89UD	332	$ .01	$ .07
Reardon, Jeff	90UD	417	$ .01	$ .07	Robinson, Jeff	90UD	403	$ .01	$ .07
Redus, Gary	89UD	419	$ .01	$ .07	Robinson, Ron	89UD	187	$ .01	$ .07
Redus, Gary	90UD	248	$ .01	$ .07	Rochford, Mike	90UD	694	$ .01	$ .07
Reed, Jeff	89UD	276	$ .01	$ .07	Rogers, Kenny	90UD	606	$ .01	$ .10
Reed, Jeff	90UD	165	$ .01	$ .07	Romero, Ed	89UD	40	$ .01	$ .07
Reed, Jerry	89UD	529	$ .01	$ .07	Romine, Kevin	89UD	524	$ .01	$ .07
Reed, Jerry	90UD	210	$ .01	$ .07	Romine, Kevin	90UD	441	$ .01	$ .07
Reed, Jody	89UD	370	$ .01	$ .15	Roomes, Rolando	89UD	6	$ .01	$ .25
Reed, Jody	90UD	321	$ .01	$ .07	Roomes, Rolando	90UD	170	$ .01	$ .07
Renteria, Rich	89UD	547	$ .01	$ .15	Rose, Bobby	90UD	77	$ .01	$ .50
Reuschel, Rick	89UD	194	$ .01	$ .07	Rosenberg, Steve	89UD	715	$ .01	$ .10
Reuschel, Rick	90UD	696	$ .01	$ .07	Rosenberg, Steve	90UD	522	$ .01	$ .07
Reuss, Jerry	90UD	96	$ .01	$ .07	Roysler, Jerry	89UD	433	$ .01	$ .07
Reynolds, Craig	89UD	284	$ .01	$ .07	Rucker, Dave	89UD	436	$ .01	$ .07
Reynolds, Harold	89UD	249	$ .01	$ .07	Ruess, Jerry	89UD	151	$ .01	$ .07
Reynolds, Harold	90UD	179	$ .01	$ .07	Ruffin, Bruce	89UD	319	$ .01	$ .07
Reynolds, R. J.	89UD	315	$ .01	$ .07	Ruffin, Bruce	90UD	580	$ .01	$ .07
Reynolds, R. J.	90UD	540	$ .01	$ .07	Runge, Paul	89UD	55	$ .01	$ .07
Rhoden, Rick	89UD	56	$ .01	$ .07	Russell, Jeff	89UD	461	$ .01	$ .07
Rhoden, Rick	90UD	504	$ .01	$ .07	Russell, Jeff	90UD	638	$ .01	$ .07
Rice, Jim	89UD	413	$ .01	$ .15	Russell, John	89UD	532	$ .01	$ .07
Rice, Jim	90UD	373	$ .01	$ .07	Ryan, Nolan	89UD	145	$ .05	$1.00
Richie, Rob	90UD	76	$ .01	$ .10	Ryan, Nolan	89UD	669	$ .01	$ .25
Righetti, Dave	89UD	59	$ .01	$ .07	Ryan, Nolan	89UD	774	$ .50	$3.00
Righetti, Dave	90UD	479	$ .01	$ .07	Ryan, Nolan	90UD	34	$ .01	$1.75
Rijo, Jose	89UD	619	$ .01	$ .10	Ryan, Nolan	90UD	544	$ .01	$ .75
Rijo, Jose	90UD	216	$ .01	$ .07	Saberhagen, Bret	89UD	37	$ .01	$ .10
Riles, Ernie	89UD	497	$ .01	$ .07	Saberhagen, Bret	90UD	326	$ .01	$ .10
Riles, Ernie	90UD	378	$ .01	$ .07	Sabo, Chris	89UD	180	$ .15	$1.00

Player	Year	No.	VG	EX/MT	Player	Year	No.	VG	EX/MT
Sabo, Chris	89UD	663	$ .10	$ .50	Smith, Bryn	89UD	78	$ .01	$ .07
Sabo, Chris	90UD	181	$ .01	$ .15	Smith, Bryn	90UD	579	$ .01	$ .07
Salas, Mark	89UD	460	$ .01	$ .07	Smith, Dave	89UD	302	$ .01	$ .07
Salazar, Angel	89UD	222	$ .01	$ .07	Smith, Dave	90UD	448	$ .01	$ .07
Salazar, Luis	89UD	136	$ .01	$ .07	Smith, Dwight	89UD	780	$ .01	$1.00
Salazar, Luis	90UD	6	$ .01	$ .07	Smith, Dwight	90UD	376	$ .01	$ .75
Samuel, Juan	89UD	336	$ .01	$ .10	Smith, Lee	89UD	521	$ .01	$ .07
Samuel, Juan	90UD	583	$ .01	$ .07	Smith, Lee	90UD	393	$ .01	$ .07
Sanchez, Israel	89UD	326	$ .01	$ .20	Smith, Lonnie	89UD	731	$ .01	$ .15
Sanchez, Israel	90UD	384	$ .01	$ .07	Smith, Lonnie	90UD	215	$ .01	$ .07
Sandberg, Ryne	89UD	120	$ .01	$ .15	Smith, Ozzie	89UD	265	$ .01	$ .10
Sandberg, Ryne	89UD	675	$ .01	$ .10	Smith, Ozzie	89UD	674	$ .01	$ .10
Sandberg, Ryne	90UD	324	$ .01	$ .15	Smith, Ozzie	90UD	225	$ .01	$ .10
Sanders, Deion	90UD	13	$ .01	$ .45	Smith, Pete	89UD	412	$ .01	$ .10
Sanderson, Scott	89UD	342	$ .01	$ .07	Smith, Pete	90UD	613	$ .01	$ .07
Sanderson, Scott	90UD	39	$ .01	$ .07	Smith, Roy	90UD	284	$ .01	$ .07
Santana, Rafael	89UD	216	$ .01	$ .07	Smith, Zane	89UD	71	$ .01	$ .07
Santiago, Benito	89UD	165	$ .01	$ .10	Smith, Zane	90UD	607	$ .01	$ .07
Santiago, Benito	90UD	12	$ .01	$ .07	Smithson, Mike	89UD	38	$ .01	$ .07
Santiago, Benito	90UD	325	$ .01	$ .15	Smithson, Mike	90UD	610	$ .01	$ .07
Santovenia, Nelson	89UD	380	$ .01	$ .15	Smoltz, John	89UD	17	$ .05	$ .40
Santovenia, Nelson	90UD	432	$ .01	$ .07	Smoltz, John	90UD	535	$ .01	$ .15
Sasser, Mackey	89UD	561	$ .01	$ .10	Smoltz, John	90UD	84	$ .01	$ .07
Sasser, Mackey	90UD	185	$ .01	$ .07	Snider, Van	89UD	23	$ .01	$ .10
Sax, Steve	89UD	53	$ .01	$ .10	Snyder, Cory	89UD	170	$ .01	$ .10
Sax, Steve	89UD	748	$ .01	$ .15	Snyder, Cory	89UD	679	$ .01	$ .10
Sax, Steve	90UD	172	$ .01	$ .07	Snyder, Cory	90UD	126	$ .01	$ .07
Sax, Steve	90UD	18	$ .01	$ .07	Sosa, Sammy	90UD	17	$ .01	$ .75
Schiraldi, Calvin	89UD	82	$ .01	$ .07	Speier, Chris	89UD	206	$ .01	$ .07
Schiraldi, Calvin	90UD	643	$ .01	$ .07	Spiers, Bill	89UD	745	$ .01	$ .20
Schmidt, Dave	89UD	447	$ .01	$ .07	Spiers, Bill	90UD	237	$ .01	$ .20
Schmidt, Dave	90UD	641	$ .01	$ .07	St. Claire, Randy	89UD	29	$ .01	$ .07
Schmidt, Mike	89UD	406	$ .01	$ .35	Stanicek, Pete	89UD	592	$ .01	$ .10
Schmidt, Mike	89UD	684	$ .01	$ .25	Stanley, Bob	89UD	411	$ .01	$ .07
Schmidt, Mike	90UD	20	$ .01	$1.75	Stanley, Bob	90UD	654	$ .01	$ .07
Schofield, Dick	89UD	201	$ .01	$ .07	Stanley, Mike	89UD	579	$ .01	$ .07
Schofield, Dick	90UD	669	$ .01	$ .07	Stanton, Mike	90UD	61	$ .01	$ .10
Schooler, Mike	89UD	28	$ .01	$ .15	Stapleton, Dave	89UD	304	$ .01	$ .07
Schooler, Mike	90UD	214	$ .01	$ .10	Steinbach, Terry	89UD	256	$ .01	$ .10
Schroeder, Bill	89UD	627	$ .01	$ .07	Steinbach, Terry	90UD	246	$ .01	$ .07
Schroeder, Bill	90UD	149	$ .01	$ .07	Stewart, Dave	89UD	185	$ .01	$ .07
Schu, Rick	89UD	490	$ .01	$ .07	Stewart, Dave	90UD	272	$ .01	$ .10
Scioscia, Mike	89UD	116	$ .01	$ .07	Stieb, Dave	89UD	383	$ .01	$ .07
Scioscia, Mike	90UD	298	$ .01	$ .07	Stieb, Dave	90UD	605	$ .01	$ .07
Scott, Mike	89UD	295	$ .01	$ .15	Stillwell, Kurt	89UD	616	$ .01	$ .07
Scott, Mike	90UD	125	$ .01	$ .07	Stillwell, Kurt	90UD	361	$ .01	$ .07
Scott, Mike	90UD	88	$ .01	$ .07	Stone, Jeff	89UD	486	$ .01	$ .07
Scudder, Scott	90UD	164	$ .01	$ .20	Stottlemyre, Todd	89UD	362	$ .01	$ .15
Scurry, Rod	89UD	208	$ .01	$ .07	Stottlemyre, Todd	90UD	692	$ .01	$ .07
Searcy, Steve	89UD	764	$ .01	$ .15	Straker, Les	89UD	83	$ .01	$ .07
Searcy, Steve	90UD	575	$ .01	$ .10	Strawberry, Darryl	89UD	260	$ .05	$ .35
Seitzer, Kevin	89UD	510	$ .05	$ .30	Strawberry, Darryl	89UD	681	$ .01	$ .25
Seitzer, Kevin	90UD	363	$ .01	$ .07	Strawberry, Darryl	90UD	182	$ .01	$ .20
Service, Scott	90UD	35	$ .01	$ .25	Stubbs, Franklin	89UD	91	$ .01	$ .07
Sheets, Larry	89UD	254	$ .01	$ .07	Stubbs, Franklin	90UD	550	$ .01	$ .07
Sheets, Larry	90UD	287	$ .01	$ .07	Sundberg, Jim	89UD	331	$ .01	$ .07
Sheffield, Gary	89UD	13	$ .25	$2.00	Surhoff, B. J.	89UD	343	$ .01	$ .07
Sheffield, Gary	90UD	157	$ .01	$ .35	Surhoff, B. J.	90UD	159	$ .01	$ .07
Shelby, John	89UD	75	$ .01	$ .07	Sutcliffe, Rick	89UD	303	$ .01	$ .10
Sheridan, Pat	89UD	652	$ .01	$ .15	Sutcliffe, Rick	90UD	109	$ .01	$ .07
Sheridan, Pat	90UD	460	$ .01	$ .07	Sutter, Bruce	89UD	414	$ .01	$ .07
Show, Eric	89UD	171	$ .01	$ .07	Sveum, Dale	89UD	421	$ .01	$ .07
Show, Eric	90UD	587	$ .01	$ .07	Sveum, Dale	90UD	499	$ .01	$ .07
Sierra, Ruben	89UD	416	$ .01	$ .25	Swift, Bill	89UD	623	$ .01	$ .07
Sierra, Ruben	89UD	686	$ .01	$ .10	Swift, Bill	90UD	313	$ .01	$ .07
Sierra, Ruben	90UD	355	$ .01	$ .20	Swindell, Greg	89UD	250	$ .01	$ .25
Simmons, Ted	89UD	570	$ .01	$ .07	Swindell, Greg	90UD	574	$ .01	$ .07
Sisk, Doug	89UD	261	$ .01	$ .07	Tabler, Pat	89UD	233	$ .01	$ .07
Skalski, Joe	89UD	716	$ .01	$ .10	Tabler, Pat	90UD	142	$ .01	$ .07
Skinner, Joel	89UD	328	$ .01	$ .07	Tanana, Frank	89UD	391	$ .01	$ .07
Skinner, Joel	90UD	369	$ .01	$ .07	Tanana, Frank	90UD	516	$ .01	$ .07
Slaught, Don	89UD	178	$ .01	$ .07	Tapani, Kevin	90UD	87	$ .01	$ .20
Slaught, Don	90UD	152	$ .01	$ .07	Tartabull, Danny	89UD	329	$ .01	$ .15
Smiley, John	89UD	516	$ .01	$ .07	Tartabull, Danny	90UD	656	$ .01	$ .07
Smiley, John	90UD	387	$ .01	$ .10	Tekulve, Kent	89UD	207	$ .01	$ .07

Player	Year	No.	VG	EX/MT
Templeton, Garry	89UD	297	$ .01	$ .07
Templeton, Garry	90UD	288	$ .01	$ .07
Terrell, Walt	89UD	475	$ .01	$ .07
Terrell, Walt	89UD	703	$ .01	$ .10
Terrell, Walt	90UD	661	$ .01	$ .07
Terry, Scott	90UD	260	$ .01	$ .07
Tettleton, Mickey	89UD	553	$ .01	$ .07
Tettleton, Mickey	90UD	297	$ .01	$ .07
Tettleton, Mickey	90UD	60	$ .01	$ .07
Teufel, Tim	89UD	277	$ .01	$ .07
Teufel, Tim	90UD	492	$ .01	$ .07
Thigpen, Bobby	89UD	647	$ .01	$ .07
Thigpen, Bobby	90UD	269	$ .01	$ .07
Thomas, Andres	89UD	144	$ .01	$ .07
Thomas, Andres	90UD	212	$ .01	$ .07
Thompson, Milt	89UD	317	$ .01	$ .07
Thompson, Milt	90UD	278	$ .01	$ .07
Thompson, Rob	89UD	172	$ .01	$ .07
Thompson, Robby	90UD	169	$ .01	$ .07
Thon, Dickie	89UD	258	$ .01	$ .07
Thon, Dickie	89UD	704	$ .01	$ .10
Thon, Dickie	90UD	439	$ .01	$ .07
Thurman, Gary	89UD	347	$ .01	$ .07
Thurmond, Mark	89UD	571	$ .01	$ .07
Tibbs, Jay	89UD	655	$ .01	$ .07
Toliver, Fred	89UD	64	$ .01	$ .07
Tolleson, Wayne	90UD	320	$ .01	$ .07
Torve, Kelvin	89UD	177	$ .01	$ .07
Traber, Jim	89UD	294	$ .01	$ .07
Traber, Jim	90UD	268	$ .01	$ .07
Trammell, Alan	89UD	290	$ .01	$ .15
Trammell, Alan	89UD	690	$ .01	$ .15
Trammell, Alan	90UD	554	$ .01	$ .15
Treadway, Jeff	89UD	393	$ .01	$ .15
Treadway, Jeff	90UD	141	$ .01	$ .07
Trevino, Alex	89UD	262	$ .01	$ .07
Trevino, Alex	90UD	205	$ .01	$ .07
Trillo, Manny	89UD	127	$ .01	$ .07
Tudor, John	89UD	66	$ .01	$ .07
Tudor, John	90UD	396	$ .01	$ .07
Upshaw, Willie	89UD	157	$ .01	$ .07
Uribe, Jose	89UD	181	$ .01	$ .07
Uribe, Jose	90UD	188	$ .01	$ .07
Valenzuela, Fernando	89UD	656	$ .01	$ .10
Valenzuela, Fernando	90UD	445	$ .01	$ .07
Valle, Dave	89UD	320	$ .01	$ .07
Valle, Dave	90UD	451	$ .01	$ .07
Van Slyke, Andy	89UD	537	$ .01	$ .10
Van Slyke, Andy	89UD	685	$ .01	$ .15
Van Slyke, Andy	90UD	536	$ .01	$ .15
Varoho, Gary	89UD	321	$ .01	$ .20
Vaughn, Greg	90UD	25	$ .01	$1.75
Velarde, Randy	89UD	189	$ .01	$ .07
Ventura, Robin	90UD	21	$ .01	$ .65
Viola, Frank	89UD	397	$ .01	$ .15
Viola, Frank	89UD	658	$ .01	$ .15
Viola, Frank	89UD	691	$ .01	$ .10
Viola, Frank	90UD	626	$ .01	$ .10
Virgil, Ozzie	89UD	104	$ .01	$ .07
Vizcaino, Jose	90UD	44	$ .01	$ .35
Vizquel, Omar	89UD	787	$ .01	$ .10
Vizquel, Omar	90UD	233	$ .01	$ .10
Walewander, Jim	89UD	454	$ .01	$ .07
Walk, Bob	89UD	438	$ .01	$ .07
Walk, Bob	90UD	596	$ .01	$ .07
Walker, Greg	89UD	231	$ .01	$ .07
Walker, Greg	90UD	350	$ .01	$ .07
Walker, Larry	90UD	466	$ .01	$ .45
Wallach, Tim	89UD	102	$ .01	$ .07
Wallach, Tim	90UD	273	$ .01	$ .07
Walling, Denny	89UD	327	$ .01	$ .07
Walter, Gene	89UD	604	$ .01	$ .07
Walton, Jerome	89UD	765	$1.00	$5.00
Walton, Jerome	90UD	345	$ .01	$1.50
Ward, Duane	89UD	551	$ .01	$ .07

Player	Year	No.	VG	EX/MT
Ward, Duane	90UD	653	$ .01	$ .07
Ward, Gary	89UD	98	$ .01	$ .07
Washington, Claudell	89UD	310	$ .01	$ .10
Washington, Claudell	89UD	794	$ .01	$ .10
Washington, Claudell	90UD	395	$ .01	$ .07
Washington, Ron	89UD	519	$ .01	$ .07
Wayne, Gary	90UD	372	$ .01	$ .15
Webster, Mitch	89UD	65	$ .01	$ .07
Webster, Mitch	90UD	153	$ .01	$ .07
Wegman, Bill	89UD	445	$ .01	$ .07
Wegman, Bill	90UD	629	$ .01	$ .07
Weiss, Walt	89UD	374	$ .10	$ .60
Weiss, Walt	89UD	660	$ .01	$ .25
Weiss, Walt	90UD	542	$ .01	$ .07
Welch, Bob	89UD	191	$ .01	$ .07
Welch, Bob	90UD	251	$ .01	$ .07
Wells, David	90UD	30	$ .01	$ .07
West, David	89UD	7	$ .05	$ .50
West, David	90UD	15	$ .01	$ .07
Weston, Mickey	90UD	683	$ .01	$ .15
Wetherby, Jeff	90UD	611	$ .01	$ .15
Wetteland, John	90UD	377	$ .01	$ .25

Lou Whitaker

Player	Year	No.	VG	EX/MT
Whitaker, Lou	89UD	451	$ .01	$ .10
Whitaker, Lou	90UD	327	$ .01	$ .07
Whitaker, Lou	90UD	41	$ .01	$ .07
White, Devon	89UD	110	$ .01	$ .15
White, Devon	90UD	129	$ .01	$ .07
White, Devon	90UD	5	$ .01	$ .07
White, Frank	89UD	350	$ .01	$ .07
White, Frank	90UD	382	$ .01	$ .07
Whited, Ed	90UD	447	$ .01	$ .20
Whitehurst, Wally	89UD	737	$ .01	$ .10
Whitehurst, Wally	90UD	564	$ .01	$ .07
Whitson, Ed	89UD	453	$ .01	$ .07
Whitson, Ed	90UD	308	$ .01	$ .07
Whitt, Ernie	89UD	118	$ .01	$ .07
Whitt, Ernie	90UD	148	$ .01	$ .07
Wilkerson, Curtis	89UD	465	$ .01	$ .07
Wilkerson, Curtis	90UD	147	$ .01	$ .07
Williams, Eddie	89UD	790	$ .01	$ .10
Williams, Eddie	90UD	289	$ .01	$ .10
Williams, Frank	89UD	449	$ .01	$ .07
Williams, Frank	90UD	539	$ .01	$ .07

Player	Year	No.	VG	EX/MT	Player	Year	No.	VG	EX/MT
Williams, Ken	89UD	506	$ .01	$ .07	Wilson, Mookie	89UD	199	$ .01	$ .07
Williams, Ken	89UD	714	$ .01	$ .10	Wilson, Mookie	90UD	481	$ .01	$ .07
Williams, Kenny	90UD	249	$ .01	$ .07	Wilson, Steve	89UD	799	$ .01	$ .10
Williams, Matt	89UD	247	$ .01	$ .35	Wilson, Steve	90UD	341	$ .01	$ .10
Williams, Matt	90UD	577	$ .01	$ .25	Wilson, Trevor	89UD	733	$ .01	$ .10
					Wilson, Trevor	90UD	637	$ .01	$ .07
					Wilson, Willie	89UD	244	$ .01	$ .07
					Wilson, Willie	90UD	349	$ .01	$ .07
					Winfield, Dave	89UD	349	$ .01	$ .15
					Winfield, Dave	90UD	337	$ .01	$ .10
					Winningham, Herm	89UD	636	$ .01	$ .07
					Winningham, Herm	90UD	589	$ .01	$ .07
					Winters, Matt	90UD	524	$ .01	$ .15
					Witt, Bobby	89UD	557	$ .01	$ .07
					Witt, Bobby	90UD	636	$ .01	$ .07
					Witt, Mike	89UD	555	$ .01	$ .07
					Witt, Mike	90UD	548	$ .01	$ .07
					Woodson, Tracy	89UD	108	$ .01	$ .07
					Worrell, Todd	89UD	512	$ .01	$ .07
					Worrell, Todd	90UD	467	$ .01	$ .07
					Worthington, Craig	89UD	725	$ .01	$ .15
					Worthington, Craig	90UD	444	$ .01	$ .10
					Wrona, Rick	90UD	582	$ .01	$ .10
					Wynne, Marvell	89UD	154	$ .01	$ .07
					Wynne, Marvell	90UD	14	$ .01	$ .07
					Yelding, Eric	90UD	427	$ .01	$ .20
					Yett, Rich	89UD	728	$ .01	$ .10
					Yett, Rich	90UD	595	$ .01	$ .07
					Youmans, Floyd	89UD	459	$ .01	$ .07
					Youmans, Floyd	89UD	730	$ .01	$ .10
					Young, Curt	89UD	392	$ .01	$ .07
					Young, Curt	90UD	4	$ .01	$ .07
					Young, Gerald	89UD	135	$ .01	$ .07
					Young, Gerald	90UD	196	$ .01	$ .07
					Young, Mike	89UD	649	$ .01	$ .07
					Youngblood, Joel	89UD	458	$ .01	$ .07
					Yount, Robin	89UD	285	$ .01	$ .15
					Yount, Robin	90UD	567	$ .01	$ .25
					Yount, Robin	90UD	91	$ .01	$ .07
					Zeile, Todd	89UD	754	$ .05	$4.50
					Zeile, Todd	90UD	545	$ .01	$2.50
					Zuvella, Paul	89UD	236	$ .01	$ .07

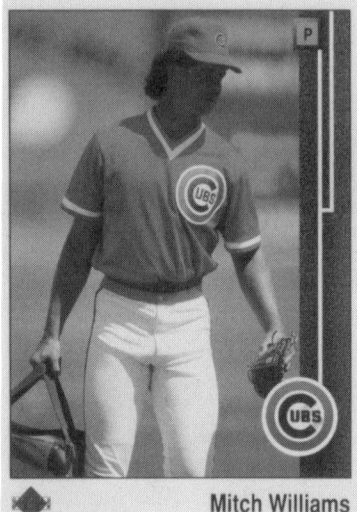

Mitch Williams

Player	Year	No.	VG	EX/MT
Williams, Mitch	89UD	778	$ .01	$ .10
Williams, Mitch	89UD	95	$ .01	$ .07
Williams, Mitch	90UD	174	$ .01	$ .10
Williamson, Mark	90UD	173	$ .01	$ .07
Wilson, Glenn	90UD	410	$ .01	$ .07

Schroeder's Antiques Price Guide

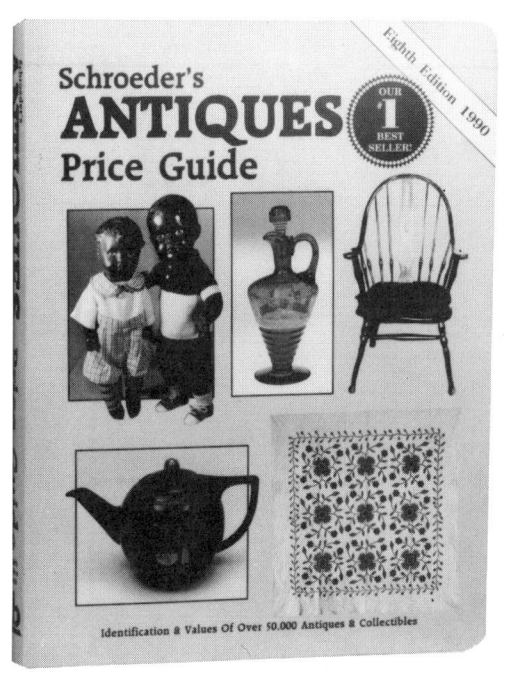

Schroeder's Antiques Price Guide has climbed its way to the top in a field already supplied with several well-established publications! The word is out, *Schroeder's Price Guide* is the best buy at any price. Over 500 categories are covered, with more than 50,000 listings. From ABC Plates to Zsolnay, if it merits the interest of today's collector, you'll find it in Schroeder's. Each subject is represented with histories and background information. In addition, hundreds of sharp original photos are used each year to illustrate not only the rare and the unusual, but the everyday "fun-type" collectibles as well. All new copy and all new illustrations make Schroeder's THE price guide on antiques and collectibles. We have not and will not simply change prices in each new edition.

The writing and researching team is backed by a staff of more than seventy of Collector Books' finest authors, as well as a board of advisors made up of well-known antique authorities and the country's top dealers, all specialists in their fields. Prices are gathered over the entire year previous to publication, then each category is thoroughly checked. Only the best of the lot remains for publication. You'll find the new edition of *Schroeder's Antiques Price Guide* the one to buy for factual information and quality.

No dealer, collector or investor can afford not to own this book. It is available from your favorite bookseller or antiques dealer at the low price of $12.95. If you are unable to find this price guide in your area, it's available from Collector Books, P.O. Box 3009, Paducah, KY 42001 at $12.95 plus $2.00 for postage and handling.